D1541492

The Rorschach: A Comprehensive System, in two volumes
by John E. Exner, Jr.

Theory and Practice in Behavior Therapy
by Aubrey J. Yates

Principles of Psychotherapy
by Irving B. Weiner

Psychoactive Drugs and Social Judgment: Theory and Research
edited by Kenneth Hammond and C. R. B. Joyce

Clinical Methods in Psychology
edited by Irving B. Weiner

Human Resources for Troubled Children
by Werner I. Halpern and Stanley Kissel

Hyperactivity
by Dorothea M. Ross and Sheila A. Ross

Heroin Addiction: Theory, Research and Treatment
by Jerome J. Platt and Christina Labate

Children's Rights and the Mental Health Profession
edited by Gerald P. Koocher

The Role of the Father in Child Development
edited by Michael E. Lamb

Handbook of Behavioral Assessment
edited by Anthony R. Ciminero, Karen S. Calhoun, and Henry E. Adams

Counseling and Psychotherapy: A Behavioral Approach
by E. Lakin Phillips

Dimensions of Personality
edited by Harvey London and John E. Exner, Jr.

The Mental Health Industry: A Cultural Phenomenon
by Peter A. Magaro, Robert Gripp, David McDowell, and Ivan W. Miller III

Nonverbal Communication: The State of the Art
by Robert G. Harper, Arthur N. Wiens, and Joseph D. Matarazzo

Alcoholism and Treatment
by David J. Armor, J. Michael Polich, and Harriet B. Stambul

A Biodevelopmental Approach to Clinical Child Psychology: Cognitive Controls and Cognitive Control Theory
by Sebastiano Santostefano

Handbook of Infant Development
edited by Joy D. Osofsky

Understanding the Rape Victim: A Synthesis of Research Findings
by Sedelle Katz and Mary Ann Mazur

Childhood Pathology and Later Adjustment: The Question of Prediction
by Loretta K. Cass and Carolyn B. Thomas

Intelligent Testing with the WISC-R
by Alan S. Kaufman

Adaptation in Schizophrenia: The Theory of Segmental Set
by David Shakow

Psychotherapy: An Eclectic Approach
by Sol L. Garfield

Handbook of Minimal Brain Dysfunctions
edited by Herbert E. Rie and Ellen D. Rie

Handbook of Behavioral Interventions: A Clinical Guide
edited by Alan Goldstein and Edna B. Foa

Art Psychotherapy
by Harriet Wadeson

Handbook of Adolescent Psychology
edited by Joseph Adelson

Psychotherapy Supervision: Theory, Research and Practice
edited by Allen K. Hess

Continued on back

THE PSYCHOLOGICAL
ASSESSMENT OF CHILDREN

The Psychological Assessment of Children

SECOND EDITION

James O. Palmer, Ph.D.
Associate Professor Emeritus
University of California
at Los Angeles

JOHN WILEY & SONS, INC.

New York • Chichester • Brisbane • Toronto • Singapore

Quotations from A.S. Kaufman, *Intelligence Testing with the WISC-R* (New York: Wiley, 1979) are used with permission.

Library of Congress Cataloging in Publication Data:
Palmer, James O.
    The psychological assessment of children.

    (Wiley series on personality processes, ISSN 0195-4008)
        Includes bibliographical references and index.
        1. Clinical child psychology.   2. Mental illness—Diagnosis.   I. Title.   II. Series.   [DNLM: 1. Child development.   2. Child psychology.   3. Psychological tests—In infancy and childhood. WS 105 P174p]

RJ503.3.P34   1983   618.92′89075   82-23910
ISBN 0-471-09765-9

Printed in the United States of America

10 9 8 7 6 5 4 3

To Minerva, Jeffrey, and Darren

Series Preface

This series of books is addressed to behavioral scientists interested in the nature of human personality. Its scope should prove pertinent to personality theorists and researchers as well as to clinicians concerned with applying an understanding of personality processes to the amelioration of emotional difficulties in living. To this end, the series provides a scholarly integration of theoretical formulations, empirical data, and practical recommendations.

Six major aspects of studying and learning about human personality can be designated: personality theory, personality structure and dynamics, personality development, personality assessment, personality change, and personality adjustment. In exploring these aspects of personality, the books in the series discuss a number of distinct but related subject areas: their nature and implications of various theories of personality; personality characteristics that account for consistencies and variations in human behavior; the emergence of personality processes in children and adolescents; the use of interviewing and testing procedures to evaluate individual differences in personality; efforts to modify personality styles through psychotherapy, counseling, behavior therapy, and other methods of influence; and patterns of abnormal personality functioning that impair individual competence.

IRVING B. WEINER

University of Denver
Denver, Colorado

Preface to the Second Edition

In the 12 years since this book was first published in 1970, there have been major changes in the field of clinical and counseling psychology and in the specialty of assessment. Interest in this field has grown enormously, and the number of students has multiplied several times. Undoubtedly, the most important change has not been just the doubling of professional psychologists but the introduction of new theories and new techniques in psychotherapy. The primary concern of clinical psychologists today is in changing behavior, and often the welter of approaches seems confusing to the beginning student, who should choose the appropriate treatment for the client at hand. Some resolution of this confusion is offered by an eclectic theory (see my text *A Primer of Eclectic Psychotherapy* [1980]), but an eclecticism does require a careful assessment of the client. Assessment to determine the choice of treatment remains the primary goal of this book.

It is my impression that the developments in assessment has not kept pace with the overall field of clinical and counseling psychology. Research on assessment techniques is not popular and has expanded little. A few new tests have been accepted, but some old standbys are no longer available. Thus, there is a greater strain on the popular techniques to answer questions— especially about treatability—for which they were not particularly designed.

The whole diagnostic system has been redesigned in the *Diagnostic and Statistical Manual of Mental Disorders* (DMS-III, 1980) but this nosology remains essentially medical and "disease" oriented. I am impressed that fewer and fewer psychologists and psychiatrists use these antiquated diagnostic labels except for filling in insurance forms. Thus, assessors are more free to discuss the traits, dynamics, behavior, and social factors for which tests *are* designed.

Specialties within specialties have sprung into being. Three new assessment situations are discussed in this edition in three new chapters: Chapter 17 on the assessment of developmental and learning disabilities and traumatic brain damage; Chapter 18 on assessment of minority-status children; and assessment for the courts. The first edition was published before there was recognition of the sexist bias in psychological writing—when all children were referred to as "he" and all teachers as "she." The use of she/he or he/she may seem clumsy to the reader at first, but soon it will seem not only more acceptable but more natural. The most important change has been not just the wording, but more important the recognition that sexist attitudes and behavior have long been major emotional and social factors in the disturbances in the lives of both sexes. Moreover, the needed alterations in these customs will create even more confusion for both the current and future generations— until a nonsexist society is established.

This second edition is thus intended to reflect these changes in clinical and counseling psychology, especially in the specialty of assessment. In order not to increase the length of the book too much, I have coalesced the theoretical introduction so as to expand the discussion of these new developments. Additional research has been noted where it is pertinent, but as stated in the original work, no attempt has been made to review the research literature. It is to be hoped that the research-minded clinician will find many unsolved problems in this volume, which is essentially a "how-to" practitioner's manual.

JAMES O. PALMER

Berkeley, California
March 1983

Contents

List of Figures and Plates

List of Cases

PART ONE

The Hypotheses
of Assessment

CHAPTER 1

A Developmental–Social Orientation

A. THE SCIENTIST–CLINICIAN DILEMMA

1. A Definition and Its Implications

Psychological assessment is the use of scientific knowledge and methods in order to study the behavioral problems of an individual child. The overall purpose of this book is to demonstrate how this knowledge and these methods may be applied to the individual case. An examination of the implications of this definition may serve to clarify this purpose.

In addition, the chief reason for considering this definition in some detail is that for many psychologists it poses a major dilemma—that of the "scientist–clinician." On the one hand, a child's behavior usually requires clinical attention because that behavior is socially and personally disruptive. Assessment thus has both a social purpose and context, which places a social obligation on psychologists. A scientist, on the other hand, has the formulation of general laws as a prime concern, rather than the study of individual cases. Nor can the scientist be limited by social demands and purposes. An examination of the purposes both of assessment and of science might make a resolution of this dilemma possible. These considerations provide the rationale for the organization of this book.

2. The Purpose of an Assessment

By definition, the purpose of an assessment is "to study" behavior. In this sense an assessment has the same goal as any scientific investigation. However, the problems that confront clinical psychologists differ in several important respects. Scientists are relatively free to select and define those general problems that attract their interest and whet their curiosity. Clinicians, however, receive their problems from those who are concerned with the behavior of the child: parents, teachers, physicians, or other responsible authorities. These social authorities define the problem—at least initially. What is most significant is that they delegate to the psychologist the responsibility for "studying the child's behavior." It is this social obligation that most sharply distinguishes the problems that face the scientist–clinician.

Since these are personal and social problems, parents usually try to answer them on the basis of their own knowledge and experience. Normally, parents accept responsibility for the child's behavior, and—as will be discussed in subsequent chapters—many parents are loath to admit they may have failed and have to seek help. At least they see that the child is disturbing to them, and usually by the time they decide to seek psychological help, they also perceive that the child is emotionally disturbed. School authorities also usually attempt a variety of educational techniques and arrangements for the child before they seek outside advice. When parents and school turn to the courts, the child may be subjected to a series of legal warnings and remedies in an effort to alter his/her behavior. Assistance with these problems is still sought from the minister, priest, or rabbi, who attempt to reply with a combination of religious law, moral dictum, and humane wisdom. These problems have been referred increasingly to the physician, especially the pediatrician, who seeks answers

3

in terms of the physical health and development of the child.

Sometimes (perhaps more often than psychologists may imagine) parents are able to solve these problems on their own. Or the teacher, judge, minister, or pediatrician—in combination with one another and with parents—is able to help the child without further specific knowledge. Usually it is only after all efforts to alter the child's behavior have been ineffective that the parents and other authorities turn to the psychologist with the question ''What is to be done with this child?''

Although the ultimate question is ''What is to be done?,'' the initial question, ''What is wrong with this child?,'' must be answered first. In fact, it is usually because no one has understood the causes of the child's disturbance that the methods of handling and changing his/her behavior are ineffective. Thus *the essential purpose of a psychological assessment is to determine the nature and extent of the disturbance in order to select and formulate the model(s) of behavioral change.*

Note that this statement presumes that there *are* different modes of treatment, different ways of altering behavior, and different milieus in which the child may be placed. If one presumes that *all* behavioral problems can be handled by a single form of treatment, for example, by psychoanalysis, by operant conditioning, by nondirective counseling, or by foster-home placement, then there is no need for assessment. In fact, the orthodox adherents of some of these ''schools'' of behavioral change have seen no necessity for assessment. However, in this book it is assumed that there are many different ways of altering the child's behavior and environment. Children's problems commonly call for a combination of approaches.

This statement of the rationale for assessment thus would seem to imply a relationship between ''what is wrong'' and ''what is to be done,'' so that if the problem is defined carefully enough, the remedy will be obvious. Unfortunately, the relationships between the problems of childhood and methods of behavioral change are far from clear. (This will be discussed in detail in Part 4.) However, the contention of this rationale is that, by defining the problem by means of a thorough assessment, it is at least easier to examine the potentialities of various approaches to behavioral change. Most of all, a thorough assessment provides the data for planning treatment so that a general mode of behavioral change can be made specific to the child and family, and to their difficulties.

B.   THE UTILIZATION OF SCIENTIFIC KNOWLEDGE AND METHODS

This second key phrase in the definition of assessment leads to a consideration of the relationship between these clinical goals of assessment and the goals of science. Such consideration is necessary because the goals of society are not necessarily the goals of the scientist. Scientists have the expansion of knowledge as their chief goal, especially in terms of general laws. Their motivation is a personal, scientific curiosity. They are relatively disinterested in the practical, immediate questions of individual behavior, except as these may provide some hints or leads to the broader theoretical questions to be explored. As a citizen, the ''pure'' scientist may be cognizant of the importance of the social-personal question. As a scientist, however, this may seem irrelevant.

Although the goals of the clinical psychologist cannot be limited to those of the pure scientist, the task of seeking answers to the questions posed by the personal problems of the individual child is often an intriguing challenge to his/her scientific curiosity. This type of scientific satisfaction is only a token, however, if the knowledge gained from the case in question cannot be used as a basis for the understanding of future cases. Often the clinical psychologist's appetite for research is whetted as he/she gains new knowledge from an individual case, or as he/she is able to generate new hypotheses. It is in this sense that the goals of "pure" and "applied" science converge. Of course, the clinical psychologist receives her/his greatest personal satisfaction whenever an assessment aids the child. Thus long-range satisfactions are realized in helping the community to think scientifically and humanely about children.

The social responsibility of assessing disturbed children places severe demands on the psychologist's scientific knowledge and acumen. This responsibility becomes even more awesome when the problems presented by the child extend beyond available knowledge and techniques. Despite the extensive upsurge of research on child development and behavior over the past decade, many of the common behavioral and social disturbances presented by children remain more a matter of "expert opinion" than of scientific knowledge. For example, we have little more than accumulated clinical hypotheses (and biases) about such prevalent phenomena as school phobias, adolescent sexual promiscuity, or even that much discussed but little researched annoyance—enuresis. More alarming is the ignorance about suicide in children, although it is currently one of the major causes of death among adolescents. Research has not yet determined why children attempt to kill themselves, nor has it provided any reliable technique of predicting the possibility of suicide. Many major emotional states such as revenge, hatred, happiness, vanity, and the like remain totally unexplored.

In view of these social responsibilities and the relative paucity of research findings, every clinical psychologist must ask this question: How is it possible to make assessments of the individual child that are at all valid and significant? The answer proposed and elaborated on in this book lies in the clinician's development and utilization of three equally important and interconnected scientific assets. The *first* is a comprehensive and integrated knowledge of fact and theory derived from the behavioral sciences. The *second* basic scientific tool that the psychologist can bring to bear on the clinical question is the ability to observe behavior carefully and accurately. Such training in methods of collecting, sampling, and collating behavioral data requires skills not possessed by the layman or by other professionals. This knowledge and these skills need to be combined with yet a *third* faculty that is fundamental to all scientists: the ability to reason logically—both deductively and inductively.

1.   The Value of "Laws"

As to the first asset, even though "general" psychology (as distinct from applied psychology) is not primarily concerned with the problems presented by an individual child, the general laws that have been developed about learning, perception, motivation, and other psychological functions do provide the basic core of knowledge for the work of the scientist–clinician. Very often, when the clinician seeks to understand a new and complicated problem in the personal life of an individual child, knowledge of these scientific laws provides the only resource. Even more directly pertinent are research studies in developmental psychology. Insofar as these clinical questions involve social as well as personal problems—and to some extent there is a social aspect to all personal problems—social psychology, sociology, anthropology, and even history and economics are fundamental to the basic knowledge of the clinical psychologist.

In practice unfortunately, the clinical psychologist too often goes through the motions of an assessment with little recognition that the data being gathered are, in fact, related to or made comprehensible by the seemingly abstruse theories or research studies he or she learned in graduate school. In a survey of the attitudes of clinical psychologists, Wildman and Wildman (1967) reported that a majority appear to operate without much reference to any one particular theory of personality.

It would seem unlikely that clinicians ignore theory altogether, but it appears probable that they use a variety of theories— without making their theorizing explicit. Most often the student needs an integration of this background in behavioral science with the clinical tasks and techniques of assessment. A complete analysis and integration of this general knowledge is beyond the scope of this book. To attempt even to state the principal relationships between the clinical assessment of children and the rest of psychology and the other behavioral sciences is an admittedly ambitious undertaking. Yet the techniques of assessment and its procedures are not understandable nor applicable without at least a recognition of other behavioral-science principles. The remainder of this chapter is intended as an outline, painted with a broad brush, of the basic hypotheses underlying assessment. It draws on general psychology, on developmental psychology in particular, and on the social sciences.

However, these "theoretical considerations" are intended chiefly as a review and reminder, since it is to be hoped that the student already possesses much of this background knowledge. In the long run, the focus of this book is on the *utilization* of assessment. Thus, only passing references will be made to the pertinent research and theories, mainly to illustrate how they can and must be used by the clinician.

2.   The Scientific Training of the Clinician

As to the second of the clinician's assets derived from scientific training, Part 2 of this volume is concerned with the methods of systematic collection, recording, and analysis of data. The methods of a scientific investigation should be logically derived from the theoretical framework within which the scientist is operating. As will be discussed in further detail, one of the main difficulties for the scientist–clinician is that the techniques of assessment have arisen from a variety of seemingly unrelated theories, many of which were never made explicit in the first place and which often have since been replaced by other concepts. Whether such a variety of theories can be integrated is doubtful, but at least an attempt will be made to relate the rationale behind the most commonly used techniques to the general theoretical framework of child development discussed in these initial chapters. Often it is through the presence of an exception to the rule, or the absence of what is expected, that the clinician begins to find some explanation for the question "What is wrong with this child?"

To the beginning student a case history and a handful of responses to a few "tests" may not even seem to be "data"—in the sense that term is used in general psychology. That these seemingly discrete pieces of information and responses are indeed "data" may be more easily recognized and accepted when the student learns how to find commonalities and interrelationships among them. In order to assist the student in recognizing and using clinical data, the main evidence offered in support of many of the concepts discussed in this volume will be life histories and responses of individual children rather than citations of experimental or actuarial studies.

One other aspect of clinical observation that should be noted at the outset is that the attitudes and feelings of the observer are intimately involved. Particularly in work with children, it is often quite difficult to remain entirely emotionally neutral and "unbiased"—even if such neutrality is desirable. "Observer bias" has of course long been recognized in many fields of science, and it has been regarded largely as an extraneous but almost unavoidable variable in the study of human behavior by human scientists. Yet in clinical studies this observer bias can be used—in fact it needs to be used—as part of the observation, but psychologists first must be aware of bias within themselves. Preparation for the clinical assessment of children should include an assessment of oneself. Such self-recognition thus enables the psychologist to recognize similar feelings and attitudes in others in an objective, nondefensive fashion.

3. The Ability to Reason

As to the third asset of the clinician's scientific heritage, it is in studying human behavior in general that the psychologist learns to reason deductively—by checking hypotheses against the data provided from observations. Such deductive reasoning is often required in clinical assessment when the clinician is called upon to investigate possible reasons for a child's behavior. However, this behavior often poses questions for which there are are no ready hypotheses, and the data frequently seem relatively meaningless and inexplicable. The clinician, like the naturalist, must learn to construct hypotheses, to think *inductively*, or, to use the more usual clinical term—*interpret* data. Such inductively determined interpretations then become the "working" hypotheses for use in treatment. It should be noted that deductively formed conclusions also are seldom complete, that the behavior of the individual child seldom fits a general law exactly, and that the conclusions so drawn are, in effect, also working hypotheses.

Moreover, the clinician—like any other scientist—should not and cannot be limited exclusively to purely formal logic. As the physicist Robert Oppenheimer pointed out in an address to the American Psychological Association (1956), scientific thought and discovery often involve the use of analogy, which is equally a traditional form of logic. Argument by analogy often enables the clinician to derive meaning and form for data, and thus to begin to formulate hypotheses about them. Last but not least, the scientist–clinician depends on a thought process common to all science—intuition. This "aha!" experience, as Helmholtz labeled it over a century ago, remains the essential element for creative insight necessary to all scientific discovery.

C. WHAT IS A "BEHAVIOR PROBLEM?"—A DEVELOPMENTAL DEFINITION FOR "PSYCHOPATHOLOGY"

The third aspect to be considered in this definition of assessment is the term *behavioral problem*. As was indicated before, initially this "problem" is defined socially by the complaints of the parents or others responsible for the child. However, there is often the question of whether these complaints and concerns are justified. Is there "something wrong with this child," or are the parents unduly alarmed? The fact that either a parent or child is subjectively distraught *in itself* constitutes a problem. In effect, the parent or other social authority requests that the psychologist further define the nature of this problem. This request is typically phrased by the common question "Is *that* normal?"

1. Prescientific Definitions

Before considering the scientific criteria for defining behavior problems, a brief historical aside concerning concepts about personal distress may be in order, for these attitudes out of the past continue to affect how people regard assessment and the relief of behavioral disturbances. Scientific psychology itself began a little over a century ago, and the history of clinical psychology can be counted in decades. According to Kanner (1962), scientists gave little recognition to psychological disturbances in children until shortly before the twentieth century. Moreover, it is only in the latter half of this century that the clinical psychologist has been considered as a possible resource for problems of personal distress.

Up until about the nineteenth century, the mind of a child—if children were deemed to possess a mind—was considered to be so ephemeral that it could be understood only by the poet. When it was recognized that the child was disturbed, he/she was thought to be "accursed," and the priest was called upon to exorcise the "devils," or a magic potion or talisman was secretly sought from the local witch doctor. Much more often, the child who demonstrated what would now be considered a psychological problem was thought "willful" and disobedient. When such a "headstrong" child could not be managed by his/her parents legal authorities stepped in, and the child's socially disturbing behavior was deemed criminal and subject to legal punishment, which was often quite harsh. These century-old concepts have never been completely discarded, and—far more than psychologists like to think—they continue to be used in our modern society. At times they even become part of the attitudes of psychologists. The legal concepts have been considerably modified to take into account psychological concepts about children's behavior. Yet such legal concepts as *delinquent, insane,* and *incorrigible* are in current use—even among psychologists. Many legal authorities, as well as others, continue to regard psychologists' explanations of children's behavior as attempts to excuse the disturbance to society. When psychologists become righteously defensive and disregard the socially disrupting effects of children's behavior, they only serve to justify the view that they do not believe in "discipline."

Nor have witchcraft and magic been completely abandoned. In this past decade, some ancient panaceas for human misery have been reintroduced; for example, rauwolfia as a legal tranquilizer and cannabis (marijuana) as an illegal, magical escape. Many parents become impatient with scientific deliberations over their distresses and fear that the psychologist will blame them. Frequently they regard their children's behavior as a curse for their own sins and wish that the psychologist could provide some magical invocation to sweep away their guilt. In the 1970s the so-called behavior drugs, such as Ritalin and others, have been introduced almost as a cure-all for a wide variety of the social and emotional difficulties of children. Although research has thrown doubt on the efficacy and even the ethics of prescribing these drugs (Schrag and Divoky, 1975), they continue to be promoted by neurologists and pediatricians. These professionals argue that these drugs continue to be used to preserve the "medical model" of "illness," in hope of some magical relief from the difficulties parents and teachers endure—without exposing their guilt feelings. At times, under the pressure of such clients, psychologists have been known to cut short their scientific assessments and respond to the client's request that they "play God" and provide immediate relief by giving them some advice or decision, without further investigation.

2.   The Medical Model

The first attempts to understand behavioral disturbances scientifically were made by physicians around the end of the eighteenth century. When scientific medicine began to show some promise of ameliorating physical ailments, people began to look to the physician for relief from psychological distress also. In the nineteenth century diseases began to be categorized using symptom patterns, and when physicians began to assess and treat behavioral disorders, they naturally used the conceptual framework with which they were then familiar. In addition, since most of their patients were adults, these diagnostic terms referred to adult symptoms. As physicians they concentrated on those behaviors that appeared to be associated with physiological disturbances, and they tended to assume a physiological basis for others, even when no disease process was obvious. The newly born science of psychology was developing out of philosophy at that time, and it was concerned chiefly with the general nature of the mind. "Mental disease" thus became the province of a branch of a medicine—psychiatry. As psychiatry became more sophisticated, many physicians began to recognize that they were dealing with psychological rather than primarily physiological phenomena. The theories of such psychiatrists as Freud, Bleuler, Jung, and Adolph Meyer—to name only a few—were primarily psychological, even though these theories often had a biological reference point. Freud frequently referred to himself as a psychologist. Nevertheless, the basic disease schema and its terminology have remained as the conceptual framework in psychiatry.

As psychologists turned their attention to behavioral disorders, they too adopted the available medical model of "mental illness." Thus Hathaway and McKinley (1943) used the then-current Kraepelin nosology for the MMPI. The original criterion upon which attempts were made to validate the Rorschach Technique was the "diagnosis" of psychiatric and neurological diseases. Psychologists continue to investigate a set of behavioral disorders labeled "schizophrenia." Their research adds to the psychological knowledge about the behavioral disorders covered by this medical label, but few if any of these investigators question the medical model underlying their studies.

As evidence accumulates concerning the behavioral nature of these so-called "diseases," the adequacy of this disease model has come to be questioned. For example, the psychiatrist Szass (1961) challenged what he termed "the myth of mental illness." Szass was soon joined by psychologists such as Albee (1966). In essence, they argued that this medical model failed to account adequately for the fact that much of the behavior subsumed under these medical concepts was not primarily physiological, but was essentially learned behavior. The fact that most psychiatrists have used mainly a psychological treatment, that is, psychotherapy, lends some support to Szass' argument. Many psychologists began to substitute the term *behavioral change* for *psychotherapy* or *treatment*, and Szass and others also argued that these behavioral disorders should no longer remain chiefly in the medical domain. At the present time behavioral

problems are being handled in a variety of settings—often without medical involvement. Nevertheless, the major responsibility for relief of personal distress and socially disturbing behavior often remains assigned to, and it is claimed by, the medical profession. This debate continues, and probably it will increase in intensity.

The inadequacies of the disease model are most marked when it is applied to children's behavior. First, it has long been recognized that children do not demonstrate many of the symptoms usually associated with the disease syndromes used to categorize behavior disorders among adults. In the psychiatric literature there has been considerable disagreement about what patterns of symptoms in childhood should be included in even the broader categories of psychoses and neuroses. When the term *schizophrenia* was first applied to children, many psychiatrists thought it was inappropriate, since these children did not commonly demonstrate such classic symptoms as hallucinations, delusions, or confused thought processes. Thus schizophrenia, when used to describe children's behavior, was modified considerably. The classic symptoms were no longer the main criteria, and greater emphasis was given instead to the child's lack of affective spontaneity and to his/her failure to relate to others. As the term *childhood schizophrenia* finally evolved, it referred mainly to a difficulty in interpersonal relationships, which is a purely psychological phenomena. Incidentally, this change in the concept of schizophrenia during childhood has led to considerable research about the nature of adult schizophrenia, and that concept has also been altered.

Second, children present many symptoms that are not included in the medical categories used to describe adult "diseases," such as enuresis, school failures, and speech disorders. The American Psychiatric Association's *Manual for Diagnostic Classification* (1951) listed only seven classifications for emotional disorders among children—aside from "mental deficiency." The latest revision of this manual (1979) has enlarged and detailed these categories, indicating in many instances that the category is "behavioral" or "social." As a result, health-insurance companies, which cover only "medical illness," have notified both clients and providers that they will not pay for treatment of these "behavioral" disorders.

Third, the symptoms that children manifest often seem relatively less stable than those suffered by adults. Although observers may agree that the child shows various signs of disturbance in general over a period of years, the symptoms often change. During one child's life, she/he may suffer a variety of "illnesses." For example, she/he may have "colic" as an infant*, subsequently be enuretic, and then demonstrate a school phobia on entering school. Later the same child may have an "alexia" when she/he tries to learn to read, and afterward may have a "behavioral problem," being a "delinquent" or "psychopath" as an adolescent. Although such series of symptoms are often interrelated and—as will be discussed throughout this book—consist of an accumulation of developmental difficulties, such a shifting set of symptoms makes it difficult to subscribe to the disease model.

Fourth, in applying the adult "disease model" to children's behavior problems, one of the greatest difficulties lies in differentiating between "normal" and "abnormal." For example, adult people who have difficulty in distinguishing reality from fantasy, who use neologisms, who are often quite illogical, who appear unaware of social amenities, who occasionally exhibit themselves sexually, and who are unable to perform any useful work would certainly be regarded as *abnormal* and *mentally ill* but it is questionable whether these terms are applicable if one is only 4 years old. The

*Contrary to popular notion, this layman term does not denote any particular physiological disorder but, instead, a generalized infantile reaction to stress and discomfort.

behavior of many normal 8-year-old children is decidedly "compulsive" at times, and much of the behavior of a normal adolescent might be described as "manic." Yet the repetitive behavior so characteristic of 8-year-olds and the rapid changes of mood and the impulsiveness of adolescence are "normal" for these respective age groups. The use of these terms from the disease model to describe such behavior creates an unnecessary and misleading pathological bias.

3. A Developmental Model

The basic fallacy of the disease model is that in using it there is a tendency to gloss over the constantly accumulating mass of evidence that these disturbances of childhood—and for the most part, also among adults—are learned social interactions rather than physiological disturbances. The disease model does not account for this learning process in a developing child.

Such a bias toward psychopathology is created when the problem is placed in the "normal"-versus-"abnormal" dichotomy. The problem to be assessed is more effectively and pertinently conceptualized by reformulating the question: *To what extent and in what ways is the child's development deterred?* This question focuses on development, and the child's difficulties are thus seen in the perspective of changes acccompanying his/her growth. In order to clarify what is meant by this developmental model, the next two sections of this chapter are devoted to a discussion of "the laws of growth" and "varieties of learning." One of the important reasons for adopting this developmental point of view in assessing children's behavior is that the purpose of assessment is to determine the possibilities of changing that behavior. The very fact that children's patterns of behavior are not yet completely determined usually increases the possibility of change. This possibility is made greater sincee growth often continues despite the barriers of stresses and impediments. In fact, at times the child's growth may be hastened or strengthened by stress, if it is not too overwhelming and if opportunities exist for surmounting impediments. In contrast, the alteration of adult patterns of behavior often involves changing long-established habit patterns—both the extinction of chronically reinforced attitudes and the learning of new methods—at a time of life when the individual normally does not accumulate new habits.

Admittedly in shifting from the disease model to an undisguised use of a psychological model based on development, it is not easy and perhaps not altogether necessary to discard the familiar terms associated with the old model. Some of these terms do describe definite psychological mechanisms, but the central point is the shift in conceptual framework. Perhaps the most noticeable change in terms is the use in this book of the term *assessment* itself. Assessment of development is not the same as *diagnosis,* which implies a pathology. Even the hybrid term *psychodiagnosis* is not appropriate, for it usually implies that a "psychopathology" is present. Both terms mainly are used to describe a disturbance in a mature organism, and they do not allow for the concept of growth. The term *assessment* is also broader than *testing* or *examination* or even *evaluation,* for it includes all of these. *Tests,* as will be seen, are only one form of data collection. *Examination* has the implication of being routine and of lacking the planned and thoughtful data-collection process of assessment. Assessment involves not only a planned, purposeful examination pertinent to the clinical question at hand, but also analysis of the data—an evaluation of results. However, the term *evaluation* does at times carry with it the sense of "social value judgment," which the scientist might consider inimical to objective analysis of data. As will be seen, the clinician often cannot avoid the consideration of social values, for these social

judgments usually play some role in the child's functioning. However, such value judgments form part of the data, not part of the analysis of it.

D.   A DEVELOPMENTAL HYPOTHESIS FOR ASSESSMENT

1.   The Nature of Growth

A child often seems to grow in spurts, to be far behind or to be advanced in comparison to her/his peers. She/he may never go through a certain "stage," or the child may continue with behavior that other children have long outgrown. A child may seem unaware of some fact or be quite incapable of a specific act one day and then—suddenly and almost miraculously—recognize that fact or perform that act. In assessing the individual child it is necessary of course to recognize what these variations mean. Are they random, chance events, or do they follow some recognized scientific laws? The term *random* implies that the order of nature is unknown, and the phrase *scientific law* merely means that an order in nature has been conceptualized on the basis of fact and logic. Assessment of the individual child has evolved from and been made possible by the scientific accumulation of facts about development, studies of the interrelationships between such facts, and finally, evolvement of higher-order constructs or "laws." Over the past century many facets of child development have been studied in detail, and a plethora of theories advanced—far more than can be covered in this section. In order to make the meaning of a developmental framework more explicit, it may suffice to review two familiar and well-accepted generalizations about development, especially because they set the guidelines for assessment.

The first principle is that the child's functioning develops from diffuse, gross, overall reactions to increasingly coordinated and finely differentiated functions.* This diffusion-to-differentiation principle is initially manifested in the child's perceptual-motor devlopment. Newborns, lying on their backs, flail both their arms and legs and arch their backs if stroked on their stomachs or in response to a sudden noise. They show no sign of focusing their eyes on objects, and it is often necessary to place the nipple in their mouths to feed them. Within a very few weeks, however, they make definite grasps at objects over their heads, follow moving objects with their eyes, and search actively for their mother's nipple when held to the breast. Within only a few more months infants—first supported in a sitting position, then able to sit on their own—make increasing strides in observing and reaching for their world. Scales for assessment of behavioral development during the first year of life are based on this differentiation of perceptual-motor functioning (Cattell, 1940; Gesell et al., 1940).

This principle is demonstrated in all subsequent functioning, locomotion, speech, toilet training, and learning of other socially imposed demands, pre-school interpersonal and group relationships, acquisition of formal training in intellectual and motor skills at school and on the playground, and later the adolescent's groping for social and sexual maturation. To cite only a few commonplace examples, children stand before they walk, intone sentences before they use words, are more likely to explore a nursery-school room, its objects, and inhabitants in seemingly aimless fashion be-

fore adopting specific play and companions. They can draw a circle before drawing a square and a square before a diamond (see the Stanford-Binet Intelligence Scale, age levels II, IV, and VII). On the Rorschach inkblots pre-school children respond chiefly to the whole blot, often ignoring or confusing even the main details, but by age 8 the children are much more cautious about making such overall generalizations and more aware of the irregularities in the form.

Even to the beginning student of child development, this diffusion-to-differentiation principle may seem so obvious as to require only passing mention. Unfortunately, this basic principle is too often ignored and violated by the authorities responsible for training the child—and sometimes it is forgotten even by the clinical psychologist. The classic example of course is toilet training. In the early decades of this century, soon after psychologists became acutely aware of the miracles of conditioning, they began to advise mothers that routine habits of defecation and urination not only could but should be instilled in the child at the earliest possible age. Since it is quite possible to establish such conditioned reflexes quite early, mothers began to boast that their babies could follow a toilet routine and control the relatively small muscles of the anal sphincter, even before the child had mastered control of the larger muscle systems needed to sit securely on a toilet. Also this social stress—one of the first major interchanges between the child and the social group (parents in this instance)—was imposed before the child learned the first major technique of interpersonal exchange: speech. Subsequently psychologists discovered that such premature conditioning of relatively complex behavior too often led to undesirable side effects, to overgeneralized attitudes about emotional control, and even to compulsive habits.

Before discussing and illustrating further the utilization in assessment of this whole-to-differentiation principle of development, it is necessary to consider a second overall

*To be precise, two growth processes may be distinguished: a whole-to-differentiation process, in which the child learns to separate out particular perceptions, thoughts, or feelings from very global or generalized impressions, and a diffuse-to-integrated process, in which the child learns to control reactions to such impressions more specifically and effectively. This distinction will be discussed in more detail in Section 4, using the terms *input* and *output*. However, since these processes constantly interact on one another and thus may be considered as a set of interactions, it is possible to discuss them as one in this introductory section.

pattern. The unfolding of behavior from wholes to parts does not proceed at an evenly regulated pace, and to comprehend and use it the rates of growth must be taken into account. The age at which children develop certain specific skills in motor activity, in intellectual tasks, and in emotional and social controls has been a frequent subject of study in the field of child development. A knowledge of these research studies is essential in the interpretations of data from an individual child. These studies of growth rates of specific skills are seldom interrelated, however, except in major longitudinal studies. The fact that the differentiation process of each skill does have unique features makes any generalization hazardous. To provide a schematic background for the subsequent consideration of specific assessment of the different functions of the ego, it may be helpful to disregard these differences for the moment and to posit a single hypothetical developmental curve.

The generalization that applies to most growth curves may be summed up as an "accumulation–integration" process, or more precisely, as "accelerated accumulation–crisis integration." As is shown in many studies of learning of various kinds, children usually accumulate many basic aspects of a skill at an increasingly accelerated rate, but not at all evenly, to a point where they seem to cease to learn further. Then during the so-called "plateau" of the learning curve, it has been observed that children go over, repeatedly practicing, or to use a term from psychoanalytic therapy, *work through,* and integrate what they have learned, polishing the skill and eliminating conflicting habits and attitudes before rising to new heights on the learning curve and perfecting the skill.

By combining these two "laws" of development, it is thus possible to project some order in the constantly changing life of the child. This combination is illustrated in diagrammatic form by the hypothetical curve of the rate of development of the ego shown in Figure 1.1. During the first six years of life, infants* develop extremely rapidly, accumulating a variety of ego functions and subfunctions or details. They acquire in this brief period most of the major tools and techniques of ego functioning. They develop the major part of their muscular controls, begin to think logically, assimilate the basic mores of the culture, and pass through the most important formative stages of "psychosexual" development. At no other time in life will the child learn so much and so rapidly. The variability of this rate of ego development is also more extreme than at any other point in the child's life. Almost no pre-school child seems to develop at a steady rate, and the differences between children during these years are often extreme. Nor do all the ego functions develop evenly. A child may be quite advanced in language development but be slow in motor proficiencies, or he/she may be quick to develop controls over affect but remain socially overdependent. Data from all longitudinal studies confirm this variability. It is for this reason that predictions from infant behavior to later childhood or adolescence have little validity—no matter how refined the measurements. Admittedly this very generalized curve does not indicate the variations within these three stages, such as the rapid spurts of growth between ages 4 and 6.

Somewhere around age 6 the overall rate of children's development becomes less precipitous, and while it does not actually form a flat plateau, the curve is not as steep. Also during this central period of childhood, the variability both between children and within the individual child is less extreme. At this time children develop more evenly, in not quite so many leaps and bounds. The reason is that they are no longer accumulating as many new functions. Although latency children learn some

---

*In the ensuing discussion, the term *infant* is used more broadly than is common in developmental psychology, and it includes all the pre-school years as distinct from the central period of childhood or "latency," ages 6–12.

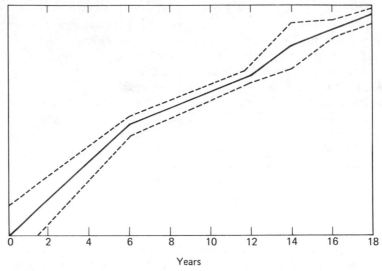

Years

Figure 1.1 Normal (hypothetical) curve of the growth of the ego. Dotted lines show variability.

new skills at school, they do not develop new basic functions. Instead, they integrate, practice, and refine the previously learned functions.

With the onset of puberty the curve of development again rises sharply, at least for a brief period, while children struggle to develop methods to cope with new physiological stresses and to learn new social behaviors in order to meet the demands for achieving the final steps into adulthood. Again the variability in the rate of development is obvious even to the casual observer. Adolescents are precociously adult one moment and infantile the next. Asked the age of her son, one mother replied quite accurately, "He's 10 going on 20!" The data available on late adolescence suggest that as the child enters into young adulthood, the curve again slacks off, and the variability in development is again less extreme. The pace of development still varies considerably, however, in the last years of high school and the early years of college or young-adult life. These last steps of adolescence are also usually integrative.

These shifts from one stage of development to another are critical periods in children's lives during which they change social milieus as well as their place of de-

velopment. On entering school they not only begin a regime of practiced learning, but also they take the first steps toward breaking family ties and loosening the heretofore relatively complete dependency on parents. The anxieties arising from such separation need to be allayed and resolved before children can proceed to the status of schoolchild. Moreover, such separation anxiety is repeated at pubescence, as the adolescent struggles for independence and for identification with his/her peer group. The final, critical period of shift and separation takes place when the adolescent leaves the parental nest altogether and becomes a young adult.

The main reason for restating these principles of development is to emphasize the fact that change and crisis are a normal and necessary part of childhood. This is not to say that extremes of behavior—of stultifying tension or of utter lack of control, often analogous to adult emotional and social disturbances—are not signs of emotional and social disturbances in childhood. Such extremes cannot be dismissed as "something the child will outgrow" (Work and Call, 1965). The chief signs of "abnormality" in childhood are the absence of growth, the failure to change, and the retreats from the critical shifts from one stage of childhood to the next. *Unmanageable stress during childhood results chiefly in disruptions of the growth process.*

Psychological assessment of a child thus begins with assessment of the nature and rate of development, and it proceeds to an investigation of possible factors that may be deterring (or overaccelerating) growth. The principal biological and cultural factors that delimit growth will be discussed subsequently in this chapter. However, *psychological* assessment is not concerned primarily with the biological or social environments per se but rather *with the learning processes* of the human organism in a defined culture. Thus, before examining the factors affecting growth and learning, it may be helpful to consider briefly the relationships between assessment and the theories of learning.

2.   Assessment and Learning

In assessment of children a knowledge of the facts and theories of human learning processes is essential. The plural *theories* needs to be emphasized because no single learning theory has been promulgated that is complete and comprehensive enough to cover the complexities of the developing life pattern of an individual child. In assessment one needs to be aware that—as Tolman (1952) in his classic paper has pointed out—there are "many kinds of learning." Learning during infancy, for example, consists largely of simple conditioning, of repetitive stamping in and stamping out of response patterns. The accumulation of habit patterns of varying strengths arising from a complexity of drives occurs throughout childhood. Yet learning through one single traumatic conditioning is so often reported in emotional disturbances that the clinician often looks for such an incident. Such a single vivid experience may be generalized to other experiences, or it may be a culminating event, triggering other behavior.

The question of how a child has learned is thus essential to every assessment. Most if not all of our assessment tools deal with learned behavior almost exclusively. The behavior they sample is learned, even if the intent is to make inferences from such learned behavior about "native potential," "inherited traits," or "brain damage." For example, an IQ test consists of graded series of learned achievements from which the assessor may attempt inferences about the learning potential of the child. Similarly, responses to projective techniques consist of attempts to fit learned responses to unstructured stimuli. Much of case-history taking is also aimed at the question of *how* a child has learned and adapted.

Nevertheless, learning theories derived from comparative research often seem to be unrelated to the task of assessment. The gap between learning theory and clinical assessment is to a great measure an artifact, resulting from a failure in the training of clinical psychologists. However, it is also true that the term *learning theory* and the research studies on learning have traditionally focused on only one question about learning—and that is *how* the child learns. The assessing clinician must be concerned however, with several other equally important questions dealing with learning. Thinking in developmental terms, the clinician also needs to know "when" the child learns, because "when" in the developmental sequence may be a more important question than "how." "When" may also be thought of as "under what circumstances," that is, "when" in a sequence of the child's experience. "Why" the child is learning is only vaguely included in traditional learning theory (which is still grappling theoretically with the problems of motivation), but in clinical assessment the drives, motivations, avoidances, rewards, and the like need to be spelled out. Often these motivations are central to the child's rehabilitation. The question of "what" is learned is considered to be of little or no import in traditional learning theory. Yet the content of learning is central to the study of human behavior. Parents, school authorities, and society at large are upset by the "bad" habit the child has learned or the "good" habit he/she has failed to learn. And although they may ask "However did my child learn that!" they do not really care about the method by which the child learns or even how something becomes unlearned. Moreover, traditional learning theory does not differentiate between learning varius types of tasks. For example, there may well be a difference between learning to handle such behaviors as sexual excitement, excessive vomiting, or fire setting, or what is more important— the learning of more socially and personally acceptable patterns. Perhaps the extinguishing of fire setting (whatever the motivation) does involve the same learning processes as the control of vomiting—but this is not known.

Central to the clinical inquiry and yet also relatively ignored by the traditional learning theorist is the question of "who" is learning. Interested almost solely in the general problem of learning processes per se, the comparative psychologist has not been concerned with individual differences in learning. Yet there is considerable evidence from educational as well as clinical psychology that individuals differ widely, not only in overall learning ability, but in their ability to utilize various learning processes. Some children and adults condition more easily than others; some generalize quickly; others not at all. What is more important is the fact that new learning by the child does not take place on an empty slate. Each task, habit, or attitude is learned by a child who already has an accumulation of other learned tasks, habits, and attitudes—to say nothing of unsatisfied drives and frustrations or conflicting emotional investments. It might be difficult, for example, to teach a starving child to use a fork!

An equally important corollary of this question of "who" is learning is the question "from whom" is the child learning? Psychologists—especially clinical and social psychologists—are becoming aware in-creasingly that learning does not take place completely inside the child. Rather, most learned behavior occurs in a social setting as part of a social interaction. In most instances some adult or peer acts as teacher to the child, and how well the child learns is dependent in part on her/his relationship to this instructor or group of instructors. Very often the motivating force is the child's dependency—both physical and emotional—upon the adult or the approval of and status in his/her peer group. Even the natural curiosity of children needs to be stimulated or at least encouraged by adult authority. Nor does the relationship necessarily have to be "positive." Children learn from those they fear or dislike or are rebelling against, although the question of "what" they learn in such relationships again arises. Thus some children learn how *not to learn* at school, to spite their ambitious parents. A close examination of how some children avoid learning is often quite revealing, for it takes an active effort on the child's part to avoid paying attention to the teacher and the class.

E.   BIOLOGICAL DETERMINANTS OF BEHAVIOR

It is widely accepted that the outer limits of learned behavior are set by the child's physiological structure, which itself is limited by genetic factors, congenital events during the fetal period, and the forces of physiological maturation that proceed through adolescence. Equally recognized is the fact that within these limits there is a great deal of variability of behavior—the result of an interaction of sociocultural stress—and of accumulated, individual experience upon this physiological organism. It would be presumptuous, however, to assume that these determinants play an equal or even proportionate role in every child's life pattern. Thus it may be helpful to consider the relevancy to the task of assessment of each of these determinants of development.

1. The Relation of Genetic Determinants of Development to Assessment

At the beginning of scientific psychology when the first systematic studies of behavior were being conducted, the scientific world of the nineteenth century was in a philosophic ferment over the discovery of the evolution of the species. It is noteworthy that Darwin was also interested in the development of behavior in the human species and that he included his observations of childhood development in his theory of evolution. The new science of psychology was further influenced at the turn of the century by the advent of the Mendelian theory of genetic transmission of physiological traits. Thus it was natural that the concept of inherited psychological traits appeared to be promising, even though this concept was based chiefly on speculation or on very simple and indefensible research. This concept—as a major explanation of human behavior—was even more acceptable, since until the early part of the twentieth century no other major theories had been conceived. As Freud began developing his psychoanalytic theory, he also accepted the general concept of inherited traits or "instincts." The new concept of learned behavior, beginning in Pavlov's laboratories and spreading to the United States after World War I, became the major alternative, and from the contrasts between these two theories came the many "nature–nurture" studies of the subsequent decades. Despite this increased understanding of the role played by postnatal learning in development, the interest in and acceptance of the concept of inherited behavioral traits has never completely waned. It has indeed received new research impetus over the past decade (Jackson, 1964).

At one time the genetic inheritance of traits was the major consideration in clinical assessment of children. When a "mental disorder," particularly all mental retardation (or "feeble-mindedness" as it was then known), was thought to be inherited, the only answer was preventive—sterilization. At one California hospital alone nearly all retarded patients were sterilized between 1920 and 1950. As psychologists began to recognize the multiple causes of behavior, including intellectual retardation and the possibilities of other therapies and rehabilitation measures, the use of sterilization became quite restricted. Today most psychologists agree that the genetic inheritance of physiological structure is only one of the many complexities determining behavior and child development. The nineteenth-century rule *structure determines functioning* has been modified to be *structure interacts with stress to determine functioning*. Also with the intensely increased mobility of the world population, the pockets of generations of inbred isolates are fast disappearing. Liverant (1960) in an incisive and critical review of genetic factors in intellectual development pointed out that geneticists are far more skeptical of the inheritance of such complex behavior than are some psychologists!

Inheritance of traits rarely becomes a major variable in assessment today. While most psychologists might be tempted to regard the extremes of behavior—especially in intellectual functioning—as possibly genetic, they are cautious about the logical error of arguing that whenever other determinants cannot be established, a trait is therefore deemed inherited. Instead, objective data are required before any conclusion can be drawn, and when the data are sparse or unreliable, then the psychologist can only report that no conclusion is supported. One main reason that clinical psychologists are slow to attribute behavioral disturbances—even in infants—to inherited traits is that there are no exact methods for assessing this factor. Most of our psychological tests are basically measures of learned achievements or reactions. Observers of infants during their first few months of life often do note obvious signs of nascent emotional and intellectual behaviors that are remarkably similar to the more fully developed traits in their parents. Even so, it is difficult to attribute even this behavior entirely to inheritance. The possibility both of conditioning during these first days of life and of congenital influences needs to be considered.

2. The Relationships of Congenital Determinants of Development to Assessment

Dating from antiquity, the idea has persisted in many cultures that events impinging on a pregnant woman could mark her child for life. Pregnant women were protected from scenes of violence; sexual intercourse during pregnancy is still frequently tabooed; touching or wearing certain talismans or repeating specific incantations was encouraged; and special diets and regimes of exercise were prescribed— all intended to affect the future character as well as the health of the child. Although such taboos are often unfounded superstitions, scientific evidence has been accumulated gradually concerning the effects of both biological and psychological stress on fetal development. For example, the effects on the child of certain diseases such as measles suffered by the pregnant mother are known, and the deleterious effects of various toxins have been established. In addition, several studies have shown that anxieties or stress endured by the mother may affect her pregnancy. Zemlich and Watson (1953), for example, discovered that those primipara women who had strong feelings of rejection toward the unborn child suffered excessive and continued bleeding, nausea, and the like more often than did mothers who accepted the pregnancy. The occurrence of miscarriages during emotional stress is commonly noted by both physicians and laymen. Yet there is little research on the possible effects of the mother's emotional condition during pregnancy on the subsequent development of her child, and this aspect of the congenital determinant of development remains speculative.

The defects in development usually attributed to congenital stress appear to be primarily physiological and secondarily psychological. Most important to psychological functioning are those traumata during fetal development that affect either the sensorimotor system or the central nervous system. Similar traumata may occur from injuries at birth when the anxieties and tensions of the mother may also result in somatic accidents that seriously affect the child. In contrast to genetically determined physiological defects, these congenital deterrents to future development are both more definable and more within the realm of possible prevention. With more research on the relationship between maternal tensions and the course of pregnancy and gestation, assessment and treatment of the anxious pregnant mother may become more possible and more frequent.

As with hereditary factors, the most important aspects of congenital determinants to assessment are the personal emotional attitudes held by children and parents. Adjusting to and overcoming handicaps that begin before or at birth are often difficult for both the disabled child and his/her family. Although few such families are entirely free from some feelings of continued fear, resentment, and guilt, the children who are referred to psychological assessment are only a small minority of the handicapped. Very probably there are at least an equal number who are not so overwhelmed by their emotional attitudes as to need psychological attention. A few years ago I participated in a nationwide survey of congenitally brain-damaged children who had lived continuously at home and attended daycare educational and rehabilitation centers (Cain and Levine, 1961). A large majority of these children and their parents showed no marked emotional disturbances, even though many of the children were severely handicapped. On the other hand, there are many congenitally damaged children in clinics and hospitals who are the objects of an overanxious, ambivalent concern by their parents and who do develop emotional disturbances. Often this results in or is demonstrated in more disability than can be accounted for physiologically, as can be illustrated by the following two cases.

CASE 1

Mandie, age 7, was born six weeks prematurely. Both of her knee sockets, her hip sockets, and the roof of her mouth had failed to develop completely, and she suffered double hernias. During the first four years of her life, she endured six major operations, and half of her body was almost continuously encased in a cast. The usual motoric exploration of her environment had been denied her. Her speech then consisted of hollow grunts, intelligible only to her mother, although Mandie responded to speech with rapt attention and often with appropriate reactions. Repair of her palate was the final surgical correction. Thereafter, with intensive rehabilitation work and speech therapy both at the hospital and at home, she made rapid progress. By age 7 she could walk without crutches, albeit with an unsteady balance and a halting gait, and her speech—hollow and slow—was understandable to everyone. Her responses on IQ tests indicated above-average to superior intelligence. Placement in a regular first-grade class at public school was recommended. Mandie and her mother seemed overjoyed, and they celebrated by a shopping spree in which they purchased matching mother–daughter outfits.

Scarcely six months later Mandie was referred again for psychological study. Her achievement at school was far below what had been expected. Previously a bubbling, happy, and compliant child, she had become listless, irritable, and inattentive. Frequently she was absent from school with brief, minor, undiagnosed complaints. Although completely toilet trained soon after her body casts were removed, she had had a series of daytime soiling "accidents," which were the final reason for suspending her from school.

Mandie's mother, Mrs. B, appeared sorely disappointed and wept as she sought some explanation for this turn of events.

"I've tried my best, done everything, spent every minute and every cent just for her. She's been my whole life these past seven years." She explained that her husband had deserted her shortly before Mandie's birth, leaving her almost destitute and alone. "It was horrible—I almost went out of my mind." In a subsequent interview, she confessed that she had known her husband only briefly, that Mandie was conceived before their marriage, which she now believed he had entered into only because of his guilt over the pregnancy. The pregnancy and marriage had been angrily disapproved of by her parents, and she had rebelled and left home at age 17. Over the past seven years she had been able to work only at odd hours, since Mandie had to be taken to the clinic almost daily, and only because she had some personal funds—"my savings for my college education"—was she able to support herself and Mandie. "When Mandie started school," she said, "I'd hoped I could get a better job or even go back to school myself." However, she did not immediately seek full-time employment because "I didn't know whether Mandie might still need me at home." Gradually her fears were more than realized, when Mandie complained of weakness and seemed disinterested in school.

Mandie claimed to want to go to school but was not as disappointed as her mother. She recited her physical complaints and even complained about her disability. Although she had never actually complained about school, she averred that the work was "too hard." (The speech drills in prior years had been much more intensive and tiring than public-school classes.) Finally she launched into a tirade against another disabled classmate—a girl she considered to be the teacher's favorite. Mandie's responses to the projective tests were full of anger, frustration and depression. Her fantasies indicated considerable ambivalence toward maternal figures, who were portrayed as evil witches who made constant bizarre demands on their victims and held them captive by unknown magic, only to be released by the "good fairy." Or, in her most elaborate tale, "a handsome prince appeared from the sky to claim the heroine as his daughter."

CASE 2

Willis, age 12, had been blind from birth because of a "retrolineal fibroplasia," the result of overuse of oxygen at his birth.* Both of his grandfathers were physicians; one was the director of the hospital where he was born. From the time of his birth his mother—a professor of education—abandoned her career and "sacrificed" her life to seeking care for Willis. With constantly conflicting counsel from the grandfathers, she brought Willis to the attention of most of the major medical and educational centers for the blind in the United States and Europe, but she was never satisfied. Willis never remained in any school longer than six months. He was a major "behavior problem," excessively demanding, destructive, restless, and inattentive. His father, an outstanding professional tennis star ("a tennis bum," his wife called him—in front of Willis), remained uninvolved in his wife's desperate search for an answer to Willis' disability. When Willis was 6, his parents divorced, and Willis' father obtained custody of his two older daughters. Willis then became his mother's sole companion.

At age 12 Willis was blatantly psychotic. He chattered away in almost meaningless sentences, rocking back and forth in the chair. Reports from various schools for the blind and private tutors indicated that at one time he appeared to have superior intelligence, was curious about everything, was eager to learn, and was rapidly becoming proficient at reading Braille. Willis now could not respond to tests, and he scarcely could be drawn away from his personal world of fantasy into even momentary conversation. His confused outpouring of

words suggested an admixture of overwhelming depression, loneliness, and despairing rage, uttered in a high-pitched, flat singsong.

His mother—a tense, tight-lipped woman—recited Willis' history in a monotone, with precise details of dates, places, and names in chronological order. She was well aware of Willis' present condition, citing the psychiatric diagnosis. She reported that Willis had received "extensive psychiatric care," mentioning the names of several well-known psychoanalysts, but it was evident that he had never remained in treatment for more than three months. When she was asked about her present situation her composure faded, and she began to weep. During the past year she and Willis had floated from one hotel to another across the world until she had run out of money. She had exhausted a large fortune and was now penniless and in debt. She could find no employment in her profession, and there was no one to care for Willis if she did take a job. She was entirely separated from all friends and family. Also, she felt she was in danger of becoming an alcoholic, since drinking was the only answer she had found for her own depression. She knew that Willis probably should be hospitalized, but she could not bear to part from him. Twice in the past month she had made plans to kill him and herself. With some encouragement from the psychologist, she accepted arrangements to admit both Willis and herself to a public mental hospital. Four months later she was able to leave the hospital, although Willis remained there—unimproved. She obtained a sales job, supporting herself, and returned to the clinic for an extended period of psychotherapy.

In both of these cases the intense compensatory "sacrifice" of the mother overshadowed and determined the course of the child's congenital disability and consequent development. Only drastic intervention kept Willis and his mother from complete tragedy, and Willis had become more disabled psychologically than physically.

---

*This iatrogenic disorder has now been eradicated as a result of the discovery of the effect of this practice.

Mandie and her mother needed only a brief period of counseling before Mandie could continue on the spectacular course of development she had manifested since age 4.

Admittedly these two cases are gross deviations from the usual course of development of children with congenital handicaps. Yet far too often, similar parental emotional reactions and interrelationships with the child interfere with the most expert rehabilitation and educational efforts. The import of the disability can only be assessed in the perspective of all other life factors (see Chapters 16 and 17).

3. The Relevance of Physiological Maturation to Psychological Assessment

Although genetics and congenital events set the limits on the physiological environment of children, the most important biological factor relevant to their psychological assessment is the continued, progressive maturation of their physiological structure and its functioning. The study of the relationships between this physiological maturation and the development of psychological functions has long been a major scientific interest and effort—especially in developmental psychology. Although it is not possible to review this research in this volume, knowledge of these studies is very important to the clinical psychologist, for it is from a familiarity with this research that the psychologist is able to relate the biological and psychological growth of the individual child. There are, however, several general conclusions from this body of research that need to be mentioned.

First, although the relationship between biological and psychological development is far from a perfect correlation, the overall trend is quite similar in both, as is illustrated in Figure 1.1. Second, these general parallels between biological and psychological growth suggest the possibility of an underlying general "growth" or maturational factor. However such a growth factor may be conceptualized, there can be little doubt that the main phenomenon distinguishing childhood from adult maturity is this fact of a continually growing and developing organism. Third—with some rare exceptions—this biological development proceeds without interruption and in relatively regular order. Even though a child may not mature psychologically, his/her biological development is not halted. Thus although a child may remain intellectually or emotionally retarded, he/she nevertheless develops physiologically into an adult. This fact is sometimes ignored, especially in the assessment of retarded children. One of the conflicts for any adolescent is that she/he has to deal with biological maturity. This conflict can be particularly acute for the emotionally immature or intellectually retarded child.

Although lags or accelerations in biological development may not be as devastating and disabling as some of the traumata occurring during the fetal stage or at gestation, such variations in postnatal biological development are much more common and probably have much more effect on psychological development than is commonly recognized in clinical assessment. For example, children who are slowly developing biologically may not be capable of performing the skills expected of them by their environment. As will be discussed, these skills include motor functions, perceptual and intellectual functioning, and affective control and expression as well. Similarly, children whose physiological maturation is accelerated may find themselves forced to handle biological stress that they are as yet psychologically unprepared to handle.

F. SOCIAL DETERMINANTS

Children's sociocultural "inheritance," like their physiological genetic "inheritance," has its beginnings many generations before birth. Whole sets of predetermined attitudes and expectations await children at birth, and they may even determine whether they will be born at all! For example, if a child is conceived out of wedlock, abortion may be considered or attempted (even though abortion may also be taboo), since the guilt surrounding illicit, premarital sexual relationships is often intense. In addition, even if the parents are subsequently married, they often continue to feel guilty and resentful toward the child who forced them into a marriage they felt unprepared to accept. Frequently in such instances, the grudge against the child is increased by secretly blaming all further marital dissension on him/her, thus creating a scapegoat who consequently becomes emotionally disturbed. Such a pattern of attitudes is wholly culturally determined. In contrast, among some preliterate tribes, conception of a child is taken as evidence that the putative father is ready for marriage, and the pregnancy of the unmarried girl is celebrated! And even in Western culture it must be admitted that the marriage ceremony does not necessarily imbue a couple with realistic parental attitudes.

Similar but less intensely tabooed attitudes also exist regarding such factors as the racial and religious backgrounds of the parents, their ages (case histories often casually mention that the mother was "too young" or "into middle age," as if there were only certain age limits within which a woman could be an effective mother), or the number of children that is supposed to constitute a family of proper size. That a child should come from parents of similar cultural backgrounds, have been conceived after a respectable period of marriage, be born when the mother is neither too young nor too old, and be a member of a sib-ship that is neither too small nor too large—all are too often accepted as "facts" rather than as cultural norms. Seldom is recognition given to the possibility that variations from these norms may have advantages as well as create problems, or that the child whose birth meets these norms may have a restricted view of society. While these events are often important hallmarks, in the socialization of the child—which the psychologist should investigate and assess—the psychologist should also be able

to recognize them as *variations on culturally determined values*.

During the first five to six years of life an intense socialization process is conducted by the family, which is abetted by other social institutions such as nursery schools. During this period children learn the cultural values regarding food and elimination of bodily wastes; they learn a vocabulary and grammar and most of its implications; they learn social values regarding expression of anger, aggression, ambition, pleasure, and pain, and most other emotions. They learn about the roles assigned to the sexes and also to many social groups. There is considerable evidence that at least the fact of racial prejudice, if not all of its implications, is well known by most 5-year-olds of both dominant and minority groups (Trager and Yarrow, 1952).

In modern cultures, both in the United States and the USSR, reading, writing, and arithmetic are taught because they are essential to production in highly technical and competitive societies. Later the sciences are emphasized for the same reason. Learning for the sake of learning or taking science to satisfy curiosity are values of a past era—even though there is now the leisure time for such pleasures. "Dawdling" curiosity is seldom encouraged. Appreciation of the arts or artistic creativity are considered educational "trimmings," so that even when a child shows potential talent, he/she is rarely encouraged to do more than develop art as a hobby. Art of any kind is so seldom seen as a possible career that it is a wonder there are either inspired painters or good jazz saxophonists. The effects of some of these cultural values on education are of course recognized by many educational leaders, and experimental schools—such as the Montessori system—are being designed to fit children's education to their particular needs, but these attempts remain experimental and limited in scope.

The assessing psychologist must therefore constantly take into account these values in education. When children fail to learn to read but have "high IQ's," the psychologist must consider not only such factors as neurological weakness, the educational method being used, or an unconscious rebellion against parental and societal values, but also the possibility that children's intellects may be invested elsewhere and that reading per se has a secondary value to them. It is debatable whether physicists, sculptors, oil drillers, and accountants necessarily should have the verbal competency needed by political scientists, advertising men, secretaries, and clinical psychologists. It should be noted too that many intelligence tests reflect cultural values by sampling verbal skills primarily or at least requiring verbalized responses. In assessing the child's potential for creativity, the psychologist can use "IQ" as only one item of his/her data.

The complexity of the modern world and the consequent extended demands of culture on the child for socialization create many stresses on development. Although most students of clinical psychology appear to have at least a passing acquaintance with these cultural stresses, the import of cultural factors to the assessment of development is often unclear. Since all children in the same culture face similar stresses, it might seem possible to disregard cultural determinants and focus instead on the variations of individual perceptions and experience entirely. Perhaps if one were to assess children in an isolated and stable society, social stress as a determinant of development might be relatively ignored. The anthropologists of a generation ago (Kardiner, 1939; Linton, 1945), who demonstrated how culture determined personality, were comparing relatively closed societies. Even class and caste as determinants of personal identity appear to be gradually breaking down under the pressure of the "outer-directed" open-ended society of today (Reisman et al., 1950).

Both social scientists and the general public agree that American society provides the child today with fewer and fewer well-established societal identifications. The extended family—the clan or "kith and kin" with its name and membership and implications of support and guidance—has almost disappeared in the United States. One can no longer depend on "relatives." The presence of an aunt, uncle, cousin, or even a grandparent residing in the home has a far different meaning to the child today than it did a generation or so ago. In addition, with the rising divorce rate there are an increasing number of children who are growing up with shifting and multiple parents. Even the larger social "units" are less definite, and there is at least a promise that being born black in the United States will lose some of its caste limitations within this generation, and consequently so will being born white. Similarly, class identifications such as rich and poor seem to be amalgamating into one middle class—both in the United States and in the USSR—thus forming a classless society quite different from that dreamed of by Karl Marx. Sociologists and psychologists now write of the individual's search for identity in a society that no longer offers definite social-unit boundaries for individual identification.

The result of the reductions of threats to life has been not only to lessen fear but to promote growth. Not only are fewer children damaged during pregnancy and childbirth but babies are both larger and more vigorous than ever before, and they grow faster and larger. They are better fed, and their bodies, unhampered by the necessity for combatting disease, are fitted for increased activity instead. As a result, the "body image" is changing. In a sexist society being small is more than ever a "trauma" to a boy, and being large is threatening to girls. In addition, the psychologist's standards of perceptual and motor acuity may need continued revision. The chances of death during adulthood have also lessened, and children have the promise of a much longer life span. As a consequence, it has been possible to extend adolescence a bit longer. A young girl can delay marriage if she is assured there is less chance she will die in childbirth.

The foremost cataclysmic threat to life

today is that of nuclear war and extermination. Both scientific and lay authorities are of the opinion that this threat has contributed to a "let's-have-fun—tomorrow-we-may-die" attitude among many adolescents, which is less overt in the adult population whose unspoken feelings young people mirror. Violence and destruction remain a popular theme in public legend and private fantasy. "An A-bomb going off" has become almost a "popular" response to several Rorschach inkblots. Yet while this nightmare of nuclear holocaust hangs over the world, the possibility of the elimination of war has never been considered so publicly, and it has never been so close to realization. Children learn both the imminence of global destruction *and* the hope of lasting peace.

The reduction of these life threats has permitted an increasing focus on psychological and social stresses. In less technically developed societies the "neuroses" of modern society are considerably less obvious—at least to a Westerner "Mental illness" (psychological dysfunctioning) in Western cultures has been declared today's major "health" problem by all authorities. The referral of a child for psychological assessment, once considered by parents as an insult to their integrity and a matter of shame, no longer carries quite as much opprobrium. An increasing number of adults and children possess considerable information about psychological functioning and are "psychologically minded"—a factor that is changing the atmosphere in which assessment takes place.

Another effect of the scientific and technological advances of the present era on the psychological development of children has been the intense impetus to intellectual growth. The scientific complexity of modern civilization places a high value on intellectual achievement and a demand for intensified and prolonged education of the child. Very likely within a decade children will face not only the demand already present for a greater number of school years, but also of more weeks per year and hours

per week to keep up with the increased amount of knowledge required of them. Children are complaining as never before about homework and the lack of time to play. Parents and schools are consequently much more concerned with children's academic achievement and learning ability. "Slow in school" is by far the most common and desperate complaint made about children.

There is also some evidence that the overall level of intelligence is increasing, at least for such intellectual activities as information gathering, social comprehension, speed of learning, and perhaps even the ability to think abstractly (Palmer, 1964). No doubt television and the other mass media greatly add to children's information as well as to their fantasies. As a result the standardization of IQ tests grows more rapidly out of date. The Stanford-Binet, revised three times since its origin in 1917, still contains such anachronisms as a thimble and a picture of a man sawing wood! Schools are often puzzled to find that the mean IQ of their pupils is 10 to 15 points above the average on tests standardized only a decade ago.

A second major social change affecting the psychological development of children is the rapid growth of the world's population. As a result, children today grow up in a much more crowded world. Their homes are likely to be somewhat smaller and less private than in the prior generation, at least among the middle class. Children's schools are much larger, but are nevertheless more crowded—as are their playgrounds. Open places to play are vanishing in many urban and suburban areas, and the automobile has almost pushed the bicycle off the streets. In crowded apartment houses and suburban housing developments children's needs for physical activity and noise making are often repressed, if not diverted. Similarly, in a crowded classroom a child may have to learn to be quiet and to study while other children receive the teacher's attention. This is true even though as a healthier child his/her energy and activity levels may be greater than those of other students. She/he has to learn to "get along with other children" as never before, because there are fewer places for privacy and isolation and more children to "get along with." The pressure for conformity both to adult and peer standards remains intense, even though these standards are relatively less rigid and more evanescent. As with the technological stresses, the population increase focuses the attention of the child and her/his caretakers on problems of human interrelationships as never before. The self-contained "introverted" child—no matter how contented she/he may be—is often considered "maladjusted" by teachers or even by parents, while the outgoing "extrovert" may be forgiven his/her transgressions, even if he/she is under considerable tension.

A third major social pressure on children is the mobility of the society. Not only do children live in a highly technical and overcrowded world, but also they and the people about them are frequently on the move. They are likely to change residences within a city several times and to move from one city to another at least once during childhood. In these moves they must "adjust" to new neighborhoods, new playmates, and new schools, and their parents and sibs are meeting similar changes. Nor is this mobility restricted to one socioeconomic level. Even in census tracts in large cities containing privately owned, single-family dwellings, ownership has been discovered to change at least once in five years in 50% of the properties. Under these circumstances, neither neighborhoods, schools, nor peer groups can offer stable values with which the child can identify. Family life may also be interrupted; as the father moves from job to job, he may not always be able to take his family with him. Personal belongings—toys, dolls, pets—which are all so important to the child, may disappear as the family moves.

In prior generations and cultures the individual's identity was established by the mores of a relatively small and stable group from which the individual rarely moved. A child's "neurosis" consisted of a conflict between these social values and the satisfaction of her/his own needs. The child today floats in an ever-changing "lonely crowd" (Reisman et al., 1950), with which she/he may have only passing contact or conflict, but which offers little personal emotional support or contributes to a sense of "belonging." The child's struggle thus is less likely to be *against* society, but to be *for* recognition. Often children seem to be "rebels without a cause" (Lindner, 1944). Children's acts appear as meaningless, unwarranted "bids for attention," whether in adolescent delinquency or in infant asthma.

The following two cases may serve to illustrate some of these social stresses. Note that, although these two adolescents come from altogether different backgrounds, the social pressures are quite similar.

CASE 3

Jimmy B, a 15-year-old black youth, was brought in for psychological assessment from juvenile court, where he was awaiting trial for assault and battery on a policeman during a civil-rights demonstration. His act of violence had been in contradiction to the "nonviolence" discipline of the demonstrators, and they had not requested that he be released on bail. Moreover, he was well known to police and school authorities both because of his previously aggressive behavior toward authority and because until recently he had been one of the "most promising" students in his school. School records showed Jimmy's scores on achievement tests to be two to three years above grade placement, and his IQ was 134. (The average at his high school was below 100.) Yet during the past year he had done little schoolwork either in class or at home, and at the time of his arrest he had not attended school for several weeks and was facing failure in all subjects. Once a star athlete, he had been dropped from all sports activities because of poor attendance at both practice and competition games and because of his inadequate academic record. Quick-tempered, he was often the center of altercations on the school grounds, and he usually reacted to school authorities either with sullen silence or a sneering retort. He was not known to be a member of any school clique or neighborhood gang, although a majority of his classmates had such affiliations, but he appeared to be a "lone wolf" with no close friends of either sex.

Jimmy was born in a black ghetto in Chicago, shortly before his mother's sixteenth birthday. She had left her rural Mississippi home the previous year but had found no permanent employment. She was unmarried, and Jimmy knew nothing of his putative father, other than that he was allegedly white. City welfare funds and several "boyfriends" were their only sources of income for almost three years until Mrs. B's first marriage. The first permanent father owned a coffee shop in a small "downstate" city where Jimmy lived for the next three years. His mother, now 19, tired of working as a waitress and restless in the doldrums of the smaller city, left her husband and—taking Jimmy— joined her parents who had moved to Detroit. From age 6 to 8, Jimmy was cared for by his grandmother, who had six children of her own—all younger than his mother. Jimmy remembered this period as a "happy" time with "regular meals and a regular family." He had used his mother's maiden name as his family name and so identified himself with his grandparents, even to calling them "Mom" and "Dad" in imitation of his mother, whom he addressed by her first name. Jimmy had attended school two years when his mother married again. He hated his new father for taking him from his grandparents' home and moving him to a new school. In turn, the new father felt rebuffed in his friendly overtures to his new son, and he was often unnecessarily harsh in his discipline. During the next four years, the family lived in many different small apartments, and Jimmy changed schools twice more. Jimmy also "hated" his sister, who was born when Jim was 9.

After four very unhappy years Jimmy's mother returned again to her parents, who were now in Los Angeles. However, the grandparents' home no longer proved to be what Jim had hoped. With three of their own children, in addition to Jimmy, his sister, and mother, they were crowded into the two-bedrom flat of a housing development. All of the adults worked, usually at different hours and although there was usually one or another adult at home, no one assumed direct responsibility for Jim. However, according to his mother, "Jim never gave us any trouble." No one in Jim's family had completed high school, but his grandfather was very proud of Jim's scholastic achievement, and he frequently advised him to "stick to his books" as the only way to get ahead. When Jim's uncle, who was two years his senior, became active in a militant organization dedicated to civil rights for blacks, Jim joined him. Together they picketed markets demanding jobs for blacks, demonstrated at the school board for desegregated schools, and passed out leaflets demanding desegregated housing. Jim's face glowed as he spoke avidly about "Freedom now."

CASE 4

Wayne L, also 15 but white, was failing in high school. However, Wayne's schoolwork had been mediocre at best throughout his elementary-school years. Although Wayne's IQ of 95 was within the "normal range," the mean IQ at his school was 117. In temperament Wayne was a placid, good-natured boy who seemed eager to please adults but who irritated them— especially his father—by his awkward and childlike ineptitude in everything he did. Like Jimmy B, Wayne was also an isolate, but not altogether by his own choosing; he shyly sought companionship from his peers, who considered him a "spaz" (a derogatory term derived from *spastic),* but

Wayne seemed almost to enjoy their constant teasing.

When Wayne was born, his father, although 30 years old, was an undergraduate at a small state university, struggling to obtain higher education following military service in Vietnam. Indeed it seemed to Wayne that his father was always studying and could never be interrupted. Because Mr. L also had to work to eke out a marginal standard of living for his family, he could not complete his B.A. until Wayne was 4. Then Mr. L moved his family to a larger city where he worked for a year as an assistant manager in a supermarket. Discontented with a financially unrewarding and intellectually boring job, Mr. L decided to return to the university to obtain a teacher's credential. Mrs. L wearied of the family's very restricted economic existence, and she was angry at her husband's refusal to "settle down" at a job after years of "sacrifice" for his education. After considerable bitter marital dissension, the L's separated, and Wayne and his mother moved to another city to live with Mrs. L's parents.

Unlike Jimmy's relatively young grandparents, Wayne's grandparents were elderly; Mrs. L was their youngest daughter. Wayne, who had learned to be quiet in the "cracker-box" married-students' dormitory apartment while his father studied, had little trouble continuing to be quiet when Grandma was ill or Grandpa napped, or when mother came home with a headache from her job as a secretary. When Wayne was 9 his father remarried and his mother agreed to return him to his father so that she could accept a better job in an overseas government post. Wayne had completed the third grade. A year later, Mr. L—now a teacher—changed jobs, and Wayne changed schools once more. The school recommended that Wayne repeat the second semester of the fourth grade, but Mr. L's pride was offended, and he decided instead to tutor Wayne at home—to help him "keep up with his class." Two years later after Mr. L obtained his master's degree, he found an administrative position. He was then able to buy a new home for his family in a new suburb where no schools had yet been built. Wayne traveled eight miles on a school bus to attend a crowded junior high, which operated on a "double-session" basis each day. Leaving home at 6:45 A.M., he returned at 3:00 P.M. At home Wayne spent many hours "glued to the TV," while his stepmother—with whom he "got along well"—was occupied with the care of his infant stepsister. Now that Mr. L was about to complete his doctorate in education, he was very embarrassed by Wayne's academic failure, and he threatened to send him to a special boarding school for backward students. As Wayne discussed this proposal, he became tearful and admitted he had seriously contemplated suicide.

Although Jimmy and Wayne were quite different personalities and came from dissimilar socioeconomic strata, the social stresses that shaped their development were strikingly similar. Both boys were frequently moved to new locales and new schools. Both were out of step in their schools—intellectually and socially. Both had experienced severe disruptions of their family structure. Both lacked any person or social group with which they could identify—until Jimmy joined the civil-rights movement. Both were experiencing a lot of violent anger—Jimmy toward society, and Wayne toward himself in his threat of suicide.

Some of the implications for assessment of these social stresses on child development may be summarized as follows:

1. The standardization of many of our assessment procedures and information is rapidly becoming less and less meaningful. Technological improvements in health and the standard of living are creating new and changing norms in children's psychological growth, especially with regard to activity levels and intellectual development.

2. As a consequence, the assessor today is evaluating children who will probably live longer, have more leisure time, and need longer and more complex formal edu-

cation. Thus emotional spontaneity and intellectual curiosity will need to be fostered.

3. The nature of children's anxieties—as derived from their environments and culture—is changing. There is less personal threat to their lives, although they may experience a vague impersonal sense of impending nuclear doom. The child struggles less and less against the structures of social institutions, but instead he/she is a "rebel without a cause" in a search for identity. Assessment of children's emotional development may thus have to shift from merely looking at personal and familial interactions to a recognition of the broader scheme of shifting social settings and the child's sense of "belonging."

4. Assessment per se is becoming a social institution. With older, established value systems fading, parents turn to the psychologist as an expert, seeking "the right way" to rear the child. In an increasing number of cases the parents voice conflicts over changing values and shifting social stresses, and these adult conflicts are mirrored in a distorted fashion in the child. Moreover, self-revelation is probably less restricted when an individual seeks "identity." On the other hand, as parents and children become more "psychologically minded," there is a greater tendency to give socially acceptable responses to tests and interviews (Edwards, 1957).

5. Assessment is directly affected by these social stresses by the very fact that psychologists are also members of society and are therefore subject to the same shifting values. Moreover, they are assigned roles as official shamans. Most child psychologists come from the middle to upper-middle classes, and even though they may have intellectual doubts and rebellious attitudes concerning their backgrounds, they are likely to function in conformity with the values of their social groups. This conformity is reinforced also by their clients, the bulk of whom come from the same social strata. Appreciation of one's own social assumptions and social stresses is often more difficult for the beginning student than an understanding of the position of clients from other social backgrounds. Students should observe whether they expect the same values of intellectual achievement, social ambition, personal habits, personal attachments, sexual behavior, and the like from all clients, as they do of themselves. If so, the assessment of the child may be skewed and incomplete—if not invalid.

G. PERSONAL EXPERIENCE AS A DETERMINANT OF DEVELOPMENT

While these biological and social stresses shape the basic framework of a child's development, the stresses affecting his/her unique modes of functioning, which set him/her apart from other children in this culture, are his/her personal experiences during the formative years. By far the most influential of all the child's experiences are those arising from relationships within the family. As is implied in the preceding discussion, whatever may be the child's biological inheritance or the conditions of his/her birth and whatever the cultural stresses, the effects of such stresses are determined by and filtered through the attitudes and reactions of the family. Although the family in general as a social institution strives to instill cultural mores and values in the child and transmits methods of dealing with social stress, the most important aspect of family interaction on the child derives from the structure of the family itself, the nature of the interactions between family members, and the roles assigned and lived out by the child and other family members. Although the family has always constituted the central influence on children, with the gradual dissolution of other cultural memberships from which children can form an identity, the family assumes even a greater role in the child's identification process. This identification process will be discussed further in Chapter 2.

The force of family influence derives of course from the dependence of the child upon her/his parents for satisfaction of needs—not only biological needs for food, shelter, and comfort, but equally important, the satisfaction of the child's emotional needs. It is mainly through the reward and deprivation of the parents' love and approval that the parent is able to influence the child's behavior and ultimately shape her/his identity. The manner in which these satisfactions are given depends to no small degree on the child's position within the family constellation and on the roles assigned to him/her or played by him/her within the family for its common satisfactions. Most parents make at least perfunctory efforts to satisfy the child's needs—and where these efforts are *merely* perfunctory, the child feels deprived. In return, each family places on the child certain demands—demands to satisfy needs and to prevent the child from interfering too greatly in her/his dependent state with the satisfaction of the family's needs.

Many factors determine the roles assigned the child in the family, such as (1) the parents' identification of and with the child as being like or unlike themselves or one of their sibs or parents; (2) the parents' attitudes toward the first born, middle child, or lastborn; (3) the parents' preoccupation with the child because of his/her particular demands; or (4) obversely, a relative neglect of his/her needs because of the demands of his/her sibs. A very important factor is the parents' ambivalence toward having any children at all and thus toward the birth of this child in particular. Such ambivalence depends on such factors as the ages of the parents, the maturity with which they can handle their own dependency needs, and their compatibility within the marriage. Many of these parental attitudes are formed before the birth of the child, but are revised in the first years of his/her life, depending on further events, for example, if the child becomes a burden by being chronically ill, a poor eater, hyperactive, or hypersensitive. The birth of younger siblings or the reaction of older sibs may also alter the family's concept of a particular child.

Both tradition and the personal desires of each parent for a child of a certain sex influence attitudes toward her/him. The premium given male children in many cultures makes parents hope for boys, for whom they have high expectations. Thus the firstborn male in a generation may be highly valued and have a great deal to have to live up to. In contrast, the birth of a girl may be a relative disappointment, even though everyone denies it. Very often many of these attitudes toward the unborn child are reflected in the name that her/his parents select. If named after a relative, the child becomes associated in the minds of the parents and then in his/her own self-image with the relative and with attitudes toward that relative. Even where there is no such direct association, the choice of the name usually turns out to have some personal associations not only for the parent selecting it but for the other parent also. Bizarre name combinations have been noted to be much more frequent among institutionalized psychotic adults. The child's own reaction to her/his name is often a good clue to his/her own self-image as, for example, in the following case.

CASE 5

Dana, age 11, was the youngest of four daughters. Her oldest sister Dorothy, age 23, was named after their mother, but was nicknamed "Dolly." Her second sister, Doris, age 21, was named after her paternal grandmother and was called "Sis." Deanna, age 19, was named after a movie actress, but insisted on being called "Lee"—her middle name. Dana's parents denied that they had any particular reason for selecting her name. "We just liked it." One of her father's favorite jokes, which Dana dreaded to hear him repeat, was that they had about run out of girls' names beginning with "D," and if they had another girl, he'd have said "damnation," and she would have been called that. He had made it clear in many other ways also that they had really hoped for a boy when Dana was born. It seemed quite probable that Dana might well have been named after her father Dan, for throughout her infancy she was called "Danny Boy" by him and her sisters, although her mother demurred, and referred to her instead as "my little Dane . . . because she was blonde and the rest of us are so dark."

The age differences between Dana and her sisters were occasioned by the fact that the mother had had considerable difficulty in childbirth with all three of the older girls and was extremely reluctant to have another child. However, she felt very pressured to bear a son, not only by her husband but by both his parents and hers, who still maintained many of their European traditions. Once the decision was made, however, she resigned herself to it. Mrs. D remembered being more relaxed and happy during this pregnancy, and she was determined to enjoy this—her last child. However, the delivery was extremely difficult, requiring surgery, and Mrs. D made a very slow recovery. When she learned that she had given birth to a girl, she felt she had failed her husband and their parents, and she became markedly depressed. Shortly after she returned home, she made a suicide attempt and was hospitalized again for several months. Thereafter, she remained a rather grim, quiet, and withdrawn woman. Nevertheless, with Dana she tried to rally her spirits, determined to devote herself to caring for this last child. Moreover, Dana required considerable care. She seemed "allergic" to almost everything. She was a poor eater and often vomited back the carefully prepared special formulas. She slept poorly and was often "colicky." She was a frail child, and although her health was relatively good after the first year of her life, her mother remained anxious and overprotective. However, Dana was also a beautiful child, with delicate features, deep brown eyes, and blonde curls. Her father overcame his disappointment and "adored her" as did her sisters. During her pre-

school years, "We called her 'our princess' and spoiled her terribly." However, the older sisters formed a coterie of their own, and as they entered adolescence they had less time for Dana. Dana, who had "worshipped" her sisters, was fascinated by their teen-aged activities, but she felt rejected by them and would come weeping to her mother when their door was closed in her face. When Dana was 5, her father suffered a financial failure and went into bankruptcy. Although the family did not lose the home and continued to have at least a marginal income, their previously comfortable standard of living was sharply reduced. To economize, Mrs. D carefully saved leftover food from each meal and began to remodel the older sisters' dresses to fit Dana. Already sensitive about food and vain about her appearance, she complained bitterly, whereupon Lee labeled her "Little Leftover"—an epithet that would send Dana into a weeping tantrum.

At school, Dana suffered over her name again. To distinguish her from a boy in her class also named Dana, the children started calling her "Dick"—an abbreviation of her last name. Dana silently accepted this new name, but was even more uncomfortable, for as she said later, she regarded it as a "phony." Only a short time before, she had realized that her father had changed his patronym from Dreyfus to Dickson to avoid anti-Semitic discrimination in his business. Because of her slight build and her mother's constant admonitions to be careful about her health, Dana felt unable to compete in the physically active play of her peers. She withdrew, sitting hunched over on a bench in the schoolyard. In conference with her mother, one of the teachers happened to remark on Dana's slumped posture. Mrs. D became exceedingly anxious because throughout her own childhood her mother had hauled her from doctor to doctor, seeking correction of her slight curvature of the spine. In recalling this condition, Mrs. D remembered with revived embarrassment being hospitalized, and, at age 14, while immobilized in traction being examined by a series of young doctors. Despite these experiences, she unconsciously repeated her own mother's behavior, and began taking Dana to orthopedic specialists, each of whom advised her that Dana had nothing wrong with her spine. Dana became increasingly resistant to these medical examinations and finally refused all further appointments.

Shortly after Dana's tenth birthday a series of events markedly changed the D's family constellation. In rapid succession, both of her older sisters married and left home. Dana was very excited about her sisters' romances and weddings, but could not understand her parents' resistance to these events. Both parents felt the girls were too young and should have gone on to college. For the next several months Dana tried to become very close to Lee, was always in her room, asked many favors of her, and talked endlessly about Lee's boyfriends and activities. However, Lee brushed Dana aside and complained to her parents that she was becoming a nuisance. When it was discovered that Lee was illegitimately pregnant, her parents tried to keep the fact a secret from Dana and avoided all discussion of it with her, even though she was fully aware of it. However, she had only a vague idea of sexual functioning, for the topic was taboo in the family. Dana became increasingly morose, withdrew into her room, and would talk to no one. The same week that Lee ran away from home, her mother went to the hospital for a hysterectomy—another event that was not previously discussed with Dana. Three days later Dana tried to commit suicide by swallowing a handful of sleeping pills.

In the hospital Dana sat immobilized in a corner on the floor, facing the wall, and wrapped up in a large sweater that belonged to Lee. She refused to talk to anyone and would not respond to her name, but when questioned, she said her name was "Ella" because "E follows D." Much later when she began to talk with her psychotherapist, she admitted that she associated "Ella" with "Cinderella." She allowed nurses to lead her to meals, to the bathroom, or to bed, but became violently combative when they tried to remove her sweater, and she completely resisted medical examination. It took her several months to accept the daily, patient attempts of her psychotherapist to get her to discuss her problems. Then she began to pour out her intense guilt feelings—to the effect that she regarded herself as the cause of all of her family's troubles. Shortly thereafter she was able to return home and to go back to school, but she continued in outpatient psychotherapy for several years.

Although this case history illustrates how a child's identity may be affected by the preconceived attitudes of parents, by the nature of changes in the family constellation, and by the personification of these attitudes in the names given the child, it is far from complete in at least one major aspect. What needs to be spelled out is the actual nature of the emotional relationships within the family. This history suggests that the family may well have used Dana as a scapegoat, but the interrelationships with her mother and father are only barely hinted at in this recitation of events. For example, the possible effects of the mother's original ambivalence toward Dana's conception and birth on their subsequent relationship required further investigation. The data just presented suggest that both parents may have tried to cover their disappointment over her sex by making extra efforts to care for her and to demonstrate their affection for her. How Dana reacted to her father's attentions, for example, and the possible effect they had on her self-concept are not recorded. Having a name associated with her father may have intensified her relationship with him, but probably in a very ambivalent fashion, thus confusing her further as to her identity. How these relationships were perceived both by the child and by the parents became a key question in the assessment.

The nature of these affectional relationships and their effect on the personality development of the child have, of course, been the central concern and contribution of psychoanalytic theory. In this chapter, passing reference has been made to some of the developmental concepts of psychoanalysis. At this point it may be helpful to consider very briefly some of the contributions—and limitations—of psychoanalysis as a developmental theory.

Psychoanalysis as a theory has evolved from the simple biological theory of drives in Freud's earliest writings to a much more complex social theory of personal development. Psychoanalytic theory now includes *inter*personal as well as *intra*personal development. "Sexuality," even childhood sexuality, includes in psychoanalytic theory not only the biological drive per se but all the social and interpersonal associations that go with it. The tie that binds child to parent and parent to child contains an affectional bond of remarkable intensity. This affectional bond is related to physical care and protection of the child, but as can be easily demonstrated both in the overt behavior and in the fantasy of the child, it also is related to the sensual or sexual life of the child. In behavioral terms, the sexuality of this bond is established in many small ways, which demonstrate the attitudes of the parent and establish the attitudes of the child.

If children experience eating as a pleasure over and above satisfaction and relief of hunger, such pleasure is derived not only from the sensual satiation of a full stomach, but also from the comfort and warmth of being fed. When the mother is anxious, angry, or even just impersonal, the child often reacts with disappointment. Feeding may also be a means whereby mothers seek to alleviate anxiety in their children or even to "seduce" them. The mother–child relationship is also "eroticized" by such "oral" activities as kissing, biting, cooing, talking, and singing. Through these pleasurable rewards, the child becomes attached to and identified with the mother. Psychoanalysts use the term *incorporation* to describe this aspect of the emotional relationship between mother and child. As the psychoanalysts have emphasized, these activities are an essential part of the "normal" mother–child relationship. It is only when the child's needs for such affectional stimulation are chronically frustrated, or when the mother persists in infantilizing the child by continuing such behavior throughout childhood to an extreme degree, that the child's development may be deterred and disturbed (see "Case of the T Family" in *The Experience of Anxiety* by Goldstein and Palmer [1975]).

Similar interpersonal interactions constitute the data behind Freud's other stages of psychosexual development of the child and their implications for parent–child relationships. The relationship between mother and child becomes compounded when the mother begins to demand that the "pleasure" that the child finds in relieving the tension of his/her bowels and bladder be regulated through toilet training. Just as the feeding relationship becomes generalized to many other interactions between them, toilet training is usually a "prototype" of the subsequent demands of the mother for the child to conform to her wishes. If this first disciplining of the child turns into a battle, the ensuing parental demands for conformity are frequently also fraught with dissension and resistance. Data on the attitudes toward toilet training and procedures used in it are thus often important clues to the development of the mother–child relationship.

The stage that Freud regarded as the climax of infant psychosexual development is of course the "Oedipal" stage. Perhaps no other single concept in developmental psychology has received so much widespread attention and has generated such controversy. Often this concept has been blindly accepted or just as blindly rejected, with little attention to the phenomena that it seeks to explain or to the corollaries and implications of the concept. And least of all, little attention has been paid to the behavioral data necessary to establish its import to the development in an individual child or to the general development of all children. Even if it were possible to encapsulate here the discussion of and evidence for this theoretical concept, which has occupied whole volumes (Mullahy, 1948), such is not the intent of these paragraphs. However, insofar as the main purpose of this chapter is to illustrate the relationship between theory and practice in the applied task of assessment, a brief examination of this most famous of all developmental constructs may thus be in order.

Before examining this particular construct in detail, a brief aside is necessary regardingg the rules for using any such abstraction. First, before using any hypothetical construct it is necessary to understand the theory thoroughly and precisely, its purposes and limitations. A second rule is that the purpose of such theory is to *predict*, not necessarily future behavior but the existence of other behavior— either past or present—that may otherwise escape the notice of the investigator or appear inconsistent or inconsequential. The third rule for the clinical use of hypotheses is that the clinician should not demand infallibility of the hypothesis for all cases but he/she should, on the contrary, be prepared to accept a null hypothesis in some cases. Thus, there may be times when there is little evidence available or when the import of the hypothesis is inconsequential. (The complete absence of any behavior relating to the hypothesis, however, would suggest the possibility of either inadequate data gathering or an extraordinary situation.) It may be noted that acceptance of the null hypothesis in a clinical case is somewhat different than in a research experiment. The clinician is not primarily interested in the general "proof" or "disproof" of a hypothesis, but in its utility in the exploration of the single case. Acceptance of the null hypothesis in one case does not necessarily limit the usefulness of the construct in the next case, although of course should a construct be rarely applicable, it might easily fall into disuse.

The phenomenon called "Oedipal com-

plex" refers to the intense and basically erotic attraction by the child to the parent of the opposite sex. That most children form such relationships, which in some instances last for many years, has long been observed by both laymen and poets—most notably Sophocles and possibly even earlier in Egyptian legend. However, little of this phenomenon to which Freud referred is directly observable behavior. Rather, what Freud discussed is an elaborate *fantasy*, a fantasy that he maintained is derived not from any special stimuli in the parental behavior, but that arises mainly from the child's own biological impulses. In line with the general developmental hypothesis of generalized to specific functioning, this attachment may be considered to be a specification of a formerly diffuse erotic impulse or drive—the attachment being formed to the parent or parental figure of the opposite sex with whom the child has had the opportunity to form such an attachment. According to psychoanalytic theory, the fantasy of possessing the parent of the opposite sex arises inevitably in the child's imagination—no matter what his/her overt behavior. However, the child may show little or no overt attachment or may even avoid or reject that parent because of the taboo on incest and the hypothesized corollary that the fantasy of a retaliation in the form of "castration" arises.

Of what practical use then is a construct such as the Oedipal complex? First, its purpose and limits. Originally the construct had as its purpose mainly the understanding of adult behavior—specifically the syndrome labeled "hysteria." The fact that Freud generalized from the data obtained from the free associations of emotionally disturbed adult women to other adult behavior—abnormal and normal—and then to child development, often without providing much other evidence, has been one of the questionable aspects of his theory.

However, the construction of scientific laws from the observance of seemingly exceptional and heretofore unrelated phenomena is far from unusual. The immediate question is the following: What predictions or discoveries about this particular child's development can be made using the Oedipal construct? The psychoanalytic answer is that a prolonged or intense preoccupation with this fantasy may result in a wide variety of childhood behavioral disturbances, particularly if the Oedipal attachment and its fears become generalized into other situations for the child. One might expect the child to placate the same-self parent to manifest fears of destruction, to be unable to develop other social attachments outside the family, and very possibly to regress to more infantile behavior. It should be noted in this regard that this one psychoanalytic concept cannot be used in isolation from other parts of psychoanalytic theory, and that this is only part of an overall theory of childhood sexuality.

How then might the clinician explore the possibility that an Oedipal complex underlies a developmental disturbance? What kind of evidence is necessary, and how may it be sought? Here again the clinician must be aware of the specifics of the theory. The construct concerns a "fantasy" and a fantasy that is often hidden from direct observation of manifest behavior. Freud specifies that the existence of this complex is usually observable only or mostly from the child's fantasy productions and dreams, and then more often than not in disguised or "symbolic" form. The clinical value of such evidence in the child's fantasy lies not only in "explaining" the symptom, but more in focusing the clinician's attention on the behavior of the child, and of the parent, in the parent–child relationship that otherwise might escape attention. According to Freudian theory, both child and parent—insofar as the parent may exacerbate the child's fantasy—would attempt to cover any manifestation of this attachment. Thus the parent may be unaware of and fail to report ways in which his/her behavior or the nature of the family situation or other events may serve to prolong the child's

normal Oedipal attachment into a "complex."

For example, the parents might not think to report that the child is in the habit of "playing" in the parental bed every morning, or if they do think such a fact is important, they may be too embarrassed to mention it. They may not notice that their son always makes a wide circle around the room when his father is sitting there, or that he anticipates punishment from his father in unwarranted fashion. They may think it only cute that their daughter always seeks her father out to take her to the bathroom or to tuck her into bed. Also they very likely would hotly and defensively deny that such behavior was at all important or unusual. In gathering data concerning a possible Oedipal disturbance the clinician must keep in mind another specification of the theory—namely, the concept of repression.

What are some of the limitations of this construct? Recognition that it derives from and has its greatest usefulness in conceptualization about pathological states, rather than normal behavior, has already been mentioned as a limitation. However, the greatest disadvantage is the absence of any definite norms or standardization of evidence. Even if it is granted that an Oedipal attachment occurs for every child, the theory never specifies exactly at what point the normal becomes pathological. Only rough ground rules and "clinical judgments" define the difference between a normal "conflict" and a pathological "complex." Nor are there data concerning the normal variations of the age at which a child might be expected to have "resolved" such a conflict. Thus if such fantasy attachments are to be expected in all children somewhere between the ages of 3 and 6, to consider the attachment as a "complex" might require evidence of a considerably intense conflict. Or if the child was chronologically older than 6, but generally retarded in overall development, one might have to seek further evidence to see whether the Oedipal conflict was the source of the developmental retardation or just one part of it. All in all, such a construct becomes a powerful tool in assessment only when the data about the personal experiences of children are carefully and thoughtfully gathered. The use of this construct to organize the data is illustrated in many cases throughout this volume, for example, as in Case 5 in this chapter.

The pattern and sequence of personal idiosyncratic experiences are often the keys to the understanding of the development of the child. By the term *idiosyncratic* is meant those events and circumstances in the child's life after birth—aside from the normal maturational stresses and beyond the conflicts of a social group. These "personal experiences" chiefly occur as a part of family relationsnips—the personal rewards and frustrations experienced. They shape his/her "personal" (as differentiated from "social") identity. Many other events and persons may also condition the child's view of herself/himself, such as physical illness, injury or strength, achievements or failures in school or on the playground,

friendships or enmities with peers or teachers, and the like. But usually the child's ability to cope with such experiences is derived in large part from those she/he has already had during her/his preschool years in interaction with her/his family. These interpersonal interactions between the infant and his/her mother, father, and peers set the stage for the first steps in leaving the nest and coping with stresses beyond the home—at school and on the playground. Nor does the influence of these relationships cease when the child enters school, for as he/she struggles to cope with extrafamilial stresses, the family's encouragement and support or criticism and rejection of her/his behavior continue to be the central criteria and motivation, as long as he/she remains dependent on his/her family. Even in late adolescence when the young adult is seeking to divest himself/herself of the late vestiges of such influence and dependency, the desire for a final parental "blessing" is seldom more than thinly disguised, no matter how outwardly rebellious the adolescent may appear.

CHAPTER 2

The Ego as the Object of Assessment

In Chapter 1 some of the main forces that shape the development of the child were outlined: the physical body that houses him/her—and "is" him/her in a sense—the familiar and social environment that grants him/her a social identity, and the history of personal events that forms the continuity of his/her "self." As will be discussed later, all of these become gradually internalized into his/her total personality. Although information about these factors is essential in every individual case, such data serve primarily to "explain" the child's state of development. They neither describe nor predict the actual behavior of the child. The first objective in an assessment is to describe the behavior of the child, her/his abilities, achievements, and potentialities for coping with the social and physiological environments. Only with objective evidence about the child's ongoing behavior is it possible to begin to hypothesize about the possible antecedents to, or consequences of, her/his development.

That the objective of assessment is to describe behavior may seem such a simple truth as not to warrant further consideration. Yet in many instances psychologists become so concerned with the stresses on the child as to gloss over his/her actual functioning. Also psychologists too often actually confuse the external stresses with the behavior itself, and they speak of the stress (or assumed stress) as if it were the behavior! This error is typified by the term *organicity.* Psychologists commonly report that they have administered "tests of organicity," or "brain damage," even though they have not actually examined the brain—nor any other organ. With slightly more precision, they may speak of "signs"

of brain damage but this is more than a problem in preciseness of language, for such assessors also frequently fail to describe exactly what behavior the child *did* manifest. The functioning behavior per se needs to be reported because it may have more than one possible antecedent. For example, while certain behavior is often found to be associated with disturbances in the central nervous system, many of the same symptoms are also found in emotional disturbances. At times psychologists also dwell on the social and interpersonal stresses on the child as if they were describing the child's behavior. Such statements as "he is a deprived child" or "he has an overprotective mother" do not describe behavior. Neither can such facts (or conclusions) be related to the developmental problem at hand until the details of the current functioning of the child are known.

A. THE FUNCTIONS OF THE EGO*

Any assessment should begin with a study of the development of the "ego." However, ego is a rather vague concept. It is difficult to describe even in general terms and not a "unit" of behavior that can be observed or measured per se. The various aspects or functions of the ego need to be defined in as operational a fashion as possible, so that they may be related to specific measurements or other samples of behavior. Without commitment to any one theory

*Several similar terms such as *personality* or *self* might be used to indicate the overall functioning of the child, but these terms have different connotations, as will be discussed subsequently. Ego, as it is used here, is a commonly accepted term.

of personality, the ego may be conceived as consisting of six functions as is shown in Figure 2.1. These functions are not at all discrete, but they overlap one with the other—especially as the child develops. The order in which these functions are arranged around the central core of "identity" is admittedly debatable. The circles are overlapped to indicate that the interrelationships between these functions vary considerably from individual to individual. For purposes of clinical assessment, the arrangement of this circle of functions is of little practical importance. In assessing the individual case, however, it is essential to describe how these functions are interrelated.

The development of these functions over the total period of childhood will be considered more fully in the remainder of this chapter. At this point, each may be defined briefly. *Motor* refers to the variety of muscular skills that the child develops and to the sensory receptions that are interrelated with these skills, helping the child to regular her/his movements. Included under this heading are the kinesthetic aspects of other kinds of functions, such as speech, gestures, and motoric expression of affect. As will be seen, this function of the ego is far more discrete and more important during the developmental years than during adult life. *Perceptual* refers to the child's ability to discriminate and interrelate the stimulations received through sensory organs (other than in motor reactions)—to see, hear, and touch in such a fashion that what is sensed forms objects with distinct shapes, colors, textures, and sometimes sounds. This ego function is more obvious in infancy and early childhood. Perception in adult years is so much a part of cognitive

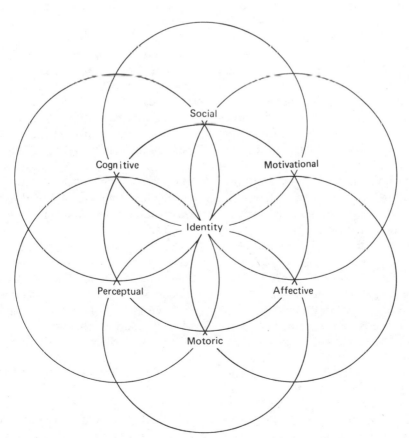

Figure 2.1 Schematic representation of the functions of the ego.

function that it is noticeable only when it does not function effectively, as in some types of central nervous system disorders.

Cognition is an admittedly old-fashioned term for *intelligence,* but the latter term is so often associated with—and thus delimited by—the IQ tests, that it may be helpful to return to the older and somewhat more inclusive term. In that respect, by cognition is meant the ability to compare and contrast the objects perceived, to abstract and generalize about them, and thus to comprehend and give meaning to them. Cognition includes the ability to remember what is once perceived and to hold perceptions as ideas to be considered after the sensation has faded. This rubric includes the perception and comprehension of social situations, emotional expressions, and feelings, as well as the perception and understanding of physical objects and the physical environment. Last but certainly not least, cognition includes constructive and creative thought and the generation of new concepts and ideas (see the discussion of cognitive output in Chapter 12).

The term *affect* designates the feeling, moods, temperaments, and emotions that the child experiences. This function might also be labeled *sensory,* in that it involves visceral, tactile, and kinesthetic sensations, in addition to tension, pain, and even tumescence and satiation. As will be seen, it is often difficult to distinguish the affective aspects of ego functioning from the motivational drives or the socializing functions of the ego. Although placed on the opposite side of the circle (Figure 2.1), affective functioning—as every clinician readily realizes—constantly interacts with and overlaps cognitive functioning.

By *motivation* is meant both the physiological needs of the child and those social drives that often become interrelated. Usually these drives are affectively loaded and are confused with the "emotions," but far more frequently than clinicians may consider, the child may have little or no feeling attached to drives, especially when need gratifications are met satisfactorily. In such instances, the child's

affects may be more attached to his/her perceptions or to his/her intellectual activities or social functionings. The chief difference between motivation and the social functioning of the ego is that the former includes only those social drives that are internalized—those the child perceives and experiences as part of the self.

Under the heading *social* are those behavioral activities that children perform as a part of the social milieu in which they exist and in which they participate. Included in these social functions of the ego are children's attempts to conform to social pressures and norms, to interact with others, to communicate, to affect their social milieus, and to obtain need gratifications from others. The overlap between social functioning and other ego functions is very considerable. Yet, during childhood social activity may—or may not—be accompanied by affect, or be a part of the child's motivations, or even be intellectually apprehended. For the young child, social activity, which is interrelated with and expressed through his/her motor activities, is more likely to be perceived than cognitively understood.

To use the term *identity* to indicate the overall interrelating of these functions is to tread on tender theoretical grounds. Some personologists refer to "identity" in the adult as "character formation," but in the child such character formation remains incomplete. However, as used here, *identity* refers mainly to children's abilities to distinguish themselves from the environment, especially from other people, to characterize themselves, and to assess their own functioning, their own needs, and their own places in society. It is in this sense of self-perception that identity can be thought of as the core of the ego.

B.   SENSORIMOTOR DEVELOPMENT

Muscular activity of the fetus precedes birth and is the first sign of life. At birth and for a brief period thereafter, gross, uncoordinated muscular and sensory activity is about the only visible behavior of the neonate. Otherwise, during the first few weeks of life, the infant is for all intents and purposes without affective, cognitive, or social behavior. Several coordinated reflexes soon appear—the startle, the grasp, orienting reflexes, visual tracking and fixation, and auditory localization, according to recent studies of neonates. The most important coordinated muscular activity is the sucking reflex, seemingly an innate behavior that allows the infant to feed and thus sustain life. However, Call's studies (1964) have suggested that even this reflex is not quite as automatic and innate as has been supposed. Usually breathing has to be given a start also with the traditional pat by the obstetrician or midwife.

These elementary muscular activities, while relatively but not entirely independent of environmental stimuli, soon become part of a sensorimotor network. Nevertheless seemingly random, exploratory movement continues to be a predominate part of the child's behavior throughout her/his infancy, childhood, and even adolescence. Wiggling, wriggling, fiddling, turning, twisting, kicking, throwing, jumping, convulsing—all are a continuing part of the behavior of children of all ages. Alternated with this muscular activity are periods of rest and sleep. Almost from birth children appear to differ in the amount and types of activities and rest they require. Whether their activity level is something "constitutional" or genetically or congenitally determined is uncertain, nor is there much

known about the effects of environmental stress and learning on the development of activity levels. However, either hyper- or hypoactivity—constant restlessness or inertness—may be a sign of either emotional or physiological disturbance, as detailed subsequently (see particularly Chapters 9 and 13). But it may be necessary to have some estimate of the usual activity level of the individual child in order to evaluate whether or not activity at any one time is either excessive or below par.

That this exploratory reaching out soon becomes purposive has been well detailed by Piaget (1954). Much of this activity is actually sensory, tactile exploration (see the following section of this chapter). However, Piaget also emphasizes that the infants begin to learn about their world through kinesthetic sensations. They discover themselves as moving and through moving, in a kind of Cartesian "I move, therefore I am." This muscular activity becomes the seeds of intelligence and later of socialization and identity formation. The measurement of infant intelligence thus consists of gradations of motor activity—developing from random reactivity to grasping, holding, and pulling coordination, and to purposeful manipulation and operation of objects outside of the body. This development is illustrated in Figure 2.2, which shows items from the Cattell Scale of Infant Intelligence and the Vineland Social Maturity Scale.

Thus the first task of the infant is to gain control over the muscular-skeletal system.

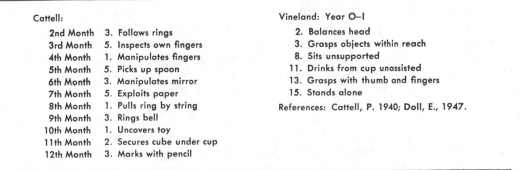

Cattell:

2nd Month	3. Follows rings
3rd Month	5. Inspects own fingers
4th Month	1. Manipulates fingers
5th Month	5. Picks up spoon
6th Month	3. Manipulates mirror
7th Month	5. Exploits paper
8th Month	1. Pulls ring by string
9th Month	3. Rings bell
10th Month	1. Uncovers toy
11th Month	2. Secures cube under cup
12th Month	3. Marks with pencil

Vineland: Year 0–1

2. Balances head
3. Grasps objects within reach
8. Sits unsupported
11. Drinks from cup unassisted
13. Grasps with thumb and fingers
15. Stands alone

References: Cattell, P. 1940; Doll, E., 1947.

Figure 2.2   Items from infant intelligence scales, illustrating the development of motor activities.

Although gaining this control depends on and in part is derived from physiological development (for the central nervous system itself is not yet reacting in a steady alpha rhythm), the development of this activity itself is distinct from physiological growth. As Jones (1949) among others has shown, muscular coordination is only partially related to skeletal development or to other indices of physiological development. Learning to hold up one's head, to turn over, to creep and crawl, to sit and stand, and to walk proceed very rapidly during the first year to 18 months in such regularity in most children that these behaviors are often regarded as entirely maturational. The many trial-and-error practice movements that the infant goes through may pass unobserved. This motor development during early infancy assumes importance when it is realized how much further motor, intellectual, social, and emotional development depend upon it. For example, much practice of arm to mouth, of finger to finger, and of balancing is required before infants can begin to feed themselves, drink from a cup, or hold a spoon. Control over large muscle systems is necessary before an infant can control throat muscles for speech, or the anal sphincter for toilet training.

This acquisition of motor skills and the coordination of perceptual and motor activities continue to be major activities of pre-school children. As they become achievements in the eyes of adults and peers and are rewarded or envied, these skills become social acts. Some of these acts such as self-feeding or bowel control are demanded of the child. Toilet training—as the psychoanalysts have emphasized—is a classic example of socialization through motor control. That eye and throat movements and other muscular activities accompany thinking in the child has been observed repeatedly by investigators of children's cognitive processes. These muscular activities are a part of the way the child learns to think. It is also true that cognitive activity requires a control over motor activity. Interesting in this re-spect is the research on the Roschach movement response (Meltzoff et al., 1953), which shows that projection of movement onto the inkblot can be significantly increased by the cessation or interruption of motor activity. Such movement responses rarely appear before age 6.

The motor control and coordination gained during the pre-school years are basic to children's school tasks such as reading, writing, and logical thinking. Not only do children have to learn to make the very fine eye-and-finger coordinations required for literacy, they have to learn how to sit still for long periods of time in a classroom and to interrupt and cease motor activity so that they can think abstractly and bring to mind the movement they have experienced. Most important, the motor activity must become internalized cognitive activity.

Throughout these school years, children continue to develop refined motor skills. With increased accuracy, they run, skip rope, bounce and catch balls, strike with fists and with bats, draw, whistle, spit, and perform many other purposeful and random acts. Again, acquisition of these skills is related to social maturation. The level of achievement draws the accolades or the derision of peers and elders. Here, social-sexual differences begin to appear regarding motor activity. The "little lady" is not supposed to achieve as extensively in these acts as is the boy. No wonder that girls achieve somewhat better in their studies than boys in the elementary grades, or that among boys there is a zero correlation between achievement in sports and grade average (Start, 1961).

The so-called "awkward" age of pubescence does not seem to refer as much to the teen-ager's motor activity as to social behavior and social self-consciousness. Often adolescents become much more aware of the social meaning of movements, but also they become much more poised, graceful, and skillful. Their walk takes on rhythm even before it is put to music in dancing. Girls are embarrassed by their elders and peers who now regard what was previously considered an innocent sprawl as "not ladylike" or "suggestive." The girl acquires postures that the boys understand as seductive, and the boys learn to walk and stand and perform feats that will attract girls. Athletic competition—already regarded as the epitome of virility—takes on even more seriousness, and the boy who cannot compete must find substitute achievements. Rhythmical activity, not only in dancing but in all forms of music and in sports, takes on extra import for the adolescent. Acquired at this age are many skills involving the use and operation of tools and machines, especially the automobile.

Thus an investigation of the child's coordination and control is often part of the assessment of her/his development. However, it is not easy to separate motor behavior from perceptual activities, and most "tests" involve both of these variables. Direct observation of the child at play or in other social situations provides the most objective data, but it is not often available to the office-bound psychologist. Psychologists should learn, however, to observe the child's motor activities and skills as these appear during contacts with the child in the examining room or playroom—that is, how the child sits, moves, handles test materials, and so forth. Interviews with the child provide a subjective report of his/her attitudes and perceptions of his/her motor activities. Most children like to talk about their play and to boast of their motor prowess. Thus the latency boy who avoids this topic or who describes only sedentary play may be suffering from some handicap—social, emotional, or possibly physiological.

The assessment of motor development and of motor handicaps is detailed in Chapter 9. It is enough to say, motor development varies considerably from child to child, depending upon inheritance, rates of physiological maturation, nutrition, and the stimulation and opportunities offered by the environment. Thus this development may be deterred by many conditions—including genetic and congenital defects, injuries and diseases, and emotional and social deprivations. In many instances failures in motor development involve several or all of these conditions. Investigation of a motor handicap requires a detailed and thorough history. Recently attention has focused on the more subtle failures in motor development, which often go unnoticed. However, a thorough psychological assessment of the motor behavior of children suffering such gross and obvious defects as cerebral palsy or muscular dystrophy is also necessary. The degree and nature of the motor handicap cannot be assumed by looking at the crippled child, nor can one depend only on the subjective reports from parents. Not only is it necessary to assess the degree of impairment, but even more important is an evaluation of an impairment's possible effects on other aspects of the child's development. For example, a child suffering from cerebral palsy may be slowed in her/his perceptual and cognitive development because she/he cannot kinesthetically explore objects or gain other basic knowledge about them through touch and manipulation. Moreover, her/his motivations may lag as she/he finds herself/himself incapacitated, and she/he comes to regard herself/himself as inadequate. Such motivational attitudes may then be affected by the responses of others to the handicap—for example, the overprotection of parents or the rejection by peers. The presence of more subtle motor handicaps, especially of lags in motor development, may go unnoticed during the pre-school years, and they come to light only when the child is unable to perform the more complex and coordinated motor tasks underlying reading of when he/she fails to control motor activity on entering school.

Obversely, disturbances of motor behavior are often indications of generalized emotional and social imbalances. Sloweddown motor behavior is one symptom of depression—even in infants. Repetitive gestures, sounds, or movements may be part of a child's obsessive fears or even of

autism. Excessive rocking, clinging, twirl-
ing, and tiptoe walking are considered by
many authorities as symptoms of childhood
schizophrenia, but these behaviors can also
be observed at moments among normal
children below age 6 (Liebowitz, Palmer,
and Colbert, and 1961). Hyperactivity also
is usually indicative of some disturbance of
development. It may arise from some disease or endocrine disbalance, such as a
thyroid disorder, but more frequently such
hyperactivity is a reaction formation—a
desperate attempt to compensate for feelings of inadequacy, either in intellectual or
social spheres or in motor skills themselves. The frequency with which children
use random motor activity as a defensive
measure against anxiety attests to its importance in children's lives. The uneasy, guilt-
ridden teen-ager also feels constantly restless, has to be "on the go" and "do something, anything" to get rid of anxiety. (For
further discussion of handicaps, see Chapter 16.)

C. PERCEPTUAL DEVELOPMENT

Although perception is derived from sensory stimulation, the psychological act of
perception is to be differentiated from the
physiological phenomenon of neural excitement. Again this is a developmental
distinction. In the neonate there appears to
be little perceptual behavior other than sensory intake. At most, eye movements and
head-turning are partially under control.
What begins as passive sensory receptivity,
however, evolves rapidly into differentiated
recognition and even an ordering of sensations, which is how perception is usually
defined. Perception may be distinguished
further from cognition in that it covers only
the awareness of sensations and the differentiation and ordering of stimuli, but not
comprehension, meaning, abstraction, or
other facets of intelligence. The importance
of these distinctions to assessment will
be seen when various handicaps and
symptoms of perceptual disturbance in development are considered.

At first these primitive sensations give
the child little or no cues for perceptual
organization. Yet they form the basis of
later intellectual, affectional, and motivational behavior patterns. Touching one's
own toes, rocking one's body—which results in kinesthetic sensations—and listening to one's own sounds are initial experiences. "Up and down and around" becomes meaningful as children become able
to lift their own heads and hold them erect
and later to sit and then stand. The warmth,
the softness, and perhaps even the odor of
the mother's body blends in with one's own
bodily sensations, but gradually these become distinct. A child soon discriminates a
mother's touch, her grasp, and her voice.
Visual discriminations, however, require
the development of the motor ability to
focus the eyes on an object. The neonate
stares and stares and turns his/her head and
stares some more.

The infant's sensations also acquire affective, motivational, and social meanings.
Certain sensations "satisfy," give pleasure
or fear, or are perceived as painful. But not
all sensations commonly thought by adults
to be uncomfortable are necessarily perceived in that way by the child. Children
may actually be more alert and quite
"happy" when slightly hungry. Being
thrown in the air by a father is not necessarily frightening, but it may bring gales of
laughter. In fact, an infant often appears to
seek new sensations. The extension of the
infant's sensory-perception experience is of
course abetted by his/her parents, who
feed, cuddle, stroke, and coo. Rocking and
singing to the baby and holding or hovering
over him/her form the basis of initial social
relationships. The importance of this stimulation to later social development has been
demonstrated by the observations of or-
phaned children by Spitz (1946) and
Goldfarb (1955) and of infant monkeys by
Harlow and Zimmerman (1958). Without
such sensory stimulation by parents, both
the human and the anthropoid infant may
become listless and less motivated to
explore the environment independently.

As infants become motorically secure

they unceasingly explore the environment, alerted by every sound and sight. As soon as they can crawl, they try to touch and grasp everything, putting things to their mouths, which seem to be particularly sensitive areas. They "see" through the ends of their fingers and their lips and tongues. As soon as they can speak they want everything identified. Their unbounded curiosity becomes a concern to adults who must rescue them from hazards. They may also become annoyed by children's demands to touch, handle, and see everything, and they may try to curtail perceptual explorations with sharp orders of "No, don't touch," whether or not the child might be hurt or whether or not adult property is endangered. Yet visual exploration alone does not quite satisfy children's curiosity throughout their development. The school-age child and the adolescent too are never quite content until they have put their hands on whatever they see. The softness, hardness, and viscosity, the warmth and coldness, the weight and motility of an object, these are just as important to the exploring child as is the visual shape and color. The child apparently first learns shape perception through handling objects. Color as a defining part of an object and discrimination of colors appear later in infancy than form perception. One measurement of an infant's alertness is his/her attention to sound, including the sound of her/his own voice. Thus on infant IQ tests the baby is asked to repeat words and word combinations.

Children who are ready for school must have already developed the ability to discriminate between simple forms and between simple sounds. They must also be able to make some groupings of visual and of auditory stimuli, to see and hear things that are identifiable as "different" or "the same." Thus on the Stanford-Binet at age 4, children must "put your fingers on the thing in the picture that is not the same as the other things." The Columbia Mental Maturity Test and the Leiter International Scale use such discrimination and grouping as the sole measures of intelligence (requir-

ing very complex discriminations and associations at the higher levels). Reading requires both letter and letter-grouping discrimination. The child who has difficulty in making perceptual groupings may well have difficulty in conceptualization of numbers, so that no matter how well he/she succeeds in memorizing multiplication tables, arithmetic will be a meaningless exercise to him/her, and mathematics will be completely incomprehensible.

In addition to being basic to children's intellectual development, perceptual development is also closely tied to social and emotional growth. Much of the infant's relationship with his/her mother, which is his/her initial social, interpersonal relationship, consists of tactile, kinesthetic, and other sensory stimulations. Throughout the period of infancy and on into childhood, it is vital that children receive sensory demonstrations of comfort and affection, since they apparently form the basis for later social trust in others when physical contact may not be present. The child finally learns that love is possible without direct sensory stimulation, having been satisfied and then weaned from it. Even more important, the petting and fondling of the child forms a foundation for her/his subsequent adult erotic experiences. Of course the sensual stimulation that the child experiences in her/his "erogenous zones," as the Freudians have labeled those sensitive parts of the body, are not usually thought of by psychologists as "perceptions." Yet, the child *does* "perceive" affection and satisfaction and love through being kissed and fondled. Slaps and spankings and loud voices and facial expressions convey anger to children, while other expressions convey tenderness, sorrow, or pain.

Genital sensations—including tumescence—can be observed early in life. In most cultures children learn to associate these sensations with taboos before they discover any other meaning to them. However, despite the taboos these sexual sensations become a part of self-perception because these perceptions are from within the child's own body. Although the taboos against childhood sexual play do teach children to control themselves publicly, they also heighten their curiosity. Even in cultures where there are few taboos against childhood sexual play, sexual stimulation appears associated with curiosity. Children peek in prohibited places—the bathroom or parents' bedroom—often without quite knowing what they are looking for. And sometimes the taboos against peeping may be generalized in children's minds, creating a suppression of all visual curiosity. "See no evil, hear no evil, speak no evil," the child is admonished. And if this warning is heavily reinforced, it may be widely generalized so that the child may be unsure of what is "evil."

Disturbance in perceptual development may thus be associated with disturbances in emotional and social development as well as the more commonly recognized and too often presumed defects in the sensory organs or in the central nervous system. In fact, the child who cannot perceive the words on the page or hear the teacher's instruction or reproduce forms on paper is as likely to be suffering from guilt feelings about seeing or hearing as from visual or auditory defects or poor neural synaptic contacts. Anger floods the nervous system and blocks perception far more frequently than cerebral hemorrhages or tumors in the child's brain. Thus in assessing perceptual development, the psychologist needs evidence about the child's emotional behavior as well as her/his physical health in order to interpret what he/she observes in the child's perceptual behavior. As will be discussed in more detail in Chapter 12, it is possible to distinguish some perceptual behavior that is more characteristic of emotional disturbance than of brain damage. Considerable perceptual material is used in assessment, such as the Draw-A-Person, Bender-Gestalt, and other "visual-motor" tests, but interest has focused mostly on either the content of the drawing (Machover, 1949) or on motor errors.

Perhaps the only major technique that has as its theoretical base the interaction between perception and other aspects of ego functioning is the Rorschach Technique. In the United States psychologists have been more concerned about the precision of their instruments and have been less clear about the theoretical base. Many users of the Rorschach therefore have given little more than lip service to the theory of perceptual modes introduced by Herman Rorschach in his original work (1921). This theory and its implications for assessing development will be discussed in further detail in Chapters 4 and 6. Suffice it to say at this point that the possibility that visual modes of perceiving form, movement, shading, and color are related to the child's development of general social and perceptual modes—or, as Rorschach is usually translated, "experience types"—is a fascinating but as yet only barely explored hypothesis (Rickers-Oviaskina, 1961; Palmer, 1955).

D.   INTELLECTUAL DEVELOPMENT

1.   What is Intelligence?

The assessment of intellectual development has of course long been a major item in studying child behavior. It remains today a central factor in assessment, though it is not the only item as it was in the earlier days of clinical work. Although intellectual achievement is certainly a major factor in the child's ability to meet his/her world, one reason that psychologists tended to give it a primary importance was the fact that for many decades the only accepted instruments for measuring any kind of child development were the "IQ" tests. During the first decades of this century IQ tests were developed that were highly objective, well-standardized, and reliable predictors of other hallmarks of intellectual behavior—especially of academic achievement. Yet despite this precision of measurement, questions continued to plague behavioral scientists: What is being measured? What is intelligence? The debates that raged in the psychological literature on these questions between 1920 and 1940 were largely concerned with what was then called the nature–nurture question. Is intelligence chiefly a genetically predetermined set of faculties, or is it a complex of learned achievements? Although this question has continued to concern psychologists (Liverant, 1960) and remains unsolved if not unsolvable, the debate has largely subsided and has been shelved with the answer *both*. Instead, psychologists have proceeded to consider operationally what they were measuring. "Intelligence is what intelligence tests measure" was the popular tautology in the 1930s. Subsequently there were the factor-analytic studies of Spearman in England and Thurston in the United States. While the general results of such factoring has been the discovery of a major overall "G" factor, running across all subtests with slightly different secondary factors and depending on the content of the scales included in the test, the problem of identifying the factors left much of the definition of intelligence unresolved.

2.   The Development of Intelligence

A developmental approach provides a more comprehensive definition to the complexities of behavior generally labeled intelligence. The nineteenth-century concept of intelligence as a unitary "faculty" is far too narrow. Rather, intelligence is a developing complexity of behaviors that are interrelated but seldom quite perfectly integrated. In rough developmental order, intelligence consists of sensory exploration, perceptual discrimination, retention and recall, associative conceptualization, and judgment and evaluation of the individual's environment (including internal stimuli). The development of this intellectual complexity is best illustrated in the widening complexity of tasks at each age level in the mental-age tests. While it is not correct that "intelligence" is what tests measure, it is true that the better tests—such as the Binet—derive their validity from the fact that they sample

this development fairly accurately. Thus a test of generalization such as "Similarities" would not discriminate among 4-year-olds (most of whom might fail it), nor would a simple test of perceptual discrimination measure intellectual capacity in 9-year-olds, most of whom would pass it.

A great deal of study has been given to the development of these patterns of intellectual behavior, and it is known when certain kinds of intellectual behaviors will appear and at what ages they begin to be consistent parts of children's functioning. During infancy there is an enormously rapid expansion of intellectual functioning, so that by age 6 nearly all of the facets of intellectual behavior are present—at least in nascent form. During the pre-school years children constantly explore the environment, comparing and contrasting experiences, naming and conceptualizing, seeking "why," and evaluating what they learn. Yet during this expansion period, children's overall intellectual functioning is quite unsteady and unreliable. It often seems that there is so much of the world for children to grasp that they never quite have the time to integrate and absorb it all. They try many forms of intellectual functioning, but they do not seem to stop to really develop any one form securely. Thus they may practice memorizing and at one moment show a phenomenal memory for some specific piece of information, such as the names of automobiles, but then not remember their own last names. They may quickly form a conceptual map of the trip across town to the nursery school, but bump their heads as they crawl out from underneath a table. This acceleration of development without concomitant integration is reflected in the relatively wide variability of IQ scores during infancy, and it results in their relatively low predictive validity.

During the later years of childhood, there is a constant working-over and practice of the thinking "games" the child has already tried. In a process analogous to kinesthetic development, children repetitiously fashion these intellectual "motions" into consistent "skills." This development of skills is of course aided, abetted, and directed by society through formal "education," but it continues also in and out of school—in contests with peers, in response to adult pressure and exasperation, and during children's own musings and private observations. Children seek out and enjoy "intellectual games." Even in societies where the achievement motive is not as extreme as in our own, children are often described as seeking knowledge faster than the teacher—parent—or wise man—can give it. Although children may say they "hate" school, often it turns out that what they hate is the boredom of waiting their turn in overcrowded classrooms, the repetitious drill of something already learned, or the repression of their curiosity in favor of some topic or skill for which they are unprepared. "Hating" school also refers to hating school authority, and the traditional resistance to school that was so much more common 50 to 100 years ago probably represented children's resistance to the authoritarian schoolmaster who drilled children on dull lessons unrelated to their own curiosity. In our modern schools, which attempt to whet children's curiosity and to present them with skills and knowledge related to practical, everyday events, the majority of children openly avow that they like school, or they only pretend to "hate" it.

With the onset of puberty, going to school and the development of intelligence assume more meaning for the child. During the childhood years intellectual activity seems relatively purposeless to children. They go to school because they have to and want to. Although they vaguely realize that this activity will serve some purpose in the future, for the moment it is mostly an exercise of their own curiosity. Adolescents discover that intellectual activity has a personal and social purpose. The skills that have been nurtured during childhood must be applied now toward an eventual vocation, toward understanding and dealing

with society, and toward an identity as an intellectually capable person. Learning, which heretofore has been fun, now becomes a responsibility. This shift is embodied in the change of relationship at school between the child and teacher when he/she leaves elementary school and enters high school or even junior high. No longer are children dependent entirely on one teacher in one settled classroom. Now they float from teacher to teacher in shifting groups. At first, courses are planned out for them, but as they proceed through high school they must make increasing numbers of decisions about what they want to learn. Homework—previously a drill of the day's lessons—now consists of seeking and integrating knowledge independently beyond the classroom. At home and in peer associations also, an increasing degree of intellectual independence is expected of a child. Parents now require children to be less "thoughtless" and to proceed with tasks without extensive, repeated instructions. In sports children have to "use their heads," plan activities, and recognize relations without extensive direction.

3. Intelligence and Motivation

Despite the excellent research on the development of intelligence, psychologists have only begun to explore the motivational "why" of intellectual development. Perhaps one should ask, as did Frenkel-Brunswik,* "Why do children fail to learn?" and accept the fact that they usually do. However, it is in looking at this question of failure, at the pathology of intellectual retardation, that it is possible at times to perceive that there is an affective, conative, and social setting within which the intellect develops. Over the past decade, psychologists have come to realize that when children are entirely preoccupied with the satisfaction of basic physiological and social needs, they may not be able to

---

*Unpublished remarks at a symposium given at the University of California in 1954.

explore and absorb the environment intellectually. It is also true that the completely satiated animal or infant may not learn. Observations of infants have shown that they are most alert and exploratory just before meals or when slightly uncomfortable. Similarly, children may be drowned by competition, but without some competition their curiosity merely wanders. Social and personal ambition—even if almost overweening—usually heightens intellectual development. Children's intellectual growth is also very likely tied in with their sexual development. Even observers who do not necessarily adopt psychoanalytic concepts have recognized the stimulus generalization of sexual curiosity—especially during late infancy. Psychoanalytic theory suggests that the intellectual work of childhood is made possible by the release of energy to the ego upon resolution of the Oedipal complex. Once children have learned to repress libidinous and aggressive drives, they can divert and sublimate these drives into schoolwork. Children who are still fighting the psychosexual battles of infancy are disinterested in and are unable to devote energy to relatively emotionally neutral problem-solving tasks.

Intellectual development in our technologically complex and achievement-oriented society possesses a high social value. Most parents desire and see as a necessity that their children are bright and achieve at school. Currently, as never before, mental deficiency is conceived of as a personal tragedy—usually for the parent more so than for the child. No doubt the high social value currently placed on intellectual achievement and education is quite realistic. In addition to the technical competency necessary for most vocations and professions, there is a need for every citizen in a democracy to be cognizant of the complications of society, both national and international. With these realistic pressures and with the stamp of institutionalized social prestige placed on intelligence, parents and society are currently putting ever-increasing pressure on the child to achieve intellectually. Thus parents who seek prestige through their children's achievements to make up "for what I never got" now have their aim justified. Almost nonexistent is the parent of only a generation ago who said, "I succeeded without education—you don't need it."

4. Social Factors and Intellectual Achievement

Often the question facing the assessor is whether or not the child is developing her/his intellect to meet these social and parental demands. Moreover, there are considerable indications that the general intellectual level of the population may be rising. For example, in the restandardization of the Shipley-Hartford Scales, it was discovered (Palmer, 1964) that the mean raw scores were considerably higher than in the original standardization of 20 years before. Educators are recognizing that the average child can absorb and comprehend far more information and with increased rapidity than was thought possible two decades ago. Moreover, children are now learning complex intellectual skills at an earlier age—skills that were previously considered possible for the young adult of superior intelligence. However, although a greater number of adolescents are now quite capable of higher education and are flooding our colleges, the intellectual requirements for college entrance—or even high-school graduation—also continue to spiral upward.

Children with average or below average intelligence often become discouraged over school achievement, especially the middle-class child, since these prestige values on achievement are strongest in that class. Feeling themselves a potential failure in the eyes of their parents and teachers, children may try to cope with this pressure by using a variety of mechanisms. Some may have the ego strength to reject the parent–teacher pressure, shrug it off, and suffer only momentary self-doubts. Many struggle valiantly to comply, and their anxiety takes the form of somatic complaints.

(Being sick is a legitimate excuse for school failure, whether the illness is feigned or unconsciously suffered.) Far too many adolescents, especially among racial-minority groups, become hopelessly disinterested in segregated, crowded, and inadequate schools. Many fight back with misbehavior at school, becoming troublemakers in the classroom although compliant children at home. Often they find surcease in those peer groups for whom school achievement has negative prestige. Some become increasingly depressed with falling self-esteem, and finally they overtly rebel after puberty.

The psychologist assessing the child's intellectual development must therefore be aware of this aura of social prestige and the stimulant of social pressure for achievement. For almost a generation, psychologists have tended to eschew intelligence testing as a routine chore—something to be handed over to the teacher or psychometrician. Assessment of emotional functioning by means of the projective techniques became the more prestigious task. The need for precise and comprehensive assessment of cognitive functioning in children, however, is now greater than ever before. It is essential both to distinguish children's strengths and weaknesses and to determine which aspects of intellectual growth may be held back by emotional or social problems and which might be altered to allow further growth.

Assessment of intellectual development is also very important because intellectual functioning is often such a hallmark of children's responses to social and emotional frustrations, over and above the frustrations entailed in intellectual achievement per se. The interrelationships between intellectual, social, and affective development have been so well recognized over the past decade as to blur the distinctions between them almost. Slow intellectual development and school failure in the early school years are often the initial signs of emotional and social immaturity. The child who is clinging to the dependency state of infancy often

resists intellectual growth and does not want to assume responsibility for independent problem-solving tasks. Such children may often appear bright enough, except when put to the test. Then they ask the questions, often trying to reverse the tester–testee roles in the assessment situation. They show spurts of idle curiosity, but they avoid actual absorption of knowledge or achievement of skills.

5.   Intellectual Achievement and Emotional Stability

Mild or moderate intellectual retardation is also often a common symptom of other emotional disturbances. Intellectual apathy is a common symptom of depression in children as well as in adults. The anxious child has difficulty concentrating, cannot remember facts, and makes hasty judgments and faulty intellectual discriminations. Although distortions in thought processes are more difficult to distinguish in the unformed intellectual functioning of the child than in the ideation of the adult psychotic, the persistence beyond the preschool years of tangential, "magical" thinking in a child's problem-solving behavior may be prodromal of schizophrenia. Similarly, it may be only in subtle signs in her/his intellectual development that weaknesses in the child's neurophysiological development are discovered. Assessment of intellectual development in children from other cultures is a special problem: Intellectual achievement is culture bound (see Chapter 16). For all these reasons assessment of children's intellectual development requires expert knowledge and skill.

E.   AFFECTIVE DEVELOPMENT

1.   What Is Meant by "Affective"

Affective behavior has its counterparts or functional expressions in sensation-like experience, in physiological and neurological functioning, in physical and social drives, and in social interaction, but not one of these exactly defines nor entirely includes emotional experience. Analogous to electricity, emotional experience seems to run through all these other behavioral phenomena and to be observable and even measurable in terms of them. Yet the phenomenon labeled "affect" is relatively independent and discrete from other psychological phenomena. There are indications that affective experience is in itself a necessary function of human existence. Such experiments as Harlow and Zimmerman's research (1958) on affectional comfort in baby monkeys or research by Spitz (1945) and others (Yarrow, 1964) on emotional deprivation in human infants strongly suggests that emotional stimulation may be a need in itself. In addition, all research and clinical observation indicates clearly that emotional expression cannot be withheld without severe repercussions to the organism's functioning, and it may even result in death.

Thus affective experience appears to serve a necessary and independent function for the individual. It gives the meaning to life; it "colors" or "moves" the form of experience—to use an analogy from Rorschach. Sex without affection or eating without pleasure or fighting without anger, while common enough, seem to most people to be somewhat empty. Even learning without curiosity becomes compulsive pedantry. Some affects appear to serve specific functions. Pain and anxiety are signals of physiological and psychological dangers, respectively. Anger and hostility prepare the individual for defense and offense. Love paves the way for affiliation, reinforcing both dependence and sex. From all of these general considerations it may be argued that a careful assessment of these affective reinforcing agents is a necessary part of the psychological understanding of the child.

The course of development of affective functioning follows in general the same pattern as the other ego functions. Temperament, which is usually defined as a proclivity to certain modes of emotional experiencing, is still considered by some psychologists to be primarily genetically determined. Insofar as hereditary factors determine the physiological structures through which the emotions operate, this hypothesis may have validity. It seems reasonable to assume that some of the temperamental differences observable in infants almost from the moment of birth may be attributable to constitutional differences, that is, they are based on even slight, "normal" differences in endocrine structure, skin sensitivity, visceral or more reactivity, or even in the structure of the reticular formation of the brain. As happens in other psychological functioning, however, the impact of environmental stress and the child's learned readjustments to this stress soon become so extensive as to mask whatever constitutional determinants may exist. Assessment necessarily deals mainly with these learned patterns of affective behavior.

2. Affect During Early Childhood

Whatever affective experience might be attributed to the newborn infant is too generalized to be distinguishable. However, within the first few weeks of life the infant's cries do appear to differ markedly in affective tone and—at least to the mother—to indicate pain, anger, or loneliness. In turn, the infant reacts differently, even before age 6 months, to angry voices or to affectionate cooing, and soon becomes able to distinguish some facial expressions. For the most part, the neonate's affective discrimination is very gross, and it consists largely of a comfort–discomfort dichotomy. Vocalizations that can be interpreted as satisfaction or happiness also are observable early in life. The first smile, usually at about ages 2 to 3 months, is the classic sign of the beginning of affective expression. Laughing usually precedes speech by a few months. Attempts to express affection by returning patting and petting can be observed in the first year of life. Rage is rather obvious in the baby's cries by 6 months. It is distinguishable from discomfort and is often accompanied by gross motor activity in full-blown "temper tantrums."

Since so much of the infant's existence is concerned with bodily functions—rather than with social interactions—it is understandable that a great deal of affective experience is derived from or is related to bodily sensations. Whether or not certain focal spots of the body are "eroticized" for the infant, as Freud maintained, there is little doubt that infants find great pleasure in putting objects into their mouths and sucking on them—a pleasure that persists through much of the child's later life in an informalized fashion into adulthood in such habits as smoking or chewing gum. At least affective life appears to begin with the mouth as the center of sensitivity or receptivity. Being cuddled and petted also bring expressions to the baby's face that can be interpreted as joyful. Whether the infant experiences sadness or depression in the adult sense is quite doubtful, but there is no doubt that the infant who fails to receive the usual emotional stimulation from the contact of a maternal figure first becomes rest-through much of the child's later life in an unresponsive, to the point of failing to eat or even of dying.

Preoccupied as infants appear to be with their own functioning, Freud's assertion that infants find pleasure in and are affectively concerned with their bowel and urinary functioning seems a reasonable possibility. (But it was shocking and disgusting to Freud's Victorian colleagues!) This assertion that bowel functioning is pleasurable is of course unacceptable to most laymen, since from the time of our bowel training everyone learns to regard these functions as "dirty," disgusting, and taboo in public discussion. Privately, however, even adults speak of "finding relief" in defecation, and, albeit with embarrassment, they may admit a pleasure in it. The "joy" of the face of the baby in defecation is readily observable, and throughout infancy most children appear to enjoy going to the toilet and to be preoccupied with the process of elimination—despite the attempts of adults to quash this affective reaction. A good deal of affective interaction does take place between the child and her/his mother before toilet training is usually attempted. Not only does the baby receive a great deal of emotional support and affection, but the mother probably has begun to condition expressions of rage negatively when she begins to wean the baby—not only from the breast and bottle, but from the total "demand" schedule. Therefore to at least a slight degree, the baby begins to experience some frustration, some moments when needs are not entirely satisfied. Prior to toilet training, however, mothers in our society make little demand on their infants to control pleasurable activities. Although in weaning the baby the mother does impose a delay in gratification, she does not usually prohibit the pleasure involved. Moreover in weaning the mother provides the control. No demand is put on the child for self-control, and no punishment is involved. In contrast, toilet training is often much more affect laden for the child than any prior experience. The resistance and anger that he/she experiences is aroused not so much by the delay in gratification but by the demand that he/she impose the control. It is at this time, therefore, that the child first experiences intense feelings of guilt, of self-recrimination for not living up to parental expectations. Imposition of guilt is the most common method of toilet training in Western culture.

Although children may have experienced some of these emotions prior to toilet training, that situation and the events surrounding it are *prototypes* of many future social interactions in which children experience strong emotions that society demands they control. Of course bowel control is not the only restriction imposed on the 2-year-old. The psychological lesson for children is self-control over affect. They learn it is required that they themselves control and delay pleasure. Moreover, with even greater intensity, they begin to learn control over their anger. At the same time they learn bowel control they are walking and learning to talk. Thus parents are not only saying "You must tell me when you need to go pottie," but they also are constantly saying "No!"—to many other things—things the baby cannot touch, things the baby cannot have, and places where she/he cannot go. Parents are asking children to feed themselves and to begin to care for their own needs in many little ways. No longer are they "King Baby" whose every want is supplied immediately. Their repetitive "No," even muttered in play, is both a practice of this self-control and a reflection of anger. Although they have experienced rage many times before, children now begin to differentiate feelings, to associate them with specific situations, and even to substitute words for motor behavior as a means of expressing affect.

During the "terrible twos" and threes infants are considerably concerned with affective experience, not only anger but tenderness as well. They can rapidly change from negativistic resistance to charming affability. They learn to give affection—exchanging kisses at random. Their play, especially with a pet or a doll, involves considerable affect and learning of affect expression and control. They take out rage on teddy bear, then kiss and cuddle it at the next moment. They project feelings and emotions onto others, and they also reflect the affection and anger between parents or sibs. Often they will naively and openly express concern over the feelings of others and the feelings exchanged between them, cutting through the adult repressions and denials of affect. It is puzzling to them that adults cover feelings. Thus their mothers may nag their fathers in angry fashion. But when the 3-year-old asks "Why are you angry at Daddy?" the mother may well deny her anger, believing that the child should be protected from it and, in adult fashion, hoping to keep her feelings about her husband private.

As children's psychological existence begins to shift from bodily functions into relationships with others, they begin to experience new emotions. Guilt and shame carry over from toilet training into other social situations. Children learn cues from mothers' faces and mothers' voices to avoid situations that might lead to these emotions. As they begin to be social individuals with possessions and privileges, they learn covetousness and jealousy. Particularly, they find they must share mothers with fathers and possibly with siblings. Feelings of murderous envy overwhelm them at times. They may invent daydreams in which the whole world blows up. Then they will be full of temporary phobias of retaliation for such destructive fantasies.

These pre-school years are also full of pleasurable excitement. Each new event and situation is greeted with wonderment. Curiosity—though often classified as a drive—also contains the affect so vital to intellectual development. Children continue to find new pleasure in the development of their bodies, motor activities, and speech. Play becomes a drive in itself, and playfulness an emotion. Many little things seem funny to children without their knowing quite why. However, humor in the more adult sense usually does not begin to be observable in any quantity until almost the end of infancy. Terman thus found that the question "What's funny about that?" was appropriate on the Binet at the 7-year level. Even the 5-year-old attempts to make jokes, however, and in late infancy children may experience moments of uncontrollable laughter over "nothing at all." All in all infancy is marked by spontaneity of feelings—both pleasurable and unpleasant.

Authorities have long argued over when children first learn fear and anxiety. The behaviorist Watson posited fear as an inborn reflex, but this was a notable exception of his overall theory that all behavior is learned through conditioning. Subsequently his students found that many infants appeared to be without fear, and they suggested that what Watson had observed in the newborn was a startle reflex. Infants under 2 or 3 years do occasionally react with fear of new objects, places, and people, but these reactions are short lived and are not as extensively demonstrated as in the 3- to 4-year-old. As infants suffer physical or psychological injury, however, they learn to become afraid. The 2-year-old has to be protected from physical and social hazards and to be kept from climbing onto the laps of strangers. By age 3, children begin to learn caution and to display brief bouts of shyness.

If anxiety is distinguished from fear and defined as the anticipation of danger rather than a direct reaction to a present hazard, then one may say that until children have built up enough experience to learn of *potential* hazards, they may not experience more than momentary anxiety. Infants react with rage or tears to an immediate stress—not in anticipation of threat. Fortunately the pangs of anxiety are not commonly experienced by infants under 2, and anxiety states in babies are rare. Some babies less than 2 years old do display expressions and behavior that are very comparable to adult anxiety. It may well be that such infants have accumulated enough experience of loss—especially of emotional support—that even in the first years of life they learn to anticipate threat from minor clues, and thus they develop a generalized state of anxiety. It is when infants begin to shift from a primarily physiological being to a more social organism that they first appear to experience any affect that is close to what is usually called anxiety in adults and older children. For anxiety, though often manifested physiologically, does seem to be mainly a social affect, which is developed and aroused in social interactions.

Psychoanalytic theory holds that while the infant may experience threat and react with rage or apathetic withdrawal, true anxiety does not develop until the infant is involved in the primary social relationship of the Oedipal conflict.* The psychoanaly-

tic definition of anxiety contains three specifications. First, anxiety is anticipatory. Although some analysts (Fenichel, 1945) compare anxiety to pain as a "warning signal," it is clear that anxiety—unlike pain—occurs before there is any danger. Second, anxiety is social, mainly involving fear of loss of love or the expression of anger. Third, anxiety is conflictual. Whereas a child *fears* danger or a threat imposed upon him/her he/she is *anxious* only about the threats that are held over him/her in reaction to what he/she wants to do. A child therefore who is beaten by a sadistic parent with no consistent pattern may be terrorized, but she/he does not necessarily experience anxiety, as it is defined here. The child, however, who is angry at the parent whom she/he also loves, will experience anxiety—lest in the expression of her/his anger she/he will lose parental love. Or in the more complicated example of Oedipal conflict, the boy who desires exclusive possession of his mother may be anxious for fear that he invoke the jealous wrath that he has projected onto his father.

Anxiety therefore, as defined here, involves the intellectual ability to conceptualize and abstract, to formulate in fantasy and imagination, and to differentiate affects so that conflicts can be anticipated. There is of course little sign of such conceptual ability before age 4. Although there is some debate about the ability of intellectually retarded children to experience anxiety, manifestations of it can be observed among the mildly retarded, but the moderately to severely retarded appear incapable of anticipating social dangers or of diffentiating conflict.

Whether or not the Oedipal fantasy is as central to the emotional development of the child as Freud thought, it is a prototype of the internalized situation in which the child experiences anxiety. The child imagines possessing the parent of the opposite sex, and she/he anticipates the anger and retaliation from the parent of the same sex—*all in fantasy*. Only the affect is real: He *is* "in

---

*That is, as it was presented by Anna Freud in 1946. Noticeably different in this respect are the concepts of Melanie Klein 1975 who posits the appearance of anxiety and guilt during the "oral" phase. However, the phenomenon that she describes as anxiety is quite different from that described by Anna Freud.

love" with his mother; he *is "jealous"* of his father; he *does "fear"* castration; and he *is "anxious."*

Thus along with an ever-widening scope of motor skills, perceptual differentiations, and cognitive processes, pre-school children accumulate a wealth of affective experiences. Since they have not as yet developed any defenses or methods of coping with affect, they experience them as "raw" feelings. Emotions are easily aroused and easily discharged. Sensitive, they wear their feelings on their sleeves. Spontaneous, they express directly what they feel in actions and in words.

3. Latency and Affect Control

As children progress from infancy into childhood, they learn to hide their feelings, delay expressions of affect, and defend themselves from overwhelming emotions. The psychoanalysts attribute the change to the "resolution" of the Oedipal conflict, wherein children abandon their dreams of a special relationship with the parent of the opposite sex, suppress sexual desires, and adopt a relatively sexless life. Certainly by age 6 children are under increasing pressure to stop acting like babies, to hold back tears, to suppress boisterous laughter, and to stop expecting to be cuddled constantly. Temper tantrums are no longer tolerated, and anger must be held within if a child is to satisfy the parental standards of Western culture. The tortuous "Why" of curiosity is now relegated to the control of the classroom. This lesson of control over affect is not easily nor quickly learned. In fact Western society provides both for the release of affect and the development of initial social controls in the pre-school years, through nursery school and kindergarten. These preparatory classes serve to teach children both to "socialize" or to "express" themselves through social interaction with children and adults other than those upon whom they depend so intensely at home. There are formal lessons in "sharing," in "cooperating," and even in competing without overt expression of anger.

The emotional "latency" of childhood, as Freud so aptly labeled it, is far from complete, and it sets in gradually. The child remains relatively spontaneous with his/her peers, but he/she is much shier and reserved in front of adults than younger sibs. Stoltz and Smith (1959) in a study of children's reactions to frustration divided the Rosenzweig Picture-Frustration Study into those situations involving frustration of the child by an adult and those involving interaction between children. In the child–child situations, children responded to the pictures with far more open expressions of aggression than in the adult–child pictures. The child, however, was much less apt to express feelings of hurt to other children than to adults. Loosli-Usteri (1931), investigating the imagination of latency children, speaks of *le conscience du hasard*—the awareness of chancing a fantasy to the Rorschach inkblots. Latency becomes a time for learning to handle and control affect—for the feelings do not actually disappear. Several childhood games merely involve the ability not to flinch, no matter what the insult or hurt. The child who loses his/her temper is taunted as a baby by his/her peers. Demonstrations of affection are limited, even with parents, and they are accompanied by embarrassment. At 8, a boy is more apt to shake hands on saying "good night" than to be kissed publicly—though a kiss in the dark from mother as the light is turned off may be acceptable.

4. Puberty and Labile Affect

With the onset of puberty the child experiences a new avalanche of affect. Whereas during latency children seem relatively carefree and insensitive, they now display moody spells and are sensitive to every emotional nuance. Girls in particular seem to be bundles of feelings at ages 12 to 13. For the junior high-school girl everything "matters." Her parents and her younger sibs find her unbearably "touchy." She is overwhelmed by romanticism and "takes everything to heart." Boys of this age seem to retain much of their practiced masculine indifference to emotional stress—at least outwardly—but also they are less obtuse and more aware of the emotional side of life than they were a few years previously. Increasingly the teen-aged boy finds it necessary to deny and repress feelings, but with greater difficulty.

During adolescence the child seems to awake from the latency of his middle childhood and re-experience the emotions of infancy with renewed vigor. In folklore the legend of Snow White epitomized this process. In this childhood fantasy the heroine is driven from the love of her father by the jealous "stepmother" who threatens her life. She becomes the companion of sexless little men, but finally is put to sleep when poisoned by the stepmother–witch. Only the kiss of the adolescent prince reawakens her. In this reawakening, adolescents again begin to resent parental controls and become anxious in the conflict between desired love from the parent and assertion of independence. Anger flares again easily against both parents and peers. Adolescents flush with embarrassment over a social faux pas or over the sudden expression of feelings. They are much more sensitive to the erotic facets of affectionate feelings. Often they feel guilty for no good reason, as if they had committed some unknown, unmentionable crime, and they are quick to feel accused and blamed. Parents, teachers, and policemen find them ready to defend themselves on every issue. Struggling with a tangle of emotions, they turn to writing poetry, joining religious and political movements, driving at high speeds—anything and everything to release the tensions and express the feelings they are experiencing. No doubt these effective experiences are aroused and spurred on by the reawakening and resurgence of sexual drives and by the new demands for personal and social independence. But the affective intensity of adolescence is also a struggle in itself. No longer can they repress emotions

as they did in latency. Now they must learn how to express their feelings in interchange with peers and adults, to use them to obtain love along with sexual satisfactions, and to aid in establishing their independent places in society. In all cultures, the puberty rites stress this achievement of emotional expression and control. Not only are deeds of daring demanded, but so too are declarations of feelings. Introspection is almost an obsession for the adolescent. Each is a Hamlet in his/her own right.

Assessment of the child's affective life is thus a goal in itself. For the development of the ability to be aware of the emotional side of life, to express one's own feelings, and to control one's emotions so as to utilize them as an enrichment of all experiences is necessary for the fulfillment of adult life. Indeed the Declaration of Independence lists "the pursuit of happiness" as one of the three aims of mankind. How well the child is learning and developing this pursuit is a major task of assessment.

5.   The Problem of Control—The Social Requirements

The most common problem in affective development lies in this assimilation of emotional controls. Some of this control, as has been implied before, seems almost inherent in the organism's course of development. After a rapid accumulation of affective experience during infancy, the child—with the aid of society—seems to need and accept a "latency" period, a period of assimilation. During adolescence the child often appears to alter between states of affective flooding and withdrawal, of "Sturm and Drang," sometimes in almost definable cycles. "We just can't understand him," one mother said of her 15-year-old son. "Last week he raged at anything we said, never sat still, seemed to be looking for a fight, or some excitement. This week he's the sweet little boy we used to know, busy with his studies, and nothing bothers him."

Most commonly the conflict for the child

arises with the controls set by society as a whole and by parental authorities in particular. Social interdictions on individual emotional behavior appear to have three main, related purposes. First, a society needs to protect the group against mass emotional outbursts that might disrupt the work of the group or lead to precipitous or irrational acts by a large part of society. Second, a society tries to protect the individual from the same thing, that is, from the disrupting effects of overwhelming outbursts of affectively loaded behavior. Third, every society seeks to instill in the child the many institutionalized forms of behavior designed to channel, sublimate, or formalize the expression of affect so that it will not be overly disturbing to either the group or the individual. For example, for the release of anger and hostility (a primary concern of society), there are such childhood activities as hostile, competitive "sports" that are accompanied by cries of "Fight, team fight" or "Kill 'em". There are war games and publicly encouraged fantasies of hostility in "fairy" tales that are full of horror, and there are sadistic comic strips and hour after hour of violent scenes shown on TV.

In contrast to the puritanical ethic of the immediately prior generations, children are now socially encouraged to enjoy life—both by words and by the actions of adults. The ideals of happiness set forth in magazine advertisements or in movies that portray everyone as having the luxuries of life and as being without serious emotional conflicts, however, are often actually depressing to economically or emotionally poverty-stricken children. They may be able to indulge themselves in fantasies of well-being and happiness for the moment only, and then have to face the harsh realities of their deprivations. Romanticism and sexual stimulation are also promoted in public fantasies, in love stories and songs, in dress and adornment, and in music and dancing. Whereas only a generation ago children were shielded from this sexually tinged emotional stimulation, much of Western culture today readily exposes not only adolescents but also younger children to a barrage of sensual stimulations and affect.

Many of the social values regarding emotional expression have been changing rapidly in Western culture during the twentieth century, accompanied by changes in the amount of stimulation given the child. At the same time rules and mores restricting emotional expression have been loosened. These changes, however, have been neither complete nor consistent. Thus side by side with the new values put on emotional freedom and expression the child learns at least to give lip service to the puritanical mores, which preach repression and denial of feelings. Frequently adolescents express considerable cynicism as to whether there are any genuine feelings at all in today's society. At the present time in American society, children are highly stimulated by socially sponsored fantasies of emotional eexpression. They are given only minimum social rules for emotional control, and they are largely left to their own individual resources to find expression.

The conflicts surrounding emotional control have also shifted. Whereas Freud wrote about a Victorian society that stifled emotion and promoted repression, the typical conflict faced by many children today is almost the opposite situation—that is, the anxiety of creating their own emotional outlets and controls, with only minimal and inconsistent social standards as guidelines. Many parents are conscious of this conflict and attempt to help their children reach some resolution of it, but they too often are even more caught up in these changing social values, since it was during their own childhoods that many of these changes began. This parental dilemma is frequently expressed by such statements as, "I don't want my child to suffer like I did under silly rules. I want him to be free to express himself. But I can't let him go wild, and he keeps testing me." It is the constant testing—not of rules but of emotional reactions in others—that is so characteristic of childhood behavior today. This testing is one of the most frequent complaints by parents, not only because it is emotionally fatiguing, but because it arouses so much guilt in the parental generation that did not itself resolve these conflicts. Typical is the parental statement ''That child almost makes me want to scream—but, of course, you're not supposed to scream.'' In a teachers' discussion of corporal punishment one teacher remarked: ''Of course, you are never allowed to spank a child in anger.'' To this another replied sardonically, ''Yes, you can only hit them in cold blood.''

6.   "Emotional Disturbance"

''Emotional disturbance'' is so much a component in all psychological disturbances that the two terms have almost become synonymous. Severe affective disturbances of psychotic proportion—such as the so-called manic-depressive psychosis or psychotic depressions—were once one of the major reasons for protecting people in institutions. But these terms are seldom used as diagnostic descriptions today, and they were almost never applied to children. Very likely such affective storms were common when our culture practiced severe emotional repression and when the psychodynamic pattern of perfectionism and family ambition, which underlies these symptoms (Gibson, 1958), were more common in our culture. However, cycles of depression and hypermanic behavior can very often be observed as one feature of children's emotional disturbances or even in normal children during the transitional phases of childhood. The hyperactive, demanding, boastful, irritable child very often has less noticeable periods when he/she is withdrawn, sullen, noncommunicative, and expressing feelings of self-doubt or even suicide. Occasionally, like some adults, such a child may be able to verbalize some of his/her feelings of sadness, inadequacy, rejection, and despondency. More frequently the child ''acts out'' these emotions

in his/her behavior, for example, as part of his school failure, in his/her social isolation from his/her peers, in a lack of interest in normal play activities, in poor appetite or sleeplessness, or even in semisuicidal behavior or ''accident proneness.'' Such a child may be masking depression by fanatic and obsessive attempts to be liked by everyone, by efforts to be perfect in schoolwork, or by an intense preoccupation with some hobby. The acting-out of guilt in violent, destructive—sometimes nearly self-destructive—behavior is a very common part of ''juvenile delinquency.'' The following case may serve as an example.

CASE 6

According to her parents, Mary had always been a ''straight A student,'' ''very obedient'' and ''well behaved,'' ''friendly though modest,'' and ''a bit shy'' and ''God fearing.'' ''Suddenly,'' at age 14, she became excessively defiant of all adult authorities, neglected her schoolwork and cut school, adopted the most extreme adolescent styles of dress and language, and became ''boy crazy.'' By age 16 she was becoming boastful of her sexual adventures so that even her parents were convinced that she was promiscuous. At first Mary defiantly denied that there was anything wrong with her behavior, insisting that her parents and other adults were unduly repressive and failed to understand teen-aged needs. By the third interview, however, she burst into tears, saying that she had always tried to be good but knew that she really was evil and that this was her inevitable fate. An adopted child, she had always felt she really could not live up to her parents' rigid moralistic standards. Although during childhood she had succeeded in meeting their demands, which had become internalized as demands on herself, she was unable to continue to meet these standards under the pressures of puberty. She had many angry feelings toward her adoptive parents, but she feared expressing them because she felt that she might be deprived of parents again. Her behavior was in a sense a substitute, indirect expression of this hostility. Moreover, she hoped that if her parents had some real reason to be angry at her and if she did something for which she would inevitably be punished, then "God would forgive me" for the greater "sin" of hating her parents.

The absence of affect or inappropriate affective response in the face of stress is as common a symptom of psychological disturbance in children as it is among adults. In classic diagnostic terms, such behavior is recognized in the "belle indifference" of hysteria, the "affect isolation" of the obsessive-compulsive, or the "bland affect" of schizophrenia. The counterphobic, whistling-in-the-dark attempt to ignore social and personal conflict is epitomized in the "What, me worry!" slogan of *Mad* magazine.* Older children and especially adolescents are often able to maintain an outward cover of affective indifference in a "Who cares?" sneer. Younger children— more dependent on others for emotional support and less experienced in emotional control—are less able to deny their feelings. A pervasive emotional blandness in a very young child may well be part of a very severe emotional disturbance, such as in the syndrome called "childhood autism."

Thus over the years a child may learn to mask sensitivity to emotional stimulations, to be inured against stress, and to reveal anxieties and depression only in behavioral manifestations. By the time she/he becomes an adult, this reaction may be so generalized a pattern to so many situations that the sources of these conflicts are unclear in her/his current situation and can be revealed only in recollections of childhood traumata during psychotherapy. In childhood, however, before such a neurotic pattern becomes fully developed, the affective aspects of the child's disturbance are more

likely to be directly *reactive* to an ongoing conflictual situation or to some loss or deprivation in the immediate past. Severe emotional deprivation—especially during infancy—can result in a very generalized psychological disturbance that lasts for many years, if it does not result in permanent disability. Yet the developing child is also emotionally quite resilient, and he/she is able to bounce back from emotional stress a little more readily than adults. Demands for emotional dependency are more acceptable socially during childhood, whereas the adult is under pressure to work and produce more independently. Last but not least, the biological and social pressures toward continued growth often force the child past an emotional trauma, helping to bypass it temporarily with perhaps only minimal disturbance at the time, giving the impression that the child has "outgrown it" or has "gone through a stage." Unfortunately, such unresolved conflict may later appear in adolescent or adult life as a neurotic disability. Such a reappearance of reactions to a childhood trauma usually occurs when the adult meets an emotional stress similar to the earlier trauma. The adult "neurosis" thus reflects the failure to learn to handle affective functioning during childhood.

F.   MOTIVATIONAL DEVELOPMENT

1.   Some Theory

It is difficult to discuss affective development without also discussing the drives, needs, and motivations of the child. In fact the distinction between a drive and the affect accompanying it is sometimes lost because the same term is used to denote both. However, both biological needs and social drives may be accompanied by various degrees and kinds of affect that differ extensively from child to child. Obversely, a child may attach the same affective valence to different drives. Thus in assessment it is important to distinguish between affect

---

Mad is a humor magazine, popular with both children and adults, that in slapstick fashion spoofs many current social problems.

and drive, for affect alone is not necessarily an indication of drive satisfaction or deprivation.

In theoretical discussions of motivation, needs and drives are often treated as if they were relatively constant or were repetitive states of the organism, which require intermittent satisfaction but have little or no individual variation. Such classical discussions also distinguish between the biological "need" and the social "drive," as if the motivations or stresses arising from within the child's physiology had little or no socialization, and as if the child's social drives had no biological origins. Perhaps these distinctions serve a theoretical or heuristic purpose, but in assessment it is difficult to treat the child's motivations as either entirely biological or social.

The so-called biological needs for oxygen, water, food, sleep, pain avoidance, relief from extremes of temperature, and sex appear to vary a great deal in intensity and frequency from child to child—even at birth. Also the strength of these needs varies over the child's life span, some being crucial for him/her at one stage of development and others assuming major importance for him/her at another age. Almost from the beginning of life, all of these needs are "socialized" in one form or another—that is, there are socially approved and tabooed forms of seeking and receiving gratification of these needs. These social modes of gratification then become motivations in themselves. There are even polite ways to breathe. For example, asthmatic breathing annoys and threatens others. The child learns that only certain foods and drinks are acceptable and that they must be consumed according to social mores—and at certain times in selected places. The same is true of sleeping and in the dress and shelter required to avoid temperature extremes. Protection against pain is highly institutionalized, not only in the institution of medicine but in safety rules and in many unwritten taboos. Social regulation of sex is so obvious as to need no comment. Yet a society has to provide a variety of possibilities and variations for need gratifica-

tion if it is to remain adaptive to the needs of its members. If a society prohibits promiscuity and polygamy, it must permit divorce and provide for the care of widows. Such societies moreover usually tolerate some degree of prostitution. A society that taboos dairy products must promote a diet full of fats and alternate sources of calcium. A society that prohibits alcoholic beverages adopts Coca-Cola.

The conditions of group living also create demands on the individual that are not always directly related to "biological" needs, although thus often affect biological functioning, and in the long run derive from the biological nature of the human species. For example, the demand that the child learn to control the elimination of bodily wastes. Strictly speaking, defecation, urination, and perspiration are physiological functions that the body performs without having to seek any gratification outside of itself—as in the search for food or for a sexual partner. Elimination of wastes becomes a "need" only when it has to be delayed and controlled. Other so-called social needs such as affiliation, achievement, and acquisitiveness appear to have their roots not so much in the physiology of the individual as in the overall biology of the species. For example, the affiliative drive becomes particularly strong in our species that has a very frequent almost continuous sexual cycle and in which the young remain dependent on the adults for almost a quarter of the life span. Achievement and acquisitiveness are fostered in a species that is biologically interdependent. Again, each culture dictates the various means by which these needs are met.

Thus each child must learn both the social regulations for need satisfactions and—within these rules—develop the skills to attain gratification. Usually these social rules involve delay of gratification or the acceptance of substitute gratifications. Assessment is concerned with these learned processes and with the affect resulting from delays in satisfaction or with partial or substitute satisfaction.

The socialization of need gratification

takes place in coordination with the development of the skills to meet the means of gratification. It is chiefly when the social lesson is out of phase with the child's development or is inadequately or inconsistently taught that the child experiences conflicts and becomes anxious. Although some social rules are "out of date" and no longer applicable following technological and demographic changes, such meaningless vestigal rules are not so much a problem for the child as they are for the whole society—even though the protest is often carried by the child in conflict with adult authority.

2. The Development of Need-Gratification Skills

Need-gratification skills develop in much the same pattern as other psychological functions. The newborn infant appears to experience needs directly and immediately. They are unable to delay or control them, and if not gratified, they react with generalized frustration and "rage." Since they are totally dependent on others, chiefly mothers, for need gratification, a need "affiliation" is immediately developed. As children become able to reach and hold, walk and talk, and develop other refined motor skills, they become increasingly able to eat without assistance or pull up a blanket over themselves or get a drink of water. An avoidance of the delay of gratifications caused when the mother cannot immediately meet the baby's needs thus begins. Insofar as such self-gratification has this reward, children develop a need for achievement. Since infants remain able to satisfy their needs only to a small degree, however, they also seek to reassure themselves that their needs will be met if they are unable to do things independently. Even in areas where they can meet their own needs independently, they may occasionally demand gratification by parents—testing their availability.

If children are assured that parents are available to meet their needs whenever necessary, they are able to progress in the development of the skills leading toward independent gratification. In the normal development of children this parental role of both insuring gratification and at the same time fostering independence is not necessarily conflictual, but indeed it is complementary. Children experience threat only when they feel that they cannot depend either on parents or on themselves to meet their needs satisfactorily and consistently. Some deprived children will make extra strides in developing skills for self-gratification, being driven into precocious independence by their anxiety—but always with an underlying feeling of insecurity. What is more common is that children who experience inconstant and insecure gratification are poorly motivated in developing self-help skills and remain "infantile." They may even appear intellectually retarded as well as socially and emotionally immature.

In effect, parental love consists of a generalized promise or symbol of need gratification to the dependent child. The parent thus offers love as a reward or a reassurance for independent behavior and threatens the withdrawal of love to insure compliance with social demands. Again these are normal parent–child relationships, and they are not necessarily conflictual. In most instances the parent has only to express momentary disapproval and then add rewards and reassurance to love as the child complies. Also the normal child perceives this compliance as further evidence of independence. Acceptance of social controls is also reinforced by the process of identification, which will be discussed more fully elsewhere in this chapter. Suffice it to say here that through this process of identifying with the adult children accept these controls as parts of themselves. They "internalize" them so that control becomes a need within them that is quite similar to their physiological drives.

In essence, children learn to approve and disapprove of their own behavior, controlling themselves with guilt independently from the actual reinforcement from the parents. As both Mowrer (1950) and Freud have pointed out, this self-reinforcement through guilt is a part of normal child development, and it is not necessarily conflictual. The child experiences conflict in establishing impulse controls mainly when (1) the parents' threats of withdrawal of love are more intense and more frequent than the rewards; (2) the demands for compliance are inconsistent with or beyond the child's skills; or (3) compliance is not sufficiently rewarded with renewed reassurance of love. Guilt similarly becomes a problem for children when the parent intimates that they are "unworthy" of love.

Children's physiological needs cannot of course be long delayed without a threat to life. Parents and society can require that children wait for food until mealtime and then that they eat slowly, using the correct feeding instruments and accepting preferred diets and menus—but they still have to be fed regularly. They must defecate in specified places and perhaps delay defecation for brief periods, but such delays may be more than can be expected from a very young child whose motor skills are still being developed. In both instances children learn that temporary control will be followed by gratification and approval. In establishing these controls moreover, parents are usually more involved in establishing affect control, especially over greed or anger, as was discussed before.

3. The Sexual Drive in Childhood

The only major physiological drive that can be delayed relatively indefinitely and the one that society is most concerned about delaying and controlling until adulthood is sex. The gradual development of sexual needs-gratification skills within the complexity of social institutions and taboos involves a network of social and personal attitudes and feelings that are interwoven with interpersonal relationships and affects. Sexual development in this broad perspective is quite frequently one of the main reasons why children are brought for assessment. In other cases, moreover, difficulties in sexual development frequently appear during the process of assessment to be major, if not central, factors in children's conflicts. Even when sexual behavior and attitudes prove not to be developmental problems in themselves, sexual gratifications are so delayed and so socially regulated that other concerns and conflicts about other developmental adjustments often become generalized to sexual development. All in all, the way in which children handle sexual drives is often a prototype of their overall motivational and affective development.

Despite the importance of the sexual drive in children's development, almost all that is known about this phenomenon comes from clinical observations. Originally knowledge of childhood sexuality was derived from the memories of adult patients during psychoanalytic treatment, but in recent decades considerable knowledge has been garnered also from the assessment and treatment of children. The absence of any other kinds of scientific investigations, either actuarial or experimental, is of course chiefly because of the taboo that still exists in our society against open discourse between adults and children regarding sex—even though both adults and children openly discuss this topic among themselves much more freely than in previous generations. The massive denial and resistance with which the scientific community as well as laymen originally met Freud's discovery of "childhood sexuality" has now largely abated. But in academic psychology a disregard of this phenomenon and sometimes even a dismissal of it as purely a psychoanalytic concept is still prevalent. Because sexual development is so complicated and because it is often given short shrift, it may be helpful to examine this particular motivational force and its relationship to assessment of children in somewhat greater detail.

In what ways and to what extent is the sexual drive manifest even during childhood? The fact is that—although children do not attain sexual maturity physiologically until puberty and even somewhat later socially—sensitivity to sexual stimulation is present at birth, and the sexual drive as an integral part of children's overall motivation continues to expand throughout their development. In newborn males genital tumescence is commonly observed when the infant is excited, even as he struggles for his first breath. Clitoral sensitivity can also be noted in female neonates. As is true for most behavioral phenomena during the first years of life, differentiation of this sensation is not immediate. When the child is bathed and diapers are changed and genitals touched, he/she will momentarily cease wiggling and his/her facial expressions will seem to express a combination of puzzlement and pleasure. As muscular control is achieved, he/she will be observed to rub the genital area against a pillow or pull at the diapers, even when dry. Manual masturbation may begin whenever the child has achieved sufficient manual dexterity and is part of his/her exploration of her/his body. However, during these initial years of life the infant's needs for food, sleep, and tactile comfort are so constant and predominant that any need for sexual stimulation seems very secondary. Children's "pleasure" understandably is derived chiefly from the satisfaction of these other drives that are so vital to rapid physiological development. Whether or not this generalized "pleasure" can properly be labeled "erotic" is questionable, since such psychoanalytic concepts were derived largely from the study of memories, associations, and dreams of adult neurotic patients. It would seem more precise to hypothesize that when these initial nonsexual drives are not satisfied in infancy it may be difficult for the child to begin to differentiate the less-vital sexual drive. Thus "pleasure" may continue to be indiscriminately experienced and generalized from one drive to the next, or it may be sought by substituting one drive for another.

In the normal progression of the child's development, however, she/he does not need either to substitute sexual gratifications for unsatisfied "primary" needs of infancy or to "eroticize" other needs. This eroticizing of other needs—particularly "oral" and "anal" activities—does appear in adult psychoneuroses, but it occurs only, as Freud was also careful to point out, when social prohibitions on sexual development are excessively and severely instilled. Otherwise, such eroticizing appears only incidentally as a part of what Freud called the "psychopathology of everyday life," that is, in the substitutes that the majority of a society accepts for sexual gratification. Thus when children's constant vital needs are met so that they are free to explore and develop other functions, they proceed to expand and refine their sexual-gratification skills—including acceptable substitutes.

Aside from the fact that sexual gratification can be delayed, it also differs from other drives in that it is by its very nature ultimately a social act. Although all needs are subject to social rules, in adulthood most of these can be satisfied without depending on others, and indeed society expects adults to obtain need gratifications relatively independently. The obverse is true for sexual gratification, however. Although children are very dependent on others for most needs and learn to become independent, the sexual need for a mate comes to the fore only with puberty and is actually realized in adulthood. Gradually throughout childhood, however, children become aware of this interpersonal aspect of sexuality and its social ramifications, which are preparatory to an eventual social and physiological maturation of their sexual drives during adolescence. At first children know "love" as gratification of their needs for food and comfort in their dependent relationship upon adults. Only gradually do they come to know love in the sense of gratification of sexual needs in an interdependent relationship with another adult. Admittedly love is seldom if ever completely defined distinctly one way or the other by either adult or child. Most adults continue to seek some gratification of their needs—other than sexual—from other adults, especially from their mates. And even in infancy the eroticization of interpersonal relationships begins to take place.

If sexual love is a generalized interdependent function in adulthood, it is understandably very generalized in the dependent child who is still learning to discriminate around various functions and feelings. Thus in infancy children may not discriminate sexual pleasure from other need gratifications, and insofar as they have need for sexual love, they look for satisfaction in a dependent fashion from the same sources they receive other gratifications— from parents. Because their sexual needs are fairly generalized and immature, they are easily satisfied by the petting, cuddling, and kissing that parents provide. Almost as soon as they have learned to locate and discriminate the source of sexual sensations in their genitalia, they also learn to discriminate between the sexes, both physiologically and socially. With mounting sexual curiosity, children of 4 to 6 peek in on parents in the bathroom, join them in bed at every opportunity, and ask embarrassing questions. They also engage excitedly in sexual exploratory play with other children of both sexes. They observe manifestations of adult sexuality between parents (if not the sexual act itself), they feel left out, and they jealously seek the attention of the parent of the opposite sex. All this exciting knowledge is reenacted in playing "house" or in kindergarten love affairs. The 4-year-old girl who announces she is going to marry her daddy soon begins to add boy playmates as her prospective mates. At the same time, children become acutely aware of social taboos. Genitalia—they discover—are the only part of the body *always* covered by clothes. Sexual parts of the body and sexual functions can only be referred to by euphemisms at best, and then only in privacy. All of sex, the child discovers, is a grand secret that everyone knows! At the same time, the child discovers that sex is part of personal identity, that a recognition of self includes being a boy or girl, and that certain types of expected

social behaviors have a sexual basis. The child uses the same-sex parent as a model, thus inadvertently reinforcing the sexual aspects of the relationship with the parent of the opposite sex.

What is seldom made clear is that children *need* to have an Oedipal relationship with parental figures in order to learn how to relate to the opposite sex, to learn that this is a prototype for future sexual relationships. Moreover, they need to learn about eroticized interpersonal relationships in a setting where there is no demand upon them to fulfill any sexual obligation beyond their skills and maturation. While the "incest taboo" has other social purposes, it also establishes this parent–child relationship as a learning situation. The taboo is a prohibition: "You must not have sexual relations with parents." But it is also a protection for the child: "You do not have to perform as a sexual adult as yet." More often than not, the chief reason that the Oedipal *relationship* becomes a neurotic Oedipal *conflict* is that the parents may unwittingly intensify this sexual aspect of the child–parent relationship—often to satisfy some of their own needs. According to psychoanalytic findings, children learn to handle the affective aspects of sexuality, the jealousy and frustration, by fantasy— particularly the fantasy of the retaliation of "castration." If the child experiences a generalized acceptance and "love" in the relationship with his parents, however, without demands for sexual behavior and with support for controls, then these fantasies and fears subside. All in all, the social taboo in childhood sexuality protects children in essence by forbidding them to enter into a relationship beyond their ability, thus reassuring them.

Infant sexuality then, as with other psychological functions, consists of a rapid accumulation of experiences in which the child learns to make very basic biosocial discriminations. By the time children are 6, they should learn that they can delay and control sexual impulses until they are past puberty. They also need to learn that these impulses are ultimately parts of an intense interpersonal relationship for which they do not yet have the skills.

Children begin this period of "latency" by engaging in a sexual social behavior outside the family circle, practicing and establishing their separate sexual roles—as boys or as girls—without the necessity of intersex involvement. Until children are sure of this social-sexual role, they are not ready to enter into sexual relationships. Although much of the latency child's sexual interest and activity is repressed, especially in contrast to infancy, her/his sexual curiosity, especially regarding sexual functioning and skills, is not altogether abated. In the current sexist culture once the boy begins to be assured of his "masculinity" and the girl of her "femininity" this curiosity can be expressed. During these central years of childhood this curiosity takes the form of becoming intellectually aware, for example, learning sexual terms and the "facts of life." Not infrequently in the later years of this period of childhood, from 10 to 12, this activity includes homosexual play and intense homosexual social relationships. That is, boys have close "buddies," and girls get "crushes" on other girls. Such eroticized interpersonal relationships are most likely to happen just before or during the initial stages of the physiological onset of puberty.

4. Sex and Adolescence

A lapse of several years, depending on the species, between the physiological maturation of sexual functioning and actual mating occurs in animals other than man. Thus "adolescence" appears to have biological as well as social roots. Most mammals— especially the anthropoids and other "social" animals—do not mate during the first season of sexual maturity, but they engage furiously in the practice of mating rituals.* Human adolescence is more prolonged than in other species partly because the whole of

human childhood and adulthood is also extended, but even more so because the human social-sexual relationship is so much more complicated and there is so much more for the adolescent to learn and practice. In contrast to other species, the human adolescent must learn to engage in a continuous sexual relationship—rather than one that is seasonal as is true of most other species—and in one that is supposed to last until the maturation of the offspring, which is again much longer than in other mammals. In preliterate and feudal societies where the life span was much briefer than now and where social behavior was much more controlled, adolescence was foreshortened also and formalized in puberty rites and in institutionalized separation of sexes until the mates could be selected by the society.

In more open societies where selection of a mate is left up to the individual much of the adolescent's time and energy is engaged in learning about mating and in preparatory practice for it. Romantic and sexual daydreams preoccupy the teen-ager's spare moments, in the classroom as well as at bedtime or in front of the TV. He/she progresses from teasing, pushing, and giggling to holding hands, kissing, fondling, and "petting," frequently proceeding on into premarital intercourse. Marriage may be delayed until the boy has learned skills for independently earning a living, but in the United States as well as in the USSR marriage is gradually being subsidized among college students, albeit indirectly and subtly by student grants and by the fact that wives also often help to support the family while the husband is still learning a trade or profession.

The fact that the adolescent is frustrated by the delay of gratifications and made guilty over the breaking of social taboos is well recognized. To a considerable degree, however, this frustration is compensated for by the fact that the teen-ager is not completely prepared for a continuous sexual relationship and is more often than not made anxious if he or she is accidently overinvolved. Currently the social taboos

---

*Kinsey, an entomologist, seems to have ignored this zoological fact in his classic study Kinsey et al., (1948) of the sexual behavior of humans, for he maintained that human sexual problems would be ameliorated if mating began immediately with the onset of puberty!

are so loosely applied and so commonly violated that they fail in their original intent—to protect children from too early release of impulses that they have not learned to gratify satisfactorily.

The more serious "sexual" conflicts of adolescence do not usually arise from repression of sexual impulses per se, but more often from the problems of attaining personal and sexual identities or from eroticized aspects of dependency needs. During the adolescent resurgence of impulses many of the lessons of infancy and early childhood are retested. The conflicts involved in these learning experiences are also often revived. The child's efforts to establish a sexual identity, a problem that had been laid aside after infancy, now again becomes of primary importance, even when the "sexism" of the society is recognized. Boys seek to prove themselves men over again with even greater intensity. Their errors embarrass them, and their failures depress them. Similarly, the young girl has to give up her sexual neutrality of latency and accept the fact of her "femininity," which appears with her first menses and her feminine figure. The achievement of an adult feminine role is particularly stressful, currently since the social role for women is in transition with the old traditional passive-receptive role no longer accepted, but with no firmly established new role as yet accepted by society.

Another major source of conflict for the emerging adult is the current recognition of the inappropriate and discriminatory sexual roles that until the latter half of the twentieth century were demanded traditionally as "natural" sex differences. No doubt these traditional masculine or feminine roles have been major sources of emotional disturbances for past generations—perhaps since the Renaissance. The conflict today is not so much over the eradication of sexism as the fact of change per se. Traditions do not disappear over night, nor do new standards become firmly established in a day. Thus teen-agers are not altogether sure what it means to be "masculine" or "feminine."

During adolescence also, children struggle to divest themselves of the last remnants of dependency on adults for need gratification in general—a struggle rife with conflict since they not only seek independence but dislike giving up the irresponsibility of childhood. Insofar as this dependency was "eroticized" in earlier years, it may appear in adolescence primarily as sexual conflict. If children are still seeking to maintain dependency on their parents for other need gratifications, they may avoid and repress sexual activities in adolescence, or they may plunge headlong into premature sexual promiscuity in an effort to find the parental love that is insufficient in heterosexual or homosexual relationships. Similarly, much of the parent–child conflict so common at this age stems from a revival of the infantile "Oedipal" relationship. Young women who were once "daddy's little girls" now reverse the field and become strangely critical of their fathers' habits and ideas—while at the same time acting toward them in a teasing and seductive manner. Toward mothers, teen-aged girls are even more intensely ambivalent, belligerently seeking conflict with them, yet all the while imitating them and seeking solace and comfort from them. To parents this is often bewildering, and they respond too often by attempting not only to reinforce the controls of childhood but also to grasp the child even tighter to their bosoms. In such instances the child experiences a double load of guilt, both over the tabooed sexual attachment to the parent and over the anger at the parent for reinforcing the dependency aspects of their relationship.

5. Other Drives

As was indicated in the preceding discussion of the development of the child's sexual drives, she/he has many other motivations to learn to handle, and sex per se does not actually become of major concern to the child until puberty. For example, the child's physiological growth constitutes a need in itself that pervades much of his/her behavior and pushes him/her past many obstacles. Curiosity—as part of his/her cognitive functioning, with roots in both motor and perceptual stimulation, in sensation, and the sexual drive—becomes a drive in itself. Many of the needs listed in Murray's (1938) need-press schemata have roots in childhood. For example, N Affiliation begins with the child's dependency on the mother for all other need gratifications, and it remains a strong need in most children throughout infancy and much of childhood. N Achievement starts with the development of motor skills, and it soon becomes basic to the child's search for identity. Murray's Thematic Apperception Test has therefore become the classic instrument for assessing need-gratification development (see Chapters 9 and 14).

6. "Need Aggression"

Aggression as a need also seems to be associated with the child's need to grow, to exercise, to defend against pain, to search for sensory stimulation, and to fend against frustration of all other needs. This concept of aggressiveness as a pushing-out into and at times against the world should be distinguished by the assessor from the affective state of anger and the accumulated generalized anger called "hostility." Anger and hostility are often expressed aggressively, but just as often in a passive, negative manner. The confusion of these concepts stems from the fact that aggression—even without anger—is often socially disapproved and repressed, since aggression may incite anger in others. In this way children may come to associate aggression with anger, and thus they may fear that their own aggression will be interpreted as an offense and an expression of anger. In our society, however, competitiveness is promoted, and many relatively nonhostile channels are provided for satisfying this aggressivity. The child learns to channel aggression into personal achievement. Children are expected to enter into aggressive games. Many aggressive fantasies are permitted, and intellectual competition is fostered. The child who is very

fearful lest his/her anger become overwhelming and result in retaliation may attempt, however, to repress all aggressive behavior even to the point of withdrawing from purely intellectual challenges and thus may appear retarded. Aggressiveness and sexual needs are often intertwined, sometimes even equated, in the child's mind. Sexual behavior often contains as much aggressive behavior as it does passive and tender behavior. Moreover, in our society almost equally strong taboos on overt expression of both needs are instilled in children during infancy. The vulgar terms for sexual acts that they learn in secret from their peers are found also to be used by peers and adults to express intense aggressive hostility. Thus, even though sex per se may not be as hush-hush as it was several generations ago, it still contains a taboo associated with aggressiveness. In many instances the so-called "sexual" problems of adolescence turn out to be more concerned with expressions of aggression and rebellion. Adolescents may withdraw from normal social-sexual behavior for fear of appearing aggressive, or obversely, they may become sexually promiscuous as a means of establishing an aggressive male or female role, while simultaneously rebelling against parents and society as a whole.

7. "Need Independence"

As may be evident from this discussion, the motivation that is most central and relatively specific to childhood is the drive toward independence—that is, relative independence from others in gaining other need gratifications. Since this drive is an integral part of all other need gratifications in childhood, it may not seem at first glance to be a "drive" in itself. However, this achievement of independent need gratification is an essential part of motivational functioning during childhood. Children's needs have to be, and usually are, supplied for them but they are under constant pressure both from society and from within themselves to become progressively more independent. The social pressures toward adult independence are obvious. However, the drive toward independence also has its biological roots in the child's overall drive toward growth. Even in infants who are completely dependent, the striving toward independence is manifested in the struggle to gain control over motor functioning and the first efforts at having wills of their own as they learn to say "No!" and in their social mastery at the toilet. They are driven from the Oedipal relationship to seek affiliative and sexual gratifications on their own among peers. They accept education as a means of gaining intellectual independence, and as children approach adulthood, independence obviously becomes an autonomous need, for as an adult it is vital. In many societies adults who remain chiefly dependent on others for need gratification may be totally rejected and in danger of their lives. Even a welfare state is unable to supply all adult needs or protect one from all hazards. Evidence from history suggests that—socially and personally—adolescents and adults will fight for independence against all odds, disregarding other needs.

For most individuals this gradual progression toward independence contains some of the most pleasurable and rewarding experiences of childhood, and some of the most intense anxieties and conflicts. Much of the pain in growing up comes from temporary failures in attempts at independent need gratification, in the frustration and embarrassment at having to depend on others. As was mentioned before, the central conflict comes from giving up the security of having needs supplied by parents, a conflict endured by all children, which is only finally resolved in adolescence when the child gains final confidence in himself. This conflict becomes a most intense deterrent to children's growth if their dependence is fostered either by neglect—so that they fear they will never be able to satisfy their own needs—or through overprotection—so that they feel that only parents can supply needs.

In a majority of cases the central question is this one: How well is the child developing need-gratification skills? or What is the strength of her/his drive toward independence? For if the drive toward independence is not fostered or is thwarted or blocked, a child may fail to progress in all other functions. If the conflict over independence becomes too intense, the child may seek to avoid anxiety by regressing to a more infantile state of dependency. Much if not all of "psychopathology" in childhood is derived from this conflict. The refusal to enter into the struggle for independence is an essential feature—if not entirely the essence of childhood schizophrenia—and many of the bizarre behaviors of the schizophrenic child appear to be attempts to invoke magically need gratification altogether independently, while simultaneously rejecting the necessary skills. Observations of the histories of such children often suggest that they may have experienced need gratification from parents in a mechanical, "magical" fashion, with little or no human contact or emotion and without regard for their struggle for independence. In the so-called "behavior disorders" of childhood the child's symptoms very often appear to be direct or indirect attempts to test out independent need gratification, particularly to see if it is socially acceptable and effective. Even in reactive depressions when a child has actually experienced a severe loss or deprivation, the very fact that she/he is depressed rather than angry derives from a realization that she/he cannot independently gratify her/his own needs.

G.   SOCIAL BEHAVIOR AS A FUNCTION OF THE EGO

The role of social and cultural forces in shaping the behavior and development of the child has already been repeatedly mentioned and emphasized. These social factors were viewed as external stresses or determinants. As has been frequently mentioned, these social stresses gradually become "internalized" so that children begin to experience these pressures as internal motivations, as parts of themselves, rather than as external stresses. What remains to be discussed at this point are several related questions: How does this socialization process take place? How do children come to experience these social values and mores as the "right" ways to behave, as parts of thier own egos? Under what circumstances and through what processes do children incorporate these social attitudes into a personal identity, and what effect do they have on a self-concept? How is the adoption of this social conscience coordinated with or in conflict with the drive toward independent need gratification? How is this process interrelated with other developmental processes? These questions need to be understood and assessed before the level of any particular child's social development can be estimated, or symptoms of social dislocation can be diagnosed.

The Process of Socialization

As was discussed before, preparations for the child's socialization begin before his/her birth. These consist of the many social institutions, formal and informal, that society has developed mainly for the purpose of transmitting these values to the child. Schools, churches, playgrounds, peer groups, childen's literature, advertisements—all aim both direct and subtle messages at the child indicating that society expects him/her not only to behave in a certain way but, in essence, to be a certain kind of person. The original and chief transmitters of these values are of course the parents and family. Indeed, the development of the child's socialization is so closely tied in with the values held and transmitted by the parents that assessment perforce usually includes some data regarding the parents' social attitudes and behavior. To a very great extent, the degree to which the child develops an internalized conscience depends upon several factors: (1) the kind of conscience developed by the parent; (2) the degree to which parents have internalized social values as part of their own identities; (3) the degree to which parents are at peace or in conflict with these internalized values; (4) the degree to which parents bow in conformity to or rebel against external social forces and rules; and (5) the manner in which parents through word and action convey these values and conflicts to the child, both directly and subtly.

Usually, parents begin planning the transmission of these values when they first contemplate having children. Even the adolescent girl or boy occasionally thinks out loud "When I have children, I want them to learn to behave (in such and such fashion)." Very often such statements concern methods of discipline or allowances for freedom, but at the same time these fantasies convey social attitudes. Young parents usually begin by perceiving children as essentially projections of themselves and their values, hopes, and ambitions. They desire a boy or a girl not only because a child of one sex or the other will expand or complement their own sexual identity, but also because they have some image of what a boy should be like or how girls should behave. Thus they may look forward to having sons because sons—in past traditionalist societies and to a great extent even today—publicly carry out society's goals and work. Or they may wish for a daughter because they fear the aggressive behavior of boys and believe girls will be more conforming. If they themselves have acquiesced to social pressures only with considerable resistance and conflict, they may dread having any children at all, for fear they may be unable to control their children and thus have their own conflicts unmasked.

Even though the mother may not be conscious of her own attitudes, she conveys them to the child from the moment of her/his birth in her tone of voice, her handling of the baby, her schedule of feeding and bathing and toileting her/him, her tenderness or roughness, and so on. If she places a high value on "discipline," she may begin by sticking to schedules, rigidly trying to avoid responding to the baby's demands, clucking sternly when the baby cries in anger. If she is convinced that cleanliness is next to godliness, she may react with disgust to baby excrement. If she is consciously or unconsciously a rebel, she may neglect the baby just to avoid conforming to society's rules for child care. If she is torn between career and children she may unconsciously convey her resentment either in halfhearted care of the baby or in an overprotective smothering as compensation for her guilt. Infants reared in public crèches and orphanage nursesries by impersonal attendants—even though they receive adequate physical attention—have been found to grow lacking a sense of humaneness and trust in others and to be very insecure in interpersonal relationships, even if they do not immediately become psychotic (A. Freud and Burlingame, 1944; Yarrow, 1964). Even before they are 1 year old, babies may learn through conditioning that an expression of anger results in rejection, or that they can threaten their mothers by holding their breath, or that just nobody cares. Since infants are completely dependent on parents for need gratifications, the manner in which these needs are met becomes the reinforcing agent in this social conditioning. If the mother frequently allows the baby's feeding to be interrupted by other things, the baby soon realizes she/he comes second in her/his mother's attention. Or vice versa, if the mother allows nothing to interrupt her attention to the child, she/he becomes "queen" or "king" until a second child enters the picture.

In the beginning the child's social world consists almost entirely of the self and mother. Indeed, there is considerable evidence to suggest that infants do not discriminate between themselves and others and that they experience the mother as an extension of themselves. In psychoanalytic terms the infant "incorporates" the mother in the feeding situation. Melanie Klein (1975) has emphasized particularly the rela-

tion between this "incorporation" and the first steps in the formation of the superego or conscience. Observers of infants more recently have come to realize that although this "oral" relationship with the mother is probably the primary or at least a very important part of the initial social experience, the child also needs tactile stimulation and sleep patterns, which are also conditioned by the mother's behavior.

Although infants are initially passive receivers of social stimulation, they soon begin to make active, aggressive demands on the social world. Even before they have developed motor controls, their cries become differentiated, thus communicating their needs to their mothers. As soon as infants can sit up, they visually explore, and then as they stand, crawl, and walk, their social worlds greatly expand not only in increased interaction with their mothers but with other family members as well. Shortly thereafter parents begin to limit what can be explored, seen, and touched, and thus to convey their value of possessions and their relationships to people. One child may learn that mother prizes property—another that possessions are not as important as people. Children begin to sense whom they can approach with impunity, who is cold and warm, and even whom their mother likes, dislikes, fears, or is angry with. Even before they learn to speak, they hear and understand "No!"— and learn whether and when "No" means "Absolutely not," "Watch out," or just "Oh, dear!" As has already been discussed, this aggressive social interaction between mother and child is epitomized in the toilet-training situation. In this and similar social training, the important fact is that children begin to discriminate fully between their own needs and the demands of society.

At this stage, however, even though children are constantly conditioned and are "incorporating" social values with mother's milk so to speak, they experience these social demands as *external* and separate from themselves. They may echo their parents' statements "*You* a bad child!" but they seldom say "*I* bad!" They learn to fear punishment or deprivation or to expect rewards and so conform to parental demands, but these values are not as yet their own. They react mainly on the basis of praise and punishment, but guilt in the sense of self-admonition is at most embryonic in infancy. The fantasies of the 4- to 5-year-old are characterized by phobias of external punishment or by magically obtained rewards from Santa Claus figures. *Thus the infant's superego is chiefly external.*

During the latency years a gradual but marked change takes place in the nature of the children's consciences. Increasingly they do what they "should" do without having to be told or punished. They begin to find reward in their own achievements. At this age much play among peers is concerned with rules and rule setting. Among 8-year-olds half the recess period at school may be taken up with the rules for the game. Social values and mores are accepted as absolutes, and variations either in the child's own behavior or in the behavior of others is perceived by the child as a threat. When a mother says "Aren't you ashamed!" to a 3-year old, she/he may cry because of mother's disapproval, but 8-year-olds who have committed a transgression hang their heads in shame and embarrassment almost before anyone mentions it. Mothers learn to become aware of the child's misbehavior because he/she looks guilty!

Exactly how this internalization of social values and demands takes place has, in my opinion, never been clearly established. It is a long-range process with some signs of internalization in the latter years of infancy, and it extends throughout childhood and into adolescence. Indeed many otherwise "mature" adults seem to operate largely on the basis of an external conscience, on the basis of a fear of punishment, or on the expectation of reward rather than on self-regulation or self-attainments. This internalization can be explained at least partially on the basis of social conditioning, that is, as "autonomous" habits wherein children learn to carry out social demands before the conditioning reward of punishment occurs. Certainly, despite latency children's concern with self-regulation, their self-control is seldom sufficient, and continued reinforcement from the parents and teachers is required.

Explanation, however, of socialization based entirely on conditioning seems incomplete, in my opinion. It explains *how* social learning takes place, but it does not account for *when*. On the basis of conditioning alone, one would expect more signs of personal guilt and shame earlier in childhood, without the marked distinction between infancy and latency. Moreover, conditioning alone does not account for the qualitative change in the child's superego. For the child's conscience is not merely an automatic habit formation and not just a well-conditioned fear of external punishment. Some factor other than simple habit formation seems present, for the children are learning to punish and reward themselves.

In psychoanalytic theory this qualitative change in the child's superego is attributed to changes in the internal sexual dynamics of the child at the onset of latency.* According to psychoanalytic theory, the child begins to internalize parental and social demands as a part of the resolution of the Oedipal situation. In essence psychoanalytic theory hypothesizes that the child, being motivated by an *internal* biological force (sex), responds with an internalized fantasy level (the Oedipal fantasy) and in turn fantasizes a punishment (castration). This internal fantasy of punishment arouses and forms the basis of most guilt feelings, according to Freudian theory. Furthermore, to escape and compensate for this guilt, the child begins to identify with the same-sex

---

*It should be noted that psychoanalytic theory does not deny the importance of social conditioning, for Freud often referred to conditioning as a *method* of learning, but instead sees this conditioning as depending upon the child's psychosexual development.

parent, and by the process of generalization, with the values of society.

If one takes the somewhat broader developmental point of view, as has been discussed throughout the past and present chapters, this psychoanalytic statement may be considered as describing a prototype of many changes taking place in and about children as they enter school. It describes what has already been stated before about children's cognitive development— that they have developed the ability to conceptualize on a fantasy level, can imagine what might happen, and can generalize from one situation to another. Latency is a period for practicing this cognitive activity and relating it to social skills, which enable children both to control impulses and to find gratification through and in these skills. Children are now more capable of delaying impulses—especially needs for erotic affection—for which they can now substitute nonerotic friendships. The internalization of social values may thus be viewed as part of children's overall drive toward independence, wherein they are seeking and practicing skills that will ultimately make them independent of their parents. The embarrassment, shame, and guilt that latency children experience when they misbehave are, according to this view, special forms of anxiety. During infancy children experience anxiety mainly when their environment fails to satisfy needs. In latency they become anxious when, in their striving toward independence, they fail themselves. As long as they depend on others, they can blame others; when they hope to do things independently, they blame themselves.

With the onset of puberty this still new and barely established internalized superego is sorely tested. The upsurge of sexual impulses creates a severe strain on the child's self-control, and it is a constant source of embarrassment and guilt to many junior high-school children. However, this struggle of teen-agers to control their sexual impulses is only one part—albeit a central factor—of the changes in their struggle for independence. During latency they sought independence by imitating and emulating adult behavior. Conformity to social rules was the means for attaining self-control and social recognition. However, this identification with the adult only partially satisfies the child's independence strivings. After they attain social skills through conforming and identifying, children begin to feel rebellious, to seek more extensive independence, which mere conformity does not permit. With these social skills they can try their own wings, formulate rules for themselves, and rebel against parental dictates. Parents at this point often despair at the seemingly negativistic behavior of their once well-mannered and well-behaved children. They may adopt unconventional dress, language, tastes, and attitudes. However, most teen-agers rebel chiefly on the "edges"—that is, against superficial conventions, seldom against the basic rules of society. The rebellion moreover is directed against the parently generation's mores, the teen-agers are overly conventional with respect to their own peer groups. Often this "rebellion" actually is provided for in social institutions. Adolescents join an "illegal" high-school "sorority" or "fraternity," become "surfers," or identify with a rebellious social movement of adults. Their clothes, haircuts, and even assertions of independence are advertised as acceptable in every adult magazine and TV commercial. In American culture, as Margaret Meade emphasized in her book *And Keep Your Powder Dry* (1942), this adolescent "rebellion" is expected and encouraged as a national virtue. It is an expected behavior as part of the preparation of an independent citizen in a democratic society. In more tradition-bound, autocratic societies this rebellion of youth—if tolerated at all—is allowed only a brief show and then in highly formalized fashion. Only in democratic societies is the drive toward rebellious independence necessary and thus fostered. Moreover, in democratic societies the choice of a mate is left up to the individual, and thus a great deal more freedom in sexual behavior is allowed and even encouraged during adolescence.

The assessment of the child's social development is among the most frequent reasons for referral, for failures in social behavior impinge directly on the parents and school, much more so than poor development in motor, perceptual, or even cognitive functioning. If the infant cannot be conditioned, if the latency child does not conform and attempt to control himself or herself, or if the adolescent oversteps the accepted boundaries of rebelliousness, parents and society take the child's failure as a mark of their own failure. When their redoubled efforts continue to fail they seek help.

In the assessment of social development, as has been emphasized in the discussion of assessment of other functions, it is necessary to keep in mind that social development is not independent of these other functions, and that failures in the child's social development may derive from and/or result in retardation of other functions. The social embarrassment suffered by the child who is slow to develop motorically or who is physically handicapped commonly causes her/him to withdraw in shyness, or to become antisocial, demanding, and rebellious. Or a handicapped child may be spurred on to develop social functioning to the point where she/he is able to be a leader or at least to manipulate the environment very successfully. The intellectually slow child is also slow to learn social behavior and social controls. Obversely, the socially immature child waits to be told what to do and what to learn. Affective, motivational, and social development are often indistinguishable aspects of the same process. The development of affective and motivational controls is a social process. Social development is motivated by need gratifications and social learning involves—and even requires—considerable affect. As Mowrer (1960) has pointed out, guilt is a powerful social catalyst.

H. THE DEVELOPMENT OF AN IDENTITY

1. Some Theory

One of the central features of clinical assessment that differentiates it from other scientific approaches to the study of behavior—the actuarial or the experimental (Goldstein and Palmer, 1966)—is that rather than studying one aspect of behavior across a sample of children or under laboratory situations, the aim of assessment is the study of the interaction of all aspects of behavior within the single individual. Indeed, the phrases *the total organism* or *the whole personality* have become shibboleths in clinical psychology, being often poorly defined and loosely applied. Allport (1948) in his classic review of the term *personality* found over 100 different definitions, many of which are still currently used. Most often in clinical parlance the term *personality* is confused with what has been distinguished previously as affective or emotional functioning. Quite often in assessment reports, there is one section on intelligence and another on personality—as if intelligence were not part of personality! Yet, as has been quite evident in this discussion, it is difficult to understand any one facet of behavior in isolation. Inversely, aspects of behavior cannot be viewed as interacting except in terms of an overall concept—that is, a personality. For most theorists, however, the term *personality* does not merely refer to a totality of functions. It would not seem sufficient to speak of a moving, sensing, perceiving, comprehending, motivated, and social organism—to sum up the developmental features discussed so far. Most students of personality posit some kind of a "unifying force," an X factor tying together and possibly regulating and amplifying all aspects of the individual's behavior. For Freud this integration was embodied in the child's sexual development, while others have posited other genetic bases or have emphasized social integration. Adolph

Meyer (1948) and Carl Rogers, in his earlier writings stressed the unifying force of biological and social growth. Maslow (1950) thought in terms of the long-range creativity of the individual, using such terms as *self-actualization* or *self-realization*. Nearly all of these theorists in discussing whatever force they posit as unifying the child's behavior use the concept and often the term *identity*—a concept also central in the theory of existentialism or in "experiential" schools of thought.

This term *identity* has particular heuristic value for two reasons. First, it focuses attention on how the phenomenon takes place, that is, the ways in which children come to perceive themselves as a unity. It thus implies and emphasizes a developmental process rather than a single force. Indeed, as will be discussed, all the forces mentioned before enter into this process of attaining an identity. The term comes closest to describing how the child experiences his/her own development, consciously and unconsciously.

Second, "identity" focuses attention on one of the primary conflicts of our time. In the historically preceding feudal millennium there was little need or concern over individual identity. Nearly all of an individual's identity was socially determined at (or even before) birth by the class and caste of the family. No mobility or change or choice was allowed. If anyone became concerned with her/his identity, it was to struggle to live up to what was socially expected. If one challenged this socially imposed identity, one was made an outcast or was likely to be killed, for example, by drinking hemlock or by being burned at the stake. In such cultures the child does not "develop" identity, but he/she "inherits" one. In assessing a child from one of the so-called "underdeveloped" countries of the world where remnants of feudalism still exist, this stress of predetermined identity would have to be taken into account. Even in contemporary Western culture vestiges of this type of identity persist.

Over the last 500 years especially during the last 200 years, the cultural changes represented in the rise and triumph of democracy, science, and technology created a new identity in which the central factor has been the struggle for personal freedom. By the beginning of this century at least in the United States, most children were taught that a man was a man not for what his father was but for what he himself achieved and accumulated.* One had to "achieve" identity in rivalry and competition with one's sibs and peers. The very fight for such achievement was an ingredient of this identity, and the failure to so struggle was considered to be both a personal and a social failure. Most of the theories of personality of the immediate past century echoed this ideology. Psychoanalysis, for example, emphasized the struggle of the child to free himself/herself from the father.† In this country behaviorism made it clear that any kind of identification was possible through conditioning and learning, although as applied in getting the child to "adjust" through "guidance," this theory went against the tide of the struggle for personal freedom. More significant and lasting were the ideas of Dewey (1938) and Mead (1932) in promulgating greater freedom for the schoolchild to learn at her/his own pace and according to her/his own motivations.

In many parts of the world and for the caste-bound black and other racial minorities in this country, this struggle for freedom continues to be the major element in personal identity. The battle cry of "Freedom now!" has been sounded by the civil-rights movement in the United States. As it has been defined by the leaders of this movement, this slogan centers upon the attainment of a personal identity. American blacks seek the same opportunities to achieve and the same individual respect that most other Americans have already

*In 1900 women still had little opportunity for an "identity."
† Freud began writing before the feminine struggle for freedom developed in Austria!

gained over the past century. The assessor working with black children needs to realize that this generation is very involved in this struggle. For the black child today identity continues to mean the *right* to be somebody, as opposed to "keeping one's place." However, for a majority of the generations of Americans since World War II, there is a relatively new question of identity (a question that has been particularly brought into focus by the black struggle for personal freedom): Who is this somebody that the individual is free to be? Essentially this question had been raised by such social novelists and poets as F. Scottt Fitzgerald (1925) and John Dos Passos (see particularly his *USA* [1938], depicting the search for identity in the 1920s), or in such books as Huxley's *Brave New World* (1946) and Orwell's *1984* (1950), which depicted the loss of identity in a world of technocracy. Psychologists were made aware of this new question through the writings of such philosopher–psychologists as Eric Fromm in his *Escape From Freedom* (1947), and then through Sartre and the existential writers and afterwards by Carl Rogers and others.

Although the process of identification had been mentioned and explored by most of the major psychoanalytic theorists from Freud on, the major work in this field is Erik Erikson's (1968) *Identity, Youth and Crisis.* Erikson expands his thesis that was introduced earlier in his now classic work *Childhood and Society* (1950)—that personality consists of a series of crises in which a child overcomes conflicts mainly concerning her or his self-controls and independence to the climactic stage of youth wherein the search for identity becomes all-important. Although Erikson emphasizes that the struggle to obtain an independent identity is most obvious during adolescence, he conceives of this identity formation as beginning in early childhood, not so much in the orthodox psychoanalytic process of "incorporation" (as does Melanie Klein) as in the mother–child relationship. This he labels the "mutuality of

recognition." Separating from the mother, the child next develops a "will to be one's self," which becomes assimilated by achievement, for example, at school and in sports.

Outwardly this question of "Who am I?" manifested itself as a protest against being a cog in a standardized world, like Chaplin in the cinema classic *The Machine Age,* or typified by the protesting student in the Student Free Speech movement at the University of California in 1964 who wore a sign saying "I am a student; do not fold, spindle, or mutilate!" But this question of identity is not merely a protest against "the man in the grey flannel suit" (Wilson, 155) or the "organization man" (Whyte, 1956). Hippies, the white "freedom fighter," the sampler of LSD, the office manager in the "sensitivity course," all began to ask these questions: "If I'm not this standardized cog, who am I?" "What kind of person am I?" "Why am I doing the things I'm doing?" "How do I relate to others?"

Because this new question of identity is most often voiced by young adults or by adolescents, it may not at first glance seem to have bearing on the assessment of children. This adult conflict, however, often mislabeled a "character neurosis," has its roots in the identity formation during the childhood of this generation that, although it was different from that of previous generations, went relatively unnoticed. At most, the older generation bewailed the fact that more children than ever before seemed not to "care about money" (or to care too much and not want to work), to be uninterested in achieving at school, to ignore set moral values and mores, and to cross and ignore lines of social institutions such as race and religion.

It would seem reasonable to suppose that this new question of identity, which is scarcely more than a generation old, will appear with even greater intensity in the coming generations, among the children who will be assessed by the clinicians reading this book. Unfortunately, since the psychologists of this generation have only begun to recognize the question, there is little in the way of scientific background nor of assessment techniques to offer as guidance. Since the question will probably continue to be central in assessment in the future, it may prove helpful to the student's thinking to review what is known about identity formation in general, at the same time speculating about the formation of this specific question of identity: Who am I?

2.   The Process of Identity Formation

In the initial phase of infancy the child does not experience herself/himself as a separate identity but as a part of his/her mother. Mothers are a child's whole world and are thus part of them. However, when the infant does not suffer any undue separation from the mother, when the physiological separation of neonate from the womb is followed by continued body contact and nurturance from her, the infant soon becomes satisfied and secure enough to begin self-exploration. Much of the sensorimotor activity of the infant constitutes in effect the first step of self-recognition. Infants find their toes and noses are part of themselves, and are different from other objects and people. Their cries and activities affect others, and others address them in tones different from those they use with older children or adults. These first steps in the development of a "body image" are followed by discoveries such as the facts that they can manipulate objects, control their body functions, delay gratifications without being destroyed, and share and compete with their siblings. All of these experiences seem essential to a child's sense of identity. For if children are restricted—for example by physical disability or illness—or held back by parents who do not want things touched or who rush to do everything for them, they may begin to feel insecure. If they experience controls over functions such as toilet training purely as externally imposed conditioning rather than as a self-rewarding achievement, then they may continue also in later life to expect some out-

side stimulus as a signal for controlling their behavior. Children need to begin to conceive of themselves as independent units capable of self-imposed controls rather than as puppets to be manipulated. The identity of children is formed by their becoming self-activating persons.

The differentiation of the self from other objects and persons in the environment during infancy takes many forms. It is practiced in play with dolls and toys. Three-year-olds use a teddy bear as a mirror, identifying the doll as "good" or "bad," as "angry" or "happy," creating a character in the image of themselves. Their identification proceeds in and through speech, as they learn the personal pronouns. The use of the first person subject is developed last, when a child finally learns to say "I" and to identity this term as the self.

The development of identity during infancy includes of course the beginnings of sexual identity, starting with the infant's discovering in the exploration of his/her body that touching the genitals gives a pleasurable sensation. Very soon he/she learns that this part of the body is something personal. In association with urinary control, the taboo of self-exposure is strengthened. These initial steps in identification as a sexual person usually only briefly precede the awareness of sexual differentiation. The ideas that "I am a boy" or "I am a girl" may or may not be associated with genital differentiation at first. In prior generations children learned these sexual distinctions by observing differences in dress, behavior, and expectations long before they had any clear idea of the physiological differences.* Now by the end of infancy most children are aware of the bodily and genital differences as well. With the change of attitudes toward sex, especially toward children's knowledge of it, this fact is perhaps a less-common mystery. Children are allowed to see naked infants of the opposite sex and to ask questions. They

---

*No longer as definite: Both sexes wear jeans and have long hair.

may even observe their parents in the nude on occasion. They go to the toilet together in nursery school and are less prohibited from bodily exploration of one another during infancy. Very likely their doubts about their sexual identity in this respect and at this age are less than in previous generations. The heightened importance once placed upon this differentiation when it was so hidden may become deemphasized. When sexual differentiation makes less difference but is a natural and accepted fact, the importance of having a phallus or the fear of being castrated may be lessened.

The formation of identity during infancy, including the child's sexual identity, comes mainly from interaction with other members of the family. These social interactions with the family, epitomized in the so-called Oedipal relationship, have already been discussed, especially the ones regarding boys. For girls, as psychoanalysts point out, this aspect of identification is slightly more complicated. Girls maintain their dependency on their mothers as objects for sexual and social identification, but they give up their fantasies of rivalry with their mothers for their fathers' affections.

Once the child makes the break from interfamily ties and enters the world of peers and adults in school, her/his identity is furthered by competition, by achievement drives and aspirations, and by social expectations and controls. During this period of childhood these other social pressures may be almost more important than any sense of sexual identity—especially in the current generation. At one time if a child could not meet social demands for achievement he or she could rely on sexual identification. Boys could disdain academic achievement and depend on being rough-and-tough males. Girls, who were not expected to be scholars, could choose to be "little ladies" and "mothers' helpers." In many other way sexual differentiations during latency are changing. Both boys and girls are now expected to achieve at school. Aggressive behavior in school-age boys is much less condoned than in prior genera-

tions, and in contrast, it is somewhat more accepted in girls. Being an expert in kickball in the third grade is almost as important to a girl as it is to a boy. School-age children must therefore seek some identity other than their sexuality. If possible, they find it in school achievement or in play skills.

A great deal of the schoolchild's sense of social importance today is derived in a struggle for social popularity. A concern with social status, which used to be chiefly an adolescent stress, seems now to be appearing at an earlier age—among grade-school children. The latency child appears to be increasingly concerned with who plays with whom, who likes whom, who knows whom, who can beat whom, and so on. In part this childhood emphasis on identity through the social "pecking order" reflects the struggle of the adult to maintain identity in a mass society. Like parents, children are members of the "lonely crowd" (Reisman et al., 1950). They live in a constantly shifting social group; neighborhood peers are always moving away (or they themselves move), and each year there are fewer and fewer children present in the class who were there in previous years. In contrast to parents, who more likely had a relatively stable school and neighborhood environment, children now have less chance to know where they stand with peers or with adults outside the family. If they are going to be "somebody," it will be on the basis of their own achievements rather than in relation to any set social group. Nevertheless, children also struggle to find where they belong in a shifting social group.

During adolescence the struggle to attain an identity comes openly to the fore with increased intensity. Seeking to form an identity, teen-agers deny ties with parents and their values, but still lacking security in themselves, they seek support by conformity to peer fads and pressures. A teen-ager's "crazy" acts and "crazy" ideas are often his/her way of testing out identity, or seeing if he/she can do things uniquely or think thoughts of his/her own. At the same time, adolescents fear being different or "crazy." If not in the "swing" of things or "in with the crowd," they may feel lonely and depressed even though they have friends with the same problem. If they are reserved, they may feel they have to defend their lack of spontaneity. If shy, they may try playing the clown. If brash, they also are overapologetic. Often the identities of adolescents are so mercurial that on the Rorschach or the MMPI their responses seem "psychotic."

This search for identity requires considerable "ego strength," that is, a sense of security and freedom. Unfortunately not all adolescents feel free enough to secure enough to test out their own possibilities. Some try to cling to childhood and attempt to maintain an identity as a child. They depend on parents for their identities. Occasionally adolescents rush into a mock adulthood, pretending that everything is solved. Sometimes the conflict is too much for an adolescent, who then becomes overwhelmed with anxiety and panic. Even children who have seemed placid or impassive in their latency period may become depressed, or they may "act out" during adolescence. The majority, however, seem to be able to rise above it all, as if it were a great adventure. They seem to be able to enjoy life and to see themselves as teenagers having fun. Although they occasionally worry about the future, they do not feel that they are under continuous pressure. Only after a fling of seeming irresponsibility are they able to accept gradually the strictures of adult responsibility. On the other hand, some adults who never identified themselves as adolescents, who withdrew from this adventure, often feel that something is missing from their identity as an adult.

3.   External Sources of Identity

As was illustrated in Case 5, one of the most important precursors of the child's identity has usually been her/his name, an identity given before or at birth. Perhaps it is less common now to name the child after some dead relative on whom the child was supposed to model. More likely modern parents pick out some fashionable name or variation of an old name—which may have the unfortunate effect of making the child feel like an oddity. Family names convey the child's cultural ancestry, imposing an identity on her or him whether or not he/she wants to accept it.

Birth order may always be one of the underlying factors in the child's identity formation. The oldest child in the family will have had a self-concept for at least a short period, of being the "one and only"—and later feel that she/he is in danger of being replaced. As the first child, she/he is subject initially, to more of the mother's anxiety—and more of the family's expectations in the long run. In contrast, once the mother has gone through childbirth and infant rearing with her first child, she is often less tense and more relaxed with subsequent children. The firstborn is always "the lead goat," but is not necessarily considered a leader by her/his sibs. The second and subsequent children never know what it is not to have to "share," but they may form an identity as "second," in terms of the mother's anxieties if not in terms of her affections. Even though they may escape the mistakes the older child makes or the parents make in rearing her/him, they realize that the older child is in some way "special." Moreover, the second child may grow up to see herself/himself as someone who is the object of envy, and who is in danger of being pushed aside by a competitor. The youngest child in a family has the advantage—and disadvantages—of the role of "baby," of whom little may be required or expected. He/she may receive an extra portion of mother's attention and affection, but also may find that the mother continues to treat him/her as an infant throughout childhood and to cling to him/her as her last child.

Complicating these patterns of identity

imposed by the sibling constellation are the attitudes of the parents toward certain family positions that they themselves have experienced. For example, a mother who herself was a middle child may have special feelings—both positive and negative—toward her middle child who in return may identify himself/herself more with the mother than with the father. Sometimes these identifications are as strong as sex identification and complicate sexual identification. Similarly a father who grew up as the oldest child may expect his oldest child, son or daughter, to be like him—an expectation that the child has to take into consideration in his or her identity formation, whether or not the child accepts and incorporates these expectations.

Furthermore, these identity pressures from the family constellation are complicated by the differences in age and sex between sibs. The oldest child who is only a year or so older than the next younger sib will have a far different identity as a competitive or envious person than if the next younger sib is 8 to 10 years younger. The intensity of such feelings and identities may be similar, but the quality of the identity as "oldest" will be different. For siblings near in age the identities of both approach a twinship. For sibs widely separated, especially when the older child has made some identification with the parents, the older child may see himself in loco parentis to his/her sib. Similarly there is more than a shade of difference to the identity "I am the oldest boy in a family of girs" from the identity "I am the older brother of a little brother or brothers." Most special is the "little princess" who has only older brothers, or the "spoiled prince" who has several older sisters.

The question of how the child is regarded by the parents has become a most important variable in children's identity formation because of changing values regarding parenthood and parental obligations toward children.

Case histories of adults and both literal and fictional autobiographies give proof that there have always been children who were at least unexpected "accidents" and unwanted interferences in their parents' lives. Such feelings and identifications inevitably arise for the child born or even conceived out of wedlock. For such a child the implication of illegitimacy hangs over his/her head, even though any conflict is consciously denied by the parents. Parents who marry very young and have children while they themselves are still growing out of adolescence into adulthood may unconsciously (or even consciously) regard the child as an imposition.

The same may be true in any marriage in which the child arrives before the parents have adjusted to each other. Parents may resent a child who arrives at an inauspicious time in their educational, vocational, or economic strivings, or when they are ill, depressed, or "too old to have any more children." Most serious is the guilt and resentment felt toward the child one or both parents plan in order to preserve a marriage that is dissolving. In such an event, even more than the others mentioned, the child may come to identify himself/herself as a pawn in parental hostilities, like a person who sticks in the craw of others. In such circumstances it would be unusual if the child did not at least occasionally wonder "Am I an accident, an unwanted person?"

In most Western socieites parents are supposed to want the children they conceive. (Strangely, only unwed mothers are given any choice!) The parents' social conscience demands that they make children feel wanted and loved, whether or not they really are. These demands are so strong that—in contrast to some other cultures—children who are legitimately conceived are rarely given to the other people to rear. Even when this is done, there is so much ambivalence about it that it is often not successful, even though there are many childless couples who seek to adopt children. This ambivalence arises within the parents, because both foster and adoptive parents, if given the opportunity, can usually reassure the child. Furthermore, there is the social standard that people should want to be parents.

The forms of family life and the functions of parents are in such a state of flux at the end of the twentieth century as to create considerable insecurity, especially for a child's developing identity. Many children are now reared in single-parent homes—mainly because of the dissolution of marriage. It is not that parents love their children less, but the working single parent has less time and energy to devote to her/his children. As a result, children from such families often wonder if anyone really cares. In many instances these children are encouraged to be as independent as possible at an early age, and they may develop an emotional and social alienation. As "latchkey" children there may be little support for a developing superego.

The rapid changes in sexual roles alter the nature of parental functions. Probably the major caretaking tasks in a majority of families are still performed by the mother, but in many families the father shares them to an increasing degree. The new roles have not as yet been clearly defined, however, nor have they been carried out consistently and without conflict between the parents. In my opinion, sexual-role conflicts are the most frequent cause of divorce. These inconsistencies and conflicts increase the child's difficulties in forming a secure identity.

How parents of the twenty-first century will regard having children remains to be seen. One can only speculate about the values they will instill into the identities of the children the readers of this book may be assessing. Very likely some of the attitudes of the past, as discussed before, will continue to prevail. Some men will continue to be too busy achieving and accumulating to be fathers, but there are indications that many men are becoming more and more aware of the distance between themselves and their offspring and are making at least tentative efforts during their increased leisure time to share with their wives the care and discipline of the children. The role of

women as mothers shows even greater signs of changing. Perhaps Betty Friedan was at least partly correct in her polemic (1963) against what she labeled the "feminine mystique"—a massive pressure by all public media and by many "professionals" for women to comform to an image of being happy but useless housewives. Employment figures indicate, however, that there is an ever-increasing number of married women working outside the home, and that they work not only to supplement the family income (often to provide "luxuries" for the family), but often with the open admission that they prefer to be away from the house and children. Usually this admission is accompanied by expressions of guilt similar to those voiced by their working husbands. More and more commonly both husband and wife believe that a woman should have satisfactions outside the home, but neither feels entirely comfortable about it—either between themselves or in the face of public opinion. If more and more mothers do tend to find employment "as soon as the children are old enough," children's attitudes toward themselves very likely will change. Perhaps there will be more children who feel deserted, unwanted, and therefore unworthy and inadequate. And perhaps more parents will see children, especially the second or third child, as inferfering with their other aims and interests. However, it is also possible that the once-bored and restless housewife can return from a job feeling "fulfilled," more appreciative of her children and husband, and feeling more justified in her demands on them to share in housekeeping activities. Under such circumstances children and husbands can no longer regard the mother as a servant—or themselves as uninvolved and thus unimportant to the family. Instead, family positions and duties may become more democratically assigned and distributed. In assessing the child's feelings of self-importance and identity, therefore, it is necessary to investigate the attitudes of the parents, especially of the mother, toward both their parental and extraparental roles. One must also assess the amount of ambivalence and guilt—or possibility freedom—involved in the fulfilling of both of these roles.

4. Summary

Perhaps the most important fact about identity formation in childhood is that it *is* in formation—that it is developing. In contrast to the identity conflicts of adulthood, which are often neurotic or even psychotic in proportion, *the identity struggles of childhood are for the most part a normal process.* Similar to the other growth processes discussed previously, the child's identity development involves times of conflict, and the course of this development is commonly erratic. Brief shifts in identity or temporary regressions are not necessarily causes for alarm, especially among adolescents. When such shifts and regressions persist, however, they are indications of a severe disturbance in development.

In nearly every case, assessment of identity development is a central factor in the overall evaluation of the child's growth. Disturbances of identity are derived from and interrelated with all other aspects of the child's development. Therefore, disturbances of identity are often clues to disturbances and deterrences in other ego functions. The child who is playing extremely different roles at home and at school, for example, may be "acting out" social, motivational, or even perceptual imbalances. If a child has a perceptual handicap, she/he may not suffer at home, and thus she/he may be able to identify as an "angel," yet be unable to function at school where she/he is a restless and resistant "devil." If the handicap is unrecognized, the child's behavior will appear as a "split" in personality—both to the parents and the school—and subjectively to the child himself/herself. Obversely, the child who is uncontrollable at home and a model of conformity at school may be working out conflicts over the control of impulses, using the school as a setting for practicing controls but demanding permission at home to relax these controls. If these imbalances in other phrases of his/her development are not corrected, the child may eventually suffer a more prolonged and definite disturbance in identity. As the child's identity forms it becomes a distinctive attitudinal core, affecting and directing all other aspects of his/her behavior. Increasingly as children mature their behavior becomes more dependent on how they see themselves. Thus disturbances in this development of identity may create disruptions in all other facets of their behavior. Children who feel they do not belong, who feel basically unworthy, who find "double messages" from parental authorities demanding dual roles, or who regard their own bodies as unacceptable may be so concerned with their identities as to be unable to function effectively in any way. Unable to obtain a clear self-perception, they are likely to distort perceptions of other people and objects. Lacking a sense of self, they are likely to see themselves as unable to control their own motivations or to obtain gratifications independently. They may even react with motoric clumsiness or regress to using motoric gestures and activities, much like a normal infant in the first stages of identity development. Such overall intensive disturbances in identity are often labeled "childhood schizophrenia" or, in infants, "infantile autism."

I. SUMMARY

In both Chapters 1 and 2 the functions of the ego have been considered in the order of their relative development, beginning with those most closely tied in with the child's physiological functioning—that is the motoric and sensory functions—and ending with a discussion of a purely psychological concept: the child's sense of identity. The primary object of the organization of this chapter has been to emphasize the need to consider all these ego functions and the core of the ego—the child's identity—in developmental framework. However, a discussion of the ego as the object of assessment might also begin with consideration of this core concept, with subsequent discussions of the various functions through which the child experiences and manifests his/her developing sense of identity. Such a perspective might be particularly meaningful in reporting an assessment because questions about identity development so often appear as part of the referral. Moreover, even when such questions are not raised a discussion of any aspect of the ego necessarily includes consideration of that function in relation to the child's concept of himself/herself. The chief reason then for focusing on the child's sense of identity in any assessment is that any disruption or deterrence of any particular ego function becomes psychologically meaningful to that particular child only insofar as it affects his/her identity. As has been mentioned repeatedly and illustrated in several case vignettes, it is quite possible for children to be subjected to considerable stress, physically or socially, without necessarily suffering a psychological disorder. Admittedly such stresses may create a temporary sense of distress. However, it is when the stresses of life create a permanent feeling of loss in children, or make them doubt their developing abilities, and most particularly their worth to others, that a psychological disturbance is created.

PART TWO

Methods of Data Collection

CHAPTER 3

The Nature and Evaluation of Assessment Techniques

A. THE HYPOTHESES AND THE TECHNIQUES

1. The Gap

In any psychological research, the experimenter usually states the hypotheses or problems and then proposes various methods or techniques to test or investigate them. She/he adopts or invents techniques that directly or indirectly sample the behaviors to be investigated, presenting as part of the scientific argument some evidence or rationale supporting the relationship between the method and the variables being sampled. If the clinical assessment of the child is to be scientific, then the techniques for data gathering should be related to the "hypotheses." Given the theoretical framework presented in Part 1 of this volume one might expect a presentation of techniques that sample the various functions of the ego and measure their development in the child. Unfortunately the relationships between the techniques commonly used in assessing children and the hypotheses that were outlined in Part 1 are quite complex and far from being specific. The purpose of this section is to explore these complexities and to attempt to relate these techniques to this particular set of hypotheses.

A brief aside on some of the reasons for this gap between hypothesis and technique may be helpful as an introduction to the subsequent discussion. In the first place, for various reasons few if any of our techniques were constructed as methods of sampling some clearly defined function.

Most clinical instruments currently in use were originated over 20 years ago on the basis of practical needs rather than theory. Intelligence tests, for example, were invented before there were theories of intelligence. "Projective techniques" were spawned while psychology was still in the process of defining "dynamics." The rationale behind "perceptual-motor" tests has been considered only recently. Much of the theory behind clinical techniques has been developed through clinical and research application. In fact, much of the general theoretical framework presented previously was derived from clinical experience using these techniques. As a result, the assessor has the advantage of a wealth of knowledge and theory provided in recent decades of experimental research and clinical experience. For example, both the Kraepelinean nosological concepts on which the MMPI was based in 1938 and the "need-press" system of the TAT of 1936 seem very old fashioned and oversimplified today. As will be discussed subsequently, the development of pattern analysis of MMPI profiles during the past decade makes a "dynamic" use of this technique in assessing adolescents possible, and the evolution of "ego psychology" over the past 20 years has greatly enhanced the usefulness of the TAT.

Nevertheless, not one of these techniques has been as extensively overhauled as they should be. A totally new or even revised set of techniques updated to meet current knowledge and theory is sorely needed. In addition, new methods of behavioral changes are being developed that will need new methods of assessment or the revision of present techniques. All in all, there should be techniques to test hypotheses, not hypotheses about tests. Without a new or revised set of tools, it is necessary to delineate with precision the nature of the stimuli presented to the child and observe the behavior elicited with increased objectivity. Most important, it is necessary to revise the interpretation of the data derived from these techniques, utilizing the knowledge and theory about child development now available. In so doing it may be possible to utilize these old tools much more effectively. By translating the findings in terms of more recent theory it may be possible to perceive new patterns from such behavior, as the students of the MMPI have done.

A second reason for the gap between theory and technique in assessment may lie in the fact that many students today seem unacquainted with the theories behind the techniques that they use. For example, students learn to administer, score, and "interpret" the Rorschach, but they seldom read Rorschach's original monograph (1921). They know little of the Jungian theory or of the theories of perception current in Rorschach's time, from which he drew his concepts. Similarly they are often unaware of Murray's *Explorations in Personality* (1938) when they use the TAT. They rarely read Wechsler's original volume (1944) or Bender's monograph (1938). Although some of the theory presented in these studies is now out of date and disputable, much of it remains valid and has been expanded, which has made it part of the conceptual framework used today in clinical psychology. In discussing these techniques in the following chapters an attempt will be made to note some of these original concepts and to examine them afresh.

A third reason for the seeming lack of relationship between theory and technique lies in the nature of manifest or observable behavior itself. If my theory of ego functions was carried to its logical conclusions in the construction of new assessment techniques, it would seem that we would need different techniques for each function. Ideally there should be techniques that tap only affect or motivation or cognitive or conative functioning, so that the assessor would not have to dig each one out from responses to various techniques. Some techniques have attempted to do this, but with little success. Intelligence tests, for example, propose to measure cognitive abilities, but the motivational aspects of these achievement scales remain enmeshed in every response. Even the latest studies on the Bender have not succeeded in disentangling the motor facets from the perceptual ones of this behavior, although such a discrimination would aid considerably in differentiating the "expressively" from the "receptively" handicapped child. *Most clinical techniques are both multipurposeful and multifaceted.* They sample a variety of behaviors relatively indiscriminately.

The difficulty lies not so much in the techniques themselves, as in the fact that *any* behavioral response is multipurposeful and multifaceted. Each contains some affect, some perception, some motivation, some intellectual task, some social aspect, and some motoric tension. Perhaps the kinds of techniques needed are those that provide stimuli that would highlight the function to be studied, while diminishing the role of other functions or at least providing means of measuring their effects. At the same time, in order to study the interrelationship and interaction of these functions in the total pattern of the ego, techniques would still be needed to stimulate systematically more than one function. For example, it might be desirable to measure "social intelligence" as well as "culture-free" intelligence, or to assess a child's motivation under conditions of both high and low affect. To assess the development of "identity" it would seem necessary to permit all of these functions to flow freely without definite stimulation. In view of these considerations it is quite probable that although these techniques should be rebuilt, whatever new techniques are derived may not be very different from those that are now extant. In the long run the important aspect of clinical techniques is neither their content nor their structure, but it is how we—the users—observe and discriminate and conceptualize the responses that the child gives.

2. Methods, Procedures, and Techniques

To examine the nature of assessment it is helpful to distinguish between "methods" and "procedures." In this chapter under the rubric *method* I will cover the sampling of behavior and the general methods of analyzing clinical data. The subsequent chapters briefly review the techniques commonly used to sample children's behavior, their rationales, and how they operate. The term *method* thus refers to an overall process and *technique* to the specific tools used in the method. Part 3 will then be concerned with the procedures of applying this method and these techniques.

No matter what techniques are used, there is an overall method of logic in every assessment. A limited sample of the child's behavior and his/her past history are obtained, using standardized techniques. Then the data are organized according to various methods of scientific analysis. Finally inferences about the child are drawn from this analysis. Although this logical process may seem almost an assumed routine to most clinicians, a closer examination of it is warranted in order to understand clearly what can be gained from clinical techniques and how to apply them.

B. THE SAMPLING OF BEHAVIOR IN ASSESSMENT

In research studies the term *sample* usually refers to the number and variety (that is, demographic characteristics) of the subjects used in the experiment. In assessment the sample in this actuarial sense consists of an N of 1—or at most of a family. However, assessment is concerned with the sampling of the different kinds and "levels" of behaviors. An assessment samples not only a number of responses of one kind but also a variety of behaviors. As in experimental designs, the way these samples of behaviors are selected and collected is also very important. In assessment, however, the usual demographic variables used to describe the sample, such as age, sex, socioeconomic status, and IQ, are not—as in experiments—"ruled out" or "held constant," but they become essential variables in the investigation.

1. The Level of Ego Functioning

The kinds of behaviors to be sampled have been roughly outlined in the attempts in Chapters 1 and 2 to give operational definitions to the functions of the child's ego. More specific relationships between the kinds of behaviors sampled by the more common clinical techniques and these ego functions will be discussed in Chapters 4 to 6. At this point it is necessary to consider the manner in which the child's functions are expressed or demonstrated or—as it is commonly designated by personality theorists—the "level" of ego functioning. Freud designated the "unconscious" and "conscious" as levels of ego functioning, adding a "preconscious" state of awareness. The fact that much of the ego functions on an unconscious or automatic level of awareness may be missed by the casual student of psychoanalysis. There is a tendency by some writers and students to confuse the unconscious with what Freud labeled the "id." (This was included in the ego schemata in Chapter 2 as biological motivations.) However, Freud makes clear that id impulses can be quite conscious at times. In fact, awareness of impulses is one of the aims of psychoanalytic treatment. Similarly, the superego or social value system also functions for the most part on an unconscious level of awareness.

It is very difficult to define operationally and utilize Freud's concepts, since whether or not a child is aware of her/his functioning and is operating on a conscious level is almost impossible to divine even if he/she is asked. If a child denies it, it is difficult to know whether this denial is *suppression* of what the child thinks we would not approve, what he/she feels anxious or guilty about, or if it is a *repression*—that is, if the motivation or other ego function is actually out of the child's awareness. Without denying the heuristic value of these psychoanalytic concepts in understanding psychotherapeutic processes, it may be more helpful for the purposes of assessment to describe these levels of behavior in terms of how they are observed.

Rosenzweig and his colleagues (1950), in classifying psychological tests, posited three "levels" at which tests sample behavior: the "objective," "subjective," and "projective." Although these terms, as Rosenzweig used them, do describe the kinds of behaviors that are covered in the terms to be used in this discussion, they were introduced to describe the tests rather than the child. These terms moreover have been so used and misused in clinical psychology that they have collective positive and negative "halos" that might confuse the reader. Therefore it may be helpful to rename these categories to indicate the three levels at which the child's ego functioning is observed: (1) *manifest* or *overt* behavior; (2) the *subjective* expression of thoughts or feelings; and (3) *associative* behavior. It may be noted that this scheme of "levels" of observation does not distinguish between levels of awareness. No assumption is made as to whether a child is conscious of what she/he is demonstrating in manifest behavior, in subjective reports, or in associations. This question of the child's awareness of herself/himself and the type of behavior is a separate consideration.

By *manifest* behavior is meant that which is directly observable, what the assessor can see children do or hear them say. It includes motor behavior—both utilitarian and random—expressive gestures and sympathetic reactions, and much of verbal behavior as well, except self-description.

For example, manifest behavior includes the child's responses to IQ test questions or the number of verbs and adjectives used on the TAT (but not the content of the TAT story itself).

Subjective, then, refers to the child's reports or opinions about her/his own behavior, verbalizations of feelings, as well as reports of the behavior of others or other people's reports about the child.

By *associative* behavior is meant those illogical, idiosyncratic reactions in which a child appears to reflect (or to use the more popular term *project)* personal feelings, motivations, and ideas. Most commonly associative behavior can be observed when the child is instructed to respond in an associative fashion to the Rorschach inkblots or the TAT, or when asked what dreams make her/him think of. Associative behavior during interviews, however, is often seen when the child or parent begins a sentence with, for example, "That reminds me. . . ." There is an associative side to a great deal of the child's behavior, but it is often difficult to sample in the few, brief contacts of the usual assessment—at least not as definitively as in the more extensive contacts of psychotherapy.

Associative behavior may be illustrated by the following sequence of events during the assessment of a 6-year-old boy who came to the clinic because of his persistent enuresis. Asked to make a drawing of his own choice, he sketched a rocket ship with red flames shooting out of the top rather than as is usual, from the rockets at the bottom. When finished he volunteered that he could write his name on the drawing and proceeded to make a large letter *P* (the first letter of his name Peter), but instead of completing it, he continued to make more *P*'s, all the while shouting "Pee, pee, pee." Excited and blushing, he began to talk about how much he loved his mother, how she "never, never" punished him, and how he "never, never" got angry with her, even though the assessor had not asked him about any of this material. This set of associations was very brief, however, thus limiting any analysis of it or inferences from it. What the assessor could note was the fact that in the treatment of other enuretic children, persistent associations have been noted between "pee pee" and excitement, as well as both angry and sexual feelings about the child's mother.

There are two major reasons why the assessor needs to be definitive about the "level" at which she/he is observing. First, each level yields somewhat different clues about the child's ego functioning. Some ego functions can be observed easily at one level, but they are difficult to observe at another. Second, the child's functioning may change, sometimes quite markedly, from level to level. For example, he/she may demonstrate one type of affect or motivation at one level and show a different, even opposite, feeling or drive at another. It is this variation in behavior from level to level that gives clues regarding the existence of conflicts, defenses, and "dynamics".

2. Manifest Behavior

This offers the best observation of a child's developing skills. Thus in manifest behavior one can easily observe a child's motor development, intellectual efficiency, and even creative abilities and intellectual achievement. The kinds of social coping mechanisms the child has developed may be observed on the playground or at home or, if such observations are not feasible, in relationship with the assessor. Some aspects of children's affect are also directly observable; for example, anger in their voices, the depression written across their faces, or the anxiety in the tremor of their hands. Children have a fairly wide variety of ways to express their affect in manifest behavior. One may express it in hyperactivity, another in remaining as rigid as a statue. Yet, reading people's faces is far from an exact or reliable way of sampling their affect. Even children may mask their expressions, tone down their voices, or otherwise hide their feelings. Most confus-

ing is the fact that in a single facial expression or gesture the child may be expressing a mixture of feelings. In summary, manifest behavior often yields well-defined clues about the motor, intellectual, social, and to varying degrees the affective functioning of the child's ego. Manifest behavior may also suggest hypotheses about children's perceptual functioning and motivations, but usually these ego functions are not easily observable from manifest behavior.

3. Subjective Behavior

Children's feelings about something or someone, their perceptions of a situation, or their motivations may be more easily discovered by the simple device of asking them. Psychologists have long used subjective reports from their subjects, adults and children, as one sample of the subject's behavior—even though psychologists recognize that both adults and children do not always "tell the truth" about either their behavior or their feelings and opinions. Both questionnaires and interviews are limited by what the subjects are *willing* to tell and what they are *able* to tell about themselves. Psychologists have discovered that children are not always good observers of their own behavior, and that many of their feelings and motivations remain below the level of their awareness. Nevertheless, subjective reports remain one of the mainstays of assessment—if for no other reason than that subjective reports do reveal the perception of the self. The degree to which the child is developing an effective and accurate self-perception may be assessed by contrasting these subjective reports with the behavior that was observed on a manifest level and through his/her associations. Manifest and associative behavior yield clues about the feelings that a child cannot or will not talk about.

Even under these limitations many children and adults are freer in discussing themselves than the skeptics would have us believe. Because children are thought not to verbalize as logically and accurately as adults there is a tendency in the assessment literature about children to emphasize non-verbal techniques, observation of free play, or associative samples, with little discussion of such subjective techniques as interviews with children or children's questionnaires. In practice, however, clinicians frequently conduct interviews with even quite young children. Also, there is more than a grain of truth in the popular notion that children by and large are "naive" or "open-faced" and "tell all." As with adults, whether children will subjectively report about themselves and their families depends a great deal on their trust in the assessor and on the intensity of their need for help. One advantage in using subjective sampling with children is that, in contrast with adults, they do not have to hide their dependency on others for approval and support. Thus quite often they will be less defensive in discussing their attitudes and feelings. Their defenses moreover are not as complex as those of an adult. The most frequent defense of children is negative and embarrassed silence. Such denial is usually so blatant that even the child cannot long countenance it. In most instances children, if encouraged and supported, will spill out subjective feelings and volunteer a great deal about themselves and their environments. Children's reports about "factual" matters certainly may be distorted either by lack of information or by the intrusion of their own associations. However, the child's reports on his/her home life, on parental behavior, and especially parental affect are not to be dismissed merely because he/she may not give an accurate chronological account or because he/she becomes confused on dates and places. Thus sampling of ego functioning on the subjective level in children can yield considerable data concerning affective, motivational, perceptual, and even social behaviors. Except insofar as one considers the logical aspects of the child's verbalization or can check the accuracy of facts and observations, subjective reports add little to assessment of intellectual functioning. The nature of a child's vocalization is of

course a manifest behavior, giving clues about motor functioning. But he/she may also describe and evaluate his/her motor behavior quite accurately.

4. Associative Behavior

Although at one time associative behavior was considered to be outside the pale of science and "childish", since Freud's discovery of the "royal road to the unconscious" by means of dreams, there has been an expanding recognition of and utilization of associative sampling of behavior in both clinical and other scientific studies of children's functioning. Many techniques have been introduced that are designed to investigate children's fantasies—in addition to the observation of free play. Unfortunately there has been too little attention paid to the rationale behind many of these techniques or to the logic of the analysis of responses to them. Nevertheless, these projective innovations have enabled the psychologist to sample the alogical ideation, the perceptual functioning, the affect, and the motivations that underlie the child's manifest and subjective behaviors.

In understanding what is meant by *associative* or *projective,* a word needs to be said about the term *alogical.* Actually, *associative ideation* in the broad sense of the term is the basis for all thinking, as has been recognized by most philosophers and their heirs—the psychologists—since the eighteenth century at least. The rules of "logic" used in Western philosophy are largely attempts to provide means for distinguishing associations that also have a basis in the extrapersonal world from those that are chiefly intrapersonal and to provide rules for communication of these extrapersonal association.* As was discussed in Part 1, the intellectual development of the child consists of learning and applying methods of distinguishing such associa-

---

*In contrast, Eastern philosophies are more concerned with intrapersonal experiences and thought, resulting in different rules of "logic." In this regard the Eastern philosophies are more *psycho*-logic.

tions, for the most part. As was also noted, a great deal of this learning about *formal* associative thinking is practiced in the child's fantasy. The child invents, imagines, fantasizes, and thus develops "creative" thinking as a necessary background to predicting and comprehending reality. If children are to learn by experience they must be able to fantasize what experiences may bring. Thus although children's associative behavior may be largely alogical, it has in it the seeds of intellectual development.

Another reason for sampling and understanding the alogical associative processes in children's functioning is that the rules of logic provide only a very limited testing of reality. Although logical reasoning is necessary for much effective problem-solving behavior, it is not the only effective way of experiencing reality. Affective, conative, and motor functioning are neither experienced nor conducted according to "rules of logic," but they are quite as much a part of the experiencing of reality as is intellectual functioning. Children usually recognize that the "rules" governing these functions often have little relation to any "logic." Adolescents are quick to spot the blatant inconsistencies of social mores and behavior. There is of course a *psycho*-logic to these functions, and children learn psychological coping methods to direct their ego functions. Sampling of this alogical associative behavior in children thus gives the assessor an opportunity to estimate how well the child is learning the psycho-logic of ego functioning. The associative behavior sampled in the child's responses to inkblots, TAT pictures, or drawings provides a wealth of data about the child's motivation and affect and his/her skills in coping with them.

C. ANALYSIS OF THE BEHAVIOR SAMPLED

The usefulness of data in any scientific study depends largely on how it is organized and analyzed. Although the actual procedures of analyzing the data come after the samples of behavior are collected, the data are not gathered in helter-skelter fashion for the most part, but in as systematic a fashion as is possible to facilitate its analysis. The clinician may gain some impressions from random or casual observations of the child. However, such observations are limited in value, because in their evaluation it is often discovered that many other facts and variables are needed in order to draw any conclusions from them. Such casual observation tends to provide data that defy analysis. For the most part, therefore, samples of behavior are most useful if drawn with some methods of analysis in mind.

Any sample of behavior may be analyzed in several different ways, and the assessor should be prepared to use more than one method, even if the specific technique is most commonly analyzed by only one method. Three such methods commonly used in as assessment may be distinguished: (1) the "metric" or "scoring" approach; (2) the analysis of "patterns" of behavior; and (3) the analysis of "themes."

1. Metric Analysis

From a strictly scientific point of view, all clinical techniques should have some form of *metric* analysis. In fact, some kinds of standardized measuring units are available for most clinical samples of behavior. Some of these scoring systems—like those for observations or for interviews—have never been developed much beyond the experimental stage, and they are therefore unknown to most clinicians. These are apt to be limited to the experimental variables for which they were built. Like most of the scoring systems for the TAT, they tend to be clumsy and require considerable time and effort to apply. Clinicians moreover seem to have an aversion to metric analysis of their data, as if in some magical fashion they destroy or contaminate their data by calculating scores. This aversion may have arisen because at one time metric analysis was the only accepted approach. Since many of the ego functions had not been sampled at all, let alone by techniques with well-developed metric analysis, the task of assessment seemed impossible if one were limited only to those techniques with scores. Then too, clinicians were entranced with the newly introduced projective techniques, which although they often had some rough scoring system, nevertheless lent themselves more easily to nonmetric methods of analysis.

The advantages of metric analysis of behavioral data are obvious: It provides operational units by which the extent and intensity of any variable can be estimated. Since a great deal of the description of and prediction about ego functioning is in terms of extent (for example, of ability or of defensiveness) and intensity (for example, of anger or depression), some form of metric analysis is invaluable. The chief disadvantage lies in the fact that a separate measure for each variable is necessary—except where two or more variables can be recategorized under some higher level of generalization. Often the problem with some of the current scales is that they try to measure several variables at once, variables that cannot logically be lumped together. If metric scores were available for every variable needed for a thorough assessment—all the IQ scores, all the perceptual scores, scores on each kind of affect and each type of social behavior, and the like—the result would be analyzable only by using a computer program, an idea that is being entertained in several quarters. Computer analysis would be required not only because of the mass of scores and "signs," but also because very few of these variables are actually discreet and independent of one another, and any actuarial analysis would have to take the intercorrelations between scores into account.

Another problem in the use of metric analysis is that some guideline is needed to establish when a score has clinical import. What is the "cutting score?" At what point on a scale can it be said that a child is developing satisfactorily? For some types of variables—for example, school achievement—it is easy enough to establish a norm for an age group. Such a norm uses an *extra*personal criterion. However, if an *intra*personal dynamic such as repression is being assessed, some other kind of criterion would have to be adopted: How much can the child repress without deterring other development? Or, how much does he/she need to repress in order to avoid being overwhelmed? In clinical work the psychologist is frequently faced with the fact that quite a few variables have a simple present/not present significance. For example, one suicidal attempt or one grand-mal seizure may be clinically "significant." This "cutting-point" problem has been interestingly conceptualized by Fisher (1959) in his "inverted-pear" diagram and critically examined further by Storms (1960). Every clinician who takes note of one inverted drawing on the Bender, of a single bizarre Rorschach response, or one TAT response should be aware of this problem. The cutting-point problem of course increases in the assessment of children since a different cutting point in a scoring system would be needed for each developmental level—if not for each year.

Perhaps the biggest complaint that clinicians voice against metric analysis is that when behavior is "reduced" to a score, one loses the richness of the personality, the dynamics of the interactions between forces in the individual and of his/her interpersonal relationships. Metric analysis, its critics say, leads quickly to "test-oriented" assessment in which the unique character of the child is ignored. However, metric analysis in itself does not mean being "test oriented," for one can become enmeshed in one's technique no matter what method of analysis is used. One can lose sight of the child and of the dynamics, and so on, if one considers metric analysis to be the *only* method and does not use it in combination with other methods. The difficulty actually lies not in the metric method itself, but in its misuse, particularly when it comes to drawing inferences from the score or sign. As will be discussed later, metric analysis is associated most commonly with "direct" inferences, although it can be the basis for other types of inferences as well.

2. Pattern Analysis

In order to avoid some of these difficulties with the metric method, clinicians and other test users have turned to analyzing *patterns* of responses. The most commonly recognized pattern analysis has been the profile of scores, for example, on the MMPI or Wechsler tests. In this way the clinician groups sets of scores together and avoids the problem of too many seemingly unrelated scores. Even on the Binet it is common clinical practice to subdivide the items into patterns and to look at success and failure on items involving verbalization, memory, or judgment, for example. On the Rorschach one needs to regard not only the individual scores but the total "psychogram"—the interrelationship between the various kinds of perceptual cues used by the child. Furthermore, Rorschach analysis includes what is known as "sequence" analysis, which means looking through the protocol to note how one response follows another. Such sequential examination of behavior is actually used in practice by many clinicians in analyzing the behavior of the child during play observations or in interviews, although it may not be as formalized or as systematic as on the Rorschach and is not labeled "sequential."

3. Thematic Analysis

Such analysis of sequential patterns leads into what may be called *thematic* analysis—a term associated of course with the Thematic Apperception Test. *Thematic* refers to the patterns of behavior or ideation *within* the protocols of test responses or of interview or observation notes, in contrast to the overall pattern of scores or sequence of scores. Such themes consist of summary statements of what the child is doing or saying in any one unit or response or behavior, such as a TAT story, a set of

interviewer–child responses in an interview, or interaction between the child and a peer on the playground, as, for example, in the following TAT story (to Picture 1, Murray series—Boy with violin):

He's trying to study his violin. He doesn't want to—or maybe he does, I don't know. It's his grandfather's violin and his father wants him to play it like he does. So does his mother. He wants to but he's tired of studying it. (What happens?) His mothers calls him back in to practice. . . . I guess he comes, 'cause he doesn't want to make his mother cry. (How does he feel then?) He feels bad.

Such a story might be analyzed along with other stories into patterns of needs and stresses of various kinds, for example, the press for achievement, the need for conformity, the need for play, and so on. The theme, however, might be summarized as "ambivalence over conformity with and identification with parents, leading toward guilt feelings in response to maternal depression."

Another example may be taken from an interview with a family. Before the interview began, the two children started playing a noisy game that did not permit conversation. Neither parent made any move to quiet the children. Finally the father—red in the face—asked the interviewer's permission to interrupt the children! After several attempts he succeeded in getting them to stop and listen. The children then began complaining to the interviewer that their father never played with them. The father denied this in a hurt voice and asked for verification from his wife that he spent considerable time with his children. The wife begrudgingly admitted that they watched TV together. The father, more flustered, declared, "This isn't the topic." He reminded his wife that they were really there to talk about the boy's enuresis. The sister, age 9, began to giggle, pointing to her brother. The son, age 7, looking hurt and embarrassed, flung himself on the floor. The mother tried to comfort the son, glaring at the father. The son then declared angrily that "father is always hurting me." The father, again on the defensive, asked, "When?" "When you're playing with us," retorted the daughter. The "theme" here appears to be one of mutual accusation and control by creation of guilt.

Finally, it is necessary to look at the overall pattern of themes—the recurrent themes and the idiosyncratic ones. To borrow still other phrases from musical analysis, one can examine *theme and variation,* noting where possible the leitmotiv— the central patterns of interaction or dynamics within the ego. Such thematic analysis is thus a method of extracting some of the interrelationships between the various ego functions, particularly between the affective, motivational, and social ones. Such thematic analysis can also be conducted to study the perceptual and cognitive reactions to social stress versus personal motivation. It helps to answer such questions as the following: How well does the child perceive and comprehend when under stress? How well can he/she perceive and understand the stresses themselves?

D. THE EVALUATION OF TECHNIQUES

Traditionally the adequacy of a technique is determined in terms of its standardization, reliability, and validity. These determinations require well-designed and conceptualized research. A thorough knowledge of such research—both actuarial and experimental—is without question necessary to the background of the assessor. Since this volume is directed mainly to the overall nature, processes, and procedures of assessment rather than being about techniques per se, a review of the research studies behind each technique is beyond its scope. The pertinent question for assessment moreover is how such research results are applied in everyday use. Thus it may be helpful to consider the relationships between such research and assessment.

1.   Standardization

In considering this question it is necessary to review at least the essential features of these traditional approaches to the evaluation of clinical techniques. These statistical evaluations are of course particularly associated with and arose out of the construction of those techniques commonly called "tests." A *test* may be defined as any standardized sample of behavior. Sometime it is forgotten that other assessment techniques, such as interviews or observational techniques, also have questions of standardization, reliability, and validity.

Standardization means three things. First, the sample of behavior is always taken in the same way, using standard instructions, standard stimuli, and a standard or uniform method of analyzing the responses. Second, standardization refers to the established range and variety of responses obtained from a defined group of children. On a well-standardized technique, responses can be identified as "normal," "usual," "frequent," "unpopular," "sterotyped," "pathological," "bizarre," "idiosyncratic," "imaginative," and so forth. Standardization establishes the number of subjects who usually "pass" or "accept" or "fail" or "reject" an item or a set of items. Third, standardization includes a reference population of which the norms are applicable. Most tests are standardized on a fairly broad range of children—from various socioeconomic backgrounds. Since assessment is concerned with development, a standardization sample needs to be stratified by age to obtain age norms. Other research studies may compare these norms of the original standardization sample with the responses of other groups of children who were not included in the original sample or with subsamples of the original. Although studies of individual differences (which are really *group* differences) are not commonly considered to be standardization, in effect they do add to the standardization by supplying further norms in terms of differences between groups.

The applicability of standardization to assessment techniques may seem so obvious as not to warrant discussion. The use of standard instructions and stimuli, the knowledge of the range and variety of responses obtained there from within the "normal" population, and the differences between these responses and those given by other kinds of children constitute the guidelines for drawing inferences about the level of development of the individual child. Such norms are basic to any estimate of the effectiveness of each of the ego functions. At one time, before much was known about "dynamics" or the interaction of ego functions, assessment consisted wholly of these "norms." Currently psychologists sometimes become so involved in "psychodynamics" that they tend to forget or ignore the basic normative data, or even deride it as "pigeonholing" the child. For example, if a child who is known to be beset by social and personal stress and to lack affective controls achieves a very low score on a standardized IQ test, some clinicians are prone to excuse the child's performance and say that "he/she is not *really* retarded because. . . ." Such statements fly in the face of the facts, for by these established standards, the child is—for whatever reason—"retarded" in intellectual development. Obversely, one may find what at first sight seems to be "pathology," for example, gross distortions on a test of visual motor functioning or repeated themes of Oedipal conflict on the TAT. But it may be forgotten for the moment that the visual motor task is more complex than a child of this age can manage, or that the child is at the age when Oedipal fantasies are at their height.

Of course it is necessary at times to alter slightly the instructions or even the stimuli of a standardized technique in order to attract a child or to enable him/her to understand what is wanted. Or sometimes it may be helpful to "inquire" further about a response the child has made than is called for by the standard procedures. However, such alterations should have a definite rationale and not be just the whim of the assessor. The assessor moreover must clearly recognize that the technique has been altered, thus affecting analyses and inferences from it. Carelessness about and ignorance of the instructions and stimuli are far too often an error of the clinical tyro, and they are characteristic of amateurish research.

2. Reliability

The reliability or consistency of a technique also involves several different questions. The first that might be mentioned deals essentially with how reliably the standardized method of analyzing the technique is used—that is, the reliability of the "scoring." Here the question is, Can several assessors score the test the same way? This is called *inter*judge reliability. Similarly there is an *intra*judge reliability: How reliable is any one assessor in scoring?*

Interjudge reliability is essentially a measure of how well assessors can communicate with one another, for if assessors do not analyze in the same way it is unlikely that they will make the same inferences. A technique with low or unknown interjudge reliability opens the door to differences in clinical impressions and results. Statements of intrajudge reliability are rare—except where a technique is being used experimentally—for this reliability varies with the assessor. In practice, each assessor should check his/her own consistency in analyzing techniques (although few assessors make such a check). For example, every once in a while an assessor should pull a sample of protocols from his/her files, have the responses copied with the scores omitted, and then rescore and check the

*Similar studies of the interjudge or intrajudge reliability of inferences can be made, but they are rare. More often, such studies are made of clinical judgment in general, rather than of specific techniques.

rescoring against the original, at least by casual inspection if not statistically. Such a personal check enables the assessor to know how consistently he/she operates and to recognize what changes he/she may be making—whether consciously or inadvertently. Such a personal, intrajudge check of course reveals only the consistency of scoring. It is still quite possible that there are consistent biases. An assessor should also cooperate with other assessors from time to time in a similar, informal interjudge reliability check. The need for such checks from time to time is illustrated by the fact that in a classroom experiment, students who had been "thoroughly" trained in the use of a standard intelligence test for over a year varied as much as 5 IQ points in scoring the same protocol!

Reliability refers more commonly to the consistency with which the child responds to the stimuli or—in test constructor's terms—the consistency with which the test "pulls" certain responses. Actually there are two such kinds of test reliability: (1) the "test-retest" correlation, which checks consistency of respondents over a specified time and (2) intratest reliability, which is commonly measured by the "split-half" or similar test correlations, which give a measure of whether the child responds to similar items in the same manner. In thinking about these kinds of reliabilities the assessor must ask both what is expected from the child and what is expected from the technique in question. For example, reliability over time in a growing and changing organism whose "mind is not yet made up" may not be expected to be as great as that in an adult. In fact, if one is interested in rate of development—that is, in changes—techniques that have a high reliability over time may not yield much information! Yet one might not gain much information from an item or a technique on which children generally responded randomly over relatively brief periods of time. Similarly, on a technique designed to sample a single trait or dimension, it might be well to have a high

split-half reliability, but on a technique designed purposefully to sample the variation of the child's perceptions, split-half or other measures of item reliability are meaningless. As Rosenzweig and his colleagues (1948) discovered in the construction of his Picture Frustration Study, it is quite possible that a child may be quite guarded at the beginning of a test, interview, or observation, and then become more expansive or self-revealing as he/she becomes more confident. On the other hand, the child may begin with naive, open-face admissions of his/her feelings and attitudes only to become anxious and guarded as he/she unconsciously realizes he/she is revealing himself/herself. Such change of test-taking attitudes or "set" may not affect the split-half reliability if the split consists of alternate items. However, children also may vary their set from item to item, following a revealing statement by an innocuous, covering, or retracting response. In fact the inventors of the TAT purposely chose picture stimuli that they believed might be innocuous or less "anxiety producing" to present to the child subsequent to those pictures believed to be more shocking stimuli. Whether or not these hypotheses about the anxiety-provoking nature of such stimuli are valid, such possibilities make the assessor think twice before accepting interitem correlations as the only measures of reliability.

The question of the internal consistency of a technique becomes slightly different when the technique is designed to sample ego dynamics. Here the reliability question might be phrased as follows: Do the items of the technique pull responses that are generally recognizable as unique to that child, or do the items draw responses from different children that are so similar or "popular" or "socially desirable" that they tell us little about the child other than his/her conformity to social norms? A brief check on the card-pull reliability of adult patients on the TAT was made in a classroom demonstration (Palmer, 1952) where naive judges were asked to match stories from different cards by the same subjects. Although most subjects were successfully matched above chance, some TAT cards were missed significantly more often than others.

3. Validity

Perhaps the most involved question asked about clinical techniques is that of validity. A full discussion of this complex topic cannot be included here, but attention may be drawn to three aspects that have particular pertinence to the practical task of assessment. First, there is the question (Jenkins, 1946), Validity of what? A validity study should begin with a careful examination of the purposes of the technique—that is, what a technique is designed to sample and measure. Any validity study should begin with a recognition and understanding of its rationale. At the same time a validation should state clearly the operations that the technique demands of both the subject and the assessor. Validation studies too often appear to be poorly acquainted with the purposes and nature of the technique under study. Sometimes validation studies even ignore the standard administration and scoring of the technique! For example, a few years ago a number of studies appeared that purported to check the validity of the so-called "color shock" on the Rorschach. None of these studies paid any attention to Rorschach's rationale for using color in his inkblots nor to what he and other Rorschach experts have given as the theoretical base for drawing inferences from the subject's response to color—or, in this instance, the failure of the subject to respond. These studies were concerned with whether more signs of shock occurred on colored cards than acromatic cards, and the results did show that such signs of shock were equally present on both. Whether the shock to achromatic cards means anything different than the shock to color—as maintained by Rorschach

theorists—was not even considered by these research studies. In some of these studies moreover, no inquiry was made to determine whether the subject's response might be based on the color, thus ignoring the fact that such inquiry is an integral part of the Rorschach operations.

Second, the assessor in reading validation studies needs to ask, What *kind* of validity? Cronbach and Meehl (1955) distinguished four types of validity studies: concurrent, predictive, content, and construct validation. As the authors pointed out, each of these aspects of validity needs to be studied. The assessor needs to know (1) whether the behavior sampled by the technique is similar to other current samples of that kind of behavior; (2) whether and to what degree one can draw inferences from (predict from) this sample of this kind of behavior with respect to other kinds of behaviors in similar or even different situations; (3) whether the sampled behavior is part of the universe of behavior to which the prediction is made; and (4) whether or not the "constructs" or rationale of the technique have been demonstrated as supportable hypotheses in experimental studies. Techniques may be quite valid in some respects and invalid in others. For example, the predictive validity of IQ's obtained from "infant" scales is zero; there is no predictable relation between the IQ obtained on, say, the Cattel at age 6 months and the IQ obtained on the same child on the Binet at 6 years. (Nor would such predictability be possible from what is known about the development of intelligence.) On the other hand, infant IQ scales do have fair descriptive validity. The infant's responses are valid representations of current intellectual development as compared with other infants of the same chronological age. Also there is considerable evidence from the experimental literature on infants that the rationale behind the items included in such scales is valid. The motor tasks and visual discriminations required in these scales correspond to what

Piaget has shown to be the "seeds" of intelligence.

4. Summary

The conscientious student who reads the research literature on clinical techniques carefully and with a critical eye is apt to be quite discouraged and disillusioned concerning both the techniques and the research. Many of the major clinical tools are inadequately and haphazardly standardized, possess only questionable reliability of any kind, and have only "face" validity or even that their validity has not been questioned. Also many of the reliability and validity studies have been inadequately thought out, poorly designed, and sloppily executed. One may justifiably ask how it is possible to carry on assessment with such tools. Many clinicians attempt to rationalize away the whole question, to try to declare that these questions of standardization, reliability, and validity have little or no bearing on "dynamic" assessment. Or—since the problems seem insoluble— some clinicians may go blithely ahead and not worry about it at all. I am not content with such arguments, and I believe it is far better to be painfully aware of the limitations of clinical techniques, constantly demanding of ourselves the required improvements in test construction and research design. Unfortunately "tool-sharpening" research is currently not considered prestigious.* It may not seem to be important research—that is, not establishing anything "basic" about behavior. But in my opinion, studies of validity often add to our general knowledge about behavior, and even routine studies of reliability or checks on standardization contain kernels of facts about development.

How then can an assessor carry out studies of the individual child with poorly

*Such studies seldom are acceptable as doctoral theses, and they are not considered as worthwhile items in a professor's bibliography.

standardized tools of doubtful reliability and unknown validity? Where such research is lacking, the answer to this question lies in an increased responsibility to examine these tools carefully and thoughtfully. It becomes essential to understand clearly the rationale and constructs underlying the technique, and to know whether such a rationale seems at least reasonable in the light of experimental research on these constructs—even though the experimental work does not directly refer to the clinical tool. There is added reason to analyze carefully the operations of the technique, to see if these operations at least appear to sample the behavior in question in a uniform, standard manner. As was suggested before, an assessor may spot check her/his consistency as a judge of the behavior sampled. And if there is no opportunity to conduct formal reliability and validity studies, an assessor must constantly scan her/his clinical studies, observing as is best possible any signs of inadequate reliabilities or of invalid descriptions, inferences, and predictions. The clinician who remains thus critical of her/his own techniques will be better prepared to make the crucial research studies.

In evaluating the techniques of assessment psychologists may well begin by reminding themselves that although they aspire to be scientists and strive to be as scientific as possible in their methods and thinking, the techniques they use are far from the accurate scientific instruments they would like them to be. Rather, these techniques are more comparable to the tools of the artisan. Their accuracy thus depends largely on the skill of the assessor, how expertly he/she uses them, how well he/she knows the nature of the material he/she is working on—that is, the developing ego—and the plans and designs he/she has in mind while working. Like the workman's tools, the assessor's techniques are not as central to his/her product as is his/her knowledge of child behavior and a skill in using the techniques to study the problem at hand. How these techniques can be put to use (the procedure of assessment) will be discussed in the next section. At this point, however, review is needed of the general purposes, operations, accuracy, and clinical advantages and disadvantages of some of the most commonly used techniques.

CHAPTER 4

Techniques Based on Samples
of Manifest Behavior

Many frequently used techniques are based on the rationale that by sampling directly observable behavior, one may predict that the child will behave similarly in other situations where such behavior is also manifestly observable. As will be seen, manifest behavior may also yield valuable clues regarding other levels of behavior. Inferences from such samples are often simple extrapolations. Included among such techniques are structured and unstructured observations of the child at play or work, structured tests of intelligence, structured tests of educational achievement, tests of visual-motor reproduction, and tests of determinants of perception.

A. UNSTRUCTURED OBSERVATION

Naturalistic observations were the beginnings of science. Before there were telescopes or even mathematics, scientists observed and recorded the movement of planets and stars while watching them from hilltops. Zoology and botany began with expeditions. Similarly scientists such as Darwin (1877) and Preyer (1881) began watching infants in daily activities. From these observations hypotheses were drawn that were later to be tested in the laboratory or in statistical studies. Both Freud and Piaget were essentially naturalists. In the assessment of individual children and in the study of the general development of children such naturalistic observation remains a revered and cherished technique that is employed widely—if not always very wisely.

The basic elements, or "operations," of

such observations are the setting and its structure and the degree of interaction between the child and the observer. How children behave in a hospital ward may well differ from how they behave in a schoolyard, and both behaviors may differ from their behavior in and around their own homes. The observer should ask, To what degree does the situation impose limits on the child's behavior? "Does it demand certain tasks of the child and/or obligate the child to specified or implied social relationships, or does it allow a relatively free choice of behavior and social interaction?" Whether the observer is part of the situation for the child also changes the nature of the child's reactions and of the observations. When children realize their behavior is under observation, they act differently than when the observer is out of sight or awareness. Thus the behavior observed during the administration of other techniques (aside from the child's responses to these techniques) contains a large element of reaction to the assessor. The child also reacts to being "put to the test." These elements may be lacking (and other factors present) when, for example, the assessor stands behind a one-way screen and observes the child at play in a nursery-school's playground that is familiar to the child. Therefore it is very necessary in reporting and drawing inferences from such "unstructured" observation to state clearly just how unstructured the situation was and to define how and where the child was observed.

Sampling of behavior by means of direct observation also requires that the frequency and length of our observations be specified. Brief, en passant, or haphazard observations are apt to yield biased or at least unreliable results. The assessor should plan these observations carefully, and— depending on the situation, the child, and the aims of the assessment—he/she should decide in advance whether a series of brief observations or several lengthy observations are needed or whether to vary the extent and frequency. These factors must be specified when drawing conclusions from direct observations.

The analysis of such observations is often more "unstructured" than the sample. In clinical practice (as distinct from research studies), the observed behavior is seldom scored or rated in metric fashion. The fairly reliable rating scales constructed in development research studies have not been adopted in clinical use. The careful assessor who makes detailed notes may be able to detect patterns of repeated reactions or sequences of reactions in the child's behavior, however. If enough observations in a variety of situations are made, an observer may be able to demarcate recurrent themes in the child's behavior. If the assessor falls back on some intuitive global impression, the conclusions are also likely to be global and nonspecific.

Because this sample is assumed to consist of "direct" manifest behavior, there may be a temptation to draw only "direct" inferences from it. There is often an aura attached to direct observation of the child that contains the implicit assumption that because one is observing the child au naturel rather than by means of a more formal "test," few or no inferences may be drawn. However, it is still quite possible to use such data inductively and to build hypotheses from it about different aspects of ego functioning. Various hypotheses may be deductively checked out using such unstructured behavior as a criterion. One may want to know, for example, what kinds of hypotheses might be drawn about the child's impulse controls from her/his playground activities. Is the murderous hostility that is blatant in her/his fantasy on the TAT represented in interactions with peers and adult authorities? If so, In what form? With what stimuli?

Perhaps the greatest difficulty in using this technique is that there is no way of firmly establishing the reliability of either samples or judgments. One reason for making a series of observations—rather than depending on just one or two long periods of observation—is that expanding the number of samples or "items" may increase this reliability. Similarly, by using a number of observations the psychologist may be able to inspect the consistency of his/her judgments. The assessor must nevertheless always keep in mind that in using unstructured observations there is considerable possibility that both the sampling and analyses of the data may be quite biased. The fact that the reliability over time of this technique is unknown and that reliability of judgment varies greatly from assessor to assessor of course limits the validity of the inferences that are drawn. It is possible to gain quite valid insights from a single casual observation, but the confidence in such validity often ranges from overweening pride in one's own intutition to scoffing distrust and disregard of such hunches—valid though they may be. Insofar as the purposes of the observations are carefully thought out in advance and the operations specific to these purposes and the data systematically analyzed, the validity of inferences is strengthened.

In considering the validity of conclusions about such "unstructured" observation it is necessary to remember that while the observation is "direct," there can be no assumption about the level of the child's behavior. When no direction or structure is laid down for a child, he/she is free to interact with the environment in a "direct" fashion—or to associate to it. Whether children are at play or taking "tests" in an office, much of their behavior may be quite "projective" or associative. Thus behavior in the sandbox or on the tricycle or even posture, gestures, and facial expression while taking an IQ test may be as much a matter of a child's "internal" associations and of projection of these associations as they are reactions to the immediate stimuli in the situation or task at hand. If the child's behavior in such situations is largely on the associative level, then inferences from it about his/her manifest behavior may be of doubtful validity. For example, if a child starts to hit another child on the playground, she/he may be reacting aggressively to something the other child has done or threatens to do, and one might be tempted to infer that this represents a sample of how this child reacts when attacked. However, if this were the only sample of the child's social behavior on the playground, the possibility could not be ruled out that the subject was projecting bottled-up feelings of hostility onto some innocent bystander. In this latter instance the manifest behavior—hitting—would not depend on a manifest stimuli, and it probably would be more frequent and less predictable. Here again, several extended observations may be needed to be able to discern to what extent the child comes into the playground ready to pick a fight, seeking attention, or feeling depressed and withdrawn, and to what extent and in what fashion he/she is reacting to the situation and the behavior of the people in it. Both aspects and their combination need to be considered in assessing the child's ego functioning.

Keeping the preceding precautions and limitations in mind, observation of the child outside of the office—on the playground, at home or in the classroom, or in the daily routine of a hospital ward—can be a very useful adjunct to assessment. Used in conjunction with other techniques it offers several possibilities that are otherwise unobtainable. First, by obtaining such a sample of the child's behavior when not under pressure to perform vis-à-vis the assessor, it is possible to estimate how much of the child's reactions to other techniques represent a "testing set." Comparing the two situations, the extent to which the child is usually anxious, uncontrolled, poorly motivated, ambitious, and so on, can be estimated. It may be possible moreover to define more clearly the degree to which the testing situation has promoted these reactions. Thus the external observation can yield another estimate of the generalizability of inferences from other techniques.

One must be very careful, however, in using such "manifest" behavior as a criterion for validating other techniques. When the same kind of behavior is observed both on the playground and during the formal testing in an office, one may be able to conclude that this is a general set the child brings to different situations. When she/he reacts differently it may be assumed at best that in the office she/he is reacting to being "tested" and distinguishes between the pressures of the adult demands for performance and the social pressures of the playground. In either instance, the psychologist will be better able to evaluate the child's responses to the tests. These test responses may also yield further information about the nature of the child's behavior outside the office. Also in the long run these correlations between overt behavior and test responses—be they strongly positive, quite negative, or even zero-older correlations—yield clues as to interactions between various ego functions and between various levels of behavior. For example, if a child who has been observed to be quite conforming, passive, and cautious on the playground tells wild tales of violence to the TAT, there is some evidence that feelings of hostility are more likely to be worked out on the fantasy level than in overt behavior. Or if the child makes a high score on an intelligence test but obtains low grades in school—where she/he "goofs off" or plays the role of the stupid clown—questions need to be raised about feelings of adequacy in social situations, dependency on others to solve problems intellectually, or resistance to authorities other than the assessor.

B.   STRUCTURED TESTS OF INTELLECTUAL ACHIEVEMENT

These thoroughly standardized and reliable tests of intellectual achievement have been so widely used and known for several decades that a general review of their composition and nature would seem almost unnecessary. A detailed inspection of their construction and composition is beyond the scope of this section. Just because these techniques are universally accepted, however, their basic rationale is seldom clearly stated. Their operations are infrequently delineated, their validity is not questioned, nor is their clinical utility evaluated. No matter how endowed these techniques may be with scientific respectability, it may be helpful to examine these questions about them in order to understand clearly their place in an assessment battery.

1. Rationale

The rationale underlying IQ tests is that they consist of direct, manifest samples of highly structured problem-solving behavior. It is assumed that these samples are so similar to problem-solving tasks in other structured situations that one 'can directly extrapolate to and predict the behavior of the child in these other situations. It may seem that this statement of the rationale of IQ tests is another way of defining intelligence as being "what IQ tests measure" (see Chapter 2). However, the only specification in this rationale about the nature of the intellectual functioning being sampled is that it is structured problem solving. These samples of intellectual behavior thus do not include problem solving in unstructured situations, which is yet another kind of cognitive behavior. The behavior is related to that sampled by IQ tests, but it is more observable in our "associative" techniques. Neither is there any assumption as to whether the child's "true" intelligence, intellectual potential, or learning capacity is being measured, or whether his/her responses represent—as is more frequently the case—current intellectual efficiency or level of achievement. These questions may be answered only by inspecting the operations and content of these scales and the nature of the responses of the child in question.

The rationale behind IQ scales is delimited further by the fact that the problem-solving tasks presented to the child are usually arranged in order of increasing difficulty. In addition the fact that the child's responses are analyzed by age norms is based on the assumption that as the child grows older, his/her intelligence also grows. That is, the assumption is that the child learns and achieves more effectively. If it can be shown by a series of such examinations (or from other data) that this intellectual growth has been fairly steady over the child's lifetime, then it would seem reasonable to hypothesize that the child's performance *at this time* represents part of an overall growth pattern—whether because of an inherent developmental rate, of a constancy in environmental factors, or both. Otherwise, these operations limit the psychologist to the statement that this IQ represents the current rate of achievement of the child as compared with other children of the same age.

2. Operations

In the operations of an IQ test the assessor is placed in the position of an authority figure questioning the ability or adequacy of the child. This is such a common situation in Western cultures that quite frequently neither the assessor nor the child questions this social aspect of the operations. As will be discussed further in subsequent chapters, there are procedures for making a child feel relatively at ease if he/she does not accept such an intellectual challenge. It should be noted, however, that in no IQ test are there any formal instructions to the child informing him/her that his/her intelligence is being challenged. Sometimes the instructions to certain subtests hint at this when the child is told, for example, "Now I want to see how many words you know" or "Now I am going to test your arithmetic." Nevertheless, there is an unspoken presumption that if a child were told "Now I am going to test your intelligence," her/his anxiety and resistance might well be increased. Perhaps it would be more definitive to say the child's anxiety would be crystallized—for most children soon become aware that that is exactly what the psychologist is up to even though both child and assessor usually conform to the social amenity of avoiding any direct statement of the challenge and pretend they are playing intellectual games.

In Western culture, which emphasizes achievement and problem solving, a child has to recognize and accept intellectual challenge by the time she/he begins school. Some children, however—for example, those who are culturally deprived—actually fail to comprehend and/or accept this social aspect of the IQ operations. They may see the situation as an enjoyable child–adult relationship in which they are receiving attention, but they do not comprehend that they are expected to achieve. Or if they do realize the demand upon them for problem solving, they may just ignore it or respond on a more associative level. Such children play "games" other than the one presented by the IQ test, often frustrating any assessor who hopes to extract an IQ from the child. Such very resistant children are admittedly exceptions. Yet many children do have at least some twinges of resentment over the implicit assumption that they accept without question a problem-solving, achievement orientation. Perhaps the most important aspect of this social assumption in IQ testing is that it is quite similar to the school situation, where it is also tacitly assumed that the child will accept intellectual challenge. Thus observations of the child's acceptance or rejection of the demand to achieve on an IQ test may give clues about her/his attitudes toward intellectual achievement in general.

Allied to this assumption of achievement orientation in IQ tests are the success–fail pattern created by the way IQ tests operate. These patterns differ from scale to scale. On mental-age-level scales, such as the Binet or Merrill-Palmer, the child experiences complete success at the basal level and complete failure at the end. On point scales, consisting of several subtests such as the Wechsler Scales or the Arthur Point Scales, complete failure occurs at the con-

clusion of each subtest, followed by success at the beginning of the next. Although the assessor may mollify the effects of this aspect of IQ scales with certain procedures (see Chapter 8), it is important to note how the achievement-oriented child (or the achievement-resistant child) reacts to this factor. The child's reactions both to the assumption of achievement orientation and to the success–fail operation are clues to the interaction between the cognitive and conative aspects of his/her ego functioning.

3.   Standardization

The original standardizations of the major IQ scales were quite thorough in most instances. However, there have been many rapid social, cultural, and educational changes in American society since these tests were constructed, and they may have seriously altered the norms. Most of the standardization samples did not include blacks or other minority groups. The oldest of these scales—the Stanford-Binet—is the only one that has been statistically revised at approximately 20-year periods, the most recent revision having been carried out in the 1970s.*

Most of the other major techniques used in assessment are at least 20 years old, and some are over 40 years; Wechsler Scale for Children [Wechsler, revised 1974], Columbia Mental Maturity Scale [Burgemeister et al., 1954], Leiter International Performance Scale [Leiter, 1948], Arthur Point Scales [Arthur, 1947], Cattell Infant Scales 1940], Merrill-Palmer Pre-School Scales [Stutzman, 1931], and the Draw-A-Man/ Woman [Harris, 1963]. As is indicated by Palmer's study (1964) of the Shipley-Hartford Scales for adolescents, it is quite

---

*Unfortunately, there seems to have been little attempt to revise the content of the Binet. It still contains objects seldom seen by children today such as a thimble, a man sawing wood on a sawhorse, and a steam locomotive, plus other vestiges of the 1917 original. The Arthur Point Scales with pictures of ladies in long dresses and high-buttoned shoes, children in knickers, and so forth is even more antiquated.

possible that the mental-age and IQ norms for these scales have changed considerably. Thus inferences from the IQ have to be limited still further to read as follows: "This IQ represents the rate of development of intelligence of this child at this age, compared to other children of the same age as of a decade or even 40 years ago!"

The size and range of behavior sampled by IQ tests varies widely from test to test. Most contain a large number of items in order to encompass the wide range of abilities called for within the age range for which the scale is intended. However, the number of items actually administered to the individual child is comparatively small! The WISC-R with 10 to 12 subtests may present the adolescent with as many as 100 separate problems, but this number is likely to drop to about 50 or less for the average 6- to 8-year-old. On the Binet the average child who passes most items on the mental-age scale a year less than his/her chronological age and fails all two years past his age level will have been presented with 48 items (some of which have several sub-items). Both the Binet and Wechsler tests have fairly varied contents, sampling different kinds of intellectual behaviors and thought processes. The Binet remains largely verbal, however, with very few nonverbal items in the older age scales. Yet the Binet has the distinct advantage of having been designed specifically for children, and its items are addressed to children, attract their interest, and hold their attention. On the other hand, the Wechsler Scale for Children—even when revised—appears to be essentially a revision of one of the adult forms (very comparable to the Army Wechsler used in the military during World War II), scaled down to children and lacking in children's items. The Grace Arthur Performance Scales, which was originally constructed for assessment of deaf and non-English-speaking children, contains only nonverbal items, and except for the Healy Picture Completion (the most old-fashioned of the subtests), it appears to be a bit more "culture free" than either the Wechsler or the Binet—both of which are obviously directed at middle-class American children. The major infant scales will be discussed in Chapter 18.

Some IQ scales sample only one intellectual activity. These scales—such as the Columbia Mental Maturity (Burgemeister, Blum, and Lorge, 1954) or the Peabody Picture Vocabulary (1965)—were designed chiefly as tests for specific handicaps (e.g., cerebral palsy or other speech and motor difficulties). The assessor using these instruments must remember that she/he is tapping only a single intellectual function. The Leiter International (Leiter, 1948), which is also a nonverbal scale, employs matching, although it is a bit more complex than the Columbia. The Draw-A-Man/Woman Scale (Harris, 1963), which scores the drawing of a human figure for detail and complexity, may seem to tap mainly visual motor coordination, but it probably involves more complex functions since it is highly correlated with social adjustment as well (Ochs, 1960). IQ's calculated from the original Goodenough Scale (1926) correlate very respectably with Binet IQ's and even higher with the Wechsler Performance Scales (Estes et al., 1961). The Goodenough Scale has the distinct advantages of being attractive to children, of being easily administered and scored, and it is quite reliable. Also the same drawing can be used as a "projective" test—even though the instructions differ.*

The preceding discussion concerning individually administered intelligence tests also applies in general to the so-called group-administered "paper-and-pencil" intelligence tests, such as Lorge-Thorndike, Thurstone PMA, Iowa, Stanford, California Mental Maturity, Otis, Detroit, and others. These tests are of course much more com-

---

*It should be noted, however, that if the usual instructions for the "Draw-A-Person" are used, rather than the specific instructions of Harris, norms cannot be applied. The child must be instructed to draw "a whole man and the best man you can draw. Make *all* of him." The instructions for Draw-A-Woman is the same, with the indicated sex change.

monly used in the public schools or similar settings where large groups of school-age children are assessed and where individual assessment of each child is not possible. Most of these tests, designed chiefly to predict academic success, are almost entirely verbal, and they are heavily dependent on education. The chief exceptions are the Henmon-Nelson (Lamke and Nelson 1958) and the Raven Matrices (1956). The latter also is used in individual assessment as a test of perception, but it has only British norms—stated in percentiles rather than the American IQ's.

The chief disadvantages of any group-administered test is that the attitudinal set of the child is difficult to estimate. If a child succeeds, one may guess that motivation was fair. If a child fails, there is little way of knowing whether he/she has an intellectual defect, poor motivation, or simply has not followed directions. Although many of these tests correlate fairly highly with the Binet or Wechsler scales, there is a tendency for the scores on these group tests to overestimate the extremes. That is, children with very low scores on group intelligence scales often seem to obtain slightly higher IQ's on the Binet or Wechsler, and vice versa, those with very superior group test scores, when tested individually, frequently fall back toward the mean by as much as 10 to 15 IQ points.

Observation of a high-achieving child during the individual test often suggests that he/she has somewhat more tension in the one-to-one testing relationship, and that he/she is especially discomforted by nonverbal visual–motor tasks (even though success on these latter tasks is also superior). In contrast, the child with an intellectual handicap or of mediocre talents—especially the immature and dependent child—may be poorly motivated on group tests, but, given some encouragement and individual support, he/she may perform much better on individually administered tests, especially on items not involving educational achievement. In sum, these group tests may be fairly effective screening devices for measuring the child's intellectual efficiency in public performance, while the individually administered test, which is more varied in content, is a measure of how the child functions in the one-to-one setting—a measurement that may be more helpful when dealing with questions of extremes of achievement.

4. Analysis of Results

Although metric analysis is built into IQ tests, that is, they have scores standardized on large samples of normal children, analysis is not necessarily limited to the total IQ score or even to scores on the subtests. However, this metric analysis is usually basic to any other kind of analysis of these techniques. In supervising advanced clinical students I have observed a tendency for the student—once he/she has become familiar with other, more complex analyses of his/her material—to become careless about the mere routine procedures, for example, in giving instructions or asking the test questions or even in scoring and adding up the scores!

Analysis of profiles of subtest scores or patterns of achievement on various kinds of intellectual tasks within the total scale is commonly the next step. Comparison is made between the success on one type of task with failure on another. Mental-age scales like the Binet or Merrill-Palmer may be analyzed in this way, as well as the point scales, such as the Wechsler or the Arthur Performance Scales (Arthur, 1947). One may compare achievement on the verbal and nonverbal tasks, on the tests of attention span and attention to detail with tasks involving more complex judgment and logic, or on tasks involving learned skills and information with tasks involving comprehension. Such analyses are most helpful in going beyond the assessment of overall level of intellectual development to a more detailed assessment of the child's cognitive functioning and its relationships with other of her/his ego functions.

Thus the 7-year-old child—one who on the Binet can repeat digits, copy a diamond, answer questions about a story, but who has less than a 6-year-old's vocabulary, who cannot make the simplest verbal similarities, and who is not able to fathom the question "What's foolish about this picture?"—may be doing well or even above-average work on tasks involving routine learning of one-to-one concrete associations. But the development of independent judgment and analysis of a situation may be quite retarded. Another child who can verbalize well about the social reasons for certain behaviors on the WISC-R "Comprehension" subtest but who becomes flustered and fumbles his/her way incomprehensibly through the social items of the "Picture Arrangement" may be said to understand social situations in the abstract. However, once she/he is involved in them, she/he may be unable to decide what they mean or how to act.

Such analysis of the child's cognitive functioning leads to inferential hypotheses about other functions—about conative, social, or affective maturity. From patterns such as the preceding on the Binet, one might want to test out the hypotheses—for example—that the first child is too dependent emotionally on others to begin to make independent intellectual judgments, or possibly that severe emotional or physiological handicaps deter more complex thought processes. Further evidence bearing on such hypotheses can of course be gathered from the quality of responses to these tests themselves, from the types of failures the child is making, as well as from other techniques designed more to test social and emotional adjustment. *Caution should be observed, however, in analyzing such profiles or patterns of subtests from IQ scales.*

Profile Analysis of the WISC-R

Since the WISC first appeared in 1949 and especially since its revision (WISC-R [1974]), many studies have been reported on analysis of the differences between the Verbal and Performance IQ's, on analysis of subtest profiles and subtest differences, and on subtest "scatter." (For a full review of these studies up to 1970 see Zimmerman and Woo-Sam [1972] and Kaufman [1979]

for more recent work.) Kaufman's book is a most comprehensive and handy reference for the user of the WISC-R. He advocates and illustrates a cautious but sensible analysis that is introduced by the following (1980, p. 11):

The limitations and assets of intelligence tests, taken together, suggest that the tests should be used by examiners who are sufficiently knowledgeable to interpret them intelligently. The burden is on test users to be 'better' than the tests they use.

Again on page 13 Kaufman notes that "a thoroughly trained professional, knowledgeable in testing and psychology, is needed when intelligence tests are used appropriately. . . ."

Thus Kaufman stresses that merely reporting the Full-Scale IQ—even with the Verbal and Performance IQ's—is insufficient information. A careful analysis of other qualitative and quantitative data is described in detail by Kaufman, which should prove most helpful to any assessor.

Yet there are strict limits to these analyses. Just *any* difference may not make a difference. "Verbal-Performance differences as large as 17 points cannot be considered 'abnormal' by any reasonable statistical standard" (Kaufman, 1976, p. 25). "The average difference in either direction is 7–9 IQ points, $S D = 7.6$" (Kaufman, 1976). Kaufman continues by saying that "virtually the entire V-P literature . . . is beset by contradictions and a lack of success in identifying characteristic patterns for various groups."

Among the major reasons for large V-P differences Kaufman discusses are the following:

1. The discrepancy may mean just what it is supposed to convey, that is, a difference in abilities. One child may be more verbal than others as a part of his/her life-style, without any real difference in overall IQ or sociocultural background.

2. The difference may reflect a right

versus left dominance of the hemispheres.

3. It may be due to a psycholinguistic deficiency.

4. It may be the result of bilingualism.

5. It may reflect the assessor's ignorance of black dialect.

6. It may be a coordination problem (V > P) in which the child is compensating for poor coordination by overemphasis on verbal learning (see the discussion in Chapter 15 on the blind).

7. The child may not work quickly enough or she/he may react negatively to time pressure. Reflective children lose time credits. Kaufman points out that a 14-year-old can solve *all* the Block Designs or *all* Picture Arrangement items, but without time credits obtain only a weighted score of 10.

8. The difference may represent a "field-dependence versus field-independence," another aspect of cognitive style in which the child's attitudes toward self and environment are reflected.

9. Last but not least "a V-P discrepancy may stem from a child's socioeconomic background. . . . children from professional families tend to score higher on the Verbal Scale, with the reverse holding true for the children of unskilled workers. . . ." (Kaufman, 1976, p. 43).

Typically, a child is administered a Wechsler Test because of a suspected abnormality—whether it is emotional, behavioral, cognitive, developmental or otherwise. Normal profiles are rarely seen or studied, and thus it is easy for a clinician or researcher to assume that observed fluctuations and patterns are in some way characteristic of the abnormal population under investigation. (Kaufman, 1976, p. 52)

As regards analysis of subtest profiles, the assessor must be acutely aware of the variability of the subtests. The SD of these subtests averages 2 scale points and thus the SD difference is at least 4. *Any difference between subtests of less than 4 is insignificant.* Similarly, when stating that a subtest is "high" or "low" as compared with the average Verbal or Performance scores, the variability should be taken into account. (see Table 4.1).

In addition to analyzing the scores on the subtests of various kinds of intelligence tests it is also well to examine the sequence of successes and failures across tests. Thus on the Binet one commonly looks at the range of success—from basal age to total failure. One may more closely examine how failure follows upon success or vice versa. Does the child, having succeeded, become overconfident, or having failed an item, seem to try harder on the next? Does she/he become increasingly confident or increasingly discouraged? It should be noted that the subtests within any mental-age group are not necessarily arranged in any order of difficulty, but they are supposed to be about equal. As Jastak (1950) has shown, the items within the subscales of the adult Wechsler I are far from being arranged in an exact order of difficulty, and inspection of the WISC-R suggests that the order of difficulty on this children's scale is also only approximate.*

Erratic patterns of success and failure across subtests that are unrelated to content may suggest lapses in attention or even conscious malingering. The bright child may be bored by simple questions, give careless or even nonsensical replies, only to become challenged by more difficult items where she/he can show off her/his intellectual talents. Such a response pattern may be important to note in making inferences from the test to behavior in other situations. Perhaps his/her behavior in the classroom is also marked by boredom, disdain for simple tasks, and utilization of talents to obtain social approval. One might ask also if such behavior is fostered consciously or unconsciously by parents. Might they reward occasional demonstrations of intellectual prowess but demand little in the way of continued intellectual labor?

Thematic analysis of these structured

---

*In fact, there appear to be large jumps in the degree of difficulty on items on the WISC-R from the very-easy to rather-difficult items with few of intermediate difficulty, particularly on Comprehension and Vocabulary.

Table 4.1. Deviations Required for Significance When Comparing a Child's Scaled Score on One Subtest with His or Her Average Scaled Score on Related Subtests[a]

Subtest	Deviation from average of six verbal subtests		Deviation from average of six performance subtests	
	$p < 0.05$	$p < 0.01$	$p < 0.05$	$p < 0.01$
Verbal				
Information	2.3	3.1	—	—
Similarities	2.6	3.4	—	—
Arithmetic	2.7	3.6	—	—
Vocabulary	2.3	3.0	—	—
Comprehension	2.7	3.6	—	—
Digit Span	2.8	3.7	—	—
Performance				
Picture completion	—	—	2.8	3.7
Picture arrangement	—	—	3.1	4.0
Block design	—	—	2.3	3.0
Object assembly	—	—	3.3	4.4
Coding	—	—	3.2	4.2
Mazes	—	—	3.3	4.4

Note: Values identical to those shown here for the six Verbal subtests should also be used when only five scaled scores are used to compute the average (Digit Span excluded). The same rule applies for the Performance Scale. In addition, the exact values in the table should be used to determine significant deviations from the average of all 12 subtests. [The values for 10 or 11 subtests are trivially smaller than the values shown here; see Sattler (1974, p. 560).]

[a] From Kaufman (1979, p. 55).

tests of intelligence is also valuable, whether or not the associative content of the child's responses are considered. The themes of intellectual processes may be considered, as well as ideational themes. In the next step beyond profile or pattern analysis one examines not only whether the child reasons well but *how* he/she reasons. Thus one might examine items from various subtests, noting when the child attempts analytic judgments or feats of concentration, and how he/she goes about it. Does the child first usually attempt a wholistic approach and then break the task down into details, or does he/she take it detail by detail, thus forming intermediate associations? For example, on the Object Assembly of the WISC-R, does the child see the auto before she/he assembles it or only afterward does she/he exclaim, "Oh, it's a car!" Does she/he on Vocabulary give a generalization and then examples, or does she/he give several concrete associations and end up with a generalization? Is her/his problem solving usually trial and error, or does this child sit back and think first? Is her/his thinking personalized? Does she/he refer the question to herself/himself, saying, "I'd do thus and thus" or "I've never seen that!" Does this child associate the task with some personal experience or object? Does she/he rush headlong into tasks, scarcely waiting for instructions, or—at the other extreme—does she/he ask for help or sit passively as if waitiing for further cues?

Along with these thought processes and behavioral themes in the quality of the child's responses to IQ tests one also finds many clues in the associative content. Although primarily designed to sample manifest problem-solving achievement, these tests often provide samples of associative behavior also in the phrasing and choice of wording the child uses on the verbal tests or in the idiosyncratic behavior accompanying nonverbal responses. Often these associative clues appear when the child is struggling with a problem she/he cannot quite fathom. Sometimes her/his associations seem to block problem solving, and she/he hides behind a "Don't know." On the other hand, the bright child may "free associate" in an imaginative, creative fashion, guessing partially or even completely successfully. Often the emotionally disturbed child carries his/her anxieties, fears, and obsessions with him/her into problem solving. Many of the items on both the Binet and WISC are concerned with social-impulse control. For example, an item might ask the following: "What is the thing to do if a child much smaller than yourself hits you?" (WISC-R), or "What should you do if someone hits you without meaning to? (Binet). Other items contain stimuli that frequently arouse association of violence or hostility: On the Binet, for example pictures of a gun on the Picture Vocabulary, or the "What's foolish?" questions such as "lost both his hands in an accident," or "the body of Christopher Columbus when he was only twelve years old," or vocabulary items calling for definitions of "knife," "nitroglycerin," "affliction," and "hara-kiri." Even seemingly neutral stimuli, such as the incomplete man or the mutilated pictures on the Binet, may evoke threatening associations to handicapped children.

5.   Inferences from Results

As to the kinds of inferences to be drawn from the behavior sampled by these techniques, the assessor's attention is usually focused initially on the direct extrapolation from children's manifest behavior to other problem-solving situations. Some of the data may also contribute to predictions about behavior in less-structured situations, such as the ability to behave rationally and test reality in social and interpersonal relationships or in anxiety-producing situations. However, the clues gained from these structured samples need to be checked out through other techniques that provide more option for independent judg-

ment and more clues about emotional-stress reactions. Rather than direct prediction, inductive inferences from the patterns and themes of the child's responses can be made, leading to hypotheses to be cross validated on other techniques. In turn, hypotheses from other techniques or from the referral question may be checked out from the data gathered from these techniques.

To cite a common example, the child's medical history or other evidence may suggest a neurological handicap,* and it is quite possible to examine the data from an IQ test to see how much behavioral evidence there may be for such a hypothesis. In such instances of course, one can only disprove the null hypothesis. How this null hypothesis is stated determines the kind of conclusion that is logically permissible. If for example the statement is "There is no evidence to support this hypothesis," then the statement can be easily disproven by any scrap of evidence. However, the only conclusion that can logically be drawn should be stated as follows: "The data are not inconsistent with or do not rule out the hypothesis." Somewhat stronger is this statement: "There is insufficient evidence to support the hypothesis that. . . ." this can be disproven only by demonstration that there is more than sufficient evidence.

C.   STRUCTURED TESTS OF EDUCATIONAL ACHIEVEMENT

Techniques designed to assess the child's level of educational achievement are a highly specialized topic that are more relevant to educational psychology than to clinical assessment, and a full discussion of these tests is beyond the aims of this book. They are much more commonly administered and interpreted by the school psychologist, and they are not a usual part of the clinic test battery. However, school achievement is one of the most common

*See further discussion in Chapters 15 and 16.

referral questions, and—in order to assess the ego dysfunctions or other factors that might underlie such school failure—the clinician frequently needs to begin with an assessment of the school achievement per se. Where records of school testing are available, the clinician should be familiar enough with these techniques to understand the scoring, the patterns of scores, and the content of tests so that she/he can relate these results to the results of his/her own assessment of the child.

Much of what has been said about the rationale, the factors of set and achievement drive, and the effects of culture regarding intelligence tests also applies to these tests of educational achievement. Also in drawing inferences from the child's performance on these tests, the clinician must take into account the child's attitudes toward school achievement. For example, the rebellious adolescent who, to use the old phrase "Doesn't care if school keeps," may resentfully dawdle his/her way through such a test even though he/she has learned the necessary skills.

Like the IQ tests, these techniques usually consist of subtests tapping various academic skills, such as reading comprehension, reading speed, arithmetic skills and reasoning, spelling, grammar, logical analysis, and so forth. Analysis of the patterns of these subscores often yields further specific information about the child's abilities and underlying attitudes, thus giving clues to be checked out in further individual assessment. Difficulty in learning to read is a most common reason for referral. Learning to read is of course basic to the acquisition of all other academic skills. Difficulties in learning to read are so often associated with the total functioning and maturation of the child that failure in this skill often becomes a question for clinical as well as educational assessment. In such instances, other techniques are usually needed in addition to the reading achievement test, such as tests of perception, assessment of motivation, and of affective controls. Since school achievement records are not always readily available, the clinician may need to administer this type of technique.

The technique most commonly used in clinical settings is the Wide Range Achievement Test, or WRAT (Jastak, Bijou, and Jastak, 1965). The WRAT has the advantage of being brief (30 minutes), and it focuses on three basic skills: spelling, arithmetic, and reading (recognition and pronunciation). It is easily scored by grade level. It's range is Grades K through 12. It should be supplemented by some standard test of reading comprehension. Any test of academic achievement should be used only in conjunction with an IQ test.

D. STRUCTURED TESTS SAMPLING VISUAL-MOTOR AND PERCEPTUAL FUNCTIONING

1. General Considerations

As I discussed previously, the child's ability to perceptually discriminate, recognize, organize, and reproduce the world about him/her is a core function of the ego. This ability is basic to intellectual development and in the long run to all other ego functions as well. Many of the items on infant IQ tests consist of direct sampling of the development of this perceptual acuity and recognition. For example, on the Cattell there are items such as visual following of a swinging ring held over the supine infant, self-recognition in the mirror, exploration of the bell, copying a line, and so on, and on the Binet, copying a circle, a square, a diamond, the three-figure form board, and a string of beads. On the WISC perceptual functioning is an integral part of most of the nonverbal subtests: perception of detail on the Picture Completion, perceptual organization and reproduction on Block Design, Object Assembly, and Digit Symbol. The Porteus Mazes, Kohs Blocks, and Sequin Form Board on the Arthur Scales also sample this ego function.

The rationale behind these samples of

visual-motor, perceptual tasks calls for somewhat more analogy than the IQ scales. Even the tasks on the IQ scales are not altogether similar to the intellectual tasks toward which the psychologist is extrapolating in her/his predictions. Although when the child is asked to copy a figure, follow a maze, or match blocks to form a board, it is not drawing ability or form-board skills per se that are being tested but instead, the perceptual functions that are posited to underlie the tasks. It is hoped that the visual-motor behavior required in copying a geometric figure is analogous to or contains the same elements of perceptual behavior as are involved in reading, driving, sorting-out objects or even people, and possibly social events and interactions. Actually this rationale is stated in a negative fashion. That is, if a child makes errors in this test sample of very simple perceptual tasks, he/she is likely to make similar errors in much more complex perceptual behavior.

Since the techniques labeled "perceptual-motor" tasks are often referred to as tests of "organic brain damage," it may be well to note that in this rationale no mention is made of the etiology of possible errors made by the child in performing these tasks. It should be emphasized that although neurophysiological handicaps may be one common deterrent to perceptual motor functioning, they are far from being the only cause of such dysfunctioning, especially in children (see Chapter 15).

The sample of behavior from these techniques is very small. The Bender contains only 8 drawings, the Graham-Kendall 15; the Porteus has 11 mazes; the Seguin contains 10 blocks (but is usually administered three times); the Kohs block consists of the reproduction of from 8 to 10 designs, depending on the form used. *The assessor should therefore never depend on any one of these techniques as the sole basis for assessing perceptual functioning* but should use more than one separate test, and in conjunction with the items on the IQ scales and with the Rorschach.

Metric analysis by means of standardized scores is available for all of these tests. Unfortunately, the standardization of the Porteus, Kohs Blocks, Seguin, and other form boards is so out of date as to be almost useless. When using them, therefore, the assessor should err on the side of caution, especially since these original norms were stated in terms of intellectual rather than perceptual growth. Thus the small errors that count against the child in estimates of intellectual development may not necessarily indicate any perceptual motor defect. On the other hand, gross failures on these techniques may be evidence of such defects, if they are consistent with other evidence.

2.   The Bender-Gestalt, the Graham-Kendall Memory for Designs, and the Frostig Tests

As regards the Bender-Gestalt, although several major attempts have been made to construct scoring methods, none has achieved popular acceptance. The simple scanning or inspection, as introduced by Loretta Bender (1938) and promulgated further by Hutt and Briskin (1960), remained the chief method of analyzing these figure drawings for many years. However, the norms given by these authorities were far too gross for application by most clinicians, and they often resulted in unreliable judgments. Koppitz's (1963) normative studies on children ages 5 to 10 provide more precise standards. Furthermore, Koppitz presents studies relating her scores on the Bender to intellectual development and school achievement. Although intellectual and perceptual functioning are so closely related during these ages, Koppitz does not provide a method whereby the perceptual functioning might be distinguished from the intellectual.

On the other hand, the Graham-Kendall Memory for Designs (1948), which has a much simpler scoring system, can be corrected for both age and IQ. Since the administration of this test involves immediate memory, however, it is more complex than the simple copying task of the Bender, and it is difficult to determine whether a failure is a result of the child's misperception of the form or a lack of concentration.

Using several such techniques, one may assess the child's performance on a slightly larger scale with a greater variety of stimuli and come up with informal patterns. For example, a child who makes no gross errors on the Graham-Kendall and who matches the Seguin blocks to the board without error and within the time limit norms, but who cannot even begin to reproduce the Kohs-block designs, would appear to have little difficulty in accurately perceiving simple form, but considerable difficulty in the analysis and reconstruction of more complex stimuli. Qualitative inspection of the way the child goes about copying the Bender or Graham-Kendall (1948) figures, placing blocks in form boards, or reproducing the Kohs designs often provides more specific cues about the child's perceptual functioning than the overall scores. For example, one may observe how important the accuracy of perception is to the child. Does she/he become preoccupied with detail, forgetting the overall gestalt, or is she/he content with a rough sketch, ignoring the details? Does she/he try to patch up her/his errors with elaborations or to add to the figure some extraneous "inner" perception of her/his own? Does she/he have to shift the materials, the design, the paper, and the blocks around for some different perspective?

Although not one of these techniques gives any rules about establishing with the child which is the top or bottom of a page, this is a very important precaution. If no top or bottom is established, rotations of the Bender figures (considered the hallmark of brain damage by the inventor of this technique) are, in my experience, quite common among normal junior high-school students! If the child is asked to "write your name at the top of the page," however, before beginning to draw, such rotations seldom occur. Nor are there precise instructions about

whether the child is to be allowed to turn the page or the drawing, as many children do. In my experience, a child frequently turns his/her paper and body at right angles to the present figure, thus drawing all figures at a 90° angle to the figure, although in line with the top of his/her drawing paper. Other children have to turn their drawing papers around in order to accomplish certain angles. Probably none of their rotations are significant in the sense of those described by Bender (1938) or by Hutt and Briskin (1960), but they may well be significant to the perceptual motor functioning of the child being observed.

As to the reliability and validity of these techniques, one is rightly disturbed and discouraged upon reading such reports as that by Goldberg (1965) who found that expert clinicians could not predict brain damage from the Bender above a base rate, or any better than most students or even nonprofessional secretarial assistants! Tamkin (1965) also found the Bender to be nondiscriminating with regard to functional disorders in adults. On the other hand, this technique does seem to have some promise—as was originally intended—in discriminating levels of perceptual motor development in children. Koppitz cross-validated her developmental norms quite successfully, and Byrd (1965), in a study of Bender differences between normal and emotionally disturbed and delinquent children, found notable differences, but that authority also remarks that "maturational effects on reproduction of designs are noted up to age sixteen." The "brain-damage" cutting scores of the Graham-Kendall have been cross-validated (1948), although unfortunately without indication of the base rate of "organicity" of the sample used in this study.

Another set of tests of visual-motor development is the Marianne Frostig Developmental Tests of Visual Perception (Frostig et al., 1966). The Frostig consists of five subtests: eye–motor coordination, figure–ground coordination, form constancy, position in space, and spatial relations. Each subtest is scored separately, and an overall total score and "PQ" quotient (age—score ratio) can be calculated. The Frostig is standardized for children ages 3—8 (but like many tests the standardization is almost all white!) The Frostig is most useful in assessing perceptual disability (see Chapter 16) or the background of learning disability (see Chapter 17).

3. Summary

In using these techniques the assessor should observe the following precautions:

1.   The restricted sampling of each of these techniques requires that more than one be used in order to obtain a wide enough sampling of the child's behavior. The use of several also permits an informal analysis of patterns of scores.

2.   Results should be analyzed on the basis of established age norms (or age should be taken into account).

3.   The inadequacy of some of these norms and the fact that reliability of the child's performance on most of these techniques is not established require that the assessor err on the side of caution and take as significant only *gross* deviations from the norm.

4.   The lack of clear-cut instructions on some of these techniques requires that the assessor adapt and take into account uniform procedures and observe and record the operations of the child in carrying out the task.

5.   The assessor should *not* assume that brain damage is the *only* possible etiology of a child's failure on these techniques nor attempt to predict brain damage from these techniques alone (see Chapter 15 for further discussion of this point).

CHAPTER 5

Techniques Based on Subjective Reports

Asking a person to report on his/her own behavior, thoughts, and feelings has long been a major technique in psychological assessment. Such subjective reports supply much of the information available concerning the person's attitudes toward the environment as well as those toward the self. However, assessors are aware that clinical subjects are often inaccurate observers of their own environments and even less accurate in describing their own behaviors. In addition, those who come as patients in a clinical setting often have considerable difficulty in expressing and objectively reporting their own emotional attitudes or evaluating the emotional attitudes of others. When they are attempting to deal with threatening and anxiety-producing data, many are quite apt to suppress or completely repress and forget about data that might make their plight more understandable. Others may exaggerate complaints in a "cry for help." Children's subjective reports in particular often seem garbled, full of inaccuracies, and interlarded with wishful thinking. For these reasons some clinicians regard children's self-reports as too unreliable to warrant consideration. Yet there may be some validity to the old saw that "out of the mouths of babes" come naive truths. Some children do seem much less inhibited in discussing their family affairs and even their own behavior and feelings than do more reserved and repressed adults. On the other hand, it is not uncommon to find children flatly denying facts about their behavior or avoiding any mention of their feelings or fantasies.

Rather than considering such reports as being either true or false, that is, as valid assessments of the actual behavior of the individual, most clinicians utilize these self-reports as sources of data about what children think of themselves, their environments, and their own behavior. Whether the subject's view is the same as another observer's is a different question. Indeed, a comparison of the subject's report and reports and observations of others forms yet another kind of data.

This latter form of data consists usually of interviews and reports from others. While such reports may be considered in some way more objective, it is necessary to keep in mind that they too are essentially subjective. Such reports from others are merely other viewpoints of the child's behavior. Even official school reports or juvenile-court documents do not necessarily reflect any more truth about the child than do the child's reports about herself/himself. For example, an 11-year-old, who was hospitalized in a psychiatric ward and who was a polite, well-behaved but depressed lad, had been labeled as "unmanageable" by the boys' home where he had been living. As evidence they cited how he "swung on the gates" after being told not to. In another instance an immense, obese 14-year-old idiot was brought to the hospital for the retarded. He was shackled to two deputy sheriffs, and was labeled a "sex maniac." Later, it turned out, he had wandered away from home, and not being toilet trained, he had urinated publicly in the park! In other instances of course, what parents and children dismiss as nothing at all turn out on school records or court findings to be serious behavior disturbances. Whatever the validity of these reports, it is important in assessing a child to have as complete a picture as possible of how the child's parents, school, and other peers and authorities may see and regard him/her. This of course strongly influences the social roles he/she may try to play or is allowed to play, and it impinges as well on his/her self-image.

In this section three types of subjective reports are to be considered: (1) unstructured interviews with the child, (2) structured questionnaires used with the child and parents, and (3) reports and observations of others about the child—both structured and unstructured.

A. UNSTRUCTURED INTERVIEWS WITH THE CHILD

The assumption or rationale for open-ended interviewing of children is that through direct, friendly, and encouraging questions, they will describe their views of their environment and of their behavior, revealing their own attitudes and feelings. The validity of this assumption depends on how the interviews are conducted. This is discussed in more detail in subsequent chapters on procedures.

1. The Operations of Interviewing

Regarding the operations of interviewing children, although this section has been labeled "unstructured," the term *open-ended* might be more advisable. *Open-ended* means that the interview can be adapted to the responses of the child, and in fact the assessor should follow through with what the child feels free to talk about. Assessment interviews however, do need structure in the mind of the assessor, who must be able to gather data and explore as many facets of the child's world as time allows. Thus the assessor needs to have in mind the questions and areas to be explored, even though she/he

may not necessarily follow any set outline nor phrase questions in a standardized form. An interviewer thus may begin with whatever the child mentions in response to the introductory statement of the purpose of the assessment and explore from there. In any case, the interviewer probably will find it necessary to change the topic from time to time—again in contradistinction to a therapeutic interview—and say, "Now I'd like you to tell me a little about. . . ."

The main reason for using such interviewing operations is of course to obtain as wide a sample as possible of the child's attitudes and feelings regarding many different situations and persons. Usually in one or two hours an accomplished interviewer can cover these general topic areas with the child, generally in the following order:

1. The child's view of the complaints, symptoms, and stresses.
2. The child's view of his/her current environment (home, peers, school) and current functioning (sleeping, eating, digestion, and elimination habits, and with an adolescent, sexual interests as well as feelings about them).
3. The child's view of his/her own development and history, including projections about the future.

Regarding the "complaints," many children are able to give some of their own reasons for coming to the psychologist's office. Their first responses to questions about complaints are frequently tentative and terse, but with encouraging exploration they can expand upon them. The assessor should not be content with a single statement, but should continue to explore for sources of psychologic discomfort other than the one mentioned initially. For example, many children begin by mentioning academic difficulties and dissension with siblings. "I hate school," a 10-year-old says, or "My sister bugs me. That's the only thing I'm ever unhappy about." As the interviewer explores these initial statements, however, it often turns out that the child has feelings of inadequacy regarding academic achievement, that his parents have high aspirations for him/her, or that there are conflicts with parents over homework and spare-time activities that are part of an overall familial dissension. Sometimes a child may initially deny any complaints or stresses. "I dunno," an 8-year-old girl says. "I haven't any problems. I'm happy. My mother just brought me here." However, she was able to discuss some of the things about her behavior that worried her mother—even though she herself maintained that she was unconcerned about them. If the child fails to speak about the complaint or difficulties mentioned in the referral, it may be necessary to ask him/her directly about them, again with emphasis on an honest exchange with the child. Quite frequently I begin the assessment with a brief interview, saying, "Let me see (looking at the referral note), your pediatrician called me and asked me to see you because you have been having a lot of headaches." Or I may say, "When your mother made this appointment for you to see me she seemed very worried over your schoolwork." After exploring the referrant's complaints with the child, however, his/her own complaints are explored by my saying, for example, "Well, those are some of the things that bother your mother or teacher, but what are some of the things that bother *you,* that are important to you?"

Usually discussion of these complaints leads easily into a description of the child's everyday life, family and home, school, recreation, and other activities. The assessor asks such questions as these: "Who is in your family? Which ones live at your house? Does anyone else live there? Describe them to me. What do you like best about them? Least about them?"

Of course children may mention these things in stating their complaint, but it is often wise to have them repeat, since they may add to the feelings hinted at earlier. Children should be asked what they do with each member of the family—with concrete examples—revealing how they relate to each. They should be asked to describe the family living quarters and their own corner of the home. To find out about their activities children may be asked to describe in detail what happened the day before the interview and how this day was different from most other days. If they describe a weekday they might also be asked to describe a weekend day. Such a description helps to get at the family relationships at the beginning of the day, the school routine, play activities, eating habits and relationships during meals, study habits, and evening family relationships and activities, ending with questions about sleep habits. "Who decides when you go to bed? What do you think of before you fall asleep? What kind of dreams do you have?" If not already discussed, the child should be questioned about the routine of his/her physiological functioning—appetitite, digestion, and elimination habits. When children mention play it is a good idea to inquire further about what they like to do for fun, when they get a chance to do what they like, who do they like to do it with, and how do they feel when restricted from what they like to do. Other aspects of their lives that should be asked about include the following: What are the things they have to do that they dislike? Who makes them do it? Do they have any ways of getting out of such tasks? Such a discussion may lead easily into methods of discipline and control used by the parents or other adult authorities, and how the child regards such discipline.

Children's views of their own developmental histories are often fascinating and revealing sets of data. Their chronology is often vague and confused, their sense of time differences is out of kilter by adult standards, and their memory of events emphasizes childhood pleasures and sorrows rather than adult crises. However, it is these very distortions that give clues about their feelings, motivations, and behavior. A 5-year-old boy's excitement and anxiety about the time the toilet bowl overflowed may reveal not only his feelings about self-controls, but, depending on his associations of the moment, they also give clues about events that are otherwise vague in his memory. In this case, it was the birth of his sister. He explained that "Mommy wasn't there. She was in the hospital, and there was nobody to fix it."

When children are initially asked to tell about their lives they often feign ignorance, but usually such a question as "What is the very first thing you can remember, from the time you were a teeny-weeny baby?" sets off a trail of memories, which can be encouraged gently by the interviewer, although he/she should avoid trying too hard to make the child be exact, or calling attention to the child's apparent inconsistencies. On the other hand, children may be much more accurate regarding family attitudes toward them and among themselves than the fact-citing adult. In the preceding example the child was telling something about which the adults may have been unaware—namely, that while his mother was hospitalized with childbirth, he felt insecure and unprotected and afraid that things might get out of control.

B.   INTERVIEWS WITH PARENTS

1.   The Parent as a Source of Data

In interviewing the child the clinician is interested in the child's attitudes, feelings, and associations, and he/she does not pretend to be getting at other kinds of facts with any validity. However, the rationale in interviewing parents as a source of data about children is not always as clear-cut. Parents were interviewed traditionally because clinicians hoped that they would supply factual, objective data. As Wenar (1961) describes the "Ideal Research Mother," the clinician also may hope that "such a mother could, (a) faithfully record events, feelings, and interpersonal relations as they happen; (b) remember with perfect fidelity; and (c) have the power of total recall upon request." In addition, anyone seeking facts from parental reports would frequently be

annoyed—if not surprised—to find several common biases. First and most obvious, the parent has considerable personal investment, consciously and unconsciously, in the child as representing and reflecting his/her efforts. Although parents usually accept overtly and intellectually the assessor's investigatory role, they often attempt in many ways to fend off any investigation that they regard as reflecting on their adequacy as parents. In such circumstances they may water down or even distort the facts, conveniently forgetting certain aspects of the development and rearing of their child or even omitting what others might regard as crucial. Even those parents who may cry "mea culpa" and describe what they regard as their failures often appear to do so because they hope that the assessor will forgive them, because they are demonstrating "insight."

Since the parents want help for the child but do not want to admit to anything but helplessness on their own part, they are also apt to enlarge upon and heavily emphasize those circumstantial pressures on the child that are beyond their own control, especially outside of the home. A clinician should take warning when the parent begins—"Perhaps I haven't been the best parent in the world, but. . . ."—and then goes on to complain about the school, the neighborhood, the child's health and physique— "despite everything I've tried to do." Such statements are intended not only to defend against self-incrimination, but also to press the psychologist to do something about those features of the child's behavior for which the parent is avoiding responsibility. Furthermore, many parents exaggerate any undesirable behavior in the child that does not directly reflect upon themselves, and they minimize anything the child does about which they feel overtly guilty. All this is not to say that parents are solely to "blame" for the child's behavior as other stresses and circumstances outside the home often do play major roles in disturbing children's development. Rather it is to emphasize that parents usually think in terms of "who's to blame," while assessors are trying to consider what kind of stresses are bearing on the child and how she/he is handling them. Thus torn between trying not to appear inadequate and yet wanting desperately to obtain help, parents often present very conflicting and confusing pictures of their child and his/her adjustment.

Next, as Wenar (1961) also points out, even parents of normal children change their attitudes toward them over the years. This affects their memories of events and the emphasis on their viewpoint about the child. Now that the child is presenting a problem to them, they remember more vividly the difficulties they had with him/her earlier, or the traumata he/she endured, and it is difficult to assess whether these earlier problems and circumstances actually led to the child's present condition or whether the parents are merely searching for something to blame.

Because of these and other biases in parental motivations during interviews some clinicians are inclined to discount the use of such interviews as a valid source of facts, and to regard them as another, entirely subjective, view. Yet the parental reports do yield considerable data about their feelings and attitudes, including their own distortions as they have come to impose them on the child. Thus one may see from these reports the kind of parental world that the child is facing. Such parental attitudes are reflected not only in their views of the facts, but even more so in the defensive biases previously discussed.

The clinician who decides to accept parental reports as another projective technique, however, runs the serious risk of having no source whatever of facts. Some clinicians assert that facts per se are not really necessary at all, since the main interest is in feelings, attitudes, and perceptions, and that the assessor's aim is to gather *psychological* facts—not historical events. This is a difficult position to maintain, however. Despite the importance of the attitudes of both the child and parents to the understanding of the child's ego development, these purely psychological phenomena are associated with and indeed are derived from nonsubjective facts—from objective events, experiences, and stresses in the child's life. Knowledge of these reality data is also essential to the assessment, for ultimately in any form of treatment or rehabilitation, one aim is to assist the child and his/her parents to test and to assess more effectively and univocally these realities for themselves.

2. Cross-Checking Data Sources

Fortunately it is possible to use the same data to assess both kinds of facts. This can be accomplished by cross-checking the data from several different sources. In fact, such a cross-check is necessary in order to be able to identify the biases in the parents' and child's accounts. First, the parental and child reports can be checked against one another. (And if each parent is interviewed separately, a third source of data is available.) Where all agree on a fact the assessor has at least some measure of reliability, although the possibility of biases running throughout the family should be kept in mind. Where there are gross inconsistencies, a second step in analysis of the data is necessary—that is, to discover the kinds of biases present in each informant. Here one can refer to the other sources of data: the observations and tests on the child and the tests administered to the parents in order to discover what kinds of defenses they are prone to utilize. Thus the Rorschach responses of the child may help tell us how accurately, in how much detail, and with what kind of distortions he/she usually perceives a situation. Or the MMPI profile on the parents can outline the patterns of defenses with which they commonly approach situations. In this cross-comparing of the data one can estimate, for example, that such and such is probably a fact since both the parents and the child report it. But it is likely that the child interprets it in one way while the parents tend to underrate or overemphasize it.

Several different kinds of data may be sampled through an interview with the parents:

1. A detailed description of the current behavior of the child is usually essential. This description should include the ways in which the parents have attempted to deal with the child's behavior and their feelings and attitudes about it.

2. In most cases the parents can supply considerable more detail about the child's past development, from conception to the present, than can the child. Such a history is vital to assessment, since it provides an estimate of both the rate of development and some of the past stresses, or continuous stresses, that may affect the child's current status.

3. In order to understand the child's history fully, at least an outline of both of the parents' backgrounds and the marital and family histories are essential. The role of this historical material in the present adjustment of the child has been outlined in the previous chapters. One technique for obtaining such material initially is the use of a biographical data sheet that the parents can be asked to fill in before being interviewed (see Figure 5.1). Such a data sheet orients the parents to the interview and can be used as a basis for discussion.

3. Analysis of Parental and Child Interviews

Although metric methods of analyzing interviewing materials have been constructed for research, they are seldom used clinically. However, when the child's developmental landmarks are compared with various reported norms, a metric analysis is being used. Thus it can be established whether the child learned to sit up, walk, talk was weaned from the bottle or breast, was toilet trained, began to speak single words and then sentences, and so on, within the period that is common to most children. These norms have been the subject of considerable research in child development, and they are spelled out in most guidebooks for parents—such as Spock (1946)—with at least some hint of the variability and of sex differences. The case-history material becomes most valuable and meaningful, however, when the clinician looks for patterns of behavior and events and for long-range trends or themes. As was suggested previously the assessor should pay particular attention to the crises or stress periods in the child's development to see how the child and his/her parents reacted, and then compare this reaction with the next crisis pattern. For example, the manner in which the child reacted to the birth of a sibling might be compared with the way he/she accepted being separated from the family when he/she began school. Patterns of family interactions and the roles the child plays with and for various members of the family need to be systematically analyzed. It is often helpful to construct a schematic chart. The following data extracted from a case history illustrate how such a schematic analysis might be drawn up.

Case 7

Billy V, age 8, was brought to the clinic with the following complaints by his parents. He was doing poorly at school and was not learning to read—although IQ tests indicated above-average intelligence. Teachers reported that he "is poorly motivated," "demands attention," and "is very immature." His mother complained that Billy "whines" and "drags his feet" when demand were made on him, and that he "always seems to want something." Mr. V stated that Billy was "babied" and overprotected by Mrs. V and Billy's sisters, ages 14 and 16. It appeared to him that Mrs. V intervened and prevented him from disciplining Billy.

The following "facts" from the interviews with the V's and Billy appeared pertinent.

1. Regarding Mr. V:

(a) He also was the youngest of three children and had two older sisters.

The following information will be helpful in understanding the answers to the tests which you are taking. Please answer *all* items. Thank you.

1. _____, _____, _____

      Last Name   First Name   Initial

_____

   Street Address   City   Zone   Phone Number

2. *Sex* (circle one): Male   Female

3. *Today's Date:* _____ _____ _____
               month   day   year

4. *Your birthdate:* _____ _____ _____
               month   day   year

5. *Your age:* _____ _____
            years   month

6. *Racial Background* (circle appropriate number):

  '1' Caucasian   '4' Mexican
  '2' Negro   '5' Other (specify)
  '3' Mongolian   _____

7. *Your religion* (circle number):

  '0' None   '3' Jewish
  '1' Catholic   '4' Other (specify)
  '2' Protestant   _____

8. *Your current marital status* (circle appropriate number):

  '0' Single   '4' Separated
  '1' Married   '5' Other (specify)
  '2' Divorced   _____
  '3' Widowed

9. *Childhood family:* Please write in the space below the year of birth and, if not now living, the year of death of your parents, brothers, and sisters: for example, 1880–1942; or if alive, 1920–. If you don't know, please write in "unknown." If you have no brothers or sisters, please write in "none."

  Father:_____

  Mother:_____

  Brothers:_____

  _____

  Sisters:_____

  _____

10. *Marital history:* Please indicate the year of your marriage. If married more than once, write in the years when married and when the marriage ended and how it ended for each marriage. For example: "1948–1952, divorced." Please include your present marriage: for example, "1955–." If you have never married, please write in "unmarried."

  _____

  _____

  _____

11. *Children:* Please write in the first name, sex, and birth year of each of your children. If you have none, please write in "none."

             Name   Sex   Birth year

  _____

  _____

  _____

12. *Head of household:* Who is usually the *main* source of your financial support (circle appropriate number)?

  '1' Myself   '5' My wife
  '2' My father   '6' Someone else
  '3' My mother   (specify)_____
  '4' My husband   _____

13. *Occupation:* Please write in the kind of work you most usually do to earn a living. Please use a "job title," indicating what you do (not merely where you work). If you are retired, what kind of work did you used to do? If you listed someone other than yourself as head of household in item 12, first put down what occupies *most* of your time, such as "housewife" or "student"; then in the spaces that follow, enter the occupation of the person you listed as head of household.

  Your occupation: _____

  Occupation, head of household: _____

  _____

14a. *Education:* Please circle the number which shows approximately how much schooling you have completed:

  '1' Post-graduate university studies
  '2' Graduate, college
  '3' Some college (not graduate), or other education beyond high school
  '4' Graduate, high school
  '5' 10th–11th grade
  '6' 7th–9th grade
  '7' Less than 7th grade
  '8' Other (specify) _____

  _____

14b. If in item 12 you indicated another person is the main source of your financial support, please circle the number which shows approximately how much education they completed.

  '0' I support myself
  '1' Postgraduate university studies
  '2' Graduate, college
  '3' Some college (not graduate), or other education beyond high school

Figure 5.1 Biographical data sheet.

‘4’   Graduate, high school
‘5’   10th–11th grade
‘6’   7th–9th grade
‘7’   Less than 7th grade
‘8’   Other (specify) _____

15. What are the main things for which you seek psychiatric help?

_____

Relatives see at the Psychiatric Clinic: *Name*   *Birth year*

Figure 5-1 *(continued)*

(b) His father died when he was 8 years old.

(c) Mrs. V regarded her mother-in-law to be overprotective of her husband, which he denied.

(d) Mr. V seldom expressed any anger except at Billy, or in arguments with his wife about Billy.

(e) Billy was named after his father.

2.   Regarding Mrs. V:

(a) Her younger and only brother had died at age 12 of a lingering illness.

(b) She had squabbled with her older sisters all of her life.

(c) She remained very close to her parents whom she visited almost daily.

(d) Mrs. V had had two miscarriages after the birth of her daughters before Billy's birth.

3.   Regarding Billy:

(a) Both parents had wished for a boy before Billy's birth.

(b) Billy's birth was normal, but he was "sickly" and a "poor sleeper and a poor eater" for the first two years of his life.

(c) Much to her despair, Mrs. V did not succeed in toilet training Billy until age 3, and he continued to have "accidents" and to wet the bed until age 6.

(d) Billy expressed many fears, especially of "monsters."

(e) Billy viewed his father as angry and his mother as "nicer."

These facts—among others—suggested the following hypothesis about the pattern of family interactions.

1.   Mr. V's relationship with Billy appeared very ambivalent. It seemed likely that he identified with his namesake, but Billy's role in the family probably reminded him of his own overprotected childhood that he wished to deny. Moreover, having lost his own father when he was 8, he might have threatening fantasies about his own role as the father of an 8-year-old son. In any event, he felt pushed out of his role as Billy's father. Last but not least, Billy was the object of all of his overtly expressed anger—including any dissension with his wife.

2.   Mrs. V probably identified Billy with her sickly brother, whose death left her the youngest in her family. Her battles with her sisters probably made her feel closer to Billy than to her daughters. Her prior miscarriages probably made Billy even more precious to her. Finally—and of the most immediate import—she was reenacting with Billy the prolonged attachment with her own parents.

3.   Thus Billy was infantilized by his mother, and he did not have to develop need-gratification skills. Since his mother regarded him as sickly, he probably felt weak and inept. Moreover, he was cowed by the explicit and singular anger of his father—who probably was the "monster" he feared—and could not compete with him directly. Indirectly he probably played one

parent off against the other. On the other hand, he was the vehicle through which disagreements between the parents were expressed.

All of these statements were of course hypotheses to be checked against other data both from the assessment and later in the treatment of the child.

Such thematic analysis is based on inductive reasoning. Admittedly it consists of seeing what can be made out of the data— post hoc. It depends largely on the scientific knowledge of fact and theory and on the clinical experience and acumen of the assessor. At the same time there is always the danger of stretching the data to fit some theoretical bias or of failing to take account of the data because of theoretical prejudice. For example, psychoanalytically oriented assessors may gladly accept any thread of evidence that might support their preconceptions, while those skeptical of Freud's concepts might ignore repeated evidence of psychosexual conflict.

Ideally an assessor should have a variety of concepts and fit them against the data, accepting those that yield the best fit for the evidence. It should be emphasized that all behavior is multidetermined and that several explanatory concepts might justifiably be entertained. Also, it is to be hoped that assessors will be free to invent new concepts if necessary for the particular child at hand. They most certainly should not merely repeat old shibboleths, but they should use their concepts in such a way and with such variation as to emphasize the uniqueness of this child. If the interpretive concept gives meaning to the child's behavior, it is also true that this child and his/her behavior and history often add to and expand upon the meaning of the theoretical concept.

Even when a case history has been so analyzed, the chief inferences are yet to be drawn. The assessor must then ask, given these patterns of behavior as shown in these data, how do they relate to the development difficulties currently presented by the child? *The purpose of reviewing the past development is to understand the present.* In making such inferences, however, assessors should be just as cautious and parsimonious as they would be in making inferences from any other kinds of data. They should be particularly careful to keep a "null hypothesis" in mind—that is, the possibility that past experiences and stresses have *not* necessarily led to the present developmental difficulties. All too often it appears easy to explain much or all of a child's current behavior in terms of history, as if current stresses were relatively unimportant. Such a tendency to argue in terms of the past is particularly tempting when analogies are used. An assessor should ask the following: Given the child's current stresses, how do the child's past experiences contribute to his/her present difficulties in a way that distinguishes him/her from other children under the same current stresses but with different histories? How might the child react to the current stress had he/she had a different background or experiences? These questions assume considerable importance when the assessor begins to make recommendations for changes in the child's behavior. Then it becomes necessary to know to what degree the behavioral changes should emphasize reorganization of current environment and relief of current stresses and to what extent it is also necessary to assist the child in healing old wounds and unlearning old habits and attitudes.

C.   CONDUCTING HOME OR SCHOOL VISITS

In clinics where there is a psychiatric "team" a visit to the client's home is traditionally conducted by the team's social worker. Observations of the home and of the interactions among the family members in their home environment offer most valuable data for the overall understanding of the family dynamics that underlie the child's symptoms.

I strongly recommend that graduate students learn to conduct home visits under the supervision of a psychiatric social worker. (In the past, psychologists were seldom introduced to this technique.) When the psychologist is practicing independently, then the home visit is her/his obligation.

Usually I conduct a home or school visit as the final step in the assessment. If a benign rapport with the child has been formed, the child is usually delighted with the prospect that the "doctor" wants to see his/her home and belongings. Parents are likely to be more anxious and guarded, especially if there is some legal possibility that the child might be removed from the home, for example, in custody cases or child-abuse cases. Even in such instances, however, parents usually yield to my request that I need to "understand the child in the natural home setting," and that I am not there to inspect the furnishings nor housekeeping. My home visits are usually brief (less than an hour). I try to visit a home just after school lets out, or in order to include both parents, after dinner. Invitations to dinner are complicated. Eating together is an intimate and emotional relationship for many people, and usually I avoid invitations to dinner.

There are many things to be observed during a home visit, and I note my observations afterward: the way you are greeted at the door and by whom; who shows you around the house; how casual or uptight the various family members are; the way the parents treat the child and, inversely, the way the child treats or reacts to the parents. The assessor can meet siblings and other family members who have not come to the office. Interaction between the child and sibs and between parents and with other family members may be directly (if briefly) observed. The way the child treats a family pet may tell you something about his/her needs for affection or for displacement of anger, for example.

Although observations of the family members and their interactions are primary, observations of the physical setting in which the child lives are also of value—

for example, the amount of living space, the possibilities for privacy or of family gathering, the comfort and feeling of warmth or coldness, and the like. It is not important whether the home is richly furnished, but rather whether a child is permitted a freedom to play, is afforded some privacy, and does not feel overly restricted, for example, by expensive furnishings or by obsessive housekeeping. Sometimes families can live happily in run-down public housing with old and broken furniture, and such poor families make every effort to provide neat, clean, and comfortable quarters. However, the assessor (who is usually from the upper middle class) can really appreciate the meaning of poverty and its impact on a child's attitudes and behavior by observing directly this kind of setting, which may allow little or no play space (even outdoors) and no privacy. Even in more well-to-do settings, children in apartments, for example, may live lives that are restricted by their neighbors or landlords, without play space, play hours, and pets.

Case 8

Lloyd (age 8) was referred by the private school because his achievement was lower than expected. His attention wandered, he disregarded his teachers' requests, responded to discipline with angry outcries or temper tantrums, fought with other children, disregarded rules of games, and in general seemed "spoiled." Lloyd's mother, Mrs. Q, had disregarded the school's complaints until the principal threatened to expel him. Mrs. Q protested to me that Lloyd was well behaved at home. She had no trouble with him, and she came to see me only at the teacher's insistence. She could not account for the school's complaints. In my interviews with her she seemed guarded and self-protective, revealing little that seemed significant. Lloyd also denied the school's accusations, retorting that the teacher was "mean" and "has it in for me," but he could not say why. His responses to the tests indicated that he was advanced intellectually and that his fantasies were replete with themes of anger and violence and strong needs for succor. Yet until I visited the home I had little idea of the sources of Lloyd's anger.

Lloyd greeted me at the door and was about to lead me in when Mrs. Q stepped between us and took over. She announced proudly that this six-bedroom home had 4500 square feet, was only two years old, and cost $500,000. She quickly led me to the living room, which had a view across the bay. But I noted that the yard outside this hillside home, while professionally gardened, was too steep for play space. The home was beautifully and expensively furnished. Lloyd sat stiffly on a plush sofa. After leading me through the main floor, Mrs. Q showed me her office and Mr. Q's gun room. Then she announced that "the child's quarters are downstairs" (she often referred to Lloyd as "the child"), and she ordered Lloyd to show me his "things." Lloyd's quarters consisted of a large bedroom, an even larger playroom, a private bath, and a 10-foot-square toy closet. These rooms too were beautifully furnished but without color or decoration, other than Lloyd's drawings that he had pinned to the wall. He explained that his mother wanted him to take them down because he had made holes in the wall, but he had put them up again to show me, defying his mother. The floor was deeply carpeted, and the walls and ceiling soundproofed so that adults upstairs would not be disturbed. A child could not make noise by racing a car across *this* floor. Lloyd's playroom had a desk, bookshelf, and chalkboard. He had his own TV and small sofa. The only plaything out in the room was a small trampoline. However, the shelves in the playroom were lined to the ceiling with expensive toys, and the floor space was taken up by three huge sacks of toys. "Wow!" I exclaimed, "You've really got a lot of things to play with!" "Yeah," he replied nonchalantly, "I got all this junk for Christmas and my birthday, and my father always brings me something when he

comes home. I hope he comes back soon." Ignoring this last remark for the moment, I asked, "Which toys do you like to play with the most?" Lloyd closed the playroom door, "I don't have much time to play. I've got to do my homework or watch TV." And he grabbed a huge stuffed animal off his bed and gave it a hug and kicked it across room.

"You said you wished your father would come back soon. Has he been away for long?" I inquired.

"I don't know," Lloyd responded morosely. "He goes away a lot on trips. For business, he says. Last time he left, he and Mommy had a big fight and she told him if he went away again he couldn't come back." In that instant Mrs. Q called down the stairs to announce that she was serving tea. Lloyd gave the stuffed animal another kick across the room.

In the living room, while tea was being served, Lloyd kept throwing pieces of new newspaper into the fire in the fireplace—causing soot to scatter into the room. Several times Mrs. Q tried to divert him, offering him cookies if he would come away from the fire. Then she asked him with a wan smile, "Dearest, please stop, won't you?" But Lloyd acted as if he did not hear her. Desperate, she grabbed him by the collar, and he turned on her, kicking and hitting. "Maybe he would obey better if he had a father around," she remarked sadly.

Thus in a brief visit of an hour, I was able to observe directly and dramatically the parents' attitudes toward possessions, creating a home that was beautifully designed and equipped but that was not child oriented, isolating the child and his playthings, which become possessions for him. Although she seemed at first to dominate the scene, in the showdown she had no real control over Lloyd's behavior. In subsequent interviews she admitted that her marriage had been deteriorating for several years and was probably nearing a total collapse. Very depressed, she was preoccupied with the loss of her husband and admitted she felt unable to deal with

Lloyd's behavior at home, even less than his behavior at school.

Children spend at least a third of their waking hours at school. A visit to the school can be very informative, particularly when the complaint comes from the school. The child can be observed directly in the classroom and on the playground. Such observations allow assessment of the child's attitudes toward learning and toward adult authority as well as how she/he interacts with other children. It is also possible to interview teachers and school authorities (who are otherwise unavailable) and to review school records more completely.

CASE 9

The vice principal at Tita's school had called her parents, stating firmly that Tita was failing at school and was such a behavior problem that it might be necessary to transfer her to another school—even though she had attended this school less than four months. The parents were shocked, because Tita had made above-average grades at her previous schools, and there had never before been complaints about her behavior. Tita's parents denied that Tita "gives us any trouble. She's the best girl in the family." This proved a family joke as Tita had three older brothers and three younger brothers, and no sisters. Tita's parents had asked the school for more details, but the school had not provided any. Sgt. F had visited the school briefly. As he phrased it, he had "received no satisfaction." Mrs. F was eight months pregnant and had been too ill recently to go to the school. Tita, age 11, described her teacher as "prejudiced" and "mean," and she complained that the teacher called her an "Army brat." She admitted that in four months she had made no close friends and had gotten into several fights on the school grounds. "They're all crybabies," Tita complained. "They don't play fair. The boys won't let me play baseball. I can hit

better than any of them. . . . The girls are always showing off their clothes. I don't like them, anyhow. They're so dumb."

Tita was a pretty child with long flowing blonde curls. She was tall for her age and had budding breasts, which showed through her Army-issue T-shirt, indicating that she was rapidly approaching puberty.

The initial interview with Tita and her parents revealed the following: Sgt. F was a "20-year" man, a professional soldier. He had entered the Army at age 18 and in five more years could retire. He admitted that Army life could be rough on families, since he was transferred from post to post almost every year, wherever the Army needed his expertise, which was organizing commissaries. He further explained that one reason that the F's had so many children was to form a family unit that did not depend so much on external friends and associates. "Tita's best friends are her brothers. We all love her." Tita rolled her eyes and grimaced at her father's remark. He brought along a collection of Tita's report cards, which verified his statement that in the previous four schools Tita had been judged a superior student and was well liked by teachers. A home visit yielded some information about Tita and her family but little that was relevant to the school complaints. Tita's father had rented a large, ramshackle farmhouse for his large brood. It was located about four miles from the "village," an unincorporated suburb of well-to-do families outside the metropolitan area. The dirt yard was full of boys, dogs, cats, and chickens. Mrs. F sat on the veranda, rocking her newborn baby boy. Tita was engaged in a game of tether ball with her next-younger brother, and she was winning. At Mrs. F's request, one of the boys interrupted his play to bring me a chair, and another brought a cup of coffee. Mrs. F had only to speak softly and firmly, and her children carried out her requests without a word of protest. She did not have to leave her chair to separate two quarreling boys and pacify each. The house—though sparsely furnished—was neat and clean.

"Everybody helps out. The boys are good housekeepers. Bill (her husband) too. He's a better cook than I." The boys showed me their garden. Tita's project was her chickens, who lived under the house. "Dad promises he'll build me a chicken house soon," she claimed. Although the boys had to share two rooms and two sleeping proches, Tita had a small attic room to herself with a dormer window box full of her collection of stuffed animals. "Maybe next year we can have a horse, a real horse!" she confided. Her ambition was to become a veterinarian.

The children all ran out to greet their father, who hugged them all. He then excused himself "to put on the beans for dinner for my troops." Later he lined them up in a mock military inspection—an evening routine for this family—checking on health, behavior, and schoolwork, and "what was fun or happy today." His voice had a military bark, but it was evident that the children enjoyed his attention and affection.

Mr. H, the vice principal, did not initially welcome the idea of the psychologist visiting the school, but he acceded since I had written permission from the parents and because he admitted that "Tita *is* a problem." He added that both he and the teacher had little free time, but that he could see me for a half hour of his lunch time, and the teacher for a half-hour of her lunchtime, and if I came a half-hour before that I could observe Tita on the school ground during her lunch. If the teacher gave her permission, I might also visit the classroom, provided I did not disrupt the class!

When I arrived, Mr. H was at lunch, but he showed me to a window where I could observe Tita. At that moment she was trying to join the boys in a baseball game, but they rejected her, calling her foul names (based on her last name, Foulks). Tita was screaming back at them, using equally obscene language, when her teacher, then on "yard duty," marched up behind her, grabbed her by the wrist, and ordered her back to where the girls were playing, just

below my observation post. "Why can't you behave like a lady" the teacher reproached her. "You're such a nasty girl." Tita sat on the bench where the teacher placed her and sobbed. The other girls turned their backs to her. I did notice that most of them wore pretty sweaters and designer jeans. Most were younger and smaller than Tita.

In an interview with Mr. H he admitted that Tita was not the school's only problem child. "We've had problems ever since the Army moved in. You see, they are a lower-class group. Many are blacks. I suppose they are nice enough, but they're just not our kind. We had such a lovely school before the Army built this base. Now we're very overcrowded and we can't ask for more taxes." He did not mention the fact that the federal government paid the local school district a subsidy for each child of a government employee—almost doubling its budget. Mr. H knew little of Tita personally other than what her teacher had complained of. He had not reviewed her record, although he knew I was coming to the school. He finally located it and held it close to his chest, checking through it. "Don't see much here," he remarked, and started to return it to the files. When I requested to see the record myself, he explained that this was a private record, not for parents or others to see. Exasperated, I rose to leave, remarking that I did not feel he was cooperative and that I would report back to the F's and "their attorney." (Here, I admit, I was fudging.) Mr. H tossed the record to me. I noted that in addition to superior grades, the record showed Tita to have made high scores on achievement tests (functioning at sixth- and seventh-grade levels) and to have an IQ of 130 on a standard group test. She had completed the fifth grade. When I asked Mr. H why Tita had been put in the fifth rather than sixth grade, he explained it was the school policy to place students from a different state a grade below that that was usual for their age "until the child proves she can succeed." Tita's poor performance, Mr. H argued, justified placing her in fifth grade. He could not explain why this bright girl might be underachieving.

Mrs. Y, Tita's teacher, had completed her half hour of yard duty and had a half hour left for lunch. She apologized for eating while we talked, explaining that since the school budget was cut, teachers no longer had a free hour "for business like this." Regarding Tita, Mrs. Y explained what Mr. H had said about the Army "brats." "She's no better or worse than the rest. They have no manners, they've never learned discipline. Look at the way she's dressed! And her language! Just like the boys. What you saw out the window happens nearly every day." Mrs. Y could not specify further on Tita's classroom behavior. "She doesn't listen. She looks bored. Her work is all right. In fact she may be very intelligent. She always has her hand up and laughs when others make mistakes. Her written work is messy. She is finished before the others, and she spends her time scribbling on the margin, decorating her paper, she says. I've tried to teach her better habits. I take off 10 points for messy papers. I can't give her all of the attention she wants. Now that the Army is here, I've 42 children in my class. I used to have less than 30. And all nice children from nice homes." Mrs. Y, white haired and in her fifties, looked weary.

Since neither my examination of Tita nor the home visit indicated any notable emotional disturbance, I concluded, on the basis of the school visit, that Tita's problems were chiefly social. She was the victim of social-class prejudice from both school authorities and peers. A large, bright, boisterous girl who lived in an all-boy family, she did not fit easily into the upper-middle-class mores of being "nice."

In a second visit, once Mr. H had the whole story, he was more amenable. He agreed that Tita was probably bored in the fifth grade, and said he was moving her to the sixth grade where the teacher was a young man who was a little more tolerant of her exuberance. This teacher assigned her extra reading or other tasks to keep her busy while slower children finished their work. In the sixth grade boys and girls participated together in sports. Obscene name-calling was labeled by this teacher as "poor sportsmanship," and violators could be banned from the game. This rule applied equally to the Army "brats" and the "nice" children from the village. Six months later I checked with Mrs. F. Tita was receiving her usual superior grades and did not complain further about the school.

D.   STRUCTURED TECHNIQUES BASED ON SUBJECTIVE REPORTS

Since the time of Galton a wide variety of structured samplings of subjective self-opinion, such as true-false or multiple-choice tests, self-rating scales, Q-sorts, and the like, have been employed by psychologists to study attitudes and feelings. Many were called "personality" tests or tests of "temperament." Most of these techniques were built for adult and adolescent literate populations, and only a few of these ever enjoyed any prolonged clinical adoption. In this section, two children's questionnaires—currently used in many clinics—will be discussed: The Rogers Adjustment Scale (1931) and the Bene-Anthony Family Attitudes Technique (1957). Also to be considered are two subjective scales used for measuring ego-functioning patterns among adolescents and adults: the MMPI (McKinley and Hathaway, 1943) and the Edwards Personal Preference Schedule (EPPS) (Edwards, 1959). The final technique to be considered will be the Vineland Social Maturity Scale.

1.   The Rationale

Often the rational behind these subjective scales is neither clearly stated nor obvious to the user. Most of them propose to measure several different variables, and no two inventories assess the same set of variables. Except for the MMPI, they appear to have been constructed on an a priori basis, that is, sets of items were selected that seemed to reflect those variables the author wished to measure. Scores were then standardized on various samples, and the interrelationships between the scores were studied. Rarely however were these studies made of the interrelationships between these scores and other kinds of behaviors. Rather, the items and thus the sets of items or scales were assumed to have a face validity. The simplest rationale behind such personality scales is that the subject's score on any one of the categorized sets of items represents a subjective opinion with regard to the variable in question, in comparison with the self-assessments of other members of the sample. If the items do form a reasonable and statistically unified category and if the subject does try sincerely to express his/her feelings about himself/herself in an objective fashion, then this type of scale may very well yield a fair measure of such subjective behavior. Except in those rare instances where there is research regarding the relationship between subjective and objective behavior, it cannot be assumed that these subjective-opinion scores necessarily reflect anything other than self-appraisal.

2. Operations

Although the instructions vary somewhat from technique to technique, in essence the operations are about the same. Except for the Vineland (and the Bene-Anthony when it is read to the child), these scales are usually self-administered. The child or adult is given the questionnaire and a pencil, and after the assessor is assured that the subject understands the directions, the subject proceeds to respond silently without the intervention or assistance of the assessor. This operation in which the subject and assessor are not in immediate contact creates several other special conditions. For some subjects the fact that they do not have to say these things aloud with someone making note of their remarks frees them to express themselves. Many adults will accept MMPI items as "true" that they do not mention in the initial interview or later deny. When given a range of choices to describe their behavior on the Rogers, children also may tend to be more frank than when asked similar questions in interviews. On the other hand, there are probably just as many children who are willing to discuss things about themselves in interviews where they can defend or explain themselves, but who are quite cautious or compulsive about committing themselves on paper with a "yes" or "no" answer. Sometimes the items will suggest to the subject things that neither the child nor the assessor has thought to discuss in the interview, thus adding to the subject's opportunity to evaluate and express herself/himself. Just as often, however, the subject may feel that many of the items are irrelevant or are out of the range of her/his experience or knowledge. Some items may only serve to intensify the child's defensiveness.

However, these other "test-taking" attitudes are not accounted for in the test scores per se. Even the MMPI "validity scores" are more concerned with other variables, such as social conformity, self-denunciation, and suppression. These variables are related to test taking, but they are at best only indirect measures of the operational conditions mentioned previously. Sometimes by inspecting the subject's responses, it is possible to make a reasonable guess as to how the subject regarded and used these operations. One can see if a disproportionate number of responses were self-derogatory (thus usually resulting in high scores on all subscales), or if the person consistently gave socially acceptable, self-approving responses, and denying any discomfort or dysfunction, which usually lowers all scores. However, this information alone does not indicate whether the subject is actually expressing a bias or whether this represents how the subject actually regards herself/himself. If the child tends to give mostly "yes" responses or to mark only on one side of the answer sheet or to show signs of responding randomly, the whole test may be held "invalid." But there is no way of discovering what made the subject decide to avoid the test—other than to ask. Following up such questionnaires with brief interviews or using them as one basis for the main interview during the assessment is therefore recommended procedure. Such a follow-up interview gives the assessor the chance to explore with the subject both his/her feelings about taking the test and some of the pertinent test items. One can also compare the defensiveness and kind of defenses used in the interview with those demonstrated or suspected on the tests.

One other limitation to these scales is the fact that they depend on the ability to verbalize feelings and attitudes, or at least to comprehend such verbalizations. Occasionally even very bright children cannot reveal how they feel, even when the task is merely to check "true" or "false." All of these scales require that the child be able to read—at the fourth-grade level or better—and that his/her intellectual development is average or better.

3. Methods of Analysis

The standardized metric scores provided by these scales lend themselves easily to pattern analysis. On the MMPI in particular, such pattern analysis of the subscales has been so intensively studied that profile analysis—as it is called—has become a complex "cookbook" art. Pattern analysis for the other scales to be discussed here has not been so finely developed, and it is still a matter of rough inspection and estimate. However, any assessor attempting such profile analysis—even on the MMPI—should take into account the nature and size of the sample, the variability of scores in the original standardization (the raw scores upon which standard scores, if computed, are based), and the intercorrelations between the scales. For no matter how exact a science one may make of profiles of scales, if the scales were constructed on small samples from limited populations, then pro-

file analysis is similarly limited. If the raw scores of the original sample were highly skewed, no amount of standardizing of this variability will change the profile's ultimate skewness. If the intercorrelations between the scales are not established, then it is impossible to know to what degree high and low spots on a profile are significant variations and to what degree they merely represent overlaps between scales. Thus when analyzing a profile of scores, the assessor should be sure that the high and low points are not merely the results of artifacts in the test standardization.

Another approach to the analysis of these techniques that is commonly used by clinicians is the qualitative inspection of the items themselves. When there are not very many items involved, it is possible to look through the subject's answer booklet and note patterns of responses that were perhaps not measured directly by the test. A test constructor seldom ferrets out all the possible factors, even if the test is constructed on a factor-analysis basis (and those in clinical use are rarely so constructed). Often subjects express—through their responses to these structured items—attitudes of their own that are not represented in the scales. The perceptive assessor may even be able to spot repetitive themes across scales by examining the individual items making up the various scaled scores. For example, on the MMPI it is quite possible for two or more subjects to obtain fairly high scores on any particular scale and yet be responding to quite different items, for each of these scales covers several different facets of a general category. Moreover, when one is examining a profile of two or more high scores, the characteristic attitudes of the individual under consideration may be hidden in the overlapping items. In any such qualitative analysis of items, however, one must be very cautious about attributing meaning to any one item, for there is no indication of what interpretation the subject placed on an item when he made his self-rating of "yes" or "no."

4. Rogers Adjustment Inventory

Turning now to some of the specific techniques, the adjustment inventory for children that Carl Rogers published in 1931 probably is not used as much as it should be, because many clinicians today may be unfamiliar with it.* This inventory consists of six sets of items. Part 1 consists of "vocations" of which the child is asked to choose the three she/he "would most like to be." Part 2 similarly asks the child to select three wishes from a list, for example, "To have my parents love me more," "To be stronger than I am," and the like. Part 3 asks the child to write the names of three companions he/she would like to have on a desert island. Part 4 asks the child to compare herself/himself with an imaginary child—for example, "Fred is the best ball player in the school"—by checking the square on a 9-point scale from "Just like him" to "Not at all like him." Simultaneously the child is also asked, using the same type of scale, "Do you want to be like him?" This part ends with this question: "Which of these children would your mother like best?" Part 5 consists of a variety of multiple-choice items of this form. "How many friends do you have? (a) hundreds, (b) quite a few, (c) several good friends, (d) no friends at all." In Part 6 the child is asked to list the members of her/his family—including himself/herself—and his/her "best boyfriend" and "best girlfriend" and then to rank this list according to whom he/she likes best. Separate forms were designed for boys and girls. From these items, Rogers derived four variables: family adjustment, social adjustment, personal adjustment, and daydreaming. Each scale draws on items from several of six parts of the test. The manual lists norms for separate age groups for each sex for ages 8 to 13. Rogers, however, was most

*Many psychologists of this generation may be surprised that Rogers ever published a test, since he is much more widely known for his nondirective and experiential approach to counseling and psychotherapy in which testing was seldom used.

concerned with the qualitative clinical use of his technique, and he cites case material illustrating this approach. The items are usually quite comprehensible to literate children in this age group who are of average intelligence or higher. Also the items are attractive to children, despite the fact that they are quite direct in approaching children's anxieties. Admittedly its standardization is now quite dated, and there has been very little research using this test subsequently. It badly needs some kind of test-taking attitude scale. In the original study, Rogers was able to distinguish "well-adjusted" from "poorly adjusted" children on the basis of the test scores, but this finding was not cross-validated nor replicated. Clinicians used to dealing with more modern "dynamic" concepts and terminology may look askance at the old-fashioned adjustment concept of these scales. Yet in using these simple measures in addition to a qualitative analysis, one can gain considerable information about the child's subjective picture of himself/herself, which can be translated into whatever set of theoretical concepts with which the assessor may be familiar.

5. The Family Relations Test

This test, constructed by Bene and Anthony (1957), is an excellent example of a well-thought-out, imaginative subjective technique. The intent—to quote from their manual—is to "indicate objectively, reliably, and rapidly the direction and intensity of the child's feelings toward the various members of his family, and, of no less importance, his estimate of their reciprocal regard for him." That these authors consider their technique a subjective approach is revealed in their statement regarding interpretation of the test results (Bene and Anthony, 1957, p. 15): "For clinical purposes, however, it is his 'psychic reality,' his own idiosyncratic concept of his emotional environment, that has operational value and is likely to be more relevant to the etiology of his symptoms than the 'objective' reality assessed through careful social enquiry.'' (When these authors speak of their test as ''objective,'' evidently they mean ''structured.'')

This technique consists of a set of statements (47 in the version for younger children, 86 for older children). In the version for younger children (age 8 or younger), the statements are subdivided into ''positive feelings coming from the child; negative feelings coming from the child; positive feelings going toward the child; negative feelings going toward the child; and dependence.'' For older children the items are further broken down into ''mild positive, strong positive (sexualized), mild negative, strong negative (hostile), maternal overprotection, paternal overindulgence, and maternal overindulgence.'' The novel feature of this technique is that as the child reads each statement (or, for younger children, as it is read to them), they are asked to consider it as a ''message'' to a member of the family and to deposit it in a little box attached to a cardboard figure that the child has previously indicated as a family member. The statements are in these forms: ''This person in the family is kind to me,'' or ''This person in the family does not love me enough,'' or ''This is the person in the family whom father spoils too much.'' Or for younger children: ''N (name of the child) wants you to come when he (she) has hurt himself (herself). Who is it N . . . wants when he (she) has hurt himself (herself)?'' If the child feels a statement does not apply to any of the members of his/her family, it can be deposited in the box attached to a figure labeled ''Nobody.'' The child also selects a figure representing the self.

In discussing these operations the authors quite carefully consider some of the problems mentioned previously regarding subjective techniques with children. For example, they note that children may well have considerable guilt and anxiety when asked to apply these statements to parents—especially those involving considerable negative feelings—and they discuss at length the necessity for establishing a supportive rapport with the child, advising that wherever possible the child should be encouraged to read the statement silently and make choices independently without interaction with the assessor. Also, although no validity score or other direct measure of defensiveness is included in the analysis of the results, a great deal of consideration is given to the kinds of defenses indicated by the distribution of the various kinds of items among the family members. For example, an overall defensiveness would be indicated if nearly all of the very negative statements were given to ''Nobody.'' Other defensive attitudes discussed in the manual are idealization, displacement, wishfulfillment/regression, projection, and reaction formation.

To analyze the child's responses, the kinds of messages that she/he sends or receives from various members of the family are to be carefully recorded and counted. Actually the number of items in each subcategory is so small, usually 8 to 10 (and their variability is not stated), that statistical differences in the distribution of any one type of response among the various family members or between the types of statements attributed to any one family member probably would be significant only when in such extreme ratios as 8:2 or greater. In fact, in all of the many examples cited in the original manual, only such extremes are mentioned. Although no one score is considered in itself and analysis is almost entirely in terms of patterns of scores, once again one might question to what degree the variability of the individual scores affects this pattern analysis. For example, if out of the 86 items 20 are attributed to the mother by the child of which 16 are positive and 4 negative, and another 15 are attributed to the father of which 12 are negative and 3 positive, the authors would probably conclude that the child sees the mother in a far more positive light than he/she sees the father. Despite the authors' psychoanalytic, development approach, no age norms are given! Nor is the possibility of sex differences even discussed. Thus despite the fascinating clinical potential of the data of this technique, the analysis of score patterns is seriously weakened by the absence of sufficient normative standards other than those provided subsequently by Frost (1969).

The inferential interpretation of this pattern analysis, as suggested by Bene and Anthony, is mainly inductive (although deductive inferences also could be as easily drawn) in terms of psychoanalytic developmental theory. From the various patterns of attitudes expressed by the child toward each of the parents and toward various siblings and other family members, the assessor can infer various psychodynamics. The authors discuss two "syndromes": "egocentric states—auto-aggressive variety" and "egocentric states—auto-erotic variety." Certainly from such data it would be quite possible to inductively infer many other kinds of syndromes of subjective attitudes and their meanings for the ego functioning of the child. Although the authors mention independent "blind" analysis and interpretation as part of their validation studies, it is evident in their discussion of case examples that in clinical use the technique is intended to be used in conjunction with other clinical materials.

The problems of validating such a technique are discussed very cogently by the authors in their manual. They cite several well-thought-out "comparisons between test results and case-history material," studying four major questions regarding the validity of their interpretations. Although the results of these studies are given in metric form in several tables, unfortunately the n of their samples is quite small, and in only one instance was it possible for them to make a statistical statement. In another study it was statistically determined that the sex of the assessor did not affect any of their variables—when testing boys. A split-half (odd-even items) reliability study on samples of fairly respectable size yielded intercorrelations ranging from .68 to .90 (corrected for attenuation), which for this

kind of material are certainly above reproach.

This technique, since it was first introduced, has excited considerable research interest, which has been reviewed by Kauffman (1970). This research has been expanded by Kauffman subsequently (1971), comparing the responses of normal and disturbed boys, and by Kauffman, Weaver, and Weaver (1971 and 1972) on age and intellectual factors and reading ability. Frost (1969) provided normative data on 190 sixth-grade children, which is most helpful in interpreting this test. A condensation of Frost's results is presented in Table 5.1. It should be noted that these norms are provided only for prepubescent children. Similar norms for children of other ages are yet forthcoming.

Distribution of these norms are obviously quite skewed. In most instances scores of zero are within the normal range, and any fairly high scores are significantly above average. Moreover, the statistical degrees of freedom are limited as each item can be attributed to only one out of five or more categories (presuming at least one sib).

6. The MMPI

Of all the structured questionnaires invented for the study of personality dysfunction, the MMPI is by far the most widely used and thoroughly studied. The normative "atlases" for analysis and interpretation of profiles both for adults (Hathaway and Meehl, 1951) and for adolescents (Hathaway and Monachesi, 1961) are standard equipment in the offices of many clinicians. Several studies have been made of the types of profiles given by parents of children brought to clinics (Marks, 1961), thus providing a basis for the MMPI's use as a technique in assessing the relationship between the emotional attitudes of parents and the developmental difficulties presented by the child. Over the past decade the considerable study that has been made of adolescent profiles has extended the clinical use of this instrument to any literate

Table 5.1.   Means for the Family Relations Test—Normal Sixth Grader (Condensed from Frost, 1969)

	Boys	Girls
Total father (N = 82)	12.06 ± 6.72 (N = 102)	11.58 ± 5.76
Outgoing +	4.80 ± 3.40	5.79 ± 3.58
Outgoing −	1.49 ± 1.83	1.04 ± 1.65
Incoming +	4.17 ± 2.93	3.87 ± 2.93
Incoming −	2.06 ± 1.51	1.38 ± 1.48
Total mother (N = 86)	13.63 ± 6.67 (N = 104)	13.23 ± 6.24
Outgoing +	5.41 ± 3.20	5.49 ± 3.19
Outgoing −	1.33 ± 2.18	1.04 ± 1.68
Incoming +	5.73 ± 3.76	5.76 ± 3.00
Incoming −	1.62 ± 1.50	1.44 ± 1.51
Next Oldest Sib (N = 47)	11.36 ± 6.76 (N = 69)	12.87 ± 7.44
Outgoing +	1.68 ± 2.37	2.54 ± 2.51
Outgoing −	4.94 ± 3.73	4.94 ± 4.02
Incoming +	1.38 ± 2.17	1.55 ± 1.99
Incoming −	3.36 ± 2.61	3.84 ± 2.65
Next Youngest Sib (N = 61)	12.05 ± 6.81 (N = 76)	12.92 ± 7.58
Outgoing +	1.72 ± 2.03	2.21 ± 2.52
Outgoing −	5.26 ± 3.87	5.08 ± 3.63
Incoming +	2.16 ± 2.36	2.81 ± 2.72
Incoming −	2.91 ± 2.33	2.82 ± 2.50
Mr. Nobody (N = 86)	22.88 ± 9.27 (N = 104)	19.80 ± 8.70
Outgoing +	5.47 ± 3.14	3.68 ± 2.78
Outgoing −	5.35 ± 4.20	5.08 ± 3.99
Incoming +	4.87 ± 3.07	4.08 ± 2.76
Incoming −	7.33 ± 3.33	6.96 ± 3.53

person over the age of 12. Because this technique is widely known and so much information is available about it in the literature, discussion will be limited to a brief review of the rationale, to some cautions concerning standardization (especially regarding adolescents), and to some remarks concerning its use with parents.

The construction of the MMPI was so strictly empirical that the term *rationale* may not at first glance seem to apply. Indeed few if any of its promulgators ever gave the rationale more than passing consideration and then only to re-emphasize this empirical approach. It is repeatedly pointed out that none of the items contained in the so-called clinical scales was selected on the basis of any theoretical premise, but instead that these scales were constructed purely by comparing the differences between samples of patients with established psychiatric diagnoses and "normals." Only

on the "Masculine-feminine" and the "Lie" scales were items arbitrarily assigned (and the rationale for the M-F scale has never been clearly stated). Thus if the MMPI can be said to have a rationale, it is the simple statement that it is the *number* of responses that a subject makes rather than the content of these responses that determines whether he/she is responding similarly to the criterion groups. The theory behind the MMPI is that any kind of item or behavior might have been used, as long as it discriminated between persons diagnosed as emotionally disturbed and those not showing such disturbance. If one holds strictly to such a rationale, interpretation of the results would be limited to the dichotomous discrimination between "mentally ill" and "normal." In fact, much of the application of the MMPI has been concerned with this dichotomy, of working out profile formulas for distinguishing "psychotic" from "nonpsychotic," and the like.

Both MMPI literature and the handbooks, however, leave no doubt that the promoters of this instrument are concerned with many more subtle personality discriminations. Consequently the rationale of the MMPI has been undergoing considerable implicit change. With the advent of complex profile analysis, from which inferences are drawn not only about diagnostic differentiations but also about personality traits and defenses, it can no longer be maintained that the content of the scales is purely empirical and meaningless. Although the items in the scales were empirically selected originally, the traits and defenses, which it is many times implicitly hypothesized these scales and scale combinations measure, *are* often based on generalizations about the item contents of the scales. Quite a few of these hypotheses have been checked out and cross-validated. Moreover, some of them concerning the content of the scales have been drawn from empirical observations—from noting and cross checking the behavior of individuals with specific profiles.

Profile analysis of this sort has greatly enriched the usefulness of the MMPI beyond the sterile differential diagnostic rationale of its origin. Profile analysis permits the expansion of the MMPI rationale, which may be stated as follows: The subjective impressions that a person expresses in judging himself/herself on their 566 items may be analyzed into traits and defenses by comparing the relative identification of these responses with each of the eight clinical standardization groups. The subtle but definite change in this rationale lies in the degree to which the test is regarded as subjective. When one merely counts responses—disregarding content—in order to make dichotomous discriminations, there is no implication that the subject necessarily is judging himself/herself in any particular fashion. How the subject interprets the item is not only unknown, but it is considered to be of no importance! Once traits and de-

fenses are attributed to the profile, however, the assumption that the meaning of the item to the subject makes no difference can no longer be maintained. In fact this assumption probably was invalid even for such dichotomies as "psychotic" versus "nonpsychotic," for even these simple distinctions carried many implied trait assumptions.

The fact that the interpretation of an MMPI profile depends in so large a part on the comparison and contrast with the traits of the criterion groups makes the constitution and definition of these criterion groups critical. In his original description of the development of the MMPI scales Hathaway (1940) emphasized that the criterion groups consisted of persons who clearly represented the diagnostic syndromes in question, and about whom there was no disagreement as to the diagnosis. Nevertheless, despite the many other studies in which it has been shown that psychiatric diagnosis is often very unreliable, there has never been any study of the reliability or homogeneity of these criterion groups. Even more serious is the absence of any discussion of the criteria upon which these diagnoses were based. Since the MMPI was devised before national diagnostic criteria were established (as in the APA *Diagnostic and Statistical Manual of Mental Disorders),* there is no indication of the kinds of behaviors, symptoms, and traits that were used to make these diagnoses. This absence of any clear-cut and detailed description of the criterion groups (other than by diagnostic label) has continued to be a major flaw in the MMPI. Even in the many subsequent studies—cross-validating and expanding on profile analysis—the characteristics of the criterion groups are rarely discussed, although many post hoc assumptions are made. When profiles based on these original criterion groups are further compared and cross-checked on new criterion groups—also undefined—the error is compounded. Fortunately in the more recent studies of the traits and defenses associated with certain profiles the following question has more frequently been asked: Are the traits and defenses that are assumed to be present in the diagnostic patterns actually reflected in the behavior of the groups being studied, regardless of diagnosis? It is where such trait patterns can be established that the MMPI gains strength and validity.

Although in the 40 years since its inception the MMPI has been administered to thousands upon thousands of subjects, the number of subjects in the original criterion groups was surprisingly small. For example, the Hypochondriasis Scale was based on a n of 30, and few of the other criterion groups exceed 100. One wonders about the stability of the enormous superstructure of profile analysis constructed on the basis of such small n's. Of course in subsequent studies many further cases have been considered, thus adding to the knowledge of the types of persons included in the criterion groups. Nevertheless, at no time has there been any revision of the original scales (apart from the addition of the K correction). It has been implicitly assumed also that the same thing is meant by the diagnostic classifications presently in use as was meant in 1937, although the standard nomenclature has twice been changed. At least two of the 1937 classifications (hysteria and psychaesthenia) no longer even exist as diagnostic categories! Admittedly the MMPI has helped to strengthen and clarify this diagnostic system in great measure by developing better definitions in terms of behavior and symptoms as part of the research. In effect, these diagnostic headings on the scales have new meanings and are personality syndromes rather than mere measures of the degree of pathology. This change is emphasized by the fact that in MMPI literature the scales are referred to by number rather than by name in the order in which they appear on the profile sheet.

Although the MMPI was originally designed for use with adults, the application of this technique to the assessment of adolescents has received considerable study over the past decade or so, culminating in Hathaway and Monachesi's *Adolescent*

Personality and Behavior: MMPI Patterns (1963) and their *An Atlas of Juvenile MMPI Profiles* (1961). Although the items and scales remain unchanged, their studies of over 10,000 adolescents in effect yield new norms. (The authors advise correcting the usual profile sheet for the juvenile means and standard deviations.) They also well recognize that emotional disturbance in this turbulent period of development does not have the same meaning as in later life. Although they do not discuss the topic of diagnostic nosology, they make no use of it and proceed directly to their "predictions" about *delinquency* and *emotional disturbance*. Both of these terms are operationally defined by their rating scales. The authors report that despite the adult psychopathological content of some of the items, the normal adolescents they tested seemed to understand the items quite well and to be unperturbed by them. My experience with the MMPI in the assessment of adolescents has convinced me continually that it is a most valuable screening device, especially for outlining the systems of defenses used by the adolescent ego.

Since the MMPI has shifted from a diagnostic technique to a set of personality scales it is possible to translate the profile patterns into terms of ego functioning. Such a dynamic approach to the interpretation of the MMPI requires a knowledge of the empirical findings regarding the characteristics of individuals who are known to produce various commonly obtained profiles. The psychologist can then combine this information with a theory of ego functioning such that it becomes possible to recognize the dynamics within the MMPI profile of symptoms.

Only a few examples can be included here. The most frequent profile among both normal and emotionally disturbed adolescents is '49 (*Pd* and *Ma* high points, between T-60 and T-70). In fact, '49 profiles are much more common today in both the adolescent and adult profiles than when the MMPI was standardized in the 1930s. This change reflects the change in personal and social value systems in the mid–twentieth-century American culture. People are becoming increasingly open about their aggressive and sexual impulses. Adolescents in particular are less inhibited affectively and are more assertive of their independence than were the good Lutherans of St. Paul and Minneapolis of 1938 upon whom these scales were standardized. Currently these scales measure—among other things—the degree to which the adolescent is participating in his/her own revolution.

Commonly the '49 profile (without a tertiary peak) from an adolescent who is referred by his parents for psychological assessment is facing a generation gap. Often the parental MMPI profiles are marked by peaks on 7 (*Pt*), indicating obsessive concerns, by high *L* scores, with excessive social conformity, or by other high-score profiles, indicating personal anxieties and the inability to accept today's normal adolescent rebellion. A '49 profile (T scores between 70 and 80) might suggest that the adolescent in question was at a peak of a rebellion normal for the current generation, while scores above 80 usually are obtained only when an adolescent is struggling with serious family and social disruptions. In this latter instance this disruption usually is represented also in other high scores, such as 8 (*Sc*) or 2 (*D*). A tertiary peak on 8 would indicate that this social struggle is accompanied by poor contact with reality—possibly by ideational and behavioral confusion. Thus a 49''8' profile, for example, would suggest that the adolescent faces this normal stress of his/her time without either internal or external guides, and is floating helplessly in the current of these stresses. In the histories of this common adolescent profile it is often found that the parents have been preoccupied with their own problems, and that they have ignored and denied the stresses on the child. A 492' profile (with 8 below 70), on the other hand, would suggest that the adolescent might be temporarily depressed by conflicts with adult authority. A tertiary peak on 7 (*Pt*) would suggest brooding guilt over the rebellion, especially

with a rise in the *F* scale. Such youngsters of the continuing ties with parents. All such hypotheses must of course be checked out against other assessment data.

The MMPI is also a very practical and helpful technique for assessing the personality functioning of the parents who bring children for assessment. Extensive assessment of parents is often prohibited both by the lack of time on the part of the clinician and by the resistance of the parents who see the child as "ill" but who are at most only half willing to admit to their roles in the child's disturbance. Most parents are willing, however, to "fill out a routine questionnaire" about "their attitudes and feelings." Quite often the parents' responses to MMPI are among the first indications of marked emotional disturbance within the parents that—when compared with the child's symptoms—may give clues as to the sources of her/his difficulties. Often these MMPI results suggest a need for further assessment of the parents. Most frequently parental scores fall within the 50–70 T-score range. Even so, variations within this "normal" range often reveal personality patterns of defenses within the parent that suggest clues about the parent–child interaction.

7. The Personal Preference Schedule

The PPS (Edwards, 1959) is another subjective technique used in many clinics to assess adolescent and adult attitudes. It consists of nine scales, each of which purports to measure the strength of a need. Although the titles of these scales are drawn from the same list of needs used by Murray in his discussion of the TAT (1938)—for example, *N* Achievement, *N* Aggression, *N* Order, and the like—they are actually defined by the content of the items within the scale, as stated in Edward's manual for the PPS (1959). It should be noted that the content of the scales, while roughly comparable to the variables discussed by Murray, are not identical with Murray's definition of these needs. Nor has there been any study of the relationship of the PPS scales to the TAT. Even if both techniques do tap the same variables, it is theoretically doubtful that there would be well-defined relationships between them, since one would not expect individuals to express their needs consistently or in the same manner on both the subjective and associative levels.

Edwards was most interested in the construction of scales that control what he has called "social desirability." As he points out, all other similar subjective tests are biased by the fact that most subjects tend to answer in a direction that they consider socially acceptable or proper. For example, on the MMPI such a tendency is measured in a gross fashion by the L scale, but exactly how a high score on the L affects other MMPI scores is unknown. In the construction of the PPS sets of statements each of which describe personal values, attitudes, and motivations were selected from a pool of similar statements in which the "social desirability of every statement had been previously agreed upon by several judges." The statements used in the final form of the schedule were selected on the basis that their social desirability ratings were equivalent.

Thus in responding to the PPS a subject indicates preferences rather than affirming or denying that the statement is true or false about her/him. In fact she/he may prefer one statement over another on one item, but on another item prefer a third statement to the first, and so on. The significance of this test-taking operation is that it results in patterns of relatively preferred *values* rather than dichotomous acceptance or rejection of self-descriptions. These responses in themselves do *not* indicate, however, whether the subject manifests such values in overt behavior or in fantasies. As with other subjective techniques, the PPS indicates only that the subject "prefers" to ascribe these values and attitudes to herself/himself. "Social Desirability" has been controlled, leaving "Personal Desirability."

Prediction from these patterns of personally preferred subjective attitudes to other behavior depends on both an acquaintance with the increasing research on the PPS and the application of the principles of ego dynamics. Over 400 research studies had been published by 1966—either studying the PPS or using it as a research instrument. Many of these studies, although only indirectly bearing on the predictive validity of the PPS, do further delineate the relationships between these patterns of preferred attitudes and other kinds of behaviors. Most pertinent for clinical use are Klett's study (1957) of high-school children and Mainords' (1956) dissertation on parents' responses.

The thorough standardization of the PPS includes percentile scores for both sexes— for both adolescents and adults. A profile of percentile scores can be drawn on the score sheet. (Standard scores are also published in the manual.) Thus the psychologist can easily spot the extreme scores, that is, where the subject differs from other members of the same sex and age, and he/she can then analyze patterns of intraindividual attitudes.

It is from these patterns of PPS scores that hypotheses about ego functioning may be conceived. For example, an adolescent boy whose preferences result in high percentile scores on N Achievement and N Order but who shows little or no preference for N Sex or N Aggression would seem to be using achievement values and orderliness as a defense against expression of sexual and aggressive impulses, especially if N Blame–Avoidance were also high. Since open expression of sexual aggressiveness does possess considerable social desirability among adolescent males in American society, this adolescent might well be in conflict with his peers and suffer some social isolation. Such a profile also would suggest that the adolescent was avoiding the development of normal coping mechanisms for these needs, and was relying on general coping methods more appropriate to latency. The obverse of such a profile would indicate that the adolescent had developed few or no controls over these drives.

8. The Vineland Social Maturity Scale

This scale is one of the most widely used techniques for assessing children's development. Based on interviews with parents, social behavior is scaled from age 1 year through adolescence. The items are grouped together in age levels much like the Binet mental-age scales, and by comparing the average "social" age to the child's chronological age a "social quotient" can be calculated. Some psychologists are tempted to consider this "SQ" as analogous to an IQ. Such an equivalence is grossly invalid. IQ tests do *not* measure social behavior and the Vineland—and similar scales—lack indicators of intelligence. Intellectually retarded children may be trained socially, and intellectually bright children may lag in developing social skills. The items in the manual (Doll, 1947) are classified into various areas of social behavior: "Self-help, Eating and Dressing, Locomotion, Occupation, Communication, Self-direction, and Socialization." As a result it is also possible to extract from the classification of these items the various kinds of social behaviors in which a child seems to be advancing and those in which he/she has not yet developed.

The chief difficulty with the Vineland is the fact that its original standardization was very inadequate. It needs restandardization on the current generation, and some of the old-fashioned items need updating. Since it is based on the parents' report, there also should be a better standard than that of a clinical hunch for estimating the reliability, defensiveness, and social desirability of the parents' responses. Little is known about the reliability or validity of this widely used technique. Although these objective items would seem to have face validity, parents of emotionally disturbed or handicapped children—and even parents of relatively normal children—often unwittingly report in a defensive manner or are poor observers of their children. Thus this face validity should be seriously questioned.

Nevertheless, the Vineland is most convenient as an *introductory* device for interviewing the parents. An extensive inquiry is necessary into the nature of the parent's observations and the parent's attitudes toward the social behavior in question, however. Only through such interviews can the validity and reliability of this particular technique be estimated for the case at hand.

CHAPTER 6

Techniques Based on Associative Behavior

A. THE NATURE OF FREE ASSOCIATION

1. "Associative" Defined

The term *associative* really has two distinct meanings in psychology. In traditional experiments on memory or judgment two stimuli are presented, and the subject is asked to "form an association." It is discovered later that even if subjects are not so instructed, the hypothesis that they do is confirmed in some fashion. It is presumed—usually correctly—that the subjects find some communality between the two stimuli and make a generalization or mnemonic so that they can remember the arbitrarily paired stimuli of the experiment, for example, between nonsense syllables, and the like. Such experiments explore the subject's ability to abstract and thus remember.

"Free association," although probably quite comparable as regards the thought processes involved, differs in that the associative link is between some presented stimuli (not always of great import to the matter at hand) and the individual's personal memories, experiences, attitudes, imagination, and feelings that those stimuli arouse. To identify this type of associative behavior, the term *projection* is often used. In a projective technique the stimuli are often purposely vague or unstructured and are not considered to be of great import to the real inquiry except to facilitate the flow of associations. The rationale is that subjects project or reflect their personal associations as stimulated by the materials of the technique.

As is discussed later in detail, the nature of the presented stimuli often *does* affect the associative processes that the psychologist seeks to elicit—sometimes considerably more than is commonly supposed. There is always the question also of how subjects form their associations (the associative linkages): Are they following whatever instructions are used to promote free association, or are they attempting to make associations of the first type mentioned before, that is, are they "stimulus bound" and analyzing rather than free associating?

Before discussing some of these problems in using and analyzing associative techniques, it may be helpful to review briefly this concept of free association. When Freud introduced what he himself labeled the "free-association *experiment,*" the novelty lay not only in a new form of treatment for hysteria, but rather in the concept that every conscious thought, manifest or subjective, also includes—like the tail of a comet—a trail of personal associations of which both the individual and others interacting with him/her might often be unaware but which are an integral part of the thought process and ideational content. Experimenting almost exclusively with emotionally disturbed adults, Freud was impressed with the extent to which his patients repressed these associations "into the unconscious"—that is, how these patients avoided focusing on their associations that were threatening, frightening, or guilt ridden. In addition, because the anxiety-producing nature of some of these associations became generalized to other associations, Freud and his colleagues discovered that in these emotionally disturbed adults the associative process per se became blocked. Such patients—although quite aware of their manifest and even subjective behavior—often could not actually account for many of their experiences, acts, or feelings because they had not taken the associative aspects of their interactions with various stimuli and situations into account. This phenomenon was most dramatically illustrated by the cases of "grande hysterie" with the fugue states, functional paralyses, and the like. Only after several decades did Freud realize that this was part of what he called the "psychopathology of everyday life." Because fairly well-adjusted persons made "slips" and appeared altogether unaware of this aspect of their their acts and thoughts, he assumed that they also were repressing some possible anxiety-ridden associations.

While this may often be the case—for everyone makes such associations—there are at least two other explanations for such behavior in the normal individual.

1. The individual may be quite conscious of the associative aspects of his/her behavior and thoughts but not speak publicly of them because of social prohibitions against verbalizing one's private thoughts or because to verbalize them would reveal his/her intentions, which for various reasons the individual would prefer to keep hidden. Freud called this "suppression," but because it played only a minor part in the types of emotional disturbances with which he was then concerned, he tended to ignore it.

2. Associative aspects of behavior may be unconscious not because of repression but merely because no one can possibly pay attention to all aspects of her/his behavior at any one moment. In this respect, a person is also often unconscious of manifest and subjective behaviors as well.

People do many things automatically because they have learned to do them without thinking, find their learned habits successful, and therefore do not need to focus awareness on them. Only when learned habits fail to bring about the desired results does a person have to stop and examine the various aspects of her/his actions, including presumptions and associations.

It should be noted therefore that the attitudes revealed by free association—even of an anxiety-provoking nature—are not necessarily repressed or unconscious. The individual responding to the Sentence Completion, the TAT, or the Rorschach may be well aware of the associative facets of her/his behavior and their relationship to other aspects of her/his deeds and thoughts. Only when there is positive evidence that the subject denies any such attitudes as may appear in his/her free associations may one speak of repression. For example, if a subject outwardly idealizes his/her mother and behaves toward her in a submissive fashion, but on the TAT tells disparaging stories about maternal figures or plots rebellion against overprotective mothers, one could posit with some reason that this anger toward the mother is repressed. However, one might speak of suppression of conscious ambivalence if the subject says, "I love my mother very much and have never raised my voice against her, but sometimes I wish that she wouldn't always wait on me and try to tell me what to do. Once I even had a dream that she died and I wasn't sorry. It sure startled me." But the associations are not unconscious.

2. Free Association in Childhood

The nature of free association during the childhood years has been more assumed than specifically formulated, even in the psychoanalytic literature. Certainly the use of play materials in psychotherapy with children and the application of the associative techniques used originally on adults to the assessment of children attest to the assumption that children can and do free associate. In fact it is sometimes assumed that because the ego of the child and its defensive systems are still in the formative stages that children free associate more openly than adults. They tend to work things out in play or appear to voice their associations openly and naively at times. However, it should be noted that the child's use of free association in everyday life (and on formal associative techniques) varies considerably, depending on the child's stage of development. During the accumulative stage of infancy (see Chapter 1), children usually engage in what to the adult appears to be uncontrolled associations. Such free-floating associative thinking is often an attempt to explore and accumulate the emotional as well as the intellectual aspects of their experiences. As they enter into the integrative stage in latency, however, this public display of associative behavior decreases sharply. Children become engaged in distinguishing fantasy from reality. Although they may enjoy fantasy, they are quick to identify it as such. Loosli-Usteri (1931) in her study of the response of 8-year-olds to the Rorschach, speaks of *la conscience du hasard*—the awareness of taking a chance, that is, in committing oneself to identifying the inkblot as being anything but an inkblot. During this period of childhood, children appear to practice "defenses," and they are relatively unaware of the associative aspects of their responses.

Adolescents in another upswing of accumulative development appear to combine their previous experiences of infancy and latency. Associative behavior reappears (often repeating some of the feelings and attitudes of early childhood), and it is usually followed by quick defensive covering. Adolescents make nonsense remarks, sing meaningless ditties, invent languages of their own, but they are embarrassed and defensive when anyone notices. Every assessor has heard teen-agers begin a TAT story with "I could tell a wild one to that picture," then make a descriptive statement, which is followed by several free associations, and conclude with defensive facetious remarks. Rarely does a teen-ager have the courage to free associate in uninhibited fashion, nor does one often meet an adolescent who has enough control to exclude completely all free association.

3. The Stimuli

Free association often seems a mystery to those untrained in this technique. Since uninhibited expression of one's associations is at least partially tabooed in Western culture (in other cultures people freely recite their dreams as part of normal communication), getting a subject to free associate without any stimuli is often difficult. Even children learn this taboo quite early in life when they embarrass their elders. Freud found that he had to train his patients to free associate.

For this reason, the instructions given the subject on projective techniques and the kinds of stimuli used to elicit free association become very important. While procedures—including the setting and instructions—will be covered in the next sections, it should be noted that there is considerable research which has been reviewed by Murstein and his colleagues (1965—see particularly Chapters 4, 5, and 11), which clearly indicated that responses to these projective techniques can be quite definitely altered by the immediate situation and stresses on the subject, by the nature of the instructions, and by the attitude, character, and even appearance of the assessor. The same is true for the objective and subjective techniques also. But assessors are usually more precise in administering intelligence tests, and subjects are more used to such techniques and are not as much at sea as on associative techniques.

When projective techniques were first introduced and became widely used, the idea was advanced that the nature of the stimulus was of little importance—that subjects if properly instructed would associate to almost any inkblot or tell stories to any picture. Rorschach in his original monograph says however, that he produced hundreds of blots before he selected the 10 he thought most suitable, but he did not reveal the criteria of selection. Murray chose his pictures similarly out of a large collection, probably on the basis of clinical intuition. Studies on the stimulus value of the Rorschach blots have been reviewed by Baughman (1965). There are indications that certain TAT pictures "draw" certain kinds of stories most frequently (Eron, 1950). There are "popular" or near-popular responses to each of the Rorschach inkblots, and certain blots are more likely to produce movement responses or to be rejected.

There are also studies of the relationship between the degree of structure in the stimulus and the freedom of the association (Lazarus, 1965). In general these studies indicate that this relationship is not exactly linear, that completely unstructured stimuli (such as the blank card, 16, on the TAT) may not give subjects quite enough to get them going, and that responses are often brief and superficial, while very structured stimuli tend to evoke stereotyped responses. Evidently the stimuli should have enough structure to start subjects associating but not enough to restrict them. Most of these studies of the nature of the stimuli have been concerned with the responses of adult subjects, and there is very little research on the question of whether these originally adult techniques are actually appropriate stimuli for children. As far as can be ascertained, it has always been assumed that Rorschach's 10 inkblots are just as appropriate for children as for adults, but it is quite possible that another set of blots could be constructed that would draw more free association from children. Murray offered the Harvard set of pictures as appropriate for children age 4 and older. However, the difficulty many young children seem to experience in telling stories to these relatively complex adult stimuli caused Bellak and Bellak (1949) to invent

the Children's Apperception Test (CAT), consisting of 10 much simpler stimuli depicting animals in various human actions and situations and concerned with such childhood stresses as sibling rivalry, separation anxiety, Oedipal conflicts, and toilet training. Numerous studies (see Murstein, 1965, pp. 525 ff.), however, have been conducted that indicate that pictures using humans instead of animals (in the same situations) draw somewhat longer and more meaningful stories—even from kindergarten children.

B. VERBAL ASSOCIATIVE TECHNIQUES

For heuristic purposes, associative techniques may be divided into those in which both the stimuli and responses are primarily verbal, those with visual stimuli and verbal responses, and those with either verbal or visual stimuli but which call primarily for a nonverbal or motor response. Although such a classification is artificial in part and purely for purposes of discussion, it does focus on the type of function that is being elicited from the child. With children it is necessary to consider the fact that their associations are not as well verbalized as adults and that they often express their fantasies in nonverbalized play.

1. Word Association and Sentence-Completion Tests

The purely verbal associative techniques, such as the Word Association and Sentence Completion, are seldom used with preadolescents. In part this is because of the level of literacy these tests require. Very possibly the Word Association could be adapted to younger children if adequate norms were available, but this grandsire of all associative techniques does not appear to be in popular use any longer—even for adults. There are, however, several well-standardized versions of the Sentence Completion for adolescents (Rotter et al., Rohde; 1965, 1957). The rationale of the

SCT is generally the same as other associative techniques, but there has been considerable discussion in the literature over the level of associative material elicited by this method, largely in terms of the amount of structure offered by the sentence "stems" that are presented as stimuli. There is the question of person reference—that is, whether the stem begins the question with "I" or "My," or whether the sentence is started relatively impersonally, for example, "When a boy. . . . or" "Most mothers . . . ." Goldberg (1965) summarizes research on this topic by stating, "What empirical evidence there is favors the first person construction. . . ." The studies that Goldberg cites were limited to adult subjects.

By far the most important aspect of the SCT stimulus stem is the nature of the content of these stems and the rationale behind this content. Goldberg (1965, p. 813) concludes that "most researchers using the Sentence Completion have seemed little bothered by the absence of a theoretical rationale underlying the use of the Sentence Completion method." But he adds, "There have been sentence completion forms that have been developed more systematically . . . ." The selection of stems has sometimes been systematized on the basis of "areas of conflict" (e.g., Forer, 1950), such as important interpersonal figures, dominant needs, environmental pressures, and aggressive tendencies. Other SCT collections seemed to have been derived—as was admitted by Holsopple and Miale (1954)—because "they seemed a good idea at the time." Rohde (1957) lists six general criteria for her selection of 65 items.

1.   The range of stimuli must be broad enough to elicit information from all areas and phases of behavior reaction.

2.   Areas likely to be foci of conflict must be stimulated.

3.   The responses must be controlled as little as possible by the stimulus phrases.

4.   The items must be arranged to lead the subject from everyday life to the more inaccessible areas of personality, in order to avoid engendering resistance.

5.   The stimuli must be comprehensible to persons of mental age 10 and up.

6.   The total time required for the method must not exceed a period convenient for the schedules of schools and other institutions."

Summing up these criteria, it appears that the aim is to stimulate associations (sometimes in specific areas) and to avoid resistance but not to control the association. Evidently the nature of the stem depends largely on the variable that the test constructor intended to assess. Forer, with his fairly structured set of stems, was evidently hoping to find associations to well-defined areas of adjustment. Rotter was interested in the single variable *degree of conflict*. Rohde describes a much broader aim—that of getting at the same interacting need-press system of variable as was originated by Murray. She is thus less concerned with the structure of her stems per se than with the variability of the responses they draw, which she illustrates at length in the description of the construction of her particular set of stems.

Both Rohde (1957) and Rotter and Willerman (1947; Rotter, Ratterty, and Schachtitz, 1965) have constructed well-standardized forms for adolescent groups. Rotter differentiates his adolescent and adult forms chiefly by content. Rohde's test was standardized on ninth-grade children, but she uses it for adults also. Both authors present data showing respectable repeat reliability and scorer reliability. Both present data that support their claims that their tests differentiate between adjusted and maladjusted children. Rohde's correlations between test scores and teachers' evaluations are among the highest I have ever seen for studies using this criterion, but her questionnaire presented to the teachers was ingeniously extensive and elaborate.

A metric method of analyzing responses to the SCT is provided both by Rotter and Rohde. Rotter's single variable measure is far simpler than Rohde's very complex scoring of needs and press. The latter requires considerable familiarity by the assessor with the Murray system and considerable practice and training to attain the level of reliability Rohde cites in her text. Rotter's test does have the advantage of a single neat score indicating the degree of conflict, but Rohde's system yields a much richer set of personality variables. Although neither author restricts analysis to this metric approach, Rohde's system does lend itself to much more extensive pattern and thematic analysis. Thus, once the need-press system is scored, it is possible to group the scores into patterns and to analyze the responses into themes sequentially.

Although almost everyone who has used and studied the SCT agrees that it is often quite successful in eliciting associative responses that provide many clues to the functioning of the adolescent, everyone agrees that this technique is also very susceptible to being neutralized by the defensive individual who realizes from the nature of the stems that his personality is being probed. Rotter and Willerman (1947), in testing a group of psychologists, found that this group in effect was saying "It's none of your business," while a college group was saying "Although it is undoubtedly your business, I will tell you only nice things about myself." Even when people come to a clinic or hospital for the purpose of studying themselves and their behavior, they often give stereotyped, neutral, seemingly meaningless, and ambiguous responses to the SCT. Adolescents in particular often respond with flippant, impudent sentences that seem to say "I dare you to make anything out of this." While such responses indicate the degree of defiance of authority and a general resistance against anxiety, they thwart the assessor who hopes to find out anything else about the adolescent's functioning.

This resistance is of course heightened by the way the test is usually administered. The subject writes out his/her responses on an answer sheet without intervention from the assessor. Although these flip responses might be less frequent if the operations were altered to have the subject dictate the responses to the assessor—thus also forcing a response from the subject and avoiding omissions—this change of operations would not only be tedious, but it would also alter the standardizations when the metric analyses were used. I use such a procedure with blind adolescents, and there appears to be no untoward restriction of their associations. (Admittedly blind adolescents often are more verbal than are the sighted.) In sum, the SCT may be thought of as a step between the subjective report and the associative process. Subjects usually realize that the stems dealing with family life, personal attitudes, and the like are asking them to report subjectively how they feel, but they do not provide the structure of the subjective questionnaire, and thus they do encourage associations.

A major shift in emphasis occurs, however, if the assessor does regard the subject's responses not only as associations but also as subjective reports. For example, if to the stem "My main trouble is . . ." an adolescent responds "my mother," the psychologist would certainly want to note that the adolescent subjectively sees his/her mother as a chief source of trouble, but the psychologist should also note several other facts about this associative report. For example, Rotter would score the response as conflictual, and Rohde might further note that the association suggests that there are probably internalized conflicts within the subject between feelings of resentment and dependency. Moreover, the subject is very possibly defending against such a conflict by externalizing the blame for this trouble and protecting his/her ego. Whether such interpretative hypotheses are tenable would depend on the appearance of similar evidence in the responses to other stems. If there were no such general themata over the whole series of responses, it would be difficult to analyze this single response without further inquiry with the child. Thus such a "conflictual" response given in isolation warrants a discussion with the child.

2. The Picture-Frustration Study

The Rosenzweig Picture-Frustration Study for Children (Rosenzweig, Fleming, and Rosenzweig, 1948) differs from most other associative techniques in that it is aimed at measuring one general variable, and it is derived from a fairly well-defined theoretical schema. Concerned with children's reactions to frustration, Rosenzweig conceived of these reactions as having two dimensions: a "direction" (extrapunitive, intrapunitive, or impunitive) and a "type" (object-dominated, ego-dominated, and need-persistent), thus providing nine possible categories to classify the responses to his cartoon situations. There is no presumption that the manner in which the child responds reflects his/her behavior in social situations. There are, however, several studies (e.g., Levitt and Lyle, 1955) that suggest that extrapunitive, ego-dominated children are more aggressive than children showing other predominate patterns on the P-F. The chief rationale of the P-F seems to be that the child's responses represent his/her views of how frustration is to be met, either in what is seen as the socially approved fashion or possibly in some idiosyncratic fashion—expressing the child's own values and attitudes toward frustration. Rosenzweig was obviously more concerned with the latter, and he sought to account for the tendency for children to respond in a socially stereotyped fashion by scoring the most frequently given responses as "popular." Evidently he hoped that by assessing the patterns of attitudes toward frustration, it might be possible to uncover relationships between such patterns and other personality variables.

The P-F stimuli consist of 24 line drawings (like cartoons) in which one figure—adult or child—addresses a child with a statement that most children are likely to interpret as socially or personally frustrating. The sex of the frustrator and that of the child are clearly indicated in most of the drawings. The subject is then asked to write in (or in the case of very young children, to dictate) "what the other person in the picture (whose "balloon" has been left empty) might say."

The structured nature of the stimulus and these instructions raise several questions for the user of this technique. Because more stimulus cues are provided the child than in most of the other projective techniques, some critics have questioned whether the P-F can be classified as projective. In addition, although the child is instructed to say "what the child in the picture" might answer, children often ask if they should say what they themselves might say, or they give some indication that they are trying to figure out the "right" or socially approved response. Rosenzweig (1950) discusses this question in his classic paper on levels of response to projective techniques. Thus the child may be attempting to be objective (looking for the right answer), subjective (saying how he/she might respond), or projective (responding with an association stimulated by the cartoon and reflecting his/her own internal attitudes rather than either a socially popular response or his own behavior).

This question is answered in part by the use of the standardized scores that Rosenzweig provides for ages 4 to 13. By using this metric method, one may distinguish the child who is attempting to be socially conforming by the fact that he/she has a high conformity or popular score. Such a child avoids direct expression of ego-defensive extrapunitive responses in favor of more impunitive defensive responses or polite submissions to adult authority (slightly higher than the mean M', I, or M). In contrast, the child who is attempting to be subjective or who is associating would be expected to come up with patterns of reactions somewhat more deviant from the norm. Of course there is the possibility that a child who is socially conforming in other everyday situations will respond in a similar manner on the test, but it is just as possible that such a child might well take the opportunity of expressing extrapunitive feelings on the test that she/he dares not to in the face of living authority or peer figures!

Thus some children may perceive that the way to handle frustration is to be conforming—whether or not they themselves can conform. Others may view frustration as calling for intrapunitive, guilt-ridden responses or for defending themselves against blame by denying—but as an ideal rather than a representation of their own behavior. *Whether children perceive themselves as behaving in the same manner as they report for the child in the cartoon cannot be answered by the test score alone.* Children may come ot the clinic with a long history of socially nonconforming, aggressive, extrapunitive behavior and not only give largely "good-boy" conforming responses to the P-F, but they may stoutly maintain that this is the way they would behave! Such children do not necessarily see any discrepancy between their test responses and their actual behavior under frustration.

Despite this problem of levels of interpreting the responses, the Rosenzweig P-F can be a clinically useful tool to assess the child's social functioning and social perceptions, especially when it is used with other materials. Because it is concerned with a rather circumscribed area of the child's ego rather than with the broader and more general dynamics of the TAT or even the Rorschach, it has not received the wide usage of these other techniques. Very likely the difficulty lies in the fact that there is not enough known about the relationship between such perceived patterns of reaction to frustration and other kinds of ego functioning. The theorists with whom Rosenzweig was associated at the time he began his studies (Dollard et al., 1939) posited that reaction to frustration or, more broadly, stress was a central variable in personality functioning, a theory to which many psychologists still subscribe. Unfortunately the exact role of reactions to

frustration—especially to the social frustration depicted in the P-F—in the ego dynamics of the child is still being explored. Most research on the P-F has been concerned either with attempts to get concensual validation or with diagnostic differentiations. Only a few scholars are concerned with the constructs underlying the technique.

3. The Blacky Pictures

Of all the structured associative techniques, the Blacky Pictures technique is unique in that it was constructed to investigate variables derived from the specific psychoanalytic theory of psychosexual development (Blum, 1949, 1950). The 10 pictures on this test represent various aspects of the psychosexual stage. These are "oral eroticism, oral sadism, anal sadism, oedipal intensity, masturbation or penis envy." Also represented are five other psychoanalytic concepts—"sibling rivalry, guilt feeling, ego ideals, and love-object." In each cartoon, the dog hero—Blacky—is depicted reacting to some other family member or combination of family members (or his "ideal"). The scene is defined by the examiner. For example in Cartoon V, "Here Blacky is discovering sex . . .," and the child is instructed to "make up a story about each picture," which is very similar to the TAT. After each spontaneous story, the child is asked several standardized questions, for example in Cartoon V, "How does Blacky feel here? (a) happy, without a care in the world; (b) enjoying himself, but a little worried, or (c) mixed up and guilty."

It should be noted that the Blacky was originally standardized for use with adults, although Blum (1950) does present a modified version for children. Here again a theoretical question arises. Psychoanalytic theory as applied to adults assumes that difficulties in emotional and social functioning are caused by reaction formations or regression of the ego to one or more of these developmental stages. It is assumed that the adult either has never passed through the psychosexual stage or has reverted to this stage under the pressure of some life stress. These concepts do not apply to children in the same fashion, however. Their reaction formations and regressions are far more fluid and temporary. As was previously noted in the introductory chapters of this book, the child who in the Oedipal stage is attempting to resolve these fantasies initially is not necessarily abnormal or maladjusted.

Moreover, not one of these psychosexual stages is resolved all at once in a precise sequence, with one stage resolved before another begins, as some readers of Freud seem to presume. Similar to the development of other psychological functions, psychosexual growth is a gradual and overlapping process. For example, a 5-year-old may be in the throes of an Oedipal conflict, while at the same time still attaining final control over her/his oral and anal impulses. Additionally, as children advance to a new stage they may at the same time, under this new stress, regress slightly and temporarily in their adjustment to previously mastered stresses. For example, a 5-year-old boy who may have achieved bladder control many months previously may suffer a relapse of a brief period of enuresis as he attempts to free himself from his initial Oedipal attachment to his mother. As has been discussed previously at several points, these psychosexual stresses of infancy are not completely resolved when the child enters latency. Rather, the latency period consists of the refinement and practice of self-controls. Finally these self-controls are tested at puberty when the psychosexual stages are revived and re-enacted. Thus in interpreting the Blacky, it is most important to take into account the overall developmental progress of the child.

The analysis of responses to the Blacky is not as structured as the theory behind it or the stimuli. There is no scoring system, and the psychologist is expected to understand and accept the theory thoroughly. This has been made more explicit subsequently by Blum (1953), and users of the Blacky should familiarize themselves with this separate volume. The spontaneous stories and responses to the inquiry are thus analyzed thematically according to the theory. The reliability of this technique is respectable (Blum, 1949), and a noteworthy study of its validity has been reported by Blum and Hunt (1952).

As to some of the advantages of this technique, its primary value does appear to be "its clinical orientation toward therapy" (Blum, 1950). Admittedly this orientation is restricted to one therapeutic method, but it is used by many clinicians. Those clinicians who use psychoanalytic theory even very broadly in eclectic fashion will find that the Blacky does assess variables relevant to their work. Like the CAT, the animal figures are attractive to children, and they are usually quite responsive.

The main value of the Blacky, however, is also its chief disadvantage. Many clinicians are unwilling to accept without modification the rather simple, orthodox psychoanalytic theory outlined by Blum. Psychoanalytic theory is no longer widely rejected as it was prior to 1940, but it is not so blithely accepted as at the time when the Blacky first appeared. Increasingly the inclination of clinicians is to merge these constructs with social-learning theory. The psychoanalytic "stage" is usually not considered separately from the ways the child is learning to cope with other stress, in addition to these primarily internal conflicts. In current use of the Blacky therefore, one might want to add into the analysis other considerations and variables—such as the nature of the family constellation, the stresses from this constellation, the past experiences of the child, and the stresses from both the immediate environment and the cultural milieu. As with other specifically oriented techniques, the Blacky is most valuable when used as one of a number of assessment tools. For example, a combined use of the Blacky and the Bene-Anthony Family Relations Test might yield valuable data on the child's view of her/his family and the effects thereof on her/his psychosexual development.

4. The Thematic Apperception Test

Of all the purely associative techniques, Murray's Thematic Apperception Test (1938) is undoubtedly one of the most widely used—both clinically and in research. Its rationale and method of analysis is a model for other associative and even subjective techniques (see the previous discussion of Sentence Completion and the Edwards Personal Preference Inventory). Although Murray advances this technique and his set of instructions and pictures as appropriate for both children and adults, there is little in the research literature to support this specific claim. Lacking such research, it may be worthwhile to raise the question of the applicability of this primarily adult technique to children (or at least its advantages and limitations when used with childern). As with the other techniques, this question may be raised separately for the rationale, the operations, the methods of analysis and inference, and the reliability and validity. The rationale is succinctly stated by Murray (1965, p. 430):

"1. In characterizing the hero of a story and in portraying his actions and reactions, the storyteller will commonly utilize some of the components, conscious or unconscious, of his own past or present personality, for example, an assumption, an expectation, an idea, a feeling, an evaluation, a need, a plan or a fantasy that he has experienced or entertained.

2. In characterizing the other major figures of the dramatic narrative and in portraying their actions and reactions, the storyteller will commonly utilize some of the personality components (as he has apperceived them) of persons—such as parents, siblings, rivals, loved objects—with whom he has had, or is having significant interactions.

3. In constructing the plot, describing the endeavors of the hero, his transactions with the other major figures, and the outcome and final consequences of these efforts and interactions, the storyteller will commonly utilize memory traces, conscious or unconscious, of some of the actual or fantasied events that have exerted a significant influence on his development."

Other authorities—for example Stein (1948)—have emphasized that each story simultaneously reflects three levels of experience in the subject's life: (1) the manifest content of the subject's interactions with the environment; (2) the feelings and attitudes of the subject about such manifest experiences; and (3) the interaction of needs and stresses *within* the individual.

Most authorities agree however that any manifest or life-history material present in TAT stories is usually masked and distorted by the associations that the subject introjects and then projects onto the characters and the plot. Subjects are not asked to tell stories about their families or their own lives and—when they do so—it is considered a special instance of the inability to get away from the self. The emphasis and the intent in the interpretation of TAT stories are on the interpersonal and intrapersonal dynamics of feelings and attitudes. Thus the TAT is aimed almost entirely at the assessment of the *internalized* associations and perceptions with which subjects view the world about them and with which they view themselves. Such associations presumably are part of the forces that guide manifest behavior.

When the TAT is used to assess children, two related questions about this rationale need to be considered. What is meant by assessment of *internalized* attitudes and feelings during that period of a person's life when such inner perspectives are still in the process of being internalized? What are the roles and purposes that fantasy plays in ego functioning during childhood, as contrasted with the uses that adults make of fantasy?

Unfortunately the answers to both of these questions are at best speculative. Turning to the first question, from the hypotheses advanced in the previous chapters we know that very little internalization takes place during infancy when children are still busy exploring their environment and mastering it in a rapid accumulation of learned skills. As a result it is a rare child under the age of 7 who can do much more with the TAT pictures than describe them, make one or two identifications of central figures, and give more than one or two associations. More involved stories from kindergarten-age children are a sign of intellectual and emotional precocity, and they frequently indicate a "forced growth"— that is, the "little-adult" phenomenon. During latency, however, when children begin to integrate and practice what they have learned during infancy, they become more able to organize some semblance of a plot to their associations to the TAT and to add voluntarily the feelings of the characters. Even the stories of most adolescents are still much less complete and involved than those told by most adults. Some children are able to weave very lengthy, wordy stories, with multiple plots and many characters, but usually such stories consist of a relatively tangential series of associations with phantasmagorical characters who shift in feelings and attitudes in chameleon fashion, much to the puzzlement of the assessor. Thus it would seem unreasonable to assume that the feelings and attitudes reflected in children's TAT stories represent permanent, established internalizations. A more tenable hypothesis would state that these associations represent the child's *attempts* to internalize experiences in addition to the conflicts encountered in this process. With children then, the TAT may be used most reasonably as an assessment of the *extent* and the *process* of internalization.

This hypothesis leads to a second set of speculations concerning the role of fantasy in the functioning of the ego. For adults, fantasy often appears to serve the purpose of the sublimation of unattainable or unacceptable wishes, feelings, and attitudes in which they experience vicariously what they cannot satisfy in overt behavior. It is infrequent, however, that adults are able to indulge themselves freely and completely and to express all wishes in fantasy. Their publicly expressed fantasies are often stopped short by defensive guards, repressions, and compensations. Children seem to learn this use of fantasy relatively early (even before the end of infancy), but for several reasons it appears neither to play such an important part nor to be quite as central a purpose in children's fantasies. Children are still learning what is attainable and what is socially acceptable. They are still attempting to test out interpersonal relationships in everyday life. They may retreat temporarily to fantasy but return to active interaction with their environment rather rapidly. In addition, a large part of the child's fantasy is of a nonverbal type and is enacted in playing games and make-believe with peers and adults. When a child retreats to solitary play and fantasy, even the layman is aware that something may be wrong. The adult use of fantasy as sublimation is relatively rare among children, for sublimation is developed much later—usually in adolescence. Before that time, children see no great need to sublimate for they still hope in dependent fashion that their needs will be satisfied and their stresses relieved by their adult protectors.

Adults may use fantasy also in a creative and imaginative fashion—in contemplation and reflection, in the introspective analysis of their experiences, and in a review of their hopes and plans for the future expansion of their lives. Even more extensively, children appear to use fantasy in an analogous but simpler fashion, that is, to review and examine what they are currently experiencing. Play and fantasy, as students of child behavior have long recognized, are among the chief methods by which children practice and integrate what they are learning. In this sense the TAT may be thought of— perhaps somewhat surprisingly—as a technique for assessing learning of concepts about interpersonal and intrapersonal experiences. It is not a learning test in the same sense of achieved skills or accumulated knowledge as intelligence tests. The affective and social functions of the ego that presumably are being tapped by the TAT do not appear to be accumulated in quite the same direct and stable fashion as are cognitive skills, but they are more tenuously and erratically learned. The TAT often does appear, however, to yield very valuable clues about *how* children learn to evaluate their social interactions and themselves. In children's TAT stories, it is possible to see evidence of the types of coping mechanisms that they are developing to handle both external and internal stress.. The TAT thus does not reveal essentially what children learn but what they are trying out. It shows how they handle their environment and how they defend themselves against both internal anxiety and external stress.

Thus the rationale of the TAT should be modified when used with children. Rather than reflecting established, internalized patterns of attitudes or feelings as with adults, it mirrors the process of internalization. For adults fantasy usually serves as sublimation and escape, but for children it is more often primarily a mode of learning. The TAT assesses this process of learning affective and social skills and controls.

The TAT is described operationally, as an unstructured technique, but there are some structural limitations set by both the instructions and the stimuli, which are especially important to note when using this technique with children. The instructions as given by Murray (1943) require more than simple free association. The subject is asked to "tell a story" and to conform to a definite story outline: "What is going on in the picture; what brought it about (the past); what is going to happen (the conclusion); and what the characters are thinking and feeling." In addition, the technique is defined for the subject as "a test of your imagination" and she/he is encouraged to be imaginative. And this instruction is repeated with renewed emphasis halfway through the test. Murray (1965) also recommended subsequently that the subject be requested to examine the picture for about

20 seconds before beginning the story, then to put the picture aside. "Also, in order to facilitate the establishment in the patient of a single individual point of orientation through identification with a preferred figure, we ask him or her to choose a proper name for the chief character before proceeding with the story" (1943, p. 427).

As Murray also says: ". . . the TAT is rarely administered as . . . it should be. . . ." Too many clinicians seem careless when administering this and other projective techniques, perhaps in the delusion that the instructions do not matter because they are dealing with an associative technique. Nevertheless, if the types of analysis recommended by Murray are to be applied—even in a gross scanning of thema—*strict adherence to these instructions is necessary*, as it is if one is to obtain stories of sufficient length to give a reasonable sample of the subject's fantasy. In his opinion, much of what is obtained is chaff or at least is not readily meaningful to the assessor, and stories of 200 words or more are what Murray believes are necessary to get at the grain. The need for a story of reasonable length is also mentioned in the instructions that tell the subject to devote about five minutes to each response.

Since children's fantasies are often fleeting and lacking in structure, the use of Murray's instructions are doubly necessary to assist the child in constructing a story. Murray recommends repeating the instructions once and only once, if the subject does not seem to understand immediately. It is often necessary, however, to encourage children several times, repeating the parts of the instructions that the child is not following. (See Chapter 8 for further suggestions on how to encourage the child.) Even so, the average length of stories told by children is usually less than Murray's requirement.

Most users of the TAT would probably agree that Murray's pictures have proved to be a most ingenious and inspired selection, providing just enough stimulation to fire the imagination yet being vague enough to permit a wide range of idiosyncratic responses. Even though most of them depict adult scenes, children are attracted and challenged by them. Of the series specified for children (marked B or G), not one seems to be too stimulating or anxiety provoking. Picture 15 (not marked either for children or adults and presumably to be used for both) does seem a bit too grim. To maintain a standardized approach Murray urges that the entire set of 20 pictures be administered in two sessions, but he himself notes that the complete set is seldom used. Even with very compliant children or those who enjoy exhibiting their fantasies, 10 to 12 pictures seem to be the limit of their endurance. Beyond that one is very apt to meet with considerable resistance or, at best, with hasty and empty responses. Although there is no rationale offered for the ordering of the Harvard series of pictures, it would seem reasonable to administer them in numerical order if only to establish and maintain a standard approach. As several critics have noted, the pictures often pull dysphoric responses because of their content and shading. Further—as Murray admits—the Harvard series does not contain "certain often critical conditions such as sibling rivalry, separation from a supporting prson, and so forth." Nevertheless, when children are concerned with these conditions, they usually appear in their themes, sometimes with little or no relation to the stimulus.

It has been shown that there are marked differences from picture to picture on the TAT on such variables as story length, variety of thema, plot construction, and "pull" for Murray's needs and press (Eron, 1950). Despite this knowledge, the stimuli have never been revised nor have norms for the various pictures ever been compiled. (Picture series designed for special age or social groups have been advanced, and these will be discussed later.) It would be helpful to know, for example, which pictures draw what kinds of themes or need-press, so that if assessors wish to investigate certain variables that might be mentioned in the referral, they would have some basis for a selection of pictures. The popular responses and their variants should be determined. When a child gives a socially popular response one may say that these associations represent the needs and press that she/he shares with a population of children. This sharing of social norms indicates the degree to which the child is internalizing these social values and stresses.

An extensive metric method of analyzing TAT stories was introduced with the technique. Knowledge and use of the details of Murray's need-press system are required to score each story or sentence within the story. (The unit of response has never been precisely specified.) This scoring system, however, has never been widely used, perhaps because it does require much detail. Moreover, this aspect of Murray's theories has not been widely accepted, even though it is quite possible to relate his schema to other approaches to personality analysis—either psychoanalysis or social-learning theory. Thus this detailed scoring appears only as a specialized research technique, such as in McClelland's N Achievement studies (McClelland, et al., 1953). It is also quite probable that Murray's schema would have to be modified somewhat if applied to children who are still in the process of internalizing needs and reacting to press. McClelland notes, for example, that N Achievement may be developed only late in adolescence, after controls have been somewhat established. A kind of N Achievement does appear quite frequently in children's TAT's, but is very probably quite different from that with which McClelland is concerned among adults.

By its title the TAT invites thematic analysis, as is described by Murray (1965) and by Stein (1948). A theme is a boiled-down restatement of the story that describes the interactions of the characters and their feelings and moods. Let us take a fairly common response to Card 1 (boy with a violin) as an example.

'This boy . . . I'll call him Alex . . . is looking at the violin. He's thinking if he wants to practice. Maybe he's thinking he might become a famous violin player.'' (The child starts to put the card away and the assessor asks, ''How does he come to be looking at the violin and thinking these things?'' ''Oh, his mother told him he'd better practice or else!'' (''How does he feel about *that?*'') ''He doesn't really want to practice but he knows he won't get any supper 'till he does!'' (''Well, what happens?'') ''I guess he practices all right,'' the child sighed, ''but then he can go play 'till suppertime.'' (''How come he thought he might become a great violinist someday?'') ''Maybe his father was a good violinist. But I guess he'll never make it. He's too little and besides he hates to practice.'

The central theme of this story is one of uncontestable compliance with maternal demands for control and learning in order to obtain immediate rewards. Along with this central theme, the storyteller, a bright 6-year-old boy, entertains the possibility of being motivated to accept emotional control, symbolized by the violin, on the basis of modeling or identification with a paternal figure, but at least in this stage of his development it seems a remote possibility to the child.

This story may be contrasted with a similar interpretation by another 13-year-old boy.

'This kid is just sitting and looking at this violin. He's 'sposed to practice but he's tired of it. He'd rather be outside playing''. (''How did this come about?'') ''Well, maybe he really wanted a violin in the first place and told his parents to get him one for his birthday. Then he found out about practicing and he hated it, but his father told him that since they bought it he's got to learn to play it''. (''What happens?'') ''I guess he has to practice, but maybe he makes so much screechy noises that his parents give up and let him trade it in on a guitar.'

Here the theme is of self-initiated attempts to learn control, of internalized ambition reinforced by adult authority, which leads to a passive-aggressive rebellion, and a search for adolescent peer identification, symbolized by the guitar.

As each story is analyzed, it is possible to note repetitive themes or variants around a central theme. One may also observe the sequence of themes from story to story. Consider, for example, the following comments of the same 13-year-old boy to three other TAT cards. To Card 2, a girl and a farm scene, he told a story about ''a girl who doesn't want to live the same kind of life as her parents . . . and leaves home as soon as she is through school.'' When presented with Card 3BM, a figure crouched against a bench with a gun on the floor, he described the figure in the following way: ''He's run away from home; now he's in jail and his mother is coming to get him.'' About Card 4—young adults, a man faced away from a young woman—he commented, ''She's always nagging at him and he's tired of it and he's going to leave and she'll be sorry.'' Gradually from these and subsequent stories, it became evident that this youngster in his fantasy was concerned with loosening ties with maternal authority, but with feelings of guilt and with insecurity concerning what the next step may be. These feelings were brought out in his story to Card 13B, a boy sitting in a rustic doorway:

'He's just sitting there doing nothing. Maybe his family has gone to town and left him behind. Or maybe he said for them to go and he didn't want to; he'd rather do something by himself for the day. But now he doesn't know what to do. Maybe he wishes he'd gone with them after all.'' (''What happens?'') ''I don't know. I guess he tries to have fun. He goes for a long walk or something. But it's no fun by yourself.'

This story focuses on the child's conflicts between a nascent need for independence and his continued need for familial affiliation, and between his need for a self-recognition as a separate identity and his inability to define that identity.

The associative material from the TAT is so impressively rich with the feelings and attitudes of the storyteller that most clinicians and even many researchers do not question its reliability or validity, but assume that each story is an adequate representation of the child's fantasy. Even in most experiments using the TAT, a kind of face validity is assumed. In most studies the reliability of the judges is not questioned, and in general it appears that given a well-defined scoring system or thematic schemata, two or more judges can easily be trained to come to the same conclusions about categorizing the stories. Whether several judges would agree as easily on the meaning or interpretation of the stories is another matter that is seldom investigated. It is probable, however, that a similar consistency could be maintained given the same theoretical constructs.

Whether the TAT provides a reliable sample of a child's fantasies is a complex question, for many different factors enter into such an overall reliability. The fact that card pull for either need-press scores or for themas has not yet been established makes it difficult to begin such a reliability study. Therefore it is impossible to study the consistency of the Harvard Pictures either by using an alternate set or by splitting the test into an odd-even series. Using the full series of 20 pictures does seem a rather exhaustive sample of a child's fantasies. Yet it is not known whether one might obtain a whole new set of themas or need-press scores on a second "equivalent" srt of pictures a week later.

In addition, fantasies that are mostly idiosyncratic inventions of a child are sometimes difficult to distinguish from those that a child has selected from what she/he has seen on television or has read and is presenting as a screen over her/his own feelings and attitudes. Perhaps in some instances it would be most reasonable to be quite conservative and limit interpretation to the assumption suggested previously for the P-F studies: That the story represents what the child thinks is socially acceptable in the way of fantasy! As with dreams told during psychotherapy, the import of the story may not always be so much in its content as in the setting or situation in which and to whom it is told. Probably any

set of TAT responses is thus strongly influenced by the fact that the child has been brought in by a parent or some other authority, and no matter how much anxiety she/he may be enduring, she/he faces a representative of parental authority who asks her/him to reveal her/his fantasies. In my experience, the TAT more than any other technique draws from the child the request "You're not going to tell my parents what I've said, are you?" TAT stories—like any other kind of response—can be masked intentionally or at least at a "preconscious" level. Thus the defiant but guilt-ridden child can, as he/she approaches some revealing material, quickly change the story, skip over parts of a plot, renege on "slips," or be so blocked as to be unable to respond. For these reasons it is recommended that the TAT be administered in the latter part of assessment after rapport has been well established.

Given these limitations about the representativeness of the sample of fantasies obtained from TAT pictures, how valid are the psychologist's interpretations? Again, most of the research on this question is based on data from adults, and very little is known about the validity of children's TAT's. The correlations between the feelings and attitudes expressed in TAT's and those assumed from observed or reported manifest behavior seldom reach any more than bare significance above zero (Samuels, 1965). One of the difficulties in such studies of course is that the criterion—the behavior observed or reported—is usually not as explicit or as well categorized as is the TAT response. It is very likely that, as is assumed in the rationale of the TAT, the attitudes and motivations expressed are relatively distinct from the behavior manifested in overt social relationships. The TAT is intended as a device to assess what cannot be directly observed or reported. It might correlate better with dreams or, as Murray suggests, with associations in a psychoanalytic therapy.

Perhaps as psychologists come to know more about the kinds of fantasy themas associated with various patterns of overt behavior, it may be possible to make predictive statements. For example, it would be helpful to know what kinds of themas are associated with enuresis, school phobias, delinquencies of various types, and suicide in children. Until such research is available, the best one can do is to lean heavily on theoretical hypotheses and assumptions about such patterns of symptoms. Thus what one can depend on is the research on these and other kinds of behavior in children, hoping that when the feelings and attitudes expressed in TAT stories appear similar to those found in research studies on a specific kind of child or childhood symptom, one can reasonably suppose a similar relation between behavior and fantasy in the child being assessed.

5. The Children's Apperception Test

Because the TAT pictures did not seem appropriate for young children, Bellak and Bellak (1949) constructed a series of 10 plates for children ages 3 to 10; known as the Children's Apperceptive Test, or CAT (see also Chapter 19). These plates use animal figures, many performing human acts, on the theory that children would be more attracted by animals, and that many childhood fantasies in literature and in the children's own productions contain such figures. Moreover it is argued that children who are engaged in testing and conceptualizing reality have more difficulty than adults in separating fantasy from reality and need the animal figures as an aid in "distancing" themselves. Bellak invented an interesting and helpful outline for analyzing CAT responses, but presents no normative data. Indeed, as Haworth (1966) reports (p. 62), "Bellak cautions that while norms may be useful as a frame of reference and as an indication of developmental trends with age, the statistical treatment of separate responses destroys their meaning as integral parts of a total universe. He maintains that norms are not essential for projective techniques and that actually, each person

and each record constitutes a sample population of needs and behavioral variables."

The CAT pictures, unlike those used in the TAT, were purposefully aimed at tapping a general aspect of childhood development and conflict. Bellak intended, for example, that the first picture, which shows three little chickens around a dining table with bowls in front off them and a vague image of an adult chicken in the background, brings out children's feelings about eating and orality, especially in relationship to a parent figure and to siblings. Similar hypotheses about each of the pictures are also advanced. Further, Bellak conceived the series as interrelated, so that the stimuli presented to the child first would influence responses to the next picture and so on through the series—somewhat according to the psychoanalytical theory of psychosexual development. Thus a set of hypotheses are present to be checked out in a study of card pull and normative data.

During the next decade a body of research on the CAT gradually accumulated, including normative data. Normative card-pull studies for various age groups, for both sexes, and for both normal and disturbed children have been thoroughly reviewed by Haworth (1966). In general, most of Bellak's hypotheses about the nature of the stimuli have been supported with some age and sex variants. Summarizing the data on thematic norms by age and sex, Haworth reviews thoroughly the studies on reliability and validity. Intrascorer and interscorer reliability have been shown to be respectable. Test-retest reliability, always a stumbling block for projective tests with children, remains an unanswered question. There seems to be a general tendency toward consistency of response by children to these pictures over time, but there remains considerable variation in stories told from one administration to another, in themes, in needs expressed, and in figures with whom the child appears to be identifying. Haworth points out some of the difficulties inherent in attempting to study reliability of the CAT, not the least of which is the rapid change and fluctuations in the functioning of children during this phase of development. She suggests longitudinal studies as models for further evaluation of reliability. At the time she wrote her book, several longitudinal studies were in progress employing the CAT. Until further evidence is provided, however, the CAT will have to be used with caution as the variables in the normal child's responses may well change as much as 50% on a second administration even a few weeks later. Whether such fluctuation in response is also true of the emotionally disturbed child or children with other developmental difficulties is unknown. One might expect that a child who give markedly deviant responses suggesting considerable emotional difficulty on the one administration of the test would likely show a great deal of the same gross signs of dysfunctioning on a second testing, if no major changes of functioning were accomplished in between the two administrations.

Validation studies of the CAT, as reviewed by Hawotth, show a similar difference between samples using normal and those using disturbed or handicapped children. Correlations between CAT scores and similar variables on other measures on normal samples are barely above zero in most studies. On other studies comparing normal and disturbed children, CAT scores usually differ markedly. Longitudinal case studies—one of which Haworth cites in detail—show "marked congruence" between CAT variables and case-history materials. Thus it appears that while the CAT may not distinguish with acceptable reliability or validity the nuances of development in the normal child, it does demonstrate and discriminate gross difficulties in development.

One factor in considering both the normative and the reliability and validity studies is the very short length of the stories (sometimes only two or three phrases) that are given by children, especially by those under age 6. Thus the data from any one story are often so brief and so sparse that

norms are difficult to accumulate, and reliability and validity depend upon an extremely narrow range of scores. In my judgment, 10 such brief samples of the child's fantasies are often insufficient for clinical-assessment purposes also. More recently Bellak has constructed an additional series of 10 pictures—the CAT Supplement (CAT-S)—for which there is some initial normative data (Haworth, 1966). Thus it is possible to double the sample of the child's fantasy by combining the two sets. To avoid fatigue and resistance, the sets probably should be administered at separate sessions.

Analysis of CAT or TAT stories told by young children is also curtailed by the fact that their stories often consist of very brief series of disconnected associative phrases rather than the relatively more integrated and sequential plots constructed by older children and adolescents. There are less clear-cut themes in the responses of children ages 3 to 8. More often children of this age group describe what they see, attributing little action to the characters, and only single-word characterizations of the "heroes." It is often difficult therefore to determine which character the child is identifying with if, indeed, the she/he seems to make any definite identification. Of course at this age the individual's thought processes in every other respect are often described as "concrete." For example, on the Stanford-Binet it is not until age 7 that one may expect a child to recognize "what's foolish about this picture," which is a "recognition" and not an "inventive" response. Neither should one expect these younger children to attribute much action to their characters, for at this stage of development they have only begun to control, internalize, and project action sequences. Their own behavior either in play or work usually consists of very simple, single, and relatively disconnected acts. To cite the Binet again, the item "Memory for a Story" (The Wet Fall) is successfully passed by 50% of children only at age 8.

In young children identification processes are just beginning to develop. Preschool children commonly use some play object, such as a favorite stuffed animal, as a means to express many of their feelings and as a substitute for practicing interpersonal relationships. While the child may seem to project onto such transitional objects—as the psychoanalysts have labeled them (Winnicott, 1953)—the nature of such projection is quite different than that shown by older children in verbal responses to the TAT . The infant's play with her/his teddy bear, although it may be accompanied by verbalization, is chiefly of nonverbal motoric responses, for example, cuddling, stroking, pounding, clinging, tossing, kissing, and biting. For the most part such transitional objects are ''security blankets,'' not so much objects to be projected upon as to be incorporated into the child's feelings. Infants use the stuffed animal as part of themselves, pulling it into their feelings. Only at the end of infancy do they begin to distinguish objects as different from themselves, as capable of having feelings different from their own, which is the essence of projection as applied to the developing child. Projection is thus a process—beginning at the end of infancy—in which children attempt to separate other people from their egomaniacal, narcissistic selves and to perceive others as having independent feelings. In the process of projection, they often attribute their own feelings to others, but the fact of projection presumes that there are recognized others onto whom the child is projecting.

Analysis of the CAT thus requires a different approach than the traditional theme analysis of the TAT. For example, while purely descriptive responses to the TAT by an older child might be considered as indicative of emotional construction, defensiveness, or ''immaturity'', for the 4- to 7-year-old accurate and detailed card description can be considered not only a fair indication of adequate intellectual development but also of a child's ability to separate objects from herself/himself and to identify them. During this latter half of

infancy, the number of confabulated, automatic, and perseverative responses to the CAT should decrease, and the number of ''accurate,'' concrete, reality-oriented responses should increase. The 4-year-old may hit the picture or gesture with it, or she/he may act out her/his stories, but such motoric expression would be much less common by age 7. Who is who is often not clear in the stories of the 4-year-old. More definite character identification may be expected by age 7, with less shifting of sex identification or mixing up of identities. In psychoanalytic terms, *''primary process'' associations,* suggesting relatively uncontrolled and generalized impulse release, might well pervade the CAT responses of the 4-year-old, but there is a gradual shift during the immediately subsequent years so that these impulses appear in the responses of the 7-year-old in much more controlled and differentiated form. In summary, the CAT used with this 4- to 7-year-old group provides much more of a sampling of the development of ego controls than of definite and differentiated internalized need systems or thematic leitmotivs.

6. The MAPS

Another variation of the TAT, which is particularly attractive to children, is the Make-A-Picture Story Test, or MAPS (Shneidman, 1952). In this technique the child is presented with 69 cardboard cut-out figures and 22 background scenes and is instructed: ''You will have figures like this one and your job is simply to take one or more of any of these figures and put them on the background picture as they might be in real life. You might start by putting the figures out on the table so that you can see each one.'' After the child has selected some figures and placed them on the background, she/he is asked to ''. . . tell a story about the situation you have made. In telling your story, tell me who the characters are, what they are doing and thinking and feeling, and how the whole thing turns out. . . .'' More movements of the figures is possible when the theater form of the test is used—where the background can be placed in a special box at right angles to the table and the figures can be mounted on small metal spools.

Shneidman maintains that the rational behind the MAPS is essentially the same as that of the TAT. Furthermore he recommends that the MAPS be used with the TAT as an extension of it. He lists five general approaches to the analysis of thematic-test interpretation: (1) the *normative* approach, using normative tabular data; (2) the *hero-oriented* approach, the classic identification with the hero hypothesis of Murray; (3) the *intuitive approach of psychoanalysis; (4) the interpersonal* approach, in which the interaction between characters is emphasized; and (4) the *formal* approach, in which formal (non-content) aspects of the story such as length, plot construction, and the like are taken into account. Shneidman emphasizes the interpretation of the particular formal aspects offered by the MAPS. He notes the process that the child goes through in selecting the figures and placing them on the background card, and he raises questions in his interpretations about why the child selected the kinds and number of figures, how these are related by the child to the background, and how they are moved about on the background. Shneidman presents no particular signs or rules for analysis of these formal aspects of the MAPS test, but he calls upon the clinician's general background in personality theory and in behavioral observation and logical speculation.

Over the past 20 years I have used the MAPS increasingly. I have found it better adapted to children than the TAT—especially for children who enjoy the figures and often let their fantasies run full, while blocking on the TAT. I always use the theater box, but I tell the child that it is like TV and ask her/him to make up a new original TV play out of her/his imagination. Because of what Shneidman calls the "formal" aspects, the MAPS seems to me to be quite different from the TAT. Often non-verbal children cannot give more than a brief explanation of the drama they construct, even if it is elaborate. The MAPS thus is not altogether a "verbal" technique. At the other extreme, some children construct elaborate four-act plays, with multiple changes of scenes. I allow children to sort over the scenes as well as the actors and to choose their own scenes and sequences. If the figures are numbered on the back, using the numbers on the figure-identification sheet, it is much easier to record the child's selections. Quite often children make up stories as they go along, changing characters and plot at will. Notes about these changes are helpful, as they illustrate some of the child's conflicts, distorted perceptions of the environment, and other confusions.

Another "formal" factor in the use of the MAPS is the figure choices. Again no norms are provided, but the psychologist who uses this test frequently will learn which figures are commonly used, with which settings, and which are rarely employed. For example, in the living-room scene, which I use as an introductory setting, most children select the father figure with a present, a surprised mother, and two children running to greet the father. (It is somebody's birthday or father has been away.) After a few such innocuous playlets, latency-age children will begin to use more aggression, threatening figures (the snake, ghost, witch, pirate) to tell tales of violence—usually with an authority figure (policeman) to control and punish the aggressive figures—an obvious portrayal of their own superego formation. In my experience, children before puberty rarely utilize the naked figures. When they do I often discover subsequently that the child has a history of being unduly sexually stimulated or even sexually abused.

7.   Other Story-Telling Techniques

A full review of all storytelling and similar techniques and methods of analysis is beyond the intent and purview of this volume. At least passing mention should be made, however, of two tests, which although not in widespread use, have been fairly thoroughly developed: The Symonds Picture Study Technique (PST) (Symonds, 1949) for adolescents and the Michigan Pictures Test (Andrew et al., 1953). Both have extensive normative data as an aid in analysis. The PST scenes have been criticized as being even more depressing than those of the TAT, and they do not, in my opinion, depict or elicit adolescent conflicts with any greater specificity than does the TAT. Furthermore, whereas the animals of the CAT do seem to attract little children, the specific depiction of adolescents in the stimuli does at times have the effect of making adolescents even more embarrassed because their problems are being investigated, and thus their defenses rise. The Michigan Pictures are directed more specifically at interpersonal relationships, consisting of photographs of families and other groups in interaction—including school situations. In these respects they leave less to the imaginative processes than the more vague TAT pictures, which permit the child to introduce characters not present in the stimuli.

8.   The Rorschach Technique

Because of the confusing mass of literature on the Rorschach, much of which fails to deal with Rorschach's original hypotheses, it may be well to restate these basic assumptions as succinctly as possible. In essence Rorschach posited the following:

1.   In making perceptual (visual) judgments, people utilize not only the outline or form but other stimuli as well, that is, the color of the stimuli, both chromatic and achromatic; the visual recognition of texture; other aspects of shading or hue, such as chianoscuro; and cues in the stimuli suggesting possible movement. Rorschach was also concerned with how much of the stimuli the person utilizes (the "location"), and how she/he organizes her/his percept.

2.   Each of these determinants of visual perception has its *analogous* counterparts (Rorschach is translated as saying "equivalents") in the ways people experience other stimuli, such as social and affective stress.

Thus Rorschach hypothesized that in projecting movement onto an inanimate inkblot, the individual puts some of his/her own kinesthetic experience into the situation and, analogously, might perceive other situations on the basis of his/her own prior experiences, sets, attitudes, values, and the like. Conversely, since the color of the blot is very much a part of the stimuli when it determines a person's response, his/her judgment in other situations would not be a projection but would be "colored" by environmental stress—that is, by the person's interactions with the environment. By similar analogous reasoning, responses determined by texture are associated with sensitivity to environmental nuances, inkblot perspectives to taking perspective viewpoints in other situations, and chiaroscuro to the "clouded sensorium." *The Rorschach is thus primarily a test of emotional perception.*

In his monograph Rorschach repeatedly distinguished between *perception* and *response*, but this distinction is often forgotten in the clinical use of this technique. Rorschach made it clear that what he believed he was sampling was how people *perceive*, but not necessarily how they behave or, in his terms, how one "experiences" *(Erlebnis)*, not how one "lives" *(Erlebens)*. Two people may perceive in quite the same manner, but their responses may be quite different, or on the other hand, two people may react or behave in the same way but on entirely different perceptual bases. Thus, reasoned Rorschach, it is necessary to divorce the perception from the response in studying perception and ask, as one does in the Rorschach inquiry: How did the person see it, and what determined the perception? What is the subject's basis of judgment? Internal or external?

Of course Rorschach did hope to be able to predict from known patterns of perceptual selection to at least broad patterns of social and emotional behavior, such as psychopathological states. Currently many clinicians continue to try to presage the behavior of the child and to decide how the child is going to act or react to events or stresses by reading the child's inkblot responses. They do not seem discouraged by the mounting research evidence to the effect that prediction from perceptual behavior to other kinds of behaviors is a risky plunge into the unknown (e.g., Bruner and Postman, [1949]). Unfortunately there is only a beginning number of studies that attempt to formulate some of the relationships between perception and behavior— that is, to what degree and in what way one's perception of a situation determines how one will react.

Even though most psychologists hold this possibility to be self-evident, until the basic details are so determined users of the Rorschach are on much safer ground if they limit themselves to *explaining* overt behavior rather than attempting to *predict* it blindly. Given this rationale, one may say that this child's "delinquent" or "schizophrenic" behavior is associated with (or to stretch the logic a bit further—is derived from) such and such patterns of perceptual behavior. In some instances research studies support a statement to the effect that these perceptual patterns are frequently present in persons diagnosed as "schizophrenic" or who are becoming "delinquent," but here also the psychologist must be logically cautious.

When, as too often happens, clinical and research studies using the Rorschach Technique falter, one of the most frequent errors is that, despite the fact that precise directions are given in most major texts for administration and scoring of the Rorschach, some clinicians seem to ignore these standard operations—or even worse, to be ignorant of them! Often clinicians who are properly meticulous in reciting the exact instructions or questions on the Binet or Wechsler and who certainly would not attempt to interpret other techniques without scoring them, strangely enough seem to regard the Rorschach as not needing any precision either in instructions or analysis. However, the Rorschach is an unstructured technique only in the sense that the stimuli are purposefully vague enough to allow a variety of responses. The situation needs to be structured for the child, and there is a definite structure for the assessor in conducting a Rorschach examination and in analyzing it.

The set of instructions given the child is quite crucial, for how the child understands the task often determines the nature of his/her responses. For example, if one merely says "Tell me what this might be" or "What does this look like," children may struggle to find some acceptable *right* answer even if they have been told "there are no right or wrong answers." If they are not also told, as recommended by Klopfer and Kelly (1942, p. 32) that "what *you* see, what it might be for *you*, what it makes *you* think of" (emphasis added), they may suppress their idiosyncratic "engrams" and voice only some "popular" response. In using the Rorschach with children, I recommend the following variant on Klopfer's directions:

Here are some cards with splotches of paint on them. I want you to look at them carefully and tell me what *you* see in the paint. What kinds of *things* (emphasizing the plural) can *you* make out of it? What kinds of things does it suggest to *you* or even just make *you* think of? Everyone sees different things on each of these. There are no right or wrong answers. I just want to know *your* ideas. You may look at it any way.

Often with children it is necessary to repeat these instructions on the second or even third card, especially if it is apparent that the child does not fully understand.

The key operation in Rorschach administration is of course the "inquiry," for it is in this operation that the essential perceptual question is posed: "What about the inkblot helped you to see. . . ." Clinical carelessness in conducting a thorough inquiry is all too common, especially among clinicians who overemphasize the associative-projective aspects in the content of the responses. For if one is only interested in the content aspects, then an inquiry only serves to gain further associative elaborations. Conducting an inquiry with children entails some special procedures that are not usually required for adults. With children under age 8 or very hyperactive or impatient children, it is most effective to ask about the perceptual determinants immediately after the response is given—before presenting the subsequent blot.* Younger children or impatient children may reject further consideration of their responses after the administration of the 10 cards, considering the test to be over. Or they tend to deny or completely revise their impressions. Sometimes such a simultaneous inquiry does run the danger of suggesting or promoting the use of the determinants on further responses, but in my experience, this is not a serious impediment.

The chief problem in conducting a Rorschach inquiry with children is getting them to specify the determinant of their response at all. Even adolescents—to say nothing of younger children—do not always comprehend the usual inquiry questions addressed to adults.* Thus if the child looks puzzled or repeats himself/herself when asked "What about the inkblot suggests that to you?" the question may be rephrased or the child may be asked "Well, tell me more about it." This latter question quite often invokes descriptive material about the concept that, in the child's words, contains the determinant. For example, children may use the terms *icky, weird-o,* or *gooey.* Such terms, however, may have to be explored just a bit further, as the child may be referring to the textural aspects of the test, but also he/she may be intimating that the concept has some chiasroscuro aspect—or even that it is moving. For example, to Card IV a 6-year-old girl said it was an "icky bear or monster!" After she outlined the form, she was asked "What's

icky about it?" "The way he might grab you. So black and all," she replied.

Many children cannot directly verbalize that the textural aspects of the blot determine their response. However, texture may be scored when the child gives a response with quite possible textural aspects and indicates by rubbing the card or pointing to the shading or uses some childhood term as *icky.* Rorschach inquiry with pre-school children has to be much more concrete and precise. Here one is usually interested in form accuracy, as other determinants are rare and usually appear spontaneously—if at all. One has to be most careful not to suggest to the child what she/he might see. Thus if the child calls Card I "a doggie," she/he may very well be perceiving the usual canine face. But should one ask "Show me the parts of the doggie," the child might feel compelled to make a complete dog even though she/he did not see it that way and end up confusing the assessor with a confabulated response. In many other situations adults receive confabulated responses because of their unconscious imposition upon the child of their perceptual functioning. An inquiry such as "Tell me about the doggie *you* see" will better allow the child to describe such perceptual limits as she/he possesses. Given such permission, the pre-schooler normally is quite free in expressing her/his own ideas. However, as children enter latency, where variations from reality are more threatening, they are less willing to take a chance, presenting *le conscience du hasard,* as Loosli-Usteri has aptly labled it (1931), that is, the child is fearful of the hazard of an independent judgment.

The reason for this detailed discussion of standardized administration and careful inquiry of the Rorschach is that the analysis of the child's responses, both metrically and qualitatively, depends on these operations.

*Sometimes children are irritated by the inquiry and retort, "It's just there! Don't you see!" "I'm not sure I see it the same as you," I reply, "Show me how *you* see it."

*Simultaneous inquiry is used by Rapport, Gill, and Shafer (1946, p. 97) for adults as well.

Since the method of scoring is so well described by Klopfer and colleagues (1956) and in other standard works, it would be presumptuous to review it here. Suffice it to say that in scoring children's Rorschachs, although one may have to depend on child language and phrasing, it is still necessary to stick closely and objectively to the evidence obtained in the inquiry. For example, most children over the age of 4 are quite capable of expressing and naming colors or specifying movements if these are part of their percept. Thus just because the child calls Card VIII a "flower," one cannot presume she/he is using the color, even if she/he adds "It's pretty." One must still inquire "What makes it pretty?"

Metric analysis of children's Rorschach responses and of patterns of scores has been immensely improved by the advent of the two volumes by Ames and associates on children's (1952) and adolescents' Rorschach responses (1959). These volumes provide the age norms and variance—subdivided by sex—which are so necessary in judging the child's perceptual growth as measured by the Rorschach. By using these norms, it is possible to answer such questions as: Is the child utilizing the perceptual cues and organizations that might be expected of him/her at this age? Is he/she learning how to respond to the emotional cues and stresses in his/her environment without undue concern? Is he/she beginning to internalize experiences and independently form attitudes and concepts upon which to judg further experiences? Are his/her impulses playing too large—or too small—a role in making judgments? Are his/her perceptions of the world more dominated by inner tension, clouded by anxiety, or denuded of emotion by repression than one might expect of the child at this age? A carefully administered, scored, and analyzed Rorschach will often give the assessor many clues toward answering these and similar queries.

The question of the size of the sample of perceptual behavior obtained by the Rorschach Technique is seldom given much concern in the literature, except for passing remarks warning against the use of records with less than 15 to 20 responses. Although among adults, such brief records may be infrequent, many normal children give only one or two responses per card, rejections are far more frequent, and often they cannot be encouraged to expand. While this small number of responses may actually mirror the limitations of their perceptual experiencing, that is, one and only one response is all they can make to most situations, analysis of the proportion of their responses among the various determinants in such limited records is per force curtailed. Thus it is not much help to know that the average 5-year-old produces .8 Fm responses per record, when one is faced with a record containing three rejections and seven responses, one of which is an Fm. This problem of how to evaluate the raw scores in the face of shifting R has always plagued Rorschach users. The usual solution has been to transpose them into proportions of the total R. Sometime, it is to be hoped, these proportions will be restated as standard scores. Increasing the number of cards used with children might also be advisable. Although an expanded set of inkblots has been developed by Holtzman and his colleagues (1961) for adults, norms on Holtzman's blots for children have not been reported. Sometimes when children do not seem to understand the possibility of giving more than one response per card, one can suggest a second turn through the cards requesting an alternative response per card. However, if this procedure is adopted, notice should be taken that the standard operations are being quite radically altered, especially if one is also using a simultaneous inquiry. Such a second set of alternative responses would then have to be interpreted as the percepts the child makes under pressure and suggestion.

Most of the reliability and validity studies on the Rorschach have dealt exclusively with adults, and the literature on children is relatively sparse. The interscorer reliability for adult records is above question (Ramzy and Pickard, 1949). Adults tend to give much the same kinds of responses with comparable patterns of determinant scores when a Rorschach is readministered after brief periods during which there are no known personality changes (Hertz, 1934). Since the stimulus value of the Behn and other sets of inkblots varies so much from Rorschach's 10 blots, there is really no comparable form for reliability comparison, nor does the usual split-half of items seem applicable to this technique. The gradual unfolding of increasing perceptual complexity and differentiation over the childhood years makes it unreasonable to expect a consistency of a child's Rorschach pattern year after year— although it would seem doubtful that major changes would appear over a few months' time, especially after year 6. The norms provided by Ames and colleagues (1952) do reveal these developmental patterns and, in this sense, indicate reliability for the Rorschach with the children.

The fact that these norms are consistent with the general observations about perceptual and emotional behavior, as Ames and colleagues (1952) have so well illustrated, also gives support to the general validity of this technique. Such clinical observation of the relationships between perceptual development and other aspects of development does not, of course, meet the more stringent demands of independent and uncontaminated validation studies. The great difficulty in conducting such studies lies in the fact that there is no independent criterion. So far, the Rorschach is the only instrument of its kind. Therefore studies are needed in which other behaviors can also be scored in the same manner as the Rorschach, that is, according to the perceptual determinants that the child seems to be using. However, whether perceptual behavior can be measured and scored from, for example, social interactions, remains to be explored. The construct validation of the Rorschach as used with adults has received increasing attention over the past decade, and there is now a considerable body of evidence to suggest that the theory that Rorschach posited in interpreting the ink-

blot responses is consistent with other kinds of behavioral observations (Meltzoff, Singer, and Korchin, 1953; Palmer, 1955, 1956, 1957; Fonda, 1960; Palmer and Lustgarten, 1962). Such studies on adult behavior do give the Rorschach user some greater confidence in applying the test to children—but the basic validation work remains to be done.

In summary, since perceptual development is so very basic to the development of all the other functions of the child's ego, the Rorschach technique—with all its limitations and unknowns—continues to occupy a central position in the assessment of children, for it is the only well-established measure of perceptual growth (see further discussion on affect and development in Chapter 10).

Because the Rorschach Technique is so commonly used purely as an associative method of estimating emotional stability, the fact that the basic operation of the subject is a perceptual analysis is too frequently forgotten. Yet the specific instructions require the child to make a visual organization out of the blot as well as an association to it. The quality of this percept (engram was Rorschach's term) has been a major concern of those interested in the "form level" of the child's response. Form-level averages for each age are given in the Ames et al. 1952 volume. As might be expected, the precision with which a child can outline his/her percepts improves from year to year. The pre-school child is apt to take one or two clues and fabricate a complete response, for example "It looks like a doggy. Here's his tail." Such a response not elaborated further would be "poor form" or a "confabulation" if given by a 9-year-old. Three- and 4-year-olds commonly repeat the same response to two or three cards in a row—which is normal perservative behavior for that age. Fanciful combinations such as a bear with boots (Card IV) are much more common and quite "normal" for children, but they might be labeled "contaminated" for adults.

Perceptual dysfunction, particularly poor

form level, has long been used as an indication of possible brain damage among adults. Z. A. Piotrowski's volume (1940) is the classic work in this field, and Fisher and Gonda (1955) in a comparison of various so-called "brain-damage" tests found the Rorschach as the most accurate predictor. Whether these indicators or "signs" can be applied to children is very questionable— especially considering the form-level norms mentioned before. On the other hand, should an older child (e.g., 10–12) yield poor form level on card after card, become markedly perplexed and unable to account for her/his responses during the inquiry, the clinician would be rightly suspicious of a possible neurological dysfunction. (For further discussion, see Chapter 17.)

Although the Rorschach Technique is basically a sampling of modes of perception, the associative content of the responses may be quite revealing of the ideation of the child. Some Rorschach authorities have put primary emphasis on interpretation of content—most notably Schafer (1954)— almost to the neglect of the perceptual approach originally proposed by Herman Rorschach. In adult records content may often play a larger part in Rorschach interpretation than in children's responses. The fact is that the 10 cards, which draw on the average only 20 to 30 responses from adults, are actually a very small sampling of ideational content, since many of the responses are often "popular" or relatively banal and sterotyped. Less than one-half, and often fewer, adult responses seem to be definitely idiosyncratic or significant in content. Children's records are even briefer on the average. With young children one response per card is quite common, and cards are more often rejected. Children's responses tend to be much less detailed and specific, replete with vague "bugs, butterflies, doggies, trees, and so on" (see Chapter 15).

Despite the limited sampling of ideational content in children's responses, in most records from disturbed children several such idiosyncratic responses or a definite set of responses usually appear that—although not unique—do carry a marked emotional edge. For example, a child may see only very passive animals and flowers, or predominately "scary" monsters, animals, and people. Clues about the psychosexual development of the child may be suggested by examining whether she/he pays attention to oral details such as animals eating, mouths, and the like, or is compulsive about detail, picking out phallic details, or concentrates on feminine genital areas of the cards. In forming hypotheses about psychosexual development from such minute clues, however, one should keep in mind not only the limited sample but the developmental level expected of the child and the relevancy of this set of hypotheses to the overall development of the child's ego.

The assessor who attempts to utilize the associative content of Rorschach responses needs also to be aware that these associations are determined to no small degree by the nature of the stimuli and of the task. The nature of Rorschach associations may be realized by contrasting them with the TAT. In contrast to the TAT, the Rorschach presents no content in its stimuli. In administering the TAT, the child is instructed to be imaginative and to utilize the picture to stimulate fantasy. He/she is not expected to describe the picture. On the Rorschach the child's task is to structure the stimuli itself, to "make something out of the inkblot." Thus the task is primarily one of structuring, with association following. The psychological meaning peculiar to Rorschach associations arises from the fact that the response is determined by perceptual factors, not by content.

The Rorschach is not a *projective* technique in the strict sense of this term. It is not designed to produce fantasy projections, for these imply an *un*reality or *non*reality process. Instead, Rorschach's instructions require a fitting of nonsense into sense, a making of reality out of a nothing, a process that is the reverse of projection. In contrast to the TAT, in which the child projects feelings, the Rorschach taps the *selective* process of the ego. The determinants are designed to show *how* the child determines perceptually the unknown realities of the world, and the content of the responses yields a sample at times of what is *selected* as associations and thus represents what the child *takes in* as regards ideas, feelings, attitudes, symbols, and so on.

As Rorschach consistently cautioned, what the child takes in or how he/she selects is not necessarily directly related to what he/she gives out—that is, how or with what he/she responds. In Rorschach's terms, these responses represent *Erleben*—experiencing or perceiving—but not necessarily *Erlieben*—living or manifest behavior. For example, the child who sees one aggressive animal or explosion or destructive association after another would appear to be experiencing his/her world (here including his/her inner world) as quite hostile and destructive. The child is responding to and selecting the hostile aspects of unstructured situations. He/she may or may not, however, project these experiences outward onto the environment or even permit them to appear in verbalized fantasies on the TAT. How the child handles these depends on the structure of his/her ego and its defensive mechanism. For example, the child may try to counteract these experiences by dreams of affection and wishes for love in his/her TAT stories.

For example, a 9-year-old girl who had been deserted by her father and lived with her psychotic mother responded to the Rorschach with associations marked by violent upheaval, clashing forces, and threats of destruction. Her TAT stories were woven around "Santa Claus" (in mid-July!). This child appeared to have been too terrified by her experiences to project them into fantasy, let alone into actual interpersonal relationships. In addition, many of her experiences came from within herself, from her own drives and impulses—as was indicated by the many movement responses in her record. Thus these feelings were not reflected in her manifest behavior *or* in her fantasies of interpersonal relationships. Conversely,

the child who fantasies violence in interpersonal relationships, who is projecting, may be quite obtuse to actual indications of violence and hostility either in the environment or on the inkblot shapes. Of course in many instances the child whose *N* Aggression and feelings of hostility are so strong that they break through defenses may be sensitive to clues of aggressive hostility on the Rorschach and also express these feelings both on the TAT and in social interactions as well.

How then may the assessor begin to judge the import of such contentual associations that seem significant on a child's Rorschach? First, one should examine the modes through which the child is perceiving and experiencing such associations. Are they stemming from within as a part of her/his instinctual life and personal attitudes and ideation, or are they chiefly stimulated by environmental contacts and interactions? Or, might they be an intellectualization—a defense against something else? In the case of the child threatened by hostility, is the feeling of hostility derived from internalized preconceptions, from aggressive impulses, from awareness of environmental threats, or from interactions with the environment? Might she/he be expressing phobic or counterphobic defenses against some other conflict or anxiety? According to the Rorschach hypotheses, the sources of the child's experiencing may be suggested by the perceptual determinants, by the inferences based on whether the child's response is dictated by color, movement, or shape. Quite often of course the child may experience the same kinds of association from several sources.

Some of the ways in which the Rorschach determinants and the associative content of the child's responses—including those on the CAT or TAT—may be used in combination will be discussed in greater detail in Chapter 10–12. It is through such combinations of perceptual mode and associative content that a beginning can be made toward an understanding of the emotional dynamics of the child. The nonverbal activity and productions of a child are essential to assessment of his/her ego functioning because they contain clues for which the child may have no verbalization. Nevertheless, they are efforts of the child to communicate to others or to work through his/her emotional interactions with the environment and within himself/herself. There are many gestures, actions, and productive expressions for which there are no adequate words in English. An assessment of children depends to a large degree on observation of nonverbal behavior because of the fact that the developing child is of necessity engaged in continuous exercise of motoric activity as part of his/her growth. Even if there were no prohibitions on verbal expression and children were taught the appropriate terms, they would probably still express many of their feelings through physical activity.

9. The Hand Test

This brief but fascinating projective technique that was introduced by Wagner (1962) has now achieved widespread use and research attention (see Appendix B of the latest edition of this manual). Based on the observation that hand gestures constitute a major form of communication, the test requires the child to interpret nine different drawings of hand gestures, plus a blank card on which the child is to "image" and describe a hand. The child may give more than one response, but the many illustrative cases show only one or two responses per card. The responses are then categorized in one of 15 headings. (Whether more than one category is used for any one response is not clear, although some responses indicate more than one attitude.)

Wagner and his colleagues (Bricklin, Piotrowski, and Wagner, 1962) are most interested in predicting what they call "acting out," that is, aggressive, asocial behavior, and they present several research studies to back up their contention that this technique can predict violence. However, as with the Rorschach (see the preceding discussion), the user of this projective test must be aware that there may be quite a gap between the cup of perception and the lip of action. *Seeing is not necessarily doing.* Thus it is safest *not* to predict violence in a child just because he/she projects violence on this or any other projective test. Used with the Rorschach, the TAT, and a detailed life history, however, it is possible to tell from this test the possibilities of "acting-out."

Acting-out is not the only variable (actually it is a ratio of 5 variables), and much more can be revealed from this test about the child's emotional and social attitudes. For example, in a study of children with learning disabilities, these children gave primarily passive-aggressive responses. The 15 categories include the following: affection, dependence, communication, exhibitionism, direction, aggression, acquisition, active, passive, tension, crippled, fear, description (or neutral), bizarre, and failure (reject). Thus a wide variation of category patterns are possible, even among normal or mildly disturbed children. Extensive norms are given for children (see Tables II, V, and VIII in the manual), such that it can be used from kindergarten through adolescence. (The test is also used for adults, with appropriate norms.)

C. NONVERBAL ASSOCIATIVE TECHNIQUES

Under the heading of direct observation, some types of children's nonverbal activities that the assessor should note during the examination have already been mentioned: the child's gait and posture, gestures and facial expressions, and the amounts and kinds of overall bodily movement. Such physical activity is also very important to note as the child is responding to associative techniques. The way children scuffle their feet, slam the card on the table, or even tilt their heads may often give more clues about their affect than the words they use.

In addition to observing such spontaneous motoric activity, the psychologist should be prepared to use techniques specifically intended to sample such behavior.

Some of these techniques—for instance, Draw-A-Person (Machover, 1949) or House-Tree-Person (Buck, 1948)—are widely employed, but there are some that are less well known such as the Make-A-Picture Story* (Shneidman, 1952), the Structured Doll Play (Lynn, 1959), and the World Test (Buhler et al., 1951) with which the assessor should also be familiar.

1. Drawings

Drawings of the human figure are one of the oldest, most clinically fascinating, and at the same time one of the least scientifically established of all associative techniques used with either children or adults. Because children need to engage in motor activity and in spontaneous creative activity, they are usually attracted to this task. Often children invest the most devotion and energy to their drawings, and in so doing they appear to express spontaneously many unspoken feelings.

The operations involved in the drawing of a person actually create several interlinked tasks for the child. I and my colleagues employ the following instructions: "Draw a picture of a person, any kind of person you want, just for fun. But make a whole person, not just a stick figure." These instructions require first that the child envision a human body, probably foremost her/his own body, although some children may be observed to try covertly to use the assessor as a model. Second, these instructions require that the child transfer this image by way of motor activity into a reproduction. The added instruction to make a whole person is intended to prevent the child's drawing only a head and shoulders. This part of the instructions does approach the distinctly different instruction for the Goodenough IQ scale ("Make the best drawing you can"), but the slight push toward an achievement motive is purposefully counteracted by the phrase *just*

*The MAPS, discovered before as a verbal technique, does not necessarily involve much verbalization. It is especially recommended for exploration of fantasy in cases when the child is relatively nonverbal.

for fun. The combined task is quite similar to that demanded by the Rorschach that also asks that a mental image or "engram," as Rorschach called it, be conceived before the actual response is given. The phrase *not just a stick figure* encourages children to go beyond any stereotyped set of symbols and to express themselves as freely as they choose.

The rational of the D-A-P is that this sample of behavior may divulge the extent to which the child has developed some image of her/his own body and the physical aspects of others. It also yields cues about the manner in which this image is transmitted into more or less controlled motor activity. It is often proposed that one may generalize from this behavior to the image that children may have of themselves as a social person or their ability to control or express themselves socially. This rationale and its second level of generalization—although not stated in these words—appears to be the basis for the use of this technique by most leading proponents of the D-A-P such as Machover (1949), Hammer (1958), and Buck (1948).

After the drawing is completed, the subsequent instructions to associate verbally to the drawing vary widely. Machover employs an extensive verbal inquiry, and she bases a great deal of her interpretation on this verbal association. Hammer discusses the D-A-P as though no inquiry were demanded of his subjects, but in discussing the House-Tree-Person Test he gives an example of the case of a child with an extensive inquiry that he notes is routine. In another case in Rabin and Haworth (1960), he does not mention such inquiry at all! In my experience, inquiry seldom yields more than few replies from children of any age, and it often meets with considerable resistance. Machover (in Rabin and Haworth, 1960, pp. 238 ff.) gives samples of the responses by a 9-year-old boy to two sets of 33 questions about his male and female drawings. Twenty to 25 of these responses are insignificant sterotypes or blanks, such as "regular" (how healthy is she?), "yes" (will she get married?), or "nothing" or "no" (to 13 questions). Twenty one of the 33 questions about the male drawings were answered similarly. Perhaps other children yield richer protocols to Machover's questions, but responses such as those quoted previously are quite typical of most children—including adolescents. The majority children present their drawings as a finished product and seem resentful when extensive inquiry is conducted, as if the assessor should be able to comprehend their unspoken graphic messages without additional verbiage. Children seem willing to answer one or two associations at most, such as age (and sex if indefinite) and "What is this person like? What kind of personality does he or she have?" Strangely enough, it is not very difficult to get a child to invent a story to the drawing, particularly if it is administered after a relatively successful TAT. It would seem that such a spontaneous association to a creative work is more acceptable to the child than a formal inquiry.

Despite the fact that Goodenough long ago devised a standardized method of scoring the child's drawing of a man as a measurement of intelligence, no such acturial measurement exists for analyzing the many other ego functions that these drawings are purported to sample. (An exception is Buck's [1948] very complicated system for obtaining an estimate of intelligence from his House-Tree-Person Test.) Most of the experts argue that a metric approach is not applicable and is even antithetical to the understanding of the overall psychodynamic operation of the ego. In practice the advocates of these drawing techniques do make use of very specific signs, interpreting them quite concretely. Indeed, some of these interpretations seem to smack of the dream-book analysis of symbols used in the early days of psychoanalysis, but which have long been discarded in current psychoanalytic practice.

For example, Levy (in Hammer, 1958) makes such statements as ". . . stroking toward the body is suggestive of introversive tendencies whereas stroking away from

the body is often associated with extroversive tendencies" (p. 110) and "the size relationship between the drawing and the available space may parallel the dynamic relationship between the subject and parent figures. Size is suggestive of the way the subject is responding to the environmental press" (p. 101). On the other hand, Hammer in the same volume says that "the size of the drawn concept contains clues about the subject's realistic self-esteem, characteristic self-expansiveness and fantasy self-inflation" (p. 64). Although these statements are not necessarily contradictory, it is difficult to tie them together. Hammer does cite research findings in support of some of his interpretive suggestions. Arbit and associates (1959), however, found that taken one at a time these signs are quite unreliable and have little predictive or even descriptive value. In defense of these experts, it should be pointed out that all consistently warn that no one sign can ever be taken as predictive in and of itself, but must be viewed in the light of the entire configuration of the child's production. Thus for example, although dark and heavy lines may suggest a depressive mood, one might be more inclined to predict that a child had a depressive outlook if the drawing were also shaded, the eyes downcast, the figure inert or listless, and the drawing as a whole carelessly constructed. As was previously discussed with respect to other associative techniques, it is my contention that greater psychometric precision—far from violating the assessment of psychodynamics—could well be introduced as a first step in analyzing these samples of behaviors. Also such precision might well help to sharpen and to specify the second- and third-level generalizations, which often appear to be so vague that they are meaningless sterotypes. In the present state of development of these drawing techniques, such overall impressions rely entirely upon the best clinical fit. Children's drawings as presently used often provide dramatic illustrations to the case histories, but the generalizations made on the basis of them are among the most tenuous and specious of all clinical predictions.

2. Free Play as an Assessment Technique

The main advantage of drawing is that it is part of the child's normal play activities. That children express many conflicts, practice many ego functions, and re-enact many social and personal-life situations in play has been well established both in research and in the clinic. Observing the child in a play setting is a classic assessment procedure. Quite frequently clinicians take children to a playroom, permit them to explore the room and its materials and play with whatever they choose, while talking to them about what they are doing and engaging them in an unstructured interview about their play in general. Such observations and conversations are intended to obtain a sample of children's freedom to play, their ability to use play materials to express themselves, and their interactions with an adult in a permissive play situation. In an hour in the playroom, the assessor should observe the following:

1. *Children's reactions when given a variety of play situations from which to choose.* Do they explore? Do they settle down immediately to play? Are they overwhelmed? How do they make choices, and with what emotions? How restless are they? How compulsive? Their responses give possible clues as to how they may make similar decisions in other situations.

2. *The use children make of the play materials they select.* Do they attempt some organized play? Do they use the materials in an appropriate fashion, recognizing them as defined objects or games? Or is their use of them primarily to express some personal feelings, for example, flinging them about in an angry, destructive fashion or pressing them to their bodies or faces as if incorporating them? Such use of play materials may give clues concerning how the child uses reality—whether as something external or

as an extension of themselves. The choice of toys or games may also provide clues about the feelings that children need to play out. They may select objects to work out objectively angry and hostile feelings, such as military toys, a ball that can be slammed against the wall, or a punching-bag doll. They may want something that they can use to show achievement and prowess, something to cuddle, or something to express sexual excitement.

3. *The manner in which children relate to the adult examiner and his/her presence in the child's play world.* In the first place, can they accept the examiner's offer to play freely and yet permit the examiner to be present? Do they allow the adult to observe their play or are they uneasy about play being observed and feelings revealed? To what extent do they involve the adult in play? Do they need the adult to play with them? How dependent on others are they in their play? What kinds of things do they seek from the adult: Assistance in decision making? Information about the play materials? Engagement in competitive play? An obedient servant? Observation of such behavior may be very helpful in direct assessment of how the child uses significant adults (or how he/she would like to use them) in everyday life.

Two major aspects of the operations involved in the observation of free play need to be considered: the nature of the stimulus (the playroom and its materials) and the activities—chiefly the structure or control offered by the examiner. First, if free play is to be observed, then the playroom should be set up to permit it. Such a room should invite play and be as free from restrictions as possible. For example, if water play is permitted, the walls and floor should be of a material that will not be harmed by water and water paints, and there should be a drain in the floor and a mop handy in case the child becomes anxious and wishes to clean up his mess. If a rubber ball is available, it should be possible to bounce it against the wall without disturbing the assessor's colleagues in the next room, or against the ceiling without danger of smashing a light fixture. All in all, the room and its materials should not require the assessor to say "I'm sorry, we cannot do that here." The rule should be the same as in play therapy: "We can do and say most anything we want here, except that no one should get hurt by anything we do. I won't hurt you and I won't let you hurt me or yourself."

The playroom should invite play. First, it should be pleasantly decorated without being so elaborate that it is stilted, and it should be free of outside distractions but should not seem altogether enclosed. For example, one very inviting playroom has long windows, letting in light from about the ceiling level, is screened on the inside to avoid breakage from overactive play, but gives a sense that the room is not completely closed in. Another very ideal play space consisted of a roofless garden court, surrounded by a high fence, which led into the examiner's office through sliding-screen doors. This could be protected against inclement weather by pulling down a canvas. The floor area should be large enough to permit some physical activity—at least 100 ft²—but should not be so large as to make the child feel lost in space. For example, it is difficult for a child to feel comfortable playing alone in a room designed to hold a whole nursery-school class.

Second, the number and kinds of play materials to be made available to the child should be carefully considered. Murphy and Krall (in Rabin and Haworth, 1960) list six types of play materials that "one will want to include".

1. *The miniature life toys:* housekeeping objects and family dolls, tiny soldiers, animals, cars, planes, and the like.
2. *Materials that will permit regressive play in conjunction with the miniature life toys:* sand, water, clay.
3. *Larger toys for more realistic play:* regular-sized dolls and trucks.

4. *Materials that permit aggressive play:* guns, rubber knives, punching bag, "Bobo the Clown".
5. junk toys containing fragments such as pegs, light switches, string, tops, balls.
6. *Materials that permit communication and expression:* a pair of toy telephones, crayons, pencils and paper, chalk, paints, finger paints.

For older children or even for young ones who need to express their feelings of competition and achievement, it is a good idea to have a few simple competitive games—such as checkers or Parchesi—or a deck of playing cards. These latter materials give the child a chance to involve the assessor in his/her play and to challenge him/her should he/she choose to do so, as well as the opportunity to express his/her feelings about rules and restrictions.

If all these materials are immediately available—especially if they are scattered about the room in a jumble—most children become overwhelmed and spend the major part of an hour sorting them over. Or they may feel that there is no need to play with anything definite since disorganization is presented to them. To avoid this, the materials should be segregated in cupboards that can be opened one at a time. If the assessor has reason to believe the child might be overwhelmed by or distracted by the number of toys, he/she can say, "All these cupboards have different kinds of toys. We won't have time to play with all of them today, but let's look in these (selecting those containing materials the assessor wishes to present), and we can look in the others the next time we get together." If the child is dissatisfied or overly curious, it is still possible to open all cupboards. In some instances the assessor may want to present a limited set of materials. Some thought should be given beforehand to the appropriateness of the play materials to the child being assessed and to the kinds of play materials that might best aid the assessment. For example, one might want to see how a compulsive child might behave if given the chance to be messy with finger paints. Or a child who is experiencing considerable familial dissension that he/she cannot voice may be able to express his/her feelings in play with the doll house or with puppets.

If free play is to be elicited, the assessor must reverse or alter the role he/she normally plays in structured assessment situations and stand back, giving little or no instructions other than the general limitation mentioned previously. As has been indicated, it is often possible to carry on a conversation with children as they play. In fact, many children invite such conversations and even seem more at ease if the adult behaves in a natural and interested way than if she/he sits silently, taking surreptitious notes. The adult need not participate in the child's play, and he/she should not do so unless invited. In some instances, when it is obvious that the child is anxious lest the adult feel hurt that she/he is not included or if the assessor wants to test the child's ability to play independently, the assessor may want to reassure the child that she/he need not be included. The conversation should *not* take the form of an inquiry as on the Rorschach or of confronting interpretive statements, for these approaches tend to inhibit the child's play. Such commentary is appropriate only after the child is definitely engaged in a play therapy, not during the assessment period per se. The playroom observation may constitute a prelude to play therapy, thus giving the child a chance to become accustomed to the clinician. The play situation forms a baseline for the clinician in subsequent efforts to alter the child's behavior.

Since a playroom, as previously described, is not always available, it is a good idea for an assessor to keep on hand some simple play materials that can be used in an office situation, for example, a doll house, a set of miniature toys (similar to those used on the World Test), and a set of hand puppets. A child might thus be invited to play with the materials on a table or on the floor or in a small sandbox for a half hour or

so after the formal testing is completed. (If these materials are presented to the child earlier in the assessment, it is often difficult to persuade the child to return to more structured tasks.)

Although several methods of scoring free-play observations with rating scales, and the like have been devised for specific research purposes, not one appears to have been adopted clinically, and most have been too specific for the more diverse multipurpose needs of clinical assessment. Murphy and Krall have stated the following

Since the child's use of play may express the most personal, idiosyncratic experience reflected in any medium, no standardized set of criteria, signs or scores can offer an adequate approach to the evaluation of play. Just as the analyst is constantly on the outlook for new experiences not previously discussed in the literature, the psychologist who evaluates the play of a child needs to be sensitive to the unforeseen events which may carry him closer to the experience of the child than scores on standard lists could do. Anyone undertaking to use play for general diagnostic purposes should be thoroughly familiar with the discussion by Erikson, Peller, Despert, Murphy, and Loomis at a minimum. . . . (Rabin and Haworth, 1960, p. 290)

The fact that there is no comprehensive scoring system for evaluating play observations does not, however, excuse the assessor from a careful recording of his/her observations nor from a thoughtful and systematic analysis of the data. Although some children are made uneasy when the assessor takes notes during the observation period, usually they are unconcerned since responses to other techniques have been written down in prior contacts. It is then possible to go over such process recordings of the child's behavior, noting the sequence of events, and then as on the TAT, the general themes. Viewing these in light of the rationale discussed previously one may obtain many clues about various aspects of the functioning of the child's ego.

There are really no established norms of

clinic playroom behavior. One can only guess by what has been reported from nursery school and other free-play observations. Even these have been largely of children playing in groups. Such norms can only be gathered through experience by the individual assessor. She/he learns, for example, not to be very impressed by the fact that an 8-year-old boy takes a couple of swings at the "Bobo" punching bag as he enters the room and a couple more before he leaves, and to be quite aware of the possible sexual implications of the behavior of an 11-year-old girl who spent most of her time wrestling "Bobo" to the floor and squirming around over him.

The reliability of such data obtained from one or two play sessions has never been established, to the best of my knowledge. The assessor should keep in mind that this sample of the child's play is probably biased by several factors—such as the relative artificiality of the setting, the fact that the child is being observed, and that children's play probably varies extremely from time to time in both the amount of expressiveness it contains and the intensity with which feelings are expressed. In addition to these unknown reliabilities of the data, there are even larger questions about the reliability and validity of the inferences drawn from these data by the assessor. The reliability of judgments depends essentially upon the assessor's experience. Unfortunately the emphasis in the training of psychologists on exact measurement is not always balanced by training in careful observation and recording of behavior. When no rating scale is provided for the novitate, she/he tends either to become lost or to overestimate and overgeneralize from the scraps of behavior she/he is trying to analyze. Only by careful practice in systematic observation can an assessor become consistent.

The validity of generalizations drawn from free play presents essentially the same dilemmas as do the projective techniques: Against what criteria does one compare the expression of unconscious feelings and

emotions? Although no validation method has univocal acceptance, at least an internal validation may be obtained by noting the consistency of the child's behavior through the comparison of these play observations with other data obtained from projective materials and from the case history. However, there are two possible fallacies in such an internal validation process:

1.   The assessor must be careful not to contaminate conclusions by selecting only those data from each set of observations that support his/her overall hypotheses. His/her hypotheses must fit a majority of the data.

2.   Conversely, the assessor should not expect that data obtained from one level of ego functioning will necessarily be consistent with that obtained from another level. In fact, it is quite reasonable to suppose that these data may actually seem at odds, especially in the ego functioning of emotionally disturbed children. For example, it would not invalidate one's hypotheses to find that a neatly dressed and well-behaved child who has a history of enuresis gives largely compulsive and stereotyped responses to most of the projective tests, with only minor signs of repressed hostility, but in the playroom becomes so involved in messy water play that she/he accidently wets the assessor, albeit with considerable signs of guilt! (Free and structured play with pre-school children is discussed further in Chapter 15.)

3.   The World Test

Although most clinicians are aware of the values and hazards of free-play observations, many do not seem as familiar with the possibilities of more structured play techniques, involving the use of more or less standardized materials, more well defined methods of analysis, and more limited rationales. Two such techniques that have received at least occasional use in clinical settings are the World Test (Buhler et al., 1951) and the Structured Doll Play Test

(Lynn, 1959). The later is discussed in Chapter 15.

The World Test consists of a set of miniature buildings and other objects that can be used to form a village, human figures to people it, military personnel and equipment, and a set of domestic and wild animals.* The child is invited to sit on the floor and open the case. Buhler used the following directions to the child: "See all these things. You may play with them and build something with them here on the floor. You may use as many as you like. Here are houses, trees, people, soldiers, cars. . . ." And the assessor points out each item, naming it. "Now you may play." She recommends that the child have an area 6 ft² in which to construct a world and that the child be allowed to play 20–30 minutes. She suggests that the examiner ask the child what she/he is making after about 5 minutes and make further inquiry after 20 minutes. Thus the elements of the child's world are identified, but the arrangement of these elements is left up to the child.

In this set of test operations the assessor withdraws after having acquainted the child with the stimuli, and the child is free to utilize them as he/she sees fit (or not utilize them, as is frequently the case). Although Buhler and her co-writers do not remark on interactions between the child and the assessor, it has been my experience that many children try to involve the assessor in the construction of the world. They frequently ask for further identification of the items, ask advice about using them, or permission to use their own ideas, or even invite the assessor to join in the play, giving directions, sharing items, and so on. One boy went so far as to divide out the entire box of toys between himself and examiner—one at a time. "This is for you, and this is for me." He directed the psychologist to play with his half on the opposite side of the room and kept coming across to see how the psychologist was proceeding! Each time he would "borrow" one of the "doctor's toys" to add to his world, so that in effect the toys he left for the psychologist were those he was omitting from his world. Although such extreme interactions are rare, the kinds of interchange that the child voluntarily creates between himself and the assessor should be noted. In this interchange the child may be demonstrating the amount and kinds of support and help she/he needs in organizing a world. Through observing this interchange the assessor may gain clues about how dependent, demanding, manipulating, seductive, or rejecting the child may be in relation to adults when she/he has to organize the elements in her/his environment.

When this technique was constructed the criterion for a clinical instrument was that it could statistically distinguish normal children from emotionally disturbed or retarded ones. Thus most of the original studies were concerned with the discriminative values of various signs, such as use of aggressive elements, the absence of human figures, the number of items used (50 or less), the number of types of items, closed versus open worlds, schematic versus disorganized worlds, and so on. Unfortunately, in these studies of signs and symptoms the basic standard data were almost forgotten, and only the barest age norms are given.

As is indicated by the cases cited in these original articles,* the World Test provides much more data than a mere discrimination between normal and disturbed children. Although there does not appear to be any further research on this technique and no systematic validation, I am continually impressed with the fit between children's use of these materials and other clinical data. More than on any other projective technique, children display on this well-named World Test how they organize the elements of the world about them, what kinds of

---

*See Appendix A.

*All were published together (see (Buhler et al., 1951).

emotional stimuli they accept and reject, the interactions of these elements, the attitudes toward them, and the methods of coping with them. Most of all the World Test shows the child in action, with a minimum of required verbalization.

As to methods of analyzing responses to the World Test, the rough classificatory signs or "symptoms" that Buhler lists are scarcely metric scores, but they do provide beginning steps. Thus the gross number of objects used does seem to be an indication of how many stimuli the child can admit and handle. This measure also reveals how empty or overcrowded the world seeeems to the child. The number of different types of elements may be taken as one measure of the complexity of his/her world. Buhler— who was a "Gestalt" psychologist—also stresses observation of the way the materials are organized by the child. As she notes, some children systematically organize the play materials into a village with an outlying farm area for the animals and a nearby military post and a zoo, and so forth. Others, particularly younger or retarded children, may line up the materials in neat rows but with little or no systematic arrangement. Still others present some partially organized sections but with disparate elements intruding in bizarre fashion, as if the child were trying to use and absorb something into his/her world that he/she does not understand or that is out of place. The content of such intrusions often gives clues to some of the child's conflicts.

Case 10

For example, Bobby, age 6, had built a relatively well-organized village and peopled it with several human figures, but he had not used any of the animals or soldiers. Then he proceeded to place a wild animal behind each of the buildings. "They all got loose from the zoo and are hiding," he explained. Then he brought in several soldiers to hunt down the animals. None of the human figures were disturbed. Questioned about this, he looked puzzled, then he decided the following: "They don't see it—they don't see all the lions, 'cause they're invisible. Only these guys (the soldiers) can see 'em." It was noted that Bobby's parents had been unable to see his aggressive behavior at school, and they openly expressed their feelings that the school authorities were unjustly critical of him.

Another variable in the child's organization of his/her world that Buhler observed was the closure or openness of the overall gestalt. Some children built very tight little worlds, with everything crowded together in a small circle. Others scattered their buildings and people loosely across the floor, freely utilizing all the available space. Some used the fences and other materials to enclose many elements. Many children made sure that the animals, domestic or wild, were corralled.

Case 11

Marlene, age 7, built two squares of four buildings facing in toward one another. Inside one square she put the boys and in another the girls. The assessor also noted that on the DAP, Marlene, after drawing a girl, specifically asked for a separate piece of paper on which to draw a male figure and that she continued to remark on and emphasize the sex differences in her drawings. In the initial interview, the assessor discovered that Marlene had four brothers, but no sisters, and that there were no girls of Marlene's age in her immediate neighborhood. However, neither Marlene nor her parents had seemed particularly concerned with the fact that Marlene's world was chiefly male. These data suggested that Marlene might be struggling to separate out and establish her feminine identity.

Another major variable—not specifically noted by Buhler—is the sequence in which the child selects the objects and inserts them in his/her world. Most commonly, children of all ages begin by selecting buildings and other inanimate objects and then adding animals and people. Most children put in houses before they use other buildings, usually placing the school, hospital, or jail last—if these buildings are used. Domesticated animals and human figures are usually inserted before the wild animals. It would not be unusual, for example, if a normally aggressive 5-year-old boy played first with the soldiers or aircraft, and then set them to one side to become occupied with building a village, finally constructing a military airport on the outskirts. The sequence of choices is most important to note when the child's world is chaotic, for the sequence of associations often reveals the defenses and conflicts that disturb his/her world. For example:

CASE 12

Lonnie, age 9, was both threatened and fascinated by the wild animals. Initially he brushed them aside, making a sound that suggested both fear and disgust. He sorted over some of the buildings but used none. He then selected the policeman and the jail, and he placed them in the center of the floor without comment. Then he added several soldiers, the "Stop" sign, and a dog. Two houses were then placed far from the first objects. He returned to examine the wild animals and asked the assessor to name

each and to tell him if they were dangerous. When he was asked to name them, he became upset and stopped playing for a second but began to identify them to himself—sotto voce—with his back to the assessor. His attention returned to other objects, and he played momentarily with cars and planes. Then he gave the monkey a ride in the car, adding a bear and a lion. He concluded by crashing the cars and wild animals into the policeman and the jail.

In the initial interviews with Lonnie's mother it was discovered that Lonnie's personal world was also chaotic. From ages 3 to 7 he had been a "football" between his parents in the divorce court, each claiming custody over him. This battle was not resolved when Lonnie's mother remarried, for his father continued to give him treats and did not discipline him. In his mother's home Lonnie responded to this discipline with temper tantrums and angry rejections of his stepfather and his mother. His reactions caused so much dissension between his mother and stepfather that their marriage was about to be dissolved. However, when Lonnie's parents quarreled he became extremely upset. During one such parental quarrel he ran screaming into the street, declaring he was going to be killed. He would have been hit by a car had not the driver quickly swerved and crashed into a neighbor's house.

PART THREE

Procedures in Assessment

CHAPTER 7

The Assessment Milieu and the Referral

A. THE ASSESSMENT MILIEU—A COMPLEX OF INTERPERSONAL RELATIONSHIPS

In clinical assessment—as in any scientific study—the procedures of data collection are dependent upon and secondary to the goals and purposes of the investigation. Children are interviewed and tested, not merely to see "what the tests show" (a phrase too often found in student reports!), but rather to determine the level and variation of the development of ego functions quantitatively and qualitatively. As in any scientific study, assessment of these functions requires a systematic, precise, and careful collection of data.

In Part 2 the methods and techniques for collecting data were reviewed. However, the setting in which these techniques are used and the procedures in administering them are also important factors. These procedures include the environmental setting in which the clinician works, the nature of the referral, the planning and preparations for the assessment, the setting of appointments and fees, the initial contact with the child, the introduction of the child to the assessment, procedures in interviewing children, procedures in testing, handling resistances during the assessment, procedures in interviewing parents and others concerned with the welfare of the child, and procedures in reporting findings and follow-up.

As the ramifications of these steps in carrying out an assessment are explored in detail, it will become obvious that the procedure as a whole involves many different variables that affect the assessor and his/her procedure of gathering data about the child and, ultimately, analysis of these data and the reporting of that analysis. As the assessment proceeds, these variables become even more complex and interwoven in interaction with one another. These variables are considered separately in the initial discussion of the environmental background in which the assessment is carried out. Thereafter, however, these assessment procedures will be examined sequentially in order to emphasize the manner in which this complex of variables does develop. A recognition of this procedural process may help the assessor to keep track of the variables, to manage them, and even to take advantage of this sequence per se as further data in evaluation of the child's behavior.

As will soon be obvious, the variables that most significantly affect assessment are most commonly called "interpersonal relationships." Before examining the procedures of *assessment* it may be helpful to define this term operationally. First, there are the interactions between the child and the assessor—how the child views the assessment and the psychologist conducting it; how the psychologist regards this particular assessment and the child; how the behavior of the psychologist affects the child and his/her motivation and achievement; how the child and his/her problems, personality, behavior, and even performance and achievement affect the psychologist; and how they interact from the moment they meet. All of these interactions taken together constitute a major variable in the assessment process.

Yet this interaction between child and assessor is seldom an isolated experience for either of them, but it is nearly always affected by and embedded in a complex of other interpersonal relationships—directly and indirectly bearing on the assessment. The most important of these sets of interpersonal relationships is the one involving the child's parents, the child, and the psychologist. How the parents' attitudes, expectations, and behavior affect those of the child—and of the psychologist—and the relationship between child and psychologist, and how these in turn condition the parents' reactions constitute a second major issue in the assessment process. (This will be discussed in detail in this chapter.)

Third, it is necessary to consider how the relationships between these central figures are affected by and have effects upon many other persons concerned with the assessment and the welfare of the child. These include the person who refers the child for assessment, other parental authorities, staff colleagues of the psychologist who may or even may not be directly involved with the assessment, school, medical, and community authorities, and even at times siblings and peers of the child—as, for example, when the child is being assessed at school or in other institutional settings.

B.   THE ENVIRONMENTAL SETTING

1.   The Community

In the broadest dimension, both the relationship between child and psychologist and the purposes and import of the assessment are delimited by the nature of the community in which the psychologist works and the community in which the child lives (which are not necessarily the same). Attitudes toward being a psychologist as a profession and toward psychology as a science vary from community to community and in different segments of any one community. Most commonly psychological assessment is a middle-class phenomenon,

sponsored chiefly by the upper-middle class, utilized by a broad span of the middle class, and conducted by middle-class professionals. Although in such communities there may be a minority that has negative views about anything associated with mental health, for the most part, psychologists and their clients will usually be in agreement that such services are worthwhile and necessary.

Some communitites, however, even those that are predominantly middle class, barely tolerate anything associated with psychology—especially where the clinic is sponsored by some agency not directly under the aegis of the community, such as a university or a state government. In such settings the child and parents who seek psychological assessment run the risk of at least silent if not vocal disapproval from their respective peers. Although driven by dire necessity to seek these services, the clients may themselves regard the psychologist with grave reserve and feel considerable shame and guilt. At the other extreme is the community that hires the professional expert as a kind of shaman to solve a hidden agenda of problems, such as those described in *Crestwood Heights* (Seeley, Sim, and Loosley, 1956).

In other institutional settings, such as in the juvenile hall or welfare agency of public hospitals and clinics largely serving lower socioeconomic clients, the services are nevertheless mainly paid for by the middle- and upper-class taxpayers, who sit on the governing boards of these institutions and who expect the institution and its employees to foster middle-class standards and behavior in their work with their clients. Even where the professional attempts to bridge the gap between the section of the community that governs the institution and the clietele it serves, the lower-class client usually recognizes—albeit covertly or unconsciously—that the institution was set up with the idea of reforming and rehabilitating them away from their mores. Thus they may come overtly with hat in hand, being cooperative and obsequious, but also they may come with unspoken suspicion and resentment. The psychologist should be quite aware of the relationships between the institution and the community and between the power structure of the community that sponsors it and the clientele served.

Sometimes, such as in the isolated state hospital or institution for delinquents, the child may not even be a member of the community where the institution is located. For example, I was once employed in an institution that was the major employer in a small rural community—so that community consisted chiefly of the employees of the hospital. Yet the power structure of the community was most hostile toward the hospital and its patients, and it carried on legal and social war to attempt to drive the institution out!

2. The Nature of the Institution

The second factor in this general environment is the nature of the institution and the psychologist's position in it. In settings where the institution is generally run on democratic principles, with little or no competition between staff members and with a general problem-solving orientation, the assessment would be treated as another and important step in service to the child. In other settings where there are intrastaff power struggles or battle lines drawn along theoretical differences or personalitites, the psychologist's work may be hampered severely. The psychologist may feel it necessary to watch her/his step in conducting and reporting an assessment. If the child under consideration presents problems that might sharpen staff differences, the psychologist may have to take care that she/he does not unconsciously treat this particular child in a defensive way that might bias the observation. Insofar as is possible, the assessor should try to prevent such intrastaff difficulties from entering her/his relationship with the child and attempt to seek solutions for these problems in a more appropriate arena. One of the most difficult positions

for a psychologist is when she/he feels that her/his work will not be appreciated or will be disregarded by other staff members, so that she/he begins to go about her/his assessments in a listless manner. On the other side of the same coin is the tyro who feels that her/his observations constitute the only answers. In fact, the novitiate sometimes actually has both opinions of himself/herself. However, the psychologist who is oriented toward problem solution rather than her/his own status wins the respect of her/his colleagues in the long run.

The nature of the institution may also directly affect the attitudes and expectations of the child and his/her parents. If the agency is part of a line of bureaus through which the client must make application before being able to get service, he/she is often very frustrated and may thus arrive on the psychologist's doorstep feeling both negativistic and hopeless. Where the client has direct access to the agency—especially where that access includes a friendly and perceptive receptionist who is not made defensive by angry or distraught parents—the child and the family's expectations are more likely to be positive.

Many other aspects of the institution's public image may also affect the client's perception of it: its professional reputation, its location, its title, and the like. The assessor should be aware of these factors, and in his initial interview when inquiring how it was that the client sought help from this particular institution, he/she should be alert for indications in the client's response as to whether these factors are playing a part. For example, the middle-class parent whose financial status prevents seeking private care and who finds herself/himself in a dingy hallway at the back of the public-welfare building in front of a door labeled "Psychiatry Clinic" may feel very let down—and defensive. Or on the other hand, the family from the lower socioeconomic strata who make a long trip across town to the seemingly palatial new buildings of a university that is located in an upper-middle-class suburb may—after paying a parking fee and lining the old car among the newer ones and entering the marble halls—wonder in embarrassment what they are doing there! Such parents may even question whether their child's needs will be considered in such a setting. Very often it is necessary for the psychologist to be sufficiently aware of these attitudes and frustrations, and to allow the parent and child at least a few minutes to rest up after their efforts to get to the office and to ventilate briefly some of their difficulties in finding and adjusting to its surroundings. A pleasant waiting room, a helpful and cheerful receptionist, and the greeting given by the psychologist usually serve to ameliorate such negative first impressions.

3. The Assessment Room

The environmental aspect of the assessment that bears most immediately on the psychologist–child relationships is the room in which they work. The setting for an assessment should be one in which both the child and assessor can work comfortably— at ease and without distraction. The room where the assessor works should be located close enough to the clinic waiting room so that the fearful child can be reassured that her/his parent is near at hand, but far enough away so that he/she knows the parents is not listening. Ideally there should also be a supervised waiting room for children where they can stay during parent interviews. Child-sized lavatories and low-level drinking fountains should be included in plans for any clinic serving children. All of these environmental details make a child feel that the assessment situation has taken account of her/his physical needs and implies to the child that her/his psychological needs may also be met.

In building a new clinic, a room should be set aside for assessment purposes that is separate from either the office or playroom. It should not be much larger than 8 ft × 10 ft, so as not to give the child too much opportunity to move about, but it should be spacious enough to contain a worktable for the assessor's materials, a chair, a table

adjustable in height for the child to work on, and a chair appropriate to the child's size. This ideal room should be free of all other distracting materials. Assessment of children in the usual office setting has the disadvantage that the child may be attracted by many other objects that she/he may want to explore or ask about and to which the clinician may want to deny the child access or about which he/she may not want to have to explain. The assessor should not have to answer the telephone or protect his/her papers and books from the hyperactive and possibly destructive child. The child should not have to feel that he/she is in the adult's domain, for example, because of the formality of desks, file cabinets, bookcases, typewriters, and dictaphone equipment. A playroom is often at least equally distracting, unless it is entirely cleared of all play materials. Doll houses, dart boards, and "Bobo" punching bags are far more fascinating than most test materials, and they offer fine targets for the child who seeks to avoid the job of assessment. This ideal room should be brightly lighted, but preferably not with any source of flickering light (which can induce seizures in brain-damaged children). A window in any room does give a sense of openness and freedom, but it is not necessary. It should be draped or shaded, both to avoid distractions from the outside and the possibility of glare. Such a room—while as devoid as possible of things other than the work materials and furniture—need not be absolutely bleak. The walls may be painted in warm colors, preferably with washable paint and decorated with simple prints—or even children's drawings. If the room abuts on other rooms where the sound of a child's voice or of kicking feet or scraping furniture might be undesirable, soundproofing may be needed. Floors need not be carpeted, but they definitely should not be waxed or slippery for, no matter how children are warned, they tend to lean back in chairs, to push on the table, or otherwise slip and slide across waxed floors. An assessment session can come to an abrupt end when a child's chair slides from under him/her as he/she moves to the front edge of it to handle test materials on the table, only to crack his/her chin on the table's edge as he/she goes down!

The temperature of a room where one is working with children should be a few degrees lower than might be comfortable for an adult without a sweater or coat. For children's body temperatures tend to run a few degrees warmer than do adults' body temperatures, and they are too warm when the adult is just warm enough. The room should have a hook on which children's coats can be hung, so they can work free of encumbrances of jacket sleeves. If the room is in a hospital or school or an institution other than a purely psychological clinic, then it should be isolated as much as possible from the sights, sounds, and smells of the institution. It should be evident to children that they are in an assessment room—not a schoolroom and not a medical examining room.

All these may seem rather petty and evident details. Too often, however, assessments are deterred unnecessarily when the assessor attempts to work in quarters where both he/she and the child are continuously distracted and where the setting so intrudes on the child's consciousness that it affects his/her responses. For example, in the usual office setting, the child has only to look around him to name 28 words in one minute as required on an item of Year X of the Stanford-Binet. IQ or Rorschach responses or interview material may be deflected or deterred when a child sits in an adult chair, is half sliding off with her/his feet dangling, and is facing a window with the sun streaming into her/his face with a ballgame going on in the playground outside. Small wonder that she/he jumps to her/his feet and peers out the window when the assessor's office phone rings. Nor should one be surprised that the next response is contaminated by the distraction.

Of course such an ideal situation is seldom attained. If one does have to assess in an office, care should be taken to keep distractions to a minimum. Admittedly there is some advantage to working in a room where the assessor feels at home. If

his/her office is his/her castle where children can invade without causing undue anxiety, he/she may feel enough at ease and accustomed to the exigencies of his/her office that he/she can account for the distractions. I personally prefer to operate ensconced in my own "cubby hole," even though hyperactive children occasionally knock over my personal possessions, stare at my books, or stand on the chair to gaze out the window. To assess a small child, the typewriter and calculator are moved out, and a child's table and chair are brought in. The drapes are drawn, and the secretary takes the phone calls. Each time I assure myself that next year I will ask the clinic for a separate room for assessment.

Sometimes it is necessary for the assessor to leave his/her setting and assess the child elsewhere, for example, at a school, in a hospital room, at juvenile hall, or in the child's home. Even in these situations, it is sometimes possible to approximate the general conditions mentioned previously. For example, on a pediatric service it may be necessary to assess a child who cannot leave the bed. Even so, one can establish the atmosphere of an assessment situation by drawing the curtains around the bed, requesting the nurse—in front of the child—that there be no disturbance, and making sure that the usual nursing operations for the child's comfort have already been performed. In such instances the child may feel more at ease and even be pleased by the assessor's visit if, during the orientation, the assessor mentions in passing that since the child could not come to the office, the assessor has made this special trip to see the child.

C. THE ASSESSOR AS AN ENVIRONMENTAL VARIABLE

Last—but certainly not least—the assessor should be considered as part of the environmental setting. The impression given by her/his appearance, demeanor, and behavior often affects the attitudes of the child and parent toward the assessment.

Although any particular initial impression may change as the assessment proceeds, the assessor should be aware of the impressions made on clients in general. She/he should also be alert for clues from any particular client about the way the client is reacting to her/him as a person and how this may be affecting and shaping the assessment. This alertness to the sensitivities of the client, so basic in every step in assessment, thus requires that the psychologist to able to see and hear herself/himself.

1.   The Motivations of the Assessor

The primary and single motivation of the assessor must be the welfare of the individual child. This rule, as expounded in the ethical-standards statement of the American Psychological Association (1963) is most practical, because if the assessor has other motives—even as some hidden agenda—most children will sense such a double bill and react to it. Nearly all assessors would probably swear that they are advocates of the child and the child alone. It is my opinion that unfortunately too many assessors fail to examine or recognize their other motives. Such is especially true of psychologists employed in special agencies. Does not the assessor in a school have the interests of the teacher and especially the school administration at heart? How easily can the school psychologist be so neutral as to consider that it just might be a poor teacher or an inadequate school that troubles the child?

The psychologist employed by the juvenile court is automatically expected by the prosecution and judge to help determine the legal question of guilt and innocence (see Chapter 17). Children—espcially those knowledgeable of the law and police—know whom such an assessor represents and respond with "soch" (socially acceptable) responses.

If the budget of a public treatment center depends on the number of clients in treatment, is the assessor employed by this clinic likely to determine that a child does not need treatment? Or does this assessor begin with the assumption that the child is emotionally disturbed just because he or she has stepped into the assessor's office? Similarly, if a child has been referred by a psychiatrist to a psychologist in private practice for assessment, how free does this assessor feel to report that the child is "normal?" If the child thinks that the assessor's motive is to remove him or her from the normal classroom to a special class for "learning disabled" ("spaz" the children call them), or if the child believes the assessor is a "cop," or if the child finds out that the assessor is going to tell her/his parents to send her/him to a "shrink" and thus all her/his friends will know that they are "weird," this child with respond to that motivation of the assessor.

How should this question of the assessor's motivations and his/her relationship with the child in various situations be handled? The first step in any case is for the assessor to examine carefully his/her motives. Who is the client? The child? The parent? The school? The hospital? The court? Or all of these? Since the welfare of the child is without question primary, to whom else is the assessor obligated? When the assessor is clear in her/his mind as to these obligations, then it is necessary for her/him to clarify these relationships with the child. Thus the assessor may begin by relating the referral source to the child. For example, "Judge _____ asked me to talk to you. He and your attorney thought because my job is understanding boys and girls that I might be able to explain things to them for you." Or, "Your teacher and the school are very dissatisfied with your behavior. I'm supposed to find out what is really wrong and advise them. But I am most interested in how I might help *you* so that you would be more happy."

These words alone are seldom completely sufficient. The assessor's interest in the welfare of the child is conveyed in the phrasing of her/his questions and in the tone of voice in which the question is asked. Empathy for the child's feelings and sympathy for his/her plight are the best ways to gain the confidence of the child. An accusatory tone or even an emotinally neutral attitude is the quickest way to discourage rapproachment. In most instances the child is feeling miserable and is hoping that someone will pay attention to his/her needs. If the assessor is open with the child as to his/her intentions, the child is more likely to respond with confidence.

Although the overall, long-term motivation of the clinician is to aid in the development and welfare of his/her client, the immediate aim during assessment is actually *investigatory*. This does not at all mean of course that the interview needs to be conducted in a cold, impersonal, or inquistiorial manner. But it does mean that at this initial stage in a clinician's contacts with the child, the clinician may ask questions and explore feelings and attitudes in a manner that she/he might not use if she/he were conducting psychotherapy. There is a cliché in clinical psychology that "therapy begins with the first contact." Probably this is true, but even so, an investigatory attitude on the part of the clinician sets the stage for therapy. Such an investigation is vital to the clinician for it provides the initial data upon which she/he can formulate therapeutic hypotheses and goals. The child—even though he/she may be unable or unwilling to respond to these questions during an assessment interview—becomes aware that in the long run therapy will be dealing with *all* feelings, even those about which he/she is most anxious. Many of the things the child mentions or the assessor asks about during the assessment interview may not come up again for discussion until much later in therapy. This "working through," or relearning process of psychotherapy, however, is definitely *not* part of the assessment, and it should be avoided at this stage even if the child seems to want to engage in it. Not only would such therapeutic exploration interfere with the assessment, but the clinician does not at this point have enough data to know where to proceed with therapy. On the other hand, if a thorough assessment is not conducted, including introductory investigatory interviews, future therapy may be seriously impeded or misguided.

CASE 13

Jonah, an 11-year-old boy, volunteered during the initial interview that he slept very restlessly and had bad dreams. The assessor asked about the child's dreams and fears, which the child willingly discussed, and on the basis of these data plus other data from other techniques hypothesized that the child's sleeplessness was related to his difficulties in controlling his anger. However, the assessor did not explore the child's sleep habits or conditions. Several months later the child revealed that he usually slept with his mother. Surprised, the therapist asked why he had not mentioned this before. "You never asked!" replied the boy. Although the question "Do you sleep with your mother?" is far from a routine inquiry during assessment, simple questions about sleep habits—for example, "Who puts you to bed?" and "Do you have a bed or a room by yourself?"—might well have brought out this important fact and given a different emphasis to and more detail for the therapeutic hypotheses.

2. The Reactions of the Child

If the purposes and procedures of the assessment have been clarified with the child before commencing with any technique, the child will be at least somewhat aware of the assessor's aims. A child should be informed that the assessor is interested in what makes children happy—and what makes them unhappy, what they like and do not like, what is easy and what is difficult, and so on. Children's reactions to such information in an assessment situation vary widely. Some are so bound up in their own anger and negativism or their own fears that they barely hear such an introduction. Undoubtedly many children initially are at least mildly threatened with the realization that their hidden anxieties may be unmasked.

Most children, however, usually recover from this initial frank exposé of the assessor's intentions, and as rapport becomes more positive the child actually begins to feel even more at ease in the face of a straightforward approach. Nevertheless, the child's own preconceptions about the assessment in general and about responding in interviews in particular may not be assuaged even if the assessor explains his/her purposes. Those children who are experiencing considerable overt anxiety, who have complaints, "problems," or "unhappiness" may be quite eager to find a sympathetic listener. Other children—especially those who have learned through bitter experience to mistrust inquiring adults—may regard the interview as an intrusion on their privacy and "take the Fifth," refusing to testify against themselves. Some children persist in this throughout the assessment, so that about all one learns is the intensity and extent of their defensiveness.

While the child may well be able to block the assessor by diversion, negativism, or tears from getting direct statements, these attitudes and other interview behaviors constitute in themselves data about the child. In addition, since the chief purpose is to gather data about feelings and attitudes rather than "facts" per se, this interchange between assessor and child, which takes place throughout the assessment but particularly during interviews, constitutes a major source of data.

3. The Assessor's Appearance

Some aspects of the assessor's appearance, such as dress and grooming, may on first thought seem too superficial or picayune to warrant much consideration. In many agencies and institutions it almost goes without saying that the professional staff should conform to relatively conservative middle-class standards in their dress and behavior, even though their clients may not themselves come from the same background, or as is often the case with adolescents, be attempting to revolt against it. On the other hand, psychologists may

well argue that a person's dress and appearance are matters of personal choice and *should* make no difference—forgetting that they themselves often make inferences about their clients from just such clues! If there is any general rule about the psychologist's manner of dress, it is largely in terms of broad limitations. Insofar as is possible, the psychologist should avoid offending or startling his/her clients with his/her dress and grooming or, on the other extreme, setting them too much at a distance by an overly formal or stiff manner of dress or uniform. The psychologist working with children can and should be a bit more informal in dress than perhaps may be required when working with adult clients. Shirtsleeves and slacks for men or a housedress or slacks for women are not only excusable, but appropriate and acceptable. It is difficult sometimes for either child or psychologist to relax when dressed up for the adult office. The psychologist who adopts the white uniform of his medical colleagues is apt to be mistaken for the fearsome laboratory technician who stabs the child with a needle.

It is inevitable, nevertheless, that some client is going to take offense at the way a psychologist wears his/her hair or at other details of grooming. For example, if a psychologist enjoys wearing a beard, he must at least recognize that children will regard him as "different" and probably expect him to be different in his behavior and attitudes as well, which may have both advantages and disadvantages. The psychologist who is pregnant has to be aware of how her clients react to her appearance. Such deviations in the appearance of the psychologist may help to make some clients feel that his/her own deviations in behavior and attitude will be tolerated, but on the other hand, the compulsive parent or phobic child may recoil.

Although the psychologist may make some adjustments in dress and appearance, the best he or she can do about his/her physical build is to be aware of the client's reactions—and of their own feelings about their body image. Such self-awareness about one's own physique and attitudes toward it has special importance when dealing with children who are just forming their own images of themselves, are quite sensitive to such impressions, and what is more, are sometimes quite frank in mentioning them. Since psychologists come in all sizes, shapes, and colors, there is no way of avoiding this factor. Even "good-looking" psychologists may be at a slight disadvantage at times when the child who is disfigured or feels ugly fears he/she will not be understood or is jealous. The young and shapely woman psychologist may find herself regarded as seductive by boys or a potential object of envy by girls. On the other hand, the psychologist who suffers some physical deformity or handicap may not be at such a disadvantage as might be thought. Strangely enough, clinics who preach "hire the handicapped" too often express doubts about hiring a psychologist in a wheelchair or one who has a sensory defect only to find that most children, including those with emotional or social handicaps themselves, usually accept such obvious defects in the assessor. The role of the assessor from a racial minority and his/her effect on the client is discussed in detail in Chapter 16.

4.   The Assessor's Speech

Children also judge adults on how they sound—the tone, pitch, and volume of their voices, the speed with which they speak, their enunciation, pronunciation, and accent, and other peculiarities of speech. While a psychologist can look in the mirror to assess dress and appearance, it is sometimes more difficult for him/her to be aware of how he/she sounds. If for no other reason, it is therefore a good idea for the student to tape and listen to her/his own interviews. At times it may be necessary to learn to modulate one's speech, both to be more comprehensible to children or even to avoid distracting them by speech mannerisms. Too often the adult who is not used to working with or being around children unconsciously adopts an artifical

manner of speech—for example, a slightly saccharin tone of voice, increased volume (with the mistaken idea that a loud voice is needed to command the child's attention), an affected enunciation, or an attempt at what is thought of as child language. One should of course modify one's college vocabulary and use words that are comprehensible to the child, but this does not require "baby talk." Children expect the assessor to speak in normal adult fashion, albeit with words they understand.

Psychologists may be even less aware of the possible cultural and subcultural differences in language between themselves and the child. Where such differences are very marked, as when either speaks with a foreign accent, the difference may be forgiven by both, just as in the case of the obvious physical handicap. However, for example, the Bronx-born and Bronx-educated psychologist may be only partly aware of his/her communication difficulties in dealing with a child from an Ozark family, even though both have emigrated to California! Again, it may not be possible or even necessary for the psychologist to alter language habits completely. An attempt to imitate the child might seem quite artificial. It is necessary that psychologists be aware of cultural language habits, so that when communicating with a child from another subcultural background they can be flexible enough to use other words and phrases. It is equally important to be able to translate a child's phraseology and pronunciation. Above all, psychologists should be aware of the subtle but definite ethnocentric and sociocentric prejudices that surround speech and language differences. Not only should they avoid being caught up in the provincialism of the academic forum, but they should be able to appreciate the possible richness of expression of the child "from the streets" or the "hill country."

5.   The Assessor's Demeanor and Physical Contacts with the Child

As to the psychologist's general demeanor, she/he should interact with the child in a relatively relaxed and informal but adult manner so that both feel comfortable. One of the most commonly discussed aspects of this interaction concerns physical contact. Since physical contact between adult and child is more common, at least in our culture, than between adults, it does leave the door open for the adult to take the child's hand, to put an arm around the child, to pick children up and comfort them when necessary, or even to take a playful poke at them. Children often use physical contact or motor behavior as one means of communication. Whether the assessor should initiate such contact or even engage in it if initiated by the child must be carefully considered in each instance. One good clue as to how the child accepts or uses such contact may be gained from the initial handshake. Some children refuse to shake hands and want no part of physical contact with a strange adult—at least to begin with. From others one may obtain every sort of handshake from a limp, wet paw that barely touches, to a vigorous yank that practically invites a wrestling match.

Some children may seem to invite such contact but then shy away from it— suddenly embarrassed—seeming to play a game of seduction and rejection. Others may use such contact as a method of detracting from and avoiding verbal communications. As a rule, the child does not necessarily expect the adult to respond to physical contact with much more than a casual recognition, that is, in adult fashion, unless the child is in dire need of physical comfort at the moment. For example, a 4-year-old was brought to my office from the pediatric ward and left for a few minutes by himself in the cold hall, dressed in his pajamas and sitting in the wheelchair. Suddenly he burst into uncontrollable tears. When he was picked up and cuddled for a moment, the storm quickly passed. This physical contact created an appropriate and warm beginning to the assessment session. In contrast, when the 5-year-old girl stood on the chair and with a sly smile jumped onto the psychologist, grabbing him with both arms around his neck and both legs

around his waist, the admittedly surprised psychologist gently set her down and asked, "Hey! What's going on here?" Although the child did not directly answer him, she showed no signs of requiring further physical contact, but accepted his friendly but businesslike approach to the assessment and became involved in the tasks set down before her.

On the part of the psychologist, some introspection is necessary concerning her/his needs and feelings about physical contact with children. Undoubtedly and quite appropriately, many psychologists work with children because they enjoy the emotional rewards children often offer, including physical contact. Normally an adult enjoys having a child take his/her hand, give him/her a hug, engage in a momentary physical tussle, or finding the child receptive to his/her overtures. Thus it is tempting to initiate such contact, and it is understandable that an adult may feel a momentary hurt if rejected. Of course the psychologist cannot depend exclusively on professional contacts for such satisfactions but instead must limit himself/herself to the needs of the child. The corollary to this rule is that the psychologist should again look at his/her own feelings if he/she cannot relax and accept physical contact from the child when it is appropriate.

In summary then, the assessor behaves most appropriately as a relaxed and comfortable adult. He/she need not speak or adopt the demeanor of a child. He/she should be prepared to offer comfort to the child—like any adult—if it is required, or to repel in adult fashion an attack on his/her person. Psychologists should be accepting of the child's natural contacts, but they should not depend on them.

D.   THE REFERRAL AND THE SPECIFIC PURPOSES OF THE ASSESSMENT

The opening key to any assessment is the nature of the referral, that is, the questions that the person who requests the assessment* has concerning the child and that the psychologist is expected to investigate. Finding out what these questions are and what kind of answers are expected is the first step. When one has a collaborative working relationship with other professional colleagues who also have some understanding of the general principles of child development, these questions may be stated clearly and relevantly, with an awareness of the advantages and limitations of assessment procedures. Referrals, however, frequently come from someone who has only passing knowledge of what assessment can and cannot answer and who may not phrase the question in the professional terms that the psychologist might prefer. Much of the time the main and only reason children are referred is that the persons dealing with them are puzzled by their behavior and symptoms and have at best some vague and ill-defined hypotheses concerning them.

Often the referrant has several questions in mind. She/he may want the psychologist to provide both some possible explanations of the child's behavior and some more clearly defined working hypotheses. Sometimes the question is even broader, for example, "How is this child progressing?" Usually the referrant also has some practical, decision-making questions. For example, should the child be placed in a special school? What kind of treatment, if any, does she/he need? What kind of care and in what kind of setting? At least a brief discussion with the referrant is usually necessary to understand what is expected and—sometimes—to clarify what pertinent information an assessment may provide.

Not infrequently a referrant has questions that cannot be answered and at the same time does not realize that an assessment might help with other aspects of the child's case that she/he has not thought to bring to the psychologist. Where the psychologist is a member of a staff that is working collaboratively on the child's prob-

lems, it is a good idea to discuss the referral in a staff conference in order to clarify the questions of everyone involved. In other situations the psychologist may have to contact several persons independently. For example, if a teacher has advised a parent about school problems the child may be having and has suggested that the child be taken to the pediatrician who then requests the assessment from the psychologist, the psychologist may need to contact physician, parent, and teacher.

Two questions face the assessor at the time of referral: (1) How does the assessor obtain the information needed in the referral? (2) What information is usually necessary? Before going into the details of these two questions, one variable that is central to both should be considered—the relationships between the referrant and the assessor.

1.   The Relationships Between Referrant and Assessor

The assessor's attitudes toward the referral are derived from interactions with the referrant. These past experiences with the referrant may well affect the assessor's initial attitudes toward the child and the assessment. A referral from the hospital superintendent or the president of the Board of Education might well be given different attention with different emotional reactions by the assessor than if the referrant were a ward nurse or a substitute teacher. A referral from a friendly colleague—one who "appreciates the contributions" of the assessor—would certainly be more welcome than an "order" to "give tests" from some administrator who never lets the psychologist know how his/her ideas and recommendations are received. The assessor may well feel freer to inquire further about the needs of the referrant who is a friendly colleague with whom the psychologist has collaborated for a number of years than some stranger with whom the psychologist has had only a single telephone contact and who initially releases little information. The psychologist

---

*For want of a better term, this person will be called the *referrant*.

thus should consider whether such natural biases, which are present in almost any referral, are possibly preventing her/him from questioning the referral further, either because the relationship with the referrant is too distant or perhaps too close. Most of all, the assessor should take pains to distinguish this relationship with the referrant from the pending relationship with his/her clients.

The relationship between referrant and psychologist may be reflected by the methods used to obtain information about the child. Most agencies and institutions have some kind of formal referral sheet or card, such as is shown in Figure 7.1. This form—in addition to asking for certain identifying data about the client and other facts that might affect the assessment—leaves space for the referrant to state some of the general and specific reasons for the referral, the working "diagnosis" or impressions, and the hypotheses that she/he hopes the psychologist will be ble to test or at least add information about. By and large, these formal written communications between referrant and psychologist are quite helpful. They are particularly helpful if the psychologist has given some thought to making up the referral card so that the referrant can understand quite clearly and definitely what the psychologist wants to know, and if the referrant knows how to and bothers to state his/her answers on this sheet equally clearly. Referral forms, however, are too often given little thought by either party. They frequently show signs of hasty construction, containing vague headings without any instructions. Understandably, the busy physician, teacher, or social worker—commonly disliking the flood of forms he/she has to fill out—may give this referral sheet only perfunctory attention.

Personal contact between psychologist and referrant is thus usually necessary, even when the generally acceptable written form has been devised. In such contacts, while using the referral card, the psychologist should make clear her/his interest in the specific problems that face the referrant. What information does the referrant

need that is not provided from other data about the child? What decisions does the referrant have to face about the client?

What is most often important and not always easy to discover is the referrant's attitudes toward the client and relationships with him/her? For example, a teacher faced with a class troublemaker, a judge who must pass sentence, a pediatrician who specializes in bone-growth problems and is uncomfortable about emotional problems of children, or possibly a minister with a missionary zeal to save this child from his divorced parents? Has the referrant already made up his/her mind about what is "wrong" with the client and what he/she is going to do, merely wanting the psychologist to confirm his/her opinion? Or might he/she only thinly veil hopes of passing the responsibility for all decisions and future care of the child to the psychologist without really releasing any authority? Quite often a referral contains some such hidden agenda, which is not recorded on any referral card and which at most is mentioned casually in passing by the referrant. In a personal contact, however, the psychologist should politely but nevertheless directly discuss such factors with the referrant. Even though the contact between them may be relatively brief, the psychologist using his/her interviewing techniques can usually establish how the referrant feels about the child and the assessment. In many instances one or both parents are involved in the referral, and in some cases they are the main or even the only referrants. Determining the nature of the referral in this instance will be discussed later in a separate section of this chapter.

2.   The Referral Data

The basic information that the psychologist needs at the time of referral is listed in Figure 7.1. This "model" referral form is admittedly much longer than that used in most agencies or institutions and would be most appropriately filled out by the psychologist in discussion with the refer-

Your file # _____   Date referred: _____

Child's name: _____
          Last   First   Middle

By what name or nickname is the child usually addressed?

_____

Date of the child's birth _____

Name of person(s) or institution with whom the child is currently residing:

_____

      Address: _____

      Telephone: _____

      Relationship to the child:_____

Father's name:

_____

      Home address: _____

      Home phone: _____

      Business address: _____

      Business telephone: _____

Mother's name:

_____

      Home address: _____

      Home telephone: _____

      Business address: _____

      Business telephone: _____

Name of the person or institution who has legal guardianship of the child:_____

_____

      Address and telephone, if different

      than above: _____

_____

Name of the school the child is currently attending: _____

      Address: _____

      Telephone: _____

      Principal: _____

      Teacher: _____

Name of the child's physician: _____

      Address: _____

      Telephone: _____

Name of any other persons concerned with the child's care and welfare who are concerned with this referral: _____

      Address: _____

      Telephone: _____

Name of person who should be contacted for appointment: _____

      Address: _____

      Telephone: _____

Who has been advised that this referral is being made:

_____

_____

What have they been advised regarding the purposes and the nature of the referral:

_____

_____

What has the child been told regarding the purposes and the nature of the referral:

_____

_____

Prior studies: Has the child been previously assessed psychologically? If so, where:

_____

Address of clinic, hospital, or psychologist

      When: _____

      Date(s) of prior assessment(s)

If copies of reports of prior assessments are available, please attach them to this referral.

Reasons for the Referral

Please summarize on the reverse of this sheet or on a separate sheet: (a) Under what circumstances and for what reasons did the child come to your attention? (b) What kinds of problems and/or symptoms does the child present? (c) What are your findings and impressions? (d) What questions are there concerning the child's care, training, treatment, and disposition? (e) What are the specific questions regarding the child's psychological functioning?

Conditions Affecting Assessment

What physical handicaps does the child have?

_____

_____

What medications is child receiving and how might they affect his responses?

_____

Figure 7.1 Model referral form.

What speech or language handicaps does the child have? _____

Who will be responsible for payment of the fees?

_____

Are there financial limitations which should be considered regarding the fees?

_____

To whom should reports of findings be sent?

_____

Has permission been obtained for the release of the assessment report?

_____

Referrant's name_____

Position_____

Address and phone_____

_____

Figure 7.1 *(continued)*

rant. To begin with, if the child is referred by any agency or institution, the assessor needs to know the file number, if any, used by that institution, so that his/her report will be properly identified. (Large agencies and schools or hospitals often have several children with the same name.) The child's exact legal name should be obtained. Sometimes a child is known by several different names. For example, he/she may legally bear the name of a divorced or deceased father, but also use the surname of a stepfather even though never formally adopted. Such information is necessary if only because it may have a bearing on the child's psychological as well as legal identity. The name or nickname by which the child is usually addressed is needed so that the psychologist will know what to call the child. An assessment can easily get off on the wrong footing if the child is inadvertently addressed by a formal name that he/she seldom uses or might even dislike. Even so, it is wisest to check this information with the child on the first meeting: "What do most people call you? What do you like to be called? Is it all right if I call you _____?"

The date of the child's birth should also be rechecked at the time of the first appointment with both parent and child. Sometimes records differ completely about birthdates, or parents' memories are vague, and such differences need to be resolved before assessment can proceed. It is of course often of interest why a birthday is in error. For example, parents who are anxious to place the child in school at an early age have been known to add an extra year to the child's age when entering him in kindergarten, giving the school a false birthdate of a few months to a year earlier; several years later, when the child is having difficulty at school or home, the parent may give the correct date to the psychologist, forgetting that the school has another date. Even if such a parent continues to falsify the child's birthdate, the child of school age will likely know and give his/her correct age and birthday (if not year).

Since many children referred for assessment may not currently be living with their parents, it is necessary on any referral form to allow space for several different addresses and names. Item 7 on this model form asks with whom and where the child is currently living, and their relationship with the child. Additionally, one may need to know the name(s) and address(es) and telephone number(s) of the parents so that they may be contacted if necessary for further information about the child. (Where the child is residing with his parents, it would not be necessary to fill in Items 8 and 9). Since legal guardianship may not lie in the hands of either parent or even in the hands of the persons currently caring for the child (as in the case of foster homes under court order), it is a good idea to note who is legally responsible for the child; in any instance it is necessary to obtain permission from the legal guardian before beginning an assessment. If the legal guardian (or, in the case of a public agency or court, a representative of the agency) does not bring the child to the psychologist in person, thus giving verbal permission, the psychologist is legally bound (in most states and countries) to obtain written permission from the guardian before examining any minor.

Identifying data about the child's school is always valuable but becomes of primary importance when the child has originally been referred by the school or is presenting school difficulties. Similarly, it is often vital to know from the very beginning of the psychologist's contacts with the child who is responsible for her/his medical care, his pediatrician or family physician. Sometimes even before assessment begins it may be necessary to contact either the school or the child's physician. In such instances, it is usually necessary for the psychologist to obtain written permission from the parent or guardian for release of school or physician records. Figure 7.2 shows a model form for obtaining permission to procure such information which, when signed by the child's legal guardian, can be mailed to the school or physician with a cover letter stating the kinds of information needed.

Not infrequently, persons are also involved in the referral other than the parents, school, or physician, such as other close relatives, ministers, attorneys, or agencies other than the one making the

To: (name of physician, school, or social agency)

This is to give my permission for the release of any or all information from your records

concerning _____
                    Name of child

to _____
        Name of the clinic or the psychologist

_____
              Parent or guardian

_____
        Date

Figure 7.2 Model for obtaining permission for the release of confidential material.

referral. Their names, addresses, telephone numbers, and relationship to the child should also be recorded.

Finally, among all these names, the one of most immediate importance is the name, address, and telephone number of the person whom the psychologist needs to contact in order to make an appointment for the child. Sometimes this person may not be any of the above! Along with this the psychologist needs to knw who has been advised by the referrant that the referral is being made and what the referrant has advised these persons about the purpose and nature of the referral.

Equally important of course is what the child has been told. Some of our professional colleagues—those used to working in close collaboration with psychologists—are aware of the necessity of clarifying with the parent and child the reasons they are asking them to come for an assessment and in general what they may expect. In instructing medical students, I suggest that the student tell both the child and the parent that she/he is making this referral and that it is to help her/him better understand the child's problems and symptoms. Further, the student is advised that he/she need not mention "tests" per se, partly because other techniques may also be used and partly because this word is so often misunderstood by both child and parent. Instead it is suggested that she/he merely ask them to see the psychologist "who is interested in how children understand and do things." If the child or parent seems anxious to know more about the examination, they should be referred to the psychologist for further information. If they ask specifically about tests, they should be told that tests may be part of the assessment, but that the psychologist is most interested in how the child is developing and "getting along." Similarly, parents may be advised to tell the child directly that he/she is going to see a psychologist, that the psychologist is a person "interested in how children do things, understand things, and the things which make children happy or unhappy."

Furthermore, the parent should tell the child the reasons he/she believes the assessment is necessary. In this regard, I usually advise parents to be fairly direct but at the same time supporting and to say, for example, "You know all the trouble you've had with _____ (school, bedwetting, stealing, etc.) which we've not really understood. Your (doctor, teacher, parole officer) tells us that a psychologist may be able to help us both understand better what is the matter and how things may be helped." Although such direct information may create other resistances or raise further questions in the child's mind, the child who has at least this general orientation is usually better prepared and less resistant than the one who is told little or nothing or is told that she/he is going "to get a mental examination."

The next item on the referral sheet— *Prior studies*—tells the psychologist whether the child has had a previous assessment, thus indicating whether the child is familiar with the procedure. If there has been such a study and the report is available to the referrant, the psychologist may want to inquire further as to why such a study needs to be repeated. What were the purposes of the prior assessment? Is it out of date? Have there been changes in the child's behavior since the previous assessment? How did the child react to the prior assessment? How might he/she feel about being reassessed? In many instances the psychologist may want to obtain a report of any prior assessments and review them in planning the reassessment.

The central and most important part of the referral is contained under the heading *Reasons for referral.* Here the psychologist hopes to obtain a concise but definitive statement of the child's problems, the referrant's view of them, and the questions that the referrant poses for the assessment. How did the child come to the attention of the referrant and for what reasons? What kinds of problems and symptoms did the referrant discover and what were her/his findings and impressions regarding them?

What decisions have to be made about the child concerning his/her care, training, treatment, or possible disposition? In these questions the psychologist seeks to get a preliminary view of the child as seen by the referrant.

None of these questions necessarily asks the referrant to pose the problems in psychological terms. For example, a probation officer might state that the child came to his/her attention because of an infraction of the law—often one of a series of such infractions. Or that he/she had found out that the child was also failing at school, was a truant frequently, and was in serious conflict with her/his parents, or that the parents were about to get a divorce, and so on. The parole officer may be requested to recommend to the court whether the child should be removed from the home, whether she/he needs to be placed in an institution for juvenile delinquents, whether she/he needs remedial education. The final question under this heading gives the referrant an opportunity to phrase those questions in psychological terms. Thus the parole officer might ask in response to this last question: "Does the child have sufficient stability to adjust in a proposed foster home? Does he/she have enough intellectual ability and motivation to succeed in public school if he/she were removed from the emotional stress at home? Does he/she show any guilt over his-her actions? Are his/her crimes a part of some overall emotional disorder?" Such questions do not necessarily limit the psychologist's investigations, but at least they will orient him/her to some of the questions that the referrant has considered and pave the way for better and continued communication between them.

The final series of questions on this model referral form is concerned with possible practical limitations on the assessment of which the assessor must be aware before beginning an evaluation. She/he needs to know whether the child has any physical handicaps, especially in vision, hearing, or motor coordination that might have to be accounted for in seection of her/his techniques. Parents should be advised that a child with even a mild visual handicap should bring his/her glasses. With the widespread use of various psychopharmaceuticals today, the psychologist needs to know if any medications are being given to the child and what kinds of effects these are having. Children vary so widely in their responses to drugs that it is always necessary to know how the child in question is reacting. Especially in a hospital situation, the psychologist should learn to check thoroughly on what medical, surgical, or other procedures the child has been experiencing during the hours prior to the assessment. Any child who has spent the morning undergoing exhaustive medical examinations—X rays, EEG's, and so forth —is usually in no condition for an afternoon of psychological tests. The child who has had a barium examination, a spinal tap, or some other extensive examination that seriously affects her/his whole system may need at least 24 hours to recover before she/he is in condition for psychological assessment.

Although this referral form does not provide space for notes regarding other kinds of stresses that the child may be experiencing, the psychologist should be alert for any indications of such stresses also. For example, in any institutional setting the psychologist as a member of the staff should be aware if the child was—for example—recently subjected to punishment, in a fight with other children, feeling very dejected because his parents failed to visit, and the like. Under such circumstances it might be best to postpone the appointment with the child for a short time. If an appointment has already been arranged, the psychologist might mention that he/she is aware of these extenuating events and offer the possibility of postponing the appointment, leaving the choice to the child. On the other hand, some children might actually see and use the assessment as a means of diverting their feelings and attention away from the immediate stress.

Information about the language the child speaks or is used to speaking at home and how well she/he speaks or understands it is of course vital to planning the assessment. Assessment procedures will be quite different when evaluating a child who speaks only a language that is foreign to the assessor or who cannot be understood clearly in any language. Many young children from bilingual homes may appear to speak the language of the community, but in fact have considerable difficulty either in understanding it or communicating in it. If the assessor has any hint that a second language is used in the home, he should inquire further about it (see Chapter 8).

The next two questions are concerned with the setting of fees. Although the fee probably will not be set on the basis of this preliminary information, the response to these items will serve to forewarn the psychologist of possible difficulties. Occasionally parents who are in financial straits or whose income is limited may fear that they cannot meet whatever fees may be charged. They may be too proud to discuss the matter and use some other excuse for avoiding an appointment. If the psychologist is aware of this difficulty, she/he may be able to bring up the matter with the parents when making the first appointment and discuss the possibilities of an adjustment or delay in fees.

The final questions in the referral deal with distribution of the psychologist's final report of the assessment. Sometimes only the referrant needs a report. In other instances, several other persons should or will want to be advised of the psychologist's findings. If persons other than the referrant are to be sent reports, the referral may have to be expanded to obtain further information about the questions and interests ofthese other persons. Moreover, if someone other than the referrant is to receive a report, the psychologist may need the permission of the child's guardian, since the report is legally confidential information. In many states the psychologist's report—like medical data—is legally the property of the client (unless it is obtained by a governmental agency). Permission to release the report to anyone, including the referrant, should be obtained in advance.

E. PLANNING THE ASSESSMENT

On the basis of the preliminary data from the referral, the assessor can construct some beginning hypotheses about the case that will in part determine subsequent procedures and his/her choice of techniques. By studying the data collected thus far, she/he can surmise what some of the important psychological variables may be. The working hypotheses may be based on the identifying information, the reasons for referral, or the circumstances surrounding the referral. The following cases illustrate how such working hypotheses are derived.

CASE 14

Dr. Smith, a staff psychiatrist, telephoned to request an assessment on Leslie, who was being considered for admission as a patient in the outpatient clinic. The date of the referral was January 15, the parents having first contacted the clinic on January 5. Leslie, who more commonly called Lee, was born on December 25, 14 years previously. He was residing with his mother and stepfather at an address in an upper-middle-class section of a large city. Business phones were listed for both the mother and stepfather, and the psychologist was advised to contact the mother at her office. The parents' last name was not the same as that used by Lee. The mother was listed as legal guardian. Lee was beginning the ninth grade in a private boys' school. The names of his teacher and principal had not been ascertained, nor was the name of the child's pediatrician known. However, both the teacher and pediatrician were interested in this referral, according to the mother, since both had urged her to seek psychiatric help for Lee.

Both Lee and his mother had been told

respectively by the psychiatrist and the social worker at the clinic that Lee would need to have an appointment with the psychologist as a further step in assessing the nature of his problems. Customarily this psychiatrist told children, "I can understand some of your problems by talking them over with you, and our social worker can similarly see how your mother feels about them. However, it is also helpful to us to see how people do things and think about things. This is why I want to meet our psychologist who will talk to you too and give you some things to work with and think out." Lee had accepted the referral without comment or question. His mother also agreed and informed the social worker that Lee had been given some psychological tests at the local children's hospital about three years ago, when he was hospitalized after being knocked unconscious in a bicycle accident.

As to the reasons for referral, Dr. Smith reported that Lee had been brought to the clinic by his mother because the school had reported to her that Lee was made very anxious by any form of competition, and that he would easily become enraged or would burst into tears during sports activities or when reciting in class. Shortly before the holidays he had become so excited and upset over a football game in which he had been the star player that despite the fact that his team won the championship he burst into tears, ran from the field, and hid for an hour. When found by the coach he seemed quite confused. He thought the team had lost and that it was his fault. His stepfather, who had encouraged him in his athletics and was extremely proud of his prowess, was very worried. The mother wondered if sports had not been overemphasized by the stepfather and if Lee perhaps should withdraw a bit from sports for the spring semester. Moreover, Lee's grades had fallen markedly over the past two years, and he had barely passed all his subjects the past semester, although he had been a slightly better student up to the sixth grade. His grades were even more of a concern since his twin brother—Lester who was known as "Les"—had maintained a B average all along. Les, however, had not matched Lee's athletic record, although he too was quite active in sports. The parents had at first ignored the school's suggestion that Lee might have a serious emotional problem and decided that the whole incident arose from too much investment in sports and the "big game."

At home they had noticed no signs of emotional disturbance in Lee, whom they saw as a model boy, usually obedient, although showing some signs of adolescent arguing back, and being mildly mischievious. "An all-around American boy," his stepfather remarked. They denied any evidence of sibling rivalry between the twins, who had always been "very close." Both were very proud of their 2-year-old half sister whom they seemed to adore. However, during the holidays Lee continued to appear morose and irritable around the house, flying off the handle" whenever his stepfather spoke to him and picking quarrels with Les. He was adamant that the family should not hold the traditional Christmas birthday party.

Finally, much to his mother's dismay, Lee secretly contacted his father, whom his mother had divorced six years previously and whom Lee had not seen for three years, and made arrangements to visit him on Christmas Day. After the holidays, Lee refused to return to school; he asked to be transferred to the local public school and hinted that if more consideration was not given to his desires, he might choose to go live with his father. Lee's mother took him first to their pediatrician who referred them to the clinic.

Dr. Smith had had two interviews with Lee. The staff social worker, Mrs. Morse, had one interview with Lee's mother. Dr. Smith found Lee unwilling to discuss any of the problems his mother had mentioned; instead, he denied that there was anything really to be concerned about and complained that his mother was making too "big a deal" out of everything. He admitted that he did get a bit excited over football, but the football season was over now and there would be no more trouble; he now could return to his studies and catch up. He did not mention his visit to his father or the birthday-party incident. When asked about them, he became a bit irritated and argued that it was just that he and Les both felt that they had outgrown "those babyish" birthday parties. As to his visit with his father, he shrugged and said he just had suddenly wanted to see his father, that he was sorry he'd upset his mother, that he had no intention of seeing his father any more. "He's just a drunk and a bum, like mother always said." He averred that he really loved his mother and "dad" (stepfather), and had no intention of leaving them, "though I really could if I wanted; the judge said so." As to the school, he admitted he had seriously considered changing to the public school where many of his neighborhood friends attended, but Les had about talked him out of it now. He added with a smile that if the psychiatrist really wanted to help him he should talk his mother out of continuing the piano lessons that the twins hated.

Dr. Smith's initial impression was that Lee had really reached some kind of impasse both at school and home just before the holidays and thereafter, but had reconstituted enough so that when faced with the possibility of having his difficulties examined, he was able to maintain that they were unimportant. Dr. Smith particularly wondered if Lee might be struggling to form some identity separate from his twin, perhaps struggling extrahard to establish his own masculine role (which might account for the visit to his father), and perhaps be indirectly beginning a rebellion against the stepfather. Dr. Smith noted that neither twin had shown much adolescent interest in the opposite sex, but suspected that this might be the real reason that Lee wanted to go to the coeducational public school. He did wonder about Lee's intellectual functioning, since the school grades had been low, but was more interested in Lee's fantasy and in his "basic personality structure and emotional development." The application for treatment was to be considered two weeks hence, at which time it was hoped the psychologist would have completed the assessment. Dr. Smith planned to have at least one more interview session with Lee, and perhaps one with Les. Mrs. Morse, the social worker, planned to continue contacts with Mrs. R, Lee's mother, especially to obtain more information about the family's functioning and Lee's developmental history. Dr. Smith said the staff would try to decide whether (1) to let the application drop at present, in view of Lee's attitudes; (2) to conduct individual psychotherapy with Lee, with perhaps intermittent collaborative contacts with the mother; or (3) perhaps to consider family therapy sessions with both parents and the twins.

The psychologist's first response to the referral was to ask if, in view of the last possibility, it might not be helpful to include Les and perhaps the parents in the psychological assessment, to which Dr. Smith readily agreed. Mrs. R had already expressed concern that Lee was was singled out for psychiatric attention, and although she had no questions about Les, had asked if he might be seen at least once so that Lee would not feel he was "different." Dr. Smith also believed that the R's would be cooperative if asked to participate in the assessment.

Next, the psychologist reviewed the referral data, particularly the findings and impressions of Dr. Smith and the questions he had posed. Considering these data, Dr. Smith's formulations seemed to the psychologist to be reasonable as tentative hypotheses, but for the purpose of assessment, it might be necessary to rephrase them slightly to permit testing of them by his techniques. Considering the problem in terms of development, Lee at 14 was at an age when adolescent "identity"—social, emotion, and biological—normally is being formed. The question could then be posed: Might there be any evidence to suggest that this normal identity formation was not proceeding smoothly for Lee? If so, what might be the nature of this possible identity crisis? What factors might be contributing to it? How severe a disruption might it be? Was it, as Lee and his family maintained, possibly a disruption related to immediate stresses for which he had now recovered? Might these stresses have caused a continued disruption? Or might the symptoms be a sign of some more long-standing developmental disturbance that came to the fore under these pressures? If no identity crisis seemed evident, what alternate hypotheses might be entertained about Lee's symptoms? The psychologist considered the possibility that Lee might have already formulated some unconscious image of himself, for example as an Esau, the nonintellectual brother whose identity depended on physical accomplishment and who was beginning to demand his "pottage." In terms of classic psychiatric diagnosis, might Lee have already developed a "character neurosis?"

Another possibility was that Lee might not yet be struggling with adolescent problems at all but instead still be psychologically in latency, perhaps even attempting to prolong the little-boy stage in order to avoid the problems of adolescence. Certainly some of Lee's reactions, his hyperexcitement and his tears, would not be considered quite so unusual on the part of a child of 7 or 8. Last, but certainly not least, was the possibility that Lee's outburst represented a release from strained but covered family relationships that though not affecting the normal development of an identity, might constitute a developmental problem per se, that is, a freeing of the self from the childhood parental and sibling bonds.

As the psychologist thought over these possibilities, he recognized that they were not necessarily alternatives, and that it was quite possible that the evidence might support more than one of them, or a combination of them. For example, it might be possible that Lee was trying to maintain a preadolescent adjustment in order to avoid the kind of identity he was already beginning to formulate in response to the family stresses.

Added to these broad developmental hypotheses were several more specific questions. Might Lee be having rather specific problems in relatively isolated or autonomous functioning, such as the handling of social stresses or in competitive situations, rather than some broad developmental progress? The question of Lee's intellectual functioning might or might not be related to his overall development or his identity but, at least in view of the practical question posed by Dr. Smith concerning Lee's academic progress, assessment of Lee's intellectual functioning did seem called for. Then there was the hint that Lee had previously needed an assessment after a head injury. Had there then been some behavioral evidence of a perceptual-motor dysfunction or other defect? If so, had it persisted and might it be playing a part in Lee's difficulties in emotional control and academic achievement?

A telephone call to the children's hospital revealed that Lee had been given several psychological tests shortly after his accident. He was found to be functioning intellectually at a low average level, but there were no indications of any gross intellectual or perceptual-motor dysfunction, and it was concluded that at least behaviorally his accident had left no immediate sequelae. A permit for release of information was signed by the parents to obtain a complete written report of these findings.

With these data and hypotheses in mind, the psychologist turned to choosing his techniques and mapping out his procedures. If he had had time to gather as much pertinent data as was feasible, identical assessment techniques for all members of the family might have been worthwhile. However, limited by time, the psychologist decided to devise a similar procedure for the twins, a more limited assessment for the parents and, unless time permitted, to bypass assessment of the half sister. For the twins, he decided to allot two two-hour sessions each. Since all family members (except the sister) were being interviewed by other staff members and their data were

available to him, he decided to keep his interviews at a bare minimum, dealing chiefly with their feelings about the assessment. For the twins he decided to begin with a structured test of intelligence, since Lee was reputed to function with a little less anxiety in structured situations. The Wechsler Intelligence Scale for Children seemed a good choice, since on the Binet a child ends in utter failure, which might be too anxiety provoking to Lee. On the other hand, several samples of Lee's reaction to failure, followed by successes on subsequent subtests, might help to evaluate his reaction to failure a bit better than on the Binet. The WISC also lends itself more readily to analysis of perceptual motor functioning and details of thought processes than the Binet. Ending the WISC on the coding subtest (where failure is less obvious), the child has the pencil in his hand, and it would be natural to go on to the Memory for Designs or the Bender-Gestalt for a further check on perceptual motor functions, perhaps adding in the Porteus Mazes.

The second session might begin with the Rorschach, both to complete the assessment of perceptual functioning and to begin study of the boys' emotional functioning. For study of their fantasies, the psychologist considered Lee's reputation for preferring motor expression over verbalization and thus decided to use the MAPS. He hoped to end this session with two self-administered techniques: the P-F Study, since there was specific question of Lee's attitudes toward frustration, and the Bene-Anthony Family Relations Test, since there was the question about the family structure. After completing these individual assessments of the twins, the psychologist planned to bring both parents and the boys together for further study of the relationships in a two-hour session. He thought it might be possible to have each family member (1) take the Edwards Personal Preference Schedule, (2) describe themselves and every other member of the family on the Leary Interpersonal Checklist, and (3) make drawings of a male, a female, and of a family. It was hoped from this latter battery of techniques to obtain data about the need patterns within the family, the perceptions each held of the other, their relative positions in Leary's ''love-dominance'' scheme, and all the perceptions of each regarding sex roles and identity both for themselves and for a family.

Another type of referral, with different complications is illustrated in the following case.

Case 15

Tina, age about 5, was referred for assessment by a children's care center operated by a religious order to whom the psychologist served as an outside consultant. No referral form was used, but the case was reviewed with the center's social worker. Tina had first come to their attention approximately five years previously when, as an infant, she was abandoned in a basket at the doorstep of the church. She appeared very malnourished and ill and was hospitalized for the next several months in the hospital operated by the church. The pediatrician estimated her age at that time to be approximately 3 to 4 months. Medical examination revealed that, in addition to the malnutrition, she was suffering from a severe amibiotic infection, disrupting her entire digestive and excretory functioning. She had not been kept clean, and her skin was covered with small sores. With special diet and medication, these conditions cleared up in about six weeks and she grew rapidly. Further medical studies indicated that the was otherwise a fairly healthy and normal infant. Her skin coloring was a light olive, her hair dark and curly, her eyes blue, and she was small boned; her nose tended to be flat and her lips large: all suggesting a mixed racial background. Her condition attracted the sympathy and attention of the nursing staff, who spent extra time playing with her and being affectionate to her. She blossomed under this care and appeared to be a happy and relatively contented baby.

The center sought to place her in a foster home but partly because of Tina's ''race'' and partly because the agency limited itself to homes practicing its religion, no immediate placement was found. Finally, one of the nurses volunteered to accept Tina in her home. This nurse had one infant of her own, was expecting a second, and planned to quit her job and devote herself entirely to caring for her children. She spoke of adopting Tina, but the agency advised her to delay this decision and accept Tina on a foster-child basis. Legal papers in Tina's case folder showed that a local court had awarded guardianship to the agency, granting it the right to place her in a home of its choosing, had designated a name chosen by the agency, and had ordered a birth certificate made out and filed in that name and stating an approximate date of birth. As was customary, the agency remained responsible for the child's medical care and offered a small stipend to the foster parents designed to cover clothing needs.

Although the agency usually tried to make periodic contacts with the children placed in foster care under its guardianship, there were only two brief notes about such contacts during the subsequent two years. At that time, the foster parents regretfully informed the agency that they were no longer able to care for Tina as the foster mother now had four children of her own including a newly born pair of twins, and their housing and finances were limited. No record was made of Tina's condition at that time nor of her reactions at being removed from this home. The social worker recalled that Tina seemed in good health. For the next eight months she remained in the center's residential institution, while a second foster placement was sought. Records were kept only of her health, physical development, and ''discipline''; her physical development and health were normal, and there was no indication that she was a discipline problem.

At approximately age 4, she was placed in the home of a middle-aged couple who had two other pre-school foster children; arrangements were made for this couple to receive monthly allotments from county funds for Tina's care. The social worker visited this home four times during the next year, and the foster mother came to the agency about Tina twice, both time to complain that the allotment checks were not forthcoming. The worker noted that the home was very neat and clean but it was very crowded and there was little play space. As far as the worker could tell, Tina seemed happy playing with the other children. However, after about six months the foster complained that Tina was becoming a "naughty" girl, would not mind, and fought with the other children. She frequently wet the bed and even soiled herself, though previously she had been completely continent. These complaints increased, and shortly after the end of the year the foster mother called to report that Tina had run away and had been picked up by the police and was being held at the juvenile hall; the foster mother refused to take her back so the worker brought Tina again to the center's home. Tina seemed very unhappy and depressed, complained that the foster parents were "mean" but could not say how. Now, three weeks later, Tina had recovered her spirits and seemed her usual self.

Several questions faced the social worker: Had Tina shown a change in attitudes and behavior that disrupted the last placement? If so, might this change make further placement difficult? Did Tina need any special kind of psychological care? Or was she merely reacting to a situation containing more stress and possibly less emotional support than the first placement? Might Tina have been reacting to the loss of the first foster mother? Tina would be old enough to start school within the year; how well might she be expected to perform? One possible placement would involve attending a public school where there were many bright children and thus expectations of high achievement. In discussing these questions with the social worker, she admitted that although she was aware of some of the variables, she had not been trained in methods of assessing them. She had tried to interview the most recent foster mother,

but had not succeeded in getting past the mother's complaints.

The psychologist in turn suggested several other possibilities. Might it be that Tina, now almost 5, had been reacting in fairly normal fashion, active, testing things out? Or might she be regressing slightly? Even running away is not altogether unusual at this age, although admittedly it is a cause for concern. If so, why was the foster mother unwilling to accept and deal with a 4-year-old's behavior? Another question concerned the sibling patterns in the two placements. How did Tina react to the birth of the children in the first home, and her eventual displacement? What was the sibling pattern in the second home? What kind of rivalries existed and on what basis? What kind of discipline and training was used in each of these homes? Most of all, the psychologist needed to know in much greater detail how Tina had actually developed if he was to make any predictions about her future placement and education.

To answer these questions, the psychologist needed data from several sources. He decided to observe Tina, first on the playground and at mealtime at the center's home, and to interview the center's matron who had known Tina before, on her return from the first placement. From this matron, he hoped to find out how she reacted after the change of placements. Then he planned to observe Tina in a playroom by herself, talking with her first about what she was doing while she played in front of him and then about herself and her placements. During one of these sessions, he planned to remove the toys and give her the Binet and some projective tests, such as the CAT and the World Test.

The psychologist hoped to obtain the bulk of his data from interviews with the two foster mothers. The social worker assured him that the first mother would undoubtedly be most cooperative, and that she had inquired about Tina from time to time and still felt a little guilty that she had not been able to keep her. The second mother might be reluctant to discuss Tina further, had seemed defensive about discussing her all along, and probably now would like to forget the whole affair. However, the agency maintained a guardianship over one of the other children placed in that home, and there was some question about continued placement of that child. Thus there was a definite reason for further contact between the agency and the second foster mother. It was finally decided that the psychologist would join the worker in making visits to both homes and interviewing both foster mothers.

In these two instances, the psychologist was acting as part of a staff, and someone other than the parent made the referral. However, in private practice or in such agencies as university psychology department clinics where all of an assessment is conducted by a psychologist, the client (parent) is often the source of referral per se. It is the mother, most usually, who calls the clinic or practitioner and asks for help with a problem concerning the child. In such instances, the questions may be about the same, but the technique of handling the referral will differ somewhat. Some clinics do have an "intake" form, essentially like the referral form in Figure 7.1. However, it is even more usual to interview the parent briefly either in phone contact or in an intake interview. The main difference of course is that the referrant is also the client and that here the client–psychologist relationship starts with the referral. How this referral is taken thus may set the tone and framework of the ensuring assessment, as is illustrated in the following cases.

CASE 16

Mrs. T telephoned the psychologist and speaking hesitantly in an anxious voice, asked if he knew anything about teen-agers and narcotics. Assured that he was interested in such problems, she went on to explain that she feared that her 15-year-old son Dale had been using marijuana. "He comes in after being with friends whom he knows I disapprove of and looks awfully funny." She had found cigarettes in his room that she believed were marijuana,

"But I really don't know for sure." Dale avoided her questions neither denying outright nor affirming her suspicions. Instead he counterattacked by accusing her of invading the privacy of his dresser drawers and calling her a "snoop." Against Dale's will, she had taken him to the family doctor for a physical examination and was told by the physician that he was in good health and that she should stop worrying because "marijuana is relatively harmless." Mrs. T appeared most worried lest Dale become involved in more harmful narcotics, get in with the "wrong" company, and be arrested. At the same time, she wondered if she were overconcerned, perhaps "making a mountain out of a molehill." She wished that her husband was home but he was away on overseas military duty. She hesitated to bother him with this problem, at least until she found out how serious the situation might be. The minister of their church suggested that she call the psychologist.

The psychologist asked if Dale was aware of her call. She replied that she had told Dale and that he was willing to go along with her request for help, "if only to get me to shut up." The psychologist assured her that her concerns were worth looking into and proceeded to make an appointment to see both Dale and Mrs. T. In this instance, he made little other inquiry over the phone, hoping to investigate in his intake interview with Dale and his mother the facts as well as the nature of each of their concerns.

His referral contact led him to guess that there might be a great deal more conflict between the mother and son than this one statement indicated. However, he realized that his first task might be to win Dale's cooperation and confidence. He decided to interview Dale first, getting his view of the situation in general and of the referral specifically before talking to the mother further.

CASE 17

Mrs. V phoned the Psychology Clinic and asked the secretary "if they gave tests."

The clinic secretary informed her politely that no staff member was immediately available to discuss this with her but that someone would return the call within the hour or at her convenience.* Mrs. V was a little annoyed, repeating her question. Assured that "testing is part of our service but that better information could be obtained from a staff member," Mrs. V left her telephone number and requested someone call before "3:00 when Bobby gets home from school." When her call was returned, Mrs. V seemed quite anxious, talking rapidly and loudly. She explained that Bobby, age 10, had not been doing at all well in school, making C's in most subjects and a D in arithmetic, that she was most concerned and had tried to help him with his homework and had conferred with the school. The school seemed to her to be unconcerned: "They have so many kids they just don't care about one." Her husband too had been no help: "After all, he's just a house painter, and he dropped out of high school to go in the Navy when he was 17. Now he says I'm nagging Bobby, that I should let the kid alone." Mrs. V added, "Bobby feels that his Dad is on his side and doesn't bother with his homework. I know Bobby is smart enough to make B's and A's, but my husband just laughs and says 'he's as dumb as his old man.' I get so mad I could kill 'em both, I really could!" When the psychologist inquired whether she had told her husband that she was going to the clinic, Mrs. V sighed and said, "He'd just laugh at me and tell me to forget it." The psychologist reflected that it sounded as if this concern caused considerable conflict between the parents and wondered if Mr. V might also like the problem cleared up. Mrs. V seemed hesitant but agreed, "They'd both like me out of their hair." The psychologist then suggested that she

discuss with Mr. V the possibility of a joint conference and, if Mr. V agreed, to ask him to call and arrange an appointment at their mutual convenience. Mrs. V remained doubtful but agreed. The next day Mr. V did call to say that he too was concerned about Bobby's achievement at school but that he felt that his wife was a chronic worrier and "makes the kid's life unbearable." He accepted the psychologist's offer of a joint conference quite readily.

In this case the psychologist was forced to make a quick analysis of the referral and some decisions about his procedures during these initial contacts. He recognized that Bobby's problem might very well be only one sample of parental differences over his training and discipline, and that he would very likely need the cooperation of both parents from the very start. Although he would very likely comply with Mrs. V's request for "tests" at some time during the assessment, it was necessary first to set the stage by inquiring further into the parents' hopes and expectations and attitudes toward Bobby's achievement now and in the future. He also wanted to explore to see if there were further questions and differences between the parents about Bobby. He hoped to establish some common concerns between them, as Mr. V had already indicated, and to use these as a basis for the assessment.

Some referrals are unacceptable. If, despite all efforts, the psychologist is unable to discover from the referrant the reasons and purposes for the referral, the referrant should be informed that the psychologist does not understand and cannot carry it out. Thus a request for "psychometric tests" with no indication of what the referrant needs to know or what decisions are going to be made on the basis of the assessment is unacceptable. Usually when this is explained to a referrant, the referral can be clarified. Occasionally the questions are posed to the psychologist in such a way as to be unanswerable.

A classic example is the "McNaughten rule," which asks whether an adult knew

*In some clinics, the initial referral information is obtained by a secretary, but in general this has not proven satisfactory even when the secretary is an experienced and trained employee. More usually, a secretary merely obtains and records the caller's name, telephone number, and address and the introductory question.

the difference between right and wrong when he/she commited a crime.* Similarly, a parent or other referrant may want to know if a child has told a lie or has performed a specific act. For example, I have been asked to decide whether a child who has accused an adult of sexual molestation is (1) falsely accusing the adult; (2) has invited the molestation and/or (3) has been psychologically damaged by this specific incident. In such instances it has been necessary to explain to the referrant that assessments give a general description of the child's development rather than specific information about particular events, but that the psychologist might contribute information about the child's behavior and development that might be pertinent to the specific behavior. For example, although the psychologist has no way of knowing if the child is lying (unless the child reports this and agrees to so inform authorities), she/he can ascertain whether the child "generally distorts reality" or "is so negativistic as to make things out of nothing." Similarly, the psychologist may not be able to discover whether a child has initiated an act, such a participating in pederasty, but he/she might estimate how much impulse control the child shows, how seductive he/she might become, or obtain other data about the child's sexual development and behavior in general.

Similarly, a referrant may ask the psychologist to make an impossible prediction, for example, "Will my 4-year-old be able to go to college?" At times considerable persuasion is necessary to convince a parent that such predictions cannot be made. Once I was asked by an anxious parent if his very bright and seemingly effeminate 6-year-old boy was in danger of becoming a homosexual. The parent finally accepted a restatement of the referral in terms of the child's current development and of questions that dealt with the care and training of an apparently precocious child.

The psychologist must also tread lightly

*See further discussion in Chapter 17.

when there is any reason to believe that the assessment might not be used in the best interests of the child or that there is some hidden agenda or unspoken reservation in the referral contract. The psychologist must make sure that the confidentiality of data and report will be maintained. The psychologist should reserve the right to decide whether certain materials might be used adversely—either at present or in the future life of the child. The classic example here is the old-fashioned school system that rigidly classified its students on the basis of IQ scores. This led a generation of psychologists to refuse to report IQ scores at all! Some physicians, who would ordinarily lean over backwards to avoid making the patient anxious by revealing any details of their own findings, have been known to bolster their own ignorance of psychological factors by reading the psychologist's report verbatim to the parent! It is to be hoped that such incidents will become less frequent as students in education, medicine, law, and the ministry now are being trained in the use of psychologists' reports. More difficult to ascertain sometimes are those occasions where the referrant—especially the parent—intends to use the assessment for purposes other than to help the child.

CASE 18

Mrs. Q brought Arlen, age 10, to the clinic to find out why he was not succeeding in school. In the initial intake contact she stated that she was "absolutely certain" that Arlen was intellectually retarded and that she hoped to be able to convince the school that he should be placed in a special class. The clinic accepted the referral with some reservations, explaining to the mother that no such assumption could be made in advance of the assessment and that there might be other reasons for the child's school difficulties. Mrs. Q seemed to accept this restatement of the referral, but became quite resistant to the clinic's request to contact the school. The assessment work with the child himself was completed before the clinic discovered that the mother had filed a formal lawsuit against the school board! Arlen reported that he had difficulties with his relationship with the teachers and principal because of his mother's constant interference with school activities. His test responses showed that he was actually above average intellectually. Mrs. Q was advised of the latter result, and an attempt was made to discuss further her relationship with the school and the child. She became enraged at the slightest suggestion that her child might be anything but retarded and demanded that the clinic write a letter to the school board confirming this. Later she included the clinic in her ultimately unsuccessful lawsuit. On court order, the clinic was forced to release its findings to the public record. Finally when the mother refused to enter the child in any public school and could not find a private school that seemed acceptable to her (or which would accept the child), the court ordered an investigation into the capability of the mother to care for the child.

Last but not least, psychologists are ethically bound not to accept a referral that is beyond their competency. Thus a psychologist who has never dealt with the case of intellectual retardation or of childhood schizophrenia or is unfamiliar with some other type of special problem should—before accepting such a referral—obtain consultation or supervision from some colleague who is knowledgeable about the specific problem. Similarly, psychologists are ethically bound to use only those techniques that they have been trained to use, and only those that they have reason to believe will contribute to the referral questions. Sometimes as the psychologist proceeds, he/she may discover hints of other kinds of disturbances than that originally suspected. For example, when asked specifically about intelligence, emotional disturbance may be discovered also. Unless an extensive investigation was requested, it is at least professional courtesy to confer with the referrant—including the parent—before proceeding. Nor should the psychologist include techniques merely out of curiosity even though it is for scientific research, unless permission of the referrant and parent has been obtained.

CHAPTER 8

Conducting the Assessment

A. ON MAKING APPOINTMENTS

It may seem that "giving" an appointment is a simple operation, which would warrant little or no discussion. In many settings arrangements for the client or patient to meet the professional person are handled by a receptionist or appointments secretary. However, in psychological work the appointment is where the patient contact begins. In essence, this is the first implementation of the assessment "contract." Quite often it is a continuation of the making of that contract, whenever the client is referred by someone else. When the appointment is made, the psychologist begins negotiations with the client—at least the parent—toward fulfilling the obligations contracted for in the referral.

For these reasons it is much wiser for the psychologist himself, rather than an appointments secretary (no matter how well trained), to arrange the appointment. The main element of this step in the assessment has to do with *time*—with the psychologist's time and with the child's time, as managed by the parent. In making this time arrangement the psychologist begins the relationship with the parent and child (even if the child is not personally contacted). In clinic settings this appointment continues and expands the client's relationship with his/her attitudes toward the clinic. In addition, the appointment contact is often used by the client and possibly by the psychologist to obtain and give additional information. In fact, the manner in which the client handles the making of the appointment may in itself yield further data about how the parent handles the child and social situations. (The position of the psychologist in private practice rather than in an agency or institution who makes the initial contact entirely on his/her own has already been discussed.) Two other situations need to be considered: the outpatient clinic or agency and the hospital or institution situation.

In the outpatient situation the psychologist has to contact the parent to bring the child to the office. She/he may arrange with a colleague to introduce the parent when the parent comes to the clinic to see the other staff member. Such vis-à-vis introductions are ideal since the client has some idea of who will be seeing the child, can think through the matter of time arrangements, and can raise any other questions that come to mind. In the everyday workings of most clinics, however, such arrangement for a personal introduction of the psychologist and client is not always feasible. Quite commonly the decision to make a full assessment may not be made until the initial contact has been reviewed by the staff. The usual practice is to review an "intake" and decide whether the clinic can possibly help the child before proceeding with further interviews and examinations. Thus the appointment for psychological assessment is made over the telephone most frequently.

Whether the contact is face to face or by means of the telephone, the psychologist should ascertain beforehand—during the referral—whether or not the client has been told that an appointment with the psychologist is to be made, and what the client has been told about the nature of the assessment. After introducing and identifying himself/herself as a member of the clinic staff, the psychologist should remind the client about the referral. For example, "Mrs. S, this is Dr. T of the Child Guidance Clinic. Mrs. J asked me to call you to make an appointment for me to see Bernie. I understand that you have already discussed this with her?" Such an introductory question–statement allows the client to introject any further questions she/he may have. When it is clear that the parent does have a general idea of why an appointment is to be made, then the psychologist may inquire about the question of time. Usually he/she begins by informing the client of approximately the amount of time that will be needed, inquiring if there are time limitations for the child and parents. For example, "Are there any times when it would be impossible for either you or Bernie to come in?" Note that such a question includes the child.

Once the limits of the client's time are established, the psychologist will want to mention his/her own availability to see if a mutually agreeable time can be set. If the psychologist has no after-school time—and after-school hours are indeed precious when one is working with children—then there should be some discussion about both the parents' and the child's feelings about missing school. The psychologist is usually able to reassure the parent that only one or two such arrangements will be required and that the child will not be missing school regularly. If an after-school appointment is being arranged, the psychologist should inquire what the child usually does on that day, with at least the suggestion that she/he is interested in how the child feels about missing some activity.

If the parent does not ask about or mention what the child has been told about the appointment, the psychologist should bring this up directly. If the parent has any doubts, the best and most honest approach that one can suggest is that the parent tell the child that the appointment will be one that is intended to help the doctors better understand some things about the "problem" for which they began going to the clinic. Suppose that Mrs. S has discussed Bernie's enuresis and night terrors with the social worker, but Bernie has not as yet come to the clinic. The psychologist discovers that Mrs. S has not told Bernie about her visit, but that Bernie has been taken to the pediatrician about these problems, who advised contacting the clinic. The psychologist should then advise Mrs. S to remind Bernie that their doctor did tell her to contact the clinic, that she has talked to one of the staff members, and that she wants him to come to the clinic next Tuesday. Since Bernie's prior experiences concerning this problem have been medical, the psychologist also should advise Mrs. S to tell Bernie that there will be no physical examination, but rather that the psychologist is a different kind of doctor who is interested in what children do and think about, and that she/he will talk to Bernie and ask him to do some different kinds of interesting things—all of which will help the doctors at the clinic understand Bernie's problem a little better. Not infrequently, parents raise other questions, such as, "What shall I tell him if he wants to know more about what he will be doing with you?" or "You mean you will be giving him some tests?" Quite often when parents ask such questions, they are voicing their own curiosity and anxieties about what the psychologist is going to do with or find out about *their* child and thus about them. Rather than enter into any extended explanation at this point, it is usually wiser to repeat gently the instructions and add that if the child does have further questions the parent tell him/her that the psychologist will be willing to talk about all this when he/she comes to the clinic.

When the child is a resident in some institution or is being seen at a school, the psychologist should begin by checking the child's schedule of activities with the institutional authority who is responsible—first with the nurse, matron, or teacher. The psychologist should also find out when the child is free and what activities may be missed if the appointment is made at one of the times the psychologist has available. One should ascertain too how the child may feel about missing whatever activity might be scheduled at that time. It is wise to inquire how the person who would be supervising the child during that time will feel about the child's being taken out of the activity. For example, if the athletic director at the hospital has nearly succeeded in getting a frightened and withdrawn child involved in a ballgame, then it might behoove the psychologist to take this into consideration—even though one might feel that a patient could miss his recreation "just this one time." Next the psychologist should meet the child and discuss the appointment briefly with her/him much in the same way one would advise the parent in an outpatient situation.

For example, "Dr. V, your doctor, has asked me to get together with you soon. I guess he talked to you a little about seeing me. I want to talk with you too and ask you to work on some things with me so that I can understand better how you think about things and work with them. This will help Dr. V to understand your problems also. Nurse R has told me that she thought you wouldn't mind missing OT tomorrow morning too much for a couple of hours. Would that be all right with you?"

Such an introduction helps to tie in the assessment procedure with the other attention the child is receiving, and it recognizes that the child's time is considered important. Of course the psychologist should be prepared to offer the child an alternative time—but not too many as this may confuse an emotionally disturbed child or give him/her too much chance to manipulate the adult. If the child asks more questions that suggest some anxiety about the assessment, the psychologist should indicate—as in the outpatient situation—that these questions can be discussed better when they meet. "Do I have to?" is the common resistant question, to which the answer is "Dr. V and I think it will help." If the child completely rejects the appointment, then it may

be necessary to contact the staff colleague who made the referral and inquire if further steps need to be taken to help the child accept the assessment, or if the assessment possibly should be delayed until the child is able to accept it.

B.   THE INITIAL CONTACT WITH THE CHILD

The relationship between the child and the assessor usually begins when they meet in the waiting hall or at the assessor's door. In this meeting there are often many subtle clues about the parent–child relationship and their attitudes about the assessment. Most commonly, when the assessor introduces himself/herself to the parent, the parent then introduces the child. If this does not happen, the psychologist should ask directly, "Are you (child's name)?" Most children appreciate being offered an adult handshake when introduced. Anxious parents frequently act as if the child was deaf and start giving additional information about him/her or instructions on how to handle him/her. The assessor should note how the child reacts to being talked about to a stranger in his/her presence as one might expect, even very young children who commonly experience such adult behavior are usually somewhat embarrassed, and they may react by hiding further behind mother's skirts or by creating some diversion so as to interrupt the parent or turn the parent's attention away from the assessor. Older children often directly show their embarrassment by blushing and remarking, "Oh, *mother!*"

In most instances the assessment should begin by having parents and child come in together for a brief introductory session. Such a family session at this first meeting emphasizes that from then on the whole family will be involved in the treatment—as is now common practice. Requiring that *both* parents attend such an initial session has become routine at many clinics. I have found such family meetings are essential when an adolescent is "charged" with "behavior problems." This introductory session serves to put the problems on the table.

I usually begin by asking the child why she/he has come. Many children respond with a shrug, turning to the parents for an answer. I do not permit parents to explain right then. Rather, I ask if the child knows "what kind of doctor I am?" If not, I explain that I deal with children's problems. "Do you have some problem a psychologist might help with?" If the child remains unable to explain, I may mention what the referrant has told me that "Dr. R has told me that you have a problem wetting the bed. I'm sure this may be an embarrassing thing to talk about, but would it be okay if I asked you some questions about it?" Or: "Your mother has told me that you were arrested for possessing drugs. Can you tell me about it?" Thus I begin by showing my concern for the child's feelings before turning to the parents. Important here is the parents' attitude toward the child and her/his problems. Such attitudes are often revealed in the manner in which the parents report and describe the problems. Do they cry "I accuse" like a prosecuting attorney, or, at the opposite extreme, do they creep mealy-mouthed around the problems, hoping not to hurt the child's feelings or to avoid his/her hostility? They may attempt to defend the child, to excuse him/her from blame, blame someone else ("It's those other older children. . . ."), or even deny that any problem exists. Parents nearly always try to exculpate themselves. The child's reactions to the parental account of the problems should be noted also. Frequently I find it necessary to interrupt the parent and ask the child for his/her feelings about what the parents are saying.

If it is my task to get a history of the child's development, I usually gather these data in such a family session also. At least a history of the complaints should be obtained. The general principle is that the child should understand the problems, as seen by the parents, and the background of the problems including her/his life history. Such a clarification is an essential start both for the remainder of the assessment and for future therapy or disposition. Only after the problems have been defined do I begin work with the child independently.

Most important to observe—especially with younger children—is how the child and parent separate. Often there is a slight delay with the pre-school child, who may hide his/her head in mother's lap for an extra second—even though a few minutes previously he/she may have been exploring up and down the hall. It may be necessary to give him/her an extra hug or kiss or go through some diversionary actions before accepting the examiner's hand. The intensity of the child's anxiety in this separation and the mother's reaction to it provide one clue about their relationship. Sometimes this is a prolonged and elaborate ceremony—or a "game" as Eric Berne (1964) would label it. Or at the other extreme, the child may desert the parent without a glance behind. Parents have their separation anxieties too. The mother who has a lot to talk about with the assessor in the hallway may be delaying separation from the child. Parents have been known to urge the child verbally to "go with the doctor" while at the same time holding tight to his/her hand. In most instances, it is usually best for the assessor to patiently step aside and let the child and parent work out the separation on their own.

Only occasionally is it necessary for the assessor to intervene by firmly requesting the parent to leave and wait "down the hall" and reassuring the child in a matter-of-fact voice that "you and I will be talking and doing some things while mother waits." In those instances where the mother abandons the child in the waiting room, the situation should be at least mentioned by the assessor to the child, with an eye to the child's reaction. Such children may be used to such maternal desertion and be able to maintain a stiff upper lip.

CASE 19

Donnie's mother pushed the child out of the car in the parking lot, scarcely stopping before she wheeled around and sped off. This 5-year-old stumbled into the lot, picked himself up, and when the psychologist rushed out to inquire what had happened, he was able to muster a noncommital "hello" as if ignoring the whole incident. When the psychologist remarked, "Your mother seemed in an awful hurry!" Donnie replied somewhat bitterly, "Yeah, she's always in a hurry!" However, he seemed rather listless and preoccupied, looking away from the psychologist toward the door. The psychologist inquired again, "Are you still thinking about how your mother was in a hurry?" At this the child burst into tears and permitted the psychologist to pick him up in her lap and comfort him. The assessment was discontinued that day, and the mother was asked to stay for an interview with the social worker during the next appointment. This time the child rushed in to greet the psychologist, sat as close to her as possible, and was eager to please and even motivated to achieve.

Some children—especially very young children—cannot make this separation from the parent easily. They may continue to cry, to demand to return to mother, or at least to need to go periodically and check to see if mother is still there. Usually some verbal recognition of the child's anxiety suffices, for example, "You seemed scared—are you afraid mother won't be out there? Shall we go see?" Of course, fear may not be the only emotion the child is experiencing over the separation. She/he may also be angry, and both feelings may have to be recognized before the child can settle down. With exceedingly anxious or shy children who do not seem to be able to make the separation at all, it may be necessary to bring the mother into the room for a brief time, and to condition the child gradually to mother's leaving. Occasionally a child may make several visits to the assessor's office in which nothing more is accomplished than that she/he permits mother to leave for increasing periods of time. The manner in which the child and mother achieve the separation under such extreme circumstances is often as revealing as any tests one might administer.

Another source of anxiety for the child is the stranger—the assessor. According to Spock (1946), a mild shyness in front of strangers is normal for the 3-year-old. Emotionally disturbed children of all ages usually show some indication of anxiety in relating to the strange doctor. Initially they may be very stiff, reserved, and guarded, or obversely, defend themselves by intrusively detracting, asking a million questions, looking out the window, playing with something, and the like. If the referrant or parent has helped to define the situation for the child, some anxiety may be deterred. However, no matter what the child may have been told, the fact that she/he expects to be observed and examined in some as yet undefined manner often creates considerable initial anxiety.

Thus once some sort of separation from the parent has been achieved, the psychologist's first job is to relieve the anxiety. One should begin by helping the child define the situation more clearly. First it is a good idea to orient him/her briefly to the room: "Why don't you sit over there. Is that chair comfortable for you? We probably will be doing some work at this table, and I'm going to sit here." Once the child is seated, one should proceed to introduce oneself a little further, repeating one's name and letting the child know how it is he/she has come to know of the child. "I'm Dr. P, and Dr. C called me the other day and told me he's been talking to you a bit and that he wanted me to meet you and do some things with you. Did he talk to you also about seeing me?" Even if the child does indicate that he/she remembers the referrant orienting him/her to the assessment, a brief discussion of what the child expects and about the nature and purpose of the assessment is usually necessary. The question "What did you think we were going to do here today?" may meet with a noncommittal shrug, but even so, the child usually gives some indication that this was exactly what was on his/her mind. If the child was referred by a physician who has physically examined and treated him/her, then it would be appropriate to ask: "Did you think I was going to do the same kinds of things with you that Dr. C does?" "What does he do?" Then the psychologist should differentiate his role for the child: "Yes, I see, Dr. C helps you when you're sick, or gives you shots" (or whatever the child mentions). Or, if Dr. C is a psychiatrist: "Of course, Dr. C is a psychiatrist, he talks with children to see how he can help them. Well, I'm a different kind of doctor. I'm a psychologist. Do you know what that is? A psychologist is interested in understanding how boys and girls think and feel about things, what they do about things, the things they like and don't like, and what makes them happy or unhappy." Such an introduction is especially needed if no family session is possible (as in inpatient services), and it might well be expanded.

As may be noted, in such a discussion the psychologist is not only introducing and differentiating himself/herself from other people dealing with the child's problems, but he/she is also beginning to relate the assessment to what the child has already experienced in the way of help. This association should be continued to assist the child in recognizing that the assessment is part of an overall effort to understand her/his problems. How such an association is made for the child depends of course on the nature of the referral. If referred by the pediatrician, one might say, for example, the following: "Dr. C told me that he had been giving you some shots for some kind of allergy, but that the shots didn't seem to help you much. Is that right?" "Why do you think Dr. C wanted to have you come see a psychologist like me?" "Perhaps if we understood more about some of the things I mentioned, it might help to solve

some of the mystery of your allergy." Such questions then might lead to a brief discussion of the child's medical complaints and of his/her current behavioral difficulties associated with being allergic, and on into his current adjustment in general. When the child is being seen by some colleague in a clinic setting, this discussion might run as follows: "I know Dr. C and you have been talking about your problems but, of course, what you talk about with her is just between you and her so she didn't tell me much about what you said. That's the rule here, you know. However, because she knew you and I were going to work together, it was necessary for me to know about the problem that brought you to the clinic. So I do know that one of the main reasons you came to see Dr. C was because of your problem in. . . ."

Depending on the child's response, one might continue, "Since you and Dr. C are already talking together about that and other things, we don't have to go into that, unless there is something more about it or some other problem you think I should know about. Talking about one's problems and the things that go with them is very helpful—after one gets used to doing it. But that's only one way we have of understanding about children and their lives. Often it helps us also to see how children do things, think about things, and look at things. That's what you and I are going to do today, so as to help you and Dr. C as you talk more together."

Such an introduction would presume that the assessor was leaving the interviewing of the child to Dr. C and was going to proceed with other techniques. On the other hand, if the interview is to be part of the assessment, then the psychologist may want to establish the relationship between the referral and the assessment a bit further, especially when the parent is the referrant. "When your mother phoned me, *she* told me that you'd been having a lot of trouble getting along at school—and with her and your father too. However, I didn't get a chance to talk with her very much about it, and besides, I really wanted to meet you first and understand how *you* saw it and what you thought about it. This gives you and me a chance to talk together in private. You see, what children and psychologists talk about together is just between them, and no one else gets to know." If necessary, the fact of the confidentiality of the assessment can be discussed further. "Of course, if psychologists told other people what they talked about with their patients, no one could trust them and tell them how they actually felt or about what was going on in their lives, 'cause sometimes it's very personal. That's why we have this rule."

For older children, the initial resistance may result not so much from separation anxiety but from both the interruption of normal activities and the prospect of facing uncomfortable, anxiety-producing topics they fear will be brought to light by the psychologist. If the psychologist has any inkling that the child is coming under protest, this resistance may have to be explored even before the introductory discussion just outlined—or at least as part of it. To the glum and glowering adolescent who does not respond to a greeting or even rise from the seat in the waiting room until his/her exasperated mother says, "Well, aren't you going with the doctor?" and who shuffles along behind down the hall and stands staring out the window at the warm afternoon sun, one might as well begin by directly recognizing that "it sure seems evident to me that you may not have wanted to come here at all this afternoon. What's the trouble?" One may then proceed directly to a discussion of the child's resistance in a sympathetic fashion. Such a recognition can usually lead into the type of introduction, as outlined before. When the resistance is less marked than in the proceeding illustration, when the child seems apathetic or bored, one might ask, the following: "On a day like this, I'd guess most young people might want to do most anything rather than come to see a doctor. What would you have been doing if you didn't have to come to see me?"

In summary, in the initial contact with the child the psychologist should (1) allow for, observe, and where necessary, recognize and deal with the child's separation from the parent; (2) introduce himself/herself and explain his/her role among those adults interested in the child's problems; and (3) investigate the child's concerns and attitudes toward the assessment, being alert to the child's fears, hopes, and resistances.

This introduction serves yet another purpose: The psychologist also meets the child. Like the child, the psychologist undoubtedly also has some preconceived notions about the type of person he/she is going to meet and deal with. He/she has heard the "complaints" (a term that has an unfortunate association with courts of law) and symptoms, knows some of the ideas that others have about the child, and has some ideas of his/her own about how children of this age should function. Also by then he/she has had at least a phone contact with the child's parent and has formed some impressions about how a child might react to "that kind of mother." The assessor may be prepared to be sympathetic, or he may be girded to meet a hostile or resistant child. Having studied the referral and made the appointment, the psychologist has made plans about the kinds of techniques to use. During this brief introduction period, he/she should silently check out his/her preconceptions. What kind of behavior does the child initially show? How is the child accepting him/her and the proposed assessment contract? What are the possibilities that he/she may run into resistance or that the child may be cooperative? How verbal is the child? How restless? How much does the child volunteer? How guarded? Observing the child's behavior during these first few minutes of the assessment will help the psychologist to decide whether the plans for the assessment can proceed or whether they need to be revised.

C.   TIMING AND SEQUENCE

This initial contact will also help the psychologist double-check two other aspects of these plans: the possible division or utilization of the time available with the child and the sequence of activities. As to the timing, under ideal situations a thorough assessment would not be time bound, and the psychologist could take as much time as needed. In practice, however, the amount of time available is limited by the psychologist's schedule, the clinic or referrant's schedule (when the assessment data are needed for the referrant's decision), and certainly by the parent and child's schedule. Early in the referral stage, the psychologist should make some rough estimate of how long it may take to gather the kinds of data demanded by the referral. Such an estimate may not be easy to make—especially for the notiviate—but as one gathers experience it becomes more possible to guess how long it might take to interview and administer a proposed set of techniques to a child of a certain age with certain characteristics and handicaps. The psychologist can also usually make a guess as to whether everything can be done in one session or in several. In negotiating the referral the psychologist should inform the referrant of this time estimate. If there is a decision pending for a certain date, will it be possible for the psychologist to complete a study by the time the referrant has to make the decision? If not, should the psychologist limit the assessment to certain essential facets of the referral, possibly continuing the rest of the assessment afterwards? Or might the decision be delayed until the psychologist has had a chance to make a complete study? If these timing elements are not worked out between the psychologist and the referrant, the psychologist may feel rushed. He/she may then rush the child and as a consequence end up with inadequate and insufficient data. Or he/she may make an excellent and thorough study of the child and write a scholarly treatise, only to find that the referrant— weary of waiting—has had to go ahead and make a decision without the benefit of the psychologist's findings.

In like manner, the time budget of the assessment needs to be discussed with the parent. In part, this is usually begun between the parent and referrant, who says, in effect, "Next I want you to take the child to the psychologist. After that we can begin to make some decisions." Some parents react with anxiety—often typical of the anxiety they experience in other, similar situations—and jump the gun, making contact with the psychologist and seeking an appointment almost before the psychologist is aware of what is going on. Others, who may be seeking to delay the opening up of their Pandora's box, seek more time before allowing an appointment.

It is during the making of the appointment that these attitudes of the parents come to light. The psychologist needs to explore with the parents their pressures about how soon they want to make a decision, and to make clear to them the clinic's time limits and flexibilities. For example, the psychologist might explain to the parents who appear to be wondering if they should put aside other obligations to meet a proffered appointment that "if you can bring your child in this week, then our staff might be able to discuss all our findings the following week, and Dr. C could advise you of our suggestions soon thereafter. However, if it is necessary for you to delay, we will understand, and you can call us when you are ready to have us see your child." At the same time, the psychologist should acquaint the parent with the prospective time budget for the assessment, the possibility that about so many hours and so many visits may be needed—a budget that may have to be tempered to meet the resistances and anxieties of the parent.

This time budget may be altered again once the psychologist meets with the child. Hopes that the child can be interviewed and administered such and such tests in a two-hour period may be dashed by the anxious child who resists either passively and silently, or by hyperactivity and a running interference with the best-laid plans of the psychologist. It is useless to barge ahead and try to obtain a history or give an IQ test in the face of a child who is either "taking the Fifth" or conducting a guerrilla war. In such instances the time is much better spent by dealing with these resistances. Often by so doing many more assessment data can be accumulated directly about the child's behavior.

Assuming that the child's anxieties are sufficiently alleviated in the initial five to ten minutes of the introductory discussion, how long may a psychologist expect to spend in contact with the child for the average overall thorough assessment? I am not aware of any time-motion study that has been reported for assessment of children. However, in an unpublished survey conducted by me (Palmer, 1957) as part of the planning for staffing the state hospitals in California, staff psychologists reported that the patient contact of their assessments of adult inpatients ranged from 2½ to 4 hours. The longer assessments were broken into two appointments. In my experience and that of my colleagues, the time needed for assessment of children is more variable, depending as it does on the age of the child as well as the nature of the referral. With younger children (under age 8), it might be possible, if they are very cooperative and involved with the procedures, to maintain their interest and cooperation for a full 2 hours. However, most pre-school and younger school-age children begin to be restless even before an hour has passed. Attention wanders, interest lags, and boredom sets in. If the assessment must be continued, then a run down the hall and a trip to the bathroom or drinking fountain is called for. It is usually wise to have a second session arranged for children in this age group.

The total time needed for the assessment of the younger child however, is usually a little shorter than that required for older children and adolescents. The overall responsiveness of the younger child is on the average more limited. Younger children may be quite verbal, but on the whole they find less to talk about than their older sibs, although some have learned at an early age how to entertain adults by being garrulous. Unless one is dealing with a very bright or unusual child, it is usually possible to ad-

minister a Binet to a 5-year-old (of about 25–30 items) in about one half to three quarters of an hour. In contrast, giving a WISC to an average 10-year-old (50–75 items) takes from an hour to 90 minutes. Similarly, the pre-schooler's responses to the Rorschach, his CAT fantasies, drawings, and other productions are briefer than those of older children. With this 3–8-year-old group, two one-hour sessions are often quite sufficient for the total assessment. (This does not include parental contacts.) "Tests" to infants under 3 years may require even less time, but often extra time is needed for general observation, and more than one session is usually required because of the variability and unreliability in the reactions of infants.* Extended assessments of older children and adolescents may require almost as much time as the assessment of adults—as many as two-hour sessions.

The previously mentioned time estimate presumes that the assessor has made at least preliminary plans regarding which techniques will be used before meeting the child. It presumes that the assessor has laid out the test materials and has checked to see that they are complete and in order so that there is no need to hunt around among them or rearrange them before presenting them to the child. It presumes the assessor is skilled in the use of these materials, that he/she does not have to flip pages of a book to read directions or questions—or even to score items—and most of all that he/she knows the tests so well that he/she can listen to and follow the child's responses and pick up clues from them without having to think about what comes next on the test.

Another skill that an assessor needs to develop is the ability to plan out the sequence for administering the techniques, which incidentally also can conserve time. Ideally one task should lead into the next, so that the child does not have to shift sets too extensively or rapidly. At the same time, the tasks should be varied enough so that the child does not become bored. For

*See Chapter 15.

example, the introductory discussion leads easily into the interview. At most one might remark, ''Perhaps I could better understand about your problem if you could tell me a little more how it began. . . .'' and then after obtaining some history of the complaint and its circumstances, lead the child into a discussion of her/his family. One might say, for example, ''You mentioned something about your mother and father. Could you tell me a little more about your family? Who else is there?'' thus leading into a gradually expanding investigation of the child's current world and history.

After 50 or 60 minutes and a short break, the assessor might remark, ''We've been talking together quite a bit, and talking helps me understand about you and your problem, but as I told you before, it also helps to see how people do things and think about things. So now I'm going to ask you to work with some materials and puzzle out some questions.'' In the normal course of events, a child's expectations about tests are on the order of the kinds of tasks included in intelligence scales. Thus he may not be surprised when the assessor says next: ''Let's begin by seeing what words you know.'' In most instances such relatively emotionally neutral problem-solving tasks are less threatening to the child than the more unstructured associative techniques. The short and varied items of the Binet are particularly designed to hold the attention of the young child, while the older child is able to stay with one type of task a little longer on the WISC-R. Although the vocabulary subtest of the WISC-R is numbered test 7, I often begin with the vocabulary—switching to test 4—or for relatively nonverbal children the mazes make an appropriate start.

If the Bender-Gestalt or Memory-For-Designs are to be used, this type of visual motor task fits in nicely with the IQ scale tasks. However, one would want to consider whether a visual motor task should be introduced after an hour of problem-solving intellectual work, or whether one should wait until the child is fresher, especially if one is dealing with a child suspected of being neurologically handicapped and quickly fatigued. In any case, at the end of an hour and a half or two hours, one should remark, ''You've worked awfully hard today, and some of the things you tried were quite difficult. Perhaps we should stop now. I do want to see you again next ——at———o'clock. When we get together again, we can do some more, slightly different things, which I'm sure you'll find interesting.''

Such a conclusion to the first session rewards the child for his/her efforts, and it lets the child know of the continuing interest of the assessor. If—to carry on this example—the assessor who decides to open the second session with a visual-motor drawing task might say, ''This time let's begin by having you use the pencil. Here are some designs.'' Subsequently, ''While you have the pencil, here's another sheet of paper. Now I'd like to have you draw me a picture of a . . .'' (and proceed to the Goodenough or to the Draw-A-Person or House-Tree-Person). Such a shift makes it easier to proceed with other associative tasks. For example, one might say the following: ''When children draw me pictures, I understand a little how they look at things. Now I want you to try a little different way to show me how you look at things. Here I have some cards with inkblots on them and I'm going to ask you to, . . .'' (giving the Rorschach instructions). Although the Rorschach instructions do not mention ''imagination,'' one can turn from the Rorschach to the TAT or CAT by saying, ''Making things out of those inkblots did require some imagination, didn't it? Now I'm going to ask you to do even more imagining, because I think imagining is pretty important for children. Here I have some other pictures, not just inkblots, and instead of just describing them to me I want you to think up a story for me, to use all your imagination. . . .'' (and continue with the TAT instructions). Often, if the Draw-A-Person has not yet been administered, I say, ''I've shown you a lot of pictures, now I'm going to end by asking you to draw me a picture.'' Or one might conclude a session with some question-naire, such as the Bene-Anthony, saying, "This time I'm going to let you read the questions and make your answers without having to say anything or having to write anything down. Here we have. . . ."

Many other sequences are quite feasible, and it depends largely on the kinds of techniques being used and the rections of the child. One might not need to give an intelligence test and wish to start directly with associative techniques. For small chil-dren, drawing is usually an attractive task and one that they often are used to doing when an adult requests them to do so. As was noted before, the shift then can be made to the Rorschach, then to the CAT. Play techniques, such as the Lynn Struc-tured Doll Play or the World Test, are best left to the end of the assessment since it is usually difficult for the child to shift back from play to a work task—even to other associative tasks. It is just as possible to begin with the Rorschach, remarking "What I'm most interested in is how *you* look at things, *your* ideas and feelings."

D.   ON HANDLING RESISTANCE—"THE GAMES CHILDREN PLAY"

Assessment carries with it some element of anxiety for nearly every child. There is the stress of having to perform, and most of all there is the anxiety—albeit often unconscious—over revealing hidden feel-ings or inadequacies. Even the very con-forming and competitive child holds back as these anxieties arise. Those children who are less driven to please or to achieve may become even more defensive when they become threatened by certain kinds of de-mands made upon them or when their se-cret fantasies are pried from them. Such defensiveness may be lowered of course by the methods mentioned before, that is, by the introductory discussion of the purposes of the assessment.

During the assessment, as the child be-comes blocked, restless, or lags and drags her/his feet, it is often necessary to give her/him a chance to recover from such moments of anxiety. The psychologist needs to recognize that there is a threat present. When the child blocks after having expressed some anxiety, it may be helpful to remark, "This is a difficult thing to talk about." Or, "That picture (or that inkblot) does make one think of some depressing things." Or, "That was a pretty scary thought," and so on. Usually such recogni-tion of the child's anxiety is sufficient to allow him/her to recover and tackle a new stimulus. Of course the way in which the child handles the anxiety engendered by the stress of the assessment is often charac-teristic of how he/she handles other similar stresses. Thus the kinds of defenses he/she uses and his/her ability to recover from anxiety during the assessment are parts of the data available for estimation of ego strength.

For some children the stress of the as-sessment is so overwhelming that they offer massive resistance. For various reasons they do not accept the assessment contract set up for them by the adult authorities. Their rejection of adult pressures to con-form and perform may be a basic part of their life problems. Usually such a child has been referred for assessment just because he or she is engaged in a battle of resis-tance with adults. These battles often take the form of what Eric Berne (1964) has labeled "games." In these games, in the transaction between child and adult, the child seeks to impose his/her own restric-tions upon the adult instead of accepting the adult's terms. Children bring the transac-tional games of their everyday lives to the assessment, and they try to renegotiate the assessment contract according to the game. In order to understand and handle such challenges to the assessment transaction, it may be helpful first to examine and define some of the common games children play in assessment—that is, the nature and man-ifestations of such resistances.

1.   The game "No!" or "Make me!" is played most commonly by younger children, consists of very open and direct negativistic verbal expressions, often with the response "No," no matter what the question. Usually this "No" is given with a smile or giggle in a seductive fashion, as if to say, "Go ahead. Make me!" The child expects the adult to play the game by responding, "Come now!" and by wheedling or cajoling. The child then repeats his "No" with even more relish, and so the game goes on in rounds of "No" and "Come now," with the child offering just enough tidbits of cooperation to entrap the adult into the game, or until the adult becomes exhausted and gives up.

2.   The game "I can't" is also played more by younger children, but also commonly by immature or passive adolescents. The aim of this game is to seek reassurance from the adult authority by claiming inadequacy. Here, the child says in effect, "I just can't," expecting the adult to respond with encouragement and reassurance, "Oh, yes you can." Often this game is played by children who really do have some doubts of their abilities and some feelings of inadequacy. Thus they seek to avoid any assessment of their functioning. If they can get the adult to reassure them by saying, "Oh, yes you can," then there is really no need to prove whether they can or not. Thus the assessment has been turned into a reassurance transaction. Although the intent is to gain reassurance against feelings of inadequacy, the player is never really reassured and must keep demanding because the reassurance per se is no proof.

3.   The game "Fifth Amendment"* is another version of the game of "No!" but is played for different reasons. Where "No!" is essentially a seductive game, "Fifth

Amendment is an attack. In this defensive tactic, the child maintains silence not to "incriminate" herself/himself. The child fears that anything she/he says may be used against her/him. It is the response of the guilty and angry child who fears that the assessor may discover how she/he feels. Just as when the Fifth Amendment is used in Congressional hearings, the refusal to respond usually incites anger in the inquirer, and the other "player" is expected to cite the child for contempt. The child argues to herself/himself that she/he has a right to privacy, while the adult seeks to "get at the truth." It is a common game between children and parents, and it is frequently brought into the assessment situation.

4.   "My game first" or "Promise me" is a game of blackmail. In this game, the child proposes an alternate activity that he/she demands that the assessor promise to permit before he/she will accede to the assessor's demands. If the adult agrees to play this game, the price is constantly raised at each step. Often the child claims the prize before cooperating, then makes new demands. If the adult refuses, the child can claim to be cheated. The child who plays this game is not accepting the assessment contract of cooperation in return for psychological understanding. Rather, she/he seeks some concrete prize for "being good." Such a child doubts the sincerity of others, cannot accept a promise on faith, but needs immediate evidence, and even when so rewarded recognizes that he/she had to be bribed and is not really loved.

5.   The game "Silly-billy" by younger children or "Flip" by adolescents is like the "No!" game. It is often seductive, but also like "Fifth Amendment," also hostile. In this game the child gives a nonsense answer, or the adolescent a flip or impudent response. The expected response is "Gee, you're cute!" or "Don't be silly!"—but with a smile. It is a teasing game, intended both to delight and irritate, but mainly to divert.

6.   Closely allied to this latter game is a

*This title is taken from the Fifth Amendment to the United States Constitution, which protects a person from testifying against himself. It has become popularized in recent years in Congressional investigations where witnesses have refused to "incriminate" themselves.

tactic known as "backward talk." Not really a game in the transactional sense, "backward talk" is really a version of simple denial in which the child gives a response entirely opposite to what she/he might say if agreeing to the assessment contract. She/he is particularly likely to deny her/his true feelings during the interview, and in extreme instances may give antonyms for synonyms on a vocabulary test or make reversals on the Bender-Gestalt or the Block Design (which have nothing to do with "organicity"). "Backward talk" does become a game when the assessor silently assents, saying in effect, "I believe you." Rorschach discovered "backward talk" when—annoyed by individuals who used the white space between the blots he had so carefully selected—he recognized that the person responding was being "oppositional." In essence, "backward talk" reverses the figure-ground of the assessment, in that the child puts the assessor on the spot to see if he/she can come up with the answer.

7. "Uproar" has been well defined by Berne (1964). In the assessment version it may start with "Silly-billy," but it proceeds to an increasing number and intensity of diversions that are no longer "cute." Like the adult game, this diversionary tactic becomes a game if the assessor roars back in the form of increasing demands on the child to "Stop it" and conform. Again, as in "backward talk," the child is reversing the assessment procedure and testing the adult. As in "No!" she/he says in effect "Make me," but this game is grimmer. Here the child defends against feelings of inadequacy by proving the adult incompetent to control the situation and thus proving himself/herself to be superior. If the child succeeds in getting the adult to lose his/her temper, the child righteously feels superior even though it be a pyrrhic victory.

8. The success of the child in any of these games depends on whether the assessor is also playing a game—which might be called "Score!" In this game, the assessor is concerned with obtaining a "scorable"

response. Rather than accepting and utilizing the response given by the child, the assessor wants the right or wrong answer. She/he is concentrating concretely on the child's verbalizations or test performance, rather than on what is going on between them. In playing the game of "Score," the assessor is in a sense also violating the assessment contract, for she/he is concerned more with technique than with the child. She/he can very easily become a victim of any of the children's games mentioned previously.

As Berne points out, a game may be disrupted by pointing out that there is a game going on. The assessor sets his pencil down and says with a knowing smile, "I know the game you're playing. It's called "No!" The 3-year-old usually screams with delight, says "No! loudly several times, and the assessor says, "Of course, I can't *make* you do anything. So I can't play the game of 'No!' But if you'd like to play my games, I'll show you what I can do. Then I'll be glad to play." Most of the time the child gives up the game of "No!" perhaps with one or more feeble attempts. If he/she persists, the assessor says sadly, "I guess you don't feel like playing anything but 'No!' Let's stop now, and we can get together again when you feel like doing something else." Since the motivation for "No!" is seductive, the child probably will feel rejected at that point, but he/she is likely to completely avoid the game at the next session. "I just can't," "Silly-billy," and even "backward talk" are likely to be denied with more backward talk and are thus more persistent. "Promise me" must be dealt with quite promptly. The assessor cannot give bribes without being caught in quicksand. The first time the child even hints that "I'll do what you say if you let me. . . ." the assessor must quickly say, "I can't play 'Promise me.' The only thing I can promise you is that I'll try to understand what you have to say and how you do things."

"Fifth Amendment" needs to be handled

with more sympathy—though no less directly. Here the assessor must let the child know that she/he realizes that the child may be afraid, or may feel that his/her privacy is being invaded. In fact, that this is true. The rationale of the assessment contract must then be discussed again and the child's fears be investigated in a kindly sympathetic manner. The assessor may say the following: "When children won't say anything to me, I often wonder if they aren't afraid to trust me. Maybe they think we'll tell their mother everything they say." "I don't care, tell her anything you want," snarls the child. "If I did that, I wouldn't have any right to ask you to do anything. The only reason I have any right to ask you anything is if I respect your rights too. And I don't even have the right to expect you to answer my questions or do any of these things unless you want me to. I think I can understand you better by asking these questions and seeing how you do things, but I need your permission if I'm to help you." The child who plays this game often needs time to think this over, and a second session may be necessary before she/he is willing to accept the assessment transactions. Where the child persists, formal assessment may have to be abandoned—with an explanation again of the reasons. Attempts may have to be made to establish some other kind of relationship with the child, that is, in therapy.

"Uproar" also calls for immediate action. "It sure seems like you want to create an uproar and get me angry. But I don't know what you're angry about." If the child can't explain, the assessor may make some guesses. "Did I interrupt something you were going to do today?"—"Are you afraid of what I may do?"—"Were you angry about something when you came today?" Again, if the child persists the assessor says, "We can't do much when you're feeling so angry and scared. I'd really like to get to know you better and have a good time talking with you and doing things. Perhaps we can get together next week when you will be feeling better."

This list of games does not begin to exhaust the defenses that children can put up against the anxieties engendered by the assessment situation. Nor are the suggested ways of handling these defenses more than illustrations. Most of all, the assessor must learn to distinguish between such defensive games and actual depression or schizophrenic confusion. Depressed children are not playing a game. Rather, feelings so overwhelm them that even though they eagerly accept the assessment contract, they are actually unable to perform. However, once the assessor recognizes the moody, depressed child, the child is usually able to discuss the things he/she is depressed about, or at least openly acknowledge the depression. The confused child who has only a tenuous hold on reality may also defend himself/herself by withdrawing and being noncommittal, but he/she is also often feeling so uncomfortable as to at least accept some offer of support and make some attempt to explain.

E.   THE ASSESSMENT OF PARENTS—THE PARENT CONTRACT

As indicated in the previous sections, the involvement of the parents in the assessment of children is necessary if only to obtain their cooperation in bringing the child in and orienting him to the assessment. In most cases also, when the child is being reared and cared for by parents or parent substitutes (other than institutional employees), it is necessary at least to interview the parents to obtain information about the child's current behavior and history. Even when the contact with the parents is focused entirely on the child, their attitudes, behavior, and personalities enter at least indirectly into the assessment—if only from the way they discuss the child. Recognizing that the development of the child's personality takes place in this parent–child interrelationship, the clinician must attempt to study the personalities of the parents and often of other immediate family members in a family assessment rather than focus entirely on the chiild's symptoms. In fact—as will be discussed later in detail—the child's symptoms and behavior usually derive from and represent a family maladjustment, such that the child constitutes a scapegoat for the neurotic interaction of the whole family. Instead of making assumptions about the behavior of other family members from the child's reports and views or from the parents' bhavior as they discuss the child, it is often necessary to obtain data directly about the parents' attitudes, behavior, and histories.* These data are obtained by asking the parents to become involved in further interviews, to take tests, and to allow observation—directly in the playroom or in the family home—of the interaction between them and the child (see Chapter 5).

The parents' acceptance of this aspect of the assessment depends largely on the manner in which the assessor handles the initial contacts with them. The predominantly middle-class parents who accept referral of their children to a psychologist or to psychological service centers often realize that they also will be subjected to assessment. Even those who may know little of assessment procedures seem aware that in some way their actions and attitudes may be related to the child's symptoms, and they expect to be questioned about it. Whether sophisticated or naive, the parents usually feel that they will be blamed or that they are at fault. In order to assuage their guilty feelings, parents may defend themselves in a variety of ways, ranging from a stiff-necked avoidance of discussion of any of their own feelings or backgrounds to an open confession—hoping thereby to gain reassurance from the assessor. Thus one of the first steps in involving the parents in the assessment is to neutralize as much as possible this blame–avoidance behavior.

Much of the parents' initial guilt can be

*Unless these data have already been obtained by some other staff member in a clinic or hospital center.

lessened by the general attitude of the assessor who seeks to understand and assist with the solution of a problem rather than to determine blame. In the initial interview with the parents, while the child's behavior and symptoms are being considered, the assessor lets the parents know that the purpose is *problem solving* rather than judgment. This is indicated by the way questions are phrased, the line of inquiry, and the tone of voice. The assessor may believe or have good evidence that the parents may have seriously mismanaged the care of the child for their own neurotic needs and feel sympathetic toward the child and be critical of the parents' failures. Nevertheless, in order to help the child in his/her contact with the parents, the psychologist must shift his sympathies and seek to understand the parents and their problems. Unless the parents are approached with a how-can-I-help-you attitude and are regarded as clients equally with the child, it is quite possible that the assessor will meet with such resistance, either overt or covert, as to be unable to help the child. Because this shift in sympathy from child to parent or from parent to child is not easily accomplished and no one is ever entirely neutral, assessment of the parent or parents is often carried out by a different assessor in collaboration with the assessor who is working with the child. Where it is necessary for one assessor to work with both parent and child, the assessor must carefully examine his/her own feelings and attempt to view the assessment task not as a purely child-centered problem, but as a family-centered one that is to be defined and resolved.

If the assessor can approach the parents with such a problem-solving attitude, she/he is then in a position to help them view their problems in the same manner. Often it is necessary to say directly to the parent who is demonstrably guilty—or defensive—that "it really isn't a question of who's to blame. Establishing blame doesn't help anybody. Rather, we need to examine in detail what the problems are and have been, and then we can think about ways of handling them more effectively. . . . Therefore, I do need to understand more of what you're up against and even some of the pressures you've been under in the past.'' Usually even the most guarded parents inadvertently mention some of their own present or past stresses while discussing the child, if only to explain and excuse what has happened. Thus it is often possible during the initial interview with the parents, while focusing on the child's behavior, to guide them into a discussion of some of their own feelings. However, merely luring the parents into discussing their roles with the child without openly recognizing that this is part of the process often results in continued resistance. Although the parents may go along with such a discussion for a while, it usually occurs to them that they are being trapped into revealing things that they may not have intended to discuss. Rather it is much wiser to let the parents know that such a discussion is proposed as part of the assessment contract. The assessor therefore might remark at the close of the initial interview, ''Some of the things that you have mentioned about your feelings and about your backgrounds do seem to help me understand your problem with your child. I wonder how you might feel about discussing these in more detail next time?'' Such a question may mobilize the parents' anxieties for the moment, but as it is discussed in more detail it is often possible to alleviate their fears of exposing themselves to blame. In like manner the assessor can say at the opportune moment, ''I can understand many of your feelings and attitudes as we talk together, but another way we have of getting your viewpoints is to ask you to fill out some questionnaires and work with some other materials I have. How do you feel about doing that?''

Once parents realize that the assessor is concerned with their problems and stresses and anxieties, they are usually more than willing to cooperate. Some may persist in maintaining that ''my child is sick, not me, but if you insist. . . .'' Others may in effect

respond, ''Yes, I'm part of the problem,'' and still others may plead, ''I am most disturbed, and it is really me and not the child who needs help.'' The assessor's response should not be to agree or disagree with any of these statements. It should be to continue to maintain that who is to be helped and how the help is to be given requires a careful and thorough assessment.

After the initial appointment and introduction, the sequence of procedures in the assessment of the parents usually begins with an interview about the child, his/her symptoms and when they began, the conditions surrounding them and their history, and then about the child's environment and his/her development. As noted before, on recognition of the importance of the parents' stresses and their feelings, it is usually fairly easy to proceed to explore their stresses. Once it is established that the parents also are the focus of the psychologist's attention and sympathy, it is possible to introduce other techniques and to ask them to take tests or to observe them in the playroom with their child or to request permission to visit the home. Preparation for either of these latter two techniques may require further exploration of both the parents' and child's feelings. For example, the assessor may say, ''It does seem important for us to understand clearly how you and your child interact. As you know, I have been observing him at play in our playroom. I think I would understand even more clearly if next time you and your child come to the clinic, you and he play together for a little while and I sit back and observe. Would that embarrass you to have me watch the two of you together?'' And, to the child, ''You and I have been having a good time in the playroom here and doing some interesting things. I wonder how you would feel if we invited your mother to join us next time, at least just once, and you could play with her. Of course, what you and I do together and talk about together is just between us, so you don't have to let her know about that unless you want to. But I'd like to see how she plays too.'' A home visit should be similarly discussed with the parents and then the child, using again the grounds that this would enable the assessor to understand the family and its interactions and settings better (see Chapter 5).

F.   PROCEDURES AND TECHNIQUES

The details of how to observe and interview children and of administering specific techniques have been discussed in Chapters 5 and 6. However, it may be helpful at this point to consider some of the general procedural problems that are common to most of these techniques. The five problems to be discussed below may be subsumed under a single question: How can the assessor maintain rapport with the child, motivate her/him to respond and achieve, and at the same time conduct a precise and systematic scientific inquiry?

1.   How Formal Should the Assessment Be?

Should the assessor and child "just talk," or should the assessor conduct a formal structured interview? Should the assessor and child engage in play, or should the assessor stay in his/her corner and observe? Should the child be told that he/she is taking tests or be invited in to "play games"? The answer to all these questions is that both are possible and necessary. It is quite possible to carry out an interview that is planned to touch at least upon many facets of the child's life but in such a fashion as to continually make the child feel that his/her interests are foremost. Such an interview is possible if (1) the assessor does not have to stick to a rigid plan or sequence of topics, but can follow the child's discussion and then introduce new material when the child has completed discussion on one topic, and (2) the assessor makes clear the reasons for asking about topics that the child has not introduced.

For example, in interviewing a 10-year-old enuretic boy, one might want to obtain data about the occurrences and circumstances of the bed-wetting, the interaction between the child and his parents regarding it (the details of training efforts and of possible feelings of shame and of the punitive actions of the parents), and about possible sexual overtones associated with the enuresis—all of which are delicate and embarrassing topics. If one begins with a restatement of the purposes of the assessment, as suggested before in the initial contact, it might be well to remark at the very beginning: "Wetting the bed! That's an embarrassing thing to talk about! At least most of the boys and girls I talk to find it embarrassing, even when they're talking to a doctor. Do you feel that way too?" If the child admits to some embarrassment, the assessor might say, "Yes, I thought you might feel that way." Or if he tries to be nonchalant and deny it: "I guess you've gotten a little used to talking about it by now. . . ." And then, in either instance, one might say, "I guess if you and I are going to understand this problem of yours, it will be necessary to think about many different things connected with it, and I may have to encourage you to talk about some more embarrassing things. But, you know, I've found that after one gets into talking about it, a lot of the embarrassment goes away, and it becomes interesting. It becomes interesting just because it's about us. However, if it gets very embarrassing, we can stop and talk about some other things until you feel easier. Okay?"

Then one might initially discuss with the child the general history of the complaint, the frequency of its occurrence—perhaps in a relatively detached fashion. If the child becomes too anxious, topics such as training and punishment might be delayed until parent–child relations are being disccussed or when sleeping habits are the topic. In fact, reintroducing the complaint at various points does help the child to maintain and recognize the purpose of the assessment. The sexual aspects of such a complaint might be investigated at several different points. For example, when discussing sleeping habits, one might ask about times the child enjoyed joining his parents in their bed, or about the circumstances when she/he is tucked in bed or awakened to go to the toilet. Or in talking about going to the toilet, one might gently inquire if the child had seen others in the family go to the toilet, his parents, for example—again mentioning that "this *is* a personal topic, isn't it!" In speaking about health and growth, one might ask a 10-year-old boy in contemplative tones if he had noticed any differences in his sexual growth, now that he "is almost a teen-ager"—since this is a time most boys do become more aware of changes in their organs and how they work. Recognition with the child that his natural bodily functions are an acceptable topic for the purpose at hand, just as other topics have been, will often help him to get by the immediate anxiety. Indeed he may be delighted to find that an adult is willing to discuss what he and his peers have been whispering about.

Testing also is both a serious challenge and a game. The general directions "I can understand from how you do things as well as talking about them" indicates the serious purpose of the assessment, but there is no need to make an inquisition out of an IQ test or to play "Score" when administering the Rorschach. Actually it is not difficult to make the challenge a game, for most assessors themselves enjoy intellectual games and fantasy—which is probably one of their own motivations for engaging in this work. If the assessor enjoys testing, his/her mood will be conveyed to the child. If the child does seem to be enjoying himself, a direct recognition of it will help to reinforce this mood. If the child is having difficulty and is obviously not having any fun, then as the assessor turns to another task he may remark, "That doesn't seem to be something you enjoyed working with. Let's try something else now." Or, to the child who appears to be struggling in perfectionist style with a drawing, one might remark, "I think you're making it like work. Why don't you just show me how you make a drawing for fun?" Similar remarks often help the

fearful or cautious child on the Rorschach or TAT.

2.   Instructions

Allied to this problem of "formality versus informality" is the problem of instructions. Certainly standardized instructions are a necessary part of scientific assessment. For the most part, these instructions appear to have been worked out with a definite rationale by the test constructor, who attempts to design them so as to orient the subject to the task without giving her/him clues as to the solution of the task. The difficulty arises when the subject does not seem to understand the directions or appears to be misconstruing them. The question arises whether one may repeat the directions or else possibly add to or reword them without so varying the task as to change its nature and thus the analysis of the response.

Some techniques do specifically allow for repetition of the instructions—for example, the Cattell Infant Scale where several illustrations and trials are standard procedures for many tasks, the Rorschach where the instructions may be repeated at least once, and the TAT where the instructions are repeated and enlarged upon as part of the standard procedure after Card 10. However, if after one repetition of instructions on the Rorschach the subject remains under the impression that she/he must interpret the whole card and find one best response to fit the whole inkblot, no further instructions are allowed, and her/his response set is interpreted as a personality variable. While such interpretation may at times be quite valid, Klopfer and associates (1956) do advise that after the inquiry in the "testing of limits," one should encourage the subject to associate to smaller pieces of the blot. He notes that some subjects then realize that the instructions did not limit them as may have been supposed.

The problem increases on techniques that do not specify what to do when the subject does not follow directions—the major intelligence tests being the most prominent examples. For example, despite the instructions on the vocabulary tests, subjects sometimes associate to the words rather than define them. Small children frequently confuse differences and similarities, particularly on the Binet, where one follows the other from Year VI to Year VIII. Except where there are definite prohibitions against giving further help, a repetition of the instructions would seem very much in order, even with a correction of the subject's misperception and a reemphasis of the correct orientation: "No, please tell me what the word *means,* not what it makes you think of." Or, "I'm not sure you have the idea here. It isn't necessary to try to find the 'right' answer to the inkblot. Merely tell me the *different* things that it looks like to you or makes you think of or even just *suggests* or brings to mind."

In the examination of deaf children* or those who do not speak English, directions are usually given by hand signals and illustrations, which usually can be repeated several times until the subject appears to comprehend or until it is obvious that no amount of illustration will suffice to communicate the instructions. If instructions are to be translated into another language or into hand signals to the deaf, the assessor should carefully check with the translator regarding any changes in meaning that might be present in the translation.

3. The Child's Perception of the Task

Since whether children understand the instructions or not can only be determined from the first responses, the next question is the following: How can one tell whether the child has understood and is giving the best response or is still trying to comprehend the task? For example, if after studying Card I of the Rorschach for 20 seconds or more, a child solemnly announces that it "looks like someone has splattered ink on this card," is this an

*See Chapter 16.

association or has he/she misinterpreted the instructions? Or similarly, if the child describes the TAT picture but does not tell a story, is she/he "blocking" and unimaginative, or has she/he failed to understand the directions? Or if on the Stanford-Binet vocabulary, the child defines *roar* as "a lion roars," is he/she defining or merely repeating? If the child just sits and stares and bites her/his lip, is this a response? Of course the assessor may repeat the instructions with gentle encouragement. Or, if puzzled, he/she may inquire further: "Tell me a little more what you mean?" Or, "Yes, it is an inkblot—what does it look like?" Or, "Yes, but what is roar like a lion roars?"

Some techniques have an inquiry as a specific part of the test, and on the Rorschach the inquiry is an essential part of operations. The TAT is less specific in its instructions, although it is common practice, particularly with children, to inquire about the essential parts of the plot if the subject has omitted them—at least on the first several cards until the child begins to realize that the instructions call for more than description or a present tense. "How did that happen?" "Well, what happens next?" "How did the person in the story feel about that?" are almost standard TAT inquiries. "Tell me a bit more what you mean?" can be used on many items on the Wechsler tests. Such inquiry should of course be voiced in a nonchallenging manner, perhaps prefaced by "I think I understand, but. . . ." Or, "I guess I'm a bit puzzled. . . ." The assessor should accept the child's wording and phrasing as long as it is comprehensible, but otherwise he/she can plead ignorance. Once the child has made an attempt to clarify her/his response—even if the response is not adequate—the assessor should praise the child for trying, to reinforce such efforts on further tasks.

How far one may carry such inquiry is a matter of clinical judgment. Obviously if one expands on the instructions or asks additional questions beyond those specified in the standardization, the task is changed.

Yet, since the purpose is not merely to obtain a score, it is often necessary to pose additional questions. One may need to inquire further on the WISC Comprehension Test or on Similarities to follow the child's logic or to see whether or not with one more clue or one more thought she/he might be able to make a more effective solution. Commonly the child is asked to "tell the story" to the Picture Arrangement Test, even though Wechsler does not include such an inquiry in his instructions—and it is quite possible that in so doing the child is helped in other PA items by the practice in verbalizing his/her logic. A similar situation arises when the child is permitted to finish the Block Design or Object Assembly puzzle after the time limit.

The answer to this dilemma is that such necessary and informative inquiry can be considered as an addendum to the test per se. Though not included in the score, it becomes part of the data, enriching the score and enabling the psychologist to understand the thought processes and ideation that accompany the response. When one allows the child to finish a Block Design or to add a response to a previously rejected inkblot, it is possible to estimate what the child may be able to do over and beyond the time limits of everyday life. Thus the score indicates what the child can do under the pressures of time, and the inquiry shows what she/he might do if given more time than usual or if encouraged.

4.   Silence and "Don't Know"

These are special responses that pose a slightly different problem. When a child quickly responds "don't know" or sits without answering, should the assessor accept this as the response or encourage the child to persist? Should the assessor let the child off the hook or sweat it out patiently, and in effect pressure the child through silence into some kind of response—if possible. The answer lies in the assessor's clinical judgment of what the child is trying to do and his/her mood and motivation.

Usually after the initial contact period and a few trial test tasks, it is possible to make some estimate of what is going on. If one has the advantage of having conducted an interview with the child before attempting tests, it is much easier to guess at what the child's silences or "don't knows" are about. The hastily shrugged "don't know" may be a version of the game of "No!" that is easily spotted beforehand in an interview. The shy, fearful, or depressed child may need support, a friendly repetition of the question, or a few more seconds of the assessor's patience. The contemplative child may need more time to respond. To the compulsively perfectionistic child who would rather say "don't know" than be wrong, one might remark gently, "I think you're making all this too hard. Just tell me in your own words what your idea is." On the other hand, the child who sits in embarrassed silence not knowing what to respond may have to be reassured that "there may be some problems you won't know the answers to, but unless you tell me that you give up, I can't tell whether you're still thinking or are ready for the next one."

G.   CONCLUDING THE ASSESSMENT

Although the total assessment involves only a brief contact between asssessor and child, it usually is a more intense emotional interaction than the child commonly experiences in contacts with strange adults. No matter how resistant, the child usually is aware that attention has been focused on his/her feelings and needs. Many of the children brought to assessment have been seriously deprived of concern and understanding. Often they are hungry for such attention—openly or secretly—but at the same time they may greet it with distrust and anxiety. Unconsciously at least, they realize that it is a temporary relationship, that it will not last, and that they should steel themselves against a false hope. The more infantile child will make obvious moves to win over the assessor, to be charming, or to begin to make demands that go beyond the assessment contract. Such children frequently try to stretch out the assessment hours and so delay the inevitable separation.

For these reasons some time is needed to allow the child to make a gradual separation rather than have it occur as a sudden impact. As was mentioned before, in making the appointment one should inform the parents of the appproximate time the appointment will involve and ask them to tell the child. This should be repeated to the child on initial contact: "We'll spend about an hour and a half together today. I don't know whether that will give us enough time to do all the things we want to, but we can always set up another appointment if necessary." If the child is anxious and wants to negotiate the time right then, one may reply, "Let's wait and see what we need." Shortly before the end of the first contact, one should warn the child, "We have about 10 minutes left," or "We've got time for one more thing. Then we can meet with your mother and see when you can return." Then at the beginning of the second—or final—contact, one can tell the child and mother, "We'll probably need another hour and a half today to finish up." The child who protests that he/she wants more time may be reassured that this does not mean he/she will not receive more attention at the clinic, but rather than this particular kind of contact or this beginning step will not need much more time.

On the other hand, the resistant child— particularly the glum teen-ager who drags his/her heels and protests that there is "nothing wrong with me" and thus does not need so much time—may be countered with raised eyebrows: "I thought you needed someone to understand, so I was giving you as much time as I could." Again, shortly before the end of the assessment the assessor should warn, "There's just one more thing I want to ask you to do before we stop." The assessor should plan to make this task one that may not be so vital to the assessment that there will be a serious lack of data if the child rushes through

it or dawdles over it to the point that it is not possible to complete it. Usually there will be little problem if it is some interesting and relatively nonthreatening task such as drawings or the World Test. Of course if the child has been rushing through things all along, the assessor should have taken note of her/his attitudes long before and raised a question about it: "You seem to be rushing and not giving yourself enough time. I wondered whether you were anxious to get through or thought you didn't have enough time?" Obversely, if a child is dawdling, interrupting, or otherwise obviously taking up more time than is necessary, it is necessary to ask some question about it: "It seems as if we have a hard time getting going on things this afternoon. I wonder if you need more time or possibly even really don't like what we're doing here today?" If the child agrees, one might inquire further about how other tasks at home or school are dealt with to see if this approach is habitual to task-oriented situations or if it is related specifically to anxiety about the assessment.

During the final task the assessor should observe in particular how the child is reacting to the announced separation. Besides observing the alacrity with which the child proceeds, one may look for such signs of anxiety as extreme carelessness or extra precision, apathy or restlessness, increase or decrease in verbalization or other extra activity, changes in facial expression and bodily movement, watching or studiously avoiding the clock, and so forth. Once the final, formal task is over, the assessor should specify that the session is ended and spend a few moments inquiring about the child's feelings and questions about it: "Well, those are all the questions I have, and all the things I planned to ask you to do. But I wonder if you have any questions you wanted to ask or anything you wanted to tell me that I may have forgotten to ask you about?" Even if the child denies that she/he has anything more to say, the assessor should reinforce whatever effort the child has made to reveal his/her feelings and to cooperate: "You've really worked awfully hard, even though I've asked you some very personal questions and asked you to do some things that were not easy. I know it's not always easy to show other people how we do things or let them know what we think about, especially when we're afraid other people will criticize us or won't understand. But I think I do understand a little bit more now. How do you feel about it?"

This question and whatever discussion follows will allow the assessor to introduce the fact that although the asessment per se is over and perhaps this particular relationship as well—unless the assessor is going to proceed with whatever treatment or disposition may be in order—the child's needs will receive further attention, and the assessment will contribute toward the planning of this attention. Thus the assessor should check with the child about his next appointment at the clinic or with the referrant: "When will you be seeing Dr. X again?" And then, "By that time I will have a chance to think over what we've done together and will be able to talk it over with your therapist. That way he can understand a bit better also. If you have more questions then about what we did here, you can ask him about it." Quite often children will show some anxiety about what the assessor will communicate to the referrant and will want to discuss it—particularly if the referrant is an authority figure for the child. "What are you going to tell my doctor?" The assessor should inquire what the child is worried might be said. Often children's replies will reveal their concern about their performance or some revelation of their feelings. "Would it help if Dr. X or the teacher or the probation officer did understand that you have difficulty doing arithmetic or that you have angry feelings sometimes toward your mother?"

Sometimes a child will admit to being puzzled or concerned about some responses. In such instances, he/she may be encouraged to contemplate—at least momentarily—what he/she has said or done and what it might mean. In general the assessor should avoid explaining or interpreting the overall results of the assessment

(particularly since there has not been an opportunity to digest them). However, if the child is trying to recognize some of his/her feelings in greater detail and is close to some insight, the assessor should permit it if only to reinforce the message that further help and understanding are in the offing. For example, a shy and retiring 10-year-old boy remarked that he was surprised how many "murder" stories he had told to the TAT. "I guess you didn't know how much murder there was in your imagination," remarked the assessor. The boy shook his head. "From what you told me about yourself you don't actually murder anybody or even hit anybody very often. But apparently these kinds of feelings are inside your thoughts, even though you don't do anything about it. Can you think of any times you feel like murdering somebody but just keep it to yourself?" The boy reminded the assessor that he had said this about his younger brother in the interview and on the Bene-Anthony Family Relations questionnaire. The assessor suggested that maybe the boy might want to think more about this and other things that had come up during the assessment and discuss them with his therapist.

More frequently the child and especially the parent pressure the assessor for some immediate advice or report of the findings. In such a situation one may tell the parent that it is not possible to answer this question before the data are analyzed. In any event, the assessor should not attempt to respond until after conferring with the referrant (before knowing how the client may use his/her opinion). This is not to say that the results of the assessment should never be conveyed to the client. On the contrary, it is to be hoped that the assessment is not performed only for the information of the referrant, but that eventually the assessment data can be used, sometimes fairly directly in further counseling or therapy. At this point, however, interpretation of the assessment findings is not appropriate.

Rather than refusing the parent's request—even with a polite explanation— the fact that the parent does want to know about the child should be reinforced. Moreover, by exploring the parent's question in more detail, the assessor may both obtain additional data and assist the parent in making a transition from the assessor back to the referrant. Thus the assessor might respond, "I am not sure I know what to recommend right at the moment, but I will be conferring with Dr. X very soon, and I know you will be in touch with him. But I wonder what ideas have occurred to you while you were talking to me and doing these things here? Has this given you a chance to consider your problem further?" Whatever response the client may give, she/he should be directed back to the referrant for further discussion. Even if the assessor himself/herself is going to carry the case, he/she should defer further discussion until there is opportunity to study the data.

After the assessor has assured the client regarding the next appointment with the referrant, the contact with the client can be concluded. The next major steps in the assessment are the analysis of the data and the formulation of a report—tasks that often take as much of the psychologist's time as the actual contact with the child and parents. As was mentioned before, the assessor should take this time factor into consideration in planning an assessment, setting time aside for it in her/his schedule, so as to be able to inform the referrant and client when the results might be ready for their use. In addition, the assessor should plan her/his own schedule so that she/he can work on the analysis of data and report as soon as possible, not only because of the client's needs, but because it is likely that she/he can do a better job while the experience is still fresh in mind—before the data get "cold." Last week's data, at the bottom of the "to-be-done" basket, too often become a chore, and the inspirations and scientific curiosity present at the end of the patient contact may fade.

Unfortunately there are those instances when—despite the efforts of the psychologist to establish an effective liaison with the referrant—she/he cannot in good faith promise the child that the assessment will definitely be used. Referrants do not always follow the psychologist's recommendations. They may not comprehend or even read the report. In such instances the psychologist should be more cautious and promise only to talk to the doctor, probation officer, or parent. Sometimes the child senses that there is difficulty in communicating with the referrant: "I don't think he'll listen to you!" The psychologist should reassure the child that he/she will do his/her best to communicate clearly.

One method to resolve such doubts, which I have found satisfactory, is to arrange for further appointments to discuss the results with the child and subsequently with the referrant—and possibly with the two together. Such an arrangement should of course be explained and be agreeable to the referrant. This method is particularly reassuring to the child if the results are to be discussed subsequently with parents or some other authority. It is also helpful to a propsective therapist.

Since children are often aware of some of their failures and successes on IQ tests or other achievement tests and of the revelations of feelings on subjective or associative techniques, such a discussion of results should center about those items that the child recognizes as meaningful. Where appropriate, the psychologist might remind the child of those tasks that the child had previously remarked were difficult. Or a seemingly "significant" TAT story might be read back to her/him to see if the child might contribute further associations. Such discussion should be limiteed to those behaviors that appear to be near the level of the child's consciousness: So-called "deep" interpretations should be avoided. For example, the child might remark that he/she found the arithmetic subtest on the WISC difficult, or at least that he/she did not like it. If appropriate, the psychologist might remark that this was understandable since the child had told him/her of difficulties with arithmetic at school, but at the same time note with the child that such difficulty might be hard to understand since his/her reasoning on other tests was above average. Even when a child has many areas of poor functioning or is performing at a retarded level, it may be quite possible to use the IQ or other tests to help her/him recognize and understand such difficulties. It is quite inappropriate to tell a child, "You did good," when she/he actually failed. On the contrary, a child should be told that the psychologist also is aware that "you have difficulty learning things and figuring things out." The psychologist might help the child speculate why this may be true. Such an interpretation may be quite anxiety provoking to the child. If there is no definite plan for the child to receive further resolution of these anxieties, then the psychologist should be most circumspect in his/her interpretations and avoid arousing more anxiety in the child than is already present. When the child succeeds beyond his/her hopes and self-estimates, the assessor certainly should inform the child. "You're really smarter than you thought." Or, "Did you know that you have a creative imagination?"

Similarly, the psychologist might ask the child which Rorschach responses or TAT stories she/he remembers and what they meant to her/him. Or the psychologist might remark, "You remember the several stories you told in which the hero got rid of his enemy. You also told me a lot about what a pest your brother can be. Could he be one of the enemies you daydream of getting even with?" Often when the psychologist connects such consciously reported feelings to the fantasies, the child will respond by making other associations on her/his own.

At the conclusion of such discussions with the child, I usually ask her/him what I should communicate to the referrant. I usually agree not to reveal anything that the child wishes kept private, but I also point out that the parent already seems aware of this or that aspect of the child's problems, and that further discussion with him/her may clarify issues. If feasible, the child can be invited to share the discussions with his/her parents, which should follow the same approach. That is, these discussions should begin with those facets of the child's behavior and functioning that they already recognize and understand, at least partially, expanding into those areas that they may be able to use or consider further. Similarly, I may ask an adolescent what would be helpful to be revealed to a probation officer or therapist. "Should your doctor know," I might ask, "that you panic easily, that you cannot think at school or on IQ tests when you are tensed up, or even that your mother confuses you? Do you think your P.O. would understand? Might this help the two of you to work out a solution of your problems?"

H. SUMMARY

Some special procedures are necessary when assessing children who are suspected of having brain damage or who have muscular, sensory, or other handicaps. These procedures will be discussed in Chapter 16. Children from other cultures or subcultures also require special attention, as is discussed in Chapter 17. However, the procedures described so far are basic to any assessment. The assessment consists of a complex of interpersonal relationships. It is vital to deal with the fears, resistances, and other feelings of both the child and his/her parents.

PART FOUR

Analysis of the Assessment: Specifications of the Ego Functions

Although the scoring and analysis of an assessment serve to organize data according to the theories of each of the assessment techniques, the focus of the analysis is not on the technique per se, but on the overall functioning of the child's ego. Thus it is necessary to examine all of the data from *all* techniques for the evidence pertaining to the development of each function. Perhaps the most difficult lesson for the beginning clinician is this task of recognizing and interpreting the evidence. The purpose of this section is to demonstrate one system by which the data of an assessment may be used as evidence of the child's ego development. In order to conduct this analysis, it may be helpful to add yet another step in this classification of ego functioning, specifying further the different aspects of each function. The categories that follow are purely heuristic and are intended only as an aid in organizing the data.

1. The *modality* of the function, that is, the bodily and social organs through which the function operates.
2. The *input* and *output* or receptive-expressive aspects.
3. The development of the ability to *focus* and to *differentiate* stimuli.
4. *Interferences* with the functioning.
5. *Coping mechanisms*.
6. The *content* or subtypes of each function. These categories may be most clearly defined by the manner in which they are applied operationally to each function.

CHAPTER 9

The Analysis of Perceptual-Motor
and Cognitive Development

A. PERCEPTUAL-MOTOR
MODALITIES

The most common modality of perceptual-motor behavior as sampled by the techniques commonly used in assessment is *visual*. Children are asked to draw what they *see* on the Bender, tell us what they *see* on the Rorschach, sort out what they *see* on Picture Completion or Picture Arrangement, or identify what they *see* on Picture Vocabulary tests (Binet or Ammons). Some of these tasks depend on hearing also—at least in the instructions—but this auditory aspect is usually a minimal part, and if a hearing deficit is suspected, the test may be given with gestures as if administered to the deaf. The Kohs Blocks subtest of the Grace Arthur is a good example of a technique that involves vision alone. On the other hand, other tests of attention, such as the Digit Span subtest of the Wechsler or Binet involve only audition. Differences in the modality of perceptual functioning may thus be evidenced in the differences in scores on tasks involving mainly one modality as opposed to another. However, the evidence may often be more qualitative than quantitative. For example, an auditory perceptual dysfunction may show up mainly in constant misperception or verbal instructions, for example, when the child asks over and over to have instructions repeated or repeats verbal problems sotto voce before proceeding. This type of dysfunction is illustrated in Case 20.

The lack of any direct assessment of tactile perception in the usual clinical battery may be excused on the grounds that tactile perception plays such a relatively small part in the overall intake of stimuli in contrast to vision and audition—except among infants. In addition, tactile dysfunctions are extremely rare and are usually compensated for by vision or hearing. On the other hand, tactile dysfunction may be one sign of brain damage, and neurologists commonly do make gross tests of the child's tactile discriminations. Inversely, the overuse of tactile perception, that is, where the child seems to have to touch everything before she/he can react to it, may be one telltale sign of a visual or auditory dysfunction. Such a child may be attempting to cope with a defect in the other senses or with an overall perceptual imbalance. Even the neurotic child who must touch things compulsively is in a sense touching for reassurance that what is seen or heard is real and permanent. Such touching behavior is fairly common among preschool children as a normal way of integrating perceptions.

The other perceptual modes are also not commonly assessed by psychologists—much for the same reason. Again, disturbances of kinesthesis are also common in some types of brain damage or are symptomatic of gross developmental lag. Differentiation between poor "balance" sense and inadequate motor coordination is sometimes difficult, and it requires close observation of the way the child moves and sits as opposed to his/her ability to perform motor tasks when his/her whole body is not reacting to gravity. The possibility of an akinesthesis should be entertained if the child can pass most of the psychologist's motor tasks, but has trouble standing erect, hopping on one foot, skipping, leaning, and the like. Dysfunction in pain perception is a rare childhood complaint. Some children do seem overly sensitive to pain and it is very rare that a child fails to experience pain with a trauma. Since pain is difficult to localize and identify even for an adult and can easily be generalized, careful interviewing of the child is often necessary to determine exactly how and where he/she does experience pain. Although such interviewing about complaints of physical pain lie chiefly within the province and skill of the pediatrician, the data from psychological interviews may be of assistance to the physician—especially when the child has difficulty distinguishing physical pain from affective experiences or when complaints of pain are heightened by emotional states. Pediatricians may also request psychological assessments of cases of childhood analgesia. Sometimes such imperviousness to pain may be part of an overall lag in perceptual development such as in the severely retarded child, or it maybe a hysterical symptom.

B.   PERCEPTUAL-MOTOR INPUT–OUTPUT

Distinguishing between input and output difficulties in perceptual-motor behavior is a crucial question in determining the type of retraining required. Since most assessment tasks involve both perceptual and motor behaviors, the evidence regarding input versus output does not come from any one set of scores or responses, but from qualitative observation of the way the child performs the task. For example, if she/he struggles in drawing the Bender figures, holding extra tight to her/his pencil, erasing and correcting, and is evidently dissatisfied with the production, Koppitz (1963) suggests such behavior is indicative of an *expressive* difficulty. The child perceives the figures but has difficulty in motorically reproducing them. On the other hand, if the child draws a figure quickly and easily but erroneously and without recognition of the error, Koppitz takes this as a sign of a perceptual or *receptive* difficulty rather than a purely motor one. Similar behavioral evidence of input-versus-output difficulties may be drawn from many other techniques such as Block Design, Object Assembly, or even on the Rorschach. For example, any child over age 5 who sees the whole of Rorschach Card II as a face with eyes at the bottom, a nose in the center, a mouth in the space, and the main D as ears, is evidently experiencing some kind of perceptual disorganization. However, another child may give the same response, but during inquiry says, "It just looks like it . . . here . . . here. . . ." This child may have an anomia or other difficulty in expression. It is possible that he/she may be able to identify the parts of the face with adequate perceptual organization when specifically asked about them.

Discrimination between receptive and expressive dysfunctions is not always easy. For example, one way children have of coping with motor difficulty is to deny it by hastily scrawling something and pushing the product aside as if content with it. Only through specific inquiry can it be determined whether or not the child actually has misperceived or if he/she has tried to avoid the motor task. In such instances, the assessor can ask, "How might your drawing be changed to look more like this?" Inversely, the child who labors in dissatisfaction over his Bender drawings may be hesitating not so much because of a motor difficulty, but because she/he has not been able to focus or discriminate perceptually.

One test specifically designed to explore this differentiation is the Goldstein-Sheerer version of the Kohs Blocks (1945). On this test the child who fails the original design is given one with the block boundaries drawn on the design, then a larger design, and finally one with both perceptual clues. Presumably, if the child can do the task with these extra clues, the difficulty is perceptual. On the other hand, if the child is given some motor training, for example by seeing how the examiner does it, and then is successful, a motor difficulty would seem more likely. Tests like the Porteus Mazes or the Arthur Scales or any of the trail-making tests (as in Part V of the Frostig [1961] also allow for observation of input-versus-output difficulties. If the child accidently gets off the path in going around the maze but corrects himself/herself, he/she most likely is having a motor difficulty in guiding the pencil. But if he/she keeps going into blind alleys becoming blocked, the difficulty would seem more perceptual. In like manner, in using any of the various aphasia test materials, if the child can name an object when it is presented separately but cannot select it from a group of objects when asked for it by name, this would seem to be evidence of a receptive agnosia—based on inability to recognize the auditory stimulus. But if she/he can select the object when given the name of it but cannot name it himself/herself, expressive anomia is presumed. It should be noted that input and output do not always develop uniformly in infancy. Thus the Binet in Years II and III contains both kinds of items. (For further discussion, see Chapters 16 and 17.)

C. PERCEPTUAL-MOTOR FOCUS AND DISCRIMINATION

The ability to screen out stimuli and focus on an object or situation is measured by quite a number of psychological tests. Focus and discrimination of the stimulus is the central task on the Rorschach. At the simplest level, focus is merely the ability to concentrate perceptually and pay attention. At the more complicated level, focusing requires sorting out and bringing together a total gestalt. The "DW," or confabulation, type of response to the Rorschach, in which the child is reminded of something by a relatively small detail of the blot but then is unable to restrict his/her response to the single detail and expands it out of proportion to the whole blot, is a classic example of a difficulty in focusing. Discriminating between several objects or situations is tested by such tasks as the Three-Figure Form Board or Aesthetic Comparison or Form Differences (on the Binet) or the Wechsler Picture Arrangement. It is central to the Raven Matrices and the Columbia Mental Maturity Scale.

On the Rorschach, difficulty in discrimination is manifest when the child cannot separate two different engrams, but contaminates two disparate associations into one, without being able to see the inconsistency of the total response. For example, the child may see Card I as a butterfly and also as a face and call it a "butterfly face." Learning to make perceptual differentiation is of course one of the tasks of the preschool child, as witness the number of differentiation tasks on the Binet between years II and IV−6. Such contaminations must be distinguished from the sometimes bizarre combinations often given by preschool children to the Rorschach, which are evidence of creative imagination and the beginning of the ability to make complex associations. For example, the following response to Rorschach Card II (inverted) was given by a very bright and imaginative 4-year-old: "It's an 'O' walking. Here's its legs. And here's its wee-wee!" Even though the combination of parts is fanciful, there is no contamination present in such a response.

Most techniques require both focus and discrimination. All the tests cited previously as measurements of focus also require some discrimination, and the tasks cited as measuring discrimination merely emphasize that aspect of the overall focus-discrimination process. Block Design on the Wechsler, for example, requires that the child make discriminatory choices between sections of the design and then focus on the section and position of the block. On the Bender or the Graham-Kendall, the child must focus on the overall gestalt but also discriminate between parts. For example, on Card A of the Bender the child may see the figure as consisting of two parts but she/he may not discriminate between the parts—drawing both as circles—or she/he may see the two parts but not be able to bring them into focus as a unity.

Motor behavior also involves both focus and discrimination. Every child has to learn how to focus on one movement while controlling or excluding others. Specificity of motor control is a task of primary importance during infancy, but it continues to be practiced throughout childhood. For example, before age 4 months, the infant may be attracted by an object held overhead and flail out with both arms and legs in an effort to grasp at it, but the average infant of this age is able at least to move both arms in coordinated fashion at the object, while holding the rest of her/his body still enough to make the grasping move. By the time a child is able to draw the Bender figures, she/he must not only focus on holding the pencil but avoid other motor movements that might make it difficult to draw. Very often the hyperactive child may make gross errors on the Bender just because he/she cannot focus on the single movements of his/her arm, but—wriggling and contorting the whole body—can only make a slapdash drawing. His/her pencil runs off the edge of the page or past the point where he/she wants to stop or begin.

Similar focusing of motor movements is required on other tasks, such as the Seguin Form Board, where the child must not only perceptually match the block to the hole, but must so control or focus his/her movements as to insert the block correctly. Typically the child who has motor-focusing problems makes a correct match between block and hole, but, unable to insert the block, he/she attempts to pound it in with both hands. The child must also learn to discriminate between movements—to choose the appropriate movement or pattern of motor behavior. Such a child first learns to use his/her hands for some things, feet for others, to make circular motions as

opposed to a straight line, and how to make arm and pencil go to the right as distinct from the left. These discriminations are qualitatively demonstrated in such tasks as drawing a square (Binet age months), on the Seguin or the Knox Blocks (of the Arthur). Sometimes even an older child has difficulty in making such motor discrimination, for example, on the Porteous Mazes, and even though she/he has figured out the pattern of the maze perceptually, still has obvious difficulty in guiding the pencil along the pathway.

D. MEASURES OF PERCEPTUAL FUNCTIONING

Among the tests most popularly thought of as measures of perceptual functioning are the Bender Gestalt and the Graham-Kendall Memory for Designs Test. Both of these techniques require the reproduction of simple designs. These tests—described in Chapter 4—have definite norms for different ages. As mentioned previously, the Bender Gestalt, using the Kopitz norms, serves as a fairly good test of perceptual accuracy for children ages 5 to 9. This test in the past has been badly misused, however, because there were no adequate norms prior to Koppitz (1963). Many younger children were misdiagnosed because they committed simple errors that were common among pre-school children but that—if made by adults—would be indicative of a perceptual-motor handicap. The Memory for Designs is for older children and takes into account the IQ and age. Moreover, it requires the child to reproduce the design from memory.

Less well recognized as a test of perception is the Rorschach Technique. Because the Rorschach does provide data regarding the individual's emotional life, it is frequently forgotten that it is in essence a test involving perception. The Rorschach basically requires that the child analyze a piece of visual nonsense. The child's ability to delineate out what Rorschach calls "engrams" is an essential part of this technique. The main question is can the child make perceptual sense of the inkblot. Actually this is a more difficult perceptual test than merely copying a design as on the Bender or the Memory for Designs. Here the child must call upon previously conceived perceptions and see how well such a memory may match the shape, color, or shading of the blot. Where a perceptual difficulty is suspected, the assessor must be most careful to conduct a detailed inquiry into the child's inkblot responses. Children with a perceptual difficulty may make what seems to be a relatively adequate or even popular response to the inkblot, but become quite hesitant and confused when asked to detail the response and explain it. In the inquiry the perceptually handicapped child begins to doubt the response and may then become quite helpless. It is this insecurity or helplessness about a response that most clearly reveals the perceptual dysfunction.

Similar feelings of helplessness and confusion are often demonstrated in children's responses to the performance side of the WISC-R. The perceptually handicapped child may slow down on the Block Design, reverse figure-and-ground, make simple errors, and be unable to correct them. Whereas the intellectually retarded child who has no gross perceptual difficulty may succeed well on the Object Assembly Test, this test is often a crucial point of failure for the perceptually handicapped. He/she does not see the whole figure, and therefore cannot assemble the jigsaw puzzle. The sequence of events on the Picture Arrangement Test is also a puzzle for the perceptually handicapped. On the Rorschach and on the WISC-R, the child may frequently turn to the examiner for help, presenting a response in a tentative fashion and asking the examiner if the answer is correct. Feelings of inadequacy and dependency and the need for succor are frequently expressed on the TAT stories of the perceptually handicapped child.

CASE 20

Lena, age 15, was referred by her pediatrician, who thought that she might be "feebleminded." She was pregnant for the scond time, and the doctor was recommending to her parents that she have an abortion. Her first pregnancy when she was 13 had ended in a miscarriage. Her parents, who were first-generation Polish Catholic, were extremely reluctant to follow the doctor's advice, although they too could see that Lena was not functioning intellectually too well, and that it was doubtful that she could care for a child. Lena was a very passive and "sweet" girl who did not seem to have much to say about her situation. Her IQ was within normal range (90), but her thinking was very concrete. She had only a very vague idea of the relationship between sexual intercourse and pregnancy. She said she was very much in love with her boyfriend, but admitted she had had intercourse with several different boys. It appears that she had discovered that boys would be friends with her if she permitted them sexual liberties. She had been only partially successful throughout her elementary school and was being kept in school only because she was going to a convent school. The sisters did not regard her as a bad girl or as intellectually retarded. They agreed to keep her in the convent, and to put her child out for adoption. Her responses to the psychological tests did show that she had a fairly severe and widespread perceptual handicap. Thus she could give concrete answers in the convent-school classes, but really failed to understand general social principles. Shortly after the birth of her child, she entered a Catholic retreat.

CASE 21

Emmet, age 17, sought the help of the clinic because of an strange job failure. He found himself unable to follow a sequence of tasks on a job. He would forget what he had to do next. He related that he had experienced such difficulties in following a sequence before, such as in playing basketball or attempting to learn chess. If he had a list to follow, he usually was able to carry out what was required. However, when hired to clean up in a hamburger stand, he would forget what he was supposed to do. In basketball he could not remember a series of plays, nor figure what one set of plays might be required as a response. He knew the rules for chess, but could not predict a series of plays. Otherwise he was doing fairly well at school—even in mathematics. However, he had had to make double the effort to memorize his geometry and did not plan to take advanced mathematics. He had taken college-entrance examinations and had scored high enough to get into the state university. He agreed that whatever handicap he had was not severely disabling in any way, but he hated to admit to himself that he had any kind of handicap.

On examination he proved to be a fairly compunctious, almost compulsive individual who was a perfectionist. Socially he was quite an isolate, and he thought that no girl would ever give him a second look. He was quite ignorant of the social mores of his generation and probably was regarded as quite "square" by his contemporaries.

Psychological testing revealed that he did have a mild to moderate perceptual handicap. He was quite panicky when he tried to reproduce the figures on the Graham-Kendall, and he was very unsure of himself in his responses to the Rorschach. He kept saying, "See, see how stupid I am?" Yet when given some support and reassurance by the assessor, he was able to explain his Rorschach responses quite adequately on the inquiry. He had no history of any neurological disorder, and the neurological examination was negative. He spent about a year in psychotherapy in which his anxiety was somewhat relieved, although he remained a rather stiff and rigid person. He was helped most by a physical-education professor, who was doing research in the field of spatial perceptual difficulties. Under this teacher's tutelage, he took up golf at which he became

quite successful and more reassured about his physical abilities. He also assisted the professor in the construction of the walk-through mazes for the blind and was able himself to follow these mazes with his eyes closed.

Although it did appear that this quite intelligent young man had a definite spatial perceptual problem, it was not really any disability, as he could have avoided some of the tasks that he found difficult. Moreover, his disability was really highly aggravated by his compulsiveness and by his extremely high self-expectations. In many ways he was such a perfectionist that he could never live up to his own goals. He was the only son of very protective parents, and he was very frightened about the prospect of leaving home and going to the university. Yet he was very angry at his mother's constantly hovering over him, and at the same time he could not identify with his father, whom he said was weak. He was afraid that he might grow up to be a weak man like his father. After graduation from high school, he decided not to leave home immediately, and he spent almost a year in psychotherapy while doing some work at the local college. He finally left town for the university in a rebellious but high-spirited mood.

E.   INTERFERENCES WITH PERCEPTUAL-MOTOR FUNCTIONING

1.   Perceptual Handicaps

In addition to children who have actual sensory handicaps, there are those who have receptive difficulty in that the sensations they receive are not organized into anything meaningful for them. They hear and see, but they do not perceive. Such children—at least in the first years of their lives—may seem quite intellectually normal, but usually their intellectual development is slowed down, at least mildly. Such children may grasp some meaning from their environments, but it may be incomplete or incorrect or oversimplified. The first recognition may come when the child fails to be able to generalize from one social rule to the next, and thus becomes a mild behavior problem. These children's thinking is thus likely to be quite concrete. They learn mainly through memorization, and they have difficulty with abstract thinking either verbally or nonverbally. Such a perceptual dysfunction may be related to the so-called mildly retarded or borderline-IQ child. However, many of these children can function about IQ = 100. By memorizing drills, they can succeed at almost everything in elementary school.

Such children usually run a cropper when they begin junior high school or high school. If they have been able to memorize their multiplication tables, they really have extreme difficulties with algebra and geometry. Learning a foreign language is also extremely difficult for them. Emotionally, they are "immature" in that they do not develop the knowledge of unspoken but accepted social rules. They remain dependent on others for interpretation of the world about them. Other children recognize that in some way these perceptually handicapped children are not socially aware, and they make fun of them and isolate them.

The precise nature of these perceptual difficulties varies considerably. Some children can get by with visual perceptions and fail at auditory. Thus they can understand what's going on from the textbook or from what the teacher writes on the board, but they fail to make sense of what she/he is saying. Other children have a great deal of difficulty with anything visual, insofar as organizing it into a meaningful whole, but they will grasp things better through their hearing. Where this perceptual difficulty is associated with an epilepsy—particularly a petit mal—the children's perceptual abilities may be quite variable from moment to moment. Petit mal epileptics suffer from frequent "shorts" in their neurological electrical systems, such that they receive pieces of sensation without ever getting any sequence of stimuli. Thus the perceptual

whole for the petit mal epileptic child is incomplete or disordered. (See Chapter 15.)

2. The Sources of Interference

The sources of interference with perceptual and motor functioning are so multiple as almost to defy description or even classification. Some may be so obvious as to seem unnecessary to mention. The perceptual-motor limitations of the blind child, for example, may seem so gross that it is possible to forget the many small ways in which it interferes with overall functioning or the implications of it for other ego functions. At the other extreme there are often interferences to the child's functioning that may be so subtle as to defy direct observation. For example, the psychologist may know that the child has been upset by something that happened just before coming to the assessment, so that he/she is unable to pay attention to the tasks presented. But the psychologist cannot always know what is going on with children or even that anything is preoccupying or pressing on them. For example, a 5-year-old girl seemed to be getting increasingly uneasy as the assessment proceeded. Her attention wandered, she wriggled about in her chair, fumbled with the test materials, and after about three Rorschach cards, seemed almost in tears. Setting the cards aside, the assessor remarked on her obvious discomfort and asked her about it. At this the child burst into tears and admitted she needed to go to the toilet but was too inhibited to have admitted it voluntarily. On returning from the bathroom, she was much more at ease, and she asked to look at the Rorschach cards "all over again." Thereafter she was able to give much more adequate responses.

Although temporarily inhibiting factors can be spotted by the astute assessor, it is often necessary to infer the presence of more long-range and constant interferences with perceptual-motor behavior from the data. Sometimes the nature of these interferences appears in the perceptual-motor responses or in the behavior accompanying them. For example, if a child with a misshapen head and spastic extremities, who is cooperative, friendly, and smiling, takes the pencil in his/her fist and attempts with glee to copy the Bender figures, but makes only very simplified, inadequate reproductions that he/she offers with satisfaction, the impression that this perceptual difficulty is related to the central nervous system* dysfunction would certainly seem quite reasonable. However, if the child was not so disabled but was very tense and glum and uneasy, openly voicing morbid and phobic ideas and elaborating his/her Bender reproductions as if to illustrate these fears, it would seem reasonable to assume that the reproductions were interrupted by severe emotional disturbances.

In most cases, however, the nature of the interference is not so blatant. All that is seen is the child's struggle to perform the perceptual-motor task and the resultant distortions in the reproductions. *To assess the nature of the interfering factors, it is necessary to examine other data from other sources.* That is, it is necessary to specify further the nature of other ego functions and their interactions with the perceptual-motor behavior. Even when the interference seems to be as "obvious" as in the preceding example, the data from the perceptual-motor tasks should be cross-checked against data from other techniques. If, for example, the placid and seemingly brain-damaged child showed signs of emotional disturbance on other kinds of tasks, or succeeded on more complex tasks involving perceptual functioning—or if the phobias of the second child were demonstrated only on the Bender, then our initial hypotheses about these children would have to be revised considerably. This assumption and other aspects of brain damage will be discussed at length in Chapter 16.

Perceptual-motor tasks have been designed and used so exclusively for the assessment of brain damage that they are commonly called "tests for brain damage," as if there were no other interferences with

perceptual-motor functioning. When attention is so focused on this one type of interference, it is often difficult even to remember that perceptual functioning is affected by other factors. In addition, there is thus a tendency to attribute all perceptual distortion to some kind of CNS dysfunction.

Although the variety of factors that interfere with perceptual-motor functioning are too extensive to be listed here and probably cannot be completely covered by any classification, most seem to fall within the following groups: (1) physiological limitations, such as brain damage, sensory deprivation, or muscular weaknesses; (2) physiological disruptions, such as injuries, illnesses, fatigue, and the like; (3) immediate and temporary environmental stress; (4) poor motivation; (5) affective disruptions; (6) intellectual retardation; and (7) social or cultural deprivations or differences from the norms used by he test.

Evidence of the presence of types of interferences other than CNS damage may be present in the perceptual-motor responses themselves, or may be inferred from them. Thus many investigators have agreed that drawings that are oversized or very tiny, that are heavily shaded or very lightly drawn, that are either too neatly aligned or organized or are drawn with no regard for organization on the page, are all signs of possible emotional interferences with perceptual-motor functioning. However, these signs may also appear in the anxious brain-damaged child as part of her/his way of coping with the task.

Sometimes the child who produces grossly distorted Bender or Graham-Kendall drawings is suffering from an as yet undetected opthalamic condition. If disruptions are noted only on visual tasks, this possibility should be seriously entertained, even though there may be evidence of alternative or additional interferences. Similarly, difficulties in motor focus and control on these tests have been known to be the first prodramata of muscular disorders such as muscular dystrophy or multiple sclerosis. When such a muscular focus

*Often abbreviated CNS.

problem stands out, the possibility of the onset of such a disease process must be ruled out before accepting some other hypothesis about the nature of the interference.

Poor motivation may result in a slapdash performance, in careless errors, even in occasional rotations (which may be an indication of negativism as well as of brain damage). The child who is preoccupied with her/his own emotional problems may "forget" more than one drawing on the Graham-Kendall. The intensely angry child may mess up the drawings just to spite the adult authority personified by the assessor. In the past decade, psychologists have come to recognize that severe cultural deprivation can also result in a developmental lag in perceptual-motor functioning (see Chapter 17). Unfortunately the signs of this kind of interference in the child's perceptual-motor responses are not well established. By and large, perceptual-motor responses do not in themselves supply sufficient evidence about the nature of these other interferences. The kinds of data bearing on these interferences from other sources will be discussed later in this chapter and in subsequent ones.

Children who are severely depressed and withdrawn and who are very disturbed emotionally or are "autistic" may do very poorly on tests of perception. It is true that brain-damaged children are often dependent on others to assist them in the interpretation of the world about them, but it is also true that not all children who are so dependent are necessarily brain damaged. Thus learned helplessness may result in perceptual confusion and perceptual dependency just as extensively and severely as does damage to brain centers.

F. COPING MECHANISMS AND PERCEPTUAL/MOTOR FUNCTIONING

The presence of interferences in perceptual-motor functioning is often not grossly evident in the distortion of reproductions themselves, but it may be inferred from the coping mechanism the child may use to overcome the interferences. Koppitz points out that the slightly brain-damaged child may seek to cover her/his perceptual disability by drawing excessively slowly and in a compulsive manner, thereby concentrating her/his total effort so that the errors are minimal and only occasional.

Case 22

Rick, age 16 years, who was being treated psychotherapeutically for his asocial acting out of his conflicts with his parents and other authority figures, suffered a massive head injury in an auto accident during a "joyride" while running away from home. After he recovered from the immediate injuries, his psychiatrist thought she noted some aphasia and possibly other perceptual-motor sequelae, although Rick averred he was completely recovered. During the therapy, Rick associated the injury with his angry and rebellious behavior and fantasied that the injury represented the punishment of fate for his wrongdoings. Nevertheless, the therapist requested psychological assessment of the possible effects of this injury both on Rick's perceptual-motor functioning and on his outlook on life in general. Rick continued to deny that he had any memory problem or speech difficulty. During the Graham-Kendall, he studied each card carefully, complained that he was not given enough time to see them, and then verbalized the shape of each design. Thus he succeeded in drawing most of them without scorable errors. When he began to have increasing difficulty in remembering them correctly, he remarked disgustedly, "I never was any good at this sort of stuff anyways!" Similarly, on the Digit Symbol subtest of the Wechsler, he verbalized each symbol as he drew it, so that he made no errors but his score was lowered because he lost time in being so meticulous. He passed the Digit Span— including the digits backwards—by whispering the numbers to himself as they were pronounced to him, but he was unable to cope with the memory passages on the

Wechsler Memory Scale in the same manner. When he could not justify his responses to the Rorschach, even some very simple "popular" responses, he would deny the response, often remarking, "Well, I don't see it that way now. Instead, it looks like. . . ." and give a new response that he often could not justify either.

Evidently Rick was suffering a perceptual-motor dysfunction. However, he was coping with it—albeit laboriously. The psychiatrist used these findings to help Rick make a more realistic appraisal of his disability and his ability to cope with it. On examination one year later, Rick demonstrated marked improvement, both in his achievement and in his self-confidence.

Another common way children cope with a perceptual-motor difficulty is by avoiding such tasks, by diverting attention, by making demands on others for help, or by rebellious, angry behavior. The avoiding of perceptual-motor tasks may take the form of refusing to go to school or neglecting schoolwork that the child cannot successfully perform. Feelings of frustration and inadequacy may be demonstrated in disruptive behavior in the schoolroom that has the secondary benefit of getting excused from lessons based on perceptual-motor functioning. Such a child may use the game of "Uproar" (see Chapter 8) during the assessment, refusing the task and attempting to divert attention away from the demands of the assessor.

CASE 23

Ole, age 7, of whom it was suspected suffered a mild cerebral defect, succeeded in avoiding the Bender altogether by the following maneuvers over a half-hour period: He broke the pencil lead four times, dropped the paper on the floor three times, erased a hole in the paper or tore it up in disgust several times, went to the bathroom twice, twice sat and "studied" the initial

figure for several minutes, complaining it was too hard, asked several times to do some other task, left his chair to look out the window, and knocked over a pile of books and insisted that he pick them up and sort them out. He finally noted that time was running out for the session, and when more time was granted claimed he was "bored" and refused to do his test altogether. His difficulties on other perceptual tasks were obvious. He guessed wildly on the Picture Completion, all the while looking at the assessor for clues and attempting to read the assessor's notes on the scoring sheet. His behavior on Object Assembly was quite similar. On Digit Span he began to be more openly frustrated, tearful, and complaining. He also made a game of the Rorschach, avoiding looking at the cards, saying, "It looks like that chair over there, doesn't it? Isn't that what you made a picture of here? Isn't it? . . . You tell me what you think it is, and I'll see if you are right!" He refused to allow any inquiry into his responses, saying, "I told you about that already. You ask too many questions. I don't want to play this game anymore. Let's play something else."

G.   THE CONTENT OF PERCEPTUAL-MOTOR FUNCTIONS

The nature of interfering factors in perceptual-motor functioning may also be indicated by the kind of task the child is trying to perform—that is, the *content* of the stimuli. Some children with severe perceptual dysfunctioning may have difficulties across the board, on all kinds of perceptual-motor tasks. However, many children can perform some of them quite successfully or at least with only mild difficulty, but they may be quite helpless and fail at others. As was noted before, some children can perform relatively simple tasks that mainly require focusing but have much more difficulty when the task involves discrimination. Whether or not the stimulus has some kind of meaningful content may also affect the child's perceptions of it. Some tasks, such as the Bender or Graham-Kendall, are in effect "nonsense" tasks. Picture Completion, Object Assembly, or even Bead Stringing (Stanford-Binet) involve a meaningful context. For some children the perceptual task is made easier when this context is provided. They can deduce what is to be done even though they may have perceptual difficulties. Without a context from which to operate, they may have no clues, and therefore their perceptual difficulty may be more obvious. Such children may try to make up an association or create a content for the nonsense task so as to keep it in mind. Other children may be hindered perceptually by complex stimuli with associative content. They are able to focus on and make discriminations among abstract forms, such as the Bender or Block Design, but when meaning is added to the task they are lost or confused.

Use of the content of the stimuli as an aid to perception is most common among older children whose perceptual-motor function has been damaged by some disease or injury to the central nervous system after infancy. They are able to call on old associations to assist them in new perceptual tasks. Children who can copy the Bender Designs or the Kohs Blocks but fail tests with a content would seem to have an associative rather than a strictly perceptual difficulty. Such a difficulty may occur among children who suffer a CNS injury or disease during the period where associative learning is occurring and after perceptual-motor learning is established, that is, after age 8. As will be discussed later, such disturbances of associative learning as a part of cognitive functioning are also characteristic of several different kinds of emotional disturbances in children. Where only certain kinds of content seem to deter perception, for example, only stimuli involving humans or only those with aggressive implications, an associative dysfunction involving affect or social functioning would seem present.

H. COGNITIVE MODALITIES

The modalities through which development of cognitive functioning takes place are commonly divided into *verbal* and *nonverbal*. The child learns to make associations, comprehend meaning, delineate, generalize, and analyze both through verbally communicating and through visualizing and manipulating objects. Most children need and use both modalities, but some think primarily with words or verbalized ideas, while others think by doing and are relatively less prone to utilize verbally expressed ideas or to put their own thoughts into words. This division of the modalities of cognition was recognized by inventors of intelligence tests long before Wechsler divided his scales into verbal and nonverbal. Arthur constructed her "Performance" scale in order to sample nonverbal thought processes. Terman and Merrill purposefully included both verbal and nonverbal terms in each of their mental-age scales, and users of the Binet have long been accustomed to examine items across the age groups according to these two modalities. (The tasks on the Binet for older children are chiefly and sometimes exclusively verbal, however). What Wechsler provided specifically was a method of measuring and comparing these two modalities within one set of scales.

Scores from the Wechsler verbal subtests, from the Shipley-Hartford (Shipley and Burlingane, 1941) (both vocabulary and abstractions), from the upper age levels of the Stanford-Binet, and from other similar scales yield and best *quantified* data about verbal intelligence. *Qualitative* evidence of cognitive process involving verbalization may come from such tests as the Rorschach, Sentence Completion, or even the TAT. In addition to scores from such formal nonverbal tests as the Wechsler Performance Scales, the Goodenough Draw-A-Man Scale, the Arthur Performance Scales, the Leiter International, the Raven Matrices, or the Columbia, the assessor should examine cognitive aspects of other drawings and manipulation of objects such as during the child's play with the World Test materials or doll play on the Lynn Structured Doll Play test or on the Make-A-Picture Story (MAPS) test. The arrangements of the materials on the World Test or of the figures in the MAPS often give clues about the child's logic and comprehension as well as information about his/her affective, motivational, and social functioning. The Merrill-Palmer Preschool Scales offer a particular advantage in that the items are about equally divided into verbal and nonverbal; items may be omitted or rejected according to the needs of the child or exigencies of the situation, and an overall estimate of intellectual development still may be obtained.

Although a preference for one cognitive modality over another during infancy may be only a temporary developmental phenomenon, a persistence of such a preference may have considerably more widespread significance as the child grows older. In the current American educational system that leans so heavily on verbal skills, a child who remains verbally retarded undoubtedly will have educational problems, even though nonverbal intellectual faculties do develop at a normal rate. However, verbal retardation may also reflect an educational deprivation or some other block connected with schooling. The inability to verbalize one's ideas or to comprehend verbally expressed ideas is also characteristic of several kinds of childhood emotional conflicts, as will be discussed later in greater detail. The child sho develops only verbally without being able to solve intellectual problems by manipulating objects may be suffering from some perceptual-motor dysfunction, as was discussed before. Being able to talk about things but not to touch and do things may also represent a motor inhibition, arising from any number of emotional conflicts or social taboos. Where there is no marked disability of either cognitive modality but merely a greater skill and preference for one modality over the other, such a difference may be part of the child's character or life-style. The nonverbal roots of the future engineer or the verbal abilities of the lawyer-to-be are often seen in the cognitive style of the child long before adolescence.

I. COGNITIVE INPUT–OUTPUT

The receptive aspect of cognition is usually labeled "comprehension" or "understanding." *Comprehension* tasks sample whether the child correctly receives not merely a perception, but also the associative connections and meaning within the perception. This is the intent of not only the Comprehension test on the Wechsler or similar items on the Binet, but also of Vocabulary and Similarities items and the Mincus Completion (Binet) and Picture Completion (WISC). These tasks all require essentially a verbal comprehension or at least some verbal expression. Picture Arrangement and Object Assembly on the WISC and "Ball in Field" on the Binet are examples of nonverbal search for the meaning provided by the stimuli. Among the best nonverbal tests of receptive cognition are the Columbia Mental Maturity and the Leiter International that depend solely on identifying the meaning of or communalities among a group of items. All of these tasks also depend to some extent on memory—that is, on how well the input was established and retained. Although there are scales for "immediate memory," that is, for attention and concentration, such as Digit Span, about the only WISC-R subtest that essentially taps memory is Information. (Note that the child does not have to understand the Information questions. He/she merely has to remember the answers.)

Although the concept of receiving the meaning from a stimulus has been central to the study of cognitive development, the act of putting-out meaning (of formulating meaning where no meaning was inherent in the stimulus) has not been commonly conceived as part of cognitive functioning per se. Rather such an act has been called "associative" or "projective thinking" and been seen as something that was somehow separate from cognition. Psychologists have occasionally tried to understand this process of inventive thought, and over the past decade there has been considerable research on creative thinking. On the other hand, philosophers have long maintained that most meaning constitutes an attribution of the mind to the object. There is not even a commonly used term to categorize this kind of thinking. This ability to formulate meaning, to pull together disparate meaningless parts into something and give them one identity, or to analyze out parts not previously identified and to speculate is, however, one of the most fascinating and unique aspects of the human mind. Psychologists are now beginning to realize that this mental faculty begins with the child's associative and imaginative thought. Since this aspect of cognition was not well recognized when intelligence tests were constructed, they do not sample it.

The intelligence tests were constructed to measure educational achievement or aptitude in an educational system that promoted mainly receptive, not inventive, thinking. This social emphasis on having the child learn what she/he is taught rather than to create ideas continues to this day. In addition, inventive, creative, imaginative fantasy was—and still often is—considered to be child's play, something that, if it persists, may be the seeds of insanity. Thus the first tests of associative and projective thinking—Jung's World Association Test (1919) and Rorschach's Inkblot Technique—were designed primarily to assess the *dis*associative aspects of associative thinking, or projective *dys*functioning.

Jung quickly began to see, however, that associative thinking had positive normal attributes. Rorschach too spoke of sampling creative thought by means of his test. The task of the Rorschach Technique is to make something out of nothing, to create and impose meaning on a situation and to structure reality. Like the task of comprehension, the task of projection calls upon previous learning and memory. (Rorschach speaks of "engrams".) Projection does not so much require the finding of

meaning out of the stimulus but rather the integration of the stimulus into conceptualizations already present in the mind. For children this is a demanding task, since their experience is as yet brief and their range of concepts with which to explain phenomena is thus limited. Moreover, prior perceptions and comprehensions are still being validated through further experience. Thus children may not be very effective nor accurate when they try to fit an unstructured situation to a limited range of not fully established engrams.

Children's Rorschach responses therefore may reveal the extent to which they can use the ideation and the organizational thinking process that they have developed to test out and formulate reality independently, rather than merely recite back what they have been taught. Their responses and explanations of the inkblots during the inquiry may be analyzed to determine the following: (1) the range of concepts used; (2) the ways the child has selected out parts of the inkblot, organized these parts together, and utilized the whole blot in order to fit some concept; and (3) the congruence that the child has selected. Projective intelligence requires that (1) the child can select out of his range of engrams the concept "doggy" to fit a selected part of the blot, for example, on Card VII; (2) the child show how the part of the detail fits the concept; and (3) the child show that these parts have beenn organized to fit the engram. When the child projects onto the blot prior motoric experiences, it is evidence that she/he has yet another dimension by which to judge the potentialities of an unknown situation—that is, the possibility that it may move just as the child moves. Similarly, if the child can integrate the more stimulating, space-filling aspects of the blot, the color, and the shading into concepts, she/he may be credited with an ability to integrate and use external affective stimuli in other unstructured situations.

Perhaps in the mythical "average" child comprehension and projective cognition develop at about the same rate. Theoretically they are complementary. The expansion of each in the child's development permits the growth of the other. The more a child comprehends, the better he/she is able to project; the more he/she can imagine, the more he/she will be able to comprehend. The fact that—on the average—these two sides of cognition are so related is shown in the significant correlations reported by several studies (Tucker, Altus, 1950; and Thompson, 1949) between various facets of Rorschach responses and various intelligence tests. The fact that these two functions seldom match one for one in a child's development is attested to by their usually low correlations. Analysis of a child's cognitive development should include a comparison of the relative development of each of these sides of his/her intelligence.

J.   COGNITIVE FOCUS AND DIFFERENTIATION

The ability to select out concepts and to name, identify, and differentiate objects is one of the chief initial cognitive tasks of the pre-school child. Among adults such concrete thinking might be viewed as inadequate, but for younger children this ability to be conrete is essential. Children must learn how to focus on one set of impressions and see them as a unit, to grasp one idea and not get it confused with other concepts. They must learn that not all women are "mamas," that 5 is different from 10 and so on. Only after they have become secure with this exclusion type of thinking can they progress to be inclusive, to make generalizations, to see similarities, to comprehend laws, and so on. Thus on the Binet the child is asked to "tell the difference between" (age VI), before grasping similarities (age VII), which is followed by a combined test at age VIII (Differences and Similarities). "Vocabulary" is also a focusing and differentiating task. The Binet vocabulary contains many generalizations or class-concept words, even at a relatively early age (for example, "brunette"). On the

other hand, the Wechsler contains mostly concrete items, even among the most difficult items. The Binet contains a variety of items at the upper age levels requiring generalization—for example, at Year X, Abstract Words and Finding Reasons; at Year XIV, Induction and Ingenuity 1 and Reconciliation of Opposites; and at Average Adult, Proverbs. Most comprehension items on both the Binet and Wechsler call for generalizations. On the Rorschach, gross, undifferentiated whole responses are the common approach among younger children. During latency, the child grows much more cautious about including every part of the blot in his/her response, and he/she begins to recognize details. In latency, children are apt to exclude or even reject parts of the inkblot that do not fit, and they find it difficult to fit everything in. This sometimes leads them to reject the whole idea. Gradually they become able to put details together to make a whole—to both analyze and reconstruct. Such a dual process of analyzing out parts and reassembling them into a whole is the central task of the Block Design and Picture Arrangement subtests of the WISC. The Object Assembly test obversely calls for grasping an overall pattern and then pulling together parts.

In analyzing the data, the assessor should note how the child goes about these tasks. For example, does she/he put the Object Assembly pieces together in trial-and-error fashion, only recognizing the whole figure when nearly finished? Or does the child stop to figure out what she/he is putting together before proceeding? The older and more sophisticated child is able to begin the more complicated Block Designs by placing the corner blocks in first. The ability to combine ideas—especially in an independent expressive fashion—is nowhere better sampled than on the TAT. The younger child tends to give only card descriptions—with little plot. She/he finds it extremely difficult to conceive of causes (the past) or consequences (the future), and if pressed, her/his plot is usually incomplete and disconnected. As children become

older, they are more able to string sequences of events together in a more integrated plot with fewer non sequiturs. Similarly, the young child's drawing of a man
may have the parts complete but poorly
arranged and disproportionate in size.
Gradually children begin to conceive of the
human figure as a whole with parts in place.
Many of the points on the Goodenough
Scales are awarded on the basis of the
placement and proportion of the details.

Although specification is the primary
concern of the younger child and generalizing is learned and developed at a later age,
these two functions do overlap considerably in developmental sequence. And to a
certain extent the age differences are determined by the complexity of the task
rather than by the nature of the cognitive
behavior. Thus, pre-school children are
making simple types of generalizations at
the same time that they are learning a wide
variety of concrete facts and discriminations. The older child—busy with constructing concepts—is still accumulating
more refined distinctions and elaborations
of his/her facts. For example, the 10-year-
old in his/her drawing of a man is not only
putting the arms and legs in the right places
and drawing them both in proportion to the
body, but he/she is adding brows to the
eyes and heels to the shoes.

The extent and nature of the development of these two aspects of cognitive
functioning often provide major clues about
the overall development of the child's ego.
For example, the child whose thinking remains very concrete and detailed and who
is unable to make generalizations may be
developing compulsive traits—that is,
isolating affect and drives by intellectualization. Such concrete thinking might also
be characteristic of a culturally deprived
child. Severe CNS trauma often interferes
with development of the ability to
generalize. Overgeneralization and intellectualization may also be symptoms of emotional conflict in children. The bright adolescent delinquent may argue with impecc-
able logic but on the basis of specious

premises. The phobic child picks out the
threatening aspect of every situation.

K. INTERFERENCES WITH
COGNITIVE DEVELOPMENT

The general factors that deter cognitive
development have been discussed at length
in Chapter 2, and they have been partially
delineated before in relation to some of the
specific aspects of intellectual behavior.
Overall retardation is covered in Chapter
16. The chief point to be emphasized is that
insofar as possible both the kind(s) of inter-
ference(s) and the kind(s) of intellectual
functioning, and the interrelationships between them should be made specific. Such
statements as "the child's intelligence is
lower than it might be because of his anxieties" or "brain damage lowers his IQ" are
of little direct help to those who may try to
treat or retrain the child.

Instead, the assessor should search for
clues in her/his data that would allow
greater specification, such as: "At times he
demonstrates an above average ability to
objectively analyze a situation or to
generalize from situation to situation, but
most of the time the potentially threatening
aspects of the situation so preoccupy him
that he can do no more than cautiously
identify it." Or, again: "Johnny loves to
talk about things, using an extensive vocabulary and demonstrating a fairly extensive fund of information for his 9 years, but
even the casual observer will discover that
he often does not really know the meaning
of the words he uses nor does he make
sense when he spouts out information.
These verbal fireworks apparently are designed to hide his sense of inadequacy over
his inability to really comprehend, which has
as its base a marked perceptual motor dysfunctioning." Or: "Diane's need to repress
any action that even smacks of being aggressive or assertive is so extensive as even
to limit her intellectual functioning at times.
Specifically, she falters when an intellectual
problem contains any kind of aggressive

content (such as the Verbal Absurdities items on the Binet). Moreover, she does not dare argue her point, she cannot explain herself when challenged, and she prefers to give the simplest response possible, hoping it will not be challenged." And again: "Mark jumps from one idea to the next, often with little connection or logic. So many things enter his mind at once that he cannot seem to sort them out. His intellectual functioning is very similar to his social and affective behavior—all of which points to a serious difficulty in self-control."

L. COGNITIVE COPING MECHANISMS

These mechanisms for handling interferences with intellectual functioning and development are extremely variable. One very common way children deal with and mask intellectual deficiencies—arising from either a physiological or a social handicap—is by compensation. They avoid those types of cognitive tasks that they cannot perform, and they overdevelop others. The classic example is the so-called "idiot savant" who cannot understand the meaning of things but tries to compensate by developing a hypertrophied memory for some trivia.*

Like the child with a perceptual-motor deficit, the child who cannot intellectually comprehend may distract from his/her disability by "acting up" or by some other behavioral reaction formation. In the classroom, such a child may keep the teacher busy with misdemeanors in the secret hope that the teacher will not realize that she/he does not understand the classwork. During the assessment such children begin getting restless each time the limit of their abilities is reached on each of the WISC subtests, or they create diversionary tactics during the Rorschach inquiry. Because such chil-

dren's behavior is so annoying, there is often a tendency by school authorities to blame their poor record of achievement on behavior alone. An analysis of the assessment data may help to determine the extent to which a child is failing because she/he is not paying attention, as opposed to trying to hide an inability to comprehend.

The opposite type of reaction formation is also very common—the masking of intellectual inadequacies by very socially conforming behavior. Teachers and parents often tend to forgive the very "sweet" child who "tries." Because they give the teacher no trouble, they may be allowed to sit hidden and neglected in the back of the class. At the end of the year, the teacher in turn compensates for the child's inadequacy by giving him/her credit for "trying," and the child is promoted into the next grade where he/she faces even greater problems. "Motherly" psychologists—of either sex—are also occasionally seduced by such well-behaved children.

CASE 24

Lillie, age 9, was a very pretty child, with long blonde hair in pigtails, soulful brown eyes, and a sweet smile, who was very polite to adults. She was thought to be very bashful by her mother and teachers, and they decided not to pressure her to recite in class, hoping she would "outgrow it." When called on to go to the blackboard, she would stand there helpless with the chalk in her hand, and even when the teacher would encourage her or attempt to help her, the tears would well up, and she would seem so petrified that she would be excused to go back to her seat. Her workbook was neatly filled with incorrect answers. During the assessment she was so demure and so helpless that the student psychologist later discovered he had not pressured her for an explanation of several of her vague Rorschach responses, and he kept looking through the data, emphasizing any adequate response he could find!

*See Case 88, "Old Sam," Chapter 16.

M. IDEATION

The content of the child's cognitive functioning (ideation) is also a very important dimension. Sometimes children have difficulty with a certain type of intellectual problem, such as arithmetic, or in judgments involving social interactions, even though their thought processes and cognitive modalities are in other respects quite adequate. Such a failure on a specific subject is often difficult to explain if one only examines the cognitive functions, as in the following case.

Case 25

The first hint of Phillip's fulminating schizophrenia came during his responses to the WISC. He was a highly verbal younster (age 10) who was considered to be potentially very bright by his teachers but was labeled as an "underachiever" because of his unsatisfactory school performance. He talked incessantly about his interest in science, and it was difficult to get him to respond to anything else. He went to great length to explain why there were four seasons in the year, but he was not clear in his explanation, he forgot the question, and actually forgot to name one of the four seasons. "What does the stomach do?" and "Why does oil float on water?" similarly set him off on a frantic flight of ideas. On other items of this and other subtests, he tended to give only perfunctory responses. All of his subtest scores were in the low-average range. Qualitatively, his failures seemed to result either from a disinterest in the topic or a highly cathectic but very confused concern with how things work and why. Associations from other techniques suggested that Phillip might be very curious and very confused about sexual functioning. His responses also indicated that he was very attached to and dominated by his widowed mother. She, however, rejected the clinic's recommendation that parent–child guidance was in order. Believing that Phillip had an educational problem, she sought private tutoring for him. Two years later information about Phillip was requested by the juvenile court that was investigating an accusation that Phillip had sexually molested several younger children of both sexes. At the court's request, Phillip was again assessed by the clinic. At this time evidence of intellectual confusion and emotional distress of psychotic proportions was rampant in his responses.

CHAPTER 10

Analysis of Affective Development

A. MODALITIES

Usually when the term *affect* is mentioned, there is a tendency to think of the outward expression of feelings—of tears or laughter, of rage or affection—openly displayed in a child's behavior. Moreover, affect is usually thought of as a reaction to something in the environment. The child cries over frustration, laughs at something funny, gets angry at someone, or shows affection toward someone. Since the control over affective expression is still developing during childhood, the experiencing of affect is predominately through *external* interactions. However, *internal* modalities of experiencing affect begin to develop very early in childhood. In fact, the initial affective states of infancy are mainly experienced internally. The baby cries because of internal physical discomforts or coos and even smiles because of satiation of physiological needs, independently of whether anyone is cooing or smiling to him/her. Only gradually do infants relate discomfort and satiation to the outside world. *Expression* of the child's affect may appear to be chiefly external, but such signs of internalization as somatization also begin early in childhood, for example, through "colic" or in asthma. It is not until children build up a bank of memories, of internal attitudes, and of contained impulses and tensions that their affective behavior can be said to be a response to internal sources rather than to whatever is going on around them immediately. Usually it is some clue to the environment that sets off these inner affective states, even though the trigger is often hard to spot. Similarly, as children learn to control and suppress affective ex-

pression outwardly, they develop means of internal expression of feelings. In addition to somatic expression, they develop a fantasy life, playing out feelings that they have learned are socially taboo or would bring undesirable responses from others.

This theoretical classification of affective experience into *external* and *internal* modalities serves to clarify some quite practical questions. For example, are children who get angry very quickly in the classroom responding mainly to some immediate social situation that may not be immediately observable to the adult observer, or do they carry a chip on their shoulders, fantasizing enemies everywhere or seeing all other children as rivals for unsatisfied dependency needs? Why is it that another child seems so nonchalant and oblivious to the same group of teasing classmates and authoritarian teachers? The treatment or the retraining of affectively disturbed children requires knowledge of how they experience affect.

How children experience affect is not easy to observe directly. Children who seem oblivious to what is going on about them may actually be quite aware of their environment, but are reacting to it on a purely internal level. Another child may be crying his/her heart out for no obvious reason, although this apparently inappropriate affective behavior may have very good reasons in the child's fantasies and fears. Much of the difficulty psychologists have encountered in understanding affective functioning—especially in children—has arisen from the attempts to assume these reasons without any idea of how the child experiences affect, except by direct observation. Some adults seem not to realize that considerable additional data may be obtained simply by asking the child for his/her subjective opinion. Many children are able to verbalize the sources of their fears, excitements, depression, joys, or anxieties—particularly if they are external. However, the child who feels sad or happy "inside" may be less able to verbalize further about it. Moreover, almost as soon as children learn to verbalize about feelings at all, they learn to cover up this private world.

Clues about the modalities through which the child experiences affect may be gained from projective techniques such as Word Association and Sentence Completion. In his original work on word association, Jung (1918) posited that behavior such as long response time or idiosyncratic responses suggested the interference of internal affect, while indicators of a dependence on external clues for affective experience might be seen in "popular" responses, in rhymes and repetitious or "clang" associations. On the Sentence Completion test, the responses to stems with personal reference that is, containing "I" or "me"—may be contrasted with relatively impersonal stems, with respect to affectivity. The child who gives predominately more affectively loaded responses to the personal stems would seem to be experiencing more affect more internally than the child who attaches his affect to the more impersonal stimuli.

CASE 26

Twelve-year-old Leona gave the following responses to a Sentence-Completion Test: "I often *feel sad*," "Mother—*I hate her*," "School—*is out tomorrow*," "Boys—*are alright*," "I get embarrassed when—*I think of some things*," "I get angry when— *EVERYTHING*." In contrast, her 10-year-old brother responded: "I often—*play ball*," "Mother—*is a klutz*," "School—*is a pain in the neck*," "Boys—*are better than girls*," "I get embarrassed when—*my father talks loud*," "I get angry when—

someone hits me." This is only a brief sample of the many responses Leona gave, indicating that her affect was chiefly internal. Her brother, however, experienced affect in response to something or somebody. The two children fought incessantly. Usually Leona began the quarrels, either by teasing her brother or by complaining about him when he fiercely claimed he was "doing nothing." He was more likely to respond by hitting her, invading her privacy, or destroying her property. When they were separated, she would continue to grouse, but he would quickly forget even the most vicious exchanges after a few moments. On the other hand, Leona was most likely to apologize, while "I'm sorry" never escaped his lips.

The one technique specifically constructed to sample modes of experiencing affect is, of course, the Rorschach Technique. Moreover, the genius of Rorschach lay not so much in his invention of the inkblot technique per se, for inkblots had been used previously as a test of form perception, but rather in his insight in connecting theory with technique. Drawing on the Jungian theory of his day, he differentiated his "intratension" and "extratension" from the social introversion—extroversion concept, focusing not onl how people behave or live (*Erleben*), but how they perceive or experience (*Erlieben*). The ideas he used are in common parlance. People speak of "being moved" by something or "moved to speak" in Quaker style, thus describing an affective state or mode in terms of motion or tension within themselves. On the other hand, when concepts and judgments are labeled "colored" by the events and people around us, it means that affect is experienced passively and receptively, through contacts with the environment.

Affect may be experienced through either or both of these modes, at various times or in various situations. Rorschach noted that many people appeared to use one mode much more than another, or to use one even exclusively. This preference of affect modality is summarized in the Experience Balance—the ratio between *M* (responses containing human movement) and *C* (responses based on color.)* Rorschach also recognized variations on these basic modes. Sometimes the movements are experienced in the form of raw impulses (*FM*), or, to use the vernacular, "animal spirits," or even pure tension, without being precisely personalized. In contrast there are shades of color, shades of affective meaning, that are the "texture" of life. Some people are stirred up by instinctual forces within them, but are impervious and insensitive to environmental clues or nuances. Others are so sensitive, are so aware of the sensuous stimuli about them that they dare not permit their own impulses to be loosened. A good deal of experience is emotionally neutral. People do not experience affect in every situation, but often attempt to consider situations purely intellectually. Approximately 30% of adult Rorschach responses are based only on the form of the blot. However, an inability to utilize and handle affect leads not only to a cold, impersonal approach to life, but also to a dangerous ignorance of the affective aspects of reality.

The development of the modes of experiencing affect and their representation in the determinents of Rorschach responses at different ages during childhood are so extensively delineated by Ames and associates (1952) that only a brief mention of the highlights need be mentioned here. Preschool children are still accumulating affective experience, and their mode of experiencing affect is largely external. They are gradually learning to control and internalize motoric experiences, but they are not "moved" by much until they enter latency. Their own animal instincts, however, may play prominent roles in their affective life. It

is during latency that the dual developmental processes of affective control and internalization are learned, practiced, and reinforced. Dependence upon the environment for affective experience is characteristic of the pre-schooler, and it is represented on the Rorschach by the predominately color-determined records. During latency, children attempt a neutralization of affect in order to integrate affective experiences. Their Rorschach records are likely to contain less color than in infancy, and the first movement responses appear. Expansion of these modes of experience is the hallmark of adolescence (Hertz, 1943a, 1943b). Adolescents go from being the victims of their environment and its stresses at one moment to imposing their will and feelings onto it in arbitrary fashion in the next. Like Hamlet, they do not know whether the reality of what they feel is within them or outside them. Ambi-equal Rorschach records are characteristic of the normal adolescent.

B. INPUT–OUTPUT

In discussing affective functioning, the distinction between mode and input–output is often blurred. When one speaks of experiencing affect internally, there is a natural tendency to assume that the stimulus is necessarily an internal one, and that the expression is also internal. Similarly, extensive experiencing of affect might be assumed to entail an environmental stimulus and an overt expression of affect. On reflection, however, it is easy to see that the manner in which the affect is experienced does not necessarily depend on the stimulus nor does it determine the nature of expression of affect. Rather, the relationships between modality and input--output may be conceptualized as two dimensional, as is shown in Figure 10.1

Thus the input may consist of such internal stimuli as spontaneous memories, dreams, values, and attitudes, or the stress and tension of physiological drives. If such stimuli are received in an intratensive

*For further definition of these modalities of the Experience Balance, a method of quantitatively distinguishing them, and some research validating these hypotheses, see Palmer (1955, 1956, 1962). See also discussion of the Rorschach in Chapter 6.

MODES

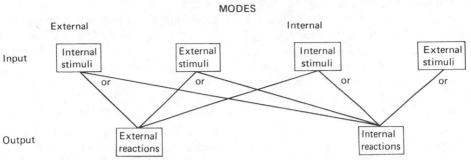

Figure 10.1   Interrelations between modalities and input—output of affect.

mode, the individual correctly identifies them as internal stimuli. The affective expression, however, is not necessarily limited to internal reactions. A child may react with further memories, more dreams, changes or expansions of value systems, feelings of tension and anxiety or guilt, or somatic reactions. But she/he can and often does also react to these inner stimuli by outward behavior that is manifest to others. The affect from dreams may be expressed in artistic productions, for example, or the values the individual has internalized regarding achievement may play a large role in the way he/she interacts with teachers or peers.

These same internal stimuli may, however, also be experienced in an extratensive fashion. If this is so, they are disassociated from the self and experienced as something external and separate. Such a disassociation is very common among children who are still forming an integrated self—or in the neurotic or psychotic adult. Thus children commonly experience dreams in the same way they experience environmental stimuli. They do not recognize themselves dreaming but rather as having a dream happen to them—much as anything else happens to them. They say, "I was scared by a bad dream" rather than "I dreamed a bad dream."

They first experience values as external, as imposed by parents and other authorities, and thus the affect connected with such externally imposed values is also experienced as external. Children may become anxious about being "naughty," but they are uneasy lest they be punished, not because they are conscious-stricken. *Naughty* is an external concept. (For further discussion of this point, see Chapter 11 on conative functioning.) Even fears may be seen as external. A 3-year-old runs from a dog and climbs in her grandfather's lap saying, "The doggie is afraid of me." Even if the internal stimuli are experienced extratensively, the output (the expression of the affect) may be internal. The younger child's superego is the external pointing finger of his/her mother, but the affect may be shown only in fantasies about being naughty. Or a child may awaken from a nightmare—screaming in terror—in the same fashion as from some external threat.

Obversely, extratensively perceiving children will correctly identify an external stimuli as something separate from themselves. They participate in the ballgame and are excited and challenged by it, but *they* do not win or lose. The *game* is won or lost. They may shout and scream or cheer or weep in chorus with others as part of the game. Yet their affect may continue and be expressed also in restless sleep or a case of the hives. Intratensive children project themselves into the external event and identify with it. When they play ball, they are concerned with what *they* do, not how the game turns out. The excitement, challenge, glory, or depression are their own—not something shared with a group. If they are challenged, they too may cheer with the group, and their external behavior would be indistinguishable from that of the extratensive child. But if they are distinterested, they do not have the need to cheer as might disinterested extratensives, who share the excitement of the crowd whether or not they like to play ball. Intratensive children also may dream of ballgames, but their dreams are likely to be of their own glory or shame, while extratensive children hear the shouts of the crowd in their dreams.

The assessment of the sources of affect is one of the most important questions in the overall study of the child with behavioral problems, and at the same time it is often one of the most difficult. Since the child's mode of experiencing affect may not be readily observable, identifying the source of his/her affect may not be easy. A potentially stimulating stress may be spotted in the situation by the adult, but the child may not see this stress as stimulating affectively, and his/her outward behavior may be in response to some inner stimulus. The 10-year-old stoic, wearing a "What, me worry" mask nevertheless experiences pride, disgust, shame, or joy, just as much as a 5-year-old sib who is shouting or crying or bubbling outwardly. But the 10-year-old is practicing containment of feelings.

The assessment of the sources of a child's affect cannot be made on the basis of any one technique, but instead it is derived from a combination of several kinds of data, for example, the determinants of Rorschach responses, the content of TAT stories, responses to Incomplete Sentences, World Test constructions, and the subjective reports given by the child and parents in the interview. Once the affective modality is established, it is possible to begin to spot the sources of affect. Looking across the board, the assessor notes the stimuli to which the child responds with anxiety, depression, exhilaration, or satisfaction.

Case 27

The assessor noted that Greg, age 8, showed poor form level on the Rorschach and gave "tension" responses (*Fm*) whenever he attempted to deal with sepa-

rate details of the inkblots. Cards II and X gave this child particular trouble, and he liked Card V best. His TAT stories were replete with themes of people who leave never to return, of persons who don't communicate, or of lost objects. His "World" consisted of a tightly packed village—fenced in. During the interview, he went into great detail about the comings and goings of the family, who leaves the house and who comes back again. His mother reported that he had to be accompanied to school throughout kindergarten and first grade, and noted that he always checks up to see who is at home when he arrives. As further data were accumulated, it became more and more obvious that separation was one source of anxiety for this child.

The meaning of separation anxiety is then established by taking into account the modality. If the child is functioning chiefly on an extraversive level, then it is likely that he/she is responding (or overresponding) to separation stresses in the environment—to threats to dependency on environmental clues. If the child is more intraversive, then this separation may be concerned with some inner struggle. He/she may need people around not for their own stimulation per se but, for example, as a protection against inner impulses, anger, sexual impulses, or fantasized fears. In this latter instance, the separation would be secondary to other affective arousals, requiring further analysis of the sources of affect. Since the developing child continues to be dependent on the environment for emotional support and at the same time is increasingly internalizing experiences, this analysis of the sources of affect is often quite complicated. If separations make a child anxious, she/he may be responding to real separations in the environment, while simultaneously working out some inner conflicts.

The reason for this complicated analysis of affective *input* is of course to understand children's affective *output*. The aim is to understand why they become so anxious when they have to go to school, why they scream at their mothers, why they seem to be hyperexcitable, or what depresses them. In studying the input it may be discovered, for example, that this affective reaction in the school situation has little to do with school per se, but that it may be aroused by fears of children's own hostility toward their parents, and that they have to stay at home to see that the awful things they have imagined and wished would happen to them do not occur. Screaming battles with mother may be directed both at her over-protective controls and at the child's need to drown out an erotic attachment to her. Sometimes the relationship between the internal sources of children's affect and their outwardly expressed affect may seem quite obvious, but often it is complicated and indirect.

For example, much of the data may give evidence that the child feels emotionally deprived in relationships with parents and family, and thus depressed, angry, and guilty. Perhaps the child may voice such feelings as subjectively and consciously experienced, and even the parents may be aware of this possibility. However, all may report that aside from an occasional sullen reaction in the face of discipline the child shows little outward manifestation of such feelings at home, rather that she/he is obedient, compliant, even outwardly cheerful in interaction with her/his family most of the time. In such an instance it might be quite difficult for anyone—child, parent, or psychologist—to explain affective outbursts, disruptive, angry, and excitable behavior in the school situation as arising from his/her depression over family interrelationships. Very often the key to understanding how the affective input and the expressed affect are related lies in analysis of yet another aspect of the child's affective functioning—namely, the kinds of interferences with affective functioning that the child experiences and the mechanisms with which she/he attempts to cope with these interferences.

Before turning to a discussion of these interferences and coping mechanisms, some further thought needs to be given to the kinds of data commonly obtained regarding affective output. Usually any direct observation of affective reactions is very brief, and it is under the very special and limited circumstances of the assessment situation itself. It is usually difficult for the psychologist to observe the child in prolonged interaction with parents, peers, or other situations. Projective techniques may yield many clues about input, but they are notoriously poor predictors of output. Therefore the chief sources of data are the subjective reports from the children and parents. However, it is in the area of affective functioning that such subjective reports are likely to be most unreliable. Children have enough difficulty admitting that they are impudent to teachers who restrict their activities or get furious at playmates who disregard them. They usually find it even less admissible at first to mention that they glower at their parents (if they even realize that they do!), or that they are panic stricken by an erotic dream (even if they remember it). At most, one can observe their affect during the interview when parental discipline is discussed or when erotic feelings are hinted at.

Case 28

Mary, age 5, who was so excitable that she had trouble sleeping, responded to the assessor's question about sleeping arrangements in her home by changing the subject and avidly reciting a rambling, disconnected spy story she had seen on TV. Her drawing of a house contained a large keyhole in the door, which she called an "eye hole." Her parents initially said nothing about the possibility that she might have considerable sexual curiosity—even when asked directly about it. Only later did it occur to Mary's mother that Mary always seemed to have to go to the bathroom when her father was there, or asked to have her father take her to the toilet or bathe her (all of which was permitted). No one noticed at first that Mary seemed to manage to be present when her mother changed the diapers of her 4-month-old baby brother or that she made frequent excuses to get into the parental bed. The possibility that the parents might well be aware of and be guilt ridden by the recognition of Mary's excitement in such situations was, however, foreseen from their responses to the Edwards PPS. Her father's responses indicated very strong N Exhibitionism and N Heterosexuality, suggesting that he might well be quite seductive. Mary's mother proved to be a very modest and compulsively orderly person who repressed sexual needs as something "dirty." For the father to report Mary's behavior would have meant admission of—or at least arousal of—guilt feelings over his own behavior. Mary's mother tried to blind herself to any indication of erotic ideation. Thus, although Mary's behavior during the assessment, as well as many of her responses to the tests, suggested that she was at least responding to erotic stimulation and curiosity, support of the hypothesis that her excitement was actually enhanced by erotic experiences was not obtained until long after the assessment—during subsequent counseling interviews with the parents.

To assess affective output, the psychologist must be most alert to small cues dropped by the child and the parents, and he/she must follow through on these side remarks or hints regarding affect. In a supportive and nonthreatening fashion, the psychologist needs to inquire further about the affective behavior of the child. Even though the informants may deny at first any affect or be unaware of it, they may reveal whatever affective reactions the child may be demonstrating in their description of the child's behavior. Often the assessor may be able to use clues gained from the child's responses to the projective techniques as a guide in conducting the interview, as was done in Mary's case.

The Bene-Anthony Family Relations Test (1957) (see Chapter 5) is designed especially to sample affective input—output. The items on this questionnaire are worded to distinguish between those feelings expressed by the child (labeled "outgoing"), and those expressed to the child by someone else in the family ("incoming"). The way in which the child distributes these two sets of items in the boxes behind the family figures is often very revealing of affective patterns. Most children tend to attribute most outgoing feelings to the parents and most incoming feelings to children. A reverse pattern would be very unusual, and it would suggest that the child sees her/his parents as depending on her/him and her/his sibs for emotional stimulation. Of special interest is the child's use of the figure "Mr. Nobody" (where children can deposit items they do not want to attribute to members of the family), and of the figure representing themselves. Some children may attribute many incoming feelings (especially negative ones) to "Nobody," thus denying that anyone is the receptor of negative affect. Children who live in a family that represses positive affect may designate "Nobody" as receiving comfort or affection. Children who feel rejected put the incoming negative items in the "Self" box. Guilt-ridden children may attribute the outgoing negative items to themselves. The very repressed child who feels alienated may not put any items in the "Self" box.

The Rosenzweig P-F Study of Children (1948)—see Chapter 6—was constructed specifically to measure the patterns of affective modality and input—output. Rosenzweig's schema is very close to that presented in Figure 10.1. Although the distribution of children's responses among the various categories of the P-F may have little relationship to their manifest behavior, such responses may be taken as evidence of children's values regarding affect. Thus some children believe that frustration should be responded to by outwardly expressed complaints, aggressive actions, or demands of assistance. Others depict internal reactions to frustration as their model.

Children who believe that all frustration has to be denied probably have considerable difficulty in maintaining these values in external behavior. Children who think that they are primarily responsible for a solution of frustrations may react outwardly with depression or compulsive behavior. Aggressive and demanding children are likely to make similar responses to these techniques, but not all children who so respond do demonstrate these feelings internally. These "false-positive" cases may be using the P-F as fantasy. As noted in Chapter 6, the level of response can only be determined by reference to other data.

C. FOCUS AND DISCRIMINATION OF AFFECTS

Very frequently the critical aspect of a child's emotional adjustment is the ability to differentiate affects. The child under stress may experience a variety of affective stimuli from the environment that are disparate and confusing. Sensitivity to such incoming affective stimuli may be compared to a radar screen. A child then has the task of sorting out and identifying the various "blips," distinguishing the friendly objects from the hostile ones. If the air is full of affect, it may be difficult to make these discriminations. Simultaneously, the child may also experience internal affects, both from struggles for need gratifications and in reaction to the external stresses.

The development of this ability to discriminate affective stimuli follows the general pattern discussed in Chapter 2, Section E. Very likely this discrimination develops parallel to perceptual discrimination. Early in life children are unable to make much more than simple pain—pleasure discriminations, but during the pre-school years they begin to experience a variety of affects and to attempt to discriminate between them. For the most part, pre-schoolers experience affect as something external to themselves, but, as they enter latency, they have already begun to sort out which are their feelings and which are the feelings of others. Although latency-age children often appear oblivious to feelings, they are actually making efforts to control and discriminate affects. They attempt to keep feelings to themselves and to appear to be obtuse to the feelings of others, but this blocking of affect allows them to practice this task of affective discrimination without becoming flooded with affect. In adolescence they are often forced to make increasingly refined affective discrimination in a variety of interpersonal relationships. They become more sensitive to the feelings of others and also more introspective.

The methods by which children cope with these affects will be discussed later. At this point consideration needs to be given to the manifestions of affective discrimination in assessment data. The child's ability to discriminate affect is often revealed in the discussion of feelings during an interview. "How do you feel about that?" and "How do you think other people feel about that?" are questions that should be interjected at every appropriate part of the interview—if the child does not voluntarily state feelings. Sometimes it seems that children are so overwhelmed by their own anger, depression, or excitement that they are unable to discriminate any other feelings. Even so, the assessor should inquire and determine the extent to which the child's affective perception is out of focus. Other children appear to have an affective tunnel vision. They cannot say how they feel nor how others feel. Others experience affective double binds. They receive two or more affective messages. Internally they experience a conflict of feelings, for example, love and hate, shame and pride, and the like (see Section F below).

Since children are still learning the difficult and imprecise language of affects, it is often not easy for them to differentiate their feelings in words. In addition, much of pre-school children's affective expression is motoric. Thus children's subjective reports of feelings normally have to be supplemented by reports from parents and by other mothers—particularly associative techniques. Some parents are acute observers of their children's affects and can report their children's efforts to differentiate them. Others who are less cognizant of their child's feelings nevertheless naively reveal the child's affective discriminations as they describe the child's behavior. For example, one mother remarked of her 10-year-old, "Why he knows I love him!" "Yes," replied her husband, "and he knows when you're out of sorts—even if you don't say anything." Or another mother speaking of her adolescent daughter, "She's so moody; it's hard to say how she feels. You can say this for her—if she's in a bad mood she keeps it to herself and stays clear of the family up in her room. If she's in a good mood, she's all over the place."

However, many parents of an emotionally disturbed child are poor observers of the child's feelings—which is usually one of the child's problems. These parents are often wrapped up in their own affective states and ignore the child. They are unaware of the emotional messages they send the child, and they react defensively to the child's confused or angry responses. Sometimes they may not even recognize the child's overt anger or depression and are only able to complain about the child's acts, much as if they were complaining about a machine.

The ability to discriminate affect is evidenced in children's Rorschach responses by the form level of their affectively determined responses. If the form level of the child's movement, texture, or color responses is markedly less adequate than in the purely form-determined ones, this may be one sign that they have difficulty in discriminating those situations that are affectively loaded. If CF is much greater than FC, the child is making less well-formed perceptions of external affective stimuli. If movement responses are largely vague whirlings or tensions rather than well-defined M or FM, it may be internal affects that are unclear to this child. When the

child gives few or no affectively determined responses, it is impossible to tell whether she/he is unable to make such discriminations or whether she/he is blocking out all affect—or both. One indication in such records is the differences in form level between the child's responses to the colored and achromatic cards. If form level drops on the colored cards, it would seem that he/she has more perceptual difficulty in responding to external stimuli. (Lower form level on the achromatic cards, which is rare, is more likely to occur as a reaction to the ideation suggested by the card, but it is also possible for the child to be confused by the shading or the achromatic coloring.) The best way to determine children's affective discrimination when they give mainly affectively neutral responses is in the "testing of limits," that is, when requested to respond specifically to the color and shading or to find movement responses or to detail a movement response pointed out by the assessor. Not infrequently the tightly defended child who has made only cautious responses will—when encouraged in the testing of limits—respond with well-defined color and movement responses. The very threatened child, however, may not be able to handle either external or internal stimuli—even when they are pointed out.

Evidence of the child's affective discriminations on the TAT or similar techniques is often more subtle but nonetheless revealing. As was previously noted, children's TAT's are more likely to be action stories, with little or no mention of the affects of the characters. Usually the feelings are revealed in the actions—much as the child expresses feelings. However, it may be possible in the TAT situation to get the child to verbalize the feelings behind the character's action. One may ask directly, "How does (the character) feel?" But the child is more likely to respond to the simpler question "How come he did that?" "He was mad," or "He was bad," the child may reply. "How can people tell?" the assessor should persist in asking.

Sentence Completion techniques often

offer a particular opportunity to test children's affective discriminations, as most SC forms contain many items that require explanation of affect: "I feel most angry when . . ." or "The things that make me uneasy are. . . ." The child who has difficulty making affective discriminations may respond, "Nothing" or "Everything" to such stems.

Last but not least, the child's drawings of human figures often illustrate very dramatically affective discriminations. Even sketchy or poorly formed drawings often contain expressions in the curve of the mouth, the glance of the eyes, the turn of the head, the gesture of the arm, the position of hands, or the overall posture of the body. In contrast, some children may produce very elaborate but lifeless mannequin figures. The overall amount of expression in the drawing may be one measure of the child's awareness of feelings—an ability to make affective discriminations. The kinds of affects illustrated in such drawings should also be noted. Affectively disturbed children often illustrate their confusion by drawing one kind of emotional expression in one part of the body and another one somewhere else. One such child who was trying to mask his anger at his parents who were in the middle of a divorce battle drew a little boy with a big smile, waving goodbye. Yet the eyes of the drawing strongly suggested anger, and the left hand of the drawing was clenched in the fist at the side of the body. Another child—struggling with the problem of controlling his hyperactivity—drew a figure that portrayed excitement, but loaded the figure down with a huge hat.

D. INTERFERENCES WITH AFFECTIVE FUNCTIONING

So many different kinds of factors can limit the child's reception of affective stimuli or block affective expression that any listing would be incomplete. Many of these factors have already been discussed in some detail throughout this volume, especially in Chapter 2 and in the immediately preceeding sections of the present chapter. This section is concerned with the ways in which such blocking of input or expression is manifested in the responses children give to our most commonly utilized techniques. For example, a child may be completely unresponsive to the color or the shading of the Rorschach inkblots; she/he may attribute all negative feelings on the Bene-Anthony Family Relations Test to "Mr. Nobody"; the feelings of TAT characters are not mentioned or even suggested. During the interview, a child may spend 15 minutes describing the pesty behavior of a younger sib but when asked if this sib is annoying, the child looks surprised and says it really doesn't bother her/him, that she/he just shrugs it off or doesn't pay any attention to the sib. To describe such behavior psychologists commonly use such terms as *denial of affect,* or *blocking,* or under special circumstances, *bland affect.*

Such terms may describe the response, but they do not indicate whether the interference lies in the reception of affect or in the expression. Does showing no affect under circumstances where most children would show affect indicate that a child is obtuse or insensitive to the normally affect-creating stimuli, or is it expression that is blocked? Often it is assumed that the child does recognize and feel but for some reason or other cannot respond outwardly. However, it is also possible that for this child the stimuli may not be affect producing. Or, she/he may actually have become so steeled against such stimuli as to actually be unable to recognize them when faced with them. In dealing here with the absence of a response, there is no easy way of knowing whether the child is unaware or just unresponsive.

Distinguishing between receptive and expressive blocking entails other aspects of the response. If a child says "ooh" and "aah" only to the colored cards of the Rorschach, or mentions that they are colored but does not use the color, or hesitates for many seconds before responding and then carefully notes that the colored parts of the blot are excluded, it may be assumed that he/she at least recognizes the presence of affect-arousing stimuli from the environment even though he/she is unable to respond to them. Similarly, if to the TAT the child describes how the antagonist does things to get the hero angry or sad, and the like but fails to mention how the hero responds, an expressive blocking can be assumed. If on the Bene-Anthony the child describes various members of the family as having incoming feelings but denies any outgoing feelings in return, it would seem likely that she/he is suppressing expression of feelings. In contrast, if the child's affective life is chiefly intratensive, if she/he is unaware of incoming feelings from the family, or if only the heroes of the TAT stories have feelings, then the blocking of feelings would seem to be more receptive. Quite frequently such a repression of affect is widely generalized, covering all sorts of feelings and blocking both the reception of feelings and their expression. As was noted before, such a "coarctate" (to use the Rorschach term) emotional neutrality is a fairly common characteristic of latency-age children. Certainly if a child's responses to the color cards of the Rorschach are given without hesitation or other signs of tension, it does not seem meaningful to speak of "color shock" even though color is not used. If the child's stories to the TAT are not only lacking in affective content but are told without affect, there is little sign of awareness of affect. If the child mentions neither personal feelings nor those of others in describing his/her everyday life, then it would appear that he/she is quite obtuse to feelings. In essence then, it is the nature of the coping mechanism that tell us whether the reception or the expression is being blocked.

Interferences with affective functioning may also result in what is known as "inappropriate affect" or in overreactivity. The child cries endlessly over what appears to be a slight hurt, is terrified by what seems an innocuous stimulus, laughs uproariously at something no one else thinks is funny, or goes into tantrums over "nothing."* In these examples, the word *seems* is important because the affect may be inappropriate in the eyes of the observer but not necessarily in the eyes of the child. It may well be that to the child the loss, the terror, the joke, or the insult may be very real. Thus it may not really be the affect that is inappropriate but rather the perception on the situation. Such hyper-affective reactions may also be displacements or counterphobic phenomena. Classic is the "laugh-clown-laugh" reaction to cover depression, or whistling through the cemetery to cover fear. One teen-aged boy wept copiously throughout the initial interviews, without being able to say what he was weeping about. There were some signs of depressive affect in his responses to the projective techniques, but the predominate affective content of his responses was anger. Only much later in subsequent psychotherapy hours did he volunteer that he himself realized his tears covered his anger. Quite commonly such inappropriate affective outbursts may be the overflow of bottled-up feelings. The previously meek and compliant child, who has never responded with even a sign of annoyance, suddenly becomes murderously enraged at the last straw, or the joking "life of the party" bursts into tears when he/she is no longer able to contain depression. Very often the affect that is being displaced, reacted against, or bottled up is revealed in the child's responses to the projective techniques, thus exposing the reaction formation.

CASE 29

Sometimes the source of the affective disturbance is very obvious. Arla, a bright 10-year-old girl who had been failing at school, told the rather unusual story on

*The term *lack of affective control* is much more a specific than the term *lack of emotional control*, which, as it is usually applied, includes conative and social functioning as well as affective.

Card 7GF that the mother and little girl were crying because the dog had died. On the Rorschach, Card IV, she saw a "dead giant," and then on the same card, D1, "a weeping cow." Finally, in drawing her family, she made a circle of her mother, brothers, and herself around a coffin and said with tears in her eyes that her father had just died. The fact that the father had died about two years before was not mentioned in the intake interview with the mother because it was later revealed that the mother felt guilty for having divorced him the year before his death. She had told the child of the father's death at the time, but had avoided showing any grief "so as not to upset the child," and the child had not seemed moved at the time by this announcement. The child's underlying grief was manifested chiefly in her apathy toward her schoolwork and in her social isolation.

Quite often the sources of affective inhibitions may be much less obvious. They may lie in unconsciously assumed taboos, possess guilt-ridden associations, or be part of a role played within the family by the child.

CASE 30

For the past month Amy Lou E, age 13, had frequently awakened in the night, tearful and shaken by nightmares that she could not recall. She had always been subject to mild attacks of uticaria, or "summer hives," and was thought to be allergic to certain foods or to summer pollens, but this year her skin rash persisted into the fall and she was continually scratching—"all through the night," her mother reported. The dermatologist could find no source for her skin outbreak and had diagnosed it as "neurodermatitis."

The possibility that Amy Lou could be emotionally disturbed seemed unimaginable to her parents or her teachers or those who knew her. They regarded her as essentially a "happy" child, who "seldom complained," was "obedient," "helpful around the house," "has many little friends," "adores her little brother," and "loves animals." Her schoolwork was generally superior. "Very neat in her work" and "well behaved," read the teacher's notes. In appearance Amy Lou was a pretty, fair-haired child, neatly and attractively dressed, who smiled sweetly and sat demurely and expectantly in her chair awaiting the psychologist's questions.

Her "problem," she decided solemnly, was that her "kitty had been put away." "Daddy put him to sleep with a little ether in a box, and we buried him in the backyard. Mother thought his fur made my skin itch but he was getting old anyway. He didn't do much but sleep most of the time." Amy Lou's eyes teared as she spoke, and as she wiped them, she continued, "One shouldn't cry over animals. They're not humans, you know. We didn't have a funeral or anything. That wouldn't have been appropriate. After all, there isn't any kitty heaven, really." And she smiled. She contrasted this incident with another, when "the neighbor's dog died . . . they all cried something awful, for days, and held a big funeral. Isn't that silly though! They're kind of awful people, but maybe I shouldn't say so." She stopped—embarrassed. Encouraged to go on, she descried how these neighbors shouted at one another. "The father swears sometimes . . . the mother has the funniest laugh, you can hear it a block away" and "they're always kissing one another, right out where you can see it. My mother says they're the kissiest family she ever saw." She described her own family, as speaking in modulated tones always. "Even when angry?" asked the psychologist. Surprised, Amy Lou denied they ever got angry. "My little brother sometimes yells and stamps his foot, but then he's only 6. He'll learn though. Daddy never puts up with *that!*" The punishment for such a display of anger in the E family was to be isolated in another room. When asked about kissing in her family, she replied that "Mommy kisses me on the cheek when she says goodnight, and Daddy gives me a little peck right here''—pointing to her forehead. Asked if her parents kissed, ''One another?'' she said in amazement, and then burst out laughing so hard that the tears ran down her face. '''Scuse me,'' she apologized in embarrassment.

That Amy Lou inwardly experienced considerable exuberance was evident from the dancing, jumping, whirling figures she saw on the Rorschach cards. However, the same figures were sometimes also described as fighting—''clawing one another until the blood drips down.'' Aside from this response (to Card II), she made no reference to the color of the blots, and she was unusually hesitant in response to the last three colored cards. On the other hand, she was quite aware of the texture of the blots, mentioning ''fur'' (Card VI), ''icy water'' (card VII), and ''sherbet'' (Card VIII) ''because it looks so creamy and drippy''—but did not mention the color and could not say what flavor it made her think of. Stories about people who were stiffly polite to one another prevailed on the first half of her TAT, but before she was through she was reciting one fantasy after another about bloody murders in which the criminal killed in anger. The murderer was always caught, tried, electrocuted, and ''went straight to you know where.'' Her drawing of a person was a svelt feminine figure dressed in an off-the-shoulder evening dress with feminine curves (although no breasts were indicated) and long flowing hair and long lashes and heavily emphasized lips, identified as a ''party girl, about 20.'' She made a grimace when asked to draw a male figure, and produced a smaller cartoon-like boy in an aggressive stance, with prominent teeth, identified as ''a little monster, about 10—all boys are really monsters, like my brother, sometimes,'' and she laughed merrily.

The affective rigidity of Amy Lou's self-righteous parents was obvious during the initial interviews with them, and it became even more manifest when Amy's concern with and conflict over affective expression were used as clues to discuss with them

affective expression within the family. An almost puritanical ethic concerning affect was revealed. In subsequent interviews with both the parents and with Amy Lou, it was discovered that her itching and uticaria occurred most severely following incidents in which affect of various kinds was almost consciously suppressed. Then she began to recall her nightmares, which contained obvious angry feelings toward authority figures, and then with considerable guilt Amy began to admit feelings of hostility, first toward her little brother, then toward her parents.

E. COPING MECHANISMS

Usually when one thinks of coping with affect it is in term of ''emotional control,'' that is, the suppression of affect demanded by the social group surrounding the child. In this sense, psychologists also speak of the uninhibited affect or spontaneity of the child is contrast to the seemingly more inhibited adult. However, certain amounts of certain kinds of affect may be a threat to the child's ego functioning. In my opinion, the real-life portrayal in full color on television of violence or of sexuality strains the ego controls of children, especially younger children. Children who are as yet still internalizing the adult inhibitions are easily overstimulated and ''flooded'' with affect. When something strikes them as funny, they may laugh until they choke, or when disappointed, they may cry without surcease. Affect can be infectious among children, as any schoolteacher knows too well. One joker can ''break up'' a whole classroom; one crying infant can set off a whole nursery. Such floods of affect may temporarily incapacitate the child, so that she/he cannot study or even play.

Children gradually learn to suppress and internalize affect, not just because society demands it, but because it disrupts the ego. One particular kind of affect problem not infrequently encountered in the clinic is the overstimulated child, for example, the child who is teased or seduced or is overly excited. The unconsciously sadistic teasing adult, the bullying older sib, or the pesty younger sib can keep a child in a constant state of tears. The parent who constantly fondles the child or unconsciously teasingly seduces the child can keep him or her in a state of erotic excitement. Families who play a constant game of ''uproar'' can wear a child into a state of affective fatigue.

CASE 31

Jay, age 11, often became so flushed with excitement on the playground or even when called on in the classroom that he could not function at all. He would fumble the ball, run into the fence, or become mute. At other times he would be so listless as to seem depressed or be fatigued and fall asleep in class. In moments of excitement, his facial muscles jerked in an uncontrollable tic. He seemed to be furtively touching the area of his penis or his rectum almost constantly. Although intelligence tests administered by the school psychometrist showed him to be a very bright boy, his schoolwork frequently was at the near-failure level.

During the assessment Jay was very tense, and his face frequently flushed bright red. His hands often dropped suddenly toward his crotch, and several times he rose suddenly from his seat as if jabbed from behind. During the Rorschach, his facial tic was most marked as he struggled for many seconds to get out some response. His Rorschach psychogram was most remarkable for an 11-year-old in that there was not a single response based exclusively on form. All of his responses contained some kind of affect—either internal or external. Often this affect had no boundary at all. It was pure sensuousness, labile reactivity, explosive tension, or free-floating anxiety. His TAT was most dramatic. He played all parts, voicing the affect of each character. These characters screamed and shouted; spoke in seductive whispers, threatened and cajoled, and wept and laughed without

end. By the time the assessment was over, both Jay and the psychologist were exhausted.

Jay's mother was an obese, large-breasted young woman, who, except for her weight, could have been fairly pretty. Her unkempt hair fell about her shoulders and she often sat sprawled in her chair, or with one leg across her knee, idly rubbing her calf. Her cheap housedress was rumpled as if she had slept in it. At one point, when giving an example of her poverty, she mentioned that she owned no brassieres or panties, but ''I hate 'em anyhow.'' During the interviews, she also displayed considerable volatile affect. As she told of how her husband had abandoned her in poverty, leaving her to care for Jay and his younger brother, she filled the air with four-letter invectives in bitter denunciation of him. Nevertheless, she revealed that even after two years of separation, her husband, who now lived with another woman, would return to visit almost weekly, supposedly to spend time with the boys. However, these visits usually consisted largely of recriminations and quarrels between the parents and concluded either in physical violence or in sexual relationships. At these times the boys either ran to the neighbors or retreated into the bedroom. In another context, she mentioned that the apartment was tiny—one bedroom, bath, living room, and kitchenette, and that the walls were so thin ''you could hear a whisper in the next room.'' It seemed quite evident that the boys were witness to the parents' quarrels and love-making. Moreover, it was discovered she and the boys shared the one bed—''because we only have one coverlet.'' When this situation and its possible relationship to Jay's affective overstimulation were questioned further, she protested, ''But I always wear something to bed; I never sleep naked!'' Unemployed, she was entirely dependent on welfare, and the severe limitations of her income also depressed her. Sometimes she would spend whole days in bed, or sit around the house depressed and in tears. Jay would try to cheer her up and comfort her, waiting on her and bringing her little things. On the other hand, when the boys disobeyed her, or particularly when they did not stay around the house when she wanted them, she would become outraged, screaming at them and striking them. However, her rage would be short lived, for the boys had learned that if they quickly apologized, kissed her, and climbed in her lap, she would melt and forgive them. All in all, it was apparent that Jay's environment was intensely affectively overcharged.

With considerable reluctance and ambivalence, she yielded to the social worker's recommendation that the boys be placed temporarily in a residential children's care center. She visited them twice weekly and received continued counseling from the social worker there. Subsequently she decided to break off all relationships with her former husband, and sued for divorce and child support. Through the State Vocational Rehabilitation Service, she received training as a nurse's aide, and after six months was fully employed. Jay's symptoms abated almost immediately after being placed in the center. When he and his brother returned to live with his mother, Jay was making above-average grades at school and presented no behavior problems. Two years later, she and the boys dropped by the center to introduce her new husband to the social worker. All seemed prospering and happy.

Coping with such external overstimulation is often very difficult for a child. Jay's tics and compulsive gestures were indicative of the tension that he felt from his highly charged environment. Another common response of the overstimulated child is some type of psychophysiological response, such as Amy Lou's uticaria or the "fainting spells" of the Victorian teenager. Every mother knows that when a child is overly excited, she/he may vomit or have a bloody nose. The asthmatic or epileptic child will be subject to an attack when under emotional stress. In assessment interviews, the assessor should particularly investigate the events and surroundings leading up to recent attacks or to psychological upsets. Sometimes the child's TAT stories or other fantasies will give leads to the possible affective antecedents to such psychophysiological reactions. Somewhat less commonly, children are able to escape the stimulating situation—as Jay tried to do at times by staying away from the apartment until forced by hunger or bedtime to return. Other children escape by busy work or even by overachievement at school.

Coping with internally experienced affect is also frequently a distressing problem for a child. In fact, what is most disturbing about external stimulations is that they arouse and exacerbate internal affective states that the child is attempting to control. Jay's tics did not serve as a method of coping with the external stimulation, but rather with the tension aroused within him. His own anger, his own anxiety, and his own sexual excitement had to be controlled. However, most children who are attempting to cope with affective stimulation are not so externally stimulated. Their affects lie dormant within them. They may be enraged or disappointed over external events, but these events in themselves may contain little affect.

The affect that is most commonly experienced internally is of course anxiety. This generalized sense of insecurity may have very definite sources in the environment. The child is anxious about something, but the anxiety itself lies within, even if she/he is reflecting the anxiety of someone else. Coping with such internally experienced anxiety is the most common trial for the latency child or the adolescent. Methods for coping with anxiety are almost as varied among children as among adults, but children's defenses are usually not as well perfected nor as much consistent and integral parts of the ego as among adults. Gross, generalized defenses such as outright intellectual and perceptual distortions are more common among children. They are less able to adopt the more subtle denials and evasions of the adult. Their evasions seem outright fantasies or "lies." The adult tries to appear "reasonable," to ignore the anxiety, or to evade it by compulsively turning his/her attention elsewhere. Only rarely is the child able to deflect anxiety through sublimation. Intellectualization of affect does occur among children—even among retarded children—but it is more commonly an adult defense.

Children's reaction formations to anxiety also are likely to be more gross and more simplified than those used by adults. Among children the most common reaction formation is some kind of physical or social activity. Children cannot endure anxiety long. They have to *do something,* anything, almost as if they hope by being active they can expend the anxiety itself in the energy used up in the activity. Such motoric release of anxiety results in such symptoms as hyperactivity, or in adolescent restlessness, in fisticuffs between sibs, and in increased masturbation (without necessarily any heightened sexuality). Often such hyperactivity occurs when the child reports subjective feelings of boredom, for it is in such periods when the child is not otherwise occupied that internal fears come close to consciousness.

CASE 32

Corey, a very emotionally constricted 14-year-old, reported that every morning he ran steadily around the block between the hours of 6:30 and 8:00 A.M., ostensibly or prepare for a track meet. However, he was frequently so exhausted that he fell asleep in class, and by afternoon had little energy left to make practice trials around the school track. He also had many fears of and considerable anger toward his rigid and distant stepfather. Later, it was discovered that by practicing for track he avoided having breakfast with his stepfather.

Corey was almost conscious of his jealousy of his mother's newly acquired husband. His biological father had deserted the family when Corey was only 3, and Corey and his mother were very close. Corey's stepfather had been in and out of the home for several years and had publicly announced their intention to marry many months before the wedding. Corey claimed the marriage was a complete surprise to him and that he had never heard them discuss it. As far as he was concerned, they were "just good friends." His unconscious denial of his mother's marriage was no longer tenable. He had to find some other escape from his own feelings of disappointment, rejection, and anger.

Restless activity is also the major coping mechanism used by children to counteract depression. Although adults may also react with "manic" activity to mask their depressions, this defense is even more common among children. Often such hyperactivity has a compulsive quality to it. The activity is intended not only to distract from or counteract the depressive affect, but often also seems to contain elements of undoing the experience of loss that underlies the depression. The child who is depressed because she/he feels neglected or rejected engages in an activity that denies these feelings.

CASE 33

Billy, age 12, was taken to a new community by his mother after she divorced his father. While she worked, she left him in the care of her maiden aunt, who disapproved of her divorce and was annoyed by boyish noises and activities. Billy tried to make friends at school but failed to get into the main clique. He was temporarily accepted by an outcast group and—as an initiation rite—was required to steal something. He elected to steal food from the market. His mother could not understand: "He gets plenty of food at home," she cried. Billy "acted out" his feelings of being abandoned.

F. AFFECTIVE CONTENT

Recognizing and specifying the feelings and moods of a child should not be, but too often seem to be, a difficult task. Children do not and cannot mask their feelings as successfully as adults, and any attentive adult and most other children can, by observing the child carefully, make a fairly reliable and valid description of the child's feelings. These emotional states of a child are such a commonplace occurrence and so much of the child's everyday behavior that it does not really take a psychologist to recognize them. The difficulty is that many adults—especially those who have to deal with the emotionally disturbed child who does mask feelings or who annoys the adult—blind themselves to the child's affects. Indeed, the central affective problem for the child quite often lies in the fact that she/he happens to live in an environment that is blind to affect, that is, among particularly insensitive adults or in a cruel peer group.

Another factor that makes this simple observation seem difficult to adults—including some psychologists—is that they are used to adults' verbalized statements, although most people know that verbalized statements of affect are often masked and evasive. In addition, because affects have not been subjected to psychometric measurement nor been the subject of much experimental research, psychologists often approach them as if they were something ephemeral, an ascientific phenomenon.

It was the work of Carl Rogers and his students that brought the feelings of the client into focus and made them a central aspect of clinical psychology. The beginning student should familiarize himself with Rogers' approach (1951). Special attention should be paid to the way that Rogers in his published interviews with clients recognizes the feelings of the client as the client describes her/his own behavior, even when the client does not specify affect in direct terms. Of course the Rogerian therapist and therapists of almost any school often ask the client to specify feelings, since clarification of affect is one of the beginning aims of therapy (Palmer, 1980). However, neither Rogers nor any other therapist considers the client's statement alone to be evidence of how the client "really feels." The therapist is interested in getting the client to explore and uncover repressed or hidden affects. Of course the assessor does not have the time nor is he/she in a position to so explore affect. He/she must be able to recognize unspoken feelings, but he/she is not in a therapeutic relationships with the child. Thus the assessor cannot demand that the child recognize feelings.

A complete catalogue of children's affective behavior and its manifestations is beyond the scope of this book. It may be helpful, however, at least to review the main affective categories—especially those of clinical concern—with some explanation of how such affective behavior may be recognized and specified in the responses of children to the most commonly used techniques. Again, in dealing with children it is necessary that these affects be considered developmentally. For this purpose, five categories of affect may be considered: (1) security–anxiety, (2) happiness–depression, (3) affection–anger, (4) pride–shame, and (5) innocence–guilt. Personalogists would probably differ as to whether these particular categories are independent and as to whether they are actually continua. The purpose here, however, is merely to provide some organization and distinctions for discussion.

1. Security and Anxiety

Certainly from infancy on children's needs for a feeling of security are obvious. As infants they particularly need to feel secure physiologically, to rest assured that their physical needs will be supplied. Gradually this need for security becomes expanded to include social needs. It should be noted that this need for security is *affective*, as distinct from conative. It is a feeling of security, not a drive per se—although getting rid of anxiety does form a motivation. (See further discussion in Chapter 11.) Thus children may have all their needs answered, but if they are not sure their needs are to be fulfilled, if satisfactions are erratic and inconsistent, or if there is some threat—real or imagined—to their fulfillment, they may be anxious. On the other hand, children may not feel insecure even if they receive only minimal satisfaction of their needs as long as they feel certain that these needs will be met consistently and without threat of deprivation. As children grow, these possible anxieties become more extended and complicated. Infants experience anxiety largely on the basis of external events—on the basis of here-and-now conditioning. As they begin to internalize experiences, to build up "sign gestalts," and to foresee the possibilities of deprivation, the source of anxiety also becomes internal.

The anxieties of older children have two main antecedents. First, they learn that they must comply with adult wishes and demands if their own demands are to be met. If they do not obey, they may be deprived. They must increasingly learn to satisfy at least some of their own needs. Thus security does not depend wholly on the environment but on the child as well. Second, there is the social demand that children delay some of their needs—particularly sexual drives—and that their needs be satisfied at particular times and in particular forms. Indirectly and gradually, the responsibility for satisfaction of needs is placed upon the child, who is concerned with his/her ability to conform to social demands. Often these anxieties are accompanied by other affects, that is, frustration and rage, depression, shame, and guilt. However, anxiety without feelings of anger, of depression, or of blame is also frequently observable. This pure anxiety is often associated with the inability to "tol-

erate ambiguity," as Frenkel-Brunswich (1948) has described it.

Three kinds of general anxiety are commonly differentiated. The term *free-floating anxiety* is used to describe those overt and generalized manifestations of insecurity that are readily observable by most of the people around the child and often by children themselves. They express apprehension in many situations: They cry easily, they tremble, sleep and appetite are disturbed, their palms perspire constantly, they look and act "afraid," their voices break.

When such manifestations of anxiety are not so generalized but occur only under specified conditions or in response to certain people, the child's anxiety is often labeled as "fixed." It should be noted that the object of such fixed anxiety may be a displacement. In the famous case of Little Hans (Freud, 1909), the child was "afraid" of horses, and he became anxious only when in the streets of Vienna—then filled with horse-drawn vehicles. Subsequently, the child's associations revealed that his real anxiety concerned his father. Such anxieties may be expressed in the form of childhood fears or phobias, but in my opinion, this term is often overused and misused. Specific phobias are actually rare among children. For example, the term *school phobia* is a misnomer. In most such instances, the child is not anxious about anything at school. Indeed, he/she seldom manifests a fear of school, but more often than not is afraid of what is going on at home, or of what he/she fantasizes might happen if not there to prevent it.

The third form in which anxiety appears in children's behavior is when it is repressed and is manifest only in otherwise inexplicable behavior, such as the hyperactivity or "acting-out" (as previously described). In this form children may not overtly experience any anxiety, and they may deny it completely. Nor will others think of them as "nervous." Their anxiety shows itself in an inability to work at school, in somatic symptoms, or in the "immaturity" of their social behavior. The presence of such repressed anxiety, however, may be noted both directly and indirectly in the nature and content of their responses to techniques such as the Rorschach or TAT. On the Rorschach such anxiety is manfest in the vagueness of responses, in the selection only of details that are obvious and clear-cut, in the hesitancy of responsiveness, in the overuse of shading—especially chiaroscuro—or of the white space, or most severely in the record devoid of any determinant except form. Although a "monster" or two appears among most latency-age children's Rorschach responses, since all such children experience some threat from within, intense feelings of anxiety are demonstrated when the child's Rorschach responses are replete with threatening content. Underlying anxiety may be demonstrated in TAT stories by themes of insecurity or themes in which everything is altogether secure, with all threat denied. Often these themes reveal the source of the anxiety, even when threat is omitted or specifically denied.

The ambiguity in the structure of TAT stories may also be a sign of anxiety. Some children cannot specify anything, but give only a series of descriptive sentences. They cannot commit themselves to any one story or make up their minds about the character of any of their heroes. The hazard of speculation is too threatening to them. Other children manifest anxiety obversely by becoming overly detailed, having to account for everything. The interference of anxiety with formal problem-solving behavior on intelligence tests has previously been noted. Thus, the inability to concentrate, as represented by low scores on the Digit Span subtests of the Wechsler or Binet, is considered traditionally as a possible sign of tension. The anxious child may be slightly more at ease on structured materials, such as those offered on IQ tests, but nevertheless require more support, express more self-doubts, be less willing to "guess" when she/he reaches the upper limits of her/his ability. On the DAP, Machover

(1949) and other authorites (Hammer, 1958) argue that extra shading in of figures—comparable to the Rorschach shading—is an indicator of free-floating anxiety, as are very sketchy or lightly done drawings. Similar interpretations are made of Bender Gestalt reproductions (Clausen, 1962).

Blocking and refusal to enter into unstructured tasks often indicate panic in the face of the unknown. For example, one very anxious 7-year-old spent a half hour with the World Test merely opening and peeking in the test case; when the psychologist opened the case wide and took out some materials for him, he became rigid with fright and quickly returned the materials, slamming the case lid shut. Although such anxiety often seems quite generalized and unattached to any specific stimulus, careful examination of the overall protocol, across techniques, often gives clues as to the specific types of situations and persons who most threaten the child. The number of signs of anxiety on any one technique may actually be insignificant, for example, perhaps one or two shading responses or only one white-space response, one prolonged response time or card refusal on the Rorschach, one or two "phobic" respones, a horror story or two on the TAT, and an anxious moment or so on the WISC. Yet, if one looks across the board at all the responses of the child, it is possible that one might find that these indices of anxiety follow some pattern, for example, that they always follow upon or substitute for associations about female or maternal figures, or about sexual symbols, or about threats of injury or of loss.

CASE 34

Jimmie F, age 10, came to the clinic because of his obstinate attitudes toward adult authority both at school and at home. He also seemed to have alientated many of his playmates by being demanding and "bossy." The initial interview with his father revealed that Jimmie's parents had divorced about five years previously and that he had been placed with his father since his mother was hospitalized for alcoholism. Two years thereafter, the mother was killed in an auto accident. A year prior to his coming to the clinic, Jimmie's father had married a much younger woman, who tried to win Jimmie over by being mildly seductive toward him.

That a great deal of anxiety underlay his behavior and that this anxiety was specifically associated with the shift in maternal figures was indicated by the following set of responses:

To the Rorschach: Car I, "A witch . . . no two witches, flying away with somebody. And he's lost his head"; same card inverted, "It's an iceberg, cold gray ice, dripping"; Card II (to D5 + D3) "a rocket ship, a jet taking off, with the exhaust flame below." Card III, "Two women, I think, pulling something apart. It looks like a skull." Card IV, "I can't see nothing, except maybe some big old boots." Card V, "Looks like a bat, doesn't it?" Card V, "A totem pole, stuck in the ground. Card VII (after a long pause, and much turning of the card), "Could be two rabbits, no . . . two women, Indian women, saying 'goodbye' "; same card inverted, "Like a cloud, a kind of unhappy cloud, all full of rain, just about to rain." Card VIII, "Two lions walking up the mountain." Card IX, after considerable pause, "Jezz, that's a 'mother' " (obviously using the word "mother" as a vulgar expression indicating that he was puzzled), but could give no further response. Card X, "A crab (D1); two beavers eating at a tree and its going to drop into the water (D8)."

In reviewing these responses, the assessor noted that Jimmie's first response, the two derogated female figures who have captured a male figure, seen as "headless" or without power, was in itself a rather unusual and anxiety-provoking concept; moreover, this response was followed by a depressing thought, stimulated by the shading of the card; the response to the space in Card II indicated a rejection of the blot itself, an escape form situation, although Jimmie was not able to completely reject the blot, being attracted by the extra stimulation of the color. Analogously, one might

suppose that when Jimmie experiences anxiety, especially concerning female figures, he tries negativistically to escape the situation, but at the same time becomes involved in it in labile fashion. His response to Card III is the popular one, but he adds in the detail that the female figures are splitting a skull apart; both female figures and a skull are commonly seen here, but this interaction that Jimmie projects onto these concepts is idiosyncratic. Again, after such a response, similar to Card I, he has some difficulty on the succeeding card. Thus, on Card IV, he notes the popularly seen "boots" but feels he is not doing justice to the possibilities of the blot. On Cards V and VI he recovers, expressing no direct anxiety and giving fairly popular responses. On Card VII, he is again struck with the feminine figures, being unable to stick with his concept of "rabbits"; again, his response is not markedly unusual, but they are depicted as Indian (suggesting again the possibility of females as aggressive), and most notably he specifies that they are "saying goodbye"; this response is again followed by a dysphoric reaction to the shading. He is subsequently able to pick out the popular response to Card VIII, but as on IV and V, he is unable to do anything further with this card. His choice of vulgarity to express his bafflement at the complexity of form and stimulation of the color to Card IX now seems most significant. Under pressure of environmental stimulus, he blocks and his anxiety is expressed with overtones of erotic hostility. Again, on Card X Jimmie is able to give a popular, everyday response, ignoring now the extra stimulation of the color. But he ends where he began with a response in which two figures are destroying or eating away at something that will fall into space.

On the TAT also, Jimmie's anxiety seemed focused on relationships with mothers, on their loss, and on their possible threat to this manhood. In Picture 1 he depicted the boy as having broken the violin and "now his mother will be broken hearted" because it was she who liked to hear him play. "Maybe his father will get him a new one," Jimmie concluded. To Picture 3BM, the boy is crying because his dog has died. His father (not his mother) comes in to comfort him and will buy him a new one, but he really wants the old one back. To Picture 5, a maid is looking in to call the family to dinner. When the assessor asked about the woman being a "maid," Jimmie explained that maybe they had a maid so that the mother wouldn't have to work too hard; maybe she is sick or something." To Card 6BM, Jimmy blocked for over two minutes, finally asking, "That's the grandmother, not his mother, isn't it?" He couldn't think of a story right away, finally decided that the young man had come to live with his grandmother "because his parents had died." He couldn't expand on this story. To Card 7BM, the young man is listening to his father, who is giving him some advice, "like about business or getting married; maybe the young man wants to get married. Or maybe he is telling him something sad. . . ." but Jimmie could not continue either of these themes. To Card 8BM, Jimmie perceived the prone figure as a woman (it is almost always seen as a male), and told a story of a boy who wanted to grow up to be a doctor and operate on people and save lives, like the doctors who are operating "on this woman." To the assessor's question, Jimmie decided that maybe the woman was having a baby or perhaps "she had been hurt in an accident." The hero in his story would grow up and be a better doctor than those shown in the picture: "He'd be able to save people's lives." On Picture 11, Jimmie described how the hero had "looked into the cave of doom" and was being chased by the dragon but would make it to safety. Then the hero would be able to "fight back." To Card 12 BM, Jimmie told a version of the Snow White fairy tale; the figure bending over the reclining figure was seen as the Prince was about to kiss and awaken the sleeping beauty (ignoring the fact that the reclining figure is wearing a necktie!). He remembered that Snow White had been poisoned by the evil

witch, but he completely forgot about the seven dwarfs and other details of this fairy tale. The hero in Jimmie's version was not Snow White, but the prince, who had "searched all over for the woman he loved." On Card 13B, the little boy is waiting for his mother to come back from the store with groceries, but she is late, and he worries that something may have happened to her. Finally, she appears and they all get to eat. On Card 17BM, Jimmie portrayed the figure on the rope as "escaping something" or "rescuing somebody"; maybe, Jimmie speculated, "he is a fireman going up the rope to rescue some woman. He saves her and everybody is happy—except the fireman's wife." And Jimmie laughed. In his final story, to Card 18BM, Jimmie decided that the hero was being helped away from the scene of an accident. "He didn't get killed but somebody else did; maybe his wife." As to how the story might end, Jimmie concluded, "Maybe he'll get married again someday—but he'll never forget her." These stories appear to contain many references to the loss of maternal figures, or their feared loss, and the need for rescue or reviving them. He is so concerned with this loss that he actually misperceives the depicted sex of some of the persons and changes the pictures to fit his concerns. Jimmie's responses strongly suggest that he was still grieving over the loss of his mother and perhaps was not too sure of the stability of the new mother, and not too willing to accept her. Yet his heroes do look for some resolution, some rescue and are able to "fight back."

A pervasive anxiety that exists in all children is the fear that the parent–child bond will be prematurely broken, leaving the child abandoned and helpless. This *separation anxiety,* as Bowlby (1969) has called it, is basic to the child's development and might be called a normal anxiety. As discussed in Chapter 1 and to be considered further in Chapter 11, a psychological and physiological drive toward growth is present in all children, even if deferred or thwarted. Yet this growth in itself is a threat to the parent–child bond, for by maturity independence is established and the symbiosis is destroyed. Since it is the bond that deteriorated, separation threatens both children and parents. Separation anxiety almost universally appears when children take steps to the leave the family—when they start school, when they go to separate recreations, when a divorce occurs, at the onset of puberty and on leaving home as young adults. This normal anxiety acts as a brake on the dissolution of this bond, preserving it sufficiently such that children can develop the abilities to cope with further independence.

By school age, children who sleep alone in their own beds, can be kissed goodnight and left to sleep alone. They should not need to have a parent by the bedside until they drop off to sleep. But they may need to peek in the parents' room on awakening just to make sure they have lasted through the night. The 6-year-old trudges off to school, but still he/she clings to parents. The 14-year-old presses for newly found freedoms, but he/she still depends on parental backing. Parents gradually but reluctantly let go. In normal durations children's separation anxieties are resolved as parents support the child's moves toward increasing independence. Although such anxiety is a normal feature of maturing, it also underlies many other anxieties. For example, failure in school often reflects the child's anxiety over being able to solve problems independently.

CASE 35

Adele, age 18, was hospitalized with the diagnosis of anorexia nervosa. She had lost weight rapidly, dropping from 150 pounds to only 77 pounds in three months. During the past two weeks she frequently vomited back what she ate. She refused to give up her starvation, fearing desperately that she would return to being "a fatso." She grew too weak to work and had to give up the apartment she had rented to live separately from her mother and new stepfather. She had enrolled in college but found she could not concentrate on her studies, although previously she was a superior student. She returned to living with her parents, but they had ony a one-bedroom apartment and no separate room for her. Her mother, exceedingly worried, quit her job to care for Adele because she was becoming so frail. The mother began to wait on Adele, hand and foot, cooking special foods and hovering over her. But Adele continued to lose weight. Adele protested that she was no "china doll" and could take care of herself if her mother would permit, and there was nothing to worry about. Adele's physician, tearful for her life, convinced her to accept hospitalization.

Adele had suffered several parental losses and separations. Her father was killed in Vietnam when she was only 4. She has been very close to him, and she and her mother wept in one another's arms for many days when they got the news. His picture always had a prominent place over her bed. Adele and her mother went to live with the maternal grandmother. Her mother went to work to support the three of them and grandmother cared for Adele. Adele became a "poor eater," finicky about food," and grandmother delighted in cooking special tidbits to tickle Adele's appetite. Previously Adele's weight had been normal for her age, but with grandmother's special dishes Adele became noticeably chunky. Adele was 11 when her grandmother died. After that Adele grieved more, eating "junk food" constantly. By age 13, Adele weighed 170 pounds and was 5'1" tall. At this time her mother remarried. Adele "adored" her new father, who treated her like a pet. She was "second" mother, keeping house and doing the cooking while both parents worked. With her parents urging her, she "tried" to diet but without success. She showed no signs of adolescence—physical, emotional, or social. Her obesity hid the normal changes in shape and breast development. She had only two menstrual periods in three years.

She had no interest in boys, and very few girlfriends. She enjoyed roller skating with prepubescent children in the neighborhood or playing with her stuffed animals. Her father built her a doll house, and she decorated it with miniatures—"as a hobby. I don't pay with dolls anymore!" In high school she was an all-A student. Yet she had no interests outside her home. In her last year of high school, she attracted one boy who told her he liked fat girls. While she lived with her parents, he hung around her home, always pressuring her to engage in sex, but she barely let him touch her. Finally he disappeared just before she moved out.

Adele's second father and her mother quarreled constantly, and after several separations their marriage dissolved when Adele was 17. Adele blamed her mother, believing that her mother was unfaithful. She planned to live with her father. She and her mother had an explosive, screaming quarrel. But the stepfather disappeared without a word. Adele, determined to separate from her mother, found her own apartment and a job and started college. At the same time, Adele's mother married a third time and moved into an apartment where there was no room for Adele. It was at this time that Adele began her severe diet.

This case illustrates the difficulties that can occur in a parent–child symbiosis. Adele was struggling to separate from her mother, but over the years the bond had become almost too strong.

2. Happiness–Depression

Jimmie's and Adele's responses not only indicate a sense of insecurity and anxiety, but perhaps even more they reflect grief and depression. In fact, these two affects—anxiety and depression—so commonly appear together that neither the oberver nor the subject can quite distinguish them. Perhaps the child who continuously feels insecure over a long period will also experience some depression, for the insecurity itself will be experienced as a loss. Children who experience a loss may also feel insecure and feel a threat of further loss. Obversely, happy chldren do not usually feel insecure. However, even children can and do distinguish between these two varieties of affect, both subjectively within themselves and in their behavior. Children's facial expressions may appear strained and tense but not necessarily clouded with depression. The apathy of children's depression is in contradistinction from the hyperactivity of their anxieties— although at times this hyperactivity may be a mask for and a reaction to the anxieties created by depression.

Depression as a reaction to a loss is not the only type of depression, but it is the most common source in children. Such depression can be noted even in infancy, as witness the severely depressive reactions of infants who are deprived of mothering (Spitz, 1946). The loss may be of a loved one, but children like adults also suffer depression when the loss is part of their own bodies, as in an operation or amputation. This loss may only be temporary in reality, for example, when a parent goes to the hospital or has to leave the home for awhile, the child may not be able to comprehend or be assured of the parent's return. Or the child may experience loss and depression when the parent is unable to care for him, so that the child feels a loss of love even though the parent is physically present. Even such a normal loss as the loss of "baby" teeth traditionally is compensated for by the parent in the ceremony of hiding the lost tooth under the child's pillow and replacing it with a coin while the child sleeps. Sometimes a child's depression derives from a single, intense loss (a single-incident learning), such as the loss of a parent through death. More often, however, such a single loss results only in a temporary grief episode, from which the child recovers, as he/she becomes again involved in and driven by the push of development.

Pervasive, extensive depressions are

more likely to occur when the child experiences a series of losses, or prolonged deprivation. Because these may be small and almost forgotten individually, careful interviewing may be necessary to elicit what does underlie the child's depressive affect.

CASE 36

Connie R, age 7, often seemed listless and unhappy, not joining other children in play, not even watching TV, which once fascinated her. She spent long periods of time just sitting and moaning slightly to herself. She frequently complained of stomach aches but refused medicine and seemed to recover rapidly; the pediatrician could find no physical reasons for these complaints and advised psychological help. Sometimes she seemed abnormally hungry and kept asking for food and at other times refused to eat altogether for a whole day. Most of all, she was completely disinterested and apathetic at school, making no effort to become involved in the work, although tests showed her to be intellectually above average. Often she tried to get out of going to school because of her stomach pains or other excuses. Although Connie's mother used the term *depressed* in describing Connie's behavior, she could think of nothing that might be depressing her. Inquiring further, the psychologist discovered that Connie's parents had been divorced about three years, partly because the father's work had kept him away from the family for many days at a time. After the divorce, Connie and her little sister were supposed to be visited by their father every other weekend, but in the last year Mr. R had not been able to visit even once a month. Mrs. R admitted that Connie "used to be" very attached to her father, but did not seem to miss him much at present. Mrs. R and her two children were living with her mother, who cared for the children while Mrs.R worked. Her father had died about a year ago. At this point in the interview, Mrs. R wept for a moment. When she recovered, she remarked, "It's been too much!"

Connie clung behind her mother's skirt and left reluctantly for the playroom only when assured that her mother would remain nearby. She stood, silent and glum, staring at the play materials until she saw a stuffed toy dog that she picked up and cuddled. On inquiry from the psychologist about doggies, she told of having to give up her dog when she moved to Grandma's because Grandma disliked dogs. Subsequently, she had a kitty, but it got run over. She spotted another doll and noted it looked like one her father had given her. At this point, she fell silent, sitting on the floor, her faced buried in the stuffed doggie. When asked further about her father, she stared straight ahead for a moment, then complained of stomach ache and demanded to return to her mother. On the next appointment, Connie was given the Binet; she responded very slowly and with little drive, but nevertheless achieved an IQ of 114. On the Rorschach and TAT, she gave brief responses that were gloomy and dysphoric.

Connie's case also illustrates another common cause of depression in children, that is, a reaction to depression in the parent, especially in the mother. Further interviews were held with Mrs. R, and she took the MMPI, the Sentence Completion, and Draw-A-Person. Despite her attempts to deny and repress, it was evident that she was experiencing considerable depression. She was angry, bitter, and had intense feelings of rebellion, but was able to hide them by keeping busy at work, yet she suffered intense headaches in the evening. Her anger and grief over her divorce had never been resolved, and had been exacerbated by the death of her father, with whom she had retained strong infantile ties. Nor could she break away from her mother, who passively dominated her by being dependent on her and making her feel guilty. Interestingly, Connie and her mother drew almost exactly the same female figure (discounting Connie's more primitive form level): a sad-looking, heavily shaded little girl!

How Mrs. R's depression was transmitted to Connie was not clear until much later in the therapy, when Connie dramatized it in doll play: The mommy doll was crying 'cause the daddy doll died, and then the girl doll cried too. At the same time, Mrs. R, who had questioned whether she spent too little time with Connie or whether she might be neglecting her, began to realize that she was most likely to cuddle with Connie and pay attention to her when she herself felt sad and lonely, or to be rejecting of Connie when she felt angry and rejected. Thus she began to see how she had treated Connie as an extension of herself and or her own depression, and to relate how Connie had responded with depression. This insight temporarily increased her guilt feelings, but she was able to look at her relationship with Connie more realistically and then to seek new and more appropriate outlets for her needs in more adult fashion, that is, with her boyfriend. Connie saw her mother's depression as a rejection, and thus as a loss.

The patten of anger, guilt, and then depression, as demonstrated in the case of Mrs. R is most common. As children begin to internalize their feelings and to experience guilt rather than loss of fear, they also can become depressed like the adult. If Connie had been slightly older, it would not be surprising to find evidence that she vaguely blamed herself for her losses. On the TAT, one might find themes in which the girl was to blame for the father's leaving, or had to be punished for murderous feelings toward the mother, or for robbery of the mother. Adolescents who have a history of losses similar to those experienced by Connie frequently relive these depressions as they struggle with the adolescent drives toward independence and sexual maturity. Symptomatically, adolescent depression is often acted out, for example, in truancy, school failure, or mild delinquencies. Thus the sullen, seemingly rebellious adolescent may give responses that spell out considerable underlying guilt and depression. Since adolescence is a time of life in which mild, temporary disappointments are normally quickly sloughed off, even slight indications of continuous

depressive affect are to be considered significant. For example, on adolescent norms for the depression score of the MMPI, as given by Hathaway and Monachesi (1961), T scores are much higher than for adult norms. Since adolescents tend to cover depression by hypermanic behavior, extremely high "Ma" T scores on adolescent MMPI Profiles may also indicate depression. On the Rorschach, the depressed adolescent may respond with use of achromatic color of shading, but more often depression at this age is maked on the Rorschach by apathy, by an absence of color, shading, or movement responses. The presence of color responses in an adolescent Rorschach is not contraindicative of depression but, in combination with other signs, may indicate a continuation of infantile dependency on the environment, an effort to reestablish and regain infantile relationships, and to compensate for the earlier losses. On the TAT, the guilt-ridden depressed adolescent is likely to respond to themes of hostility, guilt, and punishment, accompanied by depressive affect.

3. Affection—Anger

From the discussion about security—anxiety and happiness—depression, it is obvious that these two affectional dimensions become intertwined with various degrees of affection and anger. Although these affects may be highly intercorrelated and in the younger child experienced without much differentiation, they are quite distinguishable affects both theoretically and in the behavior of the child—even in infancy. For example, receiving affection may or may not lead to security and happiness. Where such affection is eroticized, as is too often the case, by either the parent or child, the child may experience anxiety rather than security and consequently feel guilty and depressed. Obversely, the anxious or depressed child may appear very affectionate, searching for love. Anger may lead to feelings of anxiety, guilt, and depression, but the child who is able to express anger—or to receive it—appropriate to the situation may feel more secure in the long run, and feelings of depression may actually be relieved.

It is easier to differentiate love from the other affects than to define it. Definitions of love have defied poets and philosophers through the ages, and most psychologists avoid the term (if not the whole concept) by using euphemisms such as "positive" feelings and the like. In using the term *affection* rather than *love*, one may be able to distinguish between the more erotic implications of adult love and the positive interactional affect between children and others. However, it is to be admitted that in so doing I also may be euphemistic and not allow for the erotic overtones present in much of the child's affectional experiences. Love is love, and it should not be diminished by other terms.

Anger too is a definite and directly experienced affect, so common a part of our experience that it may not seem to warrant description or behavioral definition. Manifestations of covert anger have been illlustrated many times in the cases in this volume. Anger is not the opposite of love. The term *hate* describes the far end of this dimension more accurately, but hate is a rather rare affect in childhood (Redl and Wineman, 1951). At least for purposes of discussion, anger may be thought of as a relatively temporary negative affective reaction to some definite person concerning some definite situation. When such anger is prolonged or becomes generalized, the term *hostility* is used. Intensified, continuous, and generalized, such hostility is commonly called "hate." While anger is on the opposite side of this dimension, children from infancy on experience the conflict of both love and anger toward the same person—almost at the same moment. A full-blown hatred seems to blanket out love, although the two commonly alternate. Affection--anger thus may be considered a "dimension," but not a continuum.

Another reason for using these terms is to distingush the affect from the drive. Such distinction needs to be made in the case of all affect, for each can become a motivation, but the need to obtain love or to express hatred is such a strong motivation that it is sometimes difficult to conceive of these drives as primarily affective, or at least experienced by the individual as affect.

Since a major concern in assessment of children is the development of interpersonal relationships, expression of affection and anger is often a focal point. Too often, however, the novice reports only the fact that the child has such feelings: "This is a very angry or hostile child" or "Johnny lacks affection." Such statements often have a taint of value judgment to them, as if there was something wrong with having angry feelings or even being hostile per se, or as if it is unusual to "lack affection" in itself. The main question is of course how the child copes with these affects. Continuous or frequent states of anger or generalized feelings of hostility may of course be draining in themselves. Even being in love is—as every teen-ager knows—both delightful and enervating at times. In most instances, children (or adults) who feel injured or insulted and can express righteous anger feel relieved. Their communication of anger is in a sense a normal human interchange, a warning to others that they will defend themselves. Similarly, the expressions of affection tell others that they seek such support and will defend and support them.

Anger or affection becomes a "problem" when such expression is blocked or is overwhelming. A conflict is created when children perceive anger as threatening a loss of love. They avoid expression of feelings of anger if these feelings are directed toward someone upon whom they are dependent or from whom they need emotional support. Similarly, they avoid making these persons angry. During pre-school years, children learn to "control their tempers" for fear of rejection. Later in childhood, when they begin to internalize, they stifle anger because of feelings of guilt. The 2- or

3-year-old tells anyone "No" if she/he feels like it; she/he also is quite free with affections. However, before reaching latency children become considerably more discriminating. They learn by then who will permit to say "No" and who will respond to offers of love. Thus it is rare to find a pre-school child who so represses anger that it becomes a generalized state of hostility. Likewise, the latency child who is indiscriminate in his/her affections would be considered "immature."

Anger also becomes a "problem" for children because it is so commonly associated and confused with aggressive impulses and behavior. The untrammeled, yet normal aggressive drives of childhood create social problems, and they make others angry. Children often interpret the efforts of others to control aggressive behavior as anger, even if these efforts are not accompanied by anger. Thus being aggressive creates anger, and it may be interpreted as such by both the child and by others. Children do learn to discriminate between aggression and anger, but often it is a fine line of distinction. Children push and pull on one another or even hit one another "just for fun." Getting ahead in line or in a game can also be a nonangry competition. But feelings of hurt and anger begin to enter in. Making these discriminations is almost a preoccupation of social relationships during latency. Children continuously test how far they can go with one another—or even with parents and teachers—until the line is crossed between aggression and anger.

As has been repeatedly illustrated in the cases cited in this volume, when children have intense conflicts about expression of anger they often throttle their aggressive drives. Thus a child who has intense and generalized feelings of hostility may be quite passive. The so-called passive-aggressive personality probably should be labeled "passive-hostile"—at least in childhood. The child's efforts to remain passive and contain hostility are seldom if ever quite successful. Hostile feelings are

likely to burst forth in aggressive form, occasionally like an erupting volcano. Even passivity may be an indirect expression of hostility if the child is unable and unwilling to take the independent steps expected by others. This passive expression of hostility often underlies such symptoms as enuresis or underachievement at school.

CASE 37

Peter, age 8, had not spoken a word to anyone at school or outside his home since he began kindergarten. His teachers were annoyed and tried to force him to speak, but he ignored them. His written work was perfect, and he was well behaved and otherwise pleasant, so until he entered the third grade his teachers wearied of trying to force him to talk. The third-grade teacher, however, advised his parents that he would fail since he did not respond to oral questions. The parents were aware of Peter's refusal to speak at school (he did talk at home), but they thought him "shy" and believed he would gradually "get over it." On nonverbal tests Peter achieved an IQ of 115. He refused to respond to any verbal test and even rejected the MAPS and World Test. Two young psychiatrists at the University Center tried to treat him with play therapy, but he just sat passively and silent in the playroom until they gave up. He was brought by the last resident psychiatrist to the teaching rounds. Peter came dressed in full cowboy regalia, with two cap pistols in side holsters. He merely glared at the chief psychiatrist, who then took the guns, pointed them at Peter, and said "BANG!" Peter's face remained impassive. The professor pointed out that Peter's silence was a method he had of evoking anger in others without commiting an offense. Interviews with Peter's mother revealed that Peter had never wanted to separate from her—nor she from him—when he became of school age.

The child who is full of repressed hostility is also likely to be very sensitive to anger in others, to easily feel hurt, rejected, and to interpret the actions of others as anger—projecting onto them her/his own hostility. A mild form of paranoia or at least feelings of persecution is common in early adolescence. Not as yet prepared to handle the normal surges of aggressive sexual impulses, the 13-year-old projects them onto others. He or she complains that adults are "picking on me" "Get them off my back" is the cry. Similarly, adolescents are "crushed" by rejections, especially of their affections.

Feelings of affection may also become loaded with anxiety or guilt for the child. Even before love has sexual overtones (in the usual sense of sexual), children begin to experience moments when those they love cannot reciprocate. Mother is not always right there at the moment the 2-year-old needs love or wants to tell her he/she loves her. Moreover, just as anger and aggression become intertwined, so do love and aggression—especially in infancy. The infant wants to hug the mother, to devour her. In fact, mothers also express their love for their babies in similar terms: "I love you so much I could eat you!" Such "oral-aggressive" love, as Freud called it, is often difficult for parents to endure. If it is expressed by the mother, it may cause panic in the child. Of course if expressed by the mother in response to the child's oral-aggressive behavior, such a statement as just quoted may also act as a reassurance to the child in that the mother in effect accepts and recognizes the child's wishes.

As sexual and aggressive impulses become stronger and even more interlaced later in infancy, the child becomes more cautious and discriminatory in his/her expressions of affection. At 4 and 5, she/he tells mother "I love you" but watches her reaction, and then does something naughty to test her, asking repeatedly, "Do you love me?" Similarly with peers she/he may bring a gift or kiss a friend one moment and hit and pull on the friend the next. Such open expressions of affection are much more repressed during latency and early adoles-

cence, while feelings of affection are being internalized. Once children learn that their affection is acceptable to others and that others will respond, they do not have to test it as extremely. They begin to accept affection as part of themselves without being rewarded constantly.

In early adolescence affectionate feelings again are tinged with sexual drive. Adolescents try to make sure that no one recognizes this and that these drives do not enter into parental or other relationships. Only after they begin to enter the state of normal heterosexual relationships can they once again permit overt expressions of affection. One mother noted that her son scarcely had said "hello" to her between ages 13 and 15. Now at age 16, "He has a steady girlfriend and they smooch for hours—but I get a good-night kiss too, for the first time since he was 10!"

Manifestations of these various patterns of affection and anger can often be gathered directly from the reports of the child or his/her parents. Where these feelings are strongly repressed, however, the child may be entirely unable to bring them up in interviews, and blocks or denies their importance when questioned. Since the difficulties in exchange of these feelings often are present in both the child and in his/her parents, the nature of the conflict may only be hinted at in the parental interviews, in subtle clues or in the tone of voice or phrasing of the subject. Thus quite commonly the referrant will remark to the psychologist, "This child seems very sweet and denies any anger, but I sense an underlying well of hostility. His mother acts this way too. Please see what you can find."

Sometimes the evidence of bottled-up rage is quite clear in the associations of the child to the projective techniques. Angry, mean, threatening faces or attacking, vicious animals appear in a child's responses to the Rorschach or in drawings. Here the psychologist must be careful to distinguish between expressions of anger and signs of aggressive impulses. Not every explosion means anger, not every powerful aggressive animal necessarily indicates hostility. For example, one 10-year-old drew a man with boxing gloves. "Who's he going to hit?" asked the psychologist. "Why, nobody," replied the child in surprise. "He isn't going to hit someone. He's just working out." "But isn't he going to hit someone some time?" persisted the psychologist. "Well, he might get into a boxing fight," admitted the child. "Who would he like to box with?" inquired the psychologist. "Oh, someone else who likes to box for fun," replied the child. The conflcts surrounding feelings of anger are often most dramatically revealed on such techniques as the CAT, TAT, or MAPS. Some sample responses from different children follow.

On the TAT, for example:

3BM: She just shot somebody. There's the gun on tthe floor . . . (?) . . .Maybe she's sorry and is going to kill herself . . . (?) It coulda been her boyfriend. He coulda told her he didn't love her anymore. . . .

6BM: They're just standing there . . . I don't see no story . . . (long pause) . . . They look kinda angry, but they don't seem to be saying anything . . . (angry about?) . . . Well, maybe he wants to leave home, or get married, something like that and doesn't want to tell his mother 'cause it'll hurt her, but she already knows and is angry anyhow. (He is angry?) Yeah . . . he wishes she'd understand and is mad 'cause she doesn't. She isn't going to say anything either, just looks out the window, mad like . . . That's all I can see. I don't know how it ends.

MAPS LIVING ROOM SCENE: This little boy is waiting for his father to come home. He's seen a Cadillac stop outside and goes to greet his father. But it isn't his father, it's this gangster, who is going to shoot everybody. His mother screams and his sister cries. He runs out the door and gets a policeman who comes and arrests the gangster. (How does the boy feel?) He's angry 'cause his father didn't come home.

MAPS STREET SCENE: Here's this man and here's his wife, and they don't see this car coming and they get runned over and get smashed to death (child laughs nervously). (How come they didn't see the car?) They were having a big fight, as usual. (What about?) . . . I don't know. Maybe she wanted something and he didn't think they had the money for it. (What did she want?) How should I know! (angrily).

CAT 1: The baby chickens have to eat their mush and they hate mush. The mother says, "Eat your mush or I'll eat you up." But they don't want to . . . (What happens?) They eat the mother instead . . . Eat 'er all up . . . They eat everybody up (child screams with laughter).

To the Rorschach:

CARD II: These two dogs . . . no, bears . . . having a big fight . . . blood all over them . . . they bit off each other's legs . . . blood shooting up in the air.

CARD III: These two cannibals . . . cannibal ladies . . . fighting over the guy they're eating . . . they're fighting over his brains . . . that's 'sposed to be the best part, isn't it?

CARD IX: It looks like a volcano exploding. Here's some people down here trying to run away but they're going to fall in and get burned up.

Affectionate feelings and the need for affection also are often dramatized in children's fantasies and associations, sometimes in the same set of fantasies expressing considerable anger. For example to the TAT:

11BM: His father comes in and sees him sleeping on the couch. He thinks maybe he's sick or something 'cause he is sleeping on this couch insead of his bed. But he isn't, he's just tired. So the father is worried over him and goes to feel his forehead. He doesn't want to wake him up, just wants to see how he is. The boy wakes up and he's scared for a minute but the father tells him it's okay and he's glad he isn't sick, and the boy isn't scared anymore. (What was he scared about?) He didn't know what his father was going to do. He thought maybe his father was mad 'cause he was sleeping on the couch, but he was glad his fahter wanted to see how he was.

7GF: This mother is trying to read the girl a story, and the little girl isn't listening very much . . . (How come?) . . . Maybe she didn't have anything to do. She was through playing with her doll and hadn't anything to do. Now she wants to go out and play 'cause she hears the other kids outdoors. (What happened?) Her mother knows she wants to go out and play and gives her a big kiss and tells her, "Okay, run out and play."

To the Rorschach:

CARD I: Two ghosts, right here in the middle . . . they're right up against one another, like they're kissing (laughs). I guess ghosts kiss! And here's two more ghosts, with wings, on the side. They look like they're patting the other ghosts on the head. (In the inquiry, the child noted that "you can see right thu 'em . . . they're ghostylike." This use of the shading suggested considerable anxiety intermixed with the affectionate feelings).

CARD III: Two people picking something up. Like each is reaching for it. Like they were saying, "Let me pick it up for you. . . ." "No, permit me!"

4.   Pride and Shame

Like anger and affection, pride and shame are also in essence social or interpersonal affects. Pride is a little more than a feeling of confidence or of self-worth. It implies that the child is expecting or receiving rewards for achievement or for some kind of socially approved behavior. Children do not know how to be proud unless they have experienced praise, or are seeking praise. Similarly, they are ashamed only with respect to what others think of them or might think of them. These affects appear relatively early in childhood, becoming first most noticeable somewhere between ages 3 to 6, when the child becomes deeply involved in self-mastery and in being rewarded for such abilities. The 4-year-old boasts of what he/she can do, with exaggerated claims of powers and prowess and constant requests for adult attention to abilities and for adult praise. At this age, children are testing not only their abilities, but what others think of them.

When they cannot control themselves, they become dreadfully embarrassed. "Aren't you ashamed!" the 3-year-old boy says to his teddy bear, echoing the parents. The 5-year-old boy bites his lip and tries not to cry when hurt, because as a boy he would be embarrassed to be seen crying. Kindergarten and first-grade children taunt one another with cries of "Shame! Shame!" Little girls at this age are also unconsciously vain little creatures. They pose and cavort in seductive fashion, enjoy dressing up and grooming (much like their teen-aged sisters, but in striking contrast to the latency "tomboy"). At other moments, both they and their little brothers in this age group are suddenly very embarrassed by their bodies, and they become quite modest. As with other stages of early childhood development, these affects of pride and shame are repeated during early adolescence. The latency child can be shamed and does exhibit pride over accomplishments, but embarrassment—particularly as a response to social failures—is most marked in adolescence.

Although in the long run shame is not usually as disturbing to the ego structure as anxiety, depression, or guilt,* it is usually acutely painful at the moment, and children as well as adults make immediate moves to

_____

*Shame or "loss of face" is a more severely disturbing emotion in such cultures as the Chinese, where the child's errors are seen principally as reflecting on the parents.

cope with it. To "face up" to errors is difficult for the child. Such admission, with the possibility of learning from the error and correcting it, has to be rewarded if the child is to learn. "Hanging one's head in shame" typifies the tendency to try to escape the pain of social embarrassment. Children quickly learn to avoid situations where they might be embarrassed. Since they do not experience social inadequacy as their fault (see the discussion on guilt below), they are more likely to be angry at the persons who embarrass them than to become depressed. Thus children who are frequently shamed are also quick to feel falsely accused. They become sensitive to the weaknesses of others and are quick to embarrass them in return. They are apt to seek out other acts of skill or positions of social status of which they can be proud and to be boastful of these.

Shame—rather than guilt—is most likely to be experienced when children do not possess the ability to perform the acts expected of them or to achieve the status that permits them entry to peer cliques. Feelings of shame are thus experienced more frequently by the novitiate, the socially and economically deprived, and by the physically handicapped or scarred. In fact, shame is the affect associated with inadequacy, whereas guilt derives from blame.

CASE 38

Vera L, age 15, was born with one leg shorter than the other, and a small but noticeable red birthmark on her face. Her mother, who had delayed having any children until age 40, was most disappointed. Her father, who really had not wanted any children in the first place, maintained a sneering attitude about Vera's disfigurement—an attitude that he commonly took toward disappointments and that characterized his lifelong and barely concealed depression. Mrs. L counteracted her disappointment by an anxious, hovering overconcern in her care of Vera. She was easily convinced that every time Vera coughed she was catching some dreadful disease, so she constantly protected her and ran to the pediatrician at every occasion. By the time she was 5, Vera was also very anxious—and very spoiled. She had already learned how to panic her mother and to control both parents by causing them to disagree about her care.

Vera's start at school was a tremendously anxiety-laden event—both for her and for her mother. Mrs. L warned Vera "not to mind" if other children made fun of her, which made Vera even more anxious. Vera did not want to separate from her mother, and Mrs. L stayed around the school until asked to leave by the teacher. At first Vera was very shy, hanging around the edge of the schoolyard and refusing to play with the other children, sitting in the back of the room, covering her face. The teacher made special efforts to introduce Vera into peer activities, and gave her a "special" seat near her desk. It was easy to praise Vera for her accomplishments, since she was bright. Vera's physical development was also somewhat precocious, and despite her slight limp, she became quite adept in gross motor coordinaton and at playing active games on the playground. Thus after only year, she changed from being shy and retreating to being a dominating leader—at times almost a bully. She tended to boast excessively and to make fun of others. Yet she still had moments of intense embarrassment, almost without provocation, during which she would giggle without being able to stop, embarrassing her further. When her mother was advised of Vera's uncontrollable giggling, she again assumed that Vera as defective in some way and carted her off to a series of neurological examinations until she found a neurologist who conceded that Vera's behavior "might" be an "epileptic equivalent." Thereafter, Vera's parents treated her as an epileptic, filling the medicine chest with anticonvulsants. Anytime that Vera became angry, anxious, or excited, her mother changed medicines. Mr. L, who had ulcers, decided that Mrs. L was mistaken in "drugging" Vera, and he insisted that the whole problem was Vera's diet.

Vera's pediatrician, now very aware of the family situation, tried desperately to stop the medication and the dieting but without effect. He pointed out that these ill-advised medications had unknown but possibly deleterious effects on Vera, both physiologically and psychologically, that her father's diet was making her anemic. The parents responded by demanding a new diet and new medications. In recalling this, Vera was quite embarrassed and tried at first to deny that her parents' concern was of any importance, but admitted that she was always fearful that other children would find out about the medications or that her mother's fears might be realized and that she would have some epileptic accident that would shame her in front of her peers.

The culmination of Vera's difficulties began with the onset of her menses, which, since her growth was generally precocious, occurred at age 11. Even at age 10 she showed marked breast and hip development that embarrassed her as other girls and boys remarked on it with giggles. Her mother tried to dress her to hide this development, but Vera quickly outgrew the loose blouses and sweaters. By age 12, Vera was already acting like an adolescent. She was in full rebellion against her parents, rejecting their attempts to control her, coming and going as she pleased, entirely neglecting her schoolwork. Painting herself with cosmetics, she joined a mildly delinquent group of older adolescents. As Vera admitted, almost defiantly, her behavior embarrassed her parents acutely.

Mrs. L continued to conceive of Vera's behavior as a defect. This time she concentrated on Vera's physical blemishes, and after more doctor-shopping, found a surgeon who agreed to try to correct Vera's leg. He warned the L's that surgical correction of this defect was risky, especially since her bone growth was almost completed, but, he admitted subsequently, he felt pressured into attempting reconstruc-

tion of her leg by the mother. For the next two years, Vera was in and out of hospitals. Several operations were required. Long periods of recuperation in bed followed each operation. Mrs. L hovered over her, granting her every request, and Vera was very demanding. Her only friends were disabled children whom she met in the hospital. At home in bed, she was very lonesome, restless, irritable, and depressed. She kept up with her studies by having a home teacher and special tutors hired by her parents. She sat like a queen in her traction bed at home, telephoning her friends on her private line and writing endless letters to various boys she had met previously. The seductive tone of these letters and phone calls worried Vera's parents, who further embarrassed her by shouting at her while she was on the telephone and by reading her letters and diaries. Vera retaliated by being most demanding and outrageously impudent whenever her parents' friends were in the house. When her parents reprimanded her, Vera screamed with anger, heaping curses on them and striking them with her crutches. Mr. L stated that he felt "ashamed" to enter his own home.

When at age 15 Vera was able to return to public school (with her leg in a cast), the separation anxiety of starting school in the first grade was re-enacted. Mrs. L demanded extra assurances from the school authorities about Vera's "safety" at school, raising questions in their minds about Vera's ability to attend. Vera's preparation for return to school consisted of dyeing her hair and buying the shortest skirt possible (which didn't fit over her cast). Within three days Vera had (1) lost her temper at a teacher, (2) vomited up her breakfast in the classroom, (3) been brought into the dean of women's office on charges of "lewd" dress and behavior. Mrs. L quoted the dean of girls as saying, "Vera says the most shameful things!"

Prior to entering public school, Vera had been attending special classes for the handicapped. Most of the children in this class were permanently handicapped in contrast to Vera's temporary disability. Many had intellectual handicaps. Vera was insulted and embarrassed at being placed with this group. Asked what irked her most, she replied, "Their boasting!" During her stay with this group, she constantly derided the other children, making fun of their handicaps and punching holes in their claims to adequacy. It was obvious that Vera resented most was that very behavior of which she herself was most guilty.

Although pride and shame are everyday affective phenomena in human behavior, especially in children, there has been almost no systematic study of these affects nor even recognition of them and their manifestations in clinical assessment. In reviewing 100 randomly selected reports of assessments on children, I found none mentioning the words *shame* or *pride;* only two referred to "embarrassment" and then only in describing the behavior of the child during the examination. Although it was not possible to check further into the data per se, it did appear that in many instances the assessor may have confused feelings of shame with more adult guilt reactions, and pride with the need for achievement or ambition. It seems inconceivable that psychologists cannot recognize these emotions in children. More likely the reason that they are not mentioned is that they are considered unimportant or only temporary affects—relatively unrelated to long-range affective development. In any event, there is no rating scale in common use to define "shame" nor any projective technique that includes this concept in its sampling of associations.

Thus the clinician is dependent mainly on the subjective reports of the child or parent or on direct observations for assessment of the child's feelings of shame or pride. However, shame is often too painful for children to report directly, and they have learned that they must soft-pedal admissions of pride, in order to avoid appearing boastful. Adults—especially those who turn for assistance in understanding their children—are often poor observers of them, and part of the problem may well be that they are obtuse to their children's feelings of embarrassment. Such parents may view the child's feelings of shame only as resistance to doing what they want the child to do, especially to achieve. In fact, if the parents admit that the child is ashamed of a failure or inadequacy, they might have to admit that they also are ashamed of the child. The same parents are also unlikely to recognize and praise the child for other accomplishments or to recognize what the child may take pride in. Too often they see these accomplishments as unimportant or as "childish."

It is usually necessary therefore during assessment interviews for the psychologist to ask the child and the parents about possible situations in which the child may experience shame or pride. The clinician should be particularly observant of the child's face and voice when topics such as physical blemishes and disabilities, school failure, or social failures are discussed. The adolescent or prepubescent child may be able to shrug off feelings of shame in discussing such failures, but the presence of this affect often shows through in his/her tone of voice, gestures, and posture. Blushing, of course, is the classic manifestation of embarrassment. The experienced interviewer will also make efforts to introduce topics in which the child may have an opportunity to talk about things she/he is proud of. Even before discussing painful topics like school failure or physical inadequacies, the assessor should inquire about what the child likes to do "for fun," what "you are good at," and the like. Some very depressed children or those who feel very inadequate may be threatened by such questions, but such an approach is welcomed by most. After talking about those things children enjoy and are proud of, they are often more able to mention—even voluntarily—the situations that embarrass them.

CASE 39

Kenny, age 10, was referred for assessment by the school primarily because he had been apprehended peeking into the girls' restrooms and gave other indications of sexual curiosity. His parents were also concerned with his continued, intermittent enuresis. Kenny was pushed into the psychologist's office by his mother, who was obviously embarrassed by his reluctance. He sat scrunched up in the chair, looking furitively about the room and out the window. The assessor remarked on his reluctance to come to see him, noting that many children were embarrassed by having to see a psychologist. "They are?" responded Kenny tentatively. "Especially when embarrassing things have happened to them," responded the psychologist. Kenny reddened and drew himself tighter up into the chair.

Asked if he knew why children came to see psychologists, he nodded, "'Cause they have problems." He only shrugged when asked if he had any problems or if his parents he had some problems. "Didn't you talk with them?" he asked suspiciously. Informed that the psychologist had heard the parents' "story" but wanted to know how he felt, Kenny fell silent. "What did you expect we might do here?" asked the psychologist. Kenny said he had been told he was to take some tests, and he thought they might be like the "Iowa" test he took at school. This opened up a discussion about tests and school. Kenny said he "hated" that achievement test but added proudly that he had been told he made a high score on it. He was embarrassed to admit that he had not made grades to match this test score. Quickly he mentioned that he had gotten an "A" on a special project and on several tests where he enjoyed the subject matter. He admitted he was often bored at school (subsequent testing re-

vealed he had an IQ of 144!) and liked to make up games to amuse himself or to tell jokes to amuse others.

"Would you like to hear some of my jokes?" Kenny asked, proceeding to tell several little jokes in a self-assured manner almost like an adult raconteur. Responding to the assessor's laughter, he became more expansive—obviously proud of his story-telling ability—ending with one story with evident sexual overtones. Realizing suddenly that he had told an "off-color" story, he blushed markedly. When the assessor noted he seemed embarrassed, Kenny said cautiously, "I'm sorry. I thought maybe you wouldn't like that one." Asked more about his joke telling, he admitted he liked to "show off" among his classmates and that he often disrupted the class by whispering stories to his buddies, "especially like that last one." "That's why I get sent to the principal's office." After further discussion Kenny agreed that he did have a problem "in keeping my lip zipped up" and "not paying attention to the teacher," saying "that's why my grades are no good." As he came to these conclusions he was much less embarrassed, but actually seemed somewhat self-satisfied that he had found a reason for seeking psychological consultation.

Children—especially adolescents—also commonly mention feelings of shame and pride in their TAT stories. Since these feelings may not be mentioned spontaneously, the assessor should inquire about the feelings of the "hero" whenever the situation in the story implies shame or pride. The experiential basis of these feelings may also appear in the Rorschach determinants. Since shame and pride are affects in reaction to and in association with environmental stimuli, one would expect these affects to be experienced by those sensitive to environmental stresses. Thus Rorschach responses that contain both shading and color, while not evidence of these affects directly, do indicate that the subject is more likely to experience shame and pride when she/he does fail. One type of response that, in my opinion, suggests the experiential basis for these social affects is when the child sees color as indicated by the shading—for example, the top of Card VI is said to "look like a bright colored flower" or "the sun rising, all orange." This projection of "coloring" into sensation is what happens when shame or pride is experienced.

These affects may also be illustrated in the stance and expression of the child's drawings. One 5-year-old, for example, drew a figure with the head off to the right, almost on the chest. When asked about this head, the child remarked, "He's hanging his head. He's ashamed," but could not decide what the figure might be ashamed of. The figure did seem to have an erect penis, but when asked about that part of the drawing, the child remarked in embarrassment that he had made a mistake and erased it. On the adolescent forms of Sentence Completions, the stems "The things that embarrass me most are. . . ." and "I was most proud when. . . ." are commonly used. Embarrassment over "goofs" and pride over achievement on IQ scales are other common indicators of children's experiencing these affects.

5. Innocence and Guilt

Innocence and guilt are so much associated with legality in our culture that even when these terms are used by psychologists to describe subjective feelings, the fact that they are subjectively experienced affects may be forgotten. Thus it may be surprising to discover that people may feel very guilty even when they have done nothing wrong. Obversely, people often are outraged when it appears a person feels very innocent even though she/he may have committed what—in the eyes of society—is a heinous crime. These reactions occur because the person's affective state is presumed to be synonymous with the value system of society. Even psychologists may fail to understand

that affects and value systems may not or need not be equated.

As noted in the discussion on pride and shame, shame and guilt are often confused in the mind of the beholder and even at times in the report of the subject. Shame is an affective response to external, environmental stimuli—that is, to social situations. Guilt and innocence relate to internal, self-actuated phenomena. People feel ashamed in response to the opinion of others. They experience guilt in response to their own opinion of their behavior. The subjective experience of shame is quite different from that of guilt. Children feel shame, particularly when accused by someone else, but at the same time they feel self-righteously innocent and thus quite angry. For example, they may be embarrassed over a social faux pas or a disability but not blame themselves at all. The confusion arises when such phrases as "ashamed of one's self" are used, which, in a sense, describe guilty feelings. When a child is told, "Aren't you ashamed?" he is really expected to feel guilt rather than merely embarrassment.

Perhaps the main reason that shame and guilt are so often confused—especiallly in regard to children's feelings—is that they are related developmentally. Shame, in a sense, is the developmental predecessor of guilt. Both do relate to blame and thus to the child's superego. Shame is the affect associated with an external control system. It occurs when children depend on others to exercise control over them or at least to assist in learning controls. Shame is thus most closely tied in with the learning and establishment of physiological controls, and it becomes generalized to other social behaviors. However, during infancy children are learning the mechanism of controls, but they do not as yet accept responsibility for independent self-control. Even during the early years of latency, children are still testing the external authorities who demand these controls.

It is during latency that the internalization of control takes place. During these years the adult sense of guilt begins to appear, but even at this time, shame is still the more prevalent affect. Guilt and shame are both experienced by the adolescent—often at the same time. Since adolescents are subjected to new lessons in social behavior, they have new things to be ashamed of. Since they have already learned to take some responsibility for themselves, they also often feel guilty over "goofs" as if they should be able to manage the things they are just learning about. Here again it may be noted that guilt and shame are not the same affect. The teen-ager may secretly be quite proud of sexual development but feel quite guilty that she/he cannot always control these urges. The affects associated with adolescent masturbation may thus be both pride and guilt.

Both guilt and shame are related to children's feelings about themselves. Children may feel ashamed when they cannot live up to what is expected of them by others. They feel shame over their disability or ignorance. They thus may feel inadequate and helpless. However, when they begin to blame themselves for such disability or ignorance, when they feel "worthless" rather than merely inadequate, they are experiencing guilt. Both shame and guilt are related to depression, but the depression felt by the ashamed child is the infantile depression of the loss of external social control. The depression experienced by the guilty person is the more adult type of depression—the feeling of worthlessness and of self-blame.

Manifestations of guilt in children's behavior, particularly in adolescent behavior, have been discussed at length at many points in this book and do not need repetition at this point. Suffice it to remind the reader that the child, like the adult, is often prone to gloss over feelings of guilt or to deny them altogether. The presence of this affect among adolescents is most often manifested in their behavior, in the actions they take to deny and avoid guilt and depression.

Evidence of feelings of guilt is also found in response to various kinds of associative techniques. As an internal affect, the experiential basis for feelings of guilt are evidence on the Rorschach movement responses. It is when children are capable of withholding and internalizing kinesthetic motor responses that they are able to experience guilt. Such movement responses do not in themselves represent or predict the subjective feeling of guilt. The tension represented in the inanimate movement response (Fm) is more likely to denote feelings of guilt, especially when the content of the response has to do with falling or being destroyed. On the TAT guilt may be specifically mentioned as the feeling of the hero but is more often represented in the behavior of the hero who "acts" guilty and in the punishment meted out by the storyteller to offending criminal "heroes." Children rarely punish heroes who are ashamed. The shame itself is enough punishment.

The presence of guilt may also be deduced from adolescent MMPI patterns. Feelings of guilt are particularly present in the "472" profile ($Pd, Pt,$ and $D,$ above 70). At first glance, "psychopathic-personality" traits may seem the opposite of guilt, but it must be remembered that adolescents respond to guilt by "acting out." At this age guilt and rebellion are closely associated. The obsessive mulling over of feelings and behavior included under the "psychaesthenia" scale is more obviously part and parcel of the experience of guilt. High depression scores are relatively rare among adolescents, who cannot endure depression. Thus even scores between 55 and 70 are more significant for the adolescent than for the adult. The "479" profile is similar, except in this instance the adolescent is masking his/her depression by manic behavior and ideation. Quite frequently K is also elevated in the profiles of guilt-ridden adolescents, representing their efforts to suppress guilt. However, as guilt mounts and becomes unbearable to the adolescent, F and Sc also tend to rise. In this pattern adolescents then begin to exaggerate complaints, often in a plea for relief, and experience increasing confusion. The hallucinatory and delusional experiences of the "schizophrenic" adolescent often reveal very open feelings of guilt.

The interpretation of manifestations of guilt in children requires some different considerations than those for adults. In the treatment of adult neuroses, the relief of neurotic guilt has been such a common problem that psychologists frequently forget the role of guilt feelings in the development of the normal child's ego—particularly the superego. Guilt is the affective component that heightens children's motivation to internalize and adopt social behavior as their own. It is the leaven in the child's rising sense of an identity. Just as anxiety is a warning signal against possible insecurity, shame is a warning signal against social injuries and guilt against loss of independence.

Thus, while children are forming a conscience and a sense of self-regard, they may show extra amounts of guilt feelings. Latency children, as has been illustrated elsewhere in this book, are involved in rules and regulations, in right and wrong, and in who is to blame. Their TAT stories therefore are often full of crime and punishment. At least two such stories may be expected in the protocol of the average 9-year-old. Unfortunately there are no norms for estimating exactly whether these themes or other signs of guilt are merely part of nor-

mal superego development or whether they represent a conflictual, hypertrophic development. Although normative data certainly would be helpful, an analysis of the details of the stories and of the sequence of stories is informative. The question is not so much the extent of the child's guilt feelings but rather what she/he feels guilty about and how she/he is handling these feelings.

For example, a 9-year-old boy who tells a series of stories about burglary, especially about women who get robbed—some ending with the apprehension and execution of the criminal hero and some with his/her escape—would seem particularly concerned with control over his needs for succor and narcissistic supplies, particularly in relation to his mother. Another latency child might still be attempting to work through intense rivalries with her/his father or sibs, fantasying "accidents" and "murders" in which who the guilty person is, is controversial. Robberies and murder stories by latency girls, although not as common, also often contain hints to the effect that they are working through and internalizing controls over their needs to possess love. Little girls also often struggle with their burgeoning "femininity" at this age, and their fantasies become concerned with giving up "masculinity." Guilt over aggressiveness is thus quite a common theme in latency girls' fantasies in our sexist society.

CHAPTER 11

Analysis of Conative Development

The main question in the assessment of children's motives is not so much the identification of the drives per se as it is the comprehension of the methods that they are developing for channelizing, controlling, delaying, and redirecting their impulses. This development of need-gratification skills constitutes one of the principal aspects of ego development. In order to spell out the kinds of evidence relative to this aspect of ego development and the interpretation of such data, some further details of this concept of conative development need to be considered. As has been considered with the other ego functions discussed in Chapters 9 and 10 the motivations of the child need to be specified as to the following: (1) modality, (2) input–output, (3) focus and differentiation, (4) interferences, (5) methods of coping, and (6) the different kinds of skills associated with specific motivational patterns.

A. CONATIVE MODALITIES

As was indicated in the discussion of modalities in the other ego functions, the primary consideration is not so much the physiological or social source of the function as it is the manner in which the child experiences the function. Since the overall aim in describing the ego functions of the child is description of the development of a sense of identity or self-concept, the first aspect to be considered about needs and drives is how the child experiences these drives in relation to the self. The chief question then is the following: Does the child experience these needs and drives as

chiefly *external* or ego alien or as chiefly *internal* or ego integrative?

Most adults—except those who are severely emotionally disturbed—generally accept without question that most of their physiological drives are a part of themselves. However, under times of stress even "normal" adults may speak of their drives in an ego-alien sense. For example, hunger or sex may be referred to as kind of homunculus or "devil" within. This external experiencing of even physiological needs is, however, much more common during early childhood. Since food and other need gratifications have to be supplied to children externally during infancy, they often act as if their needs for these supplies are also external. Even when normal children begin to be deprived temporarily of food at weaning, they do not experience internal hunger to the point that it can be identiied as a part of themselves. Similarly, as their other physiological needs—for elimination, comforting, or sex—are delayed by social regulation and by social demands for self-control, children seldom see themselves as having and experiencing needs. However, since the regulation of children's food intake and defecation of wastes and of their needs for sleep and for activity begin very early in infancy, children usually begin to recognize these needs as a part of themselves after they have words to express them.

The exception to this development of internalization of the experience of physiological needs is, of course, sexual need. Since direct gratification of this need is strictly tabooed in most cultures, one might imagine that such regulation would rapidly cause children to experience their sexual needs as a part of themselves. Even casual observation indicates, however, that for several reasons preadolescent children do not experience sexual impulses as a part of themselves. If sex is talked about, most children speak and act as if sex is something only other people experience and do. When an infant's genitalia are stimulated, either in masturbatory activity or by clothing, she/he can be observed to have a puzzled look, as if experiencing some strange force. Frequently adolescents, or adults remembering adolescence (for example, during psychotherapy), speak of their masturbation as if they were driven to it by some external force.

The reasons that sex remains experienced chiefly as external are several. First, although sexual sensations occur from birth onward, the maturation of this drive does not occur until puberty, when it becomes a primary need. Not only can sex be delayed—such delay is needed until sexual maturity. Children are not able to satisfy this drive, and society protects them from undue stimulation until puberty. For these and other reasons, children often do not differentiate sexual needs from other drives clearly (see differentiation and focus of drives). Frequently, if other needs are gratified, children may feel sexually gratified also. Obversely, their lack of sexual gratification may result in the heightening of other needs, but when these needs are gratified, sexual drives may be lessened also—in sublimated fashion. Most of all, children learn to gratify these sexual needs on an ideational level (see the discussion on input and output). In fact, as has been described in previous chapters, conceptualization of sexual need gratification has as its epitome the Oedipal fantasy. Once a fantasized solution of sexual urges has become possible, the child ceases most overt sexual behavior on a motoric level, even refusing such normal sexual contact as kissing and caressing.

When children begin to experience increased sexual urges at puberty, they begin to recognize these urges as part of themselves. Often the 12-year-old, for example, shows many signs of experiencing sexual urges—but as something ego alien. Stories of being robbed or raped, that is, of being sexually attacked by an external force, are very frequent in the TAT stories at this age. In girls' responses to 6FG, the man in the picture is commonly seen as a robber, or even blackmailer, or as making some untoward and unmentionable advance or suggestion. Girls of this age seldom see the man in 13MF as the sexual object, but rather they depict him as a lover or husband who finds the girl has been murdered or robbed—with the implication of rape. Boys of about 14 respond in a similar fashion to Pictures 4 and 13MF.

Most informative in this respect are the child's responses to the TAT primeval dragon in the cave (Picture 11). Although no "card-pull" norms are available, in my experience children before pubescence are likely to tell stories to Card 11 in which two monsters are battling for existence. During the early years of pubescence, the typical story runs as follows: The dragon suddenly appears and threatens to destory a hapless and innocent traveler who is trying to get through a strange passage in the rocks. Only after ages 15 and 16 is the following type of story common: The hero is exploring the cave, a scientist looking for the dragon, which the hero captures and preserves for humanity, being honored for his prowess. Another common response to this picture at about ages 12 to 14 is that the dragon comes out of the cave and is accidentally destroyed while searching for food. This suggests that the search for gratification of the fiery impulse may lead to destruction.

Recognition of secondary physical sexual growth as part of the self is often manifested in the adolescent's drawing of a human figure—especially in the drawing of the female figure (although such recognition may also be indicated in the clothing put on the male figure, or in his stance). Again, the presence of breasts or well-defined hips on the drawing of the female figure would suggest a precocity in a 12-year-old girl or boy. At this age they are much more likely to draw slightly younger children or parental figures. It is only after they have become comfortable with their own pubescence and accepted it as part of themselves that they project it as part of their body image in their drawings.

The fact that children have engaged in sexual relationships with each other or adults does not indicate that they necessarily experience sex as a part of themselves. Strange as it may seem on initial consideration, the 13- and 14-year-old girl who has been quite promiscuous and who even talks about it in adult nonchalant fashion usually does not see her behavior or her impulse as part of herself. Her seeming sexual precocity makes more sense when, as is commonly the case, it is discovered that her behavior is based on motivations such as a rebellion against her parents, a bid for their attention, or even counterphobic reaction to her sexual impulses themselves.

CASE 40

Sandy, age 13, was described by the juvenile-hall physician as "a well-nourished, well-developed female without signs of physical illness or distress." She had been examined to determine if she had been sexually violated after she was apprehended in a motel room in the company of three older "juvenile males." She had been reported as a missing person by her parents after she had not returned the previous Friday night. She was picked up by the sheriff the following Sunday on a report by the motel owner. The physician's report regarding possible sexual molestation was "indeterminate." Sandy refused to discuss the matter. She was released to her parents on Monday morning. They immediately called the psychologist, requesting an emergency appointment that day.

Sandy's appearance suggested that she might be quite sexually provocative. She was dressed in the current urban teen-aged style her ragged jeans were cut so short that her thighs were exposed. She was barefoot and her long streaked blonde hair fell loosely to her shoulders; she wore eye makeup but no other cosmetics, and her skin was quite tan but free of adolescent acne. In the waiting room she sat across the room from her mother, looking away at the wall, her face in a pout. Her mother, Mrs. Y, was, in contrast, plainly attired, an almost dowdy woman who showed no special attention to dress or grooming. Although only 38, her hair was beginning to gray, and the lines in her face were accentuated by her harried and depressed expression. She rose to greet the psychologist and called hesitantly to Sandy who did not respond. When the psychologist went over and introduced himself to Sandy, she silently rose, made a spiteful face at her mother and accompanied the psychologist to the office.

Soon after the interview began, Sandy's sullen hostility ignited into open expression of anger against her parents, her two younger brothers, her teachers, and even her girlfriends. She accused her mother of being too critical and always treating her like "I'm a child." "Daddy's even worse; he just agrees with everything she says! He comes home and doesn't know what it's all about and then opens his big mouth." Her chief complaints were that her parents did not accept her clothes, her friends, her use of the telephone, and so on. They did not understand the problems she was having at school with teachers whom Sandy considered prejudiced against her. Instead, her parents kept nagging her for better grades and about homework. She claimed she got "mostly B's and C's, with a D in gym." She "hated" gym because she did not want to have a change clothes, and get "all sweaty and have to shower." She had forged her parents' names to notes excusing her from classes and had been caught in her forgery by her father who told the school authorities to take whatever measures they saw fit. However, her mother had intervened when she was threatened with expulsion. She felt her parents let her brothers (ages 9 and 11) "get away with everything."

At the end of the interview Sandy was asked about the incident that landed her in juvenile hall, which, the psychologist noted, they had neglected to discuss. Sandy made a sour face, "Oh, that!" She suddenly looked quite depressed but began to talk. She had gone to a show with a girlfriend that Friday night and had met several boys there. After the show they all drove around for a while with one of the boys who was older and had a car. She realized that the hour was growing late and that she would be scolded for returning home after hours. She was also angry at her girlfriend who was flirting with the driver who was an acquaintance of Sandy's. "He wasn't my boyfriend or anything, but I'd introduced her to him and she had no right to crowd in like that." She asked the boy to drive her over to her aunt's home in the nearby small town. After he drove away she found there was no one home. She wandered down the street, met some other boys whom she did not know but who offered her a ride home. Instead, they took her still farther away to a resort town. She escaped from them, met some other adolescents and slept most of the day on the riverbank. Saturday night she joined these adolescents for a "party." "There was a lot of sex there, but I didn't do anything, honest I didn't." Later, one of the boys offered to drive her home but instead took her to the motel with two other boys. When she resisted their sexual advances, they let her alone. Very tired, she lay down to sleep, "but I got a big knife out of the kitchen and had it beside me" for protection against a possible attack.

Whether Sandy's story was fact or fantasy, her responses to the projective techniques did indicate that she was very immature for 13. Of her 14 responses to the Rorschach, 11 were based entirely on the form of the blot and 3 were rather generalized reactions to color. She saw no human figures. Card III was "a monster's face"; Card IV also "a big hairy monster"

(she was using the term *hairy* in the current teenage slang meaning "horrible"); Card VII was "clouds" and "rabbits." Cards VIII—X were, respectively, "ice-cream flavors" "some kind of flowers, all the colors," and "paint spilled over." Most remarkable in this 13-year-old's responses was the lack of FM; none of her responses showed any indication that her perceptions included her "animal instincts." On the other hand, she was overly respondent to and dependent upon emotional stimulation from the environment. This pattern of response did support the possibility that Sandy would be easily influenced by others, that she could be led astray, but that her sexual and other instinctual drives were not only part of the picture, but probably strongly repressed, as in latency.

Similarly, in Sandy's very brief TAT stories, the heroines had very few, if any, motivations of their own; rather, things happened to them that made them unhappy. The boy with the violin was forced to practice by his mother, but Sandy could not imagine what he might be doing if he was free. On card 2 the girl "had to go to school" and is "looking back to watch her father working"; on Card 4, "Her boy friend has to go in the Army and she's scared she'll be left all alone." 6GF: "He's criticizing the way she's playing the piano and she's mad." Card 11: "It's just looks like there's a lot of rock and stuff, all bare. Like the end of winter and pretty soon it's going to be all spring, but there's nothing there right now." Asked about the dragon: "Oh, that! I don't know where that goes in." Card 12F: "Looks like that old fairy story about the witch that fed the girl the poisoned apple." Asked how it turns out, "I don't remember; I guess she spits it up . . . right in the old witch's face," answered Sandy who laughed. 13MF: "Looks like she's very sick and her father, I mean her husband, thinks she's going to die, and he's very worried and crying and everything. It turns out she really isn't sick at all. Maybe she just got drunk and is sleeping if off!" These fantasies indicated that Sandy conceptualized the factors affecting her life as chiefly external, with little recognition of the play of motivations of her own. Symbolically, Sandy remained frozen in the winter of latency, and though her spring was not far away, she ignored and was unable to include the phallic symbol of the snake–dragon. Nor could she visualize or even remember that Snow White would be rescued from the witch–mother by a Prince Charming. Finally, it is the father-cum-husband who is to be made concerned when her impulses overcome her.

Mrs. Y's first remark during the interview with her was seemingly guilt-ridden, "I guess we've just done everything wrong with Sandy!" but immediately thereafter she began to describe the pressures that she was experiencing in a self-pitying martyrish fashion. Her children took up all of her time and energy, cooking what each wanted, picking up after them, driving them everywhere, and so on. Sandy particularly seemed very demanding to her, ready at a moment's notice to throw a tantrum when she thought she might be refused what she wanted, never contributing anything to the care of the house, always squabbling with her brothers, never saying "thank you." "Instead, for all your efforts you get a sneer or a snarl." Like Sandy, she felt unsupported by her husband; indeed, she felt her husband protected and spoiled Sandy. "Of course, he's very embarrassed by what has happened." Mr. Y was a city official who had risen in the ranks because of his political and community activities—which often occupied his evenings and weekends. Mrs. Y expressed the fear that Sandy's escapade might reflect on Mr. Y's reputation and damage his career. "He just got appointed on this new youth commission and now *this* had to happen," she moaned.

It was noted that Mrs. Y, like Sandy, also felt that things happened to her, rather than that she caused things to happen. It was not her motivations but those of others that concerned her. Regarding Sandy's escapade, Mrs. Y remarked, "I don't know what caused her to do something like that.

She never seemed interested in sex. She just seemed like a little girl to us. I guess we didn't realize she's almost a teen-ager." The lack of communication between Mrs. Y and her daughter, especially regarding Sandy's development, was even more evident in a subsequent interview. When Sandy's menses had begun the previous year, she had not informed her mother and had secretly helped herself to sanitary napkins from her mother's supply. "If I get cramps, the family just thinks I'm sick. My father's so funny! He tried to make me take an Alka-Seltzer. I pretended I did and then spit it up in the toilet."

The degree to which sociocultural values are being internalized by the child and the manner in which this internationalized by the child and the manner in which this internalization is taking place are often of central concern in an assessment. Although children's physical needs become part of their identity at a relatively early age (with a recurrence of this process at puberty), the acceptance of these social values as a part of the self is a continuous process throughout childhood. There seems to be no point in the child's development where the infusion of these values into personal motivations is not of active concern both for those responsible for the child's care and for the child herself/himself. The ways that these social values become personal motives have been discussed in previous chapters, and they will be considered further in Chapter 12 as part of the discussion of social development and its interpretation. Suffice it to say that this internalization of social values and mores is the hallmark of social development. As regards conative development, the important aspect is that these external social values do become motives.

At this point the question is simply whether or not the child experiences such social stress primarily as external or as coming from within. Does he/she strive at school in order to satisfy parents' ambitions or because of some personal need for achievement? Does he/she join the crowd because one is supposed to be sociable and a member of the group or because he/she likes people and wants affiliation? Does she/he do things voluntarily because of rewards or because of some personal pride in being autonomous? Where such social values concern prohibitions of behavior, control can also become a personal motivation. Thus children learn that certain kinds of aggressive behaviors (or even aggression, in general) are prohibited. At first children control their aggressive actions, whether positive or negative, because they fear punishment or desire praise. Even aggressive exploration of their environment may be curtailed. Later, in latency, this control becomes the basis of an internalized guilt.

Data about this process of the internalization of social motivations can be garnered from many of the techniques of assessment. In the interviews, the question "How did that happen?" is better than the question "Why did you . . . ?" for it allows the child a bit more freedom to choose between mentioning external pressure and personal desire. A neutral question permits an analysis of the wording used by children to explain their behavior or the situation in which they find themselves. Often such attitudes are expressed in the very first remarks in an assessment interview when the psychologist inquires, "How was it that you came to see a psychologist?" After a few shrugs of the shoulder, most children begin describing the complaints either their mother or the school has made—that is, external stresses. Fewer mention their own internal unrest, needs or guilt feelings. Further questioning is usually necessary to determine whether such statements reflect internal or external motivation for accepting the psychologist's implicit offer to help. If the child states the parents' complaints, the assessor should determine whether the child accepts these as a part of his/her behavior or whether he/she merely wants the parents to "get off my back." Inversely, complaints against the environment may be voiced as frustrations of her/his motivations, for example, of needs for narcissistic supplies or for independence. Or they may constitute a protest against the impositions placed on her/him to do things that she/he does not regard in any way as need gratifying.

Since children and even their parents may be unable to discuss the reasons for their behavior, either because they are unaware of or ashamed of them, it is often necessary to gather additional data from projective techniques such as the TAT and Sentence Completion. However, even in TAT fantasies the child may fail to include the motivations of the hero, and it is necessary in such instances to make an on-the-spot inquiry: "How come?" "What would make her/him do that?" If the child indicates that the hero was reacting in an affective state, for example, "Cause he's mad, that's why!" the assessor should continue to inquire, "What's he so mad about?" As in the analysis of interview data, it is the phrasing of the child's explanation of motives in the fantasy that is important. Compare the following stories to Picture 1 (which often draws stories about achievement), all of which were told by 10-year-old boys:

ART'S STORY: "He's just sitting there looking at this violin or something . . . (?) [in a resigned voice] He has to practice it, I guess. (He feels?) He hates it. . . . (How come?) How should I know? He just hates it. (What does he hate about it?) I guess just having to do it. (How come he has to do it?) I guess his parents or somebody. . . . (What happens?) He practices all right! Else he gets a whipping. [Art laughs in a hollow tone.] (How does it turn out in the long run?) Huh? (Does he just keep on practicing every day?) I don't know. . . . Maybe it wears out. . . ."

BOB'S STORY: "Should he have a name? I'll call him Jake. . . . That's a good name, isn't it? I don't know any boy named Jake, but I read it. Like 'everything's Jake!' [Bob laughs at his own pun.] Jake has to practice this violin here. . . . He's stopped 'cause he sees some other kids out the window playing and they want him to come out. He'd like to run out and play too, but his mother has told him to play the violin, or else. He'll make some more racket on it, and then his mother will let him out. (How does it turn out in the long run?) You mean in the future? Well, let's see. . . . We'll say his mother gets tired of making him do it and listening to him play so awful and stops making him practice.''

CHUCK'S STORY: "This kid has been practicing his violin and he's tired of it and wishes he were through so he could go out and play. (How does he come to be practicing?) Well, maybe his father gave him this violin and wants him to learn to become a great violinist. (How does he feel about that?) Well, he's too young now to appreciate it. He just wants to finish his pactice and go out. Maybe when he learns to play it better, he'll like it more.''

DAN'S STORY: "This guy's studying the violin. He's sitting there and thinking how to play it better. (How come?) He wants to become a great violinist. (?) Maybe his father or grandfather were great musicians or he's heard some famous violinist and liked it. (What happens?) He asks his teacher to show him how to play it better. (And then?) He practices a lot more and becomes very good at it.''

Art feels that controls are imposed on him for no purpose. Unlike Bob, he does not even express needs of his own. Bob has needs to gratify, but they are the needs of his environment—that is, his peers want him to play. Chuck has both sets of needs and both are his. Note he says "his" violin. Dan's need to control and achieve are almost entirely his own. Although modeled after his father, he drives himself.

If the gratifications of children's needs have been inconstant and unsure, they will feel threatened when competing with others or when required to gratify their own needs. Children will continue to seek infantile gratification from others, and their social behavior will be immature also. Such immaturity is a common cause of behavioral and educational disturbances in the elementary-school child and is often evidence in the complaint itself. For example, such children may be described by the teacher as "demanding of her attention." They do not learn anything unless the teacher hovers over them. It may often be noted—in further interviewing about schoolwork—that children perceive the teacher as the source of motivation of achieving. Their attitude is that they go to school because the teacher wants them to, not because they have any interest or curiosity of their own. Such an attitude is often blatantly displayed by the adolescent school dropout. In such cases one often needs only to scratch the surface to discover a chronic immaturity of motivational experiencing that usually begins in latency.*

B. CONATIVE INPUT AND OUTPUT

Whether children consider their needs as integral parts of themselves, or internal, or as something alien to their egos, or external, depends to a considerable extent on the *input* and *output* of the motivation. The term *input* is used here to describe the form in which the motivation is experienced by the child. *Output* refers to the manner of expressing the need. There are basically two ways in which children both receive and express their needs and drives. The first may be called "motoric," the other "ideational."

Perhaps *physiological* might be a better term than *motoric*, but the latter draws attention to the fact that many needs, particularly physiological drives, are experienced by the child in terms of visceral and

---

*I have seen college students who exhibited the same attitude! They are motivated by "grades" and by parents, not by an interest in acquiring knowledge.

skeletal sensations. Hunger comes to one's attention through a contraction of the stomach walls, and sex through a tumescence of the genital organs. Lack of oxygen results in severe muscular contractions. A drop in bodily temperature makes the child shriver and realize that she/he is cold.* Such motoric input is not limited to physiological drives. The "secondary" or social motivations are also frequently motorically instilled in the child. She/he may learn about property values by having her/his hands slapped when reaching for something she/he should not touch. He/she may learn to curb aggressive impulses by having his/her nose punched by a peer when invading the other child's activities. Such motorically induced pain may thus teach children to avoid certain activities and to conform to social norms. At the same time it is to be hoped that social motives will also be reinforced through more pleasurable motor experiences. Although children may conform partly through fear of pain, their motivations are more strongly instilled if they receive caresses or are fed or played with. Such motoric instillation of motivation does not prevent the child from perceiving the need as external. How she/he *perceives* the need and how it is actually instilled may be quite distinct.

In contrast, many motivations—especially for an adult—have little or no motoric component but are largely ideational. Adults behave in the way they do, not because of any special physiological tension or sensation, but because some concept or memory in their mind drives them.* Many adult social needs consist of such ideational values. Sometimes even physiological needs are on an ideational level. For example, adults sometimes eat because it is dinnertime when one should

eat, whether they are hungry or not. Or adults may exercise because they think exercise is good for them, even though they are fatigued. However, as parents often discover with considerable vexation, children do not readily grasp the idea of eating at a definite time, whether or not they are hungry, and they have to be taught to defecate in the proper place and to withhold defecation until a time can be allowed for it. How these essentially motoric needs become ideational, or at least attain an ideational component, is an important aspect of child-rearing and is often a focal point in assessment.

As has been discussed at several points previously, the training of the child in the control and management of these physiological drives is often the prototype of learning of the control of other, more social drives, which essentially are largely ideational. Thus if children do not learn "going to the bathroom" and "eating dinner" as ideas as well as motoric acts, it may be difficult for them to learn such concepts as "going to school," "staying out of fights," "obeying the teacher," "respecting property," or "being polite" as being other than motoric acts. One very common reason behind the referral of children for assessment is that they have learned as infants to perform these social behaviors as automatic motoric acts without any idea of why or when they are appropriate but only because they are conditioned by the punishment or praise they receive. Their social behavior in relatively unstructured situations outside the home may then be naive or even inappropriate. They may become anxious and fearful when no immediate conditioning agent is present. Moreover, in such situations they may express some of the pent-up resentment and frustration over this meaningless conditioning.

On the other hand, the input of the child's motivations may have little or no motoric base but be almost exclusively an abstract idea. Such is the case with most of children's social motivations. The child has

---

*Admittedly, children do not directly experience the contraction of sweat glands when hot, nor of salivary or other mucous glands when thirsty, but, instead, they experience dampness or dryness, respectively.
*Nevertheless, motoric sensations usually accompany the idea.

to learn what "being good" or "well be-haved" means, or what it is to "want to get ahead." Much of "how to be nice" or not "to be naughty" and what these terms mean in concrete acts is learned prior to entering school. The child must first learn the specific motor acts that are covered by the ideational term. This requires at least a modicum of intelligence, and it is part of the cognitive development of the child. Children whose intellectual development is slow will also be slow to grasp the meaning of these social motivations. A retarded child may want to be nice but not be able to comprehend exactly what "being nice" is. Sometimes, even bright but socially isolated children have difficulty in grasping the meaning of some social concepts. For example, such children may want desperately to affiliate with their peers but through lack of experience be unable to specify the kinds of behaviors that would mark them as being "in."

Motivational output may also be classified as motoric or ideational. Children of all ages, but especially pre-school children, express their wants by physical movements primarily. They touch, reach, and grab for what they want, and even their verbalizations are often accompanied by a lot of motor activity. Although this may be intended to fulfill the need, there is often much excess of nonfunctional motor activity accompanying the demands. The child almost seems to experience the need through the motor arousal and release. As the child learns to delay need gratification, this excess motor activity may increase temporarily, but it subsides as the child learns ideational expression.

As discussed in the earlier chapters of this book and as is mentioned in more detail in Chapters 12 and 13, *the development of the ability to delay gratification of needs and to control motoric release, taken together, is a keystone to all ego development*. It is the basis of abstract thinking, of affective internalization, of the comprehension of social behavior, and of the ability to meet social norms in nearly all major cul-

tures. Most of all, it is the basis for the formation of both the social and personal sense of identity. Only when children begin to conceive of need gratification as an idea rather than simply as a motor reaction are they able to begin to form other concepts and abstractions. Only when they can begin to contain and delay the need can they begin to contain and channel affects. Both of these developments are necessary for effective social functioning, and both are necessary for children to experience themselves as independently functioning persons.

Since the ability to delay and conceptualize need gratification is so important to all of ego development, attention to the data bearing on this question is usually a focal point in any assessment. As is the case with other aspects of ego development, no special technique has been designed to sample this ability specifically. Rather, evidence concerning the input and output of need gratification is present in nearly all clinical procedures and tests. Indeed, it would be difficult to construct a technique just for this purpose, since conative functioning so pervades children's behavior. It is thus necessary to focus on the need-gratification aspects of all the data collected about children's functioning.

These techniques also do not distinguish between input and output. This distinction can only be made by looking very carefully at the child's behavior and responses. As noted before, the distinction between perception and response is often very difficult. This distinction is somewhat easier to make once children are able to conceptualize at least some of their needs—and can verbally express such concepts. Direct observation of the pre-school child yields data primarily about the expression of output of needs. During these pre-school years, the input of motivation is so much a part of the parent—child relationship that assessment necessarily turns to techniques that sample parental attitudes and behaviors as well as the child's development per se.

Data concerning the manner in which a

child experiences and expresses needs may be gathered by examining concretely the kinds of skills a child is developing for need gratification. The level of development of these skills is in itself one indicator of conative development. In assessing input and output of motivations, however, the main aspect with which the assessor needs to be concerned is not the skill itself but the ways the child is experiencing and expressing these motivations. By beginning with the concrete aspect of skill development, it is often possible to expand the interview with the parent or even with the child and discuss how the skill is being taught and learned.

The Doll Vineland Social Maturity Scale—Revised (1965) is one of the earliest and most notable attempts to assess the "self-help" skills during infancy and latency. It focuses attention on the need to investigate how well the infant is learning to do things for himself/herself. It can form the basis for a more extensive interview with the mother about these behaviors and for more detailed observation of the child. This self-help development is, of course, dependent upon and intercorrelated with his/her development of motor skills. Motivation for the learning of these motor skills is, in turn, the desire for independent need gratification. In the interview with the mother, the psychologist should investigate the degree to which this motivation is fostered. How much does the mother encourage or even tolerate the child's efforts toward self-help? To what degree does she push her/him to do things independently? Is she made anxious by the child's failures? Is she easily pressured by demands that she satisfy the child's every need? Does she attempt to teach her/him how to answer her/his own needs, or does she find it easier just to go ahead and do things for the child, since he/she seems so helpless and takes so long to feed himself/herself or dawdles over dressing himself/herself?

For example, many mothers take what seems the easy way out in toilet training by conditioning the child through "establish-ing regular habits"—that is, putting her/him on the potty at regular intervals. Such a routine is admittedly very helpful at the onset of toilet training, but in the long run children have to learn to go to the toilet on their own when they need to. Despite any conditioning, children are liable to have little "accidents" in between the potty sessions. The average mother then quite appropriately loses patience, scolds the child, insisting that she/he make efforts on his/her own to control body eliminations. The mother's anger becomes the reinforcing agent for the child's independent action. It is possible, of course, with the utmost patience and suppression of anger, to toilet train the child entirely on routine conditioning. It is not uncommon to hear a mother of an emotionally disturbed child boast that the child "gave me absolutely no trouble" when he/she was toilet trained, thus describing such a pure conditioning. However, such children frequently have difficulty in learning to satisfy their needs independently. Moreover, they also learn that anger has to be suppressed as much as possible.

Toilet training is only a prototype of the mother–child relationship in self-help training. The assessor should explore other types of training as well as the mother's methods and attitudes. Does she insist that the 2-year-old attempt to feed himself/herself, using a spoon, and then reward the child for the attempts—even if he/she is sloppy? Does she foster curiosity by providing the opportunity to explore or by attempting to answer questions, rather than putting everything out of reach and "shushing"' the child when she/he interrupts her activities? Does she button buttons and tie shoes for the child rather than attempt to teach these skills, even though it takes more trouble and even involves some fuss?

As might be expected, most mothers would maintain that they do make efforts to teach their children these skills. Thus direct questioning of the mother often results in denial of any failure or of any restrictions on her part and an insistence that there is something wrong with the child since she/he is not learning. More information is gained if the interviewer inquires in a neutral tone about the efforts the mother has made and the conditions under which self-help was learned or not learned. When kindergarten children are retarded in the development of self-help skills, when they passively wait for others to take care of their needs and seem helpless, mothers very often appear physically or emotionally unable to make the efforts to teach such children to care for themselves. Another common situation is the working mother who has to leave the training of the child to a baby-sitter or to a grandmother who "spoils" the child by waiting on her/him and who does not tolerate motoric activities.

When there are no such extenuating circumstances, the psychologist should explore further to see if the mother has needs of her own to overprotect her child or is herself a passive, helpless person, relatively incapable of making the effort to train her child. The handicapped child in particular needs extended and intensive training toward self-help, and there is much more temptation to wait on the blind, crippled, or intellectually retarded child, thus inadvertently reinforcing his/her helplessness (see Chapter 15).

Such self-help training of course extends beyond the simple motor skills needed for eating, dressing, keeping clean, and avoiding physical hazards. Even before children begin kindergarten, they develop needs for social affiliation. By the time the infant has learned to walk and talk, his/her mother has also weaned him/her so that she is not the child's constant companion. If the child hangs at her skirts, she begins to brush him/her away and returns to other duties. Children have to learn to occupy themselves, with only an occasional glance and word from their mothers. If they have older sibs, they may seek companionship from them and join in their achievements and play. Mothers may also seek out other toddlers as companions for their children.

Nursery schools were invented for this purpose (not only in our culture, but also in preliterate cultures). It is the credo of nursery schools and kindergartens that they are not just for baby-sitting and entertaining infants, but rather that they are to provide a "head start"—an opportunity for activity, for socialization, and for achievement. They are aimed at creating independent goal achievement, even though they do not always obtain this ideal. In contrast, one of the adverse side effects of television is that it is too often used as a passive baby-sitter, discouraging activity, curiosity, and socialization.

In assessing the development of a preschool child, the psychologist should collect data about her/his opportunities for independent acquisition of affiliative and achievement needs. Subtle interviewing of the mother is necessary to obtain these data. If the child has not had these opportunities, she may blame the neighborhood or kindergarten. However, one must listen carefully to the mother's complaints to understand the extent to which her own attitudes may enter into the restriction of the child's opportunities in this regard. Is she reluctant to separate from the child to permit him/her to go to nursery school? Does she have undue fears about her child's health and welfare? Is she too passive to make the effort? Would it threaten her ego for someone else to care for and be close to her "baby"?

The separation of the infant from the family in the quest of these social needs is important not only because they must be gratified, but also because the child begins to develop ideational modes of gratification in satisfying them. Although these secondary needs probably have their bases in physical needs, they become autonomous and do not require physical and motoric gratifications. Thus the need itself becomes ideational in the long run. Being affiliative, for example, is a concept, not a physical hunger. Therefore, attempts to gratify such social needs force children to begin to conceptualize. They begin to discover that they cannot answer all of their needs purely by motoric responses. Instead, they have to develop concepts of human interaction and affect. The emergence of conceptualization as a mode or aspect of need gratification is evidenced in many aspects of pre-school children's behavior. Their play, for example, although still primarily motor activity, begins to include acting out fantasies, practicing social interactions, and imitating adult need gratification modes. They still spend many hours either just riding tricycles up and down, or swinging, manipulating, and hitting things. But more and more they engage in games of "pretend," usually with slightly older children. The 5-year-old begins to play house, school, store, or war, practicing concepts of human interrelationships. Through this play they begin to imagine how social needs may be gratified.

As was noted in the introductory chapters, the development of ideational modes of need gratification has as its prototype the child's development of the ability to delay and conceptualize sexual drives in what Freud labeled the Oedipal conflict. Whether one accepts the hypotheses of this psychoanalytic concept, most observers do agree that the overall bond with the mother does have to be relaxed enough by the time the child leaves the home to enter school to permit her/him to seek gratification of needs for affiliation outside the family circle. Whatever erotic component there is in the gratification of social needs has to be repressed at this time, as society forbids the child to attempt to satisfy these needs with other children—even if it were possible. Children have to learn how to get along with others outside of the family before they can enter into the more complicated social world of sexuality. Thus in assessment, it is important to gather data about the child's affective interrelationships with parents as evidence of her/his development of the ability to find social gratification on her/his own. Has he/she learned to conceive of his/her parents as individuals rather than merely as extensions of the self? Is he still a mama's boy at 7—or is she

exclusively "daddy's little girl?" Has the child broken away from this bond sufficiently to allow him/her to seek gratifications elsewhere?

Although some evidence concerning this development of internalized, conceptualized gratification can be obtained from indirect clues supplied by the mother or father in parent interviews, it is at about age 6 that the process of internalization and ideational need gratification is revealed in children's associative responses. On the Rorschach, for example, prior to age 6 children tend to respond primarily if not exclusively with vague form or nearly pure color reactions. The first M responses appear at about age 6 or even slightly later. This ability to delay kinesthetic action and to project associatively heralds the appearance of the development of ideational need gratification. As Ames and associates (1974) point out, this step in ideational modes is presaged at age 5 by the appearance in 5-year-olds' Rorschach responses of the nonhuman m response.

This development is dramatically evidenced in the changes in children's TAT stories. Prior to age 6, children generally merely describe the card, with occasional mention of affects but little or nothing regarding the motives of the hero and very little plot. At about age 7 the child is somewhat more able to answer the examiner's questions as to "why" the hero did this or felt that way. The 9- to 10-year-old voluntarily attributes motives to his/her hero in about half of the stories. Although the 7-year-old may have an outcome for a TAT fantasy, it is likely to be farfetched and unrelated to the plot. She/he cannot tell how the hero finally achieves. The 10- to 11-year-old can tell you that the boy in Card 1 becomes a "great violinist" because he practices hard, and so on.

Preoccupation with ideals is the hallmark of adolescence. The daydreaming romantic is perhaps an overdrawn stereotype, but even the most philistine "surfer" does not entirely escape the idealism of youth. Even in their seeming antithetical attitudes toward values and ideals, such adolescents reveal their concern. More than at any point in childhood—indeed in their whole lives—they are concerned with how and when needs are gratified. They outdo their 6-year-old sibs in finicky food habits. They can only dress in the fad of the moment, speak certain words, and answer their need for excitement with certain thrills. The approaching possibility of gratifying long-repressed sexual drives now haunts their every thought and deed, intermixed with aggressively charged achievement needs. Yet the morals and values surrounding need gratification become almost obsessive concerns.

Estimation of the normal development of such ideational need gratification during adolescence is often difficult. At moments when an adolescent is struggling with some specific problem, his/her ideational confusion and erratic behavior may be almost indistinguishable from what would be unhesitatingly labeled "schizophrenia" in an adult. It was not purely by accident that Kraepelin originally called schizophrenia "dementia praecox"—the dementia of the young. At other moments, however, an adolescent may evince a blasé disregard for eithics or, like a small child, demand gratification immediately. Behavioral reports from angry, disappointed, or astonished parents are likely to be quite unreliable. The adolescent may report only "crazy" thoughts or erratic behaviors and try to argue that these are normal and sane. The Rorschach of a normal adolescent may contain some mildly contaminated responses that reflect these obsessions, and some of his/her TAT stories may be "way out."

What needs to be determined is the extent to which such adolescent extremes of ideationalization actually deter the development of other functioning. Thus, in interviewing an adolescent and her/his parents, the assessor should divert them from merely reciting "crazy" ideas and behaviors and to inquire about the child's other functioning. For example, is the youth so obsessed with this particular need gratification problem that she/he cannot eat or sleep? Is she/he suffering from some somatic disturbances? Even if neglecting schoolwork, is he/she actually not absorbing what the teacher says? Are there moments when he/she does behave "sanely"? In connection with this line of inquiry the psychologist should take a look at the adolescent's responses to relatively neutral problem-solving tasks, such as those on the Wechsler. Only if this ideational concern has spread across several areas of the adolescent's functioning can one begin to think in terms of "schizophrenia."

Second, one should inquire about the history of such behavior. Unless there is a history of "prodromal" signs of a pre-pubescent throught-process disturbance, one should be extremely cautious about applying such socially pejorative labels as schizophrenia. Although psychiatry is now beginning to distinguish more definitively between the long-term ego deterioration called schizophrenia and what are now labeled "adolescent behavior disorders," in my opinion too many adolescents are still labeled schizophrenic purely on the basis of temporary need-gratification confusions. In fact, it is quite possible that this distinction is the basis for the differentiation of the "process-versus-reactive" schizophrenia. Many of these adolescents who seem to have a sudden onset of schizophrenia may actually be experiencing a need gratification crisis.

The following case may serve to illustrate some of the problems that arise in the development of need gratification input and output and how they are assessed.

Case 41

Milton G., age 10, was referred to the clinic by the school for assessment of his educational needs. For the past three years he had been placed in special classes for the "educationally handicapped," but the teacher and the school psychologist questioned this placement and requested further clinical evaluation. His mother also was dissatisfied with his educational progress, but rather than questioning his need for special classes, she was insistent that he needed even more individual instruction. Further inquiry regarding the referral revealed that although Milton had not progressed satisfactorily in the first two years in regular classes, the school authorities would not have placed him in this special class but for the insistence of his mother. She took the initiative and informed the school that Milton was a "premature" baby who had been diagnosed as "cerebral palsy" at age 3. The school records showed further that at the usual age 5 years, 8 months, on finishing kindergarten, Milton did not seem ready to enter the first grade. His score on a "reading readiness" test was below the level that predicts success in reading at the first-grade level. His kindergarten teacher noted that Milton "was very demanding of my time and attention," was "possessive of playthings," "did not socialize well," "had crying tantrums when disciplined or when other children frustrated his activities." Nevertheless, Mrs. G insisted that Milton be placed in the first grade and hinted that she regarded the kindergarten teacher as prejudiced against Milton. The first and second-grade teachers recorded very similar notes about Milton. He "insisted on pursuing his own interests, disregarding what the class was engaged in and disrupting others"; "he brought toys to class and was preoccupied with his own play." His word recognition was satisfactory, but his reading comprehension was inadequate. He seemed to be learning to add and subtract by rote memory; he memorized the sum of 5 and 6, but if these numbers were reversed, he considered it a new problem and had to learn it all over again. Similarly, he could successfully memorize a list of words for spelling but could not even guess at the spelling of a new word even though he could spell another with the same phonetic base.

Mrs. G boasted of how smart Milton appeared to be to her, citing as an example that during Sunday afternoon excursions, she and her husband would make a game of drilling Milton on his arithmetic and spelling, helping him to memorize problems and words. However, at school Milton was a resistant pupil, constantly complaining that the work was too hard and that the teacher demanded too much. When the school psychologist attempted to administer the Wechsler Scale for Children to him, Milton was similarly resistant and querulous. He needed continuous encouragement and kept expecting to be prompted. "I haven't had that yet," he would complain. "Milton refuses to try to think on his own," remarked the school psychologist. Despite this resistance, Milton achieved an overall score within the "normal" range: IQ 94. Both his verbal and performance IQ scores were within a few points of this total. He made above-average scores on subtests involving chiefly recognition of and memory for concrete details (Information, Digit Span, Digit Symbol, and Picture Completion), and his vocabulary was average for his age. However, he had considerable difficulty on any test involving abstract reasoning and conceptualization.

On initial contact at the clinic, Milton was very tense and apprehensive. Before he entered the psychologist's office, he was reassuring the psychologist of his success at school. Talking more about school, he first boasted that he was a "lot smarter than those dummies" in this special class and that he would like to be put in regular classes. At the same time he complained of how hard the work was and how tough his teacher made things and how the children in his neighborhood who were in regular classes teased him and called him a "dummy" and a "spaz." He reluctantly agreed to show the psychologist how he did think things out, but when the WISC-R materials were brought out, he cried, "Oh no! Not *that*!" His behavior during this administration of the WISC-R was similar to that previously reported by the school psychologist, and his responses and scores were practically identical. He copied the

Bender figures very slowly and meticulously, but quite accurately. After much complaint and resistance, he finally dashed off a scribbly drawing of a man who, he remarked, looked "scared and mad." Each Rorschach card looked harder than the last one to him, but he consented to "make a guess" and then demanded that the examiner affirm his response or tell him what it really was. His responses were relatively accurate as to form but did tend to be very simple, without much detail. Of his 13 responses, 10 were simple form, 2 were primarily determined by the bright color, and 1 by achromatic color. There were no movement responses of any kind.

Yet Milton did not lack a fantasy life, and his fantasy on the CAT, in contrast to the Rorschach, was full of "movement." He told fairly long and elaborate stories in which the characters did such and such and then they did something else. The actions of these characters did not follow one upon the other in any logical fashion, and it was difficult to understand why they were doing these things. Milton ignored the examiner's questions about the characters' motivations. For example, to Picture 1: "The babies are eating their dinner. The mother gave them their dinner. She brings them more dinner. Then they go out and play. Some other kids come over and play. He [pointing to one of the babies] is crying. Then they go out to play. (Why is he crying?) When they get through playing they have some more dinner. Then they go to sleep. Their father comes home and brings them a present. That's all. (What do they play?) They're asleep now."~To Picture 6: "He's asleep and he wakes up. There's nobody there. He eats breakfast and then he runs away from home. (How come?) He finds a million dollars and he's very rich now. He buys two bicycles [Milton describes the bicycles at length]. Then he goes out to play. (What does his parents think?) They go in a big fight and they're dead now. (How come?) A big gorilla came along and killed them dead." All in all, Milton's fantasies suggested that although

he experienced considerable infantile hunger for love, he had little or no idea how to gratify this need. Similarly, his need for aggressive activity was plain but he had no concept of how to achieve this need. He often felt frustrated and very angry, but these feelings seemed disconnected, random, and generalized. As Milton saw it, things just happened without rhyme or reason.

Although Milton's perceptual-motor functioning seemed intact, there was the possiblity that his inability to conceptualize (a fundamental part of his cognitive as well as of his conative functioning) might be due to some general central-nervous-system defect. Strangely, Mrs. G was somewhat resistant to the clinic's recommendation for neurological assessment. In her mind, the cause of Milton's retarded development was already established as brain damage, and she was reluctant to question it. Yet she yielded to the psychiatrist's insistence. When the neurologist reported, after extensive examination, that he could find no indications of CNS disturbance, or even of cerebral-palsy symptoms, Mrs. G remained unconvinced. However, the point was not argued with her. While she remained fixed in her opinion, she did continue to bring Milton in for psychotherapy and to discuss with the social worker her behavior and attitudes toward Millton and the interactions within the family.

Using the results of the assessment, the treatment was aimed at (1) helping Mrs. G to see how she infantilized Milton, and why, and urging her to adopt tactics designed to promote his independent need gratification and (2) exploring with Milton the possibilities of conceiving ways for such independent gratification. Both in his play and conversation, Milton soon began expressing considerable dissatisfaction and anger over his lack of gratifications and with his interpersonal relationships both with his peers and at home. He became angry with the therapist's questions regarding his role in gaining these satisfactions, derisively labeling him "Dr. Why." As

Mrs. G began refusing to wait on Milton and to insist that he do things for himself, Milton was at first even more resistant and angry but admitted he was secretly glad to find he could and wanted to do things on his own. Without parental help, his schoolwork improved markedly within a year and the following year he was placed in a regular class, only a half year behind his age level where he continued to perform successfully. He remained somewhat isolated socially from his peers until he entered junior high school two years later. The psychotherapy was discontinued when he was graduated from elementary school, but a follow-up interview was conducted two years later when Milton was 13 and in the eighth grade. At that time he was making average grades at school, seemed to have several close friends, and to be accepted by his peers. A reassessment showed that his IQ had jumped 16 points to 110. His responses to the Rorschach and TAT at this time revealed much more ideational conceptualization and need gratification. Mrs. G, a very bright woman who had quit college after two years to get married, had now returned to college to work on her teacher's credential. She remarked, "I used to really hate Milton and all the problems and care he required. None of my needs seemed satisfied, but I thought I had to do my duty and I felt so guilty hating him. Now I see I did have some real needs, and that caring for children can be fun, if you see how they can grow up. I'm proud of him now and proud of myself."

C. FOCUS AND DIFFERENTIATION

The ability to differentiate one need from another and to focus on the satisfaction of one need at a time develops slowly over the years of childhood. The neonate appears to experience all needs as a generalized tension, and it is difficult initially to discover the sources of this tension. However, it does not take most mothers very long to distinguish from the baby's cries and other behaviors whether she/he is hungry, restless, in pain, or in need of comforting. Even before children can speak they usually are able to make simple distinctions between physiological wants. They can respond to such questions as "You want something to eat?" or "You want to go potty?" By age 3 children should be able to verbalize the forms of need gratifications to these wants, as witness the Stanford-Binet item at this age level. "What do you do when you are thirsty?" Even so, when these needs arise, it is sometimes difficult for even the average child to think of anything else. These needs become generalized, affecting much of the child's behavior. For example, Sanford (1936) found in one of his early studies on the TAT that schoolchildren gave many more responses and themes concerning eating and food if the test was administered just prior to lunch. Such a generalization of a need may occur even more persistently if the child continuously or even periodically experiences deprivations.

Case 42

Angela, age 3, had been placed on a very restricted diet because of her diabetes. She became preoccupied with food. She named her stuffed animal "Candy" and was forever biting on it. She startled both the children and the teacher at nursery school when she greeted them by licking their hands, and later she became quite a problem when she began biting others.

Case 43

Norman, age 3, in the same nursery class, had just completed a prolonged battle with his mother over bowel control. However, he had learned his lesson well and was very concerned about cleanliness. As far as Norman was concerned, getting dirty was a capital crime—to the point that he was almost immobilized. Keeping immaculate made it difficult for Norman to eat and even though he was sorely tempted, he could not bring himself to participate in the admittedly sloppy afternoon snack. In the playyard he finally latched onto one tricycle and kept riding back and forth, carefully avoiding touching anything or anybody. He screamed with fear when the teacher invited him to join the others in the sandbox. Norman's impasse was finally broken when the teacher prevailed upon his mother to spend an afternoon at the school and suggested to her that she specifically give Norman permission to get dirty. Although Norman's mother at first was unconvinced and not even quite in agreement of the necessity to do this, she agreed to attempt it. At first Norman did not believe his mother when she encouraged him to abandon his tricycle and join the other children in the sandbox. What did convince him was when his teacher involved his mother in finger painting. When he saw his mother getting dirty and even enjoying it, he began to believe her. Although his mother had feared that he might revert to his previously "messy" habits and even break his recently obtained bowel training, she was relieved to find that this did not occur. In addition, Norman rapidly learned to distinguish getting "dirty" in play from defecating.

. . . .

It is in these needs that entail avoiding or in the more abstract social needs that the child has the most difficulty in differentiating motives. Freud labeled the child's initial sexual drive, which is also experienced in terms of suppression, with the rather clumsy phrase *polymorphous perverse,* by which he meant nonspecific and nonfocal. His detailed study and classification of the stages of the child's differentiation of the need for erotic stimulation and gratification is a classic model for the study of need-differentiation patterns. If there were similar studies of the child's differentiation of other needs, it might be much easier to investigate Freud's hypothesis that the differentiation of the sexual drive sets the pattern for other needs. Children's needs for affiliation, for example, although probably closely allied to the sexual drive as

Freud maintained, may not follow exactly the same pattern of development. It does seem true that the neonate will accept any mother for a brief period, thus making adoption quite feasible at an early age. However, it is not long before she/he distinguishes the affiliative bond with mother from other interpersonal relationships. Although this affiliative bond is reinforced by feeding and comforting, most observers of infant behavior agree that the child seems to need to have these wants satisfied consistently by one person. A series of mothers rather than one affiliation often appears to result in difficulties in forming meaningful relationships later in life.

Weaning away from this bond and learning that affiliative needs can be met by someone other than the mother occur in very much the same way as Freud describes the weaning from oral satisfaction of erotic needs. The child has to learn to delay satisfaction of affiliative associations, to wait until his/her mother is available or until his/her father comes home, or until a peer or sib is available. Learning to endure even brief moments of loneliness is one of the most painful lessons of childhood. Like the sexual drive, satisfaction on the ideational or fantasy level soon plays a major role. Indeed, it is during moments of social isolation and loneliness that children experience fantasy most vividly. They create imaginary playmates with whom they play imaginary games. The Oedipus complex of the affiliative drive involves not so much the parent of the opposite sex as sibs, who are rivals with the parents for the affiliative bond. This process might be better labeled the "Cain complex." By murdering the hated sibling rival in fantasy and experiencing the guilt, the child is better able to be his "brother's keeper."

CASE 44

Mike, age 5, carried about an empty gunnysack that he explained was to "pick up the pieces" just in case his 3-year-old sister, Nellie, was "run over." However, he never attacked her and was even quite protective of her when other children pushed her around. He was even disturbed when she was punished by their parents. An only child may develop more slowly in this respect and may have more difficulty in making affiliative discriminations than children who have sibs.

As may be gathered from the preceding discussion, the ability to discriminate need gratifications requires not only differentiation of needs per se but also of potenital gratifications. The child learns what is edible, who will give love, who reciprocates in her/his affiliative needs, whom he/she can compete with in his/her drives for achievement, and the like. Early in infancy the child is surprisingly flexible about the exact form of need gratifications. Most infants will eat almost anything, go to sleep anywhere, even under conditions that would preclude sleep for older children or adults. It makes little difference to them where they go "potty," and they can be comforted by any adult.

However, this stage evaporates very soon, and at least by the beginning of the third year of life, children request specific foods and reject others, are comfortable only in their own crib, have to have their *own* potty and their *own* mother to comfort them. Such rigid limitation is, in my opinion, associated with the fact that need gratification during infancy is chiefly motoric, and the association between need and gratification is learned principally through simple conditioning. Although this conditioning can be and usually is generalized, it is when children are able to conceptualize need gratifications that they also become able to make discriminative choices. For example, infants soon learn that specific foods not only satisfy but are particularly enjoyable and are associated with pleasurable eating. Other foods that may not be as tasty to the child are rejected as not satisfying hunger—very often be-

cause they are also associated with unpleasant eating circumstances.

CASE 45

A mother presented her rather pear-shaped, flaccid 10-month-old baby, Rosa, to the pediatrician in a Well-Baby Clinic, complaining that the baby had trouble sitting up and made little effort to crawl or pull herself erect. Noting the baby's obesity, the pediatrician began inquiring about her diet and was horrified to learn that she was fed mainly carbohydrates. The doctor began advising the mother to add strained vegetables and meats to the baby's diet, but he noticed the look of disgust on the mother's face. Further questioning revealed that when the mother had tried feeding "those things" to the baby, the child had regurgitated. Moreover, it was evident that the mother "could not stand the sight" of these strained baby foods and disliked vegetables in any form. Her husband also was a "meat-and-potatoes" man. When the mother first came into the examining room, it appeared as if she were pregnant. Later it was discovered she was merely obese—like the baby—and equally listless.

In the assessment of this ability to discriminate needs and their gratifications, data may be obtained from a variety of courses and techniques. For example, in the interviews with the child and also with the mother, the assessor should inquire about likes and dislikes in need gratification. One such like or dislike might be explored in some detail: How did it develop? What are the respondent's own associations concerning this particular need discrimination? What does the mother recall about the child's food finickiness and distaste for vegetables, for example? How does the child recall it and what associations does she/he bring up? Sometimes such questions may seem very far removed from the immediate complaint, but nevertheless they may be quite revealing about motivational differentiation.

CASE 46

Mrs. A was very concerned about the company 13-year-old Phyllis was keeping, and a battle ensued that reached a climax when she ran away from home for the weekend. The interviews with the mother revealed that she had never trusted Phyllis to make decisions about need gratifications in choices of food, clothes, or recreation, that she had long worried about the health and welfare of the child in an overprotective fashion. Consequently, the child did not know how to make discriminations on her own. Phyllis was very resentful that her mother tried to intervene in her choice of friends, but oddly enough did not seem even aware of the degree to which her mother had made decisions for her about need-gratification choices. She reported in a puzzled childlike tone that she had not eaten for the two days she had been away. Although she had money to buy food, she had been unable to select from a menu at a restaurant and had left in embarrassment.

Although the inability to make discriminative independent choices about gratifications is in itself a sign of immaturity, a child who confuses one need with another usually is demonstrating an extensive ego disturbance. Most often such a confusion of needs begins with the acceptance of the gratification of one need for the lack of satisfaction of another. For example, an obese child may be found to be substituting food for affection or for sex. Or, as was illustrated in Case 40, Sandy tried to substitute sexual behavior for parental affection. However, what may begin as a temporary or casual substitution often becomes such an autonomous habit pattern that, in the child's mind, one need is no longer merely substituted for the other, but they are actually equated. One depressed

and overweight 9-year-old girl denied that she was substituting food for affection. "Chicken soup *is* love!" she declared solemnly.

D. INTERFERENCES IN CONATIVE DEVELOPMENT

Many of the factors that impede the normal developmental process of the attainment of independent skills for need gratification and of the internalization and channeling of drives and impulses have already been discussed in a previous chapter and in other sections of this chapter. The anxiety and other affective factors accompanying conflicts over need gratification were also discussed in Chapter 10. In the following section of this chapter and in Chapter 12, the roles played by social taboos and compunctions and their internalization into personal guilt will be given further consideration as major factors in conative development, both as a normal developmental process in the attainment of self-control and as a principal deterrent to the development of need-gratification skills. At this point, what is most important to consider are the manifestations of these interferences in the child's everyday behavior and in the samples of his/her behavior that may be gained from the administration of psychological techniques. In general, these manifestations may be thought of as taking three major forms: (1) *hypotrophic*, (2) *hypertrophic*, and (3) *compensatory*.

1. Hypotrophic Conative Development

Some aspects of a child's conative development may lag while others progress normally or even quickly. One of the most common patterns of behavior that indicates an interference in conative development is what might be called "hypotrophic"—that is, an overall retardation of either impulse control and need-gratification skills or both. Sometimes the outward manifestation of such hypotrophic conative development takes the form of purely "impulsive" behavior, that is, the child seems to have no control over impulses, makes continuous demands, and grabs what she/he wants. Since such children have fair skills in maneuvering the environment into answering their needs, they may seem to have developed need-gratification skills. However, such a skill in maneuvering or forcing others to meet one's needs is not the same as development of skills for *independent* need gratification.

Very often such a combination of a lack of impulse control along with the development of skills at demanding and exhorting need satisfactions from others is associated with a history of severe neglect of the child by the parents, both in need gratification and in the teaching of impulse controls. Such children "grow like Topsy," as described in Stowe's *Uncle Tom's Cabin*. No one tells them what to do, but neither is anyone particularly concerned with their needs, especially with those needs involving interpersonal care. Such children are thus forced by circumstances to "scrounge" for their own satisfactions.

Although these children are quite often very aggressive in seeking their own need satisfactions, molesting and annoying those about them, they are often also quite depressed. As their efforts to supply their own gratifications become more futile and as they meet with increasing repressive reactions from social authorities, they may have periods of massive and overwhelming depression. Although such a hypotrophic growth may appear in children of very socially deprived families where very few physical or personal gratifications are available, it also can be present in any home where only perfunctory physical care is given the child and little or no attention is paid to the child's needs for affection or to her/his impulse controls.

An equally frequent manifestation of such hypotrophic development appears in the seemingly passive and even well-behaved child who, in fact, is quite dependent upon the environment for control and channelization of her/his impulses. Not knowing what to do when there is no one there to supervise, her/his behavior suddenly becomes bizarre and out of place. Very often this lack of conative development appears when such a passive, compliant, and seemingly good child enters into one of the crisis points of childhood, such as separation from the parents upon entering kindergarten, the onset of puberty, or graduation from high school. Such children, when they leave the guidance of overprotective and ever-feeding mothers, become terrors in the kindergarten and first-grade classrooms, much to the amazement of their parents. Teachers and other observers may call such children "spoiled." These children make immediate and constant demands for narcissistic supplies from the teacher and peers.

Similarly, the well-behaved but very dependent latency child, who has always made good grades and practiced the piano faithfully, may panic when she/he shifts from junior high to high school. She/he may become either so depressed as to be unable to attend school or plunge suddenly into teen-aged social and sexual activities in haphazard form, seeking the same emotional support and guidance from peers that she/he has learned to obtain in previous years from teachers and parents.

Quite commonly, such children experience considerable overt depression when they are left on their own to manage their need gratifications. Such depression may be manifested outwardly in apathy, a sudden decline in grades, or adolescent restlessness. Disappointment, hurt, and anger may be themes on the TAT, and increased use of shading or achromatic color may appear in such a child's Rorschach responses. Strangely, such children may appear to be both severely repressed and impulse ridden. As long as their needs are gratified by others, they accept the repressive forces of an external superego, and their impulse life is not outwardly manifested. However, such seemingly very well-behaved children may give Rorschach responses dominated by the animal-movement category. They relate fantasies to the TAT that are replete with scenes of uncontrolled and immediate need gratification or of guiltless anger toward those who might attempt to frustrate such impulses. Such "spoiled" children do not develop independent need gratification because their needs are constantly gratified by others. Nor do they independently control impulses because they are constantly bribed.

A most serious form of retardation of conative development occurs when the child shows repression of impulse life at all levels. As has been noted in previous chapters, such overall repression in a mild form is the hallmark of the latency child. However, even in latency most normal children show some signs of the stirrings and waxing and wanings of impulse life in their play, intellectual curiosity, and fantasies. When a child demonstrates little or no such evidence of even a latent impulse life, she/he is not progressively developing means of handling and controlling impulses, but instead she/he is developmentally stultified. Such a massive, overall repression in the child immediately before and during the onset of puberty may well be the prodromal signs of a later explosive emotional disturbance in adolescence. If such an overall repression continues for that length of time, there is the possibility that at least a very passive-aggressive character structure, if not a schizoid pattern, may develop.

A history of such repression is often seen in the person with a "schizophrenic break" in the latter years of adolescence or of early adulthood. The manifestations of such overall repression often seem benign in children's histories. Such children are often quite compulsive "grinds" at school, sometimes overachieving. They are often worried about their schoolwork, using it as an excuse for social isolation. Their parents and even teachers—far from being disturbed by these children's lack of socialization—often support their repres-

sion and in fact demand it. Unless these children become so depressed as to be physically ill, they may not be seen in psychological clinics, but their hypochondriasis is often treated by pediatricians. When they are referred for psychological assessment, their responses to projective techniques are often quite sterile, lacking in imagination, and void of signs of emotional life. Such a child frequently will compulsively strive for achievement on an intelligence test, but become quite stultified when faced with the Rorschach or TAT and be unable to do much more than describe a TAT card, apologizing profusely for a lack of imagination. The MMPI profiles of such adolescents are marked by the height of the K, or repression, scale, a general flatness of most of the other scales, with perhaps a slight rise in hypochondriasis or depression (both of which are usually lower among normal adolescents than among adults). A T score of 65 or above on schizophrenia for such a child is not unusual. In contrast to the profile of the "spoiled" child, the PD and MA scales of such repressed adolescents are usually low.

Much like impulse-ridden children, repressed children suffer from deprivation of need gratifications. It is because they have been given the hope that if they conform and achieve they will win parental support and affection and will be allowed full need gratification. Children—and adults—who have severely and chronically repressed their impulses often have grandiose dreams of gluttonous revels or sexual orgies. When the parents remain cold and distant and the dreams of need gratification fade, the repressed adolescent slumps into depression or "schizophrenia."

2. Hypertrophic Conative Development

The opposite side of the coin is the child who shows hypertrophic development of need-gratification skills and impulse controls. Such children may also show considerable academic success, but if so, they are also likely to be socially successful. They may also be quite adept in manipulating their environment, concentrating efforts on pleasing adults and wheedling things out of them or commandeering their peers, while neglecting any actual achievement in the classroom or on the playground. For example, they may organize the ballgame but avoid going to bat. They charm the teacher and make many promises but act surprised when demands for productivity are made upon them. They may be able to charm their way through elementary school but find their techniques of manipulating teachers are ineffective in junior high school with many different teachers to please. Often such children are quite able to get what they want even on their own. Mothers of such children will report that they learned to feed and care for themselves at an early age. The usual complaint against such a child is that he/she is exceedingly ''willful.'' However, such hypertrophic development of need-gratification skills often proves to be a child's defensive measure. Such rapid growth is fostered when the child feels her/his needs will not be met unless she/he makes immediate efforts to gratify them independently or to maneuver other people into meeting her/his needs. This maneuvering of the hypertrophic child is much more subtle than the screaming, demanding negativism of the impulse-ridden child.

Among children who manifest such precocious development are those who face inadequate or sick parents, or the absence of parents. For example, such behavior may be manifested by a child of psychotic parents who are unable to provide for the child's needs and who force him/her to handle a great deal of reality on her/his own—including the reality of the parents' confusion. Although some children are made psychotic by their psychotic parents, this reaction of becoming precociously able to manage their own need gratifications is also a common phenomenon. Similarly, although children in orphanages or other institutions may remain quite infantile and even retarded, it is not unusual to find an orphan who develops very rapidly and who becomes quite independently skilled in the gratification of his/her own needs—albeit in a ''psychopathic'' fashion. Such children, however, often manifest signs of being quite untrusting of others. Although they may painfully learn not to go afoul of the law, they may remain cynically aloof from society. In the long run, such children run into trouble because their dependency needs are never really effectively met. Despite their ultraindependence, they inadvertently and circuitously set up situations wherein they may test out whether they can depend on others. Basically they feel very cheated and often plot a very generalized revenge against the world that they feel has deprived them.

The Rorschach protocols of such children often are characterized by a predominance of human movement responses, but they are very cautious and restricted when stimulated by the color of the inkblots. Their confusion and blocking increase when stimulated by the texture of the blots. This latter inability to handle texture is one manifestation of their ambivalence over need gratification and dependency. In TAT stories such children emphasize the hero's ability to meet his own needs, but scenes of revenge against cheaters or robbers are also prevalent.

Although this syndrome is more commonly seen in the clinic among adolescents or latency children, such precocity is also occasionally a defensive measure in the late infancy period.

CASE 47

Andy's paranoid mother had the delusion that he was not her child. He was a very bright 5-year-old who showed every sign of rapidly developing methods to defend himself and answer his own needs. In responding to Shniedman's MAPS test, this little boy utilized the Superman figure in every one of his little plays. Superman became superego, controlling the evil characters, including naked, seductive, and confusing mother figures. Superman aided a giving and rewarding paternal figure, but this father was often removed from the stage and Superman had to protect the child. However, Andy's need for further emotional support in his confused world was also manifest by his use of another figure who assisted Superman. He called this figure the "doctor," and he seemed to understand where the child had pain. Andy was quite aware that his mother was delusional. He was very depressed, since his sense of identity was affected by her delusion, but he appeared to be maintaining his own hold on reality by this precocious development of controls over his own impulses and of need-gratification skills.

3. Compensatory Conative Development

A third general pattern of disturbance in conative development may be labeled compensatory. Rather than a simple hypotrophic absence or repression of need-gratification skills and impulses, the child may seem to neglect the gratification of some needs and hypertrophically develop skills and interests in the satisfaction of others. Such compensatory behavior may be seen in physically disabled children who become superior in their intellectual achievements. In a sense, the child who concentrates on the "good-boy" or "good-girl" role and represses impulses to obtain social rewards may also be thought of as compensating. However, such children often do not receive much reward for their good behavior, and they are constantly pressured for an increasing amount of achievement and are made to feel guilty about any manifestation of their impulses. More subtle forms of compensation may be commonly observed in what might be labeled the "cuteness" and "naughtiness" syndromes.

Children who have the good fortune to be physically attractive and who are rewarded for being socially "cute" may develop and foster these socially rewarding attributes that do gain them—at least temporarily—the need gratification they seek. The beautiful little girl or handsome boy may unconsciously depend on good looks, expecting others to reward them for being attractive. Good-looking children learn that parents, teachers, and even peers may not demand as much of them in the way of impulse control or deny them need gratification. Such children may avoid intellectual or physical competition with other children and compete only in the area of "looks." They are often referred to the clinic at about junior high-school age when their scholastic achievement is not up to par and when they begin to make extra efforts to be ostentatious in their dress and grooming. Although actually physically attractive, in their emphasis on their body image, such children begin to develop doubts of this image if only because they place so much emphasis on it.

In what might be called the "naughtiness' syndrome, children misbehave just enough to get attention without actually getting themselves into trouble. They play the clown in the classroom, often getting others into trouble as well. Their parents, although sometimes disturbed and angry at the child's mischievousness, may privately describe his/her naughtiness as "cute." It often turns out that they tolerate or even encourage such behavior, vicariously enjoying the child's antics and even boasting that he/she does things that they would not have dared to do. Such parents may complain bitterly about how much more "freedom" children of this generation are allowed in contrast to their own childhood, but often they do little to control the child. By being "naughty" the child attracts the attention of the parents, inveigles them into rewarding him/her in order to avoid further naughtiness, and then reneges on his/her promises—in a continuous cycle of defrauding the parents. This constant maneuvering through "naughtiness" eventually becomes a need-gratification skill itself, and in the long run, it compensates for the lack of development of other need-gratification skills.

Moreover, neither the "cute," "charming" nor the "naughty" child actually expresses her/his own impulses but instead represses some basic needs. For example, the very pretty adolescent girl who has always depended upon being pretty may, in fact, repress her sexual needs and be quite uncomfortable when she finds that boys are sexually attracted to her. Similarly, the naughty child—although seemingly aggressive—may actually be quite dependent and passive and never develop ways of handling needs to be aggressive and independent.

Such disproportionate or compensatory conative development is shown on such techniques as the Edwards Personal Preference Schedule or the TAT (both of which use Murray's Need-Press System). For example, a 15-year-old boy who obtains a high N Achievement and N Endurance may be compensating if, at the same time, his N Succorance, N Heterosexuality, and N Aggression are abnormally low or absent. A similar though obverse pattern is also quite common in adolescence. For example, many teen-aged girls overemphasize romanticism and utilize their newfound sexuality in quite compensatory ways to avoid independent achievements while disclaiming adult values of N Order or N Endurance.

CASE 48

For example, Adele, age 15, although of above-average intelligence, was repeating the ninth grade, and it appeared that she might fail again. She told the following stories to Cards 2 and 8GF, respectively, of the TAT:

The mother is the boss. She is making the boy work hard and has told the girl that she must go to school. The girl hates her mother for making her brother work and is thinking of running off with her boyfriend to get married. She fakes out her mother by carrying the books, but she meets her boyfriend and they go off to the city. (Examiner asks if there is no father in the story. The storyteller laughs.) I guess I just forgot him.

She's supposed to be studying but she's daydreaming about her boyfriend. [Pause] I can't think of much more. (What might she be daydreaming about?) I don't really know. I guess maybe he's foxy. She's all hot for him. (How does the heroine feel about her studies?) Maybe she thinks they're pretty feeble. She doesn't look very smart—maybe she's kind of dumb.

E. COPING MECHANISMS IN CONATIVE FUNCTIONING

As has been amply demonstrated throughout this chapter, it is almost impossible to discuss any aspect of conative development without at the same time discussing the ways in which children cope with their impulses and become skilled at meeting needs. In fact, what have been discussed as modes, input–output, differentiation, all may be viewed as various ways of coping conatively. Nor is it possible to discuss interferences in conative development without mentioning coping. The three types of interference patterns mentioned are in effect coping patterns—albeit neurotic and in the long run ineffective. The purpose of this section is to look at the underlying attitudinal "set" with which children approach coping with drives. In so doing, it is hoped the interrelationships between the various patterns of coping already discussed may be more clearly defined and delimited.

Although a theoretical formulation of the interrelationships between various coping mechanisms is beyond the scope of this book, a rough schematic model may be helpful, purely for heuristic purposes. Clinical experience suggests that coping involves at least two major attitudinal dimensions, which in the diagram of this schema (see Figure 11.1) form the axes of a circle. The horizontal axis describes the amount of energy or activity that the child deems necessary to attain need gratification. This dimension may best be understood by applying the commonly used terms *passive* and *aggressive* to the extremes. The extremely passive child waits

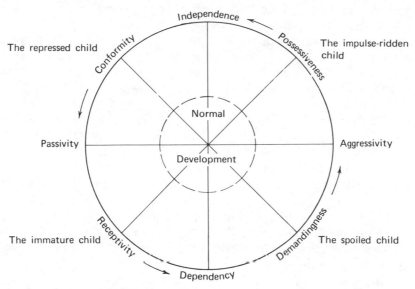

Figure 11.1   A schematic representation of interrelationships among coping attitudes toward need gratification.

for others to satisfy needs and even to stimulate drives. The extremely "aggressive"* child seeks out his/her own need gratifications without waiting for others and imposes his/her impulses and drives on the world whether or not he/she is stimulated by the environment.

The vertical axis of this diagram is intended to describe the interpersonal attitude or stance of the child in coping with his/her drives—that is, dependency on others. Because passivity and dependency are so often found together, it may seem at first glance that they are synonymous. The very passive, dependently "receptive" child is seen quite frequently in the clinic. However, it is also quite possible for the child to be passive and conforming and at the same time to try to independently seek need gratifications. This coping pattern is illustrated in what I previously labeled "the repressed child," who does what she/he is told, who is expected to achieve independently but not aggressively. Similarly, being aggressive is often associated with being independent. The extremely aggressively independent child is typified by what was described in the previous section as the "impulse-ridden" child, who in nonconformist fashion rejects any controls and seeks—often because of his/her circumstances—to gratify his/her own needs. Yet there is also the child who is both aggressive and dependent, who depends on others in demanding fashion—the "spoiled" child. These terms on the outer edge of the circle describe extremes of behavior. In the normal development of any child, all of these attitudes may be involved in the child's attempts to cope with his or her drives. The inner dotted circle denotes these "normal" limits. As those readers familiar with Leary's (1957) Interpersonal Adjective Check List will immediately note, this schema is analogous to the one Leary constructed to describe interpersonal relationships. Obviously it is also quite comparable to the schema presented by Ericson (1950) in his psychoanalytic constructs concerning need gratification.

Although it would be interesting to explore this theoretical scheme further qua theory, it may be more meaningful for as-

---

*The term *aggressive* is used in so many ways and has so many affective associates that were it not popularly used to describe coping attitudes it might almost be preferable to use some other, less-common term, such as active. In particular, the psychologist should distinguish between aggressive coping and aggressivity as a need. This will be described in the following section.

sessment purposes to review briefly what was described in more detail in previous chapters concerning development of these coping mechanisms.

Observers of neonates (Call, 1964) have noted differences in their approaches to need gratification while feeding at the breast. Some newborns have to be propped up and have the nipple pushed into their mouths. Others grab at their mother's breasts, making sucking noises and motions. Such observations have led some to propose that such passive receptivity or "aggressive" possessiveness is possible genetically or congenitally determined. However, it has also been observed that the newborn's behavior is often fostered or at least abetted by the mother. She can condition receptivity in the baby by making the breast available immediately and holding the suckling against it—or she can let the child struggle slightly for a second. In turn, such behavior on the part of the mother may reflect her own need-gratification attitudes. Those mothers who take an aggressive stance toward satisfaction of their own needs may "possess" the child, pushing her/him to her breast to satisfy her maternal needs.*

A more "receptive" mother might await the child's demands to be fed. Where very strong receptive or possessive attitudes are a part of the mother's neurotic character structure, the reactive attitudes of the infant are likely to be equally intense. Thus, coping attitudes may be formed at a very early age.

In most instances, however, the way an infant perceives and expresses need gratifications is not dependent entirely on this relationship with the mother but, in the normal course of events, is part of her/his further maturation. Unless a mother forces

*Psychotherapeutic interviews with mothers of emotionally disturbed infants often reveal that breast-feeding and comforting of the infant may serve to gratify many different needs for the mother. For example, many women are sexually stimulated during breast-feeding, and their attitudes toward breast-feeding reflect their attitudes toward sexuality.

the baby to grab at her breast continuously, she/he is most likely to begin life expecting to have needs gratified. As mother begins to regulate the baby's gratification, she fosters independence. As children become more able to satisfy needs, they accept the mother's urging of independent need gratification, and they begin to attempt to possess things for themselves. During the pre-school years this predominately receptive attitude continues. A 4-year-old who attempts in most situations to make the first move toward need gratification would be quite precocious and "hypertrophic" in a majority of situations.

By the time children start school, they can be expected not only to be able to answer many of their own needs—at least within the limits that such need gratification is available—but also to have developed a sufficiently aggressive attitude that they generally desire to take the first step toward need gratification. They should be capable of, if not responsible for, feeding themselves, keeping themselves warm, avoiding hazards, and obtaining affiliative contacts with family and with peers. Moreover, it is expected that the child take steps toward exercising these skills independently rather than waiting to be urged or merely receiving satisfactions.

This development of an aggressive attitude is necessary before children can achieve in the school situation. They can sit back and absorb some knowledge at school, but in the long run they must aggressively seek knowledge if they are to achieve. If education entailed only repetitive memorization of information, as it once did, then a passive-receptive absorption of "facts" would be all that was necessary. However, even in more authoritarian-oriented educational systems, some independent cognitive processes are required—some "possession" of an idea. Present-day American education, of course, strongly emphasizes such active possession of learning from kindergarten on. In fact this aggressive, independent attitude has so been fostered by the educational system in the current generation that many college and even high-school students rebel against teachers who expect them to memorize facts or to learn what the teacher thinks is best! Teachers also resent students who expect them to "spoon-feed" them with learning.

During the adolescent years, being receptive versus being independent frequently becomes a conflict both within the adolescent and between the adolescent and adult authorities. Teen-agers want to see themselves as being able to satisfy their own needs, they are impatient with those who try to wait on them and are embarrassed and depressed momentarily when they are unable to independently gratify needs or control impulses. At the same time they often behave as if they expect the whole world to provide for them exactly as they wish. Since being passive is so closely associated with being dependent, because they take advantage of the last chance to gratify this dependency need they may often assume that it is also necessary to be passive. For example, an adolescent may make extra efforts to earn the money to buy something that his/her parents could supply and might even be willing to buy. Then the child will turn around and make some seemingly outrageous demand on them, fully expecting them to meet it, and even argue that he/she deserves it because he/she has gratified his/her own need on the prior occasion!

Turning now to the task of assessing coping mechanisms, referrals about children seldom directly indicate that such attitudes are central and definite complaints, but the assessor should read between the lines. For example, referrals that read "poorly motivated, makes no effort at school" or "very selfish and rivalrous with sibs" would suggest that the assessor keep his/her eye out for further possible data concerning need-gratification mechanisms. Even such varied symptoms as "petty theft," "obesity," or "sexual promiscuity" might lead one to entertain the hyopthesis that coping with need gratification may be disturbed and inadequate.

Data for the assessment of these attitudes toward need gratification can be collected by a variety of techniques. Clues that there might be problems in the development of these attitudes often appear in the side remarks and descriptions of the child's behavior in interviews with the parents or with the child himself/herself. Thus, the parents may describe the child as quite capable of caring for herself/himself but note that she/he waits for others to do things for her/him or that she/he "expects too much" or "is demanding." Such clues should be followed up by the interviewer with further questions about the circumstances, descriptions of how the child "expects" or "demands," and how the parents regard and treat such behaviors. Clues regarding precocious independence often are phrased in terms describing "aggressive" behavior: "just helps himself to what he wants," "has little regard for the rights of others," "acts as if she owns the world," "hates to be waited on," "hates to be told what to do," and the like. Either overly passive or hyperaggressive attitudes may be masked in the parents' reports if they unconsciously encourage the child's attitude. Thus the parent may describe with pride how compliant the child is, how he/she accepts without complaint whatever the parent says or is always ready to take whatever is offered. Or inversely, the parent may describe how independent the child is, how she/he goes ahead and does things independently.

A child's behavior as well as his/her responses often offer opportunities to assess need-gratification attitudes. Some children sit back and wait for the assessor to approach them, volunteering little but being compliantly receptive. However, as was noted before, dependently oriented children may also be quite aggressive and demanding. Such children may reject the psychologist's requests to talk or to take test, but instead they may seek to be entertained or to be released from the situation altogether. They may perceive the assessment situation as making a demand on them that offers little for satisfaction of their needs. More independent children may also be quite cooperative, but they are likely to decide for themselves how to go about the task. If something interests or challenges them, they may put forth quite a bit of effort but slack off when their motivation wanes. Moreover, they are more likely to lead the interview to where they want it to go.

Among various techniques that offer special opportunities to observe need-gratification attitudes are the CAT or TAT and the Rosenzweig P-F Study. In CAT or TAT stories these attitudes may be observed in the manner in which the hero achieves her/his needs. For example, to Card 1, how does the hero get out of practicing the violin—or become a great violinist (whichever common plot is given)? Does he/she sneak out when parents are not listening, or does he/she wait unitl given permission? Does he/she become a great violinist overnight as if by magic, or does the storyteller explain that the hero "earned the money to buy the violin by working every night after school, then finds himself a good teacher and practices every day. . . ." Is the young man in 6BM or 7BM asking permission or hoping that his mother or father will do something for him? Or is he telling them something or "plotting a robbery?" Another indication on the CAT or TAT of these attitudes is the degree to which the child depends on the stimulus in order to invent a story. Receptive children add relatively little to the stimulus. And although they may construct a whole plot, they mainly use the clues given them. Independent children make the card their own, weaving into it some of their own fantasies. They add characters and objects not present in the card for their own ends.

Since the P-F for children deals with the frustrations experienced in social situations and the verbalized attitudes toward such frustrations, it offers specific data regarding need-gratification attitudes. Among younger children the most frequent responses to the P-F Study are the "Object-Dominance" and "Ego-Defensive"

categories in contrast to what Rosenzweig calls the "Need-Persistent" category. This suggests that children are more likely to focus on the frustration and defense of their ego (blaming others) than on resolutions of the frustration.

CASE 49

"Eddie (age 5) is so sweet," reported his mother. "He gets up in the morning and helps himself to breakfast and is out playing before I get up." "Yes," added his father. "And he can take his own bath and puts himself to bed." Only later in the interview did the parents admit that Eddie seldom obeyed them, and they failed to understand how Eddie could be so very disturbing to the kindergarten class, where he ignored the teacher, played what games he wanted to, and entirely disregarded the rights of others. The interviewer in this case noted also that these parents were "cooperative" but that they seemed to expect the clinic to "straighten Eddie out" for them and did not seem to understand their role in the proposed treatment plan for family therapy.

Eddie helped himself to a box of crayons and some paper on the examiner's desk and sat down and started to draw before the psychologist had a chance to do or say anything. He scarcely waited for the psychologist's introduction before volunteering a little story about one of his playmates and a fight he had had. Later when the psychologist stopped to answer the telephone, Eddie took off for the bathroom without saying a word. He returned on his own without so much as an "excuse me." At the end of the hour when a second session was to be arranged, Eddie considered his free time much as if the psychologist was going to make an appointment with him!

At age 5, Eddie evidently had the attitude that he possessed the world and that it was his to manage for the satisfaction of his own needs. This attitude also appeared blatantly throughout his test responses. In his drawings for the House, Tree, and Person, he drew the tree on the same page as the house. It was an enormous tree that overshadowed the small, sketchy house. It was quite elaborate for a 5-year-old. Buck, in his interpretive manual for the H-T-P (1948), suggests that the drawing of the tree represents the self as contrasted with the house, which is more associated with the home and environment. In his drawing of a person, which was superior for a 5-year-old (yielding a mental age of 7−6 on the Harris-Goodenough Scale), he added the unusual detail of muscles (indicated by round bumps on the arms and legs) and announced that this was the man who planted the tree and built the house! In responding to the Rorschach, Eddy was quite critical of the blots, announcing that he could make better blots himself. Some of his responses seemed most original and unusual for a 5-year-old, but it was difficult to assess his form level, since he disdained explaining himself in the inquiry. For example, he responded immediately to Card I, "The guy in the middle is swinging these two other guys around and around," but when asked for more details, he inverted the card and said only that it was necessary to cover the spaces in order to see what he had mentioned. Card II looked like "the same things . . . that's what I'd call it," and, after some pressure by the examiner, he decided that the space (D5) was the man in the middle and the rest of the blot (inverted) were the other two men, but he could not specify any details. He was able to persevere with the same response on Card III, using the popular human figures and becoming more precise by deciding that D8 was the head of the person in the middle, around which the other two figures were "having to dance." He associated Card IV with a "puppet doll" he had seen at school, identifying D1 as the "hand" inside the puppet and the rest as "a big monster puppet . . . with big feet." Card V was a big bird, or "no, an airplane," and he ran around the room imitating jet noises and flying the card as if

it was the plane. Reluctantly giving up his play with Card V, he made a sour face at Card VI and immediately rejected it. Urged to take a second look, he peeked at it inverted and announced it was a "hammer" pointing out D3 as the handle. Card VII, also given only a cursory glance, was "something smashed by the hammer." On VIII, he saw the popular "bears" (D1), "walking over the world." He completely rejected Cards IX and X. "It's silly," he announced, but he could not say why they looked silly. Although Ames, and Associates (1952) found that crude M and m responses are not uncommon among 5-year-olds, Eddie's perceptual attitudes were most extreme; he excluded any recognition of emotional impact from the environment (the color of the blots), and he emphasized entirely his own images, tensions, and impulses (3 M, 3 Fm, and 1FM and 1 F).

His dominating possessiveness of the world was equally dramatized in his responses to the CAT. The little chickens on Card 1 were "getting their dinner . . . while the mother chicken watched." On Card 2, which is usually interpreted as a game of tug-of-war between one parent bear and another, with the baby bear on one side, Eddie decidedly depicted one big brave bear rescuing two other bears. Eddie admired the lion on Card 3, remarking that he was the king and making roaring noises. "He makes everybody do what he wants," remarked Eddie. He did not notice the mouse in the background until it was brought to his attention. "The mouse is looking at the lion—how big he is!" Eddie decided. Eddie also identified with the tiger (Card 7) who "is going to get his dinner." On Card 8 the little monkey "is telling the big monkey something so the big monkey will know all about it."

Eddie had all sorts of solutions to the P-F situations. Twelve of his 24 responses were "need persistent." In contrast, only one could be classified as "obstacle dominated." Most unusual were his 10 "intrapunitive" responses, most of which indicated that he assumed the responsibility for the solution of the situation, scored *i*.

Although Eddie's drawings, Rorschach, and CAT all suggested that he was intellectually superior, he actually did very poorly in the Stanford-Binet. He often disregarded instructions, recast the problem, and went ahead and used the materials as he saw fit. Some of his responses were difficult to score by the strict rules of the test. For example, to the Aesthetic Choices, where the instructions are to point to the prettier one (Year V), he gave wrong answers to the first two. Then with an impish glance, he asked to see the third card and taunted the examiner, "I can show you the dumb one on that one too!"

Eddie's mother had suffered two miscarriages within the first five years of her marriage; she was 34 the following year, when at her husband's urging she agreed to adopt Eddie. The adoption was arranged through an attorney friend of Mr. B's. All the B's knew of Eddie's background was that he was born out of wedlock to a 16-year-old girl who had made good grades in high school until forced to leave because of her pregnancy. Eddie was 5 days old when they picked him up at the hospital nursery. Mrs. B admitted that she was a bit nervous, since she had had no experience whatever with babies. She had been told that infants set their own schedules and that she needed only to feed and change him when he cried or seemed uncomfortable. She found him an easy baby to care for and found herself enjoying cuddling him and playing with him. However, from the beginning he did not seem to respond to her cuddling and after a few moments would struggle out of her arms. He grew rapidly and his psychological development seemed advanced to Mrs. B, although she could not remember exactly when he began to crawl, walk, or talk. (The fact that Mrs. B did not note these hallmarks for her only child nor could not remember them only a few years later did seem unusual). To Mrs. B it seemed as though Eddie was up on his feet

and out of his crib and playpen before she had quite got used to having a child at all. However, she continued her laissez faire approach and did little to restrict him; she removed possible dangers and continued to enjoy watching him grow and answering his demands. "He seemed so cute and so spunky then (at age 2). We just adored him and couldn't refuse him any thing." To the best of her memory, he was talking fairly fluently by 24 months, without use of "baby talk." She also remembered that he loved to sit at the table and eat what the adults were eating and delighted his father by teaching himself to use a spoon by imitation. "He's a great mimic," Mr. B added proudly.

Eddie was about 3 when Mrs. B's mother visited the family. She was scandalized to find him still in diapers. Mrs. B described her mother as a dominating person who took charge of any situation in which she was involved. Mr. B nodded in agreement, making a sour face. "She took charge of Eddie, all right!" he remarked. "It was summertime and everytime he soiled himself, she stripped him and took him out in the yard and turned the hose on him, and then put him on the toilet and stood over him. He screamed like mad but he learned quick enough." Mr. B chuckled and added, "When she came back the next summer, he turned the hose on her!" Eddie continued to wet the bed for another six months but gradually ceased and had been completely toilet trained for the past year.

Until Eddie started kindergarten, the B's had considered him a well-adjusted, healthy child. They had centered their lives about him. They had led relatively socially restricted lives prior to his adoption, and for the past five years Mrs. B had not ventured far from the house except for necessary errands. Eddie usually accompanied her wherever she went. Mrs. B had thought he might have a difficult time separating from her the first day at school, and she had stayed around the school for several days, but he had quickly rushed off to explore the kindergarten and did not seem to notice that his mother was in the background. "It was harder on me (to separate) than on him," she remarked ruefully. It was only when the school authorities reported to her how disrupting Eddie's behavior proved to be that she became aware of the difficulties he was causing. Even so, she did not really seem to appreciate the school's problem. "I guess he's a little monster," she remarked at the conclusion of the first interview—but she laughed. Mr. B seemed more serious. "He should have some discipline," he said thoughtfully, "but I'm not sure how to begin."

Mrs. B had a slight build and was neatly but conservatively dressed; although not yet 40, she was graying noticeably and might be taken for several years older than her stated age. She spoke very softly, almost inaudibly at moments, with considerable hesitancy. However, as the interview proceeded, she began to volunteer information about Eddie, evidently enjoying talking about him. She was more reluctant to discuss her own life or feelings, tending to brush aside the interviewer's questions about herself as if they were unimportant. An only child, she admitted that she had always been dominated by her mother, and although she was conscious of considerable resentment over her mother's domination during her adolescent years, she had not openly rebelled, partly because of her fear of her mother's anger and partly because she did not want to hurt her father, whom she adored. She had little social life during high school. "My mother never told me that I could not go on dates, but I knew she disapproved and she kept me busy with church work." Although she made only passing marks at school, she did attend the local college for one year because she thought it would please her father. Thereafter, she went to work for her father in his real estate firm. Mr. B joined the firm three years later. "It was love at first sight," she noted. "But it took you four years to make up your mind," he responded with a smile.

However, it did appear that their courtship was cut short by the death of Mrs. B's father, when she was 25. She quit work and remained at home with her mother in what seemed like a prolonged grief reaction. She did not consent to marry Mr. B until three years later.

Mr. B, who was 12 years her senior, was the third of four sons of a "hard-rock" Missouri farmer, who believed and practiced hard work, stern discipline, and "fire-and-brimstone" religion. His mother was tubercular and died when he was 12 years of age. His two older brothers ran away during the following year. He and his younger brother kept house and helped their father on the farm for the next five years. "It was a hard and lonesome life," Mr. B said sadly. "My father seldom spoke unless necessary and never smiled after my mother's death." He completed high school and left home the next week to join the Navy. He remained in the service for the next 20 years, retiring at age 38. He tried going to college but quit after two years when he joined his father-in-law's firm. Despite this relatively harsh and unrewarding existence during his younger years, Mr. B did seem to be a warm-hearted man who evidently was quite supportive of his rather passive and dependent wife and, in turn, seemed to receive considerable affection from her. He also seemed to have a genuine affection for his son and expressed a concern for Eddie and his problems at school, openly asking for help from the clinic. "I guess I need some advice about being a father. I didn't like the way my father was, so glum and so unloving, and I thought if I just loved Eddie that would be all that was needed. . . . But maybe it isn't!" However, it seem became clear in the subsequent interviews that Mr. B, never having experienced love from his own father, did not really know how to give love to Eddie. In fact, it was Mr. B's underlying hope that he would receive the love from his son that he had so sorely missed during his own childhood. Thus, the passive dependent attitudes of the parents drove Eddie to gratify his own needs aggressively and independently, without regard for impulse controls.

F.   THE CONTENT OF CONATIVE FUNCTIONING

Earlier in this century personologists were preoccupied with the classification and measurement of different drives. At least implicit in their thinking was the assumption that differences in behavior could be explained, rather simply it may seem now, by differences in drive strength. Thus, it was assumed that some people had less sexual drive than others, or more intense appetites. Even the more socially learned and developed needs were considered as separate "traits" rather than forces within an ego structure. It was to measure these drive strengths that Murray (1938) originally constructed the TAT. But Murray envisioned even then that these needs were not entirely independent "habit strengths," but rather were enmeshed in a relatively fluid, functioning ego. The fact that when the TAT became a popular clinical instrument few clinicians bothered to utilize Murray's need–press system was not so much because the system was very cumbersome nor that clinicians disdain measurement but, instead, that clinicians were more interested in how these drives were handled by the ego than the name or strength of the drive. However, in an "ego psychology," such as that espoused in this book, there is a tendency to overlook drive strengths and to confuse drive nomenclatures.

One other reason that the amount of the drive is no longer the focus of assessment is that psychologists have learned that drives are so easily and frequently repressed or compensated for by other satisfactions that it is often difficult to distinguish what is actually motivating the child, let alone to measure the strength of the drive. The basic physiological drives of sex, hunger, and waste elimination are difficult to measure with psychological instruments, perhaps

just because they are primarily physiological. Moreover, although there may be individual differences in the strengths of these drives, for the most part their psychologic import lies in how people learn to cope with them. As was discussed in Chapter 5, even such social drives as N Aggression, N Achievement, or N Affiliation very possibly have some physiological basis, also unmeasurable by psychological techniques. These latter "secondary" drives are even more easily masked by repression and compensatorily interchanged, making precise and independent measurement extremely difficult.

Murray's contribution to psychology was not merely the ingenuous selection of a set of pictures but rather the construction of a method—the projective method. This method was based on the psychoanalytic concept of unconscious motives, but it provided a means of assessing the presence and import of these underlying motives without the extended process of therapeutic free association. Nearly all projective techniques, except for the Rorschach and the Word Association Test, followed upon Murray's invention. In these verbal associations and fantasies and in graphic free expression, it is often quite possible to see the underling motives reflected—motives that are usually masked by repression in everyday life. Subsequently, Edwards (1957) provided a means of measuring many of the same variables from subjective data by eliminating the element of "social desirability" through paired comparison of items. Any comprehensive discussion of the measurement and nature of these separate drives is far beyond the scope of this volume. Many of them have already been considered in some detail both in this chapter and in Chapter 5. For purposes of illustration, I shall discuss briefly the assessment of several principal drives.

Physiological drives are present in every child, and in assessment the concern is not with the presence of the drive but with how the child learns to channel and handle it. That such a physiological drive is of particular concern to the child may be evident in the content of various associative techniques. For example, the budding sexuality of the pubescent child, while seldom demonstrated in direct sexual content, is often quite manifest in symbols and slips of the tongue. Between ages 11 to 13 children begin to draw the human figure in profile, and although they may not indicate actual secondary sexual body features, such as breasts or hips, the overall posture of the figure often begins to take on a slightly more adult stance. By ages 12 to 13, the presence of a definite hip and chest area or of a rump is not unusual. Lips and eyes may also indicate some sensual interest. As Machover (1949) and others have noted, children of this age often show particular concern with the point where the legs are attached to the body, either having difficulty drawing the crotch or giving it special emphasis. Boys whose sexual urges and whose curiosity are rising may draw a male figure and take extra care to pencil in the fly to such an extent that it may look as if they had drawn a penis underneath the pants. In drawing the figure of a girl, boys of this age often start to draw the girls' legs up through and underneath the skirt. Girls' sexual interests are more likely to be shown in fancy clothes, breast lines, a seductive posture of the figure, or extra emphasis on hair and decorations.

The need for affection, which may actually be a physical drive as was suggested by Harlow and Zimmerman (1958), may be assessed from TAT stories, doll play, or the MAPS.

CASE 50

Letty, age 5, had spent most of her life in the middle of a marital battle and had been recently abandoned by both parents to her resentful, bitter, and depressed maternal grandmother. Letty poignantly spelled out her concern on the MAPS, arranging the adult figures so that they were being affectionate to each other and at the same time centering affection upon child figures. In-

termixed with these affectionate scenes were battles between the Superman figure and the ghost in which Superman prevented the ghost from breaking the affectionate bonds between the parents and between the parents and the child. In the concluding scene Letty picked out the backdrop of the desert and depicted a child figure wandering back and forth across the desert, weeping and afraid to be rescued by an old witch figure. The child imitated what must have been her grandmother's voice harshly ordering her to come to get food.

Whether or not aggressivity is a psychological drive, as Freud and others have maintained, the manner in which it appears and the way that the child handles it is often a crucial variable. As noted before, aggression becomes a need as children are forced to learn to seek their own need gratifications actively and independently. Such aggressivity should not be confused with the affect *anger* nor with the accumulative effects of anger that are called *hostility*. Rather, such aggressivity consists of a child's drive to explore and test out the environment, his/her imposition of needs, impulses, and feelings onto the world, and his/her assertion of his/her own identity as a separate and unique force in the environment. It is the accumulation of all these aspects of their behavior into a need or drive that particularly characterizes the shift from infancy to latency. However, as this assertion of the self takes on such an active form and becomes in effect a drive, children also find themselves increasingly in conflict both with adult authorities and with other children who are also asserting themselves. Thus "being aggressive" is often a complaint lodged against the latency child. The assessor must be particularly careful in understanding this complaint. She/he must distinguish the degree to which the complaint reflects the inability of the adult authority to accept what may be a natural developmental phenomenon.

At the same time, the possibility should be entertained that whether or not parents do accept this change, children themselves may be having difficulty with it. They may interpret even mild criticisms by the parents of their aggressivity as a threat of loss of love. They may find that aggressivity brings them into more competition with other children than they are immediately prepared to cope with. They may wish for the protection of the mother and try to retreat to a state in which she entertains them, feeds them, and keeps them safe from harm. They may find that the mother is willing to resume this role, but as their need aggression increases, their conflict with the maternal figure may also intensify. Moreover, children who withdraw from aggressive interaction with peers are likely to be the object of their attacks. They will likely find themselves alternately teased and isolated. Instead of entering into the normal games of push and pull, they attack with anger and receive anger in return. Evidence of such difficulty in handling aggression may come first from teachers' reports or parents' complaints about the way other children treat their child. The themes of such children on the TAT, Sentence Completion, or the World Test usually consist of mixed aggressivity, fear, and anger.

CASE 51

Sherry Y, age 8, in playing with the World Test, built a very neat and orderly world at first, omitting all such aggressive symbols as the military figures or the wild animals and even carefully corralling all of the tame animals. Suddenly she spotted the bull and, almost without warning, started to break down the entire world, remarking that the bull was getting even with all the bad people who were in its way. Her drawing of a person was not easy to identify by sex, but he or she carried a spear. When asked about the sex of the person she drew, Sherry added a skirt and identified the drawing as Jane from the TV series "Tarzan."

Mrs. Y had brought Sherry to the clinic because she refused to go to school where all the children teased her. In further discussions the mother agreed that Sherry was often demanding with other children who came to the house. Although Mrs. Y had given it little thought at first, she now realized that Sherry may well have isolated herself in the neighborhood because she was quick to anger, very possessive with her belongings, and was unwilling to be competitive. When Sherry had complained to her mother about other children, Mrs. Y had been quick to comfort her and divert her attention from the situation with other pleasures.

In the initial interviews it seemed that Sherry's difficulties in handling aggression might well have arisen from her jealousy over the birth of a little brother two years before. She had been particularly curious about her mother's pregnancy, and Mrs. Y had given Sherry considerable explanation about this event, including the fact that the father had "planted the seed that grew into a baby." Although these explanations did help to satisfy Sherry's curiosity, she had presumed that the baby would be a girl. When she discovered the baby was male, she was very angry and demanded that her mother take her brother back to the hospital and "exchange" him, as she had seen her exchange purchases at stores. When it was explained to Sherry that this was impossible, she asked if the doctor could operate on him so he would be a girl. For weeks after the sib was born, she was sullen and irritable and would not go near the baby.

However, Sherry's open rivalry with her male sibling did not seem to explain her particular modes of handling aggression. Mrs. Y—once she had described this sibling rivalry—was insistent that this was the source of Sherry's difficulties. She denied that Sherry had shown any tendencies to be demanding or explosive prior to the sib's birth. She argued almost defensively that Sherry had been an easy child to care for. "Perhaps we did spoil her a little since she was so sweet, but we also disciplined her when necessary." The discipline that Mrs. Y described consisted mainly of isolating

Sherry briefly in another room, whereupon she usually became contrite. At first Mrs. Y could not identify the kinds of behaviors for which she punished Sherry: "Just different little things. We seldom had to punish her," but on second thought she did remark that Sherry often was "greedy" and "grabbed at things." "I tried to teach her what was hers and what belonged to someone else." She explained that it had been difficult to keep Sherry out of Mr. Y's study, where the child might destroy books and papers. Sherry also loved to explore cupboards and drawers. "She always made such a mess."

In response to the social worker's questions, Mrs. Y provided the bare facts about her own background, but it was difficult frrom ths initial interview to obtain much information about her own attitudes and behavior. Like Sherry, she had a brother approximately five years her junior. She denied any memory of rivalry with him or jealousy toward him. "We each had our own interests and went our own ways," she explained. She remembered her own childhood as generally happy and uneventful. In contrast to Sherry, she recalled that she had many playmates and seldom quarreled with any of them. As evidence, she named two with whom she continued to correspond. Until she married Mr. Y she had always "lived in the same town in the same house." Her school achievements had been above average and she had attended two years of college when she met and married Mr. Y. For the first two years of their marriage, she had worked as a secretary while Mr. Y completed his training as an accountant. She denied that she had had any particular vocational ambitions of her own, but had attended college chiefly because "it did seem better to have some college education." Shortly after Mr. Y finished his training, the couple moved from Mrs. Y's hometown to a distant, large city where he found employment. That year she became pregnant with Sherry. She averred that her marriage was generally happy, that "Mr. Y provides a good living" and that "we seldom quarrel."

On the Edwards PPS, none of Mrs. Y's scores was excessively high. However, percentile scores around 70 on Order, Aggression, and Autonomy did suggest that Mrs. Y's own values might entail a mildly compulsive ordering of her environment in order to maintain her identity. Such a pattern was further emphasized by percentile scores below 25 on Intraception, Abasement, and Sex. Mrs. Y thus evinced little interest in the feelings of others, was not inclined to blame herself, and placed little value on sexual drives. This pattern of scores thus suggested that Mrs. Y tended to be somewhat impersonal, unresponsive to stimuli, and concerned with her own security.

As it was the clinic's policy to involve fathers in the assessment and treatment of children, Mr. Y was invited to make an appointment with the social worker. He canceled the first two appointments with the excuse that unexpected business had intervened. He appeared 15 minutes late to the third appointment, claiming again that his work day was rushed. He did seem out of breath and very tense and sat quietly for a moment before asking, "What did my wife tell you?" The worker explained that Mrs. Y had given her view of Sherry's difficulties, but that the clinic thought it might be helpful to understand how he perceived the situation. Again, Mr. Y was silent for a moment before asking, "I mean about us?" Mr. Y flushed and remained silent for several minutes. "I guess you thought I didn't want to come to see you, that I wasn't interested in Sherry," he said. "Well, I really was reluctant to come. Not because of Sherry. I'm very worried about Sherry. It's because of my wife—and me." He hesitated again and seemed depressed. "We've never gotten along well. She's a difficult woman to live with—perhaps I'm difficult too; I don't know." He went on to explain that he regarded his wife as "selfish," "demanding her own way," "sulking when she is slighted." "Sherry is just like her. She hasn't any friends either." He felt she was very jealous, complaining about and downgrading all of his friends and demanding that he spend "every spare minute at home." Now that he was working independently as a public accountant, he often needed to work evenings, which was the reason Mr. Y had arranged a study for him at home. From his description, it appeared Mrs. Y was jealous of his attentions to Sherry, often sending her off to bed early in the evening when he was playing with Sherry or scolding her when she tried to get his attention or acted seductively toward him. Their marital dissension had become so intense about three years ago that they had contemplated a separation. However, soon afterwards Mrs. Y became pregnant and there was no further discussion of their separation. Since the birth of their son, Mrs. Y had completely rejected his sexual advances. Mr. Y admitted he was very depressed at times and that he regarded this marital dissension as the chief source of Sherry's difficulties.

He was very reluctant to discuss this matter with his wife. He seemed resolved to try to maintain his marriage on its present basis and was afraid that further consideration in connection with Sherry's problems might again threaten it with dissolution. He begged the worker not to mention to his wife what he had said. He agreed that if his analysis of the situation was valid, it might be difficult to help Sherry without some further exploration of the marriage. But he adamantly refused to become involved further. Rather, he begged the clinic to try to help Sherry as much as possible—"without going into any of this!"

Mrs. Y failed to appear for her next appointment but did call later to make another, without explaining why she had not come in as scheduled. When she did appear, she seemed even more reserved than previously. She too wanted to know "what my husband told you" and seemed unsatisfied by the social worker's statement that they had discussed Sherry's problems. She agreed to the clinic's recommendation that both she and Sherry come weekly to the clinic, but she remarked that "I don't

know what more I have to tell you!" A week later Mrs. Y called to cancel further appointments, explaining that Sherry's pediatrician had prescribed a mild tranquilizer that "seems to quiet Sherry down." There was no further mention of Sherry's social and school problems. This case illustrates how a child's aggressive social behavior may actually reflect the hostilities within the family—especially marital discord.

One of the most common human motivations is the urge for revenge. Strangely, this is seldom mentioned by psychologists, even though it is often emphasized in literature and history. Retaliation as a motive is part of psychoanalytic theory—that is, the fear of retaliation for the forbidden wish to possess the mother. Perhaps revenge is ignored in psychological literature because it seems to be only another form of anger, but it is a very specific anger that is unique to human relationships. It is as real and common a motivation as achievement or affiliation. Although there are no research studies on revenge and no scales to measure it, everyday experience does suggest that it is probably quite a common motive among children as well as among adults. "I'll get even with you!" is a cry that periodically comes from every child.

Plotting revenge is a frequent theme of daydreams, and the ways in which revenge is attempted probably vary as greatly as any other comparable form of behavior. Often such plotting occupies much of the injured or insulted person's waking hours and his/her dreams as well. Revenge can become an obsession with children, as with adults. Because destruction of the offender is usually not possible—even moreso because even the thought of annihilating the enemy is often quite guilt creating—the child usually fantasies some substitute gratification, such as humiliating the offender or making her/him feel guilty and apologetic.

One of the main aims of this obsessive plotting is to avoid having the tables turned on the plotter. That is, the act of revenge should not be committed in such a way as to make the revenger look as if she/he were an offender, guilty of an act of aggression. Also, the revenger has to avoid feeling guilty; revenge is only satisfied when the revenger feels justified. The dream-of act of revenge often has to be very devious. Sometimes, in order to avoid having any finger of guilt pointed at the revenger, the whole idea of revenge itself has to be repressed and thus leaves the child's consciousness. In such instances, all that then remains is the act itself. Moreover, in seeking to avoid any blame, the child often chooses some other need gratification—consciously or unconsciously—through which to express revenge.

A few examples of how revenge becomes confused with and hidden in other need gratifications may serve to illustrate how needs can be confused by the child. One of the most common needs confused with revenge is *N* Achievement, either as underachievement or overachievement. A classic example is the underachiever who seeks revenge against parents she/he feels offer insufficient affection and succor but who place a high value on achievement. By playing the helpless, inadequate infant, the child wreaks revenge on the disappointed parents and, at the same time, subtly gains some of the attention for which she/he has longed. Most of all, achievement becomes the battlefield and the child's anger over her/his feelings of rejection remain hidden. Overachievement may be a child's means of revenge against the intrusion of a sibling rival. By overachieving, he/she seeks to show up the beloved baby. If he/she does everything correctly and properly, the sins of the younger sib will stand out.

This wearing of the halo is a very common behavior pattern in which older sisters obtain revenge against a favored younger brother. The obstreperous and less successful brother than becomes the object of the parents' concern and in the referral to the clinic becomes what Satir (1964) calls the "identified patient." The behavior of the revengeful sister is revealed in his screams of pain. Again, *N* Achievement becomes the battlefield in which family affections are the spoils of war. However, the sister's revenge is usually only briefly satisfied, for although she may win approval for her superior achievement, the offending sib actually obtains the parents' concerns. However, substituting achievement for revenge easily becomes a pattern, and the sister may go on to higher levels of achievement, seeking revenge against all offending males but always losing in the long run, for this behavior pattern seldom brings the affection and succor she seeks.

Revenge may involve physiological needs as well as other social drives. The use of sex as revenge as other social drives. The use of sex as revenge either in the form of frigidity or promiscuity is very common among adults, both women and men. Sexual "acting-out" by adolescents also can be a form of revenge against parents, as is illustrated in the case of Sandy (Case 40). Another syndrome in which a physiological need becomes substituted for revenge is the neurotic self-starvation called anorexia nervosa. Because of the obvious concern of everyone involved with eating and because children who suffer from anorexia are usually quite passive and "sweet," the underlying obsessive, seething revenge may easily go unnoticed.

CASE 52

Janet B, age 14, was transferred from the pediatric to the psychiatric ward with a diagnosis of anorexia nervosa. During the first month on the pediatric ward, her weight continued to diminish so that she weighed only 68 pounds when the transfer to psychiatric care was decided upon. At that time she vomited up all solid foods and had been placed on intravenous feeding as an emergency measure. Upon her admission to the psychiatric ward, she was extremely emaciated and weak. She looked depressed, spoke very little, and seemed slightly in a daze. Janet expressed a distaste for the intravenous feeding but became agitated when the psychiatrist assured her that this was unnecessary and that she would be maintained on a special dietetic fluid. She was not allowed to remain in bed but instead was required to join the activities of the other children on the ward including attendance at the hospital's school.

In the initial interview Janet was unable to give much information about the onset of weight loss and vomiting, except that as far as she could remember it began about the end of the prior semester and had continued throughout the summer. She was anxious to leave the hospital as soon as possible both because she missed her family very much and because she was eager to start high school the following week with her friends. There was no history of any prior major illnesses or accidents, and a thorough medical checkup had not revealed the presence of a disease. Nor was there any history of prior weight loss. In fact, Janet's mother reported that her daughter had been quite "chubby" as an infant and slightly overweight throughout her childhood, until the previous year. At that time Janet had become somewhat concerned about her weight and decided to diet, along with her mother who was considerably overweight. Her loss of weight until that spring had been quite modest; she had lost approximately 10 pounds over a six month period and had gained approximately two and one half inches in her height to her present height of five feet six inches.

Janet was the third of three daughters of a fairly well-to-do owner of a chain of bakeries. She laughed as she mentioned her father's occupation since the family name was Baker, and moreover, she had been known from infancy by the nickname "Cookie." The children at school had teased her at times about the fact that her name was "Cookie" Baker, but she claimed that she did not mind this. Her sisters were 10 and 14 years older than herself and both had been away from home since she was 8 years old, so that for many years she had been the only child in the home. As far as Janet's mother could recall,

Janet's growth and development had been entirely normal. Mrs. B and her husband had not necessarily planned to have a third child but were quite happy over Janet's arrival. Mrs. B denied that she had any particular hopes concerning the sex of the baby when Janet was expected, and that she was quite content to have a third girl. She claimed that Janet was a very pretty baby and that they were delighted with her. She had been in good health throughout her pregnancy, and her labor was brief and the delivery quite easy.

Janet was breast-fed for almost six months, "perhaps a little longer than my other children." She was given a bottle in addition to baby foods until after she was 2 years old. Mrs. B could not remember exactly when Janet learned to walk and talk but thought Janet's development had been quite comparable to that of her other daughters. She did remember that Janet seemed to be "less trouble" and "quieter" during infancy than her first two children but attributed this to the fact that she was a more experienced mother and less upset by babies.

She remembered being much more concerned with the care of her first child; as she recalled this, she smiled and added that when her two other daughters were infants, she had had the help of her mother who was living with the family. She recalled that she had resented the efforts of her mother to be helpful and had found her to be an interference. Her mother had died three years before Janet's birth and thus she had had Janet's care as an infant entirely to herself. Janet seemed to enjoy being cared for and played with, so that Mrs. B had found her a more enjoyable child than her older daughters. Even Mr. Baker, whom Mrs. B described as a somewhat distant man and not easily given to expressions of affection, was less reserved with his youngest daughter. He permitted her to climb into his lap and would even swoop her into his arms when he arrived home from work, which was something he had never done with the other two children. Even as an infant, Janet was quite sensitive to her father's moods and would cry if she thought that he disapproved of her. If he was cross over other things or preoccupied, Mrs. B would have to reassure Janet that he was not angry with her.

Mrs. Baker did not find it "necessary" to put Janet in a nursery school since she had "nothing else to do but take care of her." Janet was a bit tearful when she started kindergarten, and it took her several weeks to become accustomed to being separated from her mother. Thereafter, however, she was a model of good behavior both at school and at home and seemed very happy. Throughout elementary school she made all A's and B's. School records did show that Janet was considered a "timid" child by her teachers and that her main difficulty had been in reciting aloud. Her written work was considered exceedingly neat and always correct. Janet's grades dropped slightly as she entered junior high school, but her record of A's and B's continued on through the eighth grade. During the previous year, however, Janet did seem to have much more difficulty at school. She was placed in a slightly advanced class and seemed to have a considerable amount of homework. She pored over books in the evening and struggled to write compositions and reports. She complained about her assignments a great deal to her mother, who worried over them with her. She just could not seem to write a satisfactory essay and dreaded making verbal reports. Mrs. Baker tried to reassure her that it would be all right to get a C in her English and social-science courses, but Janet "couldn't stand the idea of having a C," perhaps because her father had been so proud of her top grades. In fact, Janet worked so hard and was so very concerned with these particular courses that she slightly neglected her work in other areas and her overall academic achievement fell during the year. Mrs. Baker had considered obtaining some psychological counseling for Janet at that point, but Mr. Baker had disapproved.

Janet was also active socially both at church and with a girls' club, and there seemed to be a party or other social event nearly every weekend. However, Janet was often too tired to go out or, if she went, she did not really enjoy herself. Mr. Baker had expressed some disapproval at the extent of Janet's social activities. He believed she might too easily become involved in what he considered the delinquent activities of adolescence, in "drinking, carousing around, and so on." Mrs. Baker tried to assure him that Janet's group of "little girls" were all very nice, that no alcohol was served at their parties, and that although there were boys and dancing, none of the girls did any individual dating. As the year progressed, Janet became worried lest her father disapprove entirely of her social activities. She particularly feared that he might believe these activities caused her decline in school achievement, although Mr. Baker never openly made such an association.

Janet became especially concerned that her father might not permit her to attend the social events during graduation week if she did not improve her school grades. During the weeks just prior to graduation, Janet was most anxious and tense and sleepless. She concentrated for hours on her schoolwork. Mrs. Baker prevailed on her husband to praise Janet for her efforts and to buy her the special clothes that she wanted for the parties. On the night of the graduation party, Janet was a pitch of excitement and tension. At the last minute, she almost did not go because her menses had occurred a week early. Nevertheless, with her mother's support she went to the party. She was particularly excited because her escort was a boy upon whom she had a particular crush. However, Janet was most disappointed at the party because this young man had not paid any particular attention to her but had chased after some other girl. Moreover, there was alcohol in the punch, and Janet became slightly inebriated and then ill. She was terrified that her father would discover this. It was that night when she arrived home that she first began to vomit. During the subsequent week, she seemed depressed and physically ill, had little appetite, and continued to vomit. The situation did not clear up the entire summer. Significantly, Janet did not remember this incident nor did Mrs. Baker herself associate it with the onset of Janet's symptom. Only later did Janet admit that she had expected this party to be "just everything."

That this very passive and sweet child could possibly be motivated by revenge seemed most unimaginable. Moreover, food was such a life-and-death struggle in which Janet involved the nurses, doctors, and her parents, that at first it seemed that this rejection of food was in itself the need. In fact, the resident physician initially posited that the problem as "an oral-aggressive fixation." Certainly the fixation was oral, and in the struggle to maintain Janet's life and in her obstinate resistance to food there was no doubt that aggression was also involved. However, the nature of this aggression was not easily definable from immediate clinical observation nor from the history. Psychological assessment was requested "to determine some of the sources of her underlying anxiety and her defenses against it, especially concerning being aggressive." In further discussion with the psychiatric resident who asked for the psychological consultation, he remarked that he guessed that Janet was probably a very angry girl but that anger made her very guilty.

When Janet was introduced to the assessment, she made a sour face and said that she had heard of "these 'psych' tests from the other kids on the ward" and that "I don't see what they have to do with my problem." However, she had consented to her doctor's request that she go through with the assessment, so she decided to accept the situation albeit with obvious distaste. Although there was no question about her intellectual functioning, she was given the Shipley-Hartford Intelligence Scale first as a "warm-up," that is, as an emotionally neutral task. Her scores on both parts of the Shipley indicated above-average intelligence with a WAIS equivalent IQ of 117. She expressed annoyance with the Abstraction Test, asking "Who thought these up anyway!" and then remarking "I must be pretty stupid!" She accepted the Rorschach with a noncommittal shrug but soon became quite involved in it so that by the time she was presented with the TAT she was relatively relaxed and was almost enjoying her own fantasies. When asked to draw a person, she wrinkled her nose in protest but said nothing and immediately became engaged in drawing, carefully selecting her colors. Given the MMPI to complete on her own in the ward, her reaction was again negative: "Do I have to?" She worked very slowly, read and reread each item carefully, stopping periodically to rest in her room until urged by the nurse to return to the task.

Janet gave the following responses to the Rorschach:*

*Locations are indicated by reference to Beck's details, by number. Scoring, however, is according to Klopfer (1956).

Administration	Inquiry
Card I 3″	
1. Ew! How ugly! Like an ugly mask.	The whole thing, Like a robber wears. Black. With mean eyes and a mean mouth. *W Fc; Fm Mask*
Card II 17″	
1. Could be two lambs, black lambs, just their heads. And they're nursing out of a bottle.	This (D1) is their heads. Here's their noses, nuzzling at this bottle (D4). Ears here and you can see their eyes. *D FM, FC' A P, O*

2. Or it could be a face, the whole thing. A real mean face.

His mouth (D5) is wide open, like he was yelling. Or it could be a she, I can't tell. Her eyes (D2) are red! Like she'd been crying or was angry. Angry, I guess. She's sticking her tongue (D3) out.
Like a nasty person.

W, S M, FC Hd

Card III 20″

1. I don't know. Looks like it might be some kind of X ray or somebody's insides.

(D1) Like the bones right here [points to own pelvis]. It's that shape. (X ray?) Dark and shadowy. I don't know what that red could be. (?) All bloody. But that wouldn't show on an X ray, would it?

D Fk At (D CF At)

2. Ick! This way (inverted) it looks like a big monster, coming right at you.

(D1) He's got his hands up (D5) like he was going to pounce right on you. Big black eyes (D8). And his mouth is open, with white teeth. (?) I don't know if it's human or animal. Like something from outer space.

D M, FC' (H)

Card IV 22″

1. Another big ol' monster. Are they all going to be monsters? With giant feet and arms like hooks.

The whole thing. Like he was clumping out like this [makes a menacing gesture] humped over, going to grab somebody. You can't see his face, just mean eyes (D1?) I don't know. A big tail? (laughs)

W M (H)

Card V 4″

1. Here it is again. All monsters. This is a monster bat.

Swooping down. Big claws (D10) on the end of his wings. Ugly. (?) So black. Big horns and curved in feet. Ugh!

W FM, FC' A P

Card VI 25″

1. I don't know what this could be really. This (D1) like some kind of skin, but this (D3) . . . I know, that (D3) could be the tail, like a beaver skin.

It's just shaped like a skin. There's where the feet were before it got skinned. And beavers have big tails don't they? (skin-like?) I don't know. Just couldn't think of anything else that shape.

W F Aobj. (P)

Card VI 8″

1. Oh, this is kind of cute. Like two puppy dogs, with their ears up. Or kitties. More like cats and they are spitting at each other, with their fur sticking out.

(D2) Their mouths are open and their eyes big like when cats fight. All their fur's one end. (de). Their paws are out like this, ready to fight. Upon on a fence (D4).

W FM A

CARD VIII 13″

1. Two dogs, one on either side. . . . Like wild dogs. . . .

(D1). They're stretching out to his hand here. Like smelling it. They look awfully fierce. You can see it in their eyes.

D FM A P

2. And here's a hand right at their noses, like reaching out to pet them or something. You'd think who-ever's trying to pet something like that'd get bit.

Here's the hand with long fingers, and part of the arm. (?) Just arm and hand.
dr M Hd

3. This red . . . could be meat . . . but it's too red for meat. Like poisoned meat. Maybe somebody put it out for the dogs. (laughs) Maybe that's why the're going to bite!

(D6) It's all pink and whitish . . . like spoiled or poisoned.
D FC, Fc Food

Card IX 52″

I. Ugh! The top (D3) might be like two witches, and they're standing over a big pot, stirring up some evil of some kind. It's all streaming up in their faces. Here's the fire down below.

(D3) They got pointed caps and long noses like horns and big fat tummies.
D, W M (H)
Here's the pot (D1). (poison?) The greenish color. Isn't that poison color?
D FC Obj
And the hot fire below, all this pink.
D CF Fire

Card X 5″

1. Crabs snatching at
2. some seaweed.

(D1) All these legs. *D FM A D* This green stuff.

3. Here's two guys up here, lifting up a big pole or pillar, standing on his cliff, like they were going to drop it on

(D8) Real weirdos. Like cave men. They're on top of the cliff (D9). They're going to destroy these guys (D6) D M (II)

4. These two other guys who are climbing up the mountain.

(D6) They got big fat bodies and big fat arms but little teeny hands. They'll get smashed.
D M, Fm H

5. And this guy down here has fallen off. Maybe the other guys got him or maybe he was dragged off by

(D) Here's his legs, and his mouth is open like he was screaming as he falls. *D M, Fm H*

6. These two big snakes. They're bigger than he is! It sure looks like a big ol' war is going on.

(D) Long, green snakes all curling up. (green?) More poison, I guess.
D FC, FM A P

7. Explosions all around.

Things bursting in different colors.
D CF, Fm Explo.

Summary, Rorschach Scores Case 52

	Main	Add		Main	Add		Main	Add
W	6	*1*	M	8	*1*	H	2	
D	15	*1*	FM	5	*1*	(H)	4	
Dr	1		Fm		*4*	Hd	2	
S		*1*	F	1		A	6	
R	22		Fc		*1*	Mask	1	
P	5	1	FC	2	*2*	At	1	*1*
O		1	FC	3	*1*	Aobj	1	
			CF	3	*1*	Food	1	

Summary, Rorschach Scores Case 52 (Cont'd)

		Main	Add
Experience Balance:	Obj	1	
8 : 4½ = I 116[2]	Fire/Explo.	2	
	Pl	1	

[2]For calculation of this Experience-Balance ratio, see Palmer, 1955.

Of Janet's 12 TAT stories, 4 were particularly pertinent to the question of the form of her anger.

CARD 2 (administered first): "This girl is going to school, but it looks like she's turning around like she was watching what was going on behind her. That must be her mother; she's watching something too . . . whatever's going on. They're watching this guy, whoever he is. He looks too young to be the father, maybe her brother or just some guy working there. They're watching to see if he's working right . . . (story?) . . . I don't know . . . maybe they're making sure he doesn't cheat 'em . . . (come about?) . . . Who knows! They just hired this guy to work on their farm. Maybe they don't really have a father. They have to watch that this guy doesn't steal whatever they're growing there. That's their food for the winter. But they don't look like they know much about farming. (Happens?) He probably takes the stuff and sells it when they aren't looking. (And then?) They starve to death! [laughs] No, don't put that down. Let's see. . . . The girl goes to town and tells the sheriff and they get a posse and chase the guy and catch him and hang him. (Girl feels then?) Oh, she'd be happy." [laughs]

3GF (second card): "She's all busted up over something. Crying over something. Probably something silly! [laughs] (What has happened?) Oh, she probably caught her boyfriend making out with some other girl, (Next?) She goes out and jumps in the lake! . . .

No, she wouldn't do anything like *that*. I know: she doesn't really jump in the lake; she just throws her clothes in and they float down the river and they find them at the bottom of the waterfall and they think she's drowned. Then her boyfriend thinks it's all his fault and he shoots himself . . . No, change that. The other girl thinks it's *her* fault and *she* shoots herself. Later this girl comes back and they find out that she didn't drown after all and she marries this guy and they live happily ever after . . . How's that for a story!"

CARD 5: "She sure looks like she's sneaking up on someone. Maybe she's looking in here to see what's going on behind her back . . . (?) Oh, maybe her daughter's in there making out with her boyfriend . . . (happens?) She screams . . . (Who screams?) [laughs] . . . I'll make it the mother screams 'cause the daughter knew her mother'd come sneaking around so she put a bucket of Water over the door and when the old lady stuck her head in she got all soaked [Janet laughs] (And then?) I don't know . . . Oh, I got a really funny ending. Let's say she really wasn't sneaking up on them at all. She was going to call them to dinner. Now the joke's on them. She won't give them anything to eat."

18GF (final story): "Oh, oh. Caught in the act. She was sneaking downstairs to get something out the refrigerator and her mother caught her. Looks like the mother's trying to choke her, make her cough it up! [Janet laughs] That's all . . . (Come about?) . . . More story? Well, let's see . . . Let's say this really isn't her mother. It's her stepmother. Her father died and her stepmother is trying to starve her to death so that the stepmother can get all the money her father left her. The stepmother has her locked up so she can't get away. If she goes down the stairs, there's a squeaky board and the stepmother'll hear her and lock her up again. So she makes a rope out of her sheets and tries to climb down out of her window. But she can't make it 'cause she's so weak and everything. She falls down but she doesn't get killed. Maybe she falls in some bushes or something. Anyway, the neighbors see her and they call the police and they see her condition and they arrest the stepmother and put her in jail. So the girl gets all the goodies from her father. The end!''

The profile of T scores obtained from Janet's MMPI was quite unusual: 216' 734-5. Her ''lie'' score was 68, K was 55, and F was 47. The amount of depression indicated in her score on Scale 2 was considerably higher than might have been expected from most adolescents. Although Janet complained bitterly about being hospitalized and kept wishing she could return home, she masked whatever other depression she might be experiencing by a set smile. Evidently she could not maintain this mask when presented with statements concerning depression; note that Scale 3 (Hysteria) at T score 60 does show use of repression and denial as a secondary defense. However, repression alone could not contain Janet's depression. Her sense of loss was projected on the one hand into somatic complaints and suffering (Scale 1) and, on the other hand, any guilt was deflected by ''paranoid ideation'' (Scale 6). The combination of these reactions with the indication of obsessive-compulsive trends (Scale 7) is consonant with the clinically observed compulsive fasting and vomiting, but in addition suggested an obsessive rumination over revenge. Her Pd score (Scale 4) was not particularly high for an adolescent, but considering Janet's history, it does indicate far more feeling of rebellion and of family discord than were mentioned in any of the initial interviews.

Janet's first drawing of a person did not seem to show any anger. It was a rather stereotyped figure of what appeared to be a chubby latency girl, with a round face and long curls and a set smile, dressed in an old-fashioned frock with bows and ribbons, colored in pastels, and wearing a little girl's black dress shoes; the figure was standing full face, with her hands behind her, rather demurely. Janet described her as a ''teenager all dressed up to go to a party.'' However, for a male figure, Janet began by drawing a horse, on which she placed a knight in full armor with his lance pointed out in front of him. ''He's all set to kill the dragon or something and rescue the princess . . . Maybe she (drawing I) is the princess.''

These data provided considerable evidence about the nature of many aspects of Janet's ego development. Evidently she was an intellectually bright and emotionally sensitive girl, whose affective life was far more extensive and expansive than seemed indicated in the initial clinical observations. Concentrating on the question in the referral, there was considerable evidence to back up the psychiatric resident's initial impression of ''fixation at an oral-aggressive stage.'' Obsession with food and with anger was present throughout Janet's Rorschach and TAT responses, until they became almost equivalent, as epitomized in the ''poison'' associations to the Rorschach. However, these responses suggested that Janet's oral aggressiveness had become more specific, that revenge had become an autonomous motive. Witness such Rorschach responses as the masked robber, the face with the tongue sticking out, the menacing monsters, the spitting cats, the dogs who bite the hand of those who feed them poisoned meat, the poisoned meat, the poisoned witches' brew, and finally the exploding battle on Card X. Revenge intermingled with food permeates

Janet's TAT stories. For example, to Card 2, the heroine seeks revenge for stolen food; on Card 3GF, depression over lost love is satisfied by an ingenuous revenge obtained by creating guilt in the offending parties. On Card 5, food becomes more important to the teen-ager than sex, and the mother obtains revenge for her insult by deprivation of food; finally on Card 18GF, Janet's fantasy equated food deprivation with being deprived by her mother of her father's love, and she found revenge by inciting the community to retaliate against her mother for her, thus saving her any feelings of guilt.

Combining these findings with the clinical history, it did seem highly probable that Janet had long felt deprived of her father's affections and although her strenuous efforts to please him had seemed futile, she had swallowed any anger she felt toward him. However, Janet's fantasies suggested that she blamed her mother. It was hypothesized that since Janet felt unappreciated by her father, it was likely that any normal jealousy she may have had toward her mother may well have remained unresolved and even magnified. The succor that mother had always so generously provided her now seemed like poison to Janet. If Janet could not reek revenge on her depriving father, she could attack her mother by refusing the mother's succor. Yet, even her revenge against her mother had to be indirect. She could, and did, make her mother feel guilty, without seeming willfully to be the cause of her mother's distress. The revenge thus became masked in the anorexia.

CHAPTER 12

The Assessment of Social Development

For many years the assessment of children was aimed almost exclusively at internal, personal behavior, with scant attention paid to the social pressures bearing upon them. However, as has been discussed previously, clinical psychologists now recognize that development of the child's ego takes place within a social ecology that gradually becomes part and parcel of the child's ego itself. Moreover, one of the central aims of a child's development is to function in an integrated manner as an individual in society. Thus no assessment, no matter what the complaint, can be considered complete or meaningful without data bearing on the social forces and the milieu in which the child is developing.

As was discussed in detail in Chapter 7, the analysis of these data about the child's particular social forces depends upon the clinical psychologist's knowledge of the social forces extant in the immediate community and the sociological makeup of society at large. Nevertheless, in the assessment proper, the psychologist must aim at least part of the data gathering at sampling the particular social forces bearing on the child and family and the ways in which they are handling and integrating these forces. Assessment is very often centered on the degree to which, and on the manner in which, the child is forming a social identity.

Although the interview often provides much data about the social situation of the child and family, evidence concerning the child's social growth is also present in nearly every other technique available to the assessor. Rather than deal with the techniques separately, this discussion will center around the various aspects of social development, citing examples of data gathered from various techniques and using the same heuristic outline applied in the previous chapters to ego development: modality, input–output, focus and differentiation, interferences, coping mechanisms, and content.

A. MODALITIES

The socialization of children takes place through an interaction with and membership in social groups that increase in size and variety. The "modality" of social development consists of the size, variety, and constitution of these groups. The initial social interaction—or, more specfically, personal interaction—is between child and mother. More strictly one may speak of socialization as beginning as a child becomes a member of a family group. The family grouping may change and increase or shrink during childhood, thus changing the perspective of the self as a group member and affecting the child's identity. One of the important pieces of data to be gathered at intake is a statement of the family constellation and a history of its changes. Such information includes the birth or death of a sibling, the presence or absence of parental figures, and data concerning any other types of family figures—either present in the home or outside the home—who exert any kind of meaningful effect upon the child's social development. Who these family members are now, what they mean now or have meant in the past to the child, how they have regarded and treated the child—

all should be explored in interviews with the parents and child.

Moreover, the child's feelings about this family group and the degree to which these various group members may have affected her/him and become part of internal feelings will be reflected in fantasies on techniques such as the TAT, CAT, MAPS, and the Family Relations Test. It must be emphasized, of course, that these associative techniques do not tell how the family *actually* behaves but rather how the child *perceives* them and the extent to which they are part of his/her social identity.

Children's social grouping begins to expand as soon as they begin to leave the family structure. Initially they may experience extrafamily groupings in neighborhood play. Their social world is perforce enlarged as they enter any kind of school situation—nursery, kindergarten, or elementary school. Here they find themselves in an extrafamilial, peer-group society that expands the original family group identity. Their relationship with and membership in this peer-group society exists alongside the original family group, and at least until adolescence, the peer group is largely secondary to the family. Few, if any, of the popularly used clinical techniques yield many data regarding the child's peer group membership and adjustment. For the most part, the psychologist learns about it from the child and parents, all of whom are biased by their family group membership.

Teachers' reports occasionally mention how the child gets along in the classroom and on the playground, but even these are likely to be child centered rather than group-centered reports. Again, it may be necessary for the psychologist practicing either in a clinic or privately to become familiar with the social makeup of the schools in the area. She/he should be familiar with the kinds of families in a specific area, what kind of social outlook the school authorities have, and what opportunities for peer interaction are offered to the child in a school setting. In some schools the child might well be a minority-group member intellectually and socially, if not in the usual sense of race or religion. Moreover, schools vary widely in the degree to which they tolerate variations in behavior. Conflicts between school authorities and students are occasionally obvious in high-school or even junior high-school settings. Such conflicts may well be present on the elementary-school level also, but they may be less obvious to the casual observer.

As a child enters adolescence, his/her peer group begins to increase in importance to him/her so that the kinds of children with whom he/she is associating and the settings in which these associations occur do become important variables in clinical assessment. Assessment interviews with children of any age should include some discussion of playmates and friends, and what they do together. In interviews with adolescents, an extended exploration of this aspect of functioning may be necessary.

Many of the children who come for help in a psychologic clinic are social isolates without friends. In such instances it is still necessary to ascertain from the child or parents how this child feels about peers, what it is that he/she dislikes about them, or whether he/she may feel disliked and rejected. For many children, the problem of isolation arises mainly because they cannot or will not give up enough of the original family grouping to allow the establishment of this extrafamilial social membership. The parents who fear that their child may be influenced by other children in some untoward and undesirable direction and who voice jaundiced and prejudiced attitudes toward other children are often threatened by the separation of the child—parent bond. The child also may be threatened, although at the same time attracted by the opportunity for greater freedom and independence and so be greatly torn between peer and parent. She/he may have to find some excuse, such as illness or devotion to studies, to help her/him escape this conflict.

In understanding the modes through

which these peer relationships are established, the psychologist should be aware not only of prevalent community attitudes and interaction but of the very size of this grouping itself. To no small degree today, the adult community's extreme concern with and prejudice toward adolescent behavior stem from the increasing size of this minority within society. It is estimated that well over one fourth of the population is between the ages of 12 and 25, and there is every indication that this percentage will increase over the next several decades. In many urban areas children attend junior high schools with populations of 2000 or 3000 students and high schools with 3000 to 5000 and then go on to colleges along with 10,000 to 20,000 young adults. Social adjustment in such massive peer communities is quite a different matter from that in small communities or rural areas. Such massive educational "factories" do, in essence, prepare the child to live in a mass society, but the pressure for existence for both the child and the adult in these circumstances is often quite extreme. Psychologists need to realize the severe difficulties created for the development of the child's individual identity by the enormity of educational institutions.

In general, children may be thought of as deriving socialization through two kinds of groups: an *ingroup* with which they identify and feel a membership and an *outgroup* (the "they" who set rules and controls over individual behavior), which children do not consider as a part of themselves and with which they have no membership identity. Although, in most instances, children are and feel themselves to be a member of the family, there are often members of the actual family group whom children do not include in their own perspective as family members and whom they consider as extragroup intruders. One of the best techniques for assessing the child's attitudes toward and inclusion of various familial members is the Bene-Anthony Family Relations Test. As is noted in the manual for this technique, the assessor should ascertain independently the constellation of the family. The child, in utilizing the Bene-Anthony, very often may leave out family members who actually reside in the home or add members who are not present. Thus, a child may fail to mention some sibling or parent or stepparent, but he/she may add parents who are not actually present in the home and with whom there is little contact. One child, for example, included in his Bene-Anthony family a baby who was not yet born, evidently because he wanted to express some feelings about this unborn sibling. Another child whose father had deserted the family several years previously and was almost unknown to the child put three fathers out on the table. Later it was discovered that two boyfriends and an "uncle" of the mother were residing in the home and were considered as fathers by the child. Children from broken homes may not consider stepparents and stepsiblings or halfsiblings to be members of the family but as a part of the "they" outside of themselves. In such multiple and often ill-defined family groups, the child often has to construct her/his own membership for what she/he considers to be her/his ingroup.

Sometimes such children are so confused about the family group to which they belong that they are unable to expand outwardly and begin to form peer-group memberships. Other such children may abandon the problem of family group identification and desperately seek identification among their peers. Thus one often finds that children who seem easily led into delinquency actually seek out delinquent children in order to find some kind of peer group that will accept them when they are confused or rejected by their family group.

One of the richest sources of data about the child's social behavior—particularly his/her interaction with his/her peers and with adult authorities—is direct observation of behavior in the classroom and activity on the playground through visits to the school. Unfortunately, not many clinics offer the opportunity for the assessor to leave his/her office and go out to the school.

Even if the psychologist is unable to make such visits on a regular basis, many teachers are trained to observe the child as a member of a group, and teachers' notes, or conversations with teachers, are a valuable substitute for direct observation.

Another way in which the child's membership within the family group may be assessed is to ask each member of the family to rate every other member on some brief scale, such as the Leary Interpersonal Check List (1957). This checklist is particularly handy because the dimensions it allegedly measures are conceived in terms of interpersonal interactions and stresses. In the assessment of one family constellation, the Leary ICL was given to all members of the family eight times. Each was asked to rate himself or herself and all other members of the family, including the potential therapist, wo was at that point assessing the family in a family group-therapy setting. The results of these interactions, plotted on the love-dominance circle of the ICL chart, revealed that the "identified" patient, an anorexic 13-year-old boy, was in the middle of a triangular power struggle between the very dominating father, the passive-angry mother, and a manipulating nurturant grandmother. Other siblings in the family had evidently taken sides with one or another of these three adult authorities, leaving the patient unable to dare accept succor from any one of the three, lest the others reject him. Although there were other factors bearing on this child's anorexic condition, an analysis of and a working through of the family power struggle proved to be one of the major therapeutic moves.

B. INPUT—OUTPUT

Classical behaviorism holds that, in essence, the child's mind is a tabula rasa to be imprinted by social forces. Very similarly, in classical psychoanalysis the child's libidinal instincts were thought to become encased in social taboos—thus creating neuroses. The fact that the child is conditioned by social foces and the fact that these social forces become internalized into a personal sense of guilt are complementary truths, but the idea that the child is merely a receptor of this input of social forces is only a half-truth. Children from birth on, if not actually when first thought of by the parents, are themselves a social force—an *effector* in whatever social group they are a member. In fact, children are actually effectors in groups in which they do not hold membership but with which they come into contact or conflict. The degree to which and the manner in which children receive social stimuli and in turn affect social groups is a core part of ego development. A great deal of the assessment is concentrated both on the child's sensitivity and awareness of his/her interpersonal environment and the ability to manipulate it, enter into it, and affect it. Assessment of the child's development as both receptor and effector of a social milieu can be made from a wide variety of techniques.

The Rorschach Technique, in particular, has as its central variables the "intratension" and "extratension" of an experience balance that describes the degree to which the respondent allows environmental stimuli to impinge upon his/her judgments and the degree to which he/she impinges his/her own personal attitudes and constructs upon the environment. As was explained in my prior discussion of the Rorschach, what is reflected in the child's inkblot responses is not his/her sociability or social introversion—extraversion but rather an attitudinal set toward this environment.

While the Rorschach gives a basic estimate of the child's interaction with the affective aspects of society, other techniques may be helpful in estimating the child's cognitive recognition of social stimuli, or as it is commonly called, "social intelligence." One commonly used estimate drawn from the Wechsler Intelligence Scale for Children consists of contrasting the child's score on the Comprehension subtest with his/her score on the Picture Arrangement subtest. The Comprehension scale yields an estimate of how well the child understands and recognizes social behavior and mores. It shows whether the child knows why things occur socially and what they mean. In contrast, the Picture Arrangement subtest samples primarily the child's understanding of how social events take place—that is, the sequence and arrangement of social situations. The instructions to this subtest require a child to manipulate the cartoon scenes into a meaningful sequence. Comprehension thus may be considered as a measure of the child's intellectual receptivity of social events in contrast to Picture Arrangement, which requires the child to manipulate the environment. Thus the verbally bright, achievement-oriented, but socially isolated child often achieves a high score on the Comprehension subtest but may have some difficulty with Picture Arrangement. In contrast, there is the equally bright but much less achievement-oriented child who concentrates efforts on social maneuvers and manipulation. Such a child makes a much higher score on Picture Arrangement than on Comprehension. Of course, this single-score difference cannot be used as an isolated index but should be treated as only one indicator in the array of evidence.*

Indications of the degree to which children see themselves as passive receptors of social stimuli or controllers of social milieu may also be found in TAT stories or the World Test materials. Thus in analyzing the CAT or TAT stories or the MAPS, the psychologist should note to what extent heroes and heroines are the objects of victims of their surroundings and to what extent they take charge, manage, or affect the plots. Of course, in drawing conclusions from such data, one must keep in mind that this is *fantasy* behavior. What one may conclude is that at least in fantasy children can imagine themselves as powerful figures managing their environments or that in fantasy they see themselves as victims. Thus, it must be remembered that some children who do suffer from being buffeted by their environment may take an opportunity in fantasy to see themselves in control through identifying with the hero or heroine of the story. Even so, such a fantasied role of being an effector does suggest that whatever the actual position the child occupies in the environment, she/he is at least able to conceptualize having some effect upon it. Obversely, the child who fantasies heroes and heroines as being passive victims of social forces may be projecting his/her own feelings of guilt rather than an objective analysis of the social situations. A guilt-ridden child may in effect manipulate the environment to a considerable degree but still feel that he/she is the victim of some outside force.

On the World Test one can see such receptor–effector behavior in the way the child selects and utilizes the materials rather than purely in the content of her/his production. Some children seem to search the materials for those items that will fit into some kind of plan or those that they are thinking of using to build a world with. Other children will pick out each piece of material and let it effect what they are doing so that the item in their hand determines what they will do next.

CASE 53

For example, Grace, age 5, had been ejected from kindergarten for being too "aggressive." Her father caustically remarked, "She's just like her mother; when they're a bitch at 5, what hope is there?" Grace immediately dumped the entire World Test case upside down and, hunting through the materials, picked out those she wished to have for a village, ignoring all other materials that did not fit into her plan. Another 5-year-old, Emma, about whom the school remarked that she did not seem quite mature enough to enter the first grade, daintily selected one piece at a time from the World Test chest, trying to find where

_____
*Differences must be 4 scale points or greater.

each might fit and continually asking the advice and support of the examiner. For this second girl, what was in the world controlled her and she was at a loss to deal with it.

Very commonly a child plays a role both as effector and receptor. Thus even when helpless, a child in effect draws support and guidance from others. When most aggressive and attempting most to manage the environment, she/he may be subject to increased pressure from adult authorities or peers. This concept of a social interaction rather than that of a purely stimulus—response pattern is sometimes ignored in assessment, particularly when there is an attempt to apply rigidly structured diagnostic categories. The primary example is childhood autism. In the controversy in the literature over the etiology of autistic behavior as summarized by Eisenberg and Kanner (1956), one school of thought maintains that autism occurs because the infant is emotionally and socially neglected by a narcissistic mother from the time of the child's birth. Much clinical material has been collected to support this argument. On the other hand, there are those who maintain that autistic behavior is a symptom of a generalized congenital central-nervous-system dysfunctioning and that such disturbances, as seen in the parents, are the effects of attempting to deal with a child who does not respond. The error made by persons holding each viewpoint is that autistic *behavior* is not necessarily a unitary syndrome with a single etiology. *Autistic behavior* (as opposed to "autism" as a diagnosis) may be observed both in children who have obvious central-nervous-system damage before birth and in children in whom such brain damage cannot be established. It is also true that in both cases there may be a narcissistic mother who rejects the child. Certainly not all brain-damaged children become autistic, nor do all mothers of brain-damaged children react by rejecting their children. It also is possible that some brain-damaged children will exhibit

autistic behavior no matter what the reactions are of mothers. Research about this behavioral syndrome could be greatly clarified if phrased in terms of the interaction between children and mothers rather than either the effects of mothers upon children or the social effects of children upon mothers. Autistic behavior is also found in blind children.

C. FOCUS AND DIFFERENTIATION

Both as receptors and effectors in social situations, children must learn to discriminate among the incoming social stimuli and to recognize differences and similarities among the people with whom they are dealing. They must also learn how to play distinct roles of their own in this interaction. For the infant, all people appear the same. They are all "mammas" or "daddies." Gradually, children learn to discriminate the roles that different people play, particularly if they have siblings or peers at nursery school or in the neighborhood. However, even a 5-year-old is not always able to discriminate other roles that people play with other people. For example, such a child may ask a grown woman about her "daddy," not distinguishing *daddy* from *husband*. This sorting out of roles played by people is an ever-expanding task for children. Such a receptive differentiation is essential if children are to be able to develop and differentiate roles for themselves.

CASE 54

Bert, a 7-year-old, was a physically handicapped child. His parents, in their depression and desperation, assigned him the role of the helpless cripple who needed constant care. Bert accepted this role insofar as it gave him the advantage of being the receptor of extra emotional support and other rewards and as being socially immune to the discipline and prohibitions applied to his siblings. Since in assigning this role to the child the mother inadvertently assigned herself the role of being an all-loving and all-protecting maternal figure—no matter what her needs and wants were—Bert also was in essence assigned the role of depriver of his mother's wants. Similarly, his father's authoritarian role was limited, and extra demands were made upon him as the provider of financial and material goods. Siblings in this family found themselves in the role of second-class citizens. Bert played this role comfortably at home for awhile, but as he entered school he discovered that his peers regarded him as helpless and unwanted. His teachers also did not give him quite the special treatment that he was afforded at home. At school he tried to compensate for his rejection by his peers by playing an almost opposite role—by denying his disability and attempting to force himself into the peer group. His fantasies at such a point contained megalomaniacal dreams of war and glory. With such disparate roles, Bert found it difficult to take any realistic, objective view of his disability or to develop a consistent image of himself.*

Both the structured tests of intelligence and the associative techniques provide data for the assessment of a child's ability to make these social determinations. Although certainly not purely intellectual discriminations, the ability to differentiate intellectually the roles that other people play is essential for children. They have to learn what the different rules are in specific situations and why people do the things they do—as is sampled on the Comprehension subtest of the WISC. However, knowledge of these general rules may not always help in specific situations, and thus children must also be able to spot what is going on in a specific situation and focus on it. This is sampled in Picture Arrangement. Both the MAPS and the World Test provide excellent opportunities for children to demonstrate their social discrimination. The MAPS with its numerous figures of all ages,

*See Chapter 16 for further discussion of this syndrome.

sexes—even races—and of both real and fantasy figures gives children a chance both to find the type of person they need for a specific fantasy situation and to assign roles to these characters. Younger children, under age 8, often do not make much discrimination among the stimuli provided by the test but assign roles in general as fantasies guide them. In contrast, the older latency children and adolescents will look for figures to match whatever fantasies they are dreaming up. However, a younger child's consistent selection of a particular figure to play one role may be quite significant.

CASE 55

Ben, a 5-year-old boy, whose recently divorced mother often took him to bed with her, consistently selected the half-dressed and naked women of the MAPS as mother figures. Halfway along in his fantasy, he began to confuse these figures with the witch figures. He became puzzled as to which figures he should include as daddies, picking one up and then another, and putting each back. At one point he even addressed the ghost figures as daddy—then apologized for his slip of the tongue.

The way that the child relates the figures to the selected scene may also give clues as to his/her ability to discriminate socially. Younger children make what seems to be almost random assignments of the MAPS figures to the scene, albeit with idiosyncratic meanings. Considerably more discrimination would be expected of older children, and thus their slips or fantasy intrusions are even more significant.

CASE 56

Vernon, a 14-year-old voyeur, decided to stage a gun battle between cops and robbers in front of the MAPS street scene. During his search for figures for this scene, he picked up the half-dressed female figure, fingered it, looked at it, and dropped it on the stage. Ignoring the female figure for the moment, he picked up other figures but then returned to the first figure and as he noticed it on the stage, remarked, "Oh, I guess I goofed putting this one in!" Still holding it, he finally decided that he would make the whole scene very silly and put this woman in the middle of it. This intrusion of sexuality in an inappropriate form into a masculine battle scene was consistent with the child's actual social behavior. He kept company with younger boys and had not started any normal heterosexual interests.

In playing with the World Test, pre-school children use very few human figures and only slightly more animals. Often they do not discriminate between the kinds of human figures or animals. Both adults and children are considered "people" and wild and tame animals are thrown together. Soldiers may be shown going to the grocery store. The world of the latency child is somewhat more populated, and as the child grows older, he/she will begin to pick out the policeman to direct the traffic, show children going to school, and build a zoo for wild animals. One 10-year-old who decided finally to conduct a street battle in his village first made certain that all of the children were tucked inside the school-house safely. Pre-school children also tend to operate most of the equipment in the test themselves. They fly the plane, run the train, push the cars. Older children are more likely to get one of the figures to run the cars, tend the railroad station, or turn the signals in the street. Younger children dive-bomb the airplane with their hands; older children have the soldiers do the shooting while they make the noises.

Most important, children have to learn to play different roles. They have to know those settings where they can play the role of baby, those where they have to be a tough guy, those where it pays to be smart, and those where it pays to act a little stupid. They find being conforming and compliant will pay off with the teacher but not with peers on the playground. They may be able to play "tough guy" with younger brothers, but they have to be prepared for considerably more competition if they play this role with peers of their size and intelligence. Children play such a variety of roles in their attempts to maneuver and test adults that their behavior might almost be classified as "psychopathic" in an adult. For example, it is not uncommon to find that a boy, who is quite disorderly and impolite at home, who battles with his parents and resists their efforts to teach him to be "mannerly," may be quite the opposite when he enters the home of one of his friends. His mother thus will be quite surprised when the mother of the other child compliments her on how well behaved her child is. A girl's mother may find also that although her child's clothes are scattered about her room and she gets angry when told to pick them up, her schoolwork may be quite neat. Her teachers may give different reports about her. She discovers which teachers she can sass back and which ones she must say "yes, mam" and "yes, sir" to. A boy may push his brothers and sisters around if permitted to do so but be considered a nice guy by his peers and may rarely squabble with them. He may learn that dad will seldom sympathize with his hurts nor give him physical comfort but that he can always gain mother's support when he is feeling ill, hungry, or even out of sorts. On the other hand, he may learn that his mother does not understand or is not in sympathy with him when he is physically aggressive, gets into mischief, or demonstrates sexual curiosity. His father may be the one who permits him to play the aggressive and sexual male role.

Even though normal children—especially around puberty—may test many of these roles, they seldom find it possible to present so many faces consistently but, instead, adopt those that are consonant with their self-image. An inability to vary roles with different situations and people results in a social naiveté and in the extreme is charactistic of the schizoid child. At the other extreme, children who constantly change faces to fit the situation and seek to maneuver others do seem to be failing to establish an identity, and the formation of "psychopathic personalities" does become a possibility. Usually these children face a very inconsistent and frequently changing social situation. They may find marked differences between the expectations of each parent. Soon they discover how to play one against the other. They may also experience considerable differences in the expectations and mores at home and school or between the school and peers. If children are confused by marked differences in these social situations and are unable to play different roles, they may withdraw in schizoid isolation. Or, inversely, they may concentrate efforts on adjusting separately to each situation, to "getting by" as best as possible without adopting any one of these roles as an identity.

Such children often spend much of their ego energy in playing such roles, almost to the neglect of other kinds of ego functioning. Their N Achievement becomes concentrated on social role-playing rather than on schoolwork or anything else. As adults and other children find themselves maneuvered by such a child, they become more cautious with her/him, and thus they are less likely to accept the roles she/he purports to play. Such children are often hypersensitive to the feelings of others and are quick to sense rejection. They rapidly change ground, renewing their efforts to manipulate people in some other direction with even more vigor. Such social role-playing and hypersocial sensitivvity is frequently found among children who are labeled "delinquent." However, not all delinquents have this facility, nor do all children who play multiple roles necessarily become delinquent. Because such children adjust themselves chameleon-like to any social situation, their difficulty may not be obvious immediately to the assessor—at least on the first contact. The assessor, however, may come to realize halfway through the hour that he/she is being closely observed and that tiny clues he/she drops

are being picked up. On the whole, the child is attempting to give the assessor what he/she wants while at the same time not giving herself/himself away.

Case 57

Bob N, age 16, was brought to the clinic by his parents after having been expelled from school because of a locker-room theft. His mother, who made the appointment, seemed grimly angry over the telephone, and it was difficult to arrange an appointment since she seemed to have so many other things to do. She finally accepted the appointment time offered her, remarking that she should be present at the PTA meeting where she was an officer but that she was so embarrassed by Bob's behavior and expulsion that she doubted she could face the other mothers. When informed that it was the clinic's policy that the fathers also be interviewed in the initial contacts, she retorted angrily that she could not account for her husband's time and advised the clinic to call him. Finally she agreed to inform him of this clinic rule and to ask him to call the clinic.

When Bob's father called, he seemed much less concerned, remarked that he didn't see why such a fuss was being made over what he evidently considered a childish prank and said that he was getting in touch with the school to "settle everything out of court." However, he agreed to an appointment with the clinic's social worker at the same time arranged by his wife.

Bob's parents had not arrived at the time of the appointment, but Bob was in the waiting room by himself. He quickly put out his cigarette and limply shook hands with the psychologist. A tall, lean, pinched-faced youth wth a bad case of acne, he followed the psychologist down the hallway, stopping several times to run a comb through his long hair and to get a drink of water. He slouched in his chair, looking around the room, fumbling with his cigarettes, but he did not light one until given permission by the examiner.

Asked why he had come, he responded

by asking if the psychologist was not aware of the reasons, since he knew that his mother had discussed the matter over the telephone. When invited to tell his own version of the problem, he replied in an offhand manner that the vice principal, whom he referred to by last name only, had made him stay out of school for a few days. Urged to explain further, he said "It was really nothing," that what had happened was that some friends of his had been playing a joke on another kid in the locker room and had hidden his wallet. Bob averred that he had been a witness but not a participant in this "joke" and that the vice principal knew this but had suspended him because he would not tell on the other boys. He made it clear that he considered the whole incident very unimportant and inconsequential. When it was suggested to him that he might not therefore regard the incident as a reason for being referred to the psychologist, he agreed but did not comment.

He suddenly asked the psychologist if he knew of several different youngsters who were being treated in the clinic. The psychologist asked him how he happened to bring up these names, and Bob claimed he had talked to them and knew that they were coming to the clinic and that they had advised him that he was likely to meet the psychologist. Further questioning revealed that Bob had tried to obtain as much information as he could about the clinic and about the psychologist beforehand. He had even taken the trouble of finding out what kind of psychological tests might be given and what kind of questions would be asked him. When asked why he was so interested in the clinic and in the procedures since he did not really see that he had any particular problem, Bob laughed and said that he had always been kind of curious about psychology and that he thought once that he might become a psychologist and so was interested in "that sort of thing." Asked further what he expected, he replied, "'I guess you want to know all about me." The psychocologist agreed that he was willing to listen to whatever Bob needed to talk about

with someone if Bob saw some reason for it.

Bob then volunteered, "Well, I guess I do have a sexual problem." And then he paused, looking at the psychologist. "Don't you want to hear about it?" he asked. The psychologist agreed that he was willing to listen. "You won't tell my parents?" The psychologist agreed that the discussion was confidential. Bob paused again, eyed the psychologist and began, "Well you see, there is this little girl I've been making out with every once in awhile, nothing really very much you know, never did really much, never went all the way, of course, but I just kind of wondered." He then paused, looking at the psychologist. When asked why he wanted to tell the psychologist about this, he replied, "I just thought you wanted to know about those things." He could not say why he thought such information might be important in his case, nor could he think of anything else important to talk about.

When the topic returned to the reasons for his referral to the clinic, Bob made a face and commented "Oh, that!" In further discussion about his school situation, Bob agreed that he did not care much for school and that although he had made fair grades in elementary and junior high school, his high-school grades had been barely passing. He quickly said that he had full intentions, in this his senior year, of making up his grades so that he could go to college and that he had been studying extra hard this first month of the school year because he knew that he did have a lot to make up.

He then began complaining about the assignment of classes, particularly mathematics, giving a history of his difficulties in that subject that he claimed were not altogether his fault. He said he was particularly bored the previous year when he had had to repeat a basic mathematics course and had almost flunked it a second time. Further questioning revealed that he was bored in most of his other classes, and he agreed that he was tempted at times to skip them altogether. At first he denied any other previous clashes with the school authorities except for occasional truancies. At the end of the hour, Bob asked anxiously again about the psychological tests and was told that these would be given when necessary.

The social worker reported that Bob's parents also had been singularly uninformative. The parents seemed to feel that Bob had never done anything "terribly bad" but always seemed to be in hot water with the school authorities. The mother continued to be angry as she talked about the number of times that teachers and vice principals had called her into the office. She complained that she received very little help or support from her husband about Bob's school behavior. Bob's father said that he did not see that Bob had done anything more than any other kid and that he was awaiting a conference with the vice principal regarding the current incident. Nevertheless, both parents seemed to agree that they felt that Bob needed some kind of psychological help. His mother deplored his recent poor academic record and contrasted it with the excellent record of Bob's older sister who was now in college. The father too voiced the hope that the psychologist could find out "What's the matter with that kid," but could not specify what he thought was the matter. "It's hard to find out what's on his mind." The parents agreed that they might have "lost touch with Bob" and that they rarely could find out what he was doing in school or anywhere else, let alone what he thought or felt. Both felt uneasy about him but said they had no cause for complaint about this behavior at home.

When they were asked about family schedules, it was revealed that the family actually spent little time together. Mrs. N was busy many afternoons a week with her community and entertainment activities and usually arrived home around 6, the same time as Bob. She often gave Bob his dinner then and waited until later to eat with her husband, who did not arrive from work until nearer 7:30. By that time Bob was usually out of the house—"studying" with some friends. On school nights he was

usually back in the house around 10, and they thought, usually asleep by 11. On weekends also, the family went separate ways. The previous summer Bob had been old enough to get a driver's license and was given a car and gas allowance. He had a generous cash allowance each week and always seemed to have plenty of money; neither parent could understand at all why he might be even interested in stealing anyone else's money. His father did remark that at times Bob did seem to have more money than could be readily accounted for, but Bob explained that he had been saving up allowance and his lunch money.

After these interviews the psychologist, with the permission of the parents, contacted the school vice principal. The vice principal confirmed that Bob had maintained that he was not involved in the theft but that the physical education teacher had found the missing wallet among Bob's possessions in his locker. Bob vehemently denied any knowledge of how the wallet came into his locker and tried to maintain that it was all a practical joke. The boy whose wallet was missing had claimed that Bob had stolen other things from him, and the two boys who were also implicated in this theft claimed that they had merely accepted money from Bob out of the wallet. The vice principal did not believe Bob's story but said that Bob told stories so convincingly that it was often difficult to know what to believe.

It was not the first time that Bob had been implicated in a theft, but there had never been any proof before that he had really been involved. Nearly all of the teachers and school authorities were, however, very suspicious of Bob. He was known as a kid who always tried to get away with things. He always seemed to have some good excuse and to be very pleasant about it; a "charmer," said one teacher. If caught red handed at some misdemeanor, he would apologize and try to make friends with the teacher or school authority. Several times it was suspected that he had forged notes to have himself excused from classes, but the school had found it difficult to contact his parents to find out if they had signed the notes.

An hour prior to the next appointment, the mother phoned to inform the clinic that she would not be able to come in because of a previous engagement but assured the social worker that Bob would appear. No information was given concerning Mr. N's appointment, and he did not appear either. When Bob was asked about the fact that his parents did not come in, he shrugged his shoulders and remarked that he guessed that they were busy. When the psychologist asked if this might mean that they did not really consider Bob's problem very important, his face flushed and he bit his lip and replied in a manner as nonchalant as possible, "Well, you might think that." But he seemed to collect himself quickly and added, "It's really my problem, of course, and I am sure that they will be able to give you any information that you wish."

However, Bob disclaimed any knowledge of what his parents might have to say or even how they might feel about the incident at school. Pressed further, Bob said that he did not think that his father was very concerned about it, adding that "Dad always seems to find ways out of things." He could not explain this statement further but backtracked to emphasize that he had never really had any brush with his father and so was under the impression that this incident probably would not bother him much. As to his mother's feelings, Bob smiled wryly and remarked that he was sorry if it embarrassed her. He realized that she was most concerned about what other people might think because of these allegiations. Asked if he thought she would be concerned if no one else heard of it, Bob said, "What do you think?"

The psychologist reminded Bob that he had remarked in the previous hour that perhaps the clinic should know "all about him" and asked Bob if there were things in his background that it might be helpful to discuss. Bob shrugged and said, "Ask me." However, it provided very difficult to get

any kind of history out of Bob. He knew very little about his family except that his grandfather was reputed to have had quite a bit of money. The most he could remember about his early childhood years was that the family had moved around to several different towns and that he had attended at least four different elementary schools by the time that he was 10 years old.

At that time his maternal grandfather died, leaving the family enough money to buy a home in a very nice district of town. His father had been a railroad engineer but at his mother's insistence had quit his job so that their life would not be quite as irregular. Bob was not even quite sure what his father did for a living, but said that it had something to do with his grandfather's business that he now operated, along with his mother's two brothers.

At age 10, Bob contracted rheumatic fever and was out of school for almost a year. He seemed to remember this year almost enjoyably; he was waited on hand and foot by his mother and sister. "I never had it so good." When he did return to school, he was restricted from most physical-education activities, and it was only in this current year of school that he was permitted to be enrolled in a physical-education class on a limited basis. He denied that this limitation on his physical activities bothered him at all, claiming that he never was interested in sports and that he considered athletes to be "stupid." He denied also that he had lost interest in school while ill or that he had fallen behind in his studies.

The junior high school that he formerly attended emphasized sports. The psychologist knew that the vice principal had been a football hero and that athletic competition had an important value among children at this school. Despite his denial of any interest in sports, Bob boasted that he had been invited several times to play basketball and that he had been one of the taller boys in the junior high school. He made further disparaging remarks about this school, and it was brought out that he really knew very few of the children there, most of whom had come from fairly stable families and had lived in the same neighborhood for many years. The student body was dominated by rather exclusive cliques. As a relative stranger, Bob had found it difficult to make friends.

Furthermore, the school district was divided rather strangely, so that when he started high school most of the children he did know at junior high school went to a different high school while his home lay within a district in which the high school was quite distant from his home. Thus he again found himself in among strangers. This school contained many children from lower socioeconomic strata. Again the sports program dominated the social scene. However, academic achievement was not held in high value by his peers. Bob denied that he lacked friends but when asked more specifically, he maintained that he preferred to go with one or two fellows. He claimed that the two boys allegedly involved in the theft were among his best friends and also named as friends two delinquent boys who were also patients at the clinic.

At this point Bob suddenly asked the assessor what he thought of what Bob had told him the previous hour about his girlfriend. The psychologist remarked that he thought that there was something there that concerned Bob but that he was not quite sure what it was. Bob smiled and remarked that what he had told the psychologist was not at all true and that he had made this all up because he had thought that psychologists were interested in "boys and girls and sex." The psychologist assured Bob that it was not necessary to make anything up just to interest him but rather that he was mainly interested in what concerned Bob. Bob suddenly admitted that he was unhappy that he did not have a girl friend, particularly since both of his friends were interested in girls and "make out all the time." The examiner agreed that this would be a definite concern and that it was only natural that one might at least pretend

publicly that he had a girlfriend so that he would not be embarrassed. He suggested that this might be somthing that Bob would like to talk over further at a later time.

Because the school was asking for some advice from the clinic about Bob, particularly regarding the possibility of readmitting him, the psychologist had been urged to complete his assessment at the earliest possible time. As part of the assessment, the psychologist had planned to use techniques other than the interview to explore Bob's social attitudes and his handling of affect and because of his recent poor school achievement, some measure of his current intellectual functioning. On the WAIS, Bob attained a Full Scale IQ of 119, a Verbal scala of 110, but a Performance scale of 128. Both his Vocabulary and Information subtest scores were quite superior and his verbal reasoning on the Similarities subtest was also above average. He made rather stumbling, hasty errors on the Arithmetic subtest, but his real difficulty proved to be on Comprehension. For example, he said, "The smart thing to do (when a person saw a fire start at a movie) was to slip out the side exit and avoid the mob." People should avoid "bad company" because "they aren't any fun." (It seemed as though he interpreted the word *bad* as meaning uninteresting.) Criminals are locked up, Bob thought, "because that's what happens when they get caught." The proverb Strike while the iron is hot did not mean much to Bob, but he speculated that perhaps it would indicate that one should hit anyone who was angry and thus cool him down. He seemed to sense that he was not doing very well on these items and remarked after the last response, "I guess I'm not doing too hot. Is that what you wanted?" In contrasting his responses to the Comprehension test with those on the Picture Arrangement, it was noted that Bob succeeded in arranging all of the sequences correctly and with full-time credit on all but the final one.

On the Rorschach Bob studied each card for many seconds before responding and then usually gave some rather stereotyped and innocuous form response. None of his responses had any human movement; only 2 of his 15 responses contained animal movement, and the balance of his responses, except for 1, was based purely on the form of his concept. The other response was the popular green worm on Card X. Out of these 15 responses, 6 were popular and none original. There were no human figures, even human detail, anywhere in his responses. In a "testing of the limits," Bob readily agreed that the two figures on Card III did look human and perhaps in movement but remarked, "I didn't know you wanted that kind of thing."

He was most uneasy with the TAT, claiming that he had no imagination and thus could not think of any stories. Again, he stared at the pictures for a long time before attempting any kind of response and then often merely described the cards. He denied that he could imagine in any way why the boy in Picture 1 had stopped playing the violin, except that perhaps he just was not interested anymore. He could not imagine why he had been playing the violin in the first place or what he might be thinking at present. "You can't tell about a guy from the way he looks." Most of his other stories were similar. To Card 6BM, he remarked, "It looks like the old lady is giving him hell for something but I can't tell what. The boy in the picture is just taking it for right now and knows that the old lady will forget it later. So he just goes and does what he wants anyhow. She gets mad, but she gets over it. Guess that tells you all about me and my mom, doesn't it?"

Bob's drawing of a person, which he was also reluctant to attempt, was somewhat bizarre. The figure looked like a child with a big head and grin. Bob spent a considerable amount of time drawing the body of a rather muscular male figure, carefully shading in the shirt and trousers and finally putting two large guns in the figure's hands. He laughed at his drawing and remarked how silly it looked but could make no associations to it, just remarking that it was a ridiculous figure. He begged off drawing any female figure, and as the hour was growing late, the examiner excused him.

A further appointment was made with the parents, but neither of them appeared. When they were called, Mrs. N apologized and explained that Mr. N had been able to settle things with the school. Since it seemed quite evident that the N's were not motivated to seek any further help, the case was closed at this point. Three years later the clinic received a letter from the dean of men at a state college requesting a report of the clinic's findings on Bob, explaining that he was currently suspended for allegedly cheating on an examination.

Another syndrome, which may be called "social retardation," is so widespread and is so commonly referred specifically to the psychologist for assessment that it warrants special consideration at this point. The model case is that of a child just entering pubescence who has always needed special help in schooling and who has been slow to learn how to take care of himself/herself. Often such children are quite capable at home and even at school in many ways. They read slowly, do some simple arithmetic even more slowly, but they are basically literate at about the third- or fourth-grade level. They find their way to and from school and can even be trusted on brief and simple errands. However, their social naiveté is obvious to all. Peers reject them because they do not recognize the unspoken relationships and rules in their peer group. In fact, in many instances they ignore the open and declared rules. Their parents are often embarrassed by their failure to learn how to "behave." They may have learned the words of politeness—even using them more compulsively and routinely than many other children. However, they remain very gauche, approaching strangers in such an open-faced manner that their parents fear that someone may take advantage of them. The family is tempted to hide them when guests come because they seem so socially childlike. Despite their relative successes at school, the parents begin to worry that they will "never grow up." They voice a fear that they will not be able to earn a living, not because they cannot work or do many simple jobs, but because others will reject them. More covertly, but with even greater intensity, the parents are fearful about the child's naiveté because she/he is approaching puberty and they realize that the child's lack of social know-how may cause problems with her/his social-sexual behavior, which will be learned on entering adolescence. Case 4, in Chapter 1 illustrates this.

This syndrome has many causes. Sometimes it is associated with a very mild central-nervous-system dysfunctioning, but in the majority of cases the neurological examination is essentially negative. Far more frequently the child has some mild physical handicap that may not even be noticeable but that makes her/him feel helpless and inadequate. In such cases there is often evidence that the child unconsciously plays the role of social inadequacy because he/she feels helpless and unable to get along socially. Most frequently such social retardation is a reaction formation against parental demands and expectations that the child act in a socially independent fashion. In this passive refusal to recognize social nuances, the child often arouses hostility and rejection and thus his/her course of action is basically hostile. The essential hostility in the parent–child relationships that underlie this social-naiveté syndrome is often demonstrated in the extremely phobic responses that the child makes to associative techniques. Even more dramatically, his/her anger becomes overt when some adult does not "play the game." Various attempts to retrain such children are often met with storms of anger. These children will scream repeatedly that they do not understand.

The compulsive, almost perseverative nature of such a child's social behavior is manifested not only in the simple and persistive responses she/he makes to everyone but in fantasies as well. TAT heroes will have few or no definite characteristics, and they behave in similar ways in story after story. It is often difficult for such children to differentiate one character from another in a TAT story. If someone is angry, the child may switch in the middle of the story and have another person be angry—then be unable to remember exactly who got angry about what. Drawings, which may score above the retarded level on the Goodenough Scale, will nevertheless look stiff and stereotyped. Sex differentiations on these drawings are usually vague. Nor are such children able to make any clear-cut identifications or personality descriptions of their drawings.

At the other end of the continuum, the child who is hypersensitive to social stimuli may be either excessively shy or precociously socially adept—or even both. A child who has been trained to be observant of others' feelings and to be aware of what others might do to him/her learns to be quite cautious. Some children who seem at first glance to be shy or withdrawn are merely standing to one side, carefully studying what is expected of them and what others are like. The training of the child to be socially perceptive is highly emphasized in Oriental cultures, especially among the Chinese. Such acuity in the observation of social rules and behaviors is taught to children—both consciously and unconsciously—by parents in any socially segregated group. Children of minority groups often have to learn several sets of spoken and unspoken rules and how to get along at several levels of society. They rapidly learn how to differentiate between life in the segregated ghetto and how to behave as they accompany their mother as a domestic in homes of the well-to-do or even when they cross town on a legally nonsegregated bus. In essence, social discrimination forces the black child to become more discriminative.

The responses of a child with a hypersensitivity to social stimuli contrast sharply with those of higher counterpart—the socially retarded child. Considering the indices mentioned before, the very socially aware child usually makes somewhat higher scores on both Comprehension and Picture Arrangement on the Wechsler but not necessarily superior scores. He/she is likely to hedge answers to the Comprehension subscale with many qualifications, sometimes to the extent that he/she may slightly contaminate the response. For example, one such child considered seriously the question "Why should one stay away from bad company?" and finally explained that he himself would not be so afraid that he would be influenced but that children who acted bad made other people angry and that he did not like to be in the middle of an angry situation. His sensitivity in interpersonal relationships also confused him when he came to the question of why women and children should be saved first in a shipwreck. His answer was that daddies might feel a lot worse if mothers and children were killed than mothers and children might feel if daddies were killed. He then thought this answer over and said that he was not sure of it because he thought that children would always feel bad if their daddies died instead of them. Thus his sensitivity prevented him from taking an objective viewpoint and illustrates how children who are quite socially sensitive can actually be somewhat stultified when it comes to making intellectual differentiations about social siuations. Similarly on the Picture Arrangement subtest, such children may get all the items correct but take an abnormally long time to sort out the cards, scrutinizing each detail and trying several arrangements before deciding on a final answer.

CASE 58

Margaret, age 10, made scale scores above 12 on all subtests of the WISC, except for Picture Arrangement. There she went beyond the time limits on most of the items, and her score was only 8. Margaret had not been referred to the clinic but was seen in an extended clinical study as part of a research project. She had been selected for this individual study out of a sociometric study of the social interactions of very bright children. It was noted in the study that Margaret was a preferred partner in one-to-one relationships but was seldom chosen as a leader. Classroom and playground observations suggested that she seldom, if ever, intruded herself into any kind of activity although she was often invited by other children to participate. Her teachers rated her as a "shy-but-strange" girl. Her TAT stories were marked with a repetitive consideration of how people treated one another and what they thought of one another's treatment. Her characterizations of her heroes were very carefully and minutely drawn. These characters interacted with one another in consideration of how the other person would feel. Her plots were actually very simple, mostly in the present tense, and she often found it difficult to say what would happen next or how things would conclude. In fact, she felt very content with an elaborate statement of the interpersonal interactions without any conclusion.

Her Rorschach experience balance was "ambi-equal" with many movement and color responses, the latter being chiefly form color. Her responses frequently contained additional use of texture, such as shading in the highlighting of human faces or seeing the dual figures (as on III and VII) as having shadows. Such use of shading to denote shadows. Such use of shading to denote shadows, which this child specified, is even rarer among children than among adults. One is reminded of the Jungian concept of the shadow as the social reflection of a person's personality.

Such children are not necessarily of superior intelligence. In fact, quite often they concentrate so much of the energy of their ego into this awareness of social stimuli that they may not achieve intellectually. However, they may have considerable interest in literature or other fine arts or, as they enter high school, in the social sciences. One would imagine that if such a child learns to control and utilize this social sensitivity, he/she should eventually become an excellent psychologist. On the other hand, some children are overwhelmed by the constant influx of such stimuli and do not develop either intellectual or other defensive measures to handle and assess it. (See Section E on coping mechanisms.)

D.   INTERFERENCES

Many of the factors that interfere with the social development of the child have been discussed previously in this chapter and in the introductory chapters and do not need to be explored further at this point. The important consideration here is the interaction between two main types of interferences: (1) those that arise from within the family grouping, and (2) extrafamilial or societal interferences. As has already been discussed, families have many ways of assigning roles to children that, in effect, keep them from developing into socially effective adults. Usually such family roles are relatively satisfactory within the family group. The difficulty arises when the child plays these same roles in society outside of his family group.

For example, in a family that places an extremely high value on achievement, order, and self-control, a child may succeed in being a model of such behavior. However, he/she may find that he/she is "being good for nothing" school. Particularly, he/she may not be appreciated by peers who may see him/her as being overly competitive in classwork, a compulsive tyrant on the playground, and as being prissy and fussy. Even some teachers may be annoyed by such behavior.

In other families with the same values, the child may be assigned a negative role in the family as a failure or scapegoat. If the parents project upon the child all their fears

of failure and make him/her into the failure figure, he/she may well act out this failure syndrome at school as well as at home. Such a child may well become the socially retarded child just described. The family history and parental responses to the Edwards Personal Preference Schedule in the following case give one example of this particular syndrome.

CASE 59

Saul H, age 12, was repeating the sixth grade and it looked as though he might fail once more. The pediatrician's referral stated that although "Solly" was rather obese, he was in generally good health and that a special neurological examination had been entirely within normal limits despite his mother's continued belief that Solly might have some neurological problem. Repeated intelligence tests at school had consistently shown Saul to be functioning at an average level, although his IQ had dropped from 113 in the first grade to 102 currently in the sixth grade. Such a drop in IQ over this period of childhood might be accounted for as a simple regression toward the mean. Saul's decreasing level of achievement had, however, been much sharper than could be accounted for by the drop in IQ. Teachers noted that Saul was "immature," "more concerned with neatness than the correctness of his answers," "quibbled often and becomes mixed up in details," and "a social isolate because of the ease with which he is frustrated."

When Saul was brought to the clinic, it was obvious that his parents had made an extra effort to have him neatly dressed and groomed. Although it was a warm day, he was wearing a jacket and tie and his shoes were highly polished. Nevertheless, he had somehow succeeded in scuffing one shoe and in messing a chocolate bar across his starched white shirt. His mother was in despair because he had messed himself and was quite apologetic to the assessor about Solly's appearance. In addition, he had a slight cold, his nose was running, and his pockets were stuffed with used Kleenex that he dropped in various parts of the lobby and in the office. Saul himself could not say what he thought was wrong but did show some vague self-concern, particularly surrounding his school failure.

Saul was more open about his negative self-concept on the Sentence Completion; for example: *"I*—am a slob" and *"My father thinks*—that I can't do anything right." To the item *"Other children . . ."* Saul wrote "Who cares?" His TAT characters were often helpless and ineffective and subject to considerable criticism. One such character, the male figure in 6BM, Saul labeled as a "nebish" (a Yiddish term roughly equivalent to "stumblebum"). On the Rosenzweig's P-F Study for Children, Saul gave an unusually high number of ego-dominated, intrapunitive responses indicating that he was considerably concerned with self-blame. On the whole, intrapunitive responses dominated his P-F. His rather negative self-image was portrayed in his drawing that was of a rather tall and very thin man (in contrast to Saul's own obesity) but obviously a very awkward figure.

His difficulty in drawing, particularly in the placement of the facial features and details of the hands and feet, was so striking that the examiner thought that Saul might have some perceptual-motor handicap but Saul's performance on the Bender-Gestalt was well within normal limits. He had particular difficulty with the Rorschach because he continually criticized his own responses and thus found himself in a bind when he tried to justify inconsistent aspects of the blot. For example, he at first called detail 1 on Card VIII "a bear," but then said that it could not be a bear because it was pink. Then he could not decide whether one detail was a tail that would really make it a chipmunk or whether that was a leg and then "Where is the tail?" He frequently described things as "messy" or as "big, old, and hairy." (Using the word *hairy* to mean ugly.) Many of his responses had at least a mild phobic quality: "nutty

people from out space" or a "big, hairy, old monster," but Saul chuckled and the tone of his voice suggested that the monster was not really frightening.

Mrs. H had brought along a written list of complaints about Saul, but before she could get very far in a discussion of them, she was already mentioning her own self-recriminations over her failure to raise Saul correctly. She accused her husband of being a failure as a parent, and he retorted that she was to blame. She was especially critical of Saul because of his sloppy eating habits, his failure to clean up his room, and his continual arguments with her and her husband in their attempts to discipline him: "He's a regular attorney, just like his father." Mr. H, stung by this remark, retaliated by describing his wife as a person who kept their home "hospital clean" and who constantly nagged when anything was out of place. Mrs. H retorted that she tried to do all of these things to keep a neat home for her husband, to have meals on time, and to do things correctly because she thought that this was what he demanded. When Mr. H shrugged off her attack, she was almost in tears, declaring that she had slaved all these years to make a "decent" home and that he did not really appreciate her. Furthermore, she remarked with acid bitterness that she thought that a great deal of Saul's problems might be laid at her husband's doorstep because it was really he who constantly nagged at Saul and set high and perfectionistic standards for the child's behavior. It was Mr. H, she concluded, who consistently corrected Saul's speech, his schoolwork, his manners at the table, and his appearance.

Mr. H, now nettled, retorted that if he had not done these things Saul would be a perfect baby, that his wife spoiled Saul constantly by picking up after him, and by stuffing him with food and cooking special dishes for him until he was excessively overweight. He accused her of undermining his own attempts to discipline Saul through comforting him and giving him treats, especially when Mr. H had imposed some restriction on Saul or required some achievement from him.

As the staff reviewed this initial interview with the parents, it seemed obvious that each parent disliked their own roles, yet feared that it would displease the other if they did not play them. In subsequent interviews, this possibility was explored with them. Mrs. H admitted that she might like to have some of the privileges of her sister-in-law who "sat in bed all morning and played bridge all afternoon." Mr. H laughed and remarked, "Thank God no!" to which she said, "See see!" Mr. H, in turn, admitted that he really hated to discipline Saul and pointed out to his wife that despite his sister's seeming neglect of the household chores, she did pay attention to her children's behavior and that he envied his brother-in-law who did not have to fuss over the kids.

Both parents had been born and reared in central Europe, had endured frightful hardships during World War II, and had lost most of their relatives in concentration camps. Mr. H had just completed his training as an attorney when the war broke out, and he had fled to Switzerland where he remained working as an unskilled laborer until he was able to come to the United States. He was past 30 and spent the next three years training as an accountant since his European legal background was not accepted in the United States. He did not marry until he was almost 40 and was 43 when Saul was born. He recounted his past with considerable depression; he was particularly bitter because he wass never able to realize his career in law, and deprecated his own profession as an accountant. Although he was making a fair living, he put in many hours at his work, often arriving home after dinner, bringing work home for the weekend. His wife was critical of his working habits, complaining that he took far more pains with his work than was appreciated by his clients and that he troubled himself unnecessarily with many details. Moreover, she complained that he had difficulty in collecting his fees because he

was not aggressive enough. She had tried many times to help him in his work, but there was so much disagreement between them that she no longer went to the office with him.

Mrs. H, who was 10 years her husband's junior, had been hidden in an attic during the war in Holland in a way similar to that described in *The Diary of Anne Frank*. This situation had required very strict compliance to routine as a life-saving measure. She had had little formal education, but her father, who was a religious scholar and teacher, had successfully carried on the education of his children during their long years of hiding. It was one of her regrets that she had never received any kind of formal certification for her education. She was very embarrassed by her European accent, which persisted despite her several years in high school in classes in English for the foreign born. Consequently, there was considerable carping in this family over the correct way to speak. Mr. H took advantage of his wife's self-concerns to note that despite her avowed efforts to speak English correctly she frequently lapsed into Yiddish when she was upset or when she wanted to discuss things with him that she did not want Saul to understand. Mrs. H complained that Saul was critical of both of them for theeir accents but that Solly had made particularly poor grades in English and grammar.

The profiles of scores on the Edwards' Personal Preference Schedule for both Mr. and Mrs. H were remarkably similar. Both had scores above the seventieth percentile on need achievement and need order and above the ninetieth percentile on need abasement. This pattern of scores, along with a relatively low score on need aggression, suggested that both set relatively high standards for themselves and were also quite self-critical and unable to really allow themselves to actively seek their goals. Both parents also made above-average scores on Nutriance, suggesting that both (particularly the mother) placed a high value on waiting on others while, at the same time, both gave only few responses placing any value on Succorance (particularly the father), suggesting that they did not allow themselves much satisfaction through receiving help from others. This latter set of scores seemed to be most important, as it indicated that both were denying themselves in an almost martyrish fashion in an attempt to find satisfaction through Saul, yet were constantly failing to meet their need achievement through him also. Saul, in turn, appeared to be acting out the needs of both parents to lower their need achievement to a more realistic level and was reflecting their own self-deprecations and need abasement. It thus seemed that Saul was a "failure" because the parents saw themselves as second-class citizens who constantly failed to meet their own high ambitions.

Saul's case thus illustrates how an intra-familial group pattern can be reflected out onto society, in this case in the classroom. However, the child also can disrupt the family group with pressures experienced elsewhere. In a sense, this also happened in Saul's case, since the kinds of demands for achievement and for interpersonal relationships that he found at school were not satisfied by the kinds of responses he had learned at home.

The backwash of social problems into the home and the working through of these extrafamilial conflicts within the family setting are very common during adolescence. A seemingly peaceful family life may be disrupted when the child attempts to insert peer mores into it that may be quite inappropriate. Whether the family accepts the adolescent's attempt to adopt and internalize these peer standards will depend upon how rigidly the family had insisted upon its own internal regulatory measures. If the family is quite rigid, then the intrusion of these new mores may be disturbing. A child who comes from a family that might be described as "close knit" may find adolescence quite unacceptable by previously approving parents, chiefly because adolescence breaks family ties. Many chil-

dren from such families seem unconsciously to recognize that their peer standards will be unacceptable to the family and thus avoid becoming engaged in them. At least they are cautious about admitting to the family that they are interested in such peer activities. On the other hand, the same child may be most fascinated by those very peer activities that might be most disturbing to the family in his/her effort to free himself/herself from the closeness of the family group.

CASE 60

The L family is a good example. All members of this family were very intelligent and energetic people. Mr. L, who made only a modest living, had nevertheless devoted all of his limited finances to his home and family, to the exclusion of any recreation for his wife or himself. Their large home with a swimming pool was obviously beyond their means. Mr L took the bus and carried his lunch to work because they could only afford the single large station wagon that Mrs. L used to transport the children. All the L's time was spent in family activities. Although each child attended a school that started at a time different from Mr. L's own work hours, the entire family was aroused early in the morning so that they spent their early morning hours and breakfast together. Similarly, dinner was delayed until the entire family could be gathered. Even homework was a family-centered activity in which the parents participated by going from room to room where each child studied. All participated actively in church activities. Although Mr. L had a "bad back," he continually strained himself by participating in the Little League with the boys and in family outings and camping and teaching his girls to dance. Each member of the family played a different musical instrument, and Mrs. L was very proud of their joint musical efforts that were displayed annually to all the L's friends in a huge Christmas party when they performed as a group. Seldom did the six L children go to other children's houses to play, but their playmates were constantly brought to their home.

When the oldest boy went away to college, he had never spent a night away from his family. The family came to the clinic when the second oldest of their two daughters, Stella, age 16, began spending many more hours with her peers than with her family. She began dressing in the most outlandish style, and she utterly refused to permit her parents to meet her boyfriends. Stella angrily declared that she would not permit her father to interrogate her boyfriends as she had seen him do with her older sister and with her older brother whom she declared "would not know what to do with a girl if he saw a live one." Her twin brothers, age 14, were also making many complaints against their father and then against their mother for supporting him. The twins also protested against their 10-year-old sister because she was playing the role of "little angel" in the family and their father held up her behavior to them as indicating a person who appreciated parental affection and family life.

The father's appeal for help from the clinic was heightened when his college son came home dressed in a very casual style, his hair uncut, and especially when he started an argument at the dinner table over the use of marijuana. Previously, intellectual discussions of the news of the world and of the daily comings and goings of the family members were commonly reported and commented upon during dinner. Much to the children's amazement, the father became outraged when this topic was brought up and forbade its discussion. Mr. L's behavior on this occasion was so unusual that even Mrs. L was quite concerned. After the initial interview with the parents, it was decided to initiate a brief series of family sessions. Only six sessions were required for the children to express more openly their need for extrafamilial identifications and for the parents to express their feelings of loss and yet to recognize that such activities and interests were to be expected.

Problems frequently arise in families, as is shown in the preceding example, because of the rigidity of the family structure in the face of extrafamilial pressures. Moreover, as described in Chapter 12, current social institutions frequently create almost overwhelming pressures on almost any family. The isolation of the nuclear family from any clan grouping, the constant mobility of the American family, the alienation of the individual in the mass culture, the new demands of technology for new skills and achievements, and the resultant alienation of the individual in the mass society all create problems for social development for every child. These problems are mentioned here for a second time to emphasize the necessity for the assessment of their effects in every case. It is necessary for the assessor to investigate how the child and his/her family are meeting these social stresses, what they mean to this particular family, and how the parents and child are coping with them. Although these stresses can disrupt development at any point in the child's life, it is more often that they become most marked at puberty. Thus one should almost routinely ask how many times the family has had to move, what has happened to family possessions and ambitions because of such moves, and how the family is meeting the problems of social and technological change.

The chief technique for assessing such stresses is, of course, the interview with the parents. However, it is often possible that the parents do not recognize the stresses that they themselves are under, and hints from the child may give clues concerning what should be explored with the parents. The following case summary may suffice as an example.

Case 61

Ricky M, age 4, had been referred for psychological assessment by the pediatrician who had examined him when his mother had become worried over his listlessness, loss of appetite, interrupted sleep habits, and behavior at nursery school where he was reluctant to separate from her and seemed unable to join spontaneously in school activities. The pediatrician found Ricky to be in good health and felt that the boy might be depressed.

The possibility that there might be extraneous social pressures on this family was noticed immediately when it was discovered that both parents were working and it was difficult for them to find time for an appointment at the clinic. Mr. M was employed full time as an electronics technician, a trade he had learned in the navy. He was also attempting to continue his education as an electronics engineer by attending university classes at night. This young couple had recently moved to Los Angeles from the Midwest where Mrs. M had been living with her parents until her husband's discharge from the navy approximately six months previously. Determined to establish a home for his wife and child, Mr. M had immediately purchased a tract house, which also demanded a considerable amount of his energy since it was not landscaped. The couple were also trying to pay for their new furnishings and to keep up the repairs on an old car. However, these facts were not immediately brought out in the interview since both parents were preoccupied with Ricky's problems and did not perceive their pressures as related to him.

In the initial playroom contact with Ricky, he preoccupied himself with the play house and dolls and enacted the parents' comings and goings and concerns. In this play Ricky had the baby left alone while the parents were preoccupied. Asked how the baby felt Ricky stopped his play and sat very quietly, looking as if he was about to cry. Among his stories to the CAT, the following responses particularly suggested that his depression might be associated with the separation anxiety he experienced because of the busy routine of his parents.

CARD 1: "The mommy is feeding the babies. Daddy isn't home yet. (How do the babies feel?) They save some for daddy."

CARD 2: "The baby is pulling on the rope. He wants to get them to come with him. (Who should come with him?) His mommy and daddy."

CARD 3: "The mouse comes out to see if the big tiger is still there." (Why?) 'Cause it's time for him to go to work."

CARD 9: "He's all alone. (How come?) Everybody's gone. All gone. (What does he do?) Cries."

Subsequently, the parents' situation was discussed with them; both admitted that they were somewhat depressed and felt under considerable pressure in their situation. Mrs. M began to talk about her feelings of loneliness in leaving her hometown and friends. Mr. M talked of his daydreams during his navy years of having a home for his wife and baby and his disappointment since he currently was almost exhausted by the strain of trying to attain them. Mrs. M reported that her parents had offered to loan the couple money to ease their house payments, but Mr. M had felt that he had already asked too much of them as they had cared for his wife and baby during his stint in the navy. He agreed that although it might hurt his pride slightly to accept this loan, it would make it possible for his wife to stop working.

After several interviews, this couple seemed to have some insight into the social pressures that they were under and were planning steps to change part of their arrangement. Mr. M decided to accept the loan from his in-laws and to register for the summer session as he had previously planned. That fall Mrs. M dropped by the clinic after a routine visit to the pediatrician to report that Ricky had blossomed during the summer while she was home and that she and her husband were attempting to lead slightly more relaxed lives although both were determined that he should continue to try to finish his college education. She did, however, plan to delay returning to full-time employment until after Ricky was well established in school. She also confided in the social worker that both of them were disappointed because they could not enlarge their family at this point. However, a year later Mrs. M again dropped by the clinic to show the social worker a new baby. She admitted that the family was again under considerable strain because Mr. M had finally decided to go to school full time on the GI Bill, which really limited their finances since she was unable to work. However, both of them were now fairly cognizant of the strains that they were enduring and were making efforts to make sure that these were not reflected in their relationships with their children. Ricky at this time was attending school and seemed "to be doing very nicely." Despite the increased social pressures, Mrs. M did not look nearly as depressed as she had when she first came to the clinic, and she reported that her husband seemed to be enjoying a very busy and strenuous life.

E.   COPING MECHANISMS

The myriad ways in which children cope with interferences in social development almost defy classification. Many of these have been described at various points throughout the previous and present chapters. A majority of these coping mechanisms reflect aspects of what has been already discussed as the process of internalization, in which children cope with social stimuli by making them parts of themselves. They adopt the family rules as their own, thus identifying with the parents. In a similar process during latency, children incorporate and internalize the extrafamilial, societal mores. Seldom if ever, however, are they able to internalize all the various stresses from this social environment and some of them therefore remain ego alien. Thus children in general handle such social stresses by either internalization or alienation or a combination of both. As children's abilities to focus upon and to discriminate various kinds of social stimuli become increasingly acute, it becomes more possible for them to accept and to internalize some parts of a social milieu and to reject others.

Sometimes children can internalize two quite inconsistent or even conflicting viewpoints that may not, however, actually become conflicting unless they encounter situations in which they must make a decision between them. For example, it is commonly believed by males in a sexist society that the only marriageable women are virgins—like one's mother. Many men holding this viewpoint also believe that any sexually approachable woman is a prostitute at heart. This virgin–prostitute attitude toward women is so widespread in Western culture, handed down as it is from father to son by looks, titters, and tone of voice, that it is well accepted by most 12-year-old boys—and many 12-year-old girls. For some teen-agers such a mythology, if accepted, can create a serious block on adolescent heterosexuality. A young man who believes both of these myths might well feel that he should abstain from any normal heterosexual activity, such as dating, dancing, or petting, for fear that on the one hand he might be guilty of "ruining" one of the virgins or, on the other, of being entrapped by one of the prostitutes. However, most young men succeed in refusing to accept one or the other side of this dilemma. Either they hysterically block out the prostitute side of the myth and thus presume that they are always pursuing only good girls, or they cynically decide there is no such thing as a virgin. Such a mythology is even more devastating to a young woman, who is often not sure which role she is expected to play and what kind of identity is being imposed on her. If she acts in a sexually provocative manner (and finds this hard to control), then she may fear that she will be looked upon as one of the prostitutes. If she does not behave in this way, then she may fear that she will be unattractive.

Another common sexist set of conflicting viewpoints surrounds aggression. Boys are urged to be competitive, to be aggressive in sports or in business, or even to be intellectually aggressive. At the same time any aggressiveness that adults may not necessarily associate with achievement is constantly dampened with "do's" and "don'ts" throughout childhood. Many children do learn rapidly to discriminate between where aggressivity is approved and where it is disapproved. Yet gross inconsistencies regarding aggression are prevalent throughout our society and are often quite confusing to children. Many teen-agers today are well aware of the biblical commandment "Thou shalt not kill" and reject the government's encouragement of young men to join the military service and to kill the enemy.

Because of these and other similar inconsistencies in the American value system, the disillusionment of the current generation of adolescents is more extreme than that experienced by other recent generations. Many brighter and more sensitive adolescents seriously question and consider alien many of the major social viewpoints held by their elders and the majority of society. However, when children find social dictums unacceptable, they also experience—anomie—and an emptiness of identity.

Children may use many other defenses when they are faced with conflicting ideologies or when they wish to hide the fact that an ideology is alien to them. Many adolescents may mask their feelings of alienation by simple suppression or repression. The surfer, for example, runs off to the beach and forgets about social problems. Others "drop out," projecting the conflict onto parents, schools, or other authorities. These adolescents view the adult as having the conflicting viewpoint—not themselves. They tend to use such conflicts of ideology that they can pick out and enlarge upon from the adult world to mask and detract from some of their own personal conflicts. The brighter and more sensitive adolescent hopes idealistically to resolve the conflicts, but she/he often admits to moments of confusion and feelings of helplessness.

Another common way children have of coping with ideological conflicts is to isolate or compartmentalize one set of values from another. A child adopts and uses an ideology when it is handy, appropriate, and approved of. But he/she may ignore it when it is inappropriate. Younger children often utilize this isolation of ideological conflicts far more readily than adults, since their internalization of ideology is still in process and is not nearly as rigidly fixed. For example, I interviewed children in the "authoritarian-personality" study of Frenkel-Brunswik (1951). On the ethnocentric scale in the interviews and on the special TAT, a 10-year-old white girl who had recently moved to California from the Deep South showed many signs of race prejudice, ethnocentrism, as well as an authoritarian viewpoint. When dismissed from the interview and permitted to attend recess on the schoolground, she was observed playing happily with a black and a Mexican American. As she returned to the classroom, I invited her back in for a few extra minutes of interview and remarked on her behavior. She replied that I did not understand; what she had told me was quite true. Yet, she said, "It is like a stoplight at the street corner. If you are there with your mother and the light is red, you stop. If the light is red and traffic is coming, you stop. If there is nobody with you and there is no traffic coming, and the light is red, you may still go on."

The way in which a child handles social inconsistency or discrepancy often is very comparable to, if not actually part of, the way he/she learns to handle any kind of perceptual inconsistency. Thus the compulsive child who is bewildered by changes in routine, imperfections, or other perceptual detractions very likely will be unable to handle socially conflicting stimuli. The child with a perceptual-motor handicap may have difficulty with social perceptions, and it is frequently difficult to decide which is primary—the social or the sensory perceptual difficulty. The child who shows a perceptual-motor blocking only after he/she enters school may actually be generalizing a difficulty in making social discriminations to making other kinds of perceptual discriminations. Such a regressive reaction to social conflicts is not uncommon in the latency child. For example, the child may be led to school, urged to achieve, and taught to honor his/her father and mother. At the same time, he/she may resent being pushed out of the nest—especially if he/she has been insecure or if a rival younger sibling is going to enjoy much more of the parents' attention. Thus, the child may unconsciously mess her/his way through a Bender-Gestalt just as she/he behaves childishly in other situations to avoid resolution of social and emotional problems. It is for such reasons that Koppitz (1963) carefully avoids designation of any particular etiology in her measures of perceptual-motor development.

When such simple perceptual difficulty arises in the context of social conflicts, the assessor should take note of the possibility of *social*-perceptual rather than merely visual-perceptual regression. For example, if "minus" responses on a latency or teen-aged child's Rorschach are present—particularly where some human figure in interaction is commonly seen—one might well suspect that this child may be having some difficulty in internalizing social perceptions. A good example here is where the child over age 8 is unable to see the common M response on Card III and gives some distorted or vague response, such as a "beetle" or "crab," to D1. Another common distortion occurs in responses to D1 of Card VIII, to which the popular response is an animal walking or climbing. Most children ignore the fact that this "bear" happens to be pink. However, the child who is concerned with the color of the bear may be indicating some difficulty in the social integration of his/her impulse life with emotional contacts with the environment. Of course, no one such response is predictive of such a difficulty, but such a clue puts the assessor on the alert to examine the data further for other possible indicators. Conflicts of ideology or of internalized social

attitudes are also commonly portrayed in TAT stories and acted out on the MAPS.

F.   THE CONTENT OF SOCIAL FUNCTIONING: ANIMISM, CONCRETIZING, AND DEPERSONALIZATION

Although there are many more kinds of childhood social behaviors than can be covered in this book, it is to be hoped that those already discussed and illustrated in this chapter and in Chapter 2 will serve the purpose of orienting the student to the recognition and understanding of this aspect of the child's ego. Instead of further attempting to catalog these social behaviors, it may be helpful to consider three common ways in which children commonly conceptualize social interactions: (1) animism, (2) concretizing, and (3) depersonalization. As will be seen, each of these forms occurs as a part of the *normal* development of most children. It is only when the child uses any one of these exclusive of reality testing or persists in using them that social development is deterred. When such conceptualizations are used by an adult, they are symptoms of a severe psychological disturbance.

1.   Animism

Animism is a term from anthropology originally used to denote the attribution of a human life to plants, stones, and other inanimate objects. As pre-school children imitate adult behavior with dolls and teddy bears, they also conceptualize the doll is alive. They may see objects as containing threats or promises, much as adults use charms or omens, but for children these objects are very much alive. It is not at all unusual for pre-school children to have toys or even trees or other objects that they talk to and treat as friends. They need a night-light to protect them from unfriendly, harmful objects who may come to life in the dark. Although adults may perceive that these are projections of children's affections and fears, to pre-schoolers they are very real. By the time they enter school, children usually no longer need these inanimate friends and enemies. Not only have they begun to repress fantasy in general and to explore and test reality, but they usually have plenty of friends and some real enemies among their peers.

Animistic conceptualizations are thus the first steps in the development of the child's formulations about social experiences. Through such animisms the child re-enacts his/her social experiences and affects. Psychologists utilize this tendency of the young child to humanize inanimate objects when they involve the child in doll play or present cards with animal subjects as stimuli, as on the CAT. On pre-school IQ scales (Merrill-Palmer, Year II), the child is instructed to "make the block walk like I did." This animation of the inanimate was recognized by Rorschach as he studied the internalization of kinesthetic experience. According to Ames and colleagues (1974), inanimate movement is a precursor of human movement and reaches a peak at age 5. Typical is the previously mentioned response of a bright 4-year-old to Card II (inverted): "It's an O walking." She saw the space D5 as the O and D2 as the feet.

The socially isolated or lonely child may persist in using animasms for many years, substituting stuffed animals or other objects for friends. So do children who have met with continued rebuff and rejection. Animistic conceptualizations are often part of the phobic child's fantasy life.

CASE 62

Maria, age 8, had an extensive and almost systematized set of objects that were either good or bad, safe or poisonous, which in effect constituted a delusional scheme. Many objects in her house were evil to her and threatened to turn her into a witch. She could not touch them, sit on them, or go near them. Other objects were safe or even constituted refuges where she could hide

from the evil objects. Objects as well as gestures could combat and destroy the evil if she become accidently contaminated. Her preoccupation with these phobias was so extensive that she could scarcely eat or sleep, let alone go to school. Often she lay awake at night in terror, lest she had accidently contaminated herself and would become an evil person who might kill someone.

Her father, a poorly educated but highly successful businessman, considered her to be a contrary and obstinate child and punished her severely for her "silly habits" and thoughts. Her older sister made fun of her and used her fears to control Maria and to gain advantage in the father's eyes. Neither the father nor the teen-aged sister seemed at all aware that Maria's phobias had set in coincident with the death of her mother. Maria had really not known her mother who had been an invalid and who was isolated in a separate room for the first four years of Maria's life.

In the initial interview, Maria recalled with tears her memories of her mother's screams in the night as she lay dying of cancer. Maria readily admitted that she associated many objects in the house with her mother, either negatively or positively. The negative objects proved to be where Maria had happened to be sitting or things she was using when she felt angry at her mother or frightened by the recognition of her mother's dying. Other objects she had touched or used when she was dreaming of her mother's returning from death. Each object seemed to take on a different part of her associations and her relationship with her mother and thus became part of her own fears and hostilities. Maria's responses to the Rorschach and other associative stimuli were similarly both highly phobic in content and distorted in form.

2. Concretizing

At other times, children conceptualize human relationships and social stimuli in a very opposite and yet analogous form, that is, as if such social stimuli were actually inanimate. For want of a better term, this form of conceptualizing social experiences may be called *concretizing*. Such concretizing, although fairly common among preschool children, does not seem as well-recognized as animistic thinking. More often concretizing appears to be merely a misunderstanding and, in fact, often originates in an inability to understand a concrete term. The child hears an adult use an abstraction or analogy to describe a person or a social experience, and then conceives of the abstraction in concrete terms. For example, one 4-year-old child heard his mother exclaim to her professor–husband, "I can read you like a book!" Later the mother discovered the boy staring at his father and discovered that he was trying to "read" him. Even after she explained her analogy, the child persisted in concretizing his relationship with his father, noting that his father "always reads books." To this child, his erudite and literate father was a book. Years later he referred to his father as "bookish" and suddenly recalled his original concretism.

CASE 63

Mark, age 6, who seemed to be having some difficulty conforming to and understanding the school rules, was asked about such rules. The child seemed at first to misunderstand the question and talked about "rulers." However, as the discussion ensued, it appeared as if Mark really perceived the school regulations in terms of the measuring stick, as if they were some kind of inanimate object. His confusion in part was explained by his association to regulations as being enforced by a slap on the wrist with the ruler. As the assessment proceeded, it was evident that he also conceived of other such social concepts in very concrete, inanimate terms. His drawing of a person had a distinct robot-like quality and on the World Test he used none of the human figures. When his attention was drawn to the fact that there were human

figures available to people his village, he remarked that these were only tin people and that he wanted real people. His own speech and gestures were also quite stiff and mechanical.

That Mark probably lacked "real people" in his environment was suggested by the appearance and behavior of his father who reminded the assessor of a mannikin and who was obsequiously formal throughout the interview. Noticeably, this father referred to his child as "it." One of the complaints of the school was that Mark did not seem to realize that anyone had any feelings and was most surprised when other children complained when he hit them or interfered with their activities. Like Maria, Mark had lost his mother at an early age and had been reared largely by a succession of part-time maids and tutors and spent most of his waking hours—outside of the classroom—wandering around a large and empty house where the servants moved like shadows.

3.   Depersonalization

Here, as in concretizing, the child detaches the affective components of a social experience but without turning the experience into an inanimate form. The child often denies social interactions and behaves in a mechanical fashion as if there was no social interaction. Much of Mark's behavior might also be described as depersonalization. Again, in mild form, depersonalization is one aspect of the normal development of the child's socialization. Latency-age children in particular use this coping mechanism to water down the myriad of social exchanges that they are experiencing so they will not be overwhelmed. Although they may consciously recognize that other children—and adults—have feelings, who arouse feelings in them, they often seek to depersonalize social relationships in order to keep this affect life under control. For the 8-year-old, anything can be excused with the phrase "I didn't mean to!" The child is also implying, "It doesn't mean anything.'' In many instances, children depersonalize human relationships and social institutions in order to avoid conflicts.

CASE 64

When Herb, age 14, was asked to draw a feminine figure, he drew a highly stylized sports car instead and handed over his production claiming that he could not draw any kind of a woman and that he liked sports cars better than women anyway. As he made this statement and looked at his drawing further, he elaborately printed the word *Mother* across the car. Further investigation revealed that his life was highly programmed by his mother in almost computer style. She had arranged his time so that he was engaged in some activity at nearly every moment of his waking life. Every afternoon he was engaged in some kind of class or recreation that she had arranged for him. Dinner was served him in front of the television rather than with his parents, and during the evening hours before he went to bed, he was firmly isolated in his own room with his school books—apart from the family. His main moments of contact with his mother were in the family car when she drove him from one activity to another.

Further interviews with the mother suggested that her programming of the child's life was designed to keep him at a distance from her while she carried on her own activities. She was also very much afraid that if he did not have such a well-mapped-out life, he would become a ''delinquent teen-ager,'' meaning that his sexual interests would come to the fore. In each of these activities arranged for him, the boy also found rather mechanical and impersonal relationships. He had few or no relationships with peers in these swimming lessons, guitar lessons, or religious classes. His only friend was the apartment-house janitor whom he knew only by the name *Stovepipe,* with whom his mother had forbidden him to associate. Thus it was not entirely surprising that Herb had very little concept of others as real people with feelings or of social rules as having any humanistic meaning. The discovery of his inability to conceptualize either individuals or social groups as anything but inanimate helped in part to explain his lack of guilt after he was apprehended firing a rifle at passing cars on a highway.

CHAPTER 13

Analysis of Ego Functioning and Identity Formation

This chapter is concerned with relating assessment data to two conceptual constructs: the function of the ego as a whole and the formation of the sense of identity. As described in Chapter 2, these concepts are highly interrelated both in theory and in their behavioral manifestations. They are also quite distinct aspects of the overall functioning of the child. Both are what might be called second-level abstractions, that is, concepts that link together and integrate the generalizations that have been labeled ego functions. Thus, the term *ego* refers to all the various functions: all modalities, all input–output mechanisms, all types of focus and differentiation, all coping mechanisms, and all the various contents of all functions. The concept *identity* is yet another across-the-board conceptualization of all ego functions. Since both of these second-level abstractions are derived from the primary classifications, they depend upon the same data from which the part functions were determined. However, merely summing the various ego functions does not result in a meaningful description of the overall functioning of the ego nor of the child's sense of identity. Rather, the assessor must integrate the data and abstract from them further. These second-level generalizations, while not requiring additional data, do necessitate additional measurements or analysis of the data and other dimensions for interrelating them.

A. DIMENSIONS OF THE TOTAL FUNCTIONING OF THE EGO

Many different approaches to overall functioning of the ego have been suggested by various theorists. No brief review could possibly do justice to these theories, and such a review is beyond the purview of this book. However, there are at least three main dimensions that many theories of personality commonly utilize. The first of these might be labeled the overall "energy level" that the child seems to display and that is distributed in various amounts and various functions of the ego. The second may be referred to by the term used by Rorschach, "the experience balance," which covers many kinds of "introversion–extroversion" or "internal–externalization" concepts. The third, dilation–constriction, is also derived from the Rorschach theory and like the experience balance appears under different names in other theories, such as "expansion and restriction" or "open–closed" systems.

Energy level refers to an overall behavior pattern that is very commonly observed and noted but that is somewhat hard to define. Perhaps the psychological concept that comes to mind first is that of Freud's "libido," by which he meant the total instinctual forces of the person. Unfortunately, libido has become so confused and identified with purely sexual energies (even by many psychoanalytic writers) that it is no longer really a useful concept. Whatever term is applied, most theorists do seem to agree that children differ considerably in the amount of physiological and psychological energy they display. Physiologically, there is a fairly wide range in normal metabolism and other body functions that create physical energy. Individual differences in drive-states have not been given much attention in experimental psychology, but everyday clinical observation suggests that there is considerable variation from child to child and at various times in the child's life. Then, of course, there is the diurnal variation of sleep and wakefulness for every individual. It has been observed that high drive-states may result in either extreme tension and wakefulness or in apathy and sleep.

As regards individual differences among children, some children are quite obviously full of energy, always on the go, seem to require considerable amounts of energy-creating foods, and a minimum amount of sleep—although they might sleep quite soundly when they do sleep. Other children eat less, are more easygoing and relaxed and require more rest. These differences also occur among children who are under stress or who are experiencing a considerable amount of tension or other disturbance. Thus, the high-energy-level child who is depressed may actually show his/her depression by increasing his/her normal activity to a point of exhaustion or his/her depression may be noticeable just by the fact that his/her normal activity level drops. The tension of a normally low-energy-level child may be easy to observe, since restlessness in such a child would be a marked change. However, a slowing down of the overall activity may also be a natural reaction under stress.

Because tension and depression often mask the basic energy level of children seen in a psychological clinic, it is sometimes difficult to assess the underlying energy level from behavioral observation alone.

One of the best indicators is the description given by the parent of the child's everyday activities and of possible changes in activity level with the onset of the child's depression or of current stress. The mother may note, for example, that her son previously was always up early, ate a "good breakfast," and was out to play almost immediately and kept active the entire day.

CASE 65

Mrs. D, discussing her 11-year-old son, came to realize that there had been marked changes in his general activity level following the death of his father six months before. She had not, until the moment of discussion within the interview, realized that he was very probably depressed. Now Fred remained sleepy in the mornings, dawdled over his food, sat for hours in front of the TV, or hung about whining and making demands that she entertain him. His rest at night was now fitful. She contrasted him with her daughter, age 8, who had been a "sleepyhead" in the family and who was quite selective about what she ate and was a dainty eater, who preferred relatively sedentary activity, and who, although a good student, seemed to need more time for her studies. Following the father's death, she also complained more about little things, ate a great deal more—gaining 20 pounds. She fell asleep during the day, even at school but was restless at night. Both had been examined physically, and there was no change in their metabolism.

Energy-level differences within the family are often a point of conflict. Most people realize that it is difficult for an aging person to have full care of a high-energy-level toddler. Even the middle-aged parent can be exhausted by the pace of teen-aged children. What may not be discernible is that where there are differences between parents themselves in adult energy level, differences that might not cause excessive conflict within the marriage, the presence of one or more children in the family with the same energy level as one of the adults may cause the family dynamics to be thrown out of balance. Thus a woman with a low energy level might marry a man with a much higher energy level, almost, it might seem, to counterbalance her pace. If, however, she is faced later with three sons whose energy level is like her husband's, she may find herself overwhelmed and her protests may seem to her husband and sons as nagging and complaining. In such circumstances the boys may have biased views of women as being extraordinarily weak, as needing protection, and as incapable of participating in male activities. An easygoing, sedentary, low-energy man who selects for contrast a wife with a high-pitched energy level and then finds himself with daughters whose energy levels are like his wife's may feel badgered and hasseled. His wife and daughters may see him as stodgy and unappreciative and lacking in affection. Such girls might grow up feeling that all men have to be pushed and pulled and tugged at.

When the assessor is faced with the complaint of the hyperactive child, she/he should be most careful to investigate the energy level of both parents. Not uncommonly, such a complaint arises from the low-energy-level parents who, hoping for a placid baby, find themselves with a child who to them appears extremely hyperactive but who, to other families, might seem quite normal or even below normal in activity. Obversely, in a family where the parents and most of the children possess a high level of energy, a more easygoing steady-paced child might actually appear slow and dull, and the child might come to feel somewhat inadequate and out of place. Thus a review of family energy-level patterns during both the parent interview and the interviews with the child is often essential in understanding family conflicts and the development of feelings of identity.

Although no one psychological test is aimed at the assessment of psychic energy level, it is possible to gain some estimate of the child's overall pace and push from his/her behavior in response to many different techniques. Classically, energy level has been considered to be tapped by the "timed" test. Thus, on the Digit Symbol Test of Wechsler, one child may attack it with vigor and consider speed the most important variable. Yet, another child may view this task as one of precision and accuracy—rather than mere speed. Of course, in looking at these variables, one needs to take into consideration the amount of tension the child also shows and discount tension and depression in estimating basic energy level. No one such test would give us the entire picture, and it is necessary to note energy level throughout the assessment. Timing and pace appear as variables in many subtests of the Wechsler, on the Bender, on the Rorschach, and even in the storytelling of the TAT. Although a high number of responses to the Rorschach or a quantity of detail in the TAT stories, for example, might indicate a high energy level, a child with a lower energy level may also be quite imaginative and productive if given enough time.

Extremes of activity and energy level may be signs of very severe disturbance in the child's development. Not only may they indicate considerable depression, as was noted before, but a child who demonstrates considerable alterations of energy level should be checked thoroughly by the pediatrician. These changes could be symptoms of endocrinological disorders or neurological dysfunctions. Even where there are psychological indications that a child may be severely depressed, if he/she shows a marked droop in energy level or becomes extremely hyperactive, a thorough physiological examination should accompany a psychological assessment.

The distribution of energy within the ego among various ego functions is another major consideration. Normal, low-energy children can concentrate their energies when need be, for example, on their schoolwork—and then to let down and relax during playtimes. However, low-energy children who are members of high-energy-level families that set an exhausting pace at home may not have the push to maintain themselves at school. Nor can they compete if placed in a high-energy-level peer group. High-energy-level children run into the opposite kind of problem. If they control and bottle up energy and sit still in the classroom, adjusting to the overall pace of the average child, they will need to burst loose once they are freed from this social constraint. I recently observed that a 12-year-old child in my neighborhood ran four square blocks every morning before breakfast and every evening before dinner. When the child was asked about this daily personal track meet, he explained cheerfully that this exercise exhausted him sufficiently so that he could sit still in class during the day and fall asleep later in the evening. This boy is a top student, an excellent musician, and an outstanding athlete. Both of his parents are active physicians and community leaders, as well as being quite successful in the rearing of five children. There is never a dull or quiet moment in their home.

The distribution of energy among the various ego functions may also be one sign of possible disturbance in the child's growth. Thus the child whose need gratifications are unsatisfied may pour much energy in an effort to meet these needs and have insufficient energy to devote to other ego functioning. In a sense such maldistribution of energy typifies—if not actually defines—depressive states in children. Such children devote much their psychological energy into compensating for whatever loss they have endured and controlling the resultant feelings of frustration and anger. Children who are depressed over a loss or a deprivation do not have the energy for normal spontaneous play or social interactions. The psychological tension they endure saps their energy level, so that they cannot achieve at school. They become too tired to think.

An even more dramatic illustration of energy imbalance is seen in obsessive chil-dren, who consume so much energy in compulsive acts and obsessive thoughts that—no matter how they may be driven to perfectionism—they may be very unsuccessful and unable to complete any task because of this exhaustion. Very often such compulsive behavior may also be viewed initially as merely hyperactive. Again, this term *hyperactivity* must be explored in detail in interviews with the parents to determine what is meant. Other children may bottle up considerable amounts of energy to conform to the demands of parents or other social authorities who consider such release of energy as "aggressive." In such instances, they may be quite inactive despite their high energy level. Such disparity between activity level and energy level may create considerable tension for the child. (For example, see the case of Wayne, Case 4 in Chapter 1, and Ricky, Case 61, in Chapter 12, among others.)

The term *experience balance* was originated by Herman Rorschach, but the concept itself is not really foreign to most theorists of the overall functioning of the ego, for example, Eysenck (1960) or Rotter (1975). Even in the traditional stimulus-response learning theory of individual functioning, allowances are made for the possibility that the stimulus may come either externally from the environment or from within—if one takes into account the function of memory as a stimulus. The focus on this dimension of the overall functioning of the ego is, however, particular to Rorschach's theory. The balances between input and output for each of the ego functionings have been discussed in the previous chapters. Whether or not there is an across-the-board balance of experience—a uniformity of input and output in all functions—may, however, be seriously questioned. At least theoretically it would seem possible that an individual could be quite dependent upon the environment for the formation of intellectual judgments but at the same time be relatively independent of the environment in his/her affective life. In fact, among adults, such a pattern of being quite sure of how one feels about something without actually being able to analyze it intellectually is a fairly common phenomenon. Equally numerous are adults who are quite capable of intellectually analyzing situations very independently but whose value judgments are easily swayed by others. These two examples alone suggest that any rigid typology cannot do justice to the variety of the input–output patterns.

Although this concept of "experience balance" does appear in many theories (usually in other terms), it has not been the subject of much rigorous research. Because it is a second-level abstraction, it is difficult to establish criteria by which to measure it, outside of the Rorschach test, as I discovered in a series of exploratory studies (Palmer, 1955, 1956, 1957, and Palmer and Lustgarten 1963). Nevertheless, these studies do suggest a constancy of input-–output in a variety of situations, such as intellectual functioning, subjective value systems, and fantasy production. Clinically it does appear that most commonly a person whose input–output balance leans toward either the internal or external on one function seems to have similar balances in other functions. Individuals whose experience balance varies from ego function to ego function seem relatively rare. In Rorschach's day it was popular to consider that such personality developments were very likely to be hereditary in origin. The developmental trends noted in the more recent studies (Ames et al., 1974; Hertz, 1943 a and b) do strongly suggest a maturational factor (see discussion in Chapter 5). However, there is some evidence that the experience balance can be altered under conditions of severe stress (Palmer, 1963). It would seem reasonable to suppose that less severe but chronic stress might also affect this overall pattern of ego functioning.

Clinical observation also indicates that among children extremes of experience balance are rather rare. Young children are, of course, quite dependent upon the environment for nearly all stimulation and are unable to effectively form concepts of their own without cues from the environment. However, after the process of internalization—beginning at the close of infancy and expanding during the early years of latency—children are likely to attempt to use both internal and external clues for assessing the world about them. Moreover, a child may use a variety of clues in formulating his/her own identity. The age at which one set of perceptual clues becomes preferred over another seems to vary so widely that no generalization can be firmly stated. One might at least hypothesize that a child who from the beginning firmly identifies with one parental image might well adopt that parent's experience balance at quite an early age and continue to view the world with the same perspective as that parent consistently throughout his/her childhood and as an adult. However, since it is much more common for a child to form some identity with each of his/her parents and more common for parents to vary at least slightly in their own experience balances, one might expect the majority of children to test a variety of patterns of experience balance until one or another becomes most effective or personally satisfying.

Although Rorschach hoped through further study to be able to identify pathological states, he made it clear in his original thesis that even the extremes of the experience balance were not in themselves pathognomic. Similarly, during childhood, neither the early onset of a particular experience-balance trend nor the lack of any definite experience balance can in itself be considered a deterrent to development or a sign of psychopathology. Certainly there are personal and social values that may be well enhanced by a very stable and early determined pattern of ego functioning. There is also much to be said of a continuing flux and flow and testing of patterns. However, an understanding of how the child's experience balance is developing may be very helpful in understanding if not predicting her/his method and ability to cope with either normal or unusual stress. For example, children who early show signs of a stable introversive experience balance and who maintain such a balance over most of the years of their childhood may present a stable front to others. Moreover, they themselves will feel secure in their patterns of behavior. However, should such introversively oriented children face marked environmental stress and change—not consonant with their particular internal schema—they might find it quite difficult to take such change into account and to alter their internal perceptual framework. Commonly such children develop quite slowly during adolescence, requiring considerable time to absorb new stresses and strains.

In contrast, many children, although they make some internalizations, never quite trust their own internal experiences, and they continue to demand empirical proof anew in each situation. Although much more flexible in the face of environmental change than their more introversive peers, such extroversive children do not feel quite confident about themselves and are more likely to be involved in an "identity crisis" during adolescence. Children who form what Rorschach called an "ambi-equal" pattern can utilize cues both from within themselves and from the environment as they attempt to meet the external and internal stresses of adolescence. Such children, however, continue to face the problem of resolving inconsistencies between these two sets of clues. Least capable of facing adolescence and entering into adulthood are those children who attempt to judge situations purely on a barebones intellectual basis, without considering either the emotional and social clues of the environment or their own set of past experiences and personal attitudes. Such "coarctate" individuals are unable to judge the behavior of others or themselves. Although a coarctate experience balance may be demonstrated from time to time—especially during latency in the normal

child—a continuation of this pattern past puberty may be taken as a sign of serious ego dysfunctioning.

Although the Rorschach Technique is the only clinical instrument specifically designed to assess experience balance, it is not the only technique that offers data in this area. In fact, in view of the limited number of responses that many children give to the 10 inkblot cards, estimations of experience balance based solely on a child's Rorschach might be of questionable reliability. Taking the $M:$ Sum C ration from the Rorschach as only one item of the data, the assessor should look at all of the various input–output patterns of each of the separate ego functions. Only if there appears to be a marked consistent trend across all functions can the assessor reasonably hypothesize that an overall experience-balance type is being formed.

The import of this rather broad generalization about the function of the ego may not seem obvious, especially in the developing child. Admittedly, it was adopted from the philosophical writings of Carl Jung and may seem a far cry from the immediate and practical problems presented in a referral for an assessment of a child. In fact, such an authority on the Rorschach as Beck (1949) states in his introductory text that the experience balance is relatively unimportant. However, most writers on personality function do accord this variable or similar concepts a major role in personality function. In regard to functioning of the child, the experience balance may be considered as a long-range indicator of the individual's relationship to her/his environment and her/his perspective on the world. Occasionally the manifest symptoms and behavior of the child may arise from an imbalance of input–output, but the main reason for considering the development of the experience balance is that it provides a glimpse of the future adult.

Even in considering extremes of input –output patterns, one should be careful about making value judgments. Becoming an introvert or extrovert is not in itself a sign of neuroticism. Rather, such trends constitute a way of life that is developed in childhood. The fact that a child at any one point shows a marked trend in either direction need not be of major concern—at least prior to adolescence. Usually during adolescence such overall personality trends are tested and revised. Very extroversive children may find that they must develop some strengths within themselves and begin to depend somewhat on their own experiences and memories. They have to clarify some of their own attitudes as being separate from those of others. They may remain essentially extroversive with just enough recognition of their own inner life to achieve an adult independence. Obversely, children who are developing an introversive balance will be challenged in adolescence to take some recognition of the emotional realities about them. Otherwise, as adults they will be battered about the ears by others who feel ignored or intruded upon. One should not be too concerned about latency children who give minimum recognition to either emotional stimuli from the environment or from within. If, on the other hand, such children are unable to expand their balance of experience and take into account such emotional stimuli, they will run into serious trouble during adolescence as they will be unable to evaluate either the world about them or the world within.

To utilize these experience-balance indicators prior to adolescence, the psychologist needs to note possible trends and their relation to the long-range development of the child. Thus one might wish to use the experience balance as a basis for recommendations to a therapist or some other person planning out a program that requires estimates concerning long-range personality development. The assessor might, for example, indicate to the referrant a need to help the child utilize and recognize inner impulses and fantasies. Or inversely, one might wish to recommend that an introversive child be placed in a milieu that might promote an exchange of emotional relationships.

The third dimension—*dilation—constriction*—is concerned with expanse or breadth of ego functioning. This ego dimension is utilized by numerous personality theorists under a variety of blueprints. Lewin (1936), for example, speaks of the size and permeability of the "life space." Even laymen distinguish between a person who "spreads himself thin" and the person who "walks a straight and narrow path," This expansiveness dimension is interrelated both with energy levels and with experience balance, but it may be distinguished from both. Thus, a person with a high energy level might be expected to live an expanded life—into everything with considerable emotional investment—but it is also quite possible for such individuals to concentrate their energies on a narrow range of activities and interests. In fact, such a pattern of high energy levels and restricted interests probably underlies much of the productive work of scientists and artists who are able to pour all their energies into a single activity, ignoring almost all other exigencies of life.

Inversely, one might expect the person with a generally introverted or personally determined outlook on life to tend to lead a relatively emotionally constricted life. However, it is quite possible that such an introverted person might have a very expansive life that, if combined with a high energy level, might lead to considerable creative productivity. Many other patterns and combinations of these ego dimensions are also possible. Prominent in the political life and the entertainment field are those persons with high energy levels who are quite extroversive and who have an expanded horizon. In contrast, a low-energy and introversive person may find adjustment much easier if she/he restricts her/his field of activities. Not all of these combinations are necessarily successful adjustments. For example, a person with a low energy level who is quite extroversive may try to be expansive but constantly be exhausted and thus easily turns to defenses, such as obsessive hypochondrical concerns. Low-energy people who are extremely introversive may float into an expansive fantasy that could become a near psychotic retreat from reality.

Such types are the extremes of what are probably normally distributed traits. Most children do not fall at either extreme; they are not altogether expansive nor altogether constricted. In considering the sizes of the life spaces of children, it may be helpful to describe them as having some set point on a continuum, but it is necessary to keep in mind that this concept describes an overall dimension that is still developing. Far moreso than adults, children swing back and forth between being very expansive and spontaneous and retreating to a restricted and single-minded little world. The "mood swings" that are commonly experienced in children are manifestations of such an overall expansion and retreat. Such dilation and constriction is also observable in the child's intellectual behavior, as was previously discussed. Children on occasion may be interested in a variety of intellectual stimuli and dabble in each one. Later they may devote themselves almost exclusively to one activity, neglecting all others. Socially, they may have times of contacts with a variety of peers at different levels of society, and at other times exclude all others except a single beloved chum. As with the experience balance, a trend toward either dilation or constriction may not be obvious prior to puberty. A consistent trend during latency does not predict with any definite accuracy the kind of overall ego functioning the child will finally evolve during adolescence.

The assessment of a child's use of her/his life space calls for a wide variety of data. As was suggested in the preceding paragraph, facts such as the spread of intellectual interests and social interactions in everyday life are one set of indicators. Remembering, however, that a child's life may be introversively expansive, one also needs to take into account the expanse and variety of her/his fantasies. Nearly every one of our

multipurpose techniques provides at least one or more measures of expansiveness. The size of the child's drawings on either the Draw-A-Person or the Bender-Gestalt is one measure of this variable. The number of objects used in the World Test, as well as their variety, is also considered by its author to be an expression of the child's dilation or construction of his/her outlook on the world. On intelligence tests items such as Digit Span on the WISC or Binet, Response to Pictures, Level I (Stanford Binet Year III-6), or Word Naming (Stanford-Binet, Year X) are indications of a child's intellectual expansiveness. Other intellectual tasks require the child momentarily to focus his/her attention on a single task or a single aspect of a problem. On the Picture Completion subtest of the WISC, for example, children must stay within the limits of a picture presented to them and the detail within those limits in order to succeed. They cannot look beyond the picture and reply that a man is missing from the coat or that there is no nail on which to hang the thermometer.

Although like the experience balance, this dimension of dilation–constriction of the ego describes a long-range personality development, the immediate import of either an extreme dilation or an extreme constriction is of much more concern. Extremes at either end of this continuum may be one indication of a severe emotional disturbance in the child. A severe constriction of all ego functions in adolescence is strongly suggestive of depression or even of the onset of a psychosis. A manic dilation of the ego may be a defense against such a depression—a phrenetic warding off of a psychotic break. Although swings between dilation and constriction do appear to be more extreme among children than among adults, a child who is functioning at either extreme should be assessed very carefully for the presence of some kind of immediate stress. Not infrequently the stress may be nonspecific and general, such as that experienced in a life crisis when the child shifts from infancy to becoming a schoolchild or turns the corner from latency into puberty.

B.   ASSESSMENT OF IDENTITY FORMATION

A child's sense of identity lies at the core of the ego and involves all ego functions. It is both a part of the overall ego and distinct from it. While the ego is a set of interacting functions, the term *identity* refers to: (1) the child's perception of these interacting functions, (2) the social roles assigned to her/ him, and (3) her/his affective evaluation of these identities. Thus, identity may be considered as that part of the ego that looks at itself, that considers how the ego is viewed by others, and in which the sense of pride and of guilt is centered. These three aspects of identity are, of course, highly interrelated. How one perceives oneself is partly a result of how much self-regard one has that in turn—especially for children—depends upon the identities imposed upon them by others, the behaviors others expect of them, and the roles assigned them. Inversely, the roles they play and what others come to expect of them depend upon their own attitudes toward themselves and their awareness of their own functioning. Which of these three aspects should be discussed first is therefore an arbitrary choice. The main reason for so dividing the subject of identity into three aspects is that it serves to organize a variety of the pertinent data.

1.   Assessment of Self-Perception and Awareness

Most students of child development and personality agree that self-awareness is a developmental phenomenon that begins in infancy and expands throughout childhood, reaching its critical point in late adolescence. Identity formation is both an unfolding and accumulative process and thus—at each stage of development—requires consideration of additional data and new criteria.

Imagine for a moment that there was a Stanford-Binet for ascertaining identity that yielded an "identity quotient." What kinds of items might each age level contain? During the earliest months of infancy children's identity formation consists of becoming aware of themselves as a physical unity. The identity "age" in terms for this infant scale might consist of observations of the degree to which the child explores her/his own body parts, such as touching and manipulating toes and fingers or experiencing overall physical sensations in rocking, stretching, and then pulling herself/himself erect. Similar items are present in the Cattell Infant Intelligence Scale and in the Vineland Scale of Social Maturity. Since identity also consists of recognizing differences between the self and others, the identity quotient scale would contain the Cattell items of recognizing and differentiating the presence of the mother. A few months later on the Cattell a child recognizes himself/herself in the mirror by patting it. Similarly, children turn over in the crib, manipulate other pieces of the environment, and see these things as being separate from themselves. Weaning is also an act in which a child separates the self from the mother and makes the first beginning toward the satisfaction of her/his own needs. Thus the child says, in effect, "I am because I can do."

Children thus begin with recognition of themselves as behaving and even accomplishing persons. This aspect of identity continues to play a prominent role in self-awareness in childhood. However, even during infancy several other elements of self-perception are present—at least in embryonic form. A second type of item of an identity-development scale would consist of simple intellectual acts. Children begin to name and recognize objects and include themselves in this naming process by differentiating the objects from their own persons. In fact, the use of a given name to identify the self precedes the use of proper pronouns. "Johnny want" appears in the child's speech before "I want."

Actually, naming other people might be one of the earliest items in the identity scale—for example, beginning with the names "mommy," then "daddy," then sibs, and himself/herself. Later the child distinguishes *mine* and *yours*, relating objects to the self. The names of objects and their possessors and the names of people are a preoccupation of the 3- and 4-year-old child.

At this age level also, a child begins to make sexual distinctions as part of his/her identity. They identify adults as "mommies" and "daddies" and themselves and other children as "boys" and "girls." Infants begin by identifying themselves with a parent—first the mother and then the father. As psychoanalytic theorists have suggested, it is during weaning that infants see themselves as separate from the mother. Perhaps it would be more precise to say that they see the mother and the self as distinct once they are involved in actively feeding themselves. However, such a separation of the child's awareness as being part of his/her mother is probably a very gradual process that still has remnants in adolescence. In any case, a child's social identity as part of the family and how he/she recognizes this would also be elements on an identity scale. By age 3, the average child recognizes her/his father and siblings as family members distinct from nonfamily members. By age 4, a child begin to use her/his patronym as a part of her/his own name and identity.

Last but not least, some of the types of items that one might include in such an identity-development scale would come out of children's affective relationships. They are not only *somebody* because they belong, but they also have an *identity* because they are loved or hated. In turn, they experience themselves as someone who loves or hates. Their identities are formed by their recognition of tender or angry feelings from others and their experiences of such feelings within themselves. This discrimination between feelings that belong to the self and feelings that come from others is

gradually learned over the entire period of childhood, but has its definite beginnings during the pre-school years.

Just as other kinds of development turn from an accumulation of experiences toward an integration and repetitive practice of learned experience in latency, so identity development proceeds in latency into a working through of the basic facts of identification that children have already learned. They have already discovered that they are separate from others, that they have names, belong socially to a family group, have a definite sex, and are both objects of and expressors of affect. However, by and large these facts about identity are imposed externally upon children in the form of roles that they are expected to play or lessons they are expected to learn. How well they learn these roles, and even more to what extent they accept them, are the questions of identity formation during latency. Thus, in this imaginary "identity-development" scale the items for the latency years would be concerned with behavior manifestations of practicing these roles and with accepting or internalizing them. Although children may begin practicing various imaginary roles during the pre-school years—for example, playing cowboy or playing various family-member roles in a game of house, and the like—this playacting is even more intensified in latency. One of the items on an identity-development scale might thus be the numbers and kinds of identities the child acts out, both in play and in various social situations. Does he/she play at being astronaut, grocer, doctor, and so on, in a game with other children? Does he/she pretend to be the various characters on TV? Does he/she try out various roles with family members or with the peer group? Does he/she try being the baby in the family or the little grown-up? Does he/she attempt to play the role of the "big shot on campus" while still in the second grade?

During latency it is traditional that boys and girls separately practice different roles. Although it is very probable that the psychoanalysts are correct in their hypothesis that children in latency have nothing to do with the opposite sex in order to resolve their Oedipal conflict, it is also probably equally true that this separation of the sexes serves to give children opportunities to practice sexist roles. These traditional sexist roles are imposed on children from infancy on. Infant-wear comes in two colors—blue and pink. "What a *pretty* little girl!" or "What a *handsome* boy!" people remark—never a "pretty boy" or a "handsome girl." Toys are defined as "feminine" (dolls) or "masculine" (guns, trains, cowboy outfits). Girls are thus prepared emotionally for a single role: housekeeper and mother. Boys, however, are given a wide choice of mostly extrafamilial and aggressive roles. Little girls are scolded for aggressive activity, reviled as tomboys, and told to "be a little lady." A boy is warned by his father to be a man, not a "momma's boy." To be labeled "sissy" by other boys is an unendurable epithet. Aggressive behavior by boys is at least covertly encouraged by most fathers. A boy who gets into fist fights may be asked by his mother, "Are you hurt?" but by his father, "Who won?" Boys learn to deprecate women as being weak and unable to endure conflict; they learn quickly to bottle up tears and cover gentle emotions. Eight-year-old boys refuse good-night kisses from guests, solemnly shaking hands. But then a boy will allow his mother a kiss when tucked into bed. Inversely, girls may weep, giggle, and swoon with "love," but they are not supposed to have angry, "nasty" feelings.

An expanding and often vehement rebellion against these sexist roles has been developing during the past 20 years, led mainly by adult women who find these roles extremely limiting—both socially and emotionally. This equal-rights movement also advocates revision of the way children are taught sexual roles in many quarters. Children of both sexes are taught to be gentle and empathetic in social relationships, but they also are allowed to participate in aggressive, competitive play (but are discouraged from hostile, violent games or toys—such as guns).

Identity development in latency is not, however, restricted entirely to children's images of themselves sexually. In fact children continue to spend much of their time practicing roles as both physical and intellectual achievers. Their sense of self as a moving and accomplishing person expands enormously between the ages of 6 and 12. Children's identities particularly derive from their activities on the playground, at home, and in their neighborhood in active physical games and play. Whether this play consists of organized sports or individual activity with peers, it is often extremely competitive. Similarly, children have expanding intellectual achievements to depend upon as a part of their identity. No longer are they merely naming things or even merely getting their relationships established, but now they are inventing ideas and making finer discriminations. Learning becomes a function that adds to a sense of identity. To a far greater extent than in their earlier years children adopt the Cartesian philosophy "cognito ergo sum."

A child begins to have a memory now, to see himself/herself as an identity that exists over time. Even at age 7, children can tell you about things that happened when "I was a little child." Although their chronology may be inexact and their sense of time quite fluid, they definitely recognize that they are the same person now that formerly existed as an infant. Yet a child differentiates his/her current identity from what he/she was like as a baby and can, on request at least, recite some of those differences. "How are you different now from what you were like when you were a baby?" might be an item on an identity scale that most 8-year-olds could easily answer.

The latency child's identity as a member of social groups also continues to expand. A child sees herself/himself as having a membership in a school tha has a name, as being part of a neighborhood, as belonging to a religious group, and as having a definite racial identification. Although 9-year-old children may not know precisely what it means to be a Catholic or a Mormon, a a Democrat or a Republican, or all the implications of being white or black, they at least are well aware that such differentiations exist in the adult world. Thus they fling these terms around and discuss them with peers. A child becomes acutely aware of his/her place within the hierarchy of his/her peer group. A child knows how each of his/her playmates and schoolmates are regarded by the group as a whole. Children may be less aware—or at least less willing to admit—how they themselves stand with their peers. In this respect, an identity-development scale might well adopt items from the Rogers Adjustment Scale (1931), which deals with the number of friends and the relationship to friends that a child is willing to talk about. In fact, much of the Rogers Scale (1931) is concerned with various identity behavior during latency.

Despite the fact that the term *latency* implies a repression of affective experience, the trying out and acceptance of various kinds of affective behaviors is very much a part of identity formation during latency. Perhaps the reason that this may not be easily recognized is that the development of affective function to the ego is concerned largely with control of affect during this stage. As a child experiences affect as being part of the self, the self becomes responsible for the control and expression of affect. It is this internalization of affect that is the hallmark of latency. To an increasing degree children are expected to withstand disappointment without becoming enraged. Also, they are expected to find some solutions to their disappointments. If there is no one to play with, they are expected to entertain themselves. If they are hungry, they may be expected to wait until the family eats again. If they need comforting, they are expected to come to parents or other adults for surcease without excessive tears. These affective self-sufficiencies become part of an advancing sense of identity.

Children's social and affective discrimination becomes more refined during these latency years also. They may have some people whom they hate without reservation and some people whom they love with abandon, but they are beginning to distinguish between the things they like about one person and the things they dislike about that same person. For the infant, "Mommy" is all good at one time or all bad at another time. Latency children are able to tell you that there are things they like about "Mom" and things that they do not like about her. They may mention some child about whom they make generally derogatory remarks, but at the same time may report that they spend time with this child occasionally in relatively peaceful play because this other child has some assets that they enjoy.

The acceleration of identity development with the onset of puberty is so remarkable that the concept is almost equated with adolescence. However, as is evident from the preceding discussion, the identity-formation process in adolescence is actually the grooming period. As adolescents rush headlong from childhood into maturity, the fulfillment of their identities becomes a critical focal point. During these final years of childhood adolescents attempt to integrate and finally establish the kinds of identities that they have been developing. All along, this identity formation has been largely — although not exclusively — an unconscious process. During latency they can talk about themselves if asked. During adolescence self-awareness and self-contemplation become much more manifest, conscious processes, at times painfully obsessive.

Beginning in high school if not in junior high school, an adolescent has to decide what kind of person she/he wants to be. Children make choices of electives in schoolwork looking toward eventual careers. They enter into extracurricular activities at school, into certain kinds of peer groups, and they make other choices about themselves that determine their identities.

A child now chooses between being an "egghead" scholar, an athlete or "surfer," or a "punk" rebel. Children may play all of these roles at various times, but they are almost consciously concerned with what they are doing and why. Peer heroes and peer causes are much more important to them now. They are even more conscious of age distinctions. They become extremely aware of the physical self: Dress, grooming, speech, language, posture, and the development of their bodies become all-important to them.

An identity-formation scale would thus have many items concerned with the awareness by the teen-ager of the various facets of identity development. Much of what is called adolescent rebellion is actually adolescent identity development. Teen-agers have to say "no"; they need to set their own patterns; they must determine their own comings and goings—all in preparation of seeing themselves entirely separate from parents and other adult authorities. They may not really expect these authorities to accept their declaration of independence, but it is necessary for them to assert it.

This action component of identity formation in adolescence is present not only in achievement in social behavior but also in the sexual role. In a traditional, sexist society a boy practices being a man among men during latency. During adolescence he has to practice being a man among women. For girls, the physical and sexual aspects of identity development in adolescence are even more marked. Although masculine virility is practiced and boasted about among latency boys, girls have few opportunities to be sexually feminine before puberty. With the onset of the menses, a girl has positive proof that she is a woman. Thereafter she is not allowed to play a tomboy role or to avoid feminine activities with impunity. Her physique reflected in her own mirror tells her that she is becoming a woman. For a girl, feelings about body image are far more of an intense core of identity than for most boys. Although a boy

may take considerable pride in or have considerable concern with his muscular development, height, and weight, or even complexion, this masculine concern with body image is seldom as intense as is the feminine concern of most girls with it. Scarcely any girl escapes altogether from this socially imposed, physical, feminine narcissism. Even the high-school girl who appears to take only minimum concern with dress and grooming, who makes little or no effort to keep up with teen-aged girl fashions or fads, and who devotes herself to studies or athletics, only barely hides her dreams and concerns about her body image. Any denial of this feminine narcissism is usually a reaction formation. Such a girl frequently does not act like a girl only because she fears that her physique is not "feminine." Acting like a boy and acting like a girl—and *acting* is a very important part of adolescent identity formation—is not merely a pose but is part of a continuous interaction with the opposite sex.

An assessor should not ignore the emotional intensity of girlfriend—boyfriend relationships, as do many adults when they refer to "mere puppy love." For the adolescent these affective relationships are extremely intense and being in love is not merely a sexual attraction but is a very essential part of "being somebody who is in love" and who is loved in return. The psychologist's identity test should take heed of what poets and philosophers have long known, namely, that the essential and complete feelings of an identity are derived through a love affair. Such affairs may be very brief and occur only once or twice before the end of adolescence, but nevertheless they are very important to the final stages of adolescent identity formation. They may not even include any actual sexual experiences. In fact, most adolescents become quite aware that there is a difference between being in love and having a sexual experience—even though the two are often combined. Currently, experiencing the full range of sexual activity before the age of 21 is often considered by the late adolescent as being essential to his or her achievement of being an adequate person. However, many late teen-agers bitterly complain that they really do not know what it means to be in love. This seems almost the reverse of the previous generation who fell madly in love but could not allow themselves sexual interaction.

With the increasing challenge to these traditional sexist roles—especially by women—adolescents are no longer presented with clear-cut, socially defined sexual "role models." Adolescent girls look forward to careers other than housewife and mother. They compete vigorously with boys in the classroom and on the playground. They disdain being "sex objects" and deride the "macho" behavior of boys. Yet the traditionalist sexist roles remain embedded in much of modern culture, and girls who want to be accepted by men frequently quell their rebellion. For adolescent boys there is as yet no complete model for change from these sexist roles. Unless both parents are androgenous, the effect of a sexually liberated mother on a growing boy is usually nil. The ultimate result, it is to be hoped, will be a relatively androgenous society in which the evils of sexism will be eradicated. Yet during this period of change it is my impression that this overthrow of sexist roles will increase the difficulties in identity formation for both girls and boys of the next generation.

One of the current results of this upheaval in sexist roles is—in my opinion—the increase in homosexuality. The myth that homosexuality is constitutionally or genetically determined is rapidly being destroyed. There is little doubt in my mind that homosexuality is a matter of choice and that this is an openly intellectual choice. Since in many urban centers a homosexual life-style is becoming openly recognized, the choice of a homosexual role is offered to the adolescent as an alternative to the traditional sexist role. Homosexuality can be especially attractive to the intellectually bright and aesthetically talented boy who fears failure in his attempts to meet "macho" standards. The possibility of such a choice looms even larger for the teen-ager who has no close identification with a father figure or whose father is derided by the mother.

CASE 66

Lance M, age 16, was brought to the hospital emergency room with a deep, self-inflicted chest wound, which he barely survived. A tall, slim, pale-skinned boy with bright red, shoulder-length hair, he was exceedingly handsome but slightly "effeminate" in appearance. This impression was reinforced by his high tenor voice and his mannerisms of speech and gesture. Lance's suicide attempt was precipitated by the marriage of his male piano teacher with whom he was in love. Lance had known for months that his teacher was going to be married. He had met his teacher's girlfriend and was invited to play the church organ at the wedding. Yet Lance secretly had doubts of his teacher's heterosexuality. Lance knew that the teacher's roommate was openly gay, and for years he had supposed that the teacher also was homosexual. Lance admitted that when he masturbated he daydreamed of his teacher as his sexual partner. He thus wondered if the marriage might be the teacher's cover for his homosexuality. The week prior to the wedding, Lance decided to test his relationship with his teacher and offered himself as a sexual partner to him. When he was gently but firmly refused, he fled in tears, disappearing from home and school, and was not seen again until the suicide attempt a week after the wedding.

Lance was a brilliant scholar, achieving all A's except in mathematics—the traditional male-achievement subject. He had no close friends, as no other adolescents shared his intellectual and aesthetic interests. Lance played the lead in the high-school Shakespeare play, and he designed the mural for the auditorium. He disdained athletics of any kind and had been excused from physical education because of an alleged heart murmur. Several girls were attracted by his good looks and his artistic interests—but Lance fled when his relationship with a girl threatened to become a love affair. Otherwise, he enjoyed the company of girls and was often surrounded by them in school projects. Yet after school he was a "loner," who spent many hours practicing his music, and he looked forward to a career as a concert pianist.

Since age 6, Lance, an only child, had lived with his mother, aunt, and maternal grandmother in the grandparents' home. For the first three years the house was dominated by his bedridden grandfather, whom Lance seldom saw but who made continuous, exacting demands on the women for physical care and comfort. Lance's grandmother had quite directly—in front of the boy—expressed her wish that the old man would die. His aunt also derided her father as a tyrant. Only Lance's mother patiently and wearily waited on her father. Lance felt he came second in his mother's love and turned to his grandmother and "old auntie" for affection. "They spoiled me rotten," Lance admitted. Nevertheless, Lance's little-boy activity and noise was hushed for his grandfather's sake, and Lance knew too that running, jumping, and yelling annoyed the older women. Thus even after his grandfather's death when Lance was 9, his activities were restricted. No TV, classical music only on the radio, "good" books to read. museums, symphonies, the ballet and opera—this adult world was imposed on and accepted by him.

Even before Lance and his mother moved to the grandparents' home, they seldom saw much of his father. When Lance was very small he remembered seeing his father, who was a cook aboard a freighter, every few weeks when he came into port. Lance thought of him as a "bear," a huge, black-bearded character who usually arrived home drunk, thrusting the boy to one side and demanding immediate sex from Lance's mother. Lance overheard his mother crying, the thrashing

about in the bedroom, and he presumed that his father was beating his mother, a scene that Lance had once witnessed. When he peeked in the window and saw his father on top of his mother, his suspicions were confirmed.

Yet Lance as a pre-schooler wanted his father's affection and often talked about him when he was absent. Lance would stand at the window all day waiting for his father to return whenever his ship was expected. His father's absences grew longer, his visits less frequent and shorter, and the parental quarrels more violent. After Lance saw his father entering a bar with another woman, he accepted his mother's continued assertions that his father was a drunken bum who wanted her only for sex and who did not love either of them. After his sixth birthday, Lance saw his father only twice. He saw him once just after his grandfather's funeral when his father dropped by to share in the inheritance — or so the women declared. They threw him out and told him never to show his face again. The second time was when Lance had just turned 15, and he met his father on the street. When his father discovered the kind of social life his son led, he invited Lance to go to a whore house. Lance fled in disgust and disappointment. Yet despite his own description of his father's behavior, Lance defended him as "not all bad" — at least as "no worse than any other man" — and he wondered if part of the blame for the break-up of his parents' marriage might not lie with his mother, whom he called a "frigid, rigid elitist." He had overheard enough of family conversations to know that his mother had married this sailor in rebellion against her well-to-do elitist parents. He also was aware that her return home and her slavelike care for her father was in the hope of gaining his forgiveness. Yet there was no doubt that Lance identified almost completely with his mother. This identification was enforced by the fact that the two looked exactly alike.

Lance's adolescent homosexual attraction to his teacher thus arose chiefly from three sources: first, the negative images of his father and grandfather, which were reinforced by his mother, grandmother, and aunt; second, by his identification physically and emotionally with his mother and grandmother (who still had red hair at age 75!); and third, by a sexist society that did not accept his talents, looks, nor interests as "masculine."

For the next two years, while in psychotherapy, Lance continued to be an isolate. In his second year of college he entered into a homosexual love affair that, to the therapist's knowledge, has lasted for over five years.

2.   Identity Formation as an Interaction Between the Ego and the Environment

In the preceding section, identity was analyzed as an accumulation of experiences leading to a sense of a separate and total self. This discussion was concerned specifically with the hallmarks of these accumulative experiences and perceptions, and only passive consideration was given to the forces that shape the identity. In contrast to intelligence tests that measure only the pace and accumulation of intellectual function but not the forces shaping or actually deterring intellectual development, an identity-formation scale should measure the interactions between the ego and the environment. An examination of some of the forces that shape identity is a necessary part of an assessment.

Since the motivational or molding forces that form the child's identity also shift in nature and intensity over the childhood years, it would be quite possible in constructing this hypothetical identity-formation scale to include items that would sample the nature and effect of these shaping forces.* During infancy the forces that shape identity are largely external to the

*In fact, had the constructors of intelligence scales been aware of the motivational forces that shape intellectual development these also might have been included at each mental-age level.

ego. Children are given a name, assigned roles in a family, and expectations of them are formed. Each child has a particular kind of body with a definite sex that develops at a certain rate. Whether she/he is adequate or inadequate, good or bad, acting like a boy or acting like a girl, or has other attributes that serve to delimit this identity, all depend partly upon what others say or how others behave toward her/him.

Although young children are largely passive receptors, the identities assigned them by others during infancy does not mean that they do not react to these roles nor that they receive them without affect. Certainly they may protest or react with depression to assigned negative roles or to disparagement of this kind of identity. They may even at times assert and test roles of their own. However, such independent assertion is not the usual way in which identity is formed. In fact, when parents say proudly, "My child has a will of her own; she is a little character," they are, in effect, according the child this role. For the most part children adopt those roles that are positively reinforced and avoid those that are rejected or denied by others. Even when they act the little monster and are publicly denounced for this by their parents, it often turns out on further investigation that the parents passively permit this role or even secretly encourage it. Whether the child plays the role of passive invalid depends not nearly so much on how physically incapacitated he/she may be but on whether this is the view taken by the parents.

Items on an identity-formation scale during infancy should thus include a sampling of the parents' attitudes toward the child and the roles they assign him/her. In assessment much of this information needs to be gathered from the interview with the parents. In such interviews they may not directly say how they regard their child or explicitly define the roles they assign him/her. If they are aware of their behavior in this respect, they may feel very defensive. Rather, the assessor obtains such information by the description of their interactions with the child, the way they compare this child with other children in the family, what they deplore about the child, and what they expect from her/him. A very important item in the interview that concerns identity is behavior for which the parents punish and reward the child—which reflects their values. At this point in a child's life, the parents' values determine the limits of the child's identity.

Young children play the roles assigned them because they are as yet almost entirely dependent on their parents for satisfaction of their needs. However, as they enter latency and develop greater and greater skills at need gratification, they are much less dependent on their parents and do not have quite as much pressure to conform to parentally imposed identification. Moreover, they are practicing these skills for extended periods of the day away from parents—in the company of peers and under the direction of other adults. They may find that the roles assigned them by parents are not appropriate away from home. They may continue to play some of these roles in order to pacify their parents or to manipulate them, but they do not necessarily see such roles as a part of themselves. Thus what they accept and internalize out of these infant roles depends on other social pressures.

Such identity formation during latency depends more upon whether the roles played gain some need gratification. Children may therefore continue to play some of the roles the family assigns them because they in turn allow a greater freedom or self-assertion in return for compliance to their image. Children may, however, play roles that an almost opposite those assigned by their parents, if in so doing they can find the freedom to do other things that serve to enhance their identities. Thus, for example, if one is the fourth boy in the family and his mother has treated him like the little girl that she wishes for throughout infancy, he may play that role until he reaches latency and then entirely reverse it when he finds it necessary to be a boy among boys. His

reversal may also constitute an independent testing of identity in order to separate himself from his mother. As was noted, latency is not merely a repression of affect but rather an independence of affect in relation to others. Children's need for emotional independence drives them further into self-assertion and thus toward internalization of an identity.

This internal motivation for identification becomes even more marked during adolescence. Adolescents have to declare their independence openly and define their own identity if they are going to be successful in leaving childhood. During adolescence they go through the process of giving up parental pressure and parental example as external sources of identity formation. They do not necessarily give up all of these values, even though at times they may seem to reject them entirely, for many of these are internalized already. What they do reject is the parental approval or disapproval of identity. Thus they come to feel that the things they want and the things they do and the person they have become are what they themselves direct. These may or may not be what the parents also desire. Adolescents may or may not imitate parents. If they are like their parents, then it is because these values and this identity have become internalized.

If for various reasons adolescents have actually internalized these values, if they do not see them as their own, then they will conitinue to be very dependent on parents and parent substitutes for direction. They will feel that they have little identity of their own, and they will seek approval or test disapproval for every act, although they may resent having to do so. This failure at internalization of values and the subsequent search for identity are currently the most critical and widespread problems among adolescents. Such a failure in the development of an identity underlies a wide variety of behavior disorders in adolescence—ranging from deression to angry rebellion to open psychosis and often including elements of all three. The prevalence and severity of this developmental lag in identity formation thus deserve further examination.

In order for internalization of identity to take place, two general conditions must be present. First, during infancy, children should receive from the environment a generally positive picture of their identity. The parents may utilize both rewards and punishment for a child's behavior to condition that child to their sets of values and attitudes. However, if the child is to proceed to an internally induced self-image, then the rewards should be received more often than punishment. Particularly there should be rewards for avoiding tabooed behavior as well as punishment for committing it. Moreover, parents should distinguish between punishment of the child's behavior and derogation of his/her identity. Children need to learn that something is a "bad" thing to do, which they may be able to internalize as a value, but they should not internalize the opinion that they are "bad." Although children may tend to believe that they are bad, they are not comfortable with such an identity and keep testing it. Children who approach latency with a feeling that the environment offers little love but mostly punishment or who have been told repeatedly that they are inadequate as persons will continue to seek external approval of their behavior and continue to attempt to revoke any externally created negative identity. Such children will then remain dependent on the environment for their identity.

The second condition necessary for internalization is that children feel free to test what they have accepted as a part of themselves. In everyday terms this means that the parents must permit children to guide their own behavior as much as possible. To internalize, children must feel trusted. Mother has to learn not to worry if Johnny, age 8, goes around the block to play because she knows that he will come home. She knows that—given the opportunity and time—he will complete his homework because he wants approval and pride for him-

self. She realizes that he will not do anything that will embarrass her because she knows it will embarrass him. Such trust does not, of course, develop overnight. But as the child enters latency, there needs to be an unspoken contract between child and parent that the child is to be given gradual increments of permission and encouragement to utilize the values that have been externally conditioned during infancy. In many little ways parents convey to a child that there are things that her/his own conscience will tell her/him to do. Certainly, this conscience, or superego, is not the same as a feeling of self-adequacy or identity, but it is an important aspect of identity during this period of internalization.

Failures of internalization and identity formation thus may arise from several situations during early childhood, either separately or simultaneously. Children may not receive adequate affection or support and rewards—especially in relationship to punishment and derogation. Often, because of this a child may not be trusted by the parents since she/he continues to test them, seeking their approval. Such children become unable to control themselves if the parents are not present. If both of these conditions for internalization are violated, it is likely that the child will present a major behavioral problem to all adults concerned—long before adolescence. Even if such a child does succeed in going through latency without any marked behavioral disturbance, it is very likely that the stresses of puberty will upset whatever uneasy balance she/he may have achieved. Such children are often unable to meet and handle for themselves the stresses of burgeoning sexual impulses and pressures for independent behavior, nor are they able to participate in a peer society. Under such conditions, some children retreat in a regressive fashion, depressed and near psychotic. Others defend themselves by massive reaction formations, by rebelling excessively, exposively asserting their independence in an effort to hide their feelings of inadequacy, their continued dependence on their parents, and their negative self-image.

Case 67

Larry G, age 15, was remanded by the juvenile court to the clinic for psychological assessment. In the past year he had twice been arrested for possession of marijuana; he had been put on probation both times and had violated this probation. Currently, he had been convicted of selling marijuana and faced the possibility of one year in prison for his crime. It was only because his family was known as "community leaders" that the court agreed to the plea of the family's attorney and granted further probation on the condition that the parents seek psychological assessment and treatment. The court records showed further that Larry had had no other brushes with the law but that he had been expelled from two different high schools in the past year. The probation officer's report, which was rather brief, revealed further that Larry's father was a businessman with an income of around $50,000, that the family owned their own home and lived in a respectable upper middle-class neighborhood. Mr. and Mrs. G were Larry's biological parents and neither had any previous marriages. In the home in addition to Larry and his parents was his sister Lisa, age 17. Larry also had an older sister, Elaine, age 20, who was married and lived away from the parental home. The probation officer noted that it was suspected that Lisa might also be using marijuana, since she associated with known users, but she had not been apprehended. He had not discussed this fact with her parents. He remarked that Larry showed no guilt over his actions. The parents appeared to him to be quite concerned about Larry's behavior and very angry at him, but the probation officer found no gross evidence of family dissention.

In appearance Larry was a very handsome lad, slight in build, with very delicate, almost feminine features. He was dressed appropriately, casually and neatly, in expensive clothes. He appeared to be trying to assume an air of nonchalance as he came into the office, but his constant wetting of his lips, his perspiring palms, and his nails, which were bitten to the core, all suggested considerable tension. He immediately lit a cigarette and started to put it out until the psychologist nodded permission. His face was drawn into a sullen sneer as he began the interview by defiantly defending an individual's right to use marijuana. The psychologist listened to his arguments, which were presented very logically and which suggested that Larry was probably quite bright intellectually. Larry ended his diatribe with a challenging "What do you think?"

The psychologist replied that he realized that Larry had very strong feelings on the topic and asked why he felt it was necessary to argue these feelings so vigorously. Larry retorted that he probably was wasting his breath, since he knew the psychologist did not agree with him. The psychologist agreed that this might be true, but he said that he considered it important that Larry had opinions of his own and that he respected him for it. Larry replied rather despondently that he felt no one agreed with him or believed him. This statement lead to further discussion about his feelings that he was not trusted by his parents and that they did not understand him. With only slightly more encouragement from the psychologist, Larry plunged ahead into a description of a negative relationship with his parents and a history of his development as he viewed it.

He was particularly bitter and depressed as he discussed his father. He felt that his father had never understood or cared what he, Larry, felt or thought. Larry saw him as interested only in exacting immediate and complete obedience, no matter what the circumstances. He first blamed his father's behavior on the fact that he had been a military officer who had retired only recently. On further reflection he became even more bitter, noting that he was acquainted with many other military families and that he had not seen other officers behave in this way toward their sons. He even thought that his father acted in a more authoritative fashion toward him than toward the troops that he had commanded. When he was younger he feared his father and stayed out of his way, which had been relatively easy since his father had usually been preoccupied with his work and social activities or had been separated from the family by his military assignments. It was only after his father's retirement that there had been serious and continued clashes between the two. Larry laughed when he recounted that he had always called his father "sir" and found himself unable to break the habit, even adding "sir" when he swore at his father. He described how teen-aged interests and activities irritated his father who countered them with absolute prohibitions. He recounted with anger how his father had forbidden him to associate with certain friends because his initial impression was that these friends were "no good." He complained that his father had refused to sign his report card the previous year because he had two C's even though the balance of the grades were entirely A's. The following semester Larry made no A's, there were two D's on the card, and he forged a report card that looked more satisfactory in order to avoid his father's wrath. The forgery was subsequently discovered by the school and he was expelled.

The second expulsion occurred upon his first arrest for use of marijuana. However, Larry's biggest complaint was that his father had promised to get him a car when he was old enough to drive, which would have been only two months away from the date of the interview, but that following his arrest the father had withdrawn his promise and told Larry he would not even be able to use the family car until he was past 18. Larry admitted that he also had a temper, that he could not contain his angry feelings and had sworn at his father and had come close to hitting him at times. He had been punished with spankings and whippings when young, but more recently he had been restricted from all social activities. He had been forbidden the use of his record player, allegedly in order to give him greater time to attend to his studies.

Larry was also very bitter because he felt his father favored Lisa, even though Lisa also had been openly defiant of him. He felt that the father did not punish Lisa and that she got away with "murder." He alleged that he had first learned about the use of marijuana from Lisa, but that she had never been "busted" (arrested). Larry was also angry at his mother but hedged his anger with many qualifications. His initial complaint was that he thought she should defend him more and that she tended to side with his father. "She has to, I guess," he added sadly. He also felt that she was full of complaints against him and that it was hard to know what to do to please her. However, he was quick to add that he guessed he had done many things to make her sad and that he did feel most badly because he had disappointed her. He contrasted her behavior with that of his father, saying that he could never remember that she had punished him for anything but he still did not feel that she had much understanding of his needs or feelings. On further reflection, he admitted sadly that he could not remember her as showing much overt affection or attention to him.

He felt much closer to his older sister, Elaine, whom he felt had received the same treatment from the hands of his father. Three years previously his father had driven Elaine from the house when it was discovered that she was illegitimately pregnant. Subsequently, Elaine had married the father of her baby only to divorce him a year later. Now Elaine had remarried and was pregnant with the second child. Larry enjoyed visiting his sister and brother-in-law and often retreated to their home when in conflict with his own parents. He felt he could confide in Elaine and receive comfort from her.

Larry was born in Germany where his father was then stationed but moved back soon to the United States while his father was on duty in Korea. When he was approximately school age, he and his mother and sisters joined his father in Japan where they remained for most of his grade-school years. During those years he was cared for largely by Japanese-speaking servants who often fed him and saw that he was bathed and put to bed when his parents were otherwise occupied. In mentioning the servants, Larry made derogatory remarks about their habits and hinted that he often "put things over on them" or even teased them in order to annoy them. In a subsequent interview, Larry revealed that unbeknown to his parents he had had his first heterosexual experience with a Mexican servant girl who currently lived in the home. As Larry discussed this period of his life further, it was evident that a great deal of his behavior was unknown and unobserved by his parents. They knew very little about his friends, his school, or about what happened at home while they were away. However, if their lives were disturbed he was punished severely.

Subsequently, Mr. and Mrs. G. were interviewed. Although Mr. G's erect bearing and set jaw did attest to his military career, he was surprisingly soft spoken and reflective as he discussed his problems concerning Larry. Mrs. G was a small but strikingly beautiful woman, very tastefully dressed with a coiffure lacquered in the latest style. For the most part, she sat quietly by while her husband talked, her face set in a drawn smile. The interviewer was not surprised to learn subsequently that she had been a professional model until the birth of her children. It was also evident that Larry inherited most of his good looks from his mother. Mr. G opened his discussion with the interviewer by announcing his views regarding marijuana, initially blaming all their problems on the fact that marijuana was so commonly used by adolescents and that it was easily obtainable. Like Larry he ended his pronouncements with the question "What do you think?" Again, the interviewer reflected the fact that very strong views were being expressed and that

Mr. G had a need to make his feelings clear.

This led to considerably more discussion of Mr. G's desperation over being unable to tell Larry how to behave and what was the proper thing to do. Mr. G readily admitted that he felt very ineffective and openly regretted that he had had so little contact with Larry during Larry's earlier childhood years. He did not openly blame his wife, but strongly hinted that he felt she had had little control over the children.

Mrs. G did not immediately comment, even though the interviewer asked her about her feelings and experiences with Larry during his childhood. However, as the discussion continued, she became very defensive, stating that she had tried very desperately to teach Larry the right things but had received very little support from her husband. Although he did not defend himself, she grew more and more direct in her accusations against him, to the effect that he had been unreasonably harsh in his discipline with Larry and that he had paid little attention to Larry's needs when Larry was younger. As she became more angry, she began to denounce her husband for his behavior toward Elaine at which time she seemed near tears. Mr. G sat hunched over with his face in his hands. Finally he seemed unable to take her accusations any further and retorted that she could have handled things better if she had not been away from the home so often and if she had tempered her use of alcohol. Mrs. G, her face now flushed with anger and her voice shrill, retorted that he always accused her of being an alcoholic when he was trying to excuse himself and if she had ever drunk excessively it was because she was lonely and neglected by him. The interviewer pointed out that apparently some very strong feelings between them underlay Larry's problems and that further discussions might be helpful—to which both parents agreed.

These interviews suggested strongly that Larry had long felt that his behavior was more punished than rewarded and that he had experienced little approval for any independent testing of his own ability to guide himself. Evidence from other techniques indicated that little in the way of self-substained controls over his behavior had ever been internalized and that Larry's sense of identity was primarily negative. For example, on the Sentence Completion Test he made responses such as: "*A mother* should show her son that she loves him," "*My father* can't be argued with," "*Who cares* if I live or die," "*I wish* I was never born." Although Larry gave 33 responses to the Rorschach inkblots, many of which were quite detailed and imaginative, only 2 could be scored as containing the human figures in action, 1 of which was the popular response to Card III. In contrast, 9 of his responses were primarily based on the color of the cards and 5 were scored CF. This experience balance indicated that Larry remained chiefly dependent on cues from his environment and that little had been internalized. Moreover, such over dependency on the environment was accompanied by considerable feelings of tension and anxiety, as was evidenced by responses such as the one to Card IX, which he described as a volcanic explosion, the dark colors showing fire and lava and the pastel shading indicating gas and clouds. Sensitivity was suggested in responses such as those to Card VI, which he saw not only as a soft and furry-bear rug but as a gasoline pump leaking a slick of oil. Other responses also suggested a considerable underlying depression and overt anxiety, such as those to Card IV, which he saw as the kind of stove used in military barracks (D1), bulging out a cloud of black smoke. In 8 different responses he was fascinated by the white space; the most significant of these appeared on Card VII (often the card that is associated with feelings about maternal figures), which Larry saw as "a gaping canyon surrounding such high cliffs that no one can possibly descend into it." The psychologist interpreted Larry's attention to the empty space as indicating not only negativism and resistance but also feelings of emptiness and depression.

On the TAT Larry tended to describe his heroes as under the influence of other people or of circumstances beyond their control. For example, to the picture depicting the boy with the violin (1), Larry did describe the boy's anger and resentment as from being forced to practice his instrument. Questioned further, he decided the boy would "put the violin down and split" when no one was watching. He decided that it had been the boy's father's decision that he play the violin and that he probably would "get hell" when the father discovered he had not practiced. Significantly, Larry made no mention what the boy himself would do. Similarly, to Card 3BM Larry decided the boy in the picture was crying against his bed because he had been punished. In this story the hero's parents had taken away his bicycle because "his teacher had given him a poor grade." To Card 6BM, Larry told the story of a woman weeping because her husband had been killed, but then he changed to decide that she was really weeping and angry because the man in the picture, her son, had done something wrong. Asked what the son had done wrong, Larry hesitated and then decided that perhaps he had gotten into bad company. As to the conclusion, he thought that maybe the mother would forgive the son but it would take a long time. Presented with Card 7BM, Larry hesitated for quite a while, remarking that he saw very little of a story in this picture and, when encouraged further, he decided that the young man in the picture had been accused of doing something wrong and was conferring with his attorney. Larry concluded that although the young man had done nothing wrong, he probably would be convicted anyhow and sentenced to 30 years in prison. In response to Card 8BM, Larry saw the man on the table as having been wounded in battle and now being operated on in primitive conditions by military surgeons. "Bad luck, they can't save him!" Larry concluded grimly. As to the figure in the foreground, Larry, when questioned, decided that he was "some character" who happened on the scene and "turned around because he couldn't stand the sight of blood." Card 11 Larry saw as depicting Dante's *Inferno*, which he had read in its entirety as a special project in high school in his English class the previous semester. He could not tell a story about it but said that it probably depicted a scene where people were being punished in hell for their sins. As to the dragon-like figure in the central background of this picture, Larry perceived it as a monster that was specially designated to devour selfish people (the psychologist subsequently cited this response as evidence that Larry did have a sense of guilt, albeit a rather infantile fear of punishment). To Card 16 Larry tried to joke. "It's an invisible man who has just disappeared." When encouraged to expand this into a story, he decided that this man was able to disappear whenever he did not want people to know what he was doing or when he wanted to escape from them. Asked what the man might want to do that he did not want other people to see, Larry could not decide but when pressured for a story, he decided that the man had been under attack from some bully and had been able to escape him by becoming invisible. He could not imagine what might happen further. Stories to the other TAT cards also suggested that people might have to escape from or bluff their way through hostile attacks from others. In no story was any hero actively seeking anything on his own or deciding anything for himself.

Finally, Larry made a drawing of a small boy with face upturned and hands stretched up and out. "It looks like he's reaching for something he really can't get," Larry remarked. He could make no further associations to his drawing but remarked that the boy was probably about age 7.

Larry's identity development thus was a result largely of a failure at internalization. Such inadequate development shows up even more strongly during the high-school years because such children commonly see high school as an imposition upon them rather than as something that they are interested in or need. They resent authority not in the sense of adolescent rebellion but rather in the sense of frustration of their needs that they themselves cannot control without an outside authority nor satisfy on their own. In contrast, adolescents with a well-developed sense of self may rebel against authority not because they feel deprived of anything but because they want to do things on their own. Both the normal and the "emotionally immature" child, as children with poor identity development are commonly labelled, may use the same words in defying adults. However, their tone of voice is different and it is obvious that the normal child wants to be encouraged toward independence, whereas the emotionally immature child is making demands for someone else to supply his/her needs.

In addition, when emotionally immature children are allowed to be on their own, they remain restless and dissatisfied and do not know what to do with themselves. Although they may want money badly to buy things, they characteristically do not seem to be able to find a job or keep one if someone else finds it for them. Although they may enjoy sports, such children usually avoid athletic competition. In fact, they often are unable to entertain themselves and go looking for "kicks and thrills," associating with similar youngsters who passively seek "a way out." Although such children do not necessarily become engaged in gross social delinquencies, they are commonly on the fringes of delinquent groups or passively accept suggestions from more actively delinquent peers. Such adolescents may easily become involved in the use of marijuana or in other behaviors that are found on the fringes of political or religious movements. However, they are not the intellectual philosophers who lead such movements. Like the boy in the preceding case history, they may initially voice an argument they have heard somewhere else for independent action, but soon they are reciting their complaints against an allegedly depriving pair of parents.

Although this identity retardation, as it might be called, is far and wide the most common type of identity problem in adolescence, the term *identity conflict,* or *identity crisis,* refers to slightly different kinds of problems. Actually these terms are used to cover a wide variety of difficulties. Sometimes a child suffers because a variety of identities are externally imposed upon him, such as was illustrated in the case of Dana (Case 5, cited in Chapter 1). As was noted, Dana's name was confusing to her from the first. She was alternately little princess and then scapegoat; she was mother's little girl and father's little girl but really neither. She attempted to identify with her sisters and was rejected by them. In her final psychotic state at pubescence, she rejected all of these identities and saw herself as a Cinderella.

The term *identity conflict,* or *identity crisis,* is most commonly associated specifically with the development of sexual identity in a sexist society. Like other aspects of identity, sexual identity has its roots in early-childhood experiences. However, a sexual-identity crisis is particularly associated with adolescence. It is then that adolescents not only accept a sexual identity as a finality but begin to practice it far more actively in interactions with others than previously. In the classic case of a sexual-identity crisis, the child finds it difficult to be actively "male" or "female," often preferring to be sexually neutral and inactive—perhaps even denying any feelings of conflict or of inadequacy. However, such children often feel quite inadequate and display such feelings in other behaviors or in their appearance. Thus, they may blame their heterosexual retirement on their size or looks, or lack of opportunity. Although such children frequently react in counterphobic fashion by suddenly becoming very sex conscious, displaying considerable sexual curiosity and alleged interest in the opposite sex, or dressing in almost bizarrely seductive fashion, they usually stop short of actually becoming socially and sexually involved with the opposite sex. Other children recognize and label such children as "phonies" and after one or two

contacts have little to do with them. Such rejection leaves these children even more lonely—with increased feelings of inadequacy. As these experiences increase, such children become more and more worried and guilt ridden over sexual impulses, angry and depressed when they find themselves masturbating, and obsessed with the possibility that they might become homosexual. In the classic case, the parent of the same sex is either physically absent or psychologically distant or inadequate, thus leaving the child without a model for sexual identification (see Case 63).

Interestingly, in such cases of sexual identity conflict, responses to the psychological tests, especially in the early years of adolescence, are often similar to those previously illustrated in the case of Larry (66). The sexual aspect of the difficulty in identity development is usually better represented in the problems the child has in everyday life, such as in her/his heterosexual contacts with peers, than it is in overtly sexual symbols or fantasies or in responses to such techniques as the Rorschach or TAT. Occasionally the older adolescent may—with some bravado—give a sexual response to the Rorschach or tell a sexy story to the TAT or intellectualize about homosexuality during the interview. If such responses are associated with sexual-identity conflict, they are usually given with considerably more anxiety and defensiveness than might be shown by relatively normal 16-year-olds whose sexual impulses are spilling over into fantasies. Such overt sexual interests are almost par for the course for the normal, bright 16-year-old.

However, any child under 16 who obsessively verbalizes about sexual anatomy and sexual functioning during the initial context of assessment often proves to be expressing a breakdown in identity formation of near psychotic extent. The obsessive element often proves to be a more important factor than the sexual content of the adolescent's ideation. In most such cases, the history often reveals that the child has used obsessive and compulsive defenses throughout childhood. Although the internal stress of burgeoning sexuality can be the precipitating cause of collapse of the child's ego functioning, the fact that the ego could be so precipitously overwhelmed does suggest that both ego development and identity formation are probably immature. Thus, such a preoccupation with sex in an adolescent would suggest that the control systems of the ego were never well formed in the first place, that they still remain largely dependent on external forces, and that they may have been successively weakened in accumulative fashion by each stress in childhood.

3. Self-Awareness

The formation of an identity includes a certain degree of self-awareness and of consciousness of ego functioning—the development of which is one of the most remarkable and most frequently noted facets of adolescent behavior. Adolescents are often uncomfortably self-conscious, aware of themselves and their functioning. At other moments they may seem to be most unconscious of themselves and behave in a completely free and straightforward manner. Yet, this awareness scarcely ever leaves them completely, and it takes most of their adolescent years for them to get used to it. A complete and continuous lack of self-awareness would suggest that the full blossoming of an identity is not yet attained. Such self-awareness may be noted at moments throughout childhood—even in the pre-school child—and becomes gradually more extensive throughout childhood, but it seldom blossoms until after pubescence. It is this factor of self-awareness that makes it possible for adolescents to assess and evaluate their own ego functioning.

For most teen-agers, this self-awareness occurs with only occasional shudders of anxiety and guilt, but when considerable guilt has been instilled in a child and when her/his self-image is quite negative, this awareness is extremely painful and has to be closed off and repressed. Because self-awareness is often used as one of the keys in psychotherapy, at least a qualitative estimate of the nature and extent of a child's recognition of her/his own functioning is frequently an essential part of an assessment.

Although there is no one well-defined instrument for measuring this variable, signs of introspectiveness and reflectiveness about the self may be seen on a variety of techniques. On the MMPI, for example, self-awareness would be indicated if the K and Hy Scales are relatively low. At least a moderately high Pt would suggest some concerns with the self. On the Rorschach, responses based on perspective or depth (FK using Klopfer's scoring or FV using Beck's scoring) are commonly considered as one index of reflectiveness. However, such "distancing" does not necessarily indicate introspectiveness. In order to interpret such vista responses as a tendency toward self-reflection, it is necessary to note the context in which they appear, for example, whether in company with internalized M responses or along with external, color responses. Not uncommonly in adolescence, responses containing perspective are associated with white space, suggesting a more oppositional perspective rather than self-awareness.

Self-awareness on the TAT may be indicated by fantasies in which the hero or heroine is reflecting upon herself/himself. Probably one of the best indications of the development of self-awareness is the degree to which the feelings of the hero are voluntarily mentioned by the storyteller. Not infrequently, the storyteller who becomes concerned with the ego functioning of the heroes or heroines will remark on this awareness of her/his own feelings and functioning. Even where this reaches the proportions of an obsessive excoriation, the very fact of this self-awareness—albeit extreme—is an indication that identity formation is reaching a climax.

CHAPTER 14

Reporting the Assessment

A. THE IMPORTANCE OF REPORT WRITING

The third and final step in assessment—after the data are collected and analyzed—is the communication of this analysis to the referrant and to others concerned with the child. The importance of effective communication of these findings cannot be overemphasized. If these findings are to be of any assistance to the referrant and are to carry any weight in the decisions that she/he needs to make in helping the child, they must be communicated as clearly and definitively as possible. Reports that are carelessly composed, that are replete with jargon, and that are a jumble of ideas without logic or organization often confuse rather than enlighten the reader. On the other hand, a report that states concisely and logically in good English the nature of the child's behavior and its causes provides a basis for the referrant in the organization of her/his work.

For many psychologists, especially those in training, the communication of their findings, especially in writing, seems an arduous task. They enjoy the contacts with the child and are challenged by the analysis of the data but shrink with distaste from writing a report. Undoubtedly, writing reports does become easier with experience. The chief difficulty for the novitiate is in bringing together her/his miscellaneous observations and formulating arguments. When a report seems particularly difficult to write, it is usually because the analysis of the data is incomplete or has not been thought through and logically organized. Thus, when one finds it

difficult to compose a report—or is writing endlessly—the best advice is to go back over the data and review one's analysis of it.

Report writing is also often difficult for psychologists—and, in fact, for many scientists—because they seldom receive any training in writing beyond their freshman English-composition courses. Unfortunately, few universities provide special training in scientific writing. There are, however, several manuals on report writing (for example, Hammond and Allen, 1953; Klopfer, 1960) that provide guidelines for the student. Rather than reviewing these texts, this chapter is intended as a supplement in which the organization and logic of the report is emphasized.

Assessment results may, of course, be communicated either orally or in writing. Very often an assessor is called upon to deliver reports in both forms. In many settings, psychologists present a report as part of a staff discussion and file a written report as part of the record. Oral reports are often easier and more satisfying because the psychologist has an opportunity to clarify his/her statements in a discussion of the findings, or he/she may even expand or revise concepts, comparing notes with colleagues who also observe the child. However, oral presentations also should be cogently organized and much of what is suggested in this chapter concerning written reports also applies to oral presentations. The written report is more exacting, since it does not allow for discussion and is part of a permanent record. Such records, although they are confidential and not to be used by any person other than the referrant or the hospital or clinic, can nevertheless be released to other persons by the permission or order of the child's parent, guardian, or a court. Children are often seen by various agencies and these reports follow them. I have had the experience of having records of children that I have assessed requested by other clinics or by the military or the courts years later after the child has become an adult. Recently the United States Congress has been concerned with the possibility that "these invasions of privacy" might become part of the public record and follow the person throughout his/her life. Thus it behooves assessors to be most circumspect and to have in mind—throughout the report—that they are writing for the welfare of the child. In clinical psychology, hasty analysis of the data and careless wording of the report are not only scientifically reprehensible but are also professionally unethical.

B.   THE REPORT AND THE REFERRANT

The first guideline for a good report is that it should be written for and to the referrant. It should reply clearly and succinctly to the referrant's questions. If these could not be answered, the reasons that they could not be investigated must be explained. However, the written report need not be this strictly confined. Very often the assessor uncovers data that may be quite important to the work of the referrant about which the referrant has not thought to inquire. However, such findings should be directly related to the questions and the purposes of the referrant's work with the child.

For example, suppose that the school is concerned with a boy's intellectual development and with his motivations toward learning. Suppose further that the data from the assessment indicate that the child is quite bright and is highly motivated to achieve but that currently he is quite depressed over the death of his father and threatened by the fact that his mother is unconsciously turning to him for emotional support in a highly seductive fashion. This latter fact may well be of little concern to the school if, indeed, it is any of the school's business at all. However, it is quite proper and necessary to convey to the school authorities that the child's problem does not lie in poor intelligence or poor motivation but rather in a depression related to his home experiences. One might suggest to the school that the child's school achievement is so severely deterred by depression that care and guidance of her/him require the assistance of facilities outside the school system. On the other hand, should the question be asked by a psychiatric colleague in a clinic, a more detailed explanation of the possible causes of the child's depression may well be in order. Similarly, if the assessor is possibly the person to proceed with treatment and the referrant is the patient's mother, conveying these findings orally might in itself constitute an initial if not an extensive part of the mother's treatment. Both the content and format of the report thus depend on whom it is written for and for what puropse. The assessor should be most flexible in communicating reports, and no strict rules for report writing can be laid down that will cover every case. The discussions that follow are intended to be generalizations mainly about written reports to other professional colleagues.

C.   THE LANGUAGE OF THE REPORT

One aspect of report writing that has been given considerable attention in various books has been the language used in the report. Sargent (1951), in particular, remarked on the use of psychological jargon. She noted, as have other commentators (Hammond and Allen, 1953; Klopfer, 1960), that there is a tendency for psychologists to speak in a technical language that often confuses those who are not psychologically trained. She warns very properly that reports of assessment must be written in a language that is comprehensible to the referrant. Even when one is writing to other psychologists, psychiatrists, or mental health workers, there should be a minimum of the use of technical terms. However, Sargent argues that there are many concepts about behavior that can be designated only by terms used mostly by psychologists. Many of these terms are at least vaguely known to most users of psychological findings, and so they are not truthfully jargon. I am more conservative on this matter and feel that even when such terms are widely used, unless they are clearly understood by both the writer and the reader, they should be avoided.

In well-functioning clinics and hospitals, part of the purpose of the staff conferences is to define clearly such terms in the communication between various staff members. Some opportunity for definition of terms is also possible in an ongoing relationship between a psychological consultant and an agency even when the agency is not primarily psychologically oriented, such as a school or an adoption service. As has been pointed out in previous chapters of this book, such common terms as *Oedipus complex* often are flung about with little recognition of their operational definition. In many instances it might be much more preferable to speak about "a prolonged and intense dependency on the parent of the opposite sex and an intense rivalry for affection of that parent with the parent of the same sex." Even a widely used and well-accepted concept such as "perceptual ability" may at times be actually unclear to members of the profession as well as to laymen. Certainly perceptual development has a different meaning to the social psychologists, psychologists studying vision, and the Rorschach user. I was once asked in court to define "perceptual functioning" and found it most difficult to explain to a jury of laymen.

Since such terms often have broad meaning and need to be specified for the case at hand, it is often helpful to accompany them with an illustration, a simile, or an analogy. Although idiomatic terms may not be formal scientific language, they often describe behavior vividly and concisely. For example, the phrase "mama's boy" conveys the meaning of Oedipal conflict, at least in part, to a great many people. A report should not be written in slang, but the vernacular need not be avoided and at times becomes the most meaningful and succinct way of communicating.

D. STEPS IN COMPOSING A REPORT

As was previously noted, the composition of a report requires a careful and detailed analysis of the data. One of the best ways to begin is to go through the data, response by response, and make notes. Such notes need not be complete sentences but merely words or phrases, itemizing the different aspects of the responses. In order to comprehend the relationships between responses and to follow the train of the child's thoughts and feelings, it is a good idea to begin with the first responses, that is, in the referring contacts and in the introduction, and take each aspect of the contact in sequence, including the final handshake. These analytic notes may refer back and forth to other responses. Thus, although each technique should be analyzed separately, one should take note of the responses that are similar—or in contrast—to responses to other techniques. The patterns of scores and overall themes should be similarly noted. A summary of these notes from each technique helps to pull together the separate findings, bringing together the different themes and defenses and characteristics. A model for such outlining is presented in the chapter on the psychological examination in Menninger (1962).

Some psychologists proceed directly from these test-by-test notes to the composition of their reports. In effect, these writers orient their report about the *techniques* rather than the child. In such reports each test is analyzed separately and in detail. Sometimes each paragraph is labeled with the test name, such as "Wechsler Results" or "Rorschach Findings." More often these test-oriented reports have subheadings such as "Intelligence" or "Personality"; their hallmark is phrases such as "the Rorschach shows," the "TAT indicates," "an IQ of 110 was obtained," or "there were such and such signs of brain damage." A thoroughgoing test-oriented report may contain some raw data cited in evidence of the analysis of findings. Because each test is handled separately, a subsequent section discussing and integrating the separate results is commonly necessary. The essence of all this analysis and discussion is then reiterated in a separate summary. These reports are thus often quite lengthy, running from four to six single-spaced typewritten pages. Such test-oriented reports may be advantageous when it is necessary to communicate much of the raw data upon which the analysis is based and the logic of that analysis. They are perhaps appropriate in the classroom setting where the student must demonstrate that each technique has been individually taken into account and thoroughly analyzed in detail and the method by which the student has drawn his/her final conclusions.

In most instances, however, the disadvantages of a test-oriented report far outweigh the advantages. In the first place, most referrants are not interested in "what the tests show" but in how the child behaves. In reading paragraph after paragraph of test findings, many of which may appear disparate and disconnected, it is often difficult to recognize how the child actually is functioning. Even though the separate findings may be subsequently integrated into a discussion, in the test-oriented report this discussion also is usually phrased in terms of test findings. Most of all, such reports reflect the test-bound

attitude of the writer. They suggest that the assessor has not been able to successfully look across and beyond his/her techniques to the essential overall functioning of the child.

In most situations, a report oriented in terms of the child's behavior rather than in test results is much more satisfactory as communication to the referrant. In such a child-oriented report, the functioning of the child's ego and his/her relationships between various ego functions may be reported in separate paragraphs, but the analysis of each ego function may be drawn from a variety of techniques. Thus in a paragraph discussing cognitive functioning, the analysis may be drawn not only from the Wechsler but from the Rorschach or even the TAT. Perceptual-motor functioning would include both the Bender-Gestalt, the Draw-A-Person, and parts of the Wechsler and the Rorschach. Such a report might contain quotes from the child's responses as illustrations of his/her behavior or report scores of subtests or from the Rorschach psychogram as supporting evidence of the kinds of behaviors seen in the child. The phraseology in child-oriented reports disregards the test. Thus, instead of saying "the Rorschach shows," the child-oriented reports states that, "Johnny's perception of the emotional stresses. . . ." The child-oriented report is replete with such phrases as "Mary understands," "Anna feels," "Bill fantasizes," "Karen avoids." The use of the child's name or the personal pronoun is thus the hallmark of the child-oriented report. Since there is no necessity to analyze each technique separately, a child-oriented report is usually briefer than the test-oriented approach. Even a very thorough assessment can be reported in less than three typewritten pages if the data have been thoroughly analyzed and integrated beforehand.

Such integration can be achieved if the psychologist goes over his/her initial notes in an effort to outline the development of the various ego functions. At this point in the analysis one may write descriptive statements about the modes of each function, the input and output, the interferences, and the methods of coping. However, these miscellaneous statements do not in themselves constitute a report. It is necessary to organize them into a logical argument.

E. THE LOGIC OF REPORT WRITING

In reporting experiments, a scientist usually states the hypothesis and reports data bearing on this hypothesis that either supports or fails to support it. In some instances, assessments utilize this form of argument. For example, it may be hypothesized that the child's functioning is deterred by trauma to the central nervous system. Data may then be presented that give evidence for such a trauma or are contra-indicative of it. Other similar hypotheses might be made concerning the effects of environmental stress or the presence of certain kinds of psychodynamics. Often, questions posed by the referrant can be phrased to state such testable hypotheses.

However, as has been suggested previously assessments are far more often exploratory studies rather than purely experimental or actuarial in nature. The clinician is asked to look across the overall behavior of the child and discover "what is wrong" or indicate "why" the child behaves in such and such a manner. The clinician, in his/her exploration of the child's development, often runs across very important facts about it that, although unknown to the referrant, may nevertheless have considerable bearing on the questions at hand. Thus the logic of reporting a clinical study usually differs from that of the experimental report. In a clinical study results are reported first and then conclusions are drawn. These conclusions actually form hypotheses for further investigation in therapy.

Most commonly, then, a clinical report begins with a description of the child's current functioning and level of development—that is, with statements about the quantitative efficiency and qualitative nature of the various ego functions. The report may begin with the "facts" of the child's perceptual-motor and intellectual functioning, the manner in which she/he expresses or fails to express affect, how she/he copes with impulses, and how she/he handles the stresses from the environment. Such introductory paragraphs may only hint at the interrelationships between these functions and the forces that are affecting them. However, they should be written so as to lead logically into a more thorough analysis of coping mechanisms and defenses and discussion of the motivating factors both from within and without the child. It is in this latter discussion that the assessor reports her/his hypotheses about the underlying dynamics and possible etiology of the child's behavior. However, such conclusions cannot be made meaningful until the reader is advised of the kind of behavior the child is actually exhibiting. In logical terms, first-level generalization should precede second-level generalizations.

If the main body of the report of the assessment follows this inductive logic, the summary need not be a mere reiteration but may be a recapitulation. Thus the summary may state the conclusions succinctly with reference to the supporting data in a more classical deductive fashion. For example, the main body of the report might begin with the description of the child's intellectual retardation and the quality of his/her thought processes. This may be accompanied by a similar description of his/her difficulties in impulse control and in the lability of his/her affect. It might be concluded that the child's ego functioning seems retarded—across the board. This introductory statement might then be followed by a discussion of some of the stresses facing the child. The relationship between these functions and a history at birth might be considered; the nature of the child's relationships with his/

her parents and other important persons in his/her environment might be discussed; and the possibilities of a relationship between environmental stresses and the child's retardation would be speculated upon. The summary, then, could begin with a restatement of these hypotheses. For examples. "Weakened at birth by his prematurity and deterred further by continuous illness during infancy, Johnny's development had probably been slowed even further by his resistance to the high level of expectations presented him by his parents. Since his parents also overprotected him, he was never really motivated to develop independent skills. Thus he remains much more invalided than is warranted by his neurological weaknesses since he plays the role of the helpless and retarded child who sees no need to succeed at school nor to control his affect or impulses in any social situation."

F.   REPORTING THE RELIABILITY AND VALIDITY OF THE ASSESSMENT

A report of a scientific study also includes some statement of the conditions under which the data were gathered and the methods of gathering those data. In research reports the appropriateness of the techniques used in the research is usually discussed and related to the hypothesis. A similar brief statement of the conditions of the assessment and the techniques used should also be included in a report of an assessment—usually preceding the main body of the report. Since in the assessment the techniques used are fairly standard and well known to other assessors (if not always to the referrant), the mere listing of the techniques usually suffices. However, a statement of the conditions under which the data were obtained usually requires a brief paragraph entitled, for example, "Behavior during Assessment." In this paragraph the assessor mentions the mood and motivation of the child, the child's understanding and acceptance of the assessment, and his behavioral reactions.

Any conditions that might have biased or otherwise affected the assessment should also be reported. Cases 65 and 66 are examples of reports about the conditions of an assessment. Admittedly, both are related in greater detail than is necessary in most reports.

CASE 68

George, age 11, was brought to the clinic by his mother whom he had not seen for several weeks, as she and his stepfather had been out of town. The referral had been arranged by his father who was to pick him up later. The assessment had been demanded by the mother, however, as part of her continued battle with the father over George's custody. The father had arranged for the mother to pick him up and bring him to the clinic, but he was due to return to the father's home that evening. If George was upset by this situation, he did not show it overtly. Rather, he appeared nonchalant for an 11-year-old, smiling and shaking my hand and did not even seem embarrassed when his mother requested that he kiss her goodbye publicly. That George was quite uneasy about the assessment was demonstrated initially when he pushed his chair up against the wall as far as possible from me. It was soon ascertained that George had not been informed at all that the assessment was to occur and had thought that he was spending the afternoon with his mother. He did admit that he had been advised by the referring psychiatrist that such an assessment would be in order. He denied that he had any idea why such an assessment would be required or even why he had even seen a psychiatrist in the first place. He averred that it was his mother's "big idea" and that she had alleged that he was not doing too well at school and that she worried about his seeming lack of friends. George completely denied that he found any problem at school at all and claimed that he was completely satisfied with his friends and had told his mother that she need not worry about him. Despite this,

George did seem eager to talk about himself and his life. He readily chatted on about his play activities and his schoolwork and mentioned his family and their comings and going voluntarily. He seemed actually to be taking an opportunity to review his life. However, any suggestion on my part that these might be of concern to him or be problems was quickly denied. Nor did he make any protest when the tests were introduced. Rather, he was most cooperative, congenial, and seemed quite challenged to achieve. His demeanor was largely serious, though there were no gross signs of depression or anxiety, and he smiled on occasion quite appropriately. Given a break in the assessment, he took the opportunity to race down the hallway jumping into the air to touch some hanging signs. All in all, a fairly reliable sample of his behavior was obtained.

Case 69

This assessment was obtained under very trying conditions that very likely affected the results. First, there was the fact that Carlos' parents were anxious to return to their home in Guatemala City after having spent an expensive and anxious two weeks while he was here in the hospital. Thus there was an atmosphere of pressure for a decision. Second, there was every evidence that Carlos had been very unhappy in the hospital; his parents had visited him as frequently as possible but this was the first time that this 7-year-old had ever been separated from his mother. Moreover, since his English was extremely limited, he often found it very difficult to make his wants known. Last, but not least, the medical staff had planned to take one more barium enema that morning. Thus Carlos had not had breakfast and the plans were only changed when it was discovered that the appointment for the assessment had been made. When this was discovered, the assessment was delayed until Carlos was fed.

When the translator told him that the doctor would wait until he finished breakfast, Carlos seemed quite mollified and thanked the translator very politiely. He was also very happy to find someone who spoke Spanish and queried the translator quite anxiously about what he might expect in the ensuing hours of the morning. He seemed a little puzzled when he was told that the doctor merely wanted to talk with him and play some games with him but was relieved to find that there were no shots or other medical procedures to be endured. Carlos also seemed embarrassed when it was requested that he leave his bedroom in his pajamas and robe, and a further delay was caused when he insisted on dressing. When he finally arrived in my office, he was dressed in a suit, white shirt, and tie, and his hair was very neatly combed. Although most of the assessment was conducted through the translator, it did turn out that Carlos' understanding of English was far greater than had been expected. Often he replied immediately in Spanish to questions that were posed to the translator in English. However, occasionally the assessment was slowed further by the fact that he used childish expressions or local patois with which the translator was not entirely familiar and that required considerable explanation. He seemed to enjoy chatting about his school, family, and playmates, but since the setting of his life was not well known to the examiner nor translator, some of it was not too comprehensible. Initially Carlos seemed rather unresponsive to the test materials until it was discovered that he was waiting for permission to reply.

None of the standard intelligence tests for Spanish-speaking people were available in our clinic, and the translation of the Binet was not entirely satisfactory, especially on those items in which the content is more familiar to North Americans than to Central Americans. Carlos was quite responsive to the CAT, although he remarked at times with amazement about animals dressed as humans and was particularly puzzled by the final card where the dog is displayed in the bathroom. Even the Rorschach, which is relatively culture free, seemed a little confusing to Carlos, and it took him a while to realize that it was quite permissible for him to express his own ideas. The history obtained later from his parents did help to explain some of his responses and the perspective with which he viewed the techniques presented to him.

G.   SAMPLE REPORTS

In the following reports the raw data are presented first, followed by a detailed analysis, in order to demonstrate the steps leading to the report.

CASE 70

Danny DeV, age 12, was brought to the clinic by his mother upon the referral of the child's pediatrician. In the initial intake interview, Mrs. DeV reported that since age 9, Danny had suffered from alternating periods of prolonged retention of feces, sometimes going without a bowel movement for up to two weeks. Quite often after a period of bowel retention, Danny would have a subsequent period in which he would have difficulty in controlling his bowels and would soil himself. Mrs. DeV was not sure as to the exact onset of these symptoms. Danny had kept hidden the fact of his constipation originally, and it was discovered only when he began to complain of "stomach aches." At first Mrs. DeV reported that his soiling had started during a bout of the flu but later remembered that several months previously she had noticed that his underclothes were stained and had scolded him about it. Following Danny's illness, he began to have an increasing number of "accidents," first at home and then at school. At the outset Mrs. DeV voiced her opinion that Danny's symptoms were "purely psychological" but could not specify at all what it was that gave her this impression. She remarked, with a smile, "that's why I brought him to you doctors here."

On further thought Mrs. DeV said that she felt Danny really had a "behavior problem" that should be "nipped in the bud." The school had reported to her that Danny always wanted to give all the answers in class, that he always seemed to be "on stage." "He needs to learn controls," the teacher had told Mrs. DeV. He refused to do routine schoolwork, which he saw as pointless. He felt picked on by some of the teachers and had been suspended for two days recently because of a fight with another boy in the classroom over a piece of paper. Mrs. DeV wondered if Danny's "accidents" might be associated with his boredom and frustrations at school, since quite often he had been sent home to clean himself up after such an incident. Over the past months he had missed an average of two half-days of school each week because of his bowel-control problem. Mrs. DeV went on to note that Danny is very easily frustrated over what seem to her quite small incidents. "He blows up over nothing. Only yesterday Danny went into a tizzy just because I had let his brother use his bedroom slippers." As Mrs. DeV described Danny's "tizzies," it appeared that they were really temper tantrums in which Danny cried and screamed, pounded his fists on the floor, and sometimes destroyed things—most often his own possessions. However, he rarely attacked anyone. At other times his "tizzies" seemed to contain little anger and consisted largely of frenzied excitement. When some special event was in the offing, Danny could scarcely "contain himself."

Danny was also interviewed briefly during his initial contact. He was a sturdily built youngster, who appeared slightly above average in height for his age. Towheaded and freckled faced with a winning smile, Danny was quite attractive. He was also very verbal, eager to talk about himself and his interests. He did not seem particularly embarrassed about discussing his symptoms but tried to slough off the topic. He could not remember when the symptoms began and tended to deny that they were of any great serious consequence or concern to him. It seemed to Danny that he always had "a little bowel trouble off and on" since he was a baby. He admitted rather nonchalantly that he had lost bowel control "once or twice" at school but denied that this had caused him any particular embarrassment. He explained that he would excuse himself from the classroom and report to the school nurse who would then send him home. By so treating this encopresis as an illness, Danny was thus able to avoid any major social embarrassment.

Danny was much more eager to discuss two of his current projects. He claimed that he was then engaged in "writing a novel" and had completed 80 pages in my "own handwriting." "It's a space murder story." Danny was even more excited about his invention of a rocket. He had carefully drawn the plans for this rocket and had painstakingly typed out a description of it and without telling his parents had mailed it to the president of the United States. He was exceedingly proud because the day prior to this interview he had received an acknowledgement of his letter to the White House.

Following this intake contact, appointments were made for Danny to return for further interviews with the psychiatrist and for a psychological assessment. The psychiatric social worker also made appointments with both parents to obtain further developmental history and data concerning the family. The psychiatrist planned to interview Danny further about his family relationships and his methods of coping with frustration. In making the referral for the psychological assessment, the psychiatrist hoped that Danny's fantasies might "uncover some of the underlying dynamics." He said he was interested in what made Danny so explosive and yet at the same time so retentive. He also wondered if Danny was as creative and imaginative as was suggested in the brief intake interview. The psychologist suggested that in addition to the assessment of Danny it might be helpful to have some brief assessment on both parents.

Subsequently the social worker arranged for the parents to return and take the MMPI.

In planning the assessment the psychologist noted that the chief questions posed in this referral concerned Danny's handling of affect but that the motivational factors that lay behind this apparent affect disturbance were probably the main points of the investigation. Further details were needed of Danny's methods of coping with frustrations, but the larger question to be dealt with concerned the kinds of need gratifications in which Danny experienced frustration. Thus it appeared that the assessment should cover Danny's development of method of coping with need gratification as well as with affect. The initial history also suggested the disturbance of affect and conation might be affecting Danny's social development as well. The question of creativeness raised by the psychiatrist indicated a need to assess Danny's intellectual functioning. There seemed no question of his perceptual-motor development. To sample these functions the psychologist planned to administer the Wechsler Intelligence Scale for Children in the initial contact and to follow this up in a second appointment or the administration of the Rorschach, the TAT, and some drawings.

Danny had been prepared for the psychological assessment during the intake interview by the psychiatrist. He remarked that he thought "tests are fun" and hoped that they were "real hard." He enjoyed showing off his intellectual prowess, although he made no particular remarks about either his successes or failures on the WISC. When an item was presented to him that was beyond his ability, he merely shrugged it off. He was even more fascinated by the projective materials and was evidently eager to display his fantasies. Words seemed to tumble out of him as he dictated a TAT story, but he would check himself from time to time, "so that you can get everything down word for word." Even so, the TAT protocol was not completely verbatim.

WISC Results

Danny DeV

Verbal Subtests	Weighted Scores	Performance Subtests	Weighted Scores
Information	17	Picture Completion	15
Comprehension	12	Picture Arrangement	11
Arithmetic	16	Block Design	17
Similarities	18	Object Assembly	13
Digit Span	12	Digit Symbol	13
Vocabulary	17	Mazes (Not given)	
	—		—
Total	92		69
Prorated	77		
Verbal IQ	134	Performance IQ	127

Full Scale Score   146
Full Scale IQ   133

Rorschach Technique*

(Response times were instantaneous and
thus not recorded)

I   ∧C∨>
1. ∨Looks like popular art.

Careless. Like thrown by some beatnik who shot down balloons of ink.

W   F,C',m,   Art

2. ∧Keeps reminding me of a cat's face.

Just the eyes and nose. (Sd. 27+30).

S   F   Ad

3. ∧Also looks like a map of Europe and Asia. On each part here.

Here's Vietnam, Korea. And Africa and Spain. (D8 + 9).

D F Geog.

4. ∧Two big pincers holding out for something.

Like some crab. (D1).

d FM Ad

II   ∧∨
1. ∧Two people that had walked all over

D2 are footmarks.

D F/C Hd

2. ∨Australia and had red ink on their feet.

D1 + D1. It's been split in half. There's red all through it.

D F/C Geog.

---

*Locations are indicated in ( ), using Beck's numbering. Scoring, however, is according to Klopfer. Additional responses are scored in ( ).

3. ∨Looks like blood splashed all over the place.

Like a big battle'd taken place. The red . . . the way it's spread out. . . .

D CF,m Blood

4. ∨The bottom looks like a dragon.

(D4) is the eyes and mouth. You could attach the head to either part (D1). Looks like a gigantic something or other.

d W F (A)

5. ∨A crab. A particular type. I can't remember what it is called.

(D3.) Two antennas. The general shape.

D F A

III
1. ∧A dissected fly.

Two big eyes (D4) and claws (D5). This could be blood all over the place.

D F, CF A

2. ∨A gigantic monster, going after something.

Like a huge fly or giant ant from a horror movie, with a trail behind him. (D1)

D FM (A)

3. >Water splashed all over the place.

[Patient holds card at right angle to his face.] At an angle, it looks like a rainy street. You can see the shine off it.

W c,m Water

4. ∧Two dogs dancing on their hind legs.

D1. The head, body and legs.

W M A (P)

IV
1. ∧A palm tree with jungle growth all around it.

The fronds. (D4) and the base. (D1). All the circular motions could (points to the shading) be leaves closing in one on another.

W Fc,m Pl.

2. ∧A king, with all the robes and everything.

(D1). The crown and face. He's throwing off his robes (D2).

W M H O

V
1. ∧A two-headed butterfly.

Antenna here and here. Big wings.

W F A P.

2. ∧Two rockets that fell over. They didn't quite work.

(D10) are the rockets and all the rest is a big cloud of smoke after blowing up.

W Fm, K Explosion.

3. ∧A raven's beak.

(D9) Sharp and well defined.

D F Ad.

4. ∧A duck's beak.

Not so well defined. Thicker (D8).

d F Ad.

VI
1. ∧A rocket that *did* work.

(D1) All the flame and smoke. (D3) is the rocket.

W Fm,K Explosion.

2. ∧Half the sun.
   . . . V . . .

(D6) It's circular, cutting off the rays going up. Dark and light shows the corona.

D Fc N

3. ∧Something in a book: It's called the two-headed, slimy-nosed bird. The Dirty Bird.

(D4) is the eyes. D6 the shoulder and beak. (dirty?) The uneven darkness.

D Fc A O

VII ∧..V. ∧
1. ∨Two girls looking at themselves in the mirror.

(D2) the hands, face and pony tail.

D M H.

2. ∨A lion with a back like a camel. A hump.

(D2). The face, mane, and hump.

D F Ad.

VII
1. ∧The phoenix rising out of the fire.

No particular bird shape, just flame and the general rising motion.

W CF, m Fire

2. >Two bears

(D1) Four legs, general shape.

D F A (P)

IX
1. ∧Two gigantic dragons battling each other.

(D3) The head, eyes, mouth. Clawing away. The mist is rising from the battle. (D1.) Cloudy.

W FM,K (A)

2. A frog.

Eyes like slits (D22).

S F Ad.

X
1. ∧A big fireworks display in the sky. A pageant with a lot of color.

Splashes of color. All the darkness implies motion too. (D11) is the director with big

2. ∧People dancing, and a

3. ∧Guy at the bottom leading.

arms, leading a choir. (D3) are two trumpets. The orange and part of the circle is the bell of the trumpet.

1. *W CF, mC' Explosion.*
2. *D M H*
3. *D M H O*

Add: *(d FC Music O)*

4. ∧A bird flying overhead.

(D10) Body and wings.

D FM A.

5. ∧A lot of animals: an owl, and
6. ∧Ogres.

(D7) More movement. Eyes and body.

D FM A

(D8) Mouth, eyes. A monstrosity. Arguing, like brother and sister.

D M (H)

7. ∧Rabbits.

(D5) Long ears and smiling mouth.

D FM Ad P.

8. ∧A flying squirrel.

(D7) All spread out.

D FM A

9. ∧The head of a cow.

The same as the owl, with horns.

D F Ad

Summary of Scores[a]

Location	Determinants		Content	
$W = 10 + 2$	*M*	$= 6$	*H*	$= 4$
$D = 20$	*FM*	$= 7$	*(H)*	$= 1$
$d = 5 + 1$	*Fm,m*	$= 2 + 6$	*Hd*	$- 1$
$S = 2$	*K*	$= 0 + 3$	*A*	$= 8$
$R = 37 + 1$	*F*	$= 13$	*(A)*	$= 4$
$P = 2 + 2$	*Fc*	$= 3$	*Ad*	$= 8$
$O = 3 + 1$	*c*	$= 1$	*Art*	$= 1$
	C	$= 0 + 2$		
	FC	$= 0 + 1$	Geog.	$= 2$
	F/C	$= 2$	Blood	$= 1$
	CF	$= 3 + 1$	Water	$= 1$
			Explo.	$= 3$
Ratios				
Experience balance =			*N*	$= 1$
6:5; 103 amb-iequal[a]o			Fire	$= 1$
FM = m: FC + c:9:4			Music	$= +1$
$F\% = 38\%; A + (A) + Ad = 59\%$				

[a]For scoring of the experience balance, see Palmer (1953).

[b]Includes additionals.

Danny DeV　TAT

1:　This guy has been trying to practice violin all afternoon. He has been playing all wrong notes and is about ready to give up. He sits and dreams, "This thing is hopeless; it's a wonder I ever got it." It had been given to him by an aunt or uncle who had money to throw around or didn't play it either. Hopeless. He thinks if he closes his eyes it'll go away. Eventually someone will wake him up and tell him to get practicing.

3BM:　This guy's been out running around town and met up with a real good cardplayer. He's just come from robbing the bank. He goes where a card sharp is and says "I can beat you again." He's also drunk. Finally, he gets wiped out; lost his $10,000. He goes around shooting in the air; everybody ducks. He grabs all the money. He runs to his house—no, to a train station. He is over the effects of alcohol.—He buys a ticket to Chicago and Ontario. He hides the strong box in a panel while the trainmen are out.—He gets away. Course, eventually he'll return to the scene of the crime; anyway they always do that—(?) He's blown all the money. Police sent out a bulletin to be on the lookout for a guy throwing around a lot of money. He wanders into the same gambling house. Bartender calls police who come just when he's winning back his $10,000.

6BM:　The "army ant"—that grows in millions—Queen comes to Los Angeles in bananas and she lays eggs—and they've been brought into customs in larva. Queen taken out—ants marching out looking for food—second stage—thrown in dump—spread into 1000s, propagated fast—to 1,000,000s—marching thru Griffith Park—National news scene—planes flying over—firemen and police out—. This guy here's a scientist talking to his great aunt. He's been working on an insecticide—has produced some that

have been shelved—. He decides to produce more. Ants are now on freeway—his home is overrun—. His great aunt evacuated—. He goes back to plant and gets packet that'll make 500,000 gallons; it is mixed in a pool in Valley—Ants march in to the Valley—now they're underground. He rushes the insecticide into the sewers—the ants dying out by 1000s—Queen is killed; found down gutter—. He mixed a second batch—he gets permission to release 1000 gallons into culverts—he kills all the ants—there's the smell of rotten meat which ants eat.

7BM:　These two guys sitting in a bar telling dirty jokes to each other. [Laughs]—One had too much. The other has sour look. He says "all these guys stealing hub caps, etc. You think that's what America's youth is coming to?" The other hiccups. They could be any two guys in America with nothing better to do—If he was not drunk, he has a look that he'd really be ashamed if anyone else heard him.

8BM:　Here's a private Army set up. Fifteen guys go around to Vietnam; they're going round sabotaging, destroying things. They got a supply of arms on top of the hill—100 men are looking for them—so when they come after them up the hill, 3 guys get up there. All are killed but 1. The commander, he gets hurt but doesn't tell the doctor. He gets hit again on other side—so now they take him to the doctor. This other guy doesn't fit in the story—He just on guard watching the battle—the other 85 going up the hill—now they're reduced to 6—(turn out?) I don't know if all are wiped out or win—like just before—reinforcements come in like in old cavalry pictures—where the cavalry comes to the rescue.

11:　A good one! [Patient almost drops the card]—Reminds me of the book I wrote, "Octa." Everything was prefaced with "8"—"Detail 1"—The characters were from various sciences and mechanics—here in Morocco—they're chasing a guy who's mugged the agent who carries secrets—who sells it to the Chinese commies. They find the guy who throws his money around—They mug him in the men's room. [Patient laughs]—They rip his clothes off and find it in his heel. The communists are determined to get it back. They chase them in the hills—they're blocked by a landslide—West hurls a homemade grenade and they climb over and get away with the secret—

12BM: This is an old man who's gone off his rocker in old age. His grandson's come over. They don't know how far off old man is but he's very rich and they bow to him like reeds in the wind. Unfortunate, since grandfather hates him—he's involved in big proxie battle, etc. The grandfather decides to kill him. He sees him sleeping on couch. The grandson is sleeping with clothes on just in case so he won't have to run out in street in pajamas. The grandfather knows karate and hits him on forehead and kills him. He drives him out and throws the body off cliff. Then he decides to destroy car by driving off pier, but fails to get out and is drowned in the tide—The stock goes to his enemies—the police never find out how grandson was killed.

13B: This is a boy who could read minds. He knows his mother didn't like him. She was a bit off. He has a dog named Bobbie—he knows Bobbie's food is poisoned by his mother who knows he can't live without dog. The dog can read boy's mind too. He throws food out after all. His mother runs to his father and yells, "He tried to kill me." The boy runs to his room. Father rushes up and pounds on door and demands he come out. They break in—Bobbie growls and rushes at his throat—the father and mother flee—Now the boy is waiting in the evening. Dog is

missing—He also had a toy Panda—(How does it end?) Just leaves him there—I can't figure out an end as I can't see it happening in the first place.

17BM: This guy's breaking out of jail. He was innocent in the first place—So he found rope and decided to break out—they got a big light on him, and are about to recapture him. (How did it come about?) He was framed. Originally he was in politics but he had powerful enemies. A quirk of fate left him in office when enemies were elected—They trump up charges against him like running around with other men's wives—this guy had a queer way of doing things like breaking out and then proving he was innocent—which he had to do to begin with—

16:   It's a white cow eating marshmallows in snow storm—That's a private joke! This bridge has a car falling off—It's a bridge noted for suicide and accidents—has highest rate of anything. You name it—but it hasn't fallen—This guy is racing off to work—he was going too fast so he ran on the walk and crashed and went into the water below—That doesn't leave any room for development, does it?

18BM: This guy doesn't look real—Hands all over and pants 20 sizes too large—He's having a dream that his pants are 20 sizes too large. His tie is all messed; hands all over; his eyes are closed and he is stumbling around in a drunken trance. He sees the face of a friend who was killed in the war. Next morning he's sitting there. There's a knock on the door and sure enough there *he* is—sitting there—"Are you the parting breath?"—This guy doesn't know what to do, but then: "Smile, you're on Candid Camera"—but he had dreamed it. Later he was at horror movie about guy eaten up by ants and it was same face. He left movie and got sick and went to hospital. In hospital a guy next to him was brought in for surgery. It was the same face! The guy was shocked—He'd been bugged all day by it—On the way home he saw a body hanging from tree—So he threw the body in the bushes and took the rope and hung himself. That was the end.

Even as the psychologist attempted to record Danny's responses, he noted with amazement the high energy level displayed in Danny's mental activity and the expansive development of Danny's ego as represented in his productivity. After the psychologist had scored the tests and made some detailed notes concerning each one, he turned to the overall task of the analysis of Danny's ego development. Although the referral raised no question regarding Danny's perceptual-motor development and these data did indicate that his perceptual-motor acuity was on the whole probably superior to most children his age, there were some interesting aspects that seemed related to the questions at hand, particularly the child's symptoms. First, as regards Danny's motor functioning, it was noted that his drawings of a man and of a woman (see Plates 14.1 and 14.2) were relatively static and even his volunteered drawing of a rocketship (Plate 14.3) was not in orbit but "landing on the moon." On the Rorschach a preponderance of Danny's movement responses were passive or, when active, the action had already taken place. For example, "the two big pincers" (see response 4 to Card I) are "merely holding out for something," the two girls on Card VII, response 1, are "looking at themselves in the mirror," and on Card VIII, response 1, "the Phoenix is rising out of fire," in a seemingly automatic "rising motion." Exceptions to this passivity, however, were present in the gigantic monster, response 2 to Card III, and in the first response to Card IX where the dragons are "battling each other." Note, however, that this latter aggressive

Plate 14.1

Plate 14.2

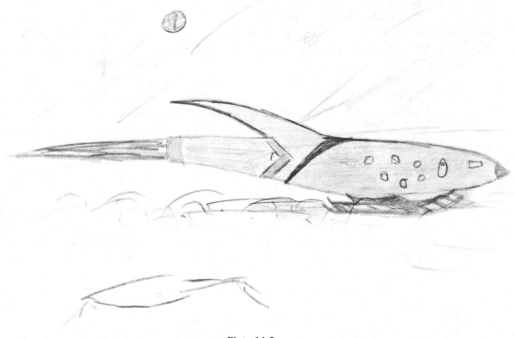

Plate 14.3

movement is accompanied by an indication of anxiety. More frequently the movement of Danny's responses was half hearted; the motion was completed or was included in something else. The inanimate movement in many of his responses was given to an act already committed such as response 3 to Card II or response 3 to Card III. Even more remarkable are comments such as response 2 to Card V and response 1 to Card VI where, in the first instance, the movement was unsuccessful and, in the second instance, the fact of success had to be mentioned specifically and the act was already complete. Certainly Danny's motor activity on the subscales of the WISC was superior for his age, but his scores on tests such as the Object Assembly and Digit Symbol where he was working against time were slightly though not significantly lower than most of his verbal responses (the psychologist wished later that he had administered the Mazes). Danny's ability to fantasy a great deal of motor activity was demonstrated in every one of his TAT stories. These data, particularly the large number of inanimate re-

sponses on the Rorschach, suggested to the psychologist that, far more than most 12-year-olds, a great deal of Danny's motor activity might well be expressed on a visceral level. Whether or not his motor functioning was also demonstrated outwardly in skeletal muscular modes could not be determined from these data alone.

In his perceptual functioning he was very accurate, being able rapidly and definitively to form percepts of incoming stimuli. By and large, his ability to perceptually differentiate was quite superior and, in general, his form level on the Rorschach was detailed and accurate. However, this made the presence of the few formless or inaccurate percepts even more remarkable. Note, for example, the relative looseness of Danny's very first response, response 1 to Card I, and his lack of precision throughout Card II. In contrast, on Card X Danny began with a gross, overall percept that he then proceeded to define in precise detail. These variations in Danny's perceptual differentiation arose because of marked affective and conative interferences. Intense, aggressive impulses and intensely angry feelings seem to be the most obvious sources of these interferences. Danny appeared to be attempting to deal with the stressful conative stimuli by becoming more and more expansive and by spewing out a wealth of detail in an effort to cover the underlying anxiety. Rather than freezing and blocking perceptually in the face of noxious stimuli, Danny actually appeared to be enlarging his perceptual field and extending his perceptual responsiveness. The psychologist wondered if by this mechanism Danny might be seeking to water down or even lose the disturbing affects and frustrations in this wealth of detail. However, handling this amount of perceptual stimuli appeared to be an arduous task even for such an intellectually bright 12-year-old.

Danny's perceptual-motor functioning could be summarized as follows. Very sensitive to all incoming stimuli, Danny attempted to absorb and analyze as much of it as possible. Although his responses to these stimuli were primarily on an external motor level, the degree to which Danny attempted to handle stimuli on an internal visceral level was indeed phenomenal for a 12-year-old. Despite the general superiority of his perceptual functioning, Danny was not successful in absorbing quite as many of the stimuli as he attempted to take in; nor was he able to contain this input and avoid external responses to it. This perceptual-motor input–output probably was part of the general high energy level and expansiveness of Danny's ego, but it also seemed to be a coping mechanism for handling anxieties involved in the perception of affective and conative stimuli.

Cognitively, Danny functioned at a very superior level. He was highly verbal but his nonverbal cognitive functions were also superior. His thought processes, though full of details, were nevertheless fairly well organized, especially for a 12-year-old. His TAT plots, for example, were very elaborate, but for the most part he did not lose sight of the overall plot. However, his ideas spilled all over and, as with his per-

ceptions, Danny seemed to have a compulsive need to include everything. There was evidence that his intense affective and conative impulses pushed his intellectual productivity rather than deterred it. It was hard for him to stop with one idea. It was easy to see how Danny would be bored with the routine of the average classroom and that he would have a need to preoccupy himself with other activities. No intellectual problem, however, failed to interest or challenge Danny. He appeared curious about everything. Yet, his ideation did tend to be morbid; he was obsessed with destruction and death; insofar as there was a disruption to his intellectual functioning, it was this intrusive and obsessive preoccupation with his own hostility. However, the intrusion of such primitive processes did not really deter Danny from intellectual testing of reality; his fantasies were extensive and bizarre at times but never reached the proportions of psychotic ideation.

If Danny's intellectual functioning was remarkable, his affective development was even more amazing. When one considers the affective obtuseness of the usual 12-year-old boy, Danny was certainly unusual in his sensitive awareness of the emotional components of his environment. Even more than most adults, Danny was immediately stimulated by the emotional aspects of his environment, and he appeared to respond to these stimuli in a highly diffuse and spontaneous fashion. Moreover, there were many signs that Danny was also beginning to be quite aware of affective stimuli coming from within him. His TAT stories depicted heroes who have inner feelings as well as being stimulated from external sources. For the most part, Danny appeared to be still in latency and thus to be keeping a lid over sensuous feelings. Yet, there were many signs throughout his record that the stresses of puberty were beginning to impinge upon him and that he reacted affectively, albeit probably quite unconsciously, to these new drives. As might be expected, these multiple affects and sensitivities are very difficult for any 12-year-old to cope with. Thus, Danny found it much more difficult to form affective boundaries than he did perceptual or intellectual boundaries. One feeling floated into the next. Many feelings came up all at once, and Danny could not differentiate or separate these feelings very easily. He was happy and depressed, anxious and fearless all at once. Yet, when one looks at the input and output of Danny's affective functioning, a pattern does appear.

The pattern appears most clearly, for example, in his story to Card 3BM of the TAT: (1) An external affective stimuli incites (2) internal anxiety, which (3) expands into external reactivity, which (4) increases embarrassment and guilt and (5) leads to further depression and a need to cover depression by (6) exuberance, which then leads back in a vicious circle to number (1). Danny's coping mechanisms for dealing with affective stimuli were in general very ineffective. He tried to avoid them, but this was almost impossible because of his voracious appetite for stimuli in general. He tried to intellectualize, but his anger and depression in particular got away from him. He tried to joke about it, but his depression was close to the surface in his humor. Most of all, he tried to handle affect on an internal fantasy level, but he remained too dependent on his environment and too wrapped up in environmental interchange for his affect to be contained in fantasy. The chief affect with which he has the most difficulty is apparently anger, which, when internalized, leads to depression. His pattern of coping with affect thus parallels his pattern of coping with defecation. He attempts to contain his affect until he almost bursts, whereupon he no longer has any control over it.

It is Danny's conative function that appears to be at the source of his difficulties in development. In contrast to the hyperdevelopment of his intellectual and affective functions, Danny's development of dealing with methods of need gratification are relatively immature. First, it is obvious that a great many of Danny's needs are external or ego alien to himself. The referring psychiatrist noted that when Danny was describing his bowel "accidents," Danny said, "I guess I just get busy and then this thing *happens to me.*" Or, in describing a situation where he was hurrying to the toilet, "*It* caught up with me." Even such a basic physiological need as defecation was in Danny's view an external force beyond his control. A detailed examination of his TAT stories reveals clearly the extent of this ego alienation of Danny's impulses. For example, on TAT 1, although he first had the hero "playing all wrong notes," the hero says, "This *thing* is hopeless." "If he closes his eyes *it* will go away." In the story to 3BM, the hero is excused from his impulsive behavior because of his use of alcohol. The overwhelming oral impulses symbolized in the marching army ants in story 6BM are also an external force. This story in particular illustrates Danny's struggle to destroy an impulse that is not part of himself. In 7BM, the hero would experience shame but only if anyone external to himself knew of his purient interests. Story 8BM shows the private internal war that Danny is experiencing, but even here it is a war between two external, impersonal destructive forces. In story 11, Danny gets carried away with this theme and cannot contain himself. Note, particularly, that the "secrets" get taken from the hero "in the men's room." In story 12 feelings of murderous rage and an impulse to possess the parents are projected outward onto the parental figure, the grandfather. On 13B the hostility is externalized to what in an adult would be considered a paranoid degree. And in 17BM the hero was "framed" and has to escape his powerful enemies, but it is necessary first to break out and then to prove innocence. In Danny's story to Card 16, even suicide is externally caused by the bridge. And finally, in 18BM, Danny's extensive feelings of guilt over his murderous impulses are also external. Since Danny experiences most of his impulses in this way, it may not be surprising to find that his guilt feelings are also separate from his ego.

It was often very difficult for Danny to separate one motivation from another. He tried to specify on the TAT why his heroes were doing things, but as he expanded these stories, it became more and more difficult to define exactly why and who does what in them. Danny did strive to cope actively with need-gratification frustrations. Initially, in each TAT story the hero does struggle with the problem independently, but quite often the story is decided not by the hero but by some kind of fate. As with his rockets on the Rorschach, these efforts do not always quite work, but Danny continued to hope that he would find some way of independent need gratification. The difficulty that Danny faced was, of course, that these impulses were not part of himself over which he had some control but were external to him. He did not appear to recognize that the satisfaction of his basic infantile needs for succor, comfort, and solace depended in part on himself. These initial dependency needs were still extremely intense for Danny and continued to threaten him. The hunger for affection that he constantly felt became a destructive "oral impulse" that, in effect, poisoned a great deal of his interpersonal relationships. This unrestricted need for an infantile type of affection was apparently the unmentionable "secret" that Danny continually had to hide.

A detailed analysis of the needs and press in Danny's stories may be helpful in understanding both the sources of his need-gratification difficulties and how he coped with them. In story 1 there is the external press of a demand for achievement that the hero cannot accept; although he feels hopeless, the pressure is unending. In story 3BM the hero, for an unstated reason, feels it is necessary to rob in order to obtain narcissistic supplies. Need gratification was a gamble for Danny, a gamble that, when he lost, drove him to

intense and destructive anger. The strength of his need for narcissistic supplies was so intense that he continued "to return to the scene of the crime." The pressure of his intense hunger in the story to 6BM affected all of society. This hunger was answered by poison, that is, it had to be met by a counterforce that, interestingly enough, considering Danny's symptoms, is poured down the sewer. In so doing, the externalized source of the hunger, the Queen Mother, is killed. In the story to 7BM, the "dirty jokes" of youth suggest that Danny was experiencing pubescent sexual drives that now were not differentiated for him from his preoccupation with oral and anal need gratifications. The motivation behind the intense battle that went on within Danny gets completely lost in story 8BM. But the chase for the secret re-enters on Card 11. This secret is revealed in 12BM where the hero, the grandson, seeks the old man's riches but loses in what is apparently an Oedipal battle, which was not a simple one for Danny. In the story to 13B, the hero feels poisoned by the food given to him by his mother, which suggests that he might feel himself poisoned by mother's love. The Oedipal nature of Danny's conflict is illustrated even further in the story to Card 17BM. There are trumped-up charges against him, like "running around with other men's wives." Evidently much of Danny's expansive ego activity was to prove his innocence. However, in the story to Card 16 it is evident that Danny, at times, felt markedly depressed and foresaw that in his manic effort to work out all his problems suicide might be a result. His murderous impulses constantly haunted him, as is illustrated in Card 18BM. In every situation he was "bugged" by his own guilt.

Some of the external pressures that Danny experienced are shown in the responses of his parents to the MMPI.*

---

*The following reports, derived from a computer analysis, were made available by Alex B. Caldwell, Ph.D., Medical Psychological Services, Los Angeles, California.

NAME. MR. DEV

MMPI SCORES (CORRECTED FOR K). *L*56, *F*50, *K*54, *Hs*59, *D*65, *Hy*55, *Pd*41, *Mf*68, *Pa*52, *Pt*53, *Sc*49, *Ma*58, *Si*50, *Es*56.

TEST-TAKING ATTITUDE. He tended to be self-favorable in responding to the MMPI and was moderately minimizing of emotional problems. The profile appears valid.

SYMPTOMS AND PERSONALITY CHARACTERISTICS. The profile indicates a mild current depression. Tension, anxieties, worry, and self-criticism are suggested. He appears particularly vulnerable to feelings of guilt, and others could easily manipulate him in this way. Psychiatric patients with similar but more elevated profiles have complained of loss of appetite and insomnia, but such symptoms may be relatively mild in his case. Despite these depressed moods, his overall functioning and practical ego strength appear fair to adequate in most areas.

The pattern suggests a few scattered physical symptoms lacking a sufficient organic basis. Symptoms such as gastrointestinal distress, headache, back pain, or fatigue are apt to be at least partly psychological in origin. The profile would indicate mildly more than average worry about bodily functioning. Psychiatric patients with similar but more elevated profiles were seen as mildly repressed and as tending "to look at the good side of things." Some complained of being sexually inhibited and "bottled up." His makeup tends mildly toward the feminine, such as verbal or esthetic interests, rather than mechanical and outdoor activities. The pattern indicates strong and solid family loyalties, and his conscience would be strict but dependable. He would internalize family distress and be overly quick to blame himself for family struggles. He tests as practical and oriented toward tangible achievements and accomplishments. In similiar cases the needs for attention and affection repeatedly interfered with the testees' capacity to act in positive and assertive ways toward loved ones, especially with problems such as misbehavior and delinquency by children and other impulsive and aggressive behaviors by loved ones.

DIAGNOSITIC IMPRESSION. The pattern suggests mild depressive trends. However, the profile is within the normal range, and it is not diagnostically definitive.

TREATMENT CONSIDERATIONS. The current level of disturbance would not indicate an urgent need for psychotherapy unless clinical symptoms handicap functioning or there was any risk of suicide. Contacts with family members or other informants could help to clarify what the current stresses are, what secondary gains there may be from his symptoms, and how such gains could be minimized. Some psychiatric patients with related profiles showed a "flight into health," both as a positive response to reassurance as well as an avoidance of exploring psychological problems. The normality of his profile and the favorable ego strength would predict a good prognosis and a positive response to treatment. He is apt to focus on his specific difficulties and distresses. Readjustment to the loss of a loved object, a recent rejection by a supporting family member, or a related loss of emotional support could be important in treatment interviews. A gradual ventilation and acceptance of aggressive feelings and sexual impulses could lead to more positive expressions of them. If a past role of hard work and self-sacrifice for his family had broken down, then he could benefit from new activities and a less-dependent role without undue family demands and frustration.

NAME. MRS. DEV

MMPI SCORES (CORRECTED FOR k). *L*42, *F*57, *K*53, *Hs*64, *D*64, *Hy*60, *Pd*64, *Mf*34, *Pa*38, *Pt*46, *Sc*59, *Si*69, *Es*64.

TEST-TAKING ATTITUDE. She was straightforward in answering the MMPI without being unduly defensive or self-critical. The profile appears valid.

SYMPTOMS AND PERSONALITY CHARACTERISTICS. The profile shows mild personality-disorder tendencies. At times she is apt to be seen as egocentric, immature, impulsive, and demanding. Recurrent family conflicts and guilt struggles are indicated. Occasionally self-defeating and self-punishing, she would then act against her own long-term interests with lapses in her judgement and forethought. Similar patients have used a variety of manipulations in order to evade difficult life situations. In some cases, the low tolerance for frustrations led to angry outbursts toward family members.

The profile indicates scattered physical symptoms and concerns on a psychological basis. Pain, weakness, and fatigue are apt to be partly psychological in origin. Such symptoms as GI pain or other GI complaints, headache, and undue menstrual distress have been associated with similar but more elevated profiles along with ulcers and histories of gastrectomies. Obesity, anorexia, nausea, or other symptoms involving eating were also typical in these cases.

The secondary depression tests as mild. Similar patients often have felt anxious, indecisive, unappreciated, and misunderstood. They saw themselves as lacking in social skills with the opposite sex. Her balance of interests is rather feminine, including esthetic, cultural, or verbal interests and sensitivities. There is apt to be some rejection of aggressive masculine activities and a hypersensitivity to sexual roles.

Some similar patients were described as oral dependent. Her father is apt to have been indifferent and lacking in affection. Family backgrounds consistently included indulgent and protective attitudes by their mothers. Difficult sibling relationships and other family conflicts were common, and the childhood homes had relatively other upheavals. As a result, the lives of these patients became home oriented with an emphasis on food and nurturant care.

DIAGNOSTIC IMPRESSION. Although the diagnoses associated with this profile among psychotherapy patients are varied, they typically have reflected personality disorder tendencies; most often these were passive-aggressive in type. The pattern also suggests mild current depressive trends. Her profile is within the normal range, however, and it is not diagnostically definitive.

TREATMENT CONSIDERATIONS. Her ego strength would predict good general effectiveness and self-sufficiency. However, the pattern predicts a future course of family struggles and of conflicts in her close relationships. It should be noted that males with this pattern are ulcer prone, and past workups on these patients have often been positive. Contacts with family members and other informants have been useful in similar cases in order to clarify what the secondary gains were and how such gains could be minimized. Such contacts could also help to evaluate possible paranoid trends. The anticipation of long-term psychotherapy is questionable, since her motivation may be mildly shallow and prompted by current pressures.

The pattern recommends the talking out of current distresses and the clarification of her immediate problems. She would seek to focus treatment onto her specific symptoms and situational difficulties so as to avoid facing the full extent of her contributions to them. The discovery and interpretations of her devices to keep others at a distance—especially as she uses them on the therapist—can be meaningful and important in treatment. She could benefit from learning to see how she aggravates these difficulties and what kinds of circumstances are personal "traps" into which she repeatedly falls.

After analyzing these data, the psychologist reviewed them in a staff conference with the psychiatrist and social worker. In this conference his observations and conclusions were compared and integrated with the data gathered by the social worker and psychiatrist. The final written report without the preliminary paragraphs read as follows.

ANALYSIS OF RESULTS. Danny is evidently an intellectually very bright youngster, who has considerable potential for emotional spontaneity and sensitivity. Currently, however, his development appears to have reached a crisis as he enters adolescence. His normal spontaneity is accompanied by clouds of depression, and his striving is accompanied by considerable tension. He faces adolescence with a great deal of ambivalent conflict. Outwardly, he piously mouths latency attitudes, like a little adult, denying interest in heterosexual peer activities and asserting independence from peer values—since they conflict with his "egghead" intellectual interests. He is secretly very curious about and excited by the prospects of adolescent activities, both sexual and rebellious. However, he perceives adolescence as a complete abandon of impulse controls, particularly as uninhibited aggression and as satiation of oral needs, but with only a hint of genital impulses. The prospect of puberty thus severely threatens his tight lid of repression and arouses considerable guilt.

Danny's difficulty in entering adolescence is much greater than normal because he is still fighting battles within himself over control of infant impulses. He has never adequately resolved the matter of control over aggression and hostility. Outwardly supermoralistic, he is preoccupied in fantasy with violence and destruction. At 12, he is still playing "cops and robbers" and "good guys versus the bad guys." Superego controls have been internalized, but Danny's superego is so rigid and so punitive that it is alien to the ego and thus not integrated into the personality structure.

Danny's fantasies provide a wealth of data about the dynamics of his conflicts. Problems in anal control are repeatedly evident, consonant with the presenting symptom. However, these fantasies suggest that underlying Danny's difficulty in accepting anal controls is a persisting oral aggression, a demanding, grasping hunger for maternal affection, which, still unsatisfied, leaves him frustrated, angry, and unwilling to accept social control. This unsatisfied and seemingly unsatiable hunger is the chief basis for his pervasive feelings of guilt. He fears that his frustration and anger would lead him to destroy the maternal bond and thus he would lose the source of succorance. To cope with his anxiety he has mounted an accumulated reaction formation, through being overconforming and by striving to please, chiefly by intellectual achievement. He then relegates his anger to the fantasy and visceral level.

The roles of the parents and their interactions, both with Danny and between themselves, is outlined by their MMPI patterns. Although all of their scores fall within normal limits, both parents show signs of neurotic struggles within themselves, which are quite similar and also quite like Danny's conflicts. Both use somatization as a method of handling anxiety; both are easily made guilty and depressed. Mr. DeV is a very passive, almost effeminate man, who is quite socially conforming and who would have little empathy with adolescent rebellion. Mrs. DeV is relatively much more aggressive and striving; she controls and manipulates, chiefly in a passive, seductive manner but sometimes without regard for reality and seldom with any insight into either her own behavior or the needs of those about her. Yet, both are conscientious parents who strive to provide for and train their children.

SUMMARY. The exciting prospect of adolescent impulse release reactivates Danny's childhood struggle over the control of both anal and oral impulses, exacerbating a well of hostility and ensuing guilt and depression. His psychodynamics reflect very similar patterns in his parents who also somaticize anxiety and are easily depressed. Danny "reads his mother's mind" and knows that behind her seductive manipulation lies considerable anger and rebellion. He is unable, except in fantasy, to separate from her and give up his infantile demands on her. Nor does he receive support from his passive and conforming father. In his most depressed moments, he sees no solution and suicidal ideas enter his fantasies.

CASE 71

Mrs. N first sought psychological consultation regarding her daughter Susan when Susan was age 11. The initial paragraphs of the first report read as follows:

SUSAN N, age 11 years, 5 months.

REFERRED BY: Mrs. N, patient's mother.

REASON FOR REFERRAL. Susan has always been unable to keep up with her school-work. She has been in special classes but is now placed in a regular fourth-grade class, two years below normal age level. She is failing still and is the subject of teasing from other children because of her slowness and because she is older and larger than her classmates. The immediate referral question was whether Susan should change schools once more and return to a special class. There had been no prior psychological study, and Mrs. N accepted the suggestion that the assessment review Susan's overall psychological development for the purpose of further planning.

METHODS OF ASSESSMENT. Interviews with Mrs. N and Susan; Wechsler Intelligence Scale for Children; Graham-Kendal Memory for Designs; Goodenough Draw-A-Person Test; Rorschach Technique; Children's Apperception Test. A neurological consultation was obtained and a follow-up interview was held with Mrs. N.

APPEARANCE AND BEHAVIOR DURING EXAMINATION. Susan was an appealing child who, with a sweet smile, looked up as if expecting approval. She was a bit tense at first but relaxed quickly. In the interview, she volunteered little; when she was encouraged, she was able to talk about things she enjoyed but evaded questions about unhappy events. She accepted the tests with no question or resistance, in passive compliance to an adult request. She was outwardly unperturbed by her failures but was reassured when successful. "That one's too hard," she would explain in matter-of-fact fashion. Her speech was clear and without noticeable defects, but her use of language was often more appropriate to a pre-school child than an 11-year-old.

Mrs. N evidently was attempting to take an objective view of Susan and of herself. Generally, she seemed a fairly reliable reporter. However, it was evident that she has many conflicting and guilty feelings about Susan's condition, which came to the fore during the interviews. It was particularly difficult for her to separate her feelings about Susan from her own anger and grief over her divorce. She came close to tears as she discussed these topics.

PRESENT SITUATION. Susan and her mother live together in an apartment which Mrs. N selected last year to be near a special school for Susan. Mrs. N supports herself and Susan by working full time as a saleswoman. Around the home, Susan is able to care for herself and help her mother like a normal 11-year-old. She comes home by herself after school, entertains herself, and often starts dinner before her mother returns. She has almost no close friends because of the present school situation and the changes of school but, with Mrs. N's encouragement, attends "Campfire" meetings. Mrs. N devotes most of her evenings and weekends to Susan, restricting her social life to a rare date.

During summer vacations and other holidays, Susan visits her father and returns to her mother for the school year. These partings, both from mother and father, are always stressful and tearful for Susan who openly says she wants to live with both parents and who urges her mother to move back to the hometown.

At school Susan is well liked by her teachers. She is compliant, well behaved, and eager to please. Mrs. N fears that because Susan is no behavior problem she may not receive the special attention she needs to improve her work.

PAST HISTORY. Shortly before Susan's birth, Mrs. N separated from her husband and filed for divorce. During her pregnancy she was very emotionally upset and physically ill. Her labor was prolonged and difficult, but Susan was considered normal at birth. At this time, Mrs. N reconciled with her husband. Throughout the first year, Susan was a continual feeding problem; she "threw up constantly" and was "always crying." Mrs. N was hospitalized for surgery when Susan was 8 months old, and Susan remained in the care of her maternal grandmother for several months. Susan's toilet training was started "immediately" when the child could sit on the "potty." Although bowel training was established quite early, Susan was quite delayed in urinary control and continued to wet the bed periodically.

Much of Susan's life has been interrupted by prolonged physical illnesses or traumata, which probably have deterred her development. Beginning at about age 3, she suffered from severe throat and ear infections that culminated in a tonsillectomy at age 6. As a result, her first year at school was interrupted. At age 7, she had a severe bout of nephritis, was out of school almost a semester, and remained physically weak for some time thereafter. A year later she injured her knee, limped badly for several months, and was unable to be on the playground. Last October she had an appendectomy. For the past year she has been receiving orthodontic treatment. She suffers frequent severe colds, keeping her home from school.

The central trauma in Susan's life was the separation of her parents, which culminated in divorce when she was about 9. To this date Susan cannot mention the divorce without tears. If Mrs. N's continued acrimony against her husband is any index, the dissension between the parents must have been very intense. At first, Mrs. N was given custody of both Susan and her brother (four years Susan's senior), but almost two years ago Mrs. N agreed to let the brother remain with her former husband, following his remarriage. Since the divorce, Mrs. N and Susan have moved several times, involving almost annual changes of school for Susan. The parents continue to disagree over Susan's care, and each tries to get her to stay with them. Mrs. N declared in tears, "She's all I've got to live for!"

Before continuing this report, it is necessary to present Susan's response to the tests. Susan's scores on the Wechsler Intelligence Scale for Children were as follows:

Susan's Scores on WISC

Verbal Tests	Scale Scores	Performance Test	Scale Scores
Information	6	Picture Completion	12
Comprehension	6	Picture Arrangement	6
Arithmetic	5	Block Design	5
Similarities	10	Object Assembly	6
Vocabulary	8	Coding	7
Digit Span	5	Mazes (omitted)	
Verbal IQ	79	Performance IQ	80
	Full Scale IQ 77		

Susan's drawing of a man shown in Plate 14.4. This drawing, when scored on the Goodenough Scale, yielded a mental age of 7 years and 3 months and an IQ of 66.

Susan's reproduction of the Graham-Kendall Designs are shown in Plate 14.5. The scoring is shown only for those designs that were inadequate. The total raw score

Plate 14.4

Plate 14.5

of 9, when corrected for age and IQ, yielded a corrected score of 5, which is in the "borderline" range between a normal performance and that considered by the au-

thors of this test to be indicative of central-nervous-system dysfunctioning.

Susan gave the following Rorschach responses. She did not turn the cards.

Free Associations	*Inquiry*

Card I—1"

1. A cat—no—

It's got big ears (D8), eyes, mouth [indicating the central spaces] (location?) [top half of card] If this [space above card] were filled in, it would be the hair.

DS   F   Ad

This [indicating the bottom half] looks like a pumpkin. These two [spaces] are the teeth.

(DS F Mask)

2. Sort of an upside-down spaceship—it doesn't look too good.

The wings and this tip and the windows. The capsule was up here and they threw it down and it blew up—(how does it seem to be now?) Oh, it's flying now.

WS Fm Obj.

Card II 5"

1. A skeleton of a butterfly or a moth.

The feelers, the wings, and the face. (detailed in D2) (including D3?) No. (What makes it look like a skeleton?) It's died or dissolved up or something tore the skin off [points to D5]. That looks like the skeleton.

WS F- A O-

Card III 3"

1. A beetle.

All around here, D1. It's the skeleton of a beetle (?) The teeth or the bones and the skin. (Are D2 and D3 a part of it?) Maybe this is the heart and the flowers. (The heart?) It's the shape of a heart (and flowers?) They're hanging from the stem or it's a face hanging there, an ugly face tormenting the beetle. Are these really beetles?

D F- A (D F At)
(D F Pl) (D Fm Hd)

Card IV 7"

1. It's a monster with a sort of small face.

The whole things. It's got one eye and two arms and this and the tail (this?) Big feet.

W F A

(D3) looks like a skunk, it's the color, the shade—the white tone and the brown tone.

(D FC' A)

Free Associations	*Inquiry*

Card V 2″

1. *That's* a bat!

Wings, feelers and pinchers that suck up blood.

W F A P

Card VI 32″

1. Not much of anything.

Nothing.

Rejected

Card VII 10″

1. A girl with no body hardly.

(D2) The legs and arms, and hair. (?) So fat and flabby and big, but I don't know what this could be [indicating D6] Oh, it could be the inside of an apple.

D F H
(di F Food)

Card VIII 10″

1. Two bears on a mountain—well, not bears—birds or hawks or something.

Mice, they're mice! It looks like the legs and the face, like a mouse.

D F A (P)

The upper half looks like the skeleton of a coyote strung up there. (Coyote?) The feet and the body. It looks like it's yelling and this is the face.

(D FM A)

Card IX 30″

Not much of anything (encouraged) Well, it looks like they—in the middle—(40″)—

1. Looks like a bone.

1. [indicates the center D] It's shape in this little things (?) Just the shape.

D F At

Card X 15″

1. A big old monster—sorta—with big blue hand and all that.

(D1) are the hands and (D11) are the two cheeks. They're monster or bugs, or something—like outer space monsters, mad at each other.

DW M, F ⟷ C (A)

Summary of Rorschach Scores, Susan N—First Assessment

Location	Determinants	Contents
W = 4	M = 1	H = 1
DW = 1	FM = + 1	Hd = − + 1
D = 5 + 6	m = 1 + 1	A = 5 + 2
di = − + 1	F = 6 + 4	(A) = 1
S = − + 3	$F\text{-}$ = 2	Ad = 1
R = 10 + 7	FC' = − + 1	At = 1 + 1
P = 1 + 1	$F\longleftrightarrow C$ = − + 1	Obj = 1
		Pl = − + 1
		$Mask$ = − + 1
		$Food$ = − + 1

Susan's responses to the Children's Apperception Test were as follows:

1. The chickies are sitting down at the table and they're starting to eat dinner and the mother is coming to check on them to see if they're eating. So they say their prayers and start eating. (How do they feel?) They think the food is good, but it's chicken feed—(and then what happens?) They eat, they go to the bathroom, they brush their teeth, they wash their hands, and kiss their mother goodnight and go to bed.

2. The papa bear is tugging with the mother bear and the baby bear. All three will fall off the mountain. (?) They go to the bottom and they hurt theyself. (How come?) They're pushing and tugging and then they have to go to the hospital. (How did it all start?)—[in a very sad voice] I don't know—(How did the baby bear feel?) He didn't like it, it was too much work and the mamma bear didn't like it, she just came out of the hospital.

3. The mouse comes out of the hole. The lion doesn't see the mouse. The lion has a cane and a chair and a pipe [continues to describe the card]—(What happens?) The mouse looks up at the lion and the mouse says to himself "Why shouldn't I go up and tell the lion he's a coward?" but he's afraid he'll get killed. The lion is thinking about the mouse. He's just getting ready to kill him. (How did it turn out?) The lion doesn't get to see the mouse and the mouse doesn't get to see the lion.

4. The baby deer is riding the mamma deer or kangaroo. The mamma kangaroo is carrying the milk home. The mamma kangaroo is carrying a baby in her pouch. There are two kids. They are going home to dinner—(?) He doesn't like it, it's too much trouble, it's tiring. He's tugging and pulling along. He's riding her on his bike. [Susan seemed to perceive the mother kangaroo as also on the tricycle.]

5. The two big bears are going to sleep. The mamma bear and the papa bear are asleep in their own beds—(What happens?) They wake up and find they have to eat breakfast. The papa has to go to work and the baby has to go to school.

6. Baby bear is going to sleep but not yet. The mamma and papa bear are already asleep—for the winter. But, the baby is just sitting thinking about the next day. Whether it's going to be raining, snowing, or sunshine. (What else might he be thinking?) He's thinking if he doesn't go to sleep, mother and papa will wake up and spank him.

7. The lion is just about to jump for the monkey. The monkey is afraid. There are lots of rocks down there. The lion can't climb and the monkey is up the tree. The lion falls down but he isn't hurt.

8. The monkey's aunt is telling him something, and the mamma monkey is telling the father monkey something. There's a

picture of grandmamma on the wall. (What is his aunt telling him?) "You'd better mind your mamma 'cause every little boy should do that." (How come?) He did something naughty. He threw her wristwatch on the floor, he was mad at his mamma 'cause his mommy wouldn't let him go to the show. (What is the mommy telling the father?)—I don't know what to make up about that.

9. —I don't know—A kangaroo—or a rabbit story: The baby rabbit is about to go to sleep but she's looking out the door to see what they're doing—(?) They're having a party—(What does she see?) A big man. No—a big fat woman. That's her teacher, she wonders what she's doing there. She thought she might have did something wrong at school so she gets up and asks her mother and her mother says go back to bed. And she asks why the teacher is there. "She wants to know how you do at home and at school." (How does the baby rabbit feel then?) She doesn't like it, she thought the teacher would say she wasn't doing so good. It takes her two years to find out. The mother says, "You were very naughty that day." She says "I wasn't either." They argue until something happens. The mother slaps the papa and the papa slaps the mamma, and the baby doesn't like it. They all settle down when the baby goes to school.

10. I don't know what he did wrong, but the mama is spanking the boy! (?) He thought he did something wrong but he didn't—I don't know what it could be.

These protocols were then reviewed with the prospective psychotherapist. The written report included the preceding reasons for referral and methods of assessment, the appearance and behavior during examination, the present situation and past history, and concluded with the following analysis of test results.

ANALYSIS OF RESULTS. Intellectually, Susan functions at a mildly retarded or "borderline" level: WISC Full Scale IQ 77, Verbal IQ 79, Performance IQ 80;

Goodenough Draw-A-Man IQ 66. Her verbal skills, particularly information, arithmetic, and vocabulary, are undoubtedly depressed by her educational deficit. Even her social judgment is below average. In contrast, her ability to comprehend verbal abstractions is quite adequate and her performance on a test of attention to detail (Picture Completion) was above average. Low scores on tests involving visual-motor coordination and memory suggested the presence of a dysfunction of basic perception, of a type commonly associated with CNS damage.

Emotionally, Susan tries to play the role of the sweet and innocent child, but behind this mask she experiences considerable tension and confusion. Although socially compliant and friendly, she cannot really allow any emotional investment in her environment and sees no possibility of trusting anyone to answer her needs. She tries to repress her inner life, her daydreams and impulses, and handle all situations in a completely neutral fashion. However, fears of being overwhelmed and destroyed often break through her defenses, adding to her tension and depression. These phobic ideas suggest considerable underlying frustration and anger. She feels starved and deprived of love, angered and ready to devour others, then guilty and afraid of being devoured. Her defense is then to remain frozen and childlike in the hope that no one will know how angry she feels.

The main cause of Susan's fear of emotional deprivation, anger, and guilt appears to be her feelings about the divorce of her parents. Her fantasies support her mother's report that Susan has never acknowledged in her own heart the reality of this divorce but keeps hoping for some restitution. Because she feels so insecure over the loss of her parents, she cannot allow herself even a normal expression of frustration—let alone her real anger at her parents. Moreover, her fantansies suggest that she has a vague feeling that she may in some way have been responsible for the divorce, that it was the result of some "bad" behavior on her part. On the other hand, she tries not to change anything, particularly not to grow up, not even to succeed at school, in order to retain the childhood state she was in when the divorce occurrred. She seems to hope that by remaining static, restitution will be more possible.

SUMMARY IMPRESSION. Susan's school failure and even her low intellectual functioning are symptoms of her general emotional withdrawal and depression that is a reaction to the divorce of her parents and her underlying confused feelings of anger and guilt. Her school failure is further compounded by the fact that she changed schools and missed school so frequently.

NEUROLOGICAL CONSULTATION. Because of the history of frequent severe illnesses and Susan's poor performance on visual-motor tests, a neurological consultation was obtained. The neurologist reports that Susan shows no signs of any neurological disorder or dysfunction.

RECOMMENDATIONS. These results, including the neurologist's report, were discussed with Mrs. N. She was advised to (1) seek psychotherapy for Susan and (2) to apply for individual tutoring or to a school for remedial educational work.

A letter summarizing these results and recommendations was sent to Susan's father at his request.

Following the original consulation and assessment, Mrs. N accepted the recommendations of the psychologist. Susan was placed in a special remedial school and began twice a week psychotherapeutic sessions with another psychologist. Approximately 20 months thereafter, Susan's therapist requested a reassessment. The therapist was discouraged by what appeared to be very slow progress. Moreover, the therapist reported that Susan's mother and father independently had requested a summary of the progess of treatment.

Second Assessment, Susan N, Case 71, Age 13 Years 1 Month Wechsler Intelligence Scale for Children

Verbal Tests	Scale Scores	Performance Tests	Scale Scores
Information	7	Picture Completion	10
Comprehension	9	Picture Arrangement	11
Arithmetic	4	Block Design	7
Similarities	9	Object Assembly	7
Vocabulary	6	Codinng	8
Digit Span	(omitted)	Mazes	(omitted)
Verbal IQ	81	Performance IQ	90
	Full Scale IQ 84		

In the second assessment, Susan was asked to "Draw-A-Person" rather than to draw a man. Her first drawing, of a female figure, is shown in Plate 14.6. Although the exact instructions for the Goodenough Draw-A-Man test were not given, when Susan's drawing of a male figure (see Plate 14.7), was scored on the Goodenough Scale, a mental age of 8 years, 6 months and an IQ of 68 were obtained.

Susan's reproductions of the Graham-Kendall Designs are shown in Plate 14.8. The raw score totals 7, which, when corrected for age and IQ, yielded a corrected score of 4.0, which again was in the borderline range.

Plate 14.6

RORSCHACH TECHNIQUE, SUSAN N, SECOND ASSESSMENT

Susan did not turn the cards.

Free Associations	*Inquiry*

Card I

I forgot what I said last time (encouraged)—50″

1. In my opinion, I think it's a cockeyed bear skin—(anything else?) Uh, uh.

There's no neck [indicating the top space] and this [indicating the center space] is all burned out—(What makes it look like a skin?) The arms (D8) and it's kind of flat on a floor like (burned?) Well, there's no skin there. (skin?) It's all black.

W, S FC′ A obj

Plate 14.7

Free Associations	*Inquiry*

Card II 25″

1. A half of a butterfly.

(D2) and (D3) are the feet and head. The feelers are right here (D22)—(What kind of a butterfly?) It's a butterfly raccoon.

D F- A

2. It's a half of a racoon, that's what I'd say.

(D1) with a piece of (D5) taken out. The feet are (D22) (Is the butterfly and racoon the same thing?) It's kinda—butterfly raccoon, just the feet.

DW F- A O- (highly contaminated)

Card III 3″

1. That's a frog!

(D7) are the feet and arms. (location?) (D7) (not a whole frog?) No.

DW F- Ad

Plate 14.8

Free Associations	*Inquiry*
Card IV 20″	
1. A lizard.	The whole thing, except for (D3). Well, maybe (D3), but not (D2). These are two monsters' feet (what makes it look like a lizard?) The spine with this tail and his head (D1) plus (D5).
	D F A
Card V 3″	
1. A bat. I know, that's what it was last time.	The whole thing, the spinal cord, the head and ears, the pinchers and wings.
	W F A P
Card VI 23″	
1. A leopard.	A spinal cord and tail. The arms and the skin (skin?) It's all spotted.
	W F, FC′ A

Free Associations	*Inquiry*

Card VII 17"

1. A bear.

Feet (D5), the arms (D21) and the fur on the head (D10). (The fur?) It's fluffy and spread out.

D Fc A P

Card VIII 33"

1. Two mountain climbing rats.

Two of them. They're pink ones and they're by a mountain (pink?). The eye and the nose (?) Yes, I've read of white ones, the pink are uncommon. (Where's the mouth?) [points out the shape of (D1)]

D FM, ⟷ C A P

Card IX 6"

1. A mouse.

The whole thing. This part, (D1) and (D3) and the spinal cord and where he's scratching his face (D21)—and his eyes and big pink ears. This fluffy part of the ink is his ears and these are the feet (D3).

DW FM-, Fc A O-

Card X 15"

From the looks of it, I'd say it's a monster. I don't know what kind.

(D9) and (D1) (?) (D1) are big hands with the fingers spread out. The nose is (D8) and the feelers; a knife sticking in his mouth. (D9?) It's a pink ink splatter, (?) Well, it's pink and spread out like fur.

DW FM, C (A)

Now it looks like crushed flowers (D's 15,7 and 13) (crushed flowers?) The green, brown and the yellow. (crushed?) That used to be a flower now it's crushed and the (D7) is the green leaf.

(D CF, m Pl)

Summary of Rorscach Scores—Susan N: Second Assessment

	Location		Determinants		Content	
W	= 3	FM	= 2	A ⟷	= 8	
DW	= 4	FM-	= 1	(A)	= 1	
D	= 4 + 1	F	= 3	Ad	= 1	
S	= − + 1	F-	= 3	Aobj	= 1	
R	= 11 + 1	Fc	= 1 + 1	Pl	= − + 1	
P	= 2	FC'	= 1 + 1			
O-	= 2	F ⟷ C	= − + 2			
		CF	= − + 1			

On this second assessment, Susan was given the TAT rather than the CAT. She gave the following responses.

2:    This is the daughter named Mary. She is wondering how she is going to earn some money to support her family and she is going to school right now. The mother is wondering how she is going to earn enough money to support the farm. (What happens?) Her son is trying to get the horse across the field to get the crop in to have enough food to eat and enough money to get things from the store. (How does it turn out?) She finds a job. She works at the store for $150 per week for enough to pay bills and stuff.

3GF: Like a show in a movie. The lady comes in drunk and doesn't know what to do. She comes home to her mother and wonders how she's going to earn enough money to pay her bills, about $300. She finds a job at a bakery. After that, she comes home and says to her mother, "I got a job at the bakery, cooking and serving. I get three million per week. I can the bills with that money." (She came home drunk?) She's an alcoholic.

4:    This man came home and says to his wife, "I'm going out and find this man and fight him if he doesn't give me a job, I'm going to kill him." The wife doesn't approve and says he should stay home. (What happens?) They start fighting and she tries to hold him back and he's trying to get out the door which she won't let him do. So her kids come home and want to know what's going on and she accidently lets him go. She tells the kids all about what he's going to do. He comes home with his shirt torn and a black eye and the wife doesn't know what to do, so they call a lawyer. That's the end. (What all happened?) Nothing, the lawyer solved it. (But what happened when the man was out?) Well, he meets this guy in the restaurant and

they go across the street and start fighting for about 15 minutes and came home. (What about the guy he was fighting?) He didn't get hurt; he was the one who started it.

5:    This lady knocks on the door of a neighbor and she wants to know what's going on. She opens the door and sees nobody's in the house and she goes in and sees somebody lying on the floor. She finds her friend is dead. She calls the police and goes in their car and goes around, and as soon as she sees this man running, she knows that it's him. She says that's it. They ask his name. He says he's her husband and he killed his wife. (Why?) "She broke a vase." "I don't understand." "I had to kill her, but I didn't mean to but I did. She threatened me." He got put in jail and got out in 10 years.

6GF: The guy comes in and knocks on the door and nobody answers. He comes in and sees a lady writing a letter. He sneaks up behind her and scares her. She sees it's her husband and wants to know why he scared her. He said it's her anniversary and he brought her a present. "What is it?" She opens it and finds a diamond ring and in small letters it says that she's going to get killed that night at 12 o'clock. So it's only 11 o'clock and at 12 o'clock she's killed. That's the end of it. (How come?) Well, she asked him if she'd done something wrong. She said he killed his mark (?). That's all—(she gets killed?) The man's wife, the two of them were fighting and this lady pulled a knife and stabbed it into her (?). He was the guy what was going to kill her. He sneaked into her bedroom while she was asleep.

9GF: The lady sees this woman. She sneaks up behind a tree and she sees her husband and he doesn't like the way he's necking with her. She goes out on the beach and recognizes her. He calls her but she doesn't come because he's jealous of the lady. He calls and she goes away. She sneaks up behind the girl and kills her. Jealous, so she just kills her.

7GF: The lady's telling her to go into the other room. She'll tell her later what she's talking about. She calls the man and tells him and he goes out and goes home. She calls her daughter in and so—she says, "What happened?" The mother said, "What?" Oh, she's reading. She tells the daughter about it and tells her not to tell anyone. If she does, 'cause she gets $100 per week. 'Cause she does all the housework so—(What does her mother tell her?) This guy is coming to the house some Wednesday. It's Tuesday already. She's going to serve cocktails with a poisonous mix. Her daughter says, "Why?" "'Cause I don't like the man." "Why?" "'Cause my mother told me never to fool around with any man that's not nice." "How is he not nice?" "He goes around collecting money. He says for a good cause, but it really gives them counterfeit money." So she says to her mother that she wants to know what's going on and her mother tells her. Her mother tells her, "How come that man's so mean?"—"He says to women that he wants to go out with them but he gives them counterfeit and they get put in jail instead of him. Then they give it to the stores and liquor places. So she kills the man and comes home late—and that's about it.

12GF: The lady is wondering how she can kill this man. This lady is a Catholic sister and she says, "Why don't you drop a poisonous stuff in his glass?" "That's a great idea"; so she did. The sister said, 'A good job you did, you are a good agent." "You're a good agent too, sister." And she says, "We've work to do and if you don't come along with me, you're going to get killed." "What for?" "Because you told me to put the poison in that

drink." "But you said it was a good idea." "Never believe what you hear, sister." That might be the screams because she gotten killed (?) The sister got killed.

17GF: These people, the men on this ship, are loading the boat. The lady is on top of them, up above them. The sun is shining on the lady and the man says, "I'll be up in a minute." The lady says, "What for?" and the man says, "So I can marry you." "But I don't want to marry you." So they don't marry each other, so they go out with one another a couple of times and then they don't go out with one another anymore. (How come she doesn't want to get married?) "'Cause he is mean."

18GF: The lady is looking at the other lady and says to the man who's married to this lady that she's going to die 'cause she has rabies. "Why don't you give her some shots?" They take her down but the doctor says it's too late. She's dead. (How come she has rabies?) This dog came up and bit her and he or it gave it to her.

APPEARANCE AND BEHAVIOR DURING EXAMINATION. Attractively dressed and neatly groomed, Susan is developing into a very pretty youth, albeit a fragile appearing, pale beauty. She was much more poised and socially outgoing than before and accepted the assessment outwardly in almost adult fashion. However, she gradually lost her composure as the tests became more and more stressful, and she became visibly anxious. Although she tried to make up excuses to herself over her repeated and obvious difficulties, she was almost in tears by the time we were through. Otherwise, her affect seemed quite blunted, especially on the TAT. Although the contents of her stories were highly emotionally charged, she told them in a flat, matter-of-fact tone.

ANALYSIS OF RESULTS. Intellectually, Susan continues to function in the dull-normal range; the increase from a Full Scale IQ of 77 to an IQ of 84 is not in itself significant. Her overall Performance IQ increased by 10 points from 80 to 90 and Verbal IQ increased only by 4 points, from 77 to 81. However, there was an increase of 2 or more weighted score points on five of the scales and none showed any significant decreases. Most marked with the 5-point increase in Picture Arrangement, suggesting considerable improvement in intellectual understanding of the sequence and meaning of social events. (Comprehension also jumped 3 points.) All told, Susan does seem to be developing intellectually at a slightly more accelerated pace.

Despite these gains in intellectual growth, Susan continues to show definite signs of a marked perceptual handicap. Her visual-motor coordination and perceptual grasp of even simple configuration is so poor that it is indeed remarkable that she has made any intellectual gains at all. Particularly in unstructured situations, as on the Rorschach, she becomes so perplexed and helpless that she is almost unable to respond. In desperation she grasps some detail and in vague fashion tries to fathom the situation but is so confused that her responses are often close to complete confabulation.

Susan's perceptual handicap results in even more confusion when she attempts to understand and deal with emotional stimuli. Outwardly, Susan has learned to mask her feelings with a socially acceptable smile and passive compliance. However, she remains very dependent on her environment for emotional support, absorbing in passive fashion any emotional stimulation and is thus easily influenced by others. Having formed little or no identity of her own, she remains in a symbiotic relationship with her mother. In mirror distortion she reflects her mother's fears and frustrations. Thus, she echoes her mother's anxieties over their tight financial status, which fits into her own anxieties over being fed and of even being able to be independent and care for herself. Similarly, she reflects her mother's continued anger at the father, which expands Susan's own conflictual anger at him for his desertion of the family. Susan's fantasies of murderous hostility now include her mother, causing her even more confusion, guilt, and depression. She envisions most interpersonal relationships as a poisonous plot of jealousy threatening to destroy everyone concerned. Although emotionally still quite infantile, Susan nevertheless is beginning to experience the normal physiological stresses of puberty and thus there is an erotic overlay in her fantasies, again reflecting her mother's sexual frustrations, all of which only serve to heighten Susan's anxiety and confuse her more.

SUMMARY IMPRESSION. Susan continues to show every sign of a moderately severe generalized perceptual handicap, which I am even more convinced probably stems from some overall neurological weakness or dysfunction. She does show signs of a slight spurt of intellectual growth that makes her a bit more capable of conforming to well-structured situations, but she seems even more disabled emotionally by stress. She remains in a symbiotic tie with her mother, in addition to facing the stress of the early years of adolescence.

RECOMMENDATIONS:

1. Susan should have another thorough neurological assessment. If, as I suspect, she does have some overall weakness, psychotherapy might have to be directed toward helping her accept and adjust to this handicap.

2. It would seem unlikely that Susan's symbiotic relationship with her mother and her mother's anxieties can be resolved unless Mrs. N can be helped to understand and deal more effectively with the situation and some of her own stresses.

3. Susan's difficulties in dealing with unstructured situations and complex prob-

lem solving suggest that her placement in regular classes in junior high school should be seriously reconsidered. In my opinion, the stresses involved may be far too great for this handicapped child. Admittedly, such a reconsideration could be quite anxiety provoking for Susan who sees this placement as a promotion, that is, a reward for "good" behavior and a denial of her handicap.

These results and recommendations were discussed with the therapist and with Mrs. N. A second neurological consultation was obtained, but again there were no findings of any gross neurological difficulty. The neurologist, after looking over Susan's perceptual-motor responses on the psychological techniques, was of the opinion that this behavior was strong evidence of a generalized but mild central-nervous dysfunctioning and hazarded that this dysfunctioning might well be the sequela of possible damage that Susan probably endured during her mother's pregnancy and prolonged gestation. The fact of her many illness also suggested a generally weak physiological organism.

Despite several consultations with Mrs. N, she remained quite resistant to any continued therapeutic consideration of her personal problems. In a matter-of-fact fashion she admitted that she had been very depressed and volunteered that she at least had intellectual insight into the possibility that her depression had been a severe stress to Susan. She openly wept as she expressed considerable guilt about the possible damage she might have done. However, she averred that her life situation was now markedly changing, that she had been actively dating one man and was seriously considering marrying him. She recognized that this relationship with her boyfriend might be disturbing to Susan but felt that with the therapist's help Susan could come to accept the fact that she was not the only person in her mother's life. The therapist continued to be of the opinion that without at least collaborative treatment of Mrs. N, the prognosis for Susan was limited. However, in view of the findings in this second assessment that suggested that Susan was in a state where she was more cognizant of, but also more confused by, many of the realities in her life, it seemed it most urgent to continue Susan's therapy.

As to Susan's school placement, she adamantly refused to continue attending any sort of special classes for the handicapped. A conference was held with the assessor, the therapist, and the school counselor, and a program was worked out whereby Susan could attend regular classes for most of the day in largely nonacademic subjects and remain in special classes for reading and arithmetic. The school reported that Susan's progress over the previous year had been very slow and that her continuation in the public schools was justified chiefly to assist her in her social adjustment and to prevent her from having an identity as a disabled person.

Mr. N was advised by letter of the progress of the treatment as seen from this assessment (without mention, of course, of the parts referring to his ex-wife). He agreed to continue to sponsor Susan's therapy.

Fourteen months later the therapist requested a third assessment of Susan's development. The therapist expressed the opinion that the intense anxiety that Susan demonstrated the year before had now largely abated, that Susan had shown no real changes in her attitudes or life situation over the past several months, that her mother's life situation continued to be a major source of stress, that there was no potential change in Mrs. N's behavior, and that generally there seemed to be little to be gained in continuing the psychotherapy. At this time Susan was 14 years and 3 months old.

Susan's responses to the Wechsler Intelligence Scale for Children on the third assessment yielded the following scores.

Susan, Case 71, WISC

Verbal Tests	Scale Score	Performance Tests	Scale Score
Information	10	Picture Completion	9
Comprehension	10	Picture Arrangement	8
Arithmetic	9	Block Design	10
Similarities	12	Object Assembly	11
Vocabulary	8	Coding	8
Digit Span	11	Mazes (omitted)	
Verbal IQ	100	Performance IQ	93
	Full Scale IQ	96	

Plate 14.9

Susan's drawing of a man on this third assessment is shown in Plate 14.9. The Goodenough Mental Age for this drawing was 6 years 9 months with an IQ of 51 (based on the Goodenough C.A. ceiling of 13-6.)*

Susan's reproduction of the Graham-Kendall Design at this time are shown in Plate 14.10. The raw score of 5, when corrected for Mental Age and Chronological Age, yielded a corrected score of 3, still in the borderline range.

Susan's third set of Rorschach responses were as follows. (Again the cards were held upright.)

---

*This test was scored before the Harris revision.

Free Associations	*Inquiry*

Card I 15″

1. A dress or coat.

The whole thing. It has a tail, arms, the back, the feet. It's a "mod" dress. These, (D5) snap together. (Mod?) The cut outs. *WS F Clo O*

Card II 15″

1. How about a caterpillar?

(D3) are the feelers, (D2) are the feet, or the feet could be (D1) or that could be ears and these are arms [indicating the little dr center at the bottom of the blot] A long nose and eyes. *W F- A*

Card III 18″

1. A lizard.

(D3) are the sharp teeth, (D5) are the arms. Here's the leg [the outer edge], and (D8) are the cheeks. *W F- A*

Card IV

I remember this one. I liked this one. 20″
1. A space monster.

It has big feet (D2) and a long tail, (D1). Here are the little arms, (D4) and the face (D3). *W F (A)*

Card V 2″

1. A bat.

The whole thing, the feet, the long arm wings, the eye feelers. *W F A P*

Card VI 10″

1. I don't know what those green bugs look like. A green bug, I'll say.

(D10) are the teeth, (D9) the arms, (D23) the legs, (D3) the tail. Here's the spine down the center. *W F A*

Card VII 8″.

1. A chipmunk.

(D4) are the big cheeks they store their food in. (D5) are the legs. Here are the arms, the little ones, and the fur. (The fur?) The puffy part [rubs the card]. *W Fc- A*

Card VIII 5″

1. Two bears climbing the mountain.

(D1) it's steep or it could be sorta like a tree. *D FM A P W F N*

Plate 14.10

Free Associations	*Inquiry*

Card IX 12″

1. A giant mouse.

The whole things. (D11) is the sharp sting like the legs, (D4) the big ears. It looks kinda mad, the way the nose is. *W F-, FM A O-*

Card X [patient sighs] 12″

1. How about a spider, no . . . a bee!

The whole thing. (D1) are big muscles and (D3) a needle. Here are the feet, legs, and the inner part of the body. [Patient points randomly at various D's]. *W F- A*

Summary of Rorschach Score: Susan N—Third Assessment

Location	Determinants	Content
W = 10	FM = 1 + 1	A = 8
D = 1	F = 5	(A) = 1
S = 1 −1	F- = 4	Clo = 1
R = 11	Fc- = 1	N = 1
P = 2 O- = 1		

Susan's responses to the TAT on this third assessment were as follows.

2: This is a man plowing the field and the girl is thinking of how it would be to be living in the big city. The lady is thinking of how it would be if it were more beautiful. (How did this all come about?) Well, she looks more like the city type. (What do the others think of the girl's idea?) They don't like it and want her to grow up and have farms of her own. (?) She goes up and tells her mother that she's going to go to the city. She marries a nice young rich baron and they live happily ever after.

3GF: Like in our modern times. They live in an apartment house. She opens the door to the apartment and she is crying. She tells her mother than she took LSD and she was on a trip and she feels horrible, crazy. She puts on her pajamas and goes to bed, then she takes some more LSD and feels bad again. She keeps taking it. Her mother says she should go to a doctor. So she wants to know what she keeps taking it. But the doctor has another patient and was terribly busy. She tells her mother and her mother says, "I'll go with you the next morning." So the doctor says, "Take pep pills." So she takes pep pills and is too busy to take LSD. Pretty soon she starts taking marijuana and the doctor says, "If you start you will never be able to stop."

4: The woman is going out with another man. She left her husband but she likes this other man too. The husband was a maniac on sex and the woman tells him not to go out and fight this other man. So he goes out anyhow and picks a fight and the woman says, "He deserved it." (What does she mean?) The other man, he forced her, so they go out in the alley. The husband wins and kills the other guy. She wasn't too happy but she was glad it was all over.

5: The lady asks the daughter what time she was going to dinner and the daughter says, "Oh, about 7 or 8." The mother asks her "What time is your date coming?" and the daughter replies "7:30." "Well, it's 6:30 now, you've only got an hour." She is dressing and a man taps on the window. She screams. Her mother comes in, "What's the matter?" and she tells her mother "There's a man at the window who wants me to come with him"— "Maybe it's a dream." Her date comes and this man is out in the alley. "Who is that," asks the date. "I don't know, just ignore him." "How can I ignore him when he's in the back seat?" They go dancing and have a good time. They stay up to 4 A.M. They decide it would be nice to get married. The daughter gets married the next day. The mother wishes the daughter could have married someone else. Someone more pleasant. And the mother gets married and went to live with her daughter. Oh, brother! But the mother moved away after three years. Then the mother died and her husband died a few years later.

6GF: —I can't say too much about that one.—They're playing a play in dark shadows. A guy comes up and asks, "Is your father dead?" "In a way he is and a way he isn't. His name is Dr. Schneider." "What does Dr. Schneider do?" "He's a doctor in physical education." "What does he do in physical education?" "He has health." "Let's drop that subject." She pulls off her right white earring. He picks it up and a white sleeping pill comes out. He said, "What the hell?" The police came and she said. "That's the man who said my father was dead." So they pick him up and the lady got married to her father.

7GF: The title is, "The Mother who Died." This is the moral: while mother is reading a story, you should never listen to the story, but you should listen to the footsteps. The mother says, "Why don't you listen to the story?" "I hear footsteps." "It might be your father." The mother opens the door, and the daughter screams like she never screamed before. A high-pitched scream. The daughter picks up the mother and finds a knife in her back. "Was that daddy?" "I can't tell." "Fix me my dinner." "I can't, I'm a dying woman." But the girl doesn't know about death and things. She tries to fix the mother up. The moral is, never read a book to your daughter unless it's important.

11: What's that? It's a bee! These men are on a safari in the jungle. The picture shows a bee coming down the mountain. There's a falling stream of acid making the bee very hot. He wants to know why he's doing this and he jumps in the acid but it doesn't burn him up. He finally gets out and he's all burning. It flies around in a cave. It wants to know why it's doing that. It lands in a trail and goes back over the cave where it belongs. The earth starts to shake and the bee is trapped 'cause a landslide closed the cave, so the world is saved.

12GF: This nun is the mother of the lady. The lady wants to know who the man is. The nun says, "Why not go see?" "You're kinda of a nut!" "You don't call me a nut!" So they pick a fight. They're in a museum. The man is her former husband. She wants to know if he is a counterespionage spy. "No." "Well, why are you following me around?" "I'm not a child anymore and I can follow anyone around I like." (How does it turn out?) The man marries the lady and the mother goes in a nun's home. The nun is the tablesetter for the sisters. After years and years the old lady dies.

17GF: —I can't make up a story—The men on the boat, the lady is standing on a bridge. The sun is shining on the lady. The men come from Japan. They are hauling in lots of goods. (How about the lady?) She's just waiting for her husband.

18GF: Oh, the lady is supposed to be killing her, egads! The lady doesn't like this other lady. "What ever happened to Baby Jane?" That's not the real story, just the end of it. The lady doesn't like Baby Jane so she crippled her. "Why did you call the people from the insane society?" So she got her arm over her neck and she wouldn't talk, so she just killed her.

During this third assessment, a brief interview was held with Susan and she was asked how she herself looked at her therapy and what she felt about continuing it. Tears came to her eyes as she considered the possibility of terminating her relationship with the therapist. She did agree, however, that such a termination would eventually have to come about. Susan remarked, "I'll be a teen-ager then."

The following report was then made to the therapist: "Intellectually, Susan continues to make marked gains. She is now developing intellectually at a rate that might be expected for her age. Her intellectual development is the more remarkable since she continues to show signs of perceptual-motor dysfunction. The perceptual-motor dysfunction is also not quite as marked as it appeared three years ago but nevertheless is quite definite. In fact, Susan's responses in this third assessment even more strongly support the hypothesis that this perceptual-motor lag is very likely the sequela of some generalized central-nervous-system dysfunctioning suffered much earlier in her life.

"Although Susan now is able to handle relatively emotionally neutral problem-solving tasks much more effectively, she remains handicapped principally when she faces the task of perceptually comprehending and handling emotional stress. It is in unstructured emotional and social situations that Susan's perceptual handicap is most marked. Under the stress of emotional pressures, she becomes confused and severely difficult, if not impossible, to handle emotional stress from her environment or from her own impulses. Her fantasies, which read like psychotic poetry, reveal a conglomeration of raw feelings and impulses for which Susan has little resolution. However, it does appear that Susan no longer feels quite as intensely deprived and depressed as she did three years ago. Rather, she is now concerned with very definite Oedipal feelings. In her fantasies she expresses murderous anger toward her mother whom, it appears, she feels deprived her of her father. In fact, in one fantasy the heroine rediscovers the father and marries him, getting rid of the mother! Moreover, Susan appears now to question her mother's poisonous anger toward men. Nevertheless, Susan is also quite confused and threatened by her own sexual urges that now press on her as she advances into adolescence. She seems to fear that if a man came into her life it might be as destructive to her as she perceives it was to her mother. Yet, she seems to continue in these fantasies hoping that nevertheless there will be a Prince Charming for her.''

SUMMARY IMPRESSIONS. Despite continued evidence that Susan is very probably mildly brain damaged, she is evidently making marked strides in her intellectual development. Moreover, although the perception of social and emotional stress is particularly difficult for her, Susan is attempting to deal with the unresolved and prolonged relationships of her childhood that have been reevoked during pubescence. In fact, Susan appears to be tackling these problems with somewhat less anxiety and depression, despite the confusion of her perceptions and the intrusion of her perceptions and the intrusion of primary processes into her ideation.

RECOMMENDATIONS. Although progress in treatment may seem very slow for this perceptually handicapped child, it certainly seems that Susan's development has been much more enhanced than could have been predicted three years earlier. Both consciously and in her fantasies, Susan pleads for continued assistance while she struggles with the adolescent stresses of sexuality. Thus, if at all possible, it would seem advisable to continue therapeutic support for the following year. It does remain questionable whether Susan can achieve a point where she can function emotionally and socially relatively independently. Nevertheless, it does seem possible that she might attain even more emotional stability and some sense of personal identity.

As might be expected, the therapist was most pleased and encouraged by these results. She remarked that she had been aware of them for some time, that Susan's Oedipal conflicts were coming to the fore, but she had felt that Susan might not be able to face these conflicts and thus had not encouraged discussion of them in the treatment. She agreed that as indicated in story 3GF, she had attempted to help Susan repress and avoid sexual excitement. However, she was now of the opinion that the problems of Susan's sexual maturation could no longer be avoided. Since Susan was determined to become a teen-ager, the therapist* agreed that Susan would need continued support.

Mrs. N was also greatly encouraged, not only by Susan's intellectual improvement, but by the possibility that Susan could, in perhaps a limited fashion, mature to the point of a relatively normal social and emotional life. She reported that Susan was no longer a placid little girl, but at times was enraged at her in a rebellious fashion, ''like any other teen-ager.'' Far from being upset by this change in Susan, Mrs. N was actually encouraged at Susan's development. She admitted that she had at times let herself daydream that Susan might enter into normal teen-aged social life. She

*Unfortunately, public credit cannot be given to this very skilled and persistent therapist, since to do so might identify the patient, who now is married, a mother of two children and a relatively independent and well-adjusted adult.

bought Susan attractive adolescent clothes in the latest fashion. However, at that time Susan had no boyfriends and only one or two casual girlfriends. Mrs. N herself seemed to be breaking the symbiotic relationship she had maintained with Susan over the past year since her divorce. She was engaged to be married, although a date had not been set for the wedding. How Susan might take this additional stress was as yet unknown, although Susan seemed fond of her prospective stepfather.

CASE 72

Cindy K, age 7 years, 8 months, was refered by her pediatrician who had been treating her continued vaginal irritation and discharge. He had been concerned after Cindy's mother had reported to him that Cindy masturbated excessively and openly around the home and that she had been engaged in sexual play with other girls and boys of varying ages. The neighbors had become quite upset and had cautioned their children against playing with Cindy. The pediatrician was most shocked to learn that Cindy had been taught to engage in sexual play by Mrs. K's stepfather who, until about two years ago, had frequently been called upon as a babysitter for Cindy and her younger brother.* Mrs. K had mentioned these facts to the pediatrician merely to explain the source of Cindy's vaginal irritation and seemed relatively undisturbed by any other aspects of them. However, when the pediatrician explained that he was concerned with the possible long-range emotional disturbances arising from the situation, Mrs. K agreed to accept his referral to the psychologist. When Mrs. K contacted the psychologist, an appointment was made for an interview with her. Subsequently Mrs. K was seen for two further interviews, and Cindy was seen in two two-

*This occurred before the law demanded that incest be reported to the police.

hour assessments sessions. During this second assessment with Cindy, Mrs. K filled out the MMPI. A follow-up interview then was held with Mrs. K to discuss the results of this assessment.

Mrs. K was a strikingly beautiful woman who was fashionably and expensively dressed. Although her constant smoking and such mannerisms as biting her lip suggested considerable tension, Mrs. K attempted to discuss Cindy and her own problems in an objective and intelligent fashion, as if she was telling a story about someone else. However, she was not able to completely contain her feelings, her voice became harsh and angry as she discussed her own relationship with her mother, and she was near tears as she recited some of her own difficulties. Although a great deal of the discussion centered around Mrs. K herself and her own background, she did seem genuinely concerned about Cindy, expressing the fear that "Cindy may turn out to be just like me."

Asked first about Cindy's symptom, Mrs. K explained that initially she had not been particularly concerned about Cindy's masturbation, as she had thought that such self-stimulation was perfectly normal among pre-school children. However, as this activity continued she had asked the advice of yet another pediatrician who had assured her that Cindy would grow out of it. When Cindy continued to masturbate every night as she went to sleep and began to rub her genitals frequently during the day in public, Mrs. K had tried to punish her by depriving her of things—but without effect. Mrs. K had wondered if punishing Cindy for masturbating might draw Cindy's attention even more to this activity and "besides I was not always around when she did it." Mrs. K was upset when she received vigorous complaints from nursery-school teachers and from the kindergarten teacher. The kindergarten teacher had advised Mrs. K that "Cindy might not really be ready for school yet," largely because of this behavior. Thus

Cindy was excluded from school until she was 6. Mrs. K was not disturbed at first when she learned of Cindy's sexual play with other children. "Isn't that normal too?" she asked. However, the complaints from the neighbors has grown to such a point that Mrs. K's landlord had refused to renew her lease and two months ago she had been forced to find another apartment. At first Mrs. K did not voluntarily mention what she had told the pediatrician about her stepfather. When asked about this, she sighed deeply and said that she had never really apprehended her stepfather sexually fondling Cindy; only recently, when Mrs. K was trying to discipline Cindy for masturbating, Cindy reported, "Grandpa used to rub me all the time and I used to rub him." Mrs. K then said in a very depressed tone that she believed Cindy's report, since both she and her sister had been similarly molested by her stepfather when they were children. After a pause, she remarked, "Maybe I had better begin at the beginning."

Throughout Mrs. K's childhood, she had lived in the home of her maternal grandfather with her mother and her sister who was two years her senior. The home was dominated by her grandfather whom she variously described as a "tyrant," "an ignorant old man who would still be a dirt farmer if oil had not been discovered on their ranch," and "a wicked old man who had nothing but sex on his mind." In regard to this last statement, she explained that her maternal grandmother had died shortly after her mother's birth and that her grandfather had had various mistresses in the home from time to time. Her grandfather and her mother often quarreled violently, but her mother had never left the home and continued to occupy the family mansion. Mrs. K's father separated from her mother shortly after Mrs. K's birth, and she had seen very little of him since. Mrs. K reflected that she thought it quite probable that her father could not live in the same house with her maternal grandfather, but that her mother had refused to leave home. She based this supposition on the fact that her mother's second marriage similarly disintegrated.

Mrs. K's mother married a third time when Mrs. K was approximately 11 years of age, and it was this second stepfather who had sexually molested her and her sister. Mrs. K boiled with anger when she recalled that when she complained to her mother about her stepfather's sexual advances, her mother had accused her of lying and refused to do anything about it. In giving this history, Mrs. K made no direct association between this sexual relationship with her stepfather and her own subsequent sexual behavior, but she did go on immediately to mention that she had developed physically very early and "started playing around" while she was still in junior high school.

When she was 17 she became pregnant in what she described as a casual sexual escapade. Her grandfather was outraged and forced her to marry Cindy's father, whose parents were socially and financially indebted to him. However, this young man refused to move into the grandfather's household and escaped from the situation by enlisting in the military service shortly before Cindy's birth. "I was really very wild after that," Mrs. K remarked, explaining that she became even more sexually promiscuous, became pregnant a second time two years later, but bore this second child, Cindy's brother, out of wedlock. At this time, her mother, with whom she constantly quarreled, demanded that she leave the house. In desperation, Mrs. K accepted a proposal from a man she had known only slightly and who had been pressuring her to marry him. At first, this second marriage seemed quite ideal; her husband was some 10 years her senior, seemed genuinely fond of Cindy and the younger brother, and had moved them away from Mrs. K's hometown and had bought them a lovely home. However, Mrs. K soon discovered that her husband was impotent. Subsequently, he apprehended her in an affair with another man and divorced her. She returned to her mother's home quite depressed.

Her depression was increased by the death of her grandfather. She remembered that she had been very surprised to find herself weeping openly at his funeral. "I guess I really did love the bastard," she remarked. She resolved to attempt to become financially independent of her mother, particularly because their quarrels became even more violent. At one point, she actually fired a pistol at her mother and spent the night in jail but was not prosecuted as her mother declined to sign the complaint. She trained as a model and soon thereafter found very remunerative employment in an adjacent metropolis. She was able to support herself and her children independently. She continued to have many boyfriends and many offers of marriage but denied that she had any further sexual affairs. "I think I've been burned enough."

Because Mrs. K had not been altogether responsible for Cindy's care and training, she was rather vague about Cindy's development. During Cindy's first years of life, she had been cared for chiefly by Mrs. K's mother or by a hired nursemaid. She had not breastfed Cindy as she found herself unable to lactate. However, she could not remember that Cindy had been any particular feeding problem. It seemed to her that Cindy had always been hungry and always ate well. "When she was little, she always seemed to have a bottle in her mouth." Mrs. K recalled that Cindy was still requesting a bottle when she was 3 years of age and that she had decided to take the bottle away because she thought it might not look right to her second husband. Later in the interview, Mrs. K remarked that Cindy had always sucked her thumb and continues to do so especially when she is tired or ill. Mrs. K was not sure when Cindy was toilet trained but believed it must have happened when Cindy was approximately 2 years of age. She could only recall that Cindy was completely toilet trained at the time that she remarried.

As far as she could recall, Cindy was relatively unaffected by the birth of her brother, David. She denied that there was any rivalry between the children, noting that Cindy actually seemed very fond of David and enjoyed trying to hold him or cuddle with him, calling him "my baby." Only recently had there been little fights between them, largely over favorite foods. Except for the vaginal irritation, which Mrs. K had first noted approximately two years ago, Cindy had been in relatively good health.

After she separated from her second husband, Mrs. K had found it difficult to obtain caretakers for her children while she worked or went on dates. Her stepfather, who had separated from her mother, lived nearby and she accepted his offer to watch over the children from time to time. About two years ago, he had returned to Mrs. K's hometown, and she was forced to try to hire other people to care for her children. Because she could not find babysitters, she frequently was unable to go to work and lost considerable income. Several times she was forced to borrow money from her mother, which always resulted in another altercation. When it was suggested to Mrs. K that her situation seemed very depressing, she admitted that occasionally she was so overwhelmed with depression that she had actively considered suicide.

A slight-built blond child who was neatly dressed and groomed, Cindy accepted the testing situation in a matter-of-fact fashion. However, it was apparent from the first that she was quite tense and apprehensive. In the initial session, the psychologist attempted to structure the situation for her, associating it as a follow-up of her medical treatment. This only caused her to be more tense and guarded. Regarding her physical symptom, Cindy said only that she "itched down there" but denied that this caused her any great concern or embarrassment. She also denied that she had ever know any other children who had a similar itch or had seen anyone else rub their genitals.

She relaxed noticeably when the discussion turned to her school and play activities. As her mother had reported, Cindy seemed to enjoy going to school and had been at least moderately successful in the first two years. Cindy described, with obvious enjoyment, some of her work at school, talked about some of her playmates, but froze perceptibly when asked what they did together. She talked excitedly about her hopes that she would receive a pet rabbit for Easter but then became sad as she remembered that her mother could not let her have a pet in the apartment. She described her brother David as "cute," but agreed that he could be "a little pest" when he got into her things. When asked about who took care of her when her mother worked, she replied that her grandpa used to, but "now we have other babysitters." She showed no particular affect when mentioning her grandfather. When asked about her father, Cindy remarked, still in her matter-of-fact tone, that he had gone away and that she did not expect him to come back. She denied that she missed him and added that she thought maybe her mother would find them another daddy later. During the administration of the tests, Cindy was quite compliant and cooperative but she remained rather guarded and required considerable encouragement at times to respond.

Because the pediatrician had expressed the opinion that Cindy seemed retarded intellectually, the Stanford-Binet Form LM was administered. Cindy passed all items at the VI-year level, four items at the VII- and VIII-year level, three at the IX-year level, one at the X-year level, which yielded a Mental Age of 8 years, 0 months and an IQ of 110. It was noted that Cindy passed "Similarities" at year VI but failed "Similarities and Differences" at year VIII. Her other failures at years VII and VIII were on "Comprehension IV." Her score of 7 on the Vocabulary was sufficient for age VI but not for age VIII. Cindy's verbalization, however, was adequate enough for her to pass such items as "Rhymes: new forms" on year IX and "Finding Reasons I" on year X. Her perceptual-motor functioning

seemed effective as she quite easily drew a diamond for year VII and passed the "Memory For Designs I" at year IX but not at year XI. However, she was not able to pass the "Paper Cutting" items at year IX.

Cindy's drawing of a man yielded a Mental Age of 8 years 6 months and an IQ of 107 when scored on the Goodenough Scale. This drawing and a subsequent drawing of a girl were quite stilted, and the overcontrol of motor activity demonstrated in the drawings did suggest the possibility of a perceptual-motor diffficulty. However, this motor behavior could also be explained in terms of the emotional restriction as was evident in Cindy's other responses.

Partly because of her age and partly because she seemed so very guarded, it was decided to inquire after her Rorschach responses as she gave them rather than subsequent to the free associations. Her responses were as follows:

Card I 40″
I can't make anything out of this one— (encouraged)—100.″ This looks like a dress, it's all I can make out of it(?) It's like this [pointing to the lower part of D4]. It's a shirt with a slip underneath it. *D Fc Clo*

Card II 4″
Rocks—and a bear—that's all. (Show me the rocks. [Cindy points to a little d in D1]. They're kinda round. (Show me the bear). This shape, D1, the nose and the body (Anything else you can show me about it?) [no response] *Di F N D F A P*

Card III 4″
A butterfly (D3), that shape and a stick (D7) that shape. *D F A P D F Pl*

Card IV 40″
Nothing out of this one—just nothing. It looks so ugly. (?)—90″ It really looks like a monster. [indicating the whole card with her finger] (?) Here's the feet, D2, and the body. (How about this, D4)? I don't know. (And D1?) His arm— (What makes it look so ugly?) The way the shape is, with his arm down here. *W F (H)*

Card V 5″
A cocoon web; a cocoon coming out of it. Here's the web [indicating the usual butterfly wings]

and here's the cocoon coming out of it [indicating the center of the card] (What makes it look like a web?) 'Cause that's what cocoons got. *D FM A*

Card VI
Oh no!—30″. Nothing out of it. The whole thing, nothing out of it [turns card over]. *Rejects.*

Card VII [sighs] 3″
A butterfly. That's all and two rabbits. The butterfly is here [points to D4 and 6] the shape and this thing here (D6). (D6?) I don't know (How about the rabbits?) [points to D2] The ear, the face, the nose, and the tail. *D F A   D F A*

Card VIII 5″
Two cats (D1) (How do they seem to be?) They look like bobcats, the face. (Anything else you can tell me about them?) No, and some mountains, this shape (D2) [outlines shape with her fingers]. *D F A (P) D F N*

Card IX 3″
Nothing—7″. Just a blob full of paint—only one thing, a bear's head. (D6) that's all (?) Here's his eyes. *W C Color   D F Ad*

Card X 5″
Two spiders (D1) and two flowers (D2). (What makes it look like flowers?) Just this shape. *D F A P   D F Pl*

Cindy told the following stories to the CAT.

1.   Some animals are eating their dinner and a rooster is up here. (What happens?) The rooster is getting at them. (Why?) 'Cause they're eating without her, 'cause they were hungry. (What happens next?) She looks like she's going to give them a spanking after dinner. (How do the children feel?) They feel happy, they look happy without her.
2.   The father is pulling away from the mother bear and the baby bear. (How come?) He's probably mad at them. (About what?) They're taking the rope away from him. (What happens?) The father bear looks disappointed. (And how does the baby bear feel?) Like he was mad, like he was going to bite his daddy. (How come?) He don't want his father to have it. He wants his mother to have the rope.
3.   The lion is smoking a pipe and a mouse is peeking out at the lion and the lion is in a chair and he has a stick by him. (What happens?) The lion is mad. (What about?) 'Cause his wife isn't cooking dinner and he doesn't have anything to put in his pipe. (What happens next?) He's just sitting there waiting for his wife. (And the mouse?) He's just staring at the lion.
4.   The kangaroo is trying to beat the other kangaroo on the tricycle and the baby kangaroo is holding onto the balloon. The kangaroo is holding a basket with milk and food in it. There is a house back here and it has smoke, and some of the trees are all burned up. (What has happened?) Maybe she's mad at him. (How is that?) 'Cause he did something wrong. He played out too long (?) He might get a spanking. (Why?) He's sad because he didn't get a ride like him.
5.   Two bears are sleeping in a crib and a father bear and a mother bear are sleeping in a bed next to them and they're asleep—(What happened?)—I can't—(encouraged). The other bear is sleeping in the crib next—(a brother or a sister?) A brother—(They're in the same room with their parents?) They're not afraid of the things that could happen to them in their own room.
6.   The mother and the father and the baby bear are sleeping in the cave. The father is sleeping next to the door so one can come in. (What happens?) The baby is awake—(what does he do?) He's just laying down; then he gets up, and he probably tries to get out and the mother and the father wake him and they say, "What are you doing?" "I'm trying to go outside." "Never do that again."
7.   The tiger is trying to get the monkey and the monkey let go of the rope, and the monkey's afraid so he'll be real afraid and he tries to get away—all I can make up about that one. (What happens?) The tiger might get the monkey.
8.   The baby monkey is in bed so the mother is being real mean to him and the other mother is talking and having coffee. (What did he do bad?) He did something wrong over at a friend's house. They're all telling him to go to bed. (How does he feel?) He's sorry he did it. (How does he feel about going to bed?) He don't want to. (What could they be talking about?) They're glad he has to go to bed; it's his next-door neighbor and he don't like it. He did it. (What did his neighbor do?) [no response]
9.   The rabbit's sleeping in his bed and he thinks something's happening. So he looks out of his room and doesn't see his parents—(?) He thought they were in the next room but they were out taking a walk—(How does he feel?) He thinks somebody took 'em away. (How does he

feel?) Bad, 'cause he has no one to take care of him.

10. The mother puppy is spanking the baby puppy 'cause he was a bad boy and he is saying ow, ow, ow. (What did he do that was bad?) He didn't come home when his mother called him.

When the World Test was opened, Cindy seemed relatively uninterested. She searched lackadaisically and apathetically through the test objects in random fashion. Once or twice she turned back to a house she had set out and peered under it as if she was looking to see what was inside. She fiddled with one that had windows and doors to open, and then placing her face down close to it, she stared into the windows. Then she shrugged as if she expected it to be empty and returned to the case. Although she picked up several of the human figures and held them for a second, she returned these to the case but became preoccupied with the animals. She smiled as she found the horses and began to search for other animals that she placed in a little pile separate from her line of houses. She seemed a little puzzled by the wild animals, quickly rejected the snake and the dinosaur, but placed some of the others in the same pile with the domestic animals. Finally she seemed to be satisfied with what she had selected and, turning around, she stood the animals up but without any particular arrangement. She did find the barn and sat that next to the animals and then sat quietly looking at what she had done. When asked what she had made, she shrugged again and said, "Nothing." Asked what the buildings were, she replied, "Some houses and stuff." Asked about the animals, she said, "They're just eating." She picked up the horses again and stared at them and then began to put things back into the case.

The following report was sent to the pediatrician:

To the casual observer, Cindy's psychological development might seem quite average for her age. Intellectually, she is functioning at a normal pace. As disturbing as her environment may be, it does not seem to affect Cindy's ability to solve intellectual problems, to learn at school, or to understand intellectually the meaning of rules of the society about her. Her choice of words is sometimes a bit immature, but she can generally say what she means even though she is not very verbal. Like most children her age, she feels that facts are facts and there is not too much need to explain them. However, she shows no special intellectual curiosity nor imagination. It is perhaps in this respect that she may, on first impression, seem slightly dull.

Although not intellectually dull, Cindy does lack the natural spontaneity one might expect of a happy and outgoing child. It seems difficult for Cindy to really become interested in or excited about anything. Although she does not openly express any sadness, for a child this age, this apathy in itself does strongly suggest an underlying depressiveness. Even more strongly than most latency children, Cindy is very emotionally guarded. She avoids the emotional aspects of a situation as much as possible. By and large, the emotional pressures and stimulations in her environment seem to have little meaning to her. Similarly she tries not to permit her own impulses to have any affect on her. Cindy's neutralizing of emotional stimuli is so extensive that it would appear probable that any kind of affective stimuli may be threatening to her. It appears as though Cindy could not become emotionally involved with others nor permit her own impulses and feelings to be openly expressed.

Behind her mask, Cindy does have some very strong affects and impulses. There are many associations in Cindy's responses that strongly suggest that the sexual stimulation that she has experienced may be very threatening and confusing to her. Cindy's actual sexual development is symbolized by one of her Rorschach responses — "a cocoon web." That is, still in latency, Cindy is like a larva encased in a cocoon, but as further indicated in her Rorschach response, things are stirring in this cocoon. Cindy experiences sexuality as "an ugly monster"; when faced directly with even a symbol of sex, she rejects it completely.

Cindy's fantasies suggest that there are other aspects of her experiences that are even more disturbing to her. One of the reasons that this child is so very emotionally guarded is that she has experienced many emotional separations. Repeatedly in her fantasies, people are rejecting or separating from one another. Sometimes Cindy seems to feel that children would be almost better off without having to depend upon parents. Nevertheless, emotional succorance is very important to Cindy. In her view, the main reason people feel angry is that they are not fed, cared for, and comforted. Cindy experiences her world as very empty and lacking in any organization or any human relationships. It would appear from both her history and her responses to the tests that the only positive emotional experience she has found has been through genital stimulation.

SUMMARY IMPRESSION. Deprived of continued and stable relationships, particularly those that supply infantile needs for comfort and affection, Cindy continues the only kind of emotional stimulation she has known. Thus, she substitutes sexual stimulation for human love and affection, albeit on a childish level. The history given by Cindy's mother suggests that this pattern probably has existed in her family for several generations.

Because Cindy's pattern of behavior is so much a part and parcel of the life led by her mother and her mother's family, it would seem extremely difficult to make much change in Cindy's behavior as long as she is part of the milieu. However, Mrs. K does show some signs of wanting to make changes in her own behavior. She experiences considerable depression regarding her own situation and, although her history and responses to the MMPI suggest considerable instability, she may be motivated to consider changes in her own ways of living.

These results were then discussed with Mrs. K in a follow-up interview. She very readily accepted the recommendations that she herself should enter into psychotherapy but asked that Cindy be seen at the same time. She accepted a referral to another psychologist for the psychotherapy, and the assessor continued to see Cindy in weekly play sessions. During the first several months, Cindy remained very guarded but seemed to be gradually edging into a relationship with the therapist. The two therapists held periodic collaborative discussions; Mrs. K's therapist reported that as she proceeded to explore her feelings, she was becoming more and more depressed whereupon she continued to "act out," for example, she frequently missed appointments with her therapist or would call desperately for extra appointments thereafter. Only twice did she fail to bring Cindy to her appointments. Six months after the assessment, Mrs. K was badly injured in an automobile accident that scarred her face and required the amputation of one arm. While recuperating from this accident, she became openly psychotic, made another attack on her mother's life, and was committed to a state hospital. At this point, Cindy's father, whom she had really never seen, reappeared and sued Cindy's grandmother for custody of both children. The court asked for the advice from the psychologist who suggested that the children be made wards of the court and that foster homes be found for them. At this point, Cindy had not seen her therapist for several months; when they met in the court antechambers, Cindy immediately rushed into his arms and wept. She could not say why she was crying but obviously saw the therapist as a comforting person.

CASE 73

Billy B, aged 3 years 9 months, was referred for psychological assessment by a neurologist who had examined Billy on referral from the child's pediatrician. Billy had two defects at birth: a "clubfoot" and a mild "ptosis," or weakening of the eyelid muscles. The foot deformity necessitated a specially built shoe. The drooping of his eyelids did give Billy a look of being sleepy or possibly dull. Billy's mother had worried that his motor development might be slowed and that he might be retarded. She revealed to the neurologist her fears that defects might be signs of trauma to the central nervous system. In referring Billy for psychological assessment, the neurologist reported that Billy's nervous system seemed quite intact, that there was no sign of any central-nervous-system disorder nor of inadequate motor functioning. He also remarked that Mrs. B seemed unduly anxious about Billy's development in general and that he had found it difficult to reassure her that in his opinion Billy's defects did not reflect any weakness of the brain. Because of this, the neurologist thought that further assessment of Billy's perceptual motor and intellectual functioning might be in order and that some assessment might be necessary of the role of Mrs. B's anxiety.

In making the appointment over the telephone, Mrs. B was full of questions and requests. She wanted to know what type of tests would be used, explaining that she was receiving training as a teacher for the mentally handicapped and was familiar with some of the tests. She wanted to be reassured that the complete examination would be given. She wanted to know from the first how many examinations would be necessary and was concerned that they be arranged at a time convenient to both her and her husband. She was very pleasant and courteous in all these questions but her concern did confirm the neurologist's impression that she had considerable anxiety about the situation. She seemed a little surprised when the psychologist requested that she and her husband come in without Billy for the first appointment, until it was explained to her that the psychologist did need information from then regarding Billy's development.

After this initial interview with the parents, Billy was seen in two subsequent one-hour sessions, accompanied first by his mother and then by his father. On each occasion each parent filled in the MMPI while waiting for the child. Both parents were then seen together in a follow-up interview. The Stanford-Binet Intelligence Test, Form LM, parts of the Merrill-Palmer Scale of Mental Tests, the Rorschach Technique, the Lynn Structured Doll Play Test, and the World Test were administered to Billy. During the initial interview with the parents, the Vineland Social Development Scale was filled out.

On the Binet, Billy passed all items at the III-6 level, five items at year IV, five items at IV-6, four items at year V, four items at VI, one item at VII, and one item at VIII. Because Billy was getting somewhat restless and expressed some feelings of disinterest in items far beyond his ability, none of the items at year IX were administered. Thus on the Binet he achieved a Mental Age of 5 years 4 months, IQ 138. On the Merrill-Palmer, Billy completed such perceptual items as the manikin, the little pink tower, the picture puzzle, the Sequin Form Board, and the buttoning of two buttons at the 4½-year level. His only actual failure below the 5-year level was the six cube pyramids (which does not appear on this test before age 4).

In administering the Rorschach to Billy, the inquiry was conducted simultaneously with the free associations. His responses were as follows.

Card I 2″
It's a mountain (?) All of it, a big mountain. *W F N*
Here's a gun, here's a gun, and here's a gun. [indicates D5 and D8] (What makes them look like a gun?) They're pointing. *D Fm obj*

Card II 2″
It's got red and that make it fire. *D CF Fire* And here's another gun, it shoots. [indicates D3] *d Fm Obj*

Card III 3″
This doesn't have any gun. Here's a butterfly (D2) and dead (?). *D F A P*

It's dead, that red stuff is the blood (D3) *D CF Blood*

Card IV 4″
There's no red, it's not dead. It's a plant 'cause it has that [points to D1] (?) The leaves. *W F Pl*

Card V 3″
It's a butterfly. —Hey! It's both sides, both the same. (?) Big wings and those things [puts fingers over his forehead indicating antennae] *W F A P*

Card VI [Billy glances at the card and then looks at the ceiling] (What do you see on the card?) [still looking at the ceiling] 20″
It's spiderish, every part of it [looking again at the card and points to D3] It's too scary. *DW F A*

Card VII 5″
Too icky! Looks like some blood (?) All icky [rubs hand across the slaps it]. *D c Blood*

Card VIII 3″
Goody, it has colors, blue, red, orange, pink, blue, and some green. *W C n Color*
Here's a stick, D1, or a fish, also D1. *D F Obj D F A*

Card IX 7″
Yellow. Why is that broke (?) The yellow is broke [points to space between D23]. *D Cn, m Color*

Card X 6″
An octopus, D1. *D F A P*
And an archer. *D F H O*
And candles. *D F Obj O*

Billy was fascinated with the Structured Doll Play materials. In the first setting he decided that the child figure should sleep in a bed: "He's a bigger boy and doesn't have to be a baby no more" and thus not in the crib. He decided that a mother and father would have their own separate bedrooms and that there was no place for either in the bed "'cause the boy's sleeping in it." He also decided that the boy would drink from a glass and not a bottle and added that "he walks around the town with the boy; they've got to move to another house 'cause it's prettier than the one they have." (Later Mrs. B explained that the family had recently moved from an

apartment to a home of their own.) On the peer choice, Billy decided that the boy should play with the boy and described the play as walking, kissing one another" 'cause they like to." Asked what else they do, he said, "They play and they fight and they open up wide." He decided that the boy would play similarly with the girl. In the fighting situation, Billy got very excited and did not at first want to join the assessor in making dolls fight but then seemed to enjoy making a bigger fight than was illustrated to him. His verbalization at this point was a little difficult to understand: "The army check, one has to go to the army check and this boy doesn't, he's going off to his car." When the parent figures were introduced into the fighting scene, Billy had the mother say, "Why did you do that?" and then the mother doll spanked the little boy. He was less sure of what father would do and, when pressed, said, "Nothing." In the feeding scene, Billy chose the father to feed the boy figure and when asked how the boy liked the food, he remarked, "He doesn't; he hates it and runs away." (What does the father do?) "He catches him; he comes back to eat." In the injury setting, Billy also selected the father to "come and take him on his arms" when the boy fell and hurt his leg. However, when the mother was introduced, Billy said in a high-pitched imitation of his own mother's voice, "I like you still but I don't like you falling," and Billy had the child reply, "I hooked you," and the mother, "I smacked you." (smacked?) "Not kissing," said Billy. In the pursuit scene, Billy chose first the mother and he had the mother and the child both fall down (?) "The mother didn't know what happened but there is a good elevator on the mommy and the boy came up," and Billy tried to place the boy doll in the mother doll's arms. When the father was introduced, the father continued to chase the boy with gales of laughter and when asked why the father was chasing the boy, he replied "'cause he likes to." In the reprimand scene he had the mother repri-

Rorschach Summary—Case 73

Location	Determinants	Content
W = 1	M = 0	H = 1
DW = 1	FM = 0	Hd = 0
D = 11	m = 2 + 1	A = 5
d = 1	F = 10	Obj = 4
R = 17	c = 1	N = 1
	CF = 2	$Fire$ = 1
	Cn = 2	$Blood$ = 1
		Pl = 2
P = 3 EB = 0.5 = 70E		$Colon$ = 2
O = 2		

mand the child because "he fell and cried" and the father reprimand the child because "you hit." In the parental relationship scene Billy had the parents face each other and decided they were going to change their clothes and go out and pick up the boy. Similarly, in the separation scene he chose the mother and had her first put on a jacket and go pick up the daddy at school. This scene was repeated when the father was introduced, that is, the boy and father went to pick up the mother at school. (Both parents were university graduate students and alternately cared for Billy while one or the other was in classes.) In the hospital scene, Billy decided that the doll boy was bad because he had cried about the shot. He had the father figure say, "You've been a bad boy at the hospital and you can hang up your jacket everyday." He had the mother doll take the boy out of the bed but remarked, "He did not get anything," indicating that the boy doll did not get any reward. In the toilet scene, Billy had the boy doll go to the toilet by himself and remarked with evident pride in his voice, "He used to go to the potty, now he goes here" (pointing to the toilet). In the bathing scene Billy did not seem to perceive any difference or show any affect regarding placing of the girl and boy dolls in the same bathtub. Time prevented the administration of the nightmare scene. Using Lynn's preliminary standards, these results suggested that Billy was maturing fairly well in his personal and social rela-

tionships. He was evidently interested in developing independent need-gratification skills. It did appear that Billy was beginning to identify with his father, that is, he saw the father as a companion, who even fed him and controlled his eating habits. Quite noticeably, Billy thought of his mother as being threatened if he was hurt, injured, or cried. Most important Billy thought that his mother equated being hurt with being "bad."

Billy was fascinated with the World Test materials and dug into the case with great glee, tossing objects out almost without glancing at them. After he had emptied most of the box, he set about arranging and rearranging them, stopping at various points to play with objects such as the cars, train, airplane, and soldiers. He lined up the buildings in several lines, asking the assessor to identify some of them. He selected some of the children and placed them around the school, and posted adult human figures at various points beside the buildings. He put the domestic and wild animals around the barn but put obviously aggressive animals such as the snake and dinosaur back in the chest. Although he played with the soldiers and some of the military equipment, he did not include these in his World but left them off to one side of his main scene. After constructing his World, he continued to move cars and the train and people up and down the streets of his village. He talked a great deal while he was working, identifying various pieces and remarking on them. He noted that the children were going to school; he had people going to the store, the hospital, and the church. He asked to have the jail identified and included it in the village but seemed to pay very little attention to it. All in all, his play seemed quite spontaneous and happy.

In the initial interview, Mrs. B seemed quite tense. She was dressed rather plainly in dark clothes, wore little or no cosmetics, and her hair was tied together at the nape of her neck with a bun. She spoke rather rapidly and sharply but nevertheless raising her voice at the end of the sentence as if asking a question. Her husband, although dressed in a suit and a tie, was so blonde and so slightly built that he appeared almost 10 years younger than his stated age of 30. Although Mr. B was an elementary-school principal, it would have been easier to imagine that he was a camp counselor. Neither parent spoke for a moment, but Mrs. B gave her husband a glance indicating that she wanted him to initiate the discussion. He remarked that "we" were worried when Billy's foot defect was discovered at birth and had become more disturbed when approximately three months later the eyelid ptosis was definitely established. He quickly added that he had not noticed any particular difficulties in Billy's development thereafter but that he thought the complete assessments currently being conducted by the neurologist and the psychologist were quite necessary. Asked why he felt the examinations to be necessary, he indicated that he hoped that the examinations would end any further concerns; pressed further to voice his concerns, he shrugged and pointed at his wife.

Mrs. B's facial expression and gesture and tone of voice suggested that she was dissatisfied with her husband's statements. When the psychologist remarked on this, Mrs. B replied tartly that she thought her husband might not always observe some of Billy's difficulties, since he was not responsible for Billy's care as frequently as she. Moreover, she thought that her husband had a general tendency to brush aside and avoid anything unpleasant. Mr. B nodded in agreement, adding that he might be trying to gloss over things and that his wife did have more opportunity to observe Bill. (The assessor noted to himself that Mrs. B referred to her son with the diminutive *Billy*, while her husband referred to him as *Bill*.) When Mrs. B tried to describe her concerns about Billy's development, she was quite vague. She remarked that he seemed somewhat clumsy and then gave as evidence that he had not been successful in riding the two-wheeled bicycle that belonged to his 6-year-old cousin. Billy was able to ride a tricycle and attempted to use skates (Mrs. B remarked on this with a note of horror in her voice) and loved to play on such equipment as slides and swings. His father quickly added that Bill enjoyed tossing and attempting to catch a ball, which he thought was possibly above average for a child not yet 4 years old. Mrs. B agreed that Billy loved to try many activities and seemed relatively successful at them, but she explained that he was always falling or scratching or bruising himself. Asked how Billy reacted when he was hurt, she voiced the opinion that maybe he had something wrong with him, since he seldom complained of any pain. She remarked further that some of his bumps and bruises had caused him to limp further. Twice she felt that he had broken his arm. Although when they went to the hospital emergency room, she was angered when the doctors informed her that the X rays were negative and that he had merely a mild "contusion." Asked if Billy's clubfoot had proved to be of any great handicap to him, she remarked immediately that "of course, one worries more about a crippled child."

The psychologist then asked Mr. B specifically what he thought about this, and after some hesitation he replied that he did not see that Bill seemed particularly handicapped but added quickly that he could understand his wife's concern. The parents were then interviewed regarding the specific items of the Vineland Social Development Scale. Both parents agreed that Billy could feed himself, dress himself, bathe himself, and tend to his needs at toilet with little or no supervision. They described him as exceedingly sociable, said that he enjoyed showing off to adults, performing little tasks and household chores, and playing with peers, almost at the kindergarten level. They remarked that he particularly enjoyed being in the company of adults, such as shopping with his parents or accompanying them on various errands. They were very proud of his behavior in public, remarking that they knew of no child who behaved himself as well as Billy did in restaurants or primarily adult settings.

As to Billy's developmental history, he was born when Mrs. B was 28 and her husband 26. They had been married approximately three years and had used birth-control methods in order to avoid having children until after Mr. B completed his master's degree at the university and had obtained a job as a school vice principal. Until that time, Mrs. B had herself been employed as a schoolteacher, but once Mr. B was working she resigned with the purpose of having a child. Thus, Billy appeared to be both a planned and wanted child. Mrs. B reported that during her pregnancy she was frequently ill and had continued mild vaginal "spotting." Her labor pains began three days prior to Billy's birth although they were not continuous. Otherwise his birth was uneventful and initially he appeared to be a normal health neonate. His clubfoot was noticed several days after birth and Mrs. B admitted that she was quite disappointed about this defect from the first and remarked that at the time she even found herself worrying that perhaps she had done something wrong in her dieting and exercise during her pregnancy that might have caused this defect. She breast-fed Billy for approximately four months, but her breasts were exceedingly tender. Due to Billy's avid hunger, nursing him

often was quite painful to her. Her obstetrician suggested that Billy be put on a bottle formula and that breast feeding did not seem necessary in view of the difficulty that she was experiencing. From the first, she was gratified that Billy seemed to be an alert and active baby, kicking and squirming, reaching and pulling, and attentive to any face that appeared over his crib or to footsteps that entered the room.

She had kept a baby book on his progress, which she had brought with her. Her notes showed that in general Billy's motor development was at least normal, if not precocious. He was sitting up almost without support by age 3 months, pulling himself erect to his feet at 6 months, and attempting to walk holding onto things at approximately 10½ months. Her notes were not definite but as far as could be ascertained, he was walking by the time he was 1 year old. Since that time, "He has always been into things, and on the go." Her notes indicated that he had spoken his first words at age 8 months, but when questioned further she agreed that these were sounds such as "mamma," but that he seemed to understand both "go" and "come" and "potty" by the time he was walking. However, he first spoke words clearly somewhere between 18 and 24 months. By the time he was 2, he was definitely speaking two- and three-word combinations. Mrs. B remarked very proudly that although she had feared that Billy might be difficult to toilet train, since he seemed to her so active and willful, it turned out that he almost toilet trained himself. He seemed to be a great imitator and had entered the bathroom and watched his father urinate whereupon he tried to ape him. He was then provided with a potty of his own and proceeded to use it almost exclusively for urination and a second potty was given him for defecation. She went on to remark that they did not realize how much children learn through imitation and that by and large Billy had acquired all his skills by observing and imitating his parents.

When the assessor remarked with some amazement on the rapidity of Billy's development of these motor and social skills and particularly in his ability to imitate without much further training, Mrs. B quickly retracted her note of pride and said she had observed similar abilities among retarded children whom she regarded also as "great imitators." Thus, she did not feel that Billy's development was any sign of intellectual development, and she was still concerned lest he might turn out to be retarded.

Both parents readily accepted the assessor's request for information about their own backgrounds. Mrs. B was the oldest of five children born and reared in a rural village in a western desert state. Both of her parents were schoolteachers. Her next younger brother suffered a spasticity of his entire left side, probably from a birth injury. His care and management was of considerable concern to Mrs. B's mother, and Mrs. B was instructed by both parents to watch out for this brother at school. However, it turned out that her brother was quite capable of caring for himself in many ways. He was a bright boy who ultimately succeeded in completing a university education and at that time was employed as a geologist, which entailed traveling over mountainous territory on horseback. One other younger brother was also frequently ill with asthma, and Mrs. B also helped her mother care for this brother as well as her baby sister who was 16 years her junior. Since both of Mrs. B's parents were employed full time, much of the care of the house and the younger children fell on Mrs. B's shoulders. She denied that she was at all concerned about this or even resented it but rather now regarded it as excellent training for becoming a mother. She added that she might have had more resentment about being tied down with home duties had it not been that she lived in a rural area where there were not as many places to go or things for a teen-ager to do. After she completed elementary school, she commuted to high school and then junior college in a nearby city, so that she did not actually leave home until age 19 when she decided to attend the university.

Mr. B was the youngest of three boys, born and reared in the city where the B's were currently living. His father also was a high-school teacher and later a high-school principal, but his mother did not work outside the home. As far as he could remember, his childhood was relatively uneventful. He remembered scrapping with his brothers but remarked that his two older brothers were more likely to fight among themselves than with him. He felt his mother was somewhat overprotective but that he and his brothers were able to avoid some of the mother's demand for cautiousness by obtaining their father's support. He remembered particularly that the mother was almost adamant that he should not play school football and was quite angry with his father, who signed the permit without further discussion. Mr. B was active in sports, earning varsity letters in both swimming and football. He remarked that he did not consider himself any great football player but that he had been quite obese and therefore had been a good block. In telling this, he seemed to enjoy this joke upon himself. He remained somewhat active in sports, although not going out for varsity teams in college. The B's had met while attending the university. Mrs. B remarked that she had first noticed him because he was an excellent dancer and she did not see how anyone as heavy set as he was, could dance so smoothly. In mentioning Mr. B's weight, he explained that he had at one time been seriously overweight but that in recent years he had been able to diet and lose weight to the point where his doctor felt he was at least within normal range for his height.

Following Billy's birth, Mrs. B had found herself bored and restless at home as Billy seemed to demand so little care. Thus she began to look for extra things to do. She had volunteered to work with intellectually retarded children and finally decided that she would return to graduate school for some training in the special education of retarded children. She thus was attending two classes weekly. At approximately the same time, Mr. B received an inheritance that enabled him to take a leave of absence from his teaching position and return full time to the university, working toward a doctorate in eduation. He, too, was particularly interested in the education of handicapped children.

On the MMPI, two of Mrs. B's scale scores were above 70 (*D* and *Pd*), and two more were between 65 and 70 (*Hy* and *Pt*). The remainder of her scores were within the normal range. Her *K* score was 60, while *L* and *F* were both just below 50. This profile suggested that Mrs. B possibly had more rebellious and angry feelings and that there might be more dissention in the B's marriage than was indicated in this initial interview. It also suggested that she was an obsessive worrier, a person who is easily affected by guilt feelings and that she tended to blame herself more than she blamed others.

In contrast, Mr. B's MMPI profile was almost unremarkable. His highest scale was at the *MA*, which was at 55, and all other scales were close to 50.

The following report was sent to the neurologist:

In all areas of psychological development, Billy is markedly precocious. Intellectually, he is functioning at the 5-year 4-month level with an IQ of 138. Although the parents raised the question of a possible perceptual-motor defect, Billy's visual-motor development is actually advanced for his age. His social development is also more comparable to kindergarten- than nursery-school level. He feeds himself, dresses himself, is completely toilet trained, and plays with peers at the kindergarten level. Emotion-

ally, also, Billy is developing very rapidly. He is already cognizant of the need for impulse control and shows signs of making efforts toward self-regulation of his impulses. He reflects his mother's anxiety over him in his doll play where his mother equates "getting hurt" with "being bad." His doll play further suggested that he is attempting to establish a masculine relationship with his father whom he also regards as a protector against injury. He playacted the busy schedule of his parents in which he is obviously involved but showed little sign that any tension arises from these family activities. Billy's father raised little question about Billy's development and the concern was largely Mrs. B's. Her responses both to the MMPI and during the interview suggested that she worries excessively and is easily upset and made anxious. Her anxiety, particularly concerning Billy's physical development, is probably based in part on the fact that she was responsible for the care of ill and disabled siblings when she was younger, a concern that is still reflected in her interest in the education of the mentally retarded. This particular preoccupation may be associated with some of Mrs. B's feelings of guilt, particulary surrounding expressions of anger or of independence. Her current situation suggests that she might very well feel guilty about continuing her own education and her professional ambitions and might be using imagined difficulties in Billy as a rationale for such guilt. In discussing these findings with Mr. and Mrs. B, the disparity between Mrs. B's concerns about Billy and the findings of the test were noted directly with her, and some of her overtly expressed feelings of tension and depression were remarked on further. She noted at this time that she had become so tense several months ago that she had requested her physician to give her a prescription for tranquilizers. He had recommended at the same time that she seek psychological consultation. This recommendation was reinforced at this current interview, and Mrs. B seemed relatively accepting of it.

PART FIVE

Special Problems

CHAPTER 15

Assessment of Infants and Pre-School Children

Although most of what has been discussed previously in this book about assessment of older children also applies to the pre-school child, there are some special theoretical considerations, some special techniques and ways of relating to pre-school children, about which the beginning assessor should be knowledgeable. This chapter opens with a discussion of that important question of prediction versus description of development in early childhood, followed in Section B by a review of problems of growth during early childhood. Section C discusses the special techniques in examining pre-school children; Section D deals with methods of relating to pre-schoolers; and the final Section, E, treats some of the purposes for which assessment of infants is or is not appropriate.

A. PREDICTION VERSUS DESCRIPTION OF DEVELOPMENT IN EARLY CHILDHOOD

1. Prediction

Up through the first half of the twentieth century many people used to wish for the prediction of development from infancy on. It was hoped that by studying the baby one could outline a life plan for the child, knowing the child's IQ and the child's "infant personality." Even after it was discovered that most of the IQ tests of infants, at least, had zero predictability for age 6—let alone any later in life—people still kept hoping that cognitive development could be discovered to be an inherited faculty. As has been noted frequently throughout this volume, the context of genetically inherited intelligence has been eroded by the fact, first, that few if any geneticists will accept the idea of the inheritance of complex behavior, and second, by continued proof that intelligence is a developmental, learned faculty.

Nevertheless, in some quarters vague genetic knowledge and grandmothers' hunches are applied to children. This too often determines their future, for this is what everyone begins to expect of them. The growth of a child is analogous to the building of a house. Although one may be able to learn something from the first foundations about the shape and nature of the house being built, the mere footings in a building scarcely outline its shape, height, and content. Even the full foundation may not be laid.

In fact, our analogy fades slightly when we think that the foundations of adulthood are being "poured" throughout childhood. For example, at approximately age 8 a full new set of foundations inside the child are established in the form of what is known as the conscience or superego. In a house, steel reinforcements are added at various times. Thus, the house may turn out to be much stronger and have a better foundation than one might see in its early stages. The same is certainly true of a child. Thus, prediction of future behaviors, habits, attitudes, intelligence, and personality should all be strictly avoided in early childhood. It is still very possible and probable that the child's life will be shaped markedly by events even after puberty.

2. Description

Description of these foundations, however, may be very essential. Or, in other terms, it should be helpful to the parent and for the child's well-being to have fairly frequent psychological assessments of growing pre-school children. Such reassessment will not predict the future but will be able to describe the present *process* of growth. Thus the pre-school tests are valid in the sense that they will compare the child fairly well with other children of the same age and describe their growth rate. Ideally, all babies should be seen frequently in baby clinics and examined by a psychologist at least once or twice prior to the end of year 1 and twice prior to the end of year two. Perhaps annual assessment thereafter will be sufficient. These periodic examinations prior to school age would be very helpful in parent guidance and prevention. Unfortunately, the cost and manpower for such examinations are not usually available.

B. GROWTH DURING EARLY CHILDHOOD

To understand further the problem of prediction and description, let us review very briefly some of the previous discussion about growth. During the period in childhood from birth to about age 4, growth is very fast and irregular, often with accelerations that make prediction very difficult. Babies are extremely flexible and pliable. Sometimes children can endure severe psychological traumata with appropriate reactions, but in the long run they can bounce back with no show of permanent harm. Nevertheless, they may and probably should be assessed.

During early childhood the most important development is largely perceptual and motor. As pre-schoolers begin to develop the ability of analyzing rather complex gestalts, their language is improved. Actually, the beginnings of language are usually one-to-one associations, and language learning continues on this one-to-one basis, with increased numbers of associations, throughout the next several years. However, children soon begin to understand grammar even though their grammatical formation during these years remains inadequate. Along with this perceptual-motor development is a rapid growth in the concept of human relations. Who is who and how to relate to various people are important learning situations in early childhood. In fact, it is quite necessary for the child to be able to form relationships outside the family before she/he can attend kindergarten. Nursery school consists almost entirely of the learning about human relationships. Thus, assessment of children in this age period should really focus on perceptual-motor developments and human relationships. Of course, the seeds of intelligence are being developed, but it does appear that intellectual functioning at age 1 has little to do with intellectual functioning at age 6.* The beginnings of independence also take place during these years, but, by and large, children remain fairly dependent on parents until just about kindergarten age or older. Despite this continued dependence of the child, the assessor should review with the mother the ways the child is attempting to achieve some signs of independence, which, it is to be hoped, the mother is fostering.

C. TECHNIQUES FOR ASSESSING PRE-SCHOOL CHILDREN

1. Interviews with the Mother

In any attempt to assess pre-school children, it is vital that the mother or mother figure be interviewed. This interview should focus on the child's current behaviors, on sleep habits, eating habits, defecation habits, motor development, speech development, and social development. During these pre-school years it is possible to ob-

---

*Yet there is this general bias in American psychology to look chiefly at cognitive factors.

tain a more precise developmental history from the mother than later because mothers' memories tend to fade. If a mother has had two or three children in a row, it may be difficult for her to remember much about the middle child, for example. Nevertheless, it is important to find out as clearly as possible about what age the child began to pick up his/her head and look around; when the child sat up unsupported; when she/he pulled on something and stood erect; when she/he began to crawl; when she/he took the first steps and how long before the child was then steady on his or her feet and really could scramble across the room; when she/he began self-feeding, either from the cup or with a spoon; when the child first began to make understandable words, even single words or "momma" and "daddy" and when she or he first began to put two words together, such as "go potty"; when the child seemed ready for potty training and when she or he completed at least day training; the kinds of motor activities the child is able to demonstrate, such as rolling a ball, pulling a toy on a string, and the like. There are many more such items that can be gained from the use of such an instrument as the Vineland Social Maturity Scale, which is much more useful as a basis for a behavioral interview with the mother than it is as a scorable scale.

Mothers should also be asked about possible illnesses and other traumata, what kinds of illnesses did the child endure during the first several years of life. How severe were they? How long did they last? Did they require medical attention? Since during the first two years the child's main world is his or her own body, such illnesses take on a particular psychological significance. For example, earaches are dreadfully painful, but the child who has not developed satisfactory speech cannot communicate the terror she or he may be experiencing. If a child merely screams continuously, the mother may become weary and unsympathetic—even though she may know that her child is suffering.

Some childhood physical disturbances are really indicators of anxiety, such as the so-called "colic." Pre-school children often show their anxieties by vomiting. Because the alpha rhythm of the nervous system is not yet established, pre-school children may occasionally have epileptic attacks, which does not mean at all that they are going to be epileptic, but which may mean that they are under considerable stress.

Interviews with the mother should also take into consideration the structure of the rest of the family. Is this the mother's first child? If so, is she a little anxious about having a first child? Is she still a teen-ager who has not completed her adolescence? Is she a woman in her early forties who is interrupting a career because she fears it may almost be too late to have a child? Or is she a woman who has had numerous children previously and may not really have wanted to have any more? Is she trying to please her husband in a sexist world by producing a son? Was this a particularly difficult pregnancy for her? If so, why? Or, is this the child that she has been anxiously hoping for and waiting for all of her life?

This is a good period in the child's life for an assessment of the family history and the cultural "baggage" that the child carries from birth on. What is the cultural background of this family? What is the father like, what does he do for a living? Do grandparents play any kind of a role in this family? Are there other siblings, and what roles do they play in the family? What is the economic outlook for this family?

2. Observation and Play

One of the most important techniques for assessing infants and pre-school children is the direct observation of their behavior— either in the crib or on the floor or in the playroom. Observation of the mother and child together—where the mother is caring for the needs of the infant, such as in feeding or bathing or rocking the baby to sleep—would be ideal. Here it is possible to see the infant in his/her most natural state of being cared for. Of course, the mother may be a bit anxious about being observed but more than one visit may put her at ease. I also like to administer whatever tests I am going to do on a pre-schooler in his or her own setting, although this may not always be feasible. Watching a child play in his/her own home (with the TV shut off) is also better than watching the child explore strange playrooms. Nevertheless, much can be learned about the child from his/her methods of exploring a playroom and the types of toys that he/she may pick out and play with momentarily. Two or three observations are much more reliable than one. As noted previously, the playroom should not be permitted to become a jumble of broken toys—a set of building blocks, a sturdy doll house with doll family, a handful of wooden trains or cars (too large to be swallowed or even carried away in children's pockets), a ball, a Bobo-clown doll (a punching-bag figure), a pair of toy telephones, and a few puppets might well suffice. Except for the doll house, these might be stuffed into a kit bag and taken along for play sessions elsewhere than an actual playroom. As described earlier, no specific instructions are given a child in this situation, but he/she is merely allowed to play at random while the observer sits to one side. Of course, should the child invite the observer to play, it is quite feasible for the observer to join the child, but only at his/her the direction.

Case 74

Tania, age 16 months, was reported to be upset because her parents were getting a divorce, and she was torn between the two parents. Her mother said that Tania was always reserved when she returned home from a weekend visit with her father. I visited the home on Sunday evening when the child was returned to her mother after visiting the father. She was delivered to the doorway by her father, and she ran across the room to greet her mother. Her mother tried to greet her cheerfully, but it was obvious the mother was emotionally upset

and fearful that the child would be disturbed. The child proceeded to whimper and asked for food. It was nine o'clock at night. She was fed a bit of her favorite babyfood and put to bed. She did not want her mother to leave the room, but her mother rocked her a bit in a rocking chair and she became drowsy and was put into the crib. Her mother continued to sit with her in the dimly lit room, and the child went off to sleep. Fifteen minutes later the child woke up crying. The mother again rocked her in the chair, gave her a bottle, and sang to her. She had indicated to me that this was proof in her mind that the father was a disturbing figure. Intellectually, the mother was aware that she was tense but said she was trying not to transmit her tensions to the child. The child went back to sleep and 20 minutes later again awoke. The process was repeated. This time the child stayed asleep almost an hour, and I was about to leave the home when Tania again awoke—vomiting. The mother said that this behavior was repeated the next evening, even though there was no visit the next day. The father alleged that no such behavior took place in his home and that the child seemed quite happy with him and his second wife. There is no doubt, however, that there was considerable, intense anger between the two parents. Observation of the child later in the week showed no such symptoms. On the contrary, she played actively, seemed quite happy, and ate without regurgitation. Her sleep in the middle of the week was undisturbed.

3.   Formal IQ Tests

There are at least a half dozen well-researched and thorough measures of intellectual development prior to age 2, the four most common of which are reviewed here. Gesell's Test of Motor Abilities emphasizes motor development from age 2 months on. It does also contain some items related to perceptual discrimination and attention. The emphasis here on a developmental diagnosis (Gesell et al., 1940) makes it, at least theoretically, one of the most useful and important instruments in studying the intellectual growth of children during infancy. On the other hand, of course, the relationship between these motor developments and perceptual-motor functioning and other elements of intelligence fade fast as the child grows older, thus making it very difficult to predict from such an instrument as the Gesell to the Stanford-Binet, which is much more verbal.

Cattell's Infant Intelligence Scale (1940) was constructed as a downward scaling of the Stanford-Binet. At the very early months, the Cattell also contains only perceptual-motor items: following an embroidery ring swung over the head of the child, grasping for it, reaching up for it; interest in objects placed near the infant in the crib and later the ability to grasp them and hold onto more than one; the baby's interest in his/her own image in the mirror; and at a slightly later age, the baby's ability to reach around a piece of glass and grab at a toy rather than to pound its way through the glass shield. But Cattell adds in verbal items at a relatively early age—not only the response to a mother's voice but even to simple sentences like "Give me the dolly"—before the child has developed responsive speech. At age 2 on the Cattell, the items become the same as the old 1937 Form M of the Binet, but one may begin using the 2-year scale of the latest edition of the Binet after the child has passed items up to age 2. In any case, items for age 2 are included in the Cattell. Thus the Cattell does have the advantage of introducing verbal items at a fairly early age and of a continuous measurement with the Binet of the child's development over the years. It may be of particular advantage when trying to examine a difficult child of about 30 months who does not pass everything at 24 months, and one may have to begin at at least 18 months to get a basic level, and advance, perhaps, into 36 or 42 months on the regular Binet to achieve a top level.

Bayley Scales of Infant Development (1969) is the culmination of Bayley's many decades of infant-development study at the University of California's Institute of Child Welfare. Bayley's scales consist of three parts: a mental scale, a motor scale, and the infant-behavior record. The mental scale is made up of 163 items, interpersonal reaction factors. One can thus attain a mental-development index and a psycho-motor index separately.

The Denver Developmental Screening Test (Frankenburg and Dodds, 1967) was constructed specifically to aid in the then-burgeoning number of pre-school educational programs, such as the Head Start program. The test was considered a helpful instrument in screening out those who would be considered poor educational risks in such programs, with the added aim of identifying those pre-schoolers who showed signs of possible neurological damage. The standardization group, however, specifically eliminated all children with any history of handicaps and utilized an almost exclusively North American white population (whereas Head Start turned out to have a large proportion of black and Latino children). The authors themselves cautioned against the use of DDST as a single-diagnostic tool and recommended close observation of qualitative aspects of test behavior in relation to motivation, dependency or hostility relation to the mother—child and examiner—child interaction, and the maintenance of optimal, standard testsing conditions. It is a practical, efficiett, dependable device, inexpensive and quick and easy to administer and evaluate with relatively little training or experience in testing.

Nevertheless, it is doubtful that the persons who use this test have been trained in psychological testing, as the test itself was made simple enough to be administered by the average clerk. It is my own fear that too many times this test may have been used by inexperienced, poorly trained examiners, to the detriment of a child labeled with such an instrument for the rest of his/her life. The results of each section of the test are categorized as to normal, abnormal, and questionable, and the child's performance in any section is considered normal if he or she passes at least one item, which is intersected by the child's age line if the child has no delays on any other items in that sector. A child's performance is considered abnormal if she/he has two or more delays in the section under question. These categorizations are to be considered as very rough, and it is necessary to keep in mind that the Denver is, as labeled, a screening device. It is not an IQ test, and predictions about future intellectual development are as unreliable as those from any other infant test.

In addition to those scales specifically for the infant range of 2 to 30 months, there are quite a few scales designed for the child 2 to 6 years old. The latest revision of the Stanford-Binet Intelligence Test in 1973 continues to capture the essence of this granddaddy of children's IQ tests in that it is specifically directed toward children in its content and children are attracted to it. The items are brief and topics change several times during one age group, so that the child is not bored. In fact, most little children enjoy a constant change of task. (This is in contrast to the WPPSI or the WISC-R.) The Binet takes the rapid growth of intelligence during these few years directly into account, and the items are divided into half-year units—at least between ages 2 and 5. The chief disadvantage of the Stanford-Binet remains its emphasis on verbalization, and thus it might not be the instrument of choice when the child has a speech or language problem. Again, one must be cautious about children from other cultures who speak English but who actually think in some other first language. Since it is possible to readminister the Binet every several years during a person's childhood, it is a good instrument for a continuous survey of a child's development.

Now growing in popularity is the Wechsler Preschool and Primary Scale of Intelligence (WPPSI) (Wechsler, 1967). This baby of the Wechsler family— designed to measure intellectual growth in children 4 years old to 6½ years old— duplicates in form the other Wechsler tests and consists of 10 subtests, 5 verbal and 5 performance. There are 2 new performance

tests. The Animal House test is analogous to the Coding, and the Geometric Designs test, an item long popular on tests for young children, involves copying of forms.

One of the chief advantages of using the WPPSI that follow-through examinations can be compared, at least roughly, by using the appropriate form of the Wechsler at later ages.* This advantage, however, is offset by the study showing that the WPPSI is not a very good predictor of IQ's on other tests. For example, according to the WPPSI manual, the WPPSI correlates with the Peabody Picture Vocabulary Test at only .58 and at .75 with the Stanford-Binet. Almost all normal children receive higher mean scores on the Binet than on the WPPSI—a difference that was found for the culturally disadvantaged as well as for gifted groups. There is no doubt that the WPPSI and other IQ tests are *not* interchangeable.

The second advantage of the WPPSI is that, like other Wechsler tests, it does not end in an experience of total failure for the child as does the Binet or other mental-age-level tests. Instead, the subject experiences more frequent failures spread out over the 10 subjects. This format of subtest scores and separate Verbal and Performance IQ's offers even more temptation for overinterpretation than do the formats of the other Wechslers. The unreliability of the subtests on the WPPSI is even greater than on the WISC-R, and thus any *interpretation of the pattern scores on the WPPSI is entirely unwarranted.* Certainly no 5-year-old should be judged to have minimal brain damage on the basis of the WPPSI alone. The WPPSI, like the WISC-R, has been noted for its limited sensitivity and discrimination at its lower age limits. For example, a 4-year-old, making no correct responses, would obtain a Verbal IQ of 56, a Performance IQ of 57, and a Full Scale IQ of 53 points. The manual recommends that the test is not usable for 4-year-olds who

*This is also one of the main advantages of using the Binet.

are suspected of having an IQ of 75 or below. Since, in this very area of slowed-down intellectual development for the 4-year-old, it has often been questioned in the use of pre-school or Head Start, it is very disappointing that the WPPSI does not serve this purpose.

The Merrill-Palmer Scale of Mental Tests (Stutzman, 1931) is a mental-age test ranging from ages 18 months through 71 months, thus covering the nursery school and early kindergarten age group. It has a variegated set of little tests in it, both verbal and nonverbal, that, although they occur in age groups, may be administered in groups of tests. However, if one does not stick strictly to the mental-age arrangement, it may be somewhat difficult to keep track of the tests passed or not passed and establish a base age. The verbal tests, which begin at the 18-month level, include repetition of words and word groups, such questions as "What does the doggie say?" "What is this?" and "What is it for?" pointing to the pencil or shoe, and a fascinating little vocabulary test called Action Agent, for example, "What runs?" "What cries?" "What sleeps?" and the like. The majority of the tests are visual-motor in nature. There is the usual peg board, a version of the Seguin, a nest of cubes, cutting with scissors, picture cubes, buttoning buttons, stacking and counting blocks, and copying a circle, square, and star. One of the major advantages of the Merrill-Palmer is that tests that are rejected by the subject can be omitted and not counted against him/her just because he/she refused to engage in the task. It is also possible to omit a test or two where the materials may be misleading. Of course, one cannot omit a test once it is given to a child who failed it. The main disadvantage of the Merrill-Palmer is that its standardization is quite out of date, but again one may raise the question as to whether there is a significant difference between the 4-year-olds of 1930 and the 4-year-olds of today. My own guess is that under the influence of television and pre-school education, the average 4-year-old in

the second half of the twentieth century would make a much higher score on this test than the standardization group.

There are, of course, other widely used IQ tests that can be used on the pre-school, kindergarten group, such as the Leiter International, which principally employs matching at that age level, the Columbia Mental Maturity, and the Peabody Picture Vocabulary Tests—all of which use only one type of item. The Columbia and the Peabody are particularly handy for quick screening when a full IQ test may not be needed.

4. Associative Techniques with Pre-School Children

As soon as children are able to converse, it is quite possible to use the usual adult or child version of adult associative techniques, such as the Rorschach and the Children's Apperception Tests. Ames and colleagues (1974) begin their classic research of child Rorschach studies with an analysis of responses of 50 children 2 years old. No doubt these were bright and verbal children, for using Binet standards, only 50% of 2-year-olds are able to combine two words in a meaningful combination. Thus, it seems doubtful to me that most 2-year-olds are able to verbalize a meaningful response and inquiry to the Rorschach. By age 3, however, the Rorschach is usually an appropriate instrument for understanding the social-perceptual development of the child. In these pre-school years, it is best to administer the test with a simultaneous inquiry after each response rather than having to run through the cards twice, since many pre-schoolers are too impatient to take a second look.

Although one must avoid giving the child any hints as to the determinant, once it is established that the determinant is primarily form it is necessary to push just a bit further to determine form level. In this age group, one does not expect anything near the form level of precision of a school-age child. Nevertheless, if a child calls the blot a "doggie," the "doggie" should be somewhat logically arranged, with a head at one end and a tail at the other and the feet at the bottom. But if no further details are given, this would not be a bad response for a 4-year-old. Gross and vague W responses are very common in this age group, but gradually children begin to carve out more distinctive parts of the inkblot and to separate them out from other parts, just as the child may do in everyday perception. Yet, there may be, at moments, marked perseverations or confabulations, which would be hallmarks of severe disturbance in older children but which occur quite frequently at ages 3−5.

Similarly, very "pathological" signs, such as gross color responses or color naming, commonly occur at this age. And while they may be indications that the child's emotional controls are still poorly formed, they are not in the true sense of the word "pathological." On the other hand, between age 4 and 5, most children do show some nascent signs of internalization and internal control of affect—beginning with the little m response, or inanimate movement response, common in the 5-year-old. A 5-year-old who still shows gross color responses, whose form level is frequently mixed up or confabulated, who perseverates from one card to the next, and who shows no signs of beginnings of any internal controls, is immature and the possibility of a rather severe emotional disturbance should be considered.

Using the contents of the pre-school child's responses to the Rorschach as indicators of emotional disturbance seems to me hazardous. The test is very short—usually less than 15 responses—and whether or not these responses contain anything significant seems to me to be fortuitous. For example, one very bright and well-adjusted little girl, aged 4½, looked at Card IV and said, "Eew! Yucky! It looks like a toilet full of boiling blood." She showed me the shape of a toilet bowl in the areas usually seen as the feet of a large animal, the center detail was "a you-know-what," indicating a bowel movement, and the back swirling, dark area of the card was the black blood. There were no other responses in the child's Rorschach like this in any way; most seemed rather innocuous. She could not associate to the response. She had never seen a toilet with blood in it, but she insisted that's what it looked like.

CASE 75

Wally, age 5, gave 13 responses: 6 butterflies, 1 flower (without any color in it), 1 cloud, 1 sunset (with color), and the popular animals of Card VIII. This child's ego development was slow. He paid little attention to the suggestions of the nursery-school teacher, and he scrapped readily with other children in the class over toys or privileges or food. When crossed, he cried desperately to go home to his mother. The mother admitted to the schoolteacher that she was having great difficulty as a single parent—without support from the child's father—and she begged the school to keep Wally, as she would have to quit her job and go on welfare if he was not in the nursery school.

The Children's Apperception Test, or CAT, is Bellak and Bellak's (1949) version of the TAT for the pre-schooler. It has become one of the most widely used of all techniques for the younger child. Preschoolers tend to tell very short and often only descriptive stories to the CAT pictures; it is difficult to get the average 4- or 5-year-old to do more than name the parts of the picture. Again, using Stanford-Binet norms, 50% of the 3-year-olds are unable to even satisfactorily name parts on the Picture Description tests. Therefore, not much more can be expected of the 4-year-olds. I often vary the instructions, helping the child by beginning the story with "Once upon a time," and proceed in each case to say, "And then what happened?" "And then how did it all end?" Even so, I do not always obtain either a beginning or an end to a story—and little characterization. Nevertheless, the descriptive choices in themselves are often interesting and give significant information about the child. For instance, there is a difference between a child who describes three chickens on Card 1 as contentedly eating dinner, as waiting for dinner, as disappointed in dinner, or ignoring the dinner and about to have a fight, and the like. Whether the mother chicken in the background is seen as a mother or is even mentioned may be significant. Thus, this card draws on oral contentment versus oral aggression and also on sibling rivalry and parental caretaking feelings. Card 2, showing three bears pulling on a rope, becomes of interest when the child is able to say which is the mommy bear, the daddy bear, and the baby bear. Who is pulling against whom and who is the loser? Card 3 is interesting in that the lion (or tiger, as children may confuse them) is certainly seen usually as a powerful and paternal figure. And whether or not this big father is going to be friendly toward the little mouse in the back is a common question. Sometimes, however, this father is seen as disabled and held back, as if the child is trying to hold back his/her own aggressive impulses, or is possibly portraying his/her father figure as a weakened and held-back figure.

Card 4 is definitely aimed at a sibling-rivalry story, but, in my experience, the sibling-rivalry theme is less frequently pulled by this card than the picnic or mother-will-feed-us scene. Card 5, which was obviously intended to draw stories about the baby's bed and parents' bed, does not, in my experience, have any particular card draw. Card 6 probably was intended to illustrate the child as separate from the parent—perhaps to draw upon the child's feelings about parents being together with the child left out. Scenes of baby bear running away or walking off and getting lost and parents coming to hunt for the child are more common. Card 7, the tiger after the monkey, does draw upon the child's fear of "eat or be beaten," but with many varia-

tions. Card 8 is, in my experience, a little complicated for even 5-year-olds, although it is probably intended to draw upon children's reactions to family secrets. Card 9 is a good picture to draw upon feelings of loneliness and night fears. And the last card, while intended primarily to deal with toileting and punishment, often does not seem to make much sense to the child. More often than not the child says that the puppy is being punished for going into the bathroom rather than for failing to use the bathroom. As mentioned in Chapter 6, the repeat reliability of the CAT is questionable, again because of the general principle that the child is developing so rapidly that emotional patterns and behaviors change almost from month to month.

5. Doll Play and Other Associative Techniques

The Make-A-Picture Story Test, MAPS, as described previously in Chapter 6, may also be used with pre-school children, but my own experience is that this complex set of paper-doll figures and scenes is usually too complicated for younger children. Much better in this respect is to use a set of "family dolls" (which can be purchased at almost any toy store) along with appropriately sized furniture, such as an adult bed, a child's crib, a toilet and sink or bathtub, TV, sofa, a dining table and three chairs. This allows for various home scenes, such as joining the family in TV, being fed at the dining table, or being bathed and toileted and put to bed. Kitchen furniture is often handy for such doll play also, as would be a dolly high chair. However, I purposely avoid having too much elaborate doll furniture about, since children become interested in the furnishings and not in the play itself. Although at times I have had a doll house—and quite successfully—it too may interfere with assessment play, as differentiated here from play therapy. The purpose of structured play is to encourage the child to utilize certain materials to obtain fantasies or reactions to life scenes, rather than to emit free and unstructured play as one might in play therapy. If the child cannot play without a playhouse, I usually have a box of painted blocks approximately 3″ × 1½″ × 4″ that can be used to build walls with doors and entrances, but with no roof so that the child can immediately move the dolly through a playhouse that the child and not the therapist constructs.

The kinds of structured situations that I have been using are based fundamentally on Lynn's Structured Doll Play Test (1959) (see Appendix B). Thus, I begin by showing the 3- or 4-year-old—or even 2-year-old—that the dolly can be walked across the tabletop, and I have the child imitate my walking movements (similar to the walking blocks in some IQ tests). Then we decide which parent the child may like to take a walk with, and then I'll ultimately have the second parent join in the walk. This sets the scene for further parent–child interactions. The child may then start some more active outdoor games, such as playing ball, and choose again which parent to play ball with. The child falls and has an "ouch." Which parent is coming to help her/him up and plant the healing kiss? Indoors, which parent joins the child watching TV? Which parent prepares dinner? Does the child sit in a regular chair at the dining table, or is the child to be fed in a high chair separate from the parents? Who gives the child a bath? Does the child sit on a potty or the regular toilet, and does a parent have to be present? Or, can the child take a bath pretty much on his/her pwn? Does the child go to bed by herself/himself, or does a parent have to be there? Or, does one or the other parent—or both—come in for good-night kisses or a story? What story and what prayers does the child use? What happens if the child has a nightmare? What happens if the child wets the bed?

Although many children seem to realize that the doll play is really about them, it is much easier for them to talk about themselves through the dollies. I often use this technique as part of an examination of custody questions for the court by ending the parents having a big fight and being placed at opposite ends of the table. Where, I ask, will the doll live?* This technique can be used with children from single-parent families. If the child says, "But I do not have a daddy (or mommy)," the examiner merely says, "Oh, let's pretend here that the dolly does." This gives an insight into the child's imagination of what a united nuclear family might be. It is, of course, quite permissible to expand any of the preceding to say, "Okay, let's have the daddy live on the other side, over here," and then find out what happens between the visiting parent and the residential parent.

The other structured family-doll situation—the Bene-Anthony Family Relations Test (1957) for younger children—is also a very appropriate investigative tool for pre-school children. Occasionally, there is a slight difficulty in the use of this technique with pre-school children, especially where they are in a conflictual family, because they believe it is a good idea to have each one of the family dolls receive a message, no matter what the message may be. If the child starts to put the message in mommy and says, "No, mommy has too many, I'll give it to little brother," one should point out to him/her child that it is not necessary to have an even distribution of the messages. Also, it is a good idea once in a while too see if the child understands the message, especially it if seems to be misappropriately placed. It is also necessary at times to remind the child that there is a Mr. Nobody—although older children often use Mr. Nobody in an attempt to get away from any kind of negative statements.

The World Test is also an appropriate technique for understanding the child's developing approach to an environment outside the family. Like the MAPS, it does have nearly too many objects for the comprehension of children prior to age 6. There are just too many things to play and too many things to arrange. However, since there is no requirement to make up any kind of story at all, the World Test is a little

*One child responded by throwing the dolls in my face.

easier than the MAPS for young children. A most common reaction from the 3- to 4-year-olds is to line up the buildings very tightly with one another and build a barnyard separate from them, enclosing the domestic animals and ignoring or discarding the wild animals. Some children of this age become preoccupied with playing with one toy—an automobile or plane—thus avoiding the rest of the materials completely. This is a reaction that probably echoes their own ability (or familiarity) to deal with the world outside their own home and their own reactions. On the other hand, a very organized village with people and activity in it would be quite rare for any child under the age of 5.

Although a 2-year-old can hold a crayon and make a straight line, copy a circle, or even a star (on the Merrill-Palmer), most children under the age of about 4 are unable to voluntarily draw any recognizable human figure. Even the 4-year-old, when asked to draw a person, is either likely to refuse or merely makes a circle with some indication of facial features for a head that may or may not be inside the circle and that at best may have lines for arms and legs coming out of the head. However, after age 4 these figures begin to improve considerably. The eyes and mouth and nose are inside the head and scribbles for hair may be added; the arms come out the side of the head and the legs come out of the bottom of the head. The child who is entering kindergarten is likely to be able to make a recognizable house with a door and chimney and a window or two. Lines in the drawing of a 5-year-old are likely to be somewhat direct and connected; the tree has a trunk and more than a scribble for leaves. People may even be doing things in the drawing of a 5-year-old. He or she may make even elaborations on his/her drawing. For example, one 5-year-old who had an IQ on the Peabody of 130 drew a house with a door and roof and chimney and then put stilts underneath so that the rushing water in the creek would not cause a flood. This child had seen pictures of a flood on the television news the night before. In another attempt, he drew Santa Claus on a sleigh with a recognizable reindeer going uphill to his home. Surprisingly, these drawings by kindergarten-age children often have expressive countenances showing anger or sadness or joy and exuberance. For example, one little girl drew a remarkable dancing girl complete in leotards, and then drew a line diagonally across the paper to a sun at the top and announced that the dancer was going to dance her way clear up to the top of the sky.

As noted in Chapter 6, the assessor must be extremely cautious in interpreting these drawings. There is a tendency to overinterpret drawings in almost dream-book fashion. Despite the extravagant claims of some authorities who have studied drawings, there are no one-to-one meanings for any kind of drawing of a bodily feature. Certainly at age 4, blank eyes put on a picture do not indicate "paranoia." The assessor should inquire about some of the odd lines or pieces that a child may add to a drawing that are not immediately recognizable. It is necessary to conduct a simple inquiry to understand the meaning of the child's drawing. Although children cannot be questioned as thoroughly as Machover suggests for adults, it nevertheless is possible to ask the child to "tell me about your drawing." Or, "If they are doing something, what would they be doing?" (This gets around the child's response, "They aren't doing anything.") Sometimes, of course, children are unable or unwilling to verbalize about their drawings other than to identify the body parts. In such instances, any interpretation of the drawing constitutes the assessor's associations.

D. ASSESSMENT PROCEDURES WITH YOUNGER CHILDREN

The extreme dependency of the pre-school child on the adult affects the performance of pre-schoolers. Often, pre-schoolers can do a task but may be reluctant to demonstrate it, not merely because of a fear of failure but because of a kind of unconscious recognition that if they can perform the task adults will no longer wait on them. A 3-year-old climbs up the steps and is capable of climbing down by himself/herself. When his/her father requests him/her to come down, however, the child sits on the top of the stairs and refuses to budge, screaming for the father to carry him/her. Thus, being dependent often decelerates the development of a need achievement. If a pre-schooler achieves, he/she may lose the parent's care. Of course, parents constantly need to praise the child for achieving and for being independent, but a real feeling of "I can do it myself" develops slowly during these pre-school years and is not even complete when the child enters school. Although the examiner of older children may promise them not to tell their parents about their responses, the examiner of pre-school children may want to tell them that "we will tell mommy how well you did." Moreover, as will be seen, some of the infant tests actually call for praise on right answers and give the child hints and help until she/he gets rolling on the test.

The personality and attitudes of the assessor play an important part in successful assessment of infants and pre-schoolers. Clinical psychologists are highly-educated and verbal people. On the other hand, people who work with children must be observers of behavior and not require extensive verbalization of the child. They must be able to unbend and be flexible, and if need be, to get down on the floor with the child. This ability to unbend with children, to relax with them, and to wait and permit them to respond is sometimes the most difficult task for the erudite scientist who hopes to become a clinical psychologist. Perhaps it is a little more difficult for the men who—by tradition at least—are not supposed to know how to deal with small children. This is, of course, one of the myths of sexism, and I would recommend that beginning clinical psychologists of both sexes should start by working with pre-schoolers and babies—for if students learn

to relax with little children, they will be more relaxed with older children and adolescents and will be less academic with their adult clients.

1. Infants

Ideally, infants should be examined in their own nursery in their own home, where they feel at ease and the situation is familiar. Of course, such a home visit may not be feasible, and most infants become used to physical examinations outside their own home. However, I would avoid what was once a common practice of including the psychological examination along with a physical examination, not only because the length of the examination might be tiring on the child (and in such medical settings the psychological examination usually comes last), but because it is a good idea to separate the psychological from the physiological in the parents' minds. A warm, comfortable crib is necessary for examining infants who are not able to sit up alone. However, other materials should not be hung from the crib that would distract the child from the test situation. Children who can sit up and hold up their heads should be put in a high chair, and the examination can then be conducted from a table to the high-chair tray. In contrast to older children, I frequently have the mother present, asking her to remain to one side, to say nothing, and to give no signal of any kind to the child. Having the mother present is usually necessary for infants in a strange situation. One should, of course, avoid trying to examine a hungry or sleepy child, and the appointment should be arranged after he/she has been napped and fed and is alert and ready for some kind of play. Once the child's attention begins to wane or he/she shows signs of boredom or fatigue, it is usually useless to proceed, and a second session should be scheduled. As babies' moods and comforts and discomforts change from hour to hour, it is a good idea to see them a second time, in any case, scheduled at a slightly different time. This also allows the baby to become more acquainted with the assessor.

2. Examination of the Pre-School Child

Some pre-school children can also be examined from a high chair, but most prefer to be in a nursery-school-sized chair at a low table. I usually say to the child, "Here I have a chair and table just for you, just for your size." The examining room should be free of other distracting toys or objects, and I usually disconnect the telephone. If necessary, the child should be allowed to explore the room briefly and then be led back to the chair at the table. One should have all the assessment materials open and ready. The child's interest is best held if each test is presented quickly and then removed and the next test presented immediately afterward, without long intervals of waiting while the examiner searches for the test materials or takes another glance at the book for instructions. I strongly advise psychologists who plan to assess infants and pre-schoolers regularly, to memorize the tests in advance so that there is no need to continually check back with the textbook while the child peers underneath the table or decides to help the examiner find the next test. With pre-schoolers, as well as with older children, I frequently tape their stories, as the children are often impatient while the examiner tries to catch up with some rapidly told tale.

Since the emotional interactions of the pre-school child are more immediate and of a less-predetermined pattern than is true of older children, the interaction between the child and the examiner during the examination is of utmost importance. How does the child behave, dealing with a strange but interested adult? How willing is the child to cooperate with this adult and in effect play the adult's game rather than the game the child wants? How insecure does the child seem to be? How much encouragement does she/he need? Does she/he helplessly wait for some adult to do the task, or does she/he jump in and attack the materials

almost without waiting for the complete instructions? How spontaneous is the child? Does he/she seem to seek any kind of affection, or does he/she shy away from any physical contact with the examiner? All these and many more questions can be answered by careful observation of the child's behavior during the examination. These should be written down almost immediately after the examination is over.

Case 76

Flora, age 3½, was having considerable difficulty getting along at nursing school. In fact, the nursery school had insisted that her mother get a psychological evaluation of the child; otherwise, they would exclude her from school. Flora had been hitting the other children—often was in tears—and complaining about them. She did not really participate in play with other children but tried to maintain a completely isolated play by herself. She rejected the teacher's encouragement to join in class activities. She often seemed to be whining and complaining and frequently wet her pants. Her mother was amazed, saying that there was no such behavior at home and that she felt perhaps it was a problem with the school. The mother was, at that point, thinking of finding another nursery school. However, she admitted that Flora had changed schools twice before, always with the same complaints. I first observed Flora in my office. She was a bit shy and initially did not want to leave her mother. In the first visit, her mother sat with her in the office while Flora and I played with some structured doll material. After about a half hour, Flora insisted on being taken home. In a second session, she permitted her mother to remain in the waiting room, greeting me cheerfully and engaging in the Merrill-Palmer test quite actively—again for a little over a half hour. I asked her if I might visit her nursery school, and she frowned, saying that she hated school but that it was all right if I came. She could not tell me what she disliked at school, except that the other children were nasty to her. The school had a one-way-screen observation room where I could see the children at play. Flora sat in one corner of the sandbox somewhat by herself. When another child approached, she threw sand in the child's face. The other child screamed in anger and retaliated with more sand, and the teacher had to intervene to stop a sand-throwing fight. Flora then marched off to the bathroom by herself. It was then time for refreshments, but Flora could not be encouraged to leave the bathroom to have cupcakes and milk. Later she told me that the teacher always discriminated against her, never giving her any cupcakes and milk. She did come out of the bathroom when the children all stretched out on mats for naps, but instead of taking a nap, she ran back to her corner in the sandbox and threw sand at the teacher when the teacher tried to get her to come and take a nap. As she left that afternoon she told her mother that she was never coming back to that school again. When I visited the home, Flora answered the door and was very excited to see me, but her mother intervened and began talking to me immediately, ignoring Flora, who was pulling on my coattails to come and see her playroom. The mother was holding Flora's sister, age 1½, in her arms, but set her down to talk with me further. Flora immediately ran over and hit her sister. There were more screams, and the mother intervened for a moment, picking up the baby again and cuddling it and ignoring Flora. At that moment, Flora's older sister, age 5, entered the room, and before anyone could notice what was going on, a fight ensued between the two sisters. Their mother did not intervene immediately, but the screams from both children were so loud that they prevented adult conversation. Their weary mother separated them, sending the older child out of the room but comforting neither. At this point I decided to pay attention to Flora, and she immediately quieted down and led me to her room, showing me all her various toys and dollies. Her older sister now entered the room and

claimed that half of the things that Flora said were hers really belonged to the older sister. The three girls shared a room, which was crowded with toys and strewn with clothes. Flora and her older sister both grabbed a stuffed animal and began to pull on it until it tore apart. There were more screams and kicks and hits. However, their mother did not appear and intervene. When I asked her about it, she said in a weary voice, "Let them fight it out." Yet the mother maintained that—as far as she could tell—her household was happy. Flora's mother was three months pregnant. "I hope it will be a boy this time; we were always looking for one."

CASE 77

Marta, age 17, did not want to have a baby. When she found herself pregnant by her boyfriend, she was afraid to tell her parents. By the time she and her boyfriend finally hoped that they could do something about it, it was too late to have an abortion. He was 19 and was able to get a job, and both sets of parents agreed that they should get married. Marta was ill throughout her pregnancy, and several times it seemed that she was close to a miscarriage. Her labor was quite prolonged and painful, and her baby finally had to be delivered by caesarean section. She felt very clumsy with the baby and kept running to her mother for advice. However, her mother was angry that Marta had become pregnant, was cold to her, and gave her little support in the care of the baby. The baby seemed to be constantly ill. Marta ran frequently to the pediatrician, who said that the baby was colicky and turned Marta over to his nurse for advice about how to care for the baby. The baby awoke frequently in the night, disturbing her husband, who was not really happy at having to get married. She was unable to nurse the baby, and the child required several different, special formulas before finally settling down to eating steadily and gaining weight. Marta was quite depressed, could not sleep well, and frequently she found herself sitting alone crying, while attempting to care for the baby. She felt the baby did not like her because the child frequently pushed away from her when Marta attempted to cuddle her. Under observation, the baby seemed relatively inert, and she paid no attention to what was going on around her. Although the baby was attempting to walk, she really was not steady at all on her feet and continued to whimper even when held. When referred to the psychologist, Marta was so depressed that she was considering suicide.

E. PURPOSES OF ASSESSMENT OF PRE-SCHOOL CHILDREN

One might wonder what reasons a person would have for attempting to measure childhood development in these years, since it is so unreliable and predictability is so poor. However, since it is possible to assess the current level of development at least, such an examination may serve several purposes.

1. Normal Development

The most common question is whether the development is normal. Is this child showing the signs of development one might normally expect at this age? Usually, of course, the question of normality comes up because there are some doubts about whether the child is really slow or not. Here one must be quite cautious, of course, since a child may slow down in development and then catch up very rapidly shortly thereafter. Thus, where there is a question of whether the child's developmental level is slowed, there should be repeated examinations every few months over a year or so. Conditions in which the child is developing may change. For example, a child's development may be slowed down by the emotional climate in the house. If the mother is extremely depressed over a death in the family or some other tragedy, the child may echo her depression and be tem-

porarily slowed down. In families where there is a divorce, the pre-schooler may lose bowel control, suffer night terrors, or sleepwalk. Another child, under similar circumstances, may revert to "baby talk" after having learned to speak quite clearly. Infants, more than older children, respond to the stresses of the environment. Parents and pediatricians worry whether the child is developing normally.

2. Pre-School Placement

Placement of a child in a program of early education also requires measurement of intellectual and emotional development. Here the question is not whether a child is going to develop into some kind of brilliant genius, but whether or not he/she at that point might benefit more from an early-education program rather than merely attending a play-school type of nursery school. In such instances, both pre-school IQ tests and projective techniques, as well as interviews and observations, may be quite helpful. Children who are going to be placed in situations where they will read and write before age 5 do need a thorough psychological examination.

3. Adoption, Foster-Home Placement, and the Neglected Child

These topics, which involve the courts and other legal authorities, are discussed in Chapter 19. Many times these assessments involve home visits or interviews with concerned adults. The assessor must take into account that in nearly every case the child is depressed and not functioning up to par—even infants who have been removed from the biological mother and placed in foster homes to await adoption. To be torn from two mothers and then be adopted is a serious disruption in an infant's life. (Adoption at birth is not so traumatic.)

The assessor of infants and pre-school children should be clear that the results of such an examination are valid only as a *description of the child* and that they have no validity for prediction. The assessor must also be aware of the unreliability of infant behavior, which advances rapidly but in spurts. Thus, the examination should be spaced over several observation periods and repeated every six moths between ages 6 months and 5 years in order to observe trends in early development. Direct observation of the infant in the crib or the preschooler on the playground is highly recommended, even though this involves the assessor leaving his/her office. The interaction between the mother and infant is the focal point of such observation.

CHAPTER 16

The Assessment of Physically Handicapped Children

A. INTRODUCTION—SOME FREQUENT BIASES

The assessment of handicapped children poses some very difficult problems for the assessing psychologist. The tools that psychologists are accustomed to use with nonhandicapped children are often quite inappropriate. Not only are such visual stimuli as the Rorschach or the performance tests on the Wechsler unuseable with the visually handicapped, but the questions asked on other tests that depend purely on auditory perception often refer to visual cues. For example, the similarity between a wheel and ball may be obvious to the sighted child, but it may be a very difficult item for a child with no vision. The blind child might have a different answer to what one should do if one "sees" fire and smoke in a theater than would a sighted child.

Not only are our instruments often inappropriate for handicapped children, but being tested in itself often becomes an anathema to a disabled child. Thus, the mentally retarded child, who often has gone through many tests and failed many times, develops such a "failure syndrome" that he/she panics when faced with another testing. In this instance, the assessment may unearth only the child's disability and fail to discover his/her other abilities that might be developed with the proper retraining or rehabilitation.

In addition to the inadequacy of the major assessing instruments and the handicapped child's attitude toward being tested, the assessor, in a sense, is also handicapped by two strong biases in American psychology, which prevail outside the specific field of assessment of handicapped children but which are nevertheless most virulent in this particular clinical-problem area. The first of these biases is the primacy in American psychology placed on cognitive behavior. By far, the majority of studies on child development deal with cognition and learning. In fact, I recently reviewed the subjects listed in the Psychology Abstracts from 1960 to 1980. I found very few references (sometimes none) to such topics as revenge, anger, affection, or even sexual drives in children. While there has been much study on the socialization of the child, these studies are dwarfed by the enormous concern with purely cognitive development. The construction of the instruments to measure intellectual development of the handicapped date nearly to the beginning of the twentieth century. Almost totally ignored, however, are the difficulties that handicapped children have in their emotional, social, and motivational development, or in their overall development of an identity. Yet for children who have any kind of sensory, motor, or neurological handicap, these latter factors may be of far greater importance than their cognitive development. In fact, blind children, for example, may become supercognitive—full of verbalization—in order to compensate for feelings of loneliness, bitterness, and anger.

The second bias of American psychology, which is perhaps related to the bias about considering only cognitive behavior, is the assumption that most psychological

461

handicaps—especially cognitive ones—arise from a disease to the central nervous system. This assumption of "brain damage'" is more prevalent among those who deal with the "developmentally disabled" as the intellectuually handicapped child is now labeled.

The functional or social, motivational, or emotional aspects of a handicap are not limited to those children who are intellectually retarded. For example, although few people today would refer to the deaf child with a speech problem as being a "dummy," nevertheless, when such a child has great difficulty in learning, there is always the underlying assumption that perhaps the child also has some brain damage. At one time many people assumed that most children who are thought to be suffering from "cerebral palsy"—another wastebasket diagnosis—had brain damage to areas other than the hypothalamus. Often children with learning disabilities are labeled with such Greek terms as *aphasia* or *alexia* when they cannot speak clearly or read easily, and these terms are assumed to designate some kind of brain damage, demonstrable or not (see Chapter 17).

A third bias of many workers in the field of the rehabilitation of the handicapped arises from the natural sympathy that may cloud the objectivity of the assessor. The assessor and therapist feel sorry for the child. Thus the assessor may gloss over many of the difficulties of such children, excusing them on the basis of disabiliity. There is often an assumption among many assessors and therapists that the handicapped child is a dear, sweet child who eagerly awaits our care. The truth is that many of these handicapped children demonstrate severe behavorial problems that repel those who attempt to train or treat them. As discussed further in Chapter 17, the actual brain-damaged child often demonstrates very poor emotional controls and has considerable difficulty in learning social rules. Deaf children are not always nice children. In fact, they often present severe behavior problems just because they do not hear

authorities and find that they can "get away with things" by using the excuse of their hearing loss. Blind children may seem quite autistic at times. Epileptic children may have explosive tempers.

These biases—and perhaps others—are taken into account when the various kinds of handicaps are discussed. Before discussing these handicaps and their assessments, we include a brief section on the principal variables present in the assessment of such handicaps. Then, follows a discussion of the receptive handicaps, namely, vision, audition, and perception. The next section deals with expressive handicaps, espccially muscular and speech. The final section deals with such illnesses as diabetes, cardiac problems, hemophilia, multiple sclerosis, and the like. In each of these sections, we attempt to show how modification of the assessing instruments may be necessary to assess both the abilities and disabilities of the child.

B.   SOME IMPORTANT VARIABLES

Dictionaries and most textbooks do not distinguish very well between the terms *handicapped* and *disabled*. However, I would like to suggest that the term *handicap* refers to the physiological injury itself. *Disability*, on the other hand, should be used to indicate the behavioral dysfunction associated with such handicaps. A person who has lost a leg or an arm, for example, has suffered a fairly high degree of handicap, but if he/she has an adequate prosthesis that he/she has learned to use, the disability may be very minor.

CASE 78

Mimi, age 20, a college student, was tetraplegic and mute. She was succeeding very well with college and later married, had two children, and took care of them and her house with only the occasional help of a housekeeper. She also worked as a counselor for the disabled. Her handicap was severe, but she had overcome a great deal of it, and thus her disability was much less than one would have imagined from meeting her initially.

On the other hand, anyone who has worked in this field at all has run across children and adults who have a minor handicap but have become quite helpless because they were waited on hand and foot and learned to expect it. Their disability in this latter instance was much greater than one might expect. Although some physiological retraining is possible in many cases, for example, in traumatic paralysis or in a severe strabismus, most rehabilitation efforts are aimed at reducing the degree of disability. The blind child learns to "travel" with or without a cane or dog; the hard-of-hearing child learns to lip read and finger talk; and the retarded child often can at least be "trained" in many aspects of self-care, and if only mildly retarded, is considered "educable." Thus, the psychologist usually does not measure the handicap, which is physiological, but he/she is responsible for measuring the degree and nature of the disability.

A second variable that should be considered when assessing any handicapped child is the point of the child's development at which the injury was sustained. A child who was blinded or deafened or brain damaged prior to being born—or within a very short time thereafter—would have an entirely different experiential background than one who was injured later in her/his childhood. A child who once saw and now is blind, who once heard and now is deaf, or who once was learning quite adequately but now has an organic handicap in learning has some advantages over the child who never saw or never heard, or who always had been a failure at learning. A memory of that previous time when the functions were adequate helps.

At the same time, there is a slightly negative factor in the case of the postnatally injured child who remembers being adequate. It is more difficult sometimes for such a child to accept her/his handicap. The child who was handicapped prior to birth is more likely to accept the handicap and deal with it, whereas the postnatally handicapped child may look for some kind of magic that will set everything back on the right track—the same "magic" that seemed to be behind the trauma or disease that caused the handicap. More important, children who are handicapped later in their childhood have at least learned some functions prior to the handicap, and very often they can retain these functions or know what they mean. For example, a boy who was blinded in a firecracker explosion at age 12 knew what colors and things looked like, even though he never saw them again. On the other hand, the child who is handicapped later in life is more likely to concentrate on the cause and to fix blame for the loss; such a blame complex does not occur quite so strongly and frequently among children who are handicapped before birth.

There is a third group of children that should be mentioned—those who suffer from a progressively increasing handicap. The young woman mentioned in Case 78, who suffered muteness and tetraplegia, sustained gradual losses in stages. At one time she could talk and had much better use of her hands and feet. She was also helped by a series of brain operations that at first resulted in considerable relief, in a slight return of functions, and in the retardation of the disorder. However, these chemothalmolotomies had to be repeated with ever-decreasing positive results. Gradually, she thus became more and more handicapped physically and died in her thirties when her children were not completely grown. She never denied her handicap as a reality in her existence, but she utilized all of her waning physiological strength and her never-weakening psychological strength to reduce the disabling effects of the handicap. Losses in vision and hearing may also be progressive—perhaps the worst example is multiple sclerosis, which comes and goes, often confusing the victim who is never sure whether or not he or she is really handicapped.

The principal importance of the point in the child's development at which the handicap occurs has to do with whether or not he/she is in one of the critical periods of development. For example, children who suffer from some disability that keeps them out of school just as they begin the first grade may have a much harder time than children who are injured a few years later. This shift over from being a pre-schooler to a school-age child is an important landmark in the child's development. Children who have a poor start or who may not make a start at all at the proper age may always feel as if they are behind. Similarly, children who are struck by some severe trauma when they are just entering puberty and are held back in social and emotional development during that period will not have a normal adolescence even if they are able to continue some special education.

The nature and severity of the handicap is a third factor to be considered by the assessor. Even though the psychological assessor does not measure the degree of physiological handicap, the psychologist should be apprised of its nature and severity. It may be helpful for the psychologist to know the general cause of the disability—although in many instances this is not clearly known, especially among children whose handicap occurred prior to birth (see Chapter 17).

Most important to the assessor is knowledge of the exact nature of the handicap. Seldom is anyone completely handicapped. There are some children who have absolutely no vision at all, but many children who are visually handicapped have some partial vision. They may see light and shadow, for example. Among the hard of hearing, hearing losses are even more variable. For example, in a pair of twins, both of whom had been deaf from birth, one twin could actually hear the telephone or doorbell but could not answer the telephone. His brother, however, did not hear the telephone ring, but he could distinguish what people were saying to him on the telephone fairly well. When I was a child, I knew a boy who had a mild paralysis and could not run; he could, however, swing a bat quite accurately. Another boy was so cross-eyed that he saw two balls coming at him and hit between them, as he described it, but he was a fairly fast runner. These two youngsters together were always winners.

Since in assessing and training the handicapped child the focus is often on the disability, many teachers and psychologists as well tend to gloss over or forget that this child is an emotional being in a social setting like any other child. Thus, as in any assessment, the assessment of a handicapped child should begin with a careful personal and social history. Just because a child has a physical handicap does not mean that he or she might not also have social and emotional deprivations. In fact, such problems are often present among handicapped children. Let me note here a few of the social problems associated with severe handicaps: The handicapped child often needs extra medical care, costing the family more money; he or she may need more physical care at home and thus be a physical burden on parents and siblings; the handicapped child often is socially left behind in the world of children and thus feels rejected and isolated; parents and others tend to "spoil" the handicapped child and fail to help him/her become more independent and self-sufficient; handicapped children tend to feel guilty when they find that they are a burden or when they are rejected by playmates; and they tend to drift off into their own private and sometimes psychotic worlds. (See Case 2 in Chapter 1, the story of Willis.)

CASE 79

Orin, age 11, had been rescued from the backwoods of the Ozark Mountains by the county social worker who had heard there was a blind boy in the woods. Orin had lived with an old man in a cabin on a hill above a river and had never been to town before. His grandfather did not know the cause of the blindness, but he presumed that Orin had always been blind. His daughter had left the boy with him when Orin was 3. Physical examination at the school for the blind in St. Louis verified that Orin probably had no vision of any kind. Yet he had been known to roam the woods and to find his way back home and to be a good swimmer and fisherman. He had never been to school; the neighbors who knew he was blind regarded him as a "dummy." Yet he could speak quite fluently and identify objects by name as he touched them, if they had been in his experience. However, in the school for the blind, he became not only helpless but a nuisance. He could not find his way around; he was not used to any kind of routine; he screamed and fought with the attendants at the school who tried to give him a bath or put shoes on him; and he sat alone in his room crying for his grandfather. He was not used to a flush toilet and therefore urinated and defecated whereever he wished. Somehow, unbeknown to the school authorities, he managed to set fire to the dormitory, which of course horrified the people in charge, since a fire in a blind school is extremely frightening to all concerned. Luckily, no one was injured. It was obvious that Orin's problem was not his blindness but rather the culture shock he experienced in being moved out of his entirely bucolic setting into one with urban expectations.

C. RECEPTIVE OR SENSORY HANDICAPS: THE BLIND AND DEAF

1. Visual Handicaps

The assessment of a visually handicapped child should begin with a thorough interview with the parents and the child. It is absolutely necessary to obtain a good description of the handicap itself, its origins and development, and its present state. One should also obtain from the parents their description of the degree of disability, because it is their understanding of the disability, their attitudes toward it, their ways of

managing it, and their hopes for the child's future that often determine the actual degree of disability. Thus, the child whose parents regard the child's blindness to be a "curse" or to be the result of some supposed mistake that they made during the mother's pregnancy, for which they cannot forgive themselves, who view their blind child as a "poor little thing," who wait on the child hand and foot and never permit the child to explore things, who with endless cheerfulness accept the endless "burden" of their child—it is this child who probably suffers the greatest inability to function successfully as a blind person. On the other hand, the parents who accept their child's visual handicap as a fact of life without assigning blame, who make every effort to train her/him to function in the most effective fashion, who regard their blind child socially and emotionally as one might regard any other child, who can be both angry and affectionate with the child—it is *this* child who is likely to have the least disability.

With respect to specific tests for the blind, intellectual functioning of the nonsighted has long been measured by the Hayes-Binet, which is roughly a combination of the verbal items on the Stanford-Binet 1937 edition, forms L and M. A similar Verbal IQ can be obtained by using the verbal tests on the WISC-R. The Haptic Intelligence Test for the Adult Blind (Shurrager and Shurrager, 1964) may also be used with adolescents. This is a nonverbal IQ Test, based on the performance scales of the WAIS. Even so, as noted previously, it is necessary to modify a few items and to take into account the visual implications of others in order to use the WISC-R appropriately. For example, the child should be permitted to feel the examiner's hand when he/she is asked the first question in Information, "What finger is this?" Although blind persons do tend to be quite verbal and fairly adept at abstract thinking, it is very likely that it is somewhat easier to make abstractions—especially for children—if one has seen the object. Not only does it help to see a wheel and a ball to recognize roundness, or a candle and a lamp to recognize light, but it would help to have seen a scale and a yardstick to know the relationship between a pound and a yard, or to have seen a mountain and a lake to recognize their similarities. Sighted children are allowed to see the vocabulary cards; blind children should be presented with a card in braille or have the word repeated and spelled if necessary. Some greater choices of action might be given to comprehension questions when using this test for the blind; for example, a blind person who found the wallet (question 2) might very appropriately ask the help of some sighted person rather than going directly to an authority. A blind person who smells smoke in a theater certainly should try to find help from some sighted person. Question 5, about losing a ball to some other child, is entirely inappropriate for the nonsighted and might be changed to losing a toy or some object commonly used by blind children. Similarly, it is doubtful that license plates (question 8) are as familiar objects to blind children as they are to sighted children. In my experience, IQ's obtained on the WISC-R verbal scales by blind children tend to underestimate their intellectual functioning.

The learning of self-help and social behavior, such as is measured by the Vineland or similar scales, is probably also underestimated. Yet, this is an important part of the development of blind children. Although being blind certainly does slow down a child's social development and self-help learning, nevertheless it is extremely important that the child develop such functioning if he or she is ever going to live any kind of an independent life. Thus, it is a good idea to use the Vineland or any other behavioral measure of social development in an interview with the parents. (Even if nothing else is accomplished by using this test, it does emphasize to the parents that one should expect the blind child to learn to do many of the self-help items on such tests.) Thus a blind child might be just a little slower in finding his or

her way around the house or out into the neighborhood—and parents should be more cautious about permitting such travel—but a blind child has to learn to go to the toilet, take a bath, brush his/her teeth, change clothes, put himself/herself to bed at night, just like any other pre-schooler. Admittedly, this takes considerably more care and training by the parents, who should, of course, consult the local agency for training of the junior blind.

Learning to get around with either a cane or dog—or without either at times—is a major learning task for blind children. Some blind children, who may be very bright intellectually, have a great deal of difficulty in finding their way around in space, particularly in dealing with streets and going across town. Other children, who may not be quite as intellectually astute, quickly become good travelers. At one time I experimented briefly with the use of an inset metal maze, hoping in that way to estimate travel by the length of time it took to learn such a maze. However, my preliminary results suggested that there was little relationship between such hand movements and broad spatial learning, and I did not pursue this experiment. Gallagher (1968) reports positive correlations between the Haptic Intelligence Scales and travel.

Blind children also need the tactile ability to learn braille, and tests have been constructed for this—which are usually administered at schools for the blind. Tests for educational achievement in braille are also available at the blind schools. Many nonsighted persons are quite capable of doing tasks that we ordinarily think of as reserved for the sighted. For example, they may be employed as typists, telephone-switchboard operators, or assemblers of electrical components—even as teachers, lawyers, and psychologists. Training for such tasks does, however, involve considerable ability to imagine spatial relationships, albeit on a smaller dimension than in travel. Since appropriate tests for such abilities are not guaranteed for the sighted, it is very difficult to predict such work abilities for the blind. Perhaps one could adapt such old, standard tests as the Purdue Pegboard or even the Seguin Form Board. In my informal experimentation with testing blind children, I found that those who were highly verbally oriented did less well on learning the Seguin than did children whose verbal ability was only modest. In using such tests—even informally—it seemed to me that a better measure was the number of trials needed to learn the board rather than timed completion. Norms for the number of trials needed to learn the Seguin are available as part of the Reitan battery for the neurologically handicapped child and might be applied to the blind.

As to assessment of emotional functioning among blind children, it is possible to adapt several of the commonly used projective techniques, such as the Thematic Apperception Test, the Word Association Test, and the Sentence Completion Test. To use the TAT, I simply read the descriptions in the manual that Murray provides that accompanies the TAT plates. This was put on tape for blind children who had learned to operate a tape recorder, and they either dictated their stories or typed them themselves. Again, it is probable that some of these test items do depend a lot on visual experience, but I was continually amazed at what seemed to me to be a high degree of imagery among the blind, perhaps because I had always considered imagery to be a visual ability. However, I discovered that many children who had been blind since birth could use words to describe scenes and interactions and feelings quite appropriately and dramatically. Most sentence-completion tests can be read to the child, who dictates an answer, as can a word-association test. The MMPI is available in braille for blind adolescents, or it can be read onto tape for their use.

CASE 80

Arnold, age 13, was brought to the local mental hygiene clinic by his teacher at the blind school where he was residing, be-cause he was always in fights with the other children, was impudent and even insulting to the teachers, and seemed to have a great deal of difficulty in learning braille. He also frightened the schoolteachers by wandering off the grounds and down the street and around town by himself. Arnie complained that the other kids were a bunch of sissies and bums, that they were not teaching him anything at the blind school, and that he wanted to return to his home.

Arnie had been blinded at age 6 when he did not drop a large firecracker when it was lit. It exploded, ruining both of his eyes and blowing off two of his fingers. For a brief period he had some light vision, but the condition of his eyes deteriorated, and each had to be removed and replaced with a glass eye. Thus, at age 12 he had no vision at all. Arnie was born and raised on a farm in northern California, and there were no facilities for education of the blind nearby. However, Arnie had started school already and was learning to read. He was evidently very bright, and neither his parents nor his teacher in the rural school considered that he should do anything other than return to school after his injuries had healed. He was accepted by the other children, and he quickly found his way around the schoolroom. Other people read his lessons to him—both at school and at home. His mother permitted him to wander around the farm almost unaccompanied, and he learned his way by bumps and bruises. He told me with a smile that his horse had been one of his best teachers, as the horse seemed to know in some way that the rider was a "different" person. He recalled that the horse would purposely ride him under the limb of a tree, where he would be hit on the head, but Arnie learned quickly to duck as they approached a tree. He could play such games as hide-and-seek, for he could hear the other children breathing. He learned to wrestle and could hold his own in a fist fight. He was almost completely self-sufficient in self-care. He had his mother, for example, attach labels of different materials to each of his socks so he could tell what color he was wearing. However, by the time Arnie was 12, his parents realized that he did need to learn some special techniques, such as braille and how to travel. Moreover, the local union high school was somewhat reluctant to accept a blind adolescent.

On the Hayes-Binet, which the school for the blind was using as an IQ test, Arnie obtained an IQ of 141. The school was very happy with his self-care and accepted him gladly. However, Arnie was used to rough-and-tumble relationships with his brothers and his friends, whereas most of the boys and girls in the school for the blind, many who had been there for many years, were far more genteel. They were not used to being given a shove just for the fun of it. Nor was the school accustomed to have such an independent lad around. Arnie disliked braille because he was used to being read to. Nevertheless, he put up a struggle trying to learn it but found himself somewhat hindered by the loss of several fingers on his right hand.

With only a brief period of counseling, Arnie was able to return to the school for the blind, behave himself, and learn braille. In his senior year a high school, he prevailed upon his mother and the local school authorities to allow him to return home and spend his senior year in a public school, where he succeeded with all A's. He took notes in braille but had a reader to read to him. An all-A student at the university, he went on to graduate school where he received a doctorate in economics. I last heard of Arnie when I read in a newspaper that he had become professor of economics at a prominent university and is an adviser to the president of the United States. He had married and was the father of three quite healthy and vigorous children.

CASE 81

Gordon, age 10, was also brought to the mental hygiene clinic by his teachers at the blind school. He, too, was getting along very poorly with the other children. He complained that they were always picking on him, but his teachers reported that he was a demanding and whining child who constantly sought their attention for any excuse and who had much difficulty in working on his own. He was learning satisfactorily but they felt he was underachieving and learning more slowly than he should. Gordon was far more interested in learning to play the piano than in learning braille. The schoolteacher was of the opinion that many of Gordon's problems with the teachers and the other children stemmed from the fact that his aged aunt, who was his caretaker, had "spoiled him." Gordon lived at home with her and attended the school only on a day basis. Most of the other children resided at the school. Gordon's aunt, Mrs. K, agreed to come and talk to the counselors at the clinic.

Gordon's retinitis had begun at birth or shortly thereafter, but he was almost a year old before his parents clearly recognized that he was visually handicapped severely. At first, they had great hopes that medication, exercise, surgery, or some other magic would halt the progression of his visual loss. He was an only child and his mother was nearly 40 when he was born, so she had great hopes for this baby. At first, she hovered over him with almost overwhelming attention, becoming increasingly anxious and depressed. She felt her husband blamed her for the child's blindness. She became very religious, attending church two or three times a day to ask for God's forgiveness. Gordon's father could not endure her behavior; he did not accept the blind child, and when Gordon was about 2 years old he abandoned them. Shortly after that, Gordon's mother became so emotionally disturbed that she was hospitalized in a local mental hospital. At this point, Mrs. K, who was Gordon's aunt, took over his care. Her husband had been killed in World War II, and she had no other children. She then devoted her every waking moment to Gordon's needs and wishes. As a result, Gordon was a relatively helpless 10-year-old. He could not dress himself; he still needed his aunt's help in washing or combing his hair; he was a very sloppy eater (in contrast to Arnie, who prided himself on polishing off a banana split without getting a drop on his clothes); and Gordon had to be guided everywhere—even around his own home which he was so familiar with. He had learned braille at school, but only when the school insisted that his aunt stop reading to him temporarily. She took him everywhere with her when he was not at school because, she explained, "Why, he might get hurt in some way if I wasn't there!"

Although quite intellectually bright, Gordon was emotionally and socially quite infantile. He cried very easily when frustrated, and other children took advantage of his babyish ways and teased him or tried to push him around. Gordon was also a somewhat angry and depressed youngster. He did not like the identity of being the "poor blind child" that his aunt fostered. In fact, he stated quite clearly that he hated himself for being blind. He wondered what would have happened if he had not been blind. He wondered if it was his fault that his mother remained mentally ill. He rarely saw her, since his aunt felt it was "not good for the child" to visit her. In his fantasies to the TAT, the heroes were extremely valiant people who rescued princesses from prison or they were supermen who accomplished miraculous tasks. Or, in one tale, the hero was not recognized for his great deeds, but when he was killed everyone was sorry.

A year of psychotherapy helped Gordon and his aunt separate. She permitted him to reside at the school for the blind and come home only on weekends, when she began to make expectations on him to care for himself. Gordon spent over half of his year in psychotherapy in an angry harangue with his therapist, accusing the therapist of making his life worse and not understanding at all what it meant to be blind. Nevertheless, the therapist kept insisting that what it meant to be blind was Gordon's task for himself to resolve, not for the therapist.

Subsequently, there were sessions between the therapist, Gordon, and his aunt, or between the therapist, Gordon, and his teacher. He was now less infantile but remained a rather cynical and prissy young man who had no close friends. He was still quite demanding of others, and after high school he returned to live with his aunt while he attended the university. He had hoped to become a jazz pianist, but he did not succeed professionally. I had no opportunity to follow him in his career, but friends of his whom I knew advised me that shortly after he received his bachelor's degree, his aunt died, leaving him a fairly large fortune. He was employed on a part-time basis as an editor for a literary magazine. Even in death, his aunt controlled him, since she designated that he would not receive the entire inheritance but would have to live off of a trust. He doubted his own abilities to care for his money and hired a business manager, who later became his homosexual companion.

Although Gordon's blindness played a part in his development and eventual adulthood life-style, nevertheless, this case should emphasize that the development of a blind person is often not remarkably distinct from that of a sighted person. Gordon's development was perhaps more influenced by the loss of his parents than by the loss of his sight. His relationship with his aunt, who became an overwhelming and dominating mother, did disable him more than his loss of sight. Just knowing that a person is blind is insufficient in understanding their development and personality.

2. Auditory Handicaps

It is even more important in the assessment of a child with a hearing loss to know the nature and history of the handicap. While there is some variation in the degree and nature of a visual handicap, the variation is even greater among those who have a loss of hearing. Seldom is the loss of hearing absolute. More frequently, people who are called "deaf" are left with some partial hearing, which allows them some kind of an auditory contact, although such contact may be really quite inadequate. Some children hear low pitches but not high-pitched sounds, and some hear the opposite pitches. Some children's hearing loss consists of a constant sound interference, like static that may occur whether or not there is any sound in the environment. Others have a loss that is easily rectified by a hearing aid that magnifies the volume. For others, volume magnification does not help at all. Others suffer from a hearing loss that varies from moment to moment, such that they may hear perfectly clearly at times, but most of the time they do not understand anything at all. As might be imagined, these latter children are often confused because they never know what to expect.

One of the most important factors to understand in the history of a deaf child is *when* the deafness was discovered and established. Far too often, the deaf infant is not known to be hard of hearing but, rather, is thought of as retarded. The first sign of deafness in a child is often the fact that he or she fails to learn to talk. The idea that the child may be intellectually retarded is given further evidence if the child *occasionally* hears. Let us suppose that a child can hear loud sounds but cannot distinguish voices or vocalizations. He or she thus may respond to sound and therefore not seem to be deaf, but he or she fails to understand speech and to develop it. Whether a child is deaf or merely mute can be easily resolved if one has palmar galvanic equipment. One merely attaches the electrode to the child's palm and if the child is hearing a spoken word or noise, the galvanator's dial will indicate a stimulus. However, a simple behavior-reward setup will also suffice. For example, the child is shown that the examiner has a piece of candy in his/her hand, and the examiner then puts his/her hands behind his/her back and exchanges the candy back and forth. The examiner then holds out one fist; if there is candy in the fist, the examiner says "candy" to the child. If the child reaches for the candy,

she/he is given it. However, if the examiner does not say the word *candy,* there is no candy in the examiner's hand. If the child hears, he/she learns soon that there is no candy when the word is not said. However, if the child does not hear, then she/he will reach for the candy every time and will fail to learn that it is associated with the word *candy*. These simple devices are often needed, since the usual audiometer test is not applicable to a child who is not yet saying anything at all or who is under the age of 3.

Since hearing losses are often missed or are misdiagnosed early in a deaf child's life, it is important to note what kinds of hypotheses are made up for the child's failure to learn. Moreover, the pre-school child who is deaf is likely to be quite disobedient and "headstrong." He or she goes ahead and does what may be satisfying to him/her without reference to adults, thus appearing to be mainly a "hyperactive," "brain damaged," or "autistic" child, rather than a child who is merely hard of hearing.

The assessor who is going to work with the deaf should learn some simple hand signals or sign language. However, he or she may be faced with some children who do not understand sign language, but many hard-of-hearing children can follow simple signs.

There are several tests specifically designed to assess intellectual development in the hard of hearing. The Arthur Point Scale (1947), one of the original tests, should be administered entirely by hand signal. The Leiter International Performance Scale (1948) is a similar, completely nonverbal mental-age scale. The Performance Scales of the WISC-R may also be used with the hard of hearing, but it should be noted here that the test should be modified because hand signals are not sufficient for some of the subtests. For example, one might have to use the first three items on the Picture Completion Scale as examples, pointing out to the deaf child that there are missing parts in each picture. Credit, then, should be given for these samples. Similarly, it may be necessary to use more than one sample on Picture Arrangement and to use the first two items on Block Design as sample items. Since the ability to use language is highly associated with abstract thinking, the non-speaking deaf child may respond with only very concrete answers. He or she may have difficulty with such nonverbal tests of abstraction as the Block Design on the Wechsler. Both the Wechsler Mazes and the Porteus Mazes, used separately, seem to be fairly definitive and fair tests of intellectual development among hard-of-hearing children. The Harris Draw-A-Man Test or Draw-A-Woman Test may be used if it is possible to communicate to the child the directions, either through hand signals or speech.

Assessment of emotional functioning of deaf children is easy enough if they can read. Thus, the instructions to the TAT or Rorschach can be typed out and handed to the child, who can then respond to each with speech, sign language, or he/she may write out the story. I found it possible to examine so-called intellectually retarded deaf children with the Rorschach merely by making up two or three samples so that the child understood that he or she was to interpret the inkblot. Since many of these children used only very rudimentary sign language, it was necessary to have the help of the teacher of the deaf.

CASE 82

Mitchell, age 12, had been placed in an institution for the mentally retarded when he was only 6 because he had not learned to talk, was a severe behavior problem, and was thought to be severely intellectually retarded. His poverty-stricken parents, who never visited him again, could no longer care for him along with their several other children. It was not known precisely when the institution discovered that he was deaf, but when he was left in the institution there was no teacher of the deaf available. Mitchell soon became a very clever boy

around the hospital. He did little errands and worked in different areas of the institution's vocation program. When a teacher of the deaf was hired, Mitchell was put in this teacher's class. He learned a very simple sign language, consisting mainly of learned signs and symbols rather than an actual hand-signal alphabet. His teacher guessed that Mitchell might be really quite bright and was not at all intellectually retarded. Mitchell enjoyed puzzles and other similar games. Therefore, he was readily challenged by the Grace-Arthur Tests, on which he achieved an IQ of 110. His Draw-A-Man likewise gave him an IQ of above 100. His responses to the Rorschach were most dramatic. He readily caught on to the idea of interpreting an inkblot. Since he communicated with very simple hand signals, the teacher of the deaf had to make guesses about what Mitchell was indicating. For example, to Card 1 he curled and flexed his fingers, indicating he thought it was a spider. He zoomed Card 2 through the air and gave every indication that he thought it was a spaceship. He acted out Card 3, standing and bowing, indicating that he thought it was a man bowing in the inkblot. Overall, his Rorschach suggested that he perceived his environment quite accurately and that his emotional development was fairly normal for a boy his age, in his situation. However, his behavior around the hospital suggested that he was quickly developing into a manipulator and thief. He was always in trouble with the attendants, and if anything was stolen one was likely to find it in Mitchell's "bag of tricks." Except for the teacher of the deaf, he had no friends among the staff, nor was he emotionally close to any of the other patients in the hospital. The social worker was unable to locate his parents, and with some doubts he was placed in a foster home where one parent was also deaf. It was explained to the foster parents that he might become a behavior problem but that they were to discipline him firmly if necessary. Mitchell did turn out to be a problem for these foster parents, and finally he ran away, returning to the hospital. The teacher of the deaf convinced Mitchell to return to the foster home, and he succeeded this time not only in adjusting to the home but in attending classes for the deaf, learning formal sign language and some lip reading. The last that the hospital heard of him is when he returned as a young adult, hoping that the hospital could help him find his original parents. At that time, he was working fairly successfully as a carpenter's helper.

CASE 83

Ava, age 30, was so severely depressed that I feared she might commit suicide at any time. Her husband, whom she had married on the rebound after a quarrel with her lover, was killed in an automobile accident within a few months after their marriage and had left her pregnant with Ramon, now age 7. Her father, a very rigid Protestant minister, had disowned her when she married a Mexican Catholic. He refused even to see his grandson. Ava was a very beautiful woman who for a while was able to earn a living as a model, but because she thought Ramon needed her every minute, she was not able to work steadily. At the time she entered psychotherapy with me, she had been earning a living largely as an expensive call girl and then as a mistress to an elderly, well-to-do man who paid all her bills. She also accepted such bizarre jobs as smuggling diamonds. She was advised by numerous doctors that her child was brain damaged, and she thought it was her fault as she had difficulty in giving birth to him. She thought it was possible she had injured him when she could not relax at his birth and had suffered greatly from labor pains. At age 7, Ramon was completely uncontrollable and was not attending any kind of school. His mother had to stay at home with him most of the time. He was very destructive had ripped up the furniture, torn up her clothes, and had even set the apartment on fire once. He had not learned to speak, but he did feed himself and go to the toilet by himself. However, he still would soil his clothes at times and was enuretic. He ate like a little animal with his hands and frequently smeared food or feces around the house.

After only a few minutes with Ramon, it was obvious to me that he was not hearing anything. A door slammed and he did not startle. Telephone bells rang and he paid no attention to them. I screamed in his ear and it made no different to him whatsoever. On the other hand, he was visually very attentive to everything and explored my office—touching everything. However, after about 5 to 10 minutes, he headed out the door and went down the hall to see where his mother was. In about five more very brief visits, I engaged him in pieces of the Arthur Test. He was fascinated by the game and seemed to understand what I wanted him to do, merely by the hand signals suggested in the Arthur. Ava was then sent to the school for the deaf, where she learned a series of behavior-modification techniques, which helped her to control Ramon to the extent that he was able to begin his studies in the school for the deaf. He made excellent progress. Relieved of his continuous care and no longer feeling guilty about his condition. Ava was able to obtain regular and legal employment. However, she remained considerably depressed, particularly because she believed no man would ever accept her and her deaf child. She might have married her elderly lover, except that she felt that he disliked Ramon and certainly would be no adequate father for him. Many men sought her sexually, but this only angered her: She really wanted someone who would help her by being a father for Ramon. Ava spent nearly three years in psychotherapy and then dropped out—still moderately depressed. She returned to psychotherapy some seven years later when Ramon was an adolescent, because he was involved in the use of street drugs. He was succeeding relatively well at school but had almost no social contacts. It appeared to me that his drug usage was largely his way of gaining entrance to groups of teen-agers who were also using drugs at that time in the early 1970s. I last heard of her on a recent New Year's Day when she telephoned me long distance to let me know how extremely lonesome she was and to say that she was again contemplating suicide. Ramon, now a young adult, was a plumber and had moved away from home. Ava admitted that there was no one else in her life and that she had become chronically alcoholic.

Both blind and deaf people do tend to band together, perhaps for no other reason than that they form friendships at the special schools for the sensory handicapped. However, such grouping together is far more common among the deaf, who form almost a separate community. Their communication problems with other people are more severe than are those of the blind, especially if they have limited speech. At least among the adult hard of hearing, there is almost a "paranoia" of deafness. However, this paranoia is not really the kind of emotional disorder that this term commonly denotes, but it is rather the uneasiness and suspiciousness of anyone who does not know whether other people are talking *to* them or *about* them. It is really more of a guardedness and slight defensiveness than a true paranoia. I have not observed this among deaf children, although deaf adults have assured me that it forms a part of the character of many deaf people early in their lives. However, deaf children who are cared for normally by their parents and learn the experience of trust, as Erikson labels it, do not suffer from any noticeable emotional difficulty in relating to others.

D. EXPRESSIVE HANDICAPS—SPEECH

There have been so many studies, both research and clinical, of children's speech difficulties that it would be impossible to cover them in a few paragraphs in this book. The assessment and treatment of speech is essentially beyond the purview of the average clinical psychologist. However, as has been emphasized in the preceding paragraphs, the handicap itself may not be the only aspect of the child's disability, and very often a child with a speech difficulty develops difficulties in other areas such that the child is not only not speaking clearly, but he/she may be emotionally upset, intellectually slowed down, and stuck motivationally in a "failure syndrome." Other children make fun of children with speech defects and isolate them socially. They become angry and depressed. Although ultimately a speech pathologist may be the professional person to examine and treat the child's specific handicap, a careful and thorough assessment by the clinical psychologist of the child's total adjustment is often necessary as the first step.

Thus, a speech difficulty should not be considered as a simple single handicap, any more so than one might regard any other symptom as merely a "poor habit" or, in the opposite extreme, as a symptom of brain damage. Rather, one must begin, just as one might with any other symptom or handicap, with interviews with the child and the parents regarding the nature of the handicap, the degree of disability ("What does this speech difficulty keep the child from doing?"), and a history of the handicap—when it began, when it is worst, and the conditions under which the child speaks most clearly. One must obtain a good description of the way the parents train and discipline the child. For example, some children may be so angry at their parents' punishment that they refuse to speak or are so waited on hand and foot by their parents that they do not need to speak. One would expect that a hearing loss had already been checked out before the psychologist sees the child, but this is not always true. One should also carefully observe the nonspeaking child to see if there are signs of that special kind of social and emotional withdrawal known as autism. If the child is able to speak but stutters badly, before he/she is sent to a speech therapist it is vital to have a good picture of the child and of his or her family and their interpersonal relationships. Most stuttering arises from psychological conflicts that must be cleared up at least concomitantly with speech training.

One special warning to the beginning psychologist who is examining a child with a speech difficulty: *Beware of Greeks bearing gifts*. At one time it was thought that all speech difficulties resulted from some neurological disease or trauma. Thus, as is the custom of physicians, these speech difficulties were given Greek names. However, these Greek names had little specific meaning, and the label in itself did not necessarily indicate any particular neurological dysfunction. However, because a neurologic label had been applied to the child, psychologists assumed far too often that the child necessarily suffered from some "brain damage" or disease. Yet terms like *aphasia* or *anomia* or *alexia* are not neurological disorders but are merely the neurologist's terms for describing or for indicating, respectively, the inability to speak comprehensively, the reaching for words, and difficulty in learning to read.

Assessment of the intellectual development of children with speech impairments can be accomplished with the same kinds of techniques used for the hard of hearing. For the cerebral palsied child without speech, the Columbia Mental Maturity is a nice addition to this performance battery. The Draw-A-Man or Draw-A-Woman can serve both as an IQ test and as a technique for understanding children's identity. Assessment of fantasy and feelings can be accomplished by use of such techniques as the World Test or the Make A Picture Story Test. Children who can write can respond to the TAT, Sentence Completion, or the Rorschach. Most of the so-called "aphasia" tests were constructed primarily for adults. Such complex and expensive techniques as the Reitan Battery (see Chapter 17) consist largely of pieces from other tests, and usually the performance tests of the WISC-R or the Grace-Arthur Point Scale are sufficient. Because many speech difficulties are perceptual as well as expres-

sive, it is often necessary to clear up this point by the use of the Bender or the Memory for Designs, as may be appropriate for the child's age.

Case 84

Felicia, age 6, was brought to the clinic mainly to assess whether she would be able to go to school. She was unable to communicate with any meaningful speech to anyone outside her family but responded with guttural noises that sometimes approached words, and in a series of tones that sounded like sentences with periods and question marks so that her family halfway understood her. Her hearing had been checked and was normal. Her history showed several facts that might be related to her speech difficulty. She was the fifteenth child of 16 children in a Mexican family where Spanish was the primary language at home. Her younger sister, Paula, was now 4 and was speaking quite clearly in both English and Spanish. No one else in the family had any speech difficulties. Because she had had so many children, Mrs. R was not clear about the conditions of her pregnancy nor gestation with Felicia, but she could not remember having any special difficulties during her pregnancy. Felicia's birth, which was at home with a midwife, was regarded as normal. However, when Felicia was about 13 or 14 months old, she suffered from a series of "colds" that were accompanied by high fevers. Her mother said that she thought that at that time Felicia might die because she was so sick. Because she was a frail baby, her mother and older sisters took special care of her. She was not really weaned from the bottle until she was almost 3 and was still in diapers at that age also. "She was like our special pet," Felicia's older sister reported. She was not placed in any nursery schools or had she as yet attended kindergarten. Everyone said she was an alert child who seemed to understand anything that was said to her in either language. Once the mother began toilet training, she was easily trained. And she quickly learned to feed and dress herself and to avoid the normal dangers around the family home. However, she was never really out of the family environment. She had no playmates other than her sisters; she was considered to be "jealous" if attention was paid to her immediately older brother or little sister. Occasionally, cousins of about her age visited, and she would have nothing to do with them. She was even jealous of the family dog. She would push others aside when the dog was being petted and pretend that she was the dog who needed to be loved. "We love her so much, what will we do," asked the family. Felicia was fascinated with the little problems on the Leiter International Scale, and her score was in the normal range for her age. Similarly, her Draw-A-Man, using the Harris scale, yielded an IQ of 100. She could copy the Bender figures accurately for a 6-year-old. She enjoyed playing with the paper dolls of the MAPS, but it was difficult to understand what was going on in her little playlets. She used many of the figures all at once, and in combinations that seemed to have little meaning. However, as far as the assessor could observe, there was no indication that the figures she picked out were in any conflict. Once or twice, if they fell over, she would take a maternal figure and pick up the fallen figure gingerly and have the mother figure give it a kiss. After a while she was merely drawing the same figures out of the file and rearranging them on the stage, regardless of the background.

Although it was possible that Felicia's speech impairment might have had its origins in the high fevers she suffered as an infant, nevertheless it was also obvious that the family, by making her a pet and not demanding any speech from her, had aggravated her situation. The child was referred to a speech therapist who believed that, based on the psychologist's results, it would be possible to train her to speak much more clearly. Prior to beginning such therapy, however, there was a session with the family members who were presented

with the assessment results. The family were advised to begin requiring clearer speech of Felicia at home. Although it was understood that they loved her—and there should be no doubt that she was loved—nevertheless, they were told they should not really make a pet of her. She was sent to a special kindergarten class for children with speech impairments so that she could experience socialization outside of her family group. Her speech improved markedly over the next six months, and she was able to enter regular school classes with only a mild speech difficulty at the beginning of the next school year.

E.   MOTORIC HANDICAPS

As is true of the other types of handicaps, there are a wide variety of impairments possible in the muscular or motor system of the child. One of the most common is called "cerebral palsy," but this is in truth a wastebasket term covering miscellaneous damages largely to the lower brain that were sustained either in utero or at birth. Many CP children also have speech difficulties due to misshapen jaws or lack of muscular control. At one time, because of the difficulties in speech that CP's often suffer they were confused with the mentally retarded. At one institution with which I am familiar, previously there had been a whole ward of over 100 women who suffered only CP but who had been stuck in this "home for the feebleminded" as children. Most of them were quite literate, and some of them were actually capable of much self-care. They had in effect been abandoned by their families. Approximately a decade ago, newspapers and magazines were full of articles on "spastic" children whose mobility was severely limited by their stiff limbs. Unfortunately, the term *spazz* became an epithet among normal children to indicate any other child who was considered by them to be abnormal. Because of their appearances and their bizarre movements (especially among the locomotor ataxia), such children become the objects of scorn of normal children and are often social isolates. Quite frequently such children develop inappropriate social mechanisms so that they will be noticed or liked.

CASE 85

Antoinette, age 16, was actually a very pretty girl. She kept her long blond hair brushed constantly; she had lovely blue eyes and flashed a nice smile and had a pretty figure. When she was sitting still it was not immediately obvious that she suffered from a cerebral palsy. Unfortunately, her speech was quite guttural, and although she had had many years of speech therapy, her efforts at speech were barely comprehensible. Because she was so very anxious about her speech, her face would writhe in almost ticlike fashion before she could open her mouth, and her arms would start to jerk and her body stiffen and her head swing back. Embarrassed, she would laugh initially in raucous fashion before she spoke, and she became known as the "laughing cow" (the name of a brand of cheese). When she rose from her chair, she looked as if she was going to pitch forward completely. Her arms would swing wildly to help her balance herself, and she appeared as if she was grasping the air for something to hold onto. She could control her bodily movements considerably better when alone or with her family than when out in public, where she was always fearful of being laughed at. Thus, at home she could do many things that would surprise people who saw her only casually on the street. She was entirely independent with respect to self-care. Sitting quietly in her own room, she could control at least her right hand to type accurately and slowly. She could even crochet. And she had become a fairly good cook, although her mother always worried that she might burn herself—which she never had. Antoinette had always attended a special school for the handicapped, but she longed to be among other teen-agers and share in the activities

of nonhandicapped youngsters. She implored her mother to allow her to attend the local public high school. She was very romantic and listened to all the popular songs on the radio, and she read many romantic novels. Her mother was afraid that Antoinette would be too socially naive and might possibly be used by the other teen-agers—especially by the boys. "But I know all that, mother," Antoinette replied, "and I've got to learn to get along. I've got to learn not to be embarrassed."

Although Antoinette had had many psychological examinations by examiners attached to the school she had attended, her mother sought my advice as a person outside the school system. I reviewed the package of reports of her school work and adjustment and of the various tests administered to her over the years. It was obvious she was a very bright child who, in this system and this handicapped society in which she had grown up, was well adjusted. She reviewed with me her expectations in high school, and I could not see that she was any more unrealistic than other girls her age. "I know that some kids will make fun of me, but they are cruel and I will tell them so. Besides, I think I can make some friends who will defend me," Antoinette said sincerely. "I will find some nice boyfriend, and he will tell them to shut up. Besides, the teachers will like me, and they won't let the other kids hurt me." The first hurdle that Antoinette faced and that she did not expect was that the school authorities did not want her in their classes and buildings. The principal shrugged and said that he was not allowed to take disabled children no matter how nice they were, that this was the school rule and that he had no authority to change it. The school superintendent's office stated that the school's insurance prohibited admission of disabled children that if Antoinette fell and hurt herself or was pushed by some other child, the school could be sued and they had no coverage. Antoinette wept, "But I never fall, even though I may look like it." At this point Antoinette's father decided to defend his daughter. He was a fairly prominent businessman in the community and was personally acquainted with some of the members of the school board. He took Antoinette to the school board where she, by merely sitting still, charmed the board members into permitting an exception so that she could be admitted to the school. School authorities were still uneasy and wondered if she should not have a wheelchair or a crutch, but the dean of girls observed her and decided that she could walk easily enough. Then, there was the objection that she could not enter into the physical-education program that was required for all children. However, she could swim quite well and "maybe I can learn to be a coach." The school authorities were delighted with her cheerful determination. The other adolescents were not nearly as abusive as she had expected, although some snickered at times, particularly when she rose to recite in class, but a teacher defended her and demanded that the children be patient with her, particularly when she spoke. Others—especially some of the girls—befriended her, ate lunch with her, and even invited her to their homes. But, by and large, she was left out of the boy–girl relationships that are the center of high-school life. She was not invited to the parties that she heard of because there was no boyfriend to take her. However, she swallowed her pride and her tears and tried to pretend that she was altogether happy. Her mother remained uneasy about her adjustment. Antoinette and I had several more counseling sessions, but she stoutly declared there was nothing wrong and that she would get along alright. In her senior year she attracted the attention of a young man from Indonesia, and it was almost love at first sight for both. Her mother again feared that she would become sexually involved, but Antoinette tried to assure her mother that there was no sexual relationship between them, mainly because he was a strict Moslem. Since Antoinette and her parents were fairly faithful Christians, this religious difference did not please the par-

ents either. But they found the young man, who visited the house frequently, to be a very polite, quiet, "nice" boy who was very respectful to them—something they did not feel they enjoyed from other teenagers. Before Antoinette's parents decided what position to take regarding this relationship, it was suddenly broken up by his parents, who discovered that Antoinette was disabled. They regarded this as an indication that she suffered from some brain damage, which made her very unacceptable to them. They had no understanding whatever of her condition. They forbade their son to see her again and removed him from the school. Antoinette was so heartbroken that she stayed at home for over a week, refusing to eat, very depressed, almost ill. She returned to school, where much to her surprise the other girls were quite sympathetic and assured her that here would be other boys who would be equally attracted. They told her she need not fall in love with the "first jerk that comes along." Antoinette's broken heart healed as rapidly as that of any other teenagers in a similar situation. I have not seen her for quite a few years, but I am a personal friend of her parents. They have told me that she went through a similar love affair in college and that shortly after she graduated she was married for several years to a man they did not care for because he used their relationship to boss her around. She had separated from this man and was living in another city, where she was earning a living as a proofreader and assistant editor to a scientific magazine.

Children with muscular dystrophy, cerebral palsy, or even locomotor ataxia can be examined with many of the same tests that are used for normal children. For children who cannot manipulate or speak, it is often possible to get them to point in such tests as the Columbia Mental Maturity or even to indicate in some way the blocks they wish moved around in many of the Leiter items. One student psychologist very ingeniously used the multiple-choice Rorschach, reading the choice possibilities to the child and having him/her nod yes or no as the response occurred to him/her. It does take much more patience to test a cerebral-palsied child with a speech handicap because one must wait for the child to gather up enough energy and control to make an answer, and the answer may not always be exactly intelligible. Such examination is usually more qualitative than quantitative. If one is predicting a young child's ability for speech or socialization training, then one needs to estimate the child's potential even though her/his funtioning may—on strict accounting—be quite retarded.

The frustration of not being able to grasp the thing you want, take the steps you want, or say the words you want is intense, and children who are motorically handicapped are often so upset by their handicap that they scream in anger or easily give up. They fling themselves on the floor in what seem to be temper tantrums, weeping in their frustration and helplessness. Such behavior often leads neurologists and parents as well to believe that the child has damage to those sections of the brain that control emotions. The child then may regret that he/she has lost emotional control and ask in a pitiful voice, "Why am I such a bad boy or girl?" Even more so than children who suffer other handicaps, the motorically handicapped tends to feel that in some way she/he brought their difficulty on themselves—that they are cursed. Indeed, at one time when people believed in witches, children who had such handicaps were believed to be bewitched or to be witches.

F.   THE EPILEPTIC CHILD

At one time, epileptic children were commonly seen by psychologists and mental health clinics because their seizures were not clearly understood by their parents or others, and because they suffered from "behavior problems" as well. However,

with the discovery of anticonvulsive drugs that can keep seizures under control, fewer and fewer epileptic children are now seeking psychologic help but are succeeding well in school, in society, and in their families. It is probable, therefore, that the "epileptic personality," which was once considered a definite syndrome, was due largely to the emotional and social difficulties that children suffered when their seizures were not controlled. However, there do remain some children whose seizures are not controlled by the conventional anticonvulsants and who must make social and emotional adjustments to their seizures.

Moreover, the drugs do have side effects. Thus, children who are on heavy medication are "dopey," their reactions slowed down both motorically and intellectually. Medication sometimes has to be changed briefly in children when the drug causes damage to the gums and teeth. Luckily, after a while many epileptic children can function on mild medication. They seem to be able to control their seizures during the daytime and suffer from them mainly at night.

The chief difficulties that I have seen in recent years are those suffered by the child who has petit mal epilepsy. Their consciousness is interrupted frequently and often without external evidence, in such a way that they grasp only a portion of the stimuli around them. They drop off for a second or two every few minutes. Thus they have great difficulty in learning, either formally in school or in social situations where they frequently lose seconds of awareness. These children develop a defense of being very passive and helpless. On IQ tests they seem to be malingering, where they seem to answer one question quite adequately, fade out on the next, and then come back and be able to answer the next question. Or, they may give a partially correct answer in a manner that seems as if they have a glimmering of the correct response. The insecurity that results from having a nervous system that goes into shock at almost unpredictable times is, in my experience, frequently revealed on the Rorchach by more than one or two responses representing explosions, destruction, or deterioration.

For example, Card 1 may be seen as Mt. St. Helens, where the top has caved in and everything is dead. Or Card 6 might be seen as a dead leaf. A rocketship on Card 2 is very popular for many children who are not epileptic, but the epileptic child is more likely to describe such a response as a spaceship that is exploding and falling apart. Similarly, epileptic children are likely to elaborate on the near-popular response of an atom bomb exploding on Card 9, saying that the whole world has gone "kaboom!" "Fireworks" is a popular response to Card 10, but one epileptic child described it as "fireworks where someone accidentally set them all off at once." This same child called Card 7 "a big hole that had been blown out by an atom bomb." And Card 4 was "a heap of ashes left over when a house had burned down." However, epileptic children—even those who suffer from grand mal and who have positive spikes on the EEG—may show no signs of "brain damage" on the Bender Gestalt or the Memory for Designs tests. Epileptic children do not necessarily suffer from perceptual losses.

Psychologists have long noted the emotional upsets and mood changes that seem to occur in persons who have convulsive seizures. Supposedly following a seizure, the epileptic individual becomes almost overcontrolled, very well behaved, almost "sticky sweet." Gradually they are supposed to build up an irritability with sudden and inexplicable flashes of temper—at times becoming openly violent just prior to having a seizure. Although some epileptic adults may show such a pattern of emotional behavior, it is not a constant pattern among epileptic children. However, I must admit that the anticonvulsive medication may break up such a sequence of emotions. There are still some neurologists who maintain that there is such a phenomenon as an

"epileptic equivalent" in which, instead of having seizures, children do such things as set fires, kill animals, or run amok. In an extensive study of the EEG pattern of 14-6 wave and spikes, which are supposed to be associated with such epileptic equivalents, no behavioral differences were found between children with or without such an EEG pattern (Walter et al. 1960). In my experience and opinion, children who are known to have seizures or who show abnormal EEG patterns have no more nor less emotional problems in reaction to and coping with frustration than do children with other handicaps or children who have family and social problems. Unfortunately, however, whatever emotional difficulties they may demonstrate are far too often blamed on the EEG pattern. It should be noted that 40% of EEG's are "false positive"; in other words, although the person's EEG may be abnormal, they do not suffer from any seizures!

Whereas epilepsy does not necessarily include any particular personality pattern or emotional reaction, it is true that emotional upset and frustration may result in a seizure for an epileptic child. Quite frequently, children may show questionable seizures early in their life, particularly before the alpha rhythm sets in completely at about age 6. Because of this, pediatricians do not always regard seizures among infants as being very serious because there is a strong likelihood that the seizures will disappear. However, if the alpha rhythm is not completely installed, children may suffer from a recurrence of seizures during puberty. One 13-year-old girl could not really distinguish between her menstrual periods and seizures, since she commonly suffered a seizure just before or just after her period. The tensions of puberty and early adolescence often are enough to set off seizures in children who have not had seizure patterns before. However, such adolescent epileptics may not suffer seizures in their adult years if they are able to find a fairly secure and routine pattern of existence.

CASE 86

Godfrey suffered his first epileptic seizure at age 15 when he rose to accept the presidency of his class. His classmates and the teacher were astounded and frightened when he fell to the podium, salivating, moaning, and convulsing. Luckily, the school nurse knew some of the first aid necessary for handling an epileptic child and prevented him from choking to death on his own tongue. Godfrey was an intellectually brilliant youngster who was extremely popular with other students, who had chosen him almost unanimously to be their president. The class was advised that he had merely suffered an illness and a fever. Godfrey was aware that his father had frequent seizures, but he had always thought they were associated with his father's alcoholism. (Epileptic's controls can be weakened by the use of alcohol quite easily.) Godfrey's grandfather, an evangelist, also suffered from epilepsy and would have seizures in front of his congregation, but these were supposedly religiously induced and were thought by the faithful to be a sign that their minister was in touch with God. Thereafter, Godfrey had several more seizures, particularly when emotionally excited or upset. However, he was soon taken to a neurologist, where it was determined that he had an abnormal EEG that was consistent with the seizure pattern, and he was placed on medication, which gave him almost total daytime relief from seizures. Although he did not meet with any further social "accidents" and most people ignored or forgot that he had ever had a seizure, Godfrey himself remained very aware that he might suddenly lose consciousness, and, as he put it, "go ape right in front of everybody." Despite his medication, he suffered another seizure during his first attempt to have sexual intercourse, frightening himself and his girlfriend. He then withdrew from attempting to have anything to do with the opposite sex and became a social isolate. He continued to devote himself to his studies and

was an all-A student in college, yet he so feared being openly known as an epileptic that he refused to report this to the draft board. Instead, he claimed to be a conscientious objector on religious grounds, did not report when drafted, and was placed in prison. In prison he became a serious student of religion, and upon being released he went to a theological school. He decided to become a missionary in India, and I have not heard of him since.

CASE 87

Arletta, age 13, had suffered her first "fainting spell" at her twelfth birthday party. The candles had just been blown out on the cake when she fell to the floor, unconscious. Her mother had tried to reassure everyone, including herself, that Arletta had merely become overexcited, but when Arletta fainted again a month later at breakfast, her mother decided that a physical examination might be wise. A pediatric examination revealed no abnormalities or disease, and the physician advised Arletta's mother that young girls do faint at this time in their life, and no one should think anything about it. However, Arletta continued to have these "fainting spells" every month, and several months later she was returned again to the pediatrician, who then advised a neurological examination. The neurological examination, including the EEG, was entirely negative; the neurologist noted that these fainting episodes were not exactly the same as the usual epileptic attacks. She did not foam at the mouth, lose her urine, nor have muscular contractions. Although she fell, she had never hurt herself, and her mother remarked that she wondered how Arletta could drop to the floor and not hit a piece of furniture. Although the neurologist doubted that she suffered from any "true" epilepsy, he nevertheless prescribed anticonvulsive medication and referred the child and mother to a psychologist, saying that he thought there must be some other kinds of emotional problems present. However, he failed to specify the nature of his suspicions.

The initial interview did not reveal anything very significant to the psychologist. Arletta lived in an intact family; her father worked at an administrative job that provided a relatively adequate income. Her mother was a costume designer for one of the local theaters but was present in the home a great deal of the time. Arletta made mostly B's at school. She had a coterie of girlfriends but told the psychologist that she considered herself too young to have boyfriends. She listened to much of the music that was popular with children her age and idolized certain musical and entertainment stars that she saw on TV or in the movies. She also "idolized" her 16-year-old brother, and her mother reported that, contrary to most brother–sister relationships, there had never been any rivalry or quarreling between them.

However, the psychologist noted that there was little discussion of the relationship between Arletta and her father, and when asked, Arletta turned away and answered curtly, "Oh, he's alright." Pressed further, she said that he was too busy and she really didn't see much of him. In a family session, the father said very little but did show concern about his daughter's "spells." He begged off a second appointment, saying that he had to be out of town at that point and would let the psychologist know when he was available again. However, he never called back. The assessor became even more suspicious that something was wrong between Arletta and her father when she gave such Rorschach responses as, to Card 4, "It's one of those big, dangerous monsters—maybe a sex fiend." Although she could point out the features of the monster, she could not say why she thought the inkblot looked like a sex fiend other than, "You know how those monsters are, they're all sex fiends." On Card 6 she saw "something biological, I'm not sure exactly what it is, but some kind of something is emerging out of some body-like," she said. She paused for a moment and then said, "You'll think I'm awful, but this looks like something sexy too. But I can't tell you why." Nor could she describe her association any further in the inquiry. To Card 9 she said, "This is someone who may be just emotionally overcome. All is colors. It's like something had gotten into them and overwhelmed them." Again, Arletta could not specify her response any further. Her TAT stories also contained many suggestions of sexual concerns. For example, on Card 2 (the farm scene) Arletta was much more concerned with the pregnancy of the woman in the background, leaning against a tree. She said, "I don't understand this. How could she be pregnant; she looks too old. And this man looks far too young to be her husband. Maybe this woman (pointing to the woman in the foreground) is shocked to find that her mother is pregnant. She cannot understand how her mother could be pregnant when there is no father." Arletta could not think of a conclusion to the story. To Card 3GF, Arletta remained concerned with the idea of pregnancy, saying that this woman had just learned that she was pregnant and she did not have a father for the baby. "It's the same situation as in the picture before." And to Card 4, she said, "This is the rest of the story that we saw in the picture before. He is her boyfriend and the father of her child, but he is leaving her. That is why she is so upset." Card 5, "The mother is looking in the door at her daughter and the daughter's boyfriend. She is shocked. They are doing something that they shouldn't (!) Oh, you know, something they really shouldn't do. I can't tell you." But it was to Card 6 GF that Arletta really suggested the core of her problem. "This is the girl's father. They have some secret and he is warning her never to reveal the secret."

At this point Arletta had tears in her eyes and set the picture down, looking away. When I asked if she and her father had some secret that she was holding all to herself and never revealing, she began to cry further and admitted then that her father had frequently molested her sexually since she was about age 8. She was afraid to ever reveal it to anyone, "My brother would kill him. It would kill my mother to know." She was afraid that if she permitted her father to continue to have intercourse with her that she would become pregnant. She did not know how to deny him, nor did she have any access to contraceptives. She knew, however, that she probably would not become pregnant until after she had had her first menses. It seemed to me that her monthly "fainting spells" were a substitute for menstruation, and when I mentioned that to her she nodded as if she almost recognized this herself. With her permission, I helped her reveal her secret to her mother, and, as was required by state law, to the child-protection agencies who must be notified of child abuse. The father was then removed from the home; he admitted almost gladly to his crime, as if relieving a burden from his soul. The court agreed to place him on probation and prohibited him from living in his home, on the agreement that he and the family enter into psychotherapy. Two weeks later Arletta had her first menstrual period, and she did not suffer from any "fainting spells" thereafter.

G.   HANDICAPPING ILLNESSES

Sometimes physiologically handicapping illnesses, such as diabetes, cardiovascular problems (e.g., rheumatic heart conditions), hemophilia, kidney failures, or other chronic, life-threatening conditions, may form the basis for a behavioral disability. Similar to the neurological handicap, these systemic disorders may also be turned into intellectual and emotional handicaps if children are infantalized by their parents, isolated from their peers, and form an identity as someone who is abnormal. Not infrequently, such children actually become unruly and undisciplined behavior problems. No one disciplines them just because they are ill. They, too, can become sweet and helpless—far beyond the limitation put on them by their illness.

In such instances, one must begin the assessment with a detailed history of the child's development and especially of the relationship between the child and parents and the parents' attitude toward the handicap. One of the more important features of children who suffer from such chronic disorders is the extent to which they permit the disorder itself to become a major aspect of their psychological identity. It is very tempting for such individuals to lose their individual identity and become a "case." They no longer are a person but are a "diabetic" or a "hemophiliac." They announce this cheerfully to you when you first meet them. They have been in and out of doctors' offices, in and out of hospitals and special-treatment centers to the extent that their physiological disorder dominates their personality.

One special technique for assessing the child's identity, which would be pertinent in this instance, is the use of a special sentence-completion test known as the "I Am Technique." This little test* consists of 10 to 15 sentence-completion items each of which begins with "I am." The child is then asked to respond with a different answer for each of these 10 to 15 blanks. (Sometimes 20 blanks are used for adults, but most children under the age of 12 can barely fill in 10.) After the child has put in his surname and family name as two entries, then the disorder as a third entry, he/she is often stuck for further evidence of his/her identity.

Children with these handicaps are often isolated from other children in the schools and put in special classes for the handicapped—whether or not these classes may be appropriate to their particular handicap. The constantly wheezing asthmatic child not only disturbs the rest of the class but may be in a poor condition for learning—both physiologically and psychologically. It is difficult for such a child to

---

*I am unable to discover the originators of this little technique, but I have seen it used in various clinics.

pay attention to anything but the asthma. Such children may actually be very bright, and if their condition can be controlled will learn rapidly. Nevertheless, their condition often continues to dominate their lives. Their concern for maintaining their medication and for avoiding stress that brings the condition back again occupies much of their time and energy and limits other activities. As with motoric handicaps, the school authorities are often reluctant to risk the admission of a sick child for fear that they will be held responsible. Thus, the child with hemophilia is not considered admissible to many public schools because of the officials' fears that he or she might be injured and bleed to death just because the school has no facilities to prevent such bleeding. Only in recent decades have children with hemophilia or other life-threatening physiological handicaps been admitted to public schools with a special condition that they do not have to enter into activities that might endanger their lives. They should have special contact with nearby hospitals in case they are disabled. Thus children who have weak hearts or who suffer from epileptic seizures, hemophilia, and the like may and should attend regular classes in public schools. They should be treated like other children who do not have such handicaps, as long as their condition is known to the school nurse and arrangements are made for their care in case they suffer some extreme injury because of their disability. In fact, because such children probably will be unable to enter into occupations that are physiologically strenuous, it is all the more important that they receive any education available that will enable them to perform intellectual tasks. Thus, the training of their intellectual and artistic abilities is doubly important for these children.

A physiological handicap thus becomes a disability only when parents, families, and teachers treat these handicapped children as invalids and fail to emphasize the development of their abilities to the highest degree rather than the limitations of their "disability." Assessment of these children must begin with a thorough history of their development, an investigation of their relationships with their parents and siblings, and a thorough assessment of their abilities and their motivation for achievement. Such a thorough psychological assessment is essential for planning the training and education of physiologically handicapped children.

CHAPTER 17

Assessment of Developmental and Learning Disabilities and Traumatic Brain Damage

A. INTRODUCTION: BACKGROUND, AND SOME COMMON ASSUMPTIONS

Clinical psychology had its beginnings in the assessment of children whose psychological development, especially cognitive, was slowed. From the early nineteenth century, when Itard studied the "Wild Boy of Averon" and Seguin experimented with his Form Board as a measure of intelligence, until World War II, most clinical psychologists functioned mainly as "mental testers" (for a more complete history of clinical psychology, see R. Watson, 1953). During the nineteenth century when genetics was a new and exciting discovery, genetics dominated the field of psychology. Thus, it was presumed that the "feebleminded" inherited their condition. Histories of families with several retarded, psychotic, or criminal members were cited as evidence of the genetic supposition—without recognition of the effect on a child of being reared by retarded, psychotic, or inadequate parents. This assumption was utilized mainly when there was no other obvious etiology.

Because some retarded children did demonstrate evidence of brain damage in their wizened or gigantic skulls, it was argued that all other retarded people must also have diseased or "deficient" brains, evidence of which was undetectable at that time. Statistics up to a decade ago showed that there was no known cause for the retardation of over three quarters of institutionalized children. These children used to be labeled "pseudoretarded," "undifferentiated," "garden variety," or they were assumed to be "familial". Many children who were put in these institutions until only a few years ago would be recognized today as suffering from "autism" or "childhood schizophrenia." Many were intellectually normal children who had been abandoned or had become, for other reasons, wards of the court and were too depressed and angry to pay attention to IQ tests. If, as too often happened, they spent their entire childhood in some home of the feebleminded, they became institutionalized and just as developmentally disabled as some child with brain damage. However, once it was established that retarded children reared in their own homes functioned much more effectively than those in institutions, many were discharged into foster-care homes.

On the basis of the intelligence tests of the day, many children were arbitrarily labeled "mental retardates" or "aments." It was assumed that these children must be brain damaged, even though there was no positive neurological evidence of any central-nervous-system disorder or dysfunction. Since many of them were believed to have inherited their disorder, they were sterilized so as not to reproduce more "morons." Although the importance of inherited traits, including intelligence, has diminished in the thinking of most psychologists there are still some theorists who hold stoutly to the idea that such complex behavior as intelligence is mostly inherited (e.g., Shields and Gottesman, 1971). On the other hand, in a very incisive review, Liverant (1960) points out that almost no geneticist really holds that any complex behavior, such as intelligence, can be accounted for on the basis of genes (see Chapter 1).

In some circles today, there is an almost religious belief that brain damage is the central cause of most intellectual retardation. These theorists use the term *pseudoretardation* to account for the majority of children in whom there is no evidence of neurological damage but who fail to develop intellectually. This term suggests that children who exhibit no evidence of brain damage are not "really" retarded. But, it is intimated, these children may in some way be malingering.

CASE 88

"Old Sam" had wandered around the institution since he was a child. His records were a blank; nothing was known of the reasons why he was placed there or of his family background. As far as anyone could remember, not one member of his family had ever visited him. The whereabouts of his family were unknown. On admission at age 4 in 1920, his IQ on the 1917 Stanford-Binet was 37, and he had never been reevaluated. There was no doubt that Sam functioned on a "moderately" retarded level. Occasionally, Sam got lost crossing the institution grounds where he had lived for 50 years. He could not tell time. He had to be reminded to care for himself at the toilet and to bathe. All attempts to teach him any kind of a task had failed, and he had not attended the institution's school. Yet somehow he had memorized the names of the presidents in historical order, the names of the states and their capitals, and the names of all the counties in California and the county seats! He was labeled an "idiot savant" and was shown off to visit-ing students like the village clown. When he died, a pathologist at a nearby medical school who was studying the brains of retarded people conducted an autopsy and found no evidence of brain damage or disease. The pathologist then argued that Sam was not truly retarded—because his brain was normal! That Sam may have been "autistic" or "schizophrenic" on admission is a likely hypothesis, but after more than 50 years of institutionalization, Sam was, in effect, just as retarded as any brain-damaged child.

The presumption that some deficiency in the brain exists in retarded children was bolstered by subsequent studies—both clinical and experimental—of children who did suffer from brain injury or disease. Because individuals known to be brain damaged frequently lost intellectual faculties, it was assumed without further question that all such losses must have neurologic bases.

Thus arose the following *illogical syllogism:* Because some brain damage results in intellectual retardation, therefore all intellectual retardation is the result of brain damage. The illogic remains even if one changes the syllogism to read as follows: Most brain damage results in retardation, therefore most retardation is the result of brain damage.

Those who cling to the purely "organic" basis for intellectual retardation ignore or discount the following facts:

1.   Many children whose development is retarded show no concrete evidence whatever of disease damage to the central nervous system (CNS). The best logic is to admit a lack of evidence, for example, "intellectual retardation, cause unknown."

2.   Not all damage to the CNS results in intellectual retardation. Witness the cerebral-palsy children who for years were lumped together with the retarded.

3.   Intelligence is not an inborn faculty but is a developing and expanding set of learned problem-solving and coping behaviors.

4. Intellectual development, especially in early childhood, is often irregular and spasmodic. The alpha rhythm of the brain is not completely established until age 6 or later. By adult standards, many pre-school children look "organic" on Wechsler tests, the Reitan battery, or EEG.

5. Further intellectual development cannot be reliably predicted from tests on pre-school children (see Chapter 15).

6. Intellectual development can be accelerated through training, education, and environmental change. Significant changes in IQ are achieved through home care, systematic conditioning of behavior, and special education. Retardation is not necessarily permanent nor regressive.

7. Even those children whose intellectual development is deterred by trauma or disease after birth sometimes spontaneously recover. Often their rehabilitation is aided through physical and psychological training and therapy.

8. Most of the presumption of a CNS deficiency fails to take into account the negative effects of severe emotional and social stress on intellectual development. For example, a ghetto child who is neglected, abused, and ill, who is separated from noncaring parents and placed in one foster home after another, may well develop a "failure syndrome" at school and on tests, and thus be labeled "retarded." Without further attention, such a child may become as intellectually disabled as some child with Downs syndrome.

A gradual change in attitude and philosophy by workers in this field is reflected in the terms they use. By the middle of the twentieth century the term *mental deficiency*, with its subterms *idiot, imbecile,* and *moron*, was being replaced by the term *intellectual* (or *mental*) *retardation*—severe, moderate, or mild. Subsequently, the genteel euphemism *exceptional child* was introduced, but this term became confused with *superior child* in many people's minds. The current term *developmental disability* is important in that it recognizes that intelligence is an expanding and changing factor in the child's growth. By dropping such terms as *mental* or *intellectual*, the emphasis has shifted to the overall development of the child—social and emotional, as well as cognitive. Most important, "developmental" has the implication of possible change—in contrast to a "deficiency" that can never be rectified. If a child is developing albeit slowly, then that development can be altered through training and education (for further discussion, see Gordon, 1970).

B. ASSESSMENT OF THE DEVELOPMENTALLY DISABLED

Sometimes, it seems quite evident that a child's intellectual retardation stems from a neurological disease, deficit, or trauma before or at the moment of birth. There may be signs of Down's syndrome or some other equally rare genetically determined neurological weakness. The child's skull may be misshapened by excess fluid or the use of forceps. Most children—but not all—who function below IQ 40 show signs of neurological damage. However, the assessor must be cautious: Not every child with a distorted skull necessarily becomes intellectually retarded.* To assign a neurological cause to a child's retardation, it is necessary to have a thorough neurological examination and documented history. One should have a history of the pregnancy and birth, not only from the mother (whose memory and perception may be hazy and distorted, as she looks for causes), but the obstetric record should be obtained.

It is becoming popular today to assess such children with so-called "neuropsychological" techniques. Some of these instruments are very brief, such as the much-abused Bender Gestalt or the Memory for

---

*While many children known to suffer Down's syndrome are retarded, it is not known how many children may have all the other features of this disorder except low intelligence since they do not come to the attention of authorities.

Designs (see Chapter 4). Although there now exist relatively solid children's norms for these instruments, assessors should be exceedingly cautious in basing a diagnosis of brain damage solely on these single-item instruments. It's best to use them as part of a battery.

Much more extensive and detailed are the Halstead-Reitan (Reitan and Davison, 1974) or the Luria batteries (Golden, 1978). The Reitan includes the WISC-R and over 150 other items in 12 subtests, most of them adopted from other short tests. According to various writers (cf. Hynd and Obrzut, 1981), this battery correctly identifies brain-damaged children—with only 5% false negatives. They admit, however, that among non−brain-damaged children this and similar techniques give false positives of 20% or higher,* thus severely weakening their predictive value.

Although either the Reitan or the Luria test batteries can be helpful in detailing specific weaknesses among children with *documented evidence of brain damage other than the test results, I have strong reservations about their use as predictors of brain damage without such independent data.* To label a child as brain damaged without further evidence may condemn her/him to false self- and social images and subject him/her to years of social isolation in "special" classes—or in institutions. There is much less harm done to children whose brain damage goes undetected. The writers in Hynd and Obrzut (1981), for example, admit that not all children failing these tests are necessarily brain damaged, but it is obvious that they believe that some kind of brain damage underlies such failures. This assumption must be avoided, and the test can be used without adopting it. Advocates of these tests do insist that specialized training in "neuropsychology" is necessary for their use.* They also emphasize the qualitative nature of interpret-

ing the results, suggesting that even though the child may not make scores indicative of brain damage, there may be signs of brain damage in the quality of responses. Again, the bias toward organicity seems evident.

In addition, I have reservations about the use of these instruments—especially with pre-school children—because they are so long (requiring up to six hours!) and boring. Young children may fail out of boredom and wandering attention—especially those "hyperactive" children who are supposed to be brain damaged and with whom these tests are used to bolster this assumption. They should not be used separately from the WISC-R or other standard IQ test. At most one errs on the side of the child's welfare to assume that children whose intellectual development is normal do not have significant brain damage. (See section C for discussion of so-called minimal brain damage and specific disabilities.) If these batteries are to be used, they should be administered in several brief sessions.

Despite Wechsler's warnings, many assessors continue to use profile analysis of subtest scores on his tests to determine brain damage. The assessor must be most aware that the SE_m of these subtests on all the Wechsler scales is at least 2 or greater; thus the SE_{diff} is more than 4. *Differences of 4 or less are insignificant and meaningless and should be ignored* (R.J. Piotrowski, 1978). Moreover, most of the studies on profile analysis have been conducted with adults on the WAIS. Children's profiles on the WISC-R should not be "adultomorphized." Children's thought processes are not the same as those of adults. Neurologic trauma and deficit in utero may not result in the same kinds of intellectual distortions or failures as does brain trauma among adults. Kaufman (1979) in a thorough review of the WISC-R, points out that extreme caution is advised not only in profile analysis of subtest scores but in the use of "scatter" as evidence of brain damage. His research

---

*This phenomonen of high false postives is explored by Fisher (1959) in what he calls the "twisted-pear" curve.)

*It seems they mean neuroanatomy, for there is little in these writings about behavior.

shows clearly that as much as 7 points scatter is normal! Moreover, these profile patterns may in fact represent differences in life-styles. The developing intellectual patterns may represent developing ways of thinking. Future dancers, engineers, mathematicians, chemists, billiard players, may have different intellectual patterns than future priests, salesman, con men or psychologists.

Texts on "neuropsychology" usually ignore the Rorschach Technique as a possible indicator of brain damage, despite the fact that it is basically a test or perception. Fisher and Goda (1955) found that the Rorschach predicted brain damage as well as most neurological signs among adults, including the EEG. However, like the other tests of neurologic deficit, there is the tendency to overpredict, seeing brain damage where it does not exist. Moreover Z.A. Piotrowski's signs (1940) are limited to adult protocols. Using these indicators, most children could be called brain damaged! Perservation, contamination, poor form, confabulation, loose, whole responses, and indecision are common in the protocols of pre-school children.

In summary, the diagnosis of brain damage as a source of developmental disability should be made only on the basis of multiple evidence. One type of evidence must be clear-cut neurological evidence. Far too many children in the past have been doomed to deadly lives in institutions because of incomplete examinations with overblown interpretations—based on the dangerous assumption that if the child has a low IQ, she/he must be brain damaged. Assessment of seemingly well-established brain damage should include the following:

1.   A prenatal history based on medical records, as well as on the mother's memory.
2.   A similarly derived birth record and postnatal history.
3.   A careful and detailed analysis of the mother–child relationship.
4.   A current and thorough neurological examination.

5.   An age-appropriate IQ test, which is analyzed both qualitatively as well as quantitatively.
6.   Appropriate tests of perception: the Bender Gestalt before age 9; the Memory for Designs after age 9; the Rorschach after age 8.

Children who suffer brain damage before birth or at birth may develop not only cognitive deficits but emotional and social problems as well. Indeed, in many cases these latter disturbances may well mask whatever intellectual talents the child may possess. Thus, in addition to cognitive tests, assessment of the brain-damaged child should include such instruments as the World Test, Structured Doll Play, and the Rorschach. Often the brain-damaged, retarded child will reveal his/her simple and undifferentiated world gestalt by lining up the World Test figures and buildings in a meaningless random line. However, there are such children whose arrangement of the World Test materials suggests a more discriminative and organized world, even though they cannot solve cognitive puzzles nor verbalize effectively. Similarly, on the Rorschach some brain-damaged children, who are also intellectually retarded, produce only very simple gestalts—responses without detail and which upon the challenge of inquiry deteriorate into confusion. Other low-IQ children with established neuronal deficits may be able to produce fairly elaborately organized gestalts.

CASE 89

Medical records showed that Lorna probably suffered some damage—to an unknown degree—to her brain at birth. She was 2½ months premature and weighed only 4 pounds. The umbilical chord was wrapped around her neck, and she was "blue," indicating anoxia. All of her subsequent development was slowed. She did not sit erect until age 10 months, only walked by age 16 months, and at age 3 did not talk and was not toilet trained. Her unmarried mother, then only age 18, abandoned her to the care of her grandmother. When entered in kindergarten her speech remained comprehensible only to her grandmother, and she still soiled herself on occasion. The other children made fun of her and rejected her, and she responded by biting and hitting them. Therefore, she was removed from the classroom. The following year she was entered in a "special class," but she remained a "behavior problem" and made little progress. When Lorna was 7, her grandmother died and she was made a ward of the court. When tested on the 1937 Binet, she obtained an IQ of only 58. She was then sent to a state institution for the mentally retarded. A more complete assessment was conducted, consisting of the WISC, the Rorschach, the Bender-Gestalt, the Harris/Goodenough Draw-A-Man and Draw-A-Woman, and the World Test. On the WISC, her Verbal IQ was 55, her Performance IQ 69, and Total IQ 59. The distribution of scores within each scale was insignificant—her highest score of 7 was an Object Assembly. Yet her responses to the Rorschach were indistinguishable from those of the average 7-year-old and her gestalt on the World Test was relatively well organized, indicating that she was not retarded in her perception of her social world. Her Bender copies did show some signs of brain damage, according to Koppitz norms, but the results were judged to be indeterminate and—at best—"borderline." Her drawings of a man and a woman were in the 6-year level, giving IQ's of 90 and 92, respectively. Her overall retardation was thus deemed to be "mild" and to be the result primarily of her birth injuries and prematurity. Yet, it seemed likely that the desertion by her mother and her grandmother's death were also basic traumata to this brain-damaged child and that these factors underlay her continued poor emotional control and social difficulties. She screamed and wept when frustrated, fought with the other children on only the slightest provocation, and frequently disregarded the hospital rules. Consequently, she was regarded as the "bad girl" of the ward, was

often placed on isolation or deprived of privileges. Yet, she could be charming and was an attractive, red-haired, freckled-faced child. At the institution's school, she made considerable progress, especially with the help of a speech teacher whom she adored. By age 12 she was learning to read and was doing simple arithmetic at the second-grade level, but her behavior had changed little. Though she remained physically tiny, she was maturing sexually. She was thought to be active in institutional homosexual activities and was attracting the interest of the older boys. Her teacher and the nurses were worried about her, and it was proposed that she be sterilized.

At this time she was reevaluated psychologically. Now, on the WISC-R her Verbal IQ was 60, her Performance IQ was 84, and her Total IQ was 70. Since only those under IQ 65 were considered legally "retarded," she could not be sterilized without permission of her mother—whose whereabouts were unknown. Her Bender-Gestalt drawings remained indicative of brain damage, but her Rorschach consisted of eight responses, all M! This suggested that she lived in a daydream world of her own fantasies, isolated emotionally from others.

Prior to this time, this institution had not been able to offer anything more than drug treatment for children with behavioral problems. Various drugs were tried on Lorna, but nothing had seemed effective. At this time a behavior modification program was started on her ward. She was eager to achieve and receive rewards, but the nurses and teachers remained worried about her sexual behavior. Although at that time it was deemed a waste of time to treat brain-damaged retarded children with psychotherapy, her progress seemed to warrant this effort. In her simple, halting verbalization she was able to go over the tragedy of her life with appropriate tears and anger. Two years later her emotional controls had improved to the point where she was able to leave the institution to go to a foster home. There, she continued classes in special schools. At age 20 she reappeared on the institution grounds on the back of a motor-cycle with her husband whom she wanted to introduce to her therapist. Later, she settled down in a nearby community and seemed to be succeeding as a housewife and mother.

In studying the "functional" or non–brain-damaged retarded child, a very careful, detailed history and description of current functioning must be obtained. Is the child failing to learn despite all efforts of parents and teachers, or is there some reason that the parents wish to keep the child infantalized? The assessor must be very careful to try to ascertain the child's abilities as well as disabilities. Quite often such mild intellectual retardation is associated with the lack of any drive toward achievement. It may be that the parents overemphasized achievement and the child is resisting, or the child seeks to remain an infant and not learn in an effort to get the attention and affection of her/his parents. Such acquired or learned helplessness results not only in a depression, but in childhood it may result in a mild-to-moderate developmental disability, especially in learning. If the only diagnostic instrument used is an IQ test, then this kind of infantalization may be missed. As noted previously, the most important aspect of this kind of developmental disability is the relationship between the parent and the child. Sometimes the child does have a mild neurological handicap, but he/she need not be disabled unless the parents overprotect him/her and unless the child accepts his/her "helplessness."

The child's position and role in the family often plays a part in her/his developing a learning disability. For example, if one child in the family is very bright and very adept and another child is not quite so bright, then family roles may emphasize the precocity of the bright child and emphasize even any imagined handicap in the not-so-bright child.

CASE 90

Millard S. age 8, was named after his father, a professor of Jewish history, and his grandfather, who had been president of a university. Junior, as he was called, had not yet begun to learn to read and had a mild-to-moderate speech difficulty, but otherwise he seemed bright and could do simple arithmetic in his head. He was born prematurely and had a very mild limp from a "clubfoot." Originally, he had had a cleft palate, but this had been surgically corrected. The pediatrician advised his parents that there was no physiological reason why Junior could not speak quite clearly, and all the speech teachers advised the parents that Junior just made no effort to learn to speak clearly. He could be understood by his parents and his closest friends, but he was incomprehensible to strangers. One speech teacher, before she was fired by the parents, told them that Junior was merely holding onto baby speech.

Junior was the first son and first grandson in the family, and they had had high hopes for him. His father frequently intimated that he thought that any defects that Junior had were due to the fact that Junior's mother did not take care of herself during her pregnancy, failed to attend religious and social occasions, and perhaps did not have the right diet. Mrs. S felt very guilty but could not imagine what she really had done. The S's had three older daughters and had hoped desperately for a son. Mrs. S was quite anxious during her pregnancy, was ill throughout, and almost had a miscarriage.

Despite the slightly twisted foot and the cleft palate, the obstetrician pronounced Junior to be normal at birth, and he was not a sick baby thereafter. But Mrs. S and the family fussed over him a great deal, "I always prayed that he would be normal," Mrs. S said.

If Junior was not the scholar that his father and grandfather hoped for, his sisters certainly were. His older sister, now 19, had graduated from high school at 15 with an all-A record. She was now about to graduate from a major West Coast university. His next oldest sister, age 16, had won the national science award, which had been presented to her on television; she too was graduating with honors from high school. The third sister was an accomplished violinist who played as soloist with the city youth orchestra. She, too, made excellent grades at school. Only Junior failed. Although his sisters received praise and support for their accomplishments, the focus of the family's attention and concern was on Junior. They went from speech teacher to speech teacher, not one of whom was successful in improving his speech to the extent that he could attend school. Tutors and special-reading teachers came daily to the home. He attended several special schools for the handicapped. Many of the family's funds were spent trying to educate Junior, but he was evidently very resistant. Teachers complained that he "fooled around" and did not concentrate on his studies. He was a sweet child who smiled happily and loved attention, but he did not pay attention to anything that was taught him. He could go through the lessons one day and then have absolutely no memory of them the next day.

Since Junior could achieve well enough at times, he frequently achieved a normal IQ on nonverbal tests—if he was praised each time he succeeded. In fact, his Draw-A-Man, when scored on the Harris scale, gave him an IQ of 115. Repeated neurological examinations were negative, yet the neurologist—because Junior did have the slightly twisted foot and been born prematurely—continually guessed that he was "brain damaged" without any further evidence.

On the basis of these data, a psychologist worked out with his parents and the school a program of behavior modification. Junior was systematically praised both at school and at home for continued achievement, his failures were ignored, and he was given no attention at all unless he continued to

achieve. He was soon learning to read under this program. His speech also improved when his entire family refused to try to understand him unless he spoke clearly. If he screamed at them unintelligibly, which was his initial reaction, they separated from him and had nothing to do with him. If he spoke clear words, they praised him, repeated the words, and told him how bright they thought he was. After only about four months, he was reading only a year below grade level and was speaking quite clearly. The following year he was able to enter regular classes, only about a year behind his age level. He also was becoming quite active at sports.

So-called learning disabilities are also commonly associated with personal and social deprivations. Children who are not personally encouraged to learn, who find no reward for achievement at school, who really have limited opportunities for schooling, may easily fail to learn. Such children, although called "developmentally disabled," show no evidence whatever of any brain damage. They are developmentally disabled only in the sense that their motivation and opportunities for learning have been squashed.

CASE 91

Harrison, age 14, came to the attention of juvenile authorities because he was arrested as an accomplice in a murder when one of his companions in a robbery shot the grocery-store owner they were attempting to rob. The psychologist at juvenile hall discovered that Harrison was entirely illiterate, although he had been attending school until approximately two months before his arrest—when he seemed to have dropped out altogether. His school attendance the previous year had been very spotty. The psychologist also discovered that Harrison had attended at least 10 different schools in his community. As were most of the students in these schools, Harrison was black but his teachers were white. Harrison was embarrassed because he couldn't read or write, but he tried to deny that it was of any importance and boasted that he was making out pretty well anyway. He had very nice clothes and seemed to have quite a bit of money and lots of possessions. At the time he was arrested, he also had several packets of drugs on him, which he admitted he had hoped to sell.

At the time of his arrest, Harrison was living with his mother and her boyfriend, who was suspected of being a pimp and dealer in illicit drugs. The boyfriend and Harrison had frequent physical fights, and Harrison had bruises from being whipped by this man. Harrison had no idea of exactly who his father was, and his mother usually had some lover who acted as husband and father for a short time. He had seven younger brothers and sisters, some of whom lived with him and his mother. When Harrison's mother did not have a current boyfriend to support her, she lived with her mother and grandmother. Harrison was very fond of his grandmother and great-grandmother, both of whom tried to get him to go to school and church. He admitted sadly that "I'd be a better guy if I did do what my grandmother said." He also admitted that it was very tempting to earn a great deal of money dealing drugs or being a male prostitute. Most of the men he had known as fathers had little or no education. On nonverbal IQ tests, he functioned in the bright-normal range. His responses to projective techniques indicated that he was more depressed than he would admit and that he was generally guarded and angry at the whole world.

Although the legal charges against Harrison were quite serious, the court took into account his age and the fact that he had not had a previous arrest. The probation officer could not locate his mother or stepfather, and he was put on probation in the care of his grandmother. The probation officer reported that Harrison did attend school and was making moderate progress in special classes for learning to read. Unfortunately, two years later he appeared before the court again with three charges of auto theft. Re-examined at this time, he was reading at about the fourth-grade level.

C.   LEARNING DISABILITIES—THE MYTH OF MINIMAL BRAIN DAMAGE

The reasons that children do not learn are multiple, ranging from social deprivation to emotional upset to physical handicap to brain damage—without considering over-crowded schools, abbreviated school hours, and poor teaching methods. Many of the sources of school failure have been discussed previously in this book. School failure is the most common symptom in childhood and often has many causes. This section examines one very highly touted assumption regarding so-called learning disabilities, namely, the assumption of "minimal brain damage" (MBD).

This assumption is proposed when:

1.   The child is failing to learn at school; particularly when not learning to read, the term *dyslexia* may be used to indicate the supposition of MBD.
2.   The child has an IQ of 80 or higher.
3.   The child has low scores on some of the Halstead-Reitan scales or the Luria battery.
4.   Strong neurological evidence of brain damage is *not* present, but there may be so called "soft signs" of motoric weakness.

Regarding the first assumption, one may say that any approach to academic failure must be multidimensional and multicausal. School failure usually results from an intersecting set of stresses on the child, one of which may (or may not) be a neurological deficit. In fact, such a deficit may not be an actual disability (as defined in Chapter 16), except for the other emotional and social stresses involved. As noted before, the clinician should not be swayed by poorly defined Greek terms, such as *dyslexia*.

With respect to the second assumption, the concept of significant brain damage at IQ 80 or above is questionable. Children whose IQ's range from 80–110 may have some perceptual difficulties that are not necessarily related to CNS dysfunction (see Chapter 9). Above an IQ of 110, the assumption of a deficit is meaningless. As noted in the previous section, this concept of MBD is often derived from misuse of the IQ, especially from unwarranted subscale profile analysis or scatter analysis of the WISC-R.

As for the third assumption, the Halstead-Reitan and Luria batteries can only be used with extreme caution. *These tests do not measure brain damage.* They are fair measures of cognitive and perceptual difficulties. They correlate well with the failure to learn to read (as do most other tests of perception), but Hynd and Obrzut (1981), in reviewing these techniques, do not report any relationship between these tests and neurological signs of brain damage, such as EEG or brain scan (see also Pihl, 1968). Children who have poor motivation, who are depressed, and who are restless (read hyperactive*) may easily become bored on these long tests that hold little interest or challenge to most children.

Regarding the fourth assumption, it should be noted that "soft signs" of motoric weakness are not necessarily indicators of either intellectual nor perceptual dysfunction. Limp handshakes do not mean brain damage, but they may be an indicator of a passive-aggressive personality. Other weaknesses may have causes other than CNS dysfunction. Poor reproduction on the Bender-Gestalt may result from slow motor development and not from perceptual lag.

Serious damage to the welfare of the child and his/her parents may result from misdiagnosis of children who fail to learn—especially from the use of the meaningless label of "minimal brain damage." The use of this label, based purely on such

*Hyperactivity is also illogically assumed to indicate MBD.

tests as the Halstead-Reitan or the Luria-Nebraska, has far too often resulted in assigning children to useless years of special education, at the cost of thousands of dollars to parents and taxpayers. On the basis of these tests alone, children have been unnecessarily drugged with amphetamines, creating a possible addiction. Worst of all, this label and its associated treatments can result in a lowered self-confidence and a distorted self-image as an inadequate person. These children all too frequently develop a "failure syndrome," remaining passively dependent on their world.

CASE 92

Bryan, age 13, had been diagnosed as having "minimal brain damage" when he was about age 5, and he had been in special classes for "learning disability" ever since. A tall, heavyset boy, with a loud voice and no manners whatever, Bryan was an offensive oaf who disgusted adults and annoyed other children, who rejected him. He brooked no discipline whatever from his mother, whom he addressed in vulgar and obscene language, and he was in continual fights with his brother who was three years younger. His mother was so desperate that she said she would either put him in an institution or that she herself would commit suicide. Bryan demanded to be waited on hand and foot, and he would become furious if his mother did not meet his demands immediately. He did obey his father, but he was rarely home and often did not defend his wife when Bryan verbally attacked her. Although, in front of his parents, Bryan protested that he was not a "spaz" and did not really need to be in a school for the learning handicapped but should be put in public school, when I interviewed him separately from his parents, he broke down almost in tears and admitted that he felt awful about himself and wished that he could really learn to read and write like any other kid. His brother teased him endlessly and instigated many of the physical altercations. Several interview sessions with the family and with Bryan by himself were necessary before he would submit to yet another set of psychological examinations. He protested that he had been "psychologized" to death but agreed to a fresh look at his abilities, on the promise that I would share the results with him openly before his parents were informed. Nevertheless, he was extremely anxious throughout the examination. Fortunately, he succeeded at an average level, or better, on the Wechsler, and I was able to give him support truthfully in the areas where he succeeded. He was even more frightened at approaching the Graham-Kendall, which had not had before, and he demanded that we recheck each drawing with the original. He moaned over his very minor errors, but I assured him—again truthfully—that they were insignificant. His responses to the Rorschach revealed a great deal of anxiety, helplessness, and insecurity, but none of the classic signs of brain damage. His Full Scale IQ was 117, with a Verbal IQ at 120 and a Performance IQ at 111. Although I saw absolutely no sign of any kind of possible brain damage on any of these standard tests, I asked a colleague who specialized in the examination of neurologically damaged patients to administer the Reitan battery. She reported that there was no sign whatever of minimal brain damage, although she noted—as have many authors—that there is no study relating the Reitan battery to the prediction of brain damage. Then, with the permission of the parents, I sought out the five previous examinations he had taken, from the time he was age 5 to the present. All the psychologists had reported that they saw no signs on the psychological tests of brain damage. Nevertheless, because he was failing to learn to read and had once been labeled "alexic," all the neurologists assumed that he had minimal brain damage.

It was true that Bryan did seem clumsy. He stumbled into a room, plopped himself into a chair, sprawled out, and seemed so ill at ease that one wondered whether he might be somewhat ataxic. He claimed that he loved sports, and he was always in front of the television set for every football, basketball, and baseball game. Nevertheless, he did not participate in any sports in the neighborhood, and his special school did not have a sports program. His brother, who never let him alone for a minute and was always upbraiding him, jeeringly said that because Bryan was such a clumsy person, he really could never play ball. He stated also that Byran did not know how to catch or kick a ball. This made Bryan so furious that he had to be restrained immediately from physically attacking his brother in the family session. Yet, aside from his nonparticipation in sports, no one could cite any definite evidence that Bryan had any type of motor difficulty. He rode a bicycle quite successfully and had learned to ski.

According to Bryan's mother, she had had no difficulty with him until he was approximately 3. Her pregnancy had been uneventful, and she had no trouble at gestation. However, when Bryan was about 3, he began to have screaming temper tantrums, refused to go to nursery school, and for a brief period at least, lost both bowel and urinary control. "It was very difficult for me to handle him then, because I was pregnant with his brother." When his brother was born, Bryan became a major behavior problem. However, his mother had never previously related the onset of his difficulties to the birth of his brother.

It was also about this time that she and her husband first separated. In fact, she had thought even before Bryan's birth of separating from her husband but felt that she could not support herself and that perhaps her marriage could be improved with counseling. However, her husband rejected the idea of counseling, and after Bryan's birth she felt even more trapped in her marriage. Her husband did supply a fair living, and there were no economic worries. However, he was seldom home, and she believed that he had a mistress.

From then on she "sacrificed everything" to Bryan's care. She admitted that she might have neglected her second son, who gave her no real problem at all except for his constant fighting with Bryan.

An intellectually bright woman who had a master's degree in history, she devoted all of her time to being a housewife and caretaker to her children, despite the fact that she hated every minute of it. There was no doubt that Bryan and his brother felt their mother's discontent and depression. To assure herself that she was really needed by Bryan, she submitted him to examination after examination, always being assured by some physician that he had "minimal brain damage."

At this point another neurological consultation was requested. The neurologist was not advised of my findings; he reported back that it was possible that Bryan had at one time suffered from a light case of poliomyelitis and that he was clumsy. The neurologist also saw no positive signs whatever of brain damage.

The results of my examination and that of the neurologist were reported back to the family in a very dramatic session. At first, they could not believe what they heard. We repeatedly went over the results of previous examinations. When they saw that there was no psychological evidence whatever of brain damage at any time, the mother remarked bitterly, "I have been f——d by the medical profession."

For the next three years, Bryan was treated with a combination of individual and family therapy. A strict behavioral regime was instituted in the family with Bryan's permission and understanding. He was to be granted privileges as his behavior improved, and was to be denied privileges when he resorted to his infantile, demanding, cursing behavior. His years of accumulated anger and depression were worked out in his individual therapy. He was shifted from the small private school to a special-education program at the university, where after one year he was able to enter a public junior high school. Here, he did participate in the sports program and became sports editor of the school paper.

Initially a very slow reader who could write only simple sentences, he was writing acceptable articles for the school paper within three years. Unfortunately, his family situation deteriorated; his mother walked out on all three men and decided to have a life of her own. Bryan did become much more depressed and angry at this point—as did his brother and father. Nevertheless, the mother's determination to sacrifice her life no longer to a child who was not really disabled seemed to sober all of them. They began to realize how very dependent they had been on her and to what degree they had made her into a slave. After a temporary setback, Bryan went on to high school, and I did not see him for several years. However, I was acquainted with members of his family who assured me that he was graduated successfully from high school and had entered junior college. The last I heard of him he had a part-time job and was living with other students at the college.

D. ASSESSMENT OF TRAUMATIC BRAIN DAMAGE

Children who suffer traumata to the central nervous system after their birth often require psychological attention. These traumata may be the result of either external injuries, internal diseases, or tumors. The chief reasons for a psychological evaluation are (1) to assess the degree and nature of the *behavioral* handicap, if any; (2) to assist in planning retraining and re-education, if needed; and (3) to assess the posttrauma progress of the child, either his/her improvement or deterioration. The nature and degree of the trauma does not necessarily determine the degree of *behavioral* limitations; the handicap does not altogether determine the disability. Some children with a major injury to their brain may become only mildly disabled, while others with seemingly a minor trauma become severely disabled. Some children may become permanently disabled, others progress slowly, and a few recover dramatically—almost overnight. Some suffer cognitive and perceptual disabilities primarily; others become disabled primarily in their social and emotional functioning. Severely brain-damaged children seem to suffer an across-the-board loss. They find themselves motorically crippled, making intellectual errors, suffering a loss of memory, and thus they become easily frustrated, depressed, and embarrassed. The injury may include both brain centers for intellectual functioning and emotional control, especially if hemorrhaging has occurred. Thus, a thorough assessment of *all* functioning—not merely intelligence—is equally required.

CASE 93

Pedro, age 9, received a severe wound when a bullet, accidentally fired by his older brother, ricocheted and struck him in the right temple, passing through his brain out the left-rear portion of his skull. Massive hemorrhaging occurred, flooding much of his brain. He was unconscious for several weeks, and it was expected he would remain vegetative or die. Miraculously, he recovered consciousness but was tetraplegic and completely aphasic—though he did seem to recognize and understand his mother and sisters who came to visit and spoke in Spanish to him. Given this hope, the physicians prescribed an intense program of physiotherapy; in less than six months, Pedro's paralysis improved markedly. He could walk—even run—with a walker and had sufficient arm function for such practical uses as feeding and partially dressing himself. However, he had no speech and barely responded to Spanish. At first, he was a placid patient with a wan smile, but as he recovered physically he became increasingly irritable, screaming in anger if frustrated, weeping when left alone even for a brief period, or giggling over nothing. He was excessively jealous of the attention given by the hospital personnel to other children, striking out at them. At these moments, he was able to shout a single vulgar word in Spanish.

A Spanish-speaking psychologist administered the Leiter International Performance Scale, the Columbia Mental Maturity Test, the Peabody Picture Vocabulary (Spanish edition), the Bender-Gestalt, and the Draw-A-Man Test. Pedro was fascinated by this adult who offered personal attention, and he seemed to struggle to achieve. The examiner, however, had doubts that Pedro clearly understood the directions at times. On the Leiter, he frequently fumbled unsuccessfully in random fashion with the blocks and returned them to the examiner with a hopeful smile. His IQ on the Leiter was only 59. He did seem to catch on to the idea of "Which doesn't belong?" on the Columbia, but his achievement was not significantly higher: IQ 64. His performance on the Picture Vocabulary was also hit-and-miss: IQ 62. Holding a pencil and drawing was a difficult task for this still partially spastic child. He knew he was failing and screamed in frustration, refusing further attempts.

The psychologist also interviewed Pedro's mother, Mrs. G. She spoke English clearly but preferred to converse in Spanish. She explained that Pedro also had learned English quickly after their arrival in the United States five years ago but that the family spoke Spanish at home. She explained that their lives had been chaotic ever since coming to the States from rural Mexico. "Once we were happy; in Jalisco we had enough to eat; we had a little farm, and a little house all our own." In the United States her husband was often unemployed, and instead of becoming rich as they had hoped, they barely eked out a living. Special funds for crippled children met Pedro's medical bills. When he went home, he had to return three times each week for physiotherapy, and Mrs. G was instructed in carrying out his exercises at home. Soon, he was running about and had regained most of his arm and hand movements. However, Pedro's speech and verbal comprehension did not return as rapidly, despite intensive speech therapy. Then it was discovered that his family did not require him to speak and had accepted his aphasia without question. His parents and sibs were then instructed to demand speech from him. His temper tantrums increased as he struggled to express himself, but gradually he began to use some Spanish phrases. Another year passed before he said anything in English. He was eager to return to school and was promised that his schooling could resume once he recovered his English. Everyone at home began to speak English to him—even his grandfather—who had recently arrived from Mexico and who told him that the two of them would learn to speak English together. Once in school, Pedro rapidly learned to read and write again, but he had lost two years that he was unable to regain. Luckily, he was a small child and thus did not appear to be older than his classmates. On a repeat of the WISC-R, Pedro now achieved a Full Scale IQ of 102. He had no errors on the Memory for Designs.

The techniques used to assess traumatic brain damage are the same as those used to assess the developmental disabilities: the appropriate-age Wechsler test, the Bender or Memory for Designs, and the Rorschach Technique. Here the Reitan or the Luria-Nebraska batteries are helpful in a qualitative if not quantitative description of any resulting disabilities. As in any other assessment, a careful and detailed description of the child's behavior should be obtained from the mother.

This description should form the baseline for deciding whether or not there has been any significant loss. One needs to know clearly what the child was like prior to the injury. This includes not only perceptual-motor and intellectual behavior but emotional and social behavior as well. It should be emphasized again that brain damage often shows up as an emotional disturbance when the child is frustrated over intellectual, perceptual, or motor difficulties—unbeknown to the mother. If at all available, this baseline should be supplemented by a review of any tests given to the child prior to the injury. Often, such tests are available from school records. Of course,

these school records may not contain scores of such individual tests as the Wechsler, but they are more likely to have educational achievement-test scores. These are not exactly IQ tests, but a gross estimate of intellectual functioning may be assumed from these scores.

Case 94

When Tara was 7, she had run out in the street chasing a ball from the schoolyard and had been struck by a truck. Like Pedro, she was unconscious for many weeks, and it was thought that she would not live. Nevertheless, with a thorough regimen of physiotherapy and speech therapy, Tara began to make a slow but steady recovery. Four years later, at age 11, she was able to achieve an IQ of 101 on the WISC-R, and the score on her reproductions on the Memory for Designs was in the "borderline" range. On the Rorschach, she did show signs of feelings of helplessness, perplexity, and insecurity, but otherwise no gross signs of distorted thoughts. She had been functioning fairly well in a school for children with learning disabilities, and it was contemplated that within a year she might be returned to regular public-school classes. Her parents' lawsuit against the trucking company had never come to trial, as the civil courts were very overcrowded. At this point the insurance company argued that Tara no longer suffered any disability and that the trucking company was liable only for her medical care. They cited the latest results of the psychological examination as proof that she was now normal again.

Fortunately, she had been tested at the school with a routine group-IQ test just a few weeks prior to her injury. She had achieved at "standard score" of 125, which placed her in the "superior" range. More important, however, as evidence in court was the baby book that her parents had kept that showed she had indeed been precocious in her infancy and early childhood. They had dated photographs showing her riding a tricycle at age 2 and of learning to swim before she was 3. They had recorded her speech at 18 months and had dated the record at that time. In court, I testified that this was evidence of precocious growth.

The attorney for the defense (for the insurance company) had done his homework; he asked me if the results of the group tests were really those of an IQ test. I told the court that, of course, this was not the same as the standard, individually ad- ministered tests, but that the results did represent the child's intellectual develop- ment in comparison to other children of her age in her school at that time. The jury accepted the evidence of her precocious growth in infancy and the scores on the school group tests as evidence of her func- tioning prior to the injury. Thus, she was awarded an extra compensation for the fact that she was functioning only at average and not at a superior level.

CHAPTER 18

Assessment of Children from Different Cultures

A. INTRODUCTION—THE REALITY OF CULTURAL DIFFERENCES

There should be no doubt in anyone's mind that in the final quarter of the twentieth century there is considerable social upheaval and strife throughout the United States and much of the Western world that is caused by the inequalities, discrimination, and prejudices among peoples of different cultural backgrounds. Such inequalities between the majority and minority cultures and subcultures have existed over many centuries and are deeply rooted in the history of the United States. It is only in the twentieth century that this discrimination has become widely recognized and contested. In only a few decades there has been considerable progress away from what was almost a caste system in which blacks, Spanish-speaking people, Orientals, Native Americans, and other minority groups were placed. Nevertheless, discrimination in action and prejudice in attitude are far from eradicated. Some of the effects of such discrimination and prejudice on the part of both the minority and majority groups have been discussed previously. The present chapter delineates more explicitly the effects of such prejudice and discrimination in psychological assessment.

Because of the intense feelings that surround the subject of prejudice and discrimination, there is often confusion between those topics and the fact of cultural differences. Because prejudice and discrimination are completely unacceptable, there is a tendency at times for people to think

that the differences in cognition and behavior that peoples of different cultures exhibit should also be eradicated. This, in essence, is the old "melting-pot" theory. However, such a melting-pot approach is in itself based in prejudice: It assumes that in the long run there will be just one culture and—without quite saying so—that the culture will be basically white, Anglo-Saxon, and Protestant (WASP). It should be emphasized that the eradication of discrimination and prejudice should include the highlighting and preservation of cultural differences.

As the reality of discrimination and prejudice and of cultural differences has begun to achieve recognition in many areas of American life, there has been specific attention paid to the fact that many of our assessment techniques have in the past been used to support these prejudices and discriminative actions and to downgrade the contributions of various cultures. Some research studies and numerous hortatory articles have appeared that show clearly that the test scores of minority groups do differ considerably from those of the majority and that these scores have been used, or rather misused, to uphold biological theories of racial differences and inadequacies. A review of these studies is beyond the scope of this book, but this chapter is devoted to a discussion of the specific ways in which these prejudices affect assessment in general—not only in test scores but in the basic interactions between the assessor and the child.

One might assume that over the past

generation and on into the next one, the members of which the readers of this book will be assessing, many of the cultural differences that I mentioned later will have gradually disappeared into the so-called melting pot. However, it is my own clinical impression, in over 40 years of psychological assessment of children, that ways of thinking and behavior that are culturally induced do not really disappear in succeeding generations. Black children who no longer live in ghettos, who no longer speak black English, and who suffer much less discrimination than in previous generations quite often continue to think as a black. The same is true of children of Latin heritage who do not speak Spanish, do not live in a barrio, and whose parents provide at least a middle-class living. Nevertheless, they inherit a set of behaviors that unconsciously permeate their thinking and reactions. I have Chinese friends who have not spoken Chinese since childhood and who cannot remember it—but they dream in Chinese. Recognition of these basic cultural and subcultural identities is not a prejudice or is it meant to support prejudice, but rather it is a recognition of a reality with which the psychologist must deal in assessing American children of different backgrounds. The recognition of these cultural differences is most important to the psychologist being trained in the final quarter of the twentieth century: The number of people from various backgrounds with cultural differences is rapidly increasing at an almost geometric rate yearly. The readers of this book will be assessing many more children with Spanish-American and Oriental backgrounds than did psychologists of previous generations. Or is this true only in the United States. In Great Britain, there is a continued and increasing influx of peoples from India, Africa, the West Indies, and other regions. In Holland, there are immigrants from Indonesia, and in France groups from North Africa and Vietnam. As in the United States, the British immigrant may speak clear English—undistinguishable almost from that of the native-

born—but he or she thinks and behaves according to the dictates of his/her own culture. Thus, it is most important for the clinical psychologist in the United States and in other Western cultures to have a clear understanding of the effects of cultural backgrounds on the children they are assessing and on the assessment process per se.

B.   CULTURALLY DIFFERENT ATTITUDES TOWARD ASSESSMENT

As has been made clear in previous chapters, the attitudes toward an assessment, and especially the relationship between the assessor and the child, form a variable in the assessment that is almost as important as are the talents and behavior of the child himself/herself. If the assessor does not understand what is going on between him or her and the child, then there may be a serious misinterpretation of a "test score" or of "facts" from the case history. These attitudes and this relationship are even more important and need to be understood more fully when the assessor comes from one cultural background and the child from another. Let us then look at some of the more important attitudinal differences that commonly arise.

1.   The Assumption of Judgment—and Misjudgment

Nearly every child who is being assessed realizes that the interviews and tests are not merely games—even though some assessors use that word in introducing them. Children know that they are being examined and assessed, and in that sense—judged. If they fear they have some disability that they have tried to keep hidden, they may try to avoid being judged. In my experience, this phenomenon of the fear of being judged and possibly misjudged is fairly common among children with minority-culture backgrounds. They have long experienced prejudice and discrimination, either directly or subtly, or they have been taught to expect it from the experiences of their parents. Thus they will be on the alert for prejudice and discrimination in a situation in which they are being assessed and judged. Children with minority backgrounds hesitate just half a second more before responding. They think the question over a little bit more. Unconsciously, they expect a hidden meaning. They usually face an adult who belongs to the more powerful majority culture and who may in some way affect their future by the way in which they respond. These attitudes may not be present in every child with a minority background, but assessors should learn to spot such feelings and take them into account.

2.   The Assumption of Inadequacy

One of the reasons that children from minority groups fear being judged is because they themselves fear they may be inadequate. As sociologists, such as Gunnar Myrdahl and others, have made clear, one of the evils of prejudice that seriously affects a minority group is that members of a minority come to believe that these prejudices are true. Although they may stoutly deny such prejudices consciously, the fear that they themselves may be actually inadequate because of their ethnic or cultural background lies deep in the unconscious of the minority-status person. Only recently has pride in being black or recognition of being a member of La Raza become a factor in the identity of people with minority backgrounds. It is as if people from such backgrounds have to go out of their way and consciously deny for themselves this fear of inadequacy. Thus, the child with a minority background is unhappier when he or she makes a mistake, is more guarded about setting out an independent opinion. Such children may want to avoid the whole process of assessment to avoid such feelings of inadequacy. These children may be labled "uncooperative" by the white assessor who does not understand their fears.

3.   Attitudes Toward Independent Expression

In my experience, children with minority backgrounds are thus more guarded about expressing their own opinions and ideas. Not only will they be judged as inadequate should the examiner disagree with their opinions, but they have learned since early in their infancy to tell "the man" (the white authority) what he wants to hear. Such a feeling would seriously impede the child from responding to the Rorschach and the TAT. Moreover, there are some cultures in which children are taught not to think independently but to repeat what is drilled into them in school. The thoughts of Confucious, or more recently the thoughts of Chairman Mao, are all that one needs to know if one is a Chinese child, and such respect for the ancestors and their thoughts is a part of Chinese life, even after several generations of living in the United States. Nor is the Chinese culture the only one whose members believe there are strictly right and wrong ways of thinking and responding, and that individual differences are to be squashed. In fact, most cultures also take this attitude.

4.   Different Attitudes Toward Expressing Feelings

The traditional white Angle-Saxon Protestant has as one of his/her basic beliefs the ideas that one should suppress, as much as possible, all emotions and ignore feelings. WASP's are put off by and shocked and prejudiced against people who openly express their emotions and who are sensitive to feelings. This WASP attitude runs through much of American psychology, especially in books on "adjustment" and "mental health." One is supposed to be well adjusted and in good mental health if one has control of emotions and intellectualizes feelings. There is, of course, a counterreaction to that in much of the "mental-health" movement today, but nonetheless much of the emphasis remains on intellectual control of emotions and intellectual appreciation of feelings rather than on the experience and expression of raw emotions or the true experience of feelings. In fact, this basic personality factor in WASP culture is so strong that according to such major studies as *The Authoritarian Personality* (Adorno et al., 1950) the "sin" of free emotional expression and emotional sensitivity is frequently projected onto minority groups. Thus, the fantasy that blacks are more emotionally free and open, more sexual, more musical, and so on is a way in which white people can divest themselves of their own emotions, feelings, and impulses. People from minority backgrounds frequently struggle to avoid appearing to be more emotionally free, and, as Myrdahl and others have shown, they attempt to identify with the majority group.

On the other hand, people from minority cultures may not necessarily have such emotional restrictions. They may allow themselves louder voices when they have feelings; they may sing with greater feeling; they may shout with greater elation or anger; they may walk and dance in a manner that expresses their emotions—not in the stilted fashion of the Puritans. This is not to say that other cultures may not have their own restrictions or their own rituals to allow expression. Thus, a WASP funeral is different from a black funeral; a black funeral is different from a Latino Catholic funeral; which is again different from a Chinese funeral.

I emphasize these factors since one of the main aims of assessment is to understand the emotions and feelings of the child and the child's development in handling and expressing and controlling these emotions. These factors seriously affect minority children's responses to projective techniques or to interviews. For example, the WASP culture places a high emphasis on the value of "facts," time, and dates—almost in obsessive fashion. Other cultures do not place the same value on the preciseness of when and how things happen. In other cultures, it is common to associate one occurrence with another, not necessarily in chronological order, but by placing emphasis on a central event that may have, in the person's own mind, affected his or her life. On the other hand, in WASP culture the importance of events may be difficult to assess immediately because each is passed over with equal weight.

CASE 95

Mrs. W, a 25-year-old black mother, was attempting to give me a history of her child. She could not remember exactly the child's birth date, but she said it was some time before Christmas. As to the year, that was the year before her mother died, but she wasn't sure because she'd had a big fight with her mother, and she wasn't living with her mother right then. Nor could she remember exactly when her mother died, but she thought it was 5 years before and she was pretty sure that her child was 6 years old. However, when I began to ask about the developmental hallmarks of the child, she was even more vague. Mrs. W explained that she had been working and then she had been arrested. When she was in jail she made peace with her mother, and her mother took over the care of the baby. Maybe it was 2 years before her mother died when the baby was born, she conceded. In any case, she thought that the baby had developed normally but wasn't sure and said that her mother had toilet trained the baby, so that when she got out of jail the baby wasn't any trouble any longer. "I think it was about 2," she said. "It couldn't have been much more because my mother died then. I'd kicked my habit and then I was able to take care of him myself. Oh, I know," she said, "I got a card in here that shows when I was put on probation." And she fished through her purse and found a card that showed that she had been put on probation approximately 4 years previously. "So," she said proudly, "that makes little Ben 6 years old, doesn't it?"

CASE 96

Mrs. R, a 25-year-old white housewife, came to the clinic with a baby book, giving the dates of each stage of her 6-year-old child's development. This book showed not only when he took his first step but when he said his first word, was toilet trained, and so on. Each illness that he had suffered and every time she called the doctor were carefully recorded, including the medications he had been given. She explained each entry in some detail, apologizing if she thought there was a lack of information. It was only in the third interview that it was discovered that her father had a lingering illness during the first year of the child's life, and it was obvious he was dying painfully. The fact that she was seriously depressed—often in tears—and spending a great deal of time at her parents' home during this year was not listed in the baby book.

Of course, not all persons with a WASP cultural background are quite so precise and rigid, nor are people from nonwhite cultures always unable to recall events chronologically. However, the beginning assessor must be careful not to criticize or look down upon the person who does not follow the white norm of historical reporting.

5.   Exposing Personal and Family Secrets

There are prohibitions in every culture against giving away family secrets. However, the reasons for keeping privacy and the kinds of secrets to be kept private vary considerably from culture to culture. Feelings of shame or personal guilt may prevent someone from the WASP culture from saying anything bad about his or her family. Similar feelings may prevent such a person also from saying anything about one's own mistakes, for fear of blame or guilt. The only excuse for misbehavior that is publicly allowed in WASP culture is physical illness or physical calamity. Thus, one's "nervous breakdown" or a child's "misbehavior" may be blamed upon some illness in child-

hood or some untoward calamity—or perhaps on the neighbors' children. Such events as marital dissension, fights with other members of the parental family, or mistakes made in child rearing would be glossed over.

CASE 97

Mrs. N, a 40-year-old housewife, was trying to explain why she thought her 12-year-old son, Herbert, had a "learning disability" and had not been able to learn to read. She was sure that he suffered some kind of brain damage at birth, but she did recognize that there had been no positive neurological findings in four or five different examinations over the years. The birth records did show that he was a breach delivery but also that there were no injuries to the child during this delivery and that he seemed normal thereafter. In fact, try as she could, Mrs. N could not remember any untoward events or any slowness in development prior to the time that Herb entered school. In fact, in kindergarten it was estimated that he was of above-average intelligence. She had two older children who were excellent students and who were well behaved. It was only several months later that Mrs. N revealed in tears that just before Herbert's birth she had discovered that her husband had a mistress whom she visited daily. She had thought of divorcing him but realized that there was no way that she could provide an income for three children, so for the following 12 years she had tolerated the fact that her husband would be away every evening and on all weekends. She was sure that her older children were aware of her husband's infidelity. Nevertheless, she called him "a good father," because he played with the children and supported them, went over their schoolwork, and was as equally concerned as she was with Herb's school failure. After the initial blow up with her husband, she said nothing to him about his behavior for the following 12 years, during which they publicly acted as the model married couple.

"But," she added, "I frequently cry myself to sleep." It also became obvious that she was very close to Herbert, closely monitored all of his behavior, and as Herbert put it, "She hovers over me like a helicopter." The working hypothesis of the assessor and therapist was that Mrs. N had, to a certain extent, substituted Herb's love for the love of her husband, or at least she had compensated for the loss of the husband's love by her overattention and overprotection of Herb. This overprotection, in turn, had kept Herb from growing up, which was demonstrated by the symptom of not learning in school. Herb's immaturity was seen in his responses to the Rorschach and TAT.

Where WASP culture emphasizes the fear of blame or shame, other cultures keep family secrets to avoid the wrath of the gods or the more realistic retaliation of the "clan." As noted previously, these fears may persist in minority-group cultures long after the family apprently has become Westernized. A French-Canadian friend of mine noted that his father had marched the children off to the British-Canadian school every morning with the admonition "Remember, you are a Briere!" (family name). Third-generation Chinese-Americans have advised me that although they are intellectually aware that their ancestors will not arise from their graves and haunt them should they talk about the ghosts in the family closet, nevertheless, this kind of fear is so imbedded in Chinese culture that it would not occur to them to reveal family secrets voluntarily. It is automatic for anyone of Chinese descent to preserve the integrity of the family. A similar reservation seems to exist between many people of Mexican descent, where the family is equally revered as a unit.

This reservation about revealing family problems or personal problems related to family relationships becomes intensified as ethnic consciousness is raised. Thus, people with minority backgrounds who are developing pride in their cultural heritages, who think that "black is beautiful," who

are proud of La Raza, are going to be defensive about reporting events that may seem to them to downgrade their cultural background in the eyes of the white assessor.

CASE 98

Mr. G, age 75, was trying to explain his difficulties in raising his grandson, Melvin, age 12. "We just don't get along on anything. He's always been such a good boy, but now he gives us trouble everywhere." However, Mr. G admitted that Melvin was doing well at school, was in no trouble with the police, and was in good health. The difficulties seemed to lie in the fact that Melvin no longer liked the food that his grandmother cooked nor would he give the absolute and unswerving obedience to his grandfather's rules as he had done previously. What seemed to hurt the grandfather most was that Melvin refused to go through the Bar Mitzvah and wanted to change his Jewish name so that people would not know that he was Jewish. The old man sighed and said that he really understood Melvin's position because he himself and his father had, to a certain extent, rebelled against the Jewish religion. "My father was a socialist atheist, and I think I am too," said the old man. "My son-in-law is Jewish too and lives in Israel, but I do not think he is religious." When I asked why having the boy study Hebrew and go through the Bar Mitzvah was important, he said that it is the only way that the child will recognize that he really is Jewish and thus appreciate his cultural heritage. As he thought of it some more, Mr. G. realized that the food and general atmosphere of his life, thoughts, and life were Jewish, despite the fact that he had rebelled against his religion as a youth. As he and his wife and Melvin thought over this question in family therapy, the grandparents decided to give Melvin a choice about what he wished.

Melvin agreed that he desired to have a cultural identity, but he wanted it to be the same as his grandfather's and great-grandfather's. What came out at this point were Melvin's intense disappointment and feelings of anger and rejection because his mother had died, and because his father had remarried and moved to Israel, leaving Melvin behind. He asked his grandfather fiercely, "My father's behavior was not Jewish, was it? Is it Jewish to desert your son?" The grandparents agreed with Melvin that they too had been angry at their son-in-law for moving away and leaving them with the child, even though they assured Melvin, "You have become our son and we your parents."

6. Fantasies and Dreams

Fantasies and dreams also play different roles in different cultures. For some people, a dream may tell you whether to bet on a horse or to avoid certain places where danger might lurk. In some families and some cultures, dreams are discussed in the morning across the breakfast table. But in the WASP culture where emotional control is more the rule than the exception, people are more likely to declare, "I never dream" or to repress dreams. Frequently, a WASP child will start to tell me a dream, look a little confused, and then deny that they really remember. Sometimes such children can draw pictures of dreams that they cannot recite. Personal privacy may also keep people from other cultures from revealing their dreams. But once rapport is established, with someone from a culture where dreams are important such people will recite dreams in far more detail and with more free association than do WASP's.

Fantasizing—which although related to dreaming—is another question. The Swiss psychologist Loosli-Usteri (1931), in reporting her experiences in giving the Rorschach to peasant children in the Alps, notes what she calls *le conscience du hasard,* or the fear of taking a chance. It is as if by making something up to fit the inkblot one might inadvertently create a reality rather than a mere fantasy. In my experience, such fears are not limited to Alpine children. Children commonly ask, "Is that what it really is?" Such cautiousness about making something up—and thereby creating a truth—is common wherever there may be a cultural background of magical thinking. (Of course, the concept of magical thinking is a WASP invention; WASP culture is no more realistic than any other culture.) For example, there are fairly obvious cultural factors in the following three stories told by 14-year-old girls to Card 2—the farm scene—of the TAT.

MARIA, A THIRD-GENERATION MEXICAN AMERICAN GIRL: "Her mother is pregnant but her father just died. Her brother must plow the fields and take care of them. The girl has many brothers and sisters. She is the oldest and must take care of them. She hates her life and would like to run away, but she knows she must stay home. She prays to God to help her. This all happens 100 years ago. (How does it turn out?) She stays there and marries someone from the neighbor's farm. She has many children. That was the story of my grandmother."

OLEATHA, A BLACK GIRL: "This is back in the days of slavery. She wants to run away and go to the north. This is her mother here; that could be her father, I don't know. She had a boyfriend and he ran away. It is all a long time ago. She does not have any money and she is afraid. Maybe she will be killed. I don't know how it turns out."

RANDY, FROM A MIDDLE-CLASS WASP FAMILY: "This happened back in the old days when they all lived on the farm. The family worked very hard, yet do not make much money. Yet they have been able to send their daughter off to college. She does not want to go because she loves her mother and her dad, but they tell her that they want her to go to college. They tell her how important it all is. She goes away to college, then she gets a good job and makes a lot of money, and brings her dad and her mother to the city where they can retire and not have to work so hard anymore.''

If Randy's story had been told by Oleatha, one might presume that Oleatha's parents were enforcing the white values of college education or that Oleatha was adopting these values in order to blend into the white culture. Similarly, Oleatha's story would have a far different meaning if told by Randy: One would have to presume that the element of slavery would have a different connotation for each. Maria's story would be an odd story to be told by either a black or a WASP teen-ager.

7. Need Achievement

As shown by McClelland and his associates (1953), the drive to achieve plays an important role in WASP culture. "Keeping up with the Jones" and getting ahead are extremely important in white Western culture. What may not be recognized is that this drive is not nearly as strong among members of minority groups. For many generations, achievement was squashed among American blacks. Blacks did not show off their prosperity in many parts of the United States because it drew the attention of discriminating whites who used their legal and political powers to quickly "hold back" any black who seemed to be "getting ahead." Keeping blacks in their place was extremely important for the threatened white. Respectable black families were always modest about their achievements (with perhaps the exception of the achievement of their children in school). However, the "conspicuous display" of possessions was a similar behavior among both poor urban blacks and poor whites. Such an attitude, lasting for several generations, affected the behavior of children in response to achievement at school or achievement on IQ tests. As a black schoolteacher friend of mine, who worked in a segregated school in a southern city, remarked, "Even children today fear being

regarded as too smart." Moreover, many children from minority groups who have had little opportunity to enter into professional or semiprofessional jobs become discouraged and do not see any value in education despite what their parents or the schools may tell them. The model for achievement in the slum areas of our enormous cities is the hustler who, through some criminal activity, owns a big Cadillac and wears fine clothes.

Fortunately, much of this is slowly but definitely changing. There are many more opportunities for blacks and other minorities to advance, but they are fewer than for WASP children. Not only that—even though the opportunities may be increasing, the attitudes underlying the need for achievement are not altering as rapidly, for changes in feelings and attitudes often lag behind the cultural realities. Thus, black and other minority adolescents do not feel nearly as hopeful of achievement as does the white child. Nevertheless, the black or other minority child may work even harder at school but always with the fear and expectation of possible failure. One reason that black children occasionally function lower on IQ tests than comparable WASP children is simply because they are uneasy about achievement, do not really expect to achieve, and grow tenser when faced with an achievement task, as are all IQ tests. Middle-class families from minority groups often place a high value on education as a means of escaping caste status, and therefore they force-feed education to their children.

Case 99

Junior, age 7, was not learning to read. His father, who was an administrator at the university, had applied to the university's Special Education Clinic to have him admitted to the special education department's School for Learning Problems, but the school was overcrowded and had denied Junior admission at that time. Mr. J sought the advice of a private psychologist, hoping to pressure the department of education into admitting Junior.

Junior was an obese boy with distinct negroid facial features and a very dark complexion. He looked exactly like his father. His three older sisters and his mother were much lighter in complexion and their facial features were less markedly negroid. During the examination, Junior was quite tense, sitting rigidly upright in his chair, wetting his lips, and staring straight ahead. He wore a fixed smile and occasionally would grin in a silly fashion. His voice was so low as to be almost inaudible. He volunteered nothing and gave only brief responses, needing constant encouragement. He was unusually unsure of himself, seeking reassurance that his answers were correct or acceptable.

On the WISC, Junior attained an IQ of 91, with the Performance IQ being 12 points above the Verbal. His Draw-A-Man was also under age norms (Harris S.S. 90), but it had a definite "Afro" haircut. His Rorschach consisted of only six responses, and his attempts at the CAT were so barren and feeble that I gave up. However, he was fascinated by the World Test. He built two villages, one on the floor and one on the table. The one on the floor contained a school, jail, hospital, stores, and a few homes. The one on the hill consisted only of houses—mainly several plastic homes that I had added to the set and that looked like mansions. Asked about his construction, he shyly explained that the white people lived on the hill and that "the others" lived "down here."

Junior's consciousness of race and its relationship to his reading problems was explained by the family history. Mr. J's family had emigrated to New York City when he was about Junior's age and had lived in the slums of Harlem. His mother, who had been a schoolteacher in the South, now worked as a domestic, but she impressed on him the value of education. As he put it, "I kept out of trouble and studied and was able to graudate from high school, even though I usually had to work as many

hours as possible to earn my share of the family income." It took Mr. J 12 years to finish 4 years of college—working his way and taking a few courses here and there at different schools. He did not marry until he was over 30, and he was past 40 when he earned his M.A. At 50, he was still hoping to obtain a Ph.D., but he was now assistant dean of housing—in effect the landlord for the university's graduate-student apartments. Mrs. J, who also worked as a minor administrator, grew up in a middle-class but segregated neighborhood in St. Louis, the daughter of a black educator. She had not known poverty or did she have to struggle for an education. But she had married Mr. J, 15 years her senior, as soon as she finished college. Though she was somewhat bitter about the fact that she had never used her education and complained that blacks and women too often have few opportunities for careers, she did agree with her husband who fiercely argued that anyone with determination and intelligence could advance—that race really did not hold anyone back. When the J's first came to the university 15 years ago, Mr. J was a student and they lived in the university apartments. Their daughters were the first black children to attend the all-white school in an upper-middle-class neighborhood. Mr. J was a hard taskmaster, especially about homework, and the girls were successful students. However, just before Junior was born, the family moved into a home of their own—a lovely house with all the amenities of middle-class standards but on the edge of a segregated all-black section of the city. The children and Mrs. J loved their home but Mr. J. hated it; he did not want to live in this racially segregated area—not because he was against segregation but because he did not want to associate with "that level of people." He continually searched for a home in an all-white section of town. But in the 1960s no real estate salesman would even show him property outside the black area.

When I checked with the public school, I discovered that Junior was not failing completely. However, he was so shy that he could not recite. But on reading tests he passed just below grade level, which was consistent with his IQ. His father continued drilling him two hours nightly, rewarding him for successes and punishing him with deprivation when he failed. "These are hours of torture for all of us," Mrs. J reported, "Junior is in tears and unable to speak, Mr. J is furious and exhausted, and I have a headache just being around them." A tutor was hired to supplement Mr. J, but to no avail.

Mr. J was advised that IQ was not a reliable measure of ability, especially for black children, but he grasped at it as evidence that Junior would never succeed. On this basis, he was able to relax his desperate attempts to drill Junior. Disappointed, he threw up his hands and declared that he would have nothing more to do with Junior's education. Three years later I met Mr. J and his wife at a memorial service on the occasion of the death of the Rev. Martin Luther King, Jr. We wept together. Several times we met informally as friends. Mr. J confided that Dr. King's death had struck him so deeply that he was for the first time in his life reviewing his own identity as a black. "All my life I've struggled not to be black. I imposed it on my son. Now I must change." Quite recently I ran across Junior on the street. At 19, he had been graduated from high school and was attending a two-year college, learning computer software. He was more verbal and cheerful, though still very soft spoken.

8.   Relationships with Authorities

Perhaps the most important variable in the assessment of minority children has to do with the relationship with authority—particularly white assessors. Experience has taught members of minority groups that authorities are not on their side nor for their benefit. These authorities include doctors, teachers, and social workers, as well as policemen. The minority-group member

has found that members of the so-called helping professions are not always really helpful but far too often treat them with disdain and disgust, failing to treat their problems adequately, neglecting their needs. For many poor minority members, the welfare worker seems to be the enemy who will curtail their benefits and even turn them over to the police. Their association with psychologists is liable to be in juvenile court or in some other institutional setting that may threaten their freedom. It is almost incomprehensible to people from minority groups to realize that a white assessor can really understand them and their feelings.

It is likely also that they will greet the black assessor as a representative of the white world—at least initially. Although some of the distrust and defensiveness of minority-group children is easing, the relationship with the white assessor remains a major factor in their assessment. Thus, the white assessor who is attempting to understand the psychological functioning of a minority-member child should keep this factor in mind as the responses of the child are interpreted. At least at this point in history, it is quite probable that a black assessor is somewhat more successful receiving the confidence of these minority-background children and in establishing a rapport with them than is a white assessor.

Sometimes a child of one minority group will trust the psychologist with a background in another minority group more than he/she will trust the white assessor, who is definitely a part of the child's vision of the enemy. Thus, a Chinese assessor attempting to assess a child of Latino or black background probably would establish a rapport more readily than would a WASP assessor. There seems to be an empathy between nonwhites, which minority children recognize. This does not mean that a white assessor cannot establish quite favorable and adequate rapport with a minority child, but it does often take a little more effort and a little more time to gain the confidence of such a child.

C. LANGUAGE DIFFERENCES

At this time, the United States, as well as other countries, is experiencing a wave of immigration of people with very different cultural backgrounds. For example, there is a large influx from southeastern Asia and from throughout Central and South America. Not only do these people have different cultures, but also they speak different languages, and even when they learn English they think in their native languages. Thus, if one tried to examine a Vietnamese child with the idea of placing him/her in school, one might find he/she spoke adequate English but was slow because he/she translated each word or sentence in his or her mind from Vietnamese into English. Children who speak Spanish at home also speak Spanish to their compatriots even though they speak adequate English to the schoolteacher. Nor is it really only a matter of translation.

Different languages have diverse grammars, which connect different words together in distinctive chains of ideas. Psycholinguists place heavy emphasis on the differences in personality constellations in different cultures because of language structure. The magic of words affects everyone in every culture. All cultures treat words as if they had a reality in themselves. One of the principal difficulties in translating any work of art or in translating any words relating to feelings and emotions has to do with the importance laid upon words, the side-meaning implications, the feelings. It is well illustrated in attempts to utilize Yiddish words in English, some of which have been adopted in America by people who are not Jewish. But *meshuga* does not quite mean crazy nor silly. It may mean not being very bright but it certainly doesn't mean stupid. There is no completely comparable English equivalent. "To schlep" something implies not only to bear a burden but, to a certain extent, it implies that one will bear such a burden almost willingly. Again, there is no exact English equivalent. English does not possess the affectionate diminutive present in other languages. It does not utilize the gender of articles. These factors affect not only translation of words per se but also translation of feelings and attitudes. Spanish "macho" sexism, in my opinion, is reinforced by the Spanish language.

The fact that different languages have different emotional connotations in their grammar and in their vocabulary makes for considerable problems in translation. As discussed at more length later, it is very difficult to translate tests directly. Words that are common in one language may be rare in another and even ideas that are verbally expressed are not equally difficult. For example, many words in English and Spanish do come from the same Latin background, but they have entirely different meanings. Moreover, the Latin base may be very commonly understood by the Spanish-speaking child, whereas the English-speaking child of northern European heritage may be much less familiar with the Latin root word. Words that are a common experience in English and derive from a Nordic or German background may be meaningless even when translated to the Spanish-speaking child.

Of equal difficulty for the WASP psychologist or even the well-educated minority-member psychologist is the street patois used by various minority members. Black children who speak black English rapidly are almost incoherent to many white assessors. In fact, the black patois is quite often used as a defensive, secret language, that enables black children to discuss things when whites are around without being understood. Teachers in Hawaii run up against the same problem. Children of Hawaiian or other mixed backgrounds use Pidgin English specifically to avoid conversations with schoolteachers. Children get into the habit of using these patois both on the streets and the playgrounds, and they do not learn the same English that is spoken by the well-educated WASP. It is as if they speak an entirely different language. Yet, very often these are the children the psychologist is called upon to assess, since they are the children who have the most difficulty in school and the most difficulty with law enforcement officials.

To avoid the language problem in tests, many nonverbal tests of intelligence have been constructed. The old Arthur Point tests were really invented for use with the deaf, but they can be applied to children who speak other languages or who are from other cultures. However, one should probably eliminate the Healy Picture Test because it is definitely designed for the white middle class and is very old fashioned. The Leiter International Scales are an improvement on the Healy, but even tests like the Leiter are not entirely culturally free as they still have the assumption of the achievement drive. Again, the normative data of such nonverbal tests come from white standardization groups. Thus the comparison is always with the white child.

Another attempt to avoid the cultural difficulties embedded in American psychological tests has been to translate these tests into other languages. As noted before, these translations are often very inadequate because of the different connotations of words in a vocabulary test, and even the nonverbal, so-called performance side may or may not tap the experience of children from other cultures. Thus, the Spanish version of the WISC, which was developed on Puerto Rican children, has been criticized by many psychologists because it ignores differences in language as well as in culture.

Another attempt to correct cultural biases—especially with respect to language differences—has been the development of tests in the cultures for which they are to be applied, such as the BARSIT or Baranquilla, which was developed in Columbia, Venezuela, and Mexico specifically for people from those countries and was standardized on various populations within those countries. While this test and others like it might be quite applicable to South and Central Americans, it is of questionable value when applied to Latinos reared in the United States, even though they may speak

and read Spanish. Children from Caracas or Mexico City do not have the same cultural backgrounds as children who grew up in the barrios of Los Angeles, Denver, or New York City. One of the worst examples of the errors of translation has been the attempts to translate the MMPI. Not only are there questions about the translation itself and the meaning of the test sentences to people from other cultures, but also one certainly cannot use the standards for the various scales, which were developed on white Minnesotans in 1930. Even the children's norms for the MMPI were developed on schoolchildren from Minnesota and North Dakota. Thus the test is of questionable value when used on Chicanos in Los Angeles, Puerto Ricans in New York, or on people from any other nonwhite or foreign culture. Yet the MMPI has been translated into many other languages, such as Italian and Japanese, with complete disregard of the differences in cultural norms.

D.   BIASES IN TESTS

It is now fairly well established that many of our psychological tests are culture bound (i.e., they are a part of WASP culture), and they do not adequately sample the intellectual, emotional, and social development of children from another culture. This is particularly true of our tests of intellectual development. Although they may contain in their standardization samples an adequate percentage of children from minority backgrounds, they do not really account in any way for differences in language or achievement drive. Moreover, in the standardization of these tests, the responses of children from minority groups have been averaged in with those from white groups as if they were the same. These statistics mask the differences in intellectual approaches of different cultures and assume in the long run that all children belong to the same group—the WASP majority. Thus, these averages with respect to the performance of minority-group children are meaningless.

Not only are the standardization groups for tests of achievement and intelligence inadequate, but the tests themselves contain biases derived from WASP culture in their contents and in their contexts (Barclay and Yates, 1969; Mumford et al., 1980). Often, the content of these tests is outside the experience of children from minority backgrounds. There has been some attention paid to this in the revision of the Wechsler Intelligence Scale for Children, such as in Picture Arrangement item 4—the plank. However, this factor is largely ignored in the Comprehension subtest. Minority children from lower socioeconomic groups do not have the same answers as middle-class WASP children as to what to do when they find a wallet on the street or when they lose a ball that belongs to someone else. If children live all their lives in housing projects or in wooden cold-water flats in the slums, they may know nothing about why one would build a house with bricks, and they may never see a letter mailed that needs a stamp. As far as I can ascertain from the contents of the Stanford-Binet, in even the latest revision there is no recognition of such differences in cultural experiences.

At one time there was a black version of the TAT called the Thompson Thematic Apperception Test, but I do not believe this was widely used. It is no longer carried by the test publishers. Shneidman's MAPS contains figures that look black, oriental and Jewish but there are no black children. Nor do children seem to recognize that these children are of different cultural backgrounds except for the black adult woman who does play the role of a maid commonly in white children's stories. As far as I can tell, black children use the MAPS as they do any other test given them by a white person. Even the Rorschach, which is supposed to be culturally free, actually has some norms based largely on white schoolchildren (Ames et al., 1952). Drawings too are not culture free (Wise, 1969). One cannot assume that the emotional development of children from minor-

ity backgrounds is necessarily the same as children from the WASP majority upon whom these norms are based.

E.   CULTURAL BIASES OF THE ASSESSOR

It should not be assumed from the preceding that the difficulties in assessing children of minority backgrounds lie in the fact that these children have problems adapting to WASP culture. On the contrary, the real problem lies in the fact that the assessment itself is part of a science dominated by white culture, with white norms, white expectations, and white values. Assessment was invented by whites to assess white children in white schools. Both the instruments and the processes of assessment thus contain some very basic assumptions of white culture. I have already spelled out some of these. First, there is the white cultural bias of need achievement. The white assessor expects children to want to achieve and strive to achieve, and he/she is disappointed when the child assumes a lackadaisical or even antiachievement stance. Even the most liberal white becomes uneasy and puzzled when a black or Hispanic child seems to "play stupid." This behavior on the part of the minority child is likely to arouse old prejudices in even well-educated whites who have tried to bury their biases. Second, the white assessor is likely to assume that children will want to demonstrate not only their achievements but also their imagination and fantasies and to relate their emotions. He or she will understand the defensiveness of some white children but not the defensiveness of children from different cultural backgrounds. Thus, the child who has the fear of fantasy or who cannot display emotions in front of a white examiner may be called "uncooperative" by the examiner.

Another basic assumption of white American psychology, as previously stated, is the primacy of cognition. Somehow American psychology has not yet learned that people from many cultures, including their own, do not necessarily behave in a rational and intellectual manner. As a matter of fact, conscious intellectual reasoning plays a very, very small part in the determination of human behavior, even though in Western culture rational thought is expected and called for, other cultures may not place such empahsis on these expectations or depend upon them. This does not mean that people from other cultures cannot be quite logical, but they do not necessarily give logic the same value or primacy. Other cultures may place a higher recognition on the factor of emotions and feelings in human behavior. Their interpersonal relationships may be based on the expectation that people will have feelings rather than that people will argue or decide logically. Children learn these values very early in life, and thus by latency age, the white majority-culture child has learned to cover over and ignore feelings, while children from other cultures may give primacy to recognition of emotions and be far more emotionally perceptive. In WASP culture, traditionally, emotional perceptivity has had almost a negative value as something weak and feminine. On the other hand, blacks who have not been allowed to compete intellectually have at times developed their emotional perspicacity to estimate white behavior.

Last but not least, there is an underlying assumption that in some way the minority-group child may be basically inadequate. This position is held openly and argumentatively by a few psychologists, such as Jensen (1980). However, Jensen's controversial arguments, in my opinion, show him to be ignorant both of the nature of intelligence tests and of genetics. Jensen and others like him assume that somehow these achievement tests that we call intelligence tests measure some kind of basic faculty with which one is born rather than learned achievement. Some studies of the development of intelligence, such as those done by Piaget and by other students of intellectual development in the United States, show concretely how intelligence is developed. The conclusions of these studies are at variance with those of Jensen. Jensen also ignores the various cultural factors mentioned previously. Last but not least, Jensen has no real concept of the nature of genetics. He does not seem to realize that such very complicated behavior as intellectual achievement is never genetically determined (Liverant, 1960). Fortunately, Jensen's ethnocentric biases are not accepted by the majority of psychologists or by the public.

However, much less recognized is the uneasiness and puzzlement of the middle-class white assessor when he or she finds a minority-member child not living up to the white-majority standards. Often the white assessor begins examination of a child from a minority background with a kind of hope that the child will succeed—a hope that in essence betrays the assessor's underlying assumption that the child is likely to be inadequate. This fear that the child will be inadequate is demonstrated when the white assessor almost leans over backwards to help him/her succeed. Such an assessor may actually gloss over the child's failures or distortions, thus not really assessing the child's strengths and weaknesses objectively. As noted before, children sense when the assessor is tense and defensive, and they become tense and defensive in turn. If they unconsciously recognize that the assessor expects them to be inadequate, it may confirm their own fears of being inadequate and they may therefore fail.

F. SOME POSSIBLE RESOLUTIONS

Although, as has been discussed in some detail already, the assessment of minority children presents many problems, an objective and meaningful assessment—even by white assessors—is not necessarily impossible. To correct these biases, it is necessary first and foremost for the assessor to understand and take into account his or her own biases. Rather than expect inadequacy in the minority child, the assessor must approach her/him without any expectations whatever and merely accept the responses given by her/him as that child's way of approaching the world. The assessor must give up his or her expectations of cognitive solutions, drives toward achievement, or need exhibitionism. In essence, the assessor must play the role of anthropologist partly or at least have a thorough background in anthropology and sociology. This latter is necessary in order to accept and understand cultural differences, particularly the kinds of cultural differences that the assessor will meet in the immigrant to Western culture in the child who belongs to a group of lower socioeconomic status, or to an ethnically different cultural group. Once the assessor understands his or her cultural biases, it is then much easier to recognize the cultural differences presented by a child from a different background. Without the assumptions of white American psychology, it is far easier to understand and appreciate the attempts of the minority-member child to perceive the world. And once the assessor is free of his or her own biases, he/she may well find that the child's approach to the world is not so very different, although it is not identical to that of the white child. Granting that the assessment of a minority child by a white assessor may never be quite as successful as would be the assessment of the same child by a minority-member psychologist, there must be an even more active prommotion of the education and training of psychologists from nonwhite backgrounds. We badly need more Black, Oriental, and Latino psychologists. This is not to say at all that we should have segregated assessment centers, but clinics that serve primarily one or two different minority groups certainly should have psychologists on the staff who are themselves minority members.

Assessors must recognize the cultural bias of the tests they are using, both in the standardization of the tests and in the words, phrases, and pictures used. In assessing minority children, the assessor may want to avoid reporting scores such as IQ's, but he/she may wish to be able to describe the thinking of the child qualitatively. Again, the clinical psychologist must also be a social psychologist to understand what might be the norms for various cultural backgrounds. Unfortunately, such norms are seldom given by the assessor with a background in social psychology.

One of the main questions to be used in the application of psychological tests to minority-group children is the purpose of the assessment. For example, if a minority-member child is to be assessed as to whether or not he or she can be placed in a public school, these tests might be quite adequate in such a case. The reason is that the school itself is a white institution, even when the majority of the children at the school may be from another cultural or subcultural background. The standards of the school board, as applied to that school, will be white. Members of the white culture are those who run the schools, set the school standards, and determine what is taught. White IQ tests were developed to assess the ability of children to succeed in such white schools. These tests may seem very "'unfair" to the black child or the Spanish-speaking child, or the Vietnamese child, but the tests are not as "unfair" as are the schools themselves. It is for this reason that special classes have been used to help the minority-member child adapt to white schools. The truth is that neither the tests nor the schools take into account the cultural differences and the needs of minority children in an adequate way.

What is needed, then, is an improvement in both the schools and in the tests so as to take into account the needs of children from different cultural backgrounds. As new tests are developed, as new schools are built, the old biases must be erased. I would not advocate that we have different tests for black children and white children or for Latino and Chinese children, and so on, as this would merely add to cultural segregation. Nor do I believe that some kind of complete integration or melting-pot approach will help us in understanding the needs of minority children. Rather, what is needed is a clearer recognition of the differences between the children of different cultures and subcultures and even an emphasis on these differences, so that children from each culture recognize their own heritage, as well as the heritages of other cultures. Such an approach should be basic in American psychology in the recognition of individual differences and even in the promotion of such differences, rather than in their repression.

CHAPTER 19

Children in the Courts

A. THE JUVENILE COURT

The juvenile courts, which were developed during the first quarter of the twentieth century in the United States, have now spread to all American states and to most of the countries of the world. The history of these courts is beyond the purview of this book, but those interested should read *The Dangerous Life* (1931) by Judge Ben Lindsey, who was one of the principal lawyers and judges who helped to develop these courts. In strict contrast to the adult courts, which, although they do protect the rights of the individual, are devoted chiefly to the welfare of the community, the juvenile court has as its main aim and interest the welfare of the minor. In so doing, of course, it is presumed that the interests of the community are also protected but not in the same sense as in the adult courts. In the juvenile court, the court aims at protecting the child and in determining what would be best for her/his welfare and development. In fact, in many cases the court assumes guardianship of the child and at least outlines a program of care for him/her. Even if such programs are not supervised directly by the judge, at least those carrying out such programs are accountable to the court. A judge in the juvenile court has at his right hand the probation officer, who investigates a case, who reports back to the court, and who generally has responsibility for carrying out the orders of the court. Most juvenile courts—at least in urban areas—have, in addition to the probation officer, the services of a guidance clinic staffed by psychiatrists, psychologists, and social workers.

These professionals also investigate, report back to the court, and they see that the proper program designed to help a child is carried out. Another arm of the court is the juvenile hall, where children who cannot be released to their parents are held pending trial or until they can be placed in some other institution or foster home. Usually the children who have committed some crime are kept separate from those who have been deserted, neglected, or abused.

The procedures in juvenile court are also quite different from those in the adult courts. Recent legal rulings have held that children are entitled to a legal defense (including children who have committed no crime), and in some areas a jury could be impaneled if anybody strongly demanded it. In most cases, the juvenile hearings are far more informal than hearings in the adult courts. The juvenile judges do not always wear the black robe or sit on a high bench, but, rather, they may be at a desk with the probation officer. Although the child usually is sworn in, the court begins by making certain he/she knows what it means to tell the truth and that he/she knows that the court is trying to be helpful. Thus, juvenile-court procedures are more of a discussion between the court and the child—especially when there is no major crime involved—than a formal questioning by attorneys.

However, as discussed later, when there are criminal charges against a minor, then the hearings tend to become more formal—with charges read by a district attorney and then explained by the court to make sure that the child understands what is going on and what she/he is charged with.

Sometimes, witnesses are heard and cross-examined, but usually the court accepts the probation officer's interviews with school officials, and the like. The juvenile offender is often returned to the community under the supervision of his/her parents, if caretaking parents are available. Only a small percentage—those who are habitual delinquents—are placed in special institutions.

The court may determine the future of deserted, neglected, or abused children, and again it may turn over the duty of carrying out the program to some social agency or probation officer. However, adults who abuse children or neglect them may be tried in adult criminal court. Whereas court records for adults are open to the public and there is a public trial, the juvenile court usually is closed to the public or the news media, and the records of the court are also not for the public eye. In many states, the media are not allowed to report the names of juvenile offenders. This restriction of records continues even after the minor becomes an adult, and the records may even be destroyed at that time. In this way juveniles do not feel that their crimes will haunt them for the rest of their lives.

Usually when the subject of the juvenile court comes up, one tends to think mostly in terms of the minor who has broken some law. Quite often such children are referred to as "juvenile delinquents," but this term has been used so broadly and so vaguely that it is really better to speak of the juvenile offender. In this book, at least, the term *juvenile delinquent* is used in a more restricted sense, to describe the child, particularly the adolescent, who becomes a habitual offender. (The dictionary does define *delinquent* as being equivalent to *offender*.)

As is discussed later, there is no single reason, even in any one case, that causes a child to be delinquent. There are many youths who do express their emotional distress chiefly by defiance of social rules and mores. I believe we should have a term for that kind of child, and I would use the term *delinquent* here, as distinct from the child whose offenses are more a part of his or her family life, or are symptoms of a neurosis or psychosis, or are those that consist of leading a deviant life-style. One may properly use the term *delinquent* if there is a history of repeated offenses, probably with each becoming increasingly more serious. For example, a child at 10 might be arrested for shoplifting some small toy or piece of candy; then a neighbor might complain that the child "borrowed" another child's bicycle and kept it for several weeks hidden away in the garage; next, the child might be arrested for trying to sneak into a movie; the same child by age 14 might be arrested for possession of marijuana; the next arrest might be for being in a stolen car; following this, might be arrests for being drunk and disorderly or further use of drugs. In some areas, the charges may be that this child is "above and beyond parental control."

The other aspect of the term *juvenile delinquent* is the question: When does a juvenile become an adult? Most courts today define a juvenile as being under the age of 18, since most legal rights are bestowed on the individual at that age. However, in many communities the youth who commits a crime before age 18 and is arrested before age 18 may be tried for that crime in juvenile court after age 18 since the crime was committed while he or she was still technically a juvenile. Moreover, such an individual may be sent to an institution for juvenile offenders and kept there for up to five years after age 18. The law is not consistent about when a person is a juvenile. In other instances, especially where a youth has committed a serious crime such as homicide or a series of major crimes such as robbery, the court may have the choice of refusing to try him or her as a juvenile, having such a youth tried in a regular adult criminal court. Thus, one 16-year-old may be tried as an adult if he or she has committed a murder and be sent to an adult institution, while another person who has committed the same crime and who is within a month of being 18 may be arrested, tried in juvenile court after age 18 and be sent to an institution for juveniles and kept there until age 23 or 24.

The causes of juvenile crime are as varied as are the causes of any other kind of crime. Among those children that I would call juvenile delinquents, the most common cause of their behavior lies in a disturbed and unstable family. There is considerable research to show that youths who are frequent juvenile offenders come from a broken home with little or no parental guidance. Although these children may not be seen as openly "neurotic" or "psychotic," they are often very angry, bitter, and depressed. They feel that no one really cares for them in any way. They are often neglected and sometimes even abused. In particular, they feel very unwanted if they happen to come from a wealthy family who shower them with money and physical goods but who show them little or no affection. More often they come from poverty-striken families where both parents have to work for a living and have little time to really pay much attention to the children. In such families, the sole method of discipline is often corporal punishment. Along with a broken or deteriorated family, these children frequently come from areas where there are many similar youths. It should be noted again that the broken family and the neglected child are not solely products of the poverty-stricken areas of the city. Broken families and neglected children exist in wealthy homes also where there is really no room for, or accounting for, children.

In some groups, being tough and rough or a member of a gang gives the individual a considerable amount of status. The youth who cannot achieve either as a student or as an athlete or as a playboy may join in some group or gang of delinquents in order to obtain such a status. In some areas, being a member of a gang is also a protection from being assaulted by other gangs. Gang membership is not restricted to the poor, although many more gangs exist in poverty-stricken parts of a city than in the more affluent areas. Gang membership appears to be much more common among minority-member youths. Here, gang membership gives one pride and status not only in the gang itself but pride in one's minority status also. Thus, a black youth who belongs to a black gang may in this way overthrow his/her identity of being an inadequate and second-class citizen. Youths of Latino background will be proud of La Raza. In poverty-stricken areas, the economically successful adult upon whom the youth may model himself/herself often becomes successful through criminal activities, such as being a pimp or prostitute or drug dealer or being involved in other types of crimes. The poverty-stricken child thus sees the adult petty criminal as very successful, wearing flashy clothes, driving a big car, and "living it up."

The crimes committed by children who come from broken homes and from poverty-stricken areas are often directed against society in general rather than against specific individuals or the carrying out of some specific kind of crime. Thus, the "juvenile delinquent" *is* likely to steal for economic gain. These children also are likely to commit acts of vandalism or violence in a desperate rebellion against what they regard as an oppressive and unrewarding society. They desecrate and shoot up the neighborhood or join in senseless gang wars and outbursts of hostility against a society that they see as offering them little opportunity and that is actually oppressing them. They do not know how else to rebel. This, of course, does not mitigate the heinous crimes they sometimes commit. Thus, the well of inner anger in such a youth might lead him or her to a violent attack on some innocent elderly person from whom they gain little economic reward. For some minority youths, an elderly white person is the enemy. Such crimes, then, are not economically motivated, but rather are emotional outbursts stemming from long-simmering hostilities or feelings of deep deprivation, of no opportunity in life, and of an inability to rebel in a more meaningful manner.   •

In addition to these social causes of juvenile crime, juveniles who have some long-standing emotional problems may also commit crimes. Those kinds of crimes are well illustrated in the novel and film *Rebel without a Cause*. In this story, the lead rebel is from an upper-middle-class home who is rebelling against his family and attempting to protect himself from other gang-member youths. However, there is also in this story an obviously psychotic lad who joins in the gang activities not as a part of rebellion but rather to have some companionship. Usually, the more bizarre crimes of youth—or adults—arise from some individual personal problem rather than from social problems. Thus one may see at times the youth who commits a murder and who also had a history of being a well-behaved scholar and athelete. Often, however, these children also have a history of divorce and lack of affection in their families.

CASE 100

Giles, age 17, drove onto the school-grounds, pulled out a gun, and murdered the school janitor for no other reason than that the janitor told him to put the gun down. This youth had alternately lived between his mother and father who were divorced. He was extremely angry at his father who had remarried. He felt his father's new wife rejected him and he hated her. There were times when he felt tempted to kill his father. He was a bright and creative boy and had done well in school. He had no previous history of any type of legal offense, or was he abusing drugs or even into the most common juvenile mischief.

CASE 101

Karl, age 16, sat on the hill one afternoon and began firing a rifle at passing cars on the freeway. When examined, he had delusions that he was ordered to shoot at those cars by some demon whom he could not resist. He had no history of previous crimes of any kind and came from a very upright and religious home. In fact, it was very likely that he had no other way to rebel against his rather strict, religious parents.

Other children might become engaged in burglary or in prostitution in order to earn enough money to support a drug habit.

In my experience, most children—or adults—become addicted to alcohol or other drugs because of an underlying depression. Adolescents, in particular, cannot endure anxiety and depression and must do something, anything, often something very desperate, to avoid experiencing guilt and depression. Drug addiction is one of the major forms of the attempt to avoid depression. Both male and female prostitution—while it does offer the juvenile offender some economic rewards—is also often part of a neurosis. The adolescent prostitute is usually trying to solve her/his problem of sexual identity. Prostitutes usually feel extremely inadequate in their sexual roles, either as a male or a female. Quite often, female prostitutes have been sexually abused as children; they hate men and sometimes actually become homosexual on the side. The male youth who is a "hustler" has usually become adapted as a homosexual and feels very inadequate as a heterosexual male.

The main reason for considering the psychological backgrounds of juvenile offenders is that the court needs to know whether or not they are exhibiting a set pattern of behavior. The determination of the disposition of the case depends on a court's being informed as to whether or not the offending behavior will be repeated. Sometimes this can be determined just by the nature of the crime. Thus, it is quite likely that a child who has learned to write bad checks or to use someone else's credit card might well continue this behavior if given the opportunity. Drug addiction or other obsessive behavior also is likely to occur again if no psychologic intervention is made. Similarly, the child who grows up in a poverty-stricken area where crime has its rewards and where the successful criminal is a model may well become a recidivist. On the other hand, the child who commits a murder or other serious crime out of a neurotic or psychotic disturbance might not be so likely to repeat such a crime.

The type of disposition needed to prevent further criminal activity and to rehabilitate the child does depend on his/her psychological and sociological makeup. It is in this respect that the psychologist performs a valuable service to the juvenile court.

The court thus asks the psychologist two major questions: (1) What is the psychological and sociological background of the child who has committed this crime? and (2) What kinds of instutitional or other treatment might be most helpful to the child to prevent him/her from continuing this pattern of behavior on into adult life? Should the child be removed from the family and social situation not only to protect society but to give him/her a chance to recover from the social and emotional pressures? Might the child need some psychotherapeutic treatment, either in the communitty or in some institution? Does the child need some further education or other training in order to be able to enter into a noncriminal job that might provide the young adult with the ability to earn a living? Because the juvenile court does aim more at rehabilitation than does the adult criminal court, it is likely to call on the psychologist for a more elaborate background history and psychological examination than would the adult court. Again, the purpose of the juvenile court is not so much the legal defense of the accused, but rather to determine what is best for the welfare of the child.

Some data required for this are gathered by the probation officer. However, in most cases the probation officer does not have the advanced and specific training of the psychologist either in gathering case-history material or in other forms of psy-

chological examination. Usually the probation officer has, at most, a master's degree, one that is not always in psychology or sociology. Most often, it is the probation officer's job to expand on the family situation and the background of the crime, but probation officers are not prepared to offer a psychological analysis of the juvenile offender and of her/his family and community. Thus, the psychologist serving the juvenile court expands considerably upon the probation officer's report, interviewing the juvenile as well as members of the family, in much more detail. The psychologist, of course, may use a variety of psychological tests in assessing the child. The psychologist is likely to review the youth's educational records and records of previous psychological or psychiatric examinations—and is even likely to make a psychological examination of the parents. The psychologist who has knowledge of community resources may investigate the possibility that these resources could be used and advise the court in that regard also. The psychologist needs to confer with the public defender or the other attorneys who are involved on behalf of the child.

Very likely, the psychologist will be called upon to advise the court whether or not the child does understand the proceedings against him or her. Youths who are poorly educated may have only street knowledge of what the court procedures are about. Psychotic children, of course, may not know what is real or unreal nor make such a distinction. Some 18-year-olds may be so immature as to be very dependent upon others and not be responsible for their own acts. Other, younger youths may be quite sophisticated, street wise, and mature in that sense so as to know full well the social rules regarding their behavior and be quite responsible for their crimes.

Even though the procedures in juvenile court are far more informal than in the adult criminal court, the psychologist must remember that he or she comes not as an advocate but, rather, merely as an adviser to the court. The psychologist may advise and recommend, but the final decision, particularly regarding legal matters, rests with the court. Most juvenile courts listen with respect to the expert testimony of the psychologist. It is the court's responsibility to decide the value of such testimony in its final decision. It is the court's responsibility to decide if the testimony of the psychologist is applicable to the law. Thus, it is principally the obligation of the psychologist to present the facts—to avoid playing lawyer and not to present arguments.

B.   THE WARD OF THE COURT: THE RUNAWAY, THE NEGLECTED, AND THE ABUSED CHILD

At one time, children who ran away from home, who were truant from school, or who stayed out at night on the streets beyond curfew were considered to be committing some kind of legal offense. However, today in most juvenile courts these behaviors are not considered to be crimes at all but rather to indicate that the child is beyond the control of the parent. These acts seldom endanger the community, but the child is in jeopardy. In such cases, the court is even more interested in the social and psychological situation that drives the child out of the home, to run away, or that leaves him/her without parental control. The court usually requests not only a probation officer's report but also a psychological study of the child and his/her family.

Some children do run away from home seeking adventure, as used to happen 200 years ago in the time of exploration in maritime countries. Tom Sawyer ran away from a home where there were no parents and where his Aunt Polly had an impossible job. Huckleberry Finn had a drunken father but no home. In the 1960s, adolescents often ran away from home looking for some kind of drug or sex adventure. It is my own personal observation that most of these runaways also came from unsatisfactory homes where there was little affection or

happiness. During the period of the late 1960s, I acted as volunteer psychologist for a church in Hollywood where these runaways were given haven. Their stories often involved homes where the parents were in constant conflict even though they might be living with one another. Thus the child felt little love from either parent, nor was any genuine attention given to his/her needs. Running away from home usually is a symptom of a disturbed family as well as of a disturbed child.

Although most children who run away are in effect emotionally neglected, the term *neglected* child is usually applied to children who are not properly cared for physically. These are children who are left to fend for themselves in filthy apartments with insufficient clothing and food. More often than not, such children are also disease ridden. They may be the children of a single parent who has to go to work and who has no money to provide for the child's care while away from the home. Sometimes such neglected children are left in the care of an irresponsible teen-ager or disabled elderly person. Other times the children may be abandoned altogether. They may be left alone in the family apartment, or they may be left with some babysitter who is not paid and who finally calls the police. In these instances, of course, no charges are made against the child, but rather the criminal charges are made against the parents who willfully neglect or abandon the child.

In these cases of neglect or abandonment, the court may ask the psychologist several questions: (1) To what degree does the child continue to suffer emotionally from such neglect? (2) What kind of program and treatment does the child require? (3) What were some of the underlying reasons that caused the parent to neglect the child so? (4) What can be done to help rehabilitate the parents so that they can resume care of the child? Thus, in cases of neglect and abandonment, assessment of both parents and children is usually necessary.

The physically or sexually abused child constitutes a much more severe parental offense. Physical or sexual abuse by other adults is not usually considered in juvenile courts, and the child, at most, is involved in the court as a witness. Although child abuse has probably gone on for centuries, it has received attention by the community and the courts only in the last decade. Certainly, many professional people who dealt with children—pediatricians, nurses, psychologists, school authorities—have long observed children who come in with severe lacerations from beatings or with broken bones or blackened eyes. But up until about 10 years ago child abuse was considered to be a private family matter, and the previously mentioned authorities seldom called in the police. When the community became aware of such physical abuse, people were horrified. Once the secret was out, the professional person felt less constrained and became obligated to report signs of physical child abuse to designated authorities. In many communities in the United States, there are recently passed laws to set up agencies, usually in the public social-welfare department, to care for such children, to investigate the causes of such abuse, and to remove children from homes where such abuse frequently occurs. In large urban centers there are now special agencies created in psychiatric institutes or in other types of child-care centers that are specifically for the treatment of both the abused child and the abusing parents. The causes of physical child abuse are probably multiple, but one consistent finding is that the abusing parent was himself/herself fairly often abused as a child. Often these families have a history of alcohol and drug abuse.

Sexual abuse of children by parents—incest—has also suddenly received the spotlight of public attention recently. Communities have suddenly become aware of sexual relationships between parents and children, although it is likely that such sexual abuse has existed for many hundreds of years. These cases of incest are quite complicated—socially and emotionally. Now that both the layman and professional worker are far more aware of the frequeny of incest, it has become a subject of investigation in many psychological centers. Incest appears to occur in every level of society and in families that, on the surface, appear to be quite stable and respectable.

Father–daughter sexual relationships seem to be the most frequent but with emphasis on relationships between a man and his stepdaughter or adopted daughter. However, sex relationships between a man and his biological daughter are not unknown. In the preliminary studies now being published about this situation, there is common agreement that such incest arises from hidden but persistent discord between the parents that often centers around marital dissatisfactions. In such instances, the natural bond between father and daughter may become atrophied. A child who is "daddy's little girl" might easily submit not only to daddy's neglected need for affection but to his need for sexual satisfaction also. Sometimes the father in such instances becomes deeply guilty and depressed. The daughter may tolerate such sexual molestation for many years before openly revealing it to someone else. In many instances, it has been discovered that the mother was probably aware of the possibility of incest but tried to dismiss it from her mind. One mother admitted subsequently that she had observed her 10-year-old daughter's playing with her father's penis several times, but she had said nothing to anyone about it. Usually, as the child grows into adolescence, she becomes more aware of the nature of this sexual realtionship with her father, more anxious about it, and thus more likely to reveal it to some other relative, friend, or authority.

Unfortunately, the community is so scandalized by the revelation of incest in a family that there is often demand for immediate separation of the child from the family and for the arrest of the father. The net result is that the child is inadvertantly punished by being taken to juvenile hall and placed in a foster home. Often the bread-winner of the family—the father—is immediately jailed and the family is thus left without income. Moreover, adult criminals are as horrified by incest as is the rest of the community, and the man who abuses children, whether his own or others, is likely to be physically attacked by other prisoners. In more humane programs, the father is removed from the home but not jailed, is allowed to go to work and support his family, and psychological treatment is provided for both the child and the adults concerned. A model program called Parents United has been set up in Santa Clara in California, which is now being copied by many cities across the nation.

Sexual relationships between a woman and her son are not unknown, but they are probably much less frequent. The psychodynamics appear to be much the same. The woman feels abandoned by her husband (many are single parents) and looks to her little boy for affection and then, ultimately, sexual relationships. Often these relationships begin with the mother encouraging her son to come to bed with her. It is probable that many cases of mother—son incest are not reported, as the boy is far too embarrassed to ever mention such a relationship to anyone else. Moreover, in our sexist society, there is less protection of the boys' sexual maturation than of girls'. Thus, a sexual relationship between a mother and her son is not considered as "evil" as is the relationship between father and daughter. However, in my opinion, the boy who is seduced by his mother suffers as much guilt and emotional disturbance as does the girl who is seduced by her father.

Sexual relationships between children in the same family are so frequent and so commonly accepted that it seldom comes to the attention of the juvenile court unless some very young child is being abused. Currently, childhood sex play is accepted as a normal part of sex exploration in most quarters, and usually it is treated by admon-

ition or light punishment—at most. The situation does become more severe when some pubescent boy molests his pre-school sister. It is probable that in this situation there is some kind of disturbance in the teen-ager or in the teen-ager's family that leads to such sex play. Usually, a teen-ager who resorts to sex play with a much younger child has difficulties making ordinary social relationships with other youths his own age. If a hue and cry is raised about such a situation, the child may grow up with considerable guilt about sex in general. On the other hand, such sex play should probably not be tolerated by the parents, and the children should at least be separated. Such molestation by an older boy of a younger girl is quite common in such places as foster homes and other kinds of institutions. Homosexual relationships between children are also fairly common, and they should probably be handled on the family level rather than as a court matter. Occasionally does one hear of homosexual relationships between parents and children, which results in serious disturbances for the child.

The effects of sexual molestation on the child are not as uniformly devastating on his/her future sexual life as is commonly feared. In fact, an unpublished study made many years ago at the University of California Medical Center revealed that less than half of the children studied showed any kind of long-range emotional disturbance after being sexually molested. On the other hand, studies of prostitutes revealed that most of them had been sexually molested as children, usually by some relative over some period of time.

In the cases that I have seen, the damage is done not only by the molestation itself (especially if it happens only once or twice) but by the amount of hullabaloo made over it. If the child is made to be a terrible victim, if there is the intimation that her/his life will be spoiled forever, if the child has to be a witness in public court and is told to relate what a horrible thing has happened to her/him, then this event may be indelibly fixed in her/his mind and may quite possibly interfere with her/his normal sexual development and maturation. On the other hand, if the situation is handled as perhaps an unfortunate but not devastating event, and if the child does not have to go through a formal cross-examination on the witness stand, then it is unlikely that this event will remain other than a dim memory when the child becomes an adult. Childhood sex play is so common that nearly everyone has a memory of such an event, with at most only a twinge of guilt about it.

Even if the child does not experience long-range emotional damage, she/he should not be subjected to experiences for which she/he is not yet prepared. Even if the molestation is not frightening or harmful, it is far too stimulating and exciting for most children. Many children do recognize that such an act is forbidden, and they feel guilty for permitting it. Thus, children who have such an experience should have some subsequent psychotherapy, at least for a brief period of time.

C. ADOPTIONS

At one time psychological studies of children who were to be adopted and the potential adoptive parents were the most frequent service offered by psychologists to the courts. Now, psychological services for adoption agencies are much less frequent because there are very few children available to be adopted. The wide use of birth-control methods has prevented people from having unwanted children. Women who do have illegitimate children often want to raise them themselves, as single parents. Moreover, the baby infant IQ tests that were once the chief method of assessing children up for adoption have been discredited because intellectual development can not be reliably predicted in infancy (see Chapter 15). On the other hand, children who are available for adoption often have physical and mental handicaps that should be assessed. There still are older children

available for adoption, and people who seek to adopt children may go to other countries where the health and psychological development of the child are often questionable. Thus, although there are far fewer adoptive studies being done by psychologists, a greater proportion of the children up for adoption do require psychologic study.

Assessment of these children is not easy, and usually it requires the best expertise of a psychologist who is experienced in the observation of infants and very young children. The main element in assessment of a child who is up for adoption has to do not only with possible intellectual development but with the general overall emotional and social stability of her/him. At the turn of this century, mental-health workers became more and more aware of the deterring effect of institutionalization on the psychological development of the infant. In fact, the death rate among infants raised in hospital settings was very high, even though they were well cared for physically and had proper nutrition. We now know that such children, if they lack normal maternal affection, become so depressed that they die in a condition known as marasmus. Thus, most children, if not adopted immediately, are put in foster homes where they receive personal care. In such situations, their development can be assessed not only by the infant IQ test but by observation of their overall behavior, such as when fed, when diapered, when they are with other infants, and certainly in their responses to foster parents. A baby who is easily pacified with food when hungry, who chirps when being bathed, who reaches out to the foster parents, and who seems to be observing everything and everyone in sight certainly is developing quite normally. On the other hand, some question should be raised if the infant is continually listless, seems "colicky," is unsatisfied when fed or frequently rejects food, who cries even when held, and who fails to reach out to a maternal figure. Any baby's behavior may change from day to day, and several observations at different times of the day on different occasions should be made.

In assessing the prospective parents, the presence of severe emotional disturbance should be ruled out. Both the obvious and possibly the hidden reasons that a couple might have to seek a child for adoption should also be explored. If the prospective parents do demonstrate a genuine affection for children and at least a basic understanding of what it means to be a parent, they may well be more than adequate parents even if their life-style happens to vary from the community norm. Thus, parents who happen to belong to some particular religious cult or who live a "hippie" life-style are not disqualified as parents solely because of this. On the other hand, people sometimes seek to adopt a child to answer their own neurotic needs or in a desperate attempt to stabilize a dissolving marriage. For example, a woman might feel very unloved and almost abandoned by her husband and seek to adopt a child to satisfy her own needs for affection.

CASE 102

Martin, age 10, was adopted by a wealthy couple who sought to adopt a child so that he/she would inherit both fortunes. This would give the appearance of a united family as well as a united corporation. Unfortunately the couple, who were married almost by arrangement, really hated one another but stayed married to please each of their parents. They, in effect, bought Martin at birth from a private agency and were doubly disappointed because he turned out to have rickets. They kept Martin, and he was reared in luxury but without any parental affection or attention. He quickly became a nuisance, and a special wing of the house was built for him and his governess. He was a bright lad and was succeeding well at school when I met him, but he was always into mischief. He was closer to the cook and chauffeur than he was to his own parents, and when this

couple retired he was allowed to go live with them and was reared by them as his parents.

D.   CHILDREN AND THE DIVORCE COURTS

It is estimated that 50% to 60% of marriages in the United States end in divorce, usually within the first 5 to 10 years of marriage. Divorce is much easier to obtain than it was a generation ago, and many couples obtain a dissolution of their marriage in an uncontested divorce with only a few moments of court hearing. Those that require an extended court hearing usually involve a dispute over property or the custody of children. Far too often these contested divorces are highly emotionally charged with hurt, disappointment, and bitterness. Quite typically the father believes that he is "being taken to the cleaners" financially by his spouse, whom he sees as an unfit mother determined to deprive him of his contact with his children—even though he may have actually had little contact with them prior to the separation. The wife in turn feels neglected by her ex-spouse, whom she feels does not care for the children and might even be harmful to them in some way. There are frequently charges and countercharges.

Children are pulled one way and then the other. As one child put it, "I feel like a Ping-Pong ball being bounced back and forth between my parents, who hate one another." Another likened his feelings to "a piece of cloth being ripped apart." The child frequently feels extremely insecure, not knowing quite what the end result of the family breakup will be. Often children feel guilty lest they in some way instigated the divorce because they have heard their parents quarreling about their care and behavior. Often these children manifest the common signs of depression, namely sleep disorders, apathy at home and at school, poor appetite, or even delinquent behavior.

CASE 103

Neal, age 14, blamed his mother because his father had packed his bags and left the house several weeks before. He became so unruly that there were almost daily quarrels between them, which sometimes ended in physical blows. Neal was a large, muscular boy, and his mother became afraid of him. Therefore she dragged him in to see a psychologist. She had a list of accusations against him—like a district attorney. Neal sat sullen and defiant, but when his mother left the room and he was asked about the divorce, he almost burst into tears. He admitted that he felt very guilty about being so angry at his mother and could not explain, even to himself, why they quarreled so frequently, except that "she bugs me." He complained that there were no real meals in the house. Even before his father had moved out, he had been accustomed to get up in the morning and leave for his stocks-and-bonds office before the rest of the family was up. Neal got himself up and grabbed something to eat since his mother and sister were still asleep when he headed off to junior high school. He was a drummer in the band, which rehearsed early in the morning before other classes. He said he was always hungry and never had enough money to buy all the food he wanted at lunch. No regular meals were served since his father didn't come home until late and his mother was on a diet. She cooked the children some dinner, but usually it was a frozen dinner eaten in front of the TV. She complained bitterly because Neal raided the refrigerator and drank gallons of milk. He had grown almost three inches in height in the past year but did not gain much weight. Because of the quarrels between his parents and the general unhappiness in the home, Neal usually avoided spending much time around the house. Yet, he did not feel very happy and was not a very good companion to his friends, and they did not encourage his presence. He felt rejected and isolated by them and would spend hours around the pinball parlor or just wan-

dering the streets until he thought that he could go home without finding his parents quarreling. The final separation occurred when his mother discovered his stash of marijuana in his bureau drawer and called the police to have him arrested—without consulting his father, who defended him.

He hated his little sister, aged 10, whom he said was a "kiss ass" who constantly made very effort to get in the good favor of his mother and who "could do no wrong." Neal also slept poorly, usually went to bed around midnight, could not get to sleep, woke up with dreams he could not remember, and awakened in the morning sleepless and unrested.

Psychological examination revealed that he had an above-average intelligence but was socially and emotionally immature. He had not really developed any inner emotional resources and remained overly dependent on his parents for emotional support. He felt not only physically hungry but emotionally starved.

Despite the continual dissension between Neal and his mother, she asked for custody of the boy, explaining that the father would really neglect him. In a conference with Neal, his father, and the psychologist, the father said that he had only a tiny apartment and did not have the time and energy to supervise Neal, but upon his son's plea, he agreed to have Neal share his apartment if he would take care of himself. The father also agreed to pay for psychotherapy for his son. Neal was not entirely successful in keeping up with his father's requirements. The father was not home to cook, and he complained about the cost of feeding this growing hulk of a boy. Nevertheless, the father and son did enjoy one another's companionship, and his father paid more attention to Neal's schoolwork and his behavior than he had prior to the divorce. For the following year, Neal's schoolwork remained below average, and he was once more arrested for loitering in the streets after curfew. His father's business took him on trips away from town several times, leaving the boy entirely on his own. At other times, the father wanted to bring home a girlfriend to stay overnight but felt uneasy about doing so with Neal sleeping on the couch in the living room.

However, after the legal formalities of the divorce were completed, the situation seemed to change markedly. Neal no longer fought with his father over the housework but actually kept house and even cooked for his father voluntarily. His father felt freer about his girlfriend when Neal started bringing his own girlfriends into the home. Neal made peace with his mother but decided not to return to her home. Much to everyone's surprise, Neal made above-average grades his senior year in high school, was graduated, and qualified to enter a local four-year state college.

As in the juvenile courts, the domestic relations or divorce courts are also concerned with "the welfare of the child." The court asks the psychologist to aid in the assessment of the child to help to determine what kind of custody and visitation arrangements would be more beneficial. The courts hope that the assessor will remain neutral in the battle between the parents and not be influenced by their vituperous accusations, but rather that they will investigate as objectively as possible the emotional stability of each of the parents, investigate the home environment, and make recommendations to the court regarding the child's future. Although the psychologist may recommend placement with one parent or the other, it is not obligatory in most courts for the psychologist to make such a recommendation. He/she should merely report the "facts" and leave the final decision—as it should be—to the judge. Sometimes, indeed, it may be the recommendation of the psychologist that neither parent is adequate to care for the child, at least at the time of the divorce, and that the child needs care over and beyond what the parents can offer. In order to obtain such an impartial assessment, it is necessary to have the

cooperation of both parents. It is my policy that when I'm called upon to make such an assessment for the domestic relations court I insist that both parents be invited to participate. However, if a parent should refuse to enter into the assessment, I may proceed, noting this to the court and advising the court of the lack of cooperation by one or the other parent. However, both parents usually will be cooperative, if only because they see it as a legal advantage.

In these assessments I usually have separate interviews with each of the parents, and I often administer such psychological tests as the MMPI and the Rorschach. I commonly make home visits to each of the homes and try to see the child in company with each parent in order to assess the relationship between the child and the parent. In addition, I make a full assessment of the child that is separate from those of the parents. This assessment usually includes direct interviews with him/her about the problem of the divorce, and the custody and visitation arrangements that the child may desire. Although at times the child's hopes for visitation or custody may be unrealistic, I make certain that the court is at least aware of the child's desires.

Often, children are unable to face the facts of the divorce directly, and they continue to hope that their parents will reunite. Children may even retain such a daydream after their parents are divorced and remarried. Parents, in turn, may continue to fight over the visitation schedule, the child-care payments (money becomes a major factor in these cases), and the parents' differing opinions about the child's education, medical and dental care, and so on. The judge often becomes weary of these complaints and countercomplaints and hopes that the psychologist can act as ombudsman and take the case out of the court's hands. This may become a legitimate psychological task if both parents are willing to cooperate and to enter into a therapy that has as its intent improvement of communication between divorced parents. However, the psychologist cannot act as a judge when parents continue to quarrel.

E.   REPORTING ASSESSMENTS TO THE COURTS

As may be seen, the actual assessment of the child before the juvenile court, the adoption courts, or the family-relations courts is no different than the assessment of any other child. The assessment regarding family relationships remains a core of such an assessment, and the psychological tests used are identical to those used for other purposes. I have found the Bene-Anthony Family Relations Test to be most helpful when assessing family relations for the domestic-relations court. With pre-school children, I use a special version of the structured doll play in which I have the child choose which parent he or she would prefer to have in certain activities. For example, I ask the child which parent the dolly wants to take a walk with, which parent the dolly wishes to watch TV with, which parent the dolly wants to be fed by or be put to bed by or to help him or her with a bath, and so forth. Then at the end, the mother and father dolly have a big fight, and I tell the child that the father is going to live over here and the mother over there. I then ask the child which parent the dolly is going to live with. Sometimes the child is able to make a choice in this latter question, but quite often he/she merely brushes all the dollies to one side—in one instance the child threw all the dollies at the examiner.

If the child is to be a witness, the court may ask the psychologist to help determine whether or not he/she is able to tell the truth and knows the difference between the truth and a lie. My attempt to answer this question consists first of administering a good vocabularly test, so that I can advise the court whether the child can verbalize appropriately. Adapting the questions from the Stanford-Binet, after having established an IQ, I may repeat these 5-year-old items, "What is a ball?" "What is a book?" Then

I will ask specifically, "What is a lie?" Most children between ages 5 and 8 can say that a lie means that something is made up, invented, is an untruth, or "isn't so." They know that people will be punished for telling a lie, that it fools people and is wrong. I often check out such simple definitions of a lie by asking the pre-school child whether or not certain facts are the truth or a lie. For example, I may say, "There is a pillow on the ceiling. Is that the truth or a lie?" I may point at their shoe and say, "That's your shoe. Is that the truth or a lie?" Then I may repeat some statement that the child has made. For example, in a case where a 4-year-old boy said that his father had sexually molested him, I repeated his statement. "Your father put his peewee in your mouth. Is that the truth or is that a lie?" The child was able to say clearly that this was the truth, after having defined with me, both in his own words and in practice, what the truth or a lie might be. Thus, I could assure the court that this child had a fundamentally correct understanding of what the truth was.

However, by and large, the difficulties in assessing children for the courts lies not in the techniques used but in clarifying what these techniques consist of for the court and of reporting the results in plain English, rather than psychological terminology. Although the language of any report should be in good English, using specific and well-understood terms with unequivocal statements, this dictum is most essential in dealing with attorneys and courts where every word and every term can and will be contested. Clarity of statement is thus most important. It is often a good idea to give examples directly from test responses or to quote the child if at all possible. The psychologist must not yield to the temptation of the scientist who speaks in terms of "perhaps" or "it may be." On the other hand, the psychologist should and can clearly specify what is speculation and what is probability. The speculations and the opinions of the psychologist will be taken in all seriousness by the court, but the court wants to know what is opinion and what is "fact." The court and the attorneys expect the psychologist to interpret the facts and give a professional opinion. This is the purpose of an expert witness. In fact, only the expert witness is allowed to give opinions and to repeat what in other cases would be hearsay. The expert's opinion is thus part of the evidence. What the attorneys and the courts need to examine when the expert is on the witness stand are vague and indefinite statements that have to be clarified. Thus, the more definitive the psychologist can make his or her statements in a written report, the less cross-examination will be necessary.

PART SIX

Assessment and Recommendations

CHAPTER 20

*Assessment for Psychotherapy—An Eclectic Approach**

A. INTRODUCTION

As stated in Chapter 1, the ultimate aim of any clinical assessment is to provide information about the child's ego development that may be useful in making decisions about her/his future. It is in this sense that an assessment is a professional activity, similar to the legal investigations preceding judicial decisions, the medical diagnosis needed before prescription of treatment, or the geodetic survey preparatory to mining operations. As was also discussed in Chapter 1, the corollary of this practical aim of assessment is that there should be a potential choice of decisions. If every problem is handled with the same treatment, assessment is superfluous.

Assessment may be used not only to make decisions regarding the methods of changing the child's behavior or relieving his/her stress, but it also is usually necessary to plan the variations within the method of change as selected. Thus, for example, should one decide that psychoanalytically oriented therapy is the preferred method, the assessment data should also be used in planning this psychotherapy, for example, its frequency, the problems that should be explored first, the nature of the child's defenses, the degree of anxiety that might motivate — or overwhelm — the child, and the like. If one is planning to seek a foster home for a child, a survey of the child's ego functioning is essential in order to know what kind of

home she/he may need or how she/he may adjust to a proposed home. Assessment thus implies that any treatment or change in the child's milieu should be planned to fit his/her needs. Logically, this fitting of the treatment to the diagnosis has two requirements: (1) there should be a method of treatment possible for the problem, and (2) the treatment should be relatively specific as to that problem.

In practice, unfortunately, neither of these criteria is ever completely satisfied. There are major problems in child development for which no method of behavioral or environmental change has had notable success. For example, no single method of treatment or even combinations of methods has yet been found that makes any major changes in the ego functioning of a chronically retarded child—even where this failure to develop has little or no organic component and is demonstrably psychogenic and sociogenic. Similarly, that hypertrophied and distorted growth of the ego known as childhood schizophrenia seldom yields to the best-planned and best-implemented treatment programs. These statements are not intended to discourage plans for treating childhood schizophrenia or functional retardation. On the contrary, when such major disturbances do severely limit the child's development, attempts to stimulate growth should be carefully planned. In fact, in the assessment of a severely disturbed or retarded child, the question is seldom merely one of diagnosis, but is one in which the central concern is for signs of any potential growth or rehabili-

---

*See Palmer, 1980.

tation. A careful assessment often makes it possible to plan some practical relief for a child, even when the future looks entirely hopeless.

Case 104

Sam, age 16, had been completely blind since birth and was considered to be severely retarded. For almost 10 years he had been cared for in what was called a "school" but which was really a private nursing home. Neither of the parents could emotionally accept Sam's severe disabilities, but both felt guilty over having rejected him. Both attempted to maintain the delusion that Sam was not intellectually retarded, even though over the years several psychologists had previously advised them that his intellectual development was extremely slow and the prognosis very poor. The school provided excellent physical care and comforts, but such training program as was available was quite superficial. He had been taught to sing kindergarten songs in a childish voice—but at 16 he was not toilet trained and could not feed himself nor find his way across a room he had lived in for 10 years—much less go from one building to the next unguided, as one might expect. The attendants at this little institution waited on Sam had and foot in a kindly, motherly fashion. In effect, they infantilized him.

As evidence of Sam's intelligence, his mother cited the fact that he remembered songs, remembered his parents (although they visited scarcely every 60 days), and even fantasized about his life prior to being at the school. When Sam was seen by the assessor, it seemed as if he did not recognize that anyone was in the room, even though spoken to several times. However, upon being touched, he did gradually begin to explore the assessor's arm and then his face. All the time he rocked back and forth in the chair, muttering something unintelligible or singing snatches of the songs he had learned. When objects were handed to him, he felt them momentarily and threw them on the floor. However, when candy was

handed to him, he recognized it and quickly popped it in his mouth, making noises of enjoyment. Obviously, the formal methods of testing intelligence were out of the question. The assessor continued to hand each of the inserts to the Seguin Form Board to Sam, to give him an opportunity to become familiar with their shape—even though they ended up on the floor. This process was repeated several times. Then the empty board was placed in front of Sam and his fingers were placed into the slots and run around their contours one at a time for several times. Then he was shown how an insert fitted into the slots, beginning with such simple forms as the circle, square, and triangle. Each time Sam succeeded in making a correct response, he was rewarded with candy. In approximately an hour and a half, Sam had learned to complete the entire Seguin without error. He seemed overjoyed with this new game and kept playing with it for another half hour. Each time he was successful, although he needed over five minutes for each completion. For each successive, correct response, he was rewarded.

Although the only data that were available regarding Sam's intellectual functioning were the alleged facts that he "had a long-range memory" and that he could learn to perform very simple tasks, it did seem quite feasible that some attempt could be made to teach him a great deal more in the way of self-help skills. When this was discussed with the school, the director was pessimistic and quite defensive. Finally, she admitted that she and her elderly staff had no knowledge of or time for such methods of training. She felt that Sam had outgrown this school and was insistent that he be removed. Finally, she admitted with considerable embarrassment that since he had reached puberty, he occasionally masturbated in front of the other, younger children.

Sam's parents were intially quite upset over the recommendation that he be put in a state hospital where there was a behavior training program. To accept such a recommendation was an open admission of his severe retardation. Moreover, they could no longer merely assuage their guilt by the monthly payments to the school. However, the director readily agreed with this recommendation and insisted that the parents find some other living situation for Sam. Six months later he was admitted to the hospital for the retarded, and within the following year, according to his mother's report, Sam was toilet trained and was feeding himself. "The last time I saw him," she said with amazement, "he wouldn't even let me help him put on his coat!"

Even where a child's developmental problems do seem remediable, the fact remains that in many instances there is no treatment nor environmental treatment specifically designed for particular problems. Most psychotherapies, most environmental manipulation, and even most psychotropic drugs are not specific antedotes, but are, rather, general methods of attempting to ameliorate a wide variety of human problems. The adherents of most forms of treatment claim that their approach is applicable to many forms of behavioral disturbances. Moreover, therapists are inclined to try the form of treatment at which they are most skilled—even if there are indications that some other approach with which they are unfamiliar might be more effective. Although there are some indications that skill may be almost more important than the therapeutic theory (at least as regards treatment of adults with verbal interviews), such a viewpoint does discourage the introduction of and experimentation with new approaches. Of course, many of the disorders of development are fairly generalized, and most children present a variety of symptoms. Assessment usually reveals that although there may be a major disturbance of one function of the ego, other functions are consequently imbalanced. Thus, in many cases the use of an approach that does seem to be effective with a wide variety of problems might be justified.

As will be discussed subsequently, it is possible to derive the general criteria for using each of the various therapeutic approaches. Far too often these criteria are stated only vaguely by the advocates of the particular approach or have to be drawn from the literature. Even less frequently do the proponents of any particular method specify the contraindications for use of their approach. The fact that psychoanalytically oriented therapy proved not to be the complete and only possible treatment of emotional disturbances, as was once claimed by some of Freud's followers, led to the development of other methods of treatment, such as client-centered counseling and behavior modification. Until more research is carried out on the specific processes and results of each of these various treatments, the most practical way of resolving the question of the treatment of choice is through a thorough assessment. Although each of these methods of therapy is based on somewhat different theories and deals with slightly different aspects of behavior, within their theoretical and practical limits, there is considerable variation in practice. Thus, it is quite possible to spell out from an assessment the needs and defenses of a child, so that direction may be given to any kind of treatment. The cases of two quite different "juvenile delinquents" may serve as examples of how assessment aids in selection of treatment.

CASE 105

The assessment indicated that Kevin was a bright, sensitive, and extremely angry 15-year-old who seemed bent on destroying both himself and his family by his repeated clashes with the law. Like the hero of the movie *Rebel without a Cause* this boy ached for a struggle with a male figure in order to free himself from the guilt aroused in his relationship with his overprotective, ill mother. These internal "dynamics" were so well defined in Kevin's responses that a psychoanalytic approach seemed most applicable. Although the prognosis for a psychoanalytically oriented therapy seemed poor for any boy who had been on probation for numerous offenses for three years and who, at the point of the assessment, was being seriously considered by the court of placement in a state reformatory, the assessor nevertheless recommended that such treatment be attempted with a therapist with whom the boy had made an initial contact and with whom he seemed to enjoy sparring. Further, the assessor suggested that there should be some limits on behavior agreed upon between the boy and therapist and that the therapist should be alert to warn Kevin against acting-out when he felt threatened by depression or was angry at the therapist. Even so, it was predicted that the therapist probably would not be able to begin much uncovering of the boy's conflicts for quite some time until there was evidence that the boy felt comfortable and accepted by the therapist. Six months later, Kevin was still in twice-weekly therapy sessions, and there had been only one critical incident; he had left the therapist one evening, depressed and angry, because he thought the therapist had "made a crack about" his mother. At 2:00 A.M. the next morning, the patient called the therapist to announce he was going to commit suicide, but he allowed himself to be talked into meeting the therapist in his office. After 18 months, Kevin's rebellion seemed to slow down. He had had no further brushes with the law and was talking about going to college.

CASE 106

Stanley, who was about the same age as Kevin and whose delinquencies were similar, proved—during the assessment—to be almost unapproachable through any verbal contacts. Although of at least average intelligence, he was almost retarded when he tried to verbalize his feelings or ideas, and he had equal difficulty in comprehending what others were trying to express. Unlike Kevin, Stanley was far less rebellious and much more amenable to the firm settings of limits and discipline. Unfortunately, these limits could not be set

by his kindly but passive grandmother, who was responsible for his care. Based on this assessment, Stanley's probation officer was able to find a foster home that accepted the boy's needs and at the same time provided the regulation that he sought. When limits were placed on him, he conformed without question.

Kevin would have attempted to disrupt any foster home in the same fashion in which he wreaked havoc in his own family. Stanley could have sat through endless hours of psychotherapy with negative results.

An individualized course of treatment planned for the specific needs of the child often entails the utilization of a mixture of methods. The needs of any one child are usually so complex that any single approach seldom suffices. Planning such treatment is not a simple task. Although it does require that a therapist be able to draw on a number of methods, "eclecticism" cannot be based on a simple random sampling of possible approaches but should involve a knowledge of the various possibilities of each.

Another variable in the planning of therapy on the basis of assessment is the limited range of skills possessed by most therapists. Ethically, psychologists are required to limit their practice to the kinds of children's problems with which they are familiar and the methods of treatment in which they are trained. However, when a child's difficulties do not appear treatable by the methods immediately available, the child is often labeled "a bad risk" or "poor candidate" for psychotherapy. For example, those child-guidance clinics whose staffs are psychoanalytically oriented often tend to reject children who are intellectually slow or brain damaged or who "act out." Little thought may be given to other kinds of remedial approaches that might help the "poor candidate." There is the implication that "poor risk" means "untreatable." Similar attitudes may be found in agencies or hospitals with other orientations. However, the assessing psychologist cannot restrict his/her considerations to the range of therapies immediately available. Rather, he/she is ethically obligated to detail the needs of the child and make recommendations about possible methods of changing the child's behavior or environment without regard to the theoretical orientation or skills of the agency. When the child's needs cannot be met by the referrant, the assessor should recommend that the child be referred to a more appropriate agency.

Unfortunately, the kinds of treatments needed by children are not available at all in many instances. Child-guidance clinics usually receive many more requests for assessment and treatment than they can possibly handle. Only a few families can afford private care. Residential treatment centers for children, public and private, are nonexistent in most communities—even in some metropolitan areas. Even the primarily custodial institutions for retarded or psychotic children have long waiting lists, dating back many months. Clinics and hospitals are likely to be located in large urban communities, and children who reside outside these areas must travel many miles if they are to receive treatment.

Thus, in recommending therapeutic or environmental interventions, the assessor has to consider the problem of the availability of resources. This "economic" question, as it may be called, may arise under several different conditions. When a clinic or hospital has a waiting list for admission, the assessor may be asked to state the urgency for treatment. Although some clinics consider each case in turn, first come, first served, most do attempt to give priority to those children who: (1) show most promise of being helped by the kinds of treatments available, (2) are most critically in need of the available treatment, and (3) cannot find treatment elsewhere. Quite often the data from an assessment can be helpful in considering each of these criteria for admission to a clinic or hospital. Whether a child's problems are "critical"

or "more critical" than those of some other applicant for treatment is often a heart-rending question for which there are no really rational, satisfying criteria. Many clinics are prone to give priority to the child and family who are experiencing a crisis, chiefly because when under stress they are likely to be highly motivated and less resistant to change. On the other hand, the child whose problems are relatively static, who does not seem likely to deteriorate rapidly or become an immediate social problem, is more likely to wind up on the waiting list. Unfortunately, if such criteria are too rigidly applied, the waiting list may consist of children whose chronic problems become gradually more severe, and whose parents, despairing of help, become less motivated or become inured to the child's behavior.

The question of whether treatment is available elsewhere may seem more the province of the social worker than the psychologist. However, the psychologist should be familiar with other resources in the community and the possibility that the family might use them. For example, a psychoanalytically oriented clinic probably should not accept an intellectually retarded child, even on a waiting list, but should take time to carefully counsel the parents and encourage them to apply at a more appropriate agency. An agency designed for treatment of juvenile delinquents might well be justified in referring a psychotic child to another agency, even though the child is on probation from a court, because the agency's staff is sorely needed by children whose problems cannot be treated elsewhere. Similarly, children should not be placed in hospitals or residential treatment centers if their problems can be handled in outpatient facilities. Nor should they be kept in an inpatient facility any longer than is absolutely necessary. Careful and repeated assessment of children in inpatient centers is often a vital part of the information needed to decide whether hospitalization should be continued.

In most instances, the fact that parents

accept a recommendation to seek psychological assessment does indicate that there
is some crucial problem to be treated or that
some change appears needed in the child's
environment. Until recently, most parents
did not accept the need for psychological
help until the child's behavior became seriously unmanageable. However, recently an
increasing number of parents have become
aware of the psychological aspects of child
development through the educational programs of television, magazines, and other
media. As a result, more parents are seeking
psychological consultations about problems
in child rearing and child behavior that most
parents formerly ignored. No doubt, if attention can be given to these relatively minor
problems, it may be possible to prevent
them from possibly becoming major deterrents to development. If treatment can be
instituted early, it may be much more possible to help many children who might otherwise become so handicapped that no treatment would be effective. The assessment of
these seemingly less severe behavioral
complaints thus assumes considerable importance.

The consciousness of the public about
psychological problems has also served to
aggravate the difficulties of already overburdened facilities. When assessing a child
whose immediate problems and development do not seem critical, the psychologist
may be called upon to make some recommendation as to whether such a child
should be put on a waiting list or whether
the parents might be encouraged to undergo
the expense of privately financed treatment. Many parents do struggle to meet
such costs, curtailing family expenses,
drawing on savings, or going into debt.
Such a recommendation by the assessor
should therefore not be made lightly or
routinely. As public and private insurance
coverage for "mental health" increases,
very likely this question of the need for
treatment will become even more crucial.
With increasing frequency psychologists
are asked the following types of questions:
Does this child need any treatment at all?

Will brief consultation with the parents
suffice? Might brief treatment, perhaps
combined with some environmental
change, be enough? If the child changes
schools (or makes some other environmental change), will his behavior change for the
better? Should the parents be encouraged
to invest considerable time and money in
treatment for the child or themselves? The
following case illustrates how these questions arise and how they may be handled.

Case 107

Mrs. B had sought consultation regarding
her son, Tony, age 7, from a public child-
guidance clinic but had been advised on the
initial contact that the clinic served only
those who could not afford private treatment. Since the B's income was over
$30,000, the clinic referred her to a
psychologist in private practice. Mrs. B
was aware of the fees currently charged by
private practitioners in the community and
when she contacted the psychologist she
mentioned—with some embarrassment—
that she was afraid that the family might not
be able to afford prolonged treatment. The
psychologist invited Mrs. B and her husband to come in for a brief initial consultation at no fee to discuss Tony's problems
and the question of the cost of treatment.

In this 20-minute meeting, the
psychologist learned that both Mr. and
Mrs. B were quite worried because Tony
was "acting up" at school and thus not
achieving. They were also concerned because Tony was very resistant to accepting
Mr. B, his stepfather, whom Mrs. B had
married two years previously. Mr. B had
completed law school just before his marriage, and although he was already becoming established in his legal practice, the
family had incurred considerable expenses
in purchasing a new home and office furnishings. Mrs. B had quit the secretarial
position that she had held before her marriage in order to devote her energies to
caring for Tony and the home—and now
her second child, Margie, born only two

months previously. The psychologist informed the B's that he could not advise them about Tony until he had an opportunity to assess Tony and the situation. This assessment, he estimated, would consist of one further discussion with them and two sessions with Tony, after which he would discuss his findings with them. The fee for this assessment was agreed upon at that time.

In the subsequent hour with Mrs. B, the psychologist inquired chiefly about the circumstances surrounding the complaint and Tony's prior development. Tony was born when Mrs. B was 20, about 16 months after her marriage to her high-school sweetheart. A year later, Tony's father, a fighter pilot, was killed in combat. Tony had barely seen his father and remembered him only as the hero in uniform in the picture on the living-room table—a picture Tony now kept in his room. Mrs. B's mother had died during Mrs. B's childhood, and she had not wanted to live with her alcoholic and dependent father, so she accepted an invitation from her husband's parents to reside with them. She had known them for many years, was fond of both of them, and was treated by them as a daughter. However, she was careful to emphasize, it had been mutually agreed that she was to have the major responsibility for Tony's care and discipline. In retrospect, she felt that they were respectful of her rights and duties as a mother. She had not gone to work until Tony was old enough to be in nursery school. She thus had taken the major responsibility for his care and training during his first three years. To the best of her memory, he was a cheerful, happy baby who developed rapidly without noticeable difficulty. Her in-laws encouraged her to date and seek a second husband. They liked Mr. B who visited the home many times before the B's were married. During their courtship, Tony once openly expressed a desire that Mr. B become his "daddy," even before Mr. B had proposed to Mrs. B. The prospective marriage was discussed with Tony, and he seemed delighted. Yet,

as the wedding date neared, Tony had become increasingly anxious, asking many questions but not waiting for answers. Several times he announced that he had decided to remain with his grandparents but then quickly changed his mind. Initially, Tony liked his new home and was friendly with Mr. B, but soon it became evident that he held back when Mr. B attempted to be affectionate and completely ignored any discipline from him. He became furious when his mother insisted that he obey his stepfather. At these moments, Tony would demand that he return to his grandparents. Mr. B felt hurt and angry, and although the B's did not openly quarrel, there was considerable tension between them over Tony. During Mrs. B's pregnancy, Tony was so resistant that they did yield and frequently permitted him to visit the grandparents over the weekends. After such visits, Tony was usually well-behaved and congenial for several days. After Margie was born, even the visits to the grandparents did not help, and they also complained that Tony was surly and disobedient.

Tony proved to be an intellectually bright and talkative youngster, who openly discussed his family situation. Although he said he liked Mr. B, he admitted that he resented his stepfather's discipline. Repeatedly in his MAPS responses, the ghost was the hero, who rescued the boy character from an intruder; Superman prevented various villans from attacking female figures; a boy who had "lost his parents on the desert" was found and cared for by an elderly couple; finally, in the graveyard scene, a military figure came out of the tomb to rejoin a grieving woman and boy! Tony's drawing of his family did not include his sister, but he added in his grandparents to one side. On the Bene-Anthony, he did admit his sister into the family—but not the grandparents. He attributed most positive feelings, both incoming and outgoing, to his mother; only three responses were given to the father figure, whom Tony clearly identified as "stepfather"; two of these were "mildly negative, outgoing" responses and one related to "paternal indulgence." Almost all negative feelings in Tony's responses belonged to "nobody." However, he did put most of the parental protection and indulgence items into the sister's box. This pattern of responses and his responses to the Rorschach did suggest that Tony tried to control his negative feelings. Very likely these negative feelings arose because Tony did not feel he was receiving his share of parental attention, although it was also possible that he overtly disdained such affection as babyish. Both of these attitudes appeared in his responses during the interviews: "Being kissed is for babies!" "They (his parents) always rush to see what *she* wants when *she* cries." There also was evidence in these and other data that Tony's struggle to hold back his anger resulted in his being at least mildly depressed. All in all, it did seem quite probable that unless Tony could resolve his confused feelings about his father's death and his new family situation, he might have continued and increasing difficulty in establishing affective controls during his latency years. Very likely these feelings of alienation would become more generalized, as was already evident in his peer relationships at school.

These results were discussed with the parents, who agreed that the psychologist's conclusions were consonant with their own observations. They also felt that Tony should have some help in resolving these conflicts but again raised the question of the cost. The psychologist admitted that it was difficult to predict precisely the extent of the treatment. However, since Tony's problems involved specific conflicts of fairly recent origin, it could be estimated that some resolution could be reached in approximately six to eight months or regular weekly sessions. Furthermore, the psychologist recommended that the parents meet with him every four weeks to review Tony's progress and discuss some of the things they might do to help him at home. The B's were relieved as they had heard of therapy that required daily sessions for several years. During the ensuing therapy,

Tony worked through much of his anger and resentment over his mother's remarriage and the birth of his sister. At the end of six months, the B's reported that Tony was much more accepting of his stepfather and no longer as openly jealous of his sister. Most significantly, his mother reported Tony had put his father's photograph in a dresser drawer—without mentioning it to anyone. At school, Tony was working hard on his lessons and was no longer a discipline problem.

Once the decision has been made that a child does need psychotherapy, the next consideration is that the child come to treatment. In many instances, even though the parents and child seem to accept the recommendation, the parents begin to have many excuses as to why the child cannot meet appointments. Studies of the rate of which adult patients continue in treatment (Sullivan, 1958) have shown that over half the adults in outpatient clinics do not attend more than 10 interviews. Although there are no studies to indicate the rate at which children continue, it is my impression that it is probably about the same. In many cases, perhaps as many as one out of three, treatment is broken off after two or three faltering sessions. Therapists often encourage those parents and children who show promise of continuing treatment and, for economical reasons, give less inducement to the family that is openly or even passively resistant. Special efforts are required to deal with these initial resistances. The child who is so anxious and guilt ridden as to be unable to express anything, or the guarded and resentful child who sits pouting in anger, may not return for treatment easily even though he/she sorely needs help. Again, such children and their parents may not initially seem to be good candidates for psychotherapy, and the data from the assessment should be reviewed for the possibility of approaches other than purely verbal interactions.

Last, in these general considerations regarding assessment for psychotherapy, it is essential that the therapist be interested in and challenged by the child's problems. Often it is maintained that the therapist has to "like" his or her patient or that it is impossible to treat someone "you do not like." Theodore Reich once remarked in a lecture I attended that this requisite that the therapist "love" his patients was an American myth. It does seem unreasonable to expect a therapist to "like" the child from the outset or even feel friendly toward her/him. He/she may and probably should be relatively sympathetic with the child's problems, but it is also quite possible that he/she does not like the child's behavior. Children's therapists are often openly unsympathetic with the behavior of the parents, as has been discussed by Loevinger (1959). Although the therapist may be a conscientious, professional person, the child may be so full of resistances as to discourage the therapist or so lackluster as to bore her/him. The therapist may be more challenged by these resistances or better able to discover the "spark" in the child if she/he can review the assessment protocols. These data may help the therapist to find the holes in the child's resistances or to promote the feelings that are nearest to the child's consciousness.

B. ASSESSMENT FOR DIRECTIVE COUNSELING

During past centuries, the chief method for attempting to change individual behavior, other than through punishment, was direct advice. On the basis of magical divination or through a native intuitive knowledge of human behavior, witch doctors and wisemen counseled parents on how to rear or rule their children. Classic is the biblical tale of Solomon, who tested the mother's love for her child—when the custody of the child was contested—by threatening to have the child cut in half. As scientific knowledge about child development began to accumulate, psychologists also attempted to inform and counsel parents

what they should and should not do about their children's behavior. Gradually, psychologists began to realize that merely advising parents and children was not altogether effective. After Rogers (1942) introduced the concept and technique of client-centered counseling and demonstrated its effectiveness, direct advice giving became a bugaboo in many psychotherapeutic circles.

The chief arguments against direct counseling may be summarized as follows:

1.   When the client receives and accepts advice, she/he is likely to become dependent on the therapist. Direct counseling thus may deter the development of independent decision making.

2.   Many clients know what they *should* do but are unable to conduct their lives in a rational fashion because of their neurosis or because of limiting factors in their environmental circumstances. In most instances, clients cannot do what they know they should do because to change their behavior would arouse overwhelming anxiety. Thus, irrational behavior serves as a defense against this anxiety. Direct counseling in such cases is not only superfluous, but it fails to assist clients in handling their anxieties.

3.   Although the psychologist may be very knowledgeable about human behavior in general, it is often difficult to apply these generalities to specific instances. Psychologists are not able to "play God" and live other people's lives for them.

Nonetheless, direct counseling does have a place in the psychotherapeutic armamentarium and, in practice, is used far more often by skilled therapists than might be supposed. Some writers (e.g., Ellis, 1962) advocate this direct approach as an exclusive method of intervention for adults—although there is less indication of its applicability with children. That some advice giving creeps into the therapeutic work of nearly all therapists—except the most orthodox Rogerians—is evident in the samples of therapy that are submitted by candidates for the diploma of the American Board of Examiners in Professional Psychology that I have reviewed as an examiner. Usually, however, such direct counseling enters as only one of a variety of interventions and plays a relatively minor role in the treatment. Moreover, it is usually modified to meet the preceding objectives. Most psychologists are likely to "inform" the client or "point out" possible alternatives to his/her behavior—leaving the decision to the client. Of course, such "informing" and "pointing out," coming as it does from a person in authority, may heavily influence the client's decisions. Psychotherapists are likely to combine direct counseling with reflection and recognition of the client's feelings and anxieties, using phrases such as, "Perhaps your anxiety has kept you from considering this alternative," or "If you did stop what you are doing, then you might have to face some of your true feelings." Although such therapeutic remarks might more properly be labeled "confrontations" or "interpretations," the therapist is strongly and directly suggesting that the client consider the "alternative" or that she/he face up to his/her true feelings. The skilled therapist does not try to give advice purely on a general knowledge of human behavior. Direct interventions are more likely to be derived from a thorough assessment followed by therapeutic investigation into the intimate details of the client's life and behavior patterns.

Direct counseling in one form or another may be indicated under the following conditions:

1. When the client is uninformed about alternative patterns of behavior or about "facts."
2. When the client is unable to formulate or conceptualize her/his own behavior—as is done by the client in other forms of verbal therapy.
3. When the client is able to carry out the psychologist's advice without suffering undue hardships or anxieties.

4. When such counseling does not interfere with the client's development of independent decision making.

Most children meet the first three criteria: They are often uninformed, they cannot easily conceptualize behavior, and they are suggestible. However, they are made anxious easily and have fewer and less well-formed defenses. Moreover, since they are not independent agents, they run realistic risks if they attempt to follow any advice that runs contrary to the dictum of their parents or other authorities. At times I have asked various adolescents, "Have you tried telling your father how you feel?" only to meet with the retort, "You don't know my old man; he'd murder me!" Helping the child face and deal with parental anger and anxiety is not easy. Most of all, independence of decision making, within the limits of the child's abilities and opportunities, needs to be fostered at each step whenever possible. This is especially true for the immature, passive, and dependent child, who is most likely to seek and be receptive to advice.

Directive counseling may be the preferred form of treatment when the chances for developing independent decision making are slim. For example, the mildly retarded adolescent often needs such direction because the chief problem for such adolescents is their inability to function independently. An assessor might recommend direct counseling when: (1) intellectual functioning is below average; (2) the child's ability to develop independent decision making cannot be developed further; and (3) when the child attempts to cope with stress by simple denial or through compulsive mechanisms. Directive counseling is most likely to be effective when the problems facing the child can be handled by concrete, explicit steps.

Various degrees of directive advice may also be in order in counseling some parents. Roughly the same criteria may be used. Parents who show little signs of insight or who are resistant to insight, parents who think concretely, and parents who are extremely passive but compulsive may need to be advised directly how to handle their children. The most important criterion for directive counseling with parents is that they be suggestible to advice from an authority. For example, it might be difficult to develop insight in an adult whose *K* and *Hy* scores on the MMPI are above 70. If these were the only significant peaks of the MMPI profile, directive counseling might be the treatment of choice. However, if there were strong signs of suspiciousness, rebellion, and confusion on the parents' MMPI, such as peaks on *Pa, Pd,* or *Sc,* the parent might be resistant and fail to carry out the therapist's recommendations.

C. ASSESSMENT FOR CLIENT-CENTERED COUNSELING

Client-centered or nondirective counseling, a method introduced by Rogers (1942), operates chiefly through the reflections of the affective components of the client's responses. However, the reflection of feelings is a common component in all verbal and even nonverbal forms of altering behavior. Before Rogers called attention to the central importance of reflection of feelings, most skilled therapists who attempted either to advise or to condition their patients or to interpret their unconscious also attempted to understand the child's affect and to indicate their empathy to the child. Today, nearly all therapists recognize that neither advice nor interpretation will be accepted unless the child realizes that the therapist understands her/his feelings and unless some of these feelings are clarified. Rogers' chief contribution in these earlier works was the recognition he gave to such reflection of feelings and his insistence that such reflection constitutes one of the primary therapeutic elements.

Originally, Rogers introduced this reflection of feelings purely as a technique with little theroretical basis. Later, he introduced his general theory that continued

emotional growth could be encouraged in the adult as well as in the child. He posited that growth was encouraged by the therapist's "warmth," which is expressed through a recognition of the client's feelings.

This particular approach to behavioral change proved not quite as simple as it first appeared. For one thing, most clients tend to express several, and even contradictory, feelings at the same time. Therapists found that it was not possible to reflect all feelings and—consciously or unconsciously—they had to respond selectively to certain feelings. Rogers' theory proved to be too vague to give precise guidance to the therapist about this necessary selection of feelings. The theory that Rogers finally propounded did include the feelings between client and therapist, but there was little indication as to whether or not this client–therapist relationship played any particular part toward changing the client's behavior.

As with any form of treatment that emphasizes one therapeutic technique exclusively, it gradually became clear that this was not equally successful with all clients. It did seem to be particularly applicable to the bright and verbal college students who came to Rogers' counseling centers. However, there were many adult patients who seemed to be either threatened or frustrated by the therapist's constant repetition and mirroring of their affect. Many clients had anger to express, including anger at the therapist, but they felt stifled because Rogerian therapists responded only with "warmth."

Nondirective counseling appears to be used chiefly with adults. However, Axline (1947) reports on the use of this approach in treating adolescents and even younger children. There is some question whether children can assume the introspective attitude toward affect that client-centered counseling utilizes. Children do not verbalize their feelings in the same fashion as do adults, but they are more prone to act on them. However, reflection of feelings is very much a part of most psychotherapy with children. The therapist remarks on the child's feelings but does not expect the child himself/herself to make the verbal recognition to the degree one might expect from adults.

Children do listen to the reflections of the therapist. For example, I watched a 9-year-old boy build a tomb of blocks in which he buried the mother doll and sealed it with clay. I remarked, "You must be very angry about something your mother has done." The child said nothing but continued with the funeral. A week later, he looked up from some other play and said, "You were stupid. I wasn't angry at nothing my mother *did*. I just hate her."

Although reflection of feelings is an important part of therapy with children, the fact that the child's affect is still in a stage of development does have to be taken into account. The affects of a child of pre-school age are likely to be quite labile, momentary, and immediate responses to the environment. At this stage in life, children figuratively wear their feelings on their sleeves, and their affect is short lived. As has been discussed at some length in prior chapters (see Chapters 1 and 10), latency-age children are engaged in developing control over their impulses and affect and try to mask them. Adolescents, facing surges of affect, also try various controls but are easily aroused, moody, and "sensitive." Thus, reflections of feelings in the young child refer chiefly to feelings of the moment. Since the young child's affects are dominated by external stimuli, the therapist's reflections may determine, rather than clarify, what the child feels. The latency child, although not unaffected by the therapist's remarks, may respond by tightening defenses. Reflection of the feelings of the child during this stage of development may result in silence and withdrawal rather than in the opening up of feelings. Such children do need permission to express affect but may not be able to be confronted with their feelings. Reflection of feelings to an adolescent requires considerable therapeutic sensitivity. The choice of which

of an adolescent's affects to reflect and the phrasing of the reflection require all the skill a therapist can muster.

To orthodox client-centered therapists, assessment was unnecessary since they believed that they merely had to await an expression of feeling from the client and reflect it. However, a thorough assessment, especially of affective development, is very necessary in preparation of the use of this technique in the treatment of children. Assessment can inform the therapist about: (1) the overall level of affective development in the child, (2) the degree of sensitivity to affect—and the defenses against such sensitivity, and (3) the kinds of feelings that it might be most important to reflect, that is, the question of selection.

Assessment of the overall level of affective development has already been discussed in Chapter 10. The degree of sensitivity and defensiveness against affect may be estimated from several sources of data. A classic sign of sensitivity to emotional nuances is the use of the texture of the inkblot on the Rorschach. More than one or two texture responses by a prepubescent child would suggest an unusual receptivity to affect. An absence of texturally determined responses before ages 12 to 13 is not unusual, but most prepubescent children are not "shocked" by the texture. They respond with some form-determined response to the textured card. They usually see the popular "bearskin" on Card VI, although without verbalizing any recognition of the texture. Children who retreat defensively from affect-creating stimuli are unable to respond effectively to the shaded cards: They either cannot respond at all, or they give some evasive or confused response. Some children confuse sensitivity to affect with affective involvement. They equate *feeling* with *doing*. One sign of such confusion on the Rorschach is the response in which shading is interpreted as color by the child. For example, the child may see the top D (D3) of Card VI as "the sun . . . because it is red and flaming," pointing out the differences in shading as indicating color. Children who focus their attention on the textural aspects of the colored cards without using the color are, inversely, attempting to avoid affective interaction by merely recognizing affect without using it. They are what the layman designates as the "sensitive" child.

Sensitivity to feelings and conflicts over such sensitivity may also be indicated in responses to the TAT, MAPS, or the Sentence Completion. It is unusual for latency-age children to remark extensively on the feelings of the characters in their fantasies, and it is more common for children in this age group to shrug off any inquiry about the hero's feelings. Prepubescent children assume that the central figure's feelings are reflected in actions and, if pressed, may retort, "Of course he's sad! What do you think? He'd be happy?" Children whose awareness of affect is unusually acute are likely to mention feelings in their stories or incomplete sentences, but with some hesitation or mild confusion. Frequently, latency-age children mention feeling at one moment and deny it at the next. Adolescent sensitivities and defenses are usually much more varied. After pubescence, children cannot blanket out sensitivity to affect so easily, and thus they are more likely to comment voluntarily on the feelings of TAT characters or to blurt out feelings on the Sentence Completion. However, adolescent efforts to suppress or deflect such sensitivity are also likely to be more varied and more desperate. Confusion of feeling with action is more common in the adolescent years. If affect is attributed to the hero in an adolescent TAT story, then the hero is likely to be portrayed as taking some action to relieve the affect—often some illogical action. As noted in Chapter 10, shame and guilt are prominent affects of this age group.

Associative techniques also serve as the major instruments for assessment of the kinds of affect that are most important to the child. The affective content of the child's responses to the Rorschach, TAT, World Test, or Sentence Completion yield valuable information as to the kinds of affective conflicts that the therapist should be prepared to meet. These responses help to pinpoint the setting and nature of the affective conflict as well as identifying the affect itself. TAT stories reveal not only that the child feels hungry for love or is angry, but that these feelings are associated with certain figures in her/his life and in specific types of interactions with them. Thus, the therapist may be prepared to reflect the feelings of the child in respect to certain interactions. "Guesses" about affective aspects of the child's actions in the playroom will thus be more accurate.

D. ASSESSMENT FOR PSYCHODYNAMIC THERAPY*

Admittedly, no brief account can possibly do justice to this complex therapy nor the theory on which it is based. This theory has already been discussed in previous chapters, chiefly in an attempt to relate it to other theories and to the practice of assessment of ego functioning. Moreover, psychoanalytic treatment, as Freud predicted, has been expanded and revised considerably since he propounded his original theses. Rather than review this theory and its changes, psychoanalytically based therapy will be considered as it is currently conceived and practiced. To relate this current therapeutic approach to assessment does require the following: (1) a summary of the general goals, (2) a brief overview of current practices—particularly as regard children, (3) some consideration of its limitations, and (4) a list of the general criteria that need to be considered when this approach is contemplated in the treatment of a child.

As to the goals of brief psychodynamic treatment, many people—including some

*Psychodynamic, as used here, includes not only Freudian psychoanalytic therapy but also such varied types as Kleinian, gestalt, transactional, and humanistic therapies.

psychologists—seem to view it mostly from secondhand summaries of Freud's earliest writings; they believe that this treatment consists chiefly of an uncovering of unconscious motivations. However, this is only one of the goals of psychodynamic therapy, and in work with children it is seldom the principal goal. Theorists have come to recognize that these motivations are part of the ego and that this treatment therefore deals chiefly with ego functions. The main goal of psychoanalytically oriented treatment, particularly with children, is the *strengthening* of ego functions and their development. Such uncovering of unconscious motivations as may be attempted is to allow children to recognize their needs and drives so that they may develop independent methods of need gratification. Mere interpretation of drives has no purpose in itself. The second general goal of psychodynamic treatment of children is to assist them in recognizing and coping with their impulses and needs. In strengthening ego development and assisting children to cope with impulses, psychodynamic treatment has as its third and long-range goal the fostering of the child's sense of identity as a unique, independent, and worthwhile person.

The techniques used to achieve these goals have also been altered and vary considerably from setting to setting. Classic psychoanalysis, in which the patient—prone on the couch—free-associates and the analyst responds with interpretations, day after day over several years, may be the popular conception, but in actual practice only a tiny percentage of adult patients receive this intensive treatment. Children are seldom if ever treated in this manner; the analyst most often treats the child in a playroom setting. Far more commonly psychodynamic treatment of children consists of one or two sessions weekly over a period ranging from 6 to 20 months. It is this brief and less intensive form of psychodynamic therapy with which this discussion is concerned.

Currently, psychodynamic treatment of children also includes the involvement of the parents in the therapy. There remain some orthodox Freudian analysts who regard the parents somewhat as intruders and who interview them only occasionally to obtain information about the child's home life or to instruct them about the care of the patient. Precedent for including the parents in the treatment of the child comes, of course, from Freud's (1909) classic case of a phobic boy, wherein he advised the father and actually saw the child only once or twice. Most psychodynamic therapists today work very closely with the parents. Either they collaborate with colleagues who treat the parents separately or as a couple, or they themselves have regular personal interviews with the parents. Family group therapy (which will be discussed subsequently in this chapter) was developed by psychoanalytically oriented therapists (Ackerman, 1958, 1962). Psychoanalytic concepts and techniques are often a part of psychodynamics, even though they may not be labeled "psychoanalytic." Such factors as defenses, resistances, and the relationship between the therapist and patient—all originating in psychoanalysis — have now become public property in psychotherapy and are necessary considerations in any form of treatment.

The techniques used in these psychoanalytically based therapies also have expanded far beyond the classic interpretation of free association, fantasies, dreams, and slips of the tongue. In actual practice, psychodynamic treatment begins with much reflection of feelings, very much like the client-centered therapy of Rogers, in what is known as the "cathartic" or "abreaction" stage. The child is encouraged to talk about her/his current life and the relevant events leading up to the present situation. The therapist remarks on the child's affective reactions to these situations, especially regarding parents, other important persons, and himself/herself. Once the child sees the therapist as a comforting and sympathetic person, it is possible to confront her/him with the irrational aspects of her/his behavior, both as the child reports it from everyday life and as it occurs in the playroom. Gradually, the therapist interrelates these feelings, motivations, and concrete behaviors into the generalizations called interpretations. Dreams, fantasies, and the child's play activities are an essential part of the data used by the psychoanalytic therapist, but they are not the only sources of data.

Increasingly, these therapists are concerned with the ongoing behavior of the child as well as with his/her past experiences. It should be emphasized that the only reason for considering these past experiences is to understand the present. As the treatment proceeds, these reflections, confrontations, and interpretations are repeated, each time with a slightly different reference and emphasis—much like the theme and variation of a symphony. This repetition of the theme and its meanings is commonly referred to as "working through." Those who are more familiar with behavior-modification therapy will recognize this "working through" as a complex form of verbal reinforcement.

The central element in psychodynamic therapy with adults is the systematic use of the relationship between patient and therapist as an instrument to effect changes in the client's behavior. In classical psychoanalysis, this core aspect of the treatment is known as "transference." The analyst purposefully emphasizes those aspects of the adult patient's interactions with the therapist that appear as a repetition and reformulation of prior relationships—in particular, the client's childhood relationships with her/his parents. Confronted with these infantile reactions that are inappropriate to the therapeutic situation and to the client's current adult life, the adult becomes able to recognize the inconsistencies in his/her behavior and to seek more appropriate, independent, and self-satisfying modes. In working through the transference, the client uses the therapist as a model on which to form an independent identity. To establish such an intimate relationship and to examine the transference in detail often requires considerable time, which is the main reason that a complete psychoanalysis may continue for several years. This transference phenomenon is also used in brief psychoanalytic therapy with adults, but it is not quite so intense and is not explored in as much detail.

In the psychodynamic treatment of children, the transference has had to be reconsidered and altered (A. Freud, 1946). Children have but relatively short pasts over which to build up relationships, and their memories are recent and brief. Most of all, they usually are still residing in the parental home. Thus, in contrast to the adult patient, it is realistic and appropriate for children to react to the therapist as an adult authority and even to relate to her/him much as they relate to their parents. Children have an ongoing parental relationship that currently and continuously influences their relationships with other adults. Children thus transfer an ongoing parent–child relationship. The working through of this transference in the psychodynamic treatment of a child thus consists of an examination of current affects, motivations, coping techniques, and conflicts. Such working through of the transference is not aimed at the eradication of infantile relationships but at the strengthening of effective coping mechanisms. The analyst seeks to help the child recognize and deal with her/his parents in as realistic a fashion as possible.

The remarkable insights that Freud possessed about human nature in general and human maladaptations in particular have led many therapists, including most analysts, to regard psychoanalysis as the ultimate and ideal therapy for all human ills. Moreover, there is a popular mythology that seems to equate the intensity or "depth" of treatment with the intensity of illness. Freud was more cautious. His original successes were with neurotic adults—especially those labeled hysterics. For many years he cautioned his followers that psychoanalytic treatment might not be as effective with other forms of maladaptive behavior, such as psychotic states or the so-called character neuroses. However, therapies based on psychoanalytic theory have been devised that have had at least moderate success with these other kinds of psychological disorders. This author, from reading the psychoanalytic literature and from my own experience as a therapist, has come to the conclusion that the applicability of psychoanalytic treatment depends not so much on the diagnosis of the patient as on the developmental stage and strength of the ego. The working through of feelings, motivations, and conflicts and the transference require a relatively intact ego. Thus, it is possible to treat a "schizophrenic" adult or adolescent where the ego is at the moment severely disturbed or "shattered" if the client at one time has been able to function relatively effectively. The acute or reactive "schizophrenic" patient may be a potentially fair candidate for psychodynamic treatment, but the chronic, or progressive, life-long schizoid character is less likely to respond. Psychodynamic therapy is similarly more successful with those client whose neurotic symptoms or characteriological distortions, even though acute, do not affect the entire ego. On the other hand, the very immature and overly dependent adult may remain unaffected by psychoanalytic therapy. In fact, such adult patients may transfer all their dependency needs onto the therapist in what Freud (1937) called an "interminable analysis."

Psychodynamic therapy involves considerable verbalization. It is an extremely wordy therapy. The client must be able to put feelings, experiences, and memories into words ad infinitum (and even ad nauseum!), until the full meaning is clear. Moreover, she/he must be able to comprehend the therapist's abstractions when the therapist interprets the relationships between these feelings and behavior. Psychodynamic therapy thus requires a verbal sophistication and an ability to abstract and generalize. Therefore, it is not applicable to the intellectually dull patient, whether

adult or child. In practice, psychoanalytic treatment is most often used with intellectually precocious and older children.

Because even brief psychoanalytic treatment often entails many hours over many months, the biggest practical limitation of this form of treatment is its cost in time and money. Privately purchased, it is so expensive that only the well-to-do person can afford it. Many public child-guidance clinics attempt to provide this form of therapy for those whose incomes are below average. (It is almost unavailable to those of "average" income!) However, this treatment requires so much time for each child that with the limited personnel available in most clinics, only a small percentage of the large number of children who need treatment can receive it. If a clinic or private practitioner is to serve the needs of the community effectively, this treatment should be reserved for those who will benefit most, and other, more appropriate types of therapies should be used for other children. The selection of the children for whom this treatment is to be used is a frequent reason for assessment.

On the basis of the preceding discussion, the major criteria for the applicability of psychoanalytic therapy may be summarized as follows.

1.   The child's ego development should be past the earliest formative stage. She/he should be able to internalize some feelings and motivations and to be making some steps toward independent gratification.

2.   In particular, the child's intellectual development should be advanced, so that she/he verbalizes fluently and can understand simply abstractions and generalizations.

3.   Psychoanalytic treatment is more effective if the child resides with an intact family. Therapy is slowed or blocked if she/he tries to satisfy natural dependency needs by using the therapist as a substitute for a missing parent.

4.   The time and money required for this treatment might best be invested in a child

who shows more than an average potential for developing into a creative and productive adult.

When psychoanalytic therapy is being contemplated for a child, a thorough assessment of ego functioning is very necessary. Since assessment of ego functioning has been the major topic of the previous chapters, suffice it at this point to review briefly those accessment methods and data that are pertinent to the previously outlined criteria. First, as regards ego strength and internalization, the MMPI contains an "Ego Strength" scale, designed specifically to measure adaptibility to psychoanalytic therapy (Barron, 1953). Although the norms on this scale were based on an adult sample, it would seem logical that an adolescent with a T score above 50 could be considered as having an ego strength equivalent to the average adult. Internalization is beginning in the child if the "experience balance" on the Rorschach is ambi-equal or intratensive. The internal stirring indicated by the inanimate movement response to the Rorschach (*Fm, m*) is also a positive sign of nascent internalization.

Ego strength can be seen in the everyday behavior of a child. For example, if a child is misbehaving at school and at home, one should try to discover in the interviews with her/him and her/his parents the nature of such misbehavior. If this behavior proves to be chiefly regressive, that is, consists of an increasingly dependent demandingness and a retreat from growth, then it might be concluded that the child's ego development is being blocked. However, a child who is rebelling, who is rejecting parental demands in order to gain independence, or who is seeking to establish new methods of need gratification may be a "good candidate" for psychodynamic treatment.

The child's history should show some capacity for entering into human relationships. She/he should not be markedly withdrawn. If the child does not get along with peers, she/he should have at least one or two friends—peers or adults whom she/he half-way trusts and enjoys. If the child is rebelling against authority, he/she should have peer allies. Even if the child is engaged in a vendetta with parents and teachers, this can be a sign that she/he is able to engage in interpersonal relationships, albeit hostile ones. Strange as it might seem at first glance, the development of neurotic defenses in a child is a positive sign of ego development. For example, the ability to deny frustration, as might be measured on the P-F Study, shows at least some tendency to withstand anxiety, as opposed to direct and aggressive attacks on the frustrating object. Children who give predominately need-persistent responses to the P-F are precocious in coping with frustration. They do seem ready at least in their attitudes to take responsibility for their own behavior.

As regards the second criterion, verbal intelligence may be measured by a number of standard techniques. Using the WISC-R for example, the Verbal IQ should be higher than the Performance IQ if psychodynamic treatment is to be favorably considered as the treatment of choice. The child should have an extensive and superior vocabulary. Similarities and Comprehension subscale scores should also be above average. If weighted scores on these three tests are 13 or higher, it may not matter too much if the child stumbles on some other verbal scales, such as Arithmetic or Digit Span. It would seem unlikely that any child who is markedly deficient in perceptual-motor development would be able to achieve an above-average Verbal IQ. However, mildly retarded perceptual-motor development would not in itself seem to be a contraindication to dynamic treatment of a child. The level of verbalization, sentence construction, and generalization may also be assessed from response to techniques such as the TAT and Sentence Completion. Some bright and verbal children react negatively to IQ scales but demonstrate their verbal competency on these other techniques.

Psychodynamic therapy requires special investigation into family attitudes and habits regarding time and money. Many attempts at treatment of a child have been short lived because neither the parents nor the therapist was aware of the changes in the lives of the family demanded by the treatment. Moreover, very frequently part of the child's disturbance may be based on these factors. The parents, consciously or unconsciously, may be too busy for the child and unable themselves to decide clearly what he/she needs—as opposed to their own needs. It is not necessary to "sell" the treatment to the parents nor to argue with them. Usually a review of their time schedules and their financial habits and problems will reveal to them the possibilities of working the treatment into their schedules and budgets. The "sacrifices" that the treatment of the child may mean to them should be recognized if it seems to the assessor that they can realistically afford the time and money. In many instances, this aspect of the assessment should be conducted by the prospective therapist if the assessor is not to conduct the treatment. Even so, some investigation of this factor may be carried on as part of the assessment, at least to gather data for further consideration by the therapist.

As to the fourth criterion, many data necessary for assessment of the other criteria can also be used to evaluate the creative potential of children. Imaginative productivity on the associative techniques, intellectual advancement, even aggressive strivings for independence, are all signs of future productivity. It should be noted once more that precocity in itself can create problems and conflicts. Psychoanalytic therapy is particularly the treatment of choice for such children. As in the Biblical story of Jacob, they are ready to give up the potage of their childhood and wrestle with the angel. Often they need special help in this struggle.

E.   ASSESSMENT AND BEHAVIOR-MODIFICATION TECHNIQUES

To judge from some research, such as summarized in Bergin and Garfield (1971), the various therapeutic techniques that are commonly labeled "behavior modification" have opened up the possibility of rapid relief for many childhood problems. These range from difficulties in child training to severe behavior disturbances that heretofore seemed implacable to any approach. Because of these possibilities, these methods quickly attracted the attention of many clinical psychologists. However, behavior modification is such a relatively recent innovation that there are as yet no well-established criteria nor techniques by which one may assess whether it is the treatment of choice for any particular child. The discussion that follows is therefore admittedly largely speculative. It may be justified, if for no other reason, on the grounds that methods of assessment appropriate to the treatment should be conceived or adapted as the therapeutic method develops—rather than as an afterthought as has been the case with other therapies. It is to be hoped that this discussion will serve to stimulate further consideration of assessment methods for the behavior-modification techniques.

Any innovation in methods of changing behavior seems bound to be not only fascinating but also challenging and controversial. Some of those who are most enthusiastic about the possibilities of behavior modification have been overly quick to contrast it with other therapies and to allege that the theoretical bases of other therapies are inadequate (Lovass et al., 1965).* Still others are openly skeptical regarding what appears to be an overly simple and limited approach. Such views make it difficult to discuss this therapy objectively. It is only natural that I would attempt to relate behavior modification to the general framework of ego development used throughout this book.† As will be seen, these two sets of concepts are not necessarily antithetical. Rather it is hoped, both may be clarified by an attempt to relate them.

*Lovass' comments refer to the treatment of childhood schizophrenia.

†Such interrelation is attempted in my book *Primer for Eclectic Psychotherapy* (1980).

The theory of operant conditioning upon which most behavior modification is based* is not new nor is its application in clinical approaches to behavioral change (Freud, 1908). As has been demonstrated repeatedly in prior chapters, social reinforcement is one—but only one—of the determinants of ego development. Verbal and nonverbal approval has been used—or withheld—in nearly every form of therapy in order to influence children's behavior, even though few therapists may have recognized their own behavior as operant conditioning. The innovation of behavior modification is the exclusive and systematic use of this one form of learning as a therapeutic technique, disregarding other theories, forms of learning, or techniques of behavior change.
of behavior change.

This theory focuses on children's immediate interactions with their environment, on the ways in which the physical and social environments affect them, rather than on past influences or internal motivational and affective states. In this approach, it is the child's responses and their consequences that need to be changed. The etiology of the behavior is of little importance to the behavior-modification therapist. To quote Meyerson, Kerr, and Michael (in Bijou and Baer, 1967):

Most rehabilitation psychologists will accept the formula $B = f(P,E)$, or behavior is a function of a person's interaction with his environment. In concentrating on the P term in the formula, however, it is easy to neglect the fact that the formula has three terms and that B and E can be independent variables also.

Behavior modification thus attempts to change B through altering E—but presumably without altering P. The alteration in E consists of changes in the reactions of E to the child's behavior. Desired behavior is rewarded; undesirable behavior is ignored or punished.

The typical childhood difficulties for which this therapy is used consist of simple behavioral acts, for example, speech pat-

terns, motor habits, tantrums, and fears and anxieties concerning specific objects or situations. As described by the users of behavior modification, the child is initially observed through a one-way screen in interaction with a parent or other caretaker. A baseline study of the patterns of rewards and punishments used to reinforce the child's pretreatment behavior is most essential since it is generally the behavior of the reinforcing parents that is to be altered. The parent, nurse, or teacher is then instructed how and when to reward, ignore, or punish the child regarding the act in question. The conditioning stimuli are often nonverbal, for example, candy, toys, or smiles of approval as rewards, and personal rejection, isolation, or even mild electric shock as punishment. However, these nonverbal operants may also be accompanied by verbalizations of approval or discouragement. Most behavior-modification therapists seem to agree that if the newly acquired behavior is to be sustained, there must be continued intermittent reinforcement. Thus, the training of the parent, nurse, or teacher is an important part of the therapy.

Although those experimenting with operant conditioning as a therapy have not as yet specified criteria for the types of childhood difficulties for which this therapy is most appropriate, some general criteria may be drawn from the preceding discussion.

First, the behavior to be changed should be primarily determined or influenced by reward and punishment from the environment. Because there is some reaction to external stress in nearly every act and because these external stimuli are the most visible variables, it is often assumed that such stress is always the most important and the most dependent variable. However, as has been repeatedly argued and illustrated in this volume, not all stimuli come from the environment. Internalized memories, attitudes, fantasies, affects, and motivations (the P in the previously mentioned formula) also stimulate children's behavior.

This difference may be further understood by making a distinction between the terms *habit* and *symptom*. A habit may

---

*Some work is also being attempted using respondent conditioning.

be thought of as behavior that does arise primarily from operant conditioning, from the rewards and punishments of everyday life. They may become almost autonomous or consist of circular reinforcements (as when the child's behavior invites more reward or punishment), but they may be extinguished at any time by a change in the environmental stress. Usually, habits consist of rather simple acts, which are not generalized beyond the particular environmental system that stimulates them. In contrast, the term *symptom* suggests that the behavior arises principally from within *P*. A symptom is a reaction to something other than the immediate environment, that is, to *generalized internal* states. Symptoms are inappropriate and unrealistic responses as regards the immediate environment. Symptoms are more likely to be relatively complex behaviors and to be generalized from situation to situation. On the basis of this distinction, behavior modification is most appropriately used and is most effective in changing habits rather than symptoms.

Second, the behavior in question must be susceptible to change through operant conditioning. As was discussed in Chapter 1, there are many kinds of learning, of which operant conditioning is only one. This is not to deny that operant conditioning is probably the most common nor that it is often very effective. Rather, the point is that not *all* behavior is learned by means of this method. For example, although in some instances children may generalize from one operant situation to another, for the most part they are learning concrete acts. They do not learn to generalize or think abstractly through operant learning alone. Moreover, they remain dependent on the reward or punishment. Operant conditioning may free a child from an annoying or debilitating habit or it may help her/him to learn, by means of other methods, how to think abstractly or act independently.

Third, the child in question must be susceptible to learning by means of operant conditioning. Because operant conditioning

is so pervasive in the learning process of most children, it might be assumed—as, indeed, the advocates of behavior modification appear to assume—that all children are equally affected by reward-and-punishment schedules. Unfortunately, little attention has been paid to individual differences in learning approaches. The concept of "cognitive styles" does suggest that different children may have different and preferred styles of learning. That there are individual differences in response to operant conditioning by different children is evident from the research reports by experimenters using this technique. For example, many of the children in the studies collected by Bijou and Baer (1967) show a marked response to this technique, but others show only a slight or even negative reaction.

It is also well recognized that adults differ widely as to suggestibility, dependency on their environment, or hypnotizability. Although children in general appear to be more suggestible and dependent on their environment than adults, there may well be differences among them in "conditionability." As might be expected, the subjects in reports on behavior modification with children are mostly under the age of 7, that is, in the age group in which children are most dependent on environmental guidance and support and before they begin to internalize.

Behavior-modification therapists do not seem to use the term *resistance,* but they occasionally describe behavior in which the child is resistant to the treatment. Children occasionally reject the reward or ignore the punishment. For example, some autistic children drop anything placed in their hands, or they may even fail to swallow candy placed in their mouths. They are used to being isolated and even seem to prefer isolation. As Orlando and Bijou (in Bijou and Baer, 1967) have remarked about operant conditioning of discrimination, "If an individual fails to show a discrimination . . . under these conditions, the question then becomes: What is unusual about this organism?" These authors then list some reasons why a child may not respond to operant conditioning: "He may be color blind, he may not respond to the reinforcer in question as positive, he may be physically ill, or even emotionally upset, he may have a past history making extinction a condition in which he has often been reinforced for perservering long enough." To this list may be added the fact that some children, especially brighter and older children, may feel that they are being bribed or "taken in." Such children regard the reinforcement as an insult to their intelligence and independence. Assessment of all of the factors is necessary so that if behavior modification is to be used, the therapist will be prepared to meet the resistances.

Fourth, the attainment of or elimination of the behavior should be desirable. Certainly, the kinds of behavior to which operant conditioning is most commonly applied do seem to be most undesirable to the adult conducting the experiment, usually also to the parents, and very possibly to the child. It does seem hard to imagine that children do not desire to walk or talk or that they like injuring themselves. Most children will aver that they would like to stop stuttering or wetting the bed or losing their temper. Yet, it is often observable that such behaviors serve definite purposes for the child in her/his interactions with the environment. For example, a child's stuttering may help to keep him/her from saying what he/she is fearful of saying. Another child may use enuresis to disturb parents; academic failure may serve the purpose of disappointing parents or of retaining the status of infancy. This is one reason why enuresis does not always respond to the variety of operant techniques specfically designed for this "habit." Martin and Kulby (1955), who followed up the effects of one such technique, concluded: "The greater investment that the child has in the enuresis as an interpersonal expression—for example, as a passive way of expressing hostility and defiance toward the parents—the less likely that the habit training procedures will be effective."

Parents or caretakers should also want

the child's behavior to be changed. As illustrated in the cases of Eddie, Case 49, and Cindy, Case 72, the parents were willing to tolerate the children's behavior until the school and other community forces objected. In other instances, parents are also resistant to change in the child, particularly those parents who may unconsciously desire and foster the behavior. They may need to infantalize the child or otherwise use the child for their own neurotic ends.

Fifth thus, the parents should be normal and cooperative. Operant-conditioning techniques can be a boon to the well-meaning but inexperienced parent or to the caretaker of a mentally retarded or otherwise disabled child. However, if behavior-modification techiques are to be successful, the parents or caretaker should not foster the undesirable behavior, either consciously or unconsciously. They should not find their own rewards in the child's failure. The child should not be playing the role of the "identified patient" (Satir, 1964), as is discussed subsequently in the section on family group therapy. For example, if a father finds his revenge against his wife when she is upset by their child's mannerisms, if the mother uses the child's behavior to try to involve the father in the discipline of him/her, and if the siblings know how to instigate the child's disturbance for their advantage, then attempts at behavior modification will be rapidly sabotaged.

Sixth, the behavior should have a rate that is frequent enough to allow opportunity for modification, that is, a sufficient number of pretreatment learning trials. If the behavior occurs, for example, only once (as in the case of fire setting), it would be difficult to work with because there is little opportunity to observe and condition it.* Some other kind of therapy, which deals with incidental behaviors or with symptoms, might be in order.

Seventh, for behavior modification to be effective, an exceedingly clear and precise description of the desired terminal behavior,

---

*I am indebted to Dr. Martha Bernal for this point.

as well as a careful description of the reinforcement contingencies that maintain the current undesired behavior, are essential. This requirement is one of the main advantages of the approach for the clinician. It requires a concise and communicable definition of the problem behavior and its antitheses at the outset. However, to arrive at such a definition, far more careful and detailed interviews with the parents or other authorities who are to follow the modification program are necessary than is usually illustrated in the literature. For example, Bernal (private communication) teaches her students to list the parents' complaints, obtaining if possible the order of importance the parents place on each complaint; these are then restated in *positive* terms, and are written down on a checklist sheet for the parents, who are asked to observe the frequency of the *positive* behavior daily during three-hour periods. For example, if the parents state that the child hits other children, the parent is asked to check those three-hour periods when the child plays quietly with sibs and peers. If the child wets the bed or refuses to go to bed, the parents are to note those nights when the child is dry or goes to bed without undue clamor. This procedure orients both parent and child toward the desired behavior, beginning in the assessment.

To summarize these criteria and counterindications: Behavior modification may well be the treatment of choice for altering simple habits or behavioral acts in young or in retarded children. Through operant conditioning, it is possible to eradicate very disturbing and destructive behavior (Bernal et al., 1968). It also has inestimable promise in the training of retarded or physically handicapped children to perform simple but essential acts. The case of Sam, Case 104, illustrates how the lack of such training constituted severe disability in itself, and how after such training, this blind adolescent was beginning to take some responsibility for his own care. Through focusing attention on operant conditioning, it may be possible to modify considerably the lives of many children heretofore thought beyond any possible rehabilitation. Moreover, it is to be hoped that other types of treatment based on other learning theories can be developed.

Although behavior modification does appear to open new vistas in rehabilitation and training, it is not a substitute for other therapies that deal with other kinds of problems. It is unlikely to be the treatment of choice for those older and brighter children who are less susceptible to simple reward and punishment. Other kinds of treatment are needed when the child's behavior is a complex symptom of internalized conflicts, attitudes, and memories. Such symptoms may be eliminated by operant conditioning, but the child's general state of disturbance remains unchanged. Some reports on behavior modification (Yates, 1958) claim that following such elimination of a symptom, the disturbed child does not develop other symptoms, but a thorough follow-up is lacking. I observed one such child before and after treatment by operant conditioning. The child's tic was no longer present, but he remained a severely anxious, withdrawn, and compulsive child, who walked, talked, and behaved in a machine-like fashion. However, his parents were satisfied with the eradication of the tic and sought no further treatment for several years thereafter, until he became almost psychotic and failed at school.

The assessment technique that behavior-modification experimenters describe in their own procedures consists, as noted previously, of a very thorough and systematic observation of the child, usually in interaction with a parent, caretaker, or even a peer. In these observations, the responses of the child are carefully counted and chartered, sometimes using special laboratory equipment or television tapes (Bernal et al., 1968). Since these therapists are interested primarily in the behavior itself, rather than causes, they often take little or no history—despite the previously quoted remarks of Orlando and Bijou. Moreover, many behavior modification therapists see no utility in other kinds of assessment. Meyerson, Kerr, and Michael (in Bijou and Baer, 1967) argue that the other commonly used assessment techniques may possibly be misleading. It is understandable that in introducing a new and explicit therapeutic technique, it is tempting to disregard and even denounce those assessment techniques that, in the past, have been associated primarily with other therapies. As was noted before, such was also the case when Rogers introduced client-centered counseling. However, scientific clinicians must resist such a temptation, for the aim of science is the integration of knowledge, and science is weakened by the isolation of ideas.

Thus, a more varied assessment may be helpful and, in my opinion, is necessary before behavior modification is selected as the treatment of choice. This assessment should be concentrated on the immediate behavior at hand. As has been discussed at length at various places (see particularly Chapter 4), direct observation of the child—plus in interaction with a parent, with peers on the playground or at school, or with sibs at home—all are extremely valuable sources of data and are used by behavior-modification therapists. In any assessment for any therapy, it is necessary to observe the interactions between the child and the environment. However, direct observations in such settings are not the only assessment techniques that provide data about interpersonal interactions. In fact, responses to most of the techniques discussed in this book can be viewed as behavioral operations, and data regarding interactions can be derived from them. Although many assessment techniques have long been used with children who were subsequently treated by psychodynamic methods and interpreted for that purpose in a dynamic framework, assessment techniques and the data they provide are not in themselves psychodynamic. The responses of the child to these assessment techniques are behaviors, and they may be utilized and interpreted by advocates of any theoretical construct. For example, several writers on the Rorschach Technique (Gibby, 1952; Gibby, Miller, and Walker, 1953) have established that this method—long considered the epitome of investigation into internalized attitudes—also can be viewed as an interaction process between assessor and subject. Moreover, the reliability and validity of direct observations of behavior when used exclusively as a method of assessment are quite doubtful, as was pointed out in Chapter 4. As illustrated throughout this book, it is usually necessary to supplement such observations with other kinds of techniques.

The necessity for using a variety of assessment techniques prior to instituting behavior modification can be seen in the preceding criteria and contraindications. First, to establish that the behavior in question is in fact a habit or a response aroused primarily by the environment, it is necessary not only to discover the stimulus-response sequences but also to investigate the degree to which the behavior may also be symptomatic of internalized conflict. This assumes that any behavior may have elements of either kind of responding. Further, data regarding the relation of the behavior in question to the environment might be derived, for example, from the World Test. Some children play by themselves, not involving the assessor. Others—especially younger children—ask for varying degrees of help and participation, which suggests they depend on others to structure the environment. The main purpose of the Rorschach Technique is the determination of the degree to which the child is responding in general to the environment and to internalizations. A detailed history would be essential, with emphasis on the kinds of stimuli that have influenced the behavior in question. A model of such a history is presented by Bernal and associates (1968). To assess the degree to which the behavior is embedded in the personality as a symptom, one might use the CAT or TAT. Lynn's (1959) Structured Doll Play (see Chapter 10) lends itself particularly well to assessment of parent–child interaction—as does the

Bene-Anthony. As was noted, the child often remarks on and imitates parental stimuli and acts out responses to the doll-play situations.

Second, whether the behavior in question is susceptible to change through operant conditioning depends, in part, on how it was established. Thus, a history of the "cause," in this sense, is necessary. Behavior modification is not necessarily limited to altering behavior previously established through operant conditioning, but it probably is most successful in readjusting such habits. However, other therapies might be more appropriate for other kinds of learned behaviors. For example, a more verbal reflection of feelings and affective support might be the treatment of choice for a child reacting to grief, even though the reaction is a specific symptom. Assessment of a grief reaction may require more than simple observational techniques.

Third, the kinds of learning that the child prefers or responds to most easily may be assessed from both intelligence tests and from the Rorschach. From responses to these techniques, one can determine whether the child learns mainly through one-to-one associations or whether she/he responds more easily to abstractions and generalizations. Operant conditioning deals chiefly with one-to-one responses. For example, one might not require the candidate for behavior modification to be able to verbalize a response to "What do you do when you are thirsty?" (Stanford Binet, Year III-6), but if she/he at least recognizes which forms belong in which inserts on the Seguin, the beginnings of such one-to-one associations are evidenced. Copying a block tower or "bridge," imitating a hand movement, and reproducing or attempting to reproduce the Bender drawings are all measurements of such learning. On the Rorschach, responses based on a simple and immediate reaction to the whole lot (as opposed to built-up or elaborated W responses), or those based on specific details, suggest that the child is using an immediate response to stimuli, without analysis of

abstraction. On the other hand, the child who attempts to respond to the whole world at one moment, who gives markedly confused and contaminated responses to the Rorschach, might not respond easily to conditioning. Such contaminated or confabulated W responses are likely to come from children who experience a global, nonspecific set of stimuli, and extensive conditioning might be required to help them make meaningful discriminations.

Fourth, whether the contemplated change in the child's behavior is desirable also necessitates a more extensive assessment than is described in most articles on behavior modification. The purposes—conscious and unconscious—of the child's acts may be assessed from interviews with him/her and with the parents, from the child's interactions and "games" with the assessor, from TAT fantasies and Sentence Completion associations, and even from reactions to intelligence tests. Although both parents and the child may be unable or unwilling in subjective interviews to state their respective purposes in maintaining the child's acts, they often reveal their motivations in slips of the tongue, in inconsistencies in their reports, and in the evasiveness and vagueness of their statements. Such data may be obtained by asking the child or parent to give a blow-by-blow detailed description of a recent incident involving the behavior in question: What happened before it occurred? What happened next? When did the child demonstrate the act in this sequence of interchanges? How did the parent react? How did the child respond to the parent's reactions? CAT stories are often very revealing of the child's purposes in carrying out the act in question. The child may state directly that the CAT hero wanted to upset or destroy the parent figure or that the parent figure in the story permitted or encouraged the hero to misbehave.

Finally, assessment is necessary to determine whether the parent is "normal" and capable of carrying out the reinforcement. Most important here is the emotional stability of the parents. Psychotic parents or even depressed parents may be so wound into their own affective states as to be unable to reinforce the child consistently. On the other hand, a highly suggestible but emotionally naive parent, such as would be indicated by a high *Hy* score on the MMPI, might be most likely to comply. One might be reassured that the parent would carry out instructions if the MMPI profile "high points" were 3 and 7—and if 8 and 2 were low. The Leary Interpersonal Check List would seem most applicable for assessing parental interpersonal reactions. A set of ICL profiles on each member of the family (including the child if she/he can read) and their projected attitudes toward other members (including the child) might serve to pinpoint those kinds of interactions between the parent and child that have to be modified—especially those that might be dealt with by behavior modification.

Further use of assessment techniques for planning behavior modification has been suggested by Greenspoon and Gersten (1967). According to these authors, assessment of four factors is required: classes of contingent stimuli, the selection of contingencies, self-control, and control by others. At least the last two are comparable to the criteria discussed before. These writers give examples of the techniques that might be used, but they insist that the relationship between test data and this therapy are yet to be established. They also emphasize that a shift in orientation about assessment for behavior modification is required.

F. HYPNOSIS WITH CHILDREN

During the latter half of the twenith century, hypnotic techniques have been reintroduced as a major form of treatment both for children and adults. Like behavior modification, hypnosis can be most effective in amelioration of unwanted habits, such as enuresis, nail biting, tics, stuttering, night terrors, or general anxiety. In fact, Kroger (1979) argues that hypnosis is merely an extention of behavior modification. A conditioning by use of repetitive statements positively phrased and with the promised freedom from the symptom as a reward is heightened and intensified by perceptual focus provided by the hypnotic states. However, as with behavior modification, there is always the chance of "symptom substitution" wherein the child, deprived of one expresion of anxiety, may well develop another symptom as a substitute expression of fears and conflicts.

CASE 108

Irene, age 7, began choking with asthma at age 4 shortly after her sister was born. The allergist could find no definitie allergen but concluded that she might be allergic to urine since the baby, who slept in Irene's room, was not toilet trained. Irene's allergy did lessen when her sister was moved to another room, but it persisted and gradually increased over the next three years to the point that Irene had an attack almost every morning so severe as to prevent her from going to school. Irene had always been a socially shy and emotionally withdrawn child, which also worried her parents. Treated with a brief series of hypnotic suggestions, Irene's asthma soon abated almost completely. Moreover, she became more self-confident at school and socialized with her peers in the neighborhood. However, within six months, she was returned to the therapist with the complaint that this previously well-behaved child was now "out of hand." She was now fighting with and biting her sister, and even some other children. Her mother reported that Irene was becoming disobedient and "sassy" and if scolded she screamed and burst into uncontrollable tears. A reassessment of the child and her parents indicated the need for family therapy.

Hypnosis is also frequently used as an adjunct to psychodynamic therapy. The client learns to react under hypnosis and free associates more easily. The therapist may suggest structured daydreams that the client completes. Clients can become very involved in this treatment, as repressed emotions surge forth in the hypnotic state. Hypnosis also intensifies the attachment of the client to the therapist. Often, even for the most rational client and therapist, it seems like magic. It is strong medicine even for adults. Thus, I am most cautious in using this therapy with children. I would make sure that the child can consciously distinguish clearly between fantasy and reality; I make sure that the child has sufficient ego strength to withstand the assault of repressed feelings under hypnosis.

Case 109

Abel, age 12, refused to dress for his gym class. He would panic and run or stand frozen with fear at the gymnasium doorway. He had no other symptoms nor behavioral difficulties. He attained an IQ of 134 on the WISC-R and was attending special classes for the superior student in the eighth grade (one year advanced). He was tall for his age and plump—so he also looked a year older. He could not explain his fear of undressing in front of other boys. In fact, in his own home he swam naked with his family, sometimes with neighbor children present. He denied his fear was associated with anything sexual. He said he knew "all about sex" but did not care to relate what he knew, as it was nasty! He specifically denied masturbation, saying, "I wouldn't be caught doing anything like that!" Nor did he exchange general talk and jokes with the other boys, as is common at his age. In fact, he had no close male friends, but he did play chess and music with a girl next door, "but she's not my girlfriend!" His parents, both well-educated professionals, said that Abel had always been shy, "introverted," but relatively happy. They agreed that they themselves had few friends and spent all recreation hours with their three children and one another, usually in intellectual activities and music. They had discussed the "facts of life" with Able at various times, as he

asked questions; he had been most curious after the birth of his sister, when he was 8.

Abel's responses to the Rorschach and the TAT revealed no sign of gross anxiety or confusion, but they seemed representative of a normal but prepuberty 12-year-old boy. Alleviation of his symptom through hypnosis was deemed feasible.

Abel proved to be easily hypnotized at a fairly deep level. In fact, he invented his own induction scheme. But this relaxation plus suggestion that the undressing was harmless was to no avail. The hypnotherapy was then extended to include guided daydreams, leading toward participation in play with others and finally toward suggestions of masturbation. After the latter daydream, Abel became very anxious and refused further hyponsis. He claimed he had no memory of his daydream but accused the therapist of "a dirty mind—always thinking about sex" and avowed that "sex had nothing to do with it." He droped out of treatment for the summer, during which he attended a Boy Scout camp. He had no trouble dressing with the boys in camp and on return to school the following year his symptom had completely abated.

Assessment for the therapeutic use of hypnosis should focus on three issues:

1. The behavior to be altered should be more of a "habit" than a "symptom," the habit should be relatively isolated behavior, not merely one symptom of a generalized emotional disturbance.

2. The child should demonstrate sufficient ego strength as to withstand the emergence of specific anxiety under hypnosis.

3. The child should at least consciously consider the relief of the habit to be desirable.

Although no one technique has been invented that covers all three factors, they can be investigated using the usual test battery plus case-history interviews. A careful and detailed description and history of the "habit" and associated situations sets the stage for the hypnosis by concentrating the child's attention on it. The Rorschach provides an overall survey of the child's ego strength. The TAT also supplies the therapist with guidelines for the use of guided daydreams. The MMPI is also useful for adolescents in the assessment of ego strength, generalization of anxiety, and specificity of the "habit."

In summary, hypnosis can be a very useful technique for treating annoying habits or specific fears of children. Before using this technique, a thorough assessment of the child is necessary to determine the applicability of this treatment and to assist in planning the process.

G.   ASSESSMENT AND GROUP THERAPIES

Of all the variations of group therapy, two forms are most commony used with children: peer groups and conjoint family groups.

For those not familiar with this form of treatment, it should be emphasized that treating children in groups is distinctly different from individual therapy. It has a different purpose and is a different technique. The essential feature of group psychotherapy lies not in the behavior of single individuals within the group but in the *interaction* between individuals and ultimately in the action of these group members as a group. Only the novice gathers together several people and attempts to conduct individual interviews with each person in front of the others. The therapeutic catalyst is the behavior of the group as a whole. In terms of behavior modification, it is the group who administers the rewards and punishments.

Thus, group psychotherapy is concerned with the dynamics of the individual only insofar as the individual's behavior affects others. As with behavior modification of an individual, group psychotherapy is less concerned with causes than with consequences. A group may be initially sympathetic toward a member's problems and exchange support. Yet, after awhile, most groups become impatient with a member's explanations and excuses and demand change. Group therapy thus puts stress on the social functioning of the individual's ego. A group may accept and even support disability in other ego functions, but not in social behavior.

The general criteria for group psychotherapy may be summarized as follows.

1.   The child's disturbance should in some way involve his/her social functioning. At first glance, this might seem true of every case. However, the degree of such social involvement does vary considerably. A large majority of children do manifest their disturbances in inadequate social relationships. Yet, some disturbed children are quite adept socially, so that their difficulties are not so obvious to others. Eventually, other children in a group may feel manipulated by or shown up by the child whose social development is hypertrophic, but such a child may not contribute much to a group of peers. Another type of child who may not overtly demonstrate social inadequacy is the one who suffers internally. She/he may not reach out to others, and thus she/he may be a relatively passive, withdrawn, or silent group member. Such a child also may subsequently be drawn out by a group but contribute little initially.

2.   The child should be susceptible to social pressure. Again, this criterion may appear to be universal, but there are also variations in the degree to which children do respond to groups. Some children are overwhelmed with anxiety in the presence of others. They are so easily embarrassed that they become mute. Other children have learned to inure themselves to group pressures. They shrug off what people say. At both extremes of this continuum of social involvement, children can ultimately be drawn into groups. The shy, embarrassed child can be made to feel accepted and the

hard-shelled child can be opened up. Yet, such children do not make it easy to form a cohesive group.

3. The type of social pressure—the "contingent stimuli" (Greenspoon and Gersten,1967)—should be appropriate to the child's needs. The group in which the child is to be placed should attract him/her and stimulate him/her to become involved. It is possible to bring together a miscellanous set of chldren, but if they have little in common or too many antagonisms, they may never form a cohesive group. It is much more difficult to form and maintain a children's group than an adult group. The dropout rate is especially high in outpatient adolescent groups. Even in groups on a hospital ward where attendance is nearly compulsory, adolescent or younger children find ways of escaping the group meetings. Thus, it becomes important to select group members who are halfway congenial, who have some problems in common, and who possibly will stimulate one another. However, it is also possible to have a group that is too homogenous. If all members are depressed or all "act out," the group may fail to congeal or become so disruptive that no therapeutic work can be carried on. It is possible to mix neurotic and psychotic children in the same group. However, one neurotic child in a group of psychotic children may become more disturbed by the raw outpouring of psychotic feelings.

In peer groups, a relatively narrow age range is usually the rule, since the 16-year-old has little in common with the 12-year-old and vice versa. However, the age range may depend as much on mental, social, and emotional maturation as on chronological age. A socially precocious 14-year-old may fit better into a group averaging age 16 than in one averaging 14. However, prepubescent children do not belong in adolescent groups. Sexually mixed groups of any age create special problems. Latency children and even junior high-school children are much more compatible and open if grouped with the same sex. As was discussed at length in previous chapters, the latency-age child is avoiding sexual stimulation. Having mixed groups of boys and girls of high-school age is somewhat more feasible, but embarrassment runs high even at this age.

If group therapy is to be the treatment of choice, then the child should be able to enter into peer relationships to at least a slight degree. The child who remains ensconced entirely in his/her family may need peer relationship, but he/she may be unable to engage in them and thus be rejected by his peers. Such a child may need some individual or family group therapy before being put in a group. Often, the parents are also treated in a concurrent group. However, the selection of the group should be based on the characteristics of the children, not of the parents. Some or all of the children in a group may also be in some form of individual therapy. This variable may have to be taken into account in forming the group. The child who has little or no prior therapeutic experience may seem naive to those who have "graduated" from individual therapy. Those in individual therapy may retreat from the group, or they may use the group to act out their transference from the individual treatment. Although such differences in therapeutic experience may be worked through in the group sessions, it is usually wiser to avoid such extraneous problems by selecting group members with roughly equal experience. For example, it is not wise to do a favor for a colleague and accept one of his/her long-term patients into an inexperienced group. Of course, the amount of time a child has spent in individual treatment is not in itself a reliable indication of her/his level of ego development. In the long run, groups should be equated on their level of ego development rather than on the basis of therapeutic experience, age, or even diagnosis.

In assessing a child for whom peer-group therapy is considered, data collection should thus include information regarding his/her social functioning. In interviews with the child and with his/her parents, the assessor should be sure to inquire about his/her behavior with peers. For example, does he/she have friends? How old are they? Are they mostly acquaintances or are some close friends? How much time does he/she spend with them? What do they do together? Does he/she confide in them, telling them things he/she would not reveal to adults? Even if he/she has no close confidantes among his/her peers, does he/she try to conform to peer standards and join in the groups at school or in the neighborhood? If the child is relatively socially isolated, is this by choice, or is he/she kept out of peer groups by his/her mother or by the fact that no schoolmates or children of the same age live in the neighborhood? Some very lonely and isolated children desire peer-group contacts even though they have little opportunity to engage in group activities.

Case 110

Kurt R, age 9, was most obstreperous at school, playing the clown and disrupting the class. Although the children laughed at him, they had little to do with him. He neglected his schoolwork and was sullen and impudent to the teacher. The teacher, however, was sympathetic, noting that Kurt was rejected by other children. When the parents were called to the school they were most embarrassed. The teacher tried to convince Mr. R that whipping Kurt was not likely to be effective and that the R's should seek psychological consultation.

The R's complied with the teacher's advice, but it was evident that they had little faith in psychology. Both spoke with heavy European accents and began the interview by stating that they deplored the way Americans rear children—the "lack of discipline" and "lack of respect" for authority. Yet, they admitted that Kurt behaved at home much as he did in the classroom. He was impudent to his father, called him names, made fun of his accent and foreign ideas and habits. Although Mr. R roared and made threats, he found himself impotent to carry out any form of discipline. Kurt was less hostile toward his mother,

merely ignoring her plaintive urgings. Both parents were quite passive and dependent people. Neither had married until relatively late in life. Mr. R was 55, a short, plump, balding man who tried to earn a living as a cantor. He had fled Vienna when Hitler came into power. Prior to his emigration to the United States at age 30, he had lived with his family and earned a living as a concert singer. After coming to the United States, he was often unemployed since he refused to do anything but sing and would not sing popular music. Mrs. R, also a refugee from the last Nazi regime, had remained with her famly until age 35, when the marriage to Mr. R was "arranged." At home, the R's spoke only German and Kurt also had a German accent when he first started school. Sometimes when excited at school, he would burst out with German expletives, for which he was teased by his schoolmates. He often threw out the school lunch his mother packed for him—"'cause it was only old black bread and cheese!" Despite Kurt's behavior at home, it was evident that these aging parents spoiled their only son and could not really bear to discipline him.

In the initial interview, Kurt was very careful not to criticize his parents in any way. "My parents are nice," he reported, evasively. He was much more open in his criticism of the teacher, but he watered down his remarks by apologizing, "I should not say so, but. . . ." He excused his lack of friends by saying that his parents "didn't care for the type of children" who lived in the neighborhood, but he denied that he disagreed with their judgments. He admitted that he did often play with one boy who lived nearby, whom his parents criticized but tolerated. Asked what he and his friend did together, he replied, "Oh, nothing much—just mess around and stuff—I like to go to his house 'cause they have such good stuff to eat." However, Kurt denied that the food his friend had was any better than his at his own home—"Just different, you know." He did explain, "We have Jewish food at home. I like it but it's fun to have something different sometimes.'' Later, he revealed that his friend's family were also Jewish but were not recent immigrants. He added that he and his "buddy" like to talk "about stuff." Asked for an example, he shrugged and blushed, "Just kid stuff, you know!" He admitted that he would like to have more friends but was quick to blame his schoolmates for forming "cliques." "They're a bunch of snobs and kooks."

Kurt possessed above-average intelligence—IQ, 115. His Rorschach responses showed him to be more sensitive to environmental stimuli than most latency boys (3 of his 14 responses contained references to the texture of the blot), but his actual involvement was rather restricted (2 FC's). His psychogram was introversive (M:C = 3:1). There were no indications on these Rorschach responses of any gross perceptual difficulty (F+ = 70%). Nor were there indications of excessive anxiety or depression. Kurt's TAT stories consisted of one fantasy after another in which "secret agents" succeeded in confusing and disrupting tyrannical authorities or in which the hero escaped punishment for some misdemeanor. For example, to Card 6BM, Kurt responded, "His grandmother caught him stealing some food from the icebox—but she probably won't do anything if he apologizes. So he apologizes. (Why did he steal?) Just for the fun of it. It wasn't serious or anything. (What will happen?) Oh, nothing. He just won't get caught next time, that's all''—and Kurt laughed.

Kurt eagerly accepted the invitation to join a male peer group that was just starting. Initially, he was the leader in disrupting the group members, all of whom had difficulty in sitting still and talking. However, the group soon tired of his giggling, his faces, and his other antics, and they told him in no uncertain terms to "cool it." However, they were most sympathetic when he talked about his parents and home life. The group quickly saw through his difficulty and told him directly, "You just act up because you can't take it at home."

His parents, who attended a parent group, were much more silent and withdrawn. Finally, Mr. R grew irritated and shouted at another group member who kept pestering him and announced that she was determined to "open him up." In his anger, he revealed his feelings about "loud Americans who spoil their children." Accusations swung back and forth but quieted down when Mrs R, near tears, confessed that she was having as much trouble with Kurt as other mothers had mentioned they had with their children. Thereafter, the group was much more sympathetic and full of advice. In fact, they were most sympathetic as the R's story came out. Mr. R seemed to remain unmoved, but Mrs. R seemed a bit more insightful as the parents compared notes. "Perhaps we have been mistaken and did not know what Kurt needed," she pleaded with her husband. Gradually, Mr. R decided that Kurt did need more play with his peers. He also was determined that Kurt "respect" him. With great reluctance, he accompanied Kurt to the Boy Scouts. He admitted that he was ignorant of baseball and embarrassed by Kurt's knowledge of American sports. However, he had been an expert skier and soccer player. He organized a soccer team among the Scouts, took Kurt to the professional games and taught him to ski. He bought Kurt a set of drums (something Kurt had yearned for), and taught him rhythm, revealing that he had once played drums in a band. Kurt responded by dropping his disdain and insults, and Mr. R remarked ironically, "The trouble with being a father is that I enjoy it!"

H.   ASSESSMENT OF FAMILIES

The concept of conjoint family therapy gained its impetus in the 1950s as an outgrowth of research on the family structure of young-adult schizophrenics (Ackerman, 1958; Jackson and Weakland, 1961). Because the group in conjoint family therapy is a natural group with a historically determined structure with affective bonds, attitudes, and interests that have developed prior to treatment—in contrast to the peer groups who are strangers both before and after treatment—authorities on conjoint family therapy (Bell, 1961; Framo, 1965; Wynne, 1965) insist that it is quite distinct from peer-group treatment. Like other group therapies, it focuses on the interactions between the group members rather than on the intrapsychic conflicts of the individual. The fact that these interactions, or transactions, have been built up prior to the onset of therapy, and that such transactions, hopefully revised, will continue in the family group thereafter does create a far different setting than in other kinds of groups. Nevertheless, most of the criteria for peer-group treatment listed before also apply to family groups.

In refreshing contrast to most advocates of a particular form of therapy, Wynne (1965, p. 290), in a chapter entitled "Some Indications and Contraindications for Exploratory Family Therapy," begins as follows:

I approach this problem with an investigative spirit, not with the intent of making doctrinaire pronouncements or promulgating an ideological, family therapy party line. Let me state at the outset that I do not regard family therapy as a psychiatric panacea, but as a valuable addition to our psychiatric repertory. On the one hand, I consider family therapy as the treatment of choice which I shall attempt to specify. On the other hand, certain limitations, some of which are intrinsic to family therapy and others of which are imposed are imposed by external, practical considerations, restrict the range of problems for which this treatment approach is appropriate.

Subsequently, Wynne states as "a general indication for . . . family therapy: . . . the clarification and resolution of any structured intrafamilial relationship difficulty." As do other writers on this topic, Wynne advocates the use of another therapy for the intrapsychic problems of the individual—usually a psychodynamic approach, since most writers on conjoint family therapy base their treatment on psychoanalytic theory. In fact, the use of conjoint family treatment in conjunction with individual psychodynamic treatment and the indications and contraindications for such combinations form an important section of Wynne's article. Conjoint family therapy is viewed by Boszormenyi-Nagy and Framo (1965) as an extention of psychoanalysis, in which the patient's interactions with his/her family, usually reported in individual therapy by the patient from his/her memories, are actually demonstrated and resolved in vivo by treating the family rather than merely the "identified patient." In fact, all authorities agree that it is the family and not any individual member that is disturbed and that is the object of treatment.

As a very specific form of group therapy, conjoint family therapy requires the following conditions.

1. The child's disturbance should be centered in a difficulty within a structured family relationship. As was pointed out in a discussion of some of the criteria for other therapies, this criterion seems applicable to nearly all children's problems. From the theoretical considerations of Section 1 to be considered later, it is obvious that I thoroughly agree with the proponents of conjoint family therapy that wherever a child lives in a family setting, the interactions and attitudes of the family toward the child and of the child toward his family, and in a third dimension (as Framo, 1965, indicates), the total pattern of family interaction and values constitute a major determinant of the degree and nature of the children's disturbances—including intrapsychic physiological disturbances. Nevertheless, the fact that there are other determinants does have to be taken into account. Obviously, a physiological disease or trauma requires medical attention, even though family counseling may well be in order just to maintain a medical regime. Learning problems, extrafamilial problems, developmental crisis, body image, and other identity problems, for example, all may require other therapeutic considerations in addition to the family interaction pattern.

Most important is the distinction made by the advocates of family therapy themselves, that is, between family interaction difficulties and intrapsychic conflicts. Certainly in most instances, intrapsychic conflicts are associated with family conflicts; often they are an internalization of the family interaction patterns, albeit distorted and distilled. Yet, many family interaction difficulties also may be viewed as arising from the internalized, intrapsychic conflicts of one or more members of a family, as has been long recognized in the old concept of *folie à deux*. This distinction between intrapsychic and intrapersonal familial disturbance is in fact usually a matter of degree. In most childhood problems, there is both family disturbance and an intrapsychic conflict within the child. The conjoint family therapists rightly do not regard the family disturbance as necessarily the cause of the child's intrapsychic conflicts, but rather use the disturbance within the family as a focal point for the treatment. Assessment for this criterion thus should be centered about the questions: *To what degree is the family interaction pattern disturbed? And, to what extent and in what ways do these family interaction patterns play a part in the child's internal conflicts?*

2.   The child should be susceptible to family pressures and respond to family interaction patterns. Again, this may seem to be a universal condition. However, on even slight reflection, one may remember that many children today, especially adolescents for whom this treatment is particularly designed, are often influenced as much by their peers and other extrafamilial stresses as they are by their parents. As was pointed out before, adolescents are very much a part of Reissman's "lonely crowd" (Reissman et al., 1950), perhaps even more so than their parents. Family ties and influences appear to be decreasing in strength with each generation. Although the proponents of conjoint family therapy do recognize that the kinship or family clan no longer exists in most cases, they do not seem to realize that the nuclear family also may be changing, and that the

family's influence on the adolescent is much different than in the immediately preceding generations. Assessment should thus take into account the strength and influence of the family structure in question. The fact that an adolescent spends a great deal of his/her time outside the family or even that he/she no longer has strong affective and cognitive ties with his/her family may not necessarily indicate a disturbance of family interactions. In the rapid currents of today's society, social and emotional separations from the family occur much earlier than in prior generations. Such separations may disrupt the family but do no necessarily indicate that the family interaction patterns were disturbed prior to this separation. Some form of conjoint family therapy may aid in easing this separation, but it seems unreasonable to expect this or any therapy to stem a social tide.

3.   In most instances, the social structure of the family should (if revised by treatment) serve the needs of the child. Dependent as the child is on the family, it is this group to which she/he turns for nearly all her/his needs. However, as was pointed out in the preceding paragraphs, as the child enters adolescence, an increasing amount of need gratifications are obtained from extrafamilial sources. In fact, it is essential for the adolescent's development into an independent adult that he/she learn to seek need gratification on his/her own, outside of his/her childhood family. Again, conjoint family therapy may be needed to ease this separation—particularly in very tight-knit families—but the goal of this therapy should be to foster the eventual separation, not to maintain the nuclear childhood family structure.

Because much of the impetus for conjoint family therapy originated in the treatment of young adult schizophrenics and with the separation problems of adolescence, there is little discussion of the use of this treatment with families in which the children are pubescent or prepubescent. In fact, writers on this therapy question whether such younger family members should be included in the group. However, since younger children are far more dependent on their families and thus far more under their influence than older adolescents, this would seem much more applicable to their families. Perhaps the emphasis is purely verbal treatment, utilizing psychoanalytic generalizations, and the like is the reason doubts are raised about treating younger children in family groups. However, I and several of my students and colleagues have had fairly successful experiences using conjoint family treatment with younger children. In fact, one such family included an 11-month-old baby, whose presence and activities were very much a part of the family interactions and of the problems of the "identified" patient (age 8). It was the birth of this baby that disrupted the previously precarious balance of family interactions, a disruption that was manifested in the behavior of the 8-year-old brother, who had theretofore been the baby in the family, much to the disgust of his father and sister and the not-too-secret delight of his mother.

Wynne (1965) lists four types of family patterns to which conjoint therapy is particularly applicable. They are: (1) "adolescent separation problems"; (2) "the trading of dissociations," that is, a mutual and interlocking set of projections of blame; (3) "collective cognitive chaos and erratic distancing"—in essence, a "schizophrenic" family; and (4) "amorphous communication" or a pattern of incomplete and vaguely implicit transactions. In treating families with preadolescent children, one might add at least two further categories (that are not mutually exclusive): (5) the adulto-morphic family wherein all members of the family are expected to conduct transactions on an adult level, with little or no allowance for normal preadolescent communication; and (6) the infantilizing family, wherein all members of the family expect to be treated as children.

Despite his laudable intentions, Wynne is much less specific regarding the contraindications for conjoint family therapy. He lists

among "other factors affecting the indications": (1) "the family constellation available for therapy," that is, the question of precisely who constitutes the family group and who should be included in the treatment. He also discusses the important topic of the relative motivation of the various members of the family; (2) "phase of the psychotherapeutic process," that is, in regard to other aspects of psychoanalytic treatment of individual family members; and (3) "kind of available therapies" in which he discusses the behavior of the therapist. The most important contraindication, according to Wynne, is the inability of the therapist to control the "countertransference."

In addition to these considerations, there are some family patterns and some family patterns that are not easily approachable by conjoint family therapy and for which family therapy may actually be contraindicated. First, as to what Wynne calls the family constellation available for therapy, there are many children whose disturbances arise chiefly from the lack of a definite family constellation. Most common of these are the children of divorced and remarried parents, who float between two antagonistic households and are unwelcome reminders or ghosts of the prior marriage for both of the original parents. This pattern is illustrated in the following case.

CASE 111

Marie, age 8, constantly demanded attention and rejected adult controls both at home and at school. She was born a year before her parents separated in what her mother openly admitted was an effort to force her husband to stay in the marriage. Thereafter, the mother withdrew from Marie, leaving her care to various maids and governesses and attempting to buy the child off with a constant flow of expensive presents and clothes. Even after seven years of psychoanalysis, the mother remained a depressed and schizoid woman. Marie's father was also depressed and had little to do with this child and her sibs for the next five years, until he remarried. At the time treatment began, Marie spent three days and four nights with her father, stepmother, and their children and four days and three nights with her mother and adolescent sibs. Twice a week, one parent delivered her to the therapist and the opposite parent retrieved her. The fact that the therapist's playroom was in effect a passageway between the two households was used to assist Marie in attempting to handle the very depressing fact that she had no real home. Neither parent could be involved in this treatment. Over a can of hot chicken soup, which Marie purchased each therapy session from a food dispenser, she worked through the despair, anger, and depression of her family situation. At first, she played out a fantasied reunion of the parents, with fits of rage at the therapist when this was identified as fantasy. Then she spent months destroying and reviving each parent in play. She demanded the therapist become a parent and, failing in this fantasy, destroyed and revived him. Finally but gradually she came to accept the reality of her separation; she sought the counsel and comfort of her young-adult sister, who accepted her recognition that the mother was depressed. In her own fashion, Marie sought to comfort her mother and received some comfort in return. At the same time, Marie began to play the role of oldest child in her father's family, as a helpmate to her stepmother in the care of the younger step-sibs, and thus found rewards from her stepmother and her father. At this time, her school problems disappeared and her academic achievement rose to a superior level. Despite her three years' diet of chicken soup, Marie lost her excess weight and was developing into a lovely and charming prepubescent girl when treatment was discontinued.

Perhaps Marie's father and stepmother could have been involved in a conjoint family therapy, but Marie's mother would certainly have protested as she had adamantly refused to permit the father to obtain custody of Marie, and Marie's father was content with the division of the child between two households. The mother's analyst, who was consulted, advised that she was in no condition to be involved in any other kind of treatment at that time, although periodic conferences were held with the mother.

In addition to considering the social membership of the family, one must assess its affective and conative structure. It is not enough to assume that consanguinal ties constitute an affective bond that motivates the members of a family. Especially in disturbed families, the nature of this bond needs close examination and observation. Some families are bound together by affection, others by a mutual dependency, still others by almost open erotic ties, by a common need achievement or need aggression, or even by mutual hatreds. Perhaps all of these are elements in most family ties, but the degree and nature of these bonds should be assessed. Conjoint family therapy may well be the treatment of choice when these family ties are particularly ambivalent. As the experts on family therapy point out, an intense and prolonged marital dissension between the parents often underlies the disturbed behavior of the child. If the marriage does rest on the child's disturbance, or if having attention focused on the child masks the marital tension, then it may be very difficult to treat the child separately from the family. Every time the child improves, such parents do something consciously or unconsciously to reinstate the child's disturbance. A careful and thorough assessment often serves to warn the therapist of such an eventuality.

In my experience, there is one type of family bond or dynamics where conjoint therapy seems contraindicated, that is, when the family seems held together primarily by a sadomasochistic relationship; as Dr. Walter Raine* states it: "when the hostility in the family is highly eroticized." In such families, each member is a whipping boy for

*Personal communication.

the other, and the passions aroused in these mutual beatings, both physical and verbal, are tinged with sexual arousal. In such marital battles, each marital partner may, for example, accuse the other of impotency. Each may fight to obtain demonstrations of affection from the child. Often the battles are focused on the adolescent's sexual behavior, real or imagined, and each parent may vicariously live out their sexual frustrations through the child's behavior. Such families use conjoint therapy as another battleground, often attempting to involve the therapist or focus their erotic projections onto her/him. Usually this sadomasochistic relationship is the very basis of the marriage. In such instances, it is often better to try to get the parents to permit the placement of the child outside the home, in a foster home or a residential treatment center. Individual treatment of the child, if she/he remains with her/his parents, is usually constantly sabotaged by the parents. The chief exception is when the adolescent is nearly ready to leave home. If the adolescent can recognize the nature of the parents' relationship, it may be possible to help her/him recover from depression and to separate from the family's sadomasochism. In such instances, assessment of the child's ego strength is most essential, for if the child's identity has been overwhelmed by the family, it will be very difficult for him/ her to withdraw on her/his own.

CASE 112

The Z family's eroticized hostility was evidenced in the initial session, when Mr. Z tried to rip off Luisa's blouse to show the therapist that she was not wearing a bra. Her mother did not intervene but Luisa kicked her father in the genitals and her brother and younger sister pushed him to the floor, where he sat moaning in pain. Mr. Z, an immigrant Italian restaurant owner, was a voluble, histrionic man, who burst easily into tears or screamed in anger, calling Luisa a "slut" and "whore" because of the way she dressed. Luisa, age 14, a full-breasted

girl with the figure of a 19-year-old, had recently adopted a "punk-rock" dress of leather pants and coat and boots, and dyed half of her chopped-off hair purple and half green. She had promptly been expelled from the all-girl Catholic high school. She had run away from home twice in the past month but returned each time within 24 hours. She denied belonging to any "punk-rock" group, but she had paraded up and down the streets where other "punk-rock" teen-agers gathered.

Mrs. Z was a social worker, a dowdily dressed, harried, graying woman who looked 10 years older than her stated age of 36. However, she, too, was full of anger and—like a district attorney reciting a list of alleged crimes to the court—accused her husband of being a hypocrite because of his numerous and flagrant extramarital affairs. She wept as she revealed that she felt inadequate in his eyes, that she was not "sexy" enough for him, and that he gave her no acknowledgement for her professional activities. She reported that he expected her to be entirely responsible for all the children's behavior as well as the care of the home.

Luisa chimed in to complain that since both parents worked full time, much of the burden of the home had fallen on her shoulders. In fact, Mr. Z often called Luisa his "little mother" or even "my second wife"! Peter, age 12, and Rosa, age 9, fought with one another and with Luisa incessantly. The girls jeered at Peter, calling him a "fag" and giggling about his masturbation, which they said they frequently observed because he did not lock the bathroom door. Peter, red in the face, jumped to his feet, threatening them with his fists, but Mrs. Z intervened. Rosa seemed a shy and sweet-mannered child who looked like she had stepped out of a Renoir painting. Yet she made little remarks that needled her sibs or parents and was quick to recite injuries or to tattle on the misbehavior of others. She suffered from night terrors and frequently spent half the night in her parents' bed. Her father referred to her as "my angel," and her sibs accused him of favoring her.

Unfortunately, no formal assessment of this family was conducted. The therapist gave the excuse that the family presented so many "crises" that there was no opportunity for an assessment. He also argued that the dynamics were so obvious that no assessment was necessary. After three family meetings, Mr. Z adamantly refused to attend. Mrs. Z and the children came to two more sessions, still quarreling, teasing, and complaining. Then Luisa ran away and did not return. Mrs. Z and the other children rejected further treatment. Several months later a Catholic family-service agency contacted the clinic, asking for a summary of the contacts with the Z's. Luisa had been found and was placed in a foster home. Several months later, Mrs. Z returned to the clinic seeking individual treatment. She had separated from her husband but still was quite depressed and angry. Luisa had abandoned her "punk-rock" appearance, seemed adjusted to the foster home, and was attending a public high school without difficulty. All of them avoided contact with Mr. Z.

Most experts on conjoint family therapy agree that a thorough assessment is required. The usual techniques employed to assay ego-strength development in individuals are most helpful. However, the assessment of the individual members does not in itself provide the data needed to comprehend the interaction between members. It is possible to hypothesize about how one personality might interact with another on the basis of two sets of comparable protocols. However, the interactions within a whole family are so complex as to require a computer program—if a computer program could be formulated. The computer analysis of MMPI profiles, now being developed for individual profiles, might well be expanded in the future to allow for such prediction of family interactions. Even so, some tests of these hypothesis would be helpful before conjoint family therapy is instituted.

Considerable thought has been given to methods for assessing these family interaction patterns. Obviously, one of the most direct methods is to conduct one or more conjoint family interviews during the assessment. The case-history material is often gathered in joint interviews with the parents, in any case. If these data are gathered in a conjoint family interview, the exchange between parents and children about events in the family history may be very revealing. Not only may the memories of one member supplement those of another, but the conflicting memories and viewpoints that frequently come to the fore reveal the dissonance in the family. It is a good idea in such conjoint family interviews to involve other siblings or important relatives, in addition to the parents and the identified patient. Such initial involvement sets the stage for identifying the problem as a family interaction, rather than merely as the behavior of the child, and thus it paves the way for conjoint treatment.

Other approaches to assessment of family interactions consist chiefly of involvement of the family in a common task (Hurwitz, Kaplan, and Kaiser, 1962; Elbert, Rosman, Minuchin, and Guerney, 1964). The latter authors also devised a method for having the family construct a common fantasy, comparable to the TAT. Levy and Epstein (1964) designed a method for a family Rorschach in which family decisions were required as to the possible interpretations of the inkblots. The use of Leary's (1957) Interpersonal Check List has already been mentioned. Particularly informative in the study of interaction patterns are the description each family member makes of each of the others on the ICL. In some instances, a family member may be assigned different roles by each member of the family, and in other cases a family member may be assigned a common role by all. Whether the family member accepts these roles may be assessed from his/her description of himself/herself on the ICL.

One of the problems commonly discussed by authorities on conjoint family treatment is the inclusion of "well" siblings. The question of how one child can develop schizophrenia while others do not appear to be disturbed has plagued those who maintain that this and similar patterns of behavioral disturbance arise from family interactions. Some authorities maintain, with some evidence, that the other siblings do manifest considerable disturbance, even though no immediate complaint is made about their behavior. In other instances, siblings do seem to escape with only mild disturbances at most. The practical import of this question is that very often neither the parents nor these siblings see any reason that anyone other than the identified patient should be included in the assessment. In settings where conjoint family therapy is employed, parents should be advised that assessment of all family members is routine. Furthermore, they may be informed that assessment of the parents and other siblings is necessary to understand the disturbances of the identified patient.

CASE 113

In discussing her 11-year-old daughter, Betsy, Mrs. S complained angrily that Betsy gave her "no satisfaction whatever. . . . She is always demanding, demanding, demanding, and never gives up," said Mrs. S wearily. For example, if she bought something for Betsy's sister, Adele, age 14, then Betsy would pout and whine endlessly unless she too was allowed a purchase. Every gift Betsy received was compared jealously with something Adele received—even though months had intervened. Betsy was resistant to any demands made on her. Mrs. S had to "nag" continuously to get Betsy to make her bed, take a bath, brush her teeth, and she was so slow in completing any household chores that Mrs. S had given up assigning them to her. Adele, however, was most cooperative. The biggest squabble between Betsy and her mother was over Betsy's schoolwork and behavior in the classroom. Betsy was barely making passing grades, yet she would claim that she had no homework. Subsequently Mrs. S would discover that Betsy was two weeks or more behind in her assignments. Betsy's behavior in the classroom was very similar to that at home. She was frequently at the teacher's desk for further help, even though the teacher had thought she had explained the work thoroughly moments before. She constantly complained about the behavior of other students, how they bothered her, got her in trouble, or tried to cheat. She talked out of turn constantly. If reprimanded, she burst into tears, denying her behavior and accusing other children, and claiming the teacher was unfair and biased against her. Several times after such an outburst, Betsy rushed from the classroom and telephoned her mother, who would panic at Betsy's incoherent tearful voice and come running to the school. Mrs. S was embarrassed by these disturbances at school and would blame variously Betsy, the teacher, the other children, and the educational system. Most of the children at school and in the neighborhood seemed to dislike Betsy and teased her unmercifully. Much larger than her peers, Betsy was known as "Betsy the Buffalo" but even the boys respected her strength. She responded in kind, often with socially unacceptable language, tattling on the others, or kicking, jabbing, and pummeling them.

Mrs. S also complained about the strain of the routine in her home. Although she usually had household help, no domestic remained in her employ for more than a few months. Everything about the home seemed burdensome to her. The S's lived several miles from the school and shopping area; much of Mrs. S's time was consumed in driving the girls to and from different schools, music lessons, and other errands. Often she was exhausted or ill. An extremely obese woman, she had had several operations for varicose veins and had been advised that she might develop heart trouble. But when she tried to rest, Betsy would arouse her with some request or complaint, or the girls would begin to fight. All of these problems had been present for many years but had come to a climax when the school authorities notified Mrs. S that Betsy might be held back a grade.

Mr. S had said little during this initial interview and, when asked to comment, he remarked that Betsy's insistence on buying things also bothered him and that he did not see why the girls always compared presents and clothes. "I can't afford this constant buying. I tell them they just have to be content with what they have." "You just don't know how much it costs to run a house or what girls need," Mrs. S retorted. She then complained that her husband seldom gave her any help in disciplining Betsy except when she pressured him or when he lost his temper. Mrs. S, now aroused, replied that she would have much less trouble with the girls if she was more organized and budgeted her time and money more effectively. Mrs. S glared at him and pouted, but did not pursue the topic, nor did Mr. S elaborate at that time.

Neither parent mentioned the reason for which Betsy's pediatrician had referred them for psychological consultation, that is, her extreme obesity. When asked about Betsy's weight problem, each parent glanced at the other. Both of them were also obese. "I guess it's a family problem," Mr. S sighed. Mrs. S quickly explained that she had a "glandular problem," but Mr. S interrupted, "No! We're just fat. There's no physical problem. Our doctor has told us that many times." Again Mrs. S pouted angrily, "I've tried to diet but no one else tries." Only Adele had succeeded in reducing to within normal limits.

When asked what she had done to discipline Betsy, Mrs. S replied, "Everything!" She had shouted and screamed and nagged; she had restricted Betsy from such pleasures as TV or shut her in her room; she had promised rewards if Betsy obeyed, but Betsy seldom was able to please Mrs. S; she had even persuaded Mr. S to whip Betsy. All to no avail.

Betsy looked and acted very much like her mother. Her voice was equally shrill and she also frequently pouted, bit her lip, and gestured with her fist as she raged on about the injustices she endured at home and at school. Her chief complaints were that no one payed any attention to her needs or her feelings and that everyone expected too much of her. She regarded Adele as her chief enemy, as Adele was favored by "everyone." The present Adele received last year for her birthday was much nicer and more expensive than the one Betsy had received recently. Moreover, she did not really get what she wanted even though she had clearly specified it. Adele did not do her share of the work and Betsy was expected to do "everything." Her mother "always" screamed at her, but "never" at Adele. Her father whipped her "with a big belt" but "never touched" Adele. Adele "got away with everything," and Betsy always was blamed. The teachers at school blamed Betsy for "everything," and Betsy cited in detail incident after incident in which others started trouble but she was caught. She was bored with class assignments, "baby work" she called them—or they were too hard and the teacher never explained. Her mother took the teacher's side. The kids at school were all mean.

Since Betsy was so unsuccessful with her schoolwork, it was decided to assay her intellectual development with the WISC. Betsy made a sour face when the test was introduced and was resistant throughout. "That's too hard!" she would complain, or "How should I know!" With praise and encouragement, she often succeeded even when she had initially rejected a task. Her Total IQ was 113, with a Verbal IQ of 115 and a Performance IQ of 110. She achieved scale scores of 12 on Similarities, Vocabulary, and Block Design, indicating that her reasoning and verbalization were more than adequate. Her top score of 16 on the Picture Arrangement showed her acute perception of the social scene. In contrast, several of her responses to the Comprehension subtest were self-centered. She sputtered over the Arithmetic questions, asking for pencil and paper and to have the questions repeated, then claimed that she never had problems like that in school. She dawdled over the Digit Symbol subtest, biting her pencil and looking up at the examiner as if expecting some kind of help.

Similarly, on the Rorschach, she protested in helpless fashion that she could not tell what the blot was supposed to be or criticized the uneveness or incompleteness: Card I, "It couldn't be a butterfly, 'cause it's got those holes . . . I don't know . . . I can't tell." Most of her responses were vague and stereotyped reactions to the whole blot. She was irritated at having to explain her responses in the inquiry, and it was difficult to ascertain exactly what determinants she was using in several instances. She saw no human figures, and of the 5 animal responses, there were 2 that she indicated might be moving or at least alive. However, she was quite responsive to the color: 2 *FC* and 2 *CF*. Four of her 14 responses dealt with food: Card VII, "fried chicken," and Card VIII, "a banana split." This pattern of responses indicated that Betsy felt helpless and resentful when faced with making decisions on her own, that she had not as yet begun to internalize concepts upon which to make such judgments, and that she remained very dependent emotionally on others.

Betsy found the TAT even more difficult. She described the cards, sometimes attributing some action or reactions to the characters but was seldom able to hazard a guess about the preceding events or the outcome. She rejected several of the pictures outright. After six attempts at storytelling, she was given the MAPS as a substitute, but her reaction was the same. Her first MAPS story did seem significant: In the living-room scene, she placed a maternal figure and two girls, all rushing to the door to meet the male figure carrying a present. "They want to see who it is for," she explained, but could not decide who did receive the present.

Betsy's feelings of being blamed and persecuted, her desires for retaliation, and her unwillingness to commit herself or take independent action all might be labeled "paranoia" if she had been an adult. However, it did appear that her mother fed Betsy's sense of being persecuted and, even more, that Betsy used her "paranoid" behavior as a means of manipulating her environment. Because Betsy did appear so dependent on her environment and because so many of Mrs. S's complaints involved family interactions, it was decided to continue the assessment with three family interviews, to explore the possibility of conjoint family therapy. It was carefully explained to Betsy and her parents that these meetings were a part of the assessment, that is, to understand more clearly the family interactions, and that Adele was to be included. However, Adele did not appear at the first session. Mrs. S had excused her so that she could attend a neighbor child's birthday party. Betsy immediately accused her mother of favoritism, pointing out that she also had been invited to the party. Mrs. S tried to calm her, saying that this meeting was to help *her*, not Adele, and that her father had taken time off from his business just because of her. "You hate me! You both hate me!" Betsy screamed. "That's why you brought me here. You think I'm crazy." Mrs. S shrugged and looked helplessly at the psychologist. Mr. S then attempted to reason with Betsy, assuring her that their concern for her indicated their love. Betsy then buried her head in her father's lap, sobbing loudly. Now Mr. S looked helpless. Asked how he felt about Betsy's feelings, Mr. S was puzzled. "I don't know how she can say we hate her. She gets everything she wants!" Betsy sat bolt upright and told him, "You didn't get the bike I wanted, and you promised!" "But you have a bike—two bikes," Mr. S responded. "But not the one I wanted," Betsy sniffled. The hour continued much in the same vein, with Betsy complaining and the parents defending themselves. Neither parent seemed able to face Betsy with their complaints.

Adele appeared at the next session. Her face was tear stained and clouded with anger. The meeting began in silence, broken by the psychologist's inquire into Adele's feelings about coming to this session. Mr. S chuckled, "She's playing the martyr." "She's a hell cat!" snapped Mrs. S. This remark brought forth an anguished scream from Adele: "You think you're so damn smart! Well! *I* don't have to come here. *I'm* not the one who needs to be psyched out. It's *her!* She's the one who's failing at school. She's the one who causes all the trouble. I *hate* her!" Betsy stuck out her tongue, kicked Adele in the knee, and snuggled up to her father. Adele reached to grab Betsy, but her mother intervened. "You see! You see!" Mrs. S exclaimed, "That's what I have to put up with all the time!" Adele continued to attack Betsy verbally, repeating many of the complaints that Mrs. S had voiced in the initial interview. Betsy continued to ignore her, looking appealingly at her father. However, when Adele mentioned Betsy's behavior at school and her lack of friends, Betsy retorted, "That's none of your business!" and began to cry. Mrs. S scolded Adele, who continued, "I've got to be known as *her* sister!" and related more incidents at school in which Betsy allegedly attacked other children. Mrs. S tried to change the topic, saying, "We're here to talk about the family. Betsy's problems at school are a different thing. We can't all be smarties like you." "No they aren't!" Adele argued. "She behaves at school just like she does at home. Everything has to go her way or she acts like a baby and screams."

In the last session, Adele quickly sat herself between her father and mother, leaving Betsy to sit between her mother and the psychologist. Betsy began to demand "her chair." This time it was Mr. S who told her to "Shut up! I'm tired of your fighting—both of you!" "But you and mother fight all the time," Adele retorted. "That's none of your business, Miss Smarty," her mother responded. "You do! You do!" chimed in Betsy. Mrs. S glared at her husband who shifted uneasily in his chair. "She wanted to buy a new sofa." Adele went on, pointing at her mother, "And he wouldn't let her. He's such a tightwad." Mr. S then repeated his demand that Mrs. S stick to his budget before he would allow her to incur further debts. Mrs. S retorted that he was a poor businessman and that the reason the girls felt neglected was that she had to spend so much time at this office going over his accounts, trying to collect from his debtors. While the parents quarreled, the girls winked at each other, giggled, and yawned. Mrs. S suddenly noticed Betsy's derision and slapped her across the face. Both Betsy and her mother began to sob. Mr. S mopped his brow, and Adele smiled sweetly.

Sometimes, even after sessions similar to the preceding, it is difficult to convince a family that the problem lies in their interactions rather than in the behavior of the identified patient. If television equipment is available, a family can often be helped to recognize the processes of their interaction when the videotape of such sessions is played back to them. In the case of the S family, the psychologist pointed out that all family members played a "game of accusation," and seldom communicated their feelings or responded to the feelings of others. Whether the S's understood or accepted this interpretation, they did seem to find some relief from these meetings and accepted the psychologist's offer to continue.

Although there were positive indications that conjoint family therapy might be the treatment of choice in this case, the decision was not clear cut. It might have been wiser, for example, to begin with a program of behavior modification in the hopes of retraining Betsy and thus easing some of the intensity of the family disruptions. However, Mrs. S appeared so overwrought and infantile herself that it seemed doubtful that she could carry out a reinforcement program in the home. Moreover, it did seem necessary to begin by relieving some of the emotional overtones before such a behavior modification could be instituted. The possibility of treating the parents separately and of individual treatment of Betsy was also considered, but it did not seem that the parents would accept the role of being patients for they continued to regard Betsy as the problem. As might be expected from the foregoing, the course of family treatment for the S's did not go smoothly. After about four months, the marital dissension was so open and so intense that the parents were treated separately for a brief period and Betsy was treated by another therapist. Then the family group was reinstituted. Communication within the family gradually improved, and the parents were then able to conduct a program of behavior modification in the home encompassing both girls. This program was continually discussed in the family sessions.

INDIVIDUALIZED THERAPY—A SUMMARY

In the previous sections of this chapter, the question has been asked: Do the problems and needs of this child fit the goals and criteria of this form of treatment? However, only occasionally do the child's needs correspond to the stated goals and criteria of any one therapeutic approach. There are often as many contraindications as indications. Rather than ask whether the child fits any particular therapeutic mold, it would seem much more reasonable to use the data from the assessment to design an individualized program to fit the needs of the child. In this section, an attempt will be made to outline the ways in which therapy might be so programmed to the child.

To design such individualized treatment requires a careful and thorough assessment and thoughtful planning. Individualized therapy does not consist merely of a random sampling of therapeutic techniques. The design should systematically take into account the following factors.

1. The needs and problems of the child.
2. The basic principles common to all forms of therapy.
3. The variations in techniques needed for the individual needs of the child.
4. The time sequence of the therapy.
5. The economic aspects of the therapy.
6. Some difficulties in implementing a plan for therapy.

1. As was discussed in Chapter 1, the overall need of every child is growth, that is, the development of a unique identity with an ego that is capable of independent need gratification. The raison d'être of any therapy is to promote such growth. Therapy, of course, does not create the urge to grow; this drive is a central aspect of the biological and social nature of the child. Rather, therapy is aimed at eliminating the obstacles and limitations to the child's growth, and thus deals with those specific behavioral stresses and conflicts that impede the child's development.

If therapy is to be planned to meet these impediments, then the first step is a comprehensive assessment. The assessment should not be limited to the questions asked by the referrant, but should explore in depth all ramifications of the child's ego development, and should contain a list of the various problems, that is, the manifest disturbing behaviors. Next, it should specify the different ways in which development is being impeded, the stresses and conflicts that underlie the disturbances. There should follow some reasonable hypotheses about the possible interrelationships of these factors, the dynamics or interacting forces. To plan therapy, an assessment should uncover and delineate the leitmotiv of the child's development, the core patterns of events and conflicts. These dynamics should be stated in terms of the child's stage of development. In particular, the assessment should specify the degree and nature of the child's dependency on others and the process of internalization. The kinds of therapy to be used depend in part on the stage of development of the child's experience balance. The assessment should also contain a summary estimate of the overall ego strength of the child, again in terms of development, for the kinds of therapy and their implementation depend on the ability of the child to absorb and use the treatment.

2. As repeatedly pointed out in the previous sections of this chapter, there are certain aspects of psychotherapy that all forms have in common and that appear to be

fundamental to behavioral change. The therapeutic "couch" need not be a Procrustean bed, but even though it comes in various shapes and sizes and designs, there are some basic elements. Any therapy must include, to some degree and fashion, the following:

(a) *A reflection or recognition of the child's affective states or feelings.* In behavior modification, which focuses on the environment, this recognition consists of the affective elements of the behavior of others in the environment and the affective responses of the child.

(b) *The relationships between these affects and the environment.*

(c) *The relationships between these affective states and the internal operations of the child.* In both client-centered therapy and behavior modification, this element of therapy is admittedly underestimated, since it is regarded as a constant.

(d) *The relationship of these affective states to the motivations of the child* and of his/her parents and other authorities. All therapies are concerned with what children are trying to do, learn, achieve, or obtain. Their affective states reflect the frustration of these goals.

(e) *The relationship between the child and the therapist.* In this relationship, the child both acts out the frustrations of everyday life onto the therapist and uses the therapist as a model.

(f) *All therapists repeatedly reinforce* various aspects of the child's behaviors, in a working-through process, sometimes using simple operant rewards and punishments, sometimes using very complex verbal and behavioral situations.

(g) Based chiefly on the therapeutic relationship, *all therapies use the therapeutic situation as a microcosm of everyday life.*

3. To design a therapeutic "couch" to fit the child, it is necessary to specify the variations needed in these basic dimensions of therapy. First, one must determine from the assessment which affective states need to be recognized and reflected. Which affective responses should be stressed? Which, possibly, ignored? Which are closest to the child's consciousness and are thus most available for reflection? Which feelings are hidden at all costs? How much spontaneity and lability are demonstrated? How much does the child limit affective awareness and expression? How sensitive is he/she? All these questions can and should be answered as best as possible if the reflection of affect is to be planned.

Second, the assessment should specify the relationships between these affects and observable environmental stresses. Are these affects a response to the environment, and to what degree? What stimuli set off these affective reactions? What stimuli inhibit them? Third, the assessment should specify the degree to which these affective responses reflect the internal state of the child. What memories, fantasies, impulses, and drives trigger off these feelings? Are these generalized affective states, or are they specific to certain external or internal stimuli? Assessment of these factors is basic to planning the degree to which the external and internal facts of behaviors are to be manipulated. Fourth, the therapist needs to be advised of the specific motivational patterns that drive the child to act and feel as she/he does. Where and why is the child frustrated in meeting need gratifications? How does she/he react to deprivation of needs? With knowledge of these motivational patterns, the therapist can make plans to help the child cope with frustrations and to find effective means of gaining need satisfactions. Usually, the behaviors that require altering are these coping mechanisms. In other instances, the child may be very adept at coping but needs to redirect his/her efforts.

The kinds of interactions that the therapist may initially expect from the child are those that the child currently conducts with other adults. These interactions appear during assessment—directly with the assessor and indirectly in the child's responses to various techniques—and parents may openly or inadvertently mention them. From assessment of these patterns, the assessor may be able to predict how the child may react to the therapist. Finally, on the basis of the assessment, it is possible to plan out the kinds of reinforcements that may need to be used for the child under consideration. One may also estimate the frequency of these reinforcements and how they should be varied. With these variables in mind, the therapeutic situations or microcosms may be selected.

4. In all therapies, the timing and sequence of reinforcements are a major factor. Some learning has to be spaced; some consists of a rapid repetition of rewards and punishments. The question facing all therapists is this one: What is to be done first? Most often, therapy proceeds step by step from one element to the next, in the order listed previously in paragraph 2: The therapist initially reflects the child's feelings, relating them to his/her environment and then to his/her own internal stresses. At the same time, the therapist begins to explore the child's motivations and their relationships to these affects. As these patterns of behavior are demonstrated in the therapy hour, the therapist uses her/his relationship with the child as a reinforcement. These and other reinforcements are repeated to obtain specific modifications of the child's behavior, externally and internally.

However, it is not possible to conduct all therapy in this exact order. Sometimes a program of operant conditioning has to be instituted before the child will respond to anything as, for example, in the case of so-called autistic children. With other children, for example, delinquent adolescents, a direct confrontation of motivations may be necessary, even before very much affect is dealt with. The planning of therapeutic strategy is made possible by the assessment of the child's modes of operation. If all of the child's functioning is overwhelmed by a habit, it may be necessary to begin with a program of hypnosis; thereafter, the motivations underlying the habit may be attacked. If the child has retreated to his/her daydream world, an exploration of that world may have to precede any alteration of his/her social environment, which then might be attacked through some form of group treatment. In other instances, it may be necessary to focus on the family and its interactions if that is where the child is operating, before turning to treatment of internal conflicts and affects.

5. The cost of the treatment in time and money also should be estimated. Unfortunately, there is no known basis for budgeting the cost of treatment. This important facet of treatment planning has yet to be studied. At best, one can make rough estimates of the number of sessions, the number of months over which these sessions will be spread, and the consequent cost in therapist's fees or salary. However, if the other aspects of treatment are systematically planned according to the assessment, and if these plans are effectively implemented, then it may be possible subsequently to determine the time and cost of various plans, much as the construction of buildings or highways are budgeted. The cost in terms of dropouts from treatment should decrease, and planned treatment should motivate more patients to remain. Conversely, the average length of treatment for those who do continue should also decrease. The number of wasted hours and misdirected efforts should be decreased by planning. The overall cost in terms of money spent on treatment may increase, but so should the number of successful outcomes.

6. If therapy is planned to meet the needs of the child, then there are no contraindications in the usual sense of the word. Each separate therapeutic endeavor is designed to be the indicated treatment of choice. However, this is not to deny that planning of therapy, in the present state of scientific development, is often very difficult. Admittedly, the preceding concepts of individually designed treatment are in

many ways quite idealistic and only roughly outlined. Certainly, they are less specific than those proposed by advocates of other set plans, which do not take the variations of the individual into account. The only answer to this objection is that plans are necessary if treatment is not to be a hit-and-miss affiar. Moreover, every expert in any kind of treatment does attempt to plan the therapy to fit the exigencies of the individual child. This proposal is intended to broaden such planning, so that by using the assessment, these individual variations may be made more definite and the opportunities for varying treatment may thus also be widened.

A second objection is that such individually designed treatment is, in effect, no treatment at all, but a potpourri of therapies. It does not seem to allow any one therapeutic technique to be completed. Admittedly, any plan must run its course to be effective. One might hesitate to cut a course of behavior modification short to begin a peer group or drop an individual psychoanalytic treament in midstream to begin a conjoint family treatment. Any planned treatment has to allow for a completion of any component approach. However, these approaches may be considerably shortened by the very fact that more than one is being employed. Very often, any one approach is prolonged by the fact that there are other problems that cannot be handled easily by this single one. Moreover, it is often possible to conduct several therapeutic approaches at once—especially if a program is planned in advance. Reductio ad absurdum, a child might come daily for a therapeutic hour, but instead of receiving psychoanalytic treatment only, she/he might have such treatment only on Mondays; Tuesdays, the child and mother might be engaged in a behavior-modification session; Wednesdays, she/he might meet in a peer group; Thursdays might be parents' day, for separate or joint sessions; and on Fridays, the whole family might gather for exploration of family interactions. Unlikely as it is that any child should need such a mixture of treatments all at once, there is no reason that several approaches might not be used at once or in overlapping sequence. Moreover, through such a multiplex of treatment, the total time needed might well be reduced.

Although some therapists are skilled at several different approaches, it is rare that any one therapist can treat all the problems of a child. When therapists are practicing alone, they usually use the methods that they know best, hoping these will make sufficient changes in the child's behavior. If the child needs other forms of treatment, she/he may be referred elsewhere. Sometimes a child may be receiving a psychoanalytic treatment plus a conjoint family therapy from one therapist, but be attending some school or institute for learning difficulties where some form of operant conditioning is used. Unfortunately, in private practice, these forms of treatment are rarely coordinated. As a result, both in private practice and in public agencies there is an increasing trend toward the use of multiple therapies.

Private practice is now being conducted by groups of several therapists with diverse training. The private clinic attempts to have several kinds of therapy available, or the individual practitioner is associated with several colleagues or a private clinic. The implementation of a plan of therapy calls not only for a variety of therapists, but for continuous administrative supervision and direction. Any such five-ring circus needs some kind of ringmaster. On the hospital ward, where such multiple treatment programs have long been used, the administrative director, usually a psychiatrist, is responsible for coordination of these treatment programs. However, the coordination of the treatment program for the individual child, within this milieu of treatments, is usually delegated to the individual therapist—the person who is working individually with the child. It is she/he who determines, in consultation with the staff, which treatments the child needs.

Outpatient clinics seldom coordinate their treatment programs quite as closely, and more responsibility is placed on the individual therapist. Far too often, even in the best of clinics, one therapist has only a slight idea of what is going on in other treatments of the child. Such miscellaneous, uncoordinated treatment can be avoided if there is careful planning by the whole staff prior to instituting any therapy. The assessment should be available to the whole staff and be used by all in a coordinated plan.

Finally, it may be objected that no plan of treatment can possibly meet the many exigencies that arise. Even if one can detail all the current stresses and conflicts that the child is enduring, it can be predicted with a high level of certainty that other stresses will occur. For example, the therapist may leave the clinic; the groups will change in membership; the child may be expelled from school; one of his/her parents may leave home; the child may fall ill or be injured. Often, these emergencies call for a rapid change in plans. In many instances, such emergencies are visibly imminent, and it may seem that no planning is possible. In fact, some families present one crisis after another for the therapist to solve, playing a long-range game of family uproar, which in effect prevents therapy from even beginning. However, treatment needs to be planned if only to prevent the therapy from being overwhelmed by crises. In a carefully outlined plan of treatment, it is possible to include these events as natural experiences to be worked through in treatment. Such treatment plans have to be flexible enough to allow for emergencies. Moreover, when the treatment is interrupted or disrupted by a crisis, there is no reason why the child's situation should not be reassessed. Case 27 illustrates such a reassessment when the delinquent adolescent suffered a head injury. If a family operates by creating one crisis after another, this fact usually is revealed in the assessment, and plans can be made for approaching this mode of operation.

These modes of treatment do not exhaust all the possibilities of changing children's behaviors. Often, it is necessary to make changes in the child's environment as well as in his/her actions and attitudes. The following chapter considers assessment for such environmental alterations and the manner in which they also may be integrated into an overall plan of behavioral change.

CHAPTER 21

Assessment for Physiological and Environmental Interventions

A. INTRODUCTION

Assessment can be extremely helpful when there are decisions to be made about possible changes in the child's environment or about proposed physiological interventions. In assessing the possible changes in the child's psychological functioning that might be affected either by changes in the environment or in medical or surgical interventions, there are at least four general considerations: (1) the nature and purposes of the proposed changes, (2) the attitudes of the child toward the changes, (3) the child's ability to use the changes for further growth, and (4) the need for someone to act as a "change agent" to assist the child in accepting and using the changes.

The assessment of a child reveals only how he/she views the social environment and his/her physical being. It does not usually provide much data about the realities of these environments unless parent interviews, home visits, and school and medical reports are included in the data. In order to make any estimate of the effects of possible environmental changes on the child, one needs to know the nature of the present environment and of the proposed alterations. One needs to know, for example, what the present school and new school are like, or what the current home situation is like and the nature of the proposed foster home, or the child's current physical condition and what kinds of surgery, prosthetics, or drugs are proposed, and the possible results thereof. All in all, what needs to be done in the prediction of possible effects of such

external changes is an assessment of the environment or of the proposed physiological change. Thus, before the assessment results can be viewed in the light of these proposed changes, it is necessary to have as precise data about them as possible.

Very often this assessment is accomplished by someone other than the psychologist. For example, if the psychologist works in collaboration with a social worker, it may be the social worker who visits the home, school, or the foster home. However, it is often very helpful for the psychologist also to join in such home or school visits. Where the question is of a proposed medical intervention, the psychologist should discuss the nature of this intervention with the physician so that data are obtained regarding the procedures the child will face and the nature of the expected physiological changes.

The second question to be asked is whether the proposed change is pertinent to the problems and needs of the child. In the referral, the parent, physician, teacher, or probation officer may propose major changes in the child's environment, but whether such changes really have any bearing on her/his problems is often questionable. For example, a parent may believe that the child's behavior arises from conflicts with peers in a certain school or in a certain neighborhood; they may even be willing to go to the extent of selling their home and making a move in order to help the child. Or a physician may believe that surgical intervention, altering the child's physique, appearance, or muscular abilities might change her/his attitudes. The representative of a court may ask whether removing the child from the home and putting him/her in an institution would not change his/her behavior. Once one has investigated the nature of these proposed changes, then it is necessary to see in what way such changes would be pertinent.

Occasionally, as is discussed, the referrant's proposed change does fit very well with the child's needs, and thus is quite appropriate. Too frequently, the proposed change is actually an act of desperation that has little relevance to the child's needs. For example, parents frequently insist that the child be placed in a boarding school, but the assessment data may suggest that her/his problems have little to do with school adjustment but, rather, are the result of tensions within the family. In such instances, further investigation and discussion with the parents may reveal that they are attempting to avoid any recognition of family tensions and are hoping secretly that, by further rejecting the child and expelling her/him from the home, their problems will be solved without any uncovering of their own behaviors. In other instances, where changes are proposed by physicians or by courts, one must take into account that the referrant may be proposing only those changes that he/she is familiar with. For example, it is quite understandable that a physician would propose physiological changes, such as the use of drugs or surgery. A teacher may be inclined to hope for changes in the child through changes in the school or the teaching method. The court may be alarmed over a child's delinquency but consider only the possibility of institutionalization or punitive measures.

If these proposed changes have little to do with the child's frustrations, then the results of the changes will probably be negligible. In many instances, the child merely continues to be disturbed. Far too often, the change adds to the child's miseries. A foster-home placement may actually increase the child's feeling of rejection, rather than relieve it. Even physiologically successful surgery or quieting drugs may make little or no change in the child's behavior if the physiological condition was not the main problem in the first place. Most courts are now well aware that placing a retarded or psychotic child in a state institution for delinquents may be of little effect and may possibly be harmful.

Once it is determined that the proposed change may be relevant to the child's problems, the next question is whether she/he will accept and use the change. Where a change does seem pertinent, the hope is that the child's tensions will be relieved, since the environmental stresses are different. However, it is often true that there is a considerable lag between the shift in the tensions the child is experiencing and the hoped-for changes in her/his coping mechanisms. When a child is put in a new situation, she/he usually does not immediately give up old, ineffective neurotic habits or psychotic behavior. The child may not experience the situation as a change for some time and thus will continue these old behaviors. One needs to investigate whether the new environment will accept ineffective or disturbing behavior for at least a brief period. For example, a new school or a new foster home would need to be advised about the child's behavior and helped to recognize that there may not be an immediate change.

Furthermore, consideration should be given to the nature of the child's disturbing behavior. For example, in the treatment of the anorexia, the child's refusal to eat is not only a way of manipulating his/her parents, but it usually also masks considerable depression. If the child is put in the hospital and the anorexic symptoms no longer make the authorities guilty and disturbed, it is very likely that the child will then be unable to hide the depression. Such depression following diets also is common. These problems are illustrated in the following case.

CASE 114

Between ages 2 and 5, Allen gradually lost his vision as cataracts developed. The effect of their surgical removal on his behavior at age 5 was quite marked. Previously he had been a very dependent child who had been very well behaved. However, once he was able to see, he no longer could use his blindness as an excuse to be cared for. Furthermore, he now was able to do many things that were impossible before. As a result, he became very angry when people did not wait on him any longer. He also got into a lot more mischief than he did when he could not see. However, the surgeon had suspected that the child might be emotionally immature and had asked for psychological assessment before the surgery was instituted. Thus, the possibility of the child's reaction to the surgery was predicted and was discussed with the parents beforehand. They were therefore somewhat prepared for the change in the child's behavior. They were able to appreciate, rather than be thrown by his anger when they insisted that he could now care for himself in many ways. They were not shocked but were actually encouraged when they found him exploring and even damaging things that he had not been able to see or know about before.

The child's ability to accept and utilize a proposed change often requires that there be some person whose specific role is to help him/her during the period of change. It may be that the authorities in the new environment will play this role. If the new teacher or foster parent is advised of the child's behavior and needs, she/he may be able to help the child accept and utilize the new environment. Sometimes, if there is no one person in the environment who can do this, a child may need another person to act as counselor regarding the change.

CASE 115

Robert, age 12, had reacted in normal fashion with depression to the death of his father. However, the assessment revealed he had found the new relationship with his mother very conflictual. He shared her depression and became much closer to her, but at the same time, this relationship threatened his approaching pubescence. He often reacted in negative fashion, especially to her offers of affection and succor. He could not explain his behavior exactly, but he did state with a burst of insight, "My mother and I are too close." The father's death had also necessitated that the mother take a job outside the home. Moreover, it was very likely that she would not be able to afford the home in which they had been living. Both for economic and psychological reasons, she was about to move in with her parents. She very much feared that Robert would not accept this change.

Robert himself asked if it would not be possible for him to go away to a boarding school. His grandfather offered to finance this schooling. Nevertheless, it was obvious that Robert was very ambivalent concerning this change. It did seem as though the proposed boarding school would offer Robert considerable support in his masculine development. It would also relieve him of the immediate, strained relationships with his mother and his maternal grandparents. To make this change, several counseling interviews were conducted with him in which the nature of the change and the reasons for making it were discussed very openly. Robert was a fairly intelligent boy and able to explore his own feelings quite readily. He thus was much more prepared to meet the new school and saw it as a potential for relieving some of his depressed and angry feelings. He promised to write the psychologist about his feelings at the school. He sent several letters indicating that he was homesick but that he found many new attractions that kept him quite preoccupied. After about three months, fewer letters were received from Robert, but his mother reported that he seemed "a changed boy" when he came home on vacation.

B. ASSESSMENT FOR POSSIBLE PHYSIOLOGICAL CHANGES

Although at one time there was little or no

consideration given to the psychological effects of medical interventions, over the past several decades physicians have become increasingly aware that medical or surgical interventions that might be considered routine, at times have marked effects on the child's behavior. For example, several decades ago tonsillectomies were performed fairly routinely, often in the physician's office. However, some children seemed to react very negatively in their behavior to what might be considered a simple operation. Sometimes they were discovered to be very depressed or quite phobic afterward. Psychological assessment of such children, even years after the surgery, sometimes reveals that they still fantasized that their lives were threatened.

Physicians now know to prepare children in advance for surgery, advising them in very simple language of the nature of the operation, the reasons for it, and what is to be expected from it. Physicians are now more aware also of the possible negative effects of a surgical or medical intervention on an emotionally disturbed child. Thus, pediatricians or surgeons are increasingly prone to request psychological assessment of a child preoperatively when they feel that she/he will be so disturbed by the prospect or the results of an operation that it may be better to delay the surgery.

Although it is known that surgical interventions of almost any kind do constitute a potential threat as well as a potential benefit, there is little or no research to indicate the specific kinds of threats or hopes children may have regarding a particular type of surgery. Of course, where children receive a physiological trauma, such as a broken bone, severe lacerations, or an injury, they are likely to see any type of surgical intervention as being beneficial and are not particularly threatened. However, where the proposed surgery may affect a part of the body about which the child has particular conflicts, repair of the trauma might also require psychological assessment and assistance.

CASE 116

Vincent, age 14, whose leg was badly smashed in an automobile accident, was advised by his surgeon that it probably would be necessary to amputate it. He was told that a prosthetic limb would make it possible for him to ambulate. The surgeon also told Vincent that if the leg was not amputated, he could walk with a crutch, but that there was danger of further complications or of possible infections. Upon receiving this advice, Vincent became markedly depressed and confused and was unable to make any kind of decision. His parents were also very worried as Vincent tried to have them decide for him. However, his father, realizing that this would affect much of Vincent's future, insisted that the boy should be involved. Because of his depression and confusion, psychological assessment was requested.

In brief, the results of the assessment showed that this boy was very motorically oriented, that he usually expressed his feelings in motor behavior, and that he was far more dependent on doing things with his arms and legs than in verbalizing. Moreover, he was in the middle of pubescence when active sports and social activities such as dancing were most important to him. In Vincent's responses to the associative techniques, there was considerable evidence that the injury had rearoused old fears of castration and deprivation of masculinity, and that the prospect of amputation reactivated his childhood fears.

The nature of the boy's fears were then discussed with the surgeon and the boy's parents. Further consultation with the physiatrist and the rehabilitation department revealed that Vincent could be quite mobile when fitted with a prosthetic limb. The boy was advised of this, was taken to the prosthetics department where he saw people dancing on artificial limbs, and even watched a basketball game with young men in wheelchairs. He was then able to accept the probability that the amputation and prosthetic limb were the best possible choices. He remained somewhat depressed, but a further consultation following the amputation and fitting of the prosthesis showed that he was much less depressed and was eager to try out his new limb.

Psychological assessment is even more imperative when the proposed surgery is not an emergency for the child's life or immediate well-being, but is "elective"—for example, for "cosmetic purposes." A pediatrician might advise a parent that the child needed a tonsillectomy, but also recognize that he/she seemed emotionally immature or otherwise emotionally disturbed and suggest that, if necessary, the proposed surgery be delayed.

Case 117

Lisa, age 4, had suffered from recurring bouts of tonsillitis with increasing frequency and severity. Both Lisa and her mother knew that a tonsillectomy seemed imminent. However, Lisa had also been showing many signs of behavioral disturbance that were in all probability associated with the recent divorce of her parents. The pediatrician therefore requested a psychological consultation. The assessment revealed that Lisa fantasized that she was the cause of her parents' separation and that she felt very guilty about it. Moreover, some of her fantasies suggested that she saw the impending operation as a punishment for her misbehavior. In consultation with the psychologist, the pediatrician decided that Lisa's infection might be controlled by medication for at least another year. A year and a half later, Lisa was again referred to the psychologist. At this time, the tonsillectomy no longer could be delayed. However, in the meantime Lisa's mother had remarried, and Lisa seemed less fearful and more at ease. The necessity of the operation and the nature of it were discussed very frankly with her by the pediatrician. Following the operation, the psychologist visited Lisa very briefly in the hospital, and there was no

indication that the surgery had in any way upset her. Several months later, the child was again brought to the psychologist by her mother, as had been suggested by the pediatrician. The mother reported no untoward effects of the operation, and Lisa seemed quite happy and voluntarily said she was glad to be relieved of her continual sore throat.

Cosmetic surgery for children—as for adults—has even more psychological implications. For example, it is sometimes proposed a child's big and flabby ears be altered or that a short limb or a disfigured face be repaired. Again, there is little or no research regarding the general psychological effects of such surgery on children. In each case it must be assessed separately. In these instances particularly, the psychologist should be aware of possible hidden motivations for the proposed surgery (Jacobson, 1961). Thus, a parent or even a child himself/herself may look forward to the operation as a fantasied panacea for all anxieties. The bashful, withdrawn schizoid child whose face is disfigured or distorted may seek cosmetic surgery in the hope that then she/he will be welcomed among her/his peers or accepted by her/his parents. However, assessment quite frequently shows that the child's appearance is not the chief reason that she/he is rejected. In such instances, it is very often helpful to delay cosmetic surgery until other psychological interventions can be made to make the psychological outcome of the surgery more realistic.

A prime example is Case 38 in Chapter 10. In this case, the child was born with one leg shorter than the other. There was no evidence that her disturbances at age 13 had any relation to this mild defect. The girl's mother, however, was firmly convinced that all the girl's behavioral difficulties arose from her reaction to this defect and ignored all of her other psychological difficulties. Several surgeons advised the mother that surgical intervention at this late age might not necessarily be successful. It was pointed out to her that the child's bone growth was almost complete, and that the possibility of lengthening the leg was not favorable. Nevertheless, the mother persisted until she found a surgeon who asked to attempt to repair the leg. The girl was unaware of the degree of pain involved in this surgery and the length required for rehabilitation. A total of four different surgical interventions proved to be necessary. Moreover, the child was in bed and out of school for almost two years. Further investigation revealed that the mother, unconsciously, was trying to separate the girl from peer activities and to keep this adolescent as a helpless child under her control. Although the child was able to walk more comfortably at the end of the rehabilitation period, she remained an excessively angry and rebellious girl who blamed her mother for the loss of her adolescence.

In most major rehabilitation centers, psychological assessment and consultation are considered essential parts of the total rehabilitation program for the child. Although the psychological aspects of physiological rehabilitation of disabled children constitute a specialty within the field of clinical psychology, any psychologist should at least be aware of some of the problems involved. In the assessment of a disabled child, special attention needs to be given to the ways in which she/he views the loss of a limb or a paralysis, and how she/he handles the depression that accompanies such a loss.

In my experience, the "phantom-limb" phenomenon noted among adult amputees (Roser, A., in Bellak, 1952) is not quite as marked among children, although they also may refuse to recognize that the paralyzed or amputated member will not reappear or be repaired as "magically" as it was injured and lost. The adult who clings to this delusion is also likely to deny feelings of depression and pretend that everything is going to be all right. Such adult patients do very poorly in rehabilitation because of the lack of motivation. In general, children, whose defenses are less developed, are more apt to experience a normal grief reaction to the loss of a limb or to a paralysis. Once this grief has subsided, they are highly motivated toward rehabilitation. However, children are easily swayed by denying adults. The mother who bleats, "Don't worry, dear, everything is going to be all right," convinces the child that some magic is going to happen and that she/he is not obligated to do anything about it. Thus, assessment of disabled children should include a careful study of the attitudes of the parents toward the disability—for example, the possibility that they may have hidden feelings of guilt regarding the cause of the child's loss, or unexpressed anger toward the child who is no longer "perfect." Where there are such attitudes on the part of the parents, the prosthesis itself becomes the magical answer. The parents, and consequently the child, come to regard the prosthesis as the total answer and fail to understand the necessity for learning to use it and for continued physical and occupational therapy. In addition, when a child suffers a traumatic and disabling injury or disease, he/she is naturally more dependent on, and demanding of, the adult, and adults tend to become guilt stricken and more likely to reinforce the child's dependency. In such instances, the prosthesis, rather than being regarded positively as an aid toward the further growth of the child, becomes a symbol in the eyes of both parent and child of her/his disability. Thus, in the assessment of a disabled child, special attention needs to be paid to his/her feelings of dependence and independence, both in general and in relation to the prosthesis.

Assessment is rarely requested regarding the use of the much more common minor prostheses, such as glasses, hearing aids, or orthodentures. But such prostheses often arouse considerable social embarassment and even feelings of self-doubt for a child. Although having braces on one's teeth is a very common event for the latency child or young adolescent, for the child who already may feel inadequate and socially on the outs, braces or spectacles may become just another sign that they are not considered adequate, beautiful, or even loved. The following case is an example.

Case 118

Lana's schoolwork had been going downhill for almost two years. Although she had made above-average grades during the first three years of elementary school, now in the sixth grade, she was failing almost completely. Her parents were quite concerned, since Lana appeared to be studying quite hard, at least up until the current semester. Her teachers also reported that Lana was an attentive student and until recently there had been no behavior problems. In this first semester, Lana seemed excessively tense and nervous in the classroom, began to stutter and cry when she was called on to recite, and was extrasensitive to any teasing by her peers. She even began to complain that her teachers did not like her and, when corrected, she would run from the room in tears. She was defiant when the teachers tried to find out what was upsetting her, and her negativism got her into more trouble with school authorities. Moreover, Lana, although only 11, was at least a foot taller than any other child in her class, weighed nearly 150 pounds, and was beginning to develop breasts and hips. Her size and behavior made her the target of other children, especially the boys who dubbed her "Lana the Horse."

In considering the possible source of Lana's difficulties, it did appear to both the parents and teachers that Lana might need glasses, since she did appear to squint at the blackboard and to hold books fairly close to her face. The teacher noted that if the instructions were given orally, Lana always understood, but she did not seem to read rapidly. Thus, she was succeeding much better at oral arithmetic than in problems from the textbook. Prior to seeking psychological consultation, her parents had taken her to an opthalmalogist who examined her and who reported that her vision seemed within the normal limits.

During the psychological assessment, Lana was having obvious difficulties on such tests as the Bender-Gestalt and the visual items of the WISC, such as Picture Completion, Picture Arrangement, and Block Design. Her Verbal IQ was 117, but the Performance IQ was only 83. However, further qualitative analysis of both her Wechsler and Bender performances as well as her Draw-A-Person (which was, in contrast, quite adequate for her age) suggested that Lana did have a marked visual handicap. Her visual-motor coordination as such was not inadequate, and her high achievement on tests such as arithmetic appeared to contraindicate possible brain damage. She went through the Rorschach, peering closely at each card, and the perceptual aspects of her responses were quite within normal limits. During the assessment, Lana became increasingly aware of her failures, biting her lips, making remarks like "Boy, am I stupid!"

After the assessment, the question of her "stupidity" was brought up with her. The assessor assured her that he did not see her as stupid, but guessed that she did have some kind of visual problem. Lana responded, "I hate *glasses.*" When asked about the eye examination, Lana admitted to the assessor that she had failed to tell the opthalmologist how blurred her vision became and about her diplopia. Her eye muscles ached and she suffered headaches whenever she read, even for brief periods. She never told her parents any of this. Lana confessed also that she felt badly about the names that the boys called her, that she wished she was petite and pretty like the other girls. Although her friends were mostly 11 and 12, they were already fantasying boy–girl relationships. She harbored considerable fears that she would never be accepted by boys, and the threat that she might have to wear glasses only added to her apprehensions. After further discussion of this problem, Lana decided to repeat the ophthalmological consultation, and her accommodation problem then became quite clear. The ophthalmologist felt that contact lenses might be too painful for her at first, and that it would be better for her to start off with regular glasses. However, at this time, Lana's mother was contemplating changing from glasses to contact lenses, and it was agreed to let Lana try them at the same time her mother did. The mother and daughter thus bore the difficulty of getting used to contact lenses together and, after a briefer period than usual, Lana had grown quite used to the discomfort of wearing them. Her school achievement rose markedly thereafter.

Another type of physiological intervention used mainly to control behavior is the psychotropic drug or tranquilizer. When first discovered, just after World War II, these drugs seemed very promising. Through their use, many very disturbed hospital patients who theretofore had been completely out of contact were able to carry out their daily activities with minimum supervision, and thus were more amenable to care and treatment. Calmed by these drugs, many chronically disturbed patients were able to enter into psychotherapy and begin to consider the reality of the world about them. This approach was so promising that an increasing number of new drugs were introduced and were prescribed for many different emotional conditions.

Soon it became obvious that the reactions—and particularly the side effects—could not be predicted easily, since they often differed from person to person and the dosages had to be altered for each individual. The research on many of these drugs was often inadequate or entirely absent. Although these drugs continue to be used with both adults and children when they are very depressed or hyperactive, they are no longer regarded as a panacea. They have seldom been used as extensively with children as they have been with adults. Moreover, there is even considerable controversy about the use of drugs with children. Fritz Redl, in his presidential address to the American Orthopsychiatric Association, lashed out against their use, labeling this practice "chemical warfare against children."* Nevertheless, proper use of

*This remark was not included in the publication of his address.

these drugs can calm very psychotic children so that they do not pound their heads against walls, pull out their hair, or scratch themselves bloody. Antidepressant drugs may rouse the completely withdrawn and lethargic adolescent, so that she/he can be engaged in a rehabilitation program.

Although psychologists have participated in research on the effects of these drugs, little or no relationship has been established between psychological assessment and the clinical use of drugs. Rarely, if ever, does a referrant request assessment for the use of this type of intervention. In some instances, the drugs are prescribed partly on the basis of an assessment, but for the most part, they are used as an emergency treatment. Moreover, since the effects are so variable, it is difficult to imagine how one might predict the possible outcome, on the basis of the data of a psychological assessment.

However, psychological assessment is related to these drugs in at least two ways. First, if a child who is being medicated is referred for assessment, the psychologist needs to know about the possible effects of the drug on the child's behavior, particularly the possible effects of the drug on the child's performance on the techniques to be used in the assessment. Although these drugs usually slow down the child's reactions (except for antidepressants), there is no precise knowledge of how any one child may be affected. The nurse's notes are one of the best sources of data, or, if the child is not in the hospital, a report from the physician. The observations from the child's parents may also be helpful. When a child is known to be using such medication, the psychologist should be most observant of the child's behavior. It is wise to ask about the type of medication being used, the dosage, and how much time has elapsed between the most recent dose and the beginning of the assessment. Very often, a child who is using these drugs will be very drowsy for the first several hours after he/she has taken them and more alert just before the next dose is scheduled. This information is most important, since these drugs do temporarily affect the central nervous system, and as a result, the responses of a sedated child often correspond to those given by children who have some generalized brain damage. Thus, if the psychologist is not aware that the child is sedated, her/his responses may seem at least puzzling, and the assessor may be misled into predicting the possibility of brain damage. The psychologist should also inquire whether the referrant needs a description of the child under the influence of the medication or when the child is least affected.

Second, psychologists may be requested to assess the effects of the clinical use of these drugs on a particular child. Most commonly, this request is made rather indirectly or implicitly. For example, a child may be very disturbed when admitted to a hospital, appearing severely psychotic and unmanageable. At that time, the child may be incapable of cooperating in an assessment. Or her/his responses may only mirror the psychotic affect and lack of contact with the immediate surroundings. After the child has been treated with drugs for a week or so, another assessment may be requested. By this time, the drug dosage may have been decreased and the child may be calmed down considerably. Although the referral may not directly request an evaluation of the effects of the drugs, actually such a post-treatment assessment may reflect the results of the drug therapy. Usually the pretreatment psychotic state has been behaviorally ameliorated. However, one should ask the following question: Are the child's thought processes and underlying affective states still very disturbed? Since the drug affects the child's motor functioning mainly, it may be presumed that there is usually little effect on the ego as a whole. This presumption, however, needs to be assessed. Thus, the psychologist may be asked, "Now that the child is motorically calmed down, what is the rest of her/his ego functioning like? Is she/he still basically psychotic or was her/his psychotic behavior a temporary state?"

C.   CHANGES WITHIN THE MILIEU

The central and most important environment of the child is, of course, the family.

Any environmental change that removes children from that family setting is thus a very drastic and major alteration in their environment. Before any such major change in the child's environment is contemplated, one should consider the possibility of other changes within the child's milieu that do not remove her/him from the family circle. When a child is so emotionally disturbed as to be unable to function in his/her environment, changes within the family living structure and arrangements or in family living habits, a change of school, or even a move by the family to a new neighborhood are usually considered before contemplating removing the child from the home.

As mentioned before, very often such proposals are made out of desperation, and they may have little relevance to the child's actual problems. However, in many instances, the possibility that such a change would at least make life a little easier for the child should be seriously considered. Even where it is fairly obvious that such a move will not clear up at all the major problems facing the child and the family, there is often the possibility that he/she may be much more able to work out the problems if the immediate stress of this environment is lessened. Thus, a child who has been failing badly in school and who has been a disrupting factor in the classroom might well be considered for a transfer to another school, even though her/his emotional disturbance is obviously a reflection of tensions within the home. Any such change would very likely require that the child and his/her family also begin some form of psychotherapy to work out these family tensions. Otherwise, the child might very well repeat the same behavior in the new school and be threatened again with expulsion.

Therefore some person should act as "change agent"—that is, the parents, the therapist, or some representative of the clinic where the child is being seen should contact the school. Conferences should be held between the school authorities and this change agent so that the school may be better prepared to handle, for at least a while, the child's continued disturbing effects. At the same time, as part of therapy with the child, she/he should be helped to see the new school as an opportunity for a fresh start.

However, such changes are not easy to effect. In most school systems, the child's behavior as well as his/her scholastic achievement are recorded on an accumulated record and passed from school to school. Thus, the authorities at the new school are quite aware that they are receiving a difficult child. Sometimes it is almost impossible to negotiate and implement any kind of education rehabilitation program for an individual child in a new school once she/he has had an appreciable history of failures. Some parents and children are quite willing to receive the assistance of a psychologists outside their system. It should be remembered, however, that in an overcrowded and overburdened school system, it is often difficult to give special attention to the single child, even though she/he may sorely need it. This is not to say that a realistic and reasonable change of schools with the intervention of a change agent is impossible, but rather that the possibility that such a change can be carried out successfully—both by the child and his/her parents—should be carefully assessed before any decision is made.

CASE 119

Larry, age 11, had a long history of a variety of school difficulties that had already resulted in two shifts in schools. A third change was now contemplated. Although IQ tests at these schools had consistently indicated that he was of superior intelligence, his actual achievement had been extremely erratic. He would become fascinated for some time with a subject and would do superior work, but, for the most part, he seemed to pay little attention to the assignments and dawdled over them. Sometimes, when teachers recognized that he was bored and disinterested, they would try to give him extra projects and motivate him—often with fair success.

The school that Larry first attended was very overcrowded, and there had been frequent changes of teachers, so that Larry's special needs were inadvertently neglected. Larry was an excessively restless child who amused and teased other children and often succeeded in getting the class into an uproar. He was angry, resentful, and impudent to school authorities when they attempted to correct him.

After the first two years of school, during which time his mother had had numerous conferences with his teachers, she decided to put him in a parochial school. His behavior continued to be much the same in the parochial school, and after less than a year and a half he was expelled because of his loud and vulgar language—specifically because he wrote sexual words on the school wall.

He was then placed in another public school, a half year below his normal grade level, since his record of achievement had been so poor. Again, his mother was frequently contacted by school authorities who complained of his classroom behavior, and his grades remained far below what might have been expected of him. During the most recent semester in the fifth grade, Larry had frequently wandered off the school grounds, without returning.

The assessment of Larry revealed that he was very angry and guilt ridden and felt very rejected because his father had deserted his mother and him five years previously. Moreover, his mother now had to work full time to support the two of them, and she was often too tired and too depressed to deal effectively with Larry's emotional needs. She had not even been aware of his truancies because she had not been at home during the day. There were often indications in Larry's responses to the assessment that the bond between him and his mother was intensely conflictual and ambivalent. There were signs that he felt that his mother's anger at his father was also directed at him. At the same time, he felt pressured to take his father's place, which was threatening to him. It was agreed that both Larry and his mother needed psychotherapeutic help, but there remained the immediate and acute problem of where Larry should attend school.

The school authorities were adamant that

Larry be transferred to another school, and Larry himself was quite vehement in saying that he would not return to this school. Although in most instances the mother might have expected to conduct the negotiations with the school, she was extremely distraught and despaired of being able to communicate Larry's needs to the school authorities. The assessor, who was not the therapist for either Larry or his mother, agreed to assist her in negotiations with the school. A conference was then held between the psychologist, the mother, the principal, and the teacher at the school to which Larry was to be assigned. The exact nature of Larry's problems within his family were not discussed, although it was indicated that family circumstances were the source of Larry's behavioral difficulties. The teacher volunteered that he had a special interest in the motivation of bright boys. He added that he would consider the possibility of working out methods of dealing with Larry's boisterousness and other disrupting activities in a way that would not necessarily threaten Larry, but he would nevertheless aid Larry in controlling himself.

Larry was then brought into the conference also. The principal explained that he was aware of Larry's problems in the previous school—whereupon Larry made a sour face—but, the principal added, he also understood that Larry's behavior was to be helped by the clinic and that the authories at the new school thus hoped that they could offer Larry a fresh start. The teacher mentioned that he would help him with his classroom behavior if Larry so desired. Larry did seem genuinely pleased by this offer of help. The principal pointed out, however, that it would be necessary to limit this program to a single semester, and that his mother would have to consider that this was a trial period.

For the following three months, the teacher conferred over the telephone with the psychologist almost biweekly. At first, it was necessary for the teacher to spend a considerable amount of time and energy with Larry, constantly warning him when his behavior started to get out of hand. Almost weekly, Larry stayed after school to discuss his school behavior with the teacher. The teacher was able to work out a "warning signal" with him, which only he and Larry understood, that designated the times when he needed to exercise some control over himself. At the same time, Larry's mother received some extra help in the home from her mother. Although this created considerable conflict between the two women, it did mean that there was someone at home when Larry arrived from school. At the end of three months, his behavior at school had improved remarkably, and Larry himself felt very encouraged.

Frequently, there are possibilities of making changes within the milieu of the home or even the home structure that might relieve considerable pressure on the child. However, parents may be so upset by the child's behavior that they may fail to recognize these possibilities.

CASE 120

Marty, who was 8, fussed constantly with his 9-year-old sister, whined about his mother's skirts, and annoyed his father by making many demands and failing to carry out his assigned household chores. He always wanted to be first at everything, monopolized the television, never seemed to want to go to bed, always forgot to brush his teeth, and disrupted family meals so frequently with his demanding and petulant behavior that he was often excluded from meals or other family activities. The list of complaints that his parents and sister had against Marty seemed inexhaustible. Marty himself complained that the family paid no attention to his needs, that his sister was always teasing him, and that his father was too strict with him. In the first two interviews, which were held with these four members of the family, Marty would burst into tears and fling himself on the floor as his father pointed out that the family could never go anywhere because Marty was always late. It was only at the end of the second interview that it was discovered that there was another member of the family, namely, Marty's younger brother, who was 11 months old. As the assessment proceeded both in the family discussions and individually with Marty, it became increasingly apparent that many of Marty's disturbances were associated with the birth of his younger brother. Marty himself voiced no complaint about the baby at first. However, several of his TAT stories and other associative materials strongly suggested that he felt very displaced and might be very resentful of the attention given to the new baby. The parents did date the onset of Marty's disturbing behavior as approximately a year ago, but they failed to notice that this coincided with the mother's pregnancy and birth of the baby. When this possibility was raised with Marty's mother, she seemed somewhat surprised, noting that Marty had seemed to look forward to a brother whom he envisioned as a potential companion. She said that at times he seemed to enjoy playing with the baby. On further reflection, she remarked that he sometimes seemed annoyed because the baby got into his things.

It was at this point that it was revealed that Marty was sharing a room with the baby. When Marty was asked about his young brother he readily volunteered that the baby messed his things up and kept him awake by his crying. He felt the baby had taken over his room. The fact that Marty had to share his room with his new baby brother seemed the crowning insult. This was clear enough evidence that Marty was no longer "the baby in the family"—a remark his father frequently flung in his face when Marty failed to use proper manners at the dinner table or to carry out his chores exactly as his father demanded. In pursuing this topic further in the family discussions, the father agreed that perhaps he had begun to expect more from Marty "since he is no longer the baby in the family."

Although there were several other aspects of this family that required further discussion, one possible change that struck everyone concerned, as soon as the situa-

tion was clearly understood, was that Marty needed a room that he could call his own. It seemed possible that such a change would restore Marty's position within his family. The parents had considered that their home would have to be expanded in the future, but they now realized how important this might be for Marty. Plans were then laid to convert the family garage into an extra room as soon as possible. In further discussion, it was revealed that Marty had known that such plans were afoot and had felt very disappointed when he understood that they might be delayed, since his father wanted to spend the family savings on a new car instead of the new room. Marty's father was somewhat taken aback by this, and he volunteered that the baby should be moved immediately from Marty's room to the parents' room. Marty's behavior began to change almost as soon as a decision was made. The family continued in weekly discussions with the therapist for another six weeks, at which time Marty was moved into the new room. By this time, much of Marty's disturbing behavior had disappeared. The family feared that Marty would feel displaced by the fact that he would have to move from his room to another, and it was decided to give him a choice. Marty chose to exchange rooms. Although it is quite possible that the change of rooms in itself was not the main factor in Marty's change of behavior, at least it was a symbol to him that his parents were aware of his needs and would attempt to gratify them "even though he was no longer the baby of the family."

Sometimes there are changes within the child's immediate family milieu that, although they do not mean that the child is actually removed from the family, do involve very major changes in the family constellation. Contemplated divorces are the most common instance. Children of parents who are thinking about separation and divorce are often referred for psychological assessment by marital counselors, attorneys, or courts. In such instances, the following question may be asked, "Should the couple be kept together for the 'good' of the child?'' Although no assessment can answer this particular question phrased in this way, an assessment of the tensions within the family and their effect upon the child may be very helpful to the couple in making a decision about their marriage. The role of an assessment in such a case is illustrated by the following case.

CASE 121

Mr. and Mrs. V, who were contemplating divorce, sought psychological consultation and assessment of their children, Anna, age 14, and Don, age 12, on the recommendation of their attorney. The V's had been on the brink of divorce several times previously but had ''stayed together for the sake of the children.'' Mrs. V felt that she no longer could stand the embarrassment and hurt of Mr. V's relations with other women, which he did not deny and which were common knowledge in the community. Mr. V complained bitterly that his wife was sexually frigid and neurotic, so that he no longer could live with her. Both of the V's had been previously married and divorced. Mr. V, now age 50, had first married at age 25 and had a 23-year-old daughter by this marriage who was not living with the V's. He had divorced his first wife allegedly because of her alcoholism. He had married Mrs. V four years later, and their marriage had always been a stormy one. Mrs. V, who was 15 years younger than her husband, had married first at age 17 to a high-school boyfriend by whom she was pregnant. However, she aborted this first child. Her first marriage ended in a divorce a year later, and at age 20, she married Mr. V. Their daughter Anna was born a year later.

Although many of the disagreements had been building up over the entire 15 years, they had seldom quarreled openly in front of the children. They readily agreed, however, that the children were well aware of the general tension between them, especially in the more recent years. However, this tension was never discussed with the children. As far as they were aware, the children had no knowledge of Mr. V's extramarital affairs. They had not even told the children that a divorce was being contemplated. In spite of their intense differences, both the V's were quite concerned with the welfare of their children, and both stated that they would be willing to continue the marriage if they thought a divorce would markedly disturb the children.

They reported that Anna seemed particularly tense and sensitive, easily given to tears over even slight disappointments or failures, and recently seemed to have difficulty in sleeping. Don, they described as showing almost no disturbance. He seemed to be succeeding at school and continuing his daily activities and peer associations in a spontaneous and undisturbed fashion. Both parents agreed that there was a bond between Don and his father. For example, they were currently beginning golf lessons, and Don had participated in the selection of the new family car. Don also seemed to be somewhat sensitive for a 12-year-old boy; he had once or twice found his mother in tears and had attempted to comfort her without asking at all about the source of her distress. Anna seemed particularly upset when her father criticized or disciplined her. Previously she had been very much ''daddy's little girl,'' but over the past year had seemed to grow quite distant and aloof from him. Mr. V was quite hurt by her behavior. Anna also was much more apt to flare up against her mother than she had been in previous years.

One of the initial questions was what to tell the children about the purpose of the assessment. Both parents were adamant that the children should not be told about the contemplated divorce. The psychologist agreed that since the decision for the divorce was not yet completely made, it probably should not be mentioned to the children at this point, but that the fact of the family tension probably could not be hidden from the children much longer. The parents argued further that even if the children were told that the purpose of the assessment was to evaluate the effects of tension, they might immediately be threatened and the assessment thus would be contaminated. Finally, the psychologist agreed to the suggestion that Anna be seen because of her recent emotional disturbances and that Don might come to an assessment just because his sister was coming.

Anna, a tall, slim girl whose feminine figure was rapidly developing, was dressed appropriately in the teen-aged fashion. She said that she understood that she had come to the psychologist because of her "nutty" behavior, which she described as "easily flying off the handle" and "crying over nothing." She could not immediately think of any particular things that disturbed her, but remarked, "My whole family is nutty." She did complain mildly about Don whom she said teased occasionally or disregarded her rights in the family, but she did not seem particularly upset, adding with a laugh, "You're going to see him and you'll see what kind of nut he is." When reminded that she said her whole family was "nutty," Anna's demeanor became markedly depressed and she said, "I know; I love them both and they both are swell to me, but something is wrong in my family but I don't know what it is." She seemed almost near tears and remarked very solemnly, "I think they are almost going to get a divorce." When asked what gave her that impression, she replied that they always talked as if they seemed quite angry with one another, that they seldom went anywhere together, that her father always seemed very busy at work and was away very frequently on weekends, and that her mother often referred to her father in a "sarcastic way." Anna, however, denied that she worried much about her parents but admitted that she had begun to think about this quite a bit when she knew she was coming to see the psychologist and was introspecting about her own behavior.

She said that she was worried about other things such as succeeding in school, a girlfriend with whom she had recently quarreled and stopped seeing, and a boyfriend whom she had hoped to attract but who seemed to be paying little attention to her.

Despite these things, Anna said she frequently felt quite happy and often had good times. She particularly enjoyed the activities in her girls' club, and she had recently become interested in sewing and, with her mother's help, had made the dress she was wearing. She usually went to the movies or to some other entertainment with her peers, but she particularly enjoyed the occasional but recently rare attention she received from her father who would take her and her brother to a show and dinner—"but mother never comes along." She said she had been worried about her mother, since her mother seemed to have frequent sick headaches, especially when any family affair was planned. This, too, made Anna suspicious that all was not right between her parents.

The assessment revealed that Anna was intellectually very bright and emotionally quite sensitive. In general, Anna's ego functioning seemed to be developing quite normally and even slightly precociously. Her responses did confirm her mother's impression that Anna's sensitivity to the emotional nuances of her environment more at times slightly overwhelming her, that she was aware of more emotional aspects of her environment than she was immediately able to cope with and understand. Although from Anna's responses one could not say that she was openly depressed, there was a depressive and dysphoric aspect to many of her responses. Her TAT's were filled with repeated themes of threatened separation. For example, on TAT Card 2, Anna thought the girl was afraid to leave home to go away to school because her home might no longer be there when she returned. However, Anna could not decide why the girl might think this. On Card 3GF, Anna thought the girl in the doorway had just discovered that her boyfriend had just left her, "maybe because he saw some other girl who was prettier or maybe because she's a witch." On Card 4, Anna decided that the young man in the foreground was leaving for the army and that his wife was in despair. On Card 5, Anna saw the woman in the doorway as looking in on "her dead husband."

She could not think how the husband died or what the woman might do next. Finally, she added with a laugh, "The old gal might commit suicide." She similarly saw the couple on Card 6GF as contemplating a separation and the two figures on Card 12 GF as mourning over the death of the father and husband.

In reviewing Anna's responses, the psychologist looked for any signs that Anna might feel involved or guilty over what she apparently realized as a near separation of her parents, but there was no evidence that there was anything more than a realistic and somewhat depressed appraisal of her family situation.

Don, a tall, husky lad, shrugged in noncommital fashion when asked why he thought he had been brought to see the psychologist. He admitted that he knew that psychologists "deal with people's problems," but added with a broad smile that he did not believe that he had any more problems "than any other kid." He said that he knew that his sister had also previously seen the psychologist and that he thought maybe she had some problems but could not say what they were or even why he suspected that she might have any emotional difficulty. In the discussion initiated by the psychologist about his general life pattern, Don talked freely and with enjoyment about his sports activities, mentioning the golf lessons with his dad. He claimed that he got along pretty well with Anna except that he too had noticed she seemed very "touchy." Asked next about his mother, Don paused briefly and added that she too seemed "touchy," but again he could not describe what about his mother's behavior made him describe her with this term.

The assessment data showed that Don also was intellectually advanced for his age, but he showed little or none of Anna's emotional sensitivity. In fact, Don seemed particularly unaware either of emotional aspects in his environment, or in his own impulse life. His perception of the world was so very matter-of-fact that he seemed to be making extra efforts to neutralize and avoid any kind of emotional involvement. Whenever his own impulses began to play a part in his conceptualization of a situation, he quickly denied them. For example, on Card 5 of the Rorschach, he first described the "bat" as "flying" but then denied this, saying, "How could an inkblot fly?" Despite the fact that he was just passed 12 years of age, Don showed no signs of internalization of any model for behavior. It seemed as though he made his judgments on the basis of what was immediately present. He blocked excessively on the TAT, apologizing that he had no imagination and could not think of stories. For example, he saw the boy with the violin, TAT Card 1, as wishing he could stop practice and go outside and play ball with the other fellows but could not say who required him to practice or how it would turn out. Pressed for a conclusion, he decided the boy would continue to "squeak away" until the assigned practice hour was finished. Similarly, he saw the figure on the Card 3 BM as a guy who had fallen asleep on the edge of his bed. He could not think of why the figure had fallen asleep in this position except that "he must have been real tired." As for a conclusion, Don finally decided, "He'll wake up with a sore neck." As to the object in the left foreground of this card, Don studied it for a minute and decided that it was something that had dropped out of the boy's pocket. Only on Card 11 did Don become any more expansive. He groaned, "Oh boy! The whole world seems to be falling part, and here's a dinosaur coming out of the cliff; he's been exposed by the earthquake, and this boy down here (pointing to a figure in the center) doesn't know what's going on at all. He's just knocked silly by a rock and he doesn't even see the dinosaur. The dinosaur will probably come down and kill this guy before he even knows what's happened." Thereafter, Don's stories did become more morbid and depressive. He saw the standing figure in Card 12 BM as about to attack and murder the reclining figures. He decided that the murderer was a madman who had crept into the boy's bedroom and concluded the story by deciding it was all a dream. The boy would wake up and nothing would have happened. To 13B, Don responded that the boy was hungry and deserted by his parents, and that the boy was sad because "he didn't know what his parents were up to." Because the boy's surroundings looked so "poor," Don though maybe they were on welfare and that the boy would be rescued by some welfare worker. Next, Don saw the silhouette figure in Card 14 as about to commit suicide, adding quickly, "I don't know why anybody would do that, maybe it's just that he's confused and doesn't know anything at all. I saw a TV story about that one time, but I don't remember it." Don claimed he couldn't think of any story to tell for the blank card, 16, and then added, "Oh yes, it must be a picture of that little kid story about Chicken Little, this is where the sky fell in." And finally, on Card 17, Don saw the figure climbing down a rope to escape a ship that was exploding and all on fire: "He'll have to swim through the oil and fire and all the water; he may be all burned up if he's lucky—I mean if he's *unlucky*."

In reviewing Don's responses, it did seem as if he was relatively much less mature than his sister and much less prepared to meet a severe emotional trauma such as the threatened divorce. Nevertheless, there were hints in several of the TAT stories quoted before that Don, at least unconsciously, recognized some kind of impending doom. It was hypothesized that Don's emotional constriction might well be his defensive wall against this unconsciously recognized threat. While Anna was already almost aware of what was going on with her family consciously and might even be somewhat relieved if it should come out in the open, Don might be expected to avoid open recognition of the tension and attempt to guard himself even further against the feelings aroused by it.

These assessments were then discussed with the parents. Both agreed that the psychologist's appraisal was very consonant with what they themselves had thought.

It was then planned to have a series of family meetings where at least some of the tensions between the parents might be gradually discussed with the children. Each family discussion was followed immediately by individual interviews with the children in which their feelings about their parents' dissension were explored further and where they were given further support. As was predicted, Anna cried openly during the first of these family discussions, begging the parents not to get a divorce, but at the same time seemed somewhat relieved. She remarked during the individual hours with the psychologist that she felt better about the situation now that everybody knew what was going on, and that she guessed that she could "live" even if her parents decided to get a divorce.

Don, on the other hand, sat very quietly during the initial family discussions, responding very briefly only when a question was directed at him. He denied that he had had any indication that his parents were disagreeing so strongly and so frequently. When subsequently asked how he felt about it, he shrugged and said, "How is a fellow supposed to feel?" He tried at first to deny everything, claiming that whatever his parents did was "their business." However, he agreed that he would be very "sad" if they divorced. As the family discussions continued, Don became obviously more depressed. In the individual interviews, he became quite angry at the psychologist, claiming that the psychologist was at fault for bringing him into the situation at all and that the psychologist was "all wet." He remarked, "This might drive me bugs," whereupon he began to sob.

Thereafter, Don and his sister were able to express considerable anger toward both of their parents, blaming each of them for the tension within the family. Both parents expressed considerable guilt and depression and tried to reassure their children that their contemplated separation had nothing to do with them. "How can you say that?" exclaimed Anna. "It has to do with us because you are our parents and we need parents and you can't separate." However, in the final session, the parents informed the children that they had decided to live separately at least, and that Mr. V would visit the home weekly. Although both children expressed some further sadness and anger regarding their parents' decision, they seemed markedly relieved that a decision had been made and that everyone's feelings had been explored about it.

D.   CHANGES WITHIN THE CHILD'S EDUCATIONAL MILIEU

Perhaps the most common question asked in a referral for assessment deals with the child's schooling. For example, a parent or pediatrician may ask whether the child needs some sort of remedial work at school, whether he/she should have a tutor, whether he/she should be placed in a special class or in a special school. These questions arise because a deterrent in the child's ego development is manifested very often in lowered academic achievement. The reasons for poor schoolwork, as they have been described throughout this volume, are varied and multiple. Whatever the cause, some decision usually has to be made regarding the possible remedial steps to be taken, for example, if the child is to need tutoring, special class assignments, or a special school. Thus, even if one does discover, for example, that the child is failing to read because of some emotional block, this finding in itself is only part of the step in making some decision about how the child may be taught to read.

Remedial education is a specialty that is usually beyond the knowledge of most clinical psychologists, and assessment to determine the specific *methods* of retraining or training lies in the purview of the educational psychologist. However, the data about ego development that the clinical psychologist gathers and analyzes are often very pertinent background to the specific decisions about the need for such educational remedial methods, the general effects of placing a child in a separate educational milieu, and the considerations that a remedial teacher might have to make about aspects of the child's ego functioning, other than his intellectual advancement. Thus, a clinical assessment should provide data regarding the specific nature of the child's psychological disabilities, so that the remedial teacher will be able to estimate the limits of the child's abilities and recognize his/her special talents and interests.

Moreover, as with any change of milieu, it is necessary to know how the child will react to the prospective change. In this instance, one needs to know how a child will feel if she/he is removed from a regular classroom and placed where children are receiving remedial aid—a situation that is often regarded by a child as indicating inadequacy and that socially isolates her/him or lowers her/his social status among peers. Children who are in special classrooms and who are behind in their work are often referred to as "dummies" by their peers in regular classrooms. Perhaps the most important considerations for the remedial schoolteacher are the child's motivations and affective responses, which must be considered before a teacher can approach any learning problem. This is especially true whenever the child has experienced failure and is discouraged and angry. It is in regard to these affective and social-behavior problems that the teacher turns to the clinical assessment.

One of the main difficulties in relating a psychological assessment of the child to educational needs is that educational philosophies, as well as methods, have been changing and developing rapidly in recent years. Educators vary considerably in their views on the content and even the aims and philosophies of such programs. Variations are almost as extensive as there are school systems.

One of the difficulties in relating the assessment of a child to such programs is the fact that, in most instances, educators think in terms of "programs," rather than in terms of the individual. The psychologist deals with one child at a time, but the educator per force must deal with relatively large groups of children. There is no doubt that those responsible for the formation of educational programs do have "the individual child" in mind, but theirs is an average or idealized child, whereas the psychologist is dealing with an actual child's very specific needs. Many educators today do advocate that the "system" approach to education be scrapped, that such institutions as classes, grades, and the like be forgotten, and that an educational program be evolved for and tailored to the needs of each child. However, until such an ideal is realized, the clinical psychologist must attempt to fit individual assessment to the realities of an educational system.

Thus, a clinical psychologist should become familiar with the educational programs available in the immediate community. She/he should know what kinds of programs and classes are available, their aims, and how they are constituted. Many of the programs in larger areas are quite varied. It usually is possible in such centers to find a program that fits the needs of the specific child fairly closely. Usually there are classes for children who are so disabled that they need to be separated entirely from those who are not disabled. However, there may be other situations where a disabled child can be accepted into a regular classroom. Most educational systems are flexible enough so that a child may attend one or two special classes or have some extra tutoring while attending a majority of the same classes as other children.

However, even in large urban centers, it is rare to find special classes adapted to very special problems. In many systems, there are special classes for the "educationally handicapped." This phase includes the emotionally disturbed child, the retarded child, and the physically or sensorily handicapped. Although at first glance this throwing of all handicapped children into one group seems very unreasonable and possibly even undesirable, I have seen such classes, especially where they were fairly small, that have

worked very well. There is at least the advantage that the source of the problem tends to be temporarily forgotten, and the focus is on the immediate recovery of educational losses. There are, however, difficulties that sometimes outweigh this advantage. For example, in so mixing a variety of handicapped children together, it may be very difficult to meet the special needs of each child. Moreover, the child who has a severe motor handicap resents being put in a class with those who are retarded or with those who are "bad kids." Similarly, the emotionally disturbed child does not see himself/herself as a "dummy" or a "spasz," which are common names for the retarded and the crippled child, respectively. Thus, wherever possible, school systems do at least try to separate these three groups.

The fact that the child is segregated at all from other children is one of the first considerations the assessor should take into account. Most children who have educational handicaps do not want to have this difference pointed up—especially to their peers. In fact, most of them are unwilling to admit the handicap or difference to themselves. Thus, the assessor should look at the child's responses to see whether she/he can accept and use this separation from the stresses of the normal classroom, or whether it might be better to permit her/him at least to sit in the regular classroom and offer this remedial work on the side. Moreover, when treated in a special manner and put in a role of being inadequate, many disabled children quickly tend to become more dependent and less adequate. One of the very untoward results of the old special schools for the blind, the deaf, and the retarded was that these extremely segregated schools created individuals who belonged, in effect, to a minority group. The graduates of many of these schools often continued to live together in small groups, apart from the rest of society, communicating only with other deaf or blind people. In the past, the retarded adult continued to live in the institution. If disabled children are not to become members of a minority group based on physical and mental handicaps, then school programs need to be instituted that integrate these minorities into the school—programs that are similar to the integration of racial minorities. Although there are probably as many deaf and blind children or children with braces and wheelchairs as there are disabled adults, it is indeed amazing to find how many nondisabled children have never seen a disabled child, because they seldom meet them in the classroom.

These social and philosophical considerations aside, the practical problems of communication between the clinical psychologist and school authorities need to be considered.* In the United States, the authorities who deal with the psychological problems of the child and those who are responsible for her/his education usually belong to two separate institutional systems. There are problems in communication, for no other reason than that their schedules and paths do not adequately cross.† In addition, the psychologist has a telephone on his/her desk and someone to assist in correspondence, whereas the schoolteacher has much more limited access to a telephone and very often little or no assistance with correspondence. I used to be very frustrated in attempting to contact the schools because it was difficult to get the child's teacher on the phone, and weeks would go by before a letter written to a school would be answered. However, a message left for a teacher to return a phone call at her/his convenience usually brings results. A good example of communication between the clinical psychologist and the school system was given in Case 118 in this chapter. Since, in most situations, the psychologist and teacher are not in a direct line of communication, the psychologist's written report assumes even greater importance. In writing reports for the school, the clinical psychologist should make extra efforts to state the results clearly and to make the findings relevant to the school situation.

There are, of course, quite a few similarities between the child's behavior in the classroom and in the assessment situation that help to make it possible to translate the psychologist's observations into statements that would be helpful to the teacher. As was mentioned before, the psychologist—like the teacher—is interested in the child's intellectual development, in her/his motivations, and in the ability to cope with stress and affect. In fact, children often are likely to see an assessment situation in terms of their school experience. Although the child may discover quite soon that the psychologist is not trying to teach anything, the place where the child has experienced being tested before is usually in the classroom. Thus, it is very likely that the teacher has met with many of the same "games" that the child plays with the assessor, and the motivation and affect that the child displays during the assessment may not be far different from what is displayed in the classroom when she/he is called upon to recite her/his lessons. Thus, the psychologist obtains a small sample of how the child relates to teachers and educational authorities.

The psychologist, of course, has the skill and opportunity to observe what the teacher may not—namely, the ego system behind the defensive "games" and other manifest behaviors of the child. The value of the assessment thus lies in the psychologist's ability to communicate these findings so that the teacher can utilize them in applying his/her special skills.

CASE 122

Patty, age 15, presented several school difficulties that had accumulated over the years and that, by the time of her first year in high school, seemed almost insurmountable. Her school record showed that her intellectual functioning, while not grossly retarded, was, at best, at the lower edge of the normal range. Her academic achievement through-

*See Case 9, Chapter 5.
†In the more closed society of the Soviet Union, clinics for children are part of the educational system.

out elementary school had been mediocre. However, teachers had at least noted her "fair" effort and good "work habits and cooperation." There was no note, prior to her entrance into junior high school, of any kind of behavior problem. However, after she left the structured classroom environment of elementary school, Patty had an increasing number of difficulties. For the past four years, she had been just above the failing mark in all subjects. The school counselor now advised her father that there was serious question whether it was wise to attempt to keep Patty in school past the compulsory age of 16. Patty had become resistant to the usual classroom routine and discipline. In junior high school she had been consistently difficult to handle because of her impudence and because she ignored the teachers' requests. During the tenth grade, Patty had become even more defiant of school rules and even somewhat disruptive in the classroom. She would outrage teachers by calmly and deliberately turning her back on them when they addressed her. If she did not care to do what they requested, she would rise and leave the classroom without any of the usual social amenities. She was frequently in conflict with the dean of women because of her dress and grooming. Her hair, which seemed untended, grew almost to her waist, and she overused cosmetics in an amateurish fashion. She paid no attention to the rules for dress set down by the girls' student-body counsel and, instead, defiantly dressed in a teen-aged fashion that often appeared to be sexually provocative. The dean of women was particularly upset at one point when she discovered that although Patty had come to school fully dressed, by lunchtime she had taken off her underclothes and stuffed them in her purse. It was this total school problem that caused Patty's father to seek psychological consultation.

In the initial interview, Patty's father was most apologetic, saying that he was afraid that it was his fault that the child's problems had gone so long unattended. He explained that his wife had died about four years previously and that he had found it very difficult to maintain communication with Patty's school, since he was employed full time. Moreover, he had four younger children who also made demands on his attention. He said that he thought he had particularly neglected Patty, since she presented no problem at home whatever, but actually had assumed a great deal of responsibility for the care of their home and of her younger brothers and sisters. He was quick to point out that there were no demands made on Patty to assume any of these obligations. He employed a full-time housekeeper. He was present in the home each evening and over the entire weekend. Patty, however, delighted in helping to clean the house, to cook and to care for the little ones. Her father had attempted to correct her when he noticed that she left the house inappropriately dressed, but admitted that she always looked so crushed when he criticized her that often he did not have the heart to intervene. He had been more worried about Patty in recent months since she had seemed to be more sensitive, to "mope around the house," to avoid her friends, and to devote herself even more energetically to the household chores. He had recently taken her to the family doctor, wondering if she might not be suffering from some kind of "anemia," but had been advised by the physician that Patty was in good general health. He had tried to encourage her to "go places and do things," but to no avail. Until the beginning of this year, Patty had had many peer friends of both sexes who came to her home; she also frequently visited in the other children's homes. She had even been on a couple of "double dates," and during the ninth grade, he had made extra efforts to see that she went to the school dances. He wondered again if she might not be "mixed up over some boy" but when he tried to inquire about this, Patty assured him almost curtly that she was "not interested in boys now."

Patty's father was also concerned about Patty's situation since he was planning to remarry in the very near future. He hoped that having a mother again in the home would be helpful to Patty, and that his new wife would not have to face the problems that Patty presented in regard to the school. Patty and his fiancée had met many times and they seemed to like one another a lot. He noted, as an example, that Patty had urged him to redecorate his room and had suggested some feminine touches that he might not have thought of on his own. "You don't think she could be jealous?" he asked with a laugh.

When Patty's father brought her to the clinic, her appearance contrasted sharply with that described by the school. Her long black hair was the only bizarre feature. Otherwise, she was dressed very modestly in a simple but casual sheath dress, and she wore no cosmetics whatever. A slim, delicately built child, she showed few signs of secondary sexual development and might easily have been taken for three or four years younger than her stated age. She was quite tense and guarded, sitting upright in the chair and frequently wetting her lips. She volunteered little, and her responses were very terse. Yet, there was considerable and appropriate affect in what she did have to say. She sighed deeply as she admitted that she knew she had been brought to the psychologist "because I'm so stupid in school." Her eyes blazed as she stated that she did not care what anybody thought of her schoolwork, or what school authorities might do if she continued to dress and act as she pleased. She relaxed noticeably and spoke spontaneously when talking about her home and her brothers and sisters. Her face froze again into a mask when the psychologist told her that he was interested in her school achievement among other things, and part of his job would be to help understand what these difficulties were in order that some further and more satisfying plans might be made for her. She remained quite tense throughout all the tests, but was cooperative.

Patty's Full Scale IQ of 81 was consistent with the scores obtained in previous years. Her difficulty in verbalizing was most acute (Verbal IQ 71), whereas she had somewhat greater degree of success on several of the Performance subtests of the Wechsler I (Performance IQ 98). Throughout the Wechsler, Patty did try to shrug off failure, but it was obvious that she felt very badly about it, nor was she reassured by her successes. Qualitatively, Patty appeared to have a very practical mind; she did better on tasks where she did not have to think through abstractions but could go and do things, such as the Picture Completion, Digit Symbol, and Block Design. She did well on the Object Assembly Test also, except for the Hand, which provides no immediate clues. Her intellectual functioning on the unstructured materials of the Rorschach and TAT were similarly rather simple and uncomplicated. She selected the large, usual details of the Rorschach inkblots, eliminating or ignoring those details of the test that did not fit precisely with her immediate impression. Her TAT plots consisted of a series of actions with little explanation of how one event led to another. When Patty had to explain or justify her percepts, she became uncomfortable and even resistant. Sometimes she would shrug and say, "I don't know," but there were occasions where she made no response at all when asked for further explanation. Patty's perceptual-motor development seemed quite normal for her age, and there were no signs of any difficulty in this area. Affectively, Patty's responses suggested that she was severely constricted and considerably depressed. Her associations to both the Rorschach and TAT indicated that she was exceedingly cautious about allowing any emotional investment in her environment. Similarly, she attempted to block out or avoid any internal feelings. She was, however, somewhat more sensitive to other people's feelings and showed signs of being easily hurt. Her chief defense against affect seemed to be a mild but definite negativism. Patty almost seemed to be defending herself against her sensitivity by pretending that she did not care at all. By defying others and obstinately ignoring a situation, she could hide the fact that she felt hurt. Patty also used her "I-don't-care" negativism to hide her depression.

Her associations strongly suggested that she probably was still grieving over the loss of her mother and that she was trying very hard to suppress her longings for a dependent relationship with a maternal figure. In fact, at one point Patty did say very directly that she loved to care for her younger brothers and sisters because she knew how much they missed having a mother. Patty's feminine interests also suggested that her identification with her mother had been fairly strong. Nevertheless, several of Patty's TAT stories also indicated that while she might look forward to having a mother, it was very likely that she did not look forward to sharing her father's affections with anyone else. For example she could not tell a story to Card 8GF, except to remark that the girl looked like she might be about to go to a wedding and, after a pause, Patty added, "She looks rather sad." On Card 18GF, Patty reversed the usual relationship attributed to the two women and described the "daughter as choking the stepmother." However, Patty could not expand on these remarks.

These results suggested that there were many problems with which Patty needed help and about which the school could do little. Yet, there were some features of these results that did seem particularly pertinent to the decision that would have to be made in the near future regarding Patty's attendance in school. For example, the school was apprised of not only Patty's slow intellectual development but also of the nature of her intellectual functioning. It was suggested to the school that emphasis might be made on her practical interests, and that further development of verbal skills or subjects involving abstract thinking might be relatively futile. The school was also advised of Patty's interest in homemaking and feminine activities. It was suggested that any program in which she could be engaged in physical or manual activities would probably fascinate her. The school was not told of the sources of Patty's depression, but the fact that she was depressed and that much of her negativism served to counteract her depression was made explicit. In discussing these results with Patty's counselor, it was discovered that the classes in which her behavior was most disturbing were those that were least adapted to her abilities, such as history, mathematics, and English composition. Her, "work habits and cooperation" were considered quite adequate in home economics, typing, and physical education. Unfortunately, the school that Patty was attending placed strong emphasis on preparing for college work and offered only a minimum program for anyone with Patty's particular needs.

Taking these results into account, the high-school counselor worked out a program with Patty as follows: Since it seemed very likely that she would be finishing her education when she was graduated from high school, it was decided she could drop most of the "academic subjects" and emphasize the more practical courses in her curriculum. In addition to the home economics courses, Patty was enrolled in a special class for expressive dancing. Patty's situation was discussed with the drama teacher who offered to try to interest her in costuming, stage designing, and makeup, since Patty's poor verbal ability did not give much promise for actual stage performances. Finally, Patty was enrolled in a practicum course two afternoons at another high school where the entire class time was spent in the care of nursery-school children. The dean of women was involved in this planning, and it was readily agreed that further punitive action regarding Patty's dress and even her behavior might be of little avail. The dean remembered that she had had some success the previous year with a girl who was very similar to Patty by assigning her duties in the office. The other girl had made extra efforts to conform to the school rules, largely because of the special attention given her.

During the ensuing year, Patty was seen in weekly psychotherapy sessions by a woman therapist. These sessions were largely supportive, with much discussion about the day-to-day events at home and school. A recheck with the school during this year showed that Patty responded well to this program and that there was every indication that in the following year she would receive a high-school diploma.

E.   MAJOR ENVIRONMENTAL CHANGES

When a change in the child's environment that involves removal from the family milieu appears necessary, a thorough assessment is in order. Such a complete change of environment is seldom contemplated unless the parental home contains so much stress and offers so little in the way of emotional support that the child's further development would be severely restricted. Usually, in such instances, the child is already somewhat disturbed and is likely to carry some of that disturbance with her/him to any new situation—at least temporarily. Moreover, the uprooting of the child from her/his home, however unstable, is likely to be a depressing event, adding to whatever feelings the child may already have of being rejected and guilty. Even where the child has shown no previous emotional disturbance and separation from the family is caused by an event such as the parents' death or their illness, the trauma of such a separation is not to be underestimated. The first step in the assessment of such a situation is a careful understanding of the exact circumstances that appear to necessitate a removal of the child from the home. In fact, the question of necessity itself should be considered.

CASE 123

It appeared necessary for Jerry, age 10, and his brother, Tim, age 5, to move to another town to live with their grandparents when both of their parents were convicted of a felony and imprisoned. However, the grandparents, after consultation with the psychologist, spontaneously attempted to preserve the home structure by closing their own home and moving into the residence in which the boys had been living for most of their lives. Thus, although the boys were rudely shocked by the separation of their parents from the home, for reasons that they did not understand, their home routine could be largely maintained.

CASE 124

The five children of the A family, including an adolescent girl, first lost their father, who abandoned them, and then their mother, who had to be hospitalized for a psychotic breakdown. Rather than place the children in an institution or separate them out into foster homes, the county welfare office was able to use the same funds to pay a foster parent to live in the home during the six months of the mother's hospitalization. Arrangements were even made for this foster mother to continue to be in the home when the mother returned from the hospital and was recuperating. Although several of the children did show signs of possible emotional disturbance and were having some difficulty in school, it appeared that this rather extraordinary and experimental move on the part of the welfare office prevented any of these children from suffering unduly because of this major disturbance in their lives. The mother was subsequently able to work and care for her children without further assistance.

In other instances, a complete separation of the child from the family may be quite necessary if the chain of interactions within the family that brought about the child's disturbance is to be broken. For example, Bettelheim (1950) found such a separation necessary for the treatment of the schizophrenic children with whom he was working. In my experience and in that of my colleagues in the residential treatment of the severely anorexic child, it is often necessary to prohibit contact between the child and parents for as long as three months. Such a separation almost inevitably results in the child's becoming severely depressed, but since such children have previously sealed off all affective reactions, the appearance of this induced depression makes it possible to make contact with their affective life.

Where such a treatment plan does seem inevitable, the assessment usually proves to be invaluable, since it provides clues as to the nature of the child's possible reactions. Thus, in two of the three recent cases of anorexia admitted to the hospital to which I was attached, the assessment data strongly suggested the possibility of a psychotic reaction, in addition to the usual depression and grief. The staff members decided to proceed with the treatment, but they were prepared to handle the children's behavior and thought processes, as well as the depression. Because the staff are aware of the fragility of the ego of such children, they are able to offer special support and thus assuage the child's confusion, so that an open psychotic break is avoided. In one such case, there was some evidence in the child's history that she had at least come close to an open break with reality a year prior to the hospitalization. The staff members were not surprised by her attempt to retreat to the corner of the ward in catatonic fashion, and they supported all her efforts to maintain contact and were able to limit this behavior. After several weeks, the child's depression lifted entirely, and she joined in ward activities.

Where the assessor does not work in a residential center or is otherwise not familiar with the kind of setting proposed for the child, the prediction of how the child will react to placement away from her/his parents is more difficult. As with other proposed environmental changes, the psychologist who hopes to make predictions about the child's reaction to changes needs to have some data concerning a possible foster home, residential institution, or boarding school. The data about such a placement is gathered most expertly and is analyzed by the psychiatric or medical social worker. However, whenever possible,

the clinical psychologist should join the social worker in appraising these placement settings. Where such collaboration is not possible, the psychologist should make every effort to obtain as much evidence as possible about the situation. Very often, of course, no specific placement is as yet proposed, although the possibility of placement is being seriously considered. In these instances, the assessment data are usually very helpful in indicating the kinds of placements that might be preferable. Thus, the psychologist may be able to give some suggestions to social-work colleagues as to the type of foster home or placement that would be most likely to relieve the stresses that the child has experienced and thus possibly promote psychological growth. The same is true when a psychologist is advising a court that may have a choice of institutions or placements for a delinquent child. An example of such a study is given in the case of Tina, Case 15 in Chapter 7.

When the placement of the child outside the home is contemplated, information is needed at the outset of an assessment concerning the kinds of behaviors that may have led directly to such a consideration or at least may be associated with it. In most instances, separation of the child from the home is not considered unless there is overwhelming evidence that he/she is unable to live there. Sometimes the child's reaction to the environment might be considered a fairly effective method of coping—even though sociably unacceptable. For example, truancy is often the best possible choice a child may make to a very disruptive home. It certainly indicates less disturbance and a greater effort to deal realistically with the situation than such reactions as depressive withdrawal, somatic reactions, or suicide.* Moreover, by frequent truancy, the child communicates to society at large that all is not well in his/her family; even if the child does not otherwise state it, this possibility usually occurs to the most casual observer.

*To remove a child from the home *only* because she/he is truant would seem to be reinforcing her/his behavior!

Quite often, the immediate and manifest reason for considering a child's placement outside the home is that her/his behavior is far too disturbing for the family, school, or the rest of society to endure. In such instances, the assessor should pay attention to the level of tolerance of the child's social environment as well as to the child's actual behavior. Such acceptance or rejection of the child's behavior by the social milieu often has little to do with the actual degree of disturbance within the child. For example, surveys of public schools suggest that schools often tolerate very overt psychotic behavior on the part of children to the point that they are learning absolutely nothing and are even a mild-to-moderate disturbance to the rest of the class. This behavior will be tolerated as long as it does not openly violate the public mores of the classroom. On the other hand, most school systems are unable to tolerate continued asocial behavior on the part of a child even though such behavior may be periodic, directed only against school authorities, and is relatively nondisturbing to the classroom. Even a single public acting-out of sexual conflicts may panic a school or a neighborhood to the point that explusion of the child from his/her milieu is demanded by a band of voices.

Cases 125 and 126

Roger, age 10, was so emotionally disturbed that he appeared almost unable to communicate. He sat in the back of the class making noises to himself or stood gesturing on the playground, completely out of contact with his peers or the rest of his environment. Yet, he was permitted to return to the classroom yearly and was brought to the attention of the psychologist only with pressure from the family physician. Immediately across the street from Roger lived Anabelle, age 14, who had been a top student, very well behaved, and liked by her teachers and peers, but whose immediate expulsion from school was demanded by all concerned when she became illegitimately pregnant. Anabelle's parents were able to use the

school's rejection of her to aid in rationalizing their own anger at her and their need to reject her. The school and Roger's parents' acceptance of his behavior, although it might well have contributed to his continued disturbance, did make it possible to involve both the school and family in his treatment. On the other hand, the combined rejection of school, peers, and parents caused Anabelle to commit suicide before plans could be implemented for caring for her outside the home.

Quite often, once the child is removed from the environment, the social group becomes so relieved from the stresses caused by that child that even after her/his behavior changes, it becomes very difficult for society to accept the child's return. A classic instance of such a problem is, of course, the law violator who, although quite rehabilitated, often finds that she/he is not accepted back in the community. Similarly, once a family and a school have successfully expunged a disturbing child and have placed her/him in the role of being "sick," they are often unable to tolerate the child's return, even though her/his behavior may have become much less disturbing.

Case 127

Dorcey, age 16, was remanded by the juvenile court for psychological assessment since the boy's mother had asked the court to declare him "incorrigible" and "a ward of the court" so that placement outside the home could be considered. This move by the mother had been precipitated when Dorcey had fired a pistol several times at his mother's common-law husband. Investigation further showed that Dorcey was also not considered acceptable at school, for although his academic achievement had been fair, he often was openly resentful of school authorities, and ignored school rules regarding behavior and dress. It was also suspected that he used marijuana, which was then widespread in the student body. Certainly, Dorcey's long hair, the dark glasses he constantly wore, and his unkempt clothes and boots all gave him a bizarre appearance. In the minds of many of the adults he met, including officials of the court, his appearance was associated with potential delinquency.

Dorcey's mother said that she had barely been able to tolerate his appearance and attitudes prior to the shooting incident, and that now she was frightened lest some further act of violence occur. Yet, she upheld Dorcey's story that he had fired the shots at her husband only because the man had been beating her and had dared Dorcey to defend her. This man had immediately left home and had not returned. Dorcey said openly that he wondered if he would not be better off somewhere else since—in his words—his mother was a "stinking bitch." However, the very fact that he had tried to protect her did suggest that their relationship was at least ambivalent. Dorcey also regarded his school environment as barely tolerable, but said that he hoped to be able to graduate in another year and that he was depressed at the prospect of leaving his girlfriend and other peer companions.

The assessment revealed that Dorcey did seem to be attempting to resolve his conflicting relationship with his mother through the social acting-out at school. Nevertheless, his abilities to appraise reality and even to control his own behavior were such that if the environment could continue to tolerate him, outpatient treatment seemed much more preferable than institutionalization. Upon receiving this report, the court also took notice of the fact that Dorcey had no previous record of actual arrests. Since he was quite ready to accept the psychotherapy offered at the clinic, the court accepted him as a ward, but decided to continue to place him with his mother. A transfer to another high school was arranged.

All these data about the circumstances leading to consideration of placement of a child outside his/her home are necessary, so that in gathering and analyzing the assessment data it is possible to relate the child's level of ego development to his/her relationship to that specific environmental setting. By combining these environmental data with those obtained from the assessment proper, an estimate can be made of the degree to which the environment may be contributing to a child's disturbances. Thus, it becomes more possible to decide how much the interaction between the child and the environment does necessitate her/his being removed from it. It also becomes more possible to foster those elements in this interaction that might make it possible for the child to remain. Moreover, a knowledge of the child's past and prospective environments provides the background for understanding his/her fantasies, coping mechanisms, and affective reactions.

Next, it is very important to be able to assess the child's reaction to the possibility of separation. Any assessment of such a case should be directed at the child's feelings about this separation, to see how she/he perceives it, what tensions it arouses within him/her, and what possible coping mechanisms he/she may make in response to it. For some children, the removal from the scene of tension, although it may be accompanied by an almost inevitable feeling of depression, at the same time is experienced as a relief.

Moreover, it is common to find that the child also is experiencing much guilt. For most children, the fact that they are being removed from their home immediately suggests that they have done something awful to warrant such a rejection. These feelings of guilt are often present even when the actual reasons for considering removal have little to do with the child. For example, nearly every child whose family breaks up because of divorce feels at least some twinge of guilt, believing that in some way her/his behavior may have caused the parental separation. Fantasies that emphasize guilt feelings or feelings of being responsible also are quite common among children whose parents die quite suddenly. Sometimes, even the display of depression and grief is inadmissable to a family or to a child.

CASE 128

A 40-year-old woman and her 15-year-old daughter, Myra, endured the death, funeral, and social reception after the funeral of their 70-year-old husband and father—not only without tears but by maintaining an outward show of social graciousness. Four months later, the girl, who had been a successful student, began failing at school and withdrew from her friends and social activities. It was only then that her depression was recognized. Assessment, first of the girl and then of the mother, revealed that they had readily accepted the supposed disapproval of their religion against any show of grief in order to hide their feelings of disappointment and even anger against the dead man because he had been unable to satisfy their needs for almost a decade. The girl's subsequent tears were of anger, as well as of grief.

The chief reason for paying special attention to the possible feelings of guilt involved in separation of a child from the family is that, quite often, this subsequent disturbing behavior turns out to be an attempt to cope with guilt.

CASE 129

Ceila, age 11, was admitted to the residential treatment center after having failed to adjust to two different foster homes. She had originally been removed from her home the previous year, after her father's death. Her mother, who was partially paralyzed from poliomyelitis, was unable to care for her as the mother's depression exacerbated her disability. Ceila had run away several times from the foster homes, had been very disobedient, fought with the other children, and started fires. It was evident from the assessment data that Ceila considered herself very inadequate and worthless. She openly called herself such names as "stupid" and "evil," but she could not explain why she so derogated herself. Some of her remarks in the initial interviews openly suggested that she, in some way, felt responsible for both her father's death and her mother's polio, although she initially denied any such feelings. Strong feelings of guilt and depression pervaded her associations on the projective techniques. In a subsequent interview, Ceila did admit that her mother's polio was thought to be the result of an accidental use of a live serum used in the polio vaccine. Ceila believed if she had not taken these innoculations herself, her mother would not have done so either. Ceila's father, who was reputed to be a very emotionally distant man, had died of cirrhosis of the liver, probably as the result of a mild but lifelong alcoholism.

Ceila's TAT fantasies revealed ambivalent feelings toward father figures, including both anger against being ignored and rejected by them and a guilt over the murderous wishes directed at them. In one story, the heroine committed suicide after the death of the father because she had been very angry at him. In another story, a witch was captured and killed by the community because she had caused the death of the community leader. The witch, Ceila explained, had caused the death of the man because he "didn't pay any attention to her." The fact that Ceila's responses to the Rorschach were replete with associations of explosive tensions suggested she might well handle guilt feelings by acting-out. Moreover, there were other associations on Ceila's TAT fantasies that suggested that she needed to continue to test whether people would accept her. Frequently, the heroes of her TAT stories initially escaped punishment for their crimes only to be apprehended and severely punished for minor infractions. For example, in Ceila's response to Card 3GF, the herione was depicted as having just killed her unfaithful boyfriend. She was subsequently arrested for crossing the street against the stop sign and was "thrown into jail for life."

On the basis of this assessment, it was decided to keep Ceila in the hospital until these guilt feelings could be ameliorated, possibly through psychotherapy. A further search for a foster home was thus delayed.

Assessment was also made of Ceila's mother, and it was discovered that she, too, harbored intense feelings of anger and guilt. Not only did she feel rejected by and angry toward her deceased husband, but she had also been disappointed when she had tried to find support for her needs and affection in her relationship with Ceila. Her fantasies suggested that she saw her polio as a curse that had been inflicted upon her because of her previous anger toward her husband and daughter. She was so depressed that she had contemplated suicide. It seemed likely that much of Ceila's depression was a reflection of her mother's attitudes. Ultimately, through psychotherapy with both Ceila and her mother, it was possible to reconstitute their relationship and to return Ceila to her own home.

CASE 130

Richard, age 12, had been suspended from junior high school after the school janitor had complained that Richard had threatened him with a knife. Richard was extremely defensive, charging that he thought the janitor was "after him," and that he needed to protect himself because the janitor was continually spying on him. Richard had made similar charges against several classmates, complaining that they had picked on him, threatened him with violence, and constantly called him names. The principal had been concerned because Richard seemed so withdrawn from his peers. The principal observed that Richard had in truth been the object of considerable teasing because he was quick to rise to the bait and because of his prissy ways. Richard also liked to show up his teachers at any possible point, going to the extent of spending many hours in the library to prove that they were wrong about something they said in class. Richard was positive that the teachers and principal "have it in for me."

Richard was backed up in his feelings by his mother who hired an attorney to sue the school board. Even in the initial interview, it was evident that she was extremely suspicious and probably a paranoid woman. She had previously been involved in litigious disputes with her neighbors. In front of Richard she openly referred to the peers at his school as "hoodlums" and hinted broadly that she thought the janitor was probably homosexual. Although she was adamant that Richard was purely a victim of circumstances, with no emotional problems whatever, she did follow her attorney's advice to seek psychological consultation "if only to prove him innocent." In the same vein, she herself submitted to the assessment. Her responses supported the impresssion that she was a very paranoid, confused, angry, and guilt-ridden woman. Although Richard's responses to the assessment suggested that he was experiencing many of the same feelings, it did appear that his disturbance was not nearly as extensive as his mother's. Thus, it seemed quite possible that he was echoing many of her concerns in a folie à deux.

Richard's father, an internationally famous scientist, had apparently extricated himself from the situation by devoting himself entirely to his work, which kept him away from the home much of the time. In fact, it appeared that the father's absence from the home served to reinforce the symbiotic bond between Richard and his mother. In an interview with the father, he openly admitted that his wife's paranoia had been evident even before their marriage, although he had not been aware of it at the time, and that her condition had grown steadily worse over the years. He had hoped that having a child would change his wife's attitude toward life, but when he found that this did not occur, he purposely avoided having any further children. He was conscious stricken and wept openly as he related how he felt he had badly neglected Richard in his absences from the home. Yet, he felt that if he had been forced to remain in the situation constantly, there would have been so much marital dissension that a divorce would have probably occurred. He had tried to "make up" for his absences from Richard by devoting as much time as possible with him on those weekends when he was at home and by taking the boy on camping trips and buying him presents, and so on. However, his wife had been so full of precautions and fears that his efforts to be a companion to Richard often went awry. The previous summer he had taken Richard abroad with him, but their trip had been cut short when he was notified that his wife was ill in the hospital. Subsequently, her physician had advised him that his wife's illness was "imaginary," and that she had rejected his suggestion that she seek psychiatric help.

Despite strong objections from Richard's mother, his father accepted the staff's recommendation that Richard be temporarily hospitalized in a residential treatment center. Separated from his mother, Richard's symptoms abated very rapidly. In group therapy, his peers advised him that "we all have our hang-ups, and yours is your suspiciousness." Richard thus began to perceive his behavior as something that could be resolved, just as the other children were attempting to resolve their conflcts. Furthermore, the other children and the staff noticed that Richard's symptoms were always strongest on Mondays after his mother had visited him over the weekend. Thus, they helped him to see the relationship between his symptoms and his mother's behavior. In individual interviews, Richard almost immediately revealed that he himself had been the subject of his mother's suspicions. When he heard other children talk about their relationships with their parents, he began to reveal how he had felt spied upon and unjustly accused of many things by his mother.

Richard's responses to the assessment also suggested that the bond with his mother severely threatened the development of his masculine identity. In part, such behavior as carrying a knife, quarreling with his peers, and his attempts to show up his teachers were Richard's way of asserting his virility and his independence from his mother. Although he was a sturdily built boy, he had never particpated in athletics because of his

mother's overprotectiveness; she constantly feared that he would be hurt. During his brief stay in the residential treatment center, Richard became skilled at basketball and spent many hours punching the punching bag. He became particularly close to one of the male attendants who was an expert at wrestling and judo, and he declared that he wished to take up judo when he left the hospital.

The staff gave serious consideration to the possibility that Richard should not be returned to live with his mother. These plans were discussed with Richard, who made only a slight protest. Richard's father also readily agreed. Richard's mother was extremely upset by this suggestion and responded that she regarded the hospital as a collaborator with the school, her husband, and her attorney in a huge plot against her. The following week, after a violent quarrel with her husband, she attempted suicide and was subsequently hospitalized in a psychiatric hospital. Richard and his father were intensely guilt ridden, and some of Richard's symptoms returned. However, a week later, plans were reinstituted for Richard's discharge from the hospital. With his father's help, Richard was placed in a boarding school at quite a distance from his home but close to the center of his father's work.

F.   TREATMENT OF THE PARENTS

Last of the environmental changes to be considered is the possibility of relieving the stresses upon the child by assisting the parents in changing their attitudes and ameliorating their anxieties. Since simultaneous treatment of parents and children in family group therapy has already been considered, the discussion here will be limited to treatment of the parents, with little or no treatment of children. There are several situations in which only the parents might be treated, among which are the following:

1.   The child's symptoms are temporary and mild, and the parents' emotional disturbances are quite open. Usually, in such

circumstances, the parents almost seem to forget about the child's behavior immediately and begin discussing their own anxieties and openly ask for help. In such instances, they are apparently using the child's behavior as an excuse to find help for themselves, as "their key to treatment," as it is commonly phrased.

2. When a child is very young and relatively nonverbal, and when, as is usually the case, the child's symptoms are fairly obviously the result of the parents' anxieties, treatment of the parents may be the preferred approach, even though the child's disturbance may be fairly severe.

3. Treatment of the parents or counseling them may be the main possibility when the child is completely resistant to any treatment approach or is otherwise unavailable. Such an approach is almost necessitated when the child refuses to come to treatment or becomes a captive audience. Again, it is usually found that the parents' reactions and fears have played a major role in the child's symptoms. Under these circumstances, it is often possible to involve the child in the treatment at a later point; the fact that the parents are attempting to make changes in themselves may motivate him/ her to become more cooperative. Moreover, when the neurotic imbalance in the family shifts, the child frequently becomes so anxious as to be more motivated toward receiving help.

CASE 131

Esther, age 14, who originally had stoutly declared that "there is nothing wrong with me except that my parents are nuts," and who absolutely refused to meet any further appointments with the psychiatrist, appeared three months later, after her parents had been seen in weekly interviews, and demanded to talk with the psychiatrist, to "find out what he's been telling my parents." She was extremely angered that her parents were beginning to deal with her in a more realistic manner, that they no longer ignored her poor achievement, that they

were concerned about her social behavior, and even that they were less threatened by some of her somatic symptoms. She continued to make appointments with the psychiatrist—even appeared without an appointment on occasion—almost weekly for the following year.

4. Counseling with parents may be the preferred approach when dealing with the behavior and learning problems of retarded or other disabled children. Such counseling is often needed to clarify the attitudes and reactions of the parents.

The assumption in all of the preceding conditions is that in some way the child's disturbing behavior is related rather directly to the parents' anxieties, fears, and attitudes. Such a relationship is present so very frequently that many mental-health workers presume that it is the core to all psychological disturbances in children. Although it is probable that the parents' anxieties do play some part, it is not true that they are always the central factors. As has been illustrated in many cases throughout this volume, there are many other factors that play a part in development disturbances. Not infrequently, the parents' behavior is found to be a reaction to the child's behavior or to circumstances that are beyond the immediate power of the parent to alter. Moreover, as was pointed out in the section on family group therapy in Chapter 19, even where the child's disturbance is probably based primarily on the interaction between him/her and the parents, there are many instances where separate treatment of the child is very much in order—particularly when these family interactions have begun to be internalized as part of the child's identity and are intermingled with and confused with his/her developmental struggles. In such instances, treatment of the parents without treatment of the child might be a very prolonged—if not unsuccessful— approach.

Obviously, when treatment of the parents with or without parallel treatment of the child is to be considered, assessment of the parents is in order. The first reason for such an assessment is to determine whether treatment of the parents will be a major assistance in relieving the child's disturbances. It is quite possible, for example, that the parents may need treatment for their own neuroses, but that the child's problems are relatively separate from those of the parents, and thus that parallel treatment is in order. Second, the assessment of the parents may assist in answering the question of whether their treatment should be oriented chiefly toward resolution of their own problems, or should it consist of counseling that is oriented mainly to their attitudes about the child and care of him/her. Even where the child does appear to be "the parents' key" to treatment, they may be so defensive in the beginning that they can be led into consideration of their own problems only by a discussion of their child-rearing practices. In other instances, assessment may reveal that the parents' compulsive introspection may be a mask for their refusal to consider their interactions with the child. Other parents may be puzzled and even irritated by questions about the child's behavior since they are motivated chiefly to resolve some of their own conflicts. Such assessment of the parents is, of course, a prerequisite to the further planning of their treatment.

Although many of the principles and techniques for assessment of children that have been discussed in this book are also applied in the assessment of adults' problems, the assesment of the adult does have many other aspects to it that are beyond our purview and have been discussed elsewhere (Pope, 1967). The aspect that is peculiar to this situation is that the assessment includes both parent and child, plus a comparison of these results. Several illustrations of how such comparisons are made have already been given in previous chapters, and a brief additional illustration may suffice here.

CASE 132

Mrs. R, age 40, brought her 5-year-old

daughter, Julie, to the clinic because Julie was unable to separate from her mother and thus would not attend kindergarten. At the suggestion of the teacher, Mrs. R had tried remaining on the school grounds for brief periods and leaving a few minutes earlier each day, but Julie continued to scream in terror if she discovered her mother was not nearby. Julie also stayed close to her home when playing and would not allow her mother to leave the house unless she accompanied her.

Julie's responses to the assessment indicated that she was an intellectually precocious child and also very sensitive emotionally. She did appear to have a few more fears than the usual 5-year-old; witches and monsters permeated her Rorschach associations, all in human-like movement. Her drawing of a person was a "big, big, big mother," which finally occupied three pages of paper. Julie's responses to the CAT also indicated that she perceived her environment as dominated by her mother; the infant figures in her stories "got lost" or otherwise became unhappy without ther mother's constant protection.

In the initial interview with Mrs. R, she began by announcing brightly that she was well aware that Julie's symptom was probably related to her own "neurosis." She went on immediately to describe her "migraine headaches," her inability to sleep, her feelings of restlessness and boredom in the home, her quarrels with her own mother, and a recent anxiety dream she had experienced—almost in breathless sequence. Subsequently, while Julie was being assessed, the MMPI, a Sentence Completion Test, and Draw-A-Person Test were administered to Mrs. R. Her responses to the initial assessment techniques did confirm the initial impression from the interview that she was obsessively concerned with many of her own anxieties, that she tried to defend herself by much rationalization and intellectualization, but nonetheless was experiencing considerable free-floating anxiety.

During the subsequent interview with

Mrs. R, while she was conducting a monologue about her relationships with her mother, the assessor glanced down at the drawing she had made, a very artistic sketch of a young and voluptuous woman in a seductive pose, and then glanced up at Mrs. R, an obese gray-haired, drab-looking woman, and wondered to himself the relationship between the drawing and Mrs. R's appearance. Mrs. R noticed the assessor looking at the drawing and suddenly burst into tears. She revealed that on the completion of high school, she had won a scholarship to a well-known institute of art, but her family had been unable to supply the needed additional financial assistance because their funds were then tied up in the medical education of her older brother. Later, she had earned her own way through college, including a master's degree in social work, and had been employed as a medical social worker for three years subsequently in order to support her husband while he finished his doctorate. After her husband had obtained his present teaching position, she stopped work and had devoted all her energies to the rearing of three children of whom Julie was the youngest. The personal isolation of this intellectually bright and artistically talented woman was extreme. She had no social life whatever and devoted herself almost entirely to the care of her home and children. Her sons, ages 14 and 13, had separated themselves from her several years ago by forming a close association with their father, who had repeatedly made it clear that they were not to be "mama's boys." She had almost consciously decided to have a third child when she found the boys separating from her. For almost a year prior to her pregnancy with Julie, she had been quite depressed. Now, she admitted she had conflictual feelings about Julie since "I had hoped that when I became 40, I could begin to live a life of my own." On the basis of the assessment, it was decided to treat Mrs. R without seeing Julie. Julie was pressed to attend kindergarten for the subsequent three weeks of the semester. The following fall, the relationship between Julie and her mother had relaxed sufficiently to the point that Julie began the first grade with no disturbance whatever.

CHAPTER 22

"Ergo Sum" — An Epilogue

One of the chief problems facing the clinical psychologists in this, the last quarter of the twentieth century, is that they live in a rapidly changing society. The children whom psychologists attempt to help live in an exploding and mobile population where the technology is capable of relieving many of the major stresses of past centuries, while also creating new social pressures. The turmoil throughout this changing society is nowhere better illustrated than in the problems encountered in rearing and educating children. In fact, the "youth" problem is a central issue in all nations today. These social evolutions and revolutions are creating intense conflicts between parents, teachers, and other adult authorities and the generation whom they are attempting to rear and educate. These conflicts are popularly termed "the generation gap." Some such gap has always existed between generations. As Margaret Mead (1942) has so cogently pointed out, this has been fostered by American ideals and values. Yet, at no time has this gap of understanding between adult and child seemed so strikingly apparent and so intensely conflictual.

Even the basic psychological problems of children are different than those of a generation ago. The question of identity, the "Who am I?" was voiced by a few members of the literati at the beginning of the century, but it has now become a central issue for the current generation. Moreover, it is a question that is poorly understood and that is almost inconceivable to many parents and teachers.

Clinical psychologists may attempt to take an unbiased perspective of their society, but their values, attitudes, methods, and training often are embedded in their social milieu. These social changes also create a generation gap in the training of clinical psychologists, stemming from the fact that the current generation has to deal with problems that were unknown to their teachers. "Identity crisis," for example, is as new a concept to the professors of psychology as it is to the other parent figures of the current generation. To students, the concepts and techniques now being taught often appear to have little bearing on these new social and personal problems. Certainly, the concepts and research developed in scientific psychology in its first 100 years were not aimed at the solution of the unforeseeable problems of the twenty-first century. Nevertheless, the concerns of scientific psychology have too often been rooted in the past rather than in the present or future. Teachers are inclined to teach what they have been taught or are interested in, and too often they are less concerned with, or are even unable to instruct and guide the student in attempting to solve current social problems. As in the greater society, the generation gap in the rearing and educating of psychologists is more acute than ever before. Many of the current differences between teacher and student appear to be magnifications of the unresolved problems of the teacher's own generation. The concepts of the 1920–1940 era had little bearing on the new field of clinical psychology in the 1940–1960 period. Both clinical and academic scientists attempted to salvage what they could of the ideas and methods of the previous 50 years in order to understand and solve the human problems of today. Because they found the previous theories inadequate, they created new ones, for example, the dynamic personality theories and projective techniques and the interest of psychologists in psychotherapy both as a practical solution to the problems of their clients and as a naturalistic scientific exploration into unknown territory.

Yet, these had scarcely been introduced — let alone tested — before new demands were presented by both clients and students for new theories and techniques to solve new problems. For example, the effects of current social problems on individual behavior are now recognized to be so extensive that the approach of individual psychotherapy often appears to be analogous to attempting to build a dam with a teaspoon. Projective techniques may reveal a great deal about the inner experiences of the individual child, but they seem hopelessly inadequate in the study of interpersonal interactions.

As is probably true of any text, this book has dealt with established practice, that is, with the theory and practice of assessment as it has been developed since 1940. Some of the recent innnovations have not been discussed because they are as yet purely exploratory. Yet, the problems currently facing psychologists urgently require rethinking of theory and revision and innovation in technique and practice. Considering the discontent that many young psychologists currently express with the state of their science, it is relatively safe to predict that there will be at least attempts at major changes both in research and practice. Some of the techniques described herein should be thoroughly revised if not altogether scrapped. Moreover, the personal and social problems of the upcoming generation may so overshadow the concerns of the past generation that the many approaches described in this book may prove no longer applicable, and new forms of assessment and treatment will be needed for a wholly new set of conflicts.

Although these changes may need to be radical in order to meet the social upheavals, neither the human scene nor the scientific study of behavior is likely to be altered so extensively that all previous knowledge and skills will be discarded. Such revolutions in theory and practice as will occur may appear to erase prior concepts and to change the focus of scientific interests, but the history of scientific change suggests that revolutions usually are only an extruding crisis in a more gradual, ongoing evolution of thought. Thus in part, the new psychology of the latter half of the twentieth century is being influenced by and even generated out of extant approaches. The extent to which this book may serve the student and contribute toward the expansion and change of psychology depends on the nature of these changes and their relationship to current theory and practice. Although the exact nature of these changes cannot be predicted precisely, some general trends may be foreseen by reviewing in broad outline the ways in which psychologists have met the problems of their generation—and have mirrored their times. Such a historical perspective has been interjected in prior chapters, but it may bear some restatement at this time.

Developing out of philosophy and as a part of education, psychology has long been associated with the climate and thought of the university. Franklin Murphy (1968)* designated three trends of thought in the development of the modern university that also seem to be appropriate in considering the development of the study of the behavioral sciences and of particular import to the current question of identity formation. The modern university, according to Murphy, developed under the influence of the Cartesian dictum "cognito ergo sum"—"I think, therefore I am." University life up until the middle of the nineteenth century was dominated by the search for knowledge per se, with little concern about its practical application. However, Murphy pointed out, with the advent of the industrial revolution and the flowering of capitalism, there was an increasing demand for technical knowledge with practical applications, as witness the establishment of teachers' colleges and agricultural colleges under governmental

*In his farewell address on his resignation as chancellor of the University of California at Los Angeles.

sponsorship. This change in the philosophy of the university, he called, "facere ergo sum"—"I do, therefore I am." Finally, Murphy viewed the changes now going on within the society as creating a new set of values, also pressing on the university. This new set of values Murphy epitomized as "sentio ergo sum"—"I feel, therefore I am." This new philosophical motto is at the heart of the current student revolution throughout the world, which in turn is part of a widespread expression of many people for a new sense of personal worth and dignity. Although a great deal of this social revolution is concerned with political rights and power, embedded in it is the cry for recognition of personal feelings.

Hubert Humphrey (1968) states this demand for personal recognition as follows: "And what's really being said by the student protester, surely by the poor and surely by the Negro is: 'Establishment here I am! Don't card-index me. My name is Joe Jones. Joe L. Jones.' They even give the middle initial. And, they say, 'I count. Don't take me for granted. I'm not to be had.' " In race relations, there is as much focus on prejudice as on discrimination, for the acts of discrimination reflect these prejudices. Similarly, the students are as concerned with the attitudes of the university and with the social "establishment" as they are with the actual practice of education. Moreover, the philosophy, music, and art of the current student generation reveal their concern with feeling and experiencing life, rather than with either knowledge seeking or achievement. Instead of dulling weary senses with alcohol, young people exhilerate themselves with psychedelic drugs, music, and lights. Murphy gives a pungent example of this change in attitude in the definition of obscenity: for the parent generation, obscenity has referred to the bathroom or brothel; for students, obscenity has to do with senseless hatred and violence. Youth would define as obscene, for example, the statement of the American military officer in Vietnam that he had to "destroy the village in order to save it."

These changes in the university and the world in which it exists may also be seen in the science of human behavior. A concern with cognition and the nature of thought dominated the metaphysics and epistemology of prescientific psychology and has continued, quite appropriately, to be a central area of theory and research throughout the past century. Most of the major psychological treatises, other than in psychoanalysis, have been based on the assumption that man is essentially a rational being and that the chief, if not the exclusive, subject of psychology should be the nature of this rationality. Moreover, prior to World War I — and even thereafter — the application of psychological research to human problems was considered beneath the dignity of the scholar and antithetical to the purposes of scientific psychology. Prior to World War II, chairs in industrial psychology existed chiefly at the major universities, but the subject of clinical psychology was rarely taught. Among psychologists, knowledge was sought for its own sake, and the problems of the individual were left by default to medicine (see Chapter 1).

Nevertheless, even before psychology had much opportunity to establish itself as a pure science, there existed increasing pressure from the society outside of the academic halls for a more practical orientation. For example, in the land-grant colleges, "child-welfare" institutes or "stations" were established, very comparable to the agricultural or business administration centers. Although these child-welfare institutes were altogether research oriented and not clinics, their studies dealt with the practical problems of nurturing, disciplining, and educating of the child (often they were part of a school of education). They were concerned only peripherally with the nature of the child's thought and seldom with the child's feelings. During the first half of this twentieth century, the dictum "facere ergo sum" became a part of the identity of most scientists, including the psychologist. Being a wise teacher or an understanding counselor meant little toward promotion on the academic ladder or even in the eyes of one's colleagues. Psychologists, like other scientists, were valued according to their research productivity, often with little regard for the contribution of this research toward knowledge in the field. Covertly, many psychologists began to recognize that such forced productivity too often led to little or no real knowledge. Even today, the focus of psychological research remains on method rather than results, as any Ph.D. candidate can testify. Only those behaviors that can be measured are considered de rigueur in psychological research, and descriptive or explorative investigations into such unknown territory as human motivations or emotions are usually avoided or ignored as if outside the pale of science. For example, although Freud, at the beginning of the century, introduced the topic of dreams as a fascinating phenomenon wherein one might possibly understand the nature of man's motivations, feelings, and even cognitive processes, to date there has been almost no other significant study of this common human behavior. Even at this writing, the chief approach in dream research is essentially methodological and physiological, that is, the rapid-eye-movement sleep studies.

Although "facere ergo sum" continues to be the most widespread identity among psychologists, the concern for men's sensibilities and motivations has not been entirely ignored and has gradually increased. In 1905, some American scholars were interested enough in the ideas of Freud and Jung to invite them to Clark University. Yet the Victorian mores of those times did not allow American psychologists to consider the tabooed topics of sex, love, anger, or other private thoughts of individual men. Nevertheless, not *all* American psychologists limited themselves to studies of sensation, perception, learning, intelligence, and the central nervous system. They did invent paper-and-pencil questionnaires on "temperament," or observed children at play, for example. Perhaps the major breakthrough in the study of human emotions was the Harvard studies in the 1930s that resulted in the classic *The Exploration of*

Personality (Murray 1938), and in such techniques as the TAT and later the P-F. Outside university halls, clinical attention to the social and emotional problems of children also dates back to the beginning of the century, as, for example, Healy's clinic in Chicago and the first juvenile courts. A few of the "schools" for the "feebleminded" employed psychologists, but psychologists were seldom on the staffs of mental hospitals, Wooster State Hospital and St. Elizabeth's in Washington, D.C. being notable exceptions. However, prior to World War II, the involvement of psychologists in such activities was negligible. In such clinics for children as did exist, the psychologist "tested" and "diagnosed" with a label, but the child's problems were seldom investigated in the manner described in this book.

Since World War II, the number of psychologists who are interested primarily in affective and social behavior has increased enormously. For example, the membership of Division 12, the Division of Clinical Psychology, of the American Psychological Association increased over 250% between 1950 and 1965, (from 1148 to 2899).* Members calling themselves counseling psychologists have also increased in number, as have those interested in the Society for the Psychological Study of Social Issues (SPSSI). New divisions of the APA have been added for those interested in rehabilitation and in psychotherapy. Psychologists have become integral staff members in every major hospital and clinic in the United States. In metropolitan centers, there is an increasing number of psychologists in private practice of assessment and psychotherapy.

---

*During this period, the total membership of APA increased from approximately 7300 to 23,500, according to the membership directories for these respective years. The proportion in Division 12 remained the same. However, fewer APA members were affiliating with divisions, and Division 12 had special membership requirements. Therefore, many younger clinicians did not join. In the subsequent decade the APA membership has almost tripled.

This marked increase in the interest of psychologists in the social and emotional aspects of behavior and their involvement in clinical practice are often attributed to the fact that World War II created a demand for understanding and treating the cataclysmic injuries to the sensibilities of those who participated in that human holocaust. The Veterans Administration helped to train many of the current generation of psychologists and channeled their research interests into unexplored fields. Yet wars alone cannot account for the continued and expanding concentration by psychologists in the study of conative, affective, and social aspects of behavior and in creating methods of altering such behavior. Their focus on human problems has been sustained and fostered by the growing demands of society for such understanding and for methods of relieving conflicts. The nature of these social and individual conflicts has been discussed at length in the introductory chapters. The chief aspect of this social change of pertinence here is the growing awareness that society is made up of individuals, as expressed so pungently in the previously cited quotation from Hubert Humphrey. Although psychologists, like other members of society, are becoming aware of the importance of human sensibilities and human experience, the youth and the racial minorities who are speaking most cogently and forcefully of these topics and of the values of "sentio ergo sum" did not learn them from professors of psychology. Indeed, the psychologists are learning from their students and clients, and from excursions into the community.

Although there exists this ever-increasing adaptation of psychologists to the demands by their society, it cannot be said that the majority has changed their identity to Murphy's "senito ergo sum." Perhaps it is too much to expect that matured scientists or even a majority of their students would alter their identities altogether, especially toward a set of values and attitudes that are as yet being defined and remain foreign to the white middle class to which most psychologists belong. Yet many do recognize that these changes in values are going on around them, and they seek to learn more about them. Some psychologists do appear to be adapting these values personally, and they participate as faculty members in the unrest and change in the university and as citizens in the public protest movements. Within psychological circles there are developments such as "sensitivity training" and a philosophic approach labeled "humanistic" psychology (Bugental, 1965; Watts, 1966; Jouard, 1968). Yet others appear to be retrenching, to demand even stricter adherence to scientific rigor both in theory and research. For example, the increasing interest in such topics as brain research and in conditioning approaches to child-behavior problems—both undoubtedly worthy topics—does not seem to fall under the rubric "sentio ergo sum." In fact, during the past 25 years, there has developed a sharp division of opinion among psychologists as to the directions to which their science and practice should turn. This division has been marked by an intensely emotional rather than rational argument. Some psychologists whose identities are almost exclusively *cognito* or *facere* have been so disturbed by the growth of clinical psychology and other groups interested in the human scene that they have threatened to leave the APA. In many universities, the clinical and social psychologists appear to live separate lives, scientifically and personally, from the other psychologists who are engaged in nonclinical research and teaching. In some universities, clinical training has been sharply curtailed, while in others, new and expanded clinical training facilities and staff are being built. Even within clinical psychology there exists a highly emotionally charged divisiveness between those who advocate behavior modification and those who seek to develop a humanistic approach. All in all, there appears to be an identity crisis within the body of psychology, very comparable to that experienced by other social groups and individuals.

As was discussed previously (see Chapter 2), these identity conflicts had their beginnings early in the century, but have only come to the forefront of social consciousness currently. The generation gap is the more acute because the upcoming generation makes obvious the problems denied and avoided by their parents and teachers. Of particular import to psychologists is the fact that both generations, parents and their offsping, recognize as never before that these conflicts are psychological. The immediately prior generations were preoccupied with developing technology and with war. Personal and social psychological problems were sloughed aside; one could not waste time with "silly" psychological problems when there were "things to be done," that is, "facere ergo sum." Moreover, recognition of psychological conflicts involved for prior generations an admission of weakness and consequently of shame and guilt. Even though psychologists themselves were actually identified with the *facere* values, laymen generally were suspicious that psychologists were going to uncover the *sentio* in them. The shift in emphasis toward the *sentio* now going on in society is already putting considerable pressure on psychologists to reconsider their attitudes and values. Since there is a growing recognition of the psychological aspects of the human scene, more and more is being expected of psychologists. Whereas psychology in the past has been regarded as a relatively minor science, the study of human behavior is increasingly being considered as possibly the most necessary. This historically youthful science is being thrust into the limelight, with expectations and responsibilities it is often not prepared to meet.

These social and personal conflicts in society will undoubtedly require further major changes both in the attitudes of psychologists toward their science and in the focus of their interests and concerns. First and foremost, the affective and motivational aspects of human behavior, the *sentio*, can no longer be pushed aside, ignored, or denied. Any research study that fails to mention or take into account these aspects should be considered incomplete. *Sentio* will have to be recognized and, for awhile, be given primary consideration by psychologists. A psychology of *persons* (not merely *personality*) needs to be developed, in which methods of describing and even measuring the behavior of an *individual* are constructed, so that predictions about that *individual* can be made lawfully. Such predictions may or may not apply to any other individual. Such a psychology of persons would be in contrast to the more traditional psychology of individual differences. This latter field, although labeled "individual," has actually been concerned with differences between groups, in which the individual is considered an "error" variable. These group differences have been emphasized almost in the same manner that the society in which it flourished emphasized group differences. This psychology of individual differences can be useful in the study of the person when it is used in a profile analysis of the individual's behavior, that is, to mark the variations in an individual's functioning. However, even this approach is at most a beginning step in the study of a person.

One of the chief objections made against the development of a scientific study of the individual has been that there were no methods. Since the psychology of individual differences depended chiefly if not exclusively on actuarial (statistical) methods, other possible techniques of analyzing data have seemed unacceptable. Imagine, if you can, a doctoral committee accepting a dissertation in psychology that did not contain any statistics. Strangely, many psychologists who have sought to study persons have ignored the fact that the experimental approach often deals with trials rather than subjects, with results expressed in curves or graphs about that subject or even statistical analysis of the trials (not the individuals).

Nor are psychologists lacking in tools and techniques for assessing the affective behavior of the person. One reason that so much attention was given to projective techniques in this book is the fact that, however primitive, they do represent a step away from the group difference techniques into the study of individual affects and motives. Moreover, the rejection of the study of *sentio* has been epitomized in the fact that these projective techniques remain outside the pale of the psychological establishment. The theory represented by them has not been integrated into the body of psychological knowledge. Now that psychologists are turning to the study of human experience, that is, of emotional perception, the theoretical concepts of Herman Rorschach may acquire renewed importance, even if his technique is limited.

Such a psychology of individual sentiments and experiencing will not, however, meet the expectations of society unless it is accompanied by another allied field of study of interindividual relationships. In fact, many psychologists have already become cognizant that the functioning of the individual is interdependent with his relationships with other individuals. Again, this fact has been a major theme throughout this book. However, scientific research on interindividual relationships is only beginning. The recognition of this factor has come chiefly from the practice of psychotherapy, particularly the group therapies, and has been represented in research in the last decade in the studies of family relationships. In social psychology, these interindividual relationships have been partly recognized — but only partly — in the studies of role playing or in the theories of social learning. However, social psychology has tended to emphasize the nature of groups and group interactions, that is, the place of the individual within a group, rather than the ways in which one person communicates and interacts with another.

The development of a science of interindividual behavior will require even greater integration of the fields of social and clinical psychology. This alliance is the more necessary because of yet another expectancy of society. Even though primary emphasis is being given to the status of the individual,

there is simultaneously a demand for study of and intervention in the emotional conflicts of groups of individuals, often fairly sizeable groups such as communities. The problem is not merely the general question of how groups behave, but the specific question of how affects and motivations shared by a group can be expressed and satisfied without sacrificing the needs of individuals within the group. Equally critical is the question of how emotional conflicts between groups can be resolved. As noted before, psychologists have been awed by the seeming enormity of these problems, but, even though they have only scraps of theory and research regarding them, they are responding and engaging in these clinical-social tasks.

The fact that psychologists are taking action in unexplored fields with ill-defined problems and using untried tools again reflects the nature of the times. Action *now*, epitomized in "Freedom *now*," is the temper of the youthful society and the socially deprived. Murphy noted that *sentio* calls for immediate satisfaction. When students or minority groups confront a governmental body, they disdain "another survey." They see no need to be studied and seek immediate redress or resolution. Psychologists are learning that they must combine action and research. Just as the clinical psychologist has learned about individual functioning through the practice of assessment and psychotherapy, so the psychologist involved in community problems can learn from the processes and results of his efforts. Later, psychologists may conduct more traditional research studies, bringing back some of their findings into the laboratory for further verification and analytic refinement, as has now been started with hypotheses formulated in clinical practice.

Murphy, in concluding his address to his students, expressed the hope that in emphasizing *sentio,* they would not exclude *cognito* and *facere* in their "ergo sum." Even though it is time that the *sentio* be recognized, he advised that *sentio* without rational practice results in social chaos. Certainly, an individual who operates on affect alone, disregarding reason or the effects of his/her behavior, also is chaotic. Nor, as Murphy also pointed out, can affective needs always be satisfied immediately, for either individuals or groups. As Jung reasoned in his *Modern Man in Search of a Soul* (1947), a modicum of dissatisfaction, even anxiety, serves as a ferment of life for both the individual and society.

Some psychologists behave as if they feared that by studying *sentio,* they would in some way have to lose their traditional *cognito* and *facere* identities. The affective side of human behavior threatens them, as if they could not know about it or deal with it without being overwhelmed by it. At the same time, some younger psychologists have proclaimed that all one has to do is be "sensitive" and "feel" and that cognitive comprehension and planned action somehow destroy pure "experience" of the individual or interpersonal emotional involvements. Since the tradition of cognitive comprehension and the practical application of knowledge are so entrenched in the identities of psychologists, it seems highly improbable that they would either entirely lose or abandon these aspects of their functioning when they become engaged in the study of *sentio*. Rather, as was noted previously, it seems both probable and possible that psychologists would and could maintain these traditional identities as they add in the *sentio* values. This does not mean that affective behavior can be reduced to or explained in terms of intellectual functioning or by sets of "facts." *Sentio* requires experiencing, becoming involved, and interacting. The psychologist cannot study it or do anything about it unless he comes out from behind the laboratory screen and the clinical couch. It is through such "gut-level" interaction with the subject, patient, group, or community that the psychologist can begin to comprehend and deal with the affective side of behavior.

APPENDIX A

The World Test

(For Children Ages 3−12)

This test is no longer available, but materials for it may be assembled from a toy store or hobby shop. The figures and buildings should be approximately proportional in size, so that people can enter the buildings and the animals can be put in the barn. Figures should be large enough (over 1″) so as not to be easily swallowed.

BUILDINGS

A school, hospital, firehouse, jail, super-market, service station, church (non-denominational), barn, airport, outdoor toilet, 6−8 houses of various sizes, and a barn.

PEOPLE

Six to 8 male and 6−8 female figures (with occupational identity where possible, for example, doctor, postman, policeman, fireman, and the like); 6−8 children of both sexes; 8−10 military figures, armed in attack poses, with guns and cannons, and so forth.

ANIMALS

Eight to 10 domestic animals (dog, horse, sheep, cow, pig); 8−10 wild animals (lion, snake, monkeys, gorilla, bear).

OTHER OBJECTS

Two to three airplanes (one military), three to four cars, fire truck, ambulance; stop signs or stop lights; fences (to build corral or zoo); trees, swimming pool, fish pond. The materials should be stored in a carrying case, with the small pieces in separate "see-thru" plastic boxes, so the child may easily spot the kind of figure he/she desires.

SPACE

A kindergarten tabletop (approximately 2′ × 3′) or a space on a hard surface floor (2′ × 3′) is usually sufficient, but the child may be allowed more space if he/she wishes.

INSTRUCTIONS

Open the box and say, "Look at all these things. Let's see what you can make with all these things. You can make anything with them you want." Permit the child to use the materials as he/she wishes without further comment. Do not assist or encourage the child further. Allow about 30 minutes or stop when the child seems to have completed his or her construction. If the child plays only with one or to objects (such as the car or airplane), repeat the instructions, encouraging him/her to "make something."

RECORDING THE DATA

Buhler did not offer any scoring system, but was most interested in the "gestalt" of the child's world, the arrangement of materials, the compactness, or closure, the orderliness, the logic, and so forth of the construction. Important also are the child's procedures, the sequence of choices, the pieces selected, and those not included—with special attention to the child's use of aggressive or threatening figures. A photograph of the final configuration is a handy record.

APPENDIX B

A Structured Doll Technique

(After Lynn, 1959; for Children Ages 2–6)

This technique, as Lynn originally designed it, is no longer available, but materials for it may be assembled from any toy store or hobby shop. They consist of the following: a doll family—approximately 2″ high—including a mother, a father, a girl and boy (not baby figures), and the following pieces of furniture: a crib, an adult bed, a "potty" chair, an adult toilet, a dining table with three chairs, a high chair, a sofa, a TV, a baby-doll bottle, plates and forks, and a doll-sized ball.

SPACE

A kindergarten table. (I find a dollhouse too confining for these activities.)

INSTRUCTIONS

Keep materials covered and away from the child until needed. Begin as follows: "Here's the little girl/boy doll (same sex as child). Here's her/his mommy and daddy (setting parents to one side but in reach of child). Now the little girl/boy is going to take a walk." Walk doll toward child. "Now you make him/her walk." Have child walk the doll. "Now who is going to walk with him/her? The mommy or the daddy?" After the child has made a choice—"Can other parent come now?" Parent dolls are then retrieved, and the following activities are initiated:

1. Ball play. "Which parent comes to play?" "Can the other parent come too?"

2. Child is hurt. "The dolly gets a bad ouch! Who is coming to care for her/him?"

3. The child misbehaves. "The dolly is naughty. What did he/she do that was naughty?" "What does the mommy do?" "What does the daddy do?"

4. The child is angry. "The dolly feels very angry. Show me how the dolly gets angry." . . . "What is the dolly angry about?'" . . . "What do the parents do when the dolly gets angry?"

5. Set out sofa and TV. "Time to watch TV. The dolly wants to watch TV. Who is going to watch TV with her/him?" . . . "Can /other parent/ watch too now?"

6. Set out dining table, chairs, dinnerware, high chair, bottle. "Dolly is hungry. Time to eat. Where does the dolly sit? . . . Who brings the food? . . . Where do the parents sit? . . . Who feeds the dolly?"

7. Set out toilet and potty. "Now the dolly has to go bathroom. Show me how the dolly goes bathroom. . . . Does he/she need any help? . . . Who helps the dolly?"

8. Bathtub and baby bath. "Now dolly needs a bath. Does she or he need help? . . . Who helps the dolly take a bath?"

9. Bed and crib. "Time for bed. Show me how the dolly goes to bed? Does he/she need any help? Who helps dolly go to bed?"

10. Dream scene. Dolly in bed or crib as placed by child. "Now it is all dark and the dolly has a bad, scary dream. What does the dolly dream? . . . The dolly wakes up and is scared. Now what does the dolly do?"

In cases where the parents are divorcing and one wishes to know the child's attitudes toward custody and visitation: "The mommy and daddy are having a big, mean fight. (Knock parent dolls together several times.) They don't love one another anymore. The daddy is going to live over here and the mommy over here—but *they both love you.* (Place dolls at opposite ends of table with child doll in center.) "Where will the girl/boy doll live? . . . Can the girl/boy visit the /other parent/? . . . When? . . . How often?" If child cannot make a choice, do *not* pressure her/him for a response but reassure," You don't have to choose. They both love you."

RECORDING THE DATA

Lynn was interested chiefly in the child's attitudes toward social growth and independence, for example, in whether she/he looked to the mother for help and companionship almost to the exclusion of the father, or whether the child could include the father at times or even do things independent of either parent; whether the child used the infant equipment (high chair, bottle, crib, potty) or the adult bed, chairs, and so on. The assessor should also note the child's psychosexual interests and identification, whether age appropriate, regressed, or advanced. Parent choices in scenes 1–11 may also indicate parent choice in custody or visitation questions.

Note. Although this play is "structured," free play need not be inhibited. Additional personal feelings are often elicited where fantasy runs free. Each structured situation should be introduced only when the child seems finished with the prior scene. Having the child engage in the action with the dolls is the sine qua non of this technique.

References

Ackerman, N. W., 1962, Family psychotherapy and psychoanalysis: The implications of difference. *Family Process,* **1**, 30−43.

Adorno, T., Frenkel-Brunswik, E., Levinson, D., and Sanford, N., 1950, *The Authoritarian Personality.* New York: Harper.

Albee, G. W., 1966, The dark of the top of the agenda. *Clin. Psychol.* **20**, 7−9.

Allport, G. W., 1948, *Personality: A Psychological Interpretation.* New York: W. W. Norton.

Altus, W. and Thompson, G., 1949, The Rorschach as a measure of intelligence. *J. Consult. Psychol.,* **13**, 341−347.

American Psychiatric Association Committee on Nomenclature and Statistics, 1968, *Diagnostic and Statistical Manual of Mental Disorders.* DSM-II. 1980, DSM-III. Washington, DC: American Psychiatric Association.

American Psychological Association, 1963, *Ethical Standards of Psychologists.* Washington, DC: American Psychological Association.

Ames, L. B., Metraux, R., Rodell, J. and Walker, R. N., 1974, *Child Rorschach Responses.* Rev. Ed. New York: Brunner/Mazell.

Andrew, G., Hartwell, S. W., Hutt, M. L., and Walton, B. E., 1953, *The Michigan Picture Test.* New York: Science Research Association.

Arbit, J., Lakin, M., and Mathis, A., 1959, Clinical psychologists' diagnostic utilization of human figure drawings. *J. Clin. Psychol.,* **15**, 325−327.

Arthur, G., 1947, *A Point Scale of Performance Tests. Rev. Form II.* New York: Psychological Corp.

Axline, V. M., 1947, *Play Therapy.* Boston: Houghton Mifflin.

Barclay, A., and Yates, A. C., 1969, Comparative study of the WPPSI and Stanford-Binet L-M among culturally deprived children. *J. Consult. & Clin. Psychol.,* **33**, 257.

Barron, F., 1953, An ego-strength scale which predicts response to psychotherapy. *J. Consult. Psychol.,* **17**, 327−333.

Baughman, E. E., 1965, The role of the stimulus in Rorschach responses in Murstein, B. (Ed), 1965, *Handbook of Projective Techniques.* New York: Basic Books.

Bayley, N., 1969, *Bayley Scales of Infant Development.* New York: Psychological Corp.

Beck, S. J., 1949, *Rorschach's Test, Vol. I and II.* New York: Grune and Stratton.

Beck, N., and Herron, W., 1969, The meaning of the Rorschach cards for children. *J. Pers. Assess.,* **32**, 150−153.

Bell, J. E., 1961, *Family Group Therapy.* Washington, DC: Public Health Monogr. 64.

Bellak, L., 1952, *The Psychology of Physical Illness.* New York: Grune and Stratton.

Bellak, L., and Bellak, S. S., 1949, *Manual of Instructions for the Children's Apperception Test.* New York: The American Orthopsychiatric Association.

Bender, L., 1938, *A Visual Motor Gestalt Test and Its Clinical Use.* New York: The American Orthopsychiatric Association.

Bene, E., and Anthony, J., 1957, *Manual for the Family Relations Test.* London: National Foundation for Educational Research in England and Wales.

Benedict, P. R., and Jacks, I., 1954, Mental illness in primitive societies. *Psychiatry,* **17**, 379−390.

Bergin, A. and Garfield S. (Eds.), 1971, *Handbook of Psychotherapy and Behavior Change.* New York: Wiley.

Bernal, M., Duryee, J., Pruett, H., and Burns, B., 1968, Behavior modification and the brat syndrome. *J. Clin. Consult.,* **32**, 447−455.

Berne, E., 1964, *Games People Play*. New York: Grove Press.

Bettelheim, B., 1950, *Love Is Not Enough*. Springfield, IL: Free Press.

Bijou, S. W., and Baer, D. M. (Eds.), 1967, *Child Development: Readings in Experimental Analysis*. New York: Appleton-Century-Crofts.

Blum, G., 1950, *The Blacky Pictures: A Technique for the Exploration of Personality Development*. New York: Psychological Corp.

Blum, G., 1953, *Psychoanalytic Theories of Personality*. New York: McGraw-Hill.

Blum, G., and Hunt, H., 1952, The validity of the Blacky pictures. *Psychol. Bull.*, **49**, 238–250.

Boszormenji-Nagy, I., and Framo, J. 1965, *Intensive Family Therapy*. New York. Hoeber.

Bowlby, K., 1969, *Attachment and Loss* (Vols. 1 and 2). London: Hogarth Press.

Bricklin, B, Piotrowski, Z. T., and Wagner, E. E., 1962, *The Hand Test*. Springfield, IL: Charles Thomas.

Breidenbaugh, B., Brozovich, R. I., and Matheson, K., 1974, The Hand Test and other aggression indicators in emotionally disturbed children. *J. Pers. Assess.*, **38**, 332–334.

Brodsky, S. L., and Brodsky, A. M., 1967, Hand Test indicators of antisocial behavior. *J. Pers. Assess.*, **31**, 36–39.

Bruner, J., and Postman, L., 1949, Perception and cognition and behavior. *J. Pers.*, **18**, 14–31.

Buck, J. N., 1948, The H-T-P technique: a quantitative and qualitative scoring manual. *J. Clin. Psychol. Monogr. Suppl.*, *5*.

Bugental, J., 1965, *The Search for Authenticity*. New York: Holt-Rinehart-Winston.

Buhler, C., Lumry, B. R., and Carrole, J. S., 1951, World Test standardization studies. *J. Child Psychiatr.*, **2**, 1–81.

Burgemeister, B., Blum, L., and Lorge, I., 1954, *Columbia Mental Maturity Scale*. New York: World Book Co.

Byrd, E., 1965, The clinical validity of the Bender-Gestalt Test with children: a developmental comparison of children in need of psychotherapy and children judged well-adjusted. In Murstein, B. (Ed.), *Handbook of Projective Techniques*. New York: Basic Books, 751–765.

Cain, L. F. and Levine, S., 1961, A study of the effects of community and institutional school classes for trainable mentally retarded children. San Francisco State College. Mimeo.

Call, J., 1964, New-born approach behavior and early ego development. *Int. J. Anal.*, **45**, 2–3.

Cattell, P., 1940. *The Measurement of Intelligence of Infants and Young Children*. New York: Psychological Corp. (Rev. 1960).

Claussen, A., 1962, *The Bender Visual-Motor Test for Children: a Manual*. Beverly Hills, CA: Western Psychological Services.

Coleman, J. C., 1968, Rorschach content as a means of studying child development. *J. Proj. Tec.* **32**, 435–442.

Cronbach, L., and Meehl, P. E., 1955, Construct validity in psychological tests. Psychol. Bull., **52**, 281–302.

Currie, C., 1969, Evaluative functions of mentally retarded children through use of toys and play activities. *Am. J. Occup. Ther.* **23**, 35–42.

Darwin, C., 1887, A biographical sketch of an infant. *Mind*, **11**, 286–294.

Dewey, J., 1938, *Experience and Education*. New York: Macmillan.

Doll, E. A., 1965, *The Vineland Social Maturity Scale—Revised*. Circle Pines, MN: American Guidance Service.

Dollard, J., Doob, L. W., et al., 1939, *Frustration and Aggression*. New Haven: Yale University Press.

Dos Passos, J., 1938, *USA*. Boston: Houghton Mifflin.

Dunn, L. M., and Dunn, L. M., 1981, *Peabody Picture Vocabulary Test—Revised*. Circle Pines, MN: American Guidance Service.

Durfee, R., 1969, The misdiagnosis of mental retardation. *J. Rehabil.* **35**, 22–24.

Edwards, A. L., 1957, *The Social Desirability Variability in Personality Assessment and Research*. New York: Dryden Press.

Eisenberg, L. and Kanner, L., 1956, Early infantile autism. *J. Am. Orthopsychiat.*, **26**, 556–566.

Edwards, A. L., 1959, *Edwards Personal Preference Schedule*. New York: Dryden Press.

Elbert, S., Rosman, B., Minuchin, S., and Guerney, F., 1964, A method for the clinical study of family interaction. *Am. J. Orthopsychiat.*, **34**, 885–894.

Eldefonso E., 1973, *Law Enforcement and the Juvenile Offender*. New York: Wiley.

Ellis, A., 1962, *Reason and Emotion in Psychotherapy*. New York: Stuart.

Ericson, E. H., 1950, *Childhood and Society*. New York: W. W. Norton and Co., Inc.

Erikson, E., 1968, *Identity, Youth and Crisis*. New York: W. W. Norton.

Eron, L. D., 1950, A normative study of the Thematic Apperception Test. *Psychol. Monogr.*, **315**, 64, 9.

Estes, B. W., Curtin, M. E., DeBurgor, R. A., and Denny, C., 1961, Relationships between 1960 Stanford-Binet, 1937 Stanford-Binet, WISC, Raven and Draw-A-Man. *J. Consult. Psychol.*, **25**, 388–391.

Eysenck, H. J., 1960, *The Structure of Human Personality*. London: Methuen.

Fenichel, O., 1945, *The Psychoanalytic Theory of Neuroses*. New York: W. W. Norton.

Fisher, J., 1959, The twisted pear and prediction of behavior. *J. Consult. Psychol.*, **23**, 400–405.

Fisher, J., and Gonda, T. A., 1955, Neurologic techniques and Rorschach Test in detecting brain pathologies. *AMA Arch. of Neurol. and Psychiatr.*, **74**, 117–124.

Fitzgerald, F. S., 1925, *The Great Catsby*. New York: Scribner.

Fonda, C. P., 1960, The white space response. In Rickers-Ovsiankina, M. A. (Ed.), *Rorschach Psychology*. New York: Wiley, 80–105.

Forer, B. R., 1950, A structured sentence completion test. *J. Proj. Tech.*, **14**, 15–29.

Framo, J. L., 1965, Rationale and techniques of intensive family therapy. In Boszormeny-Nagy, I., and Framo, J. L. (Eds.), *Intensive Family Therapy*. New York: Harper & Row, 143–212.

Frankenburg, W., and Dodds, J., 1967, The Denver Developmental Screening Test. *J. Pediatr.*, **71**, 181–191.

Frenkel-Brunswik, E., 1951, Patterns of social and cognitive outlook in children and parents. *Amer. J. Orthopsychiat.*, **21**, 543–558.

Freud, A., 1946, *The Ego and Mechanisms of Defense*. New York: International University Press.

Freud, A., and Burlingame, D., 1944, *Infants without Families*. New York: International University Press.

Freud, S., 1909, Analysis of a phobia in a five year old boy. In *Collected Papers*, Vols. III, 1948, London: Hogarth Press, 149–289.

Freud, S., 1937, Analysis terminable and interminable. In *Collected Papers*, Vol. V, 1950. London: Hogarth Press, 316–357.

Friedan, B., 1963, *The Feminine Mystique*. New York: W. W. Norton.

Friedman, R., 1970, Utility of the concept of brain damage for the school psychologist. *J. School Psychol.*, **7**, 29–32.

Fromm, E., 1947, *Escape from Freedom*. New York: Farrar and Rinehart.

Frost, B. P., 1969, The Family Relations Test, a normative study. *J. Proj. Tech.*, **33**, 409–413.

Frostig, M, Maslow, P., Lefever, D. W., and Wittlesen, J. R. B., 1966, *The Marianne Frostig Developmental Test of Visual Perception*. Palo Alto, CA: Consulting Psychology Press.

Gallagher, P., 1968, A correlation study of Haptic subtest scores and travel rating skills of blind adolescents. *New Ortr. Blind*, **76**, 240–246.

Gesell, A., Halverson, H. M., Thompson, H., Ilg, F. L., Castner, B. M., Ames, L. B., and Amatrudo, C. S., 1940, *The First Five Years of Life: A Guide to the Study of the Preschool Child*. New York: Harper & Brothers.

Gibby, R. G., 1952, Examiner influences on the Rorschach inquiry. *J. Consult. Psychol.*, **16**, 449–455.

Gibby, R. G., Miller, D. R., and Walker, E. L., 1953, The examiner's influence on the Rorschach. *J. Consult. Psychol.*, **17**, 425–428.

Gibson, R. W., 1958, The family background and early life experiences of the manic-depressive patient: a comparison with the schizophrenic patient. *Psychiatry* **21**, 71–90.

Goldberg, L. R., 1965, The effectiveness of clinicians' judgments: the diagnosis of brain damage from the Bender-Gestalt Test. In Murstein, B. I. (Ed.), *Handbook of Projec-*

tive Techniques. New York: Basic Books, 771–821.

Goldberg, P. A., 1965, A review of sentence completion methods in personality assessment. In Murstein, B. (Ed.), *Handbook of Projective Techniques.* New York: Basic Books, 777–821.

Golden, C. J., 1978, *Diagnosis and Rehabilitation in Clinical Neuropsychology.* Springfield, IL: Charles C. Thomas.

Golden, C. J., 1980, *Luria-Nebraska Neuropsychological Battery for Children.* (Available from Author, University of Nebraska Medical Center.)

Goldfarb, W., 1955, Emotional and intellectual consequences of psychologic deprivation in infancy: a re-evaluation. In Hock, P., and Zulsin, J. (Eds.), *Psychopathology of Childhood.* New York: Grune & Stratton, 105–119.

Goldstein, K. and Scheerer, M., 1945, *Goldstein-Scheerer Cube Test.* New York: Psychological Corp.

Goldstein, M., and Palmer, J. O., 1975, *The Experience of Anxiety.* New York: Oxford University Press.

Goodenough, F., 1926, *Measurement of Intelligence by Drawings.* New York: Harcourt, Brace & World.

Gordon, S., 1970, Sense and nonsense about brain-injury and learning disabilities. *Acad. Ther., 5,* 249–250.

Graham, F., and Kendall, B., 1948, Further standardization of the Memory for Designs Test. *J. Consult. Psychol., 12,* 349–354.

Greenspoon, J., and Gerstan, C. D., 1967, A new look at psychological testing from the point of view of a behaviorist. *Amer. Psychol., 22,* 848–853.

Hammer, E. F., 1958, *The Clinical Application of Projective Drawings.* Springfield, IL: Charles C. Thomas.

Hammond, K., and Allen, J., 1953, *Writing Clinical Reports.* Englewood Cliffs, NJ: Prentice-Hall.

Harlow, H. F., and Zimmerman, R. R., 1958, Affectional responses in the infant monkey. *Science, 130,* 421–432.

Harris, D. B., 1963, *Children's Drawings as Measures of Intellect.* New York: Harcourt, Brace & World.

Hartlage, L. C., 1970, Differential diagnosis of dyslexia, minimal brain damage and emotional disturbance. *Psychol. in the Schools, 7,* 405–406.

Hathaway, S. R., 1940, A multiphasic personality schedule (Minnesota): I Construction of the Schedule. *J. Psychol., 10,* 240–254.

Hathaway, S., and McKinley, J., 1943, *Manual for the MMPI.* New York: Psychological Corp.

Hathaway, S. R., and Meehl, P. E., 1951, *An Atlas for the Clinical Use of the MMPI.* Minneapolis: University of Minnesota Press.

Hathaway, S. R., and Monachesi, E. D., 1961, *An Atlas of Juvenile MMPI Profiles.* Minneapolis: University of Minnesota Press.

Hathaway, S. R., and Monachesi, E., 1963, *Adolescent Personality and Behavior: MMPI Patterns.* Minneapolis: University of Minnesota Press.

Haworth, M. B., 1966, *The CAT: Facts about Fantasy.* New York: Grune & Stratton.

Hertz, M. R., 1934, The reliability of the Rorschach Ink-Blot Test. *J. Appl. Psychol., 18,* 461–477.

Hertz, M. R., 1943a, Personality patterns in adolescence as portrayed by the Rorschach Ink-Blot Method. III: the "Erlebnistypus" (a typological study). *J. Gen. Psychol., 29,* 3–45.

Hertz, M. R., 1943b, Personality patterns in adolescence as portrayed by the Rorschach Ink-Blot Method. IV: The Erlebnistypus" (a normative study). *J. Gen. Psychol., 28,* 225–276.

Holsopple, J. Q., and Miale, F. R., 1954, *Sentence Completion: Projective Method for the Study of Personality.* Springfield, IL: Charles C. Thomas.

Holtzman, W., Thorpe, J., Swartz, J., and Herron, E. W., 1961, *Inkblot Perception and Personality.* Austin, Texas: University of Texas Press.

House, P. H., and Silvern, L. E., 1981, Behavioral observation of children during play: preliminary development of a research instrument. *J. Pers. Assess., 45,* 168–182.

Humphrey, H., 1968, This process of growth and freedom. *Sat. Rev., 51,* 22–25, 69–70.

Hurwitz, S. I., Kaplan, D. M., and Kaiser, E., 1962, Designing an instrument to assess parent coping mechanisms. *Soc. Casework.*, **43**, 527–532.

Hutt, M., and Briskin, G. J., 1960, *The Clinical Use of the Revised Bender-Gestalt Test*. New York: Grune & Stratton.

Huxley, A., 1946, *Brave New World*. New York and London: Harper & Brothers.

Hynd, G. W., and Obrzut, J. E., 1981, *Neurological Assessment and the School Age Child. Issues and Procedures*. New York: Grune & Stratton.

Jackson, D. D., 1964, *Myths of Madness*. New York: Macmillan.

Jackson, D. D., and Weakland, J. H., 1961, Conjoint family therapy: Some considerations on theory, technique, and results. *Psychiatry*, **24**, 30–45.

Jacobson, W., 1961, Screening of rhinoplastic patients from the psychologic point of view. *Plast. and Reconstr. Surg.*, **28**, 279–281.

Jastak, J., 1950, An item analysis of the Wechsler-Bellevue Tests. *J. Consult. Psychol.*, **14**, 88–94.

Jastak, J., Bijou, S., Jastak, S., 1965, *Manual for the Wide Range Achievement Test*. New York: Psychological Corp.

Jensen, A. R., 1980, *Bias in Mental Testing*. New York: Free Press.

Jenkins, J. G., 1946, Validity for What? *J. Consult, Psychol.*, **10**, 93–98.

Joesting, J., 1977, Correlation of scores on Bender Visual-Motor Gestalt Test and WISC-R. *Percept. and Mot. Skills*, **45**, 980.

Jones, H. E., 1949, *Motor Performance and Growth*. Berkeley: University of California Press.

Jourard, S., 1968, *Disclosing Man to Himself*. New York: Van Nostrand.

Jung, C. G., 1918, *Studies in Word Association*. London: Wm. Heinemann.

Jung, C. G., 1947, *Modern Man in Search of a Soul*. New York: Harcourt, Brace.

Kanner, L., 1962, Emotionally disturbed children: a historical review. *Child Dev.*, **33**, 97–102.

Kardiner, A., 1939, *The Individual and His Society*. New York: Columbia University Press.

Kauffman, J., 1970, Validity of the Family Relations Test: A review of research. *J. Proj. Tech.*, **34**, 186–189.

Kauffman, J., 1971, Family Relations Test responses of disturbed and normal boys: Additional comparative data. *J. Pers. Assess.*, **35**, 128–138.

Kauffman, J., Weaver, S., and Weaver, A., 1971, Age and intelligence as correlates of perceived family relationships of underachievers. *Psychol. Rep.*, **28**, 522.

Kauffman, J., Weaver, S., and Weaver, A., 1972, Family Relations Test responses of retarded readers: reliability and comparative data. *J. Pers. Assess.*, **36**, 352–360.

Kaufman, A. S., 1976, Verbal-performance discrepancies on the WISC-R. *J. Consult. & Clin. Psychol.*, **44**, 739–744.

Kaufman, A. S., 1979, *Intelligence Testing with the WISC-R*. New York: Wiley.

Kinsey, A. C., Pomeroy, W., and Martin, C., 1948, *Sexual Behavior in the Human Male*. Philadelphia: Saunders.

Klein, M., 1975, *The Psychoanalysis of Children*. New York: Dell.

Klett, C. J., 1957, Performance of high school students on the Edwards Personal Preference Schedule. *J. Consult. Psychol.*, **21**, 68–72.

Klopfer, B., Ainsworth, M. D., Klopfer, W. B., and Holt, R. R., 1956, *Developments in the Rorschach Technique* (Vols. 1 and 2). New York: World Book Co.

Klopfer, B. and Kelly, D., 1942, *The Rorschach Technique*. New York: World Book Company.

Klopfer, W. G., 1960, *The Psychological Report*. New York: Grune & Stratton.

Koppitz, E., 1963, *The Bender-Gestalt for Children*. New York: Grune & Stratton.

Kroger, W. S., 1979, *Clinical and Experimental Hypnosis (Rev. Ed.)*. Philadelphia: Lippincott.

Lamke, T. and Nelson, M., 1958, *The Henmon-Nelson Tests of Mental Ability*. New York: Houghton-Mifflin.

Lazarus, R. S., 1965, Ambiguity and non-ambiguity in projective testing. In Murstein, B. (Ed.), *Handbook of Projective Techniques*. New York: Basic Books, 89–93.

Leary, T., 1957, *Interpersonal Diagnosis of Personality*. New York: Ronald Press.

Lebowitz, R. G., Colbert, E. G., and Palmer, J. O., 1961, *Schizophrenia in children. Amer. J. Dis. Child.*, **102**, 25–27.

Leiter, R. G., 1948, *Leiter International Performance Scale*. Chicago: C. H. Stoelting Co.

Levitt, E., and Lyle, W. H., Jr., 1955, Evidence for the validity of the children's form of the Picture-Frustration Study. *J. Consult. Psychol.* **19**, 381–386.

Levy, J., and Epstein, W. B., 1964, An application of the Rorschach Test in family investigation. *Fam. Process*, **3**, 344–376.

Lewin, K., 1936. *Principles of Topological Psychology*. New York: McGraw-Hill.

Lindner, R. M., 1944, *Rebel without a Cause*. New York: Grune & Stratton.

Lindsay, B., 1931, *The Dangerous Life*. New York: Liveright.

Linton, R., 1945, *The Cultural Background of Personality*. New York: Appleton-Century-Crofts.

Liverant, S., 1960, Intelligence: a concept in need of reexamination. *J. Consult. Psychol.*, **24**, 101–110.

Loevinger, J., 1959, Patterns of parenthood as theories of learning. *J. Abnorm. and Soc. Psychol.*, **59**, 148–150.

Loosli-Usteri, M., 1931, La notion du hasard chez l-enfant. *Arch. Psychol. Geneve*, **23**, 45–66.

Lovass, O. I., Simmons, J., and Schaeffer, B., 1965, Building social behavior in autistic children by the use of electric shock. *J. Exp. Res. in Pers.*, **1**, 99–109.

Lynn, D. B., 1959. *Structured Doll Play Test (SDP). Manual of Instructions*. Boulder, CO: Test Developments.

Mainord, F. P., 1956, *Parental Attitudes in Schizophrenia*. Unpublished doctoral dissertation, University of Washington.

Machover, K., 1949, *Personality Projection in the Drawing of a Human Figure*. Springfield, IL: Charles C. Thomas.

Marks, P. A., 1961. An assessment of the diagnostic process in a child guidance setting. *Psychol. Monogr.*, **75** 3, Whole No. 507).

Martin, B. and Kirbly, D., 1955, Results of treatment of enuresis by a conditional response method. *J. Consult. Psychol.*, **19**, 71–73.

Maslow, A., 1950, Self-actualizing people: a study of psychological health. *Personality Symposia*, No. 1, 11–34, New York: Grune and Stratton.

McClelland, D. C., Atkinson, J. W., Clark, L.

A., and Lowell, E. L., 1953. *The Achievement Motive*. New York: Appleton-Century-Crofts.

McKinley, J. C., and Hathaway, S. R., 1943, The identification and measurement of the psychoneuroses in medical practice. *J. Am. Med. Assoc.*, **122**, 161–167.

Mead, G. H., 1932, *The Philosophy of the Present*. Chicago: Open Court.

Mead, M., 1942, *And Keep Your Powder Dry*. New York: Morrow.

Meltzoff, J., Singer, J. L., and Korchin, S. J., 1953, Motor inhibition and Rorschach movement responses: A test of sensory-tonic theory. *J. Pers.*, **21**, 400–410.

Menninger, K., 1962, *A Manual for Psychiatric Case Study*. New York: Grune and Stratton.

Meyer, A., 1948, *Common Sense Psychiatry*. Lief, A. (Ed.). New York: McGraw-Hill.

Mowrer, O. H., 1960, *Learning Theory and Personality Dynamics*. New York: Ronald Press.

Mullahy, P., 1948, *Oedipus, Myth and Complex*. New York: Grove Press.

Mumford, P. R., Meyerowitz, B., and Mumford, M., 1980, A comparison of black and white children's WISC/WISC-R differences. *J. Elem. Psychol.*, **36**, 471–475.

Murphy, F., 1968, The state of the university. *UCLA—From the Chancellor's Desk*, **10**, 2–4.

Murray, H. A., 1938, The *Explorations in Personality*. New York: Oxford University Press.

Murray, H. A., 1943, *Thematic Apperception Test Manual*. Harvard College.

Murray, H. A., 1965, Uses of the Thematic Apperception Test. In Murstein, B., (Ed.), *Handbook of Projective Techniques*. New York: Basic Books, 425–432.

Murstein, B. (Ed.), 1965, *Handbook of Projective Techniques*. New York: Basic Books.

Ochs, E., 1960, Changes in the Goodenough drawings associated with changes in social adjustment. *J. Clin. Psychol.*, **6**, 282–284.

Oppenheimer, R., 1956, Analogy in science. *Am. Psychol.*, **11**, 127–135.

Orwell, G., 1949, *1984*. New York: Harcourt, Brace.

Palmer, J. O., 1952, A note on the intercard reliability of the Thematic Apperception Test. *J. Consult. Psychol.*, **16**, 473–474.

Palmer, J. O., 1955, Rorschach's experience balance: the concept, general population characteristics and intellectual correlations. *J. Proj. Tech.*, **19**, 138–145.

Palmer, J. O., 1956, Attitudinal correlates of Rorschach's experience balance. *J. Proj. Tech.*, **20**, 207–211.

Palmer, J. O., 1957, Some relationships between Rorschach's experience balance and Rosenzweig's frustration aggression patterns. *J. Proj. Tech.*, **21**, 137–141.

Palmer, J. O. Alterations in Rorschach's Experience Balance under conditions of food and sleep deprivation: A construct validation study. *J. Proj. Tech.*, **27**, 2:208–213, 1963.

Palmer, J. O., 1964, Restandardization of adolescent norms for the Shipley-Hartford. *J. Clin. Psychol.*, **20**, 492–495.

Palmer, J. O., 1980, *A Primer of Eclectic Psychotherapy*. Monterey, CA: Brooks/Cole.

Palmer, J. O., and Lustgarten, B. J., 1962, The prediction of TAT structure as a test of Rorschach's experience balance. *J. Proj. Tech.*, **26**, 212–220.

Palmero, D. A., and Jenkins, J. J., 1964, *Word Association Norms: Grade School Through College*. Minneapolis: University of Minnesota Press.

Panek, P., and Stover, S., 1979, Test–retest reliability of the Hand Test with normal children. *J. Pers. Assess.*, **43**, 135–137.

Piaget, J., 1954, *The Construction of Reality in the Child*. New York: Basic Books.

Pihl, R. G., 1968, The degree of verbal-performance discrepancy on WISC and WAIS and severity of EEG abnormality in epileptics. *J. Clin. Psychol.*, **24**, 418–420.

Piotrowski, R. J., 1978, Abnormality of subtest score differences on the WISC-R. *J. Consult. & Clin. Psychol.*, **46**, 569–570.

Piotrowski, Z. A., 1940, Positive and negative Rorschach organic signs. *Rorschach Res. Exch.*, **4**, 147.

Preyer, W., 1881, *Die Seele des Kindes* (translated as *Mind of the Child*, 1889). New York: Appleton.

Rabin, A. I., and Haworth, M. R. (Eds.), 1960, *Projective Techniques with Children*. New York: Grune & Stratton.

Rapaport, D, Gill, M., and Shafer, R., 1946, *Diagnostic Psychological Testing* (Vol. 2). Chicago: Yearbook Publ.

Raven, J. C., 1956, *Coloured Progressive Matrices*. London: H. K. Lewis.

Reissman, D., Glazer, N., and Denny, R., 1950, *The Lonely Crowd*. New Haven, CT: Yale University Press.

Reitan, R. M., and Davison, L. A., 1974, *Clinical Neuropsychology. Current Status and Applications*. Washington, DC: Winston.

Rogers, C. R. 1931, *A Test of Personality Adjustment*. New York: Association Press.

Rogers, C. R., 1942, *Counseling and Psychotherapy*. New York: Houghton-Mifflin.

Rogers, C. R., 1951, *Client-Centered Therapy*. Boston: Houghton -Mifflin.

Rohde, A. R., 1957, *The Sentence Completion Method: Its Diagnostic and Clinical Applications to Mental Disorders*. New York: Ronald.

Rorschach, H., 1921, *Psychodiagnostik*. Bern: Bircher. (Translation: *Psychodiagnostics*. New York: Grune & Stratton, 1951).

Rosenzweig, S., 1950, Levels of behavior in psychodiagnosis, with special reference to the Picture Frustration Study. *Amer. J. Orthopsychiat.*, **20**, 63–72.

Rosenzweig, S., Fleming, R., and Rosenzweig, B., 1948, The children's form of the Rosenzweig Picture-Frustration Study. *J. Psychol.*, **26**, 141–191.

Rotter, J. B., Rafferty, J. E., and Schachtitz, E., 1965, Validation of the Rotter Incomplete Sentence Test for college screening. In Murstein, B. (Ed.), *Handbook of Projective Techniques*. New York: Basic Books, 859–872.

Rotter, J., 1975, *Personality*. Glenview, IL: Scott-Foresman.

Rotter, J. B., and Willerman, B., 1947, The incomplete sentence test as a method of studying personality. *J. Consult. Psychol.*, **11**, 43–48.

Samuels, H., 1965, The validity of personality trait ratings on projective techniques. In Murstein, B. I. (Ed.), *Handbook of Projective Techniques*. New York: Basic Books, 163–187.

Sanford, R. N., 1936, The effect of abstinence from food on imaginal processes. *J. Psychol.*, **2**, 129–136.

Sargent, H. D., 1951, Psychological test reporting: an experiment in communication. *Bull. Menninger Clinic*, **15**, 175–186.

Satir, V., 1964, *Conjoint Family Therapy*. Palo Alto, CA: Science and Behavior Books.

Schafer, R., 1954, *Psychoanalytic Interpretation in Rorschach Testing: Theory and Applications*. New York: Grune & Stratton.

Shields, J., and Gottesman, I. (Eds.), 1971, *Man, Mind and Heredity. Selected Papers of Eliot Slater on Psychiatry and Genetics*. Baltimore: Johns Hopkins Press.

Seeley, J. R., Sim, R. A., and Loosley, E. W., 1956, *Crestwood Heights*. New York: Basic Books.

Shipley, W. C., and Burlingame, C. C., 1941, A convenient self-administering scale for measuring intellectual impairment. *Amer. J. Psychiatr.*, **97**, 1313–1324.

Shneidman, E. S., 1952, *Manual for the Make-A-Picture Story Method. Proj. Monogr. 2.* Portland, OR: The Society for Projective Techniques and Rorschach Institute.

Shurrager, H. C., and Shurrager, P., 1964, *The Haptic Intelligence Scale for the Adult Blind*. New York: Psychology Research.

Spitz, R. A., 1946, Anaclitic depression: An inquiry into the genesis of psychiatric condition in early childhood. *Psychoanal. Study Child.*, **2**, 313–342.

Spock, B., 1946, *Baby and Child Care*. New York: Duell, Sloan and Pearce.

Start, K. B., 1961, The relationship between the games performance of a grammar school boy and his intelligence and streaming. *Br. J. Educ. Psychol.*, **31**, 208–211.

Stein, M. I., 1948, *The Thematic Apperception Test*. Cambridge, MA: Addison-Wesley.

Stoltz, R., and Smith, M., 1959, Some effects of socio-economic age and sex factors on children's responses to the Rosenzweig Picture Frustration Study. *J. Clin. Psychol.*, **15**, 200–203.

Storms, L. H., 1960, Rationales for the "twisted pear." *J. Consult. Psychol.*, **24**, 552–553.

Stutzman, R., 1931, *Guide for Administering the Merill-Palmer Scale of Mental Tests*. New York: Harcourt, Brace & World.

Symonds, P. M., 1949, *Adolescent Fantasy: An Investigation of the Picture Story Method of Personality Study*. New York: Columbia University Press.

Szass, T., 1961, *The Myth of Mental Illness*. New York: Hoeber-Harper.

Tamkin, A., 1965, The effectiveness of the Bender-Gestalt Test in differential diagnosis. In Murstein, B. I. (Ed.), *Handbook of Projective Techniques*. New York: Basic Books, 741–745.

Tolman, E., 1952, A cognition motivation model. *Psychol. Rev.*, **59**, 5, 389–400.

Trager, H. and Yarrow, M. R., 1952, *They Learn What They Live: Prejudice in Young Children*. New York: Harper & Brothers.

Tucker, J., 1950, Rorschach human movement responses in relation to intelligence. *J. Consult. Psychol.*, **14**, 283–286.

Vance, H. B., Hawkins, N., and McGee, H., 1980, A preliminary study of Black and White differences on the WISC-R. *J. Clin. Psychol.*, **35**, 815–819.

Wade, T. C., and Baker, T. B., 1977, Opinions and use of psychological tests. *Amer. Psychol.*, **32**, 874–882.

Wagner, E. E., 1962, *Hand Test Manual for Administration, Scoring, and Interpretation*. Springfield, IL: Charles C. Thomas.

Walter, R., Colbert, E., Koegler, R., Palmer, J., and Bond, P., 1960, A controlled study of the 14 and 6 per second EEG pattern. *Arch. Gen. Psychiatr.*, **2**, 559–566.

Wanderer, Z. W., 1969, Validity of clinical judgments based on human figure drawings. *J. Consult & Clin. Psychol.*, **33**, 143–150.

Watson, R. I., 1953, A brief history of clinical psychology. *Psychol. Bull.*, **50**, 321–346.

Watts, A., 1966, *The Book: On the Taboo Against Knowing Who You Are*. New York: Pantheon.

Wechsler, D., 1944, *The Measurement of Adult Intelligence*. 1974, Rev. Ed. Baltimore: Williams and Wilkins.

Wechsler, D., 1967. *Manual for the Preschool and Primary Scale of Intelligence*. New York: Psychological Corp.

Wenar, C., 1961, The reliability of mothers' histories. *Child Dev.*, **32**, 491–500.

Wenar, C., Handlon, M., and Garner, A., 1959–1960. Patterns of mothering in psychosomatic disorders and severe emotional disturbances. *Merrill-Palmer Q. Behav. Dev.*, **6**, 165–170.

Whyte, I. W., 1956, *The Organization Man*. New York: Simon & Schuster.

Wildman R. W. and Wildman, R. W., Jr., 1967, The practice of clinical psychology in the

United States. *J. Clin. Psychol.* **23,** 293–295.

Wilson, S., 1955, *The Man in the Grey Flannel Suit.* New York: Simon & Schuster.

Winnicott, D. WW., 1953, Transactional objects and transitional phenomena. *Int. J. Psychoanal.,* **35,** 89–97.

Wise, J. H., 1969, Self-reports by negro and white adolescents to the Draw-A-Person. *Percept. Mot. Skills,* **28,** 193–194.

Work, H. H. and Call, J., 1965, *A Guide to Preventive Child Psychiatry: The Art of Parenthood.* New York: McGraw-Hill.

Wynne, L., 1965, Some indications and counter-indications for exploratory family therapy. In Boszormenyi-Nagy, I., and Framo, T. L., (Eds.), *Intensive Family Therapy.* New York: Harper & Row, 289–322.

Yarrow, L. J., 1964, Separation from parents during early childhood. In Hoffman, M. L., and Hoffman, L. W. (Eds.), *Review of Child Development Research* (Vol. 1). New York: Russell Sage Foundation, 89–137.

Yates, A. J., 1958, The application of learning theory to the treatment of tics. *J. Abn. Soc. Psychotl.,* **56,** 75–182.

Yates, A C., Barclay, A. G., and MacGilligan, R., 1969, Intra-rater reliability of scoring Goodenough-Harris drawings by disadvantaged school children. *Percept. Mot. Skills,* **28,** 281–282.

Zemlich, M., and Watson, R. I., 1953, Maternal attitudes of acceptance and rejection during and after pregnancy. *Amer. J. Orthopsychiat.,* **23,** 570–584.

Zimmerman, I. L., and Woo-Sam, J. M., 1972, Research with the Wechsler Intelligence Scale for Children. 1960–1970. *Psychol. Schools,* **9,** 232–271.

Index

Psychology and Psychiatry in Courts and Corrections: Controversy and Change
  by Ellsworth A. Fersch, Jr.
Restricted Environmental Stimulation: Research and Clinical Applications
  by Peter Suedfeld
Personal Construct Psychology: Psychotherapy and Personality
  edited by Alvin W. Landfield and Larry M. Leitner
Mothers, Grandmothers, and Daughters: Personality and Child Care in
Three-Generation Families
  by Bertram J. Cohler and Henry U. Grunebaum
Further Explorations in Personality
  edited by A. I. Rabin, Joel Aronoff, Andrew M. Barclay, and Robert A. Zucker
Hypnosis and Relaxation: Modern Verification of an Old Equation
  by William E. Edmonston, Jr.
Handbook of Clinical Behavior Therapy
  edited by Samuel M. Turner, Karen S. Calhoun, and Henry E. Adams
Handbook of Clinical Neuropsychology
  edited by Susan B. Filskov and Thomas J. Boll
The Course of Alcoholism: Four Years After Treatment
  by J. Michael Polich, David J. Armor, and Harriet B. Braiker
Handbook of Innovative Psychotherapies
  edited by Raymond J. Corsini
The Role of the Father in Child Development (Second Edition)
  edited by Michael E. Lamb
Behavioral Medicine: Clinical Applications
  by Susan S. Pinkerton, Howard Hughes, and W. W. Wenrich
Handbook for the Practice of Pediatric Psychology
  edited by June M. Tuma
Change Through Interaction: Social Psychological Processes of Counseling and
Psychotherapy
  by Stanley R. Strong and Charles D. Claiborn
Drugs and Behavior (Second Edition)
  by Fred Leavitt
Handbook of Research Methods in Clinical Psychology
  edited by Philip C. Kendall and James N. Butcher
A Social Psychology of Developing Adults
  by Thomas O. Blank
Women in the Middle Years: Current Knowledge and Directions for Research and Policy
  edited by Janet Zollinger Giele
Loneliness: A Sourcebook of Current Theory, Research and Therapy
  edited by Letitia Anne Peplau and Daniel Perlman
Hyperactivity: Current Issues, Research, and Theory (Second Edition)
  by Dorothea M. Ross and Sheila A. Ross
Review of Human Development
  *edited by Tiffany M. Field, Aletha Huston, Herbert C. Quay, Lillian Troll,
  and Gordon E. Finley*
Agoraphobia: Multiple Perspectives on Theory and Treatment
  edited by Dianne L. Chambless and Alan J. Goldstein
The Rorschach: A Comprehensive System, Volume III: Assessment of Children and Adolescents
  by John E. Exner, Jr. and Irving B. Weiner
Handbook of Play Therapy
  edited by Charles E. Schaefer and Kevin J. O'Connor
Adolescent Sexuality in a Changing American Society: Social and Psychological Perspectives
for the Human Service Professions (Second Edition)
  by Catherine S. Chilman
Failures in Behavior Therapy
  edited by Edna B. Foa and Paul M.G. Emmelkamp
The Psychological Assessment of Children (Second Edition)
  by James O. Palmer